21st EDITION

Government by the People

TEXAS VERSION

David B. Magleby
Brigham Young University

David M. O'Brien
University of Virginia

Paul C. Light
New York University

James MacGregor Burns
University of Maryland, College Park
and Williams College

J.W. Peltason
University of California

Thomas E. Cronin
Whitman College

L. Tucker Gibson, Jr.
Trinity University

Clay Robison
Houston Chronicle

PEARSON
Prentice
Hall

Upper Saddle River, New Jersey 07458

Library of Congress Cataloging-in-Publication Data

Government by the people.—Texas version, 21st ed./David B. Magleby . . . [et al.].
   p. cm.
   Includes bibliographical references and index.
   ISBN 0-13-192157-6 (alk. paper)
   1. United States—Politics and government—Textbooks. 2. Texas—Politics and
government—Textbooks. I. Magleby, David B.

JK276.G68 2006f
320.4764—dc22

2004054155

VP, Editorial Director: Charlyce Jones Owen
Acquisitions Editor: Glenn Johnston
Production Editor: Rob DeGeorge
Development Editor: Betty Gatewood
Editorial Assistant: Suzanne Remore
Director of Marketing: Heather Shelstad
Marketing Manager: Kara Kindstrom
Copy Editor: Sylvia Moore
**VP, Director of Production
  and Manufacturing:** Barbara Kittle
Prepress and Manufacturing Manager:
  Nick Sklitsis
Prepress and Manufacturing Buyer:
  Sherry Lewis
Creative Design Director: Leslie Osher
Interior and Cover Designer: Carmen
  DiBartolomeo
Director, Image Resource Center:
  Melinda Reo

Manager, Visual Research: Beth Brenzel
Manager, Rights and Permissions:
  Zina Arabia
**Manager, Cover Visual Research and
  Permissions:** Karen Sanatar
Image Permission Coordinator:
  Michelina Viscusi
Photo Researchers: Kathy Ringrose
  and Elaine Soares
Illustrations: Mirella Signoretto
Cover Art: EyeWire Collection/Getty
  Images–Photodisc
Composition: Pine Tree Composition
Printer/Binder: Courier Companies, Inc.
Cover Printer: The Lehigh Press, Inc.
Text: 9/12 Utopia

Credits and acknowledgments borrowed from other sources and reproduced, with permission,
in this textbook appear on appropriate page within text or, in the case of photographs, on p. C-1.

Pearson Education LTD.
Pearson Education Singapore, Pte. Ltd
Pearson Education, Canada, Ltd
Pearson Education—Japan
Pearson Education Australia PTY, Limited

Pearson Education North Asia Ltd
Pearson Educación de Mexico, S.A. de C.V.
Pearson Education Malaysia, Pte. Ltd
Pearson Education, Upper Saddle River,
  New Jersey

10 9 8 7 6 5 4 3 2 1
ISBN 0-13-192157-6

BRIEF CONTENTS

CONTENTS

APPENDIX

A Message from the Authors

The United States emerged from the 2004 election divided not only on the war in Iraq and how best to pursue the war on terror, but also on issues like stem cell research, same-sex marriage, future funding for Social Security, and how to revitalize the economy. The country is also divided along party lines. The intensity of the partisan division is explained in part by the differing perceptions of the fairness of the vote count in the 2000 presidential election. Democrats won the popular vote and believe that the decision to deny them Florida's electoral vote was driven by partisanship. Republicans believe they won the presidency fairly. While the two sides in the 2004 election did not agree on much, they did and do agree that elections matter and that there are real policy consequences to elections. What is also undisputed is the importance of government and politics in people's lives.

The political parties and interest groups made voter registration and turnout—getting voters to the polls—a major priority in 2003 and 2004. While the surge in new-voter registration was most concentrated in the presidential battleground states, it was evident elsewhere as well. Some groups concentrated on getting young citizens to register and vote while other groups focused on other issues. Federal legislation was also a factor in this dynamic election environment since voters could cast provisional ballots if their registration was uncertain, a provision that resulted in multiple legal challenges. Ballot initiatives on minimum wage and same-sex marriage gave citizens additional reasons to exercise the franchise and vote. An enduring dispute in American government is how hard or easy the act of voting should be for citizens.

The war on terror not only has changed electoral politics but also has prompted recommendations about reform of our intelligence agencies, fostered a debate about defense priorities and expenditures, and led to the creation of a Department of Homeland Security. Citizens expect their government to provide security. How can government achieve this fundamental objective in light of the reality of terrorists who target America and Americans? To what extent do we pursue countries producing weapons of mass destruction? Is preemptive war a good idea given these potentially lethal weapons that could kill millions of Americans? Should the war on terror be waged by the United States alone if allies are not willing to join us? More broadly, what is the proper balance between providing security and protecting liberty? In many chapters of this edition we compare public opinion in the United States with opinions in other countries, including opinions on items like the institutions and policies of democracy in the United States. Why is the United States perceived in such a negative way in so many countries? Are there ways the United States can improve its global image?

The economy is another policy area that illustrates the importance of government at all levels. At the national level the issue has centered on whether we could pursue a global war on terror and at the same time cut taxes. The alternative of funding the war through borrowing and raising the federal budget deficit poses its own tradeoffs. Additionally, there is dispute over what kinds of taxes are most fair and beneficial to the economy. Economic factors also impact state and local governments, who generally must balance their budgets by either cutting spending or raising taxes in difficult economic times.

Constitutional democracy—the kind we have in the United States—is exceedingly hard to achieve, equally hard to sustain, and often hard to understand without rigorous study. Our political history has been an evolution toward an enlarged role for citizens and voters. Citizens have more rights and political opportunities in 2005 and 2006 than they had in 1800 or 1900. The framers of our Constitution warned that we must be vigilant in safeguarding our rights, liberties, and political institutions. But to do this, we must first understand these institutions and the forces that have shaped them.

Many U.S. citizens take for granted civil liberties, civil rights, free and fair elections, the peaceful transfer of power, and economic freedom and prosperity. Yet many people live in places where these freedoms are nonexistent. This is a time of testing for new democracies as well as old ones. Contempt for government and politics is being expressed in the United States and abroad, yet politics and partisan competition are the lifeblood that enables free societies to achieve the ideal of government by the people.

Although we constantly turn to government and to our elected officials with problems and requests, we are critical of their shortcomings. A recurrent theme of this book is the absolute need for politics and politicians, despite the widespread tendency to criticize nearly everything political. In many chapters, we showcase examples of people in politics who have made a difference. These politically active individuals have divergent parties, ideologies, and agendas, but they share a common trait of engagement in democracy. The reality is that our political system should not be taken for granted, even as we seek ways in which it can be improved.

We want you to come away from reading this book with a richer understanding of American politics, government, and the job of politicians. We hope you will participate actively in making this constitutional democracy more vital and responsive to the urgent problems of the twenty-first century.

Reviewers

The writing of this book has profited from the informed, professional, and often sharp, critical suggestions of our colleagues around the country. This and previous editions have been considerably improved as a result of reviews by the following individuals, for which we thank them all:

James E. Anderson, Texas A&M University
Alan Balboni, Community College of Southern Nevada
Thad Beyle, University of North Carolina
Robert R. Bland, University of North Texas
Wendell S. Broadwell, Georgia Perimeter College
Mark Cassel, Kent State University
Ray Christensen, Brigham Young University
Douglas Crane, Georgia Perimeter College
James Decker, Macon State College
Veronica D. DiConti, American University
Cecile Durish, Austin Community College

Jeff Fox, Fort Lewis College
Russell Arben Fox, Arkansas State University
Earl H. Fry, Brigham Young University
Bill Gangi, St. Johns University
G. David Garson, North Carolina State University
John Green, University of Akron
Yoram Haftel, Ohio State University
Kenneth G. Hartman, Longview Community College
Paul Herrnson, University of Maryland
Heidi Hobbs, North Carolina State University
Terry Jack, Gulf Coast Community College

Ronald F. King, Tulane University
Gary Moncrief, Boise State University
Ron Pettus, St. Charles Community College
John R. Phillips, Springfield College
Saundra J. Reinke, Augusta State University
Michael W. Sonnleitner, Portland Community College
Grier Stephenson, Franklin & Marshall College
Regina Swopes, Northeastern Illinois University
Robert A. Taylor, Florida Institute of Technology
Lois Duke Whitaker, Georgia Southern University
Frank L. Wilson, Purdue University

Acknowledgments

This book builds on a long tradition of clear and accessible writing, sound scholarship, and currency. James MacGregor Burns and Jack Peltason, the founding authors of the book, and Tom Cronin, who later joined them, set a high standard in these areas. As additional authors have joined the book we have worked hard to maintain this legacy while at the same time extensively revising each new edition to maintain its tradition of currency. Writing this book requires teamwork—first, among the coauthors, who converse often about the broad themes, features, and focus of the book and who read and rewrite each other's first drafts; then with our research assistants, who track down loose ends and give us the perspective of students; and with the editors and other professionals at Prentice Hall. Important to each revision are the detailed reviews by teachers and researchers, who provide concrete suggestions on how to improve the book. We are grateful to all who helped with this edition.

Research assistants for the current edition of *Government by the People* are Susan Christiansen, Stephanie Curtis, Yale Layton, Jeffrey R. Makin, Emily McClintock, Ryan Mehner, R. Chad Pugh, Dustin Slade, Peter Stone, and Paul V. Russell at Brigham Young University and Cindy Bolyes at the University of Virginia. Donna Jones and JoAnn Collins at Whitman College provided secretarial assistance. Shara Merchant at the Brookings Institution was also of assistance.

Books for major college courses like this feature state-of-the-art teaching and learning tools. Web-based items for students and instructors are some examples of these ancillaries. Learning is reinforced though simulations like those found in the "Make It *Real*" simulations at the end of each chapter. We thank the professionals who produced the supplements.

We gratefully acknowledge the professionalism and commitment of Political Science Editor Glenn Johnston. Our production editor, Rob DeGeorge, kept us on schedule and orchestrated the production of this edition. Currency has always been a hallmark of this book and Rob did a superb job of facilitating our updating of text and tables right up to the point of publication. Our thanks, too, to Suzanne Remore, who assisted Glenn Johnston in the numerous tasks involved in publishing a book of this scope. Others at Prentice Hall we wish to thank for their continued support are Yolanda de Rooy and Charlyce Jones Owen.

Many skilled professionals were important to the publication of this book. They include Pine Tree Composition for page layout, Kathy Ringrose for photo research, Mirella Signoretto for line art creation, Carmen DiBartolomeo for interior and cover design and design supervision, and Betty Gatewood for text development.

We also want to thank you, the professors and students who use our book, and who send us letters and e-mail messages with suggestions for improving *Government by the People*. We welcome feedback and suggestions from you. Please write us in care of the Political Science Editor at Prentice Hall, 1 Lake Street, Upper Saddle River, New Jersey 07458, or contact us directly:

David B. Magleby   Distinguished Professor of Political Science and Dean of FHSS, Brigham Young University, Provo, UT 84602 david_magleby@byu.edu

David M. O'Brien   Leone Reaves and George W. Spicer Professor, Department of Government and Foreign Affairs, University of Virginia, Charlottesville, VA 22903 dmo2y@virginia.edu

Paul C. Light   Paulette Goddard Professor of Public Service at New York University and Douglas Dillon Senior Fellow at the Brookings Institution pcl226@nyu.edu

James MacGregor Burns   Academy of Leadership, University of Maryland, College Park, MD 20742.

J. W. Peltason   School of Social Sciences, University of California, Irvine, CA 92717-5700 jwpeltas@uci.edu

Thomas E. Cronin   Office of the President, Whitman College, Walla Walla, WA 99362 cronin@whitman.edu

A MESSAGE FROM THE PUBLISHER

Always one step ahead . . .

Prentice Hall is extremely proud to publish the book that remains the most reliable, responsive, and respected text for use in colleges and universities in every state of the nation. For over fifty years, this is the book that has always remained one step ahead of all the others by anticipating your needs as an educator and your students' needs as learners. Now in its twenty-first edition, Magleby, O'Brien, Light, Burns, Peltason, and Cronin's *Government by the People* continues this tradition.

We are entering a very complex political era and there is no better text poised to take students from being simple onlookers to knowledgeable participants in the American political experience. The level of scholarship of the *Government by the People* author team, as well as the way in which they treat each new edition as a fresh challenge, is clearly represented in this latest edition. That is why, time and time again, *Government by the People* remains the most current, respected, and reliable book on the market and remains . . . one step ahead.

New to this Edition

■ *New! Late-Breaking, Up-to-Date Content* This new edition has been thoroughly updated and revised with coverage of the 2004 elections. Almost all chapters have undergone revisions to reflect the many changes and events in the last two years. This text is right on top of the demographic changes that are remaking society before our eyes. Special attention is given to presenting the key trends in diversity that matter in American politics, including a focus on the people in politics who are the movers and shakers that are making a difference on issues related to managing the increased diversity of America. There is an increased focus on comparative and global issues to introduce students to the increasing globalization of American politics. The rulings of the Supreme Court have been thoroughly updated and highlight changes and controversies over affirmative action, the separation of religion and government, the rights of homosexuals, searches and seizures, and the Rehnquist Court's recent rulings on federalism. There is also great coverage of the impact of campaign finance reform as well as coverage of the voter mobilization drive in 2004.

■ *New! Global Perceptions Features* This brand new feature utilizes the most current data from the Pew Research Center to show students how public opinion in various nations compares with public opinion in the United States as well as how people throughout the world view the United States. Topics covered include the spread of American ideas and customs throughout the world, attitudes throughout the world toward immigrants, and attitudes throughout the world toward unions.

■ *New! Chapter Opening Time Lines* Each chapter begins with a chapter-specific historical time line to help students place significant historical moments into context with what they are studying—as they are studying—making an otherwise difficult concept more manageable and, therefore, more meaningful.

Enduring Features of the Text

Among the many attributes of *Government by the People* are the features that have come to support the balanced presentation of topics within the text. Each of these features has been appropriately revised to reflect those issues that are most significant within our political environment today.

■ *In Comparative Perspective* This boxed feature uses data, maps, and figures to show students how the United States compares to other nations throughout the world with regard to a variety of topics, including: The British and American Systems: A Study in Contrasts, and Registration and Voting in the World's Democracies.

■ *People and Politics: Making a Difference* This thoroughly revised boxed feature provides students with short profiles of influential political figures, some of historical importance as well as some contemporary figures. Many focus on the positive contributions of America's public servants and ordinary citizens, including: Joan Blades and Wes Boyd of MoveOn, Stephen Moore and the Club for Growth, Blaise Hazelwood, Karl Rove, Sean Hannity, and Steve Rosenthal of America Coming Together.

■ *You Decide/Thinking It Through* Provides broader discussion on current topics. This participatory question-and-answer feature is designed to strengthen students' critical thinking skills as well as introduce interesting and challenging issues and ideas about American politics.

■ *Changing Face of American Politics* This feature addresses the diverse nature of the American political system. These unique boxes are designed to reflect the concerns and experiences of ethnic and minority groups in American politics, giving students tangible examples of the key trends in diversity on the American political landscape, including such topics as whether there is a relationship between race and trust.

Teaching and Learning Resources

- *Practice Tests*   This study resource includes chapter outlines, study notes, a glossary, and practice tests designed to reinforce information in the text and help students develop a greater understanding of American government and politics.
- *Instructor's Resource CD-ROM*   New from Prentice Hall, the Instructor's Resource CD-ROM allows you maximum flexibility as you prepare your lectures and manage your class. For presentation use, this CD-ROM contains a database that includes the Instructor's Resource Manual, Test Item File, line art from the text, video and audio segments of classical and contemporary political science footage, and Powerpoint™ presentations.
- *Instructor's Resource Manual with Test Item File*   For each chapter, a summary, review of concepts, lecture suggestions and topic outlines, and additional resource materials—including a guide to media resources—are provided. An electronic version is also included on the Instructor's Resource CD-ROM.

  The **Test Item File** has undergone extensive review and revision, so instructors can have more confidence than ever in the quality of test questions. This edition presents the highest level of quality and accuracy, with over 2,000 questions in multiple choice, true/false, short answer, and essay format covering factual and conceptual material from the text.
- *Prentice Hall Test Manager*   A computerized test bank contains the items from the Test Item File. The program allows for full editing of questions and the addition of instructor-generated items. Suitable for Windows and Macintosh operating systems.
- *Government by the People Transparencies*   This set of full-color transparency acetates reproduces illustrations, charts, and maps from the text as well as from additional sources.
- *Prentice Hall Custom Video: How a Bill Becomes a Law* This 25-minute video chronicles an environmental law in Massachusetts—from its start as one citizen's concern to its passage in Washington, D.C. Students see the step-by-step process of how a bill becomes a law, complete through narrative and graphics. Available to qualified college adopters. Please contact your local Prentice Hall representative for details.
- *Films for the Humanities and Social Sciences*   Qualified college adopters may select from a high quality library of political science videos from Films for the Humanities and Social Sciences. Please contact your local Prentice Hall representative for details on qualifying orders and a complete listing.
- *Choices: An American Government Custom Reader* Exercise freedom of expression by creating an American government reader that truly reflects your teaching style, your course goals, your perspective! *Choices: An American Government Custom Reader* delivers quality scholarship, pedagogy, and exceptional source materials. You choose the readings and the sequence. You can even add your own work or other favorite materials to create a reader that fits your course precisely. The price of your reader is determined by its length. Your students pay for what they need—no more. Over 250 articles, documents, book excerpts, and speeches—representing classic pieces as well as current articles and covering over 20 topical areas—are available. Visit the *Choices* Website: www.choices reader.com and learn about updates.

New and Improved Technology

As in previous editions, *Government by the People* leads the industry in providing creative, innovative electronic solutions for your classroom. Whether in the form of tools that enable more effective communication or by providing dynamic presentation of content via the World Wide Web, Prentice Hall continues to anticipate your needs.

- *New!* OneKey   For instructors who would like to implement the use of course management software to organize their course and communicate with their students, Prentice Hall is pleased to offer access to *OneKey*, an exclusive new resource for instructors and students. *OneKey* provides you access to the best online teaching and learning tools—all available 24 hours a day, 7 days a week. *OneKey* means that all of your resources are in one place for maximum convenience, simplicity, and success. *OneKey* features a host of organizational tools for both students and instructors for Blackboard, WebCT, and CourseCompass. Students can be better prepared for class and instructors can save time preparing for lectures and managing their course by utilizing the available online resources such as multimedia, tests, quizzes, and research through *Research Navigator*™, as well as gradebooks for grading and tracking student progress and success. Access to *OneKey* is available to qualified college adopters. Please contact your local Prentice Hall representative for more information.
- *New!* **Make It Real**   Available as part of *OneKey* or by itself, *Make It Real* is a new Web-based resource that enables students to take concepts discussed in the text and put them to practical use. Simulations based on real data give students a hands-on experience based on real election results; real demographics, including gender, age, education level, race, and income; real score cards from actual Senate members showing their votes on public interest issues; and real maps, including political persuasion in different regions. *Make It Real* also includes activities that enhance and promote civic participation and visual literacy. This program incorporates Census 2000 data and primary source documents. In addition, there are chapter-based assessments, flashcards, crossword puzzles, and interactive maps and time lines. Access codes are available free when packaged with *Government by the People*.
- **Evaluating Online Resources for Political Science with Research Navigator™**   Our newest addition to the

reliable Internet guide for political science, Prentice Hall's *Research Navigator*™ keeps instructors and students abreast of the latest news and information and helps students create top quality research papers. From finding the right articles and journals to citing sources, drafting and writing effective papers, and completing research assignments, *Research Navigator*™ simplifies and streamlines the entire process. Complete with extensive help on the research process and three exclusive databases full of relevant and reliable source material, including EBSCO's *ContentSelect*™ Academic Journal Database, *The New York Times* Search-by-Subject Archive, and *Best of the Web* Link Library.

A unique access code for *Research Navigator*™ is provided on the inside front cover of the booklet. *Evaluating Online Resources for Political Science with Research Navigator*™ is free for qualified college adoptions when packaged with *Government by the People* and available for stand-alone sale. Take a tour on the web at www.researchnavigator. com

■ **Companion Website**™ (www.prenhall.com/magleby) Students can take full advantage of the World Wide Web to enrich their study of American government through the *Government by the People Companion Website*™. The site features interactive practice tests, chapter objectives, and overviews. Web destinations provide a valuable source of supplemental information.

Supplemental Texts and Readings for American Government

The following books feature specialized topical coverage, allowing you to tailor your American government content to suit the needs of your course. Featuring contemporary issues or timely readings, any of the following books is available to qualified college adopters at a discount when bundled with *Government by the People*. Please visit our online catalog at www.prenhall.com/magleby for additional details.

Government's Greatest Achievements: From Civil Rights to Homeland Security, 20th ed.
Paul C. Light, New York University
ISBN: 0-13-110192-7 © 2004

21 Debated: Issues in American Politics, 2nd ed.
Gregory Scott, University of Central Oklahoma
Loren Gatch, University of Central Oklahoma
ISBN: 0-13-184178-5 © 2005

Strategies for Active Citizenship
Kateri M. Drexler
Gwen Garcelon
ISBN: 0-13-117295-6 © 2005

The Political Science Student Writer's Manual, 4th ed.
Gregory M. Scott, University of Central Oklahoma
Stephen M. Garrison, University of Central Oklahoma
ISBN: 0-13-040447-0 © 2002

Real Politics in America Series

This series is another resource for contemporary instructional material that can be used to bridge the gap between research and relevancy. More descriptive than quantitative, more case study than data study, these books cut across all topics to bring students relevant details in current political science research. From exploring the growing phenomenon of direct democracy to who runs for the state legislature, these books show students that real political science is meaningful and exciting. Individual titles are available at a significant a discount when bundled with *Government by the People*. Please see your Prentice Hall representative or access www.prenhall.com for more details on the titles in the series. A complete listing of the titles in this series can be found on page xxii.

RELIABLE. RESPONSIVE. RESPECTED.

That's GOVERNMENT BY THE PEOPLE.

BUILDING ON A LONG TRADITION OF CLEAR AND accessible writing, sound scholarship, and currency, GOVERNMENT BY THE PEOPLE **has become the most reliable, responsive, and respected text for today's American Government course.** Its distinguished author team has revised each edition with one steadfast commitment—to address your needs and the needs of your students with the most innovative response to teaching trends, as well as trends in the discipline.

As students become active participants in the study of American government, they will learn to understand and appreciate the crucial role of government and politicians—as well as their own vital role as voters and contributors to America's constitutional democracy. With this essential foundation, students will be set to respond—as involved American citizens—to the political issues facing their country, and their world, in the twenty-first century.

RELIABLE. RESPONSIVE. RESPECTED.

That's **GOVERNMENT BY THE PEOPLE.**

■ *Changing Face of American Politics*

These boxed features appear in context with topics presented in every chapter, exemplifying the ever-increasing level of diversity in the American political landscape. By involving students on a personal level, this text engages them in a more meaningful, memorable study of politics as it affects their own lives.

CHANGING FACE OF AMERICAN POLITICS

PRESIDENTIAL APPOINTEES

Presidents Bill Clinton and George W. Bush both promised to appoint administrations that were as diverse as the country. Although both presidents came surprisingly close on race, neither approached the 50 percent mark on gender. According to detailed analysis of every executive branch appointee nominated for Senate confirmation in the first year of the first term of both administrations, 30 percent of the appointees in Clinton's first year were women, compared to just 23 percent in Bush's first year.

Although the numbers seem disappointing given the changing face of the federal bureaucracy discussed in the next chapter, both administrations did much better than their predecessors—less than 15 percent of the appointees in Carter's first year (1977) were women, compared to just 8 percent in Reagan's first year (1981).* And the fact that both Clinton and Bush were both able to recruit many women and minority appointees at lower levels suggests that future administrations will be even more successful. Past research shows that the higher-level jobs almost always go to appointees with prior appointee-service at lower levels. By increasing the numbers of women and minorities in the pipeline, the Clinton and Bush administrations increased the odds that there will be more women and minority candidates

for the top jobs for future Democratic and Republican administrations alike.

*The Carter and Reagan numbers come from Gary King and Lynn Ragsdale, *The Elusive Executive: Discovering Elusive Statistical Patterns in the Presidency* (CQ Press, 1988), pp. 236–237.

	Clinton Administration, 1993	Bush Administration, 2001
Gender		
Women	30%	23%
Men	70	77
Race		
African-American	14%	9%
Hispanic	6	8
Asian-American	3	3
White	77	80

SOURCE: Data collected by the Presidential Appointee Initiative, analysis by authors.

■ *People & Politics: Making a Difference*

Politically active people represent divergent parties, ideologies, and agendas—but share the common trait of engagement in the political process. This feature reinforces the importance of being an active participant in—and contributor to—political change.

PEOPLE & POLITICS *Making a Difference* ★ ★ ★

GENERATION X IN CONGRESS (HAROLD FORD, JR., AND ADAM PUTNAM)

As the two youngest members of Congress, Adam Putnam (R.-Fla.) and Harold Ford, Jr. (D.-Tenn.) care deeply about reengaging young Americans in politics. Both were elected in part on promises to give young Americans a stronger voice in debates about the future of programs such as Social Security, and both continue to work hard to connect with their generation on jobs and access to education.

Putnam was just 26 years old when he was elected to Congress in 2000. "I want to energize a whole new generation of young people to reengage in politics," Putnam says. You, know, Kennedy did it, Reagan did it, probably Clinton '92 did it. We've got to do a better job talking across generational lines."

Ford was just 26, too, when he was elected to Congress in 1996. Young people were a central part of his first campaign. He visited more than 100 schools and spoke to an estimated 40,000 to 50,000 high school students en route to a landslide victory. "We've grown up in a

different world," his chief of staff explained to reporters when asked about Ford's view of politics. "We're more comfortable with diversity, with change, with new ideas and new attitudes."

Age does not create a shared agenda, however Putnam opposes many of the issues that young Americans support, including abortion rights. He also rejected MTV's request to film his first campaign by saying he didn't want any "purple-hair yahoo" asking whether he wore "boxers or briefs." But he does support Social Security reform, which is a key issue for young Americans who do not believe the program will still be alive when they retire.

Putnam and Ford do believe they can make a difference in showing that age is no barrier to participation. "I'm not invited to a high school class to articulate

Adam Putnam   *Harold Ford, Jr.*

the merits of permanent normal trade relations with China," Putnam says. "I'm invited to classes to talk about why it's important for young people to get involved and how they can do it." Ford agrees. "Once you get young people to pay attention, you find that you've turned on a faucet that's hard to turn off." The fact that these two Gen X'ers are in Congress is no small part of showing young Americans that age is not a barrier to involvement at the very top of American politics.

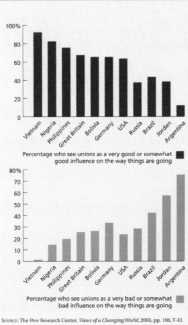
■ *Global Perceptions*

Understanding America's global image in today's world is critical to understanding the impact of its policies on both a national and international level. New to this edition is *Global Perceptions*, with data from the Pew Research Center that shows students how citizens around the world view not only the United States, its policies, institutions, and leaders, but also issues that affect their daily lives, like the Internet and crime.

■ *In Comparative Perpective*

The emphasis on providing a global context for understanding American politics is reinforced with *In Comparative Perspective* boxes. Through this feature, students learn more about foreign political structure and process, and also how these similar and/or differing approaches can affect—and be affected by—American politics.

TIME LINE

CAMPAIGNS AND ELECTIONS

1781	John Hanson is elected "President of the United States in Congress Assembled"
1789	Constitution is ratified and George Washington is elected "President of the United States"
1800	House of Representatives chooses Thomas Jefferson over Thomas Pinckney
1824	House of Representatives chooses John Quincy Adams over Andrew Jackson when the electoral college fails to elect a president
1860	Southern secession following election of Abraham Lincoln
1876	Samuel Tilden wins the popular vote but loses the Electoral College to Rutherford B. Hayes
1932	Realigning election creates a "New Deal" coalition behind the Democratic Party
1951	Constitution amended limiting president to two terms
1960	First televised presidential debates benefit the Kennedy campaign
1974	"Watergate class" creates liberal majorities in both the House and the Senate
1992	Carol Mosley-Braun becomes the first African American woman elected to the Senate
2000	George W. Bush wins the electoral college in an outcome determined by the Supreme Court
2002	Congress passes Bipartisan Campaign Reform Act, doubling individual contribution limits

RELIABLE. RESPONSIVE. RESPECTED.
That's GOVERNMENT BY THE PEOPLE.

■ *Timelines*

New *time lines* at the beginning of each chapter trace the historical development of American politics and institutions by highlighting key people, events, and documents that helped shape them. Each time line focuses specifically on historical events that are pertinent to the content of the chapter. This historical context helps students appreciate the dynamics of politics and government today and how history will continue to shape government and politics of tomorrow.

These visually-clarifying *time lines* come to life with interactivity in **OneKey** for students who want to explore further as they learn to place significant historical moments into context with what they are studying, making an otherwise difficult concept more manageable and, therefore, more meaningful.

Also available with GOVERNMENT BY THE PEOPLE—

Introducing *Make It Real*

Students will experience the power of politics through multimedia simulations featuring real data in American government. With abundant—and authentic—material tied to the text and designed to bring every chapter to life, *Make It Real*, includes:

- Civic participation activities and exercises.
- Video clips of key events that shaped American government and politics.
- Interactive maps.
- Audio speeches.
- Primary source documents.
- Census data to illustrate real, recent statistics that have an effect on—or are affected by—government and politics.

Fully integrated activities and assessment tools in *Make It Real* tie its content to the text material and offer an easy way to test students' comprehension.

Make It Real is available FREE when packaged with GOVERNMENT BY THE PEOPLE. Please contact your local Prentice Hall sales representative for more information.

One**Key** *The new, all-inclusive online resource for students*

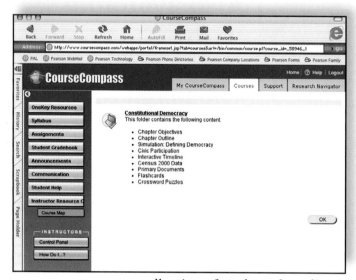

RELIABLE.
RESPONSIVE.
RESPECTED.
That's GOVERNMENT BY THE PEOPLE.

Designed and presented to accompany this new edition, Prentice Hall's exclusive **OneKey** is a unique website that offers students access to all of their learning resources—all in one place. A robust collection of study and application tools, **OneKey** enables students to enjoy a more in-depth learning experience.

■ *Students will study smarter and perform better.*

Chapter-by-chapter outlines, review quizzes, and essays, as well as interactive flashcard and crossword puzzle activities, reinforce text material. These tools are linked to an e-book version of the text, allowing students to immediately link to appropriate pages for help and feedback where they need it most.

■ *Students will experience the power of politics.*

Also included in **OneKey** is *Make It Real*. With activities, speeches, video, and documents directly tied to the text, *Make It Real* brings politics to life for your students by engaging them to become involved, active learners.

For more information, or to request **OneKey** for your students, please contact your local Prentice Hall sales representative or visit **www.prenhall.com**.

One**Key** *The new, all-inclusive online resource for instructors*

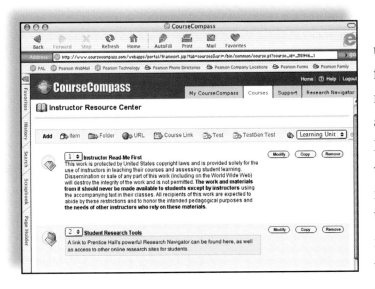

Prentice Hall's exclusive **OneKey** is a unique website that offers instructors free access to all of their teaching resources—all in one place. It contains all of the resources from the printed **Instructor's Manual** and **Test Item File**, as well as PowerPoint™ slides of all art and images from this text . . . and much more. With **OneKey** for instructors, preparing for lectures, testing, and communication with students will be easier and more convenient than ever before.

■ *Present more powerfully than ever before* using text-tied audio, video, and PowerPoint™ slides, organized by chapter of this text, to bring concepts to life for students.

■ *Assess your students' comprehension* of the major concepts and the specific chapters of this text using your choice of reliable test questions from the Test Item File.

■ *Assign your students* chapter-by-chapter, self-graded quizzes or choose essay questions and activities tied to each chapter for use as homework or relevant in-class activities.

Use the *Make It Real* simulations and activities in **OneKey**—all tied to the text—to reinforce material by involving students in the political process through active learning. Use these activities as homework assignments—or in class to spark debates among students as they experience real situations using real data from American government and politics.

Introducing **SafariX:** This new Pearson Choice offers students an online subscription to the same content online at a 50% savings. With the **SafariX WebBook**, students search the text, make notes online, print reading assignments that incorporate lecture notes, and bookmark important passages. Ask your Prentice Hall sales representative for details on available versions of this text, or **visit www.safarix.com.**

REAL POLITICS IN AMERICA

Paul S. Herrnson, Series Editor, *University of Maryland*

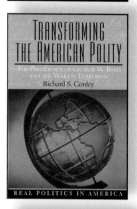

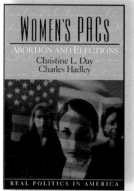

PRESIDENTIAL CAMPAIGN QUALITY:
Incentives and Reform
Buchanan
© 2004, 160 pp., paper (0-13-184140-8)

TRANSFORMING THE
AMERICAN POLITY:
The Presidency of George W. Bush and
the War on Terrorism
Conley
© 2005, 160 pp., paper (0-13-189342-4)

WOMEN'S PACS:
Abortion and Elections
Day/Hadley
© 2005, 160 pp., paper (0-13-117448-7)

THE MEDIUM AND THE MESSAGE:
Television Advertising and
American Elections
Goldstein/Strach
© 2004, 256 pp., paper (0-13-177774-2)

WAR STORIES FROM CAPITOL HILL
Campbell/Herrnson
© 2004, 160 pp., paper (0-13-028088-7)

REFORMING THE REPUBLIC:
Democratic Institutions for the
New America
Donovan/Bowler
© 2004, 224 pp., paper (0-13-099455-3)

NO HOLDS BARRED:
Negativity in U.S. Senate Campaigns
Kahn/Kenney
© 2004, 144 pp., paper (0-13-097760-8)

CONGRESS AND THE POLITICS OF
FOREIGN POLICY
Campbell/Rae/Stack
© 2003, 194 pp., paper (0-13-042154-5)

CONGRESS AND THE INTERNET
Thurber/Campbell
© 2003, 198 pp., paper (0-13-099617-3)

CITIES AND PRIVATIZATION:
Prospects for the New Century
Greene
© 2002, 178 pp., paper (0-13-029442-X)

STEALING THE INITIATIVE:
How State Government Responds to
Direct Democracy
Gerber/Lupia/McCubbins/Kiewiet
© 2001, 128 pp., paper (0-13-028407-6)

PLAYING HARDBALL:
Campaigning for the U.S. Congress
Herrnson
© 2001, 160 pp., paper (0-13-027133-0)

WHO RUNS FOR THE LEGISLATURE?
Moncrief/Squire/Jewell
© 2001, 144 pp., paper (0-13-026608-6)

CLICKER POLITICS:
Essays on the California Recall
Bowler/Cain
© 2006, paper (0-13-193336-1)

Prentice Hall is pleased to provide adopters with an opportunity to receive significant discounts on these titles when packaged together with GOVERNMENT BY THE PEOPLE. Please contact your local Prentice Hall sales representative for details.

About the Authors

David B. Magleby

David B. Magleby is nationally recognized for his expertise on direct democracy, voting behavior, and campaign finance. He is dean as well as Professor of Political Science at Brigham Young University and has taught at the University of California, Santa Cruz, and the University of Virginia. His writings include *Direct Legislation* (1984), *The Money Chase* (1990), and *Myth of the Independent Voter* (1992), and he is editor of *Financing the 2000 Election* (2002) and co-editor of *The Last Hurrah? Soft Money and Issue Advocacy in the 2002 Congressional Elections* (2004). He was president of Pi Sigma Alpha, the national political science honor society, has received numerous teaching awards, and was a Fulbright Scholar at Nuffield College, Oxford University.

David M. O'Brien

David M. O'Brien is the Leone Reaves and George W. Spicer Professor at the University of Virginia. He was a Judicial Fellow and Research Associate at the Supreme Court of the United States, a Fulbright Lecturer at Oxford University, held the Fulbright Chair for Senior Scholars at the University of Bologna, and a Fulbright Researcher in Japan, as well as a Visiting Fellow at the Russell Sage Foundation. Among his publications are *Storm Center: The Supreme Court in American Politics*, 6th ed. (2005); a two volume casebook, *Constitutional Law and Politics*, 5th ed. (2005); an annual *Supreme Court Watch;* and *Animal Sacrifice and Religious Freedom: Church of Lukumi Babablu Aye v. City of Hialeah* (2004). He received the American Bar Association's Silver Gavel Award for contributing to the public's understanding of the law.

Paul C. Light

Paul C. Light is currently the Paulette Goddard Professor of Public Service at New York University's Wagner School of Public Service and Douglas Dillon Senior Fellow at the Brookings Institution. Professor Light has a wide-ranging career in both academia and government. He has worked on Capitol Hill as a senior committee staffer in the U.S. Senate and as an American Political Science Association Congressional Fellow in the U.S. House. He has taught at the University of Virginia, University of Pennsylvania, and Harvard University's John F. Kennedy School of Government. He has also served as a senior adviser to several national commissions on federal, state, and local public service. He is the author of 15 books on government, public service, and public policy.

James MacGregor Burns

James MacGregor Burns is a Senior Scholar at the Academy of Leadership, University of Maryland, College Park. He has written numerous books, including *The Power to Lead* (1984), *The Vineyard of Liberty* (1982), *Leadership* (1979), *Roosevelt: The Soldier of Freedom* (1970), *The Deadlock of Democracy: Four-Party Politics in America* (1963), and *Roosevelt: The Lion and the Fox* (1956). With his son, Stewart Burns, he wrote *A People's Charter: The Pursuit of Rights in America* (1991); with Georgia Sorenson, *Dead Center: Clinton, Gore, and the Perils of Moderation* (2000); and with Susan Dunn, *The Three*

Roosevelts (2001). Burns is a past president of the American Political Science Association and winner of numerous prizes, including a Pulitzer Prize in History.

J.W. Peltason

J.W. Peltason is a leading scholar on the judicial process and public law. He is Professor Emeritus of Political Science at the University of California, Irvine. As past president of the American Council on Education, Peltason has represented higher education before Congress and state legislatures. His writings include *Federal Courts in the Political Process* (1955), *Fifty-Eight Lonely Men: Southern Federal Judges and School Desegration* (1961), and with Sue Davis, *Understanding the Constitution* (2000). Among his awards are the James Madison Medal from Princeton University, the Irvine Medal from the University of California, Irvine, and the American Political Science Association's Charles E. Merriam Award.

Thomas E. Cronin

Thomas E. Cronin is a leading student of the American presidency, leadership, and policy-making processes. He teaches at and serves as president of Whitman College. He was a White House Fellow and a White House aide and has served as president of the Western Political Science Association. His writings include *The State of the Presidency* (1980), *U.S. v. Crime in the Streets* (1981), *Direct Democracy: The Politics of Initiative, Referendum, and Recall* (1989), *Colorado Politics and Government* (1993), and *The Paradoxes of the American Presidency* (1998). Cronin is a past recipient of the American Political Science Association's Charles E. Merriam Award.

L. Tucker Gibson, Jr.

L. Tucker Gibson, Jr., is chair and professor of political science at Trinity University, where he teaches introductory courses in American national and state government as well as courses on U.S. legislatures, political parties, and interest groups. He has served on the Civil Service Commission of the city of San Antonio; assisted local governments across central and south Texas in redistricting their government bodies; and conducted public opinion research for political candidates, businesses, and corporations. Gibson is the coauthor of *Government and Politics in the Lone Star State: Theory and Practice*, 5th ed.

Clay Robison

Clay Robison has covered state government and politics in Texas for more than 30 years as a journalist, first for the *San Antonio Light*, and then, since 1982, for the *Houston Chronicle*. He is the *Houston Chronicle's* Austin bureau chief, and in addition to covering daily news events, he writes a weekly column that appears on the newspaper's Sunday editorial page. He has covered many of the personalities and events that are incorporated in the chapters on Texas government. Robison is the coauthor of *Government and Politics in the Lone Star State: Theory and Practice*, 5th ed.

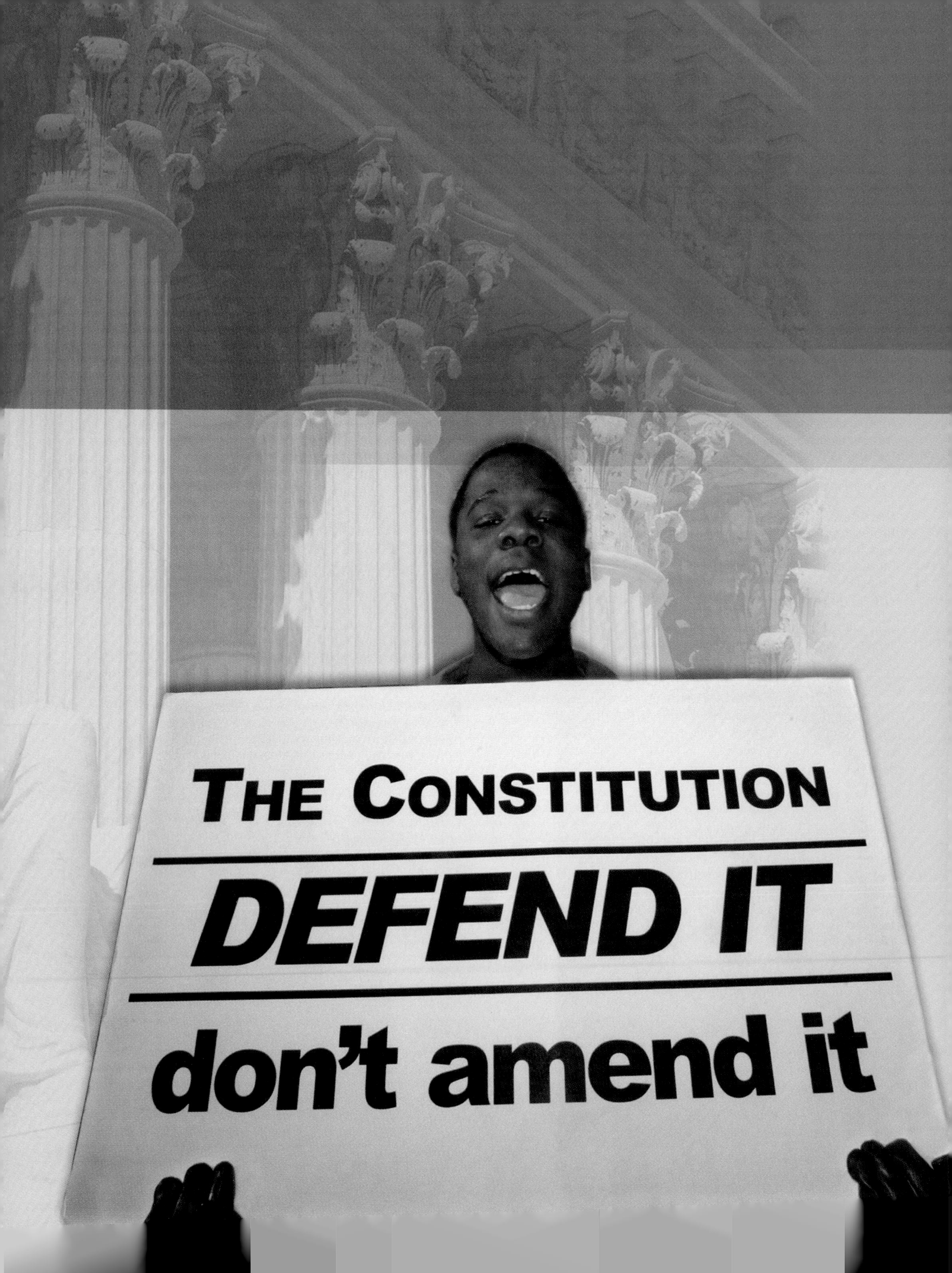
THE CONSTITUTION
DEFEND IT
don't amend it

CONSTITUTIONAL DEMOCRACY

1

The oldest constitutional democracy in the world, the United States of America, has survived for more than two centuries, yet it is still an experiment and a work in progress. We think of it as an enduring, strong government, but in a real sense, our constitutional political system is built on a fragile foundation. The U.S. Constitution and Bill of Rights survive not because the parchment they were written on is still with us but because each generation of Americans respects, renews, and works at understanding the principles and values found in these precious documents. Different generations have faced different challenges in preserving, protecting, and defending our way of government. Some have faced depressions, others world wars; most recently, Americans have confronted foreign attacks on domestic soil, terrorism around the world, and protracted war in Iraq and Afghanistan.

Terrorism on a global scale has become part of the daily news and a major concern of the American government. Before September 11, 2001, terrorist attacks seemed sporadic and far removed from the United States. The catastrophic attack on the World Trade Center in New York City and the Pentagon in Washington, D.C., made terrorism and security a preoccupation for many Americans. When asked to identify the most important problem facing our nation, terrorism and the economy are the most often mentioned problems. Voters are also concerned about moral values, as evidenced by the debate over same-sex marriage. But the war on terrorism and how best to wage it was the central theme of the 2004 election. The terrorist attacks of September 11, 2001, also changed our perceptions of domestic and international security. The government created the new Department of Homeland Security, increased spending on intelligence and security, and launched preemptive wars against terrorists and governments believed to pose a threat to the United States.

TIME LINE

CREATING THE REPUBLIC

1620	Mayflower Compact established the first basis in the new world for written laws
1775	Revolutionary War begins with battles at Lexington and Concord
1776	Declaration of Independence
1781	Articles of Confederation ratified—establishing the United States
1783	Revolutionary War ends with peace treaty with Great Britain
1786	Annapolis Convention calls for revision of the Articles of Confederation
1786–1787	Shays' Rebellion—poor farmers defy courts and state militia
1787	Constitutional Convention in Philadelphia
1787	Delaware becomes first state to ratify the Constitution
1788	Constitution ratified, replacing the Articles of Confederation
1789	Congress proposes the first amendments: the Bill of Rights

Let us define some of the basic terms we'll be using throughout this book. *Government* refers to the procedures and institutions (such as elections, courts, and legislatures) by which a people govern and rule themselves. *Politics* is the process by which people decide, at least in our system of government, who shall govern and what policies shall be adopted. Such processes invariably involve discussions, debates, and compromises over tactics and goals. *Politicians* are the people who fulfill the tasks of an operating government. Some politicians—legislators, mayors, and presidents—come to office through an election. Nonelected politicians may be political party officials or aides, advisers, or consultants to elected officials. *Political science* is the study of the principles, procedures, and structures of government and the analysis of political ideas, institutions, behavior, and practices.

In the aftermath of September 11, 2001, the United States took the offensive against Al-Qaeda by attacking its bases as well as removing the Taliban government in Afghanistan, which had supported Osama bin Laden. The war in Afghanistan successfully eradicated most terrorist camps and captured or killed many of the organization's leaders, but it failed to kill or capture bin Laden. The ability of bin Laden to evade U.S. forces and to periodically issue video or audio tapes calling for continuing hostilities highlights the problems of fighting individuals and groups like Al-Qaeda.

President Bush, who gained stature and public approval in the aftermath of the September 11 attacks on the United States, linked those attacks to the war in Afghanistan. Less than two months after the attacks on New York and Washington, D.C., President Bush said, "I have called our military into action to hunt down the members of the Al-Qaeda organization who murdered innocent Americans. I gave fair warning to the government that harbors them in Afghanistan. The Taliban made a choice to continue hiding terrorists, and now they are paying a price."[1] In a later speech he broadened the international dimension of the war on terrorism by referring to an "Axis of Evil" consisting of Iraq, Iran, and North Korea. All three of these totalitarian governments were thought to possess weapons of mass destruction and, in the cases of Iraq and Iran, were believed to be sponsoring terrorism. The U.N. weapons inspectors had been trying to determine whether Iraq possessed weapons of mass destruction. Frustrated with their inability to gain U.N. support, the United States and Britain went to war with Iraq largely on their own. Whether the United States should have waited until it had the endorsement and support of the United Nations or several more nations before going to war in Iraq will be debated for years to come.

Both the tone and style of President Bush's leadership alienated some European leaders, most notably in France and Germany. Great Britain, especially Prime Minister Tony Blair, was steadfast in support of the American approach of preemptive war in Iraq. More important to President Bush than his popularity abroad was securing his reelection in 2004, and a cornerstone of his reelection campaign was national security and his efforts to enhance it.

For the Democrats, the terrorist attacks of September 11 made criticizing President Bush much more difficult. A bipartisan coalition enacted legislation creating a homeland security department, authorizing the president to take action in Afghanistan and later Iraq, and appropriating the many billions of dollars to fund the military and nation-building expenses in Afghanistan and Iraq. Democratic presidential candidates were faced with the challenge of criticizing President Bush's policies without seeming to criticize our troops. One tack was to criticize the president's priorities in pursuing Saddam Hussein in Iraq rather than Osama bin Laden and Al-Qaeda. Some expressed support for the removal of Hussein; others opposed the war in Iraq. A common criticism among all the Democratic candidates was that President Bush and his administration had badly underestimated the challenges of establishing order and installing a new democratic government in Iraq. The steady stream of attacks on American and allied forces after President Bush had prematurely declared, "In the battle of Iraq, the United States and our allies have prevailed," underscored the Democrats' criticisms.

The Bush doctrine of using preemptive war against governments believed to pose a substantial risk to the United States and doing so even when others in the international community oppose the action will be much debated in the future. Also debated will be the extent of risk posed by Iraq, especially since the much feared weapons of mass destruction supposedly held by Iraq could not be found after the war; the impact on civil liberties of legislation like the U.S.A. Patriot Act, passed soon after September 11, 2001; who was responsible for the prison abuse in Iraq and Afghanistan; and questions about how to treat foreign nationals captured in the war on terrorism are also important topics.

One challenge for the United States in the post-Iraq war period is the way much of the rest of the world perceives us. In this book we will incorporate our analysis of innovative surveys of citizens from a large number of countries around the world on how our government and country are perceived. Americans like to think of themselves as popular around the world, especially in places like Germany and France where our government played a substantial role in the liberation of France in 1945 and in the reconstruction of the economies of both countries following World War II. We now find, however, that the differences in foreign policy approach between the United States and what Defense Secretary Rumsfeld labeled "old Europe" are substantial and may be enduring. In the minds of citizens in large parts of the Middle East, we are closely linked to Israel and therefore seen as an enemy.

The role of the United States and other prosperous countries in the international economy has also engendered backlash and protest. Because the U.S. economy is the world's largest, it has been the primary target of those concerned over the loss of local economic independence and the growing power of U.S. corporations and their products. Globalization concerns also include workers' rights and compensation and lower environmental standards in the developing world. Globalization is linked in part to the thinking of Osama bin Laden, who sharply criticizes the growing Western/American influence in the Islamic world and the impact this influence has had on culture and beliefs.

The terrorist threat raises important questions for American government. Should the response to terrorism and the threat of terrorism involve the United Nations or at least several countries? Should there be a multilateral approach, or should the United States go it alone if other countries choose not to participate, i.e., a unilateral approach? The Bush administration took the unilateral approach until the going got tough in Iraq and then seemed to shift to a more multilateral approach. The problem with a multilateral approach is that the United States will not have as much control as it does when it acts unilaterally. The problem with a unilateral approach is that the United States is left with the entire burden and expense of the operation, and should it fail the United States will be blamed.

Another consequence of the wars in Iraq and Afghanistan is their cost. Deficit spending, which had become the norm in American politics, ended during the Clinton years, and in the 2000 presidential election the candidates debated how to spend the budget surplus. President Bush, who campaigned promising a tax cut if elected, delivered on that promise. The "Bush" tax cut lowered individual income taxes by 1.3 trillion dollars over ten years. The wisdom of cutting taxes at the same time the nation was fighting a costly global war on terrorism was much debated before the 2004 election. The growing budget deficit and whether to make the "Bush" tax cut permanent were also debated. President Bush campaigned on the idea of making his tax cuts permanent to keep the economy expanding, estimating that the deficit would be cut in half within five years. Democratic standard-bearer John Kerry promised tax relief for the middle class while rolling back the Bush tax cut for high-income individuals. He also promised to reduce the deficit by half in five years.

More generally, economic issues were central to the 2004 election. Here the Republicans and President Bush were put on the defensive about the loss of jobs and the overall state of the economy. Several of the most competitive states in 2004 had experienced severe job loss. Ohio, Pennsylvania, Wisconsin, and Iowa were competitive in part because of the job loss issue. On domestic issues, Democrats and Republicans see things quite differently and the country is evenly divided. Republicans took credit for their success in enacting in 2003 a prescription drug benefit for older Americans, a program many Democrats criticized for its limitations and costs to seniors. Both parties in recent years have pushed a social policy initiative, often one long claimed by the other party. Bill Clinton's 1996 campaign touted his role in enacting welfare reform, and George W. Bush did the same with his "No Child Left Behind" education legislation and prescription drug benefits for seniors in 2002 and 2004.

Social issues, which were important to American politics in the 1970s and 1980s, were also important in 2004. Abortion and gay marriage were galvanizing issues on both the left and right. These issues also served to underscore the importance of the Supreme Court, which has ruled in recent years on these questions, often by narrow majorities. With several Supreme Court justices possibly considering retirement, the Court's future composition was the subject of campaign communications by both conservative and liberal groups.

Events of the past few years have reinforced the importance of government in setting priorities and making policies. It is also clear that who holds power makes a substantial difference in what government does or does not do. At the same time, the country's sharp divisions in partisanship and ideology, and the presence of constitutional checks and balances, make abrupt changes in direction unlikely.

AMERICAN GOVERNMENT AND POLITICIANS IN CONTEXT

The American Republic, founded on enduring values, has shown resiliency and adaptability. We have held 109 presidential and midterm elections (including the 2004 election), and we have witnessed the peaceful transfer of power from one party to another on dozens of occasions. The United States has succeeded in large part because Americans love their country, revere the Constitution, and respect the free enterprise system. We also believe that our differences are best reconciled by debate, compromise, and free elections. From an early age, we practice democracy in elementary school classrooms, and even though we may be critical of elected leaders, we recognize the need for political leadership. We also know that there are deep divisions and unsolved problems in the United States. Many people are concerned about the persistence of racism, about religious bigotry, about the gap in economic opportunities between rich and poor, and about the gun violence that disproportionately afflicts children and minorities. And we want our government, in addition to providing a defense against terrorism and foreign enemies, to provide basic health care and education as well as to address other domestic problems.

But what is this government of which we expect so much? The reality is that "government" is merely a shorthand term to refer to tens of thousands of our fellow Americans: the people we elect and the people they appoint to promote the general welfare, provide for domestic tranquillity, and secure the blessings of liberty for us.

More than any other form of government, the kind of democracy that has emerged under the U.S. Constitution requires active participation and a balance between faith and skepticism. Government by the people, however, does not require that *everyone* be involved in politics and policy making. Many citizens will always be too busy doing other things, and some people will always be apathetic toward government and politics. Government by the people does require a substantial segment of the public to be attentive, interested, involved, informed, and willing, when necessary, to criticize and change the direction of government.

Thomas Jefferson, one of our best-known champions of constitutional democracy, believed in the common sense of the people and in the flowering possibilities of the human spirit. Jefferson warned that every government degenerates when it is left only in the hands of the rulers. The people themselves, Jefferson wrote, are the only safe repositories of government. His was a robust commitment to popular control, representative processes, and accountable leadership. But he was no believer in the simple participatory democracy of ancient Greece or revolutionary France. The power of the people, too, must be restrained from time to time.

Government by the people requires faith concerning our common human enterprise, a belief that if the people are informed and caring, they can be trusted with their own self-government and an optimism that when things begin to go wrong, the people can be relied on to set them right. But a healthy skepticism is needed as well. Democracy requires us to question our leaders and never trust a group or institution that holds too much power. And even though constitutional advocates prize majority rule, they must remain skeptical about whether the majority is always right.

Constitutional democracy requires constant attention to protecting the rights and opinions of others, to ensure that our democratic processes are effectively serving the principles of liberty, equality, and justice. Thus a peculiar blend of faith and skepticism is warranted when dealing with the will of the people.

Thomas Jefferson.

Constitutional democracy is necessarily government by representative politicians. A central feature of democracy is that those who hold power do so only by winning a free election. In our political system, the fragmentation of powers requires elected officials to mediate among factions, build coalitions, and work out compromises among and within the branches of our government to produce policy and action.

We expect a lot from our politicians. We expect them to operate within the rules of democracy and to be honest, humble, patriotic, compassionate, sensitive to the needs of others, well informed, competent, fair-minded, self-confident, and inspirational. They must be candidates of all the people, not just of the ones with money.

Why does such a gap persist between our image of the ideal politician and our views about actual politicians? The gap exists in part because we have unrealistic expectations. We want politicians to be perfect, to have all the answers, and to have all the "correct" values (as we perceive them). We want politicians to solve our problems, yet we also want them to serve as scapegoats for the things we dislike about government: taxes, regulations, hard times, limits on our freedom. It is impossible for anyone to live up to these ideals. Like all individuals, politicians live in a world in which perfection may be the goal but compromise, ambition, fund raising, and self-promotion are necessary.

Americans will never be satisfied with their political candidates and politicians. The ideal politician is probably a fictional entity, for the perfect official would be able to please everyone, make conflict disappear, and not ask us to make any sacrifices. Politicians become "ideal" only when they are dead.

But the love of liberty invites disagreements of ideology and values. Politicians and candidates, as well as the people they represent, have different ideas about what is best for the nation. That's why we have politics, candidates, opposition parties, heated political debates, and elections.

"The Athenians are here, Sire, with an offer to back us with ships, money, arms, and men—and, of course, their usual lectures about democracy."

DEFINING DEMOCRACY

The word "democracy" is nowhere to be found in the Declaration of Independence or in the U.S. Constitution, nor was it a term used by the founders of the Republic. It is both a very old term and a modern one. It was used at the time of the founding of this nation to refer to various undesirables: mobs, lack of standards, and a system that encourages leaders to gain power by appealing to the emotions and prejudices of the rabble.

The distinguishing feature of democracy is that government derives its authority from its citizens. In fact, the word comes from two Greek words: *demos* (the people) and *kratos* (authority or power). Thus **democracy** means *government by the people*, not government by one person (a monarch, dictator, or priest) or government by the few (an oligarchy or aristocracy).

Ancient Athens and a few other Greek city-states had a **direct democracy** in which citizens came together to discuss and pass laws and select their rulers. These Greek city-states did not last. Most degenerated into mob rule and then resorted to dictators. When the word "democracy" came into use in English in the seventeenth century, it denoted this kind of direct democracy. It was a term of derision, a negative word, a reference to power wielded by an unruly mob.

James Madison, writing in *The Federalist,* No. 10, reflected the view of many of the framers of the U.S. Constitution when he wrote, "Such democracies [as the Greek and Roman] . . . have ever been found incompatible with personal security, or the rights of property; and have in general been as short in their lives, as they have been violent in their deaths" (*The Federalist,* No. 10, is reprinted in the Appendix at the back of this book).

Over time our democracy has become more and more of a combination of representative and direct democracy. The most important examples of direct democracy were added roughly a century ago and include the direct primary, which selects who may run for office; the initiative and referendum, which allow citizens to put to a vote of the people laws or constitutional amendments; and the recall, which allow voters to remove

democracy
Government by the people, either directly or indirectly, with free and frequent elections.

direct democracy
Government in which citizens vote on laws and select officials more directly.

elected officials from office between elections. There has been substantial growth in use of the initiative since the mid-1970s, and 2003 saw the first governor recalled in 82 years when California voters recalled Gray Davis and replaced him with Arnold Schwarzenegger.

Today it is no longer possible, even if desirable, to assemble the citizens of any but the smallest towns to make their laws or to select their officials directly from among the citizenry. Rather, we have invented a system of representation. Democracy today means **representative democracy**, or, to use Plato's term, a *republic*, in which those who have governmental authority get and retain authority directly or indirectly as a result of winning free elections in which all adult citizens are allowed to participate. The framers preferred to use the term "republic" to avoid any confusion between direct democracy, which they disliked, and representative democracy, which they liked and thought secured all the advantages of a direct democracy while curing its weaknesses. Today, as in this book, *democracy* and *republic* are used interchangeably.

In defining democracy, several other terms need to be clarified. **Constitutional democracy**, as used here, refers to a government in which the individuals who exercise substantial governmental powers do so as the result of winning free and relatively frequent elections. *It is a government in which there are recognized, enforced limits on the powers of all governmental officials.* It also generally involves a written set of governmental rules and procedures, a constitution.

Constitutionalism is a term we apply to arrangements—checks and balances, federalism, separation of powers, rule of law, due process, a bill of rights—that require our leaders to listen, think, bargain, and explain before they make laws. We then hold them politically and legally accountable for how they exercise their powers.

Like most political concepts, democracy encompasses many ideas and has many meanings. Democracy is a way of life, a form of government, a way of governing, a type of nation, a state of mind, and a variety of processes. We can divide these many meanings of democracy into three broad categories: a system of interacting values, a system of interrelated political processes, and a system of interdependent political structures.

Democracy as a System of Interacting Values

Belief in representative democracy may be as near a universal faith as the world has today. Respect for human dignity, freedom, liberty, individual rights, and other democratic values is widespread. The ideas of personal liberty, respect for the individual, equality of opportunity, and popular consent are at the core of democratic values. As the Taliban government in Afghanistan demonstrated, there are governments that not only suppress democratic values but find them threatening enough to terrorize governments that embrace them.

PERSONAL LIBERTY   Liberty has been the single most important value in American history. It was for "life, liberty, and the pursuit of happiness" that independence was declared; it was to "secure the Blessings of Liberty" that the Constitution was drawn up and adopted. Even our patriotic songs extol the "sweet land of liberty." The essence of liberty is *self-determination*, meaning that all individuals must have the opportunity to realize their own goals. Liberty is not simply the absence of external restraint on a person (freedom *from*); it is the individual's freedom and capacity to act positively to reach his or her goals (freedom *to*). Moreover, both history and reason suggest that individual liberty is the key to social progress. The greater the people's freedom, the greater the chance of discovering better ways of life.

RESPECT FOR THE INDIVIDUAL   Popular rule in a democracy flows from a belief that every individual has the potential for common sense, rationality, and fairness. Individuals have important rights; collectively, those rights are the source of all legitimate governmental authority and power. These concepts pervade all democratic thought. They are woven into the writings of Thomas Jefferson, especially in the Declaration of Independence: "All men . . . are endowed by their Creator with certain unalienable rights" (the Declaration of Independence is reprinted in the Appendix). Constitutional

representative democracy
Government that derives its powers indirectly from the people, who elect those who will govern; also called a *republic*.

constitutional democracy
A government that enforces recognized limits on those who govern and allows the voice of the people to be heard through free, fair, and relatively frequent elections.

constitutionalism
The set of arrangements, including checks and balances, federalism, separation of powers, rule of law, due process, and a bill of rights, that requires leaders to listen, think, bargain, and explain before they act or make laws. We then hold them politically and legally accountable for how they exercise their powers.

GLOBAL *Perceptions*

QUESTION: Which of these statements comes closer to your view: I like American ideas about democracy, OR I dislike American ideas about democracy?

Constitutional democracy as we practice it is not universally valued or appreciated around the world. In 2002, the Pew Charitable Trusts supported a worldwide public opinion survey of how people think about democracy, government, and public policy, generally. These studies help us appreciate how people in many nations view freedom, liberties, and democracy as well as other related topics. The Pew Global Survey asked representative samples of people in 44 countries whether they liked or disliked American-style democracy (see question at the beginning of this box).

China and Egypt were the only countries in which the researchers were not allowed to ask the question. American-style democracy was most liked in Africa, where the proportion saying they liked it exceeded the proportion saying they disliked it in all countries surveyed. In Kenya and Nigeria over 86 percent said they liked it. People in most Asian countries also tended to like it more than dislike it. However, in France 53 percent said they disliked it, and in Europe as a whole, the public was split fairly evenly. U.S. citizens tend to assume that our democracy is the envy of the world. In fact that is not the case. Countries in which 50 percent or more of the public disliked American ideas about democracy include: Jordan (69), Pakistan (60), Bolivia (60), France (53), Brazil (51), Turkey (50), and Argentina (50).

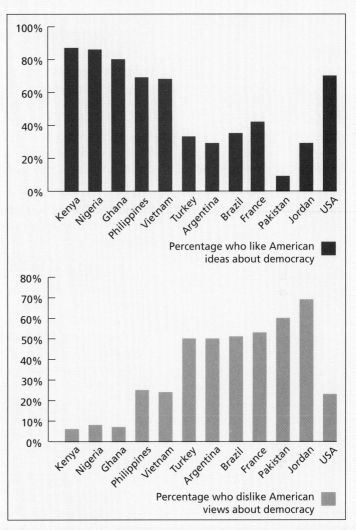

Source: Pew Research Center, *What the World Thinks in 2002*, p. T-55.

democracies make the *person*—rich or poor, black or white, male or female—the central measure of value.

Not all political systems put the individual first. Some promote **statism**, a form of government based on centralized authority and control, especially over the economy. Examples of countries with this approach include China and Cuba. In a modern democracy, the nation, or even the community, is less important than the individuals who compose it.

EQUALITY OF OPPORTUNITY The importance of the individual is enhanced by the democratic value of *equality:* "All men are created equal and from that equal creation they derive rights inherent and unalienable, among which are the preservation of liberty and the pursuit of happiness." So reads Jefferson's first draft of the Declaration of Independence, and the words indicate the primacy of the concept. Alexis de Tocqueville and other international visitors who have studied American democracy were all struck by the strength of egalitarian thought and practice in our political and social lives.

statism
The idea that the rights of the nation are supreme over the rights of the individuals residing in that nation.

But what does equality mean? Equality for whom? For blacks as well as whites? For women as well as men? For Native Americans, descendants of the Pilgrims, and recent immigrants? And what kind of equality? Economic, political, legal, social, or some other kind of equality? Equality of opportunity? Does equality of opportunity simply mean that everyone should have the same place at the starting line? Or does it mean an effort should be made to equalize the factors that determine how well a person fares economically or socially? These enduring issues arise often in our study of American politics.

POPULAR CONSENT   The animating principle of the American Revolution, the Declaration of Independence, and the resulting new nation was **popular consent**, the idea that a just government must derive its powers from the *consent of the people it governs.* A commitment to democracy thus entails a community's willingness to participate and make decisions in government. These principles sound unobjectionable intellectually, but in practice they mean that certain individuals or groups may not get their way. A commitment to popular consent must involve a willingness to lose when most people vote the other way.

DEMOCRATIC VALUES IN CONFLICT   The basic values of democracy do not always coexist happily. Individualism may conflict with the collective welfare or the public good. Self-determination may conflict with equal opportunity. For example, the right of a homeowner to add another floor to her home may conflict with the right of her neighbor to have an unobstructed view. Or the right of a person to smoke an after-dinner cigar in a restaurant may conflict with the right of others not to have to breathe tobacco smoke.

Much of our political combat revolves around how to strike a balance among democratic values, how to protect the Declaration of Independence's unalienable rights of life, liberty, and the pursuit of happiness while trying to "form," as the Constitution announces, "a more perfect Union, establish Justice, insure domestic Tranquility, provide for the common defence, promote the general Welfare, and secure the Blessings of Liberty to ourselves and our Posterity" (see the Preamble to the Constitution on page 46). Over the years, the American political system has moved, despite occasional setbacks, toward greater freedom and more democracy.

Expansion of democracy in the United States and elsewhere was in many ways a twentieth-century idea. Although on dozens of occasions in the past century, democracies collapsed and gave way to authoritarian regimes, even more democracies triumphed. Indeed, "the global range and influence of democratic ideas, institutions, and practices has made [the last century] far and away the most flourishing period for democracy."[2]

Democracy as a System of Interrelated Political Processes

Far more people dream about democracy than ever experience it, and many new democracies fail. To be successful, democratic government requires a well-defined political process as well as a stable governmental structure. To become reality, democratic values must be incorporated into a political process, most importantly in the form of free and fair elections, majority rule, freedom of expression, and the right to assemble and protest.

FREE AND FAIR ELECTIONS   Democratic government is based on free and fair elections held at intervals frequent enough to make them relevant to policy choices. Elections are one of the most important devices for keeping officials and representatives accountable.

We previously described representative democracy as a government in which those who have the authority to make decisions with the force of law acquire and retain this authority either directly or indirectly as the result of winning free elections in which the great majority of adult citizens are allowed to participate. Crucial to modern-day definitions of democracy is the idea that opposition political parties can exist, can run candidates in elections, and can at least have a chance to replace those who are currently

popular consent
The idea that a just government must derive its powers from the consent of the people it governs.

Free and fair elections are an important characteristic of democracies; however, participation requires time and patience, as is evident by these citizens standing in line to vote.

holding public office. Thus *political competition and choice* are crucial to the existence of democracy.

Although all citizens should have equal voting power, free and fair elections do not imply that everyone must or will have equal political influence. Some people, because of wealth, talent, or position, have more influence than others. How much extra influence key figures should be allowed to exercise in a democracy is frequently debated. But in an election, each citizen—president or plumber, corporate CEO or ditch digger—casts only one vote.

MAJORITY (PLURALITY) RULE **Majority rule**—governance according to the expressed preferences of the majority—is a basic rule of democracy. The **majority** candidate or party is the one that receives *more than half* the votes and so wins the election and takes charge of the government until the next election. In practice, however, majority rule is often **plurality** rule, in which the candidate or party with the *most* votes wins the election, even though it may not constitute a true majority of more than half the votes. About a third of our presidents have won with pluralities in the popular vote rather than majorities.[3] Once elected, officials do not have a right to curtail the attempts of political minorities to use all peaceful means to become the new majority. Even as the winners take power, the losers are at work to try to get it back at the next election.[4]

Should the side with the most votes prevail in all cases? Americans answer this question in a variety of ways. Some insist that majority views should be enacted into laws and regulations. However, an effective representative democracy involves far more than simply ascertaining and applying the statistical will of most of the people. In a constitutional democracy, the will of a majority of the people may not contradict the rights of individuals. For example, the Supreme Court stuck down a 1964 California initiative which would have allowed discrimination against minorities.[5] It is a more complicated and often untidy process in which the people and their agents debate, compromise, and arrive at a decision only after thoughtful deliberation.

The framers of the U.S. Constitution wanted to guard society against any one faction of the people acting unjustly toward any other faction of the people. The Constitution reflects their fear of tyranny by majorities, especially momentary majorities that spring from temporary passions. They insulated certain rights (such as freedom of speech) and institutions (such as the Supreme Court) from popular choice. Effective representation of the people, the framers insisted, should not be based solely on parochial interests or shifting breezes of opinion.

majority rule
Governance according to the expressed preferences of the majority.

majority
The candidate or party that wins more than half the votes cast in an election.

plurality
Candidate or party with the most votes cast in an election, not necessarily more than half.

FREEDOM OF EXPRESSION   Free and fair elections depend on access to information relevant to voting choices. Voters must have access to facts, competing ideas, and the views of candidates. Free and fair elections require a climate in which competing, nongovernment-owned newspapers, radio stations, and television stations can flourish. If the government controls what is said and how it is said, there is no democracy. Without free speech, there are no free and fair elections.

THE RIGHT TO ASSEMBLE AND PROTEST   Citizens must be free to organize for political purposes. Obviously, individuals can be more effective if they join with others in a party, a pressure group, a protest movement, or a demonstration. The right to oppose the government, to form opposition parties, and to have a chance of defeating incumbents is more than vital; it is a defining characteristic of a democracy.

Democracy as a System of Interdependent Political Structures

Democracy is, of course, more than values and processes. It also entails political structures that safeguard these values and processes. The Constitution and its first ten amendments (the Bill of Rights) set up an ingenious structure—one that both grants and checks government power. This constitutional structure is reinforced by a system of political parties, interest groups, media, and other institutions that intercede between the electorate and those who govern and thus help maintain democratic stability.

The U.S. constitutional system has five distinctive elements: *federalism,* the division of powers between the national and state governments; *separation of powers* among the

PEOPLE & POLITICS *Making a Difference* ★ ★ ★

JOAN BLADES AND WES BOYD AND MOVEON

One of the surprises of the 2004 election cycle was a group founded by a husband–wife team from Berkeley, California. The couple, Joan Blades and Wes Boyd, was not always politically active. Before founding MoveOn in 1998 as an e-mail campaign opposing the impeachment of President Clinton, the couple had been more concerned with software for handicapped persons and developing popular screen savers. In the 2000 campaign, MoveOn raised more than $2 million for Democratic candidates. But it was in the 2004 election cycle that MoveOn became more visible and important. As with the campaign of Howard Dean, Blades and Boyd tapped into a passionate public who were reachable through the Internet. Dean built his own Internet campaign on the MoveOn model.[*]

What Blades and Boyd demonstrated through MoveOn is that people could be organized for political purposes on a large scale through the medium of the Internet. The membership of MoveOn more than doubled during the months prior to the war in Iraq, a war MoveOn opposed, and continued to grow thereafter. MoveOn does not require a membership fee but does have a subscriber list which permits it to communicate messages and show its attention-getting ads. One major donor to MoveOn was George Soros, who pledged to provide the group with $2.5 million.[†] The group has fed off of controversy, including an ad criticizing President Bush that it tried unsuccessfully to run during the Super Bowl.[§]

Regardless of whether or not you agree with Boyd and Blades, their use of the Internet for organizing citizens, petitioning government, and raising political contributions has had an impact on American politics.

[*]Dan Gilgoff, "The Democrats' Internet Gain," *U.S. News and World Report,* October 6, 2003: p. 27.
[†]Editorial, "Mr. Soros' Millions," *The Washington Post,* November 23, 2003: p. B06.
[§]Jim Rutenberg, "Ad Rejections by CBS Raise Policy Questions," *The New York Times,* January 19, 2004: p. 7.

executive, judicial, and legislative branches; *bicameralism,* the division of legislative power between two institutions — the House of Representatives and the Senate; *checks and balances* in which each branch is given the constitutional means, the political independence, and the motives to check the powers of the other branches; and a judicially enforceable, written, explicit *Bill of Rights* that provides a guarantee of individual liberties and due process before the law.

Conditions Conducive to Constitutional Democracy

Although it is hard to specify the precise conditions that are essential for the establishment and maintenance of a democracy, here are a few things we have learned.

EDUCATIONAL CONDITIONS   The exercise of voting privileges takes some level of education on the part of the citizenry. But a high level of education does not guarantee democratic government, as the example of Nazi Germany readily illustrates. And there are some democracies, such as India, where large numbers of people are illiterate. Still, voting makes little sense unless a considerable number of the voters can read and write and express their interests and opinions. The poorly educated and illiterate often get left out in a democracy. Direct democracy puts a further premium on education. Better educated persons are more able to understand and participate in policy making through initiatives and referendums.[6]

ECONOMIC CONDITIONS   A relatively prosperous nation, with an equitable distribution of wealth, provides the best context for democracy. Starving people are more interested in food than in voting. Where economic power is concentrated, political power is likely to be concentrated. Well-to-do nations have a greater chance of sustaining democratic governments than those with widespread poverty do. The reality is that extremes of wealth and poverty undermine the possibilities for a healthy constitutional democracy. Thus the prospects for an enduring democracy are greater in Canada or France than in Rwanda, Zimbabwe, or Mongolia.

Some measure of private ownership of property and a relatively favorable role for the market economy are also related to the creation and maintenance of democratic institutions. Democracies can range from heavily regulated economies with public ownership of many enterprises, such as Sweden, to those in which there is little government regulation of the marketplace. But there are no democracies with a highly centralized government-run economy and little private ownership of property, although there are many nations with a market economy and no democracy. There are no truly democratic communist states, nor have there ever been any.

SOCIAL CONDITIONS   Economic development generally makes democracy possible, yet proper social conditions are necessary to make it real.[7] In a society fragmented into warring groups that differ fiercely on fundamental issues, government by discussion and compromise is difficult, as we have seen in the Balkans and more recently in Afghanistan and Iraq. When ideologically separated groups consider the issues at stake to be vital, they may prefer to fight rather than accept the verdict of the ballot box.

In a society that consists of many overlapping associations and groupings, however, individuals are not as likely to identify completely with a single group and give their allegiance to it. For example, Joe Smith is a Baptist, an African American, a southerner, a Democrat, an electrician, and a member of the National Rifle Association, and he makes $50,000 a year. On some issues, Joe thinks as a Baptist, on others as a southerner, and on still others as an African American. Sue Jones is a Catholic, a white Republican, an auto dealer, and a member of the National Organization for Women (NOW); she comes from a Polish background, and she makes $150,000 a year. Sometimes she acts as a Republican, sometimes as an American of Polish descent, and sometimes as a member of NOW. Jones and Smith differ on some issues and agree on others. In general, the differences between them are not likely to be greater than their common interest in maintaining a democracy.[8]

IDEOLOGICAL CONDITIONS   **Ideology** refers to basic beliefs about power, government, and political practices—beliefs that arise out of the educational, economic, and social

ideology
A consistent pattern of beliefs about political values and the role of government.

★★ YOU DECIDE

In 2003 California voters decided to remove Governor Gray Davis from office. Davis had been elected in 2002, only eleven months before the recall. The process of recall is triggered by voters signing petitions, and if enough valid signatures are gathered to meet a specified threshold, a recall election is held. U.S. Representative Darrell Issa, a wealthy conservative from Southern California, spent $2 million of his own money to hire signature collectors, which greatly helped the 2003 recall effort meet the signature threshold. Proponents of the recall contend that it provides a means for voters to maintain greater control over politicians while opponents of the recall contend that the normal election process provides ample opportunity to remove politicians from office. What do you think? Does the recall enhance or detract from constitutional democracy?

conditions individuals experience. Out of these conditions must also develop a general acceptance of the ideals of democracy and a willingness of a substantial part of the people to agree to proceed democratically. This acceptance is sometimes called the *democratic consensus.*

THE CONSTITUTIONAL ROOTS OF THE AMERICAN EXPERIMENT

Americans often take democracy for granted. Most of us probably consider it inevitable. We take pride in our ability to make it work, yet we have essentially inherited a functioning system. Its establishment was the work of others, nine or ten generations ago. The challenge for us is not just to keep it going but to improve it and make it adapt to the challenges of our times. To do so, however, we must first understand it, and this requires systematic consideration of our democratic and constitutional roots.

The Colonial Beginnings

There were many reasons one might have expected our democratic experiment to fail. The 13 original states (formerly colonies) were independent and could have gone their separate ways. Sectional differences based on social and economic conditions, especially the southern states' dependence on slavery, were an obvious problem. Religious, ethnic, and racial diversity, which challenges so many governments around the world today, existed to a substantial degree in the United States during its formative years.

Given these potential problems, how did democracy survive? How did this nation establish democratic principles for its government? How did it limit potential abuses? These questions are of importance not only to Americans but also to all others who value freedom and democracy. The United States has been a world leader in promoting the use of democratic institutions, in effect universalizing its successful experiment.

In 2003, Californians voted in a recall election to remove Democratic Governor Gray Davis from office and to replace him with Republican Arnold Schwartzenegger (left). U.S. Representative Darrell Issa (right) spent $2 million of his own money to spearhead the recall effort.

The framers of the U.S. Constitution had experience to guide them. For almost two centuries, Europeans had been sailing to the New World in search of liberty—especially religious liberty—as well as land and work. While still aboard the *Mayflower,* the Pilgrims drew up a compact to protect their religious freedom and to make possible "just and equal laws." In the American colonies, editors found they could speak freely in their newspapers, dissenters could distribute leaflets, and agitators could protest in taverns or in the streets.

But the picture of freedom in the colonies was mixed. The Puritans in Massachusetts soon established a **theocracy**, a system of government in which religious leaders claimed divine guidance and in which certain religious sects were denied religious liberty. Dissenters were occasionally chased out of town, and some printers were beaten and had their shops closed. In short, the colonists struggled with the balance between unity and diversity, stability and dissent, order and liberty. Puritans continued to worry "about what would maintain order in a society lacking an established church, an attachment to place, and the uncontested leadership of men of merit."[9] Nine of the 13 colonies eventually set up a state church. Throughout the 1700s, Puritans in Massachusetts barred certain men from voting on the basis of church membership. To the Anglican establishment in Virginia, campaigns for toleration were in themselves subversive. Women and slaves could not vote at all.

The Rise of Revolutionary Fervor

As resentment against British rule mounted during the 1770s and revolutionary fervor rose, Americans became determined to fight the British to win their rights and liberties. A year after the fighting broke out in Massachusetts, the Declaration of Independence proclaimed in ringing tones that all men are created equal, endowed by their Creator with certain unalienable rights; that among them are "life, liberty, and the pursuit of happiness"; that to secure those rights, governments are instituted among men; and that whenever a government becomes destructive of those ends, it is the right of the people to alter or abolish it. (Read the full text of the Declaration of Independence in the Appendix.)

We have all heard these great ideals so often that we take them for granted. Revolutionary leaders did not. They were deadly serious about these rights and willing to fight and pledge their lives, fortunes, and sacred honor for them. Indeed, by signing the Declaration of Independence they were effectively signing their own death warrants if the Revolution failed.[10] Bills of rights in the new state constitutions guaranteed free speech, freedom of religion, and the natural rights to life, liberty, and property. All their constitutions spelled out the rights of persons accused of crime, such as knowing the nature of the accusation, being confronted by their accusers, and receiving a timely and public trial by jury.[11] Moreover, these guarantees were set out *in writing*, in sharp contrast to the unwritten British constitution.

Toward Unity and Order

As the war against the British widened, the need arose for a stronger central government that could pull the colonies together and conduct a revolutionary war. For a time, the Continental Congress, which had led the way toward revolution, tried to direct hostilities against the British, but it took a man of George Washington's iron resolve to unify and direct the war effort. Sensing the need for more unity, Congress established a new national government under a written document called the **Articles of Confederation**. At first hardly worthy of the term "government," the Articles were not approved by all the state legislatures until 1781, after Washington's troops had been fighting for six years.

This new Confederation was a move toward a stronger central government, but a limited and inadequate one. Having fought a war against a strong central government in London, Americans were understandably reluctant to create another one, so the Articles established a fragile league of friendship rather than a national government. From

★★ THINKING IT THROUGH

The California recall effort and all the media attention to it highlighted the reality that large numbers of Californians, including many Democrats, were disappointed with Gray Davis and his lack of leadership. The high turnout demonstrated that voters will participate in a high profile recall election held at a time different from other elections. While it placed a new governor in office it did not allow voters to change other elected offices at the same time, and thus the new Governor must work with the previously elected legislature and other state officials.

One concern about the recall process is that it may make elected officials timid and indecisive because of the fear that if they act they might trigger a recall against them. Another concern is that interest groups on all sides that have resources can hire signature gatherers to force a recall election. But to be successful, a group must not only qualify a recall for the ballot, it must get a majority to vote to remove the incumbent.

Understanding the recall process and choosing from among so many possible candidates in an election like the 2003 California recall election is difficult and may have been confusing for some. The intense media coverage and the presence of a high-profile movie star candidate in 2003 mitigated these problems, but if recall elections become commonplace they could be a concern in the future.

theocracy
Government by religious leaders, who claim divine guidance.

Articles of Confederation
The first governing document of the confederated states, drafted in 1777, ratified in 1781, and replaced by the present Constitution in 1789.

**WEAKNESSES OF THE
ARTICLES OF CONFEDERATION**

1. Congress had no direct authority over citizens but had to work through the states; it could not pass laws or levy taxes to carry out its responsibilities to defend the nation and promote its well-being.
2. Congress could not regulate trade between the states or with other nations. States taxed each other's goods and even negotiated their own trade agreements with other nations.
3. Congress could not forbid the states from issuing their own currencies, further complicating interstate trade and travel.
4. Congress had to handle all administrative duties because there was no executive branch.
5. The lack of a judicial system meant that the national government had to rely on state courts to enforce national laws and settle disputes between the states. In practice, state courts could overturn national laws.

Annapolis Convention
A convention held in September 1786 to consider problems of trade and navigation, attended by five states and important because it issued the call to Congress and the states for what became the Constitutional Convention.

Constitutional Convention
The convention in Philadelphia, May 25 to September 17, 1787, that framed the Constitution of the United States.

Shays' Rebellion
Rebellion by farmers in western Massachusetts in 1786–1787, protesting mortgage foreclosures; led by Daniel Shays and important because it highlighted the need for a strong national government just as the call for the Constitutional Convention went out.

1777 to 1788, Americans made progress under the Confederation, but with the end of the war in 1783, the sense of urgency that had produced unity began to fade. Conflicts between creditors and debtors in the various states grew intense. Foreign threats continued; territories ruled by England and Spain surrounded the new nation, which, internally divided and lacking a strong central government, made a tempting prize.

As pressures on the Confederation mounted, many leaders became convinced it would not be enough merely to revise the Articles of Confederation. To create a union strong enough to deal with internal diversity and factionalism as well as to resist external threats, a stronger central government was needed.

In September 1786, under the leadership of Alexander Hamilton, supporters of a truly national government took advantage of the **Annapolis Convention**—a meeting in Annapolis, Maryland, on problems of trade and navigation attended by delegates from five states—to issue a call for a convention that would have full authority to consider basic amendments to the Articles of Confederation. The delegates in Annapolis asked the legislatures of all the states to appoint commissioners to meet in Philadelphia on the second Monday of May 1787, "to devise such further provisions as shall appear to them necessary to render the Constitution of the Federal Government adequate to the exigencies of the Union." The convention they called for became the **Constitutional Convention**.

For a short time, all was quiet. Then, late in 1786, messengers rode into George Washington's plantation at Mount Vernon with the kind of news he and other leaders had dreaded. Farmers in western Massachusetts, crushed by debts and taxes, were rebelling against foreclosures, forcing judges out of their courtrooms, and freeing debtors from jails. Washington was appalled. "What, gracious God, is man?" he exclaimed. Ten years before, he had been leading Americans in a patriotic war against the British, and now Americans were fighting Americans!

Not all Americans reacted as Washington did to what became known as **Shays' Rebellion** after Daniel Shays, its leader. When Abigail Adams, the politically knowledgeable wife of John Adams, sent news of the rebellion to Thomas Jefferson, the Virginian replied. "I like a little rebellion now and then," noting also that the "tree of liberty must be refreshed from time to time with the blood of patriots and tyrants. It is its natural manure."[12]

Shays' Rebellion petered out after the farmers attacked an arsenal and were cut down by cannon fire. Yet this "little rebellion" sent a stab of fear into the established leadership. It also acted as a catalyst. The message was now plain: Action must be taken to strengthen the machinery of government. Seven states appointed commissioners to attend the Philadelphia convention to strengthen the Articles of Confederation. Congress finally issued a cautiously worded call to all the state legislatures to appoint delegates for the "sole and express purpose of revising the Articles of Confederation." The suspicious congressional legislators specified that no recommendation would be effective unless approved by Congress and confirmed by all the state legislatures, as provided by the Articles.

THE CONSTITUTIONAL CONVENTION OF 1787

The delegates who assembled in Philadelphia that May had to establish a national government powerful enough to prevent the young nation from dissolving but not so powerful that it would crush individual liberty. What these men did continues to have a major impact on how we are governed. It also provides an outstanding lesson in political science for the world.

The Delegates

Seventy-four delegates were appointed by the various states, but only 55 arrived in Philadelphia. Of these, approximately 40 actually took part in the work of the convention. It was a distinguished gathering. Many of the most important men of the nation were there: successful merchants, planters, bankers, lawyers, and former and present governors and congressional representatives (39 of the delegates had served in Congress). Most had read the classics of political thought. Most had participated vigorously in the practical task of constructing local and state governments. Many had also worked hard to create and direct the national Confederation of the states. And 8 of the 56 signers of the Declaration of Independence were present at the Constitutional Convention.

The convention was as representative as most political gatherings at the time: The participants were all white male landowners. These well-read, well-fed, well-bred, and often well-wed delegates were mainly state or national leaders, for in the 1780s, ordinary people were not likely to participate in politics. (Even today, farm laborers, factory workers, and truck drivers are seldom found in Congress, although a haberdasher, a peanut farmer, and a movie actor have made their way to the White House.)

Although active in the movement to revise the Articles of Confederation, George Washington had been reluctant to attend the convention. He accepted only when persuaded that his prestige was needed for its success. He was selected unanimously to preside over the meetings. According to the records, he spoke only twice during the

PEOPLE & POLITICS *Making a Difference* ★ ★ ★

ALEXANDER HAMILTON AND JAMES MADISON

In the Constitution of the United States, the framers offered perhaps the most brilliant example of collective intellectual genius (combining theory and practice) in the history of the Western world. How could such a sparsely populated country by today's standards produce several dozen men of genius in Philadelphia and probably another hundred or so equally talented political thinkers who did not attend? The lives of two prominent delegates, Alexander Hamilton and James Madison, help explain the origins of this collective genius.

Alexander Hamilton had been the engineer of the Annapolis Convention, and as early as 1778, he had been urging that the national government be made stronger. Hamilton had come to the United States from the West Indies and while still a college student had won national attention for his brilliant pamphlets in defense of the Revolutionary cause. During the war, he served as General Washington's aide, and his experiences confirmed his distaste for a Congress so weak it could not even supply the Revolution's troops with enough food or arms.

James Madison was only 36 years old at the time of the convention, yet he was

Alexander Hamilton.

James Madison.

one of its most learned members. He had helped frame Virginia's first constitution and had served both in the Virginia Assembly and in the Continental Congress. Madison was also a leader of those who favored the establishment of a stronger national government.

Like most of the other framers, Hamilton and Madison were superbly educated. Both had extensive private tutoring—a one-to-one teacher–student ratio. Like scores of other thinkers of the day, both combined extensive practical experience with their schooling. Both

were active in their political and religious groups; both took part in political contests and electoral struggles; both helped build political coalitions.

Both men were "moral philosophers" as well as political thinkers. They had strong views on the supreme value of liberty as well as on current issues. Instead of simply sermonizing about liberty, they analyzed it; they debated what kind of liberty, how to protect it, and how to expand it.

Representing different constituencies and different ideologies, the Constitutional Convention devised a totally new form of government that provided for a central government strong enough to rule but still responsible to its citizens and to the member states.

deliberations, yet his influence was felt in the informal gatherings as well as during the sessions. Everyone understood that Washington favored a more powerful central government led by a president. The general expectation that Washington would likely be the first president played a crucial role in the creation of the presidency. "No one feared that he would misuse power. . . . His genuine hesitancy, his reluctance to assume the position, only served to reinforce the almost universal desire that he do so."[13]

The proceedings of the convention were kept secret. To encourage everyone to speak freely, delegates were forbidden to discuss the debates with outsiders. It was feared that if a delegate publicly took a firm stand on an issue, it would be harder for him to change his mind after debate and discussion. The delegates also knew that if word of the inevitable disagreements got out, it would provide ammunition for the many enemies of the convention. There were critics of this secrecy rule, but without it, agreement might not have been possible.

Consensus

The Constitutional Convention is usually discussed in terms of its three famous compromises: the compromise between large and small states over representation in Congress, the compromise between North and South over the regulation and taxation of foreign commerce, and the compromise between North and South over the counting of slaves for the purpose of taxation and representation. There were many other important compromises; yet on many significant issues, most of the delegates were in agreement.

Although a few delegates might have privately favored a limited monarchy, all supported a republican form of government based on elected representatives of the people. This was the only form seriously considered and the only form acceptable to the nation. Equally important, all the delegates opposed arbitrary and unrestrained government.

The common philosophy accepted by most of the delegates was that of *balanced government*. They wanted to construct a national government in which no single interest would dominate. Because most of the delegates represented citizens who were alarmed by the tendencies of desperate farmers to interfere with the property rights of others, they were primarily concerned with balancing the government in the direction of protection for property and business.

Benjamin Franklin, the 81-year-old delegate from Pennsylvania, favored extending the right to vote to all white males, but most of the delegates believed that owners of land were the best guardians of liberty. James Madison feared that those without property, if given the right to vote, might combine to deprive property owners of their rights. Delegates agreed in principle on limited voting rights but differed over the kind and amount of property one must own in order to vote. Because states were in the process of relaxing qualifications for the vote, the framers recognized that they would jeopardize approval of the constitution if they made the qualifications to vote in federal elections more restrictive than those of the states. As a result, each state was left to determine the qualifications for electing members of the House of Representatives, the only branch of the national government that was to be elected directly by the voters.

Within five days of its opening, the convention—with only the Connecticut delegates dissenting—voted that "a national government ought to be established consisting of a supreme legislative, executive, and judiciary." This decision to establish a supreme national government profoundly altered the nature of the union from a loose confederation of states to a true nation.

Few dissented from proposals to give the new Congress all the powers of the old Congress plus all other powers necessary to ensure that the integrity of the United States would not be challenged by state legislation. The framers agreed that a strong executive, which had been lacking under the Articles of Confederation, was necessary to provide energy and direction. An independent judiciary was also accepted without much debate. Other issues, however, sparked considerable conflict.

Conflict and Compromise

There were serious differences among the various delegates, especially between those from the large and small states. The conflict between the large and small states ensued before the Constitutional Convention. With the success of the War of Independence, the United States gained the formerly British land west of the colonial borders. States with large western borders like Virginia claimed that their borders should simply be extended further west, as depicted in the accompanying map. Landlocked colonies like New Jersey and Connecticut took exception to the claims of colonies with western borders like Virginia, reinforcing the tension between the colonies. The matter was resolved in the Land Ordinance of 1785 and Northwest Ordinance of 1787 when all states agreed to cede the Western lands to the national government and permit the newly acquired land to become part of new states rather than expand the border of preexisting states. But the rivalries between the former colonies were very much a part of the politics at the Convention in Philadelphia in 1787. For example, the large states also favored a strong national government (which they expected they could dominate), while delegates from small states were anxious to avoid being dominated (see Figure 1–1).

This tension surfaced in the first discussions of representation in Congress. Franklin favored a single-house national legislature, but most states had had two-chamber legislatures since colonial times, and the delegates were used to the system. **Bicameralism**—the principle of the two-house legislature—reflected delegates' belief in the need for balanced government. The Senate, the smaller chamber, would represent the states, and to some extent the aristocracy, and offset the larger, more democratic House of Representatives.

THE VIRGINIA PLAN The Virginia delegation took the initiative. Its members had met before the convention, and as soon as it was convened, they presented 15 resolutions. These resolutions, known as the **Virginia Plan**, called for a strong central government with a legislature composed of two chambers. The members of the more representative chamber were to be elected by the voters; those of the smaller and more aristocratic chamber were to be chosen by the larger chamber from nominees submitted by the state legislatures. Representation in both houses would be based on either wealth or

"Remember, gentlemen, we aren't here just to draft a constitution. We're here to draft the best damn constitution in the world."

bicameralism
The principle of a two-house legislature.

Virginia Plan
Initial proposal at the Constitutional Convention made by the Virginia delegation for a strong central government with a bicameral legislature, the lower house to be elected by the voters and the upper chosen by the lower.

FIGURE 1–1 Western Expansion, 1791.

numbers, which would give the wealthier and more populous states—Massachusetts, Pennsylvania, and Virginia—a majority in the national legislature.

The Congress thus created was to be given all the legislative power of its predecessor under the Articles of Confederation, as well as the right "to legislate in all cases in which the separate States are incompetent." Further, it was to have the authority to veto state legislation that conflicted with the proposed constitution. The Virginia Plan also called for a national executive with extensive jurisdiction who would be chosen by the legislature. A national Supreme Court, along with the executive, was to have a qualified veto over acts of Congress.

THE NEW JERSEY PLAN The Virginia Plan dominated the discussion for the first few weeks. But by June 15, additional delegates from the small states arrived, and they began a counterattack. They rallied around William Paterson of New Jersey, who presented a series of resolutions known as the **New Jersey Plan**. Table 1-1 outlines the key features of both plans. Paterson did not question the need for a strengthened central government, but he was concerned about how this strength might be used. The New Jersey Plan would give Congress the right to tax and regulate commerce and to coerce states,

New Jersey Plan
Proposal at the Constitutional Convention made by William Paterson of New Jersey for a central government with a single-house legislature in which each state would be represented equally.

TABLE 1–1   THE VIRGINIA AND NEW JERSEY PLANS

Virginia Plan	*New Jersey Plan*
Legitimacy derived from citizens, based on popular representation	Derived from states, based on equal votes for each state
Bicameral legislature	Unicameral legislature
Executive size undetermined, elected and removable by Congress	More than one person, removable by state majority
Judicial life-tenure, able to veto state legislation	No power over states
Legislature can override state laws	Government can compel obedience to national laws
Ratification by citizens	Ratification by states

and it would retain the single-house unicameral legislature (as under the Articles of Confederation) in which each state, regardless of size, would have the same vote.

The New Jersey Plan contained the germ of what eventually came to be a key provision of our Constitution: the *supremacy clause.* The national Supreme Court was to hear appeals from state judges, and the supremacy clause would require all judges— state and national—to treat laws of the national government and the treaties of the United States as superior to the constitutions and laws of each of the states.

To adopt the Virginia Plan—which would create a powerful national government dominated by Massachusetts, Pennsylvania, and Virginia and eliminate the states as important units of government—would guarantee that many of the other states would reject the new constitution. Still, the large states resisted, and for a time the convention was deadlocked. The small states believed that all states should be represented equally in Congress, especially in the smaller "upper house" if there were to be two chambers. The large states insisted that representation in both houses be based on population or wealth and that national legislators be elected by voters rather than by state legislatures. Finally, the so-called Committee of Eleven was elected to devise a compromise. On July 5, it presented its proposals.

THE CONNECTICUT COMPROMISE   Because of the prominent role of the Connecticut delegation in constructing this plan, it has since been known as the **Connecticut Compromise**. It called for one house in which each state would have an equal vote and a second house in which representation would be based on population and in which all bills for raising or appropriating money would originate. This proposal was a setback for the large states, which agreed to it only when the smaller states made it clear this was their price for union. After equality of state representation in the Senate was accepted, most objections to a strong national government dissolved.

NORTH-SOUTH COMPROMISES   Other issues split the delegates from the North and South. Southerners were afraid a northern majority in Congress might discriminate against southern trade. They had some basis for this concern. John Jay, secretary of foreign affairs for the Confederation, had proposed a treaty with Great Britain that would have given advantages to northern merchants at the expense of southern exporters. To protect themselves, the southern delegates insisted that a two-thirds majority be required in the Senate before the president could ratify a treaty.

Differences between the North and South were also evident on the issue of representation in the House of Representatives. The question was whether to count slaves for the purpose of apportioning seats in the House. The South wanted to count slaves, thereby enlarging its number of representatives; the North resisted. After heated debate, the delegates agreed on the **three-fifths compromise**. Each slave would be counted

Connecticut Compromise
Compromise agreement by states at the Constitutional Convention for a bicameral legislature with a lower house in which representation would be based on population and an upper house in which each state would have two senators.

three-fifths compromise
Compromise agreement between northern and southern states at the Constitutional Convention that three-fifths of the slave population would be counted for determining direct taxation and representation in the House of Representatives.

as three-fifths of a free person for the purposes of apportionment in the House and of direct taxation; this fraction was chosen because it maintained a balance of power between North and South. The issue of balance would recur in the early history of our nation as territorial governments were established and territories applied for statehood.

OTHER ISSUES   Delegates found other issues to argue about. Should the national government have lower courts, or would one federal Supreme Court be enough? This issue was resolved by postponing the decision. The Constitution states that there shall be one Supreme Court and that Congress may establish lower courts.

How should the president be selected? For a long time, the convention accepted the idea that the president should be chosen by Congress, but the delegates feared that Congress would dominate the president, or vice versa. Election by the state legislatures was rejected because the delegates distrusted the state legislatures. Finally, the electoral college system was devised. This was perhaps the most novel and most contrived contribution of the delegates and has long been one of the most criticized provisions in the Constitution.[14] (See Article II, Section 1, of the Constitution, which is reprinted between Chapters 2 and 3.)

After three months, the delegates stopped debating. On September 17, 1787, they assembled for an impressive ceremony of signing the document they were recommending to the nation. All but three of those still present signed; others who opposed the general drift of the convention had already left. Their work well done, delegates adjourned to the nearby City Tavern to celebrate.

According to an old story, Benjamin Franklin was confronted by a woman as he left the last session of the convention.

"What kind of government have you given us, Dr. Franklin?" she asked. "A republic or a monarchy?"

"A republic, Madam," he answered, "if you can keep it."

★★ IN COMPARATIVE PERSPECTIVE ★★

THE NEW CONSTITUTION IN AFGHANISTAN: BALANCING ISLAM AND DEMOCRACY

In December 2001, following the collapse of the Taliban regime in Afghanistan, several Afghan groups met under United Nations guidance to begin planning for democracy in Afghanistan. Their agreement, called the Bonn Agreement, set in motion the election of a transitional government, a nine-member Constitutional Drafting Commission and a larger Constitutional Commission of thirty-five members which revised the draft constitution and conducted hearings in the provinces and among refugees.

The new constitution ratified by Loya Jirga in 2004 combines Islamic and democratic values, and guarantees basic liberties, with elections to follow. Examples of the Islamic nature of the new constitution are that it declares Afghanistan an Islamic Republic and makes Islam the official religion of the country. The constitution mandates that laws under the new constitution may not be contrary to Islam. An example of

the pervasiveness of Islam in the new constitution is the mandate that a school curriculum must be "based on the provisions of the sacred religion of Islam, national culture, and in accordance with academic principles."[*]

At the same time, the new Afghan constitution guarantees fundamental rights and promises government "based on the people's will and democracy." It notes that Afghanistan is committed to the United Nations Charter and Universal Declaration of Human Rights. The new constitution ensures that women will make up at least 16.5 percent of the membership of the upper legislative house and otherwise guarantees women's rights against discrimination. While Islam is the official state religion, the constitution allows non-Muslims to practice their religion.

This blending of Islam and democracy breaks new ground in the Middle East. Turkey, which has a largely Muslim population, has a largely secular government. The lessons learned in Afghanistan may one day be applied elsewhere in the region.

[*]AfghanGovernment, n.d, "Afghan Draft Constitution: 2004," http://www.afghangovernment.com/2004constitution.htm. 30 December 2003.

TO ADOPT OR NOT TO ADOPT?

The delegates had gone far. Indeed, they had wholly disregarded Congress's instruction to do no more than revise the Articles. They had ignored Article XIII of the Articles of Confederation, which declared the Union to be perpetual and prohibited any alteration of the Articles unless agreed to by Congress and by *every one of the state legislatures*—a provision that had made it impossible to amend the Articles. The convention delegates, however, boldly declared that their newly proposed Constitution should go into effect when ratified by popularly elected conventions in nine states.

They turned to this method of ratification for practical considerations as well as for reasons of securing legitimacy for their newly proposed government. Not only were the delegates aware that there was little chance of winning approval of the new Constitution in all state legislatures; many also believed the Constitution should be ratified by an authority higher than a legislature. A constitution based on approval *by the people* would have higher legal and moral status. The Articles of Confederation had been a compact of state governments, but the Constitution was based on the people (recall its opening words: "We the People . . ."). Still, even this method of ratification would not be easy. The nation was not ready to adopt the Constitution without a thorough debate.

Federalists Versus Antifederalists

Supporters of the new government, by cleverly appropriating the name **Federalists**, took some of the sting out of charges they were trying to destroy the states and establish an all-powerful central government. By calling their opponents **Antifederalists**, they pointed up the negative character of the arguments of those who opposed ratification.

The split was in part geographic. Seaboard and city regions tended to be Federalist strongholds; backcountry regions from Maine (then a part of Massachusetts) through Georgia, inhabited by farmers and other relatively poor people, were generally Antifederalist. But as in most political contests, no single factor completely accounted for the division between Federalists and Antifederalists. Thus in Virginia, the leaders of both sides came from the same general social and economic class. New York City and Philadelphia strongly supported the Constitution, yet so did predominantly rural New Jersey.

The great debate was conducted through pamphlets, papers, letters to the editor, and speeches. The issues were important, but with few exceptions, the argument about the merits of the Constitution was carried on in a quiet and calm manner. Out of the debate came a series of essays known as ***The Federalist***, written (using the pseudonym Publius) by Alexander Hamilton, James Madison, and John Jay to persuade the voters of New York to ratify the Constitution. *The Federalist* is still "widely regarded as the most profound single treatise on the Constitution ever written and as among the few masterly works in political science produced in all the centuries of history."[15] (Three of the most important *Federalist* essays, Nos. 10, 51, and 78, are reprinted in the Appendix of this book. We urge you to read them.) The great debate stands even today as an outstanding example of free people using public discussion to determine the nature of their fundamental laws.

The Antifederalists' most telling criticism of the proposed Constitution was its failure to include a bill of rights.[16] The Federalists believed a bill of rights was unnecessary because the proposed national government had *only* the specific powers delegated to it by the states and the people. Thus there was no need to specify that Congress could not, for example, abridge freedom of the press because the states and the people had not given it power to regulate the press. Moreover, the Federalists argued, to guarantee some rights might be dangerous, because it would then be thought that rights not listed could be denied. The Constitution already protected some important rights—trial by jury in federal criminal cases, for example. Hamilton and others also insisted that paper guarantees were weak supports on which to depend for protection against governmental tyranny.

The Antifederalists were unconvinced. If some rights were protected, what could be the objection to providing constitutional protection for others? Without a bill of rights,

Federalists
Supporters of ratification of the Constitution whose position promoting a strong central government was later voiced in the Federalist party.

Antifederalists
Opponents of ratification of the Constitution and of a strong central government generally.

The Federalist
Series of essays promoting ratification of the Constitution, published anonymously by Alexander Hamilton, John Jay, and James Madison in 1787 and 1788.

what was to prevent Congress from using one of its delegated powers to abridge free speech? If bills of rights were needed in state constitutions to limit state governments, why was a bill of rights not needed in the national constitution to limit the national government? This was a government farther from the people, they contended, with a greater tendency to subvert natural rights.

The Politics of Ratification

The absence of a bill of rights in the proposed constitution dominated the struggle over its adoption. In taverns and church gatherings and newspaper offices up and down the eastern seaboard, people were muttering, "No bill of rights—no constitution!" This feeling was so strong that some Antifederalists, who were far more concerned with states' rights than individual rights, joined forces with bill of rights advocates in an effort to defeat the proposed Constitution.

The Federalists were first to begin the debate over the Constitution that opened as soon as the delegates left Philadelphia in mid-September 1787. The Federalists' tactic was to secure ratification in as many states as possible before the opposition had time to organize. The Antifederalists were handicapped. Most newspapers were owned by supporters of ratification. Moreover, Antifederalist strength was concentrated in rural areas, which were underrepresented in some state legislatures and difficult to arouse to political action. The Antifederalists needed time to perfect their organization and collect their strength, while the Federalists, composed of a more closely knit group of leaders throughout the colonies, moved in a hurry.

In most of the small states, now satisfied by equal Senate representation, ratification was gained without difficulty. Delaware was the first state to ratify, and by early 1788, Pennsylvania, New Jersey, Georgia, and Connecticut had also ratified (see Table 1-2). Reports were coming in from Massachusetts, however, that opposition was broadening. The position of such key leaders as John Hancock and Samuel Adams was in doubt. The debate in the ratifying convention in Boston pitched some of the most polished Federalist speakers against an array of eloquent but plainspoken Antifederalists. The debate raged for most of January 1788 into February. At times it looked as though the Constitution would lose, as Antifederalists raised the cry of "Why no bill of rights?" and other objections. But in the end, the Constitution was narrowly ratified in Massachusetts, 187 to 168.

The struggle over ratification continued through the spring of 1788. By June 21, Maryland, South Carolina, and New Hampshire had ratified, putting the Constitution over the top in the number (nine) required for ratification. But two big hurdles remained:

TABLE 1–2 RATIFICATION OF THE U.S. CONSTITUTION	
State	*Date*
Delaware	December 7, 1787
Pennsylvania	December 12, 1787
New Jersey	December 18, 1787
Georgia	January 2, 1788
Connecticut	January 9, 1788
Massachusetts	February 6, 1788
Maryland	April 28, 1788
South Carolina	May 23, 1788
New Hampshire	June 21, 1788
Virginia	June 25, 1788
New York	July 26, 1788
North Carolina	November 21, 1789
Rhode Island	May 29, 1790

Patrick Henry's famous cry of "Give Me Liberty or Give Me Death!" symbolizes the underlying spirit of optimism in the United States. This spirit has endured throughout this country's history, despite the many problems the country has experienced.

Virginia and New York. It would be impossible to begin the new government without the consent of these two major states. Virginia was crucial. As the most populous state, the home of Washington, Jefferson, and Madison, it was a link between North and South. The Virginia ratifying convention rivaled the Constitutional Convention in the caliber of its delegates. Madison, who had only recently switched to favoring a bill of rights after saying earlier it was unnecessary, captained the Federalist forces. The fiery Patrick Henry led the opposition. In an epic debate, Henry cried that liberty was the issue: "Liberty, the greatest of earthly possessions . . . that precious jewel!" But Madison quietly rebutted him and then played his trump card, a promise that a bill of rights embracing the freedoms of religion and speech and assembly would be added to the Constitution as the first order of business once the new government was established. At a critical moment, Washington himself tipped the balance with a letter urging ratification. News of the Virginia vote, 89 for the Constitution and 79 opposed, was rushed to New York.[17]

The great landowners along New York's Hudson River, unlike their southern planter friends, were opposed to the Constitution. They feared federal taxation of their holdings, and they did not want to abolish the profitable tax New York had been levying on trade and commerce with other states. When the convention assembled, the Federalists were greatly outnumbered, but they were aided by Alexander Hamilton's strategy and skill and by word of Virginia's ratification. New York approved by a margin of three votes. Although North Carolina and Rhode Island still remained outside the Union (the former ratified in November 1789, the latter six months later), the new nation was created. In New York, a few members of the old Congress assembled to issue the call for elections under the new Constitution. Then they adjourned without setting a date for reconvening.

Summary

1. The response to the terrorist attacks of September 11, 2001, expanded to wars in Afghanistan and Iraq. The cost of these wars and the domestic homeland security efforts is substantial and has helped, along with major tax cuts, to greatly expand the budget deficit and national debt. President Bush made national security a major theme of his 2004 election,

while Democrats criticized the president on the lack of planning for the aftermath of the war in Iraq and the inability to eliminate Al-Qaeda as a threat. Other important issues in 2004 included the economy, jobs, and such social issues as gay marriage.

2. Americans have long been skeptical of politicians and politics. Yet politics is a necessary activity for a democracy. Indeed, politics and politicians are indispensable to making our system of separated institutions and checks and balances work.

3. "Democracy" is an often misused term, and it has many different meanings. We use it here to refer to a system of interacting values, interrelated political processes, and interdependent political structures. The vital principle of democracy is that a just government must derive its powers from the consent of the people and that this consent must be regularly renewed in free and fair elections.

4. The essential democratic values are a belief in personal liberty, respect for the individual, equality of opportunity, and popular consent. Essential elements of the democratic process are free and fair elections, majority rule, freedom of expression, and the right to assemble and protest.

5. Stable constitutional democracy is encouraged by various conditions, such as an educated citizenry, a healthy economy, and overlapping associations and groupings within a society in which major institutions interact to achieve a certain degree of consensus.

6. There has recently been some concern about a decline in *social capital*—the experiences people gain in working together in community groups. Lessons about compromise, accommodation, and participation are important building blocks for democracy. Some observers say we have experienced a decline in civic engagement, while others see a healthy level of voluntary and charitable engagement that is making our communities and our nation better.

7. Constitutionalism is a general label we apply to arrangements such as checks and balances, federalism, separation of powers, rule of law, due process, and the Bill of Rights that force our leaders and representatives to listen, think, bargain, and explain before they act and make laws. A constitutional government enforces recognized and regularly applied limits on the powers of those who govern.

8. Democracy developed gradually. A revolution had to be fought before a system of representative democracy in the United States could be tried and tested. It took several years before a national constitution could be written and almost another year for it to be ratified. It took another two years before the Bill of Rights could be adopted and ratified. It has taken more than 200 years for democratic institutions to be refined and for systems of competition and choice to be hammered out. Democratic institutions such as free and fair elections and equal protection of the laws in the United States are still in the process of being refined and improved.

KEY TERMS

democracy
direct democracy
representative democracy
constitutional democracy
constitutionalism
statism

popular consent
majority rule
majority
plurality
ideology
theocracy

Articles of Confederation
Annapolis Convention
Constitutional Convention
Shays' Rebellion
bicameralism
Virginia Plan

New Jersey Plan
Connecticut Compromise
three-fifths compromise
Federalists
Antifederalists
The Federalist

FURTHER READING

BERNARD BAILYN, ED., *The Debate on the Constitution: Federalist and Antifederalist Speeches, Articles, and Letters During the Struggle over Ratification*, 2 vols. (Library of America, 1993).

LANCE BANNING, *The Sacred Fire of Liberty: James Madison and the Founding of the Federal Republic* (Cornell University Press, 1995).

WILLIAM J. CROTTY, ED., *The State of Democracy in America* (Georgetown University Press, 2001).

ROBERT A. DAHL, *On Democracy* (Yale University Press, 1998).

S.N. EISENSTADT, *Paradoxes of Democracy: Fragility, Continuity and Change* (Johns Hopkins University Press, 1999).

ALEXANDER HAMILTON, JAMES MADISON, AND JOHN JAY, *The Federalist Papers*, ed. Clinton Rossiter (New American Library, 1961). Also in several other editions.

SAMUEL P. HUNTINGTON, *The Third Wave: Democratization in the Late Twentieth Century* (University of Oklahoma Press, 1991).

DANIEL LESSARD LEVIN, *Representing Popular Sovereignty: The Constitution in American Political Culture* (State University of New York Press, 1999).

AREND LUPHART, *Patterns of Democracy: Government Forms and Performance in Thirty-Six Countries* (Yale University Press, 1999).

DREW R. McCOY, *The Last of the Fathers: James Madison and the Republican Legacy* (Columbia University Press, 1989).

RICHARD B. MORRIS, *Witnesses at the Creation: Hamilton, Madison, and Jay and the Constitution* (Holt, Rinehart and Winston, 1985).

PIPPA NORRIS, ED., *Critical Citizens: Global Support for Democratic Institutions* (Oxford University Press, 1999).

JACK N. RAKOVE, *Original Meanings: Politics and Ideas in the Making of the Constitution* (Vintage Books, 1997).

MICHAEL J. SANDEL, *Democracy's Discontent: America in Search of a Public Philosophy* (Belknap Press, 1996).

MICHAEL SCHUDSON, *The Good Citizen: A History of American Civic Life* (Harvard University Press, 1998).

THEDA SKOCPOL AND MORRIS P. FIORINA, EDS., *Civic Engagement in American Democracy* (Brookings/Russell Sage, 1999).

CASS R. SUNSTEIN, *Designing Democracy: What Constitutions Do* (Oxford University Press, 2001).

ALEXIS DE TOCQUEVILLE, *Democracy in America*, 2 vols. (1835).

GARRY WILLS, *A Necessary Evil: A History of American Distrust of Government* (Simon & Schuster, 1999).

GORDON S. WOOD, *The Creation of the American Republic, 1776–1787* (University of North Carolina Press, 1969).

See also the *Journal of Democracy* (Johns Hopkins University Press).

THE LIVING CONSTITUTION

2

The Constitution of the United States is the world's oldest written constitution and one of the shortest. The original, unamended Constitution, which went into effect in 1789, contains just 4,543 words. Yet it established the framers' experiment in free-government-in-the-making that each generation reinterprets and renews. The Constitution remains a document Americans revere. Optimists read it as expressing their hopes; pessimists put faith in its protections against tyranny and other abuses.

Why, after more than 218 years, have we not written another constitution—let alone two, three, or more, like other countries around the world? Part of the answer is the widespread acceptance of the Constitution by optimists and pessimists alike. But also part of the answer is the Constitution's brilliant structure for limited government and the facts that the framers built into the document the capacity for adaptability and flexibility.

As the Constitution won the support of citizens of the early years of the Republic, it took on the aura of **natural law**—law that defines right from wrong, law that is higher than human law. "The [Founding] Fathers grew ever larger in stature as they receded from view; the era in which they lived and fought became a Golden Age; in that age there had been a fresh dawn for the world, and its men were giants against the sky."[1] This early Constitution worship helped bring unity to the diverse new nation. Like the crown in Great Britain, the Constitution became a symbol of national loyalty, evoking both emotional and intellectual support from Americans, regardless of their differences. The framers' work became part of the American creed and culture.[2] It stood for liberty,

TIME LINE

THE LIVING CONSTITUTION

1788	*Federalist Papers* provide political arguments for ratifying the Constitution
1789	Judiciary Act establishes the structure of the federal judiciary
1801	Federalists relinquish control over the federal government
1803	*Marbury* v. *Madison* asserts the power of judicial review
1835	Chief Justice John Marshall dies—most influential Supreme Court Justice
1868	President Johnson impeached but not convicted over reconstruction
1920	19th Amendment grants women the right to vote
1972	Equal Rights Amendment (ERA) proposed
1974	Nixon becomes first president to resign
1982	Deadline passes and ERA fails
1998	President Clinton impeached but not convicted
2000	Supreme Court ends recount of presidential election.

7-4

"And there are three branches of government, so that each branch has the other two to blame everything on."

© Tribune Media Services. All rights reserved. Reprinted with permission.

natural law
God's or nature's law that defines right from wrong and is higher than human law.

separation of powers
Constitutional division of powers among the legislative, executive, and judicial branches, with the legislative branch making law, the executive applying and enforcing the law, and the judiciary interpreting the law.

equality before the law, limited government—indeed, for just about whatever anyone wanted to read into it.

Even today, Americans generally revere the Constitution, even though many do not know what is in it. A poll by the National Constitution Center found that nine out of ten Americans are proud of the Constitution and feel it is important to them. However, a third think the Constitution establishes English as the country's official language. One in six believes the Constitution establishes America as a Christian nation. Only one out of four could name a single First Amendment right. Although two out of three knew that the Constitution creates three branches of the national government, only one in three could name all three branches.[3]

The Constitution is more than a symbol, however. It is a supreme and binding law that both grants and limits powers. "In framing a government which is to be administered by men over men," wrote James Madison in *The Federalist,* No. 51, "the great difficulty lies in this: you must first enable the government to control the governed; and in the next place oblige it to control itself." (See *The Federalist,* No. 51, in the Appendix of this book, or go on the Web to www.law.ou.edu/hist/federalist/.) The Constitution is both a positive instrument of government, which enables the governors to control the governed, and a restraint on government, which enables the ruled to check the rulers. In what ways does the Constitution limit the power of the government? In what ways does it create governmental power? How has it managed to serve as a great symbol of national unity and at the same time as an adaptable instrument of government? The secret is an ingenious separation of powers and a system of checks and balances that check power with power.

CHECKING POWER WITH POWER

It may seem strange to begin by stressing the ways in which the Constitution *limits* governmental power, but keep in mind the dilemma the framers faced. They wanted a stronger and more effective national government than they had under the Articles of Confederation. At the same time, they were keenly aware that the people would not accept too much central control. Efficiency and order were important concerns, but they were not as important as liberty. The framers wanted to ensure domestic tranquillity and prevent future rebellions, but they also wanted to forestall the emergence of a homegrown King George III. Accordingly, they allotted certain powers to the national government and reserved the rest for the states, thus establishing a system of *federalism* (whose nature and problems we take up in Chapter 3). Even this was not enough. They believed they needed additional means to limit the national government.

The most important way they devised to make public officials observe the constitutional limits on their powers was through *free and fair elections;* voters would be able to throw out of office those who abuse power. Yet the framers were not willing to depend solely on political controls, because they did not fully trust the people's judgment. "Free government is founded on jealousy, and not in confidence," said Thomas Jefferson. "In questions of power, then, let no more be heard of confidence in man, but bind him down from mischief by the chains of the Constitution."[4]

No less important, the framers feared that a majority might deprive minorities of their rights. "A dependence on the people is, no doubt, the primary control on the government," Madison argued in *The Federalist,* No. 51, "but experience has taught mankind the necessity of auxiliary precautions." What were these "auxiliary precautions" against popular tyranny?

Separation of Powers

The first step was the **separation of powers**, the distribution of constitutional authority among the three branches of the national government. In *The Federalist,* No. 47, Madison wrote, "No political truth is certainly of greater intrinsic value, or is stamped with the authority of more enlightened patrons of liberty, than that . . . the accumulation of all powers, legislative, executive, and judiciary, in the same hands . . . may justly be pronounced the very definition of tyranny."[5] Chief among the "enlightened patrons of liberty" to whose authority Madison was appealing were John Locke and Montesquieu, whose works were well known to most educated Americans.

The intrinsic value of the principle of dispersion of power does not by itself account for its inclusion in our Constitution. Dispersion of power had been the general practice in the colonies for more than 100 years. Only during the Revolutionary period did some of the states concentrate authority in the hands of the legislature, and that unhappy experience confirmed the framers' belief in the merits of the separation of powers. Many attributed the evils of state government and the lack of energy in the central government to the fact that there was no strong executive both to check legislative abuses and to give energy and direction to administration.

Still, separating power was not enough. In the framers' view, there was the danger that different officials with different powers might pool their authority and act together. Separation of powers by itself might not prevent governmental branches and officials from responding to the same pressures—from the demand of an overwhelming majority of the voters to suppress an offensive book, for example, or to impose confiscatory taxes on rich people. If separating power was not enough, what else could be done?

Checks and Balances: Ambition to Counteract Ambition

The framers' answer was a system of **checks and balances**. "The great security against a gradual concentration of the several powers in the same department," wrote Madison in *The Federalist*, No. 51, "consists in giving to those who administer each department the necessary constitutional means and personal motives to resist encroachments of the others: . . . Ambition must be made to counteract ambition." Each branch therefore has a role in the actions of the others (see Figure 2–1). Congress enacts laws, but the president can veto them. The Supreme Court can declare laws passed by Congress and signed by the president unconstitutional, but the president appoints the justices and all the other federal judges, with the Senate's approval. The president administers the laws, but Congress provides the money. Moreover, the Senate and the House of Representatives have an absolute veto over each other in the enactment of laws, because both houses must approve bills.

Not only does each branch have some authority over the others, but each is politically independent of the others. Voters in each local district choose members of the House; voters in each state choose senators; the president is elected by the voters in all the states. With the consent of the Senate, the president appoints federal judges, who remain in office until they retire or are impeached.

The framers also ensured that a majority of the voters could win control over only part of the government at one time. Although in an off-year (nonpresidential) election a new majority might take control of the House of Representatives, the president still has at least two more years, and senators hold office for six years. Finally, independent federal courts, which exercise their own powerful checks, were also provided.

Modifications of Checks and Balances

Distrustful of both the elites and the masses, the framers deliberately built inefficiency into our political system. They designed the decision-making process so that the national government can act decisively only when there is a consensus among most groups and after all sides have had their say. "The doctrine of separation of powers was adopted by the convention of 1787," in the words of Justice Louis D. Brandeis, "not to promote efficiency but to preclude the exercise of arbitrary power. The purpose was not to avoid friction, but, by means of the inevitable friction incident to the distribution of the governmental powers among three departments, to save the people from autocracy."[6] Still,

THE EXERCISE OF CHECKS AND BALANCES, 1789–2003

vetoes The president has vetoed more than 2,500 acts of Congress. Congress has overridden presidential vetoes more than 100 times.

judicial review The Supreme Court has ruled some 174 congressional acts or parts thereof unconstitutional. Its 1983 decision striking down legislative vetoes (*INS* v. *Chadha*) affects another 200 provisions.

impeachment The House of Representatives has impeached two presidents and 15 federal judges; of these, the Senate has convicted seven judges but neither president.

confirmation The Senate has refused to confirm nine cabinet nominations, and many other cabinet and subcabinet appointments were withdrawn because of likely Senate rejection.

For additional resources on the Constitution, go to www.prenhall.com/burns.

checks and balances
Constitutional grant of powers that enables each of the three branches of government to check some acts of the others and therefore ensure that no branch can dominate.

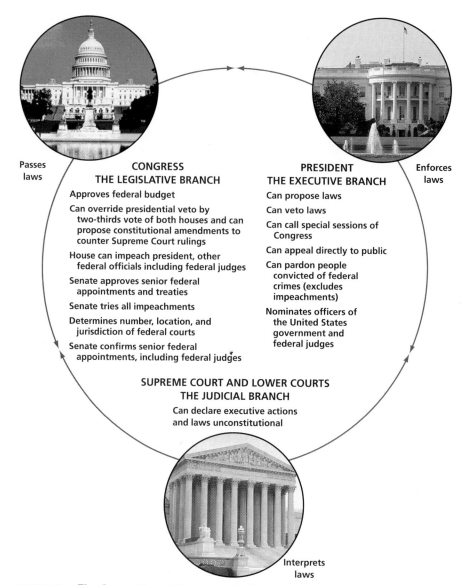

Passes
laws

CONGRESS
THE LEGISLATIVE BRANCH

Approves federal budget

Can override presidential veto by
two-thirds vote of both houses and can
propose constitutional amendments to
counter Supreme Court rulings

House can impeach president, other
federal officials including federal judges

Senate approves senior federal
appointments and treaties

Senate tries all impeachments

Determines number, location, and
jurisdiction of federal courts

Senate confirms senior federal
appointments, including federal judges

PRESIDENT
THE EXECUTIVE BRANCH

Can propose laws

Can veto laws

Can call special sessions of
Congress

Can appeal directly to public

Can pardon people
convicted of federal
crimes (excludes
impeachments)

Nominates officers of
the United States
government and
federal judges

Enforces
laws

SUPREME COURT AND LOWER COURTS
THE JUDICIAL BRANCH

Can declare executive actions
and laws unconstitutional

Interprets
laws

FIGURE 2–1 The Separation of Powers and Checks and Balances.

even though the fragmentation of political power written into the Constitution remains, several developments have modified the way the system of checks and balances works.

THE RISE OF NATIONAL POLITICAL PARTIES   Political parties can serve as unifying factors, at times drawing together the president, senators, representatives, and sometimes even judges behind common programs. When parties do this, they help bridge the separation of powers. Yet parties can be splintered and weakened by having to work through a system of fragmented governmental power, so they never become strong or cohesive. Moreover, when one party controls Congress or one of its chambers and the other controls the White House (**divided government**), as has generally been the case since the end of World War II, the parties may intensify checks and balances rather than moderate them, to the point that action on some important issues may be difficult.[7]

Divided government may lead to so much competition between the legislative and executive branches that we find "each institution protecting and promoting itself through a broad interpretation of its constitutional and political status, even usurping the other's power when the opportunity presents itself."[8] Thus we have had battles over presidential impoundment of funds appropriated by Congress, budget gridlock, and unseemly and angry confirmation hearings for the appointment of justices of the Supreme Court and even lower federal courts and members of the executive branch. Divided

divided government
Governance divided between the parties, especially when one holds the presidency and the other controls one or both houses of Congress.

government also makes it difficult for the voters to hold anybody or any party accountable. "Presidents blame Congress . . . while members of Congress attack the president. . . . Citizens genuinely cannot tell who is to blame."[9]

Still, when all the shouting dies down, political scientist David Mayhew concludes, there have been just as many congressional investigations and just as much important legislation passed when one party controls Congress and another controls the presidency as when the same party controls both branches.[10] And Charles Jones, a noted authority on Congress and the presidency, adds that not only is divided government not that important in determining how our government responds to crises, but divided government is precisely what the voters appear to have wanted through much of our history.[11]

EXPANSION OF THE ELECTORATE AND THE MOVE TOWARD MORE DIRECT DEMOCRACY   The framers wanted the president to be chosen by the electoral college—wise, independent citizens free from popular passions and hero worship—rather than by ordinary citizens. Almost from the beginning, however, that is not the way the electoral college worked.[12] Rather, voters actually do select the president, because presidential electors chosen by the voters are pledged in advance to cast their electoral votes for their party's candidates for president and vice president. Nevertheless, presidential candidates may very occasionally win the national popular vote but lose the vote in the electoral college, as demonstrated in Al Gore's winning the popular vote in the 2000 presidential election but losing the electoral college with 266 votes to George W. Bush's 271.

The kind of people allowed to vote has expanded from white property-owning males to all citizens over 18 years of age. In addition, during the past century, American states have expanded the role of the electorate by adopting **direct primaries**, in which the voters elect party nominees for the House and Senate and even for president; by permitting the voters in about half the states to propose and vote on laws (**initiatives**); and by allowing voters to reconsider actions of the legislature (**referendums**) and even to remove elected state and local officials from office (**recall**). And with the passage of the Seventeenth Amendment, senators are no longer elected by state legislatures but are chosen directly by the people.

ESTABLISHMENT OF AGENCIES DELIBERATELY DESIGNED TO EXERCISE LEGISLATIVE, EXECUTIVE, AND JUDICIAL FUNCTIONS   When the national government began to regulate the economy, it found that it was impossible to legislate precise and detailed rules on complex matters such as railroad safety, mass communications, the health and safety of working conditions, and environmental protection. Consequently, in assigning these regulatory responsibilities, Congress provides administrative agencies with the power to make and apply rules and to decide disputes. Beginning in 1887, Congress created *independent regulatory commissions* such as the Interstate Commerce Commission (which went out of business in 1995, although many of its functions were transferred to the Surface Transportation Board within the Department of Transportation) and later the Federal Communications Commission. More recently, it has established *independent executive agencies* such as the Environmental Protection Agency.

CHANGES IN TECHNOLOGY   The system of checks and balances operates differently today from the way it did in 1789. Back then, there were no televised congressional committee hearings; no electronic communications; no *Larry King Live* talk shows; no *New York Times, Wall Street Journal, USA Today,* CNN, or C-SPAN; no nightly news programs with national audiences; no presidential press conferences; and no live coverage of wars and of Americans fighting in foreign lands. Nuclear bombs, television, computers, cellular telephones, fax machines, the Internet—these and other innovations create conditions today that are very different from those of two centuries ago. We also live in a time of instant communication and polls that tell us what people are thinking about public issues.

In some ways, these new technologies have added to the powers of presidents by permitting them to appeal directly to millions of people and giving them immediate access to public opinion. And these new technologies have also added leverage to

direct primary
Election in which voters choose party nominees.

initiative
Procedure whereby a certain number of voters may, by petition, propose a law or constitutional amendment and have it submitted to the voters.

referendum
Procedure for submitting to popular vote measures passed by the legislature or proposed amendments to a state constitution.

recall
Procedure for submitting to popular vote the removal of officials from office before the end of their term.

In Comparative Perspective

THE EUROPEAN UNION

The European Union grew out of a succession of alliances formed after World War II to promote economic integration and cooperation. Through a series of treaties, the union has grown to include 25 countries, with the addition of 10 Central and Eastern European countries in 2004. One of the most important institutions created by the union is the European Court of Justice (ECJ). The ECJ has the power to declare national laws invalid when they conflict with treaty obligations and has created a uniform system of law that takes precedence over national laws and constitutions. The member states of the European Union also signed the European Convention on Human Rights, which establishes a long list of civil liberties. They are subject to the jurisdiction of the European Court of Human Rights, which resolves allegations of human rights abuses and has invalidated national laws that contravene provisions of the convention.

For the most part, the issues coming before the ECJ have been economic and commercial in nature, but it has struck down laws based on gender discrimination and advanced the right to equal pay for equal work. Critics of the ECJ complain that it has become too activist and compare it to the U.S. Supreme Court in the early nineteenth century under Chief Justice John Marshall, whose rulings striking down state trade barriers promoted the growth of our unified economy.

Due to the success of economic integration, additional treaties, the introduction of the euro as the common currency, and the enlargement of the EU, a Treaty Establishing a Constitution for Europe was submitted for ratification by all 25 member states in 2004–2005. The Constitution strengthens the powers of the European Parliament, creates a President of the Council of Ministers, and includes a Charter of Fundamental Rights for EU citizens; it also clarifies the competences of other EU supranational institutions and those member states.

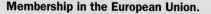

Legend:
- Member of European Union
- Member in 2004
- Hoping for membership in 2007
- Yet to begin negotiations

Membership in the European Union.

For more information on the European Union, go to www.userpage.chemie. fu-berlin.de/adressen/eu.html and www.lib.berkeley.edu/gssi/eugde.html. The ECJ maintains a site at www.europa.eu.int/cj/en containing recent decisions and other information.

organized interests by making it easier to target thousands of letters and calls at members of Congress, to organize the writing of letters to the editor, and to organize and mobilize on the Internet. New technologies have also given greater independence and influence to nongovernmental institutions such as the press. They have made it possible for rich people like Ross Perot and religious leaders like Pat Robertson, who have access to ample financial resources, to bypass political parties and carry their message directly to the electorate.

THE GROWTH OF PRESIDENTIAL POWER   Today problems elsewhere in the world—Afghanistan, Israel, Pakistan, North Korea, Iraq—often create crises for the United States. The need to deal with perpetual emergencies has concentrated power in the hands of the chief executive and the presidential staff. The president of the United States has emerged as the most significant player on the world stage, and media coverage of summit conferences with foreign leaders enhance his status. Headline-generating events give the president a visibility no congressional leader can achieve. The office of the president has on occasion served to modify the system of checks and balances and provide some measure of national unity. Drawing on constitutional, political, and emergency powers, the president is sometimes able to overcome the restraints imposed by the Constitution on the exercise of governmental power—to the applause of some Americans and the alarm of others.

JUDICIAL REVIEW AND THE "GUARDIANS OF THE CONSTITUTION"

The judiciary has become so important in our system of checks and balances that it deserves special attention. Judges did not claim the power of **judicial review**—the power of a court to strike down a law or a government regulation that in the opinion of the judges conflicts with the Constitution—until some years after the Constitution was adopted. From the beginning, however, judges were expected to restrain legislative majorities. "The independence of judges," wrote Alexander Hamilton in *The Federalist,* No. 78 (which appears in the Appendix), "may be an essential safeguard against the effects of occasional ill humors in the society."

Judicial review is a major contribution of the United States to the art of government, a contribution that has been adopted at an increasing pace by other nations. In Germany, France, Italy, and Spain, constitutional courts are responsible for reviewing laws referred to them to ensure constitutional compliance, including compliance with the charter of rights that is now part of their constitutions.[13] (See also the box on the growth of judicial power in the European Union.)

Origins of Judicial Review

The Constitution says nothing about who should have the final word in disputes that might arise over its meaning. Whether the delegates to the Constitutional Convention of 1787 intended to give the courts the power of judicial review is a question long debated. The framers clearly intended that the Supreme Court have the power to declare state legislation unconstitutional, but whether they intended to give it the same power over *congressional* legislation and the president is not clear. Why then didn't the framers specifically provide for judicial review? Probably because they believed the power could be inferred from certain general provisions and the necessity of interpreting and applying a written constitution.

The Federalists—who urged ratification of the Constitution and controlled the national government until 1801—generally supported a strong role for federal courts and favored judicial review. Their opponents, the Jeffersonian Republicans (called Democrats after 1832), were less enthusiastic. In the Kentucky and Virginia Resolutions of 1798 and 1799, respectively, Jefferson and Madison (who by this time had left the Federalist camp) came close to the position that state legislatures—and not the Supreme Court—had the ultimate power to interpret the Constitution. These resolutions seemed to

judicial review
The power of a court to refuse to enforce a law or a government regulation that in the opinion of the judges conflicts with the U.S. Constitution or, in a state court, the state constitution.

CHANGING FACE OF AMERICAN POLITICS

THE CIVIL RIGHTS MOVEMENT AND JUSTICE THURGOOD MARSHALL

In 1909, the National Association for the Advancement of Colored People (NAACP) was founded to protest various forms of racial discrimination—discrimination in the criminal justice system, in voting rights, and in education and employment. In the 1920s and 1930s, one of the NAACP's major initiatives was to lobby Congress to enact a federal law against lynching, as well as to bring lawsuits challenging racial segregation. But, because the NAACP was involved in lobbying it was denied tax-exempt status, and in 1938 under the direction of Thurgood Marshall the NAACP's litigation activities were separated and carried forth with the formation of the NAACP Legal Defense and Education Fund, Inc. (LDF).

Justice Thurgood Marshall.

As a leader in the civil rights movement in the 1940s and 1950s, Thurgood Marshall was a crusading lawyer for the NAACP's LDF. He argued before the Supreme Court and won a companion case with the landmark ruling in *Brown* v. *Board of Education of Topeka* (1954), which held that segregated public schools were unconstitutional. President John Kennedy appointed him to the federal appellate bench in 1961. President Lyndon Johnson then persuaded Marshall to become solicitor general of the United States, and he was appointed to the Supreme Court in 1967. As the first African American on the Supreme Court, Justice Marshall served until 1991 and continued to champion the cause of civil rights throughout his career.

At the time of the Bicentennial of the Constitution, he spoke out in dissent and defended his view of our "living Constitution":

> I do not believe that the meaning of the Constitution was forever "fixed" at the Philadelphia Convention. Nor do I find the wisdom, foresight, and sense of justice exhibited by the framers particularly profound. To the contrary, the government they devised was defective from the start, requiring several amendments, a civil war, and momentous social transformation to

attain the system of constitutional government, and its respect for the individual freedoms and human rights, that we hold as fundamental today. When contemporary Americans cite "The Constitution," they invoke a concept that is vastly different from what the framers barely began to construct two centuries ago.

For a sense of the evolving nature of the Constitution we need look no further than the first three words of the document's preamble: "We the People." When the Founding Fathers used this phrase in 1787, they did not have in mind the majority of America's citizens. "We the People" included, in the words of the framers, "the whole Number of free Persons." On a matter so basic as the right to vote, for example, Negro slaves were excluded, although they were counted for representational purposes—at three-fifths each. Women did not gain the right to vote for over a hundred and thirty years. . . .

And so we must be careful, when focusing on the events which took place in Philadelphia two centuries ago, that we not overlook the momentous events which followed, and thereby lose our proper sense of perspective. . . . If we seek, instead, a sensitive understanding of the Constitution's inherent defects, and its promising evolution through 200 years of history, the celebration of the "Miracle at Philadelphia" will, in my view, be a far more meaningful and humbling experience. We will see that the true miracle was not the birth of the Constitution, but its life, a life nurtured through two turbulent centuries of our own making, and a life embodying much good fortune that was not.[*]

[*]Remarks at the annual seminar of the San Francisco Patent and Trademark Law Association, Maui, Hawaii, May 16, 1987. In David M. O'Brien, ed., *Judges on Judging*, 2d ed. (C.Q. Press, 2004).

question whether the Supreme Court even had final authority to review state legislation, something about which there had been little doubt.

When the Jeffersonians defeated the Federalists in the election of 1800, it was still undecided whether the Supreme Court would actually exercise the power of judicial review. Logical reasons to support such a doctrine were at hand, and some precedents could even be cited; nevertheless, judicial review was not an established power. Then in 1803 came *Marbury* v. *Madison,* the most pathbreaking Supreme Court decision of all time.[14]

Marbury Versus Madison

The election of 1800 marked the rise to power of the Jeffersonian Republicans. President John Adams and fellow Federalists did not take their defeat easily. Indeed, they were greatly alarmed at what they considered to be the "enthronement of the rabble." Yet there was nothing much they could do about it before leaving office—or was there? The Constitution gives the president, with the consent of the Senate, the power to appoint federal judges to hold office during "good Behaviour"—basically, lifetime tenure, subject to removal only by impeachment. With the judiciary in the hands of Federalists, thought Adams and his associates, they could stave off the worst consequences of Jefferson's victory.

The outgoing Federalist Congress consequently created dozens of new federal judgeships. By March 3, 1801, Adams had appointed and the Senate had confirmed loyal Federalists to all these new positions. Adams signed the commissions and turned them over to John Marshall, his secretary of state, to be sealed and delivered. Marshall had just received his own commission as chief justice of the United States, but he continued to serve as secretary of state until Adams's term as president expired. Working right up until nine o'clock on the evening of March 3, Marshall sealed, but was unable to deliver, all the commissions. The only ones left were for the justices of the peace for the District of Columbia. The newly appointed chief justice left the delivery of these commissions for his successor, James Madison.

This "packing" of the judiciary angered Jefferson, now inaugurated as president. When he discovered that some of the commissions were still lying on a table in the Department of State, he instructed a clerk not to deliver them. Jefferson could see no reason why the District needed so many justices of the peace, especially Federalist justices.[15]

Among the commissions not delivered was one for William Marbury. After waiting in vain, Marbury decided to seek action from the courts. Searching through the statute books, he came across Section 13 of the Judiciary Act of 1789, which authorized the Supreme Court "to issue writs of mandamus." A **writ of mandamus** is a court order directing an official, such as the secretary of state, to perform a duty about which the official has no discretion, such as delivering a commission. So, thought Marbury, why not ask the Supreme Court to issue a writ of mandamus to force James Madison, the new secretary of state, to deliver the commission? Marbury and his companions went directly to the Supreme Court and, citing Section 13, they made the request.

What could Marshall do? On the one hand, if the Court issued the writ, Jefferson and Madison would probably ignore it. The Court would be powerless, and its prestige, already low, might suffer a fatal blow. On the other hand, by refusing to issue the writ, the judges would appear to support the Jeffersonian Republicans' claim that the Court had no authority to interfere with the executive. Would Marshall issue the writ? Most people thought so; angry Republicans even threatened impeachment if he did so.

On February 24, 1803, the Supreme Court delivered its opinion. The first part was as expected. Marbury was entitled to his commission, said Marshall, and Madison should have delivered it to him. Moreover, the proper court could issue a writ of mandamus, even against so high an officer as the secretary of state.

Then came the surprise. Section 13 of the Judiciary Act appears to give the Supreme Court the power to issue a writ of mandamus in cases of original jurisdiction, such as this one in question. But Section 13, said Marshall, is contrary to Article III of the Constitution, which gives the Supreme Court original jurisdiction only when an ambassador or other foreign minister is affected or when a state is a party. Even though this is a case of original jurisdiction, Marbury is neither a state nor a foreign minister. Under the Constitution, wrote Marshall, the Court had no power to issue a writ of mandamus in cases on original jurisdiction.

Marshall then posed the question in a more pointed way: Should the Supreme Court enforce an unconstitutional law? Of course not, he concluded. *The Constitution is the supreme and binding law,* and the courts cannot enforce any action of Congress that conflicts with it, even if it expands the power of the Court. Thus by limiting the Court's power to what is granted in the Constitution, Marshall gained the much more important power to declare laws passed by Congress unconstitutional. It was a brilliant move.

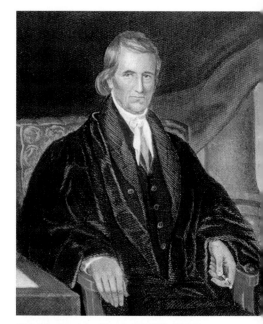

Chief Justice John Marshall (1755–1835), our most influential Supreme Court justice. Appointed in 1801, Marshall served until 1835. Earlier he had been a staunch defender of the U.S. Constitution at the Virginia ratifying convention, a member of Congress, and a secretary of state. He was one of those rare people who served in all three branches of government.

writ of mandamus
Court order directing an official to perform an official duty.

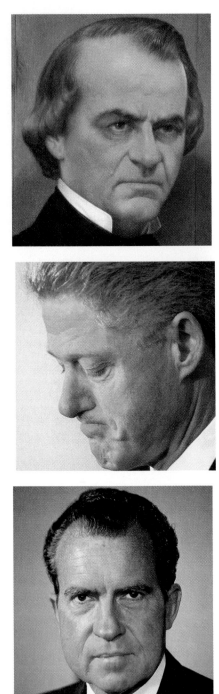

Two U.S. presidents, Andrew Johnson and Bill Clinton, have been impeached by the U.S. House of Representatives. In both cases the U.S. Senate did not muster a two-thirds majority vote, which would have been needed to convict these two presidents. President Richard Nixon almost surely would also have been impeached by the House of Representatives in 1974 but he resigned and left the presidency, and this decision preempted the House's action.

impeachment
Formal accusation against a public official, the first step in removal from office.

Marbury v. *Madison* might have been interpreted by subsequent generations in a very limited way. It could have been interpreted to mean that the Supreme Court had the right to determine the scope of its own powers under Article III, but Congress and the president had the authority to interpret their powers under Articles I and II. But over the decades, building on Marshall's precedent, the Court has taken the commanding position as the authoritative interpreter of the Constitution.

Several important consequences follow from the acceptance of Marshall's argument that judges are the official interpreters of the Constitution. The most important is that people can challenge laws enacted by Congress and approved by the president. Simply by bringing a lawsuit, those who lack the clout to get a bill through Congress can often secure a judicial hearing. And organized interest groups often find that goals unattainable by legislation can be achieved by litigation. Litigation thus supplements, and at times even takes precedence over, legislation as a way to make public policy.[16]

THE CONSTITUTION AS AN INSTRUMENT OF GOVERNMENT

As careful as the Constitution's framers were to limit the powers they gave the national government, the main reason they assembled in Philadelphia was to create a stronger national government. Having learned that a weak central government was a danger to liberty, they wished to establish a national government within the framework of a federal system with enough authority to meet the needs of all time. They made general grants of power, leaving it to succeeding generations to fill in the details and organize the structure of government in accordance with experience.

Hence our formal, written Constitution is only the skeleton of our system. It is filled out in numerous ways that must be considered part of our constitutional system in a larger sense. In fact, it is primarily through changes in the informal, unwritten Constitution that our system is kept up to date. These changes are found in certain basic statutes and historical practices of Congress, presidential practices, and decisions of the Supreme Court.

The Unwritten Constitution

CONGRESSIONAL ELABORATION Because the framers gave Congress authority to provide for the structural details of the national government, it is not necessary to amend the Constitution every time a change is needed. Rather, Congress can create legislation to meet the need. Examples of congressional elaboration appear in such legislation as the Judiciary Act of 1789, which laid the foundations for our national judicial system; in the laws establishing the organization and functions of all federal executive officials subordinate to the president; and in the rules of procedure, internal organization, and practices of Congress.

A dramatic example of congressional elaboration of our constitutional system is the use of the impeachment and removal power. An **impeachment** is a formal accusation against a public official and the first step in removal from office. Constitutional language defining the grounds for impeachment is sparse. Look at the Constitution (reprinted between this chapter and the next) and note that Article II (the Executive Article) calls for removal of the president, vice president, and all civil officers of the United States on impeachment for, and conviction of, "Treason, Bribery, or other High Crimes and Misdemeanors." It is up to Congress to give meaning to that language.

Article I (the Legislative Article) gives the House of Representatives the sole power to initiate impeachments and the Senate the sole power to try impeachments. In the event the president is tried, the chief justice of the United States presides, as Chief Justice William H. Rehnquist did in the impeachment of President Bill Clinton. Article I also requires conviction on impeachment charges to have the agreement of two-thirds of the senators present. Judgments shall extend no further than removal from office and disqualification from holding any office under the United States, but a person convicted

THE BRITISH AND AMERICAN SYSTEMS: A STUDY IN CONTRASTS

Our political system is based on the Constitution; the United Kingdom of Great Britain and Northern Ireland has no such single document. Yet both systems are "constitutional" in the sense that the rulers are subject to well-defined restraints. Parliament is the guardian of the British constitution. In the United States, it is the courts—ultimately, the Supreme Court—that are the keepers of the constitutional conscience, not Congress or the president. The limitations in our written Constitution and the practices in the unwritten British constitution rest on underlying national values and attitudes toward government.

In the British system, voters elect members of the House of Commons from districts, much as we elect members of our House of Representatives. Like us, the party with the most votes in a district wins the seat, so that even with three or more parties, a plurality of the popular vote usually results in a majority of the parliamentary seats. So long as the parliamentary majority stays together, it can enact into law the ruling party's program.

In British politics, parties are cohesive and disciplined; party members vote together and support their parliamentary leaders. In Britain, the party that wins an election has a very good chance of seeing its policies enacted. By contrast, our system depends on the agreement of many elements of society. The party that wins a presidential or congressional election or even one that controls both these branches may still have a tough time carrying out its campaign promises.

Leaders of the majority party in the House of Commons serve as executive ministers who collectively form the cabinet, with the prime minister at its head. The majority selects the prime minister. If the ruling party loses the support of the majority in the Commons on a major issue, it must resign or call for new elections. The House of Commons, when it chooses to act, has almost complete constitutional power. By tradition, there was no high court with the power to declare acts of Parliament unconstitutional, and the prime minister cannot veto them, although he or she may ask the crown to dissolve Parliament and call new elections.

In recent years, the British system has been substantially modified, however. In 2000, Britain forged sweeping constitutional reforms with the passage of the Human Rights Act, incorporating the European Convention on Human Rights as part of its domestic law and giving citizens their first American-style bill of rights. Besides introducing elements of federalism by devolving power to regional parliaments in Scotland, Wales,

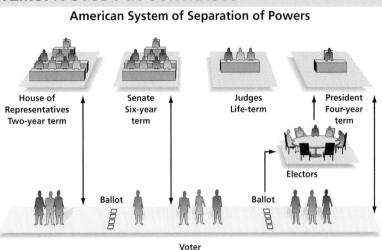

American System of Separation of Powers

House of Representatives Two-year term · Senate Six-year term · Judges Life-term · President Four-year term · Electors · Ballot · Ballot · Voter

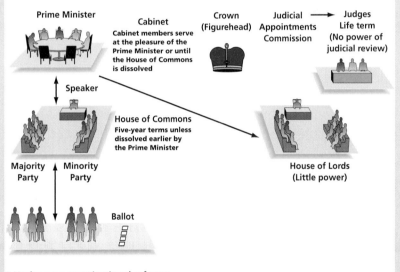

British Parliamentary System of Concentration of Responsibility*

Prime Minister · Cabinet — Cabinet members serve at the pleasure of the Prime Minister or until the House of Commons is dissolved · Crown (Figurehead) · Judicial Appointments Commission → Judges Life term (No power of judicial review) · Speaker · House of Commons — Five-year terms unless dissolved earlier by the Prime Minister · House of Lords (Little power) · Majority Party · Minority Party · Ballot

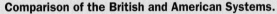

*** Under new constitutional reforms.**

Comparison of the British and American Systems.

and Northern Ireland, the House of Lords was stripped of its hereditary peers (members who served as a result of hereditary titles). The House of Lords now consists only of people appointed by the prime minister for their accomplishments in the arts, business, and public service. The 800-year-old office of the Lord Chancellor, who served as speaker of the House of Lords but also exercised executive and judicial powers in overseeing the administration of the courts, was abolished. A separate supreme court was proposed and the power to appoint justices and judges was to be given to an independent judicial appointments commission. The addition of a bill of rights, the devolution of power, and the judicial reforms creating a separation of powers are the most important changes in the British constitutional system in more than 300 years.

may also be liable to indictment, trial, judgment, and punishment according to the law. Article I also exempts cases of impeachment from the president's pardoning power. Article III (the Judicial Article) exempts cases of impeachment from the jury trial requirement. That is all the relevant constitutional language about impeachment. We must look to history to answer most questions about the proper exercise of these and other powers.[17]

Fortunately, past experience has triggered few acute constitutional disputes about the interpretation of impeachment procedures, so there is little history to go on. The House of Representatives has investigated 67 individuals for possible impeachment and has impeached 15 (two presidents—Andrew Johnson and Bill Clinton—and 13 federal judges). The Senate has held 15 impeachment trials and convicted only seven, all federal judges.

Presidential Practices

Although the formal constitutional powers of the president have not changed, the office is dramatically more important and more central today than it was in 1789. Vigorous presidents—George Washington, Thomas Jefferson, Andrew Jackson, Abraham Lincoln, Theodore Roosevelt, Woodrow Wilson, Franklin Roosevelt, Harry Truman, Lyndon Johnson, Bill Clinton, and George W. Bush—have boldly exercised their political and constitutional powers, especially during times of national crisis like the current war against international terrorism. Their presidential practices have established important precedents, building the power and influence of the office.

A major practice involves **executive orders**, which carry the full force of law. They may make major policy changes, such as withholding federal contracts from businesses engaging in racial discrimination, or they may simply be formalities, such as the presidential proclamation of Earth Day.

Other practices include **executive privilege** (the right to confidentiality of executive communications, especially those that relate to national security), **impoundment** by a president of funds previously appropriated by Congress, the power to send our armed forces into hostilities, and most important, the authority to propose legislation and work actively to secure its passage by Congress.

Foreign and economic crises as well as nuclear age realities have expanded the president's role: "When it comes to action risking nuclear war, technology has modified the Constitution: the President, perforce, becomes the only such man in the system capable of exercising judgment under the extraordinary limits now imposed by secrecy, complexity, and time."[18] The presidency has also become the pivotal office for regulating the economy and promoting the general welfare. Plainly, the president has become a leader in sponsoring legislation as well as the nation's chief executive.

Custom and Usage

Custom and usage round out our governmental system. The development of structures outside the formal Constitution—such as national political parties and the expansion of suffrage in the states—has democratized our Constitution. Other examples of custom and usage are in televised press conferences and presidential and vice presidential debates. Through such developments, the president has become responsive to the people and has a political base different from that of Congress. Consequently, the constitutional relationship between the branches today is considerably different from that envisioned by the framers.

Judicial Interpretation

As discussed earlier, judicial interpretation of the Constitution, especially by the Supreme Court, plays an important role in keeping the constitutional system up to date. As social and economic conditions change and new national demands develop, the Supreme Court has changed its interpretation of the Constitution accordingly. Because the Constitution adapts to changing times, it does not require frequent formal amendment. The

executive order
Directive issued by a president or governor that has the force of law.

executive privilege
The power to keep executive communications confidential, especially if they relate to national security.

impoundment
Presidential refusal to allow an agency to spend funds authorized and appropriated by Congress.

advantages of this flexibility may be appreciated by comparing the national Constitution with the rigid and often overly specific state constitutions. Many state constitutions are so detailed that they tie the hands of public officials and must be amended or replaced frequently.

CHANGING THE LETTER OF THE CONSTITUTION

Many people are disturbed by the idea of a constantly changing system. How, they contend, can you have a constitutional government when the Constitution is constantly being twisted by interpretation and changed by informal methods? This view fails to distinguish between two aspects of the Constitution. As an expression of *basic and timeless personal liberties,* the Constitution does not, and should not, change. For example, a government cannot destroy free speech and still remain a constitutional government. In this sense, the Constitution is unchanging. But when we consider the Constitution as an *instrument of government* and a positive grant of power, we realize that if it does not grow with the nation it serves, it would soon be irrelevant and ignored.

The framers could never have conceived of the problems facing the government of a large, powerful, and wealthy nation of over 285 million people at the beginning of the twenty-first century. Although the general purposes of government remain the same—to establish liberty, promote justice, ensure domestic tranquillity, and provide for the common defense—the powers of government that were adequate to accomplish these purposes in 1787 are simply insufficient more than 218 years later. Through its remarkable adaptability, our Constitution has survived democratic and industrial revolutions, the turmoil of civil war, the upheavals of major depressions, and the dislocations of world wars.

The framers knew that future experiences would call for changes in the text of the Constitution and that some means for formal amendment was necessary. In Article V, they gave responsibility for amending the Constitution to Congress and to the states. The president has no formal authority over constitutional amendments; presidential veto power does not extend to them, although presidential political influence is often crucial in getting amendments proposed and ratified.

Proposing Amendments

The first method for proposing amendments—and the only one used so far—is by *a two-thirds vote of both houses of Congress.* Dozens of resolutions proposing amendments are introduced in every session. Thousands have been introduced since 1789, but few make any headway. Throughout our history, Congress has proposed only 31 amendments, of which 27 have been ratified—including the Twenty-Seventh, which was originally part of the Bill of Rights but took more than 200 years to be ratified (see Figure 2–2).

Recent decades have seen a flurry of congressional attempts at constitutional amendments.[19] Congress has considered more than 11,000 proposals and the states have filed close to 400 petitions for calling a constitutional convention to consider amendments. Why is proposing amendments to the Constitution so popular? In part because interest groups unhappy with Supreme Court decisions seek to overturn them. In part because groups frustrated by their inability to get things done in Congress hope to bypass Congress. And in part because scholars or interest groups (not necessarily mutually exclusive categories) seek to change the procedures and processes of government to make the system more responsive.

The second method for proposing amendments—*a convention called by Congress* at the request of the legislatures in two-thirds of the states—has never been used. Under Article V of the Constitution, Congress could call for such a convention without the concurrence of the president. This method presents some difficult questions.[20] First, can

★★ THINKING IT THROUGH

Justice Scalia, a staunch conservative, contends that departing from the original intent of the Constitution undermines the legitimacy of the Court and leads to judicial legislation. In his view: "A democratic society does not, by and large, need constitutional guarantees to insure that its laws will reflect 'current values.' Elections take care of that quite well. The purpose of constitutional guarantees—and in particular those constitutional guarantees of individual rights that are at the center of this controversy—is precisely to prevent the law from reflecting certain changes in original values that the society adopting the Constitution thinks fundamentally undesirable." "Originalism," according to Justice Scalia "establishes a historical criterion that is conceptually quite separate from the preferences of the judge himself."[*]

By contrast, Justice Brennan, a leading liberal on the Court from 1956 to 1990, emphasized the problems with appealing to original intent: "It is arrogant to pretend that from our vantage [point] we can gauge accurately the intent of the framers on application of principle to specific, contemporary questions. Typically, all that can be gleaned is that the framers themselves did not agree about the application or meaning of particular constitutional provisions and hid their differences in cloaks of generality." Moreover, Justice Brennan maintained that "current justices read the Constitution in the only way that we can: as [contemporary] Americans. We look to the history of the time of framing and to the intervening history of interpretation. But the ultimate question must be: What do the words of the text mean in our time? For the genius of the Constitution rests not in any static meaning it might have had in a world that is dead and gone, but in the adaptability of its great principles to cope with current problems and current needs."[**]

[*]Antonin Scalia, "Originalism: The Lesser Evil," *University of Cincinnati Law Review* 55 (1989), p. 894.

[**]William J. Brennan, Jr., "The Constitution of the United States: Contemporary Ratification," lecture delivered at Georgetown University, October 12, 1985.

THE AMENDING POWER AND HOW IT HAS BEEN USED

Leaving aside the first ten amendments (the Bill of Rights), the power of constitutional amendment has served a number of purposes:

To Add or Subtract National Government Power

The Eleventh took some jurisdiction away from the national courts.

The Thirteenth abolished slavery and authorized Congress to legislate against it.

The Sixteenth enabled Congress to levy an income tax.

The Eighteenth authorized Congress to prohibit the manufacture, sale, or transportation of liquor.

The Twenty-First repealed the Eighteenth and gave states the authority to regulate liquor sales.

The Twenty-Seventh limited the power of Congress to set members' salaries.

To Expand the Electorate and Its Power

The Fifteenth extended suffrage to all male African Americans over the age of 21.

The Seventeenth took the right to elect their United States senators away from state legislatures and gave it to the voters in each state.

The Nineteenth extended suffrage to women over the age of 21.

The Twenty-Third gave voters of the District of Columbia the right to vote for president and vice president.

The Twenty-Fourth outlawed the poll tax, thereby prohibiting states from taxing the right to vote.

The Twenty-Sixth extended suffrage to otherwise qualified persons 18 years of age or older.

To Reduce the Electorate's Power

The Twenty-Second took away from the electorate the right to elect a person to the office of president for more than two full terms.

To Limit State Government Power

The Thirteenth abolished slavery.

The Fourteenth granted national citizenship and prohibited states from abridging privileges of national citizenship; from denying persons life, liberty, and property without due process; and from denying persons equal protection of the laws. This amendment has come to be interpreted as imposing restraints on state powers in every area of public life.

(cont.)

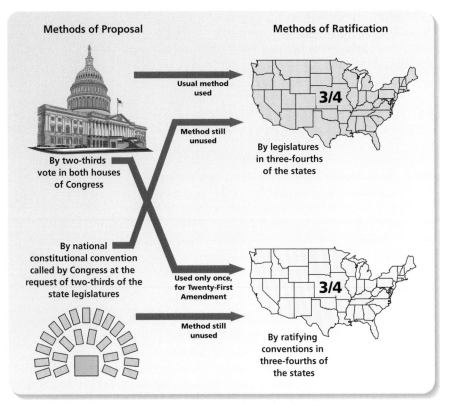

FIGURE 2–2 Four Methods of Amending the Constitution.

state legislatures apply for a convention to propose specific amendments on one topic, or must they request a convention with full powers to revise the entire Constitution? How long do state petitions remain alive? How should delegates be chosen? How should such a convention be run? Congress has considered bills to answer some of these questions but has not passed any, in part because most members do not wish to encourage a constitutional convention for fear that once in session it might propose amendments on any and all topics.

Under most proposals, each state would have as many delegates to the convention as it has representatives and senators in Congress. Finally—a crucial point—the convention would be limited to considering only the subject specified in the state legislative petitions and described in the congressional call for the convention. Scholars are divided, however, on whether Congress has the authority to limit what a constitutional convention might propose.[21]

Ratifying Amendments

After an amendment has been proposed, it must be ratified by the states. Again, two methods are provided by the Constitution: approval by the legislatures in three-fourths of the states or approval by specially called ratifying conventions in three-fourths of the states. Congress determines which method is used. All amendments except one—the Twenty-First (to repeal the Eighteenth, the Prohibition Amendment)—have been submitted to the state legislatures for ratification.

Seven state constitutions specify that their state legislatures must ratify a proposed amendment to the U.S. Constitution by majorities of three-fifths or two-thirds of each chamber. Although a state legislature may change its mind and ratify an amendment after it has voted against ratification, the weight of opinion is that once a state has ratified an amendment, it cannot "unratify" it.[22]

The Supreme Court has said that ratification must take place within a "reasonable time." When Congress proclaims an amendment to be part of the Constitution, it must decide whether the amendment has been ratified within a reasonable time so that it is "sufficiently contemporaneous to reflect the will of the people."[23] However, Congress approved ratification of the Twenty-Seventh Amendment, which had been before the nation for almost 203 years, so there seems to be no limit on what it considers a "reasonable time." Because of the experience with the Twenty-Seventh Amendment, Congress will probably continue the current practice of stipulating in the text of a proposed amendment that the necessary number of states must ratify it within seven years from the date of submission by Congress. In fact, ratification ordinarily takes place rather quickly (see Figure 2–3).[24]

Ratification Politics

The failure of the Equal Rights Amendment to be ratified provides a vivid example of the pitfalls of ratification. First introduced in 1923 and frequently thereafter, the Equal Rights Amendment (ERA) did not get much support until the 1960s. An influential book by Betty Friedan, *The Feminine Mystique* (1963), challenged stereotypes about the role of women. The National Organization for Women (NOW), formed in 1966, made passage of the ERA its central mission. By the 1970s, the ERA had overwhelming support in both houses of Congress and in both national party platforms. Every president from Harry Truman to Ronald Reagan, and many of their wives, endorsed the amendment; however, in 1980 the Republican party adopted a neutral stance on the ratification of the amendment. More than 450 organizations with a total membership of more than 50 million were on record in support of the ERA.[25] The ERA provided:

> *Section 1.* Equality of rights under the law shall not be denied or abridged by the United States or by any State on account of sex.
>
> *Section 2.* The Congress shall have power to enforce, by appropriate legislation, the provisions of this article.
>
> *Section 3.* This amendment shall take effect two years after the date of ratification.

Soon after passage of the amendment by Congress in 1972 and submission to the states, many legislatures ratified it quickly—sometimes without hearings—and by overwhelming majorities. By the end of that year, 22 states had ratified the amendment, and it appeared that the ERA would soon become part of the Constitution. But opposition organized under the leadership of Phyllis Schlafly, a prominent spokesperson for conservative causes, and the ERA became controversial.

THE AMENDING POWER AND HOW IT HAS BEEN USED (*CONT.*)

To Make Structural Changes in Government

The Twelfth corrected deficiencies in the operation of the electoral college that were revealed by the development of a two-party national system.

The Twentieth altered the calendar for congressional sessions and shortened the time between the election of presidents and their assumption of office.

The Twenty-Fifth provided procedures for filling vacancies in the vice presidency and for determining whether presidents are unable to perform their duties.

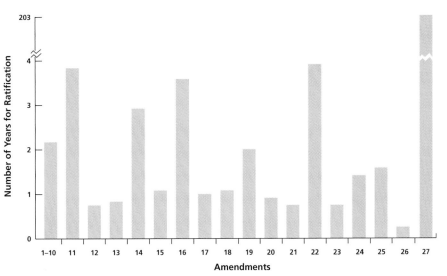

FIGURE 2–3 The Time for Ratification of the 27 Amendments to the Constitution.

PEOPLE & POLITICS *Making a Difference* ★ ★ ★

GREGORY WATSON

As a student at the University of Texas writing a paper on the Equal Rights Amendment in 1982, Gregory Watson came across an amendment proposed in 1789 as part of the Bill of Rights. It would prohibit a pay raise for members of Congress until the intervention of an election for members of the House. He also found that only six of the original 13 states had ratified it and that during the intervening years only three more states had done so.

Watson decided to start a ratification movement. He got some publicity for his efforts and, with the help of Texas Republican State Representative Don Mielke, persuaded six more state legislatures to ratify this long-forgotten proposed amendment. (By the way, Watson got only a C on his paper, although he is credited with starting a grass-roots movement to persuade 26 state legislatures to ratify the Twenty-Seventh Amendment.)*

After members of Congress tried unsuccessfully in 1989 to avoid public anger by delegating their decision to increase their own salaries to an independent commission, anti-Congress sentiment began to grow, and the ratification movement picked up steam. On May 7, 1992, the Michigan legislature became the thirty-eighth state to ratify the amendment.

The first reaction of some congressional leaders was to question this action because the Supreme Court had made it clear that amendments must be ratified within a "reasonable time." However, when members of Congress realized that the issue could be used against them in the next election, they declared the Twenty-Seventh Amendment to be "valid as part of the Constitution of the United States." The vote was 99 to 0 in the Senate, 414 to 3 in the House.

*Ruth Ann Strickland, "The Twenty-Seventh Amendment and Constitutional Change by Stealth," *PS: Political Science and Politics* (December 1993), p. 720.

People came from every state in the union to march in support of the passage of the Equal Rights Amendment.

Opponents argued that "women would not only be subject to the military draft but also assigned to combat duty. Full-time housewives and mothers would be forced to join the labor force. Further, women would no longer enjoy existing advantages under state domestic relations codes and under labor law."[26] The ERA also became embroiled in the controversy over abortion. Many opponents contended that its ratification would jeopardize the power of states and Congress to regulate abortion and would compel public funding of abortions.[27]

After the ERA became controversial, state legislatures held lengthy hearings, and floor debates became heated. Legislators hid behind parliamentary procedures and avoided making a decision for as long as possible. Opposition to ratification arose chiefly in the same cluster of southern states that had opposed ratification of the Nineteenth Amendment, which gave women the right to vote. As the opposition grew more active, proponents redoubled their efforts.

In the autumn of 1978, it appeared that the ERA would fall three short of the necessary number of ratifying states before the expiration of the seven-year limit on March 22, 1979. After an extended debate, and after voting down provisions that would have authorized state legislatures to change their minds and rescind prior ratification, Congress, by a simple majority vote, extended the time limit until June 30, 1982. Nonetheless, by the final deadline, the amendment was still three states short of the 38 needed for ratification.

The framers intended that amending the Constitution should be difficult, and the ERA ratification battle demonstrates how well they planned. Still, through interpretation, practices, usages, and judicial decisions, the Constitution has proved an enduring and adaptable governing document.

MAKE IT REAL SIMULATIONS ✓

THIS CONSTITUTION: WHAT IF YOU WERE A FOUNDING FATHER?

You have seen in this chapter that constitutions require trade-offs among competing principles and entail some form of checks and balances. The Make It Real feature for this chapter allows you to see how constitutional principles and changes that you favor would conflict with and require modifications of the Constitution.

Go to Make It Real: "The Constitution: What If You Were a Founding Father?"

S U M M A R Y

1. The U.S. Constitution, adopted in 1789, is the world's oldest. It has lasted because it is adaptable and flexible. It both grants and limits governmental power. The Constitution's separation of powers distributes authority among three branches of government: the legislative, executive, and judicial. Checks and balances limit the power of each branch.

2. Political parties may sometimes overcome the separation of powers, especially if the same party controls both houses of Congress and the presidency. Typically, this is not the case, however, and a divided government intensifies checks and balances. Presidential power, which has increased over time, has sometimes been able to overcome some restraints imposed by the Constitution.

3. Judicial review is the power of the courts to strike down acts of Congress, the executive branch, and the states as unconstitutional. It is one of the unique features of the U.S. constitutional system. The Supreme Court's power of judicial review was established in the 1803 case of *Marbury* v. *Madison*.

4. The Constitution is the framework of our governmental system. The constitutional system has been modified over time, adapting to new conditions through congressional elaboration, presidential practices, custom and usage, and judicial interpretation.

5. Although adaptable, the Constitution itself needs to be altered from time to time, and the framers provided a procedure for its amendment. An amendment must be both proposed and ratified: proposed by either a two-thirds vote in each chamber of Congress or by a national convention called by Congress on petition of the legislatures in two-thirds of the states; ratified either by the legislatures in three-fourths of the states or by specially called ratifying conventions in three-fourths of the states.

6. The Constitution has been formally amended 27 times. The usual method has been proposal by a two-thirds vote in both houses of Congress and ratification by the legislatures in three-fourths of the states.

K E Y   T E R M S

natural law	direct primary	judicial review	executive privilege
separation of powers	initiative	writ of mandamus	impoundment
checks and balances	referendum	impeachment	
divided government	recall	executive order	

FURTHER READING

LANCE BANNING, *The Sacred Fire of Liberty: James Madison and the Founding of the Federal Republic* (Cornell University Press, 1995).

CAROL BERKIN, *A Brilliant Solution: Inventing the American Constitution* (Harcourt, 2002).

JAMES BRYCE, *The American Commonwealth,* 2 vols. (Macmillan, 1889).

JAMES MACGREGOR BURNS, *The Vineyard of Liberty* (Knopf, 1982).

GERHARD CASPER, *Separation of Powers: Essays on the Founding Period* (Harvard University Press, 1997).

NEIL H. COGAN, *The Complete Bill of Rights: The Drafts, Debates, Sources, and Origins* (Oxford University Press, 1997).

CHRISTOPHER L. EISGRUBER, *Constitutional Self-Government* (Harvard University Press, 2001).

MICHAEL KAMMEN, *A Machine That Would Go of Itself: The Constitution in American Culture* (Knopf, 1986).

PHILIP B. KURLAND AND RALPH LERNER, *The Founders' Constitution,* 5 vols. (University of Chicago Press, 1987).

LIBRARY OF CONGRESS, CONGRESSIONAL RESEARCH SERVICE, *The Constitution of the United States of America: Analysis and Interpretation,* Senate Document 100–9 (U.S. Government Printing Office, 1991). Updated at www.findlaw.com/case_code.

WILLIAM NELSON, Marbury v. Madison: *The Origins and Legacy of Judicial Review* (University Press of Kansas, 2000).

J. W. PELTASON AND SUE DAVIS, *Understanding the Constitution,* 16th ed. (Wadsworth, 2004).

CHARLES H. SHELDON, *Essentials of the American Constitution: The Supreme Court and Fundamental Law,* ed. Stephen L. Wasby (Westview Press, 2002).

CASS SUNSTEIN, *Designing Democracy: What Constitutions Do* (Oxford University Press, 2001).

JOHN R. VILE, ED. *Proposed Amendments to the U.S. Constitution: 1787-2001* (The Lawbook Exchange, 2003).

★★ *On Reading the Constitution* ★★

More than 218 years after its ratification, our Constitution remains the operating charter of our republic. It is neither self-explanatory nor a comprehensive description of our constitutional rules. Still, it remains the starting point. Many Americans who swear by the Constitution have never read it seriously, although copies can be found in most American government and American history textbooks.

Justice Hugo Black, who served on the Supreme Court for 34 years, kept a copy of the Constitution with him at all times. He read it often. Reading the Constitution would be a good way for you to begin (and then reread again to end) your study of the government of the United States. We have therefore included a copy of it at this point in the book. Please read it carefully.

The Constitution of the United States

The Preamble

We the People of the United States, in Order to form a more perfect Union, establish Justice, insure domestic Tranquility, provide for the common defense, promote the general Welfare, and secure the Blessings of Liberty to ourselves and our Posterity, do ordain and establish this Constitution for the United States of America.

Article I—The Legislative Article

Legislative Power

Section 1   All legislative Powers herein granted shall be vested in a Congress of the United States, which shall consist of a Senate and House of Representatives.

House of Representatives: Composition; Qualifications; Apportionment; Impeachment Power

Section 2

Clause 1.   The House of Representatives shall be composed of Members chosen every second Year by the People of the several States, and the Electors in each State shall have the Qualifications requisite for Electors of the most numerous Branch of the State Legislature.

Clause 2.   No Person shall be a Representative who shall not have attained to the Age of twenty five Years, and been seven Years a Citizen of the United States, and who shall not, when elected, be an Inhabitant of that State in which he shall be chosen.

Clause 3.   Representatives and direct Taxes[1] shall be apportioned among the several States which may be included within this Union, according to their respective Numbers, which shall be determined by adding to the whole Number of free Persons, including those bound to Service for a Term of Years, and excluding Indians not taxed, three fifths of all other Persons.[2] The actual Enumeration shall be made within three Years after the first Meeting of the Congress of the United States, and within every subsequent Term of ten Years, in such Manner as they shall by Law direct. The Number of Representatives shall not exceed one for every thirty Thousand, but each State shall have at least one Representative; and until each enumeration shall be made, the State of New Hampshire shall be entitled to chuse three, Massachusetts eight, Rhode-Island and Providence Plantations one, Connecticut five, New-York six, New Jersey four, Pennsylvania eight, Delaware one, Maryland six, Virginia ten, North Carolina five, South Carolina five, and Georgia three.

Clause 4.   When vacancies happen in the Representation from any State, the Executive Authority thereof shall issue Writs of Election to fill such Vacancies.

Clause 5.   The House of Representatives shall chuse their Speaker and other Officers; and shall have the sole Power of Impeachment.

Senate Composition: Qualifications, Impeachment Trials

Section 3

Clause 1.   The Senate of the United States shall be composed of two Senators from each State, chosen by the Legislature thereof,[3] for six Years; and each Senator shall have one Vote.

Clause 2.   Immediately after they shall be assembled in Consequence of the first Election, they shall be divided as equally as may be into three Classes. The Seats of the Senators of the first Class shall be vacated at the Expiration of the second Year, of the second Class at the Expiration of the fourth Year, and of the third Class at the Expiration of the sixth Year, so that one third may be chosen every second Year; and if Vacancies happen by Resignation, or otherwise, during the Recess of the Legislature of any State, the Executive thereof may make temporary Appointments until the next Meeting of the Legislature, which shall then fill such Vacancies.[4]

Clause 3.   No person shall be a Senator who shall not have attained to the Age of thirty Years, and been nine Years a Citizen of the United States, and who shall not, when elected, be an inhabitant of that State for which he shall be chosen.

Clause 4.   The Vice President of the United States shall be President of the Senate, but shall have no Vote, unless they be equally divided.

Clause 5.   The Senate shall chuse their other Officers, and also a President pro tempore, in the Absence of the Vice President, or when he shall exercise the Office of President of the United States.

Clause 6.   The Senate shall have the sole Power to try all Impeachments. When sitting for that Purpose, they shall be on Oath or Affirmation. When the President of the United States is tried, the Chief Justice shall preside: And no Person shall be convicted without the Concurrence of two thirds of the Members present.

Judgment in Cases of Impeachment shall not extend further than to removal from Office, and disqualification to hold and enjoy any Office of honor, Trust or Profit under the United States; but the Party convicted shall nevertheless be liable and subject to Indictment, Trial, Judgment and Punishment, according to law.

Congressional Elections: Times, Places, Manner

Section 4   The Times, Places and Manner of holding Elections for Senators and Representatives, shall be prescribed in each State by the Legislature thereof; but the Congress may at any time by Law make or alter such Regulations, except as to the Places of chusing Senators.

---

[1]Modified by the 16th Amendment
[2]Replaced by Section 2, 14th Amendment

[3]Repealed by the 17th Amendment
[4]Modified by the 17th Amendment

The Congress shall assemble at least once in every Year, and such Meeting shall be on the first Monday in December, unless they shall by Law appoint a different Day.[5]

Powers and Duties of the Houses

Section 5

Clause 1. Each House shall be the Judge of the Elections, Returns and Qualifications of its own Members, and a Majority of each shall constitute a Quorum to do Business; but a smaller Number may adjourn from day to day, and may be authorized to compel the Attendance of absent Members, in such Manner, and under the Penalties as each House may provide.

Clause 2. Each House may determine the Rules of its Proceedings, punish its Members for disorderly Behaviour, and, with the Concurrence of two thirds, expel a Member.

Clause 3. Each House shall keep a Journal of its Proceedings, and from time to time publish the same, excepting such Parts as may in their Judgment require Secrecy; and the Yeas and Nays of the Members of either House on any question shall, at the Desire of one fifth of those Present, be entered on the Journal.

Clause 4. Neither House, during the Session of Congress, shall, without the Consent of the other, adjourn for more than three days, nor to any other place than that in which the two Houses shall be sitting.

Rights of Members

Section 6

Clause 1. The Senators and Representatives shall receive a Compensation for their Services, to be ascertained by Law, and paid out of the Treasury of the United States. They shall in all Cases, except Treason, Felony and Breach of the Peace, be privileged from Arrest during their Attendance at the Session of their respective Houses, and in going to and returning from the same; and for any Speech or Debate in either House, they shall not be questioned in any other Place.

Clause 2. No Senator or Representative, shall, during the time for which he was elected, be appointed to any civil Office under the Authority of the United States, which shall have been created, or the Emoluments whereof shall have been encreased during such time; and no Person holding any Office under the United States, shall be a Member of either House during his Continuance in Office.

Legislative Powers: Bills and Resolutions

Section 7

Clause 1. All Bills for raising Revenue shall originate in the House of Representatives; but the Senate may propose or concur with Amendments as on other Bills.

Clause 2. Every Bill which shall have passed the House of Representatives and the Senate, shall, before it becomes a Law, be presented to the President of the United States; if he approve he shall sign it, but if not he shall return it, with his Objections to that House in which it shall have originated, who shall enter the Objections at large on their Journal, and proceed to reconsider it. If after such Reconsideration two thirds of that House shall agree to pass the Bill, it shall be sent, together with the Objections, to the other House, by which it shall likewise be reconsidered, and if approved by two thirds of that House, it shall become a Law. But in all such Cases the Votes of both Houses shall be determined by yeas and Nays, and the Names of the Persons voting for and against the Bill shall be entered on the Journal of each House respectively. If any Bill shall not be returned by the President within ten Days (Sundays excepted) after it shall have been presented to him, the Same shall be a Law, in like Manner as if he had signed it, unless the Congress by their Adjournment prevent its Return, in which Case it shall not be a Law.

Clause 3. Every Order, Resolution, or Vote to which the Concurrence of the Senate and House of Representatives may be necessary (except on a question of Adjournment) shall be presented to the President of the United States; and before the Same shall take Effect, shall be approved by him, or being disapproved by him, shall be repassed by two thirds of the Senate and House of Representatives, according to the Rules and Limitations prescribed in the Case of a Bill.

Powers of Congress

Section 8

Clause 1. The Congress shall have Power To lay and collect Taxes, Duties, Imposts and Excises, to pay the Debts and provide for the common Defence and general Welfare of the United States; but all Duties, Imposts and Excises shall be uniform throughout the United States.

To borrow Money on the Credit of the United States;

To regulate Commerce with foreign Nations, and among the several States, and with the Indian Tribes;

To establish an uniform Rule of Naturalization, and uniform Laws on the subject of Bankruptcies throughout the United States;

To coin Money, regulate the Value thereof, and of foreign Coin, and fix the Standard of Weights and Measures;

To provide for the Punishment of counterfeiting the Securities and current Coin of the United States;

To establish Post Offices and post Roads;

To promote the Progress of Science and useful Arts, by securing for limited Times to Authors and Inventors the exclusive Right to their respective Writings and Discoveries;

To constitute Tribunals inferior to the supreme Court;

To define and punish Piracies and Felonies committed on the high Seas, and Offences against the Law of Nations;

To declare War, grant Letters of Marque and Reprisal, and make Rules concerning Captures on Land and Water;

To raise and support Armies, but no Appropriation of Money to that Use shall be for a longer Term than two Years;

To provide and maintain a Navy;

To make Rules for the Government and Regulation of the land and naval Forces;

To provide for calling for the Militia to execute the Laws of the Union, suppress Insurrections and repel Invasions;

To provide for organizing, arming, and disciplining, the Militia, and for governing such Part of them as may be employed in the Service of the United States, reserving to the States respectively, the Appointment of the Officers, and the Authority of training the Militia according to the discipline prescribed by Congress;

Clause 2. To exercise exclusive Legislation in all Cases whatsoever, over such District (not exceeding ten Miles square) as may, by Cession of particular States, and the Acceptance of Congress, become the Seat of the Government of the United States, and to exercise like Authority over all Places purchased by the Consent of the Legislature of the State in which the Same shall be, for the Erection of Forts, Magazines, Arsenals, dock-Yards, and other needful Buildings;—And

Clause 3. To make all Laws which shall be necessary and proper for carrying into Execution the foregoing Powers, and all other Powers vested by this Constitution in the Government of the United States, or in any Department or Officer thereof.

Powers Denied to Congress

Section 9

Clause 1. The Migration of Importation of such Persons as any of the States now existing shall think proper to admit, shall not be prohibited by the Congress prior to the Year one thousand eight hundred and eight, but a Tax or Duty may be imposed on such Importation, not exceeding ten dollars for each Person.

Clause 2. The privilege of the Writ of Habeas Corpus shall not be suspended, unless when in Cases of Rebellion or Invasion the public Safety may require it.

---

[5]Changed by the 20th Amendment

Clause 3.   No Bill of Attainder or ex post facto Laws shall be passed.

Clause 4.   No Capitation, or other direct, Tax shall be laid, unless in Proportion to the Census or Enumeration herein before directed to be taken.[6]

Clause 5.   No Tax or Duty shall be laid on Articles exported from any State.

Clause 6.   No Preference shall be given by any Regulation of Commerce or Revenue to the Ports of one State over those of another; nor shall Vessels bound to, or from, one State, be obliged to enter, clear, or pay Duties in another.

Clause 7.   No Money shall be drawn from the Treasury, but in Consequence of Appropriations made by Law; and a regular Statement and Account of the Receipts and Expenditures of all public Money shall be published from time to time.

Clause 8.   No Title of Nobility shall be granted by the United States; And no Person holding any Office of Profit or Trust under them, shall, without the Consent of Congress, accept of any present, Emolument, Office, or Title, of any kind whatever, from any King, Prince, or foreign State.

Powers Denied to the States

Section 10

Clause 1.   No State shall enter into any Treaty, Alliance, or Confederation; grant Letters of Marque and Reprisal; coin Money; emit Bills of Credit; make any Thing but gold and silver Coin a Tender in Payment of Debts; pass any Bill of Attainder, ex post facto Law, or Law impairing the Obligation of Contracts, or grant any Title of Nobility.

Clause 2.   No State shall, without the Consent of the Congress, lay any Imposts or Duties on Imports or Exports, except what may be absolutely necessary for executing its inspection Laws: and the net Produce of all Duties and Imposts, laid by any State on Imports or Exports, shall be for the Use of the Treasury of the United States; and all such Laws shall be subject to the Revision and Controul of the Congress.

Clause 3.   No State shall, without the Consent of Congress, lay any Duty of Tonnage, keep Troops, or Ships of War in time of Peace, enter into any Agreement or Compact with another State, or with a foreign Power, or engage in War, unless actually invaded, or in such imminent Danger as will not admit of Delay.

ARTICLE II—THE EXECUTIVE ARTICLE

Nature and Scope of Presidential Power

Section 1

Clause 1.   The executive Power shall be vested in a President of the United States of America. He shall hold his Office during the Term of four Years and, together with the Vice President, chosen for the same Term, be elected as follows:

Clause 2.   Each State shall appoint, in such Manner as the Legislature thereof may direct, a Number of Electors, equal to the whole Number of Senators and Representatives to which the State may be entitled in the Congress: but no Senator or Representative, or Person holding an Office of Trust or Profit under the United States, shall be appointed an Elector.

Clause 3.   The Electors shall meet in their respective States, and vote by Ballot for two Persons, of whom one at least shall not be an Inhabitant of the same State with themselves. And they shall make a List of all the Persons voted for, and of the Number of Votes for each; which List they shall sign and certify, and transmit sealed to the Seat of the Government of the United States, directed to the President of the Senate. The President of the Senate shall, in the Presence of the Senate and House of Representatives, open all the Certificates, and the Votes shall then be counted. The Person having the greatest Number of Votes shall be the President, if such Number be a Majority of the whole Number of Electors appointed; and if there be more than one who have such Majority and have an equal Number of Votes, then the House of Representatives shall immediately chuse by Ballot one of them for President; and if no person have a Majority, then from the five highest on the List the said House shall in like Manner chuse the President. But in chusing the President, the Votes shall be taken by States, the Representation from each State having one Vote; A quorum for this Purpose shall consist of a Member or Members from two thirds of the States, and a Majority of all the States shall be necessary to a Choice. In every Case, after the Choice of the President, the person having the greatest Number of Votes of the Electors shall be the Vice President. But if there should remain two or more who have equal Vote, the Senate shall chuse from them by Ballot the Vice President.[7]

Clause 4.   The Congress may determine the Time of chusing the Electors, and the Day on which they shall give their Votes; which Day shall be the same throughout the United States.

Clause 5.   No Person except a natural born Citizen, or a Citizen of the United States, at the time of the Adoption of this Constitution, shall be eligible to the Office of President; neither shall any Person be eligible to that Office who shall not have attained to the Age of thirty five Years, and been fourteen Years a Resident within the United States.

Clause 6.   In Case of the Removal of the President from Office, or of his Death, Resignation, or Inability to discharge the Powers and Duties of the said Office, the same shall devolve on the Vice President, and the Congress may by Law provide for the Case of Removal, Death, Resignation, or Inability, both of the President and Vice President, declaring what Officer shall then act as President, and such Officer shall act accordingly, until the Disability be removed, or a President shall be elected.[8]

Clause 7.   The President shall, at stated Times, receive for his Services, a Compensation, which shall neither be encreased nor diminished during the Period of which he shall have been elected, and he shall not receive within that Period any other Emolument from the United States, or any of them.

Clause 8.   Before he enter on the Execution of his Office, he shall take the following Oath or Affirmation:—"I do solemnly swear (or affirm) that I will faithfully execute the Office of President of the United States, and will to the best of my Ability, preserve, protect and defend the Constitution of the United States."

Powers and Duties of the President

Section 2

Clause 1.   The President shall be the Commander in Chief of the Army and Navy of the United States, and of the Militia of the several States, when called into the actual Service of the United States, he may require the Opinion, in writing, of the principal Officer in each of the executive Departments, upon any Subject relating to the Duties of their respective Offices, and he shall have the Power to grant Reprieves and Pardons for Offences against the United States, except in Cases of Impeachment.

Clause 2.   He shall have Power, by and with the Advice and Consent of the Senate to make Treaties, provided two thirds of the Senators present concur; and he shall nominate, and by and with the Advice and Consent of the Senate, shall appoint Ambassadors, other public Ministers and Consuls, Judges of the supreme Court, and all other Officers of the United States, whose Appointments are not herein otherwise provided for, and which shall be established by Law: but the Congress may by Law vest the Appointment of such inferior Officers, as they think proper, in the President alone, in the Courts of Law, or in the Heads of Departments.

Clause 3.   The President shall have Power to fill up all Vacancies that may happen during the Recess of the Senate, by granting Commissions which shall expire at the End of their next Session.

[6]Modified by the 16th Amendment

[7]Changed by the 12th and 20th Amendments
[8]Modified by the 25th Amendment

Section 3   He shall from time to time give to the Congress Information of the State of the Union, and recommend to their Consideration such Measures as he shall judge necessary and expedient; he may, on extraordinary Occasions, convene both Houses, or either of them, and in Case of Disagreement between them, with Respect to the Time of Adjournment, he may adjourn them to such Time as he shall think proper; he shall receive Ambassadors and other public Ministers; he shall take Care that the Laws be faithfully executed, and shall Commission all the Officers of the United States.

Section 4   The President, Vice President and all civil Officers of the United States, shall be removed from Office on Impeachment for, and Conviction of, Treason, Bribery, or other High Crimes and Misdemeanors.

ARTICLE III—THE JUDICIAL ARTICLE

Judicial Power, Courts, Judges

Section 1   The judicial Power of the United States, shall be vested in one supreme Court, and in such inferior Courts as the Congress may from time to time ordain and establish. The Judges, both the supreme and inferior Courts, shall hold their Offices during good Behaviour, and shall, at stated Times, receive for their Services, a Compensation, which shall not be diminished during their Continuance in Office.

Jurisdiction

Section 2   The judicial Power shall extend to all Cases, in Law and Equity, arising under this Constitution, the Laws of the United States, and Treaties made, or which shall be made, under their Authority;—to all Cases affecting Ambassadors, other public Ministers and Consuls;—to all Cases of admiralty and maritime Jurisdiction;—to Controversies to which the United States shall be a Party;—to Controversies between two or more States; between a State and Citizens of another State;[9]—between Citizens of different States;—between Citizens of the same State claiming Lands under Grants of different States, and between a State, or the Citizens thereof, and foreign States, Citizens, or Subjects.

In all Cases affecting Ambassadors, other public Ministers and Consuls, and those in which a State shall be Party, the supreme Court shall have original Jurisdiction. In all the other Cases before mentioned, the supreme Court shall have appellate Jurisdiction, both as to Law and Fact, with such Exceptions, and under such Regulations as Congress shall make.

The Trial of all Crimes, except in Cases of Impeachment, shall be by Jury; and such Trial shall be held in the State where the said Crimes shall have been committed; but when not committed within any State, the Trial shall be at such Place or Places as the Congress may by Law have directed.

Treason

Section 3   Treason against the United States, shall consist only in levying War against them, or in adhering to their Enemies, giving them Aid and Comfort. No Persons shall be convicted of Treason unless on the Testimony of two Witnesses to the same overt Act, or on Confession in open Court.

The Congress shall have Power to declare the Punishment of Treason, but no Attainder of Treason shall work Corruption of Blood, or Forfeiture except during the Life of the Person attainted.

ARTICLE IV—INTERSTATE RELATIONS

Full Faith and Credit Clause

Section 1   Full Faith and Credit shall be given in each State to the public Acts, Records, and judicial Proceedings of every other State. And the Congress may by general Laws prescribe the Manner in which such Acts, Records and Proceedings shall be proved, and the Effect thereof.

Privileges and Immunities; Interstate Extradition

Section 2

Clause 1.   The Citizens of each State shall be entitled to all Privileges and Immunities of Citizens in the several States.

Clause 2.   A person charged in any State with Treason, Felony or other Crime, who shall flee from Justice, and be found in another State, shall on Demand of the executive Authority of the State from which he fled, be delivered up, to be removed to the State having jurisdiction of the Crime.

Clause 3.   No person held to Service or Labour in one State, under the Laws thereof, escaping into another, shall, in Consequence of any Law or Regulation therein, be discharged from such Service or Labour, but shall be delivered up on Claim of the Party to whom such Service or Labour may be due.[10]

Admission of States

Section 3   New States may be admitted by the Congress into this Union; but no new State shall be formed or erected within the Jurisdiction of any other State; nor any State to be formed by the Junction of two or more States, or Parts of States, without the Consent of the Legislatures of the States concerned as well as of the Congress.

The Congress shall have Power to dispose of and make all needful Rules and Regulations respecting the Territory or other Property belonging to the United States; and nothing in this Constitution shall be so construed as to Prejudice any Claims of the United States, or of any particular State.

Republican Form of Government

Section 4   The United States shall guarantee to every State in this Union a Republican Form of Government, and shall protect each of them against Invasion; and on Application of the Legislature, or of the Executive (when the Legislature cannot be convened) against domestic Violence.

ARTICLE V—THE AMENDING POWER

The Congress, whenever two thirds of both Houses shall deem it necessary, shall propose Amendments to this Constitution, or, on the Application of the Legislatures of two thirds of several States, shall call a Convention for proposing Amendments, which, in either Case, shall be valid to all Intents and Purposes, as Part of this Constitution, when ratified by the Legislatures of three fourths of the several States, or by Conventions in three fourths thereof, as the one or the other Mode of Ratification may be proposed by the Congress; Provided that no Amendment which may be made prior to the Year One thousand eight hundred and eight shall in any Manner affect the first and fourth Clauses in the Ninth Section of the first Article; and that no State, without its Consent, shall be deprived of its equal Suffrage in the Senate.

ARTICLE VI—THE SUPREMACY ACT

Clause 1.   All Debts contracted and Engagements entered into, before the Adoption of this Constitution, shall be as valid against the United States under the Constitution, as under the Confederation.

Clause 2.   This Constitution, and the Laws of the United States which shall be made in Pursuance thereof; and all Treaties made, or which shall be made, under the Authority of the United States, shall be the supreme Law of the Land; and the Judges in every State shall be bound thereby, any Thing in the Constitution or Laws of any State to the Contrary notwithstanding.

Clause 3.   The Senators and Representatives before mentioned, and the Members of the several State Legislatures, and all executive and judicial Officers, both of the United States and of the several States, shall

---

[9]Modified by the 11th Amendment

[10]Repealed by the 13th Amendment

be bound by Oath or Affirmation, to support this Constitution; but no religious Test shall ever be required as a Qualification to any Office or public Trust under the United States.

ARTICLE VII—RATIFICATION

The Ratification of the Conventions of nine States, shall be sufficient for the Establishment of this Constitution between the States so ratifying the Same.

Done in Convention by the Unanimous Consent of the States present the Seventeenth Day of September in the Year of our Lord one thousand seven hundred and Eighty seven and of the Independence of the United States of America the Twelfth In Witness whereof We have hereunto subscribed our Names.

AMENDMENTS

The Bill of Rights

[The first ten amendments were ratified on December 15, 1791, and form what is known as the "Bill of Rights."]

Amendment 1—Religion, Speech, Assembly, and Politics

Congress shall make no law respecting an establishment of religion, or prohibiting the free exercise thereof; or abridging the freedom of speech, or of the press; or the right of the people peaceably to assemble, and to petition the government for a redress of grievances.

Amendment 2—Militia and the Right to Bear Arms

A well-regulated Militia, being necessary to the security of a free State, the right of the people to keep and bear Arms, shall not be infringed.

Amendment 3—Quartering of Soldiers

No Soldier shall, in time of peace be quartered in any house, without the consent of the Owner, nor in time of war, but in manner to be prescribed by law.

Amendment 4—Searches and Seizures

The right of the people to be secure in their persons, houses, papers, and effects, against unreasonable searches and seizures, shall not be violated, and no Warrants shall issue, but upon probable cause, supported by Oath or affirmation, and particularly describing the place to be searched, and the persons or things to be seized.

Amendment 5—Grand Juries, Self-Incrimination, Double Jeopardy, Due Process, and Eminent Domain

No person shall be held to answer for a capital, or otherwise infamous crime, unless on a presentment or indictment of a Grand Jury, except in cases arising in the land or naval forces, or in the Militia, when in actual service in time of War or public danger; nor shall any person be subject for the same offence to be twice put in jeopardy of life or limb; nor shall be compelled in any criminal case to be a witness against himself, nor be deprived of life, liberty, or property, without due process of law; nor shall private property be taken for public use, without just compensation.

Amendment 6—Criminal Court Procedures

In all criminal prosecutions, the accused shall enjoy the right to a speedy and public trial, by an impartial jury of the State and district wherein the crime shall have been committed, which district shall have been previously ascertained by law, and to be informed of the nature and cause of the accusation; to be confronted with the witnesses against him; to have compulsory process for obtaining Witnesses in his favor, and to have the Assistance of Counsel for his defense.

Amendment 7—Trial by Jury in Common Law Cases

In Suits at common law, where the value in controversy shall exceed twenty dollars, the right of trial by jury shall be preserved, and no fact tried by a jury shall be otherwise re-examined in any Court of the United States, than according to the rules of the common law.

Amendment 8—Bail, Cruel and Unusual Punishment

Excessive bail shall not be required, nor excessive fines imposed, nor cruel and unusual punishments inflicted.

Amendment 9—Rights Retained by the People

The enumeration in the Constitution, of certain rights, shall not be construed to deny or disparage others retained by the people.

Amendment 10—Reserved Powers of the States

The powers not delegated to the United States by the Constitution, nor prohibited by it to the States, are reserved to the States respectively, or to the people.

Amendment 11—Suits Against the States

[Ratified February 7, 1795]

The Judicial power of the United States shall not be construed to extend to any suit in law or equity, commenced or prosecuted against one of the United States by Citizens of another State, or by Citizens or Subjects of any Foreign State.

Amendment 12—Election of the President

[Ratified June 15, 1804]

The Electors shall meet in their respective states, and vote by ballot for President and Vice-President, one of whom, at least, shall not be an inhabitant of the same state with themselves; they shall name in their ballots the person voted for as President, and in distinct ballots the person voted for as Vice-President, and they shall make distinct lists of all persons voted for as President, and of all persons voted for as Vice-President, and of the number of votes for each, which lists they shall sign and certify, and transmit sealed to the seat of the government of the United States, directed to the President of the Senate;—The President of the Senate shall, in presence of the Senate and House of Representatives, open all the certificates and the votes shall then be counted;—The person having the greatest number of votes for President, shall be the President, if such number be a majority of the whole number of Electors appointed; and if no person have such majority, then from the persons having the highest numbers not exceeding three on the list of those voted for as President, the House of Representatives shall choose immediately, by ballot, the President. But in choosing the President, the votes shall be taken by states, the representation from each state having one vote; a quorum for this purpose shall consist of a member or members from two-thirds of the states, and a majority of all states shall be necessary to a choice. And if the House of Representatives shall not choose a President whenever the right of choice shall devolve upon them, before the fourth day of March next following, then the Vice-President shall act as President, as in the case of the death or other constitutional disability of the President.[11] The person having the greatest

---

[11]Changed by the 20th Amendment

number of votes as Vice-President, shall be the Vice-President, if such a number be a majority of the whole numbers of Electors appointed, and if no person have a majority, then from the two highest numbers on the list, the Senate shall choose the Vice-President; a quorum for the purpose shall consist of two-thirds of the whole number of Senators, and a majority of the whole number shall be necessary to a choice. But no person constitutionally ineligible to the office of President shall be eligible to that of Vice-President of the United States.

Amendment 13—Prohibition of Slavery

[Ratified December 6, 1865]

Section 1   Neither slavery nor involuntary servitude, except as a punishment for crime whereof the party shall have been duly convicted, shall exist within the United States, or any place subject to their jurisdiction.

Section 2   Congress shall have power to enforce this article by appropriate legislation.

Amendment 14—Citizenship, Due Process, and Equal Protection of the Laws

[Ratified July 9, 1868]

Section 1   All persons born or naturalized in the United States, and subject to the jurisdiction thereof, are citizens of the United States and of the State wherein they reside. No State shall make or enforce any law which shall abridge the privileges or immunities of citizens of the United States; nor shall any State deprive any person of life, liberty, or property, without due process of law; nor deny to any person within its jurisdiction the equal protection of the laws.

Section 2   Representatives shall be apportioned among the several States according to their respective numbers, counting the whole number of persons in each State, excluding Indians not taxed. But when the right to vote at any election for the choice of electors for President and Vice President of the United States, Representatives in Congress, the Executive and Judicial officers of a State, or the members of the Legislature thereof, is denied to any of the male inhabitants of such State, being twenty-one[12] years of age, and citizens of the United States, or in any way abridged, except for participation in rebellion, or other crime, the basis of representation therein shall be reduced in the proportion which the number of such male citizens shall bear to the whole number of male citizens twenty-one years of age in such State.

Section 3   No person shall be a Senator or Representative in Congress, or elector of President and Vice President, or hold any office, civil or military, under the United States, or under any State, who, having previously taken an oath, as a member of Congress, or as an officer of the United States, or as a member of any State legislature, or as an executive or judicial officer of any State, to support the Constitution of the United States, shall have engaged in insurrection or rebellion against the same, or given aid or comfort to the enemies thereof. But Congress may by a vote of two-thirds of each House, remove such disability.

Section 4   The validity of the public debt of the United States, authorized by law, including debts incurred for payment of pensions and bounties for services in suppressing insurrection or rebellion, shall not be questioned. But neither the United States nor any State shall assume or pay any debt or obligation incurred in aid of insurrection or rebellion against the United States, or any claim for the loss or emancipation of any slave; but all such debts, obligations and claims shall be held illegal and void.

Section 5   The Congress shall have power to enforce, by appropriate legislation, the provisions of this article.

Amendment 15—The Right to Vote

[Ratified February 3, 1870]

Section 1   The right of citizens of the United States to vote shall not be denied or abridged by the United States or by any State on account of race, color, or previous condition of servitude.

Section 2   The Congress shall have power to enforce this article by appropriate legislation.

Amendment 16—Income Taxes

[Ratified February 3, 1913]

The Congress shall have power to lay and collect taxes on incomes, from whatever source derived, without apportionment among the several States, and without regard to any census or enumeration.

Amendment 17—Direct Election of Senators

[Ratified April 8, 1913]

The Senate of the United States shall be composed of two Senators from each State, elected by the people thereof, for six years; and each Senator shall have one vote. The electors in each State shall have the qualifications requisite for electors of the most numerous branch of the State legislatures.

When vacancies happen in the representation of any State in the Senate, the executive authority of such State shall issue writs of election to fill such vacancies: Provided, That the Legislature of any State may empower the executive thereof to make temporary appointment until the people fill the vacancies by election as the legislature may direct. This amendment shall not be so construed as to affect the election or term of any Senator chosen before it becomes valid as part of the Constitution.

Amendment 18—Prohibition

[Ratified January 16, 1919. Repealed December 5, 1933 by Amendment 21]

Section 1   After one year from the ratification of this article the manufacture, sale, or transportation of intoxicating liquors within, the importation thereof into, or the exportation thereof from the United States and all territory subject to the jurisdiction thereof for beverage purposes is hereby prohibited.

Section 2   The Congress and the several states shall have concurrent power to enforce this article by appropriate legislation.

Section 3   This article shall be inoperative unless it shall have been ratified as an amendment to the Constitution by the legislatures of the several states, as provided in the Constitution, within seven years from the date of the submission hereof to the States by the Congress.[13]

Amendment 19—For Women's Suffrage

[Ratified August 18, 1920]

The right of the citizens of the United States to vote shall not be denied or abridged by the United States or by any State on account of sex.

Congress shall have power, by appropriate legislation, to enforce the provision of this article.

---

[12]Changed by the 26th Amendment

[13]Repealed by the 21st Amendment

Amendment 20—The Lame Duck Amendment

[Ratified January 23, 1933]

Section 1   The terms of the President and Vice President shall end at noon on the 20th day of January, and the terms of the Senators and Representatives at noon on the 3rd day of January, of the years in which such terms would have ended if this article had not been ratified; and the terms of their successors shall then begin.

Section 2   The Congress shall assemble at least once in every year, and such meeting shall begin at noon on the 3rd day of January, unless they shall by law appoint a different day.

Section 3   If, at the time fixed for the beginning of the term of the President, the President elect shall have died, the Vice President elect shall become President. If a President shall not have been chosen before the time fixed for the beginning of his term, or if the President elect shall have failed to qualify, then the Vice President elect shall act as President until a President shall have qualified; and the Congress may by law provide for the case wherein neither a President elect nor a Vice President elect shall have qualified, declaring who shall then act as President, or the manner in which one who is to act shall be selected, and such person shall act accordingly until a President or Vice President shall have qualified.

Section 4   The Congress may by law provide for the case of the death of any of the persons from whom the House of Representatives may choose a President whenever the right of choice shall have developed upon them, and for the case of the death of any of the persons from whom the Senate may choose a Vice President whenever the right of choice shall have devolved upon them.

Section 5   Sections 1 and 2 shall take effect on the 15th day of October following the ratification of this article.

Section 6   This article shall be inoperative unless it shall have been ratified as an amendment to the Constitution by the legislatures of three-fourths of the several States within seven years from the date of its submission.

Amendment 21—Repeal of Prohibition

[Ratified December 5, 1933]

Section 1   The eighteenth article of amendment to the Constitution of the United States is hereby repealed.

Section 2   The transportation or importation into any State, Territory, or Possession of the United States for delivery or use therein of intoxicating liquors, in violation of the laws thereof, is hereby prohibited.

Section 3   This article shall be inoperative unless it shall have been ratified as an amendment to the Constitution by conventions in the several States, as provided in the Constitution, within seven years from the date of the submission hereof to the States by the Congress.

Amendment 22—Number of Presidential Terms

[Ratified February 27, 1951]

Section 1   No person shall be elected to the office of the President more than twice, and no person who has held the office of President, or acted as President, for more than two years of a term to which some other person was elected President shall be elected to the Office of the President more than once. But this Article shall not apply to any person holding the office of President when this article was proposed by the Congress, and shall not prevent any person who may be holding the office of President, or acting as President, during the term within which this Article becomes operative from holding the office of President or acting as President during the remainder of such term.

Section 2   This Article shall be inoperative unless it shall have been ratified as an amendment to the Constitution by the legislatures of three-fourths of the several states within seven years from the date of its submission to the States by the Congress.

Amendment 23—Presidential Electors for the District of Columbia

[Ratified March 29, 1961]

Section 1   The District constituting the seat of Government of the United States shall appoint in such manner as the Congress may direct:
 A number of electors of President and Vice President equal to the whole number of Senators and Representatives in Congress to which the District would be entitled if it were a State, but in no event more than the least populous State; they shall be in addition to those appointed by the States, but they shall be considered, for the purposes of the election of President and Vice President, to be electors appointed by a State; and they shall meet in the District and perform such duties as provided by the twelfth article of amendment.

Section 2   The Congress shall have power to enforce this article by appropriate legislation.

Amendment 24—The Anti-Poll Tax Amendment

[Ratified January 23, 1964]

Section 1   The right of citizens of the United States to vote in any primary or other election for President or Vice President, for electors for President or Vice President, or for Senator or Representative in Congress, shall not be denied or abridged by the United States or any State by reason of failure to pay any poll tax or other tax.

Section 2   The Congress shall have power to enforce this article by appropriate legislation.

Amendment 25—Presidential Disability, Vice Presidential Vacancies

[Ratified February 10, 1967]

Section 1   In case of the removal of the President from office or his death or resignation, the Vice President shall become President.

Section 2   Whenever there is a vacancy in the office of the Vice President, the President shall nominate a Vice President who shall take the office upon confirmation by a majority vote of both houses of Congress.

Section 3   Whenever the President transmits to the President pro tempore of the Senate and the Speaker of the House of Representatives his written declaration that he is unable to discharge the powers and duties of his office, and until he transmits to them a written declaration to the contrary, such powers and duties shall be discharged by the Vice President as Acting President.

Section 4   Whenever the Vice President and a majority of either the principal officers of the executive departments, or of such other body as Congress may by law provide, transmit to the President pro tempore of the Senate and the Speaker of the House of Representatives their written declaration that the President is unable to discharge the powers and duties of his office, the Vice President shall immediately assume the powers and duties of the office as Acting President.
 Thereafter, when the President transmits to the President pro tempore of the Senate and the Speaker of the House of Representatives his

written declaration that no inability exists, he shall resume the powers and duties of his office unless the Vice President and a majority of either the principal officers of the executive departments, or of such other body as Congress may by law provide, transmit within four days to the President pro tempore of the Senate and the Speaker of the House of Representatives their written declaration that the President is unable to discharge the powers and duties of his office. Thereupon Congress shall decide the issue, assembling within forty-eight hours for that purpose if not in session. If the Congress, within twenty-one days after receipt of the latter written declaration, or, if Congress is not in session, within twenty-one days after Congress is required to assemble, determines by two-thirds vote of both houses that the President is unable to discharge the powers and duties of his office, the Vice President shall continue to discharge the same as Acting President; otherwise, the President shall resume the powers and duties of his office.

Amendment 26—Eighteen-Year-Old Vote

[Ratified July 1, 1971]

Section 1   The right of citizens of the United States, who are eighteen years of age, or older, to vote shall not be denied or abridged by the United States or by any State on account of age.

Section 2   The Congress shall have power to enforce this article by appropriate legislation.

Amendment 27—Congressional Salaries

[Ratified May 7, 1992]

No law, varying the compensation for the services of the Senators and Representatives, shall take effect, until an election of Representatives shall be intervened.

AMERICAN FEDERALISM

3

Responding to opposition to the Massachusetts supreme court's ruling that its state constitution forbids discrimination against same-sex couples seeking to marry, President George W. Bush said "if necessary" he would "support a constitutional amendment which would honor marriage between a man and a woman." But he added that the issue was basically a state matter, not a federal one, and he would not oppose "whatever legal arrangements people want to make."[1] That disappointed some of his conservative supporters because Vermont and California already recognize "civil unions" and "domestic partnerships" that confer the same legal benefits—health, insurance, and death benefits—for gay couples as for heterosexuals.

Although the Massachusetts court's decision may be overridden by a proposed state constitutional amendment in 2006, it renewed a national debate over the U.S. Constitution's full faith and credit clause. In 1996, Congress passed and President Bill Clinton signed the Defense of Marriage Act (DOMA), which relieves states of any obligation to recognize same-sex marriages even if they are recognized in other states and stipulates that the national government only recognizes heterosexual marriages for federal benefits such as Social Security.[2] Supporters of the law argue that the Constitution gives Congress the responsibility for prescribing the manner in which states are to comply with the full faith and credit clause. But the DOMA is likely to be challenged in the courts for going beyond the power of Congress to provide states with an exemption from their constitutional obligation under the full faith and credit clause.

The Supreme Court has not addressed the issue squarely and precedents provide no clear answer. The Court has held that states must comply with other states' judicial decisions,

TIME LINE

AMERICAN FEDERALISM

1781	Articles of Confederation establish state as preeminent over federal government
1788	Constitution ratified, replacing the Articles of Confederation
1791	Bill of Rights ratified by the states
1803	Louisiana Purchase greatly expands the size of the United States
1819	*McCulloch* v. *Maryland* interprets "necessary and proper" clause broadly
1824	*Gibbons* v. *Ogden* establishes congressional control over interstate commerce
1860	South Carolina is the first state to secede from the United States
1865	Civil War ends
1877	End of Reconstruction
1916	Federal Highway Act is first large-scale cash grant to states
1965	Voting Rights Act ends racial discrimination in voting practices in the states
1972	General revenue sharing increases funds available to state
1995	Congress prohibits "unfunded mandates," costing over $50 million
1996	Welfare reform reduces restrictions on states' use of welfare funds
2004	Massachusetts become first state to allow marriage of same-sex couples

devolution revolution
The effort to slow the growth of the federal government by returning many functions to the states.

but not necessarily with their other laws or administrative decisions. In light of recent Court rulings tilting toward states' rights and, as one scholar argues, "the fact that marriage has traditionally been an almost exclusive sphere of state authority, the Court would likely maintain the noncentralized and dual nature of American domestic relations that exist today, and allow the states to decide whether to recognize same-sex marriages."[3] However, similar DOMA laws in 38 states are likely to be challenged as well,[4] in light of the ruling in *Lawrence* v. *Texas*[5] invalidating state laws criminalizing homosexual sodomy, dissenting Justice Antonin Scalia has warned that states may no longer be able to ban same-sex marriages.

The controversy over same-sex marriages underscores the continuing debate over federalism. How do states interact with each other and with the national government? What is the proper balance of power between the national government and the states on providing homeland security, combating illegal immigration, improving education, and fighting corporate corruption and environmental pollution?

Since the founding of the Republic, Americans have debated the relationship of the national government to the states.[6] In 1787, the Federalists defended the creation of a strong national government, whereas the Antifederalists warned that a strong national government would overshadow the states. More recently, Republicans have led the charge against big government, urging the return of many functions to the states—a **devolution revolution**[7]—and they have had some success, such as when President Bill Clinton agreed to turn over more responsibilities for welfare to the states.

Federalism has recently emerged as a hot topic in other countries as well. Western European countries have formed the European Union (EU), with member nations giving up considerable authority over the regulation of businesses and labor, adopting a common monetary policy and currency (the euro), the addition in 2004 of ten Central and Eastern European countries, and debates over the ratification of a Treaty Establishing a Constitution for Europe.[8]

Heightened interest in federalism also comes from demands for greater autonomy for ethnic nationalities. The Canadian federal system strains under the demands of the French-speaking province of Quebec for special status and even independence. In the United Kingdom, devolution has occurred with Scotland, Northern Ireland, and Wales gaining their own parliaments or assemblies with considerable authority and, in the case of Scotland, limited power to tax. Belgium, Italy, and Spain have been devolving powers from their central governments to regional governments.

In contrast to some countries, the United States has had a relatively peaceful experience with the shifting balances of power under federalism. Since the New Deal in the 1930s, power and responsibility have drifted from the states to the national government. Although presidents from Richard Nixon to Bill Clinton slowed the growth of the national government, it was not until the late 1990s that the Republican-controlled Congress sought major reforms that heated the debate over federalism. As with welfare reform in 1996, Congress promoted decentralization in education with the Educational Flexibility Partnership Demonstration Act of 1999, authorizing the secretary of education to grant states waivers from federal rules setting educational goals. Still, in spite of such moves toward decentralization, Congress continues to expand federal law by making such offenses as the burning of churches, carjacking, and acts of terrorism federal crimes, even though they are already state and local crimes.

After more than half a century, the Supreme Court has placed some constraints on congressional powers in the name of federalism.[9] Like Congress, however, the Court's recent record on federalism is mixed. In spite of recent rulings holding that Congress exceeded its powers and may not authorize individuals to sue states to enforce federal laws,[10] the Court nevertheless ruled that state welfare programs may not restrict benefits to new residents to what they would have received in the states from which they moved[11] and that Congress may restrict states from selling drivers' personal information.[12]

Debates over federalism resemble those over whether "the glass is half-empty or half-full."[13] People who think they can get more of what they want from the national

Supporters applaud the announcement of a ruling by the Massachusetts Supreme Judicial Court on November 18, 2003, confirming that the state constitution does not bar same-sex couples from marrying. The issue of same-sex marriage illustrates how the debate over federalism is still a vital issue in the United States today. Proponents of same-sex marriage argue that the issue should remain in the hands of the individual states, whereas opponents want the federal government to propose an amendment to the Constitution defining marriage as a union specifically between a male and a female.

government usually advocate national action. Those who view states as more responsive and accountable argue for decentralization. Although Republicans generally favor action at the state level and Democrats tend to support action by the national government, neither party is consistent in its positions on the balance of power between the national government and the states. It depends on the issue at stake.

In this chapter, we first define federalism and its advantages. We then look at the constitutional basis for our federal system and how court decisions and political developments have shaped, and continue to shape, federalism in the United States.

DEFINING FEDERALISM

Scholars argue and wars (including our own Civil War) have been fought over what federalism means. One scholar counted 267 definitions.[14]

Federalism, as we define it, is a form of government in which a constitution distributes powers between a central government and subdivisional governments—usually called states, provinces, or republics—giving to both the national government and the regional governments substantial responsibilities and powers, including the power to collect taxes and to pass and enforce laws regulating the conduct of individuals.

The mere existence of both national and state governments does not make a system federal. What is important is that a *constitution divides governmental powers between the national government and the subdivisional governments,* giving clearly defined functions to each. Neither the central nor the subdivisional government receives its powers from the other; both derive them from a common source—the Constitution. No ordinary act of legislation at either the national or the state level can change this constitutional distribution of powers. Both levels of government operate through their own agents and exercise power directly over individuals.

federalism
Constitutional arrangement whereby power is distributed between a central government and subdivisional governments, called states in the United States. The national and the subdivisional governments both exercise direct authority over individuals.

At the official opening of Scotland's parliament on July 1, 1999, Queen Elizabeth was presented with the Scottish crown. The 129-member assembly is Scotland's first parliament in nearly 300 years.

Our definition of federalism is broad enough to include competing visions of it and the range of federal systems around the world. The following are some of the leading visions of federalism.

- *Dual federalism* views the Constitution as giving a limited list of powers—primarily foreign policy and national defense—to the national government, leaving the rest to sovereign states. Each level of government is dominant within its own sphere. The Supreme Court serves as the umpire between the national government and the states in disputes over which level of government has responsibility for a particular activity. During our first hundred years, dual federalism was the favored interpretation given by the Supreme Court.

- *Cooperative federalism* stresses federalism as a system of intergovernmental relations in delivering governmental goods and services to the people and calls for cooperation among various levels of government.

- *Marble cake federalism,* a term coined by political scientist Morton Grodzins, conceives of federalism as a marble cake in which all levels of government are involved in a variety of issues and programs, rather than a layer cake, or dual federalism, with fixed divisions between layers or levels of government.[15]

- *Competitive federalism,* a term first used by political scientist Thomas R. Dye, views the national government, 50 states, and thousands of other units as competing with each other over ways to put together packages of services and taxes. Applying the analogy of the marketplace, Dye emphasizes that at the state and local levels, we have some choice about which state and city we want to "use," just as we have choices about what kind of automobile we drive.[16]

- *Permissive federalism* implies that although federalism provides "a sharing of power and authority between the national and state government, the states' share rests upon the permission and permissiveness of the national government."[17]

GLOBAL *Perceptions*

QUESTION: Please indicate whether you completely agree, mostly agree, mostly disagree, or completely disagree with the following statement: The government controls too much of our daily lives.

The United States has more governments (federal, state, local, school districts, and special authorities) than any other country in the world. Yet, Americans are no more likely than citizens of other western democracies to believe that government in general controls too much of their daily lives. In fact, they have become less likely to agree with the statement since the early 1990s, even though the number of U.S. governments has increased.

The Pew survey suggests that people respond more to what government does by way of regulating their daily lives than the number of governments. Thus, Russians were the most likely to say that government has become less involved in their daily lives, which reflects the change from communism to a more democratic process.

SOURCE: Pew Global Attitudes Project, 2003

Completely agree that government controls too much of our daily lives   1991 ■

Completely agree that government controls too much of our daily lives   2002 ▪

SOURCE: Pew Global Attitudes Project, p. 110

■ *"Our federalism,"* championed by Ronald Reagan, Justices Sandra Day O'Connor, Antonin Scalia, and Clarence Thomas, along with Chief Justice William Rehnquist, presumes that the power of the federal government is limited in favor of the broad powers reserved to the states.

Federal nations are diverse and include Australia, Canada, Germany, Russia, and Switzerland. Although their number is not large, they "cover more than half of the land surface of the globe and include almost half of the world's population."[18] Federalism thus appears well suited for large countries with large populations, even though only 21 of the world's approximately 185 nation-states claim to be federal.

Constitutionally, the federal system of the United States consists of only the national government and the 50 states. "Cities are not," the Supreme Court reminded us, "sovereign entities." But in a practical sense, we are a nation of almost 88,000 governmental units, from the national government to the school board district. This does not make for a tidy, efficient, easy-to-understand system; yet, as we shall see, it has its virtues.

Government Under the Articles of Confederation, 1781–1788

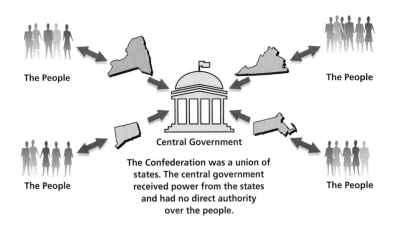

The People

The People

The People

The People

Central Government

The Confederation was a union of states. The central government received power from the states and had no direct authority over the people.

Government Under the U.S. Constitution (Federation) Since 1789

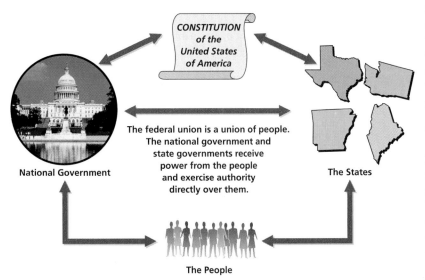

CONSTITUTION of the United States of America

National Government

The States

The federal union is a union of people. The national government and state governments receive power from the people and exercise authority directly over them.

The People

FIGURE 3–1 A Comparison of Federalism and Confederation.

Alternatives to Federalism

Among the alternatives to federalism are **unitary systems** of government, in which a constitution vests all governmental power in the central government. The central government, if it so chooses, may delegate authority to constituent units, but what it delegates it may take away. France, Israel, and the Philippines have unitary governments. In the United States, state constitutions usually create this kind of relationship between the state and its local governments.

At the other extreme from unitary governments are **confederations**, in which sovereign nations, through a constitutional compact, create a central government but carefully limit the power of the central government and do not give it the power to regulate the conduct of individuals directly. The central government makes regulations for the constituent governments, but it exists and operates only at their direction. The 13 states under the Articles of Confederation operated in this manner (see Figure 3–1), as did the southern Confederacy during the Civil War. The European Union is another example, though debates over its integration continue.[19]

Why Federalism?

In 1787, federalism was an obvious choice. Confederation had been tried but proved unsuccessful. A unitary system was out of the question because most people were too deeply attached to their state governments to permit subordination to central rule. Federalism was, and still is, thought to be ideally suited to the needs of a heterogeneous people spread over a large continent, suspicious of concentrated power, and desiring unity but not uniformity. Federalism offered, and still offers, many advantages for such a people.

FEDERALISM CHECKS THE GROWTH OF TYRANNY Although in the rest of the world, federal forms have not always been notably successful in preventing tyranny, and many unitary governments are democratic, Americans tend to associate freedom with federalism.[20] As James Madison pointed out in *The Federalist*, No. 10: If "factious leaders . . . kindle a flame within their particular states," national leaders can check the spread of the "conflagration through the other states" (*The Federalist*, No. 10, appears in the Appendix of this book). Moreover, when one political party loses control of the national government, it is still likely to hold office in a number of states. It can then regroup, develop new policies and new leaders, and continue to challenge the party in power at the national level.

Such diffusion of power creates its own problems. It makes it difficult for a national majority to carry out a program of action, and it permits those who control state governments to frustrate the policies enacted by Congress and administered by federal agencies. To the framers, these obstacles were an advantage. They feared that a single interest group might capture the national government and suppress the interests of others. Of course, the size of the nation and the many interests within it are the greatest obstacles to the formation of a single-interest majority—a point often overlooked today

unitary system
Constitutional arrangement in which power is concentrated in a central government.

confederation
Constitutional arrangement in which sovereign nations or states, by compact, create a central government but carefully limit its power and do not give it direct authority over individuals.

but emphasized by Madison in *The Federalist,* No. 10. If such a majority were to occur, having to work through a federal system would check its power.

FEDERALISM ALLOWS UNITY WITHOUT UNIFORMITY   National politicians and parties do not have to iron out every difference on every issue that divides us, whether it be abortion, same-sex marriage, gun control, capital punishment, welfare financing, or assisted suicide. Instead, these issues are debated in state legislatures, county courthouses, and city halls. But this advantage of federalism is becoming less significant as many local issues become national ones and as events in one state immediately affect policy debates at the national level.

FEDERALISM ENCOURAGES EXPERIMENTATION   Supreme Court Justice Louis Brandeis pointed out that state governments provide great "laboratories" for public policy experimentation; states may serve as proving grounds. If they adopt programs that fail, the negative effects are limited; if programs succeed, they can be adopted by other states and by the national government. Georgia, for example, was the first state to permit 18-year-olds to vote; Wisconsin experimented with putting welfare recipients to work; California pioneered air pollution control programs; Oregon and Hawaii created new systems for the delivery of health care. Nevada is the only state, so far, to legalize statewide gambling, but aspects of legalized casino gambling are now found in more than half the states. Not all innovations, even those considered successful, become widely adopted. Nebraska is the only state to have a unicameral legislature, although in recent years both Minnesota and California considered adopting one.

CHANGING FACE OF AMERICAN POLITICS

MINORITIES AND WOMEN ARE GAINING GROUND IN THE WORKFORCE

In the last few decades minorities and women have made significant gains in prestigious professions, especially as physicians and lawyers, but white males still dominate in certain highly visible occupations like police and firefighters.

Civil Workforce by Gender and Race—As a Percentage of Total Occupation

Occupation	Year	Men	Women	White	Black	Hispanic	Other	Total
Lawyers	1980	86%	14%	95%	3%	2%	1%	468,378
	1990	76	24	93	3	2	1	697,272
	2000	71	29	89	4	3	2	871,115
Physicians	1980	87	13	83	3	4	10	421,985
	1990	79	21	81	4	5	11	571,319
	2000	73	27	74	4	5	17	705,960
Firefighters	1980	99	1	89	6	4	1	186,867
	1990	97	3	84	9	5	2	216,914
	2000	96	4	82	8	6	3	242,395
Police Officers	1980	93	7	85	9	4	1	379,758
	1990	87	13	79	12	7	2	492,107
	2000	87	13	76	12	9	4	597,925

SOURCE: Census Bureau, 2000 Census; D'Vera Cohn and Sarah Cohen, "Minorities, Women Gain Professionally," *The Washington Post* A1 (December 30, 2003).

NUMBER OF GOVERNMENTS IN THE UNITED STATES

National	1
States	50
Counties	3,034
Municipalities	19,431
Townships or towns	16,506
School districts	13,522
Special districts	35,356
Total	87,900

SOURCE: U.S. Bureau of the Census, *Statistical Abstract of the United States,* available at http://wwwcensus.gov/prod/2003pubs/02statab/stlocgov.pdf.

FEDERALISM KEEPS GOVERNMENT CLOSER TO THE PEOPLE By providing numerous arenas for decision making, federalism involves many people and helps keep government closer to the people. Every day, thousands of Americans are busy serving on city councils, school boards, neighborhood associations, and planning commissions. Since they are close to the issues and have firsthand knowledge of what needs to be done, they may be more responsive to problems than the experts in Washington.

We should be cautious, however, about generalizing that state and local governments are necessarily closer to the people than the national government. True, more people are involved in local and state politics than in national affairs, and confidence in state governments has increased while respect for national agencies has diminished. A majority of the public often appears dissatisfied with the federal government. Yet national and international affairs are on people's minds more often than state or local politics. And fewer voters participate in state and local elections than in congressional and presidential elections.

THE CONSTITUTIONAL STRUCTURE OF AMERICAN FEDERALISM

Dividing powers and responsibilities between the national and state governments has resulted in thousands of court decisions, hundreds of books, and endless speeches to explain them—and even then the division lacks precise definition. Nonetheless, a basic understanding of how the Constitution divides these powers and responsibilities and of what obligations are imposed on each level of government is helpful (see Table 3–1).

The formal constitutional framework of our federal system may be stated relatively simply:

1. The national government has only those powers delegated to it by the Constitution (with the important exception of the inherent power over foreign affairs).

2. Within the scope of its operations, the national government is supreme.

3. The state governments have the powers not delegated to the central government, except those denied to them by the Constitution and their state constitutions.

TABLE 3–1 THE FEDERAL DIVISION OF POWERS

Powers Delegated to the National Government	Some Powers Reserved for the States	Some Concurrent Powers Shared by the National and State Governments
• Express powers stated in the Constitution	• To create a republican form of government	• To tax citizens and businesses
• Implied powers that may be inferred from the express powers	• To charter local governments	• To borrow and spend money
• Inherent powers that allow the nation to present a united front to foreign powers	• To conduct elections	• To establish courts
	• To exercise all powers not delegated to the national government or denied to the states by the Constitution	• To pass and enforce laws
		• To protect civil rights

4. Some powers are specifically denied to both the national and state governments; others are specifically denied only to the states; still others are denied to the national government but not the states.

Powers of the National Government

The Constitution, chiefly in the first three articles, delegates legislative, executive, and judicial powers to the national government. In addition to these **express powers**, such as the power to regulate interstate commerce and to appropriate funds, Congress has assumed constitutionally **implied powers**, such as the power to create banks, which are inferred from the express powers. The constitutional basis for the implied powers of Congress is the **necessary and proper clause** (Article I, Section 8, Clause 18). This clause gives Congress the right "to make all Laws which shall be necessary and proper for carrying into Execution the foregoing Powers, and all other Powers vested . . . in the Government of the United States."

In the field of foreign affairs, the Constitution gives the national government **inherent powers**. The national government has the same authority to deal with other nations as if it were the central government in a unitary system. Such inherent powers do not depend on specific constitutional provisions. For example, the government of the United States may acquire territory by purchase or by discovery and occupation, though no specific clause in the Constitution allows such acquisition. Even if the Constitution were silent about foreign affairs—which it is not—the national government would still have the power to declare war, make treaties, and appoint and receive ambassadors.

Together, these express, implied, and inherent powers create a flexible system that allows the Supreme Court, Congress, the president, and the people to expand the central government's powers to meet the needs of a modern nation in a global economy and confronting threats of international terrorism. This expansion of central government functions rests on four constitutional pillars.

These four constitutional pillars—the *national supremacy article,* the *war power,* the *commerce clause,* and most especially, the *power to tax and spend* for the general welfare—have permitted a tremendous expansion of the functions of the national government, so much so that despite the Supreme Court's recent declaration that some national laws exceed Congress's constitutional powers, the national government has, in effect, almost full power to enact any legislation that Congress deems necessary, so long as it does not conflict with the provisions of the Constitution designed to protect individual rights and the powers of the states.

THE NATIONAL SUPREMACY ARTICLE   One of the most important pillars is found in Article VI of the Constitution: "This Constitution, and the Laws of the United States which shall be made in Pursuance thereof; and all Treaties made . . . under the Authority of the United States, shall be the supreme Law of the Land; and the Judges in every State shall be bound thereby; any Thing in the Constitution or Laws of any State to the Contrary notwithstanding." All officials, state as well as national, swear an oath to support the Constitution of the United States. States may not override national policies; this restriction also applies to local units of government, since they are agents of the states. National laws and regulations of federal agencies *preempt* the field so that conflicting state and local regulations are unenforceable.

THE WAR POWER   The national government is responsible for protecting the nation from external aggression, whether from other nations or international terrorism. The government's power to protect national security includes the power to wage war. In today's world, military strength depends not only on troops in the field but also on the ability to mobilize the nation's industrial might as well as to apply scientific and technological knowledge to the tasks of defense. The national government has the power to do whatever is necessary and proper to wage war successfully. Thus the national government has the power to do almost anything not in direct conflict with constitutional guarantees.

THE POWER TO REGULATE INTERSTATE AND FOREIGN COMMERCE   Congressional authority extends to all commerce that affects more than one state. Commerce includes

---

express powers
Powers specifically granted to one of the branches of the national government by the Constitution.

implied powers
Powers inferred from the express powers that allow Congress to carry out its functions.

necessary and proper clause
Clause of the Constitution (Article I, Section 8, Clause 18) setting forth the implied powers of Congress. It states that Congress, in addition to its express powers, has the right to make all laws necessary and proper for carrying out all powers vested by the Constitution in the national government.

inherent powers
The powers of the national government in the field of foreign affairs that the Supreme Court has declared do not depend on constitutional grants but rather grow out of the very existence of the national government.

AN EXPANDING NATION

A great advantage of federalism—and part of the genius and flexibility of our constitutional system—has been the way in which we acquired territory and extended rights and guarantees by means of statehood, commonwealth, or territorial status, and thus grew from 13 to 50 states, plus territories.

Louisiana Purchase	1803
Florida	1819
Texas	1845
Oregon	1846
Mexican Cession	1848
Gadsden Purchase	1853
Alaska	1867
Hawaii	1898
Philippines	1898–1946
Puerto Rico	1899
Guam	1899
American Samoa	1900
Canal Zone	1904–2000
U.S. Virgin Islands	1917
Pacific Islands Trust Territory	1947

commerce clause

The clause in the Constitution (Article I, Section 8, Clause 3) that gives Congress the power to regulate all business activities that cross state lines or affect more than one state or other nations.

the production, buying, selling, renting, and transporting of goods, services, and properties. The **commerce clause** (Article I, Section 8, Clause 3) packs a tremendous constitutional punch; it gives Congress the power "to regulate Commerce with foreign Nations, and among the several States, and with the Indian Tribes." In these few words, the national government has been able to find constitutional justification for regulating a wide range of human activity, since very few aspects of our economy today affect commerce in only one state and are thus outside the scope of the national government's constitutional authority.[21]

The broad authority of Congress over interstate commerce was affirmed in the landmark ruling of *Gibbons* v. *Ogden* in 1824. There, in interpreting the commerce clause, Chief Justice John Marshall asserted national interests over those of the states and laid the basis for the subsequent growth in congressional power over commerce and activities that affect interstate commerce.

Gibbons v. *Ogden* arose from a dispute over a monopoly to operate steamboats in New York waters that was granted to Robert Livingston and Robert Fulton. They in turn licensed Aaron Ogden to exclusively operate steamboats between New York and ports in New Jersey. Ogden sued to stop Thomas Gibbons from running a competing ferry. Gibbons countered that his boats were licensed under a 1793 act of Congress governing vessels "in the coasting trade and fisheries." New York courts sided with Ogden in holding that both Congress and the states may regulate commerce, just as each has the power to tax. Congress, therefore, had not preempted New York from granting the monopoly. Gibbons appealed to the Supreme Court.

The stakes were high in *Gibbons* v. *Ogden,* for at issue was the very concept of "interstate commerce." May both Congress and the states regulate interstate commerce? And when conflicts arise between national and state regulations, which prevails?

Chief Justice Marshall asserted that national interests prevail and astutely defined "interstate commerce" as "intercourse that affects more states than one." Unlike the power of taxation, Congress's power over interstate commerce is complete and overrides conflicting state laws.[22]

Gibbons v. *Ogden* was immediately heralded for promoting a national economic common market in holding that states may not discriminate against interstate transportation and out-of-state commerce. Chief Justice Marshall's brilliant definition of "commerce" as *intercourse among the states* provided the basis clause for national regulation of an expanding range of economic activities, from the sale of lottery tickets[23] to prostitution[24] to radio and television broadcasts,[25] and telecommunications and the Internet.

The commerce clause has also been used to sustain legislation that goes beyond commercial matters. When the Supreme Court upheld the Civil Rights Act of 1964, forbidding discrimination because of race, religion, gender, or national origin in places of public accommodation, it said: "Congress's action in removing the disruptive effect which it found racial discrimination has on interstate travel is not invalidated because Congress was also legislating against what it considers to be moral wrongs."[26] Discrimination restricts the flow of interstate commerce; therefore, Congress could legislate against discrimination. Moreover, the law applies even to local places of public accommodation because local incidents of discrimination have a substantial and harmful impact on interstate commerce. The Court, however, has recently limited congressional power to address some other similar harms because it did not find a substantial connection with interstate commerce.[27]

THE POWER TO TAX AND SPEND   Congress lacks constitutional authority to pass laws solely on the grounds that they will promote the general welfare, but it may raise taxes and spend money for this purpose. For example, Congress lacks the power to regulate education or agriculture directly, yet it does have the power to appropriate money to support education or to pay farm subsidies. By attaching conditions to its grants of money, Congress may thus regulate what it cannot directly control by law.

When Congress puts up the money, it determines how the money will be spent. By withholding or threatening to withhold funds, the national government can influence or control state operations and regulate individual conduct. For example, Congress has stipulated that federal funds should be withdrawn from any program in which any person is denied benefits because of race, color, national origin, sex, or physical handicap. Congress also used its power of the purse to force states to raise the drinking age to 21 by tying such a condition to federal dollars for highways.

Congress frequently requires states to do certain things—for example, provide services to indigent mothers and clean up the air and water. These requirements are called **federal mandates**. Often Congress does not supply the funds required to carry out these mandates—called "unfunded mandates"—and its failure to do so has become an important issue as states face growing expenditures with limited resources. The Supreme Court has also ruled that Congress may not compel states through "unfunded mandates" to enact particular laws or require state officials to enforce federal laws, such as, requiring checks on the backgrounds of handgun purchasers.[28]

Powers of the States

The Constitution *reserves for the states all powers not granted to the national government,* subject only to the limitations of the Constitution. Powers not given exclusively to the national government by provisions of the Constitution or by judicial interpretation may be exercised concurrently by the states, as long as there is no conflict with national law. Such **concurrent powers** with the national government include the power to levy taxes and regulate commerce internal to each state.

In general, a state may levy a tax on the same item as the national government does, but a state cannot, by a tax, "unduly burden" commerce among the states, interfere with a function of the national government, complicate the operation of a national law, or abridge the terms of a treaty of the United States. Where Congress has not preempted the field, states may regulate interstate businesses, provided that these regulations do not cover matters requiring uniform national treatment or unduly burden interstate commerce.

Who decides what matters require "uniform national treatment" or what actions might place an "undue burden" on interstate commerce? Congress does, subject to final review by the Supreme Court. When Congress is silent or does not clearly state its intent, the courts—ultimately, the Supreme Court—decide if there is a conflict with the national Constitution or if there has been federal preemption by law or regulation.

Constitutional Limits and Obligations

In order to ensure that federalism works, the Constitution imposes certain restraints on both the national and the state governments. States are prohibited from:

1. Making treaties with foreign governments
2. Authorizing private persons to prey on the shipping and commerce of other nations
3. Coining money, issuing bills of credit, or making anything but gold and silver coin legal tender in payment of debts
4. Taxing imports or exports
5. Taxing foreign ships
6. Keeping troops or ships in time of peace (except the state militia, now called the National Guard)
7. Engaging in war, unless invaded or in such imminent danger as will not admit of delay

The national government, in turn, is required by the Constitution to refrain from exercising its powers, especially its powers to tax and to regulate interstate commerce, in such a way as to interfere substantially with the states' abilities to perform their responsibilities. Today, the protection states have from intrusions by the national government comes primarily from the political process because senators and

federal mandate
A requirement imposed by the federal government as a condition for the receipt of federal funds.

concurrent powers
Powers that the Constitution gives to both the national and state governments, such as the power to levy taxes.

representatives elected from the states participate in the decisions of Congress. However, the Court has held that Congress may not command states to enact laws to comply with or order state employees to enforce unfunded federal mandates; for example, as noted earlier, Congress may not require local law enforcement officials to make background checks prior to handgun sales.[29] It has also ruled that the Eleventh Amendment's guarantee of states' sovereign immunity from lawsuits forbids state employees from suing states in federal and state courts in order to force state compliance with federal employment laws.[30] Although Congress may not use those sticks, it may offer the carrot of federal funding if states comply with national policies, such as establishing a minimum drinking age.

The Constitution also requires the national government to guarantee to each state a "republican form of government." The framers used this term to distinguish a republic from a monarchy, on the one side, and from a pure, direct democracy, on the other. Congress, not the courts, enforces this guarantee and determines what is or is not a republican form of government. By permitting the congressional delegation of a state to be seated in Congress, Congress acknowledges that the state has the republican form of government guaranteed by the Constitution.

In addition, the national government is obliged by the Constitution to protect states against *domestic insurrection.* Congress has delegated to the president the authority to dispatch troops to put down such insurrections when so requested by the proper state authorities. If there are contesting state authorities, the president decides which is the proper one. The president does not have to wait, however, for a request from state authorities to send federal troops into a state to enforce federal laws.

Interstate Relations

Three clauses in the Constitution, taken from the Articles of Confederation, require states to give full faith and credit to each other's public acts, records, and judicial proceedings; to extend to each other's citizens the privileges and immunities of their own citizens; and to return persons who are fleeing from justice.

FULL FAITH AND CREDIT   The **full faith and credit clause** (Article IV, Section 1), one of the more technical provisions of the Constitution, requires state courts to enforce the civil judgments of the courts of other states and accept their public records and acts as valid.[31] It does not require states to enforce the criminal laws or legislation and administrative acts of other states; in most cases, for one state to enforce the criminal laws of another would raise constitutional issues. The clause applies especially to enforcement of judicial settlements and court awards.

INTERSTATE PRIVILEGES AND IMMUNITIES   Under Article IV, Section 2, states must extend to citizens of other states the privileges and immunities granted to their own citizens, including the protection of the laws, the right to engage in peaceful occupations, access to the courts, and freedom from discriminatory taxes. Because of this clause, states may not impose unreasonable residency requirements, that is, withhold rights to American citizens who have recently moved to the state and thereby have become citizens of that state. For example, a state may not set unreasonable time limits to withhold state-funded medical benefits from new citizens or to keep them from voting. How long a residency requirement may a state impose? A day seems about as long as the Supreme Court will tolerate to withhold welfare payments or medical care, 50 days or so for voting privileges, and one year for eligibility for in-state tuition for state-supported colleges and universities.

Financially independent adults who move into a state just before enrolling in a state-supported university or college may be required to prove that they have become citizens of that state and intend to remain after finishing their schooling by supplying such evidence of citizenship as tax payments, a driver's license, car registration, voter registration, and a continuous, year-round off-campus residence. Students who are financially dependent on their parents remain citizens of the state of their parents.

full faith and credit clause
Clause in the Constitution (Article IV, Section 1) requiring each state to recognize the civil judgments rendered by the courts of the other states and to accept their public records and acts as valid.

IN COMPARATIVE PERSPECTIVE

THREE DIFFERENT APPROACHES TO FEDERALISM

There is no single model for dividing authority between national and state governments or for power sharing in intergovernmental relations. The federal systems in Canada, Germany, and Switzerland are illustrative.

Canada combines a federal system with a parliamentary form of government that has authority to legislate on all matters pertaining to "peace, order, and good government." The system was established in 1867, in part to prevent conflicts similar to those between the states that led to the American Civil War. In each of the ten provinces, the lieutenant governor is appointed on the advice of the prime minister and must approve any provincial law before it goes into effect. The legislative powers of the provinces are thus checked and limited. However, the provinces retain residual powers, and unlike the U.S. Supreme Court, the Canadian judiciary has generally encouraged decentralization in recognition of its multicultural society. Thus Canadian provinces exercise greater power and the national government is weaker than in the United States. In addition, the special status claimed by French-speaking Quebec has led to intergovernmental relations that alternate between periods of centralization and decentralization.

The Federal Republic of Germany, whose Basic Laws of 1949 became the constitution with the reunification of East and West Germany in 1990, is often referred to as an example of cooperative federalism. Its 16 states, or Länder, exercise a great deal of power, far more than states do in the United States. The central government has a president and a bicameral parliament composed of an upper house, the

Federal Council, and a lower house, the National Assembly, as well as an independent judiciary. The central government has exclusive authority over foreign affairs, money, immigration, and telecommunications. But the Länder retain residual powers over all other matters and have concurrent powers over civil and criminal law, along with matters related to education, health, and the public welfare. Moreover, national legislation does not become law unless approved by a majority of the Federal Council, whose members are selected by legislatures in the Länder, not by popular elections.

Switzerland established a confederation on the basis of regional governments (cantons). The cantons reflect the ethnic and linguistic differences of their German-, French-, and Italian-speaking populations. All three languages are officially recognized by the central government. But of the 22 cantons, there are 18 that are unilingual, three that are bilingual, and one that is trilingual. They exercise most lawmaking powers and are represented in the National Council, a bicameral legislature, and the Council of States. Recent constitutional reforms further entrenched a tripartite federalism by expressly recognizing the autonomy of cities and munipalities, along with that of cantons and the federal government. As a result, cities and municipalities, unlike in the United States where they are agents of the states, have constitutional status.

For more information on comparative federalism, go to the Web site of the International Political Science Association's Section on Comparative Federalism at www.iu.edu/~soeaweb/IPSA and to the site of the Forum on Federations at www.forumfed.org.

EXTRADITION In Article IV, Section 2, the Constitution asserts that when individuals charged with crimes have fled from one state to another, the state to which they have fled is to deliver them to the proper officials upon the demand of the executive authority of the state from which they fled. This process is called **extradition**. "The obvious objective of the Extradition Clause," the courts have claimed, "is that no State should become a safe haven for the fugitives from a sister State's criminal justice system."[32] Congress has supplemented this constitutional provision by making the governor of the state to which fugitives have fled responsible for returning them. Despite their constitutional obligation, governors of asylum states have on occasion refused to honor a request for extradition.

INTERSTATE COMPACTS The Constitution also requires states to settle disputes with one another without the use of force. States may carry their legal disputes to the Supreme Court, or they may negotiate **interstate compacts**. Interstate compacts often establish interstate agencies to handle problems affecting an entire region. Before most interstate compacts become effective, congressional approval is required. After a compact has been signed and approved by Congress, it becomes binding on all signatory states, and its terms are enforceable by the federal judiciary. A typical state may belong to 20 compacts dealing with such subjects as environmental protection, crime control, water rights, and higher education exchanges.[33]

extradition
Legal process whereby an alleged criminal offender is surrendered by the officials of one state to officials of the state in which the crime is alleged to have been committed.

interstate compact
An agreement among two or more states. The Constitution requires that most such agreements be approved by Congress.

★★ **YOU DECIDE**

DO WE NEED A MORE RESTRICTED GOVERNMENT IN WASHINGTON?

Whereas in the 1980s President Ronald Reagan pressed to abolish the Department of Education, President George W. Bush signed into law his "No Child Left Behind" education bill, which among other things mandates annual standardized testing of elementary school children by 2005–2006. Some states objected to this legislation. In the aftermath of 9/11 and continuing threats of international terrorism, the Bush administration also increased the government's role in the area of homeland security, including the expanded use of state agencies as "first responders," and in combating illegal immigration. Yet, many states object to the increased financial costs and to the burden of having to track down and report on illegal immigrants in their communities.

Do we need federal standards or can states and localities be trusted to handle most domestic problems in their own way? If the national government sets standards, should it provide the funds but leave the details to the states? Should responsibility for education and welfare be given back to the states? Should states be forced to assume a greater role in improving education, maintaining homeland security, and reporting on illegal immigrants?

THE ROLE OF THE FEDERAL COURTS: UMPIRES OF FEDERALISM

Although the political process ultimately decides how power will be divided between the national and the state governments, the federal courts—and especially the Supreme Court—are often called on to umpire the ongoing debate about which level of government should do what, for whom, and to whom. This role for the courts was claimed in the celebrated case of *McCulloch* v. *Maryland*.

McCulloch Versus *Maryland*

In *McCulloch* v. *Maryland* (1819), the Supreme Court had the first of many chances to define the division of power between the national and state governments.[34] Congress established the Bank of the United States, but Maryland opposed any national bank and levied a $10,000 tax on any bank not incorporated within the state. James William McCulloch, the cashier of the bank, refused to pay on the grounds that a state could not tax an instrument of the national government.

Maryland was represented before the Court by some of the country's most distinguished lawyers, including Luther Martin, who had been a delegate to the Constitutional Convention. Martin said that the power to incorporate a bank was not expressly delegated to the national government in the Constitution. He maintained that the necessary and proper clause gives Congress only the power to choose those means and to pass those laws absolutely essential to the execution of its expressly granted powers. Because a bank is not absolutely necessary to the exercise of its delegated powers, he argued, Congress had no authority to establish it. As for Maryland's right to tax the bank, the power to tax is one of the powers reserved to the states; they may use it as they see fit.

The national government was represented as well by distinguished counsel, including Daniel Webster. Webster conceded that the power to create a bank is not one of the express powers of the national government. However, the power to pass laws necessary and proper to carry out Congress's express powers is specif-

There have been times throughout U.S. history when federal law has superseded state and local law. One example of this in recent history is the Voting Rights Act of 1965, which enforced the voting rights of African Americans in the South. In this photo, African American citizens in Montgomery, Alabama, are registering to vote for the very first time following a march that took place during one of the many voter registration drives of 1964 and 1965.

ically delegated to Congress. Therefore, Congress may incorporate a bank as an appropriate, convenient, and useful means of exercising the granted powers of collecting taxes, borrowing money, and caring for the property of the United States. Although the power to tax is reserved to the states, Webster argued that states cannot interfere with the operations of the national government. The Constitution leaves no room for doubt; in cases of conflict between the national and state governments, the national government is supreme.

Speaking for a unanimous Court, Chief Justice John Marshall rejected every one of Maryland's contentions. He summarized his views on the powers of the national government in these now-famous words: "Let the end be legitimate, let it be within the scope of the Constitution, and all means which are appropriate, which are plainly adapted to that end, which are not prohibited, but consist with the letter and spirit of the constitution, are constitutional." Having thus established the doctrine of *implied national powers,* Marshall set forth the doctrine of **national supremacy**. No state, he said, can use its taxing powers to tax a national instrument. "The power to tax involves the power to destroy. . . . If the right of the States to tax the means employed by the general government be conceded, the declaration that the Constitution, and the laws made in pursuance thereof, shall be the supreme law of the land, is empty and unmeaning declamation."

The long-range significance of *McCulloch v. Maryland* in providing support for the developing forces of nationalism and a unified economy cannot be overstated. The contrary arguments in favor of the states, if they had been accepted, would have strapped the national government in a constitutional straitjacket and denied it powers needed to deal with the problems of an expanding nation.

Federal Courts and the Role of the States

The authority of federal judges to review the activities of state and local governments has expanded dramatically in recent decades because of modern judicial interpretations of the Fourteenth Amendment, which forbids states from depriving any person of life, liberty, or property without *due process of the law.* States may not deny any person the *equal protection of the laws,* including congressional legislation enacted to implement the Fourteenth Amendment. Almost every action by state and local officials is now subject to challenge before a federal judge as a violation of the Constitution or of federal law.

Preemption occurs when a federal law or regulation takes precedence over enforcement of a state or local law or regulation. State and local laws are preempted not only when they conflict directly with federal laws and regulations but also if they touch a field in which the "federal interest is so dominant that the federal system will be assumed to preclude enforcement of state laws on the same subject."[35] Examples of federal preemption include laws regulating hazardous substances, water quality, clean air standards and many civil rights acts, especially the Civil Rights Act of 1964 and the Voting Rights Act of 1965.

Over the years, federal judges, under the leadership of the Supreme Court, have generally favored the powers of the federal government over the states. In spite of the Supreme Court's recent bias in favor of state over national authority, few would deny the Supreme Court the power to review and set aside state actions. As Justice Oliver Wendell Holmes of the Supreme Court once remarked: "I do not think the United States would come to an end if we lost our power to declare an Act of Congress void. I do think the Union would be imperiled if we could not make that declaration as to the laws of the several States."[36]

The Great Debate: Centralists Versus Decentralists

From the beginning of the Republic, there has been an ongoing debate about the "proper" distribution of powers, functions, and responsibilities between the national government and the states. Did the national government have the authority to outlaw slavery in the territories? Did the states have the authority to operate racially segregated

★★ THINKING IT THROUGH

Centralists argue that state and local officials are often less competent than national officials and tend to be concerned only with the narrow interests of their constituents. State and local governments are more apt to reflect local racial and ethnic biases as well as the biases of dominant local industries. State and local governments are also unable or unwilling to raise the taxes needed to carry out vital governmental functions.

Decentralists counter that increased urbanization has made states more responsive to the needs of communities, and they have become as sensitive to the needs of the poor and minorities as the national government. In recent years, state and local governments have also shown a greater willingness to raise taxes than the national government, and they have reformed and modernized in order to become more effective.

The great debate over which level of government best performs functions continues to rage. The Republican party started its history as the party of the National Union, while the Democrats were then the champion of states' rights, but over the past several decades, there have been changes. After winning control of Congress in the mid-1990s, Republicans led the charge against Washington, demanding the return of functions to the states. Democrats were reluctant to remove all federal standards, especially with respect to regulation of the environment and the workplace, and they generally favored providing minimum standards for programs, especially welfare and health care. More recently, President Bush and Republican leaders in Congress have pushed for expanded federal powers to counter threats to national security, to improve educational standards, and to expand Medicare coverage to include some of the costs of prescription drugs. Democrats in turn have countered that some homeland security programs do not go far enough and others go too far, that funding for education remains inadequate, and that prescription drug coverage will fall short when it takes effect in 2006.

national supremacy
Constitutional doctrine that whenever conflict occurs between the constitutionally authorized actions of the national government and those of a state or local government, the actions of the federal government prevail.

preemption
The right of a federal law or regulation to preclude enforcement of a state or local law or regulation.

schools? Could Congress regulate labor relations? Does Congress have the power to regulate the sale and use of firearms? Does Congress have the right to tell states how to clean up air and water pollution? Even today, as in the past, such debates are frequently phrased in constitutional language, with appeals to the great principles of federalism. But they are also arguments over who gets what, where, when, and how.

During the Great Depression of the 1930s, the nation debated whether Congress had the constitutional authority to enact legislation on agriculture, labor, education, housing, and welfare. Only 40 years ago, some legislators and public officials—as well as some scholars—questioned the constitutional authority of Congress to legislate against racial discrimination. The debate continues between **centralists**, who favor national action, and **decentralists**, who defend the powers of the states and favor action at the state and local levels.

THE DECENTRALIST POSITION   Among Americans favoring the decentralist or **states' rights** interpretation were the Antifederalists, Thomas Jefferson, John C. Calhoun, the Supreme Court from the 1920s to 1937, and more recently, Presidents Ronald Reagan and George H.W. Bush, the Republican leaders of Congress, Chief Justice William H. Rehnquist, and Justices Sandra Day O'Connor, Antonin Scalia, and Clarence Thomas.

Most decentralists contend that the Constitution is basically a compact among sovereign states that created the central government and gave it very limited authority. As Justice Clarence Thomas, an ardent advocate of states' rights, wrote in a dissenting opinion supporting the argument that a state has the power to impose term limits on members of Congress, "The ultimate source of the Constitution's authority is the consent of the people of each individual State, not the consent of the undifferentiated people of the Nation as a whole."[37] Thus the national government is little more than an agent of the states, and every one of its powers should be narrowly defined. Any question about whether the states have given a particular function to the central government or have reserved it for themselves should be resolved in favor of the states.

Decentralists hold that the national government should not interfere with activities reserved for the states. The Tenth Amendment, they claim, makes this clear: "The powers not delegated to the United States by the Constitution, nor prohibited by it to the States, are reserved to the States respectively, or to the people." Decentralists insist that state governments are closer to the people and reflect the people's wishes more accurately than the national government does. The national government, they add, is inherently heavy-handed and bureaucratic; to preserve our federal system and our liberties, central authority must be kept under control.

THE CENTRALIST POSITION   The centralist position has been supported by Chief Justice John Marshall, Presidents Abraham Lincoln, Theodore Roosevelt, and Franklin Roosevelt, and throughout most of our history, the Supreme Court.

Centralists reject the whole idea of the Constitution as an interstate compact. Rather, they view the Constitution as a supreme law established by the people. The national government is an agent of the people, not of the states, because it was the people who drew up the Constitution and created the national government. They intended that the central government's powers should be defined by the national political process and is denied authority only when the Constitution clearly prohibits it from acting.

Centralists argue that the national government is a government of all the people, whereas each state speaks only for some of the people. Although the Tenth Amendment clearly reserves powers for the states, it does not deny the national government the authority to exercise, to the fullest extent, all of its powers. Moreover, the supremacy of the national government restricts the states, because governments representing part of the people cannot be allowed to interfere with a government representing all of them.

The Supreme Court and the Role of Congress

From 1937 until the 1990s, the Supreme Court essentially removed federal courts from what had been their role of protecting states from acts of Congress. The Supreme Court broadly interpreted the commerce clause to allow Congress to do whatever Congress thought necessary and proper to promote the common good, even if the federal laws and

centralists
People who favor national action over action at the state and local levels.

decentralists
People who favor state or local action rather than national action.

states' rights
Powers expressly or implicitly reserved to the states and emphasized by decentralists.

regulations infringed on the activities of state and local governments. The Court went so far as to tell the states that they should look to the political process to protect their interests, not to the federal courts.[38]

In the past decade, however, a bare majority of the Supreme Court has signaled that federal courts should no longer remain passive in resolving federalism issues.[39] The Court declared that a state could not impose term limits on its members of Congress, but it did so only by a 5 to 4 vote. Justice John Paul Stevens, writing for the majority, built his argument on the concept of the federal union as espoused by the great Chief Justice John Marshall, as a compact among the people, with the national government serving as the people's agent. By contrast, Justice Clarence Thomas, writing for the dissenters, espoused a view of federalism not heard from a justice of the Supreme Court since prior to the New Deal. He interpreted the Tenth Amendment as requiring the national government to justify its actions in terms of an enumerated power and granting to the states all other powers not expressly given to the national government.[40]

The Court also declared that the clause in the Constitution empowering Congress to regulate commerce with the Indian tribes did not give Congress the power to authorize federal courts to hear suits against a state brought by Indian tribes.[41] Unless states consent to such suits, they enjoy "sovereign immunity" under the Eleventh Amendment. The effect of this decision goes beyond Indian tribes. As a result, except to enforce rights stemming from the Fourteenth Amendment, which the Court explicitly acknowledged to be within Congress's power, Congress may no longer authorize individuals to bring legal actions against states in order to force their compliance with federal law in either federal or state courts.[42]

Building on those rulings, the Court continues to press ahead with its "constitutional counterrevolution"[43] in returning to an older vision of federalism not embraced since the constitutional crisis over the New Deal in the 1930s. Among other recent rulings, the Court struck down the Violence Against Women Act, which had given women who are victims of violence the right to sue their attackers for damages.[44] Congress had found that violence against women annually costs the national economy $3 billion, but the Court held that Congress exceeded its powers in enacting the law and intruded on the powers of the states.

These Supreme Court decisions—most of which split the Court 5 to 4 along ideological lines, with the conservative justices favoring states' rights—may signal a major shift in the Court's interpretation of the constitutional nature of our federal system. Chief Justice Rehnquist, joined by Justices Scalia, Thomas, O'Connor, and frequently Justice Anthony M. Kennedy, have pushed the Court back to a decentralist position. President Clinton's two appointees, Justices Ruth Bader Ginsburg and Stephen Breyer, joined by Justices David Souter and John Paul Stevens, are resisting this movement back to a states' rights interpretation of our federal system. Consequently, federalism issues are likely to come up in future Supreme Court confirmation hearings, and the outcome of presidential elections—which greatly influence who gets appointed to the Supreme Court—could well determine how these and other federalism issues will be decided.

REGULATORY FEDERALISM: GRANTS, MANDATES, AND NEW TECHNIQUES OF CONTROL

Congress authorizes programs, establishes general rules for how the programs will operate, and decides whether and how much room should be left for state or local discretion. Most important, Congress appropriates the funds for these programs and generally has deeper pockets than even the richest states. One of Congress's most potent tools for influencing policy at the state and local levels has been federal grants.

Federal grants serve four purposes, the most important of which is the fourth:

1. To supply state and local governments with revenue.
2. To establish minimum national standards for such things as highways and clean air.

PEOPLE & POLITICS *Making a Difference* ★ ★ ★

CHIEF JUSTICE WILLIAM H. REHNQUIST

When asked his career plans by his elementary school teacher, William H. Rehnquist recalls saying, "I am going to change the government."[*] After serving in the army during World War II, he majored in political science at Stanford University and later graduated first in his class from Stanford Law School. He then clerked for a Supreme Court justice and went into private legal practice, while becoming active in Republican politics.

As an assistant attorney general in the administration of President Richard M. Nixon, he was appointed associate justice of the Supreme Court in 1972. In his early years on the Court he emerged as a champion of federalism, limiting the power of the national government and returning power to the states. However, he could not persuade a majority to go along with his views and earned the nickname "Lone Ranger" for writing more dissenting opinions than any other justice at the time. In 1986, President Ronald Reagan elevated him to chief justice. With subsequent changes in the Court's composition, Chief Justice Rehnquist was able to command a bare majority for changing the direction of the Court and reinvigorating debates over federalism.

A major legacy of the Rehnquist Court (1986–) is how it has curbed Congress in defense of the states. Besides resurrecting the rhetoric of states' rights and the Tenth Amendment, Chief Justice Rehnquist has commanded a majority for holding that:

■ Congress must make a "plain statement" of its intent to pre-empt state laws; otherwise the Court will defer to the states.[†]
■ Congress's power over interstate commerce has inherent limits, and it may not compel states to enact laws in compliance with federal standards or compel them to enforce federal laws.[‡]
■ Congress's power under the commerce clause permits it to regulate noneconomic activities but only if they "substantially affect interstate commerce."[§]
■ Congress's power to enforce the Fourteenth Amendment's guarantee of equal protection of the law is limited to remedying violations that the Court recognizes and does not extend to creating rights.[‖]
■ States' immunity from lawsuits, under the Eleventh Amendment, bars lawsuits against them, without their consent, in federal and state courts and by citizens of other states as well as of their own state who seek state com-

pliance with federal laws forbidding, for example, discrimination on the basis of age or disability.[¶]

In short, Chief Justice Rehnquist has presided over a Court that has curbed the expansion of congressional powers and federal regulations in a renewed defense of the boundaries of federalism.

[*] Quoted in Craig Bradley, "William H. Rehnquist," in Clare Cushman, ed., *The Supreme Court Justices* (C.Q. Press, 1993), p. 496.
[†] *Gregory* v. *Ashcroft,* 501 U.S. 452 (1991).
[‡] *New York* v. *United States,* 505 U.S. 144 (1992), and *Printz* v. *United States,* 521 U.S. 898 (1997).
[§] *United States* v. *Lopez,* 514 U.S. 549 (1995), and *United States* v. *Morrison,* 529 U.S. 598 (2000); but see *Nevada* v. *Hibbs,* 538 U.S. 721 (2003).
[‖] *City of Boerne* v. *Flores,* 521 U.S. 507 (1997), and *United States* v. *Morrison,* 529 U.S. 598 (2000).
[¶] See, e.g., *Alden* v. *Maine,* 527 U.S. 706 (1998).

3. To equalize resources among the states by taking money from people with high incomes through federal taxes and spending it, through grants, in states where the poor live.
4. To attack national problems yet minimize the growth of federal agencies.

Types of Federal Grants

Three types of federal grants are currently being administered: *categorical-formula grants, project grants,* and *block grants* (sometimes called *flexible grants*). From 1972 to 1987, there was also *revenue sharing*—federal grants to state and local governments to be used at their discretion and subject only to very general conditions. But when budget deficits soared in the second Reagan administration (1985–1989) and there was no revenue to share, revenue sharing was terminated—to the states in 1986 and to local governments in 1987.

CATEGORICAL-FORMULA GRANTS   Congress appropriates funds for specific purposes, such as school lunches or the building of airports and highways. These funds are allocated by formula and are subject to detailed federal conditions, often on a matching basis; that is, the local government receiving the federal funds must put up some of its own dollars. Categorical grants, in addition, provide federal supervision to ensure that the federal dollars are spent as Congress wants. There are hundreds of grant programs, but two dozen, including Medicaid, account for more than half of total spending for categoricals.

PROJECT GRANTS   Congress appropriates a certain sum, which is allocated to state and local units and sometimes to nongovernmental agencies, based on applications from those who wish to participate. Examples are grants by the National Science Foundation to universities and research institutes to support the work of scientists or grants to states and localities to support training and employment programs.

BLOCK GRANTS   These are broad grants to states for prescribed activities—welfare, child care, education, social services, preventive health care, and health services—with only a few strings attached. States have great flexibility in deciding how to spend block grant dollars, but when the federal funds for any fiscal year are gone, there are no more matching federal dollars.

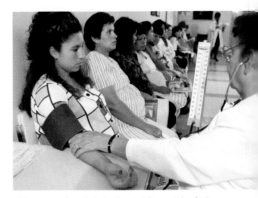

This maternity clinic is funded in part by federal block grants, which provide federal money to states for various services, such as health care, education, and welfare. States have great flexibility in deciding how to spend block grant dollars.

The Politics of Federal Grants

Republicans "have consistently favored fewer strings, less federal supervision, and the delegation of spending discretion to the state and local governments."[45] Democrats are generally been less supportive of broad discretionary block grants, favoring instead more detailed, federally supervised spending. The Republican-controlled Congress in the 1990s gave high priority to the creation of block grants, but it ran into trouble by trying to lump together welfare, school lunch and breakfast programs, prenatal nutrition programs, and child protection programs in one block grant.

Republicans, however, with President Clinton's support, succeeded in making a major change in federal-state relations—a devolution of responsibility for welfare from the national government to the states. The Personal Responsibility and Work Opportunity Reconciliation Act of 1996 put an end to the 61-year-old program of Aid to Families with Dependent Children (AFDC), a federal guarantee of welfare checks for all eligible mothers and children. The 1996 act substituted for AFDC a welfare block grant to each state, with caps on the amount of federal dollars that the state will receive. It also put another big federal child care program into another block grant—the Child Care and Development Block Grant (CCDBG).

Welfare block grants give states flexibility in how they provide for welfare, but no federal funds can be used to cover recipients who do not go to work within two years, and no one can receive federally supported benefits for more than five years. In order to slow down the "race to the bottom" in which states may try to make themselves "the least attractive state in which to be poor,"[46] Congress also stipulated that in order for states to receive their full share of federal dollars, they must continue to spend at least 75 percent of what they had been spending on welfare.

The battle over the appropriate level of government to control funding and to exercise principal responsibility for social programs tends to be cyclical. As one scholar of federalism explains, "Complaints about excessive federal control tend to be followed by proposals to shift more power to state and local governments. Then, when problems arise in state and local administration—and problems inevitably arise when any organization tries to administer anything—demands for closer federal supervision and tighter federal controls follow."[47]

Federal Mandates

Fewer federal dollars do not necessarily mean fewer federal controls. On the contrary, the federal government has imposed mandates on states and local governments, often without providing federal funds. State and local officials complained, and protests from state and local officials against unfunded federal mandates were effective. The Unfunded Mandates Reform Act of 1995 requires the Congressional Budget Office (CBO) and federal agencies to issue reports about the impact of unfunded mandates. The act also imposed some mild constraints on Congress itself. A congressional committee that approves any legislation containing a federal mandate must draw attention to the mandate in its report and describe its cost to state and local governments. If the committee intends any mandate to be partially unfunded, it must explain why it is appropriate for the cost to be borne by state and local governments.

Whether the Unfunded Mandates Reform Act significantly slows down federal mandates remains to be seen. So far, it has had little effect. The Americans with Disabilities Act (1990), for example, called on state and local governments to build ramps and alter curbs—renovations that are costing millions of dollars. Environmental Protection Agency regulations require states to build automobile pollution-testing stations and take other actions to reduce pollution, but without corresponding federal dollars. Still, state officials praise the law for increasing congressional awareness of unfunded mandates. It has forced members of Congress to take into account how a bill would affect state and local governments.[48]

New Techniques of Federal Control

In recent decades, Congress has used several other techniques in establishing federal regulations, including *direct orders, cross-cutting requirements, crossover sanctions,* and *total and partial preemption.*

DIRECT ORDERS   In a few instances, federal regulation takes the form of direct orders that must be complied with under threat of criminal or civil sanction. An example is the Equal Employment Opportunity Act of 1972, barring job discrimination by state and local governments on the basis of race, color, religion, sex, and national origin.

CROSS-CUTTING REQUIREMENTS   Federal grants may establish certain conditions that extend to all activities supported by federal funds, regardless of their source. The first and most famous of these is Title VI of the 1964 Civil Rights Act, which holds that in the use of federal funds, no person may be discriminated against on the basis of race, color, or national origin. Other laws extend these protections to persons because of gender or disability status. More than 60 cross-cutting requirements concern such matters as the environment, historic preservation, contract wage rates, access to government information, the care of experimental animals, and the treatment of human subjects in research projects.

CROSSOVER SANCTIONS   These sanctions permit the use of federal money in one program to influence state and local policy in another. For example, a 1984 act reduced federal highway aid by up to 15 percent for any state that failed to adopt a minimum drinking age of 21.

TOTAL AND PARTIAL PREEMPTION   Total preemption rests on the national government's power under the supremacy and commerce clauses to preempt conflicting state and local activities. Building on this constitutional authority, federal law in certain areas entirely preempts state and local governments from the field.[49] Sometimes federal law provides for partial preemption in establishing basic policies but requiring states to administer them. Some programs give states an option not to participate, but if a state chooses not to do so, the national government steps in and runs the program. Even worse from the states' point of view is *mandatory partial preemption,* in which the national government requires states to act on peril of losing other funds but provides no funds to support state action. The Clean Air Act of 1990 is an example of mandatory partial preemption; the federal government set national air quality standards and required states to devise plans and pay for their implementation.[50] Homeland security legislation is another example of the national government providing some funds but requiring states to provide services as "first responders" that cost more than federal funds cover.

THE POLITICS OF FEDERALISM

The formal structures of our federal system have not changed much since 1787, but the political realities, especially during the past half-century, have greatly altered how federalism works. To understand these changes, we need to look at some of the trends that continue to fuel the debate about the meaning of federalism.

The Growth of Big Government

Over the past two centuries, power has accrued to the national government. "No one planned the growth, but everyone played a part in it."[51] How did this shift come about? For a variety of reasons. One is that many of our problems have become national in scope. Much that was local in 1789, in 1860, or in 1930 is now national, even global. State governments could supervise the relations between small merchants and their few employees, but only the national government can supervise relations between multinational corporations and their thousands of employees, many of which are organized in national unions.

As industrialization proceeded, powerful interests made demands on the national government. Business groups called on the government for aid in the form of tariffs, a national banking system, subsidies to railroads and the merchant marine, and uniform rules relating to the environment. Farmers learned that the national government could give more aid than the states, and they too began to demand help. By the beginning of the twentieth century, urban groups in general and organized labor in particular pressed their claims. Big business, big agriculture, and big labor all added up to big government.

The growth of the national economy and the creation of national transportation and communications networks altered people's attitudes toward the national government. Before the Civil War, the national government was viewed as a distant, even foreign, government. Today, in part because of television and the Internet, most people know more about Washington than they know about their state capitals. People are apt to know more about the president than about their governor and more about their national senators and representatives than about their state legislators or even about the local officials who run their cities and schools.

The Great Depression of the 1930s stimulated extensive national action on welfare, unemployment, and farm surpluses. World War II brought federal regulation of wages, prices, and employment, as well as national efforts to allocate resources, train personnel, and support engineering and inventions. After the war, the national government helped veterans obtain college degrees and inaugurated a vast system of support for university research. The United States became the most powerful leader of the free world, maintaining substantial military forces even in times of peace. The Great Society programs of the 1960s poured out grants-in-aid to states and localities. City dwellers who had migrated from the rural South to northern cities began to seek federal funds for—at the very least—housing, education, and mass transportation.

Although economic and social conditions created many of the pressures for expansion of the national government, so did political claims. Until federal budget deficits became a hot issue in the 1980s and early 1990s, members of Congress, presidents, federal judges, and federal administrators actively promoted federal initiatives. Even with the return of deficit spending in the 2000s, Congress appears willing to actively promote some federal programs, at least in the areas of homeland security and prescription drug coverage. True, when there is widespread conflict about what to do—how to reduce the federal deficit, adopt a national energy policy, reform Social Security, provide health care for the indigent—Congress waits for a national consensus. But when an organized constituency wants something and there is no counterpressure, Congress "responds often to everyone, and with great vigor."[52] Once established, federal programs generate groups with vested interests in promoting, defending, and expanding them. Associations are formed and alliances are made. "In a word, the growth of government has created a constituency of, by, and for government."[53]

The politics of federalism are changing, however, and Congress is being pressured to reduce the size and scope of national programs, but at the same time to deal with the demands for homeland security. Meanwhile, the cost of entitlement programs such as Social Security and Medicare are going up because there are more older people and they are living longer. These programs have widespread public support, and to cut them is politically risky. "With all other options disappearing, it is politically tempting to finance tax cuts by turning over to the states many of the social programs . . . that have become the responsibility of the national government."[54]

The Devolution Revolution: Rhetoric Versus Reality

Recent Congresses, like their predecessors, have increased the authority of the national government in many areas. To be sure, the Republican-controlled Congress in the 1990s returned some functions, especially welfare, to the states. President Clinton also proclaimed, "The era of big government is over," though he tempered his comments by saying, "But we cannot go back to the time when our citizens were left to fend for themselves." Congress and the president came together for a major overhaul of welfare and, to a lesser degree, education. Congress also freed the states to set their own highway speed limits, changed the Safe Drinking Water Act to allow states to operate certain programs, and gave states a greater role over how federal rural development funds may be used.

In the aftermath of the attacks on the World Trade Center and the Pentagon and in confronting the continuing threats of terrorism, the role of the federal government in defending homeland security has expanded. Congress also established national criteria for state-issued drivers' licenses, forbade states from selling drivers' personal information, ended state regulation of mutual funds, nullified state laws restricting telecommunications competition, and made a host of offenses federal crimes, including carjacking and acts of terrorism. Appropriation bills pressured states to keep criminals behind bars by threatening to take grants away from states that fail to meet federal standards. Indeed, the only two major achievements of the devolution revolution remain the 1996 reform of welfare and the repeal of a national speed limit.[55] As one reporter concluded, "The 'devolution' promised by Congressional Republicans . . . has mostly fizzled. Instead of handing over authority to state and local governments, they're taking it away."[56]

THE FUTURE OF FEDERALISM

In 1933, during the Great Depression, with state governments helpless, one writer stated, "I do not predict that the states will go, but affirm that they have gone."[57] Such prophets of doom were wrong; the states are stronger than ever. During recent decades, state governments have undergone a major transformation. Most have improved their governmental structures, taken on greater roles in funding education and welfare, launched programs to help distressed cities, expanded their tax bases, and are assuming greater roles in maintaining homeland security and fighting corporate corruption. Able men and women have been attracted to the governorship. "Today, states, in formal representational, policy making, and implementation terms at least, are more representative, more responsive, more activist, and more professional in their operations than they ever have been. They face their expanded roles better equipped to assume and fulfill them."[58]

After the civil rights revolution of the 1960s, segregationists feared that national officials would work for racial integration. Thus they praised local government, emphasized the dangers of centralization, and argued that the protection of civil rights was not a proper function of the national government. As one political scientist observed, "Federalism has a dark history to overcome. For nearly two hundred years, states' rights have been asserted to protect slavery, segregation, and discrimination."[59]

Today the politics of federalism, even with respect to civil rights, is more complicated than in the past. The national government is not necessarily more favorable to the claims of minorities than state or city governments are. Rulings on same-sex marriages and "civil unions" by state courts interpreting their state constitutions have extended more protection for these rights than has the Supreme Court's interpretation of the U.S. Constitution. Other states, however, are passing legislation that would eliminate such protections, and opponents are pressing for a constitutional amendment to bar same-sex marriages.

States are also increasingly aggressive in addressing economic and environmental matters. State attorneys general are prosecuting anticompetitive business practices, as they did in joining the suit against Microsoft and, more recently, as New York attorney general Eliot Spitzer did in suing the mutual fund industry and spammers. After the Bush administration abandoned 50 investigations into violations of the Clean Air Act and changed policy on the regulation of power plants, Spitzer and several other state attorneys general sued the Bush administration and power plant companies to force them to make pollution-control improvements.[60] Business interests have argued that conflicting state regulations unduly burden interstate commerce and have sought broader preemptive federal regulation in order to save them not only from stringent state regulations but also from the uncertainties of complying with 50 different state laws. As a lawyer representing trade groups in the food and medical devices industries observed: "One national dumb rule is better than 50 inconsistent rules of any kind."[61]

The national government is not likely to retreat to a pre-1930 posture or even a pre-1960 one. Indeed, the underlying economic and social conditions that generated the demand for federal action have been altered substantially by international terrorism, the war in Afghanistan and Iraq, and rising deficits. In addition to such traditional issues as helping people find jobs and preventing inflation and depressions—which still require national action—countless new issues have been added to the national agenda by the growth of a global economy based on the information explosion, e-commerce, advancing technologies, and combating international terrorism.

New York Attorney General Eliot Spitzer was one of several state attorneys general to sue the Bush administration and power plant companies over pollution control.

Most Americans have strong attachments to our federal system—in the abstract. They remain loyal to their states and show a growing skepticism about the national government. Yet, evidence suggests the anti-Washington sentiment "is 3,000 miles wide but only a few miles deep."[62] The fact is that Americans are pragmatists: We appear to prefer federal-state-local power sharing[63] and are prepared to use whatever level of government necessary to meet our needs and new challenges.

S U M M A R Y

1. A federal system is one in which the constitution divides powers between the central government and subdivisional governments—states or provinces. Alternatives to federalism are unitary systems, in which all constitutional power is vested in the central government, and confederations, which are loose compacts among sovereign states.

2. Federal systems check the growth of tyranny, allow unity without uniformity, encourage state experimentation, permit power sharing between the national government and the states, and keep government closer to the people.

3. The national government has the constitutional authority, stemming primarily from the national supremacy clause, the war powers, and its powers to regulate commerce among the states to tax and spend, to do what Congress thinks is necessary and proper to promote the general welfare and to provide for the common defense. These constitutional pillars have permitted tremendous expansion of the functions of the federal government.

4. States must give full faith and credit to each other's public acts, records, and judicial proceedings; extend to each others' citizens the privileges and immunities it gives its own; and return fugitives from justice.

5. The federal courts umpire the division of power between the national and state governments. The Marshall Court, in decisions such as *Gibbons* v. *Ogden* and *McCulloch* v. *Maryland,* asserted the power of the national government over the states and promoted a national economic common market. These decisions also reinforced the supremacy of the national government over the states.

6. Today, debates about federalism are less often about its constitutional structure than about whether action should come from the national or state and local levels. Recent Supreme Court decisions favor a decentralist position and signal shifts in the Court's interpretation of the constitutional nature of our federal system.

7. The major instruments of federal intervention in state programs have been various kinds of financial grants-in-aid, of which the most prominent are categorical-formula grants, project grants, and block grants. The national government also imposes federal mandates and controls some activities of state and local governments by other means.

8. Over the past 218 years, power has accrued to the national government, but recently Congress has been pressured to reduce the size and scope of national programs and to shift some existing programs back to the states. Although responsibility for welfare has been turned over to the states, the authority of the national government has increased in many other areas.

K E Y   T E R M S

devolution revolution	**implied powers**	**concurrent powers**	**preemption**
federalism	**necessary and proper clause**	**full faith and credit clause**	**centralists**
unitary system	**inherent powers**	**extradition**	**decentralists**
confederation	**commerce clause**	**interstate compact**	**states' rights**
express powers	**federal mandate**	**national supremacy**	

F U R T H E R   R E A D I N G

SAMUEL H. BEER, *To Make a Nation: The Rediscovery of American Federalism* (Harvard University Press, 1993).

CENTER FOR THE STUDY OF FEDERALISM, *The Federalism Report* (published quarterly by Temple University; this publication notes research, books and articles, and scholarly conferences).

CENTER FOR THE STUDY OF FEDERALISM, *Publius: The Journal of Federalism* (published quarterly by Temple University; one issue each year is an "Annual Review of the State of American Federalism"; and has a Web site at www.lafayette.edu/~publius).

TIMOTHY J. CONLAN, *From New Federalism to Devolution: Twenty-Five Years of Intergovernmental Reforms* (Brookings Institution, 1998).

DANIEL J. ELAZER AND JOHN KINCAID, *The Covenant Connection: From Federal Theology to Modern Federalism* (Lexington Books, 2000).

JOHN FEREJOHN AND BARRY WEINGAST, *The New Federalism: Can the States Be Trusted?* (Hoover Institute Press, 1998).

FRANK GOODMAN, ED., *The Supreme Court's Federalism: Real or Imagined?* (Sage, 2001).

NEIL C. MCCABE, ED., *Comparative Federalism in the Devolution Era* (Rowman & Littlefield, 2002).

FORREST MCDONALD, *States' Rights and the Union: Imperim in Imperio, 1776–1876* (Univeristy Press of Kansas, 2000).

KALYPSO NICOLAIDIS AND ROBERT HOWSE, EDS., *The Federal Vision: Legitimacy and Levels of Governance in the United States and the European Union* (Oxford University Press, 2001).

JOHN T. NOONAN, *Narrowing the Nation's Power: The Supreme Court Sides with the States* (University of California Press, 2002).

DAVID M. O'BRIEN, *Constitutional Law and Politics: Struggles for Power and Governmental Accountability,* 6th ed. (Norton, 2005).

LAURENCE J. O'TOOLE JR., *American Intergovernmental Relations,* 3d ed. (CQ Press, 2000).

PAUL J. POSNER, *The Politics of Unfunded Mandates: Whither Federalism?* (Georgetown University Press, 1998).

WILLIAM H. RIKER, *The Development of American Federalism* (Academic, 1987).

POLITICAL CULTURE AND IDEOLOGY

4

For many Americans, the first experience with democracy is a school election, often in an elementary school. What are the expectations of these young voters, and what do these expectations teach us about our political culture? Were we to observe such an election, we would see recurrent patterns. For example, it would be considered unfair if someone suggested that some students' votes count more than others' or that some students should not be allowed to vote at all. It is likely that the candidates will be asked to speak, and they may even make a few campaign promises. When the votes are counted, the young participants expect the person with the most votes to be elected. Many important elements of our political culture are widely shared, others are evolving, and some are in dispute. Our assumptions, beliefs, and values about politics, government, participation, freedom, and liberty are the central focus of this chapter.

The specifics of a nation's political culture can be discovered not only by what people believe and say but also by how they behave. A nation's political culture is the underlying

beliefs, assumptions, attitudes, and patterns of behavior people have toward government and politics. Political culture involves such fundamental issues as who may participate in political decisions, what rights and liberties citizens have, how decisions are made, and how people view politicians and government generally. Some elements of our political culture—like our fear of concentrated power and our reverence for individual liberty—have remained constant over time. In other respects, our political culture has changed from a belief that only property-owning white men should be allowed to vote to a conviction that all adults should have the right to vote, and that participation should include a wider range of political activities. Thus, citizens now vote in party primaries to select nominees for office, whereas previously, party leaders determined who would run for office. The surge in citizen activity on the Internet in the 2004 election may be a harbinger of a more interactive political culture in the future where citizens interact with candidates, contribute money, and mobilize each other to political action.

The idea of people coming together, listening to each other, exchanging ideas, learning to appreciate each other's differences, and defending their opinions is sometimes called deliberation and builds what has been called **social capital**. Such interaction is thought to build community and relationships in ways that do not happen when citizens only cast ballots. Political scientist Robert Putnam has defined social capital as "features of social organization such as networks, norms, and social trust that facilitate coordination and cooperation for mutual benefit."[1] Because of a decline in public participation in town council meetings, community groups, the PTA, labor unions, business associations, and other civic groups, Putnam believes that we as a people are losing the skills and learning people can develop in such settings. Not all political scientists agree with Putnam's assessment that social capital is in decline.[2] More recently, Putnam found evidence of expanded civic engagement in the weeks after the terrorist attacks of September 11, 2001, but not a growth in volunteering.[3]

The social capital debate has rekindled an interest in the nature and viability of the American political culture and has spurred an examination of how it is changing. Americans have conflicting ideas and beliefs about the proper role of government and where and how political power should be exercised. These attitudes and beliefs, when coherent and consistent, are what political scientists call *ideology*. In this chapter, we look at our political culture and ideology.

THE AMERICAN POLITICAL CULTURE

Political scientists use the term **political culture** to refer to the widely shared beliefs, values, and norms concerning the relationship of citizens to government and to one another.

American political culture centers on democratic values like liberty, equality, individualism, democracy, justice, the rule of law, patriotism, optimism, and idealism. There is no "official" list of American political values, however, and as we noted in Chapter 1, these widely shared democratic values overlap and sometimes conflict.

Shared Values

social capital
Democratic and civic habits of discussion, compromise, and respect for differences, which grow out of participation in voluntary organizations.

political culture
The widely shared beliefs, values, and norms concerning the relationship of citizens to government and to one another.

natural rights
The rights of all people to dignity and worth; also called *human rights*.

Before the American and French Revolutions of the late eighteenth century, discussions about individual liberty, freedom, equality, private property, limited government, and popular consent were rare. Europe had been dominated by aristocracies, had experienced centuries of political and social inequality, and had been ruled by governments that were often arbitrary in their exercise of power. Liberal political philosophers rebelled against these traditions and proclaimed the principles of classical liberalism. They claimed individuals have certain **natural rights**—the rights of all people to dignity and worth—and that government, as a primary threat to those rights, must be limited and controlled. During this same period, the economic system was changing from a mercantile to a free market system. People began to think they could improve their lot in life and own property. Radical new ideas like these influenced the thinking of the founders of our nation.

CHANGING FACE OF AMERICAN POLITICS

TRUST IN AMERICA

Not all Americans have the same level of social trust, an important element in social capital. With less time spent interacting with one another and more time in social isolation, social trust has declined.* Public perceptions about crime and concerns about personal safety are some reasons people are less trusting.† Political Scientist Wendy Rahn examined variations in the extent to which people trusted their fellow citizens across 49 communities.‡ She defines generalized social trust "as a 'standing decision' to give most people—even those whom one does not know from direct experience—the benefit of the doubt."§

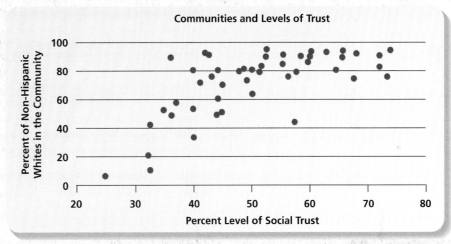

Communities and Levels of Trust

Samples from different communities were asked: "Generally speaking, would you say that most people can be trusted or that you can't be too careful in dealing with people?" Those that said you can trust most people were coded as trusting.

Across the 49 communities Rahn surveyed she found the mean level of social trust was 52 percent, with the high being 74 percent in Brown County, South Dakota, and the low being Camden, New Jersey, with 25 percent. The chart plots the percent expressing generalized social trust against the percent of non-Hispanic whites in the community. You will note there is a clear correlation between the racial composition of a community and the level of generalized social trust.

As the United States becomes more diverse, are we likely to have less trust in one another? Or is the level of trust related to socio-economic factors that are not directly related to racial diversity? As we discuss in this chapter and the next, there are other cultural forces that may pull us together.

*Robert D. Putnam, "The Decline of Civil Society: How Come? So What?" (presented at the Canadian Centre for Management Development, Ottawa, Ontario, February 1996), 11. www.collection.nlc-bnc.ca/100/200/301/ccmd-ccg/john_manion-e/jmlp66e.pdf.
†Francis Fukuyama, *The Great Disruption: Human Nature and the Reconstitution of Social Order* (New York: Touchstone, 1999).
‡Wendy Rahn, et al, *Geographies of Trust: Examining Variation in Generalized Social Trust Across Knight Communities* (American Institutes for Research, 2003). www.polisci.umn.edu/faculty/wrahn/KST7C473.doc.
§Rahn, Wendy M. and John E. Transue, "Social Trust and Value Change: The Decline of Social Capital in American Youth, 1976–1995," *Political Philosophy* 19 (March 1998): 545.

LIBERTY   No value in the American political culture is more revered than liberty. "We have always been a nation obsessed with liberty. Liberty over authority, freedom over responsibility, rights over duties—these are our historic preferences," wrote the late Clinton Rossiter, a noted political scientist. "Not the good man but the free man has been the measure of all things in this sweet 'land of liberty'; not national glory but individual liberty has been the object of political authority and the test of its worth."[4] This predominance of freedom and individualism over virtue and the public good is not universally accepted by students of American thought, and in reality both perspectives are built on some mix of the two views.[5]

EQUALITY   Jefferson's famous words in the Declaration of Independence express the primacy of our views of equality: "We hold these truths to be self-evident, that all men are created equal, that they are endowed by their Creator with certain unalienable rights, that among these are life, liberty, and the pursuit of happiness." Americans have always believed in social equality. In contrast to Europeans, our nation shunned aristocracy, and our Constitution explicitly prohibits governments from granting titles of nobility.

VALUES WE SHARE—
NEW DATA BOX

The political values and attitudes of the American public provide insights into the American political culture. While there is some variability depending on how pollsters ask questions, these data are generally reflective of public opinion.

	Percent Agree
Elected officials in Washington lose touch with the people pretty quickly.	75%
Voting gives people like me some say about how government runs things.	73
Success in life is pretty much determined by forces outside our control.	30
I admire people who get rich by working hard.	90
As Americans we can always find a way to solve our problems and get what we want.	66
Our society should do what is necessary to make sure that everyone has an equal opportunity to succeed.	91
It is the responsibility of the government to take care of people who can't take care of themselves.	66
I am very patriotic.	91
Prayer is an important part of my daily life.	80

SOURCE: The Pew Research Center for the People and the Press, *Evenly Divided and Increasingly Polarized: 2004 Political Landscape.* Data collected in August, 2003.

In addition to social equality, Americans believe in *political equality,* the idea that every individual has a right to equal protection under the law and equal voting power. Although political equality has always been a goal, it has not always been a reality. In the past, African Americans, Native Americans, and women were denied the right to vote and otherwise participate in the nation's political life.

Equality encompasses the idea of *equal opportunity,* especially with regard to improving our economic status. Americans believe that social background should not limit our opportunity to achieve to the best of our ability, nor should race, gender, or religion. The nation's commitment to public education programs like Head Start for underprivileged preschool children, state support for public colleges and universities, and federal financial aid for higher education reflect this belief in equal opportunity.

INDIVIDUALISM   The United States is characterized by a persistent commitment to the individual. Under our system of government, individuals have both rights and responsibilities. Policies that limit individual choice generate intense political conflict. The debate over legalized abortion is often framed in these terms. Although Americans agree with individual rights and freedoms, they also understand that their rights can conflict with another person's rights or with the government's need to maintain order.

RESPECT FOR THE COMMMON PERSON   Most Americans have faith in the common sense and collective wisdom of ordinary people. Most prefer action to reflection. We are often anti-expert and sometimes anti-intellectual. The emphasis on practicality and common sense has become part of our national image. Poets like Walt Whitman and Carl Sandburg and storytellers like Mark Twain, Will Rogers, Eudora Welty, and Garrison Keillor have helped shape this tradition. This reverence for the common people helps explain our ambivalence toward power, politics, and government authority. Politicians from backgrounds of privilege often downplay their past in an effort to relate more to typical voters.

DEMOCRATIC CONSENSUS   An important feature that binds most of us together is **democratic consensus**, a fairly widespread agreement on fundamental principles of

democratic consensus
Widespread agreement on fundamental principles of democratic governance and the values that undergird them.

Vivica Fox autographs photographs for fifth-grade elementary school students in Lynwood, California, as part of Teach For America Week, an annual event in which successful Americans discuss their career with schoolchildren with the hope of inspiring them to realize their own goals and ambitions.

Americorps National Service crew members remove tree limbs from the yard of a woman whose home was damaged after ice storms caused a tree to fall on it.

governance and the values that undergird them. We are a people from many different cultural and ethnic backgrounds, histories, and religions. Despite these differences, our political culture includes widely shared attitudes and beliefs about principles of government, procedures, documents, and institutions. Americans have strong opinions about who has power to do what, how people acquire power, and how they are removed from power. These are fundamental "rules of the game" in which widespread consensus is important. At the same time, this commitment to core elements of who has power and what limits exist on the exercise of that power does not necessarily mean people vote in elections, are current in public affiars, or believe government is always fair or just.

Elements of the democratic consensus are majority rule and popular sovereignty. We believe in **majority rule**—governance according to the expressed preferences of the majority at regular elections. Yet we also believe that people in the minority should be free to try to win majority support for their opinions. Despite the fact that large numbers of Americans lack strong party attachments, we favor a two-party system. Our institutions are based on the principles of representation and consent of the governed. We believe in **popular sovereignty**—that ultimate power resides in the people. Government, from this perspective, exists to serve the people rather than the other way around. The means by which the government learns the will of the people is through *elections,* perhaps the most important expression of popular consent. But there are instances when popular sovereignty and majority rule must be limited by other fundamental rights, as in the case of referendums limiting civil rights.[6] Examples include California's 1964 vote, subsequently overturned, to permit people to discriminate in the sale of residential housing and the same state's 1996 vote to prohibit affirmative action in state governmental bodies, including universities and colleges.

Many of the limits on governments are specified in the Constitution, especially in the first ten amendments (the Bill of Rights) and the Thirteenth, Fourteenth, Fifteenth, and Nineteenth amendments. The Constitution is revered as a national symbol, yet we often differ over the framers' original intentions. We honor many of these rights more in the abstract than in the particular. More than half of us, for instance, think that books with dangerous ideas should be banned from public school libraries (see Table 4–1). Intolerance of dissenting or offensive views is amply demonstrated in many public opinion polls and is observed on college and university campuses. Still, Americans can ordinarily be characterized as affirming support for democratic and constitutional values.

majority rule
Governance according to the expressed preferences of the majority.

popular sovereignty
A belief that ultimate power resides in the people.

TABLE 4–1   WHAT DO YOU MEAN BY RIGHTS AND FREEDOMS? IT DEPENDS . . .

	Agree	Disagree	Don't Know
Freedom of speech should apply to groups that are sympathetic to terrorists.	45%	50%	5%
There has been real improvement in the position of African Americans.	57	35	8
Books that contain dangerous ideas should be banned from public school libraries.	50	47	3
Protection rights should apply to the unborn.	72	24	4
The police should be allowed to search the houses of known drug dealers without a court order.	44	54	2
School boards ought to have the right to fire teachers who are known homosexuals.	33	62	5

SOURCE: The Pew Research Center for the People and the Press, *Evenly Divided and Increasingly Polarized: 2004 Political.* Data collected in August, 2003.

JUSTICE AND THE RULE OF LAW   Inscribed over the entrance to the U.S. Supreme Court are the words "Equal Justice Under Law." The rule of law means that government is based on a body of law applied equally and by just procedures, as opposed to rule by an elite whose whims decide policy or resolve disputes. Chief Justice John Marshall succinctly summarized this principle: "The government of the United States has been emphatically termed a government of laws, not of men."[7] Americans believe strongly in the principle of fairness: All individuals are entitled to the same legal rights and protections.

For government to adhere to the rule of law, its policies and laws should follow these five rules:

- *Generality:* Laws should be stated generally, not singling out any group or individual.
- *Prospectivity:* Laws should apply to the future, not punish something someone did in the past.
- *Publicity:* Laws cannot be kept secret and then enforced.
- *Authority:* Valid laws are made by those with legitimate power, and the people legitimate that power through some form of popular consent.
- *Due process:* Laws must be enforced impartially with fair processes.

PATRIOTISM, OPTIMISM, AND IDEALISM   Americans are highly nationalistic, sharing a sense of values and identity. This nationalism was reinforced by the terrorist attacks of 2001, which illustrated that unity under threat is a widely shared value. As President George W. Bush said, "We are a different country than we were on September 10th: sadder and less innocent; stronger and more united; and in the face of ongoing threats, determined and courageous."[8] We are proud of our past and our role in the world today. We are optimistic, though far more about people than about government.

We believe in opportunity, choice, individualism, and most of all, the freedom to improve ourselves and to achieve success with as little interference as possible from others or from government. As Table 4–2 indicates, U.S. citizens are more satisfied with their democratic government than are the citizens of other countries.

We know that our system is imperfect, yet we have an abiding faith in government by the people. We often grumble that elected officials have lost touch with us, we are disgusted by scandals, and we are impatient with the slowness of the system to solve problems like health care, crime, drug abuse, and terrorism. Despite the dissatisfactions, a remarkable belief persists that this nation is better, stronger, and more virtuous than other nations. Like every country, the United States has interests and motives that are selfish as well as generous, cynical as well as idealistic. Still, our support of human needs and rights throughout the world is evidence of an enduring idealism.

Where We Learn the American Political Culture

One important source of political culture in the United States, as in other nations, is the family. Children are taught from an early age what it means to be an American. They are curious about why people vote, what the president does, and whether Grandpa fought in World War II or Korea. The questions may vary somewhat from family to family, yet the themes of authority, freedom, equality, liberty, and partisanship are common. Families are the most important reference groups, and compared to families in other cultures, American families are much more egalitarian.[9]

Public schools are another source of the American political culture. Children and teachers often begin the school day by saluting the flag, reciting the Pledge of Allegiance, or singing the national anthem. Teaching American political and economic values is part of the curriculum. Not only are values taught in American history classes, but they are put into practice in school elections and newspapers and in encouraging students to participate in small-scale economic ventures.[10]

TABLE 4–2 SATISFACTION WITH THE WAY DEMOCRACY WORKS		
	Satisfied	**Dissatisfied**
United States	64%	27%
Canada	62	24
Germany	55	27
Iceland	54	23
Thailand	54	27
Costa Rica	52	25
Chile	43	31
France	43	32
Dominican Republic	40	38
United Kingdom	40	43
Japan	35	32
India	32	43
Spain	31	30
Venezuela	28	59
Taiwan	25	18
Hungary	17	50
Mexico	17	67

SOURCE: "People Throughout the World Largely Satisfied with Personal Lives," *Gallup Poll,* June 1995, p. 6.

Colleges and universities also play a role in fostering the American political culture. Students who attend college are often more confident than other persons in dealing with bureaucracy and politics generally, more likely to participate in politics and to vote, and more knowledgeable about government.[11] Many states require students at state colleges and universities to take courses in American government or state government, in part to instill a sense of civic duty while imparting knowledge about state and national governance.

Religious freedom and diversity have played a part in the formation and maintenance of the American political culture. American churches, synagogues, and mosques have long fostered a common understanding of right and wrong. Freedom, including freedom of religion, individualism, pluralism, and civic duty, have all been fostered by churches. As churches do not all take the same positions on political issues, their impact is sometimes mitigated, but they have been important to such major social and political movements as the abolition of slavery, the expansion of civil rights, and opposition to war. Civic organizations like the Boy Scouts, 4-H, League of Women Voters, Rotary Club, and Chamber of Commerce encourage citizen participation and pride in community and nation.[12]

In modern times, the mass media have taken over some functions previously performed by the family. By the time children leave high school, they will have spent more time watching television than in conversation with their parents. They may have had more political instruction from MTV than from their parents or their schools.[13] Finally, Americans educate each other about political values in the workplace, at the PTA meeting, or in more expressly political activities.

The American Dream

Many of our political values come together in the **American dream**, a complex set of ideas holding that the United States is a land of opportunity and that individual initiative and hard work can bring economic success. Whether realized or not, this American dream speaks to our most deeply held hopes and goals. The essence of the American dream can be found in our enthusiasm for **capitalism**, an economic system

American dream
The widespread belief that the United States is a land of opportunity and that individual initiative and hard work can bring economic success.

capitalism
An economic system characterized by private property, competitive markets, economic incentives, and limited government involvement in the production and pricing of goods and services.

GLOBAL *Perceptions*

QUESTION: Which of the following phrases comes closer to your view: It's good that American ideas and customs are spreading here, OR it's bad that American ideas and customs are spreading here?

American culture includes not only our democratic or political culture but also our popular culture, which includes such things as clothes, movies, food, and music. While the United States government may be unpopular abroad, our popular culture is ubiquitous. Blue jeans, Kentucky Fried Chicken, Starbucks, and the Terminator are international in popularity. While popular at one level, how do people respond when asked about the spread of American culture generally?

In other countries American popular culture is seen as a threat to the culture of that region, country or religion. The Pew Global Attitudes Project asked people their views on American popular culture. Interestingly, "people around the world object to the wide diffusion of American ideas and customs." Africa is the region most positive about American popular culture and the Middle East the least. Across all countries the range is wide, from 69 percent seeing American popular culture as good to only 2 percent having that view in Pakistan.

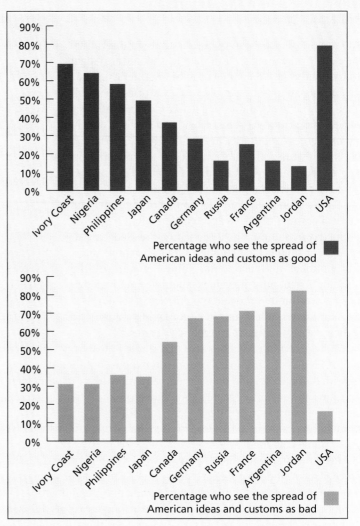

SOURCE: The Pew Research Center for the People and the Press, *What the World Thinks in 2002*. Data collected in 2002, pp. 63, 67, T-54.

characterized by private property, competitive markets, economic incentives, and limited government involvement in the production and pricing of goods and services.

The concept of *private property* enjoys extraordinary popularity. In many European democracies, the state owns and operates transportation systems and other businesses that are privately owned and operated in the United States, although there has been some privatization of communications systems like telephone companies and broadcast media in Europe. Americans cherish the dream of acquiring property. Moreover, most Americans believe that the owners of property have the right to decide how to use it

The right to private property is just one of the economic incentives that cement our support for capitalism and fuel the American dream. This is the land of opportunity for the enterprising. Here the competitive, practical go-getter can make a fortune, build a dream home, and retire early. We assume that people who have more ability or who work extremely hard will get ahead, earn more, and enjoy economic rewards. We also believe that people should be able to pass most of what they have accumulated along to

IN COMPARATIVE PERSPECTIVE

POLITICAL CULTURE IN MEXICO

In the past decade Mexico experienced the first transfer of power from one party to another in 71 years when Vicente Fox of the National Action Party (PAN) won the 2000 election defeating the Institutional Revolutionary Party (PRI). Three years earlier PRI lost the majority in Congress as well. Given these changes and the limited experience with competitive elections in the past, how do Mexicans see democracy? Had their view changed with the peaceful transfer of power between parties? Alejandro Moreno and Patricia Mendez, drawing from data from the World Values Surveys from 1995–97 and 2000–01, attempt to answer these questions.*

The political culture of Mexico remains less supportive of democracy than in the more experienced democracies. Those surveyed in Mexico were roughly twice as likely to say having a strong leader is very good or fairly good (41 percent) compared to 22 percent in advanced democracies like Germany, Australia, Canada, and the United States. Even more revealing of enduring antidemocratic sentiments is the fact that one in four Mexicans say that having the army rule is very good or fairly good, compared to 6 percent in advanced democracies. Obversely, just under two-thirds of Mexicans say democracy is the best system (65 percent) compared to 86 percent in advanced democracies. Finally, in terms of social trust, 24 percent of Mexicans surveyed felt most people could be trusted, compared to 41 percent in advanced democracies like Germany, Australia, Canada, and the United States.

This research on Mexico reminds us how popular support for democracy and democratic values like trust and tolerance take time to develop and how lingering tendencies to authoritarianism, like a preference for military rule, take time to dissipate. Moreno and Mendez conclude that Mexicans "aspire to live in a better, high-quality democracy. As they learn about it we should expect changes in democratic values and attitudes in the next years."[†]

*Alejandro Moreno and Patricia Mendez, "Attitudes Toward Democracy: Mexico in Comparative Perspective." This article and information on the World Values Survey can be found at www.worldvaluessurvey.org/library/index.html.
[†]Moreno and Mendez, p. 24.

their children and relatives. Even the poorest Americans generally oppose high inheritance taxes or limits on how much someone can earn. Americans believe that the free market system gives almost everyone a fair chance, that capitalism is necessary, and that freedom depends on it. We reject communism and socialism—a rejection fortified in recent decades as most communist nations shifted toward capitalism. In the United States, individuals and corporations have acquired wealth and, at the same time, exercised political clout. Their power has in turn been widely criticized. The Enron Corporation, for example, made over $2 million in political contributions in the 2000 elections, and between January 1, 1995, and June 30, 2001, Enron ranked among the top 15 political soft-money donors.[14] Enron later filed for bankruptcy and became a notorious example of corporate mismanagement and dishonest accounting.[15] Wealthy individuals have occasionally used their wealth to fund their campaigns for public office (Jon Corzine spent $60 million on his successful New Jersey Senate race in 2000)[16] or to influence elections or public policy (George Soros gave $27 million to organizations like America Coming Together, the Media Fund, MoveOn.org, Joint Victory Campaign, Young Democrats for America, and a few other groups working to defeat George W. Bush).[17]

The conflict in values between a *competitive economy,* in which individuals reap large rewards for their initiative and hard work, and an *egalitarian society,* in which everyone earns a decent living, carries over into politics. How the public resolves this tension changes over time and from issue to issue.

As important as the American dream is to the national consciousness, Americans know it remains unfulfilled. An underclass persists in the form of impoverished families, malnourished and poorly educated children, and people living on the streets.[18] Many cities are actually two cities, where some residents live in luxury while others live in squalor. The gap between rich and poor has grown in recent years, and a sharp difference between white and black income persists tenaciously.[19] For more people than we want to admit, chances for success still depend on the family you were born in, the neighborhood you grew up in, or the college you attended.

Coming from humble beginnings, Oprah Winfrey—television host, movie actress, and one of the highest-paid people in the country—epitomizes the American dream.

★★ YOU DECIDE

IS THE AMERICAN DREAM STILL ALIVE AND IMPORTANT?

Is the American dream alive? Is it important to people? Some would argue that the wealth and prosperity so many Americans have achieved means that for most the dream has been achieved and is therefore no longer important as a motivating force or a way to explain behavior. Others would contend that for people in poverty the hopelessness of their situaion would mean that talk of the American dream seems far fetched and unattainable. What do you think, is the American dream still an important element of the political culture of the United States?

Political and Economic Change

Political values are clearly affected by historical developments and by economic and technological growth. The Declaration of Independence and the Constitution identified such important political values as individual liberty, property rights, and limited government.[20] Early in our history, we emphasized separation of powers, checks and balances, states' rights, and the Bill of Rights. It took multiple generations before we also began to take seriously the expansion of suffrage and competitive nominations and elections. Notions of political equality and effective participation emerged during the presidency of Andrew Jackson and matured in the course of the nineteenth century. By the end of the nineteenth century, populists and suffragists turned ideals into action and formed large-scale movements to achieve more democratic forms of participation and more responsive forms of governance.

THE INDUSTRIAL TRANSFORMATION   By 1900, the agrarian society the framers knew had largely been replaced by industrial capitalism and the growth of giant corporations. With these changes, ideology was irreversibly transformed. Large privately owned corporations changed the economic order, including changes in the role of government and how people viewed each other. No one captures the implications of this shift better than political scientist Robert A. Dahl:

> One of the consequences of the new order has been a high degree of inequality in the distribution of wealth and income, and far greater inequality than had ever been thought likely or desirable under an agrarian order by Democratic Republicans like Jefferson and Madison, or had ever been thought consistent with democratic or republican government in the historic writings on the subject from Aristotle to Locke, Montesquieu, and Rousseau. Previous theorists and advocates had, like many of the framers of our own Constitution, insisted that a republic could exist only if the citizen body continued neither rich nor poor. Citizens, it was argued, must enjoy a rough equality of conditions.[21]

The success of the American economy led to the accumulation of great wealth in the hands of a few—the "robber barons" or tycoons. Many had taken great risks or earned their fortunes through inventions and efficient production practices. But as disparities of income grew, so did disparities in political resources. Economic resources can be converted into political resources, as when time is spent on political campaigns and money is contributed to parties and candidates.[22] At the beginning of the twentieth century, the rise of corporations and the concentration of individual wealth in the United States created divisions and resentment. Muckraking journalists charged that the huge corporations had become **monopolies**, using their dominance of their industry to exploit workers and limit competition. Unsafe working conditions led to regulation of the workplace by the states; however, it seemed that only the national government had the power to ensure fair treatment in the marketplace. This sentiment not only gave rise to the nation's first **antitrust legislation**—federal laws that try to prevent monopolies from dominating an industry and restraining trade—but also sowed the idea that the national government could—and should—as the Constitution asserts, "promote the general Welfare" by regulating working conditions, product safety, and labor-management disputes.

THE GREAT DEPRESSION AND THE NEW DEAL   Much of our thinking about the role of government in a capitalistic system was shaped by the Great Depression of the 1930s and the near collapse of the capitalistic system. Unrestrained capitalism and an unregulated market were faulted as causes of the Depression. The collapse of the stock market, massive unemployment, and a failed banking system caused widespread suffering among the nation's citizens. Americans had no unemployment compensation, no guarantee on bank savings, no federal regulation of the securities exchanges, and no Social Security. People turned to the government to improve the lot of millions of jobless and homeless citizens. Beginning with President Franklin D. Roosevelt's New Deal, the idea gradually gained widespread acceptance that governments, at both the national and

monopoly
Domination of an industry by a single company by fixing prices and discouraging competition; also, the company that dominates the industry by these means.

antitrust legislation
Federal laws (starting with the Sherman Act of 1890) that try to prevent a monopoly from dominating an industry and restraining trade.

state levels, should use their powers and resources to ensure some measure of equal opportunity and social justice.

Roosevelt's State of the Union Address in 1944 outlined a "Second Bill of Rights" for all citizens in which he declared that this nation must make a firm commitment to "economic security and independence." Included in his Second Bill of Rights were the following:

- The right to a useful and remunerative job in the industries, shops, farms, or mines of the nation

- The right to earn enough to provide adequate food and clothing and recreation

- The right of every farmer to raise and sell his products at a return that would give him and his family a decent living

- The right of every businessman, large and small, to trade in an atmosphere of freedom from unfair competition and domination by monopolies at home or abroad

- The right of every family to a decent home

- The right to adequate medical care and the opportunity to achieve and enjoy good health

- The right to adequate protection from the economic fears of old age, sickness, accident, and unemployment

- The right to a good education[23]

Roosevelt's policies and later efforts by Presidents John F. Kennedy and Lyndon B. Johnson in the 1960s to pass civil rights and voting rights legislation and launch a "war on poverty" defined the ideological and political fights of the second half of the twentieth century. Modern-day liberalism and conservatism turn, in large measure, on how much one believes in Roosevelt's Second Bill of Rights and how much government assistance one thinks is owed to minorities, women, and others who have suffered discrimination or have been left behind by the industrial or technological revolutions of the twentieth century. Today, free enterprise is no longer unbridled. Government regulations, antitrust laws, job safety regulations, environmental standards, and minimum wage laws try to balance freedom of enterprise against the rights of individuals. Most people today support a semiregulated or mixed free enterprise

★★ THINKING IT THROUGH

The persistence of poverty in a land of plenty is perplexing, but it does not change the reality that some are able to escape it. Examples of individuals who have achieved at least a portion of the American dream arise often enough to reinforce acceptance that the dream can come true. While some achieve the dream because they win the lottery, more do so because of opportunities like an education.

More important than data on poverty is the belief that people can attain success and affluence. The American dream does not have to be achieved by everyone to be an important motivator. New immigrant groups have long been an incubator of the American dream, and they continue to be so today. Parents working multiple low-paying jobs while stressing education for their children provide an example of both the work and dream components of this aspiration. At the same time it is also clear that the American dream is less available to some than to others and that access to it can be limited by larger forces like recessions, unemployment, or illness. Some problems many middle-class individuals can take in stride can derail the hopes and aspirations of those without a safety net. The extent to which the American dream persists in our political culture, despite its limitations, is evidence of its power and importance.

Breadlines like this provided handouts of food to thousands of unemployed and destitute people during the Great Depression.

Senator Ted Kennedy (D.-Mass) has been a champion of liberal programs and legislation for many years. He is shown here at a press conference called by the consumer advocacy group Families USA to address the rising cost of the top fifty prescription drugs sold to senior citizens.

TABLE 4–3 ATTITUDES ON BUSINESS AND LABOR

The strength of this country is mostly based on the success of American business.	75%
Government regulation of business usually does more harm than good.	53
Business corporations generally strike a fair balance between making profits and serving the public interest.	38
There is too much power concentrated in the hands of a few big companies.	77
Labor unions are necessary to protect the working person.	74

SOURCE: The Pew Research Center for the People and the Press, *Evenly Divided and Increasingly Polarized: 2004 Political Landscape.* Data collected in August, 2003.

system that checks the worst tendencies of capitalism, but they reject excessive government intervention (see Table 4–3). Much of American politics centers on how to achieve this balance. Currently, liberals and conservatives agree that some governmental intervention is necessary to assist Americans who fall short in the competition for education and economic prosperity.

POLITICAL IDEOLOGY AND ATTITUDES TOWARD GOVERNMENT

Political ideology refers to a consistent pattern of ideas or beliefs about political values and the role of government. It includes the views people have about how government should work and how it actually works. Ideology links our basic values to the day-to-day operations or policies of government.

Two major schools of political ideology dominate American politics: *liberalism* and *conservatism.* Three lesser schools of thought—*socialism, environmentalism,* and *libertarianism*—also help define the spectrum of ideology in the United States. Table 4–4 provides a general distribution of political ideology in the United States.

Liberalism

In the seventeenth and eighteenth centuries, classical liberals fought to minimize the role of government. They stressed individual rights and perceived government as the primary threat to rights and liberties. Classical liberals favored *limited government* and sought ample protections from governmental harassment. Over time, the emphasis on individualism remained constant, but the perception of the need for government changed.

CONTEMPORARY LIBERALS In its current American usage, **liberalism** refers to a belief in the positive uses of government to bring about justice and equality of opportunity. Modern-day liberals wish to preserve the rights of the individual and the right to own private property, yet they are willing to have the government intervene in the economy to remedy the defects of capitalism. Liberals advocate equal access to health care, housing, and education for all citizens. They generally believe in affirmative action programs, workers' health and safety protections, tax rates that rise with income, and unions' rights to organize and strike.

On a more philosophical level, liberals generally believe in the probability of progress. They believe that the future will be better, that obstacles can be overcome. This positive set of beliefs may explain their willingness to trust government programs. Modern liberals contend that modern technology and industrialization cry out for government programs to offset the loss of liberties suffered by the poor and the weak. Liberals such as Edward Kennedy and Hillary Rodham Clinton frequently stress the need for an involved and affirmative government.

Liberals charge that conservatives usually act out of self-interest and follow the maxim "a rising tide will lift all boats." In contrast, liberals would agree with President

political ideology
A consistent pattern of beliefs about political values and the role of government.

liberalism
A belief in the positive uses of government to bring about justice and equality of opportunity.

TABLE 4–4 DIFFERENCES IN POLITICAL IDEOLOGY

	Conservative	*Moderate*	*Liberal*
Sex			
Male	44%	29%	26%
Female	47	20	32
Race			
White	47	28	26
Black	31	28	41
Age			
18–34	45	23	32
35–45	46	30	24
46–55	42	25	33
56–64	46	29	25
65+	46	32	22
Religion			
Protestant	50	27	23
Catholic	48	28	23
Jewish	17	40	43
Education			
Less than high school	39	39	39
High school diploma	43	35	35
Some college	47	27	27
Bachelor's degree	48	21	21
Advanced degree	42	25	25
Party			
Democrat	20	30	50
Independent	34	40	26
Republican	79	15	6

SOURCE: Center for Political Studies, University of Michigan, *2002 American National Election Study Guide to Public Opinion and Electoral Behavior.*

NOTE: We have combined with the moderates persons who do not know their ideology or had not thought much about it. For party identification, we have combined independent leaners with their respective parties. Rows may not add up to 100 percent due to rounding.

Harry Truman who said, "We have rejected the discredited theory that the fortunes of the nation should be in the hands of a privileged few. Instead, we believe that our economic system should rest on a democratic foundation and that wealth should be created for the benefit of all.... Every segment of our population and every individual has a right to expect from his government a fair deal."[24]

Equality of opportunity is viewed by liberals as essential, and to achieve that end, liberals believe that discriminatory practices must be eliminated. Some liberals favor the reduction of great inequalities of wealth that make equality of opportunity impossible. Most favor a certain minimum level of income. Rather than placing a cap on wealth, they want a floor placed beneath the poor. In short, liberals seek to lessen the impact of great inequalities of wealth and work to extend opportunities to all, regardless of their economic standing. If necessary they favor raising taxes to achieve these goals. If you are interested in learning more about the liberal ideology you may find www.prospect.org or www.turnleft.com/liberal.html helpful.

CRITICISMS OF LIBERALISM   Critics of liberalism say that liberals place too much reliance on governmental solutions, higher taxes, and bureaucracy. These opponents argue that somewhere along the line, liberals forgot that government, to serve our best interests, has to be limited. Power tends to corrupt, and too much dependence on government can corrupt the spirit, undermine self-reliance, and make people forget those cherished personal freedoms and property rights our Republic was founded to secure and protect. Too many governmental regulations, too much government bureaucracy, and too much taxation tend to undermine the self-help ethic that "made America great." In short, critics of liberalism contend that the welfare and regulatory state pushed by liberals will ultimately destroy individual initiative, the entrepreneurial spirit, and the very engine of economic growth that might lead to true equality of economic opportunity.

In recent elections, Republicans have made liberalism a villain while at the same time they have attempted to position their presidential candidates more in the mainstream. George H. W. Bush, in 1988, consistently referred to Michael Dukakis as from the "liberal Democratic party." Bill Clinton was careful not to label his program as liberal, focusing on the need for economic growth, jobs, and a lower budget deficit. He insisted he was a "New Democrat." Al Gore positioned himself in the tradition of Clinton as a centrist, not a liberal, but George W. Bush charged that Gore was an advocate of big government. The same charge was leveled against congressional Democratic candidates in 2002 by their Republican opponents and their allied interest groups.

The movement to the center by some Democrats and the conventional wisdom that liberal or progressive approaches are in decline is disputed by political commentator E. J. Dionne Jr., whose book on how progressives can regain power is aptly titled *They Only Look Dead*. Dionne contends that the current political upheaval should be defined less as a revolt against *big* government than as a rebellion against *bad* government—government that has proved ineffectual in grappling with the political, economic, and moral crises that have shaken the country. Dionne challenges the claims that big government is bad or even over. Pointing to past progressive or liberal successes, Dionne contends Americans want a government that eases economic transitions, helps "preserve a broad middle class," and "expands the choices available to individuals."[25]

The popularity of liberalism and conservatism and the importance of particular issues change with world events. For a time, we were preoccupied with budget deficits. With the end of the cold war, we became more concerned about domestic policy than about foreign policy. Policy concerns changed with the terrorist attacks of September 11, 2001, and the war on terrorism that followed. Budget deficits replaced projected surpluses, and Americans became focused on places like Iraq, Afghanistan, and North Korea.

The reelection of George W. Bush in 2004, along with a net loss of four U.S. Senate seats by the Democrats, was due in part to the importance of the national security issue but it also reflected public concerns with moral values. Enactment of referendums in thirteen states in 2004 defining marriage as between a man and a woman forced moral values questions onto the agenda of the presidential election. Efforts by liberals to define the same-sex marriage issue as primarily about rights failed.

Conservatism

Private property rights and belief in free enterprise are cardinal attributes of contemporary **conservatism**. In contrast to liberals, conservatives want to enhance individual liberty by keeping government small, especially the national government, except in the area of national defense. Conservatives take a more pessimistic view of human nature than liberals do. They maintain that people need strong leadership institutions, firm laws, and strict moral codes. Government, they think, needs to ensure order. Conservatives also believe that people who fail in life are in some way the architects of their own misfortune and must bear the main responsibility for solving their own problems. Conservatives prefer a reversal of laws on judicial rulings permitting abortion, affirmative action programs, and various worker protection laws.

TRADITIONAL CONSERVATIVES Traditional conservatives are emphatically pro-business. They favor tax cuts and resist all but the most necessary antitrust, trade, and environmental regulations on corporations. They believe that the functions of government should be to protect the nation from foreign enemies, preserve law and order,

conservatism
A belief that limited government ensures order, competitive markets, and personal opportunity.

enforce private contracts, foster competitive markets, encourage free and fair trade, and promote family values. Traditional conservatives favor dispersing power broadly throughout the political and social systems to avoid concentration of power at the national level. They favor having the market, rather than the government, provide services.

Until recent decades, conservatives opposed the New Deal programs of the 1930s, the War on Poverty in the 1960s, and many civil rights and affirmative action programs. Human needs, they say, can and should be taken care of by families and charities. Conservatives are more inclined to put their faith in the private sector and dislike the tendency to turn to government, especially the national government, for solutions to societal problems. Government social activism, they say, has been expensive and counterproductive. They prefer private giving and individual voluntary efforts targeted at social and economic problems rather than government programs. As noted, conservatives have come to see some social problems as needing a government response. They differ from liberals in the extent to which they see problems this way and in a preference for state and local government over national government activity when a government response is needed.

Conservatives, especially when in office, selectively advocate government activism, often while continuing to criticize government generally. Early in the 2000 presidential campaign, for example, George W. Bush said, "Too often, my party has confused the need for a limited government with a disdain for government itself." Love of country, he said, "is undermined by sprawling, arrogant, aimless government. It is restored by focused and effective and energetic government."[26] To learn more about conservative beliefs, go to www.aei.org or www.heritage.org.

SOCIAL CONSERVATIVES Some conservatives focus less on economics and more on morality and lifestyle. Social conservatives favor strong governmental action to protect children from pornography and drugs. They want stringent limits on abortions and oppose gay marriage. This brand of conservatism—sometimes called the New Right, ultraconservatism, or even the Radical Right—emerged in the 1980s. The New Right shares the traditional conservative's love of freedom and backs an aggressive effort to defend America's interests abroad. It favors the return of organized prayer in public schools and opposes policies like job quotas, busing, and tolerance of homosexuality. In sum, a defining characteristic of the New Right is a strong desire to impose various *social controls.*

A New Right or Religious Right group that supports social conservatism includes, among others, Pat Robertson, a minister who sponsors a nightly cable television program. Robertson's Christian Coalition was a major political force in the 1980s and early 1990s but has weakened in recent years.[27] Although ostensibly working in a bipartisan fashion, it is more at home in the Republican party. The Coalition endorses candidates who are profamily, antiabortion, and antigay. It favors a constitutional amendment that would guarantee the rights to organized prayer in public schools and religious symbols in public places. Without regard to denomination, nearly two-thirds (63 percent) of those who attend church regularly vote Republican, while those who do not vote just as disproportionately for the Democrats.[28]

Some conservatives are uncomfortable with the close association between the Republican party and the Christian Right. Former U.S. Senator Warren Rudman of New Hampshire has observed, "Politically speaking, the Republican Party is making a terrible mistake if it appears to ally itself with the Christian right. There are some fine, sincere people in its ranks, but there are also enough anti-abortion zealots, would-be censors, homophobes, bigots, and latter-day Elmer Gantrys to discredit any party that is unwise enough to embrace such a group."[29] Rudman's statement was later used to justify phone calls by Robertson to Christian Coalition members urging them to vote for George W. Bush in the 2000 South Carolina and Michigan primaries instead of for John McCain, whose campaign Rudman co-chaired.[30]

CRITICISMS OF CONSERVATISM Not everyone agreed with Ronald Reagan's statement that "government is the problem." Indeed, critics of conservatism point out that conservatives themselves urge more government when it serves their needs—regulating pornography and abortion, for example—but are opposed to it when it serves somebody else's. Conservatives may also have fewer objections to big government when

Grover Norquist, head of Americans for Tax Reform, is a major proponent of lowering federal, state, and local taxes. Conservatives believe that by lowering taxes, people will have more money to invest in the economy and to donate to charitable organizations.

individuals have a choice in determining how government will impact them. Vouchers for schools, choices in prescription drug benefit plans, and options to manage Social Security savings are examples of such choices proposed by President George W. Bush.[31] Critics of these proposals see conservatives as selective in their criticism of big government or supportive only when it fits their assumptions about what is the best approach.

Conservatives place great faith in the market economy—critics say too much faith. This posture often puts conservatives at odds with labor unions and consumer activists and in close alliance with businesspeople, particularly large corporations. Hostility to regulation and a belief in competition leads them to push for deregulation. This approach has not always had the intended positive effects, as the collapse of many savings and loan companies in the 1980s, the energy crisis in California in the early 2000s, and the business and accounting failures at Enron and other major corporations in 2002 revealed.[32] Conservatives counter that relying on market solutions and encouraging the free market are still the best course of action in most policy areas.

The policy of lowering taxes during the Reagan and George W. Bush administrations was consistent with the conservative hostility to big government. Many conservatives embraced the idea that if taxes are lowered on the rich, their increased economic activity will "trickle down" to the poor. This view was criticized by many Democrats, who pointed out that the growth in income and wealth in the 1980s was largely concentrated among the well-to-do.[33] They also pointed out that reduced taxes and increased government spending, especially for defense, tripled the deficit during the 1980s, when conservatives were in control. President George W. Bush pressed for tax cuts during his administration and pressed to make them permanent in his reelection campaign. Democrats and some conservative Republicans criticized Bush for wanting lower taxes at the same time the budget deficit was growing.

Liberals charge that some conservatives repeatedly fail to acknowledge and endorse policies that deal with racism and sexism. Their opposition to civil rights laws in the 1960s and to affirmative action more recently is cited. Not only have some conservatives opposed new laws in these areas, liberals charge, they have hampered the executive branch and sought to limit the courts' implementation of civil rights laws.

The selective application of government by liberals and social conservatives demonstrates the lack of consistency by some in both groups. Liberals favor vigorous governmental programs to help the poor but oppose governmental intrusion into people's private lives to protect our national security, while some social conservatives preach less government except when they consider it necessary to counter drugs, pornography, and other social evils.

Socialism

Socialism is an economic and governmental system based on public ownership of the means of production and exchange. Karl Marx once described socialism as a transitional stage of society between capitalism and communism. In a capitalist system, the means of production and most property are privately owned; in a communist system, property is controlled by the state in common for all the people, and the government is in charge of a single political party representing the working classes, with no opposition allowed. Communist countries like Cuba are ruled by one party, the Communist party. Some countries, like Sweden, have combined some aspects of government ownership and operation of business with democracy. Others have experimented with socializing medicine and telecommunications while keeping other economic sectors private.

In one of the most dramatic transformations in recent times, Russia, its sister republics, and its former eastern European satellites abandoned communism in the early 1990s and have been attempting to establish free markets. These countries had previously had a system of state ownership and centralized government planning of the economy. But political and economic failure in the Soviet Union resulted in the disintegration of its communist leadership and its empire. Once central power was loosened over the

socialism
An economic and governmental system based on public ownership of the means of production and exchange.

Soviet republics and satellites, a tide of political and economic reform left communism intact in only a few countries, such as Cuba and China. American socialists—of whom there are only a few prominent examples—favor a greatly expanded role for the government but argue that such a system is compatible with democracy. They would nationalize certain industries, institute a public jobs program so that all who want work would be put to work, place a much steeper tax burden on the wealthy, and drastically cut defense spending.[34] Most of the democracies of western Europe are more influenced by socialist ideas than we are in the United States, but they remain, like the United States, largely market economies. Many countries appear to be turning to market solutions for problems once assumed to be the responsibility of government. Debate will continue about the proper role of government and what the market can do better than government can.[35]

Environmentalism

An intense concern with the environment and related matters is **environmentalism**, an ideology that has taken root in several democracies in recent decades and led to the formation of Green parties in several countries. The Green movement has elected members of parliament in Finland, Germany, Switzerland, Sweden, Luxembourg, Austria, and the Netherlands and is part of the liberal-left coalition governing Germany today. In the United States, the Green party emphasizes such values as grassroots democracy, social justice, equal opportunity, nonviolence, respect for diversity, and feminism. In these areas, environmentalism is little different from liberalism, but it is in the emphasis on ecology and the environment that Greens are distinct.

The Web site of the U.S. Green party says, "We must practice agriculture which replenishes the soil; move to an energy-efficient economy; and live in ways that respect the integrity of natural systems."[36] Ralph Nader, the party's presidential candidate in 2000, enhanced the visibility of the party but still won less than 3 percent of the vote in the general election. In 2004, David Cobb, lacking the visibility or stature of Ralph Nader, received less than one-tenth of one percent of the vote. More broadly, the environment as an issue in 2004 was not as important as it had been in past elections and environmental groups focused less of their attention on congressional contests and more on the presidential contest. Most environmental groups supported John Kerry. The Green party endorsed gay marriage, a tougher stance on polluters, and slave reparations.

Libertarianism

Libertarianism is a political ideology that cherishes individual liberty and insists on sharply limited government. It carries some overtones of anarchism, of the classical English liberalism of the past, and of a 1930s-style conservatism. The Libertarian party has gained a small following among people who believe that both liberals and conservatives lack consistency in their attitude toward the power of the national government.

Libertarians preach opposition to almost all government programs. They favor massive cuts in government spending and an end to the Federal Bureau of Investigation, the Central Intelligence Agency, and most regulatory commissions. They oppose participation in the United Nations and favor a defense establishment that would defend the United States only if directly attacked. They oppose *all* government regulation, including, for example, mandatory seat-belt and helmet laws. Unlike conservatives, libertarians would repeal laws that regulate personal morality, including abortion, pornography, prostitution, and illicit drugs.

A Libertarian party candidate for president has been on the ballot in all 50 states in recent presidential elections, although never obtaining more than 1 percent of the vote. The Libertarian candidate for president in 2000, Harry Browne, ran on a platform that emphasized freedom from government. The 2000 Libertarian platform was committed to a smaller government, limited by the Constitution's specifications, and proposed immediate and complete removal of the federal government from education, energy,

Bernard Sanders, a self-described Socialist, represents Vermont in the U.S. House of Representatives as an Independent.

environmentalism
An ideology that is dominated by concern for the environment but also promotes grassroots democracy, social justice, equal opportunity, nonviolence, respect for diversity, and feminism.

libertarianism
An ideology that cherishes individual liberty and insists on a sharply limited government, promoting a free market economy, a noninterventionist foreign policy, and an absence of regulation in the moral and social spheres.

PEOPLE & POLITICS *Making a Difference* ★★★

RACHEL CARSON AND THE ENVIRONMENTAL MOVEMENT.

"There was once a town in the heart of America where all life seemed to live in harmony with its surroundings. . . . Then a strange blight crept over the area and everything began to change. . . . There was a strange stillness. . . . The few birds seen anywhere were moribund; they trembled violently and could not fly. It was a spring without voices."* These words of Rachel Carson, found at the beginning of her most famous work, *Silent Spring*, elicited a response that was anything but silent.

A gifted researcher and writer, Carson had worked with the U.S. Bureau of Fisheries (later the U.S. Fish and Wildlife Service) and was one of only two women then employed with the Bureau at a professional level. Her first book, *Under the Sea Wind*, demonstrated her ability to describe the natural world to her readers. During her years in government service she became alarmed by the widespread use of pesticides and their harmful effects on the

environment. She contacted *Reader's Digest* in hopes of writing an article on the subject, but was met with disinterest.† Not until many years later did alarming wildlife death rates in specific areas sprayed by pesticides serve as a catalyst for her to write and publish *Silent Spring*.

Without moral courage to go along with her academic abilities, it is doubtful that she could have made the impact that she did with *Silent Spring*. Carson overcame personal adversity, including the deaths of a niece and her mother and the discovery that she had terminal cancer.† Carson's book has been criticized by the chemical industry, the Department of Agriculture, and many in the media. In response to these attacks she said, "I have felt bound by a solemn obligation to do what I could."§ Carson's book made a difference, influencing lawmakers to pass legislation banning the use of DDT and establishing the Environmental Protection Agency.‖

*Rachel Carson, *Silent Spring* (Houghton Mifflin, 1962), pp. 1, 2.
† Peter Matthiessen, "Rachel Carson," *Time Magazine*, March 29, 1999. www.time.com/time/time100/scientist/profile/carson02.html.
‡ www.pbs.org/wgbh/aso/databank/entries/btcars.html.
§ Matthiessen. www.time.com/time/time100/scientist/profile/carson03.html.
‖ For a more detailed biography of Rachel Carson see rachelcarson.fws.gov/carsonbio.html.

Michael Badnarik, Libertarian candidate for president in 2004. Badnarik received 380,000 votes in the 2004 election—just 20,000 less than Nader and the most of all official candidates for the minor parties.

regulation, crime control, welfare, housing, transportation, health care, and agriculture; repeal of the income tax and all other direct taxes; decriminalization of drugs and pardons for prisoners convicted of nonviolent drug offenses; and withdrawal of overseas military forces. Libertarian positions are rarely timid; at the very least, they prompt intriguing political debates.[37] The Libertarian party's 2004 candidate, Michael Badnarik, received 380,000 votes, just 20,000 behind Nader. Badnarik received the most votes of the official candidates for the minor parties (Brian Faler, "A Polling Sight: Record Turnout," *The Washington Post*, November 5, 2004, p. A7). In 2004, the Libertarian party endorsed same sex marriage, legalizing drugs, repealing the Patriot Act, withdrawing from Iraq, eliminating all gun control laws, retracting business regulations, and eliminating the FDA. To learn more about libertarianism, go to www.lp.org.

A Word of Caution

Political labels have different meanings across national boundaries as well as over time. To be a liberal in certain European nations is to be on the right; to be a liberal in the United States is to be on the left. In recent elections, the term "liberal"—which back in Franklin Roosevelt's day had been popular—became "the L-word," a label most politicians sought to avoid. But liberalism is more than a label. On big questions—such as the role of government in the economy, in promoting equality of opportunity, and in regulating the behavior of individuals or businesses—real differences separate conservative and liberal groups. This does not mean, however, that people who are conservative in one area are necessarily conservative in another or that liberals always hold similar views.

It is important to appreciate that ideology both causes events and is affected by them. Just as the Great Depression resulted in a tidal wave of ideological change, so did our involvement in World War II. The attacks on the World Trade Center and the Pentagon on September 11, 2001, may also have a lasting impact. For example, World War II, with its positive example of how government can work to defend freedom, strengthened positive views about the role of the national government. The Vietnam War probably had the opposite effect, producing disillusionment with government. The antigovernment sentiment in recent presidential elections is undoubtedly related to Vietnam, the Watergate scandal, and allegations of sexual misconduct by political leaders in recent years. The surge in patriotism and sense of national unity in the war against terrorism after September 11 stands in sharp contrast to the national mood during the final years of the Vietnam War. It also reflects, at least in the short term, a view that government has an important role to play in responding to a crisis (see Figure 4–1).

POLITICAL IDEOLOGY AND THE AMERICAN PEOPLE

For some people, ideological controversy today centers on the role of the government in improving schools, encouraging a stronger work ethic, and stopping the flow of drugs into the country. For others, ideology is centered on whether to permit openly gay people into the military or sanction same-sex marriages and on the best ways to instill moral values, build character, and encourage cohesive and lasting families.

Despite the twists and turns of American politics, the distribution of ideology in the nation has been remarkably consistent (see Figure 4–2). Conservatives outnumber liberals, but the proportion of conservatives did not increase substantially with the

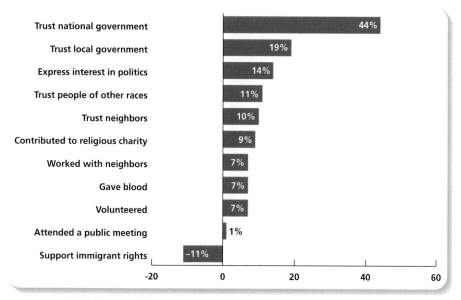

FIGURE 4–1 Net Changes in Civic Attitudes after September 11, 2001.
Source: Robert D. Putnam, "Bowling Together," *American Prospect* 13 (February 11, 2002): 20–22.

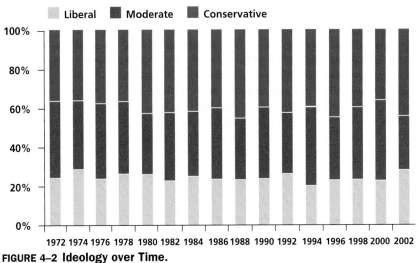

FIGURE 4–2 Ideology over Time.
SOURCE: Center for Political Studies, University of Michigan, *2002 National Election Study Guide to Public Opinion and Electoral Behavior.*

decisive Republican presidential victories of the 1980s or congressional victories of the 1990s.

Another important fact about ideology in the United States is that most people are moderates or not very ideological. In 2000 and 2002, only 2 percent of the population saw themselves as extreme liberals, while extreme conservatives ranged form 2–4 percent in these same years (see Figure 4–3). These percentages have changed very little over time. The tendency toward muted ideology is also demonstrated by the fact that more people consider themselves *slightly* liberal or *slightly* conservative than liberal or conservative. Despite claims by ideological extremes in both parties to move to the right or to the left, there are simply more votes in the middle.[38]

Both major parties targeted moderate or centrist voters in the 2000 presidential election, as reflected in the stands of the candidates on key issues, including their efforts to minimize ideological battles at the conventions. Governor Tommy Thompson of Wisconsin, who chaired the Republican Platform Committee, stated that their more conservative partisans did not push their issues because "they want to win."[39] In 2004, both presidential candidates again courted the "swing" or undecided voters in states where the race was close. But both parties also worked hard to activate more ideological voters, sometimes called the "base" vote. Kerry stressed jobs and a middle-class tax cut in an effort to secure support from working people. Bush emphasized reaching conservative Christian voters and Republicans who had moved in the last few years into outlying suburbs, sometimes called exurbs.

For those who have a liberal or conservative preference, ideology provides a lens through which to view candidates and public policies. It helps simplify the complexities of politics, policies, personalities, and programs. However, most Americans do not organize their political views systematically. A voter may want increased spending for defense but vote for the party that is for reducing defense spending because he or she has always voted for that party or prefers its stand on the environment. Or a person may favor tax cuts and balancing the budget while at the same time being unwilling to see government programs cut back substantially.

The degree to which people have ideologically consistent attitudes and opinions varies but is often relatively low. Much of the time, people view political issues as isolated matters and do not apply an overall standard of performance in evaluating parties or candidates. Indeed, many citizens find it difficult to relate what happens in one policy situation to what happens in another. This problem becomes more complex as

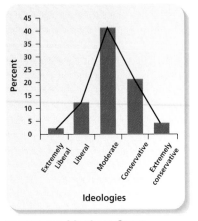

FIGURE 4–3 Ideology Curve.
SOURCE: Center for Political Studies, University of Michigan, *2002 National Election Study Guide to Public Opinion and Electoral Behavior.*

government gets into more and more policy areas. Hence many people, not surprisingly, have difficulty finding candidates who reflect their ideological preferences across a wide range of issues.

The absence of widespread and solidified liberal and conservative positions in the United States makes for politics and policy-making processes that are markedly different from those in many European and other nations. Policy making in this country is characterized more by coalitions of the moment than by fixed alignments that pit one set of ideologies against another. Our politics is marked more by moderation, pragmatism, and accommodation than by a prolonged battle among two, three, or more competing philosophies of government. Elsewhere, especially in countries where a strong Socialist or Christian Democratic party exists, like Germany or Sweden, things are different. This does not, however, mean that policies or ideas are not important elements in American politics. There has been, for instance, a shift to strongly partisan and ideological voting in the House of Representatives. Part of the explanation for the increasing importance of ideology in Congress is Republican gains in the South, with remaining southern Democrats becoming more liberal[40]; in other parts of the country where moderate Republicans were once successful, liberal Democrats now hold many seats. Perhaps even more important, congressional districts are now being drawn in such a way as to make more of them safe for one or the other party, so Republican members of Congress tend to appeal to the more conservative wing of their party, while the more liberal Democratic members of Congress tend to appeal to the more liberal wing of their party.

IDEOLOGY AND TOLERANCE

Is there a connection between the ideologies of liberalism and conservatism and support for civil liberties and tolerance for racial minorities? Some political scientists assert that conservatives are generally less tolerant than liberals.[41] This view is stoutly contested by conservatives, who have charged liberals with trying to impose a "politically correct" position on faculty and students in universities, colleges, and the media. Liberals are usually more tolerant of dissent from some quarters and the expression of some unorthodox opinions. However, liberals, too, can be intolerant—of abortion foes, for example, or the National Rifle Association or the views of Sean Hannity. On the other side, some conservatives have worked to seek dismissal of faculty members and ministers who have been critical of the war against terrorism.

Most liberals are strongly opposed to crime and lawbreaking, yet they are also concerned about the causes of crime and trying to eliminate them. Perhaps for this reason, liberals exhibit somewhat greater concern than conservatives for the rights of the accused and are more willing to expand the rights of due process. Conservatives usually take a harder line and, in recent years, have won widespread popular support for their greater concern for the victims of crime than for the rights of the accused.

Such differences are most evident in the responses of liberals and conservatives to questions of civil rights and civil liberties. In the area of free speech, conservatives are usually seen as less willing to permit speech that is out of the political or cultural mainstream. Perhaps conservatives are less tolerant because those who claim to be exercising the right of free speech often attack established values. Liberals favor limiting speech in areas like cigarette advertising or campaign spending but favor fewer restrictions than conservatives do on countercultural individuals or groups.[42]

Conservatives believe that the United States has become morally too permissive. Many conservatives, especially in the New or Religious Right, are highly critical of homosexuals, drug users, prostitutes, unwed mothers, and pornographers. They worry about what they claim has been a decline in moral standards and, interestingly, call on government to help reverse these trends. Most liberals, by contrast, generally accept nonconformity in conduct and opinion as an inescapable byproduct of freedom.[43] In this regard, liberals are like libertarians.

"It's been hell! The breakfast bagels aren't toasted, I can't sleep with a nightlight, there's no "dry hair" formula shampoo in the showers, and the guard won't get close enough for me to stab him with a spoon!"

By Steve Stack, *Minneapolis Star-Tribune*. Reprinted with permission of Star Tribune.

POLITICAL SURVEY: WHAT DO YOU BELIEVE?

Political scientists measure ideology by asking people about their beliefs and values and then placing those individual responses in a context of a broader public. The Make it Real feature for this chapter provides a sample of these polling questions, allowing you to see how you would be categorized. You can also compare your views with those of the general public.

Go to Make it Real: "Political Survey: What Do You Believe?"

Ideologies have consequences. It is these sharp cleavages in political thinking that stir opposing interest groups into action. A wide variety of groups promote their views of what is politically desirable. It is also these differences in ideological perspectives that reinforce party loyalties and divide us at election time. Policy fights in Congress, between Congress and the White House, and during judicial confirmation hearings also have their roots in our uneasily coexisting ideological values.

Our hard-earned rights and liberties are never entirely safeguarded; they are fragile and are shaped by the political, economic, and social climate of the day. In later chapters, we examine the interest groups and political parties that are battling to advance their values and compete in the American political culture. But before turning to those topics, we examine the social and economic diversity of the American political landscape in Chapter 5 and see why agreement on shared democratic values is all the more remarkable.

S U M M A R Y

1. The United States, like every other nation or society, has a distinctive political culture. It consists of a widely held set of fundamental political values and accepted processes and institutions that help us manage conflict and resolve problems. In the United States, at least in the abstract, people respect the Constitution, the Bill of Rights, the two-party system, and the right to elect officials on the basis of majority rule. Our belief in social equality has fostered acceptance of the notion that government should guarantee equality of opportunity through programs like education and job training.

2. Americans share a widespread commitment to classical liberalism, which embraces the importance of individual liberty, equality, individualism, power to the people, private property, limited government, nationalism, optimism, idealism, the democratic consensus, and justice and the rule of law. They also believe that the American dream should be something we can all pursue.

3. American political values have been and continue to be affected by historical and economic developments. Among these have been the industrial revolution, the development of large corporations and other large institutions, the Great Depression, and a global economy.

4. The sources of the American political culture include the family, schools, religious and civic organizations, the mass media, and political activities.

5. Two broad schools of thought are important in American politics today: liberalism, a belief in the positive uses of government to bring about justice and equality of opportunity; and conservatism, a belief that limited government ensures order, competitive markets, and personal opportunity. Socialism, environmentalism, and libertarianism also attract a modest following in America.

6. Most Americans are nonideological and are guided primarily by moderate pragmatism. Few Americans are extremists.

7. Ideological orientation has a bearing on how tolerant we are of the views and conduct of others. Liberals tend to be more tolerant, whereas conservatives generally favor tradition, stability, and greater levels of social control. These differences have consequences for electoral contests and policy development in our political system.

K E Y   T E R M S

social capital
political culture
natural rights
democratic consensus

majority rule
popular sovereignty
American dream
capitalism

monopoly
antitrust legislation
political ideology
liberalism

conservatism
socialism
environmentalism
libertarianism

FURTHER READING

H. W. BRANDS, *The Strange Death of American Liberalism* (Yale University Press, 2001).

JAMES W. CEASER, *Reconstructing America: The Symbol of America in Modern Thought* (Yale University Press, 1997).

E. J. DIONNE JR., *They Only Look Dead: Why Progressives Will Dominate the Next Political Era* (Simon & Schuster, 1996).

JEAN BETHKE ELSHTAIN, *Democracy on Trial* (Basic Books, 1995).

AMY GUTMANN AND DENNIS THOMPSON, *Democracy and Disagreement: Why Moral Conflict Cannot Be Avoided in Politics, and What Should Be Done About It* (Harvard University Press, 1996).

LAWRENCE E. HARRISON AND SAMUEL P. HARRINGTON, EDS., *Culture Matters: How Values Shape Human Progress* (Basic Books, 2000).

LOUIS HARTZ, *The Liberal Tradition in America* (Harcourt, 1955).

GEORGE KLOSKO, *Democratic Procedures and Liberal Consensus* (Oxford University Press, 2000).

IRVING KRISTOL, *Neoconservatism: The Autobiography of an Idea* (Free Press, 1995).

DAVID C. LEEGE, KENNETH D. WALD, BRIAN S. KRUEGER, AND PAUL D. MUELLER, *The Politics of Cultural Differences* (Princeton University Press, 2002).

HERBERT MCCLOSKY AND JOHN ZALLER, *The American Ethos: Public Attitudes Toward Capitalism and Democracy* (Harvard University Press, 1984).

LISA McGIRR, *Suburban Warriors: The Origins of the New American Right* (Princeton University Press, 2001).

CHARLES MURRAY, *What It Means to Be a Libertarian: A Personal Interpretation* (Broadway Books, 1997).

MARCUS G. RASKIN, *Liberalism: The Genius of American Ideals* (Rowman and Littlefield, 2004).

JOHN RENSENBRINK, *Against All Odds: The Green Transformation of American Politics* (Leopold Press, 1999).

JONATHON M. SCHOENWALD, *A Time for Choosing: The Rise of American Conservatism* (Oxford University Press, 2001).

ROGER SCRUTON, *The Meaning of Conservatism* (St. Augustine Press, 2001).

ALEXIS DE TOCQUEVILLE, *Democracy in America,* 2 vols. (1835).

JOHN TOMASI, *Liberalism Beyond Justice: Citizens, Society, and the Boundaries of Political Theory* (Princeton University Press, 2001).

JOHN KENNETH WHITE, *The Values Divide* (Seven Bridges Press, 2003).

GARRY WILLS, *A Necessary Evil: A History of American Distrust of Government* (Simon & Schuster, 1999).

DANIEL YERGIN AND JOSEPH STAINSLAW, *The Commanding Heights: The Battle Between Government and the Marketplace That Is Remaking the Modern World* (Simon & Schuster, 1998).

The United States is a nation of immigrants, a fact that is a source of pride. Franklin D. Roosevelt once began a speech to the Daughters of the American Revolution by saying, "You and I, especially, are descended from immigrants and revolutionists."[1] Immigrants have long been drawn to America by the hope for prosperity and freedom. However, the American dream is rarely achieved in the first generation. There are notable exceptions. Take, for example, George Soros, an international financier who is among the most successful businesspeople in the United States. Soros was born in Hungary, educated in England, and then moved to the United States. Arte Moreno, the owner of the Anaheim Angels baseball team, is the first Hispanic to own a major U.S. sports franchise. Moreno started a billboard business with a partner during college. Over time the business grew, allowing expansion into similar businesses. The conglomerate was sold in 1999 for $8.3 billion.[2] Both George

THE AMERICAN
POLITICAL
LANDSCAPE

5

TIME LINE ★★

THE AMERICAN POLITICAL LANDSCAPE

1803	Louisiana Purchase greatly expands the size of the United States
1862	Congress allows for land grant colleges, fostering growth in higher education
1892	Ellis Island opens—the entry point for millions of immigrants to America
1920	19th Amendment gives women right to vote
1929	Stock Market Crash signals the Great Depression
1945	End of World War II begins economic and population booms
1960	Kennedy elected—first Catholic President
1971	Eighteen year olds given the right to vote
1994	Proposition 187 tries to discourage immigration to California
2000	Vermont becomes first state to recognize civil unions for same-sex couples

ethnocentrism
Belief in the superiority of one's nation or ethnic group.

political socialization
The process by which we develop our political attitudes, values, and beliefs.

demographics
The study of the characteristics of populations.

political predisposition
A characteristic of individuals that is predictive of political behavior.

Soros and Arte Moreno illustrate the potential for fortunate and hardworking individuals to succeed in our political and economic system. Soros, an outspoken critic of President George W. Bush, gave $27 million in 2003–2004 to groups opposing Bush's reelection. Arte Moreno has been a contributor on a much smaller scale to predominantly Republican candidates and the Republican party. Our system not only permits immigrants and other individuals to accumulate wealth but also allows them to translate that wealth into political influence.

We have conflicting ideas about immigration. We celebrate our immigrant past and proudly recite the words of Emma Lazarus inscribed at the base of the Statue of Liberty: "Give me your tired, your poor, your huddled masses yearning to breathe free." And yet our borders are not open to all who wish to come here, and immigration is limited, with specific numbers of immigrants allowed to enter from each country each year. Hundreds of thousands avoid these limitations by crossing our borders illegally, seeking employment, refuge, and freedom.

After the terrorist attacks on the World Trade Center and the Pentagon in 2001, there was some anti-Arab and anti-Muslim sentiment, including some efforts in Congress to restrict student visas.[3] President Bush urged Americans to "treat each other with respect."[4] Disagreements about the admission of aliens into this country and about their rights and privileges have featured in political campaigns for more than two centuries. In 2004 President Bush proposed changes to the United States immigration policy that would allow illegal immigrants to receive legal status if they receive a temporary worker visa and are employed in the country.[5] His proposal and many others were debated in Congress and during the 2004 campaign.

Albert Einstein once said that most people are incapable of expressing opinions that differ much from the prejudices of their social upbringing.[6] This **ethnocentrism**—selective perception based on one's background, attitudes, and biases—is not uncommon, even among college students, who often assume that others share their economic opportunities, social attitudes, sense of civic responsibility, and self-confidence. In this chapter, we consider how our social environment explains, or at least shapes, our opinions and prejudices. We also look at our diversity as Americans and the implications of geographic, social, and economic divisions for politics and government. Specifically, this chapter explores the effects of regional or state identity on political perspectives; the implications of differences in race, ethnicity, gender, family structure, religion, wealth and income, occupation, and social class for opinions and voting choices; and the relationship between age and education and political participation.

A LAND OF DIVERSITY

Most nations consist of groups of people who have lived together for hundreds of years and who speak the same language, embrace the same religious beliefs, and share a common history. Most Japanese citizens are Japanese in the fullest sense of the word, and this sense of identity and oneness is generally the same in Germany, Sweden, Saudi Arabia, China, and France. The United States is different. We have attracted the poor and oppressed, the adventurous, and the talented from all over the world, and we have been more open to accepting these people than many other nations.

One reason so many people want to come to the United States is that it holds a promise of religious, political, and economic freedom. It is also a place of opportunity for the enterprising. Our economic system has provided widespread (but not universal) opportunity for individuals to improve their economic standing. The American dream—that anyone can find success in the United States—is widely shared.

Several elements of our diversity have political significance. Many Americans retain an identity with the native land of their ancestors, even after three or four generations. Holding on to such differences reflects socialization in families, churches, and other close-knit groups. **Political socialization** is the process by which parents and others teach children about political values, beliefs, and attitudes. This teaching occurs in the home, in school, on the playground, and in the neighborhood. In addition to fostering

GLOBAL *Perceptions*

QUESTION: **Is the influence of immigrants very good, somewhat good, somewhat bad, or very bad in your country?**

Public opinion about the influence of immigrants on society varies dramatically across different countries. The chart shows how various countries responded to the question presented above.

Immigrants are viewed most favorably in Canada, where laws favorable to immigration have long been in place. In the United States, opinion is more evenly divided: 43 percent said immigrants have a bad influence and 49 percent said they have a good influence. Economics appears related to attitudes toward immigrants in some but not most places. Even in countries with a need for workers, like Germany, there is strong anti-immigrant sentiment.

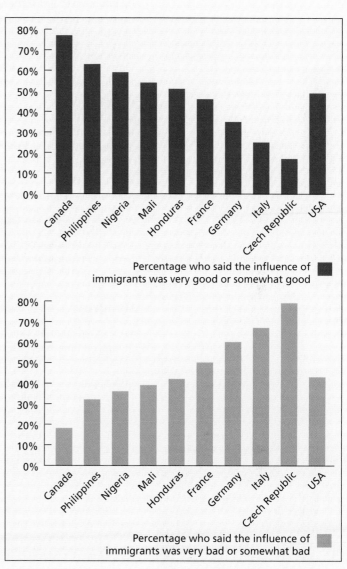

Percentage who said the influence of immigrants was very good or somewhat good

Percentage who said the influence of immigrants was very bad or somewhat bad

SOURCE: The Pew Research Center. *What the World Thinks in 2002.* p. T-36.

group identities, political socialization strongly influences how individuals see politics and which political party they prefer. Where we live and who we are in terms of age, education, religion, and occupation affect how we vote. Such characteristics of populations are called **demographics**. Persons in certain demographic categories tend to vote alike and to have certain **political predispositions** in common, and these characteristics sometimes predict political behavior. Although demographics can be important in both explaining and predicting political behavior, there are sometimes large individual differences within socioeconomic and demographic categories.

When social and economic differences coincide, they reinforce each other and make the differences between groups more important. Social scientists call these differences **reinforcing cleavages**; where these differences are reinforcing, political conflict becomes more intense and there is greater polarization in society. In Italy, for example, the regional divide between north and south is reinforced by the tendency of the north to lean toward the Socialist or Communist party and the south to be Christian Democratic and Catholic in orientation.

reinforcing cleavages
Divisions within society that reinforce one another, making groups more homogeneous or similar.

cross-cutting cleavages
Divisions within society that cut across demographic categories to produce groups that are more heterogeneous or different.

Nations can also have **cross-cutting cleavages**, instances where differences among people do not reinforce each other but rather pull in different directions. To illustrate, if all the rich individuals in a nation are of one religion and the poor of another, the nation would have reinforcing cleavages, and political conflict between the groups would be intensified. But if there are both rich and poor in all religions and if people sometimes vote on the basis of their religion and sometimes on the basis of their wealth, the divisions would be cross-cutting. American diversity has generally been more of the cross-cutting type than the reinforcing type, lessening political conflict because individuals have multiple allegiances.

In some societies, politics centers largely on passions over economic and religious differences. Although socioeconomic differences are important to understanding American government and politics, they are not as central to our politics as religion is in Bosnia or tribal identity in Rwanda. In Northern Ireland, the religious differences between Catholics and Protestants have produced centuries of violent strife that is yet to be resolved.

Despite the fact that America has been more hospitable to people from different religions, classes, and races than almost any other nation in the world, we Americans often prefer to associate only with people "like us" and are suspicious of people "like them." From hostility toward different religions in the early colonies to the anti-immigration movements of the late 1800s and early 1900s to the anti-immigration and anti–civil rights ballot initiatives of the last two decades, Americans have exhibited ethnocentrism, and for much of our history, minorities have been excluded from full participation in American political and economic life.

Geography and National Identity

The United States is a geographically large and historically isolated country. In the 1830s, French commentator Alexis de Tocqueville studied the early development of the United States and observed that the country had no major political or economic powers on its borders "and consequently no great wars, financial crises, invasions, or conquests to fear."[7] Geographic isolation from the major powers of the world during our government's formative period helps explain American politics. The Atlantic Ocean served as a barrier to foreign meddling, giving us time to establish our political tradition and develop our economy. The western frontier provided room to grow and avoid some of the social and political tensions that Europe experienced. Two great oceans also reinforced our sense of isolation from Europe and foreign alliances. American reluctance to become involved in foreign wars and controversies still emerges in debates over foreign policy.

Before the terrorist attacks of September 2001, only one foreign enemy had struck the United States on our own soil—England in the War of 1812. (The war against Mexico of 1846–1848 was fought almost entirely on Mexican land, some of which later became American land as a result of the war. The only other war fought on our soil was, of course, the Civil War.) By contrast, Poland has been invaded repeatedly and was partitioned by Austria, Prussia, and Russia in the eighteenth century and by Nazi Germany and the Soviet Union in the twentieth century. The difference is explained largely by location: Poland was surrounded by Europe's great powers. Had the United States been closer to Europe and not isolated by two oceans, it might have been overrun like Poland and our Constitution and institutions repeatedly changed or eliminated to suit the victorious invaders. The presence of powerful and aggressive neighbors impedes the development of democracy in relatively weak nations.

The ability of terrorists to promulgate war, especially if willing to die along with their enemies, as was the case with the attacks in 2001, means that isolation and national security have to be rethought. No longer does the United States have the luxury of developing our democracy behind the protection of two oceans; our newly recognized vulnerability to attacks on our own soil has changed the context in which we debate the balance between liberty and security. New York, San Francisco, and Chicago are now on the front line.

Size also confers an advantage. The landmass of the United States exceeds that of all but three nations in the world. In contrast, India has a population more than three

Slavery epitomizes the dark side of this country's national identity. During Reconstruction, some former slaves were able to purchase and work their own land while others moved north to take part in the industrial revolution of the late nineteenth century.

and a half times that of the United States on a landmass one-third the size. Geographic space gave the expanding population of the United States room to spread out. This possibility meant that some of the political conflicts arising from religion, social class, and national origin were defused because groups could isolate themselves from one another. This was what Madison hoped for in his concept of a "large republic" (see *The Federalist*, No. 10, in the Appendix). Moreover, the large and accessible landmass helped foster the perspective that the United States had a **manifest destiny** to be a continental nation reaching from the Atlantic to the Pacific oceans. Early settlers used the notion that the United States was "destined" to expand across the continent to justify taking land occupied by Native Americans and Mexicans, especially the land acquired following victory in the Mexican-American War.

The United States is also a land of abundant natural resources. We have rich farmland, which not only feeds our population but also makes us the largest exporter of food in the world.[8] We are rich in such natural resources as coal, iron, uranium, and precious metals. All these resources enhance economic growth, provide jobs, and stabilize government. As de Tocqueville observed long ago, "Yet what takes place in the United States is much less attributable to the institutions of the country than to the country itself."[9]

Geography also helps explain our diversity. Parts of the United States are wonderfully suited to agriculture, others to mining or ranching, and still others to shipping. These differences produce different regional economic concerns, which in turn influence politics. For instance, a person from the agricultural heartland may have a perception of foreign trade that is different from that of an automobile worker in Detroit. But if that automobile worker is African American, this fact may be more important to her politics than what she does or where she lives. To understand American politics, we must appreciate these differences and their relative importance.

Sectional Differences

Unlike many other countries, geography in the United States does *not* define an ethnic or religious division. All the Serbs in the United States do not live in one place, all French-speaking Catholics in another, and all German immigrants in another. Sectional differences in the United States are primarily geographic, not ethnic or religious.

The most distinct section of the United States remains the South, although the South's differences are diminishing. From the beginning of the Republic, the agricultural South differed from the North, where commerce and manufacturing were more significant. But the most important difference between the regions was the institution of slavery. Northern opposition to slavery, which grew increasingly intense by the middle of the nineteenth century, reinforced sectional economic interests. The 11 Confederate states, by virtue of their decision to secede from the Union, reinforced a common political identity, and after the Civil War, sectional differences were strengthened by the policy of Reconstruction and the problems of race relations.

The South is becoming less distinct from the rest of the United States. In addition to undergoing tremendous economic change, a large in-migration has diminished the sense of regional identity. The civil rights revolution eliminated roadblocks preventing African Americans from voting, opened up new educational opportunities, and helped integrate the South into the national economy. African Americans still lag behind whites in voter registration, but the gap is now no wider in the South than elsewhere and is explained more by differences in education than by race.[10] In economic terms, the South still falls below the rest of the country in per capita income and education, but much less so than 50 years ago. The religious and moral conservatism of the South remains notable.

Until the 1970s, political observers spoke of the "solid South"—a region that voted for Democrats at all levels. "The Civil War made the Democratic party the party of the South, and the Republican party, the party of the North."[11] The Democratic "solid South" remained a fixture of American politics for more than a century. Since 1968 that has changed dramatically, first at the presidential level and increasingly at the state and local levels. As two respected observers of the region comment, "The fall of the South

manifest destiny
A notion held by nineteenth-century Americans that the United States was destined to rule the continent, from the Atlantic to the Pacific.

Evidence of the persistent racial divide in this country can be found in the continued display of the flag of the Confederacy. Although many Southern states have finally removed this flag from state government buildings throughout the South, individuals within these states still prominently display this symbol of slavery on their vehicles and on their homes.

as an assured stronghold of the Democratic Party in presidential elections is one of the most significant developments in modern American politics."[12] "The decline of the South in the Democratic party would fundamentally reorder the American party system and realign the electorate."[13] The political alignment has shifted as African Americans have been enfranchised and become overwhelmingly Democrats and many whites have become Republicans. In 1992 and 1996, even with two southerners (Bill Clinton and Al Gore) on the ticket, Democrats won only 4 of the 11 former Confederate states. In 2000, George W. Bush carried all 11 southern states, including Al Gore's home state of Tennessee. Once again in 2004, George W. Bush carried all 11 former Confederate states, including vice presidential candidate John Edwards's home state of North Carolina.

What explains this dramatic reversal? Part of the explanation is that the Democrats' advocacy of aggressive action on civil rights in the 1960s alienated some southern whites. In addition, the debate within the Democratic party over Vietnam policy in the late 1960s and 1970s was "perceived by many southern voters as unpatriotic."[14] Democrats are aware of divisive or "wedge" issues; Howard Dean in 2004 expressed this concern "we have got to stop having the campaigns run in this country based on abortion, guns, God and gays."[15] Republican presidential candidates have more recently emphasized family values, opposition to taxes, same-sex marriage, and law-and-order issues that appeal to conservative southern voters. Republican success at the presidential level was slow to affect contests for Congress and state legislatures. Yet in recent years, Republicans had more than half of southern votes for the U.S. House of Representatives (see Table 5–1), and in 2004, they had 7 of the 11 governorships in the former Confederate states.[16] In the state legislatures of several southern states, remnants of the old "solid South" remain, but Republicans have made major inroads, and politics in the region is now predictably Republican, at least at the presidential level.

Both parties could point to successes in the South in 2002 and 2003. The Democrats picked up or retained the Governorships in Tennessee and Louisiana and the Republicans did the same in Georgia, Alabama, and Mississippi. In Georgia, this was the first GOP elected governor since Reconstruction, and in Alabama, the last Republican was elected in 1995. Overall, Republicans controlled more governorships than Democrats in the South after 2002 and 2003. In the U.S. Senate they have a much more commanding advantage, with at least 18 of the 22 U.S. Senate seats from the former confederate states in Republican hands. Because he was running for vice president, John Edwards did not run for reelection as U.S. senator in his home state of North Carolina and in November 2004, his Senate seat went to Republican Richard Burr.

Another sectional division is the Sun Belt—the 11 former Confederate states plus New Mexico, Arizona, Nevada, and the southern half of California. Sun Belt states are growing much more rapidly than the rest of the country. Arizona, California, Florida, Georgia, Nevada, North Carolina, and Texas gained 12 seats in the House of Representatives after the 2000 census.[18] Moreover, population growth in the South and West is occurring in different age groups. In the South, growth is largest among those over 65; in the West, younger persons provide the growth. Sun Belt states have also experienced greater economic growth as industries have headed south and southwest, where land and labor are cheaper and more abundant (see Figure 5–1). The shift of seats to the Sun Belt has helped Republicans as the states picking up additional seats have tended to be more Republican. That tendency was reinforced in 2003–2004 in Texas where the state legislature, after a protracted political battle, replaced the 2002 boundaries drawn by the courts with new districts aimed at defeating Democratic incumbents in the 2004 election.[19]

State and Local Identity

Different states have rather distinctive political traditions. Mention Utah, Mississippi, Oregon, New York, or Kansas, and a certain type of politics comes to mind. The same is true for many other states. Like most stereotypes, these images are often misleading, yet they reflect the fact that there is a sense of identity to states as political units that goes

TABLE 5–1 VOTING PATTERNS IN THE 11 FORMER CONFEDERATE STATES

Republican Vote for President

1980	50%
1984	62
1988	59
1992	43
1996	46
2000	54
2004	57

Republican Vote for U.S. Representatives

1980	40%
1982	39
1984	42
1986	41
1988	42
1990	43
1992	48
1994	58
1996	53[*]
1998	58
2000	53
2002	56
2004	55

Republican Share of State Legislators

	House	Senate
1980	18%	17%
1982	22	14
1984	23	17
1986	24	20
1988	27	24
1990	28	26
1992	31	31
1994	37	37
1996	44	44
1998	42	40
2000	44	42
2002	47	46
2004	50	49

SOURCE: U.S. Bureau of the Census, *Statistical Abstract of the United States,* 1993–2000. For 2004, CNN at www.cnn.com/ELECTION/2004; and *Congressional Quarterly Weekly Report,* November 11, 2000, pp. 2694–2703; and Todd Edwards, Council of State Governments, Southern Office, personal communication, December 22, 2000 and Doris Smith, Council of State Governments, Southern Office, November 10, 2004.

[*]*The 1996 Texas runoff elections are not included.*

beyond demographic characteristics and is supported by recent empirical evidence. States have distinctive political cultures that affect public opinion and policy outcomes.[20] Our electoral rules and other laws reinforce these state identities.

In American politics today, one state—California—stands out. More than one out of eight Americans is a Californian.[21] In terms of economic and political importance,

★★ **YOU DECIDE**

HOW IMPORTANT IS STATE IDENTITY TO YOU?

With national media not only presenting news but providing entertainment nationally and with substantial mobility across state boundaries, is state identity still important to Americans? Do people see enduring differences from state to state or are these differences becoming less important?

California is in a league by itself; its 53 members of the House of Representatives exceed the total number of representatives from the smallest 20 states. California's 55 electoral votes are key for any presidential candidate.[22] California's reputation for distinctive politics was reinforced in 2003 when voters replaced Governor Gray Davis with movie star Arnold Schwarzenegger in the first recall of a governor since North Dakota voters recalled Governor Lynn G. Frazier in 1921.[23]

WHERE WE LIVE

Four out of five Americans now live in central cities and their suburbs—what the Census Bureau calls *metropolitan areas*.[24] During the early twentieth century, the movement of population was from rural areas to central cities, but the movement since the 1950s has been from the central cities to their suburbs. Today the most urban state is California (over 94 percent of its population lives in cities or suburbs). Vermont is the least urban, with only 38 percent living in cities or suburbs.[25] Regionally, the West and Northeast are the most urban, the South and Midwest the most rural.

People move from cities to the suburbs for many reasons—better housing, new transportation systems that make it easier to get to work, the desire for cleaner air and safer streets. Another reason is white flight, the movement of whites away from the central cities so that children can avoid being bused for racial balance and attend generally better schools. White, middle-class migration to the suburbs has made American cities increasingly poor, African American, and Democratic. More than half of all African Americans now live in central cities, as opposed to only about one-fifth of whites, and the poverty level among blacks living in central cities is higher than among whites living in the same cities.[26] The proportions are very nearly reversed for the suburbs, where more than half of all white Americans reside. Approximately one-third of African Americans live in the suburbs, up from one-fifth in 1980.[27] In large cities such as Washington, D.C., Detroit, Baltimore, Atlanta, and New Orleans, the city population is now well over 50 percent African American (see Table 5–2). Hispanics constitute roughly three-fourths of the population of El Paso, Texas, and Santa Ana, California, and nearly two-thirds the population of Miami, Florida.[28]

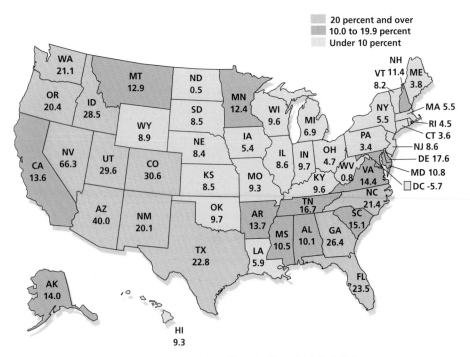

FIGURE 5–1 **Percent Change in Resident Population, 1990–2000.**
SOURCE: U.S. Bureau of the Census, www.census.gov/prod/2002pubs/01statab/pop.pdf.

As the better off have left the cities, the cities' problems have become more acute, and their tax base has not increased proportionate to their problems. Older suburban areas now face the same problems as the inner cities, as they too suffer from out-migration to newer cities and towns. High-tech and professional service companies frequently relocate to the suburbs to avoid traffic congestion and to be closer to the bedroom communities of their workers. Political boundaries, which define local governments and delineate responsibility for services, create understandable tensions among cities, suburbs, and rural areas. Tax revenues, legislative representation, zoning laws, and governmental priorities are hotly contested issues in most metropolitan areas.

WHO WE ARE

Sectional distinctions are less prominent today than they were a century or even a half-century ago. Today Americans are more likely to define themselves by a number of characteristics, each of which may influence how they vote or think about various candidates, issues, or policies.

Race and Ethnicity

Racial and ethnic differences have always had political significance. **Race** can be defined as a grouping of human beings with distinctive physical characteristics determined by genetic inheritance. **Ethnicity** is a social division based on national origin, religion, and language, often within the same race, and includes a sense of attachment to that group. In the United States, race and ethnicity issues focus on African Americans, Asian Americans, Native Americans, and Hispanics.

There are nearly 37 million African Americans in the United States, nearly 13 percent of the population. Asian Americans constitute about 4 percent of the population, and Native Americans, around 1.5 percent.[29] The Census Bureau classifies most American Hispanics as white, although Hispanics can be of any race. Hispanics are the fastest-growing ethnic group; the Census Bureau estimates that there are roughly 39 million American Hispanics, constituting over 13 percent of the population.[30] Because of differences in immigration and birthrates, whites in America will have declined to fewer than three-quarters of the population by the year 2050. The percentage of non-Hispanic whites will be about 50 percent by 2050.[31]

★★**THINKING IT THROUGH**

Despite the homogenizing tendencies of national media like Fox and CNN and federal laws that have lessened state differences, an enduring set of state differences remains in American politics. People generally take pride in the state they are from.

Part of the reason for the enduring state identities is that we elect Congress and the President at the state level. States like Iowa and New Hampshire also play important roles in narrowing the field of presidential candidates seeking their party's nomination. And some states, such as Texas and Maine, cherish their ideas of themselves as home to independent thinkers who are somehow "different" from residents of other states.

Differences in state laws relating to driving cars, drinking, gambling, and taxes also reinforce the relevance of state identity. Colleges and universities may have the same effect while reinforcing competition between different states. State identities, which are stereotypes, can be relatively innocuous, but can also play into decisions about economic development and whether or not firms locate in one state over another.[*]

[*]Jerry D. Spangler and Bob Bernick, "Is Utah's Image a Liability?" *Deseret News*, February 12, 2004, p. A1.

TABLE 5–2   CITIES WITH POPULATIONS OF 100,000 OR MORE THAT ARE AT LEAST 50 PERCENT AFRICAN AMERICAN, 2000

City	Population	Percent African American
Atlanta, Ga.	416,474	61.4%
Baltimore, Md.	651,154	64.3
Birmingham, Ala.	242,820	73.5
Detroit, Mich.	951,270	81.6
Gary, Ind.	102,746	84
Jackson, Miss.	184,256	70.6
Memphis, Tenn.	650,100	61.4
Newark, N.J.	273,546	53.5
New Orleans, La.	484,674	67.3
Richmond, Va.	197,790	57.2
Savannah, Ga.	131,510	57.1
Washington, D.C.	572,059	60.0

Source: U.S. Bureau of the Census, at www.census.gov/population/cen2000/phc-t6/tab05.pdf.

race
A grouping of human beings with distinctive characteristics determined by genetic inheritance.

ethnicity
A social division based on national origin, religion, language, and often race.

CHANGING FACE OF AMERICAN POLITICS

PERCENTAGE OF THE POPULATION BY RACE AND ORIGIN

	1990	2002	2025	2050
White	83.9%	80.7%	76.8%	72.1%
Non-Hispanic White	75.7	68.3	59.5	50.1
African American	12.2	12.7	13.7	14.6
American Indian, Inuit, Aleut	0.8	0.9	1.0	1.1
Asian and Pacific Islander	3.0	4.2	6.5	9.3
Hispanic	8.9	13.4	18.9	24.4

SOURCE: 1990 figures from U.S. Bureau of the Census, *Statistical Abstract of the United States, 2001* (Government Printing Office, 2001), pp. 16–17. All other figures from U.S. Bureau of the Census, *Statistical Abstract of the United States, 2003* (Government Printing Office, 2003), pp. 15, 18.
NOTE: Percentages do not equal 100 because Hispanics can be of any race. Figures for 2025 and 2050 are projections.

AFRICAN AMERICANS   Most immigrants chose to come to this country in search of freedom and opportunity. In contrast, African Americans came against their will as slaves. Although they were freed as a result of the Civil War, racial divisions continue as one of the enduring issues of American politics. Until 1900, more than 90 percent of all African Americans lived in the South; a century later, that figure was 55 percent.[32] Many African Americans left the South hoping to improve their lives by settling in the large cities of the Northeast, Midwest, and West. The reality for many was urban poverty. More recently, some African Americans have been returning to the South, especially to its urban areas.

Most African Americans are economically worse off than most whites in the United States. African American median family income is close to $34,000, compared to about $54,000 for whites.[33] About one-quarter of African American incomes are below the poverty level, compared to about 9 percent of the incomes of whites.[34] Poverty among Native Americans and Alaskan Natives has averaged 26 percent in recent years, a proportion quite similar to that found among African Americans and Hispanics.[35] However, some African Americans have been doing better in recent years; one-third of African American households have earnings of over $50,000 (compared to 54 percent of white households).[36] Some African Americans, like Shaquille O'Neal, a basketball player with the Miami Heat, and Oprah Winfrey, a syndicated talk show host, have risen to top earnings in their professions.

Another way to measure economic well-being is in terms of assets or wealth. *Wealth* is the economic value of the things you own (savings, stocks, property), compared to *income,* which is how much money you make from your job or investments. As a group, the median net worth of African Americans is less than one-tenth that of whites, and the median net worth of Hispanics is only slightly more than that of African Americans (see Figure 5–2).[37] As a result, most African Americans and Hispanics have fewer resources to fall back on in hard times, and they are less likely to have the savings to help a child pay for college.

Middle-class African Americans, of whom there are a growing number, are role models for the young of all races, yet their still comparatively small number serves as a reminder that most African Americans remain behind whites in an economy that relies more and more on education and job skills. About 27 percent of whites graduate from college, whereas only about 17 percent of African Americans do.[38] Among recent high school graduates, 64 percent of whites go on to college, but only 55 percent of African Americans do.[39]

Vernon Robinson, the 2004 Republican congressional candidate for the Fifth District in Greensboro, North Carolina, was the first African American to run for a congressional seat on the Republican ticket since Oaklahoma Representative J.C. Watts retired in 2002. Robinson lost the runoff election to Republican State Senator Virginia Foxx in August 2004.

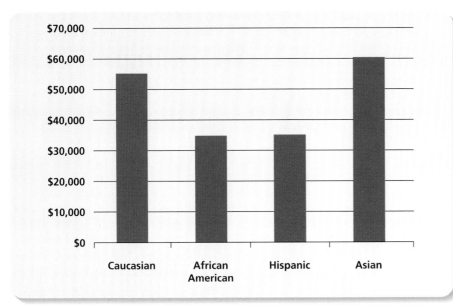

FIGURE 5–2 Wealth Distribution in the United States by Race.
SOURCE: U.S. Bureau of the Census, at <u>www.census.gov/prod/2004pubs/03statab/income.pdf.</u>

Barrack Obama, elected to the U.S. Senate from Illinois in 2004, is only the third African American senator in a century. Obama enjoyed the support of many Republicans as well as Democrats in his 2004 campaign, in part because his initial GOP opponent dropped out of the race. Obama delivered a passionate keynote address at the 2004 Democratic National Convention and is a rising star in the party.

Finally, the African American population is much younger than the white population; the median age for whites in 2002 was 37.1 years, compared to 30.5 for African Americans.[40] The combination of a younger African American population, a lower level of education, and their concentration in economically depressed urban areas has resulted in a much higher unemployment rate for young African Americans. Unemployment can in turn lead to social problems like crime, drug and alcohol abuse, and family dissolution.

African Americans had little political power until after World War II. Owing their freedom from slavery to the "party of Lincoln," most African Americans initially identified with the Republicans, but this loyalty started to change with Franklin Roosevelt, who insisted on equal treatment for African Americans in his New Deal programs.[41] After World War II, African Americans came to see the Democrats as the party of civil rights. The 1964 Republican platform position on civil rights espoused *states' rights*—at the time, the creed of southern segregationists—in what appeared to be an effort to win the support of southern white voters. Virtually all African Americans voted for Lyndon Johnson in 1964, and in presidential elections between 1984 and 2000, their Democratic vote averaged 86 percent.[42] In the 2004 election, 88 percent of African American voters voted for John Kerry.

Recently, African Americans have become much more important politically because of their increased voter participation and their concentrated population. African Americans constitute only 0.3 percent of the population in Montana and 0.5 percent in Idaho, but 37 percent in Mississippi, 33 percent in Louisiana, and 30 percent in South Carolina.[43] Southern senators and representatives cannot afford to ignore the African American vote.[44] Evidence of growing African American political power is the dramatic increase in the number of African American state legislators, which rose from 168 in 1970 to 584 in 2001.[45] Georgia has 47 African American state legislators, the most of any state. Alabama, Maryland, Mississippi, and South Carolina all have over 30.[46]

HISPANICS (LATINOS) Hispanic Americans, who generally prefer to be called Latinos, are not a monolithic group, and while they share a common linguistic heritage, they often differ, depending on which country they or their forebears emigrated from. Cuban

Ken Salazar, elected to the U.S. Senate from Colorado in 2004, is the fourth U.S. senator of Latino descent in U.S. history. Salazar replaced Ben Nighthorse Campbell, a Native American and Republican, who did not seek reelection. Salazar previously served two terms as Colorado attorney general.

Americans, for instance, tend to be Republicans, while Mexican Americans and Puerto Ricans are disproportionately Democrats.[47] Latinos are politically important in a growing number of states. Nearly two-thirds of Cuban immigrants live in Florida, especially in greater Miami; Puerto Rican immigrants are concentrated in and around New York City; and many Mexican American immigrants live in the Southwest and California. Almost 12 million Hispanics live in California.[48]

Cuban Americans are more in the upper-middle income levels, while Puerto Rican Americans and Mexican Americans are generally in lower and lower-middle income categories.[49] A recent study found differences among Latinos of Mexican, Puerto Rican, and Cuban descent in partisanship, ideology, and rates of participation, but widespread support for a liberal domestic agenda, including increased spending on health care, crime and drug control, education, the environment, child services, and bilingual education.[50] But since Hispanics are not politically homogeneous, they are not united as a voting block.

In the 1990s, America's Hispanic population grew by 58 percent.[51] This surge in growth has not, however, been accompanied by a similar surge in political participation or representation. Researchers cite many reasons for this, including redistricting, low rates of citizenship and voting, and a lack of common party commitment.

Hispanics have fared worse in redistricting than other groups. The large number of noncitizens and younger population among Hispanics diminishes their political power. For example, 9.5 million foreign-born Hispanics are not citizens, and more than half— 5.4 million—are in this country illegally. This group of Hispanics cannot vote, nor can those under 18, which is a greater percentage of the Hispanic population than for others. Language problems also reduce Hispanic citizens' voter registration and turnout. Despite their huge increase in population, Hispanic groups were disappointed by the redrawing of legislative district boundaries after the 2000 census.[52] This has spurred some lawsuits as Hispanic activists seek to eliminate gerrymandering, the drawing of district boundaries to benefit a group or party.

Given the overall growth of the Latino population, it is not surprising that both major parties are aggressively cultivating Latino candidates. Three Latinos, all from New Mexico, have won election to the U.S. Senate, although none is currently serving. Several Hispanics have been cabinet members; in the George W. Bush administration, Mel Martinez resigned as secretary of Housing and Urban Development (HUD) to run successfully for the U.S. Senate from Florida in 2004. Ken Salazar, another Latino but a Democrat, was also elected to the senate in 2004 from Colorado. Alberto R. Gonzales left the Texas Supreme Court to join the Bush administration as White House counsel. After John Ascroft's resignation in November 2004, President George W. Bush nominated Gonzales as his new attorney general. Neither party has developed an effective strategy to mobilize the Hispanic vote. The Democrats, which have historically been the party of new immigrant groups, have done somewhat better among Hispanics than Republicans. Gore carried approximately 65 percent of the Latino vote in 2000, while Kerry only carried 56 percent in 2004. This was largely attributed to Latinos' high level of religiosity and Bush's appeal among highly religious people.

ASIAN AMERICANS   Asian Americans are classified together by the Census Bureau for statistical purposes, but there are significant differences among them in culture, language, and political experience in the United States. Asian Americans include, among others, persons of Chinese, Japanese, Indian, Korean, Vietnamese, Filipino, and Thai origin, as well as persons from the Pacific Islands.

The United States is home to more than 12 million Asian Americans and Pacific Islanders, residing primarily in the western states, especially California, Hawaii, and Washington.[53] The numbers of Asian Americans grew during the 1970s and 1980s, largely as a result of immigration from Southeast Asia. Immigrants from China, India, Korea, the Philippines, and Vietnam account for five of the top ten leading countries of foreign-born persons living in this country.[54]

Many Asian Americans have done well both economically and educationally. 47 percent of Asian Americans have graduated from college, compared to 27 percent of white Americans and 17 percent of African Americans.[55] Asian Americans are becoming

Alberto Gonzales, who served as White House general counsel during George W. Bush's first term, has been a prominent advisor to the president. Bush picked Gonzales to serve as attorney general for his second term in office.

PEOPLE & POLITICS *Making a Difference* ★ ★ ★

BILL RICHARDSON: GOVERNOR OF NEW MEXICO

New Mexico Governor Bill Richardson served in Congress, as U.S. Ambassador to the United Nations, and as Secretary of Energy, before being elected governor in 2002. His breadth of experience and political drive have made him the most visible Hispanic politician in the United States. Richardson's father was American and his mother Mexican, and he grew up in Mexico City. He was drafted by the Kansas City Athletics to play baseball, but after an elbow injury, went on to college at Tufts University where he earned a B.A. and M.A. in diplomacy. Representing New Mexico in the House of Representatives, he rose to the position of chief deputy Democratic Whip, the first Hispanic to hold this positon.

Richardson has been nominated for the Nobel Peace Prize three times, in part for his work as United States Ambassador to the United Nations. Among his activities were negotiating with North Korea, Iraq, Cuba, and Sudan for the release of American hostages, mediation between Zaire's former president and rebel leaders, helping oversee a peaceful transition of power in the Congo, and working with the U.N. investigaton of ethnic massacres.

Richardson has used his tenure as governor of New Mexico to position himself as a leader of the Democratic party. In 2004, Richardson delivered the first opposition party response to a president's State of the Union message in Spanish.* He chaired the 2004 Democratic National Convention and was visible in this role. As governor of one of the battleground states in 2004, he cam-

paigned frequently with John Kerry in New Mexico, only to see the state go for President Bush, 50 percent to 49 percent for Kerry.

*www.democrats.org/news/200401210005.html

---

more politically important and more visible in politics. Gary Locke, the first Chinese American governor of a state in the continental United States, served two terms in Washington.

THE TIES OF ETHNICITY   Except for Native Americans and the descendants of slaves, all Americans have immigrant ancestors. Early settlers were generally English-speaking Protestants; even today, people of English, Scottish, and Welsh background are the largest "ethnic" group in the United States. Irish immigrants, largely Catholics, started coming before the potato famine in the 1840s and came in larger numbers after it. Upon their arrival, they experienced economic exploitation and religious bigotry. Irish Americans responded by retreating among themselves, forming a strong ethnic consciousness. Other ethnic groups that followed—Italians, Greeks, Chinese—each experienced a similar cycle: flight from their homeland and happy arrival here, then discrimination, exploitation, residential clustering, and the formation of a strong group identity.

The largest number of immigrants came between 1900 and 1924, when 17.3 million people relocated to the United States—by far the largest immigration to one country in any quarter-century in human history. From 1991 to 2000, the United States welcomed more than 9 million immigrants,[56] primarily from the Caribbean and Mexico and from Asian countries such as the Philippines, Vietnam, and China. The foreign-born proportion of the U.S. population has increased in recent years, rising from 14 million in 1980 to nearly 31 million in 2002, the largest number of foreign-born in U.S. history.[57] Recently, the proportion of Asian and Mexican immigrants has pulled even with or surpassed the number of Europeans.

Having large numbers of immigrants can pose challenges to any political and social system. Immigrants are often a source of social conflict as they compete with more established groups for jobs, rights, political power, and influence.

Transportation Secretary Norman Mineta is an Asian American, former Congressman, and the only Democrat in President George W. Bush's cabinet.

In Comparative Perspective

IMMIGRATION POLITICS IN CANADA

On a proporational basis, Canada has more immigrants each year than does the United States. Other differences between the United States and Canada in immigration policy include Canada's allowing more skilled immigrants to immigrate and the establishment of a special status for potential immigrants who are willing to invest money in a Canadian business and hire Canadian workers. Federalism is also part of Canadian immigration policy, with provincial governments having some say in whom they will allow as "independent immigrants" (not coming for family reunification or other purposes). Quebec has taken advantage of this policy because it wants to ensure that immigrants either already speak French or are willing to learn French.[*] As noted, Canadians are the most likely of any polity to view immigrants favorably.

The historic patterns of immigration to Canada and the United States also provide an interesting contrast. Both countries are world leaders in welcoming immigrants, and both countries until 1900 "absorbed large inflows from the British Isles."[†] The United States absorbed many more Irish Catholics than did Canada, while Protestants from Northern Ireland were more likely to immigrate to Canada. In the last half-century, Canada experienced a "massive demographic shift as hundreds of thousands of non-British, non-French—including many Asians—came in."[‡]

Following the terrorist attacks of September 11, 2001, Canada's immigration policies have drawn criticism as being too lax. United States and Canadian newspapers accused "the nation to the north" as being a "haven to terrorists."[§] The United States signfiicantly tightened its immigration policies as part of the war on terrorism, but Canada was criticized by the United States, in part because Canada rarely detains refugees who cannot provide identificaton.[‖] The State Department criticized Canada in 2004 as having "lax immigration laws," with implications not only for terrorism but for human trafficking and prostitution.[¶]

[*]Information provided by Earl Fry, Political Science Department, Brigham Young University. February 27, 2004.
[†]Seymour Martin Lipset, *Continental Divide*, New York: Routledge, Chapman, and Hall, Inc., p. 182.
[‡]Seymour Martin Lipset, *Continental Divide*, New York: Routledge, Chapman, and Hall, Inc., p. 185.
[§]James Neff, "Few Resources Spent Guarding Canada Border," *The Seattle Times*, September 23, 2001, p. A1; see also Bob McDonald, "Bush Showing His Toughness," *The Toronto Sun*, September 26, 2001, p. 6.
[‖]Allan Thompson, "Is Canada Really the Weak Link?" *Toronto Star*, October 6, 2001, p. A1.
[¶]Sheldon Alberts, "U.S. Raps Canadian Immigration," Ottawa *Citizen*, February 26, 2004, p. A9.

Gender

For most of U.S. history, politics and government were men's business. Women first gained the right to vote primarily in the western territories, beginning with Wyoming in 1869 and Utah in 1870, and then in Colorado and Idaho before the turn of the twentieth century.[58] The right was not extended nationally until 1920 with passage of the Nineteenth Amendment. The fears of some opponents and some proponents of *women's suffrage* (the right to vote)—that women would form their own party and vote largely for women or fundamentally alter our political system—have not been realized. During Susan B. Anthony's suffrage campaign, Jonas H. Upton, editor of the *Democratic Salem Monitor* in Salem, Oregon, contended that women, if given the right to vote, would combine to vote for war because they were exempt from the draft.[59] Others feared that women would unite to vote for prohibition.[60]

For a half-century after gaining the right to vote, American women voted at a lower rate than women in other Western democracies.[61] But in the past 20 years, slightly more women than men have voted in presidential elections, and there is no significant difference between the genders in rates of voting in midterm elections.[62] In the 2004 election, women comprised 54 percent of all voters and men comprised 46 percent. Because women outnumber men, there are more female than male voters.[63] Women have chosen to work within the existing political parties and do not overwhelmingly support female candidates, especially if they must cross party lines to do so.[64] Since 1917, less than 6 percent of representatives in the U.S. House have been women. A common way women have entered Congress have been through appointment after their husband's death. The number of women in the House of Representatives and U.S. Senate reached new highs in the 1990s. Following the 2000 elections, there were three female governors, 13 women serving in the Senate, and 58 in the U.S. House of Representatives. There were ten female major-party gubernatorial candidates in 2002, and on election day, four of them were elected. Three of the four successful candidates were Democrats. After the 2002 elections, 13 women served in the Senate during the 108th Congress. The proportion of women serving in the House of Representatives is about the same as in the Senate: below 15 percent. In contrast, some state legislative chambers are nearly 40 percent female. The number of female officeholders is rising in part because women are increasingly running in contests in which there is no incumbent.[65]

One group that has aggressively promoted female candidates is EMILY's List, a group that funds pro-choice Democrats. EMILY is an acronym for "Early Money Is Like Yeast," meaning that campaign contributions given to candidates early in their campaigns can help raise more money, just as yeast helps dough rise. EMILY's List supporters are proud of the fact that there are more women in the U.S. House than ever before. EMILY's List has also helped fund racial and ethnic female candidates, with roughly one-third of the candidates supported being African American or Latina. Republicans have duplicated EMILY's List with their own political action committee, Wish List, which gives to Republican female candidates who are pro-choice.

Is there a **gender gap**, or a persistent difference between men and women in voting and in attitudes on important issues? Women have typically divided their vote between the two major political parties. However, in recent elections, women have been more likely than men to vote for Democratic presidential candidates (see Figure 5–3). In the 2000 presidential election, Al Gore's share of the vote among women was 12 percent higher than among men.[66] In the 2004 election, Bush received 48 percent of the female vote to Kerry's 51 percent. Although women preferred Kerry over Bush by a small margin, Bush improved his standing among women by 5 percentage points compared to the 2000 election.

The women's movement in American politics encompasses a comprehensive agenda, including voting and political rights as well as extending the basic liberties of the Bill of Rights and the Fourteenth Amendment. In addition to rights and liberties, women seek equal opportunity, education, jobs, skills, and respect in what has been a male-dominated system.[67] Women are more likely than men to oppose violence in any form—the death penalty, new weapon systems, or the possession of handguns. Women, as a group, are more compassionate than men in that they are more likely to favor government that provides health insurance and family services. Women are generally more concerned than men about women's rights—enforcement of child support, punishment for sexual abuse and rape, and equal treatment in the legal system. They also identify work and family issues such as day care, maternity leave, and equal treatment in the workplace as important.[68] Other gender issues, some of them focal points in recent elections, include reproductive rights, restrictions on pornography, gun control, and sexual harassment.[69]

There are serious income inequalities between men and women. Nearly twice as many women than men have an annual income of $15,000 or less.[70] Because an increasing number of women today are the sole breadwinners for their families, the implications of this low income level are significant. Women earn on average less than men for the same work. Even among college graduates aged 25 to 34, women earn an average of 80 cents for every dollar earned by men of the same age and education. After controlling for characteristics such as job experience, education, occupation, and other measures of productivity, a U.S. Census Bureau study shows that wage discrimination is 76 cents on every dollar.[71] As age increases, the earnings gap widens. In law schools, women now constitute about half of entering classes,[72] but more generally women still lag behind men in income and opportunity.

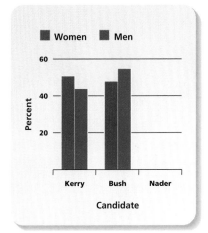

FIGURE 5–3 Gender and the Vote for President, 2004.

Source: 2004 Exit Polls from Edison Media Research and Mitofsky International at www.cnn.com/ELECTION/2004/pages/results/states/US/P/00/epolls.o.htm.

gender gap
The difference between the political opinions or political behavior of men and of women.

Rosie O'Donnell, a gay parent, is a vocal advocate for gays who want to adopt children. O'Donnell and her partner were among many gay couples that traveled to San Francisco in early 2004 to obtain a marriage license.

Sexual Orientation

Differences in sexual orientation have become important politically in recent years. The modern movement for expanded rights for gays and lesbians traces its roots to 1969, when New York City police raided the Stonewall Inn in Greenwich Village and a riot ensued.[73] Precise data on the number of homosexuals in the United States are in dispute. The gay and lesbian communities talk in terms of 10 percent; other estimates come in much lower.[74] One source estimates that 2.8 percent of men and 1.4 percent of women identify themselves as homosexual or bisexual.[75] Regardless of its overall size, the homosexual community has become important politically in several cities, most notably San Francisco. Both parties have openly professed gay members of Congress.

In 2000, Vermont became the first state to enact legislation granting gay and lesbian couples "civil union" status, which confers many of the benefits of marriage. Before this law took effect, the Vermont Supreme Court had ruled that denying gay couples the same rights and benefits as heterosexual couples was unconstitutional. In 2003, the Massachusetts Supreme Judicial Court ruled that not allowing gay couples to marry was discriminatory, and that the only remedy was full marriage rights for both heterosexual and homosexual couples.[76] This decision pushed gay marriage onto the national agenda, spurring social conservatives to argue that traditional marriage, defined as marriage between a man and a woman, needed constitutional protection, a cause that was endorsed by President Bush. In the wake of the Massachusetts ruling, mayors in cities like San Francisco, California and New Paltz, New York authorized their cities to issue marriage licenses and perform same-sex marriages. San Francisco mayor Newsom justified his policy as constitutional in the sense that it removed a form of discrimination.[77]

The political agenda for gay and lesbian advocacy groups includes fighting discrimination, including the military's "Don't ask, don't tell" policy. On some fronts, the groups have been successful. In several cities and among some employers, gays and lesbians have been able to secure health care and other benefits for domestic partners. Antidiscrimination statutes protecting people from discrimination in housing and employment on the basis of sexual orientation have been passed in several cities and states. Groups like the Human Rights Campaign are visible advocates of eliminating restrictions based on sexual orientation. Hate crimes against gays and lesbians have led the Senate to include sexual orientation in federal hate crimes legislation.[78]

Conservative groups were successful in enacting initiatives in thirteen states in 2004 defining marriage as a union between a man and a woman. Among the groups that have been active in the protest movement have been some conservative Protestants, Catholics, and Mormons. The gay marriage issue appeared on the ballots of more than a dozen states in 2004 and Congress considered a proposed constitutional amendment defining marriage as a union between a man and a woman. Democrats accused Republicans of trying to exploit the marriage issue for partisan advantage. The courts have also been drawn into the battle over sexual orientation. In a 5-to-4 decision, the Supreme Court upheld the right of the Boy Scouts of America to bar homosexuals in its organization.[79]

Family Structure

Over the past half-century, the typical American family has been transformed from a "traditional family" (mother and father married, with children in the home) to a variety of living arrangements and varying family structures. Americans are much more likely to approve of premarital sex than in the early 1970s. From 1996 to 2002, the number of Americans who cohabit (live with someone of the opposite sex without being married) increased by 50 percent.[80] Cohabitation raises public policy questions such as whether the live-in partner is eligible for employment benefits and welfare payments. Contraception is widely used and accepted, and yet one-third of all births are now illegitimate.[81] These children will often be in need of social services and financial assistance.

People now marry later in life, with men marrying on the average at age 27 and women at age 25.[82] Yet marrying later has not improved the chances of avoiding divorce. The average marriage today lasts only about 7.2 years. Before World War II, only nine

The risk of having children later in life has recently been the subject of cover stories in news magazines.

out of every 1,000 marriages ended in divorce; between 1950 and 1996, the divorce rate nearly doubled. Today it is estimated that about half of all marriages will end in divorce.[83]

Since the 1960s, birthrates have steadily declined in the United States. In the early 1960s, a woman statistically averaged about 3.5 children. By 2001, that number dropped to 2.1 children, barely meeting the 2.1 needed to replace the population. In other words, if the current trend continues, the American native-born population will actually decrease over time.[84]

Divorce is one reason why some women go to work and why the number of households headed by women has risen. Attitudes about the role of women in marriage and the family have also changed. In 1972, one-third of Americans thought that a woman belonged in the home and should not work outside the home, but in 1998, only one-sixth of all Americans felt this way.[85]

Religion

In many parts of the world, religious differences, especially when combined with disputes over territory or sovereignty, are a source of violent conflict. The conflict in Israel between Israelis and Palestinians escalated with suicide bombers willing to kill themselves while killing Israeli civilians and with Israeli troops and tanks rolling into Palestinian areas. In Iraq and Turkey, the Kurdish people have been subjected to expulsion and even genocide. The war between India and Pakistan over Kashmir is a religious and ethnic battle among Muslims and Hindus, as is the conflict between Muslims and Christians in Indonesia. Other countries like Afghanistan, Lebanon, Sri Lanka, and Sudan have also experienced intense religious conflicts in recent years. The Shi'ite–Sunni conflict in Iraq threatens the stability of the new government in Iraq.

Jews have often been the target of religious discrimination and persecution (anti-Semitism), which reached its greatest intensity in the Holocaust of the 1930s and 1940s, during which an estimated 6 million Jews were murdered.[86] The United States has not been immune from such hatred, despite its principle of religious freedom. In 1838, Governor Lilburn W. Boggs of Missouri issued an extermination order against the Mormons.[87]

Our government is founded on the premise that religious liberty is more likely when there is not one predominant or official faith, which is why the framers of our Constitution did not sanction a national church. In fact, James Madison wrote in *The Federalist,* No. 51, "In a free government the security for civil rights must be the same as that for religious rights. It consists in the one case in the multiplicity of interests, and in the other in the multiplicity of sects" (see the Appendix).

The absence of an official American church does not mean that religion is unimportant in American politics; indeed, there were established state churches in this country until the 1830s. Some observers contend that "the root of American political and social values . . . is the distinctive Puritanism of the early New England settlers."[88] Politicians frequently refer to God in their speeches or demonstrate their piety in other ways. In 2000, Democratic vice presidential candidate Joseph Lieberman, an observant Jew, made frequent references to God and religion in his speeches. George W. Bush concluded his 2004 State of the Union Address, in many ways the kickoff for his 2004 campaign, by saying "We can trust in that greater power who guides the unfolding of the years. And in all that is to come, we can know that His purposes are just and true. May God bless the United States of America. Thank you."[89] A more subtle use of religion by George W. Bush is the title he selected for his political memoir, *A Charge to Keep.* This title is also a Protestant hymn, allowing him to reinforce his connection to Protestants who will recognize the title as one of their hymns. The second verse of the hymn reads, "To serve the present age—My calling to fulfill—O may it all my powers engage—To do my Master's will."[90]

At one time, it was thought that a Catholic could not be elected president. With the election of 1960, that issue was resolved. John F. Kennedy directly confronted the question of whether a Catholic would put aside religious teachings if they conflicted with constitutional obligations. He said, "I am not the Catholic candidate for President. I am the

Democratic party's candidate for President who happens also to be Catholic. I do not speak for my church on public matters, and the church does not speak for me."[91] Nevertheless a candidate's religion may still become an issue today if the candidate's religious convictions on sensitive issues such as abortion threaten to conflict with public obligations.

During the 2004 Democratic party battle for the presidential nomination, Howard Dean initially contended that candidates should not interject religion into politics. In a town-hall meeting in New Hampshire, Dean criticized President Bush for his opposition to stem-cell research saying, "I think we ought to make scientific decisions, not theological and theoretical decisions."[92] When challenged on this comment, especially in light of the importance of religiosity in the South, he retreated to his original position. Dean's flip-flop on religion in 2004 is an example of the continuing importance of religion, at least in many parts of the country.

Religion also surfaces in political life as an important catalyst for change, as the Catholic church was in the overthrow of communism in central Europe and the leadership of black churches were in the American civil rights movement. As writer Taylor Branch explains, the black church "served not only as a place of worship but also as a bulletin board to a people who owned no organs of communication, a credit union to those without banks, and even a kind of people's court."[93] African American ministers, like the Reverend Martin Luther King Jr., became leaders of the civil rights movement; others, like the Reverend Jesse Jackson and more recently Al Sharpton, have run for national office. Hence religion can be important not only as a source of personal values and attitudes but also as a means of political activity and organization.

More recently, there has been an increase in political activity among fundamentalist Christians. Led by ministers like Jerry Falwell and Pat Robertson, they have supported political organizations such as the Moral Majority and the Christian Coalition. For two decades, they have sought to influence the national agenda, and Robertson taped telephone endorsements for George W. Bush in 2000. In 2004, Reverend Robertson generated some controversy in an interview he did on CNN when he said President Bush had originally assumed that there would be only limited casualties in the war in Iraq. They also focus their attention at the local level—school boards, city councils, mayorships, and local GOP leadership.[94] Their agenda includes the return of school prayer, the outlawing of abortion, restrictions on homosexuals, and opposition to gun control. To learn more about the Christian Coalition, go to www.cc.org. Many Americans take their religious beliefs seriously, more so than people of other industrial democracies.[95] Approximately a quarter of Americans attend houses of worship only a few times a year, 16 percent at least once a month, and 38 percent nearly every week.[96] Religion, like ethnicity, is a *shared identity.* People identify themselves as Baptist, Catholic, or Buddhist. To find out more information about religion in the United States, go to www.ipl.org/ref/RR/static/hum80. 10.00.html. Sometimes church attendance or nonattendance is more important than differences between religions in explaining attitudes. "Among both Catholics and Protestants, opposition to abortion increases with frequency of church attendance, but the percentages expressing pro-choice and pro-life sentiments are quite similar for the Catholic and Protestant groups."[97]

One defining characteristic of religion in the United States is the tremendous variety of denominations. About half the people in the United States describe themselves as Protestant (see Figure 5–4). The largest Protestant denomination is Baptist, followed by Methodists, Lutherans, Presbyterians, Pentecostals, and Episcopalians. Because Protestants are divided among so many different churches, Catholics have the largest single membership in the United States, constituting nearly a quarter of the population.[98] Jews represent 2 percent of the population.[99] Followers of Islam number more than 1,100,000.[100] Protestants came to the United States first; most Catholics and Jews immigrated after the 1840s. It was not until 1960, however, that Americans elected a Catholic president.

Religion is important in American politics in part because of the concentrations of people of particular religions in a few states. Catholics, as noted, make up nearly a quarter of the U.S. population, yet they make up nearly two-thirds of the population of Rhode Island.[101] Baptists represent 16 percent of the U.S. population, yet they account for roughly a third of the population of Mississippi and Alabama.[102] Mormons represent only 2 percent of the U.S. population but constitute two-thirds of the population of

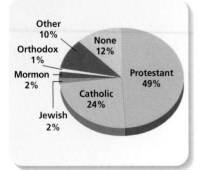

FIGURE 5–4 Religious Groups in America.
SOURCE: The Gallup Organization, at www.gallup.com/poll/focus/sr040302.asp.

Utah.[103] The state of New York has the highest percentage of Jews with 9 percent; New York City is 13 percent Jewish.[104]

In recent presidential elections, a majority of Protestants voted Republican, while majorities of Catholics and Jews voted Democratic.[105] However, in 2004, Bush received a majority of the Catholic vote and increased his majority among Protestants to 59 percent. Kerry received 75 percent of the Jewish vote. The perception among many Catholics and Jews that the Democratic party is more open to them helps explain the strength of their Democratic identification. Democrats won the loyalty of many Catholics by their willingness to nominate Al Smith for the presidency in 1928 and John Kennedy in 1960. Jewish voters' long-standing identification with the Democratic party may have been reinforced by Al Gore's selection of Joseph Lieberman to be his running mate in 2000. Southern Protestants have been Democrats for different reasons, having largely to do with the sectional issues discussed earlier. Religious groups vary in their rates of participation. Jews have the highest rate of reported voter turnout, 93 percent in 2000, while those who claim no religious affiliation have the lowest, 47 percent.[106] Catholics (62 percent) voted at a slightly higher rate than Protestants (59 percent).[107] Religion can be related to other politically important characteristics. For instance, Jews are the most prosperous and best educated of any ethnic or religious group. More than 46 percent of Jewish adults are college graduates, compared to 22 percent of Protestants and 20 percent of Catholics.[108] In this example, as in others, religion is a cross-cutting cleavage in American politics; the differences do not reinforce one another. On the basis of income and education, we might expect Jews to be Republicans, but 79 percent of American Jews voted for Al Gore in 2000.[109] Catholics had cross-pressures in 2004 because John Kerry is Catholic. This did not stop a majority of Catholics from voting for Bush. Catholics who attend church weekly were even more likely to vote against Kerry and for Bush; they gave 56 percent of their votes to Bush. Similarly, we might predict that southern Protestants would be heavily Republican, but many are Democrats.

Wealth and Income

The United States is a wealthy nation. Compared to other nations, our purchasing power is higher than that of any other advanced democracy.[110] Indeed, to some knowledgeable observers, "the most striking thing about the United States has been its phenomenal wealth."[111] Most Americans lead comfortable lives. They eat and live well and have first-class medical care. But the unequal distribution of wealth and income still results in important political divisions and conflicts.

Wealth (total value of possessions) is more concentrated than income (annual earnings). The wealthiest families hold most of the property and other forms of wealth like stocks and savings. Traditionally, one of the problems with concentrated wealth has been that it fosters an aristocracy. Thomas Jefferson sought to break up the "aristocracy of wealth" by changing from laws based on *primogeniture* (the eldest son's exclusive right to inherit his father's estate) to laws that encouraged people to divide their estates equally among all their children, resulting in smaller landholdings. Jefferson sought to encourage an "aristocracy of virtue and talent" through a public school system open to all for the primary grades and for the best students through the university level.[112]

Most college students come from the top quarter of American families in income—those earning $50,000 a year or more. Education is in turn one of the most important means to achieve upward economic and social mobility. People who go to college earn more than those who have not, and those from wealthier families are more inclined to get an education at nearly twice the rate as those positioned elsewhere on the socioeconomic ladder.[113]

College tuition and other costs have climbed substantially in recent years. Tuition, for example, climbed 113 percent, on average, at public colleges and universities and 93 percent at private institutions since 1990.[114] The impact of rising costs affects low-income students more than others. These students come from families that are less likely to be able to help with the rising costs. "College costs eat up 71% of earnings for low-income families but only 6% of the income of the top 25% of earners."[115] Low-income students have also been hurt by some college's shift away from a need-based system of scholarships.

Part of the problem for low-income students is also a success story. There are now more of them qualifying for admission, making the competition for support more intense.

The dangers of an unequal concentration of wealth were recognized in the earliest years of our history. "The most common and durable source of factions has been the various and unequal distribution of property," wrote James Madison in *The Federalist,* No. 10 (reprinted in the Appendix). "Those who hold, and those who are without property, have ever formed distinct interests in society." Madison was right. Economic differences often lead to conflict, and Americans remain divided politically along economic lines. Aside from race, income may be the single most important factor in explaining views on issues, partisanship, and ideology. Most rich people are Republicans, and most poor people are Democrats, and this has been true since at least the Great Depression of the 1930s. In terms of income, the Northeast is the most prosperous region and the South the least prosperous.

Between the 1950s and the 1970s inflation-adjusted income doubled. More recently, as shown in Figure 5–5, inflation-adjusted income has gone up and down.[116] What accounts for this pattern in contrast to the steady rise seen earlier? Economists debate the causes for this change; some cite higher energy costs, low levels of personal savings, and the worldwide slowdown in productivity growth.[117] More recent data, however, actually point to increased productivity, in part due to the more widespread use of computers and information technology.[118] While the long-term trend has been for income to rise, the bottom 10 percent of the population in terms of income has actually seen a decline in wages. At the same time, the top 10 percent has experienced substantial growth in income. Economists refer to this as *dispersion,* or the difference in growth patterns among income levels.

The bottom 12.1 percent in income is also the segment of the population that falls below the poverty line.[119] In 2003, the official poverty level for a family of four was an income below $18,660.[120] Families headed by a female are almost two times more likely to fall below the poverty line than families headed by a man, and 26.5 percent of all households headed by females fall below the poverty line.[121] Close to 16 percent of the poor are children under 18 years of age, and many appear to be trapped in a cycle of poverty (see Figure 5–6).[122] African American and Hispanic children are nearly three times as likely to be poor than white children.[123]

The definition of poverty is itself political, and a change in the definition of poverty can make it appear that there are more or fewer poor people than before. The poverty classification is intended to identify persons who cannot meet a minimum standard in such basics as housing, food, and medical care. Regardless of how one defines poverty, however, the poor are a minority who lack political power. The poor vote less than wealthier groups and are less confident and organized in dealing with politics and

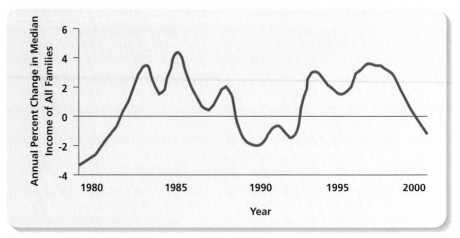

FIGURE 5–5 Median Family Income, 1980–2003.
SOURCE: Harold W. Stanley and Richard G. Niemi, *Vital Statistics on American Politics, 2003–2004* (CQ Press, 2000), p. 363–364.

government. Over the past two decades, inequality between rich and poor has been increasing, a trend quite different from the 1960s, when the gap between rich and poor narrowed.[124] Although the gap began to decrease under the first Bush administration (1989–1993), inequality between rich and poor has again been on the rise since then.[125]

The distribution of income in a society can have important consequences for democratic stability. If there is a perception that only the few at the top of the economic ladder can hope to earn enough for an adequate standard of living, domestic unrest and revolution may follow. Income is related to participation in politics. People who need the most help from government are the least likely to participate. They are also the most likely to favor social welfare programs.

Occupation

Americans at the time of Jefferson and for several generations thereafter worked primarily on farms, but by the end of World War I, the United States had become the world's leading industrial nation. This dramatic transformation also resulted in the expansion of American cities as workers moved to find jobs. Labor conditions, including child labor practices, became important political issues. Inventions and the application of technology, combined with abundant natural and human resources, meant that the U.S. **gross domestic product (GDP)** rose, after adjusting for inflation, by more than 297 percent over the period from 1960 to 2002.[126]

The United States several years ago entered what Daniel Bell, a noted sociologist, labeled the "postindustrial" phase of our development. "A post-industrial society, being primarily a technical society, awards less on the basis of inheritance or property . . . than on education and skill."[127] *Knowledge* is the organizing device of the postindustrial era. Postindustrial societies have greater affluence and a class structure less defined along traditional labor-versus-management lines.

The changing dynamics of the American labor force can be seen in Figure 5–7, which shows the percentage of the U.S. labor force in various occupations. There has been tremendous growth in the white-collar sector of our economy. This sector includes managers, accountants, and lawyers, as well as professionals and technicians in such rapid-growth areas as computers, communications, finance, insurance, and research. This shift has been accompanied by a dramatic decline in the number of people engaged in agriculture and a more modest decline in the number of people in manufacturing (the blue-collar sector). Today only 2.4 percent of working Americans are employed in agriculture, and only 13.3 percent are employed in manufacturing.[128] Governments are among the biggest employers in this country. Federal, state, and local governments produce more than 18 percent of our gross domestic product.[129]

Women and racial minorities have distinct occupational patterns. The majority of blue-collar jobs are held by men, while women hold over 62 percent of jobs in the service sector—especially in education, social services, and health care.[130] As noted earlier, women generally earn less than men of the same age and education. Occupations in which women predominate, like teaching and clerical work, are generally lower-paying than industrial or management jobs. And as women advance in their careers, especially in management, they encounter a barrier to advancement that has been referred to as the "glass ceiling."

Social Class

Why do Americans not divide themselves into social classes as Europeans do? American workers have not formed their own political party, nor does class seem to dominate our political life. Marxist categories of *proletariat* (those who sell their labor) and *bourgeoisie* (those who own or control the means of production) are far less important here than they are in Europe. Still, we do have social classes and what social scientists call **socioeconomic status (SES)**—a division of the population based on occupation, income, and education.

Most Americans, when asked what class they belong to, say "middle class." Very few see themselves as lower class or upper class. In many other industrial democracies, large proportions of the population think of themselves as "working class" rather than middle

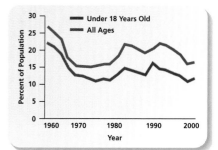

FIGURE 5–6 Percentage of Americans Living in Poverty, by Age, 1959–2000.
Source: U.S. Bureau of the Census, *Statistical Abstract of the United States, 2003* (Government Printing Office, 2003), p. 22, 28.

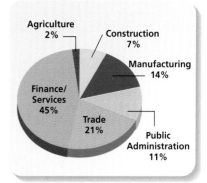

FIGURE 5–7 Occupational Groups 2002.
Source: U.S. Bureau of the Census, *Statistical Abstract of the United States, 2003* (Government Printing Office, 2003), p. 404.

gross domestic product (GDP)
The total output of all economic activity in the nation, including goods and services.

socioeconomic status (SES)
A division of population based on occupation, income, and education.

"It's like this. If the rich have money, they invest. If the poor have money, they eat."

class.[131] In England, nearly three out of five persons identify themselves as working class.[132] But Americans rarely use that designation.

What constitutes the "middle class" in the United States is highly subjective. For instance, some individuals perform working-class tasks (such as plumbing), but their income places them in the middle class or even the upper-middle class. A schoolteacher's income is below that of many working-class jobs, but in terms of status, the job ranks among middle-class fields.

One explanation for Americans' responses may be the elements of the American dream that involve upward mobility. Or their responses may reflect the hostility many feel toward organized labor. In any case, compared to many countries, class divisions in the United States are less defined and less important to politics. As political scientist Seymour Martin Lipset has written, "The American social structure and values foster an emphasis on competitive individualism, an orientation that is not congruent with class consciousness, support for socialist or social democratic parties, or a strong union movement."[133]

Age

Americans are living longer, a phenomenon that has been dubbed the "graying of America" (Figure 5–8). This demographic change is having important consequences; it has increased the demand for medical care, retirement benefits, and a host of other age-related services. Persons over the age of 65 constitute less than 13 percent of the population yet account for 31 percent of the total medical expenditures.[134] With the decreasing birthrate discussed earlier, there is some concern about maintaining an adequate workforce in the future.

Older Americans are politically aware, and they vote. Past legislative victories have changed the lives of older citizens. For instance, the poverty rate among this group dropped from 15.7 percent in 1980 to 10.1 percent in 2001, a change partly due to improved medical benefits passed during the 1960s.[135] As a group, older Americans fight to ensure that Social Security is protected; they value Medicare and favor prescription drug coverage. Despite their desire for services that benefit themselves, they also favor tax cuts.

Their vote is especially important in western states and in Florida, the state with the largest proportion of people over 65. The "gray lobby" not only votes in large numbers but also has four other political assets not found in other age groups that make it politically powerful: disposable income, discretionary time, a clear focus on issues, and effective organization. When older Americans compete for their share of the budget pie, the young, minorities, and the poor often lose out.[136] Congressional passage of a limited prescription drug benefit in 2003 is an example of the political power of the "gray lobby." While the measure was not popular with some conservative Republicans, the Bush administration pushed and cited it as an accomplishment in the 2004 campaign. Conservatives were not alone in criticizing the Bush prescription drug plan. Liberals and Democratic candidate John Kerry criticized the plan as not going far enough. The American Association for Retired Persons (AARP), which had backed the plan over the protest of some members, ran ads aimed at informing seniors about how to make use of the benefit.

Age is important to politics in two additional ways: life cycle and generational effects. *Life-cycle effects* have shown that as people become middle-aged, they become more politically conservative, less mobile, and more likely to participate in politics. As they age further and rely more on the government for services, they tend

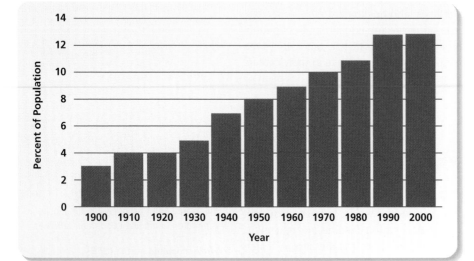

FIGURE 5–8 Percent of Population over Age 65, 1900–2000.
SOURCE: U.S. Bureau of the Census, at www.census.gov/statab/hist/HS-03.pdf.

to grow more liberal.[138] Young people, in contrast, are more mobile and less concerned about the delivery of government services.

Several groups made getting younger voters registered and to the polls a high priority in 2004. Exit polls from the 2004 election found that turnout among those 18–29 years old rose from 42 percent in 2000 to 51 percent in 2004. An estimated 4.6 million more 18–29 year olds voted in 2004. Because overall turnout was higher in 2004, the proportion of the voters aged 18–29 remained constant at 17 percent.[137]

There are also *generational effects* in politics that arise when a particular generation has had experiences that make it politically distinct. An example is the experience of those who lived through the Great Depression of the 1930s, which shaped their lifelong views of parties, issues, and political leaders. Some members of this generation saw Franklin Roosevelt as the leader who saved the country by pulling it out of the Depression; others felt he sold the country down the river by launching too many government programs. More recently and to a lesser extent, the baby boomers shared a common and distinctive political experience. These Americans came of age politically in the 1960s and 1970s during the civil rights movement and the Vietnam War.

Education

Differences in education affect not only economic well-being but political participation and involvement as well. Thomas Jefferson wrote of education, "Enlighten the people generally, and tyranny and oppressions of body and mind will vanish like evil spirits at the dawn of day."[139] The vast majority of people in the United States are educated in public schools. Nine out of every ten students in kindergarten through high school attend public schools, and more than three out of four students in college are in public institutions.[140]

Only recently has the number of college graduates in America surpassed the number of persons who did not graduate from high school.[141] Just over half of all Americans

---

TABLE 5–3 EDUCATIONAL ATTAINMENT IN THE UNITED STATES

Percent of Population—Highest Educational Level Attained

	Population (1,000)	Not a High School Graduate	High School Graduate	Bachelor's Degree	Advanced Degree
Age					
18 to 24 years old	27,313	24	68	8	—
25 to 34 years old	38,670	13	56	23	7
35 to 44 years old	44,284	12	60	20	9
45 to 54 years old	39,545	11	59	18	12
55 to 64 years old	25,874	16	57	15	11
65 to 74 years old	18,123	27	55	12	7
75 years old or over	15,647	34	51	9	5
Sex (Persons 25 years old and over)					
Male	86,996	16	55	18	10
Female	95,146	16	59	17	8
Race (Persons 25 years old and over)					
White	151,942	15	58	18	9
Black	20,359	21	62	12	5
Hispanic	19,670	43	46	8	3
Asian/Pacific Islander	7,866	13	40	31	16

SOURCE: U.S. Census Bureau, *Educational Attainment in the United States: March 2002*, at www.census.gov/population/www/socdemo/education/pp1–169.html, June 24, 2004.

Note: Percentages may not add up to 100 percent due to rounding error. "High school graduate" percentages and "some college" percentages are combined.

have not gone to college, though many college students assume that the college experience is widely shared. A little over 27 percent of whites are college graduates, compared to 17 percent of African Americans and 11 percent of Hispanics; roughly 21 percent of African Americans and 43 percent of all Hispanics stopped their schooling before completing high school (see Table 5–3).[142]

Education is one of the most important variables in predicting political participation, confidence in dealing with government, and awareness of issues. Education is also related to the acquisition of democratic values. People who have failed to learn the prevailing norms of American society are far more likely to express opposition to democratic and capitalist ideals than those who are well educated and politically knowledgeable.[143]

UNITY IN A LAND OF DIVERSITY

As remarkable as American diversity is, the existence of a strong and widely shared sense of national unity and identity may be even more remarkable. Writing about the United States some years ago, a famous reporter, John Gunther, summarized his insights from extensive travels:

> Whoever invented the motto *E Pluribus Unum* [out of many, one] has given the best three-word description of the United States ever written. The triumph of America is the triumph of a coalescing federal system. Complex as the nation is almost to the point of insufferability, it interlocks. Homogeneity and diversity—these are the stupendous rival magnets. . . . Think of the United States as an immense blanket or patchwork quilt solid with different designs and highlights. But, no matter what colors burn and flash in what corners, the warp and woof, the basic texture and fabric, is the same from corner to corner, from end to end.[144]

Social scientists sometimes speak of the "melting pot," meaning that as various ethnic groups associate with other groups, they are assimilated into American society and come to share democratic values like majority rule, individualism, and the notion that America is the land of opportunity. The melting pot idea has been criticized as assuming that differences between groups are to be discouraged. In its place, critics propose the notion of the "salad bowl," in which "though the salad is an entity, the lettuce can still be distinguished from the chicory, the tomatoes from the cabbage."[145]

As this chapter has demonstrated, regional, social and economic differences have important political consequences. They influence public opinion, participation, voting, interest groups and political parties. At the same time our country has achieved a sense of unity despite our remarkable diversity.

S U M M A R Y

1. The character of a political society and its social environment are important to understanding our politics and government.

2. As a nation of immigrants, Americans are more diverse than the citizens of most other nations. Diversity in race and ethnicity are reflected in different family structures and religions. The nation's citizens also differ in wealth and income, occupation, social class, age, and education. Divisions by gender and sexual orientation have recently become more important. This diversity is often significant in our politics, though most divisions cut across demographic categories rather than reinforce them.

3. Geography, room to grow, abundant natural resources, wealth, and relative isolation from foreign entanglements help explain American politics and traditions, including the notions of manifest destiny, ethnocentrism, and isolationism.

4. Until recently, the South was a very distinct region in the United States, in large part because of its agricultural base and its history of slavery and troubled race relations. With in-migration and the impact of the civil rights movement, it is no longer solidly Democratic. Recently, the most significant migration has been from cities to suburbs. Today large cities are increasingly poor, African American, and

Democratic, surrounded by suburbs that are primarily middle class, white, and Republican.

5. Race has been among the most important of the differences in our political landscape. Although we fought a civil war over freedom for African Americans, racial equality was largely postponed until the latter half of the twentieth century. Race remains an important issue in our politics and government. Ethnicity, including the rising numbers of Hispanics, continues to be a factor in politics.

6. Gender is important in American politics. Women have gradually acquired political rights. They now play important

roles in our government, and they differ from men in their attitudes on some issues. Sexual orientation policies, especially relating to same-sex marriage, are among the most contentious in our society.

7. Since World War II, attitudes toward sexuality, marriage, and family have changed in important ways. People cohabit at much higher rates, and those who marry are older. Divorce has also become much more commonplace. Changing family structures and attitudes affect our tax policies, child care, parental leave, and gender equality. They are also important political issues.

8. The United States has a large variety of religious denominations, and these dif-ferences help explain public opinion and political behavior. Important differences also exist between Americans who are religious and those who are not.

9. Although the United States is a land of wealth with a large middle class, not everyone has an adequate share in the American economic success. Poverty has grown over the past two decades, and it is most concentrated among African Americans, Native Americans, Hispanics, and single-parent households. Women as a group continue to earn less than men, even in the same occupations. Differences in income and wealth remain important.

10. The United States has shifted from an agricultural to an industrial and now to a postindustrial society, with consequences for occupations and politics. Governments are a major source of employment. Social class is less important in America than in other industrialized democracies.

11. Age and education are important to understanding American politics. Older citizens participate much more than young voters and are a potent political force. Education not only opens up economic opportunities in America but also explains many important aspects of political participation.

12. Despite our diversity, Americans share an important unity. We are united by our shared commitment to democratic values, economic opportunity, work ethic, and the American dream.

K E Y   T E R M S

ethnocentrism	**political predisposition**	**manifest destiny**	**gender gap**
political socialization	**reinforcing cleavages**	**race**	**gross domestic product (GDP)**
demographics	**cross-cutting cleavages**	**ethnicity**	**socioeconomic status (SES)**

F U R T H E R   R E A D I N G

DOUGLAS L. ANDERSON, RICHARD BARTNETT, AND DONALD BOGUE, *The Population of the United States*, 3d ed. (Free Press, 1996).

DAVID H. BENNETT, *The Party of Fear* (University of North Carolina Press, 1990).

EARL BLACK AND MERLE BLACK, *The Rise of Southern Republicans* (Belknap Press, 2002).

URIE BRONFENBRENNER ET AL., *The State of Americans: The Disturbing Facts and Figures on Changing Values, Crime, the Economy, Poverty, Family, Education, the Aging Population, and What They Mean for Our Future* (Free Press, 1996).

DAVID T. CANON, *Race, Redistricting, and Representation: The Unintended Consequences of Black Majority Districts* (University of Chicago Press, 1999).

MAUREEN DEZELL, *Irish America: Coming Into Clover* (Anchor Books, 2000).

LOIS LOVELACE DUKE, ED., *Women in Politics: Outsiders or Insiders?* 2d ed. (Prentice Hall, 1995).

SARAH H. EVANS, *Born for Liberty: A History of Women in America* (Free Press, 1989).

GEOFFREY FOX, *Hispanic Nation: Culture, Politics and the Constructing of Identity* (Birch Lane Press, 1996).

RODOLFO O. DE LA GARZA, LOUIS DE SIPIO, F. CHRIS GARCIA, JOHN GARCIA, AND ANGELO FALCON, *Latino Voices: Mexican, Puerto Rican, and Cuban Perspectives on American Politics* (Westview Press, 1992).

JOHN C. GREEN, MARK J. ROZELL, AND CLYDE WILCOX, EDS., *The Christian Right in American Politics: Marching to the Millenium* (Georgetown University Press, 2003).

DONALD R. KINDER AND LYNN M. SANDERS, *Divided by Color: Racial Politics and Democratic Ideals* (University of Chicago Press, 1996).

JAN E. LEIGHLEY, *Strength in Numbers? The Political Mobilization of Racial and Ethnic Minorities* (Princeton University Press, 2001).

PEL-TE LIEN, M. MARGARET CONWAY, AND JANELLE WONG, *The Politics of Asian Americans* (Routledge, 2004).

SEYMOUR MARTIN LIPSET, *Continental Divide: The Values and Institutions of the United States and Canada* (Routledge, 1990).

JEREMY D. MAYER, *Runing On Race: Racial Politics in Presidential Campaign, 1960–2000* (Random House, 2002).

NANCY E. McGLEN AND KAREN O'CONNOR, *Women, Politics, and American Society*, 2d ed. (Prentice Hall, 1998).

KEVIN PHILLIPS, *The Politics of Rich and Poor: Wealth and the American Electorate in the Reagan Aftermath* (Random House, 1990).

STANLEY A. RENSHON, ED., *One America? Political Leadership, National Identity, and the Dilemmas of Diversity* (Georgetown University Press, 2001).

RUBEN G. RUMBAUT AND ALEJANDRO PORTES, *Ethnicities: Children of Immigrants in America* (University of California Press, 2001).

ARTHUR M. SCHLESINGER JR., *The Disuniting of America* (Norton, 1992).

PETER H. SCHUCK, *Diversity In America* (Belknap Press, 2003).

JEFFREY M. STONECASH, *Class and Party in American Politics* (Westview Press, 2000).

ALEXIS DE TOCQUEVILLE, *Democracy in America*, ed. J. P. Mayer, trans. George Lawrence (Doubleday, 1969). Originally published 1835.

KENNETH D. WALD, *Religion and Politics in the United States*, 3d ed. (CQ Press, 1996).

The 2004 presidential election featured not only ads from the candidates but also ads from interest groups opposing and, less frequently, supporting one of the candidates. During the Democratic convention, John Kerry and his advocates emphasized his preparation to be Commander-in-Chief and his Vietnam War heroism. Shortly after the convention, a group called Swift Boat Veterans for Truth started running ads questioning Kerry's heroism and patriotism. The group also released a book titled *Unfit for Command*,[1] which accused Kerry of lying about his record and exaggerating the atrocities committed by U.S. troops in Vietnam. Kerry responded by calling their claims "categorically false," arguing that the Bush campaign was behind the attacks, and calling on Bush to repudiate them.[2] Bush in turn suggested that both candidates urge all interest groups to stop running ads.[3]

Individuals closely connected to key Bush political advisors or family provided early funding and support for the Swift Boat Veterans for Truth. Bob J. Perry, a longtime associate of Karl Rove, the chief political strategist for President Bush, provided $200,000 to help launch the group.[4] The veterans group also had the same attorney as the Bush campaign. A candidate campaign and interest group using the same attorney was not limited to the Bush campaign nor was it illegal, but these facts did not diffuse the Kerry campaign's claim that the Swift Boat Veterans for Truth was a front for the Bush campaign.[5]

Swift Boat Veterans for Truth was not the only interest group to run ads critical of candidates in 2004. In fact, it spent far less on ads than liberal groups opposing President Bush.[6]

INTEREST GROUPS
THE POLITICS OF INFLUENCE

6

TIME LINE ★★

INTEREST GROUPS

1833	Anti-Slavery Society founded
1890	National American Woman Suffrage Association formed
1893	Anti-Saloon League formed
1912	U.S. Chamber of Commerce is created
1920	American Civil Liberties Union is founded
1925	Passage of Federal Corrupt Practices Act
1955	AFL and CIO merge to form the largest labor union
1958	AARP is created but growth comes with the aging of Baby Boomers
1960	President Eisenhower warns against the "military-industrial complex"
1970	Common Cause represents the interests of middle-class reformers
1971	Federal Election Campaign Act passed
1976	*Buckley* v. *Valeo* ruling upholds public financing of presidential elections and contribution limits in congressional elections
2002	Bipartisan Campaign Reform Act limits "soft money"

Early in the primary season, a liberal group called MoveOn ran ads critical of President Bush. Some of these ads ran even before the Democrats had selected their nominee, reflecting the strong anti-Bush sentiment of the group. Both Swift Boat Veterans for Truth and MoveOn demonstrated that comparatively modest media buys could capture the interest of the media and greatly expand the impact of an ad. The Media Fund—a group with much more substantial advertising expenditures—also had defeating Bush as its primary objective.

All three of these interest groups were organized under Section 527 of the Internal Revenue Code. As so-called "527" organizations, these groups could raise and spend unlimited amounts of money as long as the expenditures were independent of the candidates or parties and did not use corporate or union treasury funds within thirty days of a primary election or within sixty days of a general election. Interest groups like these have long been important in electing and defeating candidates, in providing information to officeholders, and in setting the agenda of American politics. In some important respects the power and influence of interest groups has been enhanced by recent campaign finance legislation. Americans have long been concerned about the power of what some call "special interests" and the tendency of groups to pursue self-interest at the expense of less organized groups or the general public. Restraining the negative tendencies of interest groups while protecting liberty is not an easy task. Efforts to reform campaign finance and limit the potential for interest-group corruption of that process while also safeguarding electoral competition are examples of this balancing. In this chapter we examine the full range of interest-group activity as well as efforts to limit their potentially negative influences.

INTEREST GROUPS PAST AND PRESENT: THE "MISCHIEFS OF FACTION"

What we call interest groups today, the founders of the Republic called **factions**. (They also thought of political parties as factions.) For the framers of the Constitution, the daunting problem was how to establish a stable and orderly constitutional

Interest groups often use advertising to promote issues that they consider important. This advertisement, created by the National Rifle Association, is a caricature of John Kerry as a dog that "don't hunt." Judging from the animal's appearance, this dog was obviously not bred to be a hunting dog. This mailer attacks Kerry's positions on gun-related issues.

That dog don't hunt.

John Kerry says he supports sportsmen's rights. But his record says something else.

- **John Kerry voted for Ted Kennedy's amendment** to outlaw most ammunition used by deer hunters.¹
- **John Kerry supports higher taxes** on firearms and ammunition.²
- **John Kerry voted in favor of banning** semi-automatic firearms, including many firearms favored by sportsmen.³
- **John Kerry voted to allow** big city politicians to sue the American firearms industry and hold legitimate firearms manufacturers and dealers responsible for the acts of criminals.⁴

- **John Kerry voted to close** off hundreds of thousands of acres to hunters.⁵
- **John Kerry voted to commend Rosie O'Donnell's** Million Mom March, an organization calling for gun owner licensing, gun registration, and other radical restrictions on law-abiding gun owners.⁶
- **With a 20-year record of voting against** sportsmen's rights, it's no wonder John Kerry has been called a "hero" by the Humane Society of the United States, an extremist group that wants to outlaw hunting in America.⁷

If John Kerry wins, you lose.

NRA-POLITICAL VICTORY FUND

VOTE FREEDOM FIRST

faction
A term used by the founders of this country to refer to political parties and special interests or interest groups.

system that would also respect the liberty of free citizens and prevent the tyranny of the majority or of a single dominant interest. As a good practical politician and a brilliant theorist, James Madison offered both a diagnosis and a solution in *The Federalist,* No. 10 (reprinted in the Appendix). He began with a basic proposition: "The latent causes of faction are thus sown in the nature of man." All individuals pursue their self-interest, seeking advantage or power over others. Acknowledging that Americans live in a maze of group interests, Madison went on to argue that the "most common and durable source of factions has been the various and unequal distribution of property."

A Nation of Interests

As we noted in Chapter 5, some Americans identify with groups distinguished by race, gender, ethnic background, age, occupation, or sexual orientation. Others form groups based on issues like gun control or tax reduction. When such associations seek to influence government in some way, they are **interest groups**.

Interest groups are sometimes called "special interests." Politicians and the media often use this term in a pejorative way. What makes an interest group a "special" one? The answer is highly subjective. One person's special interest is another's public interest. Some interest groups claim to speak for the "public interest," yet so-called public interest groups like Common Cause or the League of Women Voters support policies that not everyone agrees with. Politics is best seen as a clash among interests with differing concepts of what is in the public interest rather than a battle between the special interests on one side and "the people" or the public interest on the other.

When political scientists call something an "interest group" or a "special interest," they are not calling it names. These are analytic terms to describe a group that speaks for some but not all of us. Much of our politics focuses on arguments about what is in the national interest. In a democracy, there are many interests and many organized interest groups. The democratic process exists to decide among those competing interests. Part of the politics of interest groups is to persuade the general public that your group's interest is better, broader, more beneficial, and more general than other groups' and at the same time label groups that oppose yours as "special interests." The term "special interest" conveys a selfish or narrow view, one that may lack credibility. For this reason, we use the neutral term "interest groups."

Social Movements

Interest groups sometimes begin as movements. A **movement** consists of a large body of people who are interested in a common issue, idea, or concern that is of continuing significance and who are willing to take action. Examples include the abolitionist, temperance, civil rights, environmental, antitax, animal rights, and women's rights movements. Each movement represents groups who have felt unrepresented by government. Such groups often arise at the grassroots level and evolve into national groups. Movements tend to see their causes as morally right and the positions of the opposition as morally wrong.

To a marked degree, our Constitution protects the liberties and independence of movements. The Bill of Rights guarantees movements, whether popular or unpopular, by supporting free assembly, free speech, and due process. Consequently, those who disagree with government policies do not have to engage in violence or other extreme activities in the United States, as they do in some countries, and they need not fear persecution for demonstrating peacefully. In a democratic system that restricts the power of government, movements have considerable room to operate *within* the constitutional system.

TYPES OF INTEREST GROUPS

Interest groups vary widely. Some are formal associations or organizations like the National Rifle Association; others have no formal organization, like Bubba's List, a group from Austin, Texas (Bubba stands for Brothers United for Building a Better America).

interest group
A collection of people who share some common interest or attitude and seek to influence government for specific ends. Interest groups usually work within the framework of government and employ tactics such as lobbying to achieve their goals.

movement
A large body of people interested in a common issue, idea, or concern that is of continuing significance and who are willing to take action. Movements seek to change attitudes or institutions, not just policies.

Some are organized primarily to lobby for limited goals such as restrictions on gun ownership, conducting research, or broadly influencing public opinion by publishing reports and mass mailings.

Interest groups can be categorized into several broad types: (1) economic, including both business and labor; (2) ideological or single-issue; (3) public interest; (4) foreign policy; and (5) government itself. Obviously, these categories are not mutually exclusive. The varied and overlapping nature of interest groups in the United States has been described as *interest group pluralism*, meaning that competition among open, responsive, and diverse groups helps preserve democratic values and limits the concentration of power in any single group.

Most Americans are represented by a number of interest groups, some of which they are aware of and others of which they may not be and often with which they differ. For instance, citizens over 50 may not be aware that the AARP (which began as the American Association of Retired Persons) claims to represent their interests, and now is open to anyone over fifty years of age. Others may not know that when they join the American Automobile Association (AAA), they are not only purchasing travel assistance and automobile towing when needed but also joining a group that lobbies Congress and the Federal Highway Administration on behalf of motorists.

Economic Interest Groups

There are thousands of economic interests: agriculture, consumers, plumbers, northern businesses, southern businesses, labor unions, the airplane industry, landlords, truckers, bondholders, property owners, and on and on.

BUSINESS   The most familiar business institution is probably the large corporation. Corporations range from one-person enterprises to vast multinational entities. Large corporations—General Motors, AT&T, Microsoft, Coca-Cola, McDonald's, Phillip Morris, and other large companies—exercise considerable political influence, as do hundreds of smaller corporations (see Tables 6–1 and 6–2). Corporate power and the implications of a changing domestic and global economy make business practices important political issues. As Microsoft and Wal-Mart have come under heightened government and public scrutiny, their political contributions have grown substantially. Wal-Mart contributed $450,000 in 2001–2002 to federal candidates or parties compared with $75,000 in 1999–2000.[7] Microsoft also donated roughly three times the amount in the 2000 and 2002 cycles than in the '98 cycle.[8]

Small business also is an important interest and can have an important voice in public policy. Within the Commerce Department there is a Small Business Administration. Small businesses are also organized into groups. An example is the National

---

TABLE 6–1   PACs THAT GAVE THE MOST TO FEDERAL CANDIDATES, 2000–2004 (MILLIONS OF DOLLARS)

	2004	*2002*	*2000*
National Association of Realtors	3.77	3.65	3.42
Wal-Mart Stores	1.65	1.08	0.46
National Association of Home Builders	2.06	1.92	1.85
Association of Trial Lawyers of America	2.17	2.81	2.66
International Brotherhood of Electrical Workers	2.33	2.22	2.62
National Auto Dealers Association	2.58	2.58	2.50
Laborers Union	2.63	2.26	1.79
Carpenters and Joiners Union	1.88	2.09	1.72
United Parcel Service	2.14	1.62	1.76
SBC Communications	1.95	1.47	1.29

SOURCE: www.opensecrets.org/pacs/topacs.asp?strid=&cycle=2004&type=C&filter=P&txt=A&Format=Print.

TABLE 6–2 TOP TEN ALL-TIME DONORS 1989–2004

	Total
American Federation of State, County & Municipal Employees	$35,408,631
National Association of Realtors	$26,276,380
National Education Association	$24,170,353
Association of Trial Lawyers of America	$24,094,416
Communications Workers of America	$22,601,816
Service Employees International Union	$22,486,475
International Brotherhood of Electrical Workers	$22,122,055
Laborers Union	$21,899,082
American Medical Association	$21,774,021
Carpenters and Joiners Union	$21,567,447

Based on data released by the FEC on October 25, 2004.

SOURCE: Opensecrets.org at www.opensecrets.org/index.asp.

Federation of Independent Business, which is involved in electing pro-business candidates, and lobbying national government on behalf of this constituency.

TRADE AND OTHER ASSOCIATIONS Businesses with similar interests in government regulations and other issues join together as *trade associations,* which are as diverse as the products and services they provide. In addition, businesses of all types are organized into large nationwide associations such as the National Mining Association, the National Association of Realtors, and the National Federation of Independent Business.

The broadest business trade association is the Chamber of Commerce of the United States. Organized in 1912, the Chamber is a federation of several thousand local Chambers of Commerce representing tens of thousands of firms. Loosely allied with the Chamber on most issues is the National Association of Manufacturers, which, since its founding in the wake of the depression of 1893, has tended to speak for the more conservative elements of American business.

LABOR Workers' associations have a range of interests, from professional standards to wages and working conditions. Labor unions are one of the most important groups representing workers. The American work force is the least unionized of almost any industrial democracy (see Figure 6–1).

Probably the oldest unions in the United States were farm organizations. The largest farm group now is the American Farm Bureau Federation, which is especially strong in the Corn Belt. Originally organized around government agents who helped farmers in rural counties, the federation today is almost a semigovernmental agency, but it retains full freedom to fight for such goals as price supports and expanded credit. As farming has grown in scale and workers are less and less likely to be members of the farmer's family, there have been efforts to organize farm workers into unions. Noteworthy here have been the efforts of the late César Chávez and others to organize migrant farm workers.

Throughout the nineteenth century, workers organized political parties and local unions. Their most ambitious effort at national organization, the Knights of Labor, claimed 700,000 members. By the beginning of the twentieth century, the American Federation of Labor (AFL), a confederation of strong and independent-minded national unions mainly representing craft workers, was the dominant organization. During the ferment of the 1930s, unions more responsive to industrial workers broke away from the AFL and formed a rival national organization organized by industry, the Congress of Industrial Organizations (CIO). In 1955, the AFL and CIO reunited into the organization that exists today.

Union membership is optional in states whose laws permit the **open shop**, in which union membership cannot be required as a condition of employment. In states with the **closed shop**, union membership may be required as a condition of employment if most employees so vote. In both cases, the unions conduct negotiations with management, and the benefits the unions gain will be shared with all workers. In open-shop states, many

open shop
A company with a labor agreement under which union membership cannot be required as a condition of employment.

closed shop
A company with a labor agreement under which union membership can be a condition of employment.

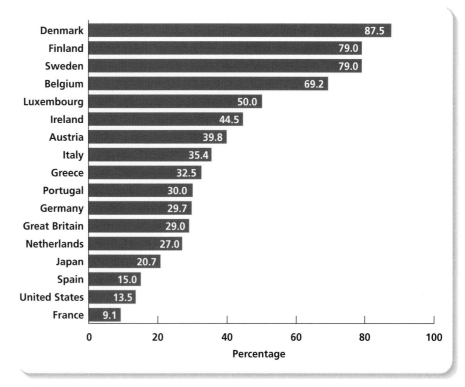

FIGURE 6–1 Union Membership in the United States Compared to Other Countries (Estimated Percentage of the Work Force).
SOURCE: European Industrial Observatory On-line, "Industrial Relations in the EU, Japan, and the US, 2001," at www.eiro.eurofound.eu.int/2002/12/feature/tn0212101f.html.

workers choose not to affiliate with a union, as they can secure the same benefits without incurring the costs associated with union membership. When a person benefits from the work or service of an organization like a union (or even a public TV or radio station) without joining or contributing, this condition is referred to as the **free rider** problem.

The AFL-CIO speaks for about 80 percent of unionized labor, but unions represent only about 14 percent of the nation's work force (see Figure 6–2).[9] The drop in the proportion of the work force belonging to unions is explained in part by the shift from an industrial to a service and information economy. Dwindling membership limits organized labor's political and lobbying muscle, and its prospects for increasing influence in the future are dim. Recently there has been growth in public sector unions, however, and even some doctors have unionized.

For some years, the Committee on Political Education (COPE) of the AFL-CIO was one of the most respected—and most feared—political organizations in the country. In the Kennedy and Johnson years, it won a reputation for political effectiveness. It encouraged and supervised grassroots political activity, and at the national level, it prepared and adopted a detailed platform that spelled out labor's position on issues. Labor contributed money to candidates, ran registration and get-out-the-vote campaigns, and otherwise supported its favorites. In recent elections, COPE has had a fairly successful record of wins for its endorsed House and Senate candidates.[10] Labor unions invested heavily in the fight against the North American Free Trade Agreement (NAFTA), claiming it would cost jobs. Labor's defeat in this battle was compounded by the 1994 election, which put Republicans in charge of the House of Representatives for the first time in forty years.

Unions have been effective in communicating with their members and organizing them for political purposes. In the 1998 elections and again in 2000 and 2002, unions sent mailings to their members, organized get-out-the-vote drives, and paid for television advertising. In the 2004 presidential primaries unions were divided; most supported former Missouri Congressman Dick Gephardt, but some—like the Service Employees International Union (SEIU) and the American Ferderation of State, County, and

free rider
An individual who does not join a group representing his or her interests yet receives the benefit of the influence the group achieves.

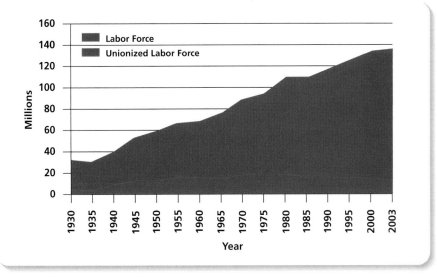

FIGURE 6–2 Labor Force and Union Membership, 1930–2003.
SOURCE: *The World Almanac and Book of Facts, 2000.* Copyright © 1999 Primedia Reference, Inc. Reprinted with permission; all rights reserved. U.S. Bureau of Labor Statistics, at www.stats.bls.gov/news.release/union2.toc.htm and www.bls.gov/cps/cpsaat40.pdf. 2003 data taken from Department of Labor, Bureau of Labor Statistics. "Press Release," January 21, 2004, at www.bls.gov/news.release/pdf/union2.pdf.

★★ IN COMPARATIVE PERSPECTIVE ★★

UNIONS IN SWEDEN

Interest groups are stronger in some countries and weaker in others. Organized labor, or unions, are a common feature of advanced democracies and industrial and postindustrial economies, but that does not mean that unions exercise the same influence over policy or politics in all countries.

In Sweden, unions are large and cohesive.* Nearly four out of five (79 percent) of the Swedish workforce is unionized,[†] compared with the United States, where less than one-seventh are unionized.[‡] In Sweden, moreover, unions form a single large labor federation, the Swedish Trade Union Confederation, which provides a powerful and cohesive voice in public policy. American unions are fragmented into several federations, and even within federations there are tensions between particular unions.

The Swedish Trade Union Confederation has a close relationship with the Social Democratic Party (SDP), with union leaders among the party leadership. One scholar has observed that in Sweden the Confederation supports the SDP with "money, manpower, and influence with the rank and file."[§] In the United States, most, but not all, unions support the Democratic party, and they are not as central to the Democratic coalition as unions are to Sweden's SDP.

Swedish unions are also more powerful in collective bargaining. In 2004, four industrial sectors agreed to a new three-year deal that would provide generally for a 6.8 percent pay raise, plus working time cuts worth a further 0.5 percent.[‖] Swedish unions are also working to further reduce the statutory normal work week, which is presently 40 hours per week.[¶] Because of the close relationship the unions have with the governing party, they can significantly influence legislation. In the United States, labor unions opposed the reelection of George W. Bush, whose administration was seen by them as hostile.** With Republicans in control of both houses of Congress and the White House in recent years, labor unions in the United States were much less involved in policy making than were Swedish unions.

*Michael Roskin, *Countries and Concepts: Politics, Geography, Culture,* 8th ed. (Upper Saddle River, N.J.: Prentice Hall, 2004), p. 205.
[†]European Industrial Relations Observatory On-line, "Overall Union Membership Declines," at www.eiro.eurofound.eu.int/2001/06/feature/se0106105f.html.
[‡]European Industrial Relations Observatory On-line, "2001–2 Annual Review for the USA," at www.eiro.eurofound.eu.int/2002/11/feature/us0211101f.html.
[§]Michael Roskin, *Countries and Concepts: Politics, Geography, Culture,* 8th ed. (Upper Saddle River, N.J.: Prentice Hall, 2004), p. 205.
[‖]European Industrial Relations Observatory On-line, "First Agreements in 2004 bargaining round concluded in Industry," at www.eiro.eurofound.ie/2004/03/feature/se0403103f.html.
[¶]European Industrial Relations Observatory On-line, "Working Time Developments–2003," at www.eiro.eurofound.eu.int/2004/03/update/tn0403104u.html.
**Steven Greenhouse, "A.F.L.-C.I.O. Plans to Spend $44 Million to Unseat Bush," *The New York Times,* March 11, 2004, p. A26.

Municipal Employees—supported former Vermont Governor Howard Dean. Finally, the firefighters supported Massachusetts Senator John Kerry. Unlike 2000, where unions were seen as important to Al Gore's securing the nomination, in 2004 they did not play that role in the Iowa caucus or other primaries.[11]

Traditionally identified with the Democratic party, unions have not enjoyed a close relationship with Republican administrations. Given labor's limited resources, one option for unions is to form temporary coalitions with consumer, public interest, liberal, and sometimes even with industry groups, especially on issues related to foreign imports. Few of labor's recent legislative initiatives have been successful, and turning to the courts has yielded mixed results.[12]

In recent elections, the AFL-CIO has mounted vigorous campaigns to elect a Democratic president and majority in Congress. Some foes of labor have proposed legislation and ballot initiatives called "paycheck protection," which would require annual authorization by union members for portions of their dues to be used for political purposes. Labor unions have successfully defeated these measures.

GLOBAL *Perceptions*

QUESTION: Is the influence of trade unions very good, somewhat good, somewhat bad, or very bad?

How do the views of people in other countries on unions compare with the views of people in the United States? The Pew Global Attitudes Project allows us to explore this question.

Unions are seen very positively in Vietnam, where 59 percent said they were a "very good" influence and 92 percent said they were a "very good" or "somewhat good" influence. People in Argentina had strongly negative views of unions, with 42 percent saying they were "very bad."

In addition to Vietnam, combining the "very good" and "somewhat good" responses found most people in these countries likely to see unions positively: Nigeria (82%), Phillipines (75%), Great Britain (67%), Uganda (67%), Bolivia (65%), Germany (65%), USA (63%), and South Korea (62%). In contrast, Unions were seen as bad in Argentina (75%) and by two-out-of five respondents or more in Russia, Brazil, Mexico, Venezuela, Italy, Poland, Slovak Republic, Jordan, and Turkey.

Unions were seen as having a good influence on a country more than did multinational corporations in the United States, Canada, and Europe (excluding Italy), but not in other parts of the world. Countries like Great Britain, Slovak Republic, and several countries in South America, Africa, and Asia saw multinational corporations as having a good influence. The positive view of unions in Vietnam does not limit the enthusiasm for multinational corporations, where 93 percent said such corporations were a good influence.

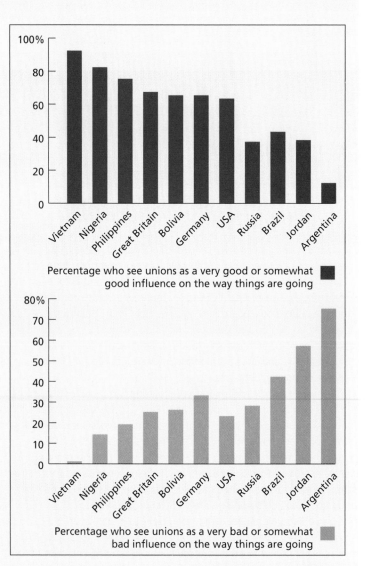

SOURCE: The Pew Research Center. *Views of a Changing World*, 2003, pp. 100, T-43.

PROFESSIONAL ASSOCIATIONS Professional people have organized some of the strongest unions in the nation. Some are well known, such as the American Medical Association and the American Bar Association. Others are divided into many subgroups. Teachers, for example, are organized into large groups such as the National Education Association, the American Federation of Teachers, and the American Association of University Professors and also into subgroups based on specialties, such as the Modern Language Association and the American Political Science Association.

Government, especially at the state level, regulates many professions. Lawyers, for example, are licensed by states, which, often as a result of pressure from lawyers themselves, have set up certain standards of admission to the state bar. Professional associations also use the courts to pursue their agendas. In the area of medical malpractice, for example, doctors lobby hard for limited liability laws, while the trial lawyers resist such efforts. Teachers, hairstylists, and marriage therapists work for legislation or regulations of concern to them. It is not surprising, then, that among the largest donors to political campaigns through political action committees are those representing professional associations such as the American Medical Association and the American Realtors Association.

Ideological or Single-Issue Interest Groups

Ideological groups behave very much like economic interest groups, although they are usually not driven by a desire to make money. Some of these groups are *single-issue groups,* often highly motivated and seeing politics primarily as a means to pursue their one issue. Such groups are often adamant about their position and unwilling to negotiate compromises. Right-to-life and pro-choice groups on abortion fit this description, as does the National Rifle Association.

Countless groups have organized around other specific issues, such as civil liberties, environmental protection, nuclear energy, and nuclear disarmament.[13] Such associations are not new. The Anti-Saloon League of the 1890s was single-mindedly devoted to barring the sale and manufacture of alcoholic beverages, and it did not care whether legislators were drunk or sober, as long as they voted dry. One of the best-known ideological groups today is the American Civil Liberties Union (ACLU), with roughly 250,000 members committed to the protection of civil liberties.[14] Religious groups are thriving in the otherwise pragmatic, pluralistic politics of today; an example is the Christian Coalition, which distributes voter guides before elections, although it has had less of a presence in recent years than it had in the 1990s.[15] African American churches have long been important politically and continue to encourage voter participation.

Public Interest Groups

Out of the political ferment of the 1960s came groups that make a specific claim to promote "the public interest." For example, Common Cause, founded in 1970 by independent Republican John W. Gardner and later led by noted Watergate prosecutor Archibald Cox, campaigns for electoral reform and for making the political process more open. Its Washington staff raises money through direct-mail campaigns, oversees state chapters, issues research reports and press releases on current issues, and lobbies on Capitol Hill and in major government departments.

Ralph Nader started a conglomerate of consumer organizations that investigates and reports on governmental and corporate action—or inaction—relating to consumer interests. Public Interest Research Groups (PIRGs) founded by Nader are among the largest interest groups in the country. PIRGs have become important players on Capitol Hill and in several state legislatures, promoting environmental issues, safe energy, consumer protection, and good government. Nader ran for president in 2000 as the nominee of the Green party and in 2004 as an independent. Despite his reputation as an advocate for consumers, he received only 3 percent of the popular vote in 2000 and one-third of 1 percent in 2004.

A specific type of public interest group is the tax-exempt public charity. Examples include the American Heart Association, the Girl Scouts of the U.S.A., and the American Cancer Society. These organizations must meet certain conditions, such as educational or philanthropic objectives, to qualify for this preferred status. Not only are public charities

The Women's Christian Temperance Union, a movement dedicated to the prohibition of drinking liquor, succeeded in passing the Eighteenth Amendment, which outlawed the manufacture and sale of alcoholic beverages. It was later repealed by the Twenty-first Amendment.

tax-exempt, but donations to these organizations are tax-deductible, and the organizations are not required to disclose information about their donors publicly. These organizations cannot participate in elections or support candidates, nor can they benefit an individual or small group. Despite these limitations, tax-exempt charitable organizations have been very active in voter registration efforts and in advertising campaigns designed to influence public opinion.

Foreign Policy Interest Groups

Domestic policy is not the only matter of concern to interest groups. Groups also organize to promote or oppose certain foreign policies. Among the most prestigious foreign affairs groups is the Council on Foreign Relations in New York City. Other groups, devoted to narrower areas of American foreign policy, exert pressure on members of Congress and the president to enact specific policies. For example, interest group pressure influenced U.S. policy toward South Africa and played a role in South Africa's decision to abandon apartheid. Groups ranging from student organizations to national lobbies like the American Committee on Africa urged divestment, sanctions, or other policy measures that ultimately promoted change in South Africa. Other groups support or oppose free trade.

The American-Israel Political Action Committee (AIPAC) has more than 50,000 members and has been very successful. Because AIPAC's primary focus is lobbying and not distributing campaign funds, it is not required to disclose where its money comes from or goes. Included in the long list of AIPAC lobbying successes are enactment of aid packages to Israel, passage of the 1985 United States–Israel Free Trade Agreement, and emergency assistance to Israel in the wake of the 1992 Gulf War. Its counterpart, the National Association of Arab Americans, lobbies for action in support of Arab causes. Efforts to secure a negotiated settlement between the Palestinians and Israel have meant that American interest groups on both sides of the dispute remain visible and important.

Public Sector Interest Groups

Governments are themselves important interest groups. Many cities and most states retain Washington lobbyists, and cities also hire lobbyists to represent them at the state legislature. Governors are organized through the National Governors Association, cities through the National League of Cities, and counties through the National Association of Counties. Other officials have their own national associations.

Government employees form a large and well-organized group. The National Education Association (NEA), for example, claims 2.7 million members.[16] Bush Administration Secretary of Education Rod Paige created controversy when he labeled the NEA a terrorist organization, a remark for which he later apologized.[17] Paige was at odds with teachers' unions because they disagreed with some of his agenda. His characterization, which caused ire among teachers, may have helped motivate teachers to participate even more in 2004 than they had in the past. Public employees are also important to organized labor, and they are the fastest-growing unions.

Other Interest Groups

Interest groups such as Greenpeace stage demonstrations to call attention to environmental issues.

Americans are often emotionally and financially involved in a variety of groups: veterans' groups such as American Legion or Veterans of Foreign Wars; nationality groups such as the multitude of German, Irish, Hispanic, Palestinian, and Korean organizations; or religious organizations such as the Knights of Columbus or B'nai B'rith. More than 150 nationwide organizations are based on national origin alone. In recent years, there has been a virtual explosion in the number and variety of interests and associations. This is especially true for environmental groups (see Table 6–3).

CHARACTERISTICS AND POWER OF INTEREST GROUPS

Groups vary in their goals, methods, and power. Among the most important group characteristics are size, resources, cohesiveness, leadership, and techniques.

Size and Resources

Obviously, size is important to political power; an organization representing 5 million voters has more influence than one speaking for 5,000. Perhaps even more important than size is the extent to which members are actively involved and fight for policy objectives. Often people join an organization for reasons that have little to do with its political objectives. They may want to secure group insurance, take advantage of travel benefits, participate in professional meetings, or get a job.

Some interest groups focus on foreign policy issues, such as U.S. aid to Israel in light of Israel's construction of a separation wall along the West Bank. Opponents argue that the wall is tantamount to apartheid and the Israeli government argues that it is a necessary security measure.

How do associations motivate potential members to join them? Organizations must provide incentives, material or otherwise, that are compelling enough to attract the potential free rider.[18] Unions are organized not just for lobbying but also to perform other important services for their members. They derive much of their strength from their negotiating position with corporations, which they use to obtain wage increases or improved safety standards. Similarly, the AARP, in addition to lobbying for prescription drug benefits and speaking out on other issues of concern to older citizens, offers incentives such as a free subscription to one of its magazines and member discounts at certain hotels. This combination of size and strength sets these groups apart from other large organizations in their effectiveness, since members derive numerous benefits from joining. The AARP was part of the coalition pushing the partial prescription drug for seniors bill that President Bush signed into law in 2003. Some AARP members, as well as former allies in Congress, expressed irritation at AARP supporting this partial benefit, which they thought was inadequate.[19]

TABLE 6–3 SOME ENVIRONMENTAL GROUPS AND HOW THEY DO BUSINESS

Group	Membership	Issues	Activities
Greenpeace USA	250,000	Forests, global warming, genetically engineered foods, oceans, persistent organic pollutants, nuclear weapons	Media events; mass mailings; grassroots activity; does not lobby government
Natural Resources Defense Council	1,000,000	Resources, energy, global warming, pollution, nuclear weapons	Lobbying; litigation; watchdog; its scientists compete with experts from agencies and industry
Sierra Club	700,000	Wilderness, pollution, global warming, human rights, population, suburban sprawl	Grassroots action; litigation; news releases
Wilderness Society	250,000	Wilderness areas, public lands, energy development	Scientific studies; analysis; advocacy group

SOURCE: Greenpeace USA at www.greenpeaceusa.org; Natural Resources Defense Council at www.nrdc.org; Sierra Club at www.sierraclub.org; Wilderness Society at www.wilderness.org.

In 2003, the AARP successfully lobbied for passage of a prescription drug plan that many seniors argued would ultimately increase the cost of their prescription medications. To protest the AARP's position, some people burned their AARP cards.

While the size of an interest group is often important, so, too, is its *spread*—the extent to which membership is concentrated or dispersed. Automobile manufacturing is concentrated in Michigan and a few other states, and as a result, the auto industry's influence does not have the same spread as that of the American Medical Association, which has an active chapter in virtually every congressional district. An association consisting of 3 million supporters concentrated in a few states will usually have less influence than another group consisting of 3 million supporters spread out in a large number of states.

Interest groups also differ in the extent to which they preempt a policy area or share it with other groups. Doctors and the AMA have effectively preempted the health care policy area because they play such an important role in the delivery of health care. But in the transportation policy area, railroads must compete with interstate trucking and even air freight companies.

Groups also differ in their *resources*, which include money, volunteers, expertise, and reputation. Some groups can influence many centers of power—both houses of Congress, the White House, federal agencies, the courts, and state and local governments—while others cannot.

Cohesiveness

Usually, a mass membership organization is made up of three types of members: (1) a relatively small number of formal leaders who may hold full-time, paid positions or devote much time, effort, and money to the group's activities; (2) people intensely involved in the group who identify with the group's aims, attend meetings, faithfully pay dues, and do a lot of the legwork; and (3) people who are members in name only, do not participate actively, and cannot be depended on to vote in elections or otherwise act as the leadership wants.[20] In a typical large organization, for every top leader there might be a few hundred hard-core activists and thousands of essentially inactive members.

Another factor in group cohesiveness is its *organizational structure*. Some associations have a strong formal organization; others are local organizations that have joined together in a loose state or national federation in which they retain a measure of separate power and independence. Separation of powers may be found as well: The national assembly of an organization establishes, or at least ratifies, policy; an executive committee meets more frequently; a president or director is elected to head and speak for the group; and permanent paid officials form the organization's bureaucracy. Power may be further divided between the organization's main headquarters and its Washington office. An organization of this sort tends to be far less cohesive than a centralized, disciplined group such as some trade unions, trial lawyers, and realtors.

Leadership

Closely related to cohesion is the nature of the leadership. In a group that embraces many attitudes and interests, leaders may either weld the various elements together or sharpen their disunity. The leader of a national business association, for example, must tread cautiously between big business and small business, between exporters and importers, between chain stores and corner grocery stores, and between the producers and the sellers of competing products. The group leader is in the same position as a president or a member of Congress; he or she must know when to lead followers and when to follow them.

Techniques

Interest groups seeking to wield influence choose from a variety of political weapons and targets. They present their case to both houses of Congress, the White House staff, state and local governments, and federal agencies and departments. They also become involved in litigation. Other techniques include protest, election activities, establishing political parties, and lobbying.

PUBLICITY AND MASS MEDIA APPEALS Interest groups exploit the communications media—television, radio, newspapers, leaflets, signs, direct mail, and word of mouth—to influence voters during elections and to motivate constituents to contact their representatives between elections. Business enjoys a special advantage in this arena, and businesspeople have the money and staff to use propaganda machinery. As large-scale advertisers, they know how to deliver their message effectively or can find an advertising agency to do it for them. But organized labor is also effective in communicating with its membership through shop stewards, mail, and phone calls.

The NRA is a large, powerful interest group with considerable political clout, dedicated to fighting all gun control legislation and to electing candidates who oppose any form of gun control.

As people communicate more and more via e-mail, this technology will become an important means of political mobilization. Howard Dean effectively used e-mail in the 2004 primary campaign to turn out crowds in Iowa, New Hampshire, and other states.[21] He also did well in raising money via the Internet.[22] John Kerry and George W. Bush also had success raising campaign funds in this way and used the Internet in their voter mobilization efforts.[23] Candidates at all levels used e-mail for fund raising and to motivate supporters. E-mail will likely become part of political communication at the workplace as management communicates information to its workers about the candidates and ballot issues.

MASS MAILING One means of communication that has increased the reach and effectiveness of interest groups is computerized and targeted mass mailing.[24] Before computers, interest groups had to cull from telephone directories and other sources lists of people to contact, and managing these lists was time-consuming. As a result, some groups sent out mailings indiscriminately. Today the computer permits easy data storage and efficient management of mailing lists. Mass mailing is now used by all kinds of interest groups. Today's technology can produce personalized letters targeted to specific groups. Such targeted direct mail can also appeal to people who share a common concern, such as environmental groups.

INFLUENCE ON RULE MAKING Organized groups have ready access to the executive and regulatory agencies that write the rules implementing laws passed by Congress. Government agencies publish proposed regulations in the **Federal Register** and invite responses from all interested persons before the rules are finalized. The *Federal Register* is published every weekday. You can find it at the library or on the Internet at www.gpoaccess.gov. Well-staffed associations and corporations peruse the *Register,* ever alert for actions that will affect their interests. Lobbyists prepare written responses to the proposed rules, draft alternative rules, and appear at the hearings to make their case. These lobbyists seek to be on good terms with the staff of the agencies so that they can learn what rules are being considered long before they are released publicly and thus have input in the early stages. Administrative rules are defined over time through legal cases and agency modifications, so even if an interest group fails to get what it wants, it can fight the rules in court or press for a reinterpretation when the agency leadership changes hands.

Finally, an interest group can seek to modify rules it does not like by pressuring Congress to change the legal mandate for the agency or have the agency's budget

Federal Register
Official document, published every weekday, that lists the new and proposed regulations of executive departments and regulatory agencies.

Taylor clipped the taxpayers by abusing student loans.

Mike Taylor made a fortune in the hair care industry. He also made up his own rules for awarding student loans.

Michael Taylor, Beauty Corner, Denver, Colorado.

Abusing Student Loans

In a hair-raising scheme to ensure the success of his "Institute of Hair Design," Mike Taylor improperly gave out thousands of dollars in federal student loan funds. Mike Taylor's "Institute of Hair Design" profited from the misuse of money that was meant for educational purposes.[1]

Ability to Directly Issue Student Loans Revoked

In 1998, based on "repeat findings" of violations, the U.S. Department of Education revoked Mike Taylor's authority to directly disperse federal student loan monies.[2] In 1999, the U.S. Department of Education followed up on this action by assessing the Institute of Hair Design about $159,000 for the numerous violations uncovered by department investigators.[3]

With Mike Taylor, There's no telling who will get clipped.

The use of both conventional and electronic mail is an effective way of reaching a large number of people during political campaigns. The Montana Democratic Party sent this ad to potential voters informing them of Republican candidate Mike Taylor's misuse of student loan money several years prior when he operated a beauty school in another state. The ad prompted Taylor to withdraw from the race.

reduced, making enforcement of existing rules difficult. In short, interest groups and lobbyists never really quit fighting for their point of view.

LITIGATION   When groups find the political channels closed to them, they may turn to the courts.[25] The Legal Defense and Education Fund of the National Association for the Advancement of Colored People (NAACP), for example, initiated and won numerous court cases in its efforts to end racial segregation and to protect the right to vote for African Americans. Urban interests and environmental groups, feeling underrepresented in state and national legislatures, turned to the courts to influence the political agenda.[26] Women's groups, such as the National Organization for Women and the American Civil Liberties Union's Women's Rights Project, also used the courts to pursue their objectives.[27] Conservative religious groups like the Washington Legal Foundation and groups identified with the Religious Right have also actively used litigation as a strategy to pursue their objectives.[28]

In addition to initiating lawsuits, associations can gain a forum for their views in the courts by filing ***amicus curiae briefs*** (literally, "friend of the court" briefs) in cases in which they are not direct parties. Despite the general impression that associations achieve great success in the courts, groups are no more likely than individuals to win their cases at the district court level.[29]

PROTEST Movements arise around particular issues but often lack widespread support. To generate interest and support for their cause, movements often use protest demonstrations. An example of a movement that used protest demonstrations to call attention to its

***amicus curiae* brief**
Literally, a "friend of the court" brief, filed by an individual or organization to present arguments in addition to those presented by the immediate parties to a case.

concerns is the diverse set of interest groups that opposed the labor, environmental, and trade practices fostered by the World Trade Organization (WTO). The 1999 protest against a WTO meeting in Seattle turned into a riot.[30] Peaceful groups like Public Citizen and the AFL-CIO were brushed aside by more violent protesters, such as the Ruckus Society and the Direct Action Network. The Seattle police, unable to contain the situation and fearful that they would be unable to protect delegates from 135 countries, resorted to riot control tactics, including tear gas, rubber bullets, and pepper spray. They also arrested more than 400 protesters.[31] Newspapers and television broadcasts around the world showed the confrontations, arrests, and destruction.

The protesters succeeded in forcing the topic of globalization and the negative consequences of increased international trade onto the political agenda. Other movements or groups that have used protest include the civil rights movement, antiwar groups, and environmental groups.[32]

ELECTION ACTIVITIES Although nearly all large organizations say they are nonpolitical, almost all are politically involved in some way. What they usually mean when they say they are nonpolitical is that they are *nonpartisan*. A distinguishing feature of organized interest groups is that they often try to work through *both* parties. Another regularity is that they want to be friendly with the winners, which often means that they contribute to incumbents. But as competition for control of both chambers of Congress has intensified and with presidential contests also up for grabs, interest groups have generally invested more in one party or the other.

Labor usually favors Democrats. The AFL-CIO has supported every Democratic candidate for president since the New Deal, although the Teamsters Union has often endorsed Republicans. In 2004, the Teamsters joined most other unions in backing John Kerry. Business groups occasionally endorse Democratic incumbents but generally favor Republicans. Some organizations are prevented from taking a firm position because of the differing views of their members. A local retailers' group, for example, might be composed equally of Republicans and Democrats, and many of its members might refuse to openly support a candidate for fear of losing business.

Ideological groups target certain candidates, seeking to change a candidate's positions or, failing that, to influence voters to vote against that candidate. Americans for Democratic Action and the American Conservative Union publish ratings of members of Congress's voting records on liberal and conservative issues; so do the U.S. Chamber of Commerce, the AFL-CIO, and other groups.

How effective is electioneering by interest groups? In general, mass membership organizations fail to mobilize their full membership in elections. Although when a group's interests are directly attacked, as was the case with the anti-union "paycheck protection" ballot initiatives in 1998 and 2000, these groups can effectively mobilize their membership.[33] More typically, there are too many cross-pressures operating in the pluralistic politics of the United States for any one group to assume a commanding role. Some groups reach their maximum influence only by allying themselves closely with one of the two major parties. They may place their members on local, state, and national party committees and help send them to party conventions as delegates, but such alliances mean losing some independence.

Numerous groups sought to mobilize their membership in the 2004 presidential election. Groups created Web sites for members to obtain information on their organization's view of candidates and provided voter registration materials and absentee ballot request forms. They also solicited contributions to help fund these efforts. One group that was especially active in this effort was the Business and Industry Political Action Committee (BIPAC).[34] Organized labor, long perceived to be the leader in voter mobilization, was also especially active in 2004, as was the National Rifle Association. The Republican party and allied groups, having learned from the techniques used by labor unions, mounted a successful voter mobilization effort in 2004.

FORMING A POLITICAL PARTY Another interest group strategy is to form a political party. These parties are organized less with the intent to win elections than to publicize a cause. The Free Soil party was formed in the mid-1840s to work against the spread of slavery into the territories, and the Prohibition party was organized two decades later to ban the sale of liquor. Farmers have formed a variety of such parties. More often, however, interest groups prefer to work through existing parties.

Today, environmental groups and voters for whom the environment is a central issue must choose between supporting the Green party, which has yet to elect a person to federal office, an independent candidate like Ralph Nader in 2004, or one of the two major parties. Sometimes minor party candidates can spoil the chances of a major party candidate. In a New Mexico congressional special election in 1997, the Green party candidate won 17 percent of the vote, taking some votes from the Democrat and thereby helping elect a Republican to what had been a Democratic seat. In the 1998 election, environmental groups campaigned aggressively for the Democrat, who obtained 53 percent of the vote, while all minor parties combined got only 4 percent.[35] In South Dakota's 2002 Senate race between Tim Johnson (D) and John Thune (R), the Libertarian candidate got more than three thousand votes. Johnson defeated Thune by just over 500 votes. In the 2000

PEOPLE & POLITICS *Making a Difference* ★ ★ ★

STEPHEN MOORE, CLUB FOR GROWTH

An interest group that first appeared on the scene in the late 1990s and became visible in 2002 in some competitive contests is the Club for Growth. One of the three cofounders of Club for Growth is Stephen Moore. Known for his candor, Moore described contributing to candidates and parties as "spitting into an ocean of money," citing contributing to his Club as a much more effective way to influence policy and "get rid of Republicans in Name Only (RINOs)."* Moore is a graduate of the University of Illinois with a master's degree in economics from George Mason University. Prior to his activity at Club for Growth he directed fiscal policy studies at the Cato Institute and worked on the Joint Economic Committee under House Republican Whip Dick Armey. He was drawn into politics by his mentor and professor, Julian Simon. Moore sees the Club as more politically involved than the "think tanks," and has patterned the Club after EMILY's List, a successful pro-Choice Democratic group that helps connect donors and candidates."†

Congressional Quarterly Today said of Moore's group, "When the supply-siders at the Club for Growth decide to back a candidate who favors the economic policies of the Reagan era, donations don't just trickle down, they gush."‡ In 2004, Club for Growth invested $2 million in the Pennsylvania U.S. Senate primary election against long-term Republican incumbent Arlen Specter and for Pat Toomey, his opponent. The group also ran ads attacking Howard Dean in the weeks before the Iowa caucuses, describing Dean's campaign as a "tax hiking, government expanding, latte drinking, sushi eating, Volvo driving, *New York Times* reading, body piercing, Hollywood loving, left wing freak show."§ The Club for Growth also invests in general elections, sometimes channeling hundreds of thousands of dollars into U.S. House or U.S. Senate races."‖

The Club for Growth seeks to pursue the "vision of limited government and lower taxes," as articulated by Ronald Reagan. The Club's home page has a photo of Reagan. Candidates endorsed by the Club support this vision and have a strong chance for electoral success. The Club invests in only a few contests where they believe they can make a difference. They do this by selecting candidates and then contacting donors who make the checks out directly to the candidate, then route the checks through the Club to enhance the Club's reputation with the candidate.¶ Electoral involvement is then linked to lobbying. Speaking of the lobbying power of the Club for Growth, Stephen Moore said, "I think we have 30 or 40 members [of Congress] who are very grateful for the help we've given them, and we've got another 30 or 40 members of Congress who think that we're a very dangerous organization that could jeopardize their political careers."**

*Stephen Moore, phone interview by David Magleby, July 21, 2004.
†Ibid.
‡Jonathan Allen, "Club for Growth Becoming a Bigger Player in Republican-on-Republican Primary Races," *Congressional Quarterly Today*, February 6, 2003.
§*National Journal Online* at nationaljournal.com/members/adspotlight/2004/01/0108cfg1.htm.
‖See Kelly Patterson, "When Redistricting Means Never Having to Say You're Sorry: Utah's Second District," David Magleby and J. Quin Monson, eds., *The Last Hurrah* (Brookings Institution Press, 2004), pp. 252–253.
¶www.clubforgrowth.org/about.php?from=about.
**www.clubforgrowth.org/what.php.

presidential election, most environmental groups supported Al Gore over Green party nominee Ralph Nader. Many Democrats, however, blame Nader for diverting votes from Gore in such battlegrounds as Florida and New Hampshire, thereby costing him the election. Democrats again worried that Nader would cost them the White House in 2004 but explicit appeals from the party and from interest groups may have helped reduce Nader's impact. Early in the campaign, Nader described Democrat John Kerry as very presidential but he later said that a vote for Kerry is "a vote for war—an endless, Vietnam-type quagmire" (see Joshua Weinstein, "Angry Ralph Nader: Scorn, Anger, and Resolve Sustain Nader," *Portland Press Herald,* October 6, 2004).

COOPERATIVE LOBBYING   Like-minded groups often join together as cooperative groups. In 1987, the Leadership Conference on Civil Rights and People for the American Way brought together many groups in the battle to defeat the nomination of outspoken federal judge Robert Bork to the U.S. Supreme Court.[36] Different types of environmentalists work together, as do consumer and ideological groups on the right and on the left. Women continue to be represented by a large variety of groups that reflect diverse interests, but the larger the coalition, the greater the chance that members may divide over such issues as abortion. Another example of a cooperative group is the Business Roundtable (BRT), an association of chief executive officers of the 200 largest U.S. corporations. The BRT, which has been in existence for more than 30 years, promotes policies that help large businesses, such as free trade and less government regulation of business.

Personal contact with and access to decision makers continue to be key elements of lobbying today, as they were at the time of President Grant's administration.

THE INFLUENCE OF LOBBYISTS

The terms "lobbying" and "lobbyist" were not generally used until around the middle of the nineteenth century in the United States. The root in these words refers to the lobby or hallway outside House and Senate chambers in the U.S. Capitol. It also refers to those who hung around the lobby of the old Willard Hotel when presidents dined. The noun "lobby" has been turned into a verb in this political context. Thus "to lobby" is to seek to influence legislators and government officials, and we call this **lobbying** even if there is no lobby in sight.

Despite their negative public image, lobbyists perform useful functions for government. They provide information for the decision makers of all three branches of government, they help educate and mobilize public opinion, they help prepare legislation and testify before legislative hearings, and they contribute a large share of the costs of campaigns. Yet many people are concerned that lobbyists have too much influence on government and add to legislative gridlock by being able to stop action on pressing problems.

Who Are the Lobbyists?

The typical image is of powerful, hard-nosed lobbyists who skillfully employ a combination of knowledge, persuasiveness, personal influence, charm, and money to influence legislators and bureaucrats. **Lobbyists** are the employees of associations who try to influence policy decisions and positions in the executive and especially in the legislative branches of our government. They are experienced in the ways of government, often having been public servants before going to work for an organized interest group, association, or corporation. They might start as staff in Congress, perhaps on a congressional committee. Later, when their party wins the White House, they gain an administration post, often in the same policy area as their congressional committee work. After a few years in the administration, they are ready to make the move to lobbying, either by going to work for one of the interests they dealt with while in the government or by obtaining a position with a lobbying firm.

Moving from a government job to one with an interest group is quite common, a practice called the **revolving door**. Despite the fact that it is illegal for former national government employees to directly lobby the agency from which they came, their contacts made during government service are helpful to interest groups. Many former members of Congress make use of their congressional experience as full-time lobbyists.

lobbying
Engaging in activities aimed at influencing public officials, especially legislators, and the policies they enact.

lobbyist
A person who is employed by and acts for an organized interest group or corporation to try to influence policy decisions and positions in the executive and legislative branches.

revolving door
Employment cycle in which individuals who work for governmental agencies regulating interests eventually end up working for interest groups or businesses with the same policy concern.

The revolving-door tendency between government and interest groups produces networks of people who care about certain issues. These networks have been called **iron triangles**, consisting of mutually dependent relationships among interest groups, congressional committees and subcommittees, and the government agencies that share a common policy concern. Sometimes these relationships become so strong and mutually beneficial that the iron triangle becomes very powerful, a sort of subgovernment. A former senior staff person from a House or Senate agriculture committee now working for an agricultural corporation as a lobbyist who has ongoing friendships with his former staff colleagues, including some who now work at the Department of Agriculture, is an example of how personal relationships work within iron triangles. Powerful iron triangles may serve to enhance the policy preferences of narrow interests and not those of the broader public interest.

Legal and political skills, along with specialized knowledge, have become so crucial in executive and legislative policy making as to become a form of power in themselves. Elected representatives increasingly depend on their staffs for guidance, and these issue specialists know more about "Section 504" or "Title IX" or "the 2002 amendments"—and who wrote them and why—than most political and administrative leaders, who are usually generalists. It is in this gray area of policy making that many interest groups and lobbyists play a vital role, as people move freely from congressional or agency staff to association staff and perhaps back again. These groups of experts are sometimes called *issue networks* and are discussed in greater detail in Chapter 18, Economic and Regulatory Policy. Like iron triangles, issue networks are made up of people with similar policy concerns; however, they differ in two important ways. First, issue networks can include more players, such as the media, than iron triangles. Second, because members of issue networks are less dependent on one another than members of iron triangles are, organization is more amorphous and less structured.[37]

What Do Lobbyists Do?

Thousands of lobbyists are active in Washington, but few are as glamorous or as unscrupulous as the media suggest, nor are they necessarily influential. One limit on their power is the competition among interest groups. Rarely does any one group have a policy area all to itself. For example, transportation policy involves airplanes, trucks, cars, railroads, consumers, suppliers, state and local governments—the list goes on and on.

To members of Congress, the single most important thing lobbyists provide is money for their next reelection campaign. "Reelection underlies everything else," writes political scientist David Mayhew.[38] Money from interest groups has become instrumental in this driving need among incumbents. Interest groups also provide volunteers for campaign activity. In addition, their failure to support the opposition can enhance an incumbent's chances of being reelected.

Some people defend lobbyists as a kind of "third house" of Congress. Whereas the Senate and House are set up on a geographical basis, lobbyists represent people on the basis of interests and money. Small but important groups can sometimes get representation in the "third house" when they cannot get it in the other two. In a nation of vast and important interests, this kind of functional representation, if it is not abused, can be a useful supplement to geographical representation.

Beyond their central role in campaigns and elections, interest groups provide another essential commodity to legislators: information of two important types, political and substantive. The *political information* provided by lobbyists includes such matters as who supports or opposes legislation and how strongly they feel.[39] *Substantive information,* such as the impact of proposed laws, might not be available from any other source. Lobbyists often provide technical assistance on the drafting of bills and amendments, identify persons to testify at legislative hearings, and formulate questions to ask of administration officials at oversight hearings.

The battle over providing a prescription drug benefit for senior citizens illustrates how lobbyists influence the electoral and legislative process. The pharmaceutical industry invested over $10 million in the 2000 election and a similar amount in 2002 in limited and disclosed contributions to candidates and parties,[40] and another $15 to $20

iron triangle
A mutually dependent relationship among interest groups, congressional committees and subcommittees, and government agencies that share a common policy concern.

million in unlimited contributions to the parties in both of these elections.[41] In addition, an estimated $65 million was spent by "Citizens for Better Medicare" in 2000 on issue ads targeted to battleground states. In 2002 "The United Seniors Association" spent an estimated $9 to $13 million on issue ads in competitive contests.[42] Lobbying was also part of the pharmaceutical industry strategy. In 2002 they spent an unprecedented $94 million on lobbying activities, hiring almost 700 lobbyists from 138 different firms."[43] Congress enacted a prescription drug benefit for seniors that had the support of the pharmaceutical industry and the largest seniors organization, the AARP. The new benefit was criticized by some as being too costly,[44] and by others as not being comprehensive enough.[45] The intense electioneering and lobbying helped define the issue and set the stage for the legislation that was enacted.

MONEY AND POLITICS

As the battle over prescription drug benefits for seniors illustrates, interest groups have several ways they can seek to influence election outcomes and policy outcomes. They can seek to mobilize voters, especially the members of the group and their families and friends. They can loan staff to candidate campaigns. They can contribute money to candidates and parties through committees they form, which are called **political action committees (PACs)**, or they can urge their members and friends to contribute directly to candidates or parties or send their checks to the group and have them delivered in a bundle, a process called **bundling**. They can raise and spend money independently through what are called **independent expenditures**. When interest groups or individuals give money to a candidate or party committee, those contributions are limited and must be disclosed to the Federal Election Commission; they are sometimes referred to as **hard money**.

Until the 2004 election cycle individuals and groups could give unlimited amounts of money to party committees. This so-called **soft money** was for many years spent only on generic party activity like get-out-the-vote drives or broad party appeals. Corporations and unions, long banned from giving to candidates and parties from their general funds for election-specific purposes, were permitted to give soft money, and they did so in large amounts. Starting in the 1996 election cycle, the party committees used this money for specific candidate attack or promotion, a topic we will explore more later. By the 2000 and 2002 election cycles, soft money had climbed to around $500 million. Soft money was banned for the 2004 election cycle.

In 1996, interest groups found another way to circumvent disclosure and contribuiton limits through **issue advocacy**. Exploiting a definition in the court case defining the kinds of communication regulated by the Federal Election Campaign Act of 1971 (FECA) as those that used words like "vote for" or "vote against," groups simply made election ads without those words and then spent millions attacking or promoting particular candidates. Corporations and unions could and did spend millions of their general funds, which otherwise would have been banned from use in elections on issue ads in 1996–2002.

The Bipartisan Campaign Reform Act of 2002 (BCRA) redefines electioneering communications to include ads aimed at a particular population (state or district) that mention a candidate by name, show the image or likeness of a candidate, or mention the election within sixty days before a general election or thirty days before a primary election. BCRA bans corporations and unions from giving general funds to parties as soft money and from using those funds to buy electioneering ads during the period before a primary and general election, and requires more disclosure of this activity. BCRA does not regulate what any of these groups may do on the phone, through the mail, or in person.

Helping elect candidates helps create a relationship between the interest group and the elected official that then is exploited in the policy process. At a minimum, substantial involvement in the election process helps provide access to policy makers.[46] Interest groups retain political and policy professionals who provide information to policy makers, individuals that are generally called *lobbyists*. We begin our exploration of the role of money and politics by examining PACs, a primary means for groups to help elect and reelect public officials.

political action committee (PAC)
The political arm of an interest group that is legally entitled to raise funds on a voluntary basis from members, stockholders, or employees in order to contribute funds to favored candidates or political parties.

bundling
A tactic of political action committees whereby they collect contributions from like-minded individuals (each limited to $2,000) and present them to a candidate or political party as a "bundle," thus increasing their influence.

independent expenditures
The Supreme Court has ruled that individuals, groups, and parties can spend unlimited amounts in campaigns for or against candidates as long as they operate independently from the candidates. When an individual, group, or party does so, they are making an independent expenditure.

hard money
Political contributions given to a party, candidate, or interest group that are limited in amount and fully disclosed. Raising such limited funds is harder than raising unlimited funds, hence the term "hard money."

soft money
Money raised in unlimited amounts by political parties for party-building purposes. Now largely illegal except for limited contributions to state and local parties for voter registration and get-out-the-vote efforts.

issue advocacy
Unlimited and undisclosed spending by an individual or group on communications that do not use words like "vote for" or "vote against," although much of this activity is actually about electing or defeating candidates.

The Growth of PACs

A PAC is the political arm of an interest group that is legally entitled to raise funds on a voluntary basis from members, stockholders, or employees in order to contribute funds to favored candidates or political parties. PACs link two vital techniques of influence—giving money and other political aid to politicians and persuading officeholders to act or vote "the right way" on issues. Thus PACs are the means by which interest groups seek to influence which legislators are elected and what they do once they take office.[47] PACs can be categorized according to the type of interest they represent: corporations, trade and health organizations, labor unions, ideological organizations, and so on.

Surprisingly, considering the explosion of PACs that has occurred mainly in the business world, it was organized labor that invented this device. In the 1930s, John L. Lewis, president of the United Mine Workers, set up the Non-Partisan Political League as the political arm of the newly formed Congress of Industrial Organizations. When the CIO merged with the American Federation of Labor, the new labor group established the Committee on Political Education (COPE), whose activities we have already described. This unit came to be the model for most political action committees: "From the outset, national, state, and local units of COPE have not only raised and distributed funds, but have also served as the mechanism for organized and widespread union activity in the electoral process, for example, in voter registration, political education, and get-out-the-vote drives."[48] Some years later, manufacturers formed the Business and Industry Political Action Committee, but the most active business PAC is the one affiliated with the U.S. Chamber of Commerce.[49]

The 1970s brought a near revolution in the role and influence of PACs—ironically, as the result of reforms intended to reduce the influence of money in elections. The number of PACs increased dramatically, from about 150 to nearly 4,000 today.[50] Corporations and trade associations contributed most to this growth; today their PACs constitute the majority of all PACs. Labor PACs, by contrast, increased only slightly in number, representing less than 10 percent of all PACs.[51] But the increase in the number of PACs is less important than the intensity of recent PAC participation in elections and in lobbying.

The BCRA campaign finance reforms that took effect in the 2004 election cycle increased the role of PACs in funding candidates and parties. Because PAC contributions are limited, they were not as attractive a means to invest in elections for those who wanted to direct a lot of money to a particular race, which groups could do with soft money before BCRA. With that option closed in 2004, interest groups made PAC fundraising and contributions a higher priority. Members of Congress also increased their efforts to raise PAC dollars, including an expanded emphasis on leadership PACs. A Leadership PAC is a PAC a member of Congress can form to raise money from individuals or other PACs, which in turn can make contributions to others. Leadership PACs were once largely a tool used by congressional leaders or those aspiring to be leaders. In 2003–2004 almost a third of all lawmakers on the hill had formed a leadership PAC.[52] Because there were again so few competitive congressional contests in 2004, safe-seat incumbents with leadership PACs were pressed by their party leaders to contribute to their party candidates in the competitive contests. Member-to-member giving has become a more important part of campaign finance in competitive races as a result of BCRA.

How PACs Invest Their Money

PACs take part in the entire election process, but their main influence lies in their capacity to contribute money to candidates. Candidates today need a lot of money to wage their campaigns. It is no longer uncommon for House candidates to spend more than $1 million and for many senators and would-be senators to spend several times that amount.[53] And as PACs contribute more, their influence grows. What counts is not only the amounts they give but also to whom they give. PACs give to the most influential incumbents, to committee chairs, to party leaders and whips, and to the Speaker. PACs give not only to the majority party but also to key incumbents in the minority party as well, because they understand that today's minority could be tomorrow's majority.

PACs, like individuals, are limited by law in the amount of money they can contribute to any single candidate in an election cycle. The Federal Election Campaign Act of 1971 (FECA) as amended in 2002 limits PACs to $5,000 per election or $10,000 per election cycle (primary and general elections). Individuals have a limit of $4,000 per candidate per election cycle. PACs have found some creative ways around this limit. They can host fundraisers attended by other PACs to boost their reputation with the candidate, or they can collect money from several persons and give it to the candidate as a bundle. Through bundling, PACs and interested individuals can increase their clout with elected officials. Two of the most important groups doing bundling in 2003–2004 were EMILY's List and Club for Growth. EMILY's List, which stands for "Early Money Is Like Yeast," raises money from individuals committed to electing pro-choice, Democratic women. It identifies candidates that fit its criteria and then solicits checks for them at an early stage in the campaign. Club for Growth, a conservative group, sees itself as applying the same bundling techniques as EMILY's List but for pro-growth and anti-tax candidates (see the box on Stephen Moore on page 146).

Soft Money and Issue Advocacy

The 1996 election was a watershed in the involvement of interest groups and individuals in financing campaigns. That year the Clinton/Gore campaign on the advice of a consultant began to use party soft money for candidate-specific electioneering. Previously soft money had been reserved for generic ads or party-building activities like building voter lists, staffing the party, and so forth. Corporations and unions were allowed to give general funds as well as PAC funds to the party soft money accounts, and there were no contribution limits on soft money. Some of the largest PAC soft money contributors were labor unions, trial lawyers, corporations, and some individuals.

Party committees had limits on how much hard money they could spend on a particular race, but there were no such limits on soft money. With soft money as an option for the party committees, they quickly started spending it in competitive settings like presidential battleground states or highly contested House or Senate contests. In some of these races, they would expend millions of dollars of soft money. We discuss the use of soft money by the political parties in greater detail in Chapter 7.

The 1996 election was a watershed in a second respect as well. The AFL-CIO decided to test the limits of the definition of what fell under the regulation of the FECA, spending an estimated $35 million against most Republican candidates.[54] The union ads avoided words such as "vote for," "elect," "support," "cast your ballot for," "Smith for Congress," "vote against," "defeat," or "reject"—the definition for what constituted a communication subject to FECA regulation according to a footnote in the *Buckley* v. *Valeo* decision.[55] Other interest groups and their consultants discovered that they also could effectively communicate an electioneering message without using words like "vote for" or "vote against." Ads that avoided these words but that were clearly about electing or defeating particular candidates became a staple in competitive elections after 1996. Groups like the pharmaceutical industry, truckers, unions, and supporters of term limits would direct hundreds of thousands of dollars or more to particular contests for Congress or presidential battleground states. These groups mounted parallel campaigns in such locales, running ads on radio and television and investing heavily in phone calls, mail, and get-out-the-vote efforts.[56] In these competitive races the noncandidate campaign generally rivaled the candidate campaign in spending.[57] For example, in one hotly contested House race in 2000, the California 27th District race, candidates spent over $11.5 million[58] while the parties through soft money and interest groups through issue advocacy spent $7.5 million.[59]

Groups especially involved in issue advocacy included groups like the AFL-CIO, Citizens for Better Medicare, National Right to Work, United Seniors Association, Americans for Job Security, U.S. Chamber of Commerce, and Planned Parenthood. The heavy investment of interest groups in these unlimited electioneering efforts became controversial in the late 1990s and through the 2002 election cycle and helped motivate passage of BCRA.

BCRA and Interest Group Electioneering

In addition to restoring the ban on corporations and unions using their general funds for election ads through soft money or issue advocacy, BCRA attempted to follow court decisions with respect to ideological interest groups. It excludes from regulation some

SHOULD CORPORATIONS AND UNIONS BE UNLIMITED IN FUNDING PARTIES AND IN RUNNING ISSUE ADS?

Does limiting the ability of corporations or unions to use their general or "treasury" funds for election-related expenditures violate the constitutional guarantee of freedom of speech? Corporations and unions, like other groups, are free to form political action committees to make contributions to candidates and parties. What was at dispute was whether they could take their profits or general funds and spend those on electing or defeating candidates or in support of party efforts. For more than a century, federal law had banned unions and corporations from spending general or treasury funds on electoral politics. Was the Supreme Court correct in upholding that precedent?

interest groups that were not established by a business or labor union, or that are funded by individuals whose purpose is to "promote political ideas and cannot engage in business activities."[60] In 2004 there were four groups that had this special status and therefore could spend unlimited amounts of money raised from individuals on competitive races. These groups were NARAL Pro-Choice America, Planned Parenthood, League of Conservation Voters, and Defenders of Wildlife. While all of these groups were active in 2004, their legal status did not have a significant impact because other groups were allowed to raise and spend unlimited individual contributions. Interest groups that had previously taken union or corporate money could not claim this status.

Although BCRA made new rules restricting how funds could be spent for advertising, it left individuals and groups free to make unlimited contributions to groups that engaged in efforts to elect or defeat candidates through the mail, on the phone, or in person. These groups are called **527 groups**, a name that is derived from the section of the Internal Revenue Code that refers to political committees, not all of which have election activity as their primary purpose. The most notable example of one of these "527" groups is America Coming Together (ACT), founded by former political director of the AFL-CIO Steve Rosenthal and former president of EMILY's List Ellen Malcolm. One of the most visible donors to this group was financier George Soros. ACT launched reportedly the largest voter mobilization project in American history,[61] utilizing voter lists and door-to-door canvassing to target voters for mobilization on election day. Their stated purpose was to "defeat George W. Bush and elect Democrats in federal, state, and local elections in 2004."[62] Another group, also partially funded by George Soros, The Media Fund, ran broadcast ads before the time frame covered by BCRA (sixty days before a general election) and then used hard money to run ads closer to the election. This group was headed by Harold Ickes, who had been assistant to the president for political affairs and deputy chief of staff to President Clinton.

During the 2004 election cycle, 527 groups were much more active on the liberal or Democratic side than on the conservative or Republican. There are several reasons for this. Democratic party activists and allied interest groups understood that the BCRA ban on soft money would leave the party and its presidential candidate at a disadvantage against the fundraising prowess of President Bush and the Republican party. They thus started early and invested heavily in their 527 groups. Republicans and conservatives were less inclined to put money behind their Section 527 groups, in part because they controlled the government and had experienced so much success in fundraising in the past. There was also real doubt on the Republican side that BCRA or the new 527 groups would survive the court challenge and Federal Election Commission review process. When both occurred, they had lost valuable time in organizing and funding their 527 organizations.

Interest groups also utilized other sections of the tax code to involve themselves in the election. Section 501 of the tax code permits groups to organize and, in the case of Section 501-C-3, donations to the group are tax deductible. Because of their tax deductible status, 501-C-3 groups avoid candidate endorsements but can be involved in voter registration and other nonpartisan activity. For groups whose contributions are not tax deductible there is wider license in what they can do in elections. In 2004 several groups were involved in the election through their 501-C-4 and 501-C-6 groups. Examples of groups active in this way and of what they did in 2004 include, but are not limited to, the National Rifle Association sending direct mail to their members, the U.S. Chamber of Commerce creating a Web site for voteforbusiness.com, and the AFL-CIO spending money on internal communications. There were examples of 501-C groups supporting both parties, but unlike the 527 groups, Republicans found more allies in the 501-C organizations.[63]

Republican-allied 527 groups were slower to start campaigning but they were visible and important later in the campaign. One group, the Swift Boat Veterans for Truth, discussed earlier in this chapter, took Kerry "off message." Another pro-Bush group, Progress for America, ran an ad, which was shown extensively in the final days of the campaign, focused on how President Bush helped the daughter of a person killed in the

527 group
A political group organized under section 527 of the IRS Code that may accept and spend unlimited amounts of money on election activities so long as they are not spent on broadcast ads run in the last 30 days before a primary or 60 days before a general election where a clearly identified candidate is referred to and a relevant electorate is targeted. 527 groups were important to the 2000 and 2004 elections.

attacks of September 11, 2001. The anti-Bush 527 organizations spent more money and focused their efforts on voter mobilization and on ads in the period between March and August when Bush had campaign money and Kerry did not.

The heavy reliance of both parties on 527 organizations and wealthy individual 527 donors raised questions about undue influence over elections from these individuals and what they expected in return if their side won the election. Regulation of 527 organizations is a topic President Bush and Senators John McCain and Russ Feingold pledged to pursue after the election.

THE EFFECTIVENESS OF INTEREST GROUP ACTIVITY IN ELECTIONS

The strong tendency of PACs to give more money to incumbents has meant that challengers face real difficulties in getting their campaigns funded. Challengers have to rely more on individual contributors. Even with the larger individual contribution limits allowed in 2004, most challengers still were largely underfunded compared to their incumbent opponents.

How much does interest group money influence election outcomes, legislation, and representation? Former U.S. Senator Alan Simpson (R-WY) testified in the court case to decide the constitutionality of BCRA that "too often, members' first thought is not what is right or what they believe, but how it will affect fundraising. Who, after all, can seriously contend that a $100,000 donation does not alter the way one thinks about—and quite possibly votes on—an issue?"[64] Another former U.S. Senator, Warren Rudman, said in the same court case that "you can't swim in the ocean without getting wet; you can't be part of this system without getting dirty."[65] In this area, as in others, money obviously talks. But it is easy to exaggerate that influence. Although a candidate may receive a great amount of interest group money, only a fraction of that total comes from any single interest. In addition, it is debatable how much campaign contributions affect election outcomes and uncertain that winning candidates will be willing and able to "remember" their financial angels or that the money in the end produces a real payoff in legislation.

Much depends, however, on the context in which money is given and received. Many campaigns—especially state and local campaigns—are small-scale undertakings in which a big contribution makes a difference. Amid all the murk of campaigning, a candidate may feel grateful for so tangible and convertible a contribution as money. Studies demonstrate a significant relationship between the frequency of lobbying contacts and favorable treatment in the Ways and Means and House Agriculture committees. Campaign contributions were found to predict lobbying patterns.[66]

One result of the recent campaign finance reforms was a surge in 2004 of interest groups communicating with voters via the mail and on the telephone. By closing down party soft money and limiting issue advocacy in television and radio ads in the weeks leading up to an election, the most recent reform makes issue advocacy via mail and telephone more attractive to individuals and groups. Examples of groups with substantially enlarged issue advocacy efforts in 2004 included the U.S. Chamber of Congress, NARAL Pro-Choice America, the National Rifle Association, and the Sierra Club. In selected

Campaign fund-raisers such as this one often charge donors $1,000 a plate or more for the privilege of meeting the candidates and mingling with influential policy makers.

Republican primaries, the NRA did issue advocacy with a higher success rate. In the 2004 general election, the most active new group was America Coming Together, also known as ACT, who spent over $55 million in 2003 and 2004. ACT spent most of their resources on a massive get-out-the-vote campaign in all key states.

CURING THE MISCHIEFS OF FACTION— TWO CENTURIES LATER

If James Madison were to return today, he would not be surprised by the existence of interest groups, nor would he be surprised by their variety. He might be surprised, however, by the varied weapons of group influence, the deep involvement of interest groups in the electoral process, and the vast number of lobbyists in Washington and the state capitals. And doubtless Madison, were he alive today, would still be concerned about the power of faction, especially its tendency toward instability and injustice.

One of the main arguments against factions is that people are not represented equally. For example, fewer interest groups represent young or low-income people than represent corporations. Further, some groups are better organized and better financed, allowing them a decided advantage over more general groups. Another problem with factions is that the existence of a multiplicity of interests often leads to incoherent policies, inefficiency, and delay as lawmakers try to appease conflicting interests. In addition, the propensity of interest groups to support incumbents in elections increases their advantage, which is often seen as undesirable. Finally, the ability of interest groups to supply needed and accurate information to government officials increases their power. Providing inaccurate information spells trouble for interest groups.

Concern about the evils of interest groups has been a recurrent theme throughout U.S. history. President Ronald Reagan in his Farewell Address warned of the power of "special interests,"[67] and President Dwight Eisenhower used his Farewell Address to warn against the "military–industrial complex."

Single-issue interest groups organized for or against particular policies—abortion, handgun control, tobacco subsidies, animal rights—have aroused much concern in recent years. "It is said that citizen groups organizing in ever greater numbers to push single issues ruin the careers of otherwise fine politicians who disagree with them on one emotional issue, paralyze the traditional process of governmental compromise, and ignore the common good in their selfish insistence on getting their own way."[68] But which single issues reflect narrow interests? Women's rights—even a specific issue such as sexual harassment—are hardly "narrow," women's rights leaders contend, because they would help over half the population. Peace groups, too, claim that they represent the whole population, as do those who support prayer in schools. These issues may seem quite different from those related to subsidies to dairy farmers, for example.

What—if anything—should be done about factions? For decades, Americans have tried to find ways to keep interest groups in check. They have agreed with James Madison that the "remedy" of outlawing factions would be worse than the disease. It would be absurd to abolish liberty simply because it nourished faction. And the existence and activity of interest groups and lobbies are solidly protected by the Constitution. But by safeguarding the value of liberty, have Americans allowed interest groups to threaten equality, the second great value in our national heritage? The question remains: How can interest groups be regulated in a way that does not threaten our constitutional liberties?

Federal and State Regulation

Americans have generally responded to this question by seeking to regulate lobbying in general and political money in particular. Concern over the use of money—especially corporate funds—to influence politicians goes back well over a century, to the Crédit Mobilier scandals during the administration of Ulysses S. Grant, when members of Congress promoted the Crédit Mobilier construction company in exchange for the right to buy shares of the company's stock below market value, on which they made huge profits.

In the "progressive" era during the first two decades of the twentieth century, Congress legislated against corporate contributions in federal elections and required disclosure of the use of the money.

In 1921, Warren G. Harding's administration allowed private companies to secretly lease naval oil reserve lands. In response to this event, known as the Teapot Dome scandal, Congress passed the Federal Corrupt Practices Act. It required disclosure reports, both before and after elections, of receipts and expenditures by Senate and House candidates and by political committees that sought to influence federal elections in more than one state. Note that these were *federal* laws applying to *federal* elections; regulation of state lobbying and elections was left to the states.

Federal legislation, including the 1925 Federal Corrupt Practices Act and the 1946 Federal Regulation of Lobbying Act, was not very effective. It was, in fact, largely unenforced. Many candidates filed incomplete reports or none at all. The reform mood of the 1960s brought basic changes. The upshot was the Federal Election Campaign Act of 1971 (FECA), which supplanted the earlier legislation.

FECA, which was amended three times, established reporting or disclosure requirements for all candidates for the U.S. House of Representatives, the Senate, and the presidency, as well as their political parties and campaign committees. It also required disclosure of the amounts spent to influence federal elections by others, including individuals and political action committees. The act established partial public financing for presidential candidates, financed by a voluntary checkoff on federal income tax forms. If candidates opted not to take the partial public funds they had no spending limitations; those who accepted the funds in the primaries had state-by-state spending limits for the primary elections. Candidates could opt out of the partial public funding for the primaries but still accept public funding and spending limits in the general election. This is what George W. Bush did in 2000 and what he and John Kerry did in 2004.[69] Bush and Kerry, like all presidential general election candidates since 1976, accepted the general election public funding and spending limit.[70]

FECA had its critics, and Congress frequently debated reforming campaign financing. In 2002, as we have seen, it enacted the Bipartisan Campaign Reform Act. There have also been significant attempts to regulate interest-group activity in elections at the state level. Some states, including Maine, Wisconsin, Minnesota, Arizona, and Hawaii, provide for public financing of state offices and state legislative races; others, including Michigan, New Jersey, and Massachusetts, provide partial public financing of gubernatorial elections; a dozen more help underwrite parties with public funds.[71]

During President Bill Clinton's first term, and after the Republicans won control of the House in 1994, Congress passed the first major overhaul of lobbying laws since 1946. Under the Lobbying Disclosure Act of 1995, the definition of a lobbyist was significantly expanded to include part-time lobbyists, those who deal with congressional staff or executive branch agencies, and those who represent foreign-owned companies and foreign entities. This act was expected to increase the number of registered lobbyists to as much as ten times its then current level.[72] In fact, the number of registered "clients" nearly doubled eight years after enactment of the act.[73] The act also included specific disclosure and information requirements.

The Effects of Regulation

Reformers for more than a century sought disclosure of money in politics. This is consistent with efforts to have more complete disclosure of conflicts of interest in potential executive branch appointees and among legislators and judges. In campaigns and elections, disclosure was often incomplete, and groups quickly found ways to avoid it. However, the disclosure provisions of the 1971 Federal Election Campaign Act, as amended in 1974, were quite effective. Until the mid-1990s, citizens, journalists, and scholars had quite a complete picture of who was giving what to whom, and who was spending money and in what ways, to influence elections. That changed with the discovery of issue advocacy as an electioneering tool in the 1996 election cycle. Disclosure of a possible **quid pro quo** between an interest group and a politician was also diminished by soft money. A large donor could give millions to a party with the expectation that it was going to a

quid pro quo
Something given with the expectation of receiving something in return.

particular U.S. Senate campaign, but such a connection is not traceable because the soft money is passed through the party before going to candidates.

The 2002 reforms enhance disclosure first by banning soft money and then by broadening the definition of electioneering to capture much more of the issue advocacy of recent election cycles. The former test for whether a communication was or was not about an election was a language test, the so-called "magic words" test, included in the *Buckley* v. *Valeo* decision discussed earlier. The new legislation defines election communication targeted to a specific audience and which includes mentioning a candidate by name, mentioning an election, or showing the image or likeness of a candidate within 60 days of a general election and within 30 days of a primary election and which makes such communications subject to disclosure.

The FECA reforms of the 1970s sought to limit the influence of large donors in federal elections. Individuals and groups were limited in what they could contribute to parties, PACs, and candidates. The Supreme Court in 1976 declared that limits on independent expenditures were unconstitutional when they were truly independent of a party or candidate. The level of independent expediture activity has always been relatively modest, and FECA had as its intended effect reducing the influence of large contributors. That changed with the surge in unlimited soft money contributions and issue advocacy in the 1996–2002 period. BCRA restores limits on large donors by banning party soft money and requiring broadcast issue advocacy in the period before primaries and general elections that targets a particular audience and mentions a particular candidate to be funded by limited contributions from individuals and groups, not from general funds of unions or corporations. Interest groups can continue to skirt disclosure should they communicate with voters through the mail, in newspaper ads, on billboards, on the phone, and by e-mail—even in the period leading up to the election.

Can groups and individuals still seek to influence the electoral process through financial contributions? BCRA permits them to make contributions to a federal candidate for a primary election and for a general election, with additional contributions allowed if runoffs become necessary. For each of these types of elections, individuals can contribute $2,000. Individuals have an aggregate two-year federal election cycle limit of $94,500 in contributions to parties or candidates. Individuals can make unlimited contributions to interest groups and other types of political actors.

The 2004 election cycle saw more invidual contributions, in part because of the larger individual contribution limits. One of the beneficiaries of these higher limits was the re-election campaign of President George W. Bush. In 2000, Bush raised about one-fifth of his total funds from two hundred individuals, who in turn raised funds from other individuals.[74] The Bush approach was similar to that of direct marketing companies that build networks of personal contacts around individuals. In the case of the Bush efforts in 2000, a person who raised $100,000 from other individuals was designated a Pioneer. In 2004, with the higher contribution limits, an individual who raised $200,000 from individuals was designated a Ranger. Overall in 2004 the Bush campaign raised $266,476,243 from individuals.

TABLE 6–4 TOP SOFT MONEY DONORS, 2001–2002

Donor (Industry)*	Republicans	Democrats	Total
Saban Capital Group	0	$9,280,000	$9,280,000
Newsweb Corp.	0	7,390,000	7,390,000
Shangri-La Entertainment	0	6,700,000	6,700,000
American Federation of State/County/Municipal Employees	500	6,586,000	6,586,500
Service Employees International Union	41,622	4,821,117	4,862,739
Freddie Mac	2,335,615	1,687,500	4,023,115

SOURCE: Opensecrets.org at www.opensecrets.org/bigpicture/softtop.asp?cycle=2002.

*Includes contributions from subsidiaries and/or executives.

Interest groups under BCRA will continue to participate through PACs. As noted, many members of Congress thrive on the present arrangements, and the leaders and members of both parties actually compete for PAC dollars (see Table 6–4). Although Republicans have generally received larger amounts, Democrats in recent election cycles put pressure on the pharmaceutical and insurance industries to give more to Democratic candidates.[75] More pragmatic PACs contribute to both parties to be in a favored position with whichever party wins the majority. One reason members of Congress become entrenched in their seats is that PACs fund them. The PAC contribution limits were not changed by BCRA, remaining at $5,000 per candidate for each of up to three elections (primary, general, and runoff).

One consequence of BCRA was that interest groups are spending more in issue advocacy. Many interest groups have already been diversifying their investment strategy. An example of diversification before BCRA is the pharmaceutical industry, whose PACs donated an estimated $5.2 million to federal candidates in 2000 and then also gave another $15.2 million in soft money to the political parties.[76] Beginning in 1999, the pharmaceutical industry contributed heavily to a group named Citizens for Better Medicare, which reported it would spend $40 million in issue advertising in 2000.[77] It ran ads in states with competitive Senate races.[78] The industry was also active in 2002.

Interest groups typically made the presidential campaign their highest priority in 2004. Some groups, like the League of Conservation Voters (LCV), in the past had invested some of their resources in presidential races but made House and Senate races higher priorities. LCV did just the opposite in 2004. With the presidential race so competitive and with so much passion behind supporting or opposing the incumbent president, the decision by interest groups to emphasize the presidential contest is not surprising.

One example of an interest group that diversified its approach in 2004 is the United States Chamber of Commerce. The Chamber did not endorse a candidate for president but strongly supported the reelection of President Bush—a position that was only strengthened when John Kerry chose as his running mate a former trial lawyer, John Edwards. But the Chamber also invested heavily in state races for state attorney general, state supreme court, and state congress in an effort to win friendlier state policies and court decisions involving business.

Some corporations had complained prior to passage of BCRA about the "shake down" by elected officials for large corporate soft money contributions. The BCRA ban on soft money gave corporations an excuse to spend less overall on politics in 2004. As noted, BCRA left other avenues open to corporations and unions. These alternative avenues included organizing the PACs, sending internal communications to members, and encouraging their employees to make individual contributions to the campaigns. It is important to remember that BCRA has only been in effect for one election and history teaches us that groups adapt over multiple elections to new rules.

What have been the effects of past reforms on interest groups? Ironically, one has been to increase the number and importance of such groups. The strategy of FECA in 1971 law was to authorize direct and open participation by both labor and corporate organizations in elections and lobbying in the hope that a visible role for interest-group activity, backed by effective enforcement, would be constitutional under the First Amendment. FECA allowed unions and corporations to communicate on political matters to members or stockholders, to conduct registration and get-out-the-vote drives, and to spend union and company funds to set up "separate segregated funds" (PACs) to use for political purposes.

TABLE 6–5   TOTAL PAC CONTRIBUTIONS TO FEDERAL CANDIDATES, 1990–2002

	2002	*2000*	*1998*	*1996*	*1994*	*1992*
Millions Contributed	282.0	259.8	219.9	217.8	189.6	188.9

SOURCE: FEC, "PAC Activity Increases For 2002 Elections", at www.fec.gov.

LOBBYING AMERICA

In this simulation, you will lobby on behalf of a fictional interest group. Your goal is to get legislation passed for your interest group. To accomplish this goal, you will research different members of Congress and finally disburse your limited resources of time and money (campaign contributions). Only if you use your resources efficiently will the legislation be passed.

Go to Make It Real "Lobbying America."

Corporations, trade associations, and unions made PACs a central part of their government relations strategy. But what changed the rules of the game for corporate interests was passage in 1974 of limits on individual contributions, something not part of the 1971 act. An explosion of corporate PACs followed this 1974 amendment.[79] In 1978, there was little difference in the level of campaign activity of PACs representing corporations, labor unions, or trade associations.[80] But that has changed, with corporate PACs spending more than the others and ideological PACs at roughly half the level of spending of trade and labor PACs.

Even with the surge in issue advocacy and party soft money contributions by interest groups in elections between 1996 and 2002, all three major types of PACs remained active in making PAC contributions to candidates. Interest groups gave PAC money to retain relationships with incumbents and candidates in relatively safe seats of parties they favored in what has long been the typical contest. PAC contributions are especially aimed at committee chairs and party leaders. To reinforce this relationship the Republicans have developed a strategy, the "K Street Project," to do even better in getting PAC contributions. K Street in Washington, D.C., houses many of the lobbying and law firms that represent trade associations and corporations that make contributions. House Republican Leader Tom DeLay, a prime mover in the K Street project, once said, "If you want to play in our revolution you have to live by our rules."[81]

With soft money largely banned in 2004 and with the uncertain legal status of some issue advocacy, many groups returned to the strategy of using their PAC as the primary means of investing in elections (see Table 6–5).

A centerpiece of past efforts to regulate interest group activity was disclosure of how politicians fund their campaigns. Disclosure permits the press and public to assess the implications of how candidates finance their campaigns. BCRA requires that the sponsors of all election-related advertising be identified in the communication, with this disclosure made prominently. This is why ads in 2004 featured the line, "I am candidate X and I approved of this ad," or something to that effect. Furthermore, BCRA requires that everything filed with the Federal Election Commission be made available to the public within 48 hours.

Candidates and some appointed officials must also disclose their personal finances, permitting voters and the press to see what investments and resources candidates have that may affect their ability to be impartial. Such public disclosure of personal assets, the value of property owned, and outstanding debts no doubt discourages some persons from entering public life, but it also makes officeholders accountable for certain obligations and actions once they enter office.

SUMMARY

1. Interest groups exist to make demands on government. The dominant interest groups in the United States are economic or occupational, but a variety of other groups—ideological, public interest, foreign policy, government itself, as well as ethnic, religious, and racial—have memberships that cut across the big economic groupings; thus their influence is both reduced and stabilized.

2. Movements of large numbers of people who are frustrated with government policies have always been with us in the United States. Blacks, women, and the economic underdogs have at various times organized themselves into movements.

3. Elements in interest-group power include size, resources, cohesiveness, leadership, and techniques, especially the ability to contribute to candidates and political parties as well as the ability to fund lobbyists. But the actual power of an interest group stems from the manner in which these elements relate to the political and governmental environment in which the interest group operates.

4. For many decades, interest groups have engaged in lobbying, but these efforts have become far more significant as groups become more deeply involved in the electoral process, especially through the expanded use of political action committees (PACs). Interest groups also take their

messages directly to the public through mass mailings and advertising campaigns. Other interest-group techniques include influencing rule making, litigation, election activities, and cooperative lobbying.

5. Concern about PACs centers on their ability to raise money and spend it on elections on behalf of endorsed candidates, typically incumbents. This concern has led to proposals to ban PACs or more strictly limit their activities. Yet their existence and rights are protected by the First Amendment.

6. Reforms of interest group excesses often include regulations that seek fairness, disclosure, and balance. All reform efforts must operate so as not to infringe on the

basic constitutional rights of individuals. The key issue today in "controlling factions" is whether to allow groups to proliferate and so balance each other, to try to regulate groups, or to seek reforms outside the groups by fostering balanced power in political parties or elsewhere.

7. Congress has enacted laws attempting to regulate and reform excesses of interest groups in electoral democracy. The Federal Election Campaign Act was passed in the 1970s in response to the Watergate scandal and the Bipartisan Campaign Reform Act was passed in 2002 in response to the soft money abuses by political parties and interest groups. The impact of these laws is debated and is often criticized for infringing on such rights as freedom of speech and freedom of association. Defenders of the reforms point to the success in removing large contributors from federal elections, at least for a couple of decades until groups found ways to circumvent the laws.

KEY TERMS

faction	*Federal Register*	political action committee (PAC)	527 group
interest group	*amicus curiae brief*	bundling	quid pro quo
movement	lobbying	independent expenditures	
open shop	lobbyist	hard money	
closed shop	revolving door	soft money	
free rider	iron triangle	issue advocacy	

FURTHER READING

SCOTT H. AINSWORTH, *Analyzing Interest Groups: Group Influence on People and Policies* (Norton, 2002).

JEFFREY M. BERRY, *New Liberalism: The Rising Power of Citizen Groups* (Brookings Institution Press, 1999).

ROBERT BIERSACK ET AL., EDS., *After the Revolution: PACs, Lobbies, and the Republican Congress* (Addison-Wesley, 1999).

JEFFREY H. BIRNBAUM, *The Money Men: The Real Story of Fund-Raising's Influence on Political Power in America* (Crown, 2000).

WILLIAM P. BROWNE, *Groups, Interests, and Public Policy* (Georgetown University Press, 1998).

ALLAN J. CIGLER AND BURDETT A. LOOMIS, EDS., *Interest Group Politics*, 6th ed. (CQ Press, 2002).

MARTHA A. DERTHICK, *Up in Smoke* (CQ Press, 2002).

KENNETH M. GOLDSTEIN, *Interest Groups, Lobbying, and Participation in America* (Cambridge University Press, 1999).

GENE GROSSMAN AND ELHANAN HELPMAN, *Special Interest Politics* (MIT Press, 2001).

PAUL S. HERRNSON, RONALD G. SHAIKO, AND CLYDE WILCOX, *The Interest Group Connection: Electioneering, Lobbying, and Policymaking in Washington* (Chatham House, 1998).

ALLEN D. HERTZKE, *Representing God in Washington: The Role of Religious Lobbies in the American Polity* (University of Tennessee Press, 1988).

KEVIN W. HULA, *Lobbying Together: Interest Group Coalitions in Legislative Politics* (Georgetown University Press, 1999).

DAVID LOWERY AND HOLLY BRASHER. *Organized Interests and American Government* (McGraw-Hill, 2004).

DAVID B. MAGLEBY AND J. QUIN MONSON, EDS., *The Last Hurrah? Soft Money and Issue Advocacy in the 2002 Congressional Elections* (Brookings Institution Press, 2004).

MICHAEL J. MALBIN, ED., *Life After Reform: When the Bipartisan Campaign Reform Act Meets Politics* (Rowman & Littlefield, 2003).

ANTHONY J. NOWNES, *Pressure and Power: Organized Interests in American Politics* (Houghton Mifflin, 2001).

MANCUR OLSON, *The Logic of Collective Action* (Harvard University Press, 1965).

DAVID VOGEL, *Kindred Strangers: The Uneasy Relationship Between Politics and Business in America* (Princeton University Press, 1996).

JACK L. WALKER, JR., *Mobilizing Interest Groups in America: Patrons, Professions, and Social Movements* (University of Michigan Press, 1991).

DARRELL M. WEST AND BURDETT A. LOOMIS, *The Sound of Money: How Political Interests Get What They Want* (Norton, 1999).

S ome years ago, a community college district in Los Angeles held a nonpartisan election for its trustees in which any registered voter could run if he or she paid the $50 filing fee and gathered 500 valid signatures on a petition. A total of 133 candidates ran, and each voter could cast up to seven votes in the election. Political parties were not allowed to nominate candidates, and party labels did not appear on the ballot to help orient voters to the candidates.

How did people vote in an election without parties? Candidates were listed alphabetically, and those whose names began with the letters A to F did better than those later in the alphabet. Being well known helped. Endorsements by the *Los Angeles Times* also influenced the outcome, as did campaigning by a conservative group. A Mexican American surname also helped. In this election, an important voting cue was absent: incumbency. Because the board of trustees was newly created, none of the candidates were incumbents. Candidates who are incumbents have an advantage because they are generally better known and have developed an identity related to the position by providing services or generating activity.[1]

Rarely do American voters face such unorganized and plentiful choices, because parties give structure to national and state elections. E. E. Schattschneider, a noted political scientist, once said, "The political parties created democracy, and modern democracy is

POLITICAL PARTIES
ESSENTIAL TO DEMOCRACY

7

TIME LINE

POLITICAL PARTIES

1796	Thomas Jefferson guides creation of "Democratic-Republican party"
1824	First partisan realigning election, others in 1860 and 1896
1828	Andrew Jackson's election ushers in the first party based on popular support
1836	Martin Van Buren is the first Democrat to be elected president
1860	Abraham Lincoln is the first Republican to be elected president
1905	Wisconsin creates the first primary election
1912	Theodore Roosevelt's "Bull Moose party" splits the Republican vote—a Democrat is elected
1932	Last partisan realigning election
1948	Strom Thurmond creates States' Rights party to combat desegregation
1968	Democratic convention in Chicago is overrun by protests and riots
1971	Libertarian party is created
1984	Geraldine Ferraro is the first woman nominated as vice president by a major party
1992	Billionaire Ross Perot creates United We Stand, predecessor of the Reform party
1994	Republicans regain control of the House of Representatives for first time in 40 years
2002	Soft money for federal party committees banned by Bipartisan Campaign Reform Act (BCRA)

political party

An organization that seeks political power by electing people to office so that its positions and philosophy become public policy.

unthinkable save in terms of the parties."[2] This provocative statement is true, but such a favorable evaluation of political parties runs counter to a long-standing and deep-seated American fear and distrust of them. Experience has taught us that free people create political parties to promote their own goals. Even though our founders hoped to discourage them, political parties quickly became an integral part of our political system.

Parties serve many functions, including the important one of narrowing the choices for voters.[3] They are both a consequence of democracy and an instrument of it. Parties need not be strong and cohesive like those in Britain and most European democracies, but there are few, if any, democratic systems that do not have political parties. Elections serve the vital task of deciding who can legitimately exercise political power, and parties are an integral part of making national and state elections work. We Americans take for granted the peaceful transfer of power from one elected official to another and from one party to another, yet in new democracies, the transfer of power following an election is often problematic. In such democracies, the holding of power may be more important than the principle of democratic competition. Well-established parties help stabilize democracy.

This chapter begins by examining the purposes parties serve that make them so vital to the functioning of democracy. We then examine the evolution of American political parties. Although American political parties have changed over time, they remain important in three different settings: as institutions, in government, and in the electorate. It is important to understand how parties facilitate democracy in all three settings. Finally, we turn to a discussion of the strength of parties today and the prospects for party reform and renewal.

WHAT PARTIES DO FOR DEMOCRACY

Party Functions

Political parties are organizations that seek political power by electing people to office so that their positions and philosophy become public policy. American political parties serve a variety of political and social functions, some obvious and some not so obvious. They perform some functions well and others not so well, and how they perform them differs from place to place and time to time.

ORGANIZE THE COMPETITION   One of the most important functions of parties is to organize the competition by designating candidates to run under their label. Parties exist primarily as an organizing mechanism to win elections and thus win control of government. For some races, parties recruit and nominate candidates for office; they register and activate voters; and they help candidates by training them, raising money for them, providing them with research and voter lists, and enlisting volunteers to work for them.[4] For more visible contests, especially ones where there is a real chance of winning, multiple candidates often compete with each other for the nomination, often without party efforts to recruit them. Recently, campaign consultants rather than party officials have taken over some of these responsibilities; we explore this topic at some length in Chapter 10.[5]

The ability of parties to influence the selection of candidates varies by the type of nominating system used in the state. A few states use a *caucus* or *convention system*, which permits party leaders to play a role in the selection of nominees by placing their selection in the hands of people willing to attend party meetings called caucuses or conventions. Most people are not willing to invest this much time in a nomination process. Other states hold *primary elections* where voters cast ballots on who the party nominees should be. As more and more states turn to primary elections, the ability of party leaders to influence who runs under their party label is reduced. Candidates with little party experience but with well-known names or ample personal funds can often win in a primary over a person with a known track record of prior party service or success in a less visible office. New Jersey Senator Jon Corzine had never run for office and was not well known in the state before spending $60 million in his successful 2000 campaign. Not all little-known, self-financed candidates win; in fact, they are often defeated. For example, Steve Forbes spent a combined $129 million in unsuccessful bids for the Republican presidential nomination in 1996 and 2000. Examples of former athletes who made successful candidates include Jim Bunning, a former baseball player and now Senator from Kentucky; Univeristy of Nebraska football coach Tom Osborne, now in the House of Representatives; and former NFL football player Jack Kemp, who served in the House of Representatives and was the Republican nominee for vice president in 1996.

A party's ability to organize the competition is also influenced by how states organize their ballots. In many states, candidates are listed in party columns—on a **party column ballot**—which makes it easier for voters to vote a *straight ticket* for all the party candidates. Straight-ticket voting is also more likely in voting systems that permit flipping one switch or punching one spot on the computer card to vote for all candidates from one party. Other states organize the ballot by office—the **office block ballot**—which makes straight-ticket voting harder. Even though many voters cast votes for candidates in more than one party, the party label of a candidate means something to most voters and is important in their voting decision.

Local and judicial elections in most states are **nonpartisan elections**, which means no party affiliation is indicated. Such systems make it more difficult for political parties to operate—precisely why many jurisdictions have adopted this reform. Proponents of nonpartisan local and judicial elections contend that party affiliation is not important to being a good judge or school board member. As with our example of the community college board at the beginning of this chapter, many voters in these nonpartisan elections rely more on how recognizable the name of a candidate is, or whether he or she now holds office (incumbency).

UNIFY THE ELECTORATE   Parties are often accused of creating conflict, but they actually help unify the electorate and moderate conflict, at least within the party. There is a strong incentive in both parties to fight out their differences inside the party but then come together to take on the opposition. Moreover, in order to win elections, parties need to reach out to voters outside their party and gain their support. This action also helps unify the electorate, at least into the two large national political parties in our system.

Parties have great difficulty building coalitions on controversial issues like abortion or gun control. Not surprisingly, candidates and parties generally try to avoid defining themselves or the election in single-issue terms. Rather, they hope that if voters disagree with the party's stand on one issue, they will still support the party because they agree with it on other issues. Deemphasizing single issues in this way helps defuse conflict and unify the electorate.

HELP ORGANIZE GOVERNMENT   Although political parties in the United States are not as cohesive as in some other democracies, parties are important when it comes to organizing our state and national governments. Congress is organized along party lines. The political party with the most votes in each chamber elects the officers of that chamber, selects the chair of each committee, and has a majority on all the committees. State legislatures, with the notable exception of Nebraska, are also organized along party lines. The 2004 election enlarged the Republican majorities in the U.S. Senate and U.S. House of Representatives. In the Senate, the GOP rose from 51 to 55 members, but this number remained below the number needed to override a filibuster. Republicans continued to control all committee chairs, but due to party rules, there was some rotation among Republicans. The Senate Judiciary Committee chairmanship, for example, switched in 2005 from Orrin Hatch (R.–Utah) to Arlen Specter (R.–Penn.).

The party that controls the White House, the governor's mansion, or city hall gets **patronage**, which means it can select party members as public officials or judges. Such appointments are limited only by civil service regulations that restrict patronage typically to the top posts, but these posts, which number about 4,000 in the federal government, are also numerous at the state and local levels. Patronage provides an incentive for people to become involved in politics and gives the party leaders and elected politicians loyal partisans in key positions to help them achieve their policy objectives. Patronage has declined dramatically over time in the United States.

party column ballot
Type of ballot that encourages party-line voting by listing all of a party's candidates in a column under the party name.

office block ballot
Ballot on which all candidates are listed under the office for which they are running, making split-ticket voting easier.

nonpartisan election
A local or judicial election in which candidates are not selected or endorsed by political parties and party affiliation is not listed on ballots.

patronage
The dispensing of government jobs to persons who belong to the winning political party.

TRANSLATE PREFERENCES INTO POLICY   One of the great strengths of our democracy is that even the party that wins an election usually has to moderate what it does in order to win reelection. For that reason, public policy does not change dramatically with each election. Nonetheless, the party that wins the election has a chance to enact its policies and implement its campaign promises.

American parties have had only limited success in setting the course of national policy, especially when compared with countries with strong parties. The European model of party government, which has been called a *responsible party system,* assumes that parties discipline their members through their control over nominations and campaigns. Officeholders in such party-centered systems are expected to act according to party wishes or they will not be allowed to run again under the party label. Moreover, candidates run on fairly specific party platforms and are expected to implement those policies if they win control in the election.

Although we lack a European-type party system, most but not all Democrats in Congress vote together, as do most but not all Republicans. There are times, however, when a president of one party receives more congressional votes from the opposing party than from his own, as President Bill Clinton did in 2000 on legislation granting China permanent normal trade relations status with the United States.[6] And when the House passed the Enhanced Border Security and Visa Entry Reform Act of 2002, which President Bush wanted, nearly twice as many Democrats voted yes—182, compared to 92 yes votes from the Republicans.[7]

Because American parties do not control nominations, they are less able to discipline members who express views contrary to those of the party.[8] The American system is largely *candidate-centered;* politicians are nominated largely on the basis of their qualifications and personal appeal, not party loyalty. In fact, it is more correct to say that in most contests, we have *candidate* politics rather than *party* politics. As a consequence, party leaders cannot guarantee passage of their program, even if they are in the majority.

Even though parties cannot exert tight control over candidates, their ability to raise and spend money has had a significant influence. Through the 2002 election, parties played an important role in competitive federal elections through their **soft money** expenditures.[9] In the 2002 South Dakota Senate race, for example, the party committees and allied interest groups spent a combined $12 million, equaling what the two major party candiates spent in that race.[10]

The Bipartisan Campaign Reform Act (BCRA), which took effect in the 2003–04 election cycle, abolished soft money donations to political parties at the federal level. Soft money consisted of contributions given to the political parties by individuals, corporations, labor unions, and political action committees (PACs) for "party-building" purposes that came to be used for candidate promotion. Because such contributions were unlimited, parties put a premium on raising them. The ads soft money paid for were often candidate centered and focused on themes important to that race.[11]

Political parties responded to the soft money ban by raising more of the limited **hard money** from individuals and political action committees. BCRA made this easier by raising the contribution limits for individuals from $1,000 to $2,000.[12] In an election cycle, an individual who wanted to give the maximum possible to candidates and parties could give $95,000, up from $50,000.[13] Both parties raised record-setting amounts of hard money in 2003–2004, surpassing what they had raised in hard and soft money combined in 1999–2000 or 2001–2002. Party hard money in 2004 was spent on a range of activities including get-out-the-vote efforts, contributions to candidates, and advertising. Parties are also allowed to contribute $5,000 of hard money to House candidates and $35,000 to Senate candidates per election cycle, and additional money in hard money coordinated expenditures. Political partes are also allowed to spend limited amounts of hard money on campaign activities that are coordinated with the candidate and in which the candidate pays part of the cost. Between 1996 and 2004, parties had scaled back their coordinated spending and contributions to candidates, instead focusing on soft money.

Political parties also could spend unlimited amounts of hard money on **independent expenditures** for or against candidates. The Supreme Court gave parties and groups the same right to independent expenditures in a 1996 Supreme Court Decision,

soft money
Money raised in unlimited amounts by political parties for party building purposes. Now largely illegal except for limited contributions to state or local parties for voter registration and get-out-the-vote efforts.

hard money
Political contributions given to a party, candidate, or interest group that are limited in amount and fully disclosed. Raising such limited funds is harder than raising unlimited funds, hence the term "hard" money.

independent expenditure
The Supreme Court has ruled that individuals, groups, and parties can spend unlimited amounts in campaigns for or against candidates as long as they operate independently from the candidates. When an individual, group, or party does so, they are making an independent expenditure.

Colorado Republican Federal Campaign Committee v. *FEC*.[14] In 2003–04, with soft money not an option and with more success in raising hard money, both parties made substantial independent expenditures. For example, in the 2004 special election in South Dakota, the two parties combined spent nearly $3 million, mostly in independent expenditures.[15]

PROVIDE LOYAL OPPOSITION Accountability in a democracy comes from the party out of power closely monitoring and commenting on the actions of the party in power. When national security issues are involved or the country is under attack, parties restrain their criticism, as the Democrats in Congress did for some time after September 11, 2001. There is usually a polite interval following an election—known as the **honeymoon**— after which the opposition party begins to criticize the party that controls the White House, especially when the opposition party controls one or both houses of Congress.[16] The length of the honeymoon depends in part on how close the vote was in the election, on how contentious the agenda of the new administration is, and on the leadership skills of the new president. Early success in enacting policy can prolong the honeymoon; mistakes or controversies can shorten it.

The Nomination of Candidates

From the beginning, parties have been the mechanism by which candidates for public office are chosen. The **caucus** played an important part in pre-Revolutionary politics. Elected officials organized themselves into groups or parties and together selected candidates to run for higher office, including the presidency. This method of nomination operated for several decades after the United States was established.

As early as the 1820s, however, charges of "secret deals" in "smoke-filled rooms" were made against this method. Moreover, it was not representative of people from areas where a party was in a minority or nonexistent, since only officeholders took part in the caucus. Efforts were made to make the caucus more representative of rank-and-file party members. The *mixed caucus* brought in delegates from districts in which the party had no elected legislators.

Then, during the 1830s and 1840s, a system of **party conventions** was instituted. Delegates, usually chosen directly by party members in towns and cities, selected the party candidates, debated and adopted a platform, and built party spirit by celebrating noisily. But the convention method soon came under criticism that it was subject to control by the party bosses and their machines.

To involve more voters and reduce the power of the bosses to pick party nominees, states adopted the **direct primary**, in which people could vote for the party's nominees for office. Primaries spread rapidly after Wisconsin adopted them in 1905—in the North as a Progressive era reform and in the South as a way to bring democracy to a region that had seen no meaningful general elections since the end of Reconstruction, due to one-party rule by the Democrats. By 1920, direct primaries were the norm for some offices in almost all states.

Today the direct primary is the typical method of picking party candidates. Primaries vary significantly from state to state. They differ in terms of (1) who may run in a primary and how one qualifies for the ballot; (2) whether the party organization can or does endorse candidates before the primary; (3) who may vote in a party's primary—that is, whether a voter must register with a party in order to vote; and (4) how many votes are needed for nomination—a plurality, a majority, or some other number determined by party rule or state law. The differences among primaries are not trivial; they have an important impact on the role played by party organization and on the strategy used by candidates.

In states with **open primaries**, any voter, regardless of party, can participate in whichever primary he or she chooses. This kind of primary permits **crossover voting**—Republicans and Independents helping determine who the Democratic nominee will be, and vice versa. Other states use **closed primaries**, in which only persons already registered in that party may participate. Some states, like Washington and California, experimented with *blanket primaries,* in which all voters could vote for any candidate, regardless of party. Blanket primaries permitted voters to vote for a candidate of one party for one office and for a candidate from another party for another office, something that is not

honeymoon
Period at the beginning of a new president's term during which the president enjoys generally positive relations with the press and Congress, usually lasting about six months.

caucus
A meeting of local party members to choose party officials or candidates for public office and to decide the platform.

party convention
A meeting of party delegates to vote on matters of policy and in some cases to select party candidates for public office.

direct primary
Election in which voters choose party nominees.

open primary
Primary election in which any voter, regardless of party, may vote.

crossover voting
Voting by a member of one party for a candidate of another party.

closed primary
Primary election in which only persons registered in the party holding the primary may vote.

permitted under either closed or open primaries. In 2000, the Supreme Court held that California's blanket primary violated the free association rights of political parties, in part because blanket primaries permit people who have "expressly affiliated with a rival" party to have a vote in the selection of a nominee from a different party.[17] In a detailed study of California's blanket primary, political scientists found that fewer than 5 percent of voters associated with one party actually voted for nominees from another party. More broadly, they concluded that the rules of a primary are important in determining the winner.[18]

Along with modern communications and fund-raising techniques, direct primaries have diminished the influence of leaders of political parties. Many critics believe that this change has had more undesirable than desirable consequences. Party leaders now have less influence over who gets to be the party's candidate, and candidates are less accountable to the party both during the election and after it.

Direct primaries are used to nominate most party candidates for most offices. Yet in some states, local caucuses choose delegates to attend regional meetings, which in turn select delegates to state and national conventions, where they nominate party candidates for offices. The Iowa presidential caucuses, in which 122,000 Iowans participated in 2004,[19] are highly publicized as the first important test of potential presidential nominees.[20]

In a few states, conventions still play a role in the nominating process for state and federal candidates. In Connecticut, for example, convention choices become the party nominees unless they are challenged. Candidates who attain at least 15 percent of the vote in the convention have an automatic right to challenge the winner at the convention, but they do not always exercise this right.[21] In Utah, if a candidate gets 60 percent of the delegate vote at the convention, there is no primary election vote for that office. Should no candidate reach 60 percent, only the top two candidates are listed on the primary ballot. In other states, convention nominees are designated as such on the primary ballot; they may or may not receive help from the party organization. Conventions are also used to invigorate the party faithful by enabling them to meet with their leaders.

In most states, candidates can get their names on the ballot as an Independent or minor party candidate by securing the required number of signatures on a nomination petition. This is hard to do, but it can be done, as Ross Perot demonstrated in 1992. He spent his own money to build an organization of volunteers who put his name on the ballot in all 50 states. Minor party gubernatorial candidates like the Minnesota Reform party's Jesse Ventura in 1998 or the Green party's presidential candidate Ralph Nader in

A precinct captain takes a head count during the caucus in Burlington, Iowa, on January 19, 2004. John Kerry easily won the precinct.

2000 secured their nominations as candidates of existing minor parties. Ralph Nader was on the ballot in 34 states and the District of Columbia as an independent candidate in 2004. Democrats successfully challenged his efforts to qualify for the ballot in Ohio, Arizona, and Pennsylvania. Some Republicans supported Ralph Nader's efforts to be on the ballot in more states, a move Democrats suspected was intended to draw support from John Kerry. Ballot access remains a major hurdle for minor party candidates.

Party Systems

Ours is a two-party system; most other democracies have a multiparty system. Although we have many minor parties, only the two major parties have much of a chance to win elections. Multiparty systems are almost always found in countries that have a parliamentary government, in contrast to our presidential system. This is, however, not always

GLOBAL *Perceptions*

QUESTION: How important is it to you to live in a country where honest elections are held regularly with a choice of at least two political parties? Is it very important, somewhat important, not too important, or not important at all?

An idea that citizens of the United States take for granted, like the need for at least two political parties, is not seen as important in all countries. For example, in countries like Bolivia, South Korea, and Jordan, less than half of the public thinks having two parties is very important. In the United States, by contrast, 84 percent say having a choice between at least two parties is important.

In the Pew Global Attitudes Project, respondents were also asked how they felt about American ideas about democracy (see Chapter 1 box). In most cases the attitudes on one question predict the attitudes in the other. But in the Philippines, Turkey, Argentina, Brazil, and Pakistan, much higher proportions say "having two parties is important" than say they "like American ideas about democracy." In Turkey, for example, 75 percent think having two parties is very important but only 33 percent like American ideas about democracy. The reverse is true in Ghana, where 80 percent like American ideas about democracy but only 58 percent think having two parties is important. This reinforces the point that in the minds of people in some countries democracy is distinguishable from their views of democracy in the United States.

SOURCE: The Pew Research Center, *Views of a Changing World,* 2003, p. T-67.

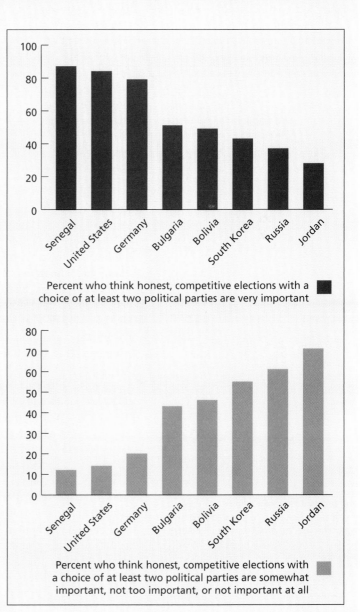

Percent who think honest, competitive elections with a choice of at least two political parties are very important

Percent who think honest, competitive elections with a choice of at least two political parties are somewhat important, not too important, or not important at all

IN COMPARATIVE PERSPECTIVE

ISRAEL'S COALITION GOVERNMENT

Israel has a multiparty system. Though Israelis vote for prime minister and parliament separately, the prime minister must still have the support of the majority of the members of parliament. If he doesn't, he is in danger of facing a parliamentary vote of no confidence. A vote of no confidence leads to new elections for prime minister and parliament. Because there are many parties, it is difficult—if not impossible—for any one party to gain a majority of the seats in the Knesset, the Israeli parliament. Usually one party can get only a plurality of the seats. A party with only a plurality of seats must form a coalition with other parties in order to maintain power. Certain concessions must be made to those parties to convince them to join. If the ruling party loses the support of its coalition partners, the prime minister and his party must form a new coalition, or else their government will be toppled by a parliamentary vote of no confidence.

The conflict with the Palestinians and disagreement over how best to coexist with them has been a source of destabilization to Israeli coalition governments. In July 2000, Prime Minister Ehud Barak, after upsetting rightist parties within his coalition by having peace talks with the Palestinians, exercised his authority to call an early election for prime minister

in order to avoid a vote of "no confidence." Ariel Sharon, an outspoken critic of Barak, soundly defeated him in the election.

The conflict between Israel and the Palestinians has escalated since 2002 and, ironically, Sharon is in a plight similar to Barak's. In early 2004, Sharon shocked rightist members of his coalition by making known that he would unilaterally withdraw all Israeli settlements from the Gaza strip along with some other settlements on the West Bank. As a result, he has faced heated opposition not only from members of the Knesset within his coalition but even within his cabinet.* In order to save his faltering government, Sharon invited the leftist Labour party to join what had been a rightist coalition.† Sharon's own Likud party voted against letting Labour into their coalition in August 2004. Sharon continued to seek help from Labour to implement his disengagement policy. This illustrates the scrambling and compromise that often occur within countries that have a multiparty system.

*Gil Hoffman, "Sharon: Settlements in Gaza Cannot Remain," *The Jerusalem Post,* February 3, 2004, p. 1.
†Greg Myre, "Sharon Invites His Favorite Dove to Help Build a Coalition," *The New York Times,* July 13, 2004, p. 4.

---

true. For example, England has a parliamentary system but also a strong two-party system.

Parliamentary systems usually have a *head of the nation,* often called the president, but they also have a *head of the government,* often called the prime minister or chancellor, who is the leader of one of the large parties in the legislature. In democracies with multiparty systems, such as Israel and Italy, because no one party has a majority of the votes, *coalition* governments are necessary. Minor parties can gain concessions—positions in a cabinet or support of policies they want implemented—in return for their participation in a coalition. Major parties need the minor parties and are therefore willing to bargain. Thus the multiparty system favors the existence of minor parties by giving them incentives to persevere.

In some multiparty parliamentary systems, parties run slates of candidates for legislative positions, and winners are determined by **proportional representation**, in which the parties receive a proportion of the legislators corresponding to their proportion of the vote. In our **winner-take-all system**, only the candidate with the most votes in a district or state takes office.[22] Because a party does not gain anything by finishing second, minor parties in a two-party system can rarely overcome the assumption that a vote for them is a wasted vote.[23] Even if a third-party candidate can keep either major party candidate from receiving more than 50 percent (a *majority*) of the vote, the candidate with the most votes (a *plurality*) wins.

In multiparty systems, parties at the extremes are apt to have more influence than in our two-party system, and in nations with a multiparty system, their legislatures more accurately reflect the full range of the views of the electorate. Political parties in multiparty systems can be more doctrinaire than ours because they do not have to appeal to masses of people. Even though parties that do not become part of the governing coalition may have little to say in setting government policy, they survive because they appeal

proportional representation
An election system in which each party running receives the proportion of legislative seats corresponding to its proportion of the vote.

winner-take-all system
An election system in which the candidate with the most votes wins.

to some voters. Under such a system, an incentive exists for third, fourth, or additional parties to run because they may win some seats. In contrast, our two-party system tends to create *centrist* parties that appeal to moderate elements and suppress the views of extremists in the electorate. Moreover, once elected, our parties do not form as cohesive a voting bloc as ideological parties do in multiparty systems.

Multiparty parliamentary systems often make governments unstable as coalitions form and collapse. In addition, swings in policy when party control changes can be quite dramatic. In contrast, two-party systems produce governments that tend to be stable and centrist, and as a result, policy changes occur incrementally.

Minor Parties: Persistence and Frustration

Although we have a primarily two-party system in the United States, we also have **minor parties**, sometimes called *third parties.* Those that arise around a candidate usually disappear when the charismatic personality does. Examples of such parties are Theodore Roosevelt's Bull Moose party and George Wallace's American Independent party. Wallace's party polled more than 13 million votes and won 46 electoral votes in 1968. Ross Perot won 19 million votes, 19 percent of the total vote in 1992.[24] He did only about half as well in 1996, despite having organized a political party. Without Ross Perot to lead it, the Reform party was badly divided in 2000. Its presidential candidate, Pat Buchanan, failed to reach 1 percent of the national popular vote and thus lost the Reform party much of the ground it had gained under Ross Perot in terms of ballot access and federal campaign funding. More visible than the Reform party was the Green party, which, although not on the ballot in seven states, mounted a major effort to reach 5 percent of the popular vote for presidential candidate Ralph Nader and thereby qualify the party for federal funding in the 2004 elections. The effort failed. The Green party mustered only 3 percent of the popular vote. In 2004, Nader, running as an independent, but endorsed by the Reform party, received one-third of 1 percent of the vote.

Minor parties that are organized around an *ideology* usually persist over a longer time than those built around a particular leader. Communist, Prohibition, Libertarian, Right to Life, and Green parties are of the ideological type. Minor parties of both types come and go, and there are usually several minor parties running in any given election.[25] Some parties arise around a single issue, like the Right to Life party active in states like New York.

Minor parties have been criticized by major parties as "spoilers," diverting votes away from the major party candidate and costing that candidate the election. Green party candidate Ralph Nader was accused of doing this to Al Gore in 2000. Interest groups identified with environmental issues ran ads urging voters not to waste their vote on Nader, who could not win the election. The closeness of the 2000 election and the perception that Nader may have cost Al Gore the White House meant that Democrats aggressively tried to block access to the ballot for Nader in 2004 and stressed his potential to be a spoiler again in 2004. Early in the campaign, John Kerry and Ralph Nader met and the candidates were on good terms. This later dissipated as Nader criticized the Democratic party and lack of differences between the major party candidates.

Minor parties have had an indirect influence in our country by drawing attention to controversial issues and by organizing such groups as the antislavery and the civil rights movements.[26] Ross Perot, for example, elevated the importance of balanced budgets in 1992 and made it more difficult for George Bush to attack Bill Clinton on character issues.[27] However, they have never won the presidency or more than a handful of congressional seats (see Table 7–1).[28] They have done somewhat better in gubernatorial elections.[29] They have never shaped national policy from *inside* the government, and their influence on national policy and on the platforms of the two major parties has been limited.[30]

Examples of minor parties operating in recent elections include the Libertarian, Green, and Reform parties. The **Libertarian party** (www.lp.org) places heavy emphasis on individual liberties, personal responsibility, and freedom from government. Its agenda calls for an end to the federal government's role in education and crime control. Libertarians believe that "if government's role were limited to protecting our lives, rights and property, then America would prosper and thrive as never before." Libertarians also

In 2004, independent presidential candidate Ralph Nader received one-third of 1 percent of the popular vote.

minor party
A small political party that rises and falls with a charismatic candidate or, if composed of ideologies on the right or left, usually persists over time; also called a *third party.*

Libertarian party
A minor party that believes in extremely limited government. Libertarians call for a freemarket system, expanded individual liberties such as drug legalization, and a foreign policy of non-intervention, free trade, and open immigration.

IS A VOTE FOR A THIRD-PARTY CANDIDATE WITH LITTLE CHANCE OF WINNING A WASTED VOTE?

In several recent close elections, including the 2000 presidential election, the vote cast for one or another minor party, if cast for the likely second choice of those voters, would have changed the outcome of the election. In such a situation, should voters care more about influencing who wins an election or more about casting a vote for a candidate whose views are closest to their own, even if that candidate has little chance of winning?

Green party
A minor party dedicated to the environment, social justice, nonviolence, and a foreign policy of nonintervention. Ralph Nader ran as the Green party's nominee in 2000.

Reform party
A minor party founded by Ross Perot in 1995. It focuses on national government reform, fiscal responsibility, and political accountability. It has recently struggled with internal strife and criticism that it lacks an identity.

believe that "every service supplied by the government can be provided better *and* cheaper by private business." Libertarians favor, in their terms, "re-legalizing" drugs and prostitiuton and also support open immigration. In 2004, a total of 278 Libertarians ran for office.[31]

The **Green party** (www.greenpartyus.org) takes its name from other pro-environment parties throughout Europe. In the United States, the Greens not only embrace pro-environment positions but are also committed to social justice, decentralization, respect for diversity, community-based economics, nonviolence, feminism, ecological wisdom, grassroots democracy, and personal and global responsibility. The party's 2004 presidential candidate, David Cobb, called for public campaign financing, greater environmental protection, and affordable housing. The party seeks to achieve social justice, eliminate discrimination, and promote self-reliance.

The **Reform party** (www.reformparty.org) was organized in 1995 by Ross Perot. It focuses on national government reform, fiscal responsibility, and political accountability. In 1996, Perot won 9 percent of the popular vote in the presidential election and qualified the party for official party status. In 2000, Pat Buchanan ran as the Reform party's presidential nominee and managed to win only 1 percent of the vote. Recently, the Reform party has been characterized by internal strife; a number of state organizations withdrew from the party, and many of the top party leaders resigned in 2002. As noted, the Reform party endorsed Ralph Nader for president in 2004.

A BRIEF HISTORY OF AMERICAN POLITICAL PARTIES

Our First Parties

To the founders of the young Republic, parties meant bigger, better-organized, and fiercer factions, and they did not want that. Benjamin Franklin worried about the "infinite mutual abuse of parties, tearing to pieces the best of characters." In his Farewell

TABLE 7–1   MINOR PARTIES IN THE UNITED STATES

Year	Party	Presidential Candidate	Percentage of Popular Vote Received	Electoral Votes
1832	Anti-Masonic	William Wirt	8%	7
1856	American (Know-Nothing)	Millard Fillmore	22	8
1860	Democratic (Secessionist)	John C. Breckinridge	18	72
1860	Constitutional Union	John Bell	13	39
1892	People's (Populist)	James B. Weaver	9	22
1912	Bull Moose	Theodore Roosevelt	27	88
1912	Socialist	Eugene V. Debs	6	0
1924	Progressive	Robert M. La Follette	17	13
1948	States' Rights (Dixiecrat)	Strom Thurmond	2	39
1948	Progressive	Henry A. Wallace	2	0
1968	American Independent	George C. Wallace	14	46
1980	National Unity	John Anderson	7	0
1992	Reform	Ross Perot	19	0
1996	Reform	Ross Perot	8	0
2000	Reform	Pat Buchanan	0	0
2000	Green	Ralph Nader	3	0
2004	Reform	Ralph Nader	0	0

Address, George Washington warned against the "baneful effects of the Spirit of Party." And Thomas Jefferson said, "If I could not go to heaven but with a party, I would not go there at all."[32]

How, then, did parties get started? Largely out of practical necessity. The same early leaders who so frequently stated their opposition to political parties also recognized the need to organize officeholders who shared their views so that government could act. To get its measures passed by Congress, the Washington administration had to fashion a coalition among factions. This job fell to Treasury Secretary Alexander Hamilton, who built an informal Federalist party, while Washington stayed "above politics."

Secretary of State Jefferson and other officials, many of whom despised Hamilton and his aristocratic ways as much as they opposed the policies he favored, were uncertain about how to deal with these political differences. Their overriding concern was the success of the new government; personal loyalty to Washington was a close second. Thus Jefferson stayed in the cabinet, despite his opposition to administration policies, during most of Washington's first term. When he left the cabinet at the end of 1793, many who joined him in opposition to the administration's economic policies remained in Congress, forming a group of legislators opposed to Federalist fiscal policies and eventually to Federalist foreign policy, which appeared "soft on Britain." This party was later known as Republicans, then as Democratic-Republicans, and finally as Democrats.[33]

Realigning Elections

American political parties have evolved and changed over time, but some underlying characteristics have been constant. Historically, we have had a two-party system with minor parties. Our parties are moderate and accommodative, meaning that they are open to people with diverse outlooks. Political scientist V. O. Key and others have argued that our party system has been shaped in large part by **realigning elections**, turning points that define the agenda of politics and the alignment of voters within parties during periods of historic change in the economy and society. Realigning elections are characterized by intense electoral involvement by the voters, disruptions of traditional voting patterns, changes in the relations of power within the community, and the formation of new and durable electoral groupings. They have occurred cyclically, not randomly. These elections tend to coincide with expansions of the suffrage or changes in the rate of voting.[34] We focus here on four realigning elections: 1824, 1860, 1896, and 1932.

1824: ANDREW JACKSON AND THE DEMOCRATS Party politics was invigorated following the election of 1824, in which the leader in the popular vote—the hero of the battle of New Orleans, Democrat Andrew Jackson—failed to achieve the necessary majority of the electoral college and was defeated by John Quincy Adams in the runoff election in the House of Representatives. Jackson, brilliantly aided by Martin Van Buren, a veteran party builder in New York State, later knitted together a winning combination of regions, interest groups, and political doctrines to win the presidency in 1828. The Whigs succeeded the Federalists as the opposition party. By the time Van Buren, another Democrat, followed Jackson in the White House in 1837, the Democrats had become a large, nationwide movement with national and state leadership, a clear party doctrine, and grassroots organization. The Whigs were almost as strong; in 1840, they put their own man, General William Henry Harrison ("Old Tippecanoe"), into the White House. A two-party system had been born, and we have had that two-party system ever since—one of few such systems worldwide.

1860: THE CIVIL WAR AND THE RISE OF THE REPUBLICANS Out of the crisis over slavery evolved a new party: the second Republican party—ultimately dubbed the "Grand Old Party" (GOP).[35] Abraham Lincoln was elected in 1860 with the support not only of financiers, industrialists, and merchants but also of large numbers of workers and farmers. For 50 years after 1860, the Republican coalition won every presidential race except

realigning election
An election during periods of expanded suffrage and change in the economy and society that proves to be a turning point, redefining the agenda of politics and the alignment of voters within parties.

FACTS ABOUT AMERICAN POLITICAL PARTIES

■ Parties began in this country as soon as people started taking sides in the debate over ratifying the U.S. Constitution, although it took a few years for them to organize into formal bodies.

■ Political parties, and especially our two-party system, have persisted over the course of our history.

■ Ours has almost always been a two-party system, differentiating us from most nations, which have a one-party or multiparty system.

■ Since 1830, we have witnessed reasonably effective competition in our national party system.

■ Our parties have historically been decentralized and fragmented. Parties are organized around states, congressional districts, counties, and cities, with state parties the most important units.

■ Winning office and power has been more important to party leaders than specific issues or platforms; political parties in the United States are primarily organized to win and hold political power.

■ Our parties can be characterized as moderate, centrist, and pragmatic, with only modest ideological cohesion and voting discipline, especially when compared to European political parties.

laissez-faire economics
Theory that opposes governmental interference in economic affairs beyond what is necessary to protect life and property.

Keynesian economics
Theory based on the principles of John Maynard Keynes, stating that government spending should increase during business slumps and be curbed during booms.

for Grover Cleveland's victories in 1884 and 1892. The Democratic party survived with its durable white male base in the South.

1896: A PARTY IN TRANSITION The Republican party's response to industrialization and hard times for farmers changed it in the late 1800s. A combination of western and southern farmers and western mining interests sought an alliance with workers in the East and Midwest to "recapture America from the foreign moneyed interests responsible for industrialization. The crisis of industrialization squarely placed an agrarian-fundamentalist view of life against an industrial-progress view."[36] The two parties also differed over whether U.S. currency should be tied to a silver or gold standard, with Republicans favoring gold and Democrats silver. William Jennings Bryan, the Democratic candidate for president in 1896, was a talented orator but lost the race to William McKinley.[37] The 1896 realignment differs from the others, however, in that the party in power did not change hands. In that sense it was a *converting realignment* because it reinforced the Republican majority status that had been in place since 1860.[38]

The Progressive era, the first two decades of the twentieth century, was a period of political reform led by the Progressive wing of the Republican party. Much of the agenda of the Progressives focused on the corrupt political parties. Civil service reforms shifted some of the patronage out of the hands of party officials. The direct primary election took control of nominations from party leaders and gave it to the rank-and-file. And in a number of cities, nonpartisan governments were instituted, totally eliminating the role of a party. With the ratification of the Seventeenth Amendment to the Constitution in 1913, U.S. senators came to be popularly elected. Women obtained the right to vote when the Nineteenth Amendment was ratified in 1920. Thus within a short time, the electorate changed, the rules changed, and even the stakes of the game changed. Democrats were unable to build a durable winning coalition during this time and remained the minority party until the early 1930s, when the Hoover administration was overwhelmed by the Great Depression.

1932: FRANKLIN ROOSEVELT AND THE NEW DEAL ALIGNMENT The 1932 election was a turning point in American politics. In the 1930s, the United States faced a devastating economic collapse. Between 1929 and 1932, the gross national product fell over 10 percent per year, and unemployment rose from 1.5 million to more than 15 million, with millions more working only part time. Herbert Hoover and the Republican majority in Congress had responded to the Depression by arguing that the problems with the economy were largely self-correcting and that their long-standing policy of following **laissez-faire economics**, a hands-off approach, was appropriate.

Voters wanted more. Franklin D. Roosevelt and the Democrats were swept into office in 1932 by a tide of anti-Hoover and anti-Republican sentiment. Roosevelt rode this wave and promised that his response to the Depression would be a "New Deal for America." He rejected laissez-faire economics and instead relied on **Keynesian economics**, which asserted that government could influence the direction of the economy through fiscal and monetary policy. After a century of sporadic government action, the New Dealers stepped in and fundamentally altered the relationship between government and society.

The central issue on which the Republicans and Democrats disagreed in the New Deal period was the role of government with respect to the economy. Roosevelt Democrats argued that the government had to take action to pull the country out of the Depression, but Republicans objected to enlarging the scope of government activity and intruding it into the economy. This basic disagreement about whether the national government should play an active role in regulating and promoting our economy remains one of the most important divisions between the Democratic and Republican parties today, although, with time, the country and both parties accepted many of the New Deal programs.

For the two decades following the 1932 election, the Republican party was relegated to watching the majority Democrats—a new coalition of union households, immigrant workers, and people hurt by the Great Depression—implement their domestic policies. During World War II, both parties cooperated in embracing a bipartisan foreign policy.

We have gone a long time since the last critical or realigning election. You will note that each realignment lasted roughly 36 years, or a couple of generations. Some political scientists anticipated that we were ripe for realignment in 1968 or 1972, but it did not happen. A shift in party allegiances among many southern whites, from the Democratic to the Republican party, coincided with the enfranchisement of southern blacks, who largely identify with the Democratic party. But this was more important regionally and did not constitute a national realignment. Now, as memories of the New Deal fade and the agenda of American politics shifts, the alignments of the 1930s and 1940s hold less and less relevance. Yet, to a surprising degree, the parties are stable and closely competitive, as recent elections demonstrated. Whether one party can seize the agenda of politics and fashion itself as the new majority party is one of the interesting political questions for the future.

Divided Government

Major shifts in the demographics of the parties have occurred in recent decades. The once "Solid South" that the Democrats could count on to bolster their legislative majorities and help win the White House has now become the "Solid Republican South" in presidential and increasingly in congressional elections as well. Republican congressional leaders—House Majority Leader Tom DeLay of Texas and Senate Majority Leader Bill Frist of Tennessee—came from states that once rarely elected Republicans. Further evidence of partisan change in the South is the sweep of U.S. Senate victories Republicans had in 2004 in Florida, North Carolina, South Carolina, and Georgia, picking up seats that had been held by Democrats going into the 2004 elections. This shift in the South is explained by the movement of whites out of the Democratic party, largely as a result of the party's position on civil rights. The rise of the Republican South reinforced the shift to conservatism in the Grand Old Party. This shift, combined with the diminished ranks of conservative southern Democrats, made the Democratic party, especially the congressional Democrats, more unified and more liberal than in the days when more of its congressional members had "safe" southern seats.

Since 1953, **divided government**, with one party controlling Congress and the other the White House, has been in effect twice as long as one-party control of both legislative and executive branches, and at other times Congress has had divided control with one party having a majority in the House and the other in the Senate. Until the 1992 and 1994 elections, the Republicans' strength had been in presidential elections, where they often won with landslide margins. Part of the explanation was their ability to attract popular candidates like Dwight Eisenhower and Ronald Reagan, but Republicans also reaped the rewards of Democratic party divisiveness and generally weaker Democratic presidential candidates. Evidence that voters are inclined to favor divided government came in the 1990s, when voters elected a Republican congressional majority in 1994 and then retained it in 1996 and 1998. Building on the Republicans' securing unified party control of government in 2002, the GOP in 2004 expanded its congressional majorities. This was especially the case in 2005 when the Republican majority in the U.S. Senate climbed to 55 Republicans versus 44 Democrats, and 1 Independent.

Republican victories in presidential elections between 1952 and 1992 were achieved with the support of some elements of Roosevelt's New Deal coalition. New Deal programs that benefited these voters had expanded the middle class and made possible the conservative "hold onto what we've got" thinking of voters in the 1980s, 1990s, and 2000. One way to interpret the closeness of the 2000, 2002, and national elections is that the country is evenly divided.

The 2000, 2002 and 2004 Elections: Into the New Century

Neither party could claim a mandate after the tightly contested 2000 elections, which resulted in a 50–50 partisan tie in the Senate, a slim Republican majority in the House, and a presidential contest whose outcome was unresolved for weeks as ballots were recounted in Florida. Although the outcome was essentially a tie, the breakdown of the vote was anything but random. The 2000 presidential results and exit polls revealed a divided nation. Al Gore carried the Northeast and Pacific states and a few urban states in

divided government
Governance divided between the parties, as when one holds the presidency and the other controls one or both houses of Congress.

the nation's midsection. George W. Bush carried the South and interior of the country, minus a few states like New Mexico. Demographically, the Democrats received large majorities of votes from African Americans, Hispanics, union households, Jews, and gays. Republicans did well among white males, religious conservatives, gun owners, and higher-income voters.[39]

The 2002 election departed from historic patterns in several respects. First, the long-standing pattern had been for the party of the president to lose seats in the House of Representatives. Since 1934, in only two elections—1998 and 2002—have the president's party gained seats. In 2002, the Republicans picked up seats in both the House and Senate, returning to the majority in the Senate and expanding their majority in the House. President George W. Bush campaigned aggressively for Republican candidates. In the last five days before the election, President Bush traveled 10,000 miles to 17 cities in 15 states. Bush and his White House political team had been deeply involved in 2002: They recruited some candidates and urged others not to run or to seek other office, they traveled to key districts and states and hosted fundraisers, and they raised party soft money for the competitive races. The net effect was a more Bush-friendly Congress, heightened political credibility, and better reelection chances in 2004. Not everything went the Republicans' way in 2002. Democrats won some key gubernatorial elections, making the number of Democratic and Republican governors nearly equal.

George W. Bush not only secured reelection in 2004 but his party picked up seats in the Senate and House. Most of the open and competitive seats in 2004 were in predictably Republican states in terms of presidential voting, such as Alaska, Oklahoma, and South Dakota. Bush carried all of these states by wide margins. In all of these states, the Senate Republican candidate won, including in South Dakota, where Senate Democratic Leader, Tom Daschle, was defeated by John Thune. Republicans also swept the open Senate seats in Florida, South Carolina, Georgia, and North Carolina. All of these seats were held by Democrats going into 2004. Democrats picked up a Republican Senate seat in 2004 with the election of Ken Salazar. Democrats also picked up a net gain of three state legislative majorities in 2004.

AMERICAN PARTIES TODAY

Americans typically take political parties for granted.[40] If anything, most people are critical or even fearful of the major parties. Parties are, in a word, distrusted. Some see parties as corrupt institutions, interested only in the spoils of politics. Critics charge that the parties evade the issues, they fail to deliver on their promises, they have no new ideas, they follow public opinion rather than lead it, or they are just one more special interest.

Still, Americans understand that parties are necessary. They want party labels kept on the ballot, at least for congressional and presidential elections as well as for statewide offices. Most voters think of themselves as Democrats or Republicans and typically vote for candidates from their party. They even contribute millions of dollars to the two major parties. Far more individual contributions go to the Republicans than to the Democrats.[41] Thus Americans appreciate, at least vaguely, that you cannot run a big democracy without parties.

Both the Democratic and Republican national parties and most state parties are moderate in their policies and leadership.[42] Successful party leaders must be diplomatic; to win presidential elections and congressional majorities, they must find a middle ground among more or less hostile groups. Members of the House of Representatives, in order to be elected and reelected, have to appeal to a majority of the voters from their own district. As more House districts have become "safe" for incumbents, the House of Representatives has become less moderate and the home of partisan ideological clashes to a greater extent than the Senate or the White House.

Although each party usually takes its extremist supporters more or less for granted and seeks out the voters in the middle, both parties retain some ideological diversity. The Democratic coalition includes the conservative Coalition for a Democratic Majority, the moderate Democratic Leadership Council (dominated by an array of southern governors and senators), a new group in 2004 called "Democrats for the West" composed of moderate western Democrats, and the liberal Americans for Democratic Action. The Democratic coalition embraces activists in the civil rights and other liberal-left movements. Republicans, while more homogeneous, have their contentious factions as well. On the more conservative side are the Religious Right, staunch supporters of the right to bear arms, and antitax activists, but also young professionals who are conservative economically but moderate or liberal on social issues like abortion and gay marriage.

As noted in Chapter 5, a gender gap exists in voting in presidential and congressional elections, with women voting Democratic more than men. As political scientist Virginia Sapiro has written, "Women and men may still be socialized to think about politics somewhat differently, or at least some groups of women and men are. The two sexes play different kinds of roles in society and family life and thus have different kinds of experiences."[43] Some interest groups also seek to reinforce the gender gap, emphasizing issues like reproductive rights, gun control, or the environment as they relate to women and often urging women to vote Democratic. Some individual Republican candidates have been successful in narrowing the gender gap.

Among Republican elected officials, the split has been between more liberal northeastern Republicans like Senator Lincoln Chafee of Rhode Island and Governor George Pataki of New York and the dominant conservative wing. Democratic officeholders also have substantial policy differences. Examples include a group of U.S. House members who are called "Blue Dog Democrats." The moniker is derived from the old reference to "yellow dog Democrats," a description of party loyalty, where a person would supposedly vote for a yellow dog before voting for a Republican. The "blue dogs" were representatives whose "moderate-to-conservative-views had been 'choked blue' by their party in the years leading up to the 1994 election."[44] Former Georgia Governor and U.S. Senator Zell Miller, also a conservative Democrat, endorsed President George W. Bush and gave an impassioned speech at the 2004 Republican National Convention. He described the Democrats running for president in a *Wall Street Journal* article as indistinguishable. He said, "Look closely, there's not much difference among them. I can't say there's 'not a dime's worth of difference' because there's actually billions of dollars' worth of difference among them. Some want to raise our taxes a trillion, while the others want to raise our taxes by several hundred billion. But, make no mistake, they all want to raise our taxes."[45]

Parties as Institutions

Like other institutions of American government—Congress, the presidency, and the courts—political parties have rules, procedures, and organizational structure. What are the institutional characteristics of political parties?

NATIONAL PARTY LEADERSHIP   The supreme authority in both major parties is the **national party convention,** which meets every four years for four days to nominate candidates for president and vice president, to ratify the party platform, and to adopt rules.

In charge of the national party when it is not assembled in convention is the *national committee.* In recent years, both parties have strengthened the role of the national committee and enhanced the influence of individual committee members. The committees are now more representative of the party rank-and-file. But in neither party is the national committee the center of party leadership.

Each major party has a *national chair* as its top official. The national committee formally elects the chair, but in reality it is the choice of the presidential nominee. For the party that controls the White House, the chair actually serves at the pleasure of the president and does the president's bidding. Party chairs often change after elections. During the 2004 election cycle the Republican National Committee (RNC) Chair was Ed Gillespie. Mr. Gillespie had been an important staff person for House Republicans, was the strategist for the Elizabeth Dole Senate campaign in North Carolina in 2002, and was the Bush spokesperson during the contentious recount in Florida in 2000.[46] He was a visible and frequently cited leader of the Republicans in 2004.

Religion is sometimes linked to partisanship. In reality, devoutly religious people are found in both major parties.

national party convention
A national meeting of delegates elected in primaries, caucuses, or state conventions who assemble once every four years to nominate candidates for president and vice president, ratify the party platform, elect officers, and adopt rules.

2004 Democratic National Committee Chairperson Terry McAuliffe.

Terry McAuliffe, the Democratic National Committee (DNC) Chair, was elected after the Democratic presidential election defeat in 2000. McAuliffe had previously served as Finance Director at both the DNC and the Democratic Congressional Campaign Committee (DCCC), the party committee for House Democratic candidates. McAuliffe chaired the Clinton/Gore reelection committee in 1996 and also chaired the 2000 Democratic National Convention. As the head of a party out of power, he was a visible spokesperson for the Democrats. He also led efforts to rebuild the party headquarters and expand its hard money fundraising base.[47]

The chair of the party without an incumbent president has considerable independence yet works closely with the party's congressional leadership. The national committee often elects a new head after an electoral defeat. Although chairs are the heads of their national party apparatus, they remain largely unknown to the voters. The chair may play a major role in running the national campaign; after the election, the power of the national chair of the victorious party tends to dwindle.

National party organizations are often agents of an incumbent president in securing his renomination. When there is no incumbent president seeking reelection, the national party committee is generally neutral until the nominee is selected. Although heated primary contests often preclude having a united party in the general election, national and state parties can attempt to dissuade candidates but in the end cannot prevent them from running.[48]

In addition to the national party committees, there are also congressional and senatorial *campaign committees.* In recent years, congressional and senatorial campaign committees have become much more active—recruiting candidates, training them, and assisting with campaign finance.[49] Senatorial campaign committees are composed of senators chosen for two-year terms by their fellow party members in the Senate; congressional campaign committees are chosen in the same manner by the House. Chairs of campaign committees are nominated by their party leadership and typically ratified by their party caucus. For information on the party committees and their leadership, go to www.nrcc.org, www.nrsc.org, www.dccc.org, and www.dscc.org. These committees have a lot of say about which candidates get party campaign funds. With the abolition of soft money, the power of the party committees was presumed to lessen. In fact, the party committees continued to be active in competitive races and battleground states through independent expenditures. While this spending did not rival the old soft money, it was substantial in 2004.

PARTY PLATFORMS   While national party committees exist primarily to win elections and gain control of government, policy goals are also important. Every four years each party formulates and adopts a platform at the national nominating convention. The typical party platform—the official statement of party policy—is often a vague and ponderous document that hardly anyone reads. Platforms are ambiguous by design, giving voters few obvious reasons to vote against the party. This generalization about party platforms does not mean that political parties do not stand for anything. Most business and professional people believe the Republican party best serves their interests, while working people tend to look to the Democrats to speak for them. The proportion of voters discerning important differences between the parties has increased sharply as the parties have become more polarized (See Figure 7–1).[50]

Many politicians contend that platforms rarely help elect anybody, but platform positions can hurt a presidential candidate. Because the platform-writing process is not always controlled by the nominee, it is possible for presidential candidates to disagree with their own party platform. But the platform-drafting process gives partisans, especially those motivated by particular issues, an opportunity to express their views, and it serves to identify the most important values and principles on which the parties are based. Once elected, politicians are rarely reminded of what their platform position was on a given issue. One major exception to this was former President George Bush's promise not to raise taxes if elected in 1988 with his memorable quote, "Read my lips— no new taxes." He was forced to eat those words when taxes were raised.[51] In reality, the winning party actually seeks to enact much of its party platform.[52]

Party platforms in 2004 were carefully controlled by the Bush and Kerry campaigns. The Republican platform played to the conservative base of the party on such issues as

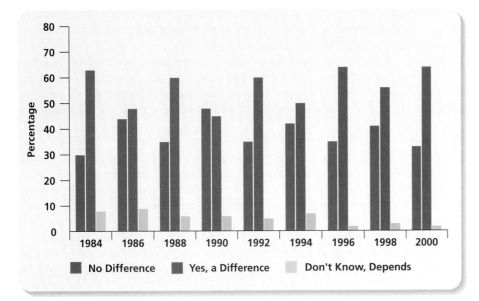

FIGURE 7–1 Important Difference in What Democratic and Republican Parties Stand for, 1984–2000.
SOURCE: *2002 National Election Study,* "Important Difference in What Democratic and Republican Parties Stand for, 1952–2000," (Center for Political Studies, University of Michigan, 2002).

abortion, gay marriage, and taxes. The Democratic platform, like the Democratic convention, sought to reassure the country that the party was strong on national security while also retaining its longstanding commitment to seniors, education, and social justice.

PARTIES AT THE STATE AND LOCAL LEVELS   The two major parties are decentralized, organized around elections in states, cities, or congressional districts. They have organizations for each level of government, national, state, and local. Party organization at the state and local levels is structured much like the national level. Each state has a *state committee* headed by a *state chair.* State law determines the composition of the state committees and sets rules regulating them. Members of state committees are usually elected from local areas. Party auxiliaries such as the Young Democrats or the Federation of Republican Women are sometimes represented as well. In many states, these committees are dominated by governors, senators, or coalitions of locally elected business and ethnic leaders. State chairs are normally elected by the state committees, although in approximately one-quarter of the states they are chosen at state conventions. When the party controls the governorship, chairs are often agents of the governor.[53]

Some powerful state parties have developed in recent years. Despite much state-to-state variation, the trend is toward stronger state organizations, with Republicans typically being much better funded.[54] In some states, third and fourth parties play a role in local elections. New York, for instance, has both a Liberal party and a Conservative party in addition to the Democratic and Republican parties. The role minor parties play in statewide elections can be important, even though they rarely win office themselves.

Below the state committees are *county committees,* which vary widely in function and power. The key role of these committees is recruiting candidates for such offices as county commissioner, sheriff, and treasurer. The recruiting job often involves finding a candidate for the office, not deciding among competing contenders. For a party that rarely wins an election, the county committee has to struggle to find someone willing to run. When the chance of winning is greater, primaries, not the party leaders, usually decide the winner.[55] Many county organizations maintain a significant level of activity, distributing campaign literature, organizing telephone campaigns, putting up posters and lawn signs, and canvassing door-to-door. Other county committees do not function at all, and many party leaders are just figureheads.

Through the 2002 election, state party organizations were the means by which millions of dollars in soft money were spent. Rulings of the Federal Election Commission made it advantageous for national parties to spend their soft money through the state parties. The focus of these expenditures was candidate promotion. In many instances, broadcast ads paid for with soft money did not even mention the party.[56] Soft money was largely banned by the BCRA enacted in 2002.

It is not clear that soft money helped build stronger parties at the state and local levels. Some soft money spending may have enhanced such party activities as building a list of active partisans in the state or district or improving the computer technology of the party offices or may have had secondary benefits when party supporters were mobilized for a U.S. Senate or House race. But for most soft money spending, state parties simply became local bank accounts for national party committee candidate-centered campaign communications. Even after the scores of millions of dollars of soft money spent by party committees, strong local party organization is rare at the city, town, ward, and precinct levels. Most local party committees are poorly financed and inactive except during the few weeks before election day.[57] In a few places, local ward and precinct leaders still do favors for constituents, from getting more police patrols in a neighborhood to organizing clambakes or obtaining horse-racing passes in a state like Arkansas.

What then was the impact of BCRA on party activity in 2004? The Democrats, who were more dependent on soft money and who had been slower to build a large hard money donor base, were the most affected. While their hard money fundraising was more successful than ever, it did not make up for the loss of soft money. Party committees for both parties spent some of their hard money in 2004 as independent expenditures in the relatively few competitive races that existed. What did make up for much of the difference was nonparty groups that raised and spent money on advertising, mail, phones, and voter mobilization. These groups, often called **527 organizations**, after the section of the tax code under which they are organized, were especially active on the Democratic side in 2004. (See Chapter 6 for a fuller disscussion of these and related groups.) Republicans had fewer allied groups campaigning for them, but they also had more hard money, which they deployed on the full range of campaign tactics, especially voter registration and mobilization. The Republican voter mobilization effort in 2002, called the 72 Hour Task Force, built on the successful mobilization effort in 2000.[58] The impact of the soft money ban was even more pronounced for the congressional campaign committees in both parties, but especially for the Democrats.

Parties in Government

Political parties are central to the operation of our government. They help bridge the separation of powers and facilitate coordination between levels of government in a federal system.

IN THE LEGISLATIVE BRANCH Members of Congress take their partisanship seriously, at least while they are in Washington. Their power and influence are determined by whether their party is in control of the House or Senate; they also have a stake in which party controls the White House. The chairs of all standing committees in Congress come from the majority party, as do the presiding officials of both chambers. Members of both houses sit together with fellow partisans on the floor and in committee.

Members of congressional staffs are also partisan. From the volunteer intern to the senior staffer, members of Congress expect their staff to be loyal first to them and then to their party. Should you decide to go to work for a representative or senator, you would be expected to identify yourself with that person's party, and you would have some difficulty working for the other party later. Employees of the House and Senate—from elevator operators to the Capitol Hill police and even including the chaplain—hold patronage jobs. With few exceptions, such jobs go to persons from the party that has a majority in the House or the Senate.

IN THE EXECUTIVE BRANCH Presidents select almost all senior White House staff and cabinet members from their own party. Presidents, however, typically surround themselves with advisers who have campaigned with them and have proved their party loyalty.

Partisanship is also important in presidential appointments to the highest levels of the federal bureaucracy. The party that wins the White House has around 5,000 noncareer positions to fill.[59] Included in these positions are cabinet-level appointments and

527 organization
Interest groups organized under Section 527 of the Internal Revenue Service code may advertise for or against candidates. If their source of funding is corporations or unions, they have some restrictions on broadcast advertising. 527 organizations were important in the 2000 and 2004 elections.

PEOPLE & POLITICS *Making a Difference* ★ ★ ★

BLAISE HAZELWOOD

During the highly contested 2004 elections the Republican National Committee (RNC) political director was Blaise Hazelwood. Her involvement in politics began at the age of 10 when she canvassed door-to-door for her father, who was running for precinct committeeman. Her interest in "grassroots" politics continued in the 2000, 2002, and 2004 election cycles, in which she was a leader in organizing the Republican voter mobilization efforts.

Hazelwood's work at the Republican National Committee began soon after she graduated from Vassar College. Ironically, after the 1994 election she and other staff were urged to seek more permanent employment. "Blaise had set her mind to stay at the RNC and began arriving at work at 6:00 A.M. and briefing Anderson (Curt Anderson, the Political Director at the time) on the news and current events. This display of determination convinced Anderson to keep her."[*] Hazelwood has played a variety of roles at the RNC, including Deputy Chief of Staff and Director of Coalitions for Victory 2000, which included work with pro-life groups, Latinos, Catholics, and many ethnic American groups.

Republicans came out of the 2000 election feeling a need to counteract the Democrats' voter mobilization strategy. Hazelwood has been instrumental in that effort. She and others organized the "72 Hour Task Force" in 2002 and 2004. This effort deployed large numbers of people, including what Hazelwood calls "paid volunteers," into key districts. Hazelwood described her approach as "fewer leaflets and more volunteers."[†] These individuals delivered person-to-person contact in the critical final phases of the 2002 and 2004 elections. In some areas the task force increased voter turnout by 2 to 3 percent.[†] According to her husband and direct mail consultant, Dan Hazelwood, "Blaise brought back the culture of grassroots campaigns into the Republican party making grassroots campaigns as important as TV, mail, and phone."[§] The Republican ground game was widely seen as having been important to the reelection of President Bush in 2004.

[*] Dan Balz, "Getting the Votes—And the Kudos: Hazelwood Helped GOP to Victory with an Emphasis on Shoe Leather." *Washington Post,* January, 1 2003, p. A17.
[†] www.abcnews.go.com/sections/politics/TheNote/TheNote_July25.html.
[‡] Dan Balz and David S. Broder, "Close Election Turns on Voter Turnout," *The Washington Post,* November 1, 2002, page A01.
[§] Dan Hazelwood, phone interview by David Magleby, August 3, 2004.

ambassadorships around the world. Party commitment, including making campaign contributions, is expected of those who seek these positions.

IN THE JUDICIAL BRANCH The judicial branch of the national government, with its lifetime tenure and political independence, is designed to operate in an expressly non-partisan manner. Judges, unlike Congress, do not sit together by political party. But the appointment process for judges has been partisan from the beginning. The landmark case establishing the principle of judicial review, *Marbury* v. *Madison* (1803), concerned the efforts of one party to stack the judiciary with fellow partisans before leaving office.[60] Today party identification remains an important consideration in the naming of federal judges. Although the party affiliation of a judicial nominee is not called for on any form, the individuals responsible for screening and evaluating candidates do take party and ideology into account. Appointees must be acceptable to certain power centers in the party. For example, Republicans in the Ronald Reagan and George Bush administrations insisted on conservative judges; Bill Clinton, although nominating Democrats, placed more importance on gender and race than on ideology in selecting judges. The confirmation process has also become increasingly partisan. Republicans claimed that Democrats were delaying hearings for George W. Bush's judicial nominees, and Democrats countered that they were responding in kind to what Republicans did to Clinton nominees when the GOP controlled the Senate.

AT THE STATE AND LOCAL LEVELS The importance of party in the operation of local government varies among states and localities. In some states, such as New York and Illinois, local parties play an even stronger role than they do at the national level. In others, such as Nebraska, parties play almost no role. In Nebraska, the state legislature is expressly nonpartisan, though factions perform like parties and still play a role. Parties are likewise unimportant in the government of most city councils. But in most states and many cities, parties are important to the operation of the legislature, governorship, or mayoralty. Judicial selection in most states is also a partisan matter. Much was made by the 2000 Bush campaign of the fact that six of the seven Florida Supreme Court justices deciding the 2000 ballot-counting case in favor of Gore were Democrats. Democrats noted that the five U.S. Supreme Court justices who decided the election in favor of Bush were Republicans.

Parties in the Electorate

Political parties would be of little significance if they did not have meaning to the electorate. Adherents of the two parties are drawn to them by a combination of factors, including their stand on the issues; personal or party history; religious, racial, or social peer grouping; and the appeal of their candidates. The emphases among these factors change over time, but they are remarkably consistent with those identified by political scientists more than 40 years ago.[61]

PARTY REGISTRATION For citizens in most states, "party" has a particular legal meaning—**party registration**. At the time voters register to vote in these states, they are asked to state their party preference. They then become registered Democrats, Republicans, Libertarians, or whatever. Voters can subsequently change their party registration. The purpose of party registration is to limit the participants in primary elections to members of that party and to make it easier for parties to contact people who might vote for their party.

PARTY ACTIVISTS Activists tend to fall into three broad categories: party regulars, candidate activists, and issue activists. *Party regulars* place the party first. They value winning elections and understand that compromise and moderation may be necessary to reach that objective. They also realize that it is important to keep the party together as much as possible, because a fractured party only helps the opposition.

Candidate activists are followers of a particular candidate who see the party as the means to place their candidate in power. Candidate activists are often not concerned with the other operations of the party—with nominees for other offices or with raising money for the party. For example, people who supported Pat Buchanan in his unsuccessful run for the presidency as a Reform party candidate in 2000 would be classified as candidate activists. Buchanan, a television commentator and unsuccessful candidate for the Republican nomination in 1996, built a personal following. Reform party members who traced their roots in the party to Ross Perot found Buchanan so repellent that they split from him and nominated their own candidate for president. Buchanan fared poorly in the 2000 election, getting less than 1 percent of the vote and as a result losing millions of dollars in federal subsidies for the 2004 elections.

Issue activists wish to push the parties in a particular direction on a single issue or a narrow range of issues: the war in Iraq, abortion, taxes, school prayer, the environment, or civil rights. To issue activists, the party platform is an important battleground because they seek party endorsement for their position. Issue activists are also often candidate activists if they can find a candidate willing to embrace their position.

Both issue activists and candidate activists insist on making their "statement" regardless of the electoral consequences. They would rather lose the election than compromise. Party activists thus include a diverse group of people who come to the political party with different objectives. It is not surprising, then, that some of the most interesting politics are over candidate selection and issue positions within the political parties. Fights over strategy and party position are conducted in open meetings and under democratic procedures. Political parties foster democracy not only by competition *between* the parties but *within* the parties as well.

party registration
The act of declaring party affiliation; required by some states when one registers to vote.

CHANGING FACE OF AMERICAN POLITICS

PORTRAIT OF THE ELECTORATE

	Republican	Democrat	Independent	Other
Sex				
Male	32%	32%	32%	4%
Female	31	35	26	7
Race				
White	36	29	30	6
Black	7	70	20	3
Hispanic	23	38	35	4
Age				
18–34	30	32	32	6
35–45	37	30	25	7
46–55	28	36	30	6
56–64	29	36	31	4
65+	32	37	27	5
Income				
$0–$14,999	20	47	27	10
$15,000–$34,999	25	41	30	17
$35,000–$49,999	29	31	33	17
$50,000–$64,999	35	31	28	12
$65,000–$84,999	36	30	26	25
$84,999+	40	27	29	16
Religion				
Protestant	46	29	22	3
Catholic	30	37	31	2
None/Atheist/Agnostic	13	38	38	13
Other/Jewish	19	40	28	13
Ideology				
Liberal	9	55	30	5
Moderate	20	35	20	5
Conservative	48	20	28	4
Region				
Northeast	30	34	33	3
North-Central	33	33	27	7
South	32	35	28	5
West	32	32	29	8
Total	31	33	28	7

SOURCE: *2002 National Election Study* (Center for Political Studies, University of Michigan, 2002). *Note: Numbers may not add up to 100 due to rounding.*

Party Identification

Party registration and party activists are important, but many voters are not officially registered with a political party. Most Americans are mere spectators of party activity. They lack the partisan commitment and interest needed for active party involvement. This is not to say that parties are irrelevant or unimportant to them. For them, partisanship is

"Very Republican. I love it."

what political scientists call **party identification**—an informal and psychological attachment with a political party that most people acquire in childhood, a standing preference for one party over another.[62] This type of voter may sometimes vote for a candidate from the other party, but in the absence of a compelling reason to do otherwise, most will vote according to their party identification. Peers and early political experiences reinforce party identification, generally acquired from parents. It is part of the political socialization process described in Chapter 4.

Party identification is the single best predictor of how people will vote. Unlike candidates and issues, which come and go, party identification is a long-term element in voting choice. The strength of party identification is also important in predicting participation and political interest. Strong Republicans and strong Democrats participate more actively in politics than any other groups and are generally more knowledgeable and informed. Pure Independents are just the opposite; they vote at the lowest rates and have the lowest levels of interest and awareness of any of the categories of party identification. This evidence runs counter to the notion that persons who are strong partisans are unthinking party adherents.[63]

Partisan Realignment and Dealignment

With the exception of the shift of southern whites to the Republican party and the enfranchisement of blacks who remain Democrats, the current system of party identification is built on a foundation of the New Deal and the critical election of 1932, events that took place nearly three-quarters of a century ago. How can events so removed from the present still be important in shaping our party system? When will there be another realignment—an election that dramatically changes the voters' partisan identification? Or has such a realignment already occurred? The question is frequently debated in the literature of political science. Most scholars believe that we have not experienced a major realignment since 1932.[64] Partisan identification has been stable for more than four decades, and even though new voters have been added to the electorate—minorities and 18- to 21-year-olds—the basic nature of the party system has trended slightly Republican but not changed dramatically. Table 7–2 presents the party identification breakdown for the period from the 1950s to 2002.

Evidence of a possible voting realignment came in the early 1980s, when Republicans won several close Senate elections and gained a majority in that body.[65] Democrats, however, won back the Senate in 1986, and until 1994 they appeared to have a permanent majority in the House. All that changed with the 1994 election, as Republicans were swept into office on a tidal wave of victories. Republicans made major inroads in the South and strengthened their share of the vote among white males.

In presidential voting, Republicans have done well, winning seven of the last ten presidential elections. Their success ratio masks a much more evenly divided electorate. Indeed, in recent years, the country has been evenly divided in partisan preferences. Democrats would also be quick to point out that their party won the popular vote in 2000, only reinforcing the point that the country is evenly divided. Why have the Republicans done better than Democrats in winning presidential elections? The answer is that they have been more effective in activating their core supporters and those few undecided voters in recent elections. Republicans also have a larger set of states they can predictably count on, forcing Democrats to win most of the populous states, which are often more competitive. The fact that Republicans have won more than they have lost in the last forty years is not yet an indication of a realignment toward the GOP.

We may therefore conclude from recent national elections that American voters overall have no consistent preference for one party over the other. In a time of such electoral volatility and low turnout, the winners and losers are determined by the basics of politics: who attracts positive voter attention, who strikes themes that motivate voters to participate, who does a better job in communicating with voters. Party identification remains important for those voters who come out to vote, and strength of partisanship remains positively correlated with turnout.

party identification
An informal and subjective affiliation with a political party that most people acquire in childhood.

TABLE 7–2 PARTY IDENTIFICATION, 1950s–2002

Decade	Strong Democrat	Weak Democrat	Independent-Leaning Democrat	Independent	Independent-Leaning Republican	Weak Republican	Strong Republican	Apolitical
1950s*	23%	23%	8%	7%	7%	15%	13%	4%
1960s	22	25	8	10	7	15	12	2
1970s	17	24	12	14	10	14	9	2
1980s	18	26	11	12	11	14	11	2
1990s	18	19	13	10	12	15	13	1
2000s	18	16	14	9	13	14	15	1

SOURCE: *2000 and 2002 National Election Study* (Center for Political Studies, University of Michigan, 2002).

NOTE: Data may not sum to 100 percent due to averaging.

*1950s percentages based on years 1952, 1956, and 1958.

Thus there are few signs of voter realignment but stronger signs of voter disengagement. Some observers feel that we are experiencing a rejection of partisanship in favor of becoming Independents, and there has indeed been an increase in the number of persons who characterize themselves as Independents. Journalist Hedrick Smith expresses a widespread view: "The most important phenomenon of American politics in the past quarter century has been the rise of independent voters, who have at times outnumbered Republicans."[66]

The **dealignment** argument—that people have abandoned both parties to become Independents—would be more persuasive were it not that two-thirds of all self-identified Independents are really partisans in their voting behavior and attitudes. One-third of those who claim to be Independents lean toward the Democratic party and vote Democratic in election after election. Another third of Independents lean toward Republicans and just as predictably vote Republican. The remaining third, who appear to be genuine Independents and who do not vote predictably for one party, turn out to be people with little interest in politics. Despite the reported growth in Independents, there are proportionately about the same number of Pure Independents now as there were in 1956.[67] There are, in short, at least three types of Independents, and most of them are predictably partisan. Table 7–3 summarizes voting behavior in recent contests for president and the House of Representatives.

Why has realignment moved so slowly? Why aren't all conservatives now happily ensconced in the Republican party and all liberals gladly lodged in the Democratic party?

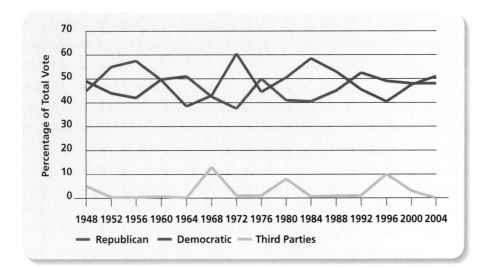

FIGURE 7–2 Presidential Vote by Party.
SOURCE: Data obtained from CQ Voting and Elections Collections, at library.cqpress.com/elections/.

dealignment
Weakening of partisan preferences that points to a rejection of both major parties and a rise in the number of Independents.

TABLE 7–3   VOTING BEHAVIOR OF PARTISANS AND INDEPENDENTS, 1992–2002

	President			U.S. House				
	1992	1996	2000	1994	1996	1998	2000	2002
Strong Democrats	93%	96%	97$	88%	87%	77%	90%	89%
Weak Democrats	68	82	89	73	70	57	73	71
Independent-leaning Democrats	70	76	72	68	69	63	73	67
Pure Independents	41	35	44	55	41	41	50	35
Independent-learning Republicans	11	20	13	25	21	24	26	27
Weak Republicans	14	20	14	21	21	25	18	25
Strong Republicans	3	5	2	7	3	7	12	8

Percent Voting Democratic

SOURCE: *2002 National Election Study* (Center for Political Studies, University of Michigan, 2002).

Americans do not casually cross party lines. If you grew up in a conservative New Hampshire family whose forebears voted Republican for a century, you are pretty much conditioned to stay with the GOP. Even if that party took a direction you disliked, you might continue to register as a Republican but quietly vote Democratic to avoid friction in the family. Or if you come from a "yellow dog" Democratic family in Texas, you might continue to vote for Democrats locally even though you disliked various Democratic candidates for president or senator. This pattern was once common throughout the South.[68]

Another reason for slow realignment is the local nature of the parties. For decades, conservative Democrats in the South have been voting for Republican candidates for president—not just George W. Bush and Ronald Reagan but also Richard Nixon and even Dwight Eisenhower—without changing their identification from the Democratic Party to the Republican.[69] Why? Partly because they still see themselves as Democrats, but also because the Democratic party remains stronger at the state and local levels in many southern states. So if candidates and voters want to have an impact on local politics, in which the only meaningful elections may be in the Democratic primaries, they retain their Democratic affiliation.

ARE THE POLITICAL PARTIES DYING?

Critics of the American party system make three allegations against it: (1) parties do not take meaningful and contrasting positions on most issues, (2) party membership is essentially meaningless, and (3) parties are so concerned with accommodating the middle of the ideological spectrum that they are incapable of serving as an avenue for social progress. Are these statements accurate? And if they are accurate, are they important?

Some analysts fear that parties are in a severe decline or even mortally ill. They point first to the long-run adverse impact on political parties of the Progressive movement reforms early in this century, reforms that robbed party organizations of their control of the nomination process by allowing masses of independent and "uninformed" voters to enter the primaries and nominate candidates who might not be acceptable to party leaders. They also point to the spread of nonpartisan elections in cities and towns and the staggering of national, state, and local elections that made it harder for parties to influence the election process.

Legislation limiting the viability and functions of parties was bad enough, say the party pessimists, but parties suffer from additional ills. The rise of television and electronic technology and the parallel increase in the number of campaign, media, and direct-mail consultants have made parties less relevant in educating, mobilizing, and organizing the electorate. Television, radio, the Internet, and telephones have strengthened the role of candidates and lessened the importance of parties. (See Chapter 10 for more on the media in this role.)

Advocates of strong parties concede that parts of this diagnosis may be correct: the demise of political machines at the local level, the decline in strong partisan affiliations, the weakness of grassroots party membership. Yet they also see signs of party revival, or at least the persistence of party. The national party organizations—the national committees and the congressional and senatorial campaign committees—are significantly better funded than they were in earlier days; they even own permanent, modern headquarters buildings in Washington, D.C., located a few blocks from the U.S. Capitol. Moreover, the parties through 2002 were capable of providing assistance to candidates in competitive races and to state and local party organizations because of their financial base, especially from soft money contributions. However, the new campaign finance reforms will likely lessen party activity. Advocates hope that strong national parties will exercise some leverage over the positions that candidates and officeholders take on party issues.[70]

Since the first years of the Reagan administration, both the Republican and Democratic parties have demonstrated a remarkable cohesiveness in Congress. This trend can be measured by the *party unity score*, defined as the percentage of members of a party who vote together on roll call votes in Congress on which a majority of the members of one party vote against a majority of the members of the other party. During the 107th Congress (2001), House and Senate Republicans voted together 90 percent of the time. Democrats were only slightly less united at 85 percent, tying their previous unity record.[71] These numbers demonstrate the growing partisanship within the two chambers. Thus while rank-and-file voters do not display strong partisan ties, party organizations and the party in government do show significant signs of strength.[72]

Reform Among the Democrats

In Chicago in 1968, the Democratic National Convention saw disputes inside the hall and riots outside, largely because of protests against the country's policy in Vietnam. Responding to the disarray and to disputes about the fairness of delegate selection procedures, members of the party agreed to a number of reforms. They established a process that led to greater use of direct primaries for the selection of delegates to the national convention and greater representation of younger voters, women, and minorities as elected delegates. Another reform was the abolition of the rule that a winner of a state's convention or primaries got all the state's delegates (the *unit rule*). This rule was replaced by a system of *proportionality* in which candidates won delegates in rough proportion to the votes they received in the primary election or convention in each state.

Chicago's former mayor Richard J. Daley, father of the current mayor of Chicago, and many other party stalwarts argued that these reforms would make the party reflective of the views of minorities within the party, such as college professors and intellectuals who would have time and resources to invest in the political process, and not working-class people, unionists, the elderly, and elected officials who depend more on group leaders to make their case. The new process also meant that elected officials who wanted a voice in determining presidential candidates had to run for delegate to the national convention. Responding to this criticism, the party created "superdelegate" positions for elected officials and party leaders who were not required to run for election as delegates.

Reform Among the Republicans

Republicans have not been immune to criticism that their party conventions and party procedures were keeping out the rank-and-file. They did not make changes as drastic as those made by the Democrats, but they did give the national committee more control over presidential campaigns, and state parties were urged to encourage broader participation by all groups, including women, minorities, youth, and the poor.

The Republican party has long had a party organization superior to that of the Democrats. In the 1970s, the GOP emphasized grassroots organization and membership recruitment. Seminars were held to teach Republican candidates how to make speeches and hold press conferences, and weekend conferences were organized for training young party professionals. The Democrats have become better organized and more professional. Both parties now conduct training sessions for candidates on campaign planning, advertising, fund raising, using phone banks, recruiting volunteers, and campaign scheduling.[73] But Republicans have cultivated a larger donor base and have been less reliant on the large-donor soft money contributions that became so controversial in recent elections.

Campaign Finance Reform and Political Parties

Following the 1976 election, both parties pressed for amendments to the Federal Election Campaign Act, claiming that campaign finance reforms resulted in insufficient money for generic party activities like billboard advertising and get-out-the-vote drives. The 1979 amendments to the act and the interpretations of this legislation by the Federal Election Commission permitted unlimited contributions to the parties by individuals and PACs for these party-building purposes. Corporations and unions could also give the parties soft money from their general funds, something they could not do in support of candidates or other party activities. With the 1996 election cycle, both parties found ways to spend this soft money in unlimited amounts to promote the election or defeat of specific candidates, effectively circumventing the campaign finance reform rules.[74]

In the 1998, 2000, and 2002 elections, congressional campaign committees, following the lead of the national party committees in the 1996 presidential election, raised unprecedented amounts of soft money. In 2000 all party committes combined raised $500 million in soft money, a figure equaled in 2002, a year without a presidential election. Soft money was spent in the most competitive races where it could help determine which party controlled Congress or the most competitive states in the 1996 and 2000 contests for the White House. This is why banning soft money became such a dedicated cause for Arizona Senator John McCain, a cosponsor of the McCain-Feingold campaign finance reform legislation. McCain, who beat George W. Bush in the New Hampshire presidential primary, in part on the basis of his challenging the party establishment on soft money, eventually lost to Bush in the 2000 nomination fight. Despite repeated defeats in one or both houses of Congress over 15 years, Congress passed the BCRA in 2002. Table 7–4 shows the effects of BCRA on the parties.

What were the implications of this surge in soft money in presidential and congressional elections? First, because soft money contributions were unlimited, the priority given to raising soft money elevated the importance of large contributors. Parties came to rely heavily on these large donors. Among the largest soft money donors to the Democrats were the Affiliated Federal State County and Municipal Employees (AFSCME), the Service Employees International Union, and the Communications Workers of America. The largest Republican soft money donors were Phillip Morris and AT&T.

Central to the arguments for BCRA was the contention that the ability of individuals and groups to donate unlimited amounts of money to the parties gives these donors extraordinary access to and influence over elected officials. Since party leaders often were the ones asking for the unlimited soft money contributions, the potential for corruption was cited by a majority of the Supreme Court as justification to uphold the 2002 BCRA legislation. The Court majority noted, "there is substantial evidence in these cases to support Congress' determination that such contributions of soft money give rise to corruption and the appearance of corruption. For instance, the record is replete with examples of national party committees' peddling access to federal candidates and officeholders in exchange for large soft-money donations."[75]

One uncertainty following BCRA was whether soft money donors would attempt to find another way to spend money on electing or defeating candidates. Some donors abandoned large donations altogether, instead making the limited and disclosed PAC or individual contributions. As we noted in Chapter 6, 2004 saw growth in PAC contributions. Other donors and some new contributors, however, pursued an alternative way to spend unlimited sums on the 2004 elections. As we have seen, they typically did this through groups formed under Section 527 of the tax code or other groups, which allowed

TABLE 7–4 EFFECTS OF THE 2002 CAMPAIGN FINANCE REFORMS

	Before 2002 Reform	After 2002 Reform
Party contributions to candidates	$5,000 per election or $10,000 per election cycle	National Party Committees are limited to $5,000 per election, although there are special limits for Senate candidates. National committees and Senate campaign committees share a contribution limit of $35,000 per campaign.
Party-coordinated expenditures with candidates	*Senate:* State voting age population times 2 cents, multiplied by the cost-of-living adjustment (COLA), or $20,000 multiplied by the COLA, whichever is greater *House:* $10,000 multiplied by the COLA; if only one representative in the state, same as the Senate limit	*Senate:* State voting age population times 7.462 cents, multiplied by the COLA, or $74,620 multiplied by the COLA, whichever is greater. *House:* $37,310 multiplied by the COLA; if only one representative in the state, the spending limit for the House nominee is $74,620, the same as the Senate limit.
Party soft money contributions to the national party committee	Unlimited	Banned
Soft money to national or state and local parties for voter registration and get-out-the-vote drives	Unlimited	Limit of $10,000 per group to each state or local party committee (Levin Amendment)
Contributions to parties for buildings	Unlimited	Banned
Party-independent expenditures	Unlimited	Unlimited, except if ad falls under "electioneering communications definition." Then source of funding is subject to FECA regulations and limits, and the ad may not be broadcast within 30 days of a primary or 60 days of a general election. Parties may choose either independent expenditures or coordinated but not both.
Individual contributions to candidates per two-year election cycle	$2,000	$4,000
Aggregate individual contribution limit to candidate or parties per two-year election cycle	$50,000	$95,000

SOURCE: www.fec.gov/pages/bcra/bcra_update.htm.

Senators John McCain (left) and Russ Feingold (right) hold a news conference to announce Senate approval of the McCain-Feingold Campaign Finance bill, aimed at reducing the influence of soft money on political campaigns.

187

THE POLITICAL HORIZON

This simulation examines party ideologies and the changes that have occurred in America's political parties. People affiliate with a party in part because of their stands on particular issues. Based on your beliefs and opinions, find out with which political party you agree most.

Go to Make It Real, "The Political Horizon."

them to spend unlimited amounts on voter registration, mobilization, mail and phone communications, and in the period prior to the two months before the general election or one month before the primary election to run ads on television. Section 527 group activity was more pronounced on the Democratic side of the 2004 election. Democratic 527 groups like the Media Fund and MoveOn advertised heavily against President Bush, especially in the period between March and September 2004. Republican groups like Swift Boat Veterans for Truth and Progress for America advertised later but were highly visible. Other groups like America Coming Together (ACT) were geared toward voter registration and mobilization of Democratic voters. Although these outside groups were more important to the Democratic effort, in the end they were important to both sides. A lot of the funding for these groups came from wealthy individuals.

Critics of BCRA had long contended that banning soft money would drive soft money to groups with less disclosure of their activity. It was clearly the case in 2004 that following Section 527 group activity was more difficult than following soft money had been in the past. Voters tend to assume that candidates are responsible for all communications in their election contests. Whether it made much difference to them if an ad was from the Ohio Democratic Party or America Coming Together is doubtful. In both cases they would have assumed that the Democratic candidate was responsible.[76]

It is unclear whether soft money had a positive effect on the parties. In competitive contests, parties have become major players, mounting their own campaigns, often against the other party's candidate. Most party spending has been on ads placed on television and radio, sent through the mail, or delivered over the telephone. To a lesser extent, parties have worked to register voters and mobilize them on election day. This latter type of activity is the only one to have an enduring effect on state and local parties. BCRA provides for limited contributions to state and local party committees; individuals and groups may donate up to $10,000 per party committee. This provision has the potential to encourage parties to continue to invest in mobilizing voters.

While the particular role parties play in financing elections may be changing, the broader roles of organizing electoral competition, simplifying voter choices, and providing an enduring psychological identification for voters have not changed. Parties are also remarkably permeable organizations that provide citizens who want to influence the course of their government an accessible and often consequential way to get involved. Finally, parties continue to reinforce federalism through the distinctive nature of many state parties.

SUMMARY

1. Political parties are essential to democracy—they simplify voting choices, organize the competition, unify the electorate, help organize government by bridging the separation of powers and fostering cooperation among branches of government, translate public preferences into policy, and provide loyal opposition.

2. Political parties help structure voting choice by nominating candidates to run for office. Before the advent of direct primaries, in which voters determine the party nominees, the parties had more control over who ran under their label. States determine the nomination rules. While most states employ the direct primary, some use a caucus or mixed caucus system where more committed partisans have a larger role in the decision of who gets nominated. Recently,

some states adopted a blanket primary in which voters could vote for a candidate from any party. These primaries were declared unconstitutional.

3. American parties are moderate. Bringing factions and interests together, they are broad enough to win the presidency and other elections. Third parties have been notably less successful. One reason for this is our single-member-district, winner-take-all election rules. In systems with proportional representation or multimember districts, there is a greater tendency for more parties to form and consequently a need to assemble governing coalitions of several parties.

4. American parties have experienced critical elections and realignments. Most political scientists agree that the last realignment occurred in 1932. In recent years, there has been divided government

and an increase in the number of persons who call themselves Independents. This trend is sometimes called dealignment, but most Independents are closet partisans who vote fairly consistently for the party toward which they lean.

5. For half a century, it has been routine to have divided government, with one party in control of the presidency and the other in control of one or both houses of Congress. Successful presidents have found ways to cope with divided government and enact important parts of their agenda. The 2002 election gave Republicans unified government with control of both houses of Congress and the White House. Republican control of national government was strengthened by the 2004 elections.

6. Parties are governed by their national and state committees, and the focal points of

party organization are the national and state party chairs. When the party controls the executive branch of government, the executive (governor or president) usually has a determining say in selecting the party chair. With the rise of soft money in recent elections, parties had more resources to spend on politics. In 2002, Congress banned soft money except for some narrowly defined and limited activities.

7. Party platforms are vague and general by design, giving the other party and voters little to oppose.

8. Parties are vital in the operation of government. They are organized around elected offices at the state and local levels. Congress is also organized around parties, and judicial and many executive branch appointments are based in large part on partisanship.

9. Parties are also active in the electorate, seeking to organize elections, simplify voting choices, and strengthen party identification.

10. Frequent efforts have been made to reform our parties. The Progressive movement saw parties, as then organized, as an impediment to democracy and pushed direct primaries as a means to reform them. Following the 1968 election, the Democratic party took the lead in pushing primaries and stressing greater diversity among the individuals elected as delegates. Republicans have also encouraged broader participation, and they have improved their party structure and finances.

11. The Bipartisan Campaign Reform Act (BCRA) significantly changed the role of

party committees by banning soft money and raising hard money contribution limits to the parties. One consequence of BCRA was a renewed emphasis on building a large individual donor base. Donors wanting to spend more than the BCRA limits did so in 2004 through a range of interest groups, many of which were allied 527 groups that ran parallel campaigns with the candidates and parties in 2004.

12. Compared to some European parties, ours remain organizationally weak. There has been some party renewal in recent years as party competition has grown in the South and the parties themselves have initiated reforms.

K E Y   T E R M S

political party	honeymoon	winner-take-all system	divided government
party column ballot	caucus	minor party	national party convention
office block ballot	party convention	Libertarian party	party registration
nonpartisan election	direct primary	Green party	party identification
patronage	open primary	Reform party	dealignment
soft money	crossover voting	realigning election	527 organization
hard money	closed primary	laissez-faire economics	
independent expenditures	proportional representation	Keynesian economics	

F U R T H E R   R E A D I N G

JOHN H. ALDRICH, *Why Parties? The Origin and Transformation of Party Politics in America* (University of Chicago Press, 1995).

PAUL ALLEN BECK AND MARJORIE RANDON HERSHEY, *Party Politics in America*, 10th ed. (Longman, 2002).

JOHN F. BIBBY *Politics, Parties, and Elections in America*, 5th ed. (Wadsworth, 2002).

DAVID BOAZ, *Libertarianism: A Primer* (Free Press, 1998).

MARY C. BRENNAN, *Turning Right in the Sixties: The Conservative Capture of the GOP* (University of North Carolina Press, 1995).

BRUCE E. CAIN AND ELISABETH R. GERBER, EDS., *Voting at the Political Fault Line: California's Experiment with the Blanket Primary* (University of California Press, 2002).

LEON EPSTEIN, *Political Parties in the American Mold* (University of Wisconsin Press, 1986).

DONALD GREEN, BRADLEY PALMQUIST, AND ERIC SCHICKLER, *Partisan Hearts and Minds* (Yale University Press, 2002).

JOHN C. GREEN AND RICK FARMER, EDS., *The State of the Parties: The Changing Role of Contemporary American Parties*, 4th ed. (Rowman & Littlefield, 2003).

JOHN C. GREEN AND PAUL S. HERRNSON, EDS., *Responsible Partisanship?: The Evolution of American Political Parties Since 1950* (University Press of Kansas, 2002).

PAUL S. HERRNSON AND JOHN C. GREEN, EDS., *Multiparty Politics in America: Prospects and Performance*, 2d ed. (Rowman & Littlefield, 2002).

WILLIAM J. KEEFE AND MARC J. HETHERINGTON, *Parties, Politics, and Public Policy in America*, 9th ed. (Congressional Quarterly Press, 2003).

BRUCE E. KEITH, DAVID B. MAGLEBY, CANDICE J. NELSON, ELIZABETH ORR, MARK C. WESTLYE, AND RAYMOND E. WOLFINGER, *The Myth of the Independent Voter* (University of California Press, 1992).

DAVID B. MAGLEBY, ED., *Financing the 2000 Election* (Brookings Institution Press, 2002).

DAVID B. MAGLEBY AND J. QUIN MONSON, EDS., *The Last Hurrah? Soft Money and Issue Advocacy in the 2002 Congressional Electons* (Brookings Institution Press, 2004).

L. SANDY MAISEL AND KARA Z. BUCKLEY *The Electoral Process*, 4th ed. (Rowman & Littlefield, 2005).

KELLY D. PATTERSON, *Political Parties and the Maintenance of Liberal Democracy* (Columbia University Press, 1996).

STEVEN J. ROSENSTONE, ROY L. BEHR, AND EDWARD H. LAZARUS, *Third Parties in America: Citizen Response to Major Party Failure*, 2d ed. (Princeton University Press, 1996).

JEFFREY M. STONECASH, MARK D. BREWER, AND MACK D. MARIANI, *Diverging Parties: Social Change, Realignment, and Party Polarization* (Westview Press, 2003).

JAMES SUNDQUIST, *Dynamics of the Party System: Alignment and Realignment of Political Parties in the United States*, rev. ed. (Brookings Institution Press, 1983).

PUBLIC OPINION, PARTICIPATION, AND VOTING

8

Undecided or "swing voters" received a lot of attention in competitive states in the 2004 presidential election. In June 2004, well before either party held its nominating convention, the proportion of undecided voters was very small compared to the same time period in earlier elections, with fewer than one-in-ten voters undecided.[1] The closeness of the 2000 presidential election in states like Florida and New Mexico reinforced the urgency of finding and converting undecided voters in 2004. Undecided voters in competitive states were courted by both sides, receiving multiple campaign communications. The 2004 election cycle saw a renewed emphasis on person-to-person contact and also targeted communications through the mail and on the telephone. In the battleground states, undecided voters received many communications about the election, often from both sides. Groups and parties were also part of this "ground war." Part of the 2004 effort included registering new voters. Republicans also concentrated on activating voters who had infrequently voted in the past. The result was a much higher turnout, especially in the competitive states, with some voters standing in line for two or more hours waiting to vote.

In a nation as evenly divided as the United States is now, candidates must also effectively mobilize their most loyal supporters, or what is often called the "base." To do this they reaffirm their support for issues or groups that matter to the base. President Bush did this by supporting a constitutional amendment defining marriage as between a man and a woman. He also committed himself to further budget and tax cuts. John Kerry had an unusually unified base, in part because four years out of power motivated

TIME LINE

PUBLIC OPINION, PARTICIPATION, AND VOTING

1870	Fifteenth Amendment guarantees the right to vote regardless of race
1920	Nineteenth Amendment gives women the right to vote
1924	Native Americans given citizenship and the right to vote
1935	First Gallup poll
1936	*Literary Digest* poll erroneously predicts FDR loss to Alf Landon
1965	Voting Rights Act forbids racial discrimination in voting practices in the states
1971	Twenty-sixth Amendment extends the vote to 18–20-year-olds
1984	For the first time, more women vote than men
1993	"Motor Voter Bill" expands the ways in which voters can register
2002	Help America Vote Act passed, modernizing voting technology

Democratic voters to unify in hopes of winning. Kerry also sent clear signals to blacks, Hispanics, union members, people who are pro-choice on abortion, and others that he was the better candidate for them.

At the individual level, likely voters in states where the outcome was close and who had already made up their minds were bombarded with postcards reminding them to vote and phone calls reminding them that it was election day and that their vote was needed. For example, in 2004, the candidates and parties mobilized voters to vote early in states where that was possible. This effort, sometimes called "banking the vote," reduced the list of people the campaigns needed to mobilize on election day. On election day, poll watchers would track who had not yet voted and those who had pledged support were again called and urged to vote.

Campaigns learn about the candidate preferences and the issue positions of potential voters through inrterviews conducted on the telephone or in person, a process called a *canvass*. Individuals who are undecided and probable voters in competitive races are likely to receive communications that persuade them to vote for one particular candidate and motivate them to vote. Interest groups and political parties may also conduct a canvass, followed by mail and phone calls, often reinforcing the same themes expressed by the candidates. In 2004, the Republican party took the lead for the Bush/Cheney campaign in mobilizing voters.

On the Democratic side a consortium of interest groups working together under the name "America Votes" shared data from the canvass and coordinated follow-up contacts. Among the groups participating in America Votes were America Coming Together (ACT), the AFL-CIO, Sierra Club, League of Conservation Voters, Planned Parenthood, NARAL-Pro Choice America, and more than 25 other groups. The focus of both the Republican Party and America Votes was highly competitive states in the 2004 presidential election, sometimes called battleground states. There were relatively few competitive Senate or House contests in 2004 and most of these were not in presidential battlegrounds. Overall, less than 10 percent of House races and only about twice that proportion of Senate races were competitive. Some of these were highly contested, such as the Senate races in South Dakota and Alaska. Most races for the Senate and House in 2004 saw much less activity.

The volume of communication in presidential battleground states was extraordinary. Voters in battleground states received unprecedented levels of contact in the 2004 presidential election. One household in Akron, Ohio, received 15 phone calls in the 24 hours before the polls closed. One home in Tallmadge, Ohio, received 11 unique pieces of mail from the Republican National Committee alone in 2004. Groups, candidates, and the parties all sent mail to voters they thought needed reinforcement or persuasion.

We learned from recent elections that a few hundred votes can determine an election outcome. Candidates cannot take any votes for granted, so in close contests voter mobilization is critical. In this chapter, we look at the nature and level of political participation in the United States, and why people vote as they do. We begin by exploring the related topic of public opinion, how to measure it, and the factors that affect the formation of opinions.

PUBLIC OPINION

All governments in all nations must be concerned with public opinion. Even in nondemocratic nations, unrest and protest can topple those in power. And in a constitutional democracy, citizens can express opinions in a variety of ways, including demonstrations, letters to their elected representatives and to newspaper editors, and voting in free and regularly scheduled elections. There are clear and direct connections between what voters want and what our governments do. In short, democracy and public opinion go hand in hand.

What Is Public Opinion?

Politicians frequently talk about what "the people" think or want. But social scientists use the term more precisely: We define **public opinion** as the distribution of individual preferences for, or evaluations of, a given issue, candidate, or institution within a specific population. *Distribution* means the proportion of the population that holds a particular opinion, compared to people with opposing opinions or those with no opinion at all. Public opinion is most commonly studied by systematic measurement through polls or survey. For instance, final preelection polls in 2004 by the Gallup Organization found that among potential voters, 49 percent reported they would vote for George W. Bush, 49 percent for John Kerry, and 1 percent for Ralph Nader. The actual vote was Bush 51 percent, Kerry 48 percent, and Nader .35 percent.

In addition to polls conducted by Gallup, Pew, and other such organizations, newspapers and TV networks conduct polls on election preferences and numerous other subjects.

TAKING THE PULSE OF THE PEOPLE In a public opinion poll, a relatively small number of people can accurately represent the opinions of a larger population through the use of random *sampling* of people to survey. In a *random sample,* every individual has a known chance of being selected. The sample of randomly selected respondents should be appropriate for the questions being asked. For instance, a survey of 18- to 24-year-olds should not be done solely among college students, since roughly three-quarters of the members of this age group do not attend college. Even with proper sampling, surveys have a *margin of error,* meaning that the sample accurately reflects the population within a certain range—usually plus or minus 3 percent for a sample of at least 1,500 individuals. The final preelection survey results in 2004 were indeed within this margin of error for the actual vote.

The *art of asking questions* is also important to scientific polling. The wording of questions can influence the answers. Question order can also alter the responses. Good questions have to be pretested to be sure that the way a question is asked does not bias how it is answered. Questions should be delivered by trained and professional interviewers, who read them exactly as written and without any bias in their voices. Questions can be worded in different ways to measure factual knowledge, opinions, the intensity of opinion, or views on hypothetical situations. Sometimes *open-ended questions* are asked to permit respondents to answer in their own words rather than in set categories. Open-ended questions are harder to record and compare, but they allow respondents to express their views more clearly and may provide deeper insight into their thinking.

In addition to random sampling and clearly worded questions, thorough *analysis and reporting of the results* are required of scientific polls. Scientific polls inform the public of the sample size, the margin of error, and when and where the poll was conducted. It is also important to realize that public opinion can change from day to day and hour to hour. Polls are really snapshots of opinion at a point in time rather than moving pictures of opinions over time.

Individual preference emphasizes that when we measure public opinion, we are asking *individuals*—not groups—about their opinions. The *universe or population* is the relevant group of people for the question. When a substantial percentage of a sample agrees on an issue—for example, that we should honor the American flag—there is a *consensus.* But on most issues, opinions are divided. When two opposing sides feel intensely about an issue, the public is said to be *polarized.* The Vietnam War in the 1960s is an example of a polarizing issue. A recent example of a polarizing issue is gay marriage. One characteristic of such issues is that it is difficult to compromise or find a middle ground. An example of a contemporary issue with polarized opinions is gay marriage. Neither those who favor legalizing gay marriage nor those who unequivocally oppose see

public opinion
The distribution of individual preferences for or evaluations of a given issue, candidate, or institution within a specific population.

How you ask a polling question makes a lot of difference in the responses people give, as demonstrated in five different polls that asked about a proposed constitutional amendment defining marriage. The first two questions were part of national surveys conducted by CBS. The third question was part of an ABC/*Washington Post* poll. The fourth question was asked by the Pew Research Center for the People and the Press.

1. Would you favor or oppose an amendment to the U.S. Constitution that would allow marriage ONLY between a man and a woman?

Favor	60%
Oppose	37%
Don't Know	3%

2. Would you favor or oppose an amendment to the U.S. Constitution that would allow marriage only between a man and a woman, and outlaw marriages between people of the same sex?

Favor	51%
Oppose	42%
Don't Know	7%

3. Would you support amending the U.S. Constitution to make it illegal for homosexual couples to get married anywhere in the United States, or should each state make its own laws on homosexual marriage?

Amend Constitution	44%
State Laws	53%
Don't Know	3%

4. Do you strongly favor, favor, oppose, or strongly oppose allowing gays and lesbians to marry legally? IF OPPOSE GAY MARRIAGE ASK: There has been a proposal to change the U.S. Constitution to ban gay marriage. Do you think amending the Constitution to ban gay marriage is a good idea or a bad idea?

Total Favor	32%
Total Oppose	59%
(For those opposed) Good idea / favor Const. amendment	36%
Bad idea / oppose Const. amendment	21%
Don't Know / Refused	2%
Don't Know / Refused	9%

SOURCE: The Pew Research Center for the People and the Press, "Reading the Polls on Gay Marriage and the Constitution," July 13, 2004, at www.people-press.org/commentary/display.php3?AnalysisID=92.

political socialization
The process most notably in families and schools by which we develop our political attitudes, values, and beliefs.

much room for compromise. The exception is those who oppose it but would favor some legal rights going to gay couples through "civil unions." (See Table 8–1.)

INTENSITY The factor called *intensity* produces the brightest and deepest hues in the fabric of public opinion. The fervor of people's beliefs varies greatly. For example, some individuals mildly favor gun control legislation and others mildly oppose it, some people are emphatically for or against it, and some have no interest in the matter at all; still others may not have even heard of it. People who lost their jobs or retirement savings because of corporate scandals likely feel more intensely about enhanced regulation of corporations and accounting firms than people who have not been directly affected by the scandals. Intensity is typically measured by asking people how strongly they feel about an issue or about a politician. Such a question is often called a *scale*.

LATENCY *Latency* refers to political opinions that exist but have not been fully expressed; they may not have crystallized, yet they are still important, for they can be aroused by leaders and converted into political action. Latent opinions set rough boundaries for leaders who know that if they take certain actions, they will trigger either opposition or support from millions of people. If leaders have some understanding of latent opinions—people's unexpressed wants, needs, and hopes—they will know how to mobilize people and draw them to the polls on election day. Many who lived in communist Poland, East Germany, Czechoslovakia, or Yugoslavia must have had latent opinions favorable to democracy—opinions supporting majority rule, freedom, and meaningful elections. The speed with which these countries embraced democratic reforms was possible when leaders encouraged widespread expression of such ideas. A more recent example of a latent opinion is the desire for security from foreign enemies, which had not been a concern before the terrorist attacks of September 11, 2001. Wanting homeland security has now became a manifest opinion.

SALIENCE By *salience* we mean the extent to which people believe issues are relevant to them. Most people are more concerned about personal issues like paying their bills and keeping their jobs than about national issues, but if national issues somehow threaten their security or safety, salience of national issues rises sharply. Saliency and intensity, while different, are often correlated on the same issue.

The salience of issues may change over time. During the Great Depression of the 1930s, Americans were concerned mainly about jobs, wages, and economic security. By the 1940s, foreign affairs came to the forefront. In the 1960s, problems of race and poverty aroused intense feelings. In the 1970s, Vietnam and then Watergate became the focus of people's attention. By the 2000s, concern about Social Security, health care, education, terrorism, and national security had become salient issues. Events like terrorist attacks or ongoing strife in Iraq tend to reinforce or elevate the importance of an issue.

How Do We Get Our Political Opinions and Values?

No one is born with political views. We learn them from many mentors and teachers. The process by which we develop our political attitudes, values, and beliefs is called **political socialization**. This process starts in childhood, and the family and the schools are usually the two most important political teachers. Children learn the content of our culture in childhood and adolescence but reshape it as they mature.[2] Socialization lays the foundation for political beliefs, values, ideology, and partisanship.

A common element of political socialization in all cultures is *nationalism,* a consciousness of the nation-state and of belonging to that entity. Robert Coles describes it this way:

> As soon as we are born, in most places on this earth, we acquire a nationality, a membership in a community. . . . A royal doll, a flag to wave in a parade, coins with their engraved messages—these are sources of instruction and connect a young person to a country. The attachment can be strong, indeed, even among children yet to attend school, wherever the flag is saluted, the national anthem sung. The attachment is as parental as the words imply—homeland, motherland, fatherland. . . . Nationalism works its way into just about every corner of the mind's life.[3]

TABLE 8–1 DIFFERING OPINIONS ON GAY MARRIAGE

	Opposed to Legalizing Gay Marriage	Opposed to Legalizing Gay Marriage but Favor Civil Unions*	Favor Legalizing Gay Marriage
Total	**61%**	**34%**	**30%**
Gender			
Men	67	32	24
Women	54	36	36
Region			
Northeast	52	46	34
Midwest	62	28	29
South	66	26	24
West	61	45	35
Age			
18–29	50	34	42
30–44	60	34	32
45–64	58	37	30
65+	81	31	12
Church Attendance			
More than once a week	82	20	10
Once a week	69	30	24
Once or twice a month	58	31	31
A few times a year	55	42	33
Never	45	50	45
Race			
Whites	62	35	31
African Americans	59	28	19
Latinos	61	37	30
Party			
Republican	74	27	18
Democrat	54	37	33
Independent	58	40	36
Political Philosophy			
Conservative	79	23	16
Moderate	57	48	32
Liberal	38	38	51
Marital Status			
Married or living as married	65	34	26
Others	54	36	35
Education			
High school or less	68	28	21
Some college	60	40	33
College degree or more	49	44	42

*Asked only of respondents who said "opposed" to legalizing gay marriage.

SOURCE: *National Annenberg Election Survey 2004,* "American Public Remain Opposed to Same-Sex Marriages as They Begin in Massachusetts, Annenberg Data Show," May 17, 2004, www.annenbergpublic policycenter.org/naes/2004_03_corrected-gay-marriage-update_05-17_pr.pdf.

"It should be 'yes' or 'no' or 'undecided'—
we don't accept a 'don't give a damn'
answer!"

Cartoon Features Syndicate.

The sources of our views are immensely varied in the pluralistic political culture of the United States. Political attitudes may stem from religious, racial, gender, ethnic, or economic beliefs and values. But we can make at least one generalization safely: We form our attitudes through participation in *groups,* and not only in groups such as families, schools, social organizations, and more political ones like the National Rifle Association or Planned Parenthood, but especially in close-knit groups like the family. When we identify closely with the attitudes and interests of a particular group, we tend to see politics through the "eyes" of that group.[4] Group affiliation does not necessarily mean that individual members do not think for themselves. Each member brings his or her own emotions, feelings, memories, and resistance to groups.

Children in the United States tend at an early age to adopt common values that provide continuity with the past and that legitimate the American political system. Young children know what country they live in, and their loyalty to the nation develops early. Although the details of our political system may still elude them, most young Americans acquire a respect for the Constitution and for the concept of participatory democracy, as well as an initially positive view of the most visible figure in our democracy, the president.[5]

FAMILY Most social psychologists agree that family is the most powerful socializing agent.[6] American children typically show political interest by the age of ten, and by the early teens their interest may be fairly high. Consider your own political learning process. You probably formed your picture of the world by listening to a parent at dinner or by absorbing the tales your older brothers and sisters brought home from school. Perhaps you also heard about politics from grandparents, aunts, and uncles. You, in turn, influenced your family, if only by bringing some of your own hopes and concerns home from school. What we first learn in the family is not so much specific political opinions as basic *attitudes* that shape our opinions—attitudes toward our neighbors, political parties, other classes or types of people, particular leaders (especially presidents), and society in general.

Studies of high school students indicate a high correlation between the political party of the parents and the partisan choice of their children. This relatively high degree of correspondence continues throughout life. Such a finding raises some interesting questions: Does the direct influence of parents create the correspondence? Or does living in the same social environment—neighborhood, church, socioeconomic group— influence parents and children? The answer is *both,* and one influence often strengthens the other. For example, a daughter of Democratic parents growing up in a small southern town with strong Democratic leanings will be affected by friends, by other adults, and perhaps by youngsters in a church group, all of whom may reinforce the attitudes of her parents.[7] What happens when a young person's parents and friends disagree? Young people tend to go along with parents rather than friends on underlying political attitudes such as party affiliation, with friends rather than parents on some specific issues like the death penalty or gun control, and somewhere in between in their actual political behavior such as votes in presidential elections.[8]

SCHOOLS Schools also mold young citizens' political attitudes. American schools see part of their purpose as preparing students to be citizens and active participants in governing their communities and nation. At an early age, schoolchildren begin to pick up specific political values and acquire basic attitudes toward our system of government. Education, like the family, prepares Americans to live in society.

From kindergarten through college, students generally develop political values consistent with the democratic process and supportive of the American political system. In their study of American history, they are introduced to our nation's heroes and heroines, the important events in our history, and the ideals of our society. Other aspects of their experience, such as the daily Pledge of Allegiance and occasional programs or assemblies, seek to reinforce respect of country. Children also gain practical experience in the workings of democracy through elections for class or school officers and student government. In some high schools and colleges, the state legislature or college trustees require students to take courses in U.S. history or American government to graduate.

Do school courses and activities give young people the skills needed to participate in elections and democratic institutions? A study of 18- to 24-year-olds commissioned

American children learn early the importance of participatory democracy.

by the National Association of Secretaries of State found that young people "lack any real understanding of citizenship . . . information and understanding about the democratic process . . . and information about candidates and political parties."[9] "Furthermore, the Secretaries of State report noted that most young people do not seek out political information and that they are not very likely to do so in the future."[10] You and your classmates are not a representative sample in part because you are taking this course and therefore have more interest and knowledge than most people.

The debate about whether there is peer pressure on college campuses to conform to certain acceptable ideas or to use particular language highlights the role higher education can play in shaping attitudes and values. How does college influence political opinions? One study suggests that college students are more likely than people of the same age who are not attending college to be knowledgeable about politics, more in favor of free speech, and more likely to talk and read about politics.[11] Is this the influence of the professors, the curriculum, the students, or the background of people attending collge? It is difficult to generalize. Parents sometimes fear that professors have too much influence on their college-age children; however, most professors doubt that they have a significant influence on the political views of their students.

MASS MEDIA   Like everybody else, young people are exposed to a wide range of media—school newspapers, national newspapers, the Internet, movies, radio, television—all of which influence what they think. They, like adults, often pick and choose the media with which they agree, so their exposure is *selective*. The mass media also serve as agents of socialization by providing a link between individuals and the values and behavior of others. The popular media help shape the attitudes and opinions of the people who watch, listen to, or read them. News broadcasts present information about our society; events that get intensive media coverage often focus our attention on certain issues. For example, the hours of TV coverage of the war in Iraq directed widespread attention to the ethnic groups there and to the difficulty of establishing a lasting peace. Similiarly, many Americans turned their attention to Islamic fundamentalism in the aftermath of the terrorist attacks of September 11, 2001.

OTHER INFLUENCES   Religious, ethnic, and racial attitudes also shape opinions, both within and outside the family. Generalizations about how people vote are useful, but we have to be careful about stereotyping people. For example, not all African Americans vote Democratic and not all Catholics agree with their church's position against abortion. It is a mistake to assume that because we know a person's religious affiliation or racial background, we know his or her political opinions.

Stability and Change in Public Opinion

Adults are not simply the sum of all their early experiences, but few change their opinions very often. Even if the world around us changes rapidly, we are slow to shift our loyalties or to change our minds about things that matter to us. In general, people who remain in the same place, in the same occupation, and in the same income group throughout their lives tend to have stable opinions. People often carry their attitudes with them, and families who move from cities to suburbs often retain their big-city attitudes for at least a time after they have moved. Political analysts are becoming more interested in the ways in which adults modify their views. A harsh experience—a war, economic depression, or loss of a job—may be a catalyst for change in attitudes and opinions

The September 11, 2001, terrorist attacks on the World Trade Center in New York, on the Pentagon in Washington, D.C., and on Flight 93 that crashed in Pennsylvania had at least a short-term impact on public trust and confidence in government. Political Scientist Robert D. Putnam has for several years been studying how the public views political institutions and community interaction. Putnam conducted a national survey in the summer of 2000. Following the terrorist attacks, he reinterviewed the same respondents to see how their views had changed. Table 8–2 shows the changes in selected dimensions. Putnam found that more than half of his sample expressed greater confidence in government after the attacks. Interest in public affairs grew by 27 percent among

The Chicago Herald Tribune *was so sure of its polling data in the 1948 election, they predicted a win for Republican Thomas Dewey before the results were final. A victorious Harry Truman displays the mistaken headline.*

GLOBAL *Perceptions*

QUESTION: Please tell me if you think that the Internet represents a change for the better, a change for the worse, or it hasn't made much difference.

The Internet is becoming a more important part of political participation. People not only learn about news, but they can engage in political conversations; contribute money to candidates, causes, and parties; and in some places even vote via the Internet. But as the Pew Global Attitudes survey data demonstrate, the world has very different attitudes toward the Internet. Some places, like Vietnam, China, Canada, and the United States, have overwhelmingly positive views of the Internet. In these places some people have ready access to this tool, while in others like China and Vietnam access is more limited. Despite this limited access, people in China and Vietnam view the Internet positively.

But the Pew data are revealing in another way as well. In many less developed countries a large number of people, and in some places a majority of people, don't know much about the Interent. There this potential democratic tool has not become familiar. Places like Uganda and Pakistan lag behind more developed countries in public awareness of the Internet. This is a helpful reminder that not everyone in the world has access to the modern tools of democracy.

SOURCE: Pew Global Attitudes Project, *Views of a Changing World* (Washington, D.C.: The Pew Research Center for the People and the Press, 2003), p. T-15.

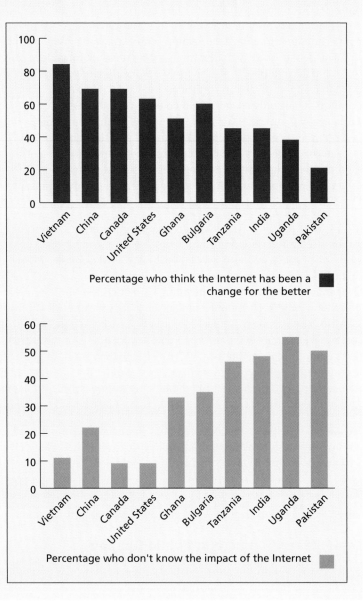

Percentage who think the Internet has been a change for the better ▪

Percentage who don't know the impact of the Internet ▪

younger people (age 35 and under) and 8 percent among older respondents. Putnam concludes, "Americans don't only trust political institutions more: We also trust one another more, from neighbors and co-workers to shop clerks and perfect strangers. Following the attacks, Americans express confidence that people in their community would cooperate, for example, with voluntary conservation measures in an energy or water shortage." The events of September 11 also appear to have led people to be "somewhat more generous."[12] How enduring these changes are is not yet clear and may be more consequential in people's private lives than in their public activities like voting, volunteering, or becoming more involved in politics. Putnam's subsequent research found that trust in community leaders, neighbors, other races, etc., declined by spring 2002, but it remained higher than before 9/11. Confidence in community cooperation also "tended to fade over time." On the other hand, civic engagement has continued at its post-9/11 level and maybe even gotten stronger.[13]

TABLE 8–2   CHANGES IN PUBLIC PERCEPTION AFTER TERRORIST ATTACKS OF SEPTEMBER 11, 2001

	Increased	Decreased	Net Change
Trust national government	51%	7%	44%
Trust local government	32	13	19
Hours watching TV	40	24	16
Interest in politics	29	15	14
Trust local police	26	12	14
Inter-racial trust	31	20	11
Trust shop-clerks	28	17	11
Support for unpopular book in library	28	18	10
Trust neighbors	23	13	10
Contributions to religious charity	29	20	9
Expect crisis support from friends	22	14	8
Trust "people running my community"	32	24	8
Worked with neighbors	15	8	7
Trust local news media	30	23	7
Gave blood	11	4	7
Volunteered	36	29	7
Expect local cooperation in crisis	23	17	6
Worked on community project	17	11	6
Attend political meeting	11	6	5
Newspaper readership	27	24	3
Visit with relatives	43	40	3
Attended club meeting	29	26	3
Attended public meeting	27	26	3
Contributions to secular charity	28	27	1
Attend church	20	19	1
Organizational memberships (number)	39	39	0
Had friends visit your home	39	45	− 6
Support for immigrants rights	21	32	−11

SOURCE: The Saguaro Seminar: Civic Engagement in America, January 15, 2002, www.ksg.harvard.edu/saguaro/press.html.

Some of our political opinions change very little because they are part of our core values. An example might be our attitudes toward abortion. Thus our views on abortion, the death penalty, and doctor-assisted suicide remain relatively stable over time. On issues that are less central to our values, such as our view of how a president is performing his job, opinions can show substantial change over time. Figure 8–1 contrasts the public opinion on President Bush with their views on abortion over time. On many issues, public opinion can change once the public learns more about the issue or perceives that there is another side to the question. It is on these issues that politicians can help shape attitudes. The decisions by Dwight Eisenhower, John Kennedy, and Lyndon Johnson to enforce school desegregation are examples of leadership of public opinion, as were the positions of Jimmy Carter on the Panama Canal Treaty and George H. W. Bush and Bill Clinton on the North American Free Trade Agreement (NAFTA).[14]

Public Opinion and Public Policy

For much of human history, it has been difficult to measure public opinion. "What I want," Abraham Lincoln once said, "is to get done what the people desire to be done, and the question for me is how to find that out exactly."[15] Politicians in our day do not face such uncertainty about public opinion; far from it.[16] Polling informs them of public

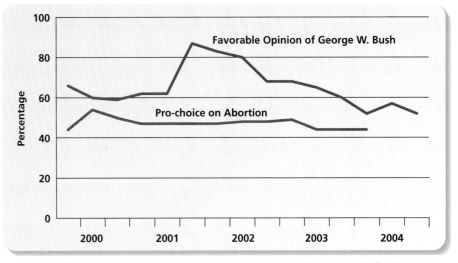

FIGURE 8–1 Comparison of Opinion of President George Bush and Attitude on Abortion Over Time.
SOURCE: Abortion/Pro-choice: Polling Report, at www.pollingreport.com/abortion.htm; Opinion of George W. Bush: Polling Report, at www.pollingreport.com/BushFav.htm9; USA Today/CNN/Gallup Poll reports, at www.usatoday.com/news/politicselections/nation/polls/usatodaypolls.htm.

opinion on all major policy issues. Politicians can commission polls themselves, or they can turn to public or media polls. More than 80 percent of newspapers and half of all television stations conduct or commission their own polls.[17]

Here are some examples of how public opinion can shape policy and in turn how policies shape opinion. During the Vietnam War, antiwar demonstrations on college campuses spread to cities all over the country. "Public opinion had a substantial impact on the rate of troop withdrawals."[18] In the Persian Gulf War, opposition to the use of U.S. forces was greatly reduced after a few days of success in the air and ground war. When American forces were dispatched to Somalia in Operation Restore Hope in January 1993, fully 79 percent of the public approved of the use of troops to ensure the delivery of humanitarian aid, food, and medical provisions. But when U.S. soldiers were killed and dragged through the streets of Mogadishu, support fell to only 17 percent in October of the same year.[19] On May 3, 2003, the day after Bush announced "Mission Accomplished" in the Iraq War on an aircraft carrier, 72 percent of Americans approved of the way Bush had handled the situation with Iraq. About a year later, after the Abu Ghraib prison torture and repeated attacks on American forces in Iraq, the Bush approval rating had fallen to 34 percent.[20]

Typically, elected officials focus on issues of importance to the public.[21] In a sense they follow public opinion. They use polls to learn how to talk about issues in ways that resonate with the public. Winning reelection is a strong motive for members of Congress.[22] "Legislators show greater attention to public opinion as election day looms," and the closeness of the fit between constituent opinion and roll call voting reflects that connection.[23] Candidates use polls to determine where to campaign, how to campaign, and even whether to campaign. The decision about which states John Kerry and George W. Bush most aggressively campaigned in was driven by the polls and a preoccupation with securing 270 electoral votes. Both campaigns lavished time and attention on Ohio, Florida, Wisconsin, Iowa, and Pennsylvania. Even smaller states like New Hampshire and New Mexico received substantial attention. Large states like New York, California, and Texas were taken for granted because one side or the other was ahead. A secondary objective was a plurality in the popular vote.

Surely polls are no substitute for elections. With a ballot before them, voters must translate their opinions into concrete decisions. They must decide what is important and what is not. Democracy is more than the expression of views, more than a simple mirror of opinion. It also involves choosing among leaders, taking sides on certain issues, and selecting the governmental actions that may follow. Democracy is the thoughtful participation of people in the political process. Elections, despite their failings, still establish the link between the many opinions "We the People" hold and the selection of our leaders.

Awareness and Interest

For most people, politics is of secondary importance to earning a living, raising a family, and having a good time; some Americans are more concerned about which team wins the World Series or the Super Bowl than they are about who wins the school board elections, who gets to be mayor, or even who gets to be president of the United States. Most people find politics complicated and difficult to understand. And they should, for democracy *is* complicated and difficult to understand. But it helps to understand the mechanics and structures of our government such as how the government operates, how the electoral college works, how Congress is set up, and the length of

These college students feel responsible to vote and line up on campus to fill out absentee ballots.

terms for the president and for members of the Senate and House of Representatives.

Details about how the government works are typically best known by younger adults, who remember learning them in school. The general adult public, however, fares poorly when quizzed about their elected officials.[24] Just over 15 percent of Americans are able to recall the name of the congressional candidates from their district.[25] With so many voters not knowing who represents them in Congress, it is not surprising that "on even hotly debated congressional issues, few people know where their Congress member stands."[26]

Although the public's knowledge of institutional and candidate issues is poor, its knowledge of important public policy issues is worse. In 1982, after approximately 59 years of debate over ratification of the Equal Rights Amendment, nearly one-third of the adults in the United States indicated they had never heard of it. The same is true for many issues.[27] In 2004, only 31.7 percent were able to correctly identify William Rehnquist as the Chief Justice of the U.S. Supreme Court, 8.6 percent incorrectly identified him, and 59.7 percent didn't know.[28] Fortunately, not all Americans are uninformed or uninterested. About 25 percent of the public is interested in politics most of the time. This is the **attentive public**, people who know and understand how the government works. They vote in most elections, read a daily newspaper, and "talk politics" with their families and friends. They tend to be better educated and more committed to democratic values than other Americans.

At the opposite end of the spectrum are *nonvoters,* people who are rarely interested in politics or public affairs and who rarely vote. About 67 percent of Americans have indicated that they are interested "some of the time," "only now and then," or "hardly at all."[29] A subset of this group might be called *political know-nothings.* These individuals not only avoid political activity but also have little interest in government and limited knowledge about it.

Between the attentive public and the political know-nothings are the *part-time citizens,* roughly 40 percent of the American public. These individuals participate selectively in elections, voting in presidential elections but usually not in others. Politics and government do not greatly interest them; they pay only minimal attention to the news, and they rarely discuss candidates or elections with others.

Democracy can survive even when a large number of citizens are passive and uninformed, as long as a substantial number of people serve as opinion leaders and are interested and informed about public affairs. Obviously, these activists will have much greater influence than their less active fellow citizens.

attentive public
Those citizens who follow public affairs carefully.

When the student pro-democracy protest was stopped by Chinese government tanks in Tiananman Square on June 5, 1989, one man stood up in defiance until he was pulled to safety by bystanders.

PARTICIPATION: TRANSLATING OPINIONS INTO ACTION

Americans influence their government's actions in several ways, many of which are protected by the Constitution. They vote in elections, join interest groups, go to political party meetings, ring doorbells, call friends urging them to vote for issues or candidates, sign petitions, write letters to the editors of newspapers, and make calls to radio talk shows.

Protest is also a form of political participation. Our political system is remarkably tolerant of protest that is not destructive or violent. Boycotts, picketing, sit-ins, and marches are all legally protected. Rosa Parks and Martin Luther King Jr. used nonviolent protest to call attention to what they saw as unfair laws (see Chapter 17). The number of Americans who participate in protests is small, but the impact of their actions in shaping public opinion can be substantial.

A distinguishing characteristic of a democracy is that citizens can influence government decisions by participating in politics. When the citizens of Belgrade turned out night after night to protest the nullification of their election, they forced Slobodan Milosevic to permit the victorious candidate, Vojislav Kostunica, to take power. But protests and demonstrations are not always peaceful or successful. In totalitarian societies, participation is very limited, forcing people who want to influence government to resort to violence or revolution. The protest of Chinese students in Tiananmen Square in 1989 failed to stop the onslaught of tanks and the repression that followed. Americans sometimes forget that our democracy was born of revolution but that maintaining a constitutional democracy after the revolution is difficult and demands public participation.

Even in an established democracy, people may feel so strongly about an issue that they would rather fight than accept the verdict of an election. The classic example is the American Civil War. Following the election of 1860, in which Lincoln, an antislavery candidate who did not receive a single electoral vote from a slave state, won the presidency, the South took up arms. The ensuing war marked the breakdown of democracy. Examples in our own time include antiabortion or animal rights groups that use violence to press their political agenda and militia groups that arm themselves for battle against government regulations.

Participation can also include less intense activity and even engaging in patriotic rituals. For example, large numbers of Americans routinely sing the national anthem or recite the Pledge of Allegiance. They communicate their views about government and politics to their representatives in Washington and the state capitol. They serve as jurors in courtrooms and enlist in the military. They express concern about the involvement of American military forces in foreign hostilities. They complain about taxes and government regulations. And many families feel it important that their children visit Washington, D.C., and other historic sights.

For most people, politics is a private activity. Some still consider it impolite to discuss politics at dinner parties. To say that politics is private does not mean people do not have opinions or will not discuss them when asked by others, including pollsters. But often politics is avoided in discussions with neighbors, work associates, even friends and family, as too divisive or upsetting. Typically, less than one person in four attempts to influence how another person votes in an election. An even smaller number actually work for a candidate or party. Only about 11 percent make a contribution to a candidate,[30] and only 11 percent of taxpayers designate $3 of their taxes to the fund that pays for presidential general elections (see Table 8–3).[31] Few individuals attempt to influence others by writing letters to elected officials or to editors of newspapers for publication. Even smaller numbers participate in protest groups or activities. Despite the small number of persons who engage in these activities, it would be a mistake to assume that small numbers of individuals cannot make a difference to politics and government. An individual or small group can generate media interest in an issue and expand the impact. Peaceful protests for civil rights, about environmental issues, and both for and against abortion have generated public attention and even changed opinions.[32]

COUNTING VOTES

Until the 2000 election, Americans took the counting of ballots for granted. But with the closeness of that election and the controversy surrounding election administration in Florida, the public became aware that counting votes is not a simple matter.

Votes are counted in the United States according to state law as administered by local officials. There has been great variability in the technology used in voting. In Florida in 2000, some counties used paper ballots, others voting machines, others punch-card ballots, and at least one used ballots that could be scanned by a computer. More recently Florida and other states have moved to computerized voting systems with touch

TABLE 8–3 POLITICAL PARTICIPATION AND AWARENESS IN THE UNITED STATES

Watched Campaign on TV	62%
Vote in presidential elections	55
Vote in congressional elections	42
Try to persuade vote of others	29
Display campaign button, sticker, or sign	9
Give money to help a campaign	11
Attend dinner, meeting, or rally for candidate	5

SOURCE: U.S. Bureau of the Census, *Statistical Abstract of the United States: 2003* (U.S. Government Printing Office, 2003), p. 269; The 2002 National Election Study, Center for Political Studies, University of Michigan. The NES Guide to Public Opinion and Electoral Behavior, at www.umich.edu/~nes/nesguide/gd-index.htm#6; See also www.census.gov.

PEOPLE & POLITICS *Making a Difference* ★★★

STEVE ROSENTHAL AND AMERICA COMING TOGETHER

One of the most important developments of the 2004 election cycle was the growth of Section 527 organizations (see Chapter 7), and the most visible and important of these groups was America Coming Together (ACT).* This group was headed by Steve Rosenthal, who previously had been the political director of the American Federation of Labor-Congress of Industrial Organizations (AFL-CIO) and Ellen Malcom, formerly of EMILY'S List, a pro-choice group that supports female Democratic candidates. The funding for ACT came from several individuals and groups who shared a commitment to defeating George W. Bush in 2004.

Rosenthal, who says he "barely made it out of High School," has deep roots in the labor movement. As a child a brick was thrown through the front window of his home to warn his father not to form a union.† Rosenthal himself became a member of the Communications Workers of America and worked for the union for twelve years. He also has consulted with numerous political candidates. During the Clinton administration he served as Associate Deputy Secretary of Labor. He has also held positions in the Democratic National Committee.

Rosenthal is best known as having returned the labor movement to its roots of person-to-person communication at the workplace, on the phone, and at the doorstep. Rosenthal describes his method as follows: "what I do when I am thinking about an election is I break it down person by person, name by name, every single voter that we talk to, and who they talk to, to connect them to what we need to do in this state."† During the 2004 election cycle ACT, under Rosenthal's direction, targeted more than a dozen states with a concerted effort to register and then turn out voters. ACT registered large numbers of new voters, many of whom voted in 2004. But it was the Republican voter mobilization that carried the day, an effort in many ways patterned after what Rosenthal had done at the AFL-CIO.

*Jeffrey H. Birnbaum, "The New Soft Money: Campaign-Finance Reform Didn't Kill Big Political Donations, It Just Changed the Rules of the Game. Meet the Players." *Fortune*, November 10, 2003, p. 155.
†Ann Gerhart, "Ground War: Steve Rosenthal Wages a $100 Million Battle to Line Up Democratic Votes," *The Washington Post*, July 6, 2004, p. C1.
‡Ibid.

screens. Another lesson reinforced by the recent ballot-counting controversies is that in every election, in every jurisdiction, and with every technology there are imperfections in voting. Touch screens are vulnerable to manipulation of the software, paper ballots are subject to human error in counting, punch cards may not always have the punches perforate, and so on. The goal in election administration is to minimize errors and eliminate bias as much as possible.

But counting votes is more complicated than the means by which we vote. There are also judgment calls that election officials have to make about incomplete or flawed ballots. In the Florida controversy of 2000, substantial attention was devoted to punch-card ballots in which the ballot did not have a completely perforated "chad" or portion of the ballot the stylus was to punch. Did a dangling chad or one that protruded but was not perforated count? These decisions mattered in an election as close as Florida's was in 2000. With the growth in absentee voting and with the law allowing military and civilians living abroad to cast their ballots and return them by mail, election officials face the possibility of a close election not being decided until days after the ballots are cast.

The issue of who may vote on election day is also important to how elections are administered. Some groups contend that the voting rolls in states like Florida were incomplete in 2000 and voters who had registered were not on the rolls. In 2004 there was some confusion, for voters who only voted in presidential elections had their voting place or precinct changed as a result of the 2002 redistricting. Voters who think they should be allowed to vote but who are not on the rolls are allowed to cast what are called provisional ballots. These ballots are only counted if it is determined that the voter was in fact registered to vote.

Congress and state legislatures in the wake of the 2000 election have invested billions of dollars in new voting technology, new rules on provisional ballots, and an effort to modernize voting methods. Florida acted soon after 2000 allocating $32 million[33] to upgrade voting machinery and banning the punch card and paper ballots. The federal government enacted the Help America Vote Act (HAVA) and authorized $3.9 billion to assist states in making voting more reliable and accessible.[34]

Interest groups, political parties, and candidates made the integrity of the 2004 voting process a high priority. Thousands of individuals were poll watchers. Groups established toll free hot lines for voters to call if they felt they were not being fairly treated, and lawyers were on call to file immediate challenges in key jurisdictions. The monitoring of voting was most intense in Ohio, where Republicans charged that Democratic-allied groups had registered Daffy Duck and Mary Poppins. Republicans also threatened to challenge the registration of many of the newly registered voters as they voted. Florida also had controversy in the period before the election regarding newly registered voters and the voting status of felons who had served their jail terms. While there were some delays on election day, they were more the result of insufficient voting booths and machines and not a large-scale challenge to the voting lists.

Voting

Americans' most typical political activity is voting. The United States is a constitutional democracy with more than 200 years of free and frequent elections and a tradition of the peaceful transfer of power between competing groups and parties.

Originally, the Constitution left it to the individual states to determine the crucial question of who could vote, and the qualifications for voting differed considerably from state to state. All states except New Jersey barred women from voting, many did not permit African Americans to vote, and until the 1830s, property ownership was often a requirement. By the time of the Civil War, the franchise had been extended to all white male citizens in every state. Since that time, eligibility standards for voting have been expanded seven times by legislation and constitutional amendments (see Table 8–4).

The civil rights movement in the 1960s, which made voting rights a central issue, secured adoption of the Twenty-Fourth Amendment and passage of the 1965 Voting Rights Act. The Voting Rights Act banned literacy tests, eased registration requirements, and provided for the replacement of local election officials with federal registrars in areas

TABLE 8–4   CHANGES IN VOTING ELIGIBILITY STANDARDS SINCE 1870

Timeline	Change
1870	Fifteenth Amendment forbade states from denying the right to vote because of "race, color, or previous condition of servitude."
1920	Nineteenth Amendment gave women the right to vote.
1924	Congress granted Native Americans citizenship and voting rights.
1961	Twenty-Third Amendment permitted District of Columbia residents to vote in federal elections.
1964	Twenty-Fourth Amendment prohibited the use of poll taxes in federal elections.
1965	Voting Rights Act removed restrictions that kept African Americans from voting.
1971	Twenty-Sixth Amendment extended the vote to citizens age 18 and older.

where the denial of the right to vote had been most blatant. Its passage resulted in a dramatic expansion of black registration and voting. Once African Americans were permitted to register to vote, "the focus of voting discrimination shifted . . . to preventing them from winning elections."[35] In southern legislative districts where blacks are in the majority, however, there has been a "dramatic increase in the proportion of African American legislators elected" (see Figure 8–2).[36]

Registration

One peculiarly American legal requirement—**voter registration**—arose in response to concerns about voting abuses, but it also discourages voting. Most other democracies have automatic voter registration. Average turnout in the United States is more than 30 percentage points lower than in countries like Australia, Austria, Belgium, Denmark, Germany, and Italy.[37] This was not always the case. In fact, in the 1800s, turnout in the United States was much like that of Europe today. Turnout began to drop significantly around the turn of the twentieth century, in part as a result of election reform (see Figure 8–3). Voter registration requirements have a substantial impact on rates of voting.[38]

American elections in the 1800s were different from those of today. Ballots were prepared by the parties, often using different colors of paper that allowed party officials to monitor how people had voted. In some areas, charges of multiple voting generated a reform movement that substituted the **Australian ballot**, a secret ballot printed by the state, for the party printed ballots This same reform period also pressed for voter

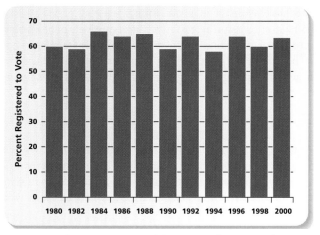

FIGURE 8–2 Percentage of African Americans Registered to Vote, 1980–2000.
Source: U.S. Bureau of the Census, *Statistical Abstract of the United States, 2001* (U.S. Government Printing Office, 2001), p. 251.

voter registration
System designed to reduce voter fraud by limiting voting to those who have established eligibility by submitting the proper form.

Australian ballot
A secret ballot printed by the state.

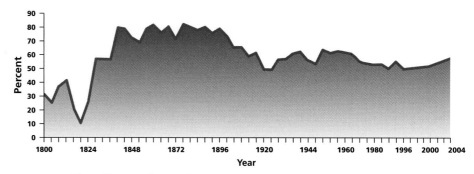

FIGURE 8–3 Voter Turnout in Presidential Elections, 1800–2004.
SOURCE: Howard W. Stanley and Richard G. Niemi, *Vital Statistics on American Politics, 1999–2000* (CQ Press, 2000). See also "National Voter Turnout in Federal Elections, 1996–2000," at www.infoplease.com/ipa/A0781453.html. 2004 update by authors.

registration to reduce multiple voting and limit voting to those who had previously established their eligibility.

Registration laws vary by state, but in every state except North Dakota, registration is required in order to vote. Six states permit election day voter registration: Idaho, Maine, Minnesota, New Hampshire, Wisconsin, and Wyoming. The most important provision regarding voter registration may be the closing date. Through the early 1970s, it was not uncommon for closing dates to be six months before the election; now, by federal law, no state can stop registration more than 30 days before a federal election.[39] Voter registration places a responsibility on voters to take an extra step—usually filling out a form at the country courthouse, when renewing a driver's license, or with a roving registrar—some days or weeks before the election and every time they move to a new address. Other important provisions include places and hours of registration.[40]

Motor Voter

The burdens of voter registration were eased a bit when, on May 20, 1993, President Bill Clinton signed the National Voter Registration Act—called the "Motor Voter" bill because it allows people to register to vote while applying for or renewing a driver's license. Offices that provide welfare and disabled assistance can also facilitate voter registration. States have the option to include public schools, libraries, and city and county clerks' offices as registration sites. The law also requires states to allow registration by mail using a standardized form. Motor Voter requires that a questionnaire be mailed to registered voters every four years to purge for death and change of residence but forbids purging for any other reasons, such as nonvoting.

The law has been successful, at least in terms of numbers of new voters registered.[41] Early data on the impact of Motor Voter suggest that neither Democrats nor Republicans are the primary beneficiaries because most who have registered claim to be Independent.[42] Yet even with the increase in registration, Motor Voter does not appear to have increased turnout.

Turnout

Americans hold more elections for more offices than the citizens of any other democracy. In part because there are so many elections, American voters tend to pick and choose which elections to vote in. Americans elect officeholders in *general elections,* determine party nominees in *primary elections,* and replace senators who have died or left office in *special elections.*

Elections held in years when the president is on the ballot are called *presidential elections,* elections held midway between presidential elections are called *midterm elections,* and elections held in odd-numbered calendar years are called *off-year elections.* Midterm elections (like the ones in 2002 and 2006) elect about one-third of the U.S. Senate, all members of the House of Representatives, and most governors and other

IN COMPARATIVE PERSPECTIVE

Registration and Voting in the World's Democracies

	Average Voter Turnout*	Compulsory Voting†	Automatic Registration‡
Australia	82.7%	Yes	No
Austria	85	No	Yes
Belgium	85	Yes	Yes
Canada	68	No	Yes
Denmark	84	No	Yes
Finland	79	No	Yes
France	67	No	No
Germany	81	No	Yes
Greece	80	Yes	No
Ireland	75	No	Yes
Israel	80	No	Yes
Italy	93	Yes	Yes
Japan	69	No	Yes
Netherlands	85	No	Yes
New Zealand	86	No	No
Norway	80	No	Yes
Spain	77	No	Yes
Sweden	83	No	Yes
Switzerland	49	No	Yes
United Kingdom	75	No	Yes
United States	48	No	No

SOURCE: Richard S. Katz, *Democracy and Elections* (New York: Oxford University Press, 1997), pp. 234–235; International Institute for Democracy and Electoral Assistance, "Voter Turnout from 1945 to Date: A Global Report on Political Participation," at www.idea.int/voter_turnout/voter_turnoutl .html.

*Percentage of turnout for total voting age population (VAP).

†In a *compulsory voting* system, registered voters are required to turn out to vote.

‡Automatic registration uses another form of citizen identification, such as an identity card or a driver's license.

In an effort to make registration easier, states have made registration forms available at motor vehicle stations, schools, public buildings, and even highway tollbooths.

statewide officeholders as well as large numbers of state legislators. Many local elections to elect city councils and mayors are held in the spring of odd-numbered years.

Turnout—the proportion of the voting-age public that votes—is highest in presidential general elections (see Figure 8–4). When examining turnout across states and over time it is best to use as the standard against which you measure turnout the Census Bureau's estimate of population over the age of 18. Because states have different voter registration requirements, the Census Bureau's estimate of eligible voters is the better baseline from which to compare state differences in turnout. Turnout is higher in general elections than in primary elections and higher in primary elections than in special elections. Turnout is higher in presidential general elections than in midterm general elections, and higher in presidential primary elections than in midterm primary elections.[43] This is due to greater interest in and awareness of presidential elections. Turnout is higher in elections in which candidates for federal office are on the ballot (U.S. senator, member of the House of Representatives, president) than in state elections in years when there are no federal contests. Some states elect their governor and other state officials in odd-numbered years to separate state from national politics. The result is generally lower turnout. Finally, local or municipal elections have lower turnout than state elections, and municipal primaries generally have the lowest rates of participation.

Turnout peaked in 1960 at more than 65 percent of persons eligible to vote, but it has since declined to just under 60 percent in 2004.[44] In midterm elections, turnout was 39 percent nationally in 2002, up 3 percent from 1998. Competition tends to encourage turnout, as was the case in Ohio and Florida in 2004 and in states like Minnesota and South Dakota in 2002. More competitive elections generate more interest in the public and more spending by the candidates which in turn stimulate participation. The number of potential voters has increased since the 1960s because the Voting Rights Act of 1965 added large numbers of African Americans to the pool of registered voters. Younger voters were also given the right to vote with the Twenty-Sixth Amendment in 1971. Our electorate has also grown richer and more educated since the 1960s. Since wealth and education are related to voting, we should have seen an increase instead of a decrease in voting. However, over 80 million eligible Americans failed to vote in the 2004 presidential election; the nonvoting figures are even higher for congressional, state, county, and local elections.[45]

Who Votes?

The extent of voting varies widely among different groups. Level of education especially helps predict whether people will vote; as education increases, so does the propensity to vote. "Education increases one's capacity for understanding complex and intangible subjects such as politics," according to one study, "as well as encouraging the ethic of civic responsibility. Moreover, schools provide experience dealing with a variety of bureaucratic problems, such as coping with requirements, filling out forms, and meeting deadlines."[46]

Race and ethnic background are linked with different levels of voting, in large part because they correlate with education. In other words racial and ethnic minorities with college degrees vote at about the same rate as whites with college degrees. Blacks in

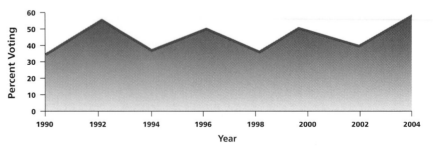

FIGURE 8–4 Voter Turnout in Presidential and Midterm Elections, 1990–2004.

Source: U.S. Bureau of the Census, *Statistical Abstract of the United States,* 1998 (U.S. Government Printing Office, 1998), p. 97; Louis V. Gerstner, "Next Time, Let Us Boldly Vote as No Democracy Has Before," *USA Today,* November 16, 1998, p. A15; www.infoplease.com/ipa/A0781453.html; National Voter Turnout in Federal Elections: 1960–2000. 2004 update by authors.

turnout
The proportion of the voting-age public that votes, sometimes defined as the number of registered voters that vote.

CHANGING FACE OF AMERICAN POLITICS

VOTER TURNOUT BY DEMOGRAPHIC FACTORS

	1992	1994	1996	1998	2000	2002
Sex						
Men	60.2%	44.4%	52.8%	41.4%	53.1%	41.4%
Women	62.3	44.9	55.5	42.4	56.2	43.0
Race						
White	63.6	46.9	56.0	43.3	56.4	44.1
Black	54.0	37.0	50.6	39.6	53.5	39.7
Hispanic	28.9	19.1	26.7	20.0	27.5	18.9
Education						
Some high school	41.2	27.0	33.8	25.0	33.6	23.3
High school graduate	57.5	40.5	49.1	37.1	49.4	37.1
Some college	68.7	49.1	60.5	46.2	60.3	45.8
College graduate	81.0	63.1	73.0	57.2	72.0	58.5
Age						
18 to 24	42.8	20.1	32.4	16.6	32.3	17.2
25 to 34	53.2	32.2	43.1	28.0	43.7	27.1
35 to 44	63.6	46.0	54.9	40.7	55.0	40.2
45 to 64	70.0	56.0	64.4	53.6	64.1	53.1
65 and over	70.1	60.7	67.0	59.5	67.6	61.0

SOURCE: U.S. Census Bureau, *Statistical Abstract of the United States, 2003* (U.S. Government Printing Office, 2003), p. 269; U.S. Census Bureau, "Voting and Registration in the Election of November 2002: Detailed Tables for Current Population Report," at www.census.gov/prod/2004pubs/p20-552.pdf.

general turn out at lower rates than whites, although this is beginning to change. African American participation in the 2004 election increased by 25 percent from the 2000 election but this still only counted for 11 percent of the electorate. Turnout among black voters surged in many states in 2000. Although nationwide, African Americans accounted for 10 percent of the total vote, the same percentage as in 1996, some states experienced exceptional increases. For example, in Florida, African American turnout increased by 68 percent, from 530,000 in 1996 to 893,000 in 2000. Missouri and Illinois also experienced exceptional turnout among black Americans. One of the major reasons was an unprecedented voter mobilization effort mounted by the National Association for the Advancement of Colored People. The NAACP's National Voter Fund spent $10 million on a get-out-the-vote campaign. Mobilization efforts can affect election outcomes in races as close as those of 2000 and 2004. In 2004, groups like America Coming Together, the NAACP, and others were especially active. Both candidates spoke to African American groups but President Bush declined the invitation to speak to the NAACP

In 2004 both parties mounted major efforts to register and mobilize Hispanic voters, a group likely to be of growing importance. Candidates, parties, and allied interest groups, anticipating another very close election in 2004, made voter mobilization a high priority. Their efforts included personal appeals, often at the doorstep, where people were invited to register to vote, efforts to get people to vote early by absentee ballot, and offers of rides to the polls on election day. The intensity of the voter mobilization in 2004 was high compared to other recent elections.

Women, another historically underrepresented group, have increased their voting levels to the point that since 1984 more women than men vote.[47] Women's recent higher turnout is generally attributed to increasing levels of education and employment.

This poster, published by the League of Women Voters, urged women to use the vote the Nineteenth Amendment had given them.

A major initiative to register young persons and encourage them to vote was undertaken in 2004. The mobilization effort appeared to work, with more than 4.6 million more voters aged 18–29 voting in 2004 than in 2000. While an impressive gain, because of generally higher turnout, young voters as a percentage of all voters did not increase in 2004. Studies of young voters before the 2004 election found that 57 percent of young adults said that the election would have a "great deal" or "quite a bit" of impact on the country's future, in contrast to the 33 percent of young adults who responded this way during the 2000 election.[48]

Income and age are also important factors in voting. Those with higher family incomes are more likely to vote than those with lower incomes. Income, of course, corresponds to occupation, and those with higher-status careers are more likely to vote than those with lower-status jobs. Poor people are less likely to feel politically involved and confident, and their social norms tend to deemphasize politics.[49] Older people, unless they are very old and infirm, are more likely to vote than younger people. The greater propensity of older persons to vote will only amplify the importance of this group as baby boomers age and retire.

How Serious Is Nonvoting?

Although Americans can hardly avoid reading or hearing about political campaigns, especially during an election as intensely fought as that of 2004, about 40 percent of all Americans fail to vote. Who are they? Why don't they vote? Is the fact that so many Americans choose not to vote a cause for alarm? If so, what can we do about it?

The simplest explanation for low turnout is that people are lazy, but there is more to it than that. Of course, some people are apathetic, but the vast majority of Americans are not. Paradoxically, we compare favorably with other nations in political interest and awareness, but for a variety of institutional and political reasons, we fail to convert these qualities into votes (see Table 8–5).

The difficulty of voting in the United States, the cost in time and effort, is higher than in other democracies. In our system, people are required to register to vote, and they must decide how to vote for a large number of offices, and in many states how to vote on ballot questions relating to public policy or constitutional amendments. Elections in the United States are held on weekdays rather than holidays or weekends as they often are elsewhere. Another factor in the decline of voter turnout since the 1960s is the Twenty-Sixth Amendment, which lowered the voting age to 18. It increased the number of eligible voters, but that group is the least likely to vote. With ratification of the amendment in 1971, turnout fell from 62 percent in 1968 to 57 percent in 1972.[50]

Some political scientists argue that nonvoting is not a critical problem. "Nonvoting is not a social disease," contends Austin Ranney, a noted scholar of politics. He points

TABLE 8–5 WHY PEOPLE DON'T VOTE	
Too busy, conflicting schedule	27.1%
Illness or disability (own or family's)	13.1
Not interested, felt vote would not make a difference	12
Out of town or away from home	10.4
Other reason, not specified	9
Did not like candidates or campaign issues	7.3
Refused or don't know	7.5
Registration problems	4.1
Forgot to vote (or send in absentee ballot)	5.7
Inconvenient polling place or hours or lines too long	1.4
Transportation problems	1.7
Bad weather conditions	0.7

SOURCE: U.S. Bureau of the Census, "Reasons for Not Voting, by Sex, Age, Race and Hispanic Origin, and Educational Attainment: November 2002," at www.census.gov.

out that legal and extralegal denial of the vote to African Americans, women, Hispanics, persons over 18, and other groups has now been outlawed, so nonvoting is voluntary. He quotes the late Senator Sam Ervin of North Carolina: "I don't believe in making it easy for apathetic, lazy people to vote."[51] Some might even contend that nonvoting is a sign of voter satisfaction.

Those who argue that nonvoting is a critical problem cite the "class bias" of those who do vote. The social makeup and attitudes of nonvoters differ significantly from those of voters and hence greatly distort the representative system. "The very poor . . . have about two-thirds the representation among voters than their numbers would suggest." Thus the people who need help the most from the government lack their fair share of electoral power to obtain it. And, it is argued, this situation is growing worse.[52]

Declining participation through voting and other political acts has puzzled some political scientists because voting rates have continued to decline even as level of education, a strong predictor of voting, has increased—part of the answer to the puzzle may be that political parties and other groups have done less voter mobilization over time. In other words, some people don't vote because no one asks them to. Furthermore, advances in technology allow parties and campaigns to narrowly target their appeals to people who are already likely to turn out.[53]

Low voting, according to those who see a class bias in voting, reflects "the underdevelopment of political attitudes resulting from the historic exclusion of low-income groups from active electoral participation."[54] In short, part of the problem of nonvoting among low-income, less-educated people is their failure to be conscious of their interests. Dynamic leadership or strong party organization, or both, would not only attract the poor to the polls but also make clear their "class grievances and aspirations."[55] Others reject this class bias argument. They admit that nonvoters are demographically different but cite polls showing that nonvoters' attitudes are not much different from voters' attitudes. One study, comparing the party identification of voters with that of all Americans, found that the proportion of Democrats was nearly identical (51.4 percent of all citizens and 51.3 percent of voters), while Republicans as voters were slightly overrepresented (36 percent of citizens and 39.7 percent of voters). All other political differences are considered to be much smaller than this 3.7 percent gap. Further, voters are not "disproportionately hostile" to social welfare policies.[56]

What effect might increased voter turnout have in national elections? It might make a difference, since there are partisan differences between different demographic groups, and candidates would have to adjust to the demands of an expanded electorate. A noted political scientist, while acknowledging that no political system could achieve 100 percent participation, pointed out that the entire balance of power in the political system could be overturned if the large nonvoter population decided to vote.[57] However, others contend more persuasively that the difference may not be as pronounced. Nonvoters are not more in favor of government ownership or control of industry, and they are not more egalitarian. Nonvoters are, however, more inclined to favor additional spending on welfare programs.[58]

Another way to think of low voter turnout is to see it as a sign of approval of things as they are, whereas high voter turnout would signify disapproval and widespread desire for change. Even on the subject of how to interpret low turnout there is disagreement.

VOTING CHOICES

Why do people vote as they do? Political scientists have identified three main elements of the voting choice: party identification, candidate appeal, and issues. These elements often overlap.

Voting on the Basis of Party

Party identification is the subjective sense of identification or affiliation that a person has with a political party (see Chapter 7). Party identification often predicts a person's stand on issues. It is part of our national mythology that Americans vote for the

party identification
An informal and subjective affiliation with a political party that most people acquire in childhood.

★★ **YOU DECIDE**

SHOULD WE ALLOW VOTING BY MAIL AND ON THE INTERNET?

During the past two centuries of constitutional government, this nation has gradually adopted a more expansive view of popular participation. Not only has the right to vote been extended to more people, but the decisions made in the voting booth have been expanded as well to include primary elections to nominate party candidates and ballot referendums in which state constitutional amendments and state laws are adopted.

It seems logical that the next step in our democratic progress is permitting voters to cast ballots through the mail or via the Internet. Not only would such a reform make voting easier, but it would permit us to have more elections. For example, when a city council wants voters to decide whether to build a new football stadium or when there is need for a special election to fill the term of a member of Congress who has died or resigned, election officials could mail out the ballots and then in two or three weeks count up those that have been returned. The state of Oregon has already conducted several general elections by mail, and other states are considering adopting the Oregon system.

What do you think? Should we move toward a system in which we replace the ballot box with the mailbox or the computer? What arguments would you make for and against such an idea?

person and not the party, but as you will see, the person we vote for is most often from the party we prefer.

As discussed, partisanship is typically acquired in childhood or adolescence as a result of the socialization process in the family and then reinforced by peer groups in adolescence. In the absence of reasons to vote otherwise, people depend on party identification to simplify their voting choices. Party identification is not the same as party registration; it is not party membership in the sense of being a dues-paying, card-carrying member, as in some European parties. Rather, it is a psychological sense of attachment to one party or another.

There has been a dramatic increase in the number of self-declared Independents since the mid-1970s. Nominally, there are more Independents in the electorate today than there are Republicans. But two-thirds of all Independents are, in fact, partisans in their voting behavior. Independent-leaning Democrats are predictably Democratic in their voting behavior, and Independent-leaning Republicans vote heavily Republican. Independent leaners are thus very different from each other and from the Pure Independents. Pure Independents have the lowest rate of turnout but generally do side with the eventual winner in presidential elections. These data on Independents only reinforce the importance of partisanship as an explanation of voting choice, because when we consider Independent-leaning Democrats and Independent-leaning Republicans as Democrats and Republicans, respectively, there were only 11 percent Pure Independents or others without a party in 2000,[59] and that proportion dropped in 2002 to 7 percent. These proportions are consistent with earlier election years. In short, the number of genuinely independent voters is relatively small and has remained so over time.

Although party identification has fluctuated somewhat in the past 40 years, it remains more stable than attitudes about issues or political ideology. Fluctuations in party identification appear to come in response to economic conditions and political performance, especially of the president. The more information voters have about their choices, the more likely they are to defect from their party and vote for a candidate from the other party.

Voting on the Basis of Candidates

While long-term party identification is important, it is clearly not the only factor in voting choices; otherwise the Democrats would have won every presidential election since the last realignment in 1932. In fact, since 1952, Republicans have been more successful in winning the White House than Democrats. The answer to this puzzle is largely found in a second major explanation of voting choice—**candidate appeal**.

The elections of the 1980s marked a critical threshold in the emergence of the candidate-centered era in American electoral politics. This change in focus from parties to candidates is an important historical trend that has been gradually taking place over the past several decades.[60] Candidate centered politics means that rather than rely on groups or parties to build a coalition of supporters for a candidate, the candidates make their case directly to the voters. In many races, the parties and groups have also made the candidate the major focus of attention, minimizing partisanship or group identification.[61]

Candidate appeal often involves an assessment of a candidate's character. Is the candidate honest? Is the candidate consistent? Is the candidate dedicated to "family values"? Does the candidate have religious or spiritual commitments? The press in recent elections has sometimes played the role of "character cop," asking questions about private lives and lifestyles. The press asks these questions because voters are interested in a political leader's background—perhaps even more interested in personal character than in a political position on hard-to-understand health care or regulatory policy issues.

Ronald Reagan's effort to generate positive candidate appeal was successful. His opponent in 1980, President Jimmy Carter, had hoped that Reagan would behave more like Barry Goldwater, who in his speech accepting the nomination in 1964 had said, "Extremism in the defense of liberty is no vice. . . . Moderation in the pursuit of justice is no virtue."[62] Lyndon Johnson, Goldwater's opponent, benefited from public perception

candidate appeal
How voters feel about a candidate's background, personality, leadership ability, and other personal qualities.

that Goldwater and those who nominated him were out of the mainstream of American politics, an idea reinforced by Goldwater's acceptance speech.

Like Barry Goldwater in 1964, George McGovern, who ran as the Democratic candidate for president in 1972, had negative appeal. He was perceived by many as too liberal, a view bolstered by images of his supporters, who by their dress and manner appeared out of the mainstream of American politics. In addition to ideological extremism, McGovern raised doubts about his judgment and leadership by how he handled his choice of a vice president. McGovern named Missouri Senator Tom Eagleton as his running mate, only to discover that Eagleton had once been hospitalized for emotional exhaustion and depression and had received electric shock therapy. McGovern initially stood behind Eagleton, but as press coverage and criticism of McGovern's lack of investigation into Eagleton's past grew, McGovern dropped Eagleton and named a new running mate, Sargent Shriver. In the end, "only about one-third of the public thought McGovern could be trusted as president."[63]

Candidate appeal or the lack of it—in terms of leadership, experience, good judgment, integrity, competence, strength, and energy—is sometimes more important than party or issues. Bill Clinton and John Edwards represent the regular working-class person rising against the odds. Dwight Eisenhower had great candidate appeal. He was a five-star general, a legendary hero of the Allied effort in World War II. His unmilitary manner, his moderation, his personal charm, and his lack of a strong party position made him appealing across the ideological spectrum. Ronald Reagan generated positive candidate appeal in part by asserting characteristics the public found lacking in Jimmy Carter—leadership and strength. In the 2004 presidential primaries, Howard Dean was initially perceived in positive terms, but that changed with his speech following the Iowa caucus. "The Scream," as it was labeled, called into question his self control.[64]

Increasingly, campaigns today focus on the negative elements of candidates' history and personality. Opponents and the media are quick to point out the limitations or problems of any given candidate. Bush was attacked in 2004 for his policies in Iraq, his failure to build broader coalitions with other countries, his tax cuts which lowered taxes for rich people as well as for others, and for rising deficits. Bush's record in the National Guard became a focus of a CBS "60 Minutes" segment, only to have CBS admit that the documents used in this critical story on Bush could not be authenticated. Kerry was attacked for flip-flopping over issues and his liberal voting record in the Senate. Kerry was also attacked for his war record by an outside group called Swift Boat Veterans for Truth. This attack put the Kerry campaign on the defensive for several days. (See Figure 8–5 for a list of which qualities mattered most to votes in 2004.)[65]

Voting on the Basis of Issues

Most political scientists agree that issues, while important, are not as central to the decision process as party identification and candidate appeal.[66] Part of the reason is that candidates often intentionally obscure their positions on issues—an understandable strategy.[67] Richard Nixon said he had a plan to end the Vietnam War in 1968, clearly the most important issue in that year, but he would not reveal the specifics. By not detailing his plan, he stood to gain votes from those who wanted a more aggressive war effort as well as those who wanted a cease-fire.

For issue voting to become of major significance, the issue must be important to a substantial number of voters, opposing candidates must take opposing stands on the issues, and voters must know these positions and vote accordingly. Rarely do candidates focus on only one issue. Voters often will agree with one candidate on one issue and with the opposing candidate on another. In such an instance, issues will likely not be the determining factor. But lack of interest by voters in issues does not mean candidates can take any issue position they wish.[68]

More likely than *prospective issue voting* (voting based on what a candidate pledges to do in the future about an issue if elected) is *retrospective issue voting* (holding incumbents,

---

★★ THINKING IT THROUGH

One of the problems with making elections more frequent is that voters will tire. Americans already vote more frequently and for more offices than citizens of any other democracy. Asking them to make voting choices even more frequently could result in lower turnout and less rational consideration. Many voters may be unaware that an election is going on. Yet the advantage of the vote-by-mail system employed by Oregon and some cities and counties is that it increases turnout, at least initially. What political scientists dispute is whether such increases in participation will continue when the novelty wears off.

Some critics of voting by mail or electronic democracy worry about fraud. Even when voters are required to sign their mailed-in ballots, the possibility of forgery still exists. Also, voting by mail or computer has the possibility of allowing people to pressure or harass voters. Another concern is late returns. Concerns about electronic voting have been reinforced by claims that the computer software is not secure and that some electronic voting fails to count all votes.*

Another criticism is that mail and electronic voting could be skewed toward participation by better-educated and higher-income voters, who routinely pay their bills by mail, make purchases on their computer, and own a personal computer with Internet access. Advocates of these new voting procedures contend that voters who do not own computers can drop off their ballots in some public building and that eventually computers will be available widely enough that access will not be a problem.†

However, if voting can be made easier and more convenient, why not do it? If the integrity of the vote can be protected and the new ways of voting become widely accessible, such changes are probably inevitable.

*E.J. Dionne Jr., "Election Dangers to be Avoided," *Washington Post*, May 25, 2004.

†Adam J. Berinsky, Nancy Burns, and Michael W. Tarugott, "Who Votes By Mail? A Dynamic Model of the Individual-Level Consequences of Voting-by-Mail Systems," *Public Opinion Quarterly* 65 (Summer 2001), pp. 178–197.

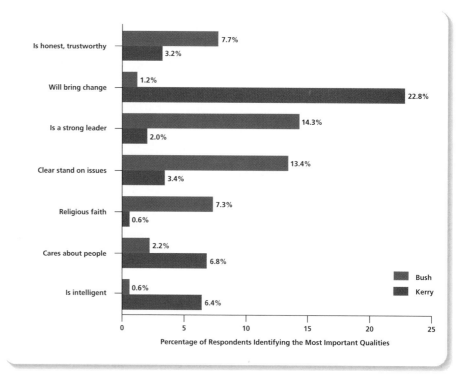

FIGURE 8–5 Which Quality Mattered Most in the 2004 Vote for President?
SOURCE: 2004 Exit Polls from Edison Media Research and Mitofsky International at www.cnn.com/ELECTION/2004/pages/results/states/US/P/00/epolls.0.html.

usually the president's party, responsible for past performance on issues such as the economy or foreign policy).[69] In times of peace and prosperity, voters will reward the incumbent; if the nation falls short on either, voters are more likely to elect the opposition.

But good economic times do not always lead to the retention of an administration, as Al Gore learned in 2000. Part of Gore's problem in 2000 was that only half the public saw their family's financial situation as having gotten better. Of these voters, Gore received 61 percent of the vote.[70] But his inability to effectively claim credit for the good economic times hurt him, especially when Republicans contended that it was the American people, not the government, that produced the strong economy. A similar debate arose in 2004 over the state of the economy and the extent to which President Bush's policies or the terrorist attacks of September 11, 2001, had resulted in job loss and other economic problems. Democrats argued that the tax cut had been irresponsible, especially when the country was at war. The Republicans countered that the tax cuts had helped stimulate the economy.

The state of the economy is often the central issue in midterm elections as well as presidential ones. Several studies have found a positive relationship between the state of the economy and "out" party gains and "in" party losses in congressional seats.[71] Political scientists have been able to locate the sources of this effect in individual voters' decision making. Voters tend to vote against the party in power if they perceive a decline or standstill in their personal financial situations.[72]

Voters see responsibility for the economy as resting with the president and Congress more than with governors or local officials.[73] In 2004, the electorate was divided over the economy, jobs, and Bush's tax cut. More voters felt the economy was "not good or poor" than felt it was "excellent or good." The view of the economy appeared to be influenced by which candidate one preferred, with Bush supporters more positive and Kerry supporters more negative.[74] Kerry often tried to make the election about the economy and jobs but the issues of security and terrorism were seen as more vital.

PUBLIC OPINION: SPIN DETECTION

Public opinion is important in a democracy because the government depends on the consent of the governed. This simulation describes survey techniques and identifies possible problems with surveys. Test your knowledge about survey research and attempt to identify problems with which surveyors deal.

Go to Make it Real, "Public Opinion: Spin Detection."

S U M M A R Y

1. Public opinion is a complex combination of views and attitudes individuals acquire through various influences from childhood on. Public opinion takes on qualities of intensity, latency, consensus, and polarization—each of which is affected by people's feelings about the salience of issues.

2. The American public has a generally low level of interest in politics, and most people do not follow politics and government closely. The public's knowledge of political issues is poor.

3. Americans who are interested in public affairs can participate by voting; joining interest groups and political parties; working on campaigns; writing letters to newspaper editors or elected officials; attempting to influence how another person will vote; donating money to a candidate, party, or group; or even protesting.

4. Better-educated, older, and party- and group-involved people tend to vote more; the young tend to vote the least. Voter turnout tends to be higher in national than in state and local elections, higher in presidential than in midterm elections, and higher in general than in primary elections.

5. Counting ballots has generated substantial controversy in recent elections. The Florida controversy in 2000 was resolved by the U.S. Supreme Court and Congress subsequently passed HAVA. In 2004, voter turnout soared, in part because of a close election and in part because of successful voter mobilization efforts.

6. Party identification remains the most important element in the voting choice of most Americans. It represents a long-term attachment and is a "lens" through which voters view candidates and issues as they make their voting choices. Candidate appeal, including character and record, is another key factor in voter choice. Voters decide their vote less frequently on the basis of issues.

K E Y   T E R M S

public opinion	**attentive public**	**Australian ballot**	**party identification**
political socialization	**voter registration**	**turnout**	**candidate appeal**

F U R T H E R   R E A D I N G

R. MICHAEL ALVAREZ AND JOHN BREHM, *Hard Choices, Easy Answers: Values, Information, and American Public Opinion* (Princeton University Press, 2002).

HERBERT ASHER. *Polling and the Public: What Every Citizen Should Know,* 6th ed. (CQ Press, 2004).

BARBARA A. BARDES AND ROBERT W. OLDENDICK, *Public Opinion: Measuring the American Mind* (Wadsworth, 2003).

M. MARGARET CONWAY, *Political Participation in the United States,* 4th ed. (CQ Press, 2000).

ROBERT M. EISINGER, *The Evolution of Presidential Polling* (Cambridge University Press, 2002).

ROBERT S. ERIKSON AND KENT L. TEDIN, *American Public Opinion: Its Origins, Content and Impact,* updated 6th ed. (Longman, 2002).

WILLIAM H. FLANIGAN AND NANCY H. ZINGALE, *Political Behavior of the American Electorate,* 10th ed. (CQ Press, 2002).

DONALD P. GREEN AND ALAN S. GERBER, *Get Out the Vote!: How to Increase Voter Turnout* (Brookings Institution Press, 2004).

ROBERT HUCKFELDT AND JOHN SPRAGUE, *Citizens, Politics, and Social Communication: Information and Influence in an Election Campaign* (Cambridge University Press, 1995).

LAWRENCE R. JACOBS AND ROBERT Y. SHAPIRO, *Politicians Don't Pander: Political Manipulation and the Loss of Democratic Responsiveness* (University of Chicago Press, 2000).

KATHLEEN HALL JAMIESON, *Everything You Think You Know About Politics and Why You're Wrong* (Basic Books, 2000).

BRUCE E. KEITH, DAVID B. MAGLEBY, CANDICE J. NELSON, ELIZABETH ORR, MARK C. WESTLYE, AND RAYMOND E. WOLFINGER, *The Myth of the Independent Voter* (University of California Press, 1992).

V. O. KEY JR., *Public Opinion and American Democracy* (Knopf, 1961).

JAN E. LEIGHLEY, *Strength in Numbers? The Political Mobilization of Racial and Ethnic Minorities.* (Princeton University Press, 2001).

MICHAEL B. MACKUEN AND GEORGE RABINOWITZ, EDS., *Electoral Democracy* (University of Michigan Press, 2004).

MICHAEL MARGOLIS AND DAVID RESNICK, *Politics as Usual: The Cyberspace 'Revolution,'* 6th ed. (Sage Publications, 2000).

MICHAEL NELSON, ED., *The Elections of 2000* (CQ Press, 2001).

RICHARD G. NIEMI AND HERBERT F. WEISBERG, *Classics in Voting Behavior* (CQ Press, 1993).

RICHARD G. NIEMI AND HERBERT F. WEISBERG, *Controversies in Voting Behavior,* 4th ed. (CQ Press, 2001).

FRANK R. PARKER, *Black Votes Count: Political Empowerment in Mississippi After 1965* (University of North Carolina Press, 1990).

THOMAS E. PATTERSON, *The Vanishing Voter: Public Involvement in the Age of Uncertainty* (Vintage, 2003).

GERALD M. POMPER, ED., *The Election of 2000: Reports and Interpretations* (Seven Bridges Press, 2001).

JAMES A. THURBER AND CANDICE J. NELSON, EDS., *Campaigns and Elections American Style,* 2d ed. (Westerview Press, 2004).

MICHAEL W. TRAUGOTT AND PAUL J. LAVRAKAS, *The Voter's Guide to Election Polls,* 3d ed. (Rowman & Littlefield, 2004).

MARTIN P. WATTENBERG, *Where Have All the Voters Gone?* (Harvard University Press, 2002).

JOHN ZALLER, *The Nature and Origins of Mass Opinion* (Cambridge University Press, 1992).

See also *Public Opinion Quarterly, The American Journal of Political Science,* and *American Political Science Review.*

CAMPAIGNS AND ELECTIONS
DEMOCRACY IN ACTION

9

Some cynics contend that elections do not matter and there is little point in voting. Strong evidence to the contrary comes from the 2000 elections, in which Al Gore won the popular vote by 539,947 votes, or only slightly more than 180 votes per county! The contest was especially close in Florida and New Mexico, where the statewide margins were 537 and 366 votes, respectively. The contest for the presidency was not the only one that required recounts. In Michigan, Mike Rogers won election to the House by 88 votes. In the 2000 election, you could truthfully say that every vote counted. In 2002, the Colorado Seventh district Congressional race was decided by 121 votes and the South Dakota Senate race was won by only 524 votes. In 2004, there were again some close elections. Senate Minority Leader Tom Daschle, a Democrat, lost by 4,535 votes in South Dakota. In the presidential race, Bush carried New Mexico by only 8,000 votes. At the state and local level, there are often races decided by only a few votes.

In the United States, citizens vote more often and for more offices than citizens of any other democracy. We hold thousands of elections for everything from community college directorsto county sheriffs. About half a million persons hold elected state and local offices.[1] In 2004, we elected a president, 34 U.S. senators,[2] all 435 members of the U.S. House of Representatives, 11 state governors, about a dozen state treasurers, nine secretaries of state, and, in many states, judges.

In addition to electing people, voters in 27 states vote on laws or constitutional amendments proposed by initiative petitions or on popular referendums put on the ballot by petition. In all states except Delaware, voters must approve all changes in the state constitution.

In this chapter, we explore our election rules. We note four important problems: the lack of competition for some offices, the complexities of nominating presidential candidates, the distortions of the electoral college, and the influence of money in our elections. We also discuss proposed reforms in each of these areas.

ELECTIONS: THE RULES OF THE GAME

The rules of the game—the electoral game—make a difference. Although the Constitution sets certain conditions and requirements, most electoral rules remain matters of state law.

Regularly Scheduled Elections

In our system, elections are held at fixed intervals that cannot be changed by the party in power. It does not make any difference if the nation is at war, as we were during the Civil War, or in the midst of a crisis, as in the Great Depression; when the calendar calls for an election, the election is held. Elections for members of Congress occur on the first Tuesday after the first Monday in November of even-numbered years. Although there are some exceptions (for special elections or peculiar state provisions), participants know *in advance* just when the next election will be. In many parliamentary democracies, such as Great Britain and Canada, the party in power calls elections at a time of its choosing. The predetermined timing of elections is one of the defining characteristics of democracy in the United States.

Fixed, Staggered, and Sometimes Limited Terms

Our electoral system is based on *fixed terms,* meaning that the length of a term in office is specified, not indefinite. The Constitution has set the term of office for the U.S. House of Representatives at two years, the Senate at six years, and the presidency at four years.

Our system also has *staggered terms* for some offices; not all offices are up for election at the same time. All House members are up for election every two years, but only one-third of the senators are up for election at the same time. Since presidential elections occur two or four years into a senator's six-year term, senators can run for the presidency without fear of losing their seat, as John Kerry did in 2004. But if their Senate term expires the same year as the presidential election, the laws of many states require them to give up their Senate seat to run for president or vice president or any other position. An example of a state that permits a candidate to run for election to two offices is Connecticut, where Joseph Lieberman was reelected to the U.S. Senate in 2000 while being narrowly defeated in his race for vice president. Had he been victorious in both campaigns, he would have resigned his Senate seat.

Term Limits

The Twenty-Second Amendment to the Constitution, adopted in 1951, limits presidents to two terms. Knowing that a president cannot run again changes the way members of Congress, the voters, and the press regard the president. A politician who cannot, or has announced he or she will not, run again is called a *lame duck.* Efforts to limit the terms of other politicians have become a major issue in several American states. The most frequent targets have been state legislators. One consequence of term limits is more lame ducks.

Term limits are popular. Voters in 15 states have enacted them for their state legislature, and in two states, the legislature imposed term limits on themselves. Even more states limit the term of governors.[3] Three-fourths of all voters favor term limits, including 9 out of 10 strong Republicans and 7 out of 10 strong Democrats.[4] Still, despite their popularity, proposals for term limits have repeatedly been defeated when they have come to a vote in Congress.

The Supreme Court, by a vote of 5 to 4, declared that a state does not have the constitutional power to impose limits on the number of terms for which its members of the U.S. Congress are eligible, either by amending its own constitution or by state law.[5] Congress has refused to propose a constitutional amendment to impose a limit on congressional terms.

Winner Take All

An important feature of our electoral system is the **winner-take-all system,** or what is sometimes referred to as "first past the post" in other countries.[6] In most American electoral settings, the candidate with the most votes wins. The winner does not need to have a *majority* (more than half the votes cast); in a multicandidate race, the winner may have only a *plurality* (the largest number of votes). In 2000, three senators and seven House members were elected by pluralities. In 2002, again there were seven House races and three Senate races decided by a plurality. One senator and one House member were elected on pluralities in 2004. Winner-take-all electoral systems have the effect of reinforcing moderate and centrist candidates because they are more likely to secure a plurality or a majority. Candidates in a winner-take-all system often stress that a vote for a minor party candidate is a "wasted vote" and that it might have the effect of helping elect the voter's least desired candidate.

Most American electoral districts are **single-member districts**, meaning that in any district for any given election—senator, governor, U.S. House, state legislative seat—the voters choose *one* representative or official.[7] When the single-member-district and winner-take-all systems are combined, minor parties find it hard to win. For example, even if a third party gets 25 percent of the vote in several districts, it still gets no seats.

The combination of single-member districts and winner-take-all is different from a **proportional representation** system, in which political parties secure legislative seats and power in proportion to the number of votes they receive in the election. Let us assume that a state has three representatives up for election. In each of the three contests, the Republican defeats the Democrat, but in one district by only a narrow margin. If you add up the statewide vote, the Republicans get 67 percent and the Democrats 33 percent. Under our single-member-district and winner-take-all system, the Republicans get all three seats. But under a system of proportional representation, in which the three seats represent the whole state, the Democrats would receive one seat because they got roughly one-third of the vote in the entire state. Proportional representation thus rewards minor parties and permits them to participate in government. Countries that practice some form of proportional representation include Germany, Israel, and Japan.

The Electoral College

We elect our president and vice president not by a national vote but by an indirect device known as the **electoral college**. The framers of the U.S. Constitution devised this system because they did not trust the choice of president to a direct vote of the people. Under this system, each state has as many electors as it has representatives and senators. California therefore had 55 electoral votes (53 House seats and two Senate seats) and Vermont three electoral votes for the election of 2004.

Each state legislature is free to determine how its electors are selected. Each party nominates a slate of electors, usually longtime party workers. Electors are expected to cast their electoral votes for the party's candidates for president and vice president. In our entire history, no "faithless elector"—an elector who does not vote for his or her state's popular vote winner—has ever cast the deciding vote. There was one faithless elector in 2000 from the District of Columbia who abstained rather than cast her vote for Al Gore in order to protest the lack of congressional representation for Washington D.C.[8] The electoral college vote in 2004 had one faithless elector: an elector from Minnesota who voted for John Edwards instead of John Kerry. This happened in spite of both parties naming party faithful on the assumption that the election would be close.

The Twelfth Amendment requires electors to vote separately for president and vice president. To demonstrate how this works, if you voted for the Republican candidate in 2000, you actually voted for the Republican slate of electors in your state who pledged

IMPORTANT FACTORS IN WINNING AN ELECTION

Uncontrollable Factors

- Incumbent running
- Strength of party organization
- National tides or landslide possibility
- Socioeconomic makeup of district

Organizational Factors

- Registration drives
- Fund-raising
- Campaign organization
- Volunteers
- Media campaign
- Direct-mail campaign efforts
- Get-out-the-vote efforts

Candidate's Personal Factors

- Personal appeal
- Knowledge of issues
- Speaking and debating ability
- Commitment and determination
- Ability to earn free, positive media coverage

winner-take-all system
An election system in which the candidate with the most votes wins.

single-member district
An electoral district in which voters choose one representative or official.

proportional representation
An election system in which each party running receives the proportion of legislative seats corresponding to its proportion of the vote.

electoral college
The electoral system used in electing the president and vice president, in which voters vote for electors pledged to cast their ballots for a particular party's candidates.

ADVANTAGES AND DISADVANTAGES OF PROPORTIONAL REPRESENTATION

The winner-take-all rule of most American elections has some advantages but also means that substantial minorities go unrepresented. In cases where there are multiple candidates and the winner only has a plurality, it means that a majority goes unrepresented.

A system of proportional representation could be applied to the allocation of electoral votes by state, or in states with more than one member of the House of Representatives, it could be applied to the allocation of seats as it is in many democracies.

Proportional representation has some advantages. It more accurately reveals the preferences of voters and gives those who do not vote for the winning candidate a sense that they have some influence as a result of their vote. In this sense, proportional representation may encourage greater turnout for people who identify with parties that rarely win elections, like Democrats in Utah or Wyoming. Proportional representation may also encourage issue-oriented campaigns and enhance the representation of women and minorities.

But there are some problems with proportional representation. It may make it harder to have a clear winner. This problem is even greater if minor parties are likely to receive representation as well. In this sense, it may encourage minor parties. Opponents of proportional representation worry that it can contribute to political instability and ideological extremism. For another example of this see the comparative perspective box on Israel in Chapter 7.

to vote for George W. Bush for president and Dick Cheney for vice president in the electoral college.

Candidates who win a plurality of the popular vote in a state secure all that state's electoral votes, except in Nebraska and Maine, which allocate electoral votes to the winner in each congressional district plus two electoral votes for the winner of the state as a whole. Winning electors go to their state capital on the first Monday after the second Wednesday in December to cast their ballots. These ballots are then sent to Congress, and early in January, Congress formally counts the ballots and declares who won the election for president and vice president.

It takes a majority of the electoral votes to win. If no candidate gets a majority of the electoral votes for president, the House chooses among the top three candidates, with each state delegation having one vote. If no candidate gets a majority of the electoral votes for vice president, the Senate chooses among the top two candidates, with each senator casting one vote.

When there are only two major candidates for the presidency, the chances of an election being thrown into the House are remote. But twice in our history the House has had to act: In 1800, before the Twelfth Amendment was written, the House had to choose in a tie vote between Thomas Jefferson and Aaron Burr; and in 1824, the House picked John Quincy Adams over Andrew Jackson and William Crawford. Henry Clay, who was forced out of the race when he came in fourth in the electoral college, threw his support behind Adams. When Adams was elected, he made Clay his secretary of state. The 1824 vote in the House was especially contentious. Jackson, winner of the popular vote, was not elected when the decision passed to the House. This outcome infuriated Jackson, who won the electoral college vote by a wide margin four years later.

As we were reminded in 2000, our electoral college system makes it possible for a presidential candidate to receive the most popular votes, as Al Gore did, and yet not get enough electoral votes to be elected president. Al Gore won the popular vote by over 500,000 votes but lost the electoral college 271 to 266.[9] This also happened in 1824, when Andrew Jackson won 12 percent more of the vote than John Quincy Adams; in 1876, when Samuel Tilden received more popular votes than Rutherford B. Hayes; and in 1888, when Benjamin Harrison won in the electoral college despite Grover Cleveland's receiving more popular votes. It almost happened in 1960 and 1976, when the shift of a few votes in a few key states could have resulted in the election of a president without a popular majority. In a year with a serious minor party candidate, the result could be the

The Electoral Commission of 1877 met in secret session to decide the controversial presidential election between Rutherford B. Hayes and Samuel Tilden. After many contested votes the presidency was eventually awarded to Hayes.

election of a president without a plurality of the vote, as some believe happened with the Nader vote in 2000. (See Chapter 7)

In two of the four elections in which winners of the popular vote did not become president, the electoral college did not decide the winner. The 1824 election was decided by the U.S. House of Representatives. In 1876, the electoral vote in three southern states and Oregon was disputed, resulting in the appointment of an electoral commission to decide how those votes should be counted. In 1888 and 2000, the electoral college awarded the presidency to the candidate with fewer popular votes.

Concern about the electoral college is renewed every time there is a serious third-party candidate for the presidency. People began to ask, if no candidate receives a majority in the electoral college and the decision is left to Congress, which Congress casts the vote, the one serving during the election or the newly elected one? The answer is the new one, the one elected in November and taking office the first week in January. Since each state has one vote in the House, what happens if a state's delegation is tied in its vote, 2 to 2 or 3 to 3? The answer is its vote does not count. Would it be possible to have a president of one party and a vice president of another? Yes, if the election were thrown into the House and Senate and each chamber were controlled by a different party.

The electoral college sharply influences presidential politics. To win a presidential election, a candidate must appeal successfully to voters in populous states like California, Texas, Ohio, Illinois, Florida, and New York. California's electoral vote of 55 in 2004 exceeded the combined electoral votes of the 14 least populous states plus the District of Columbia. The map inside the back cover of this book provides a visual comparison of state size based on electoral votes. When the contest is close, as it was in 2000, every state's electoral votes count, and so greater emphasis is given to states in which the contest is close, even less populated states.[10]

TABLE 9–1	2004 BATTLEGROUND STATES	
State	**Electoral Votes**	**% Difference in 2004 Popular Vote**
Wisconsin	10	.39% Kerry
New Mexico	5	.80% Bush
Iowa	7	.91% Bush
New Hampshire	4	1.36% Kerry
Pennsylvania	21	2.27% Kerry
Ohio	20	2.49% Bush
Nevada	5	2.62% Bush
Michigan	17	3.40% Kerry
Oregon	7	3.90% Kerry
Florida	27	5.02% Bush
Missouri	11	7.31% Bush

SOURCE: www.cbsnews.com/htdocs/politics/campaign2004/03%20battleground.pdf, and "2004 Battleground," at usinfo.state.gov/dhr/democracy/elections/battleground_states.html.

Presidential candidates do not ordinarily waste time campaigning in a state unless they have at least a fighting chance of carrying that state; nor do they waste time in a state in which their party is a sure winner. Richard Nixon in 1960 was the last candidate to campaign in all 50 states, but he lost valuable time traveling to and from Alaska, while John Kennedy focused on the more populous states in which he had a chance to win. The contest usually narrows down to the medium-sized and big states, where the balance between the parties tends to be fairly even. In 2000 and 2004, all competitive contests received extraordinary attention from the candidates, parties, and allied groups (see Table 9–1).

RUNNING FOR CONGRESS

How candidates run for Congress differs, depending on the nature of their district or state, on whether candidates are incumbents or challengers, on the strength of their personal organization, on how well known they are, and on how much money they have to spend on their campaign. We can also note several similarities in House and Senate elections.

First, most congressional elections are not close. In districts where most people belong to one party or where incumbents are popular and enjoy fund-raising and other campaign advantages, there is often little competition (see Figure 9–1).[11] Congressional districts have become less competitive on the whole in the 2000s, in large part because of the way district boundaries have been drawn by state legislatures. Districts in the 2002 redistricting were often drawn in ways that enhanced the reelection prospects of incumbents or one party, a processs called *partisan gerrymandering*. We explore this process in greater detail in Chapter 11, which deals with Congress. Those who believe that competition is essential to constitutional democracy are concerned that so many officeholders have **safe seats**. When officeholders do not have to fight to retain their seat, elections are not performing their proper role.[12]

safe seat
An elected office that is predictably won by one party or the other, so the success of that party's candidate is almost taken for granted.

QUESTION: Please indicate if you think that corrupt political leaders are a very big problem, a moderately big problem, a small problem, or not a problem at all.

In the vast majority of countries where the public was surveyed as part of the Pew Global Attitudes project, a large fraction of the people feel that corrupt political leaders are a "very big problem." In only a handful of countries did something less than a majority hold this view: the United States, Canada, Germany, Great Britain, Uzbekistan, and Jordan. The more prevailing response was for more than two-thirds of the public to report that corrupt political leaders were a large problem. In some cases, like Bangladesh and Argentina, nine-out-of-ten people said corruption was a very big problem. Even in the United States, nearly half of the respondents held this view. Places where perceived corruption is much less were once governed by monarchs and now have democracy and clean government or still have a monarchy (like Great Britain and Jordan). Countries that previously had totalitarian governments, such as Russia and Poland, have about the same distribution of opinon as countries in Africa and Asia. In short, most people in the world assume that their political leaders are corrupt.

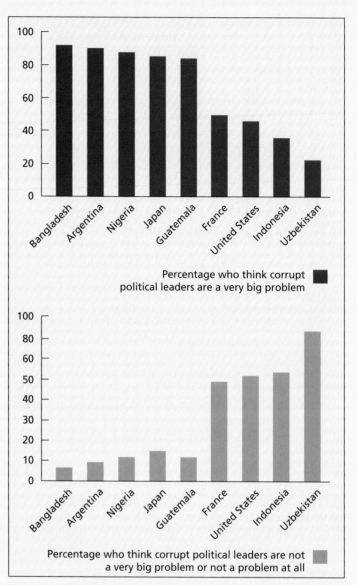

Percentage who think corrupt political leaders are a very big problem

Percentage who think corrupt political leaders are not a very big problem or not a problem at all

SOURCE: Pew Global Attitudes Project, *What the World Thinks in 2002* (Washington, D.C.: The Pew Research Center for the People and the Press, 2002), p. T-20.

Competition is more likely when funding is adequate for both candidates, which is not often the case in U.S. House elections (see Figure 9–1). Elections for governor and for the U.S. Senate are more seriously contested and more adequately financed than those for the U.S. House of Representatives.

Presidential popularity affects both House and Senate elections during presidential election years as well as midterm elections. The impact of presidential candidate popularity in a presidential election is known as the **coattail effect**, the boost candidates from the president's party get from a popular presidential candidate running in the same election. But winning presidential candidates do not always provide such a boost. The Republicans suffered a net loss of six House seats in 1988, even though George H. W. Bush won the presidency, and the Democrats suffered a net loss of ten house seats in 1992 when Bill Clinton won the presidential election. Democrats fared better in 1996,

coattail effect
The boost that candidates may get in an election because of the popularity of candidates above them on the ballot, especially the president.

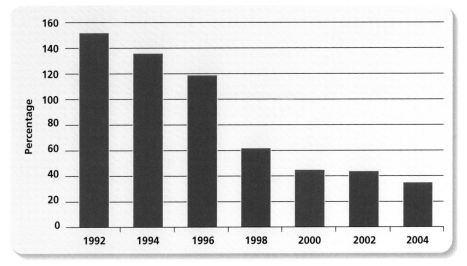

FIGURE 9–1 Competitive House Seats, 1992–2004.
SOURCE: Charlie Cook, "National Overview," *The Cook Political Report,* October 4, 2002, p. 6; "2004 Races at a Glance," *The Cook Political Report,* July 22, 2004. www.cookpolitical.com.
NOTE: Competitive races are those classified by Cook as "toss ups" or leaning toward one party.

registering a net gain of nine house seats. There were no discernible coattails in the 2000 elections. In 2004, Republicans picked up U.S. Senate seats in states carried by Bush, such as South Dakota, North Carolina, and South Carolina, and held contested seats in Oklahoma and Alaska. Overall, "measurable coattail effects continue to appear," according to congressional elections scholar Gary Jacobson, but they are "erratic and usually modest" in their impact.[13]

In midterm elections, presidential popularity and economic conditions have long been associated with the number of House seats a president's party loses.[14] These same factors are associated with how well the president's party does in Senate races, but the association is not as strong.[15] Figure 9–2 shows the number of seats in the House of Representatives and U.S. Senate gained or lost by the party controlling the White House in midterm elections since 1938. Republicans did better in 1994 than in any midterm election since 1946, picking up 53 seats. The Republican tide was not limited to the House but included a net gain of nine Senate seats.[16] In all of the midterm elections between 1934 and 1998, the party controlling the White House lost seats in the House. The range of losses, however, is quite wide, from a low of four seats for the Democrats in 1962 to a high of 71 seats for the Democrats in 1938. But in 2002, as in 1998, the longstanding pattern of the president's party losing seats did not hold. Republicans picked up a net gain of 2 seats in the Senate and 6 seats in the House. As noted, there were comparatively few competitive races in 2002, the most recent midterm election, especially for a year following redistricting.

When presidential landslides occur, as they did with Lyndon Johnson in 1964, the victorious party is especially vulnerable and likely to lose seats in the next midterm election, as the Democrats did in 1966. Given the historic pattern of the president's party's losing seats and the close party balance resulting from the 2000 elections, Democrats believed they were well positioned in 2002 to recapture control of both houses of Congress. The Democrats' hopes were dashed by a set of strong Republican candidates for the House and

Democratic Senator Barbara Boxer (center) from California debates Republican challenger Bill Jones (right) in her successful bid for reelection to the U.S. Senate in 2004.

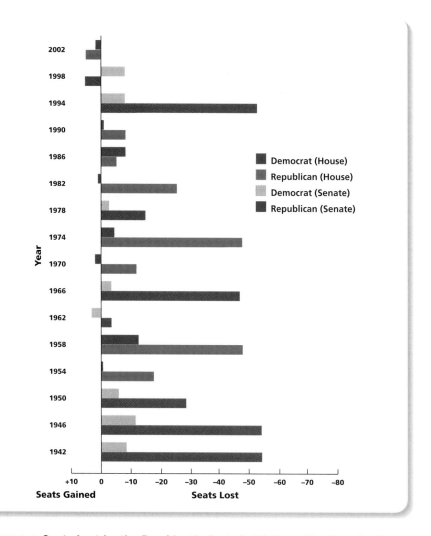

FIGURE 9–2 Seats Lost by the President's Party in Midterm Elections for the House of Representatives and the Senate, 1938–2002.

Senate, recruited in part with the assistance of the White House. President Bush invested a great deal of time and effort in helping Republican candidates in competitive races, with early visits to their states and districts to help with fundraising and an intense series of campaign stops in the last five days that more resembled the close to a presidential election than the close to a midterm election. Despite this heavy investment by President Bush, many 2002 contests revolved around more local issues. Arkansas voters rejected Republican Tim Hutchinson for another term in the Senate in part because of his private life, and South Dakota returned Democrat Tim Johnson despite five visits to the state by Bush. Johnson closely linked himself to fellow South Dakota Democrat Tom Daschle, whose power as Senate Majority Leader was at stake in 2002. In 2004, the White House was not as succesful in "clearing the field" for preferred candidates. In the Pennsylvania, Colorado, and Florida Senate races the Republicans had the kind of contested primaries they worked hard to avoid in 2002. Republicans went on to hold their seats in Pennsylvania and Florida but lost in Colorado, where the divisive primary helped the Democratic candidate.

The House of Representatives

Every two years, as many as 1,000 candidates—including approximately 400 incumbents—campaign for Congress. Incumbents are rarely challenged for renomination from within their own party, and when they are, the challenges are seldom serious. In the 1990s, for example, on average only two House incumbents were denied renomination in each election, and in 2002, 71 percent of all U.S. Representatives and 69 percent of all U.S.

Senators had no opponent in the primaries.[17] Challengers from other parties running against entrenched incumbents rarely encounter opposition in their own party.[18]

MOUNTING A PRIMARY CAMPAIGN   The first step for would-be challengers is to raise hundreds of thousands of dollars (or even more) to mount a serious campaign. This requires asking friends and acquaintances as well as interest groups for money. Candidates need money to hire campaign managers and technicians, buy television and other advertising, conduct polls, and pay for a variety of activities. Parties can sometimes help, but they shy away from giving money in primary contests. The party organization usually stays neutral until the nomination is decided.

Another early step is to build a *personal organization.* A candidate can build an organization while holding another office, such as a seat in the state legislature, by serving in civic causes, helping other candidates, and being conspicuous without being controversial.

A candidate's main hurdle is gaining visibility. Candidates work hard to be mentioned by the media. In large cities with many simultaneous campaigns, congressional candidates are frequently overlooked, and in all areas, television is devoting less time to political news.[19] Candidates rely on personal contacts, on hand shaking and door-to-door campaigning, and on identifying likely supporters and courting their favor—the same techniques used in campaigns for lesser offices. Despite these efforts, the turnout in primaries tends to be low, except in campaigns in which large sums of money are spent on advertising.

CAMPAIGNING FOR THE GENERAL ELECTION   As we have mentioned, most incumbent members of Congress win reelection.[20] Since 1970, over 95 percent of incumbent House members seeking reelection have won, and in 2000, 98 percent of incumbent House members running for reelection were successful (see Figure 9–3).[21] In 2002, again 98 percent of incumbents running in the general election won. In 2004, 99 percent of incumbents running in the general election were returned to office. Of the seven incumbents defeated, two ran against other incumbents.

One reason incumbents win so often is that they are able to outspend their challengers by roughly 3 to 1 in the House; in the Senate the difference is closer to 1.75 to 1.[22] Most challengers spend little money, run campaigns that are not significantly more visible than primary campaigns, contact few voters, and lose badly. Serious challengers in House races are hard to find. Many are scared away by the prospect of having to raise more than $1 million in campaign funds, others realize that the district has been drawn with fewer persons from their party than the incumbent's, and some do not want to face the media scrutiny that comes with a serious race for Congress. Nonetheless, in each election, a few challengers mount serious campaigns because of the incumbent's perceived vulnerability, the challengers' own wealth, party or political action committee efforts, or other factors.

Another reason most incumbents win so frequently is that their districts are predominantly Republican or Democratic. The 2002 redistricting process largely protected

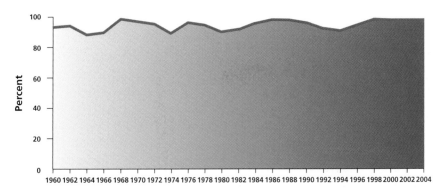

FIGURE 9–3 U.S. House Incumbents Reelected, 1946–2004.
Source: Harold W. Stanley and Richard G. Niemi, eds., *Vital Statistics on American Politics 2001–2002* (CQ Press, 2001), pp. 53–55. 2004 update by authors.

"My former opponent is supporting me in the general election. Please disregard all the things I said about him in the primary."

Dunagin's People. Tribune Media Services.

incumbents in both parties by making districts less competitive. Few incumbents were seriously challenged. Retirements and redistricting create *open seats,* which can result in more competitive elections. Potential candidates, as well as political action committees and political party committees, all watch open-seat races closely. If, however, the district is heavily partisan, the predominant party is likely to retain the seat, and once elected the incumbent then reaps the other incumbency advantages as well. But as noted, most races have incumbents and most incumbents win, lending credibility to the charge that we have a "permanent Congress." Occasionally, one party has a big victory, as the Republicans did in 1994, with a 57-seat gain in the House, securing the majority for the first time in 40 years. Large shifts like 1994 are rare in part because state legislatures through redistricting have created fewer competitive districts.

Why is keeping a House seat so much easier than gaining it? Incumbents have a host of advantages that help them win reelection. These perquisites, or "perks," come with the job of communicating with constituents and include free mailings (the *franking privilege*) and telephone calls to constituents, the free use of broadcast studios to record radio and television tapes to be sent to local media outlets, and, perhaps most important of all, a large staff to perform countless favors for constituents and send a stream of press reports and mail back to the district.[23] Representatives also try to win committee posts, even on minor committees, that relate to the needs of their districts and build connections with constituents.[24]

The Senate

Running for the Senate is big-time politics. The six-year term and the national exposure make a Senate seat a glittering prize, so competition is usually intense. Senate campaigns generally feature state-of-the-art campaign techniques; a race normally costs millions of dollars (see Figure 9–4).[25] The essential tactics are to raise lots of money, get good people involved, make as many personal contacts as possible (especially in the states with smaller populations), avoid giving the opposition any positive publicity, and have a clear and consistent campaign theme. Incumbency is an advantage for senators, although not as much as for representatives.[26] Incumbent senators are widely known, but so are their opponents, who often raise and spend significant amounts of money.[27]

When one party controls the Senate by only a few seats, as has been the case in recent years, more good candidates run, and the number of competitive elections increases. Going into the 2002 elections, the Senate had 50 Democrats, 49 Republicans, and one Independent. Jim Jeffords of Vermont was reelected as a Republican in 2000

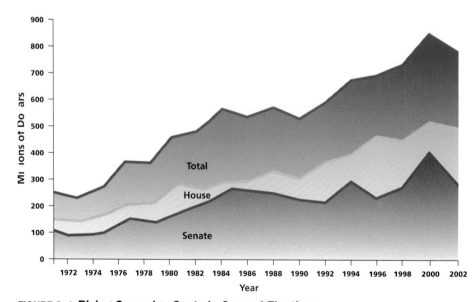

FIGURE 9–4 Rising Campaign Costs in General Elections.
SOURCE: Federal Election Commission, "Congressional Campaign Expenditures Total $772 Million," January 2, 2003, at www.fec.gov.

but switched parties in 2001, putting the Democrats in control of Senate leadership and all standing committees. The narrow margin of Democratic control meant that a net loss of one seat would put the Republicans back in the majority. The GOP mounted a major effort to reclaim the Senate in 2002, picking up a net gain of two seats and returning the Senate and all of the elected federal government to Republican control.[28] Competitive U.S. Senate races in 2004 were waged largely on Republican turf. Democrats won in Illinois and Colorado, picking up what had been Republican seats, but lost seats they had held in Florida, Georgia, North Carolina, South Carolina, and South Dakota. President Bush carried South Dakota by 60 percent to 39 percent, creating a difficult challenge for Democrats like Tom Daschle. Overall, Republicans enjoyed a net gain of four seats in the Senate, increasing their majority to 55 to 45.

The cost of Senate campaigns can vary greatly. California has nearly 70 times the number of potential voters as Wyoming; not surprisingly, running for a seat from Wyoming is much cheaper than running for a seat from California. As a result, interest groups and parties direct more money to competitive races in small states when the stakes for control of the Senate are high.[29]

RUNNING FOR PRESIDENT

Presidential elections are major media events, with candidates seeking as much positive television coverage as possible and trying at the same time to avoid negative coverage. The formal campaign has three stages: winning the nomination, campaigning at the convention, and mobilizing support in the general election.

Stage 1: The Nomination

Presidential hopefuls must make a series of critical tactical decisions. The first is when to start campaigning. For the presidential election of 2004, some candidates, like John Kerry, John Edwards, and Howard Dean, began soon after the 2000 presidential election.[30] Early decisions are increasingly necessary for candidates to raise the money and assemble an organization. Campaigning begins well before any actual declaration of candidacy as candidates try to line up supporters to win caucuses or primaries in key states and to raise money for their nomination effort.

One of the hardest jobs for candidates and their strategists is calculating how to deal with the complex maze of presidential primaries and caucuses that constitutes the delegate selection system. The system for electing delegates to the national party convention varies from state to state and often from one party to the other in the same state. In some parties in some states, for example, candidates must provide lists of delegates supporting them months in advance of the primary. The presidential campaign finance system provides funds to match small individual contributions during the nomination phase of the campaign for candidates who agree to remain within spending limitations. George W. Bush declined the federal funds in the 2000 and 2004 nomination phase, as did Democrats John Kerry and Howard Dean in 2004. Foregoing the public matching funds allows greater flexibility in when and where campaign money is spent and removes the overall limit for this phase of the process.

PRESIDENTIAL PRIMARIES State presidential primaries, unknown before 1900, have become the main method of choosing delegates to the national convention. A delegate is a person selected by local partisans to represent them in selecting nominees, party leaders, and party positions. Today, more than three-fourths of the states use presidential primaries. In 2000, some 84 percent of the Democratic delegates and 89 percent of the Republican delegates were chosen in the primaries.[31] The rest of the delegates were chosen by state party caucuses or conventions, or were party leaders who serve as "super delegates." In 2004, 85 percent of Democratic delegates and 69 percent of GOP delegates were chosen in the primaries. Several states (Arizona, Colorado, Delaware, Maine, Michigan, South Carolina, Utah, Virginia, and Washington) that held GOP primaries in 2000 switched to state caucuses or other methods in 2004 (see www.thegreenpapers.com/P04/tally.phtml).

The Iowa caucuses are an important first step in terms of media exposure for candidates running for president. Here, Democrat John Kerry speaks at a caucus site in Muscatine, Iowa, on January 12, 2004.

Presidential primaries often have two features: a *beauty contest,* or popularity vote, in which voters indicate which candidate they prefer but do not actually elect delegates to the convention, and *actual voting* for delegates pledged to a candidate. Since 1996, the Democrats require primary votes to be linked to delegate election. The Republicans allow states to separate a popularity vote from delegate selection. States which use this system include Montana, Nebraska, Illinois, New Jersey, Pennsylvania, and West Virginia.[32]

Candidates may win the beauty contest but find their opponents doing better in actual delegates elected because they failed to put a full slate of delegates on the ballot or because local notables were listed on the ballot as delegates pledged to another candidate. Different combinations of these two features have produced the following systems[33]:

■ *Proportional representation:* Delegates to the national convention are allocated on the basis of the percentage of votes candidates win in the beauty contest. This system has been used in most of the states, including several of the largest ones. The Democrats mandate proportional representation for all their primaries.[34] In some states, Republicans use this same system, but Republicans are much more varied in their delegate selection processes.[35]

■ *Winner take all:* Whoever gets the most votes wins all that state's delegates. To win all the delegates of a state like California is an enormous bonus to a candidate. Republicans still use the winner-take-all system at the state level, and in 2004, most states used this rule at either the state or congressional district levels.[36]

■ *Delegate selection without a commitment to a candidate.* New York Republicans allow the state committee to select 12 at-large delegates who are officially unpledged, as are the party chair and national committee representatives.[37]

■ *Delegate selection and separate presidential poll:* In several states, voters decide twice: once to indicate their choice for president and again to choose delegates pledged, or at least favorable, to a presidential candidate.

Voters in states like Iowa and New Hampshire, which are the first states to pick delegates, bask in media attention for weeks and even months before they cast the first ballots in the presidential sweepstakes. Because these early contests have had the effect of limiting the choices of voters in states that come later in the process, there has been a tendency for states to move their primaries up. This process is called "front loading."

California, which traditionally held its primary in June, moved it to March in 2000 so that its voters would play a more important role in selecting the nominee. Other states did the same thing. Front loading was even more prominent in 2004,[38] with Democratic National Committee Chair Terry McAuliffe's hope that the nominee would be chosen by March 2004, allowing time for the party to assist with fundraising and building party unity.[39]

In both 2000 and 2004 the nomination in both major parties was decided by March. This had the effect of compressing the nomination battle into several weeks of intense activity in the spring followed by months of much less activity before the fall general election campaign. For 2004, as in the past, states that felt overlooked in 2000 pushed for revision to the schedule, including possibly having four regional groupings (East, South, Midwest, and West).[40] States that gain visibility and importance through early primaries continue to want to maintain that advantage.

CAUCUSES AND CONVENTIONS A **caucus** is a meeting of party members and supporters of various candidates. In about a dozen states one or both parties use a caucus or convention system (or both) for choosing delegates.[41] Each state's parties and legislature regulate the methods used. The caucus or convention is the oldest method of choosing delegates and differs from the primary system in that it centers on party organization.

Delegates who will attend the national party conventions are chosen by delegates to state or district conventions, who themselves are chosen earlier in county, precinct, or town caucuses. The process starts at local meetings open to all party members, who discuss and take positions on candidates and issues and elect delegates to represent their views at the next level. This process is repeated until national nominating convention delegates are chosen by conventions of delegates throughout a district or state.

The best-known example of a caucus is in Iowa, because Iowa has held the earliest caucuses in the most recent presidential nominating contests. Every January or February in a presidential election year, Iowans have the opportunity to attend Republican and Democratic precinct meetings. Large numbers of voters attend these small town meetings and have a chance to meet and exchange views on issues and candidates, rather than merely pulling a lever in a voting booth or marking a ballot.[42]

Presidential hopefuls face a dilemma: To get the Republican nomination, you have to appeal to the more intensely conservative Republican partisans, those who vote in primaries and support campaigns. Democratic hopefuls have to appeal to the liberal wing of their party as well as minorities, union members, and environmental activists. But to win the general election, candidates have to win support from moderates and pragmatic voters, many of whom do not vote in the primaries. If candidates position themselves too far from the moderates in their nomination campaign, they risk being labeled extreme in the general election and losing these votes to their opponent.

STRATEGIES Strategies for securing the nomination have changed over the years. Some candidates think it wise to skip some of the earlier contests and enter first in states where their strength lies. John McCain pursued such a strategy in 2000, ignoring Iowa and concentrating on New Hampshire. In 2004 retired General Wesley Clark also bypassed Iowa, but unlike McCain he did not win in New Hampshire and dropped out of the race only a few weeks later. Most candidates choose to run hard in Iowa and New Hampshire, hoping that early showings in these states, which receive a great deal of media attention, will move them into the spotlight for later efforts.

During this early phase, especially important is the ability of candidates to manage the media's expectations of their performance in order to generate momentum. Lyndon Johnson actually won the New Hampshire primary in 1968, yet because his challenger, Eugene McCarthy, did better than the press had predicted, McCarthy was interpreted as the "winner." Both John Kerry and John Edwards did better than expected in Iowa in 2004, giving them momentum for New Hampshire and beyond.

Winning in the primaries thus becomes a game of expectations, and candidates may intentionally downplay their expectations so that "doing better than expected" might generate momentum for their campaign. It is also important to maintain a presidential bearing even in the primaries. In 2004, the front runner going into Iowa was Vermont Governor Howard Dean. In a speech to supporters after losing the Iowa

caucus
A meeting of local party members to choose party officials or candidates for public office and to decide the platform.

PEOPLE & POLITICS *Making a Difference* ★★★

KARL ROVE

Presidents have long had political advisors, both on their paid staff and more informally. Karl Rove has long been the chief political advisor to President George W. Bush. Rove has described his job as paying "attention to the things that affect his [Bush's] political future."* Another Bush confidant has described Rove as "the Bobby Fischer of politics," continuing that "he not only sees the [chess] board, he sees about 20 moves ahead."† Bush himself described Rove as the "boy genius."‡

Rove left the University of Utah before graduating to become chairman of the College Republicans. His interest in politics had started at an early age, when he helped campaign for Richard Nixon against John F. Kennedy. His political activism continued during high school, where he also developed an interest in debate and U.S. History. His involvement in the College Republicans helped him establish connections and enlarged his interest in politics. He was executive director of the College Republicans when George H.W. Bush was chair of the Republican National Committee. George H.W. Bush later hired Rove to help him run for president in 1980.

Rove formed his own consulting firm in Austin, Texas, where he did political and campaign consulting, including work on the successful campaign of Bill Clements, the first Texas Republican governor. Another Texas Governor became his most successful client, George W. Bush. Rove and Bush have a close working relationship. Rove, while heading the political affairs office in the White House, played an important role in recruiting candidates to run in 2002 and in talking others out of running. He also was the primary architect of the Bush 2004 reelection campaign.§ Rove heavily emphasized playing to Bush's conservative base, an effective strategy in the wake of same-sex marriage initiatives in eleven states.

*James Carney and John F. Dickerson, "The Busiest Man in the White House: As Bush Hits 100

Days in Office, His Top Strategist, Karl Rove, Is Already Eyeing 2004." *Time,* April 22, 2001, at www.time.com/time/magazine/article/subscriber/0,10987,1101010430-107220,00.html.
†Dana Milbank, "'Background' Checks," *The Washington Post,* January 28, 2003, p. A19; Dan Balz, "Team Bush; The Governor's 'Iron Triangle' Points the Way to Washington," *The Washington Post,* July 23, 1999, p. C01.
‡David B. Magleby and J. Quin Monson, eds., *The Last Hurrah?: Soft Money and Issue Advocacy in the 2002 Congressional Elections* (Brookings Institute Press., 2004), p. 102.
§www.abcnews.go.com/sections/politics/DailyNews/rove_profile001228.html.

caucuses, placing third after Kerry and Edwards, an animated Dean, attempting to rally his followers, uttered what came to be called the "Dean scream," or "I have a scream" speech.[43] As Dean learned, such a mistake, when replayed countless times on cable and broadcast news and when made the brunt of jokes elsewhere on television, becomes a defining moment and makes it difficult for the candidate to reestablish a positive campaign agenda. While Dean's ascendancy and sudden demise were both notable features of the 2004 election, a more enduring aspect of his candidacy was his extensive use of the Internet, especially for fundraising, and his demonstrating to the other Democrats the depth of anti-Bush passion among Democratic voters.[44]

Stage 2: The National Party Convention

national party convention
A national meeting of delegates elected in primaries, caucuses, or state conventions who assemble once every four years to nominate candidates for president and vice president, ratify the party platform, elect officers, and adopt rules.

The delegates elected in primaries, caucuses, or state conventions assemble at their **national party convention** in the summer before the election to pick the party's presidential and vice presidential candidates. In the past, delegates arrived at national nominating conventions with differing degrees of commitment to presidential candidates; some delegates were pledged to no candidate at all, others to a specific candidate for one or two ballots, and others firmly to one candidate only. Recent conventions have merely ratified decisions already made in the primaries and caucuses, in part because delegates are required to pledge themselves to a specific presidential hopeful (in the Democratic party) or because one candidate has been able to amass a majority of delegates. And because of reforms encouraging delegates to stick with the person to whom they are pledged, there has been no room to maneuver at conventions. National party conventions used to be events of high excitement because they determined who would be the party nominee, but in every election since the Republican convention of 1948 and the Democratic convention of 1952, the party primaries have decided who would be the nominee.

As recently as 1988, Democratic and Republican national conventions were given gavel-to-gavel coverage by the major networks, meaning that from the beginning of the first night to the end of the fourth night, television covered the conventions. Now the major networks leave comprehensive coverage to C-SPAN and CNN. National nominating conventions have ceased to dominate the national news, for the very good reason that they are no longer the place where candidates are selected.[45] The long-term trend of declining viewership and reduced hours of coverage has altered the parties' strategies. In 2004, the parties featured their most important speakers and highlighted their most important messages in the limited time given them by the networks. There were slight increases in viewership of the conventions in 2004.

Conventions follow standard rules, routines, and rituals. Usually, the first day is devoted to a keynote address and other speeches touting the party and denouncing the opposition; the second day, to committee reports, including party and convention rules and the party platform; the third day, to presidential and vice presidential balloting; and the fourth day, to the presidential candidate's acceptance speech, although in 2004 with both parties' nominees having only limited broadcast television time the foucs was on major speeches each night.[46] For sample coverage of the 2004 Republican convention go to www.2004nycgop.org, and for the Democrats see www.dems2004.org.

Because the choice of the party nominees has been decided well before the convention, there has been relatively little controversy on the floor of the conventions in recent years. The parties have turned to theatrics and celebrities in an effort to boost the audience watching the televised conventions. The networks have also shortened the proceedings on network television to only an hour or so per night of the convention.

THE PARTY PLATFORM   Delegates to the national party conventions decide on the *platform*, a statement of party perspectives on public policy. Why does anyone care what is in the party platform? Critics have long pointed out that the party platform is binding on no one and is more likely to hurt than to help a candidate. But presidential candidates as well as delegates take the platform seriously because it defines the direction a party wants to take. Also, despite the charge that the platform is ignored, most presidents make an effort to implement it.[47] For example, when President George W. Bush signed an education bill into law, he pointed to his party's commitment to "leave no child behind."[48] Neither party had a platform fight in 2004.

THE VICE PRESIDENTIAL NOMINEE   The choice of the vice presidential nominee garners widespread attention. Rarely does a person actually "run" for the vice presidential nomination, because only the president's vote counts. But there is a good deal of maneuvering to capture that one vote. Sometimes the choice of a running mate is made at the convention—not a time conducive to careful and deliberate thought. But usually the choice is made before the convention, and the announcement is timed to enhance media coverage and momentum going into the convention. The last time a presidential candidate left the choice of vice president to the delegates was for the Democrats in 1956.

Traditionally, the presidential nominee chooses a running mate who will "balance the ticket." Democratic presidential nominee Walter Mondale raised this tradition to a dramatic new height in 1984 by selecting a woman, New York Representative Geraldine A. Ferraro, to run with him. Mondale's bold decision was an effort to strengthen his appeal to women voters. But presidential candidates can also ignore the idea of a balanced ticket, as George W. Bush did when he chose another Texan from the oil industry to be his running mate. Dick Cheney moved his official residence to Wyoming and registered to vote there so that if the Bush-Cheney ticket won the popular vote in Texas, Republican Texas electors could vote for him, since the Constitution (Article II, Section 1) prohibits electors from voting for more than one person for president and vice president from their own state.

John Kerry's selection of John Edwards for his running mate in 2004 helped energize the Democratic campaign. Edwards was seen as appealing to young, rural, Southern, and moderate voters.[49] On most issues his positions were identical to Kerry's, but the two had fought aggressively against each other in the primaries despite these similarities. During the primaries, Kerry had criticized Edwards for his inexperience, especially in defense and foreign policy. Edwards helped motivate trial lawyers to contribute even more substantially to the Democratic ticket, but some parts of the business community was activated even more against Kerry because of its desire to enact limitations on damages in law suits.

THE VALUE OF CONVENTIONS　Why do the parties continue to have conventions if the nominee is known in advance and the vice presidential nominee is the choice of one person? What role do conventions play in our system? For the parties, they are a time of "coming together" to endorse a party program and to build unity and enthusiasm for the fall campaign. For candidates as well as other party leaders, conventions are a chance to capture the national spotlight and further their political ambitions. For nominees, they are an opportunity to define themselves in positive ways. The potential exists to heal wounds festering from the primary campaign and move into the general election united, but the potential is not always achieved. Conventions can be potentially divisive, as the Republicans learned in 1964 when conservative Goldwater delegates loudly booed New York Governor Nelson Rockefeller and as the Democrats learned in 1968 when the convention spotlighted divisions within the party over Vietnam as well as ugly battles between police and protesters near the convention hotels.

NOMINATION BY PETITION　There is a way to run for president of the United States that avoids the grueling process of primary elections and conventions—if you are rich enough or well known enough. John Anderson in 1980 and H. Ross Perot in 1992 met the various state requirements and made it onto the ballot in all 50 states. In 2000, Patrick Buchanan, candidate of the Reform party, was able to get his name on the ballot in all but one state and the District of Columbia, and Ralph Nader, candidate of the Green party, in all but seven states.[52] In 2004, the petition process was as simple as submitting the signatures of 1,000 registered voters in Washington State,[50] or by paying $500 in Colorado or Louisiana,[51] or as difficult as getting the signatures of currently registered voters equal to 2 percent of total votes cast in the last election in North Carolina (100,532 signatures).[53] In 2004, independent candidate Ralph Nader made the ballot in 34 states and the District of Columbia. He was excluded from 16 states, including Ohio and Pennsylvania.

Stage 3: The General Election

The national party convention adjourns immediately after the presidential and vice presidential candidates deliver their acceptance speeches to the delegates and the national television audience. Traditionally, the time between the conventions and Labor Day was a time for resting, binding up wounds from the fight for the nomination, gearing up for action, and planning campaign strategy. In recent elections, however, the candidates have not paused after the convention but launched directly into all-out campaigning. In 2004, both major party candidates campaigned aggressively from March through the general election. The intensity of the early campaign was noteworthy, with Bush spending in excess of $80 million on advertising between March and June and Kerry over $60 million.[54] Anti-Bush interest groups spent an estimated $32 million during this critical early period,[55] meaning that the Anti-Bush/Pro-Kerry spending exceeded the Bush spending during this time period. The early going in battleground states was unusually intense.

PRESIDENTIAL DEBATES　Televised presidential debates are a major feature of presidential elections. The 1960 debate between John Kennedy and Richard Nixon boosted Kennedy's campaign and elevated the role of television in national politics.[56] In 1976, President Gerald Ford debated Jimmy Carter and mistakenly said that each country in eastern Europe "is independent, autonomous, it has its own territorial integrity, and the United States does not conceive that those countries are under the domination of the Soviet Union."[57] That mistake damaged his credibility. Ronald Reagan's performance in the 1980 and 1984 debates confirmed the public view of him as decent, warm, and dignified. Bill Clinton's skirmishes with George Bush in 1992 and Bob Dole in 1996 showed him to be a skilled performer.

The 2004 presidential debates were widely watched and largely reinforced the candidate preferences of the viewers. Neither candidate made a major mistake and both candidates were able to state their positions and draw contrasts with their opponent. Challengers generally benefit more from debates and in 2004, Kerry was seen as the "winner" in public opinion surveys following all three debates. the vice pesidential debate followed the same pattern as the presidential debates, with no major mistake and few surprises. During both the presidential and vice presidential debates, mention was made by the Democrats of Vice President Cheney's daughter being a lesbian. The Republicans, and especially Mrs. Cheney, criticized the Democrats after the debate for drawing the daughter's sexual orientation into the campaign.

Since 1988, the nonpartisan Commission on Presidential Debates has sponsored and produced the presidential and vice presidential debates. The commission includes representatives from such neutral groups as the League of Women Voters. Before the commission became involved, there was often a protracted debate about debates. No detail seemed too small to the candidate managers—whether the candidates would sit or stand, whether they would be able to ask each other questions, whether they would be allowed to bring notes, and whether the questions would be posed by a single journalist, a panel of reporters, or a sample of citizens. By negotiating in advance many of the contentious details and arranging for debate locations, the commission now facilitates the presidential and vice presidential debates. In 2000, George W. Bush proposed alternative formats and locations, only to back down as it appeared he was avoiding debates.[58] The 2004 debates were again run by the Commission on Presidential Debates. The candidates again negotiated such things as whether they would be standing or sitting. An important departure from the presumed format was the use of split screens by the networks where one candidate was seen reacting while the other was speaking. President Bush, especially during the first debate, reacted with what was widely described as a "scowl" to some of the criticisms leveled by Senator Kerry. In a later debate, Bush made mention of his "scowl." The president seemed more comfortable in the format where questions came from the audience.

Minor party candidates often charge that the commission is biased in favor of the two major parties. To be included such candidates must have an average of 15 percent or higher in the five major polls used by the commission for this purpose and be legally eligible and be on the ballot in enough states to be able to win at least 270 electoral votes.[59] In 2004 Ralph Nader failed to meet these criteria for inclusion as did both he and Patrick Buchanan in 2000. In 1992, Ross Perot and his running mate, James Stockdale, had been included in the presidential and vice presidential debates, which generated large viewing audiences, averaging more than 80 million for each debate. The issue of excluding minor party candidates remains contentious. Including them takes time away from the major party candidates, especially if two or more minor party candidates are invited. Including them may also reduce the likelihood of both major parties' candidates' participating. But excluding them raises issues of fairness and free speech.

Although some critics are quick to express their dissatisfaction with presidential candidates for being so concerned with makeup and rehearsed answers, and although the debates have not significantly affected the election outcomes, they have provided important opportunities for candidates to distinguish themselves and for the public to weigh their qualifications. Candidates who do well in these debates are at a great advantage. They have to be quick on their feet, seem knowledgeable but not overly rehearsed, and project a positive image. Most presidential candidates are adept at all of these skills.

THE OUTCOME Though each election is unique, politicians, pollsters, and political scientists have collected enough information to agree broadly on a number of basic factors that they believe affect election outcomes. Whether the nation is prospering probably has the most to do with who wins a presidential election, but as we have noted, most voters vote on the basis of party and candidate appeal.[60] Who wins depends on voter turnout. The Democrats' advantage in the number of people who identify themselves as Democrats is

Presidential debates give candidates an opportunity to show how quickly and accurately they can respond to questions and outline their goals. In the debates of the 2004 elections, the consensus was that John Kerry outperformed George W. Bush in all three presidential debates; however his performance did not propel Kerry to victory in the election.

The vice presidential debate tends to be a more contentious exchange than presidential debates, providing each running mate with an opportunity to assail the opposition on various issues without the constraints that govern the presidential debates. The Iraq war, terrorism, and the economy all figured prominantly in the 2004 vice presidential debate between John Edwards and Dick Cheney.

mitigated by higher voter turnout among Republicans. Republicans also usually have better access to money, which means they can run more television ads in more places and more often.

After the votes are cast, as we saw in the last chapter, they must be counted. And the way they are counted can be a critical factor in close races. Even before the votes were counted in 2004, both parties had deployed thousands of lawyers to observe the voting and ballot counting and to launch legal challenges if necessary. The Bush victory was large enough that these challenges did not materialize. As we have been reminded, the popular vote is not necessarily the deciding vote in presidential elections. The electoral college has an important role to play and courts may have to determine if state and federal laws have been fairly applied. The peaceful transfer of power from one individual or party to another, especially after such contested elections, is the culminating event in electoral democracy.

MONEY IN U.S. ELECTIONS

Election campaigns cost money, and the methods of obtaining the money have long been controversial. Campaign money can come from a candidate's own wealth, political parties, interested individuals, or interest groups. Money is contributed to candidates for a variety of reasons, ranging from altruism to self-interest. Individuals or groups, in hopes of influencing the outcome of an election and subsequently influencing policy, give **interested money**. Concern about campaign finance stems from the possibility that candidates or parties, in their pursuit of campaign funds, will decide that it is more important to represent their contributors than their conscience or the voters. The potential corruption that results from politicians' dependence on interested money concerns many observers of American politics.

Scandals involving money's influence on policy are not new. In 1925, responding to the Teapot Dome scandal, in which a cabinet member was convicted of accepting bribes, Congress passed the Corrupt Practices Act, which required disclosure of campaign funds but was "written in such a way as to exempt virtually all [members of Congress] from its provisions."[61]

The 1972 Watergate scandal—an illegal break-in at Democratic party headquarters by persons associated with the Nixon campaign to steal campaign documents and plant listening devices—led to discoveries by news reporters and congressional investigators that large amounts of money from corporations and individuals were "laundered" in secret bank accounts outside the country for political and campaign purposes. Nixon's 1972 campaign spent more than $60 million, more than twice what it had expended in 1968. Investigators discovered that wealthy individuals and corporations made large contributions to influence the outcome of the election or secure ambassadorships and administrative appointments.

In the early 1990s, Charles Keating and his failed Lincoln Savings and Loan spotlighted the possibility that undue influence comes with large contributions. Keating had asked five U.S. senators, all of whom had received substantial campaign contributions or other perks from him, to intervene on his behalf with federal bank regulators looking into his savings and loan business. These senators came to be called the Keating Five. One of the senators was John McCain, who later became a strong advocate of campaign finance reform. The 1996 election saw aggressive fundraising by the Clinton/Gore campaign, including opportunities for donors to have meetings with the President, to fly with him on Air Force One, and to spend the night in the White House Lincoln Bedroom. A congressional investigation into these and related concerns about campaign finance in the 1996 cycle reinforced the case for reform.[62]

Efforts at Reform

Reformers have tried three basic strategies to prevent abuse in political contributions: (1) imposing limitations on giving, receiving, and spending political money; (2) requiring public disclosure of the sources and uses of political money; and (3) giving governmental

interested money
Financial contributions by individuals or groups in the hope of influencing the outcome of an election and subsequently influencing policy.

IN COMPARATIVE PERSPECTIVE

THE SOFT MONEY LOOPHOLE IN JAPAN

The Japanese strategy to combat corruption and money politics has been to create some of the most stringent campaign regulations in the world:

- Door-to-door campaigning is banned.
- Candidates may not run campaign advertisements in the media, although parties may.
- Candidates may produce only two versions of their campaign brochure, and only a limited number may be distributed; the number varies according to the number of registered voters in a district.
- Campaign posters are allowed only on government-provided poster boards that are set up in several locations across a district during the campaign.
- Direct mailing of campaign literature that mentions a specific candidate is not allowed except for a specified number of government-provided campaign postcards.
- The number of campaign offices, employees, and vehicles is restricted by law.

These regulations should make it impossible for candidates to raise and spend large sums of money in a campaign, but Japanese candidates have found a giant loophole in these restrictions by avoiding "official" campaign activities. A candidate will go door to door or mail out literature to voters or put up posters advertising a speech to be given before the official campaign period. In these precampaign activities, the candidates will be very careful never to mention the upcoming election, so their efforts are not covered by law.

Attempts to limit these activities have run into constitutional concerns. If a campaign has not begun and a person has not declared his or her candidacy, how can the Japanese government restrict the right of a citizen to speak at a meeting, discuss issues with people, mail information to people, or put up posters advertising such activities?

---

subsidies to presidential candidates, campaigns, and parties. Recent campaign finance laws have tended to use all three strategies.

THE FEDERAL ELECTION CAMPAIGN ACT   In 1971, Congress passed the Federal Election Campaign Act (FECA), which limited amounts that candidates for federal office could spend on advertising, required disclosure of the sources of campaign funds as well as how they are spent, and required political action committees to register with the government and report all major contributions and expenditures. This law also provided a checkoff that allowed taxpayers to contribute $1 to a fund to subsidize presidential campaigns by checking a box on their income tax form. The checkoff option is now $3.

In 1974, Congress passed and President Gerald Ford signed the most sweeping campaign reform measure in U.S. history. These amendments to the Federal Election Campaign Act established somewhat more realistic limits on contributions and spending, tightened disclosure, and provided for public financing of presidential campaigns.

The 1974 law was again extensively amended after the Supreme Court's 1976 *Buckley v. Valeo* decision, which overturned several of its provisions on grounds that they violated the First Amendment.[63] The *Buckley* decision emphasized limitations on contributions and full and open disclosure of all fund-raising activities by candidates for federal office, as well as the system of public financing for presidential elections.[64] The Supreme Court made a distinction between campaign spending and campaign contributions, holding that the First Amendment protects spending; therefore, legislatures may not limit how much of their own money people spend on elections, but Congress may limit how much people contribute to somebody else's campaign. Later modifications of the law and interpretations by the Federal Election Commission sought to encourage volunteer activities and party building by permitting national political parties, corporations, labor unions, and individuals to give unlimited amounts, called **soft money**, to state parties, provided that the funds were used for party-building purposes.

One of the success stories of FECA was that presidential candidates of both parties for 20 years accepted the limitations on fundraising and campaign spending that were part of the public financing provisions. In recent presidential elections the public subsidy of presidential candidates has broken down. Until 2000, presidential candidates

soft money
Contributions to a state or local party for party-building purposes.

(except wealthy, self-financed candidates) accepted the voluntary limitations that come with partial public financing of presidential nomination campaigns. George W. Bush, who raised more than $125 million for his campaign, declined federal matching funds in the 2000 primaries. In 2004, having raised over $366 million, he again turned down the matching funds in the primaries as did two of the Democrats, Howard Dean and John Kerry (Kerry raised over $322 million). In 2000 and 2004, Bush accepted the federal general election grant of roughly $75 million, along with the general election spending limit. John Kerry also accepted the public funding and spending limit in the 2004 presidential general election. Whether future candidates will also pass up some federal funds depends on how well funded their opponents are and their own ability to raise money. Beyond the problem of candidates' passing up federal funds, the number of taxpayers checking the campaign subsidy on their income tax forms has been declining, although enough did so to cover all the costs of the 2000 and 2004 elections.[65]

THE BIPARTISAN CAMPAIGN REFORM ACT (BCRA) One of the most serious problems with the campaign finance system was soft money—funds given to national parties by individuals or political action committees ostensibly for party-building registration drives, mailings, and advertising. No limits were set on the amount of such contributions. The money was called "soft" because federal law did not limit how much individuals or groups could contribute or how much parties could spend. Although soft money was supposed to benefit only parties, it was used by the parties to influence the election of federal candidates. Both parties made raising soft money a high priority, and soft money spending rose dramatically. All national party committees combined raised over $509 million of soft money in the 1999–2000 election cycle, up from $110 million adjusted for inflation in 1991–1992[66] (see Figure 9–5). In 2001–2002, all party committees combined raised over $495 million in soft money.

Soft money brought back the large donors as major players in campaign finance. It also strengthened the power of the national party committees, which allocate the money to state parties and indirectly to candidates. To the Supreme Court, which upheld the BCRA soft money ban, one of the major problems with soft money was that it

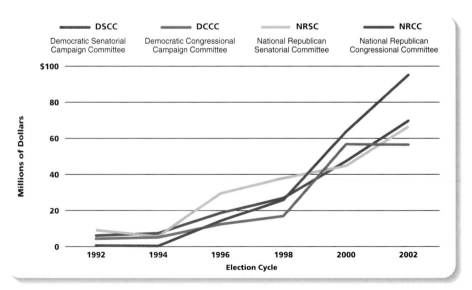

FIGURE 9–5 Congressional Campaign Committee Soft Money Spending, 1994–2002.

SOURCE: Federal Election Commission, "Party Committees Raise more than $1 Billion in 2002–2003," press release, March 20, 2002, at, www.fec.gov, April 29, 2003. Adjusted by CPI, at ftp://ftp.bls.gov/pub/special.requests/cpi/cpiai.txt, January 15, 2003.

NOTE: The totals for each party do not equal the sum of the party committee receipts because the numbers provided by the FEC have been adjusted to account for transfers between party committees so as not to double count money in the total receipts.

purchased access to elected officials and with that access came influence and the possibility or appearance of corruption.[67]

In the past, soft money had been more important in presidential than in congressional contests, but that changed in a dramatic way with the 1998 and 2000 congressional elections. The most dramatic growth in 2000 and 2002 came among Senate Democrats. Figure 9–5 plots the surge in soft money funds for the four congressional campaign committees. The 2002 election cycle also saw extraordinary soft money activity by all party committees. Overall, the parties raised nearly as much soft money in 2001–2002 as they raised in 1999–2000, which was a presidential election year. When we compare 2002 with the last midterm year, 1998, we see soft money more than doubling in four years. With President Bush leading the way, the Republican National Committee raised nearly $114 million, up from $74 million in 1998. Again in 2002, the Democratic Senatorial Campaign Committee outpaced all other committees, raising more than $95 million.

BCRA banned most forms of soft money. All soft money contributions to national party committees were banned, as was soft money spending by state parties for or against federal candidates. However, BCRA permits state and local party committees to raise and spend limited amounts of soft money for voter registration and get-out-the-vote efforts. Such activities may be funded with soft money contributions of no more than $10,000 per individual or group as permitted by state law. This provision in BCRA is called "Levin Funds," so named after Michigan Senator Carl Levin, who sponsored this as an amendment.

ISSUE ADVOCACY ADVERTISING   The 1996 election saw a surge in **issue advocacy**. Money spent on issue advocacy ads is unlimited and undisclosed because it presumably deals with issues, not candidates. Issue ad spending in some U.S. House races exceeded $1 million in recent elections; for example, in 2000, one group, the Alliance for Quality Nursing Home Care, spent more than $1 million on issue ads in the Delaware U.S. Senate race.[68] In the 1998, 2000, and 2002 elections, businesses, labor unions, health maintenance organizations, environmental groups, the Business Roundtable, pro- and anti-gun groups, pro- and anti-abortion groups, and the pharmaceutical industry ran issue ads (see Table 9–2).

TABLE 9–2   SOME FREQUENT ISSUE ADVERTISERS

Advertiser	Amount Spent*
Citizens for Better Medicare	$64
AFL-CIO	45
Coalition to Protect America's Health Care	30
National Rifle Association	25
U.S. Chamber of Commerce	15
Planned Parenthood Action Fund	14
Business Roundtable	13
Federation for American Immigration Reform	12
NAACP National Voter Fund	11
Americans for Job Security	10

SOURCE: Data from David B. Magleby, ed., *Election Advocacy: Soft Money and Issue Advocacy in the 2000 Congressional Elections* (Center for the Study of Elections and Democracy, Brigham Young University, 2001); Erika Falk, "Issue Advocacy Advertising Through the Presidential Primary, 1999–2000 Election Cycle," Annenberg Public Policy Center, press release, September 20, 2000.

*The numbers estimate total spending on issue advocacy and express advocacy; however, a large proportion went to issue advocacy.

THINKING IT THROUGH

Until BCRA, groups relied on a distinction in the *Buckley* v. *Valeo* Supreme Court decision, which defined communications that use words such as "vote for" or "vote against" as election ads and those that did not use such words as "issue ads." This distinction was not meaningful in actual campaigns, however.* BCRA defines an electioneering communication as "a communication that refers to a clearly identified candidate, is publicly distributed shortly before an election for the office that candidate is seeking, and is targeted to the relevant electorate (U.S. House and Senate Candidates only)."[†]

BCRA's new electioneering definition had only a limited impact in 2004 because the campaign started so early, well before the 60 days before the general election. Some groups simply shifted to a strategy of doing independent expenditures which are unlimited but fully disclosed. Finally, BCRA's new definition did not apply to mail, phone, or personal contact, which was a major part of the process in 2004.

Critics of the new BCRA definition point out that Congress is often in session until a few days before an election, and interest groups need to be able to inform the public about important issues that are being considered. To limit issue ads during this period may stifle the free speech of groups with a more legislative than electoral agenda. Critics also see any restriction or limitation on electioneering as a restriction on First Amendment rights, and this includes limits on corporations and unions using their general funds for these purposes.

*David B. Magleby, "Dictum Without Data: The Myth of Issue Advocacy and Party Building," at csed.byu.edu/publications/dictum.doc.

†Federal Elections Commission, "Electioneering Communications," June 2004, at www.fec.gov.

issue advocacy
Promoting a particular position or an issue paid for by interest groups or individuals but not candidates. Much issue advocacy is often electioneering for or against a candidate, and until 2004 had not been subject to any regulation.

The 2002 election saw an expansion of seniors' groups doing issue advocacy. Among those involved were 60 Plus, Seniors Coalition, United Seniors Association, and the American Association for Retired People (AARP). The AARP, by far the largest and best known of seniors' groups, urged voters to study the issues. The seniors' group that spent the most money was United Seniors, a group largely funded by the pharmaceutical industry. By masking its identity, the pharmaceutical industry could present its message without a stigma. Voters have an unfavorable impression of the pharmaceutical industry but know very little about United Seniors.[69] Other groups that engaged in substantial issue advocacy in 2002 included the Sierra Club, Planned Parenthood, and Club for Growth. These ads not only help the candidate that interest groups prefer or punish the candidate they oppose but also force candidates to discuss the interest group's agenda. Although these ads do not specifically say to vote for or against a candidate, they may contain candidates' images and names, and for voters they are indistinguishable from candidate or party ads.[70]

BCRA bans broadcast ads that show the image or likeness of a candidate, mention a candidate's name, and occur in the 60 days before a general election or 30 days before a primary election not paid for with disclosed money. This act also bans unions and corporations from using treasury funds for electioneering ads.

The use of issue ads and the growth in soft money meant that competitive congressional elections shifted from candidate-centered elections to party-centered and interest-group-centered campaigns. Soft money spending combined with interest group

Issue ads, such as this one placed by the U.S. Chamber of Commerce to promote pro-business candidates, try to influence voters to support candidates with favorable positions on the issues that are important to their sponsors.

issue advocacy spending exceeded the candidate campaigns in radio and television advertising by a margin of 2 to 1 in many of the most competitive congressional races of 2000 and 2004.[71] Parties and interest groups also spent large sums of money on mailings and telephone calls. For example, in some congressional races in 2000, targeted voters received as many as 12 pieces of political mail per day as election day approached. The intensity of issue advocacy and soft-money-funded communications in competitive races in 2002 was again extraordinary. In contests like the South Dakota Senate race, an hour of programing often had only political commercials. Because television time was sold out, some groups purchased radio time. Others turned to mail. Many groups with membership lists used these for personal contact and get-out-the-vote efforts.[72]

One of the problems with issue ads is accountability. Since interest groups using this form of electioneering are not required to disclose how much they spend or how they raise their money, voters have a hard time knowing the source of the funds. Ads by these groups also tend to be more negative.[73] Often candidates get blamed for the attacks made by these groups because voters assume that the ads are run by the candidates.

One predictable consequence of BCRA's ban on soft money was increased interest group electioneering via issue advocacy in 2004. The most visible of these new electioneering groups, sometimes called **527 groups**, is America Coming Together (ACT) which raised and spent an estimated $76 million in presidential battleground states in 2004. Much of the early money for ACT came from the wealthy investor George Soros. The advent of groups like ACT, while benefiting John Kerry and the Democrats, constitutes a shift in power toward groups and away from candidates and parties.

Republicans, in part because they were in power and had the fundraising skills of President Bush, did not see as many allied 527 groups as did the Democrats. Some examples of Republican 527 groups in 2004 included Progress for America, Leadership Forum, and the Republican Governors Association. The 527 group that may have had the greatest impact on the campaign was the Swift Boat Veterans for Truth, who attacked Senator Kerry's war record. The modest initial budget for ads generated news coverage. The message of the ads cut to the core of the persona that Kerry had presented at the Democratic National Convention. President Bush was not drawn into the controversy but former Senator Bob Dole's assertion that there may be something to the charges added to the attention the group received. Some Republican allied groups did not organize as 527 organizations but instead operated under a different section of the tax code (Section 501-C), which requires even less disclosure.[74] But it was on the Democratic side that 527 groups were most important. ACT, for example, helped organize many other interest groups in its voter registration and mobilization efforts. A related group, The Media Fund, spent $54 million in ads against President Bush up until 60 days before the election.

There are several important campaign finance-related issues that BCRA does not address. For example, it leaves intact the fund-raising advantages enjoyed by incumbents. It is not only the source of campaign money that is a problem but the pattern of unequal distribution as well. The high costs of television advertising diminish the ability of challengers to mount visible campaigns, resulting in declining competition. Only months after passage of the 2002 reforms, John McCain announced his support and sponsorship of legislation creating a "broadcast bank" where political parties would be given vouchers for free advertising time, with one-third of the time to go to challengers. Television stations, under McCain's proposal, are required to devote at least two hours per week to political coverage in which the candidates are on camera during the last month of the general election campaign.[75] For more information on broadcast time proposals, see The Alliance for Better Campaigns at www.bettercampaigns.org.

CANDIDATES' PERSONAL WEALTH Campaign finance legislation cannot constitutionally restrict rich candidates—the Rockefellers, the Kennedys, the Perots—from spending heavily on their own campaigns. Big money can make a big difference, and wealthy candidates can afford to spend big money. In presidential politics, this advantage can be most meaningful in the period before the primaries begin. There may be no constitutional way to limit how much money people can spend on their own campaigns. The 2000 New Jersey U.S. Senate race, for example, set new records for a candidate's personal spending in an

Candidates willing to spend personal wealth on their campaign enjoy important advantages. They are not subject to the contribution limitations imposed on other individuals. New Jersey Senator Jon Corzine spent $60 million of his own money on his 2000 race. Corzine was selected by the Democratic leadership to head the Democratic Senatorial Campaign Committee for 2003–2004.

527 Groups
Interest groups organized under Section 527 of the Internal Revenue Code may advertise for or against candidates. If their source of funding is corporations or unions, they have some restrictions on broadcast advertising. 527 organizations were important in recent elections.

In Comparative Perspective

CAMPAIGN FINANCING IN BRITAIN AND CANADA

United States election campaigns go on for months or even years and are very expensive. In contrast, Canadian general election campaigns are limited by law to about five weeks. Public opinion polls cannot be published during the last three days of a campaign, and the media are prohibited by law from reporting results from earlier time zones on the evening of the election in any district where voting is still taking place.

Expenditures are strictly limited for Canadian political parties and individual candidates. During the 1997 general election campaign to fill the 301 seats in the House of Commons, political parties that fielded candidates in all districts were limited by law to spending no more than approximately $8 million each for the entire election, and individual candidates could spend about $35,000 to $45,000, depending on the number of voters per district. In return, media outlets were required to sell a certain amount of airtime to the parties, and national and regional television and radio networks had to donate some free airtime to these parties. If individual candidates received more than 15 percent of the vote in their districts, the government reimbursed 50 percent of their election-related expenses. Political parties receiving at least 2 percent of the national vote or at least 5 percent of the votes cast in electoral districts where they ran candidates were reimbursed 22.5 percent of their expenses.

In the June 1997 Canadian elections, 1,672 candidates ran for office, and ten political parties received registered status. Total spending by the parliamentary candidates and political parties was approximately $70 million—less than half the $157 million spent by candidates in the United States during the 1996 election campaign ($29 million on seats in the House of Representatives and $128 million on seats in the Senate).

British general elections also offer an interesting contrast to elections in the United States. The election campaign lasts only three weeks. Candidates for the House of Commons, the most critical election in Britain, are allowed to raise and spend only $15,000. If they spend more, they are disqualified. Each candidate gets the same amount of free airtime, and each candidate is allowed one free election leaflet mailed to each voter in the constituency. About 75 percent of voters turn out, and about 95 percent of eligible voters are registered to vote. At the voting booth, the voter is handed a slip of paper with the names of three or four candidates for the House of Commons. No other offices or ballot questions are presented at the same time.

SOURCE: Adapted from Dudley Fishburn, "British Campaigning—How Civilized!" *The New York Times*, April 14, 1992, p. 25. See also, Alexancer Macleod, "Britain Leads in Campaign Finance Reform," *Christian Science Monitor*, July 30, 1999, Section: World; p. 6.

election. Wall Street investment banker Jon Corzine, a newcomer to elections, spent a total of $60 million, $35 million of it on the primary alone.[76] Corzine was elected. BCRA includes a millionaire's provision that was upheld by the Supreme Court in *McConnell* v. *FEC*. The provision allows candidates running against self-financed opponents who expend large amounts of their own wealth to have higher contribution limits for their donors.

INDEPENDENT EXPENDITURES   BCRA does not constrain **independent expenditures** by groups, political parties, or individuals, as long as the expenditures by those individuals, parties, or groups are independent of the candidate and fully disclosed to the Federal Election Commission (FEC). A group or party that does independent expenditures within a month of a primary or two months of a general election must use hard money, that is, disclosed and limited contributions to the party or group. Any 527 organization wishing to broadcast an electioneering communication within one month of a primary or two months of a general election must not use corporate or union treasury funds, it must report the expenditures associated with the broadcast, and it must disclose all funding sources since the first day of the preceeding calendar year. While contribution sources are restricted in this case, contribution amounts are not. Individuals spending their own money and not coordinating with others are also not limited. This exemption was permitted by the Supreme Court on free speech grounds. In the 1999–2000 election cycle, interest groups spent a total of $22 million on independent expenditures. The National Rifle Association (NRA) led all other interest groups with $4.2 million, mostly for Republicans, but the League of Conservation Voters ($3.2 million), the National Education Association (NEA) ($2.4 million), and the National Abortion and Reproductive Rights Action League ($2.2 million) all combined to spend $7.8 million, mostly on behalf of Democrats. Individuals can also engage in

independent expenditures
Money spent by individuals or groups not associated with candidates to elect or defeat candidates for office.

independent expenditures. In the 2000 presidential election, Stephen Adams, owner of an outdoor advertising firm, spent $2 million in support of Governor George W. Bush.[77] In 2004, billionaire George Soros, who gave millions to 527 organizations opposed to the re-election of George Bush, also spent 2.3 million in independent expenditures against the president. He used the money to run full-page newspaper ads against Bush and to fund a speaking tour during which he expressed his opposition to Bush's reelection. In addition, he maintained a Web site and sent mailings to voters in key states.

Continuing Problems with Campaign Finance

The continuing problems with federal election fund raising are easy to identify: dramatically escalating costs, a growing dependence on PAC money, decreasing visibility and competitiveness of challengers (especially in the House), and the ability of wealthy individuals to fund their own campaigns. The danger of large contributions influencing lawmakers directly or indirectly through political parties was reduced by BCRA. Large contributons, however, can still influence the outcome of elections, as the 527 and other groups [since there were groups organized under other rules, too] demonstrated in the 2004 election.

RISING COSTS OF CAMPAIGNS   The American ideal that anyone—even a person of modest wealth—can run for public office and hope to win has become more a myth than a reality.[78] And rising costs also mean that incumbents spend more time raising funds and therefore less time legislating and representing their districts. Since the Federal Election Campaign Act (FECA) became law in 1972, total expenditures by candidates for the House of Representatives have more than doubled after controlling for inflation, and they have risen even more in Senate elections (see Table 9–3). One reason

---

TABLE 9–3   AVERAGE CAMPAIGN EXPENDITURES OF CANDIDATES FOR THE HOUSE OF REPRESENTATIVES, 1988–2002 GENERAL ELECTION (IN THOUSANDS OF 2004 DOLLARS)

	Incumbent	*Challenger*	*Open Seat*
Republican			
1988	$603.1	$148.0	$1,201.8
1990	531.1	147.8	1,109.1
1992	660.7	234.6	778.2
1994	541.7	281.4	1,189.3
1996	820.3	234.9	699.0
1998	715.5	262.2	758.6
2000	944.5	331.7	1,283.6
2002	860.9	188.3	1,080.0
Democrat			
1988	$528.0	$211.9	$658.9
1990	536.2	147.4	714.3
1992	751.6	199.8	599.2
1994	711.3	186.3	684.2
1996	635.1	329.4	698.0
1998	577.1	249.1	759.3
2000	787.0	485.6	1,176.7
2002	785.1	313.4	1,020.6

SOURCE: Federal Election Commission, "Congressional Fundraising and Spending Up Again in 1996," press release, April 14, 1997, p. 13; Federal Election Commission, "1998 Congressional Financial Activity Declines," press release, December 29, 1998, p. 5; Federal Election Commission, at www.ftp.fec.gov/fec.

for escalating costs is television. Organizing and running a campaign is expensive, limiting the field of challengers to those who have resources of their own or are willing to spend more than a year raising money from interest groups and individuals.

DECLINING COMPETITION Unless something is done to help finance challengers, incumbents will continue to have the advantage in seeking reelection. Nothing in BCRA addresses this problem. Challengers in both parties are typically underfunded. House Democratic challengers averaged $198,330 in spending in 2004. In 2000 and 2002 the average for House Democratic challengers was around $350,000, while Republican challengers averaged between around $200,000 in 2002 and $250,000 in 2000.[79] In today's expensive campaigns, candidates are invisible if they only have this amount to spend.

The high cost of campaigns dampens competition by discouraging individuals from running for office. Potential challengers look at the fund-raising advantages enjoyed by incumbents—at incumbents' campaign war chests carried over from previous campaigns, which can reach $1 million or more, and at the time it will take for them to raise enough money to launch a minimal campaign—and they decide to direct their energies elsewhere. Moreover, unlike incumbents, who are being paid while campaigning and raising money, most challengers have to support themselves and their families throughout the campaign, which for a seat in Congress lasts roughly two years.

INCREASING DEPENDENCE ON PACS AND WEALTHY DONORS Where does the money come from to finance these expensive election campaigns? For most House incumbents, it comes from political action committees (PACs), which we discussed in Chapter 6. In recent years more than two-out-of-five incumbents seeking reelection raised more money from PACs than from individuals (see Figure 9–6).[80] Senators get a smaller percentage of their campaign funds from PACs, but because they spend so much more, they need to raise even more money from PACs than House incumbents do. PACs are pragmatic, giving largely to incumbents. Challengers receive little from PACs because PACs do not want to offend politicians in power. BCRA raised the individual contribution limit to a candidate in the two-year campaign cycle to $4,000, still well below the PAC contribution limit for an election cycle of $10,000. Some individuals who formerly gave $2,000 will now double their contribution to particular candidates, but politicians will continue to rely on PACs because relatively few individuals have the means to give this much money. It also often takes less time to raise money from PACs than from individuals.

To be sure, PACs and individuals spend money on campaigns for many reasons. Most of them want certain laws to be passed or repealed, certain funds to be

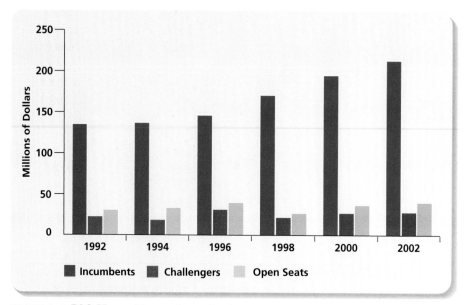

FIGURE 9–6 PAC Money Favors Incumbents.
SOURCE: FEC, "PAC Activity Increases for 2002 Elections," March 27, 2003, at www.fec.gov.

appropriated, or certain administrative decisions to be rendered. At a minimum, they want access to officeholders, a chance to talk with members before key votes.

Defenders of PACs point out that there is no demonstrable relationship between contributions and legislators' votes. But influence in the legislative process depends on access to staff and members of Congress, and most analysts agree that campaign contributions give donors extraordinary access. PACs influence the legislative process in other ways as well. Their access helps them structure the legislative agenda with friendly legislators and influence the drafting of legislation or amendments to existing bills. These are all advantages that others do not have.

IMPROVING ELECTIONS

A combination of party rules and state laws determines how we choose nominees for president. Reformers agree that the current process is flawed but disagree over which aspects require change. Concern over how we choose presidents now centers on four issues[81]: (1) the number, timing, and representativeness of presidential primaries; (2) the role of the electoral college, including the possibility that a presidential election might be thrown into the House of Representatives; (3) how we vote; and (4) how we fund presidential elections.

Reforming The Nominating Process

As noted, in 2004 once again the choice of presidential nominees was most influenced by the voteres in early primary or caucus states like Iowa and New Hampshire. The fact is that most citizens do not have a say in who the nominees are. Moreover, these early states are not broadly representative of the country or of their respective parties. Participation in primaries has been low in recent years (see Figure 9–7). In the 2004 primaries, turnout was generally under 17 percent of the voting-age population, and it declined as the primary season progressed and the field of candidates narrowed.[82] Voters in primaries also tend to be more ideological than voters generally, a further bias in the current nominating process.

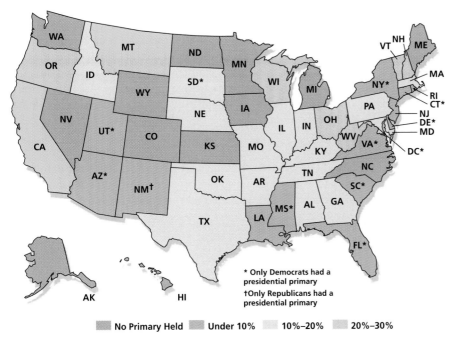

* Only Democrats had a presidential primary

†Only Republicans had a presidential primary

No Primary Held   Under 10%   10%–20%   20%–30%

FIGURE 9–7 Voter Turnout in the 2004 Presidential Primaries.
Source: Curtis B. Gans, Director, Committee for the Study of the American Electorate, facsimile to author, September 22, 2004.

None of these concerns are new. What would the critics substitute for state presidential primaries? Some argue in favor of a *national presidential primary* that would take the form of a single nationwide election, probably held in May or September, or separate state primaries held in all the states on the same day.[83] Supporters contend that a one-shot national presidential primary (though a runoff might be necessary) would be simple, direct, and representative. It would cut down the wear-and-tear on candidates, and it would attract a large turnout because of media coverage. Opponents argue that such a reform would make the present system even worse. It would enhance the role of showmanship and gamesmanship, and being enormously expensive, it would hurt the chances of candidates who lack strong financial backing.

A more modest proposal is to hold *regional primaries,* possibly at two- or three-week intervals across the country. Regional primaries might bring more coherence to the process and encourage more emphasis on issues of regional concern. But such primaries would retain most of the disadvantages of the present system—especially the emphasis on money and media. Clearly, they would give an advantage to candidates from whatever region held the first primary, and this advantage would encourage regional candidates and might increase polarization among sections of the country.

A different proposal is to drastically reduce the number of presidential primaries and make more use of the caucus system. The turnout of voters in the Iowa caucuses in recent elections shows that participation can be high, and the time participants spent discussing candidates and issues shows that such participation can be thoughtful and informed. In caucus states, candidates are less dependent on the media and more dependent on convincing political activists. By centering delegate selection in party meetings, the caucus system would also, some say, enhance the role of the party.[84]

Still another idea—used by Colorado for nominations to state offices and by Utah for nominations to federal and state offices—would turn the process around. Beginning in May, local caucuses and then state conventions would be held in every state. They would then send delegates—a certain percentage of whom would be unpledged to any presidential candidate—to the national party conventions, which would be held in the summer. The national conventions would select two or three candidates to compete in a national primary to be held in September. In this plan, voters registered by party would be allowed to vote for their party nominee in the September primaries.[85] Such a plan would likely add voter engagement in the party process but also be more expensive since candidates would mount two national campaigns, one in September and another in November.

Given the problems with the current nomination process, why has it not been reformed? Part of the answer is strong resistance from the states that benefit from the current system. In our federal system, imposing a national or regional primary is difficult.

While many voters are effectively denied a vote in determining their party's nominee, news coverage of the primaries allows them to evaluate the candidates' political qualities and their abilities to organize campaigns; communicate through the media; stand up under pressure; avoid making mistakes (or recover if they do make them); adjust their appeals to shifting events and to different regions of the country; control their staffs as well as make good use of them, and be decisive; articulate, resilient, humorous, informed, and ultimately successful in winning votes. In short, supporters of the current system claim, primaries test candidates on the very qualities they must exhibit in the presidency.[86]

Reforming the Electoral College

The Florida ballot counting and recounting after the 2000 election and the fact that the popular vote winner did not become president prompted a national debate on the electoral college. The most frequently proposed reform is *direct popular election* of the president. Presidents would be elected directly by the voters, just as governors are, and the electoral college and individual electors would be abolished. Such proposals usually provide that if no candidate receives at least 40 percent of the total popular vote, a *runoff election* would be held between the two contenders with the most votes. Supporters argue that direct election would give every voter the same weight in the presidential balloting in accordance with the one-person, one-vote doctrine. Winners would take on more legitimacy because their victories would reflect the will of the voters.

Opponents contend that the plan would further undermine federalism, encourage unrestrained majority rule and hence political extremism, and hurt the most populous and competitive states, which would lose some of their present influence. Others fear that the plan would make presidential campaigns more remote from the voters; candidates might stress television and give up their forays into shopping centers and city malls.[87]

From time to time, Congress considers proposals for a constitutional amendment to elect presidents directly. Such proposals, however, seldom get far because of the strong opposition of various interests that believe they may be disadvantaged by such a change, especially small states and minority groups whose role is enlarged by the electoral college. Groups such as African Americans and farmers, for example, fear they might lose their swing vote power—their ability to make a difference in key states that may tip the electoral college balance.

Another alternative to the electoral college is sometimes called the National Bonus Plan. This plan adds to the current 538 electoral college members another 102 electoral votes, to be awarded on a winner-take-all basis to the candidate with the most votes, so long as that candidate received more than 40 percent of the popular vote. This system would avoid elections' being thrown into the House of Representatives and would help the popular vote winner take over the White House. The most serious liabilities of the plan are that it is complicated and that it requires a runoff election if there is no winner.

Finally, two states, Maine and Nebraska, have already modified the electoral college, adopting a district system in which the candidate who carries each congressional district gets that electoral vote and the candidate who carries the state gets the state's two additional electoral votes. This quasi-proportional representation system has the advantage of not shutting out a candidate who is strong in some areas of a state but not others, but otherwise it does not address the larger concerns with the electoral college.

The failure of attempts to change the system of elections points to an important conclusion about procedural reform: Americans normally do not focus on procedures. Even after the intense focus on the outcome of the 2000 election, including the role of the electoral college, reform was not seriously considered.

Reforming How We Vote

The 2000 presidential election ended with a monthlong controversy over ballots and how to count them. While Florida became the focal point of attention with its problems with punch-card ballots, dangling chads, voter confusion over ballot formats, and when to count or not count absentee ballots, such problems are common to all 50 states. As we noted earlier, election administration is a state and local matter.

Following the 2000 election, Florida enacted legislation modernizing its election process and establishing minimum standards for polling places and voting machines. These standards include certification of electronic voting machines and requirements for the use and storage of these machines. Despite this legislation and the purchase of more than $30 million worth of new electronic machines, their first use in the 2002 primary reminded many of the problems with punch-card ballots in 2000. Some new machines failed to record votes, others had too many votes, and precinct workers were not adequately prepared to help voters with the new technology.

At the national level, both houses of Congress passed the Help America Vote Act (HAVA) providing $3.9 billion in federal funds to modernize American voting procedures, mandating that states maintain accurate statewide voter registration lists.[88] The legislation also permits voters to cast provisional ballots if there is uncertainty about their registration. Advocates of the new voting technology hope that it will improve accuracy and make voting more accessible for persons who have disabilities or who do not speak English.[89] Opponents of the changes see the funding as inadequate to the need and worry about the accuracy and security of the new systems.[90] In the days just before the 2004

The touch-screen voting machine is an example of a new way for voters to register their choice. This computerized machine prevents voters from choosing more than one candidate, as many did erroneously during the 2000 election in Florida; however, there is considerable controversy over the fact that these machines are not required to produce a paper receipt for each vote cast, making recounts impossible should they become necessary.

ELECTION IN ACTION: 2004 PRESIDENTIAL ELECTION

Try your hand as the campaign manager for either major party candidate in the 2004 presidential campaign. You will make the strategic decisions that guide your candidate to victory. As you travel through the virtual process of coordinating campaign advertisements, budgeting the available funds through election day, and deciding which states to travel to, you will better understand the impact of the electoral college and the work that goes into electing a president of the United States.

Go to Make It Real, "Election in Action: 2004 Presidential Election."

election, both parties were preparing for legal challenges to the voting process. Issues included whether or not felons could vote and whether the parties could challenge the registration of new voters at the polls. The implementation of HAVA provisional ballots was also a source of likely litigation. States like Florida and Ohio were the likely battlegrounds for this legal battle, which did not materialize because of Bush's victory margin.

The HAVA is just the start of a broader effort to modernize democracy. It is likely that state legislatures and Congress will eventually debate permitting people to vote via the Internet. The argument will be that if people can make purchases over the Internet, why not let them vote electronically as well? Some states experimented with "e-voting" on a small scale in presidential primaries in 2000 and some counties in California have also experimented with it since then. A shift to e-voting is in some respects an extension of the Oregon vote-by-mail experience since 1996. Oregon elections are now largely conducted using mail ballots, a process which reduces costs and to date has increased participation. Yet critics worry that important elements of community and democracy are lost when people do not vote collectively at the local schoolhouse or fire station. Another concern with e-voting is that it may encourage a proliferation of elections and direct democracy. If we can vote from home, why not vote on more things and more often? E-voting could also foster a political culture of more and more ballot referendums.

Reforming Campaign Finance

The incremental reforms of BCRA and the Supreme Court decision in *McConnell* v. *FEC* upholding them have not resolved the issues of campaign finance. Among the unresolved issues are how presidential campaigns will be financed, the role of interest groups campaigning as Section 527 and 501-C groups, the adequacy of disclosure, and the strength and viability of the political parties. More broadly, the inability of the Federal Election Commission to reach decisions because of its partisan deadlock, as demonstrated by its inaction on Section 527 groups, has helped generate growing pressure to reform that agency.

The 2004 election cycle, with its substantial interest group activity through Section 527 and 501-C organizations, will be seen by those who favor deregulation of campaign finance as another example of the impossibility of limiting money in elections. This school of thought will continue to push for disclosure as the regulatory aim of government in this area.

Another group of reformers will press for more aggressive reforms than those found in BCRA. Included in this agenda will be reining in the 527 and 501-C groups, restructuring the public financing of presidential elections to sustain this element of FECA, and possibly extending public financing of congressional elections. Both sides are likely to agree that change is needed at the FEC but will not agree on how to change it.

SUMMARY

1. American elections, even presidential elections, are largely governed by state law and administered by local election officials. Following the 2000 elections, governments at all levels began to look for ways to improve the system.

2. Our electoral system is based on winner-take-all rules, with typically single-member-district or single-officeholder arrangements. These rules encourage a moderate, two-party system. That we have fixed and staggered terms of office adds predictability to our electoral system.

3. The electoral college is the means by which presidents are actually elected. To win a state's electoral votes, a candidate

must have a plurality of votes in that state. Except in two states, the winner takes all. Thus candidates cannot afford to lose the popular vote in the most populous states. The electoral college also gives disproportionate power to the largest and smallest states, especially if they are competitive. It also has the potential to defeat the popular vote winner.

4. Many congressional, state, and local races are not seriously contested. The extent to which a campaign is likely to be hotly contested varies with the importance of the office and the chance a challenger has of winning. Senate races are more likely to be contested, though most incumbents win.

5. The race for the presidency actually takes place in three stages: winning enough delegate support in presidential primaries and caucuses to secure the nomination, campaigning at the national party convention, and mobilizing voters in enough states for a win in the electoral college.

6. Even though presidential nominations today are usually decided weeks or months before the national party conventions, these conventions still have an important role in setting the parties' direction, unifying their ranks, and firing up enthusiasm.

7. Because large campaign contributors are suspected of improperly influencing

public officials, Congress has long sought to regulate political contributions. The main approaches to reform have been (1) imposing limitations on giving, receiving, and spending political money; (2) requiring public disclosure of the sources and uses of political money; and (3) giving governmental subsidies to presidential candidates, campaigns, and parties, including incentive arrangements. Present regulation includes all three approaches.

8. Loopholes in federal law—including soft money and issue advocacy—led to the passage of BCRA. These loopholes grew in size and importance with the 1996 election cycle and have persisted since.

9. The rising costs of campaigns have led to declining competition for congressional seats and increasing dependence on PACs and wealthy donors.

10. The present presidential selection system is under criticism because of its length and expense, because of uncertainties and biases in the electoral college, and because it seems to test candidates for media skills less needed in the White House than the ability to govern, including the capacity to form coalitions and make hard decisions.

11. Reform efforts center on presidential primaries and the electoral college as well as on voting methods and campaign finance.

K E Y   T E R M S

winner-take-all system	safe seat	national party convention	issue advocacy
single-member district	coattail effect	interested money	527 groups
proportional representation	caucus	soft money	independent expenditures
electoral college			

F U R T H E R   R E A D I N G

R. MICHAEL ALVAREZ, *Information and Elections* (University of Michigan Press, 1998).

LARRY M. BARTELS, *Presidential Primaries and the Dynamics of Public Choice* (Princeton University Press, 1988).

EARL BLACK AND MERLE BLACK, *The Vital South: How Presidents Are Elected* (Harvard University Press, 1992).

DAVID W. BRADY, JOHN F. COGAN, AND MORRIS P. FIORINA, EDS., *Continuity and Change in House Elections* (Stanford University Press, 2000).

BRUCE BUCHANAN, *Presidential Campaign Quality: Incentives and Reform* (Pearson Education, 2004).

ANN N. CRIGLER, MARION R. JUST, AND EDWARD J. MCCAFFERY, EDS., *Rethinking the Vote: The Politics and Prospects of American Election Reform* (Oxford University Press, 2004).

RONALD KEITH GADDIE, *Born to Run: Origins of the Political Career* (Rowman & Littlefield, 2004).

RONALD KEITH GADDIE AND CHARLES S. BULLOCK III, EDS., *Elections to Open Seats in the U.S. House: Where the Action Is* (Rowman & Littlefield, 2000).

PAUL GRONKE, *The Electorate, the Campaign, and the Office: A Unified Approach to Senate and House Elections* (University of Michigan Press, 2000).

RODERICK P. HART, *Campaign Talk* (Princeton University Press, 2000).

PAUL S. HERRNSON, *Playing Hardball: Campaigning for the U.S. Congress* (Prentice Hall, 2000).

PAUL S. HERRNSON, *Congressional Elections: Campaigning at Home and in Washington*, 4th ed. (CQ Press, 2004).

GARY C. JACOBSON, *The Politics of Congressional Elections*, 6th ed. (Longman, 2003).

KATHLEEN HALL JAMIESON, *Everything You Think You Know About Politics . . . and Why You're Wrong* (Basic Books, 2000).

KIM F. KAHN AND PATRICK J. KENNEDY, *The Spectacle of U.S. Senate Campaigns* (Princeton University Press, 1999).

LOUIS SANDY MAISEL AND KARA Z. BUCKLEY, *Parties and Elections in America: The Electoral Process*, 4th ed. (Rowman & Littlefield, 2004).

DAVID B. MAGLEBY, ED., *Financing the 2000 Election* (Brookings Institution Press, 2002).

DAVID B. MAGLEBY AND J. QUIN MONSON, EDS., *The Last Hurrah?: Soft Money and Issue Advocacy in the 2002 Congressional Elections* (Brookings Institution Press, 2004).

MICHAEL J. MALBIN, ED., *Life After Reform: When the Bipartisan Campaign Reform Act . . . Meets Politics* (Rowman & Littlefield, 2003).

JEREMY D. MAYER, *Running on Race: Racial Politics in Presidential Campaigns, 1960–2000* (Random House, 2002).

WILLIAM G. MAYER AND ANDREW E. BUSCH, *The Front-Loading Problem in Presidential Nominations* (Brookings Institution Press, 2004).

STEPHEN K. MEDVIC, *Political Consultants in U.S. Congressional Elections* (Ohio State University Press, 2001).

NELSON W. POLSBY AND AARON B. WILDAVSKY, *Presidential Elections: Strategies and Structures of American Politics*, 11th ed. (Rowman & Littlefield, 2004).

SAMUEL L. POPKIN, *The Reasoning Voter: Communication and Persuasion in Presidential Campaigns*, 2d ed. (University of Chicago Press, 1994).

PAUL D. SCHUMAKER AND BURDETT A. LOOMIS, EDS., *Choosing a President: The Electoral College and Beyond* (Seven Bridges Press, 2002).

JAMES A. THURBER, ED., *The Battle for Congress: Consultants, Candidates, and Voters* (Brookings Institution Press, 2001).

JAMES A. THURBER AND CANDICE J. NELSON, EDS., *Campaign Warriors: Political Consultants in Elections* (Brookings Institution Press, 2000).

STEPHEN J. WAYNE, *The Road to the White House 2004* (Wadsworth, 2004).

See also *Public Opinion Quarterly, the American Journal of Politics*, and *American Political Science Review.*

THE MEDIA AND AMERICAN POLITICS

10

At their final number in the 2004 Super Bowl half-time show, Justin Timberlake and Janet Jackson sang "Rock Your Body." At the conclusion of this song, Timberlake removed part of Jackson's costume, exposing her left breast to 90 million viewers.[1] This incident, described by some as a "wardrobe malfunction,"[2] created substantial controversey. CBS, the network broadcasting the super bowl, claimed no advance knowledge of what occurred,[3] but was still widely criticized for not exercising more control over the half-time entertainment. The Federal Communications Commission (FCC), which regulates broadcast media, received more than 200,000 viewer complaints in eight days,[4] and FCC Chair Michael Powell stated, "We have a very angry public on our hands."[5]

Some thought too much was made of this fleeting moment, either because they did not think it so outrageous or because they thought some of the commercials aired during the Super Bowl were even more offensive. Referring to complaints that parents were blindsided by the event and citing the offensive commercials preceding it, Frank Rich of *The New York Times* said, "What signal were these poor, helpless adults waiting for before pulling their children away from the set? Apparently nothing short of a simulated rape would do."[6] Others responded that what happened in the half-time show was not all that different than what appears with some regularity on MTV or other cable networks.

Moreover, the same content on cable would not have been subject to indecency regulations. Jane D. Brown, a media researcher at the University of North Carolina at Chapel Hill and editor of *Sexual Teens, Sexual Media,* said, "For some children, this won't

mass media
Means of communication that reach the mass public, including newspapers and magazines, radio, television (broadcast, cable, and satellite), films, recordings, books, and electronic communication.

news media
Media that emphasizes the news.

have been anything out of the ordinary. If they're watching MTV, dating shows, or reality programming, this is pretty much what they see all the time."[7] One rationale for the different standards for indecency in broadcast and cable television is that broadcast television uses the airwaves and is free to the recipient, while cable broadcasts are purchased by consumers who willingly pay for them.

The controversy about the Super Bowl ads and halftime show led to action by the FCC and Congress. The FCC imposed a fine of $27,500 on each of the twenty stations owned by CBS, resulting in a total fine of $550,000. This fine was well below the $1.2 million fine levied against Fox for indecency shown on *Married by America*. The FCC did not fine CBS stations now owned by the network. It also reversed its previous ruling on Bono's use of an obscenity during the Golden Globes.[8] Subsequent to the Super Bowl incident, the House of Representatives passed legislation authorizing the FCC to impose fines up to $500,000 for indecency.[9] The media also responded to the controversy. Clear Channel Communications removed "shock jock" Howard Stern from its programming in some major markets.[10] This controversy about indecency in the media illustrates the delicate balance between free speech and broadcasters' use of the public airwaves.

THE INFLUENCE OF THE MEDIA ON POLITICS

The media, in particular the print media, have been called the "fourth estate," and the "fourth branch of government."[11] Evidence that the media influence our culture and politics is plentiful. The **mass media**—newspapers and magazines, radio, television (broadcast, cable, and satellite), the Internet, films, recordings, books, and electronic communication—are the means of communication that reach the mass public.[12] The **news media** are the mass media vehicles that emphasize the news, although the distinctions between entertainment and news

For over forty years, Americans have been getting their news primarily from television. Whenever there is a crisis, most people turn first to television for information. No event in recent history has done more to underscore the importance of television as the primary source of news in contemporary U.S. society than the terrorist attacks that took place on September 11, 2001.

are sometimes blurred. News programs often have entertainment value, and entertainment programs often convey news. Programs in this latter category include TV newsmagazines such as *60 Minutes* and *Dateline,* and talk shows with hosts like Larry King, Oprah Winfrey, Hannity and Colmes, and Jon Stewart.

By definition, the mass media disseminate messages to a large and often heterogeneous audience. Because they must have broad appeal, their messages are often simplified, stereotyped, and predictable. The mass media make money by appealing to large numbers of people. But do large audiences equal political clout? Two factors are important in answering this question: the media's pervasiveness and their role as a linking mechanism between politicians and government officials and the public.

Where do Americans get their news? Until 1960, most people got their news from newspapers. Today, although many people use several sources, they rely primarily on television. Whenever there is a crisis—from the assasination of John F. Kennedy to the *Challenger* explosion to the terrorist attacks on September 11, 2001—people are glued to their TV sets.

The Internet is becoming an increasingly important source of news for Americans, taking its place alongside print, radio, and television. The number of Americans going online for election news is growing dramatically and promises to become even more important as candidates and issue advocates pay increasing attention to the Internet as

PEOPLE & POLITICS *Making a Difference*

SEAN HANNITY

For more than a decade talk radio has been dominated by conservatives like Rush Limbaugh and more recently by Bill O'Reilly and Sean Hannity. In 2004, liberals responded by promoting Al Franken's new radio show as an alternative to the conservatives. An example of a personality who has used talk radio and cable television successfully is Sean Hannity.

Hannity attended college at New York University intermitently because of limited resources but became interested in radio in part through his involvement with college radio stations. He placed a "Job Wanted" ad in the *R&R,* a weekly newspaper covering the music industry, billing himself as "the most talked about college radio host in America."[*] His professional involvement in radio began with a station in Huntsville, Alabama. He later moved to Atlanta, where his strong local ratings attracted the attention of WABC in New York City and the Fox News Channel. He moved to New York, where he launched "Hannity and Colmes" on the Fox News Channel (cable television), reaching an estimated

audience of over one million.[†] Hannity also hosts *The Sean Hannity Show,* which is carried by 400 radio stations, reaching an estimated audience of 12 million.[†] *Talker Magazine* has rated his radio program the second most listened to talk radio show in America.[§] Hannity is also the author of two books, *Let Freedom Ring,*[||] and *Deliver Us From Evil.*[¶]

Hannity is outspoken and aggressive in his interviews and interactions with those who call into his program. He has interviewed most leading conservatives and Republicans like Dick Cheney and Donald Rumsfeld. Hannity also frequently observes that liberals like Bill Clinton have refused to appear on his program. Evidence of the impact of conservative media personalities like Sean Hannity is found in the push by liberals to have their own talk shows. Comedian Al Franken in his first broadcast described this sentiment when he said, "The radical right wing has taken over the White House, Congress, and increasingly, the courts . . . and most insidiously, the airwaves."[**]

[*] www.hannity.com/story.php?content=/about_hannity.
[†] Ibid.
[†] Ibid.
[§] Ibid.
[||] Sean Hannity, *Let Freedom Ring: Winning the War of Liberty over Liberalism* (Regan Books, 2002).
[¶] Sean Hannity, *Deliver Us from Evil: Defeating Terrorism, Despotism, and Liberalism* (Regan Books, 2004).
[**] Allessandra Stanley, "Talk Network Makes Debut, with Rage a No-Show," *The New York Times,* April 1, 2004, p. A20.

a way to get their messages to the voting public.[13] Using the Internet as a news source permits the user to obtain information on only the topics or issues desired and from multiple sources. It also means the user can access the news from multiple locations and at convenient times. It also means that some people may turn to unreliable sources, which are plentiful on the Internet.

The Pervasiveness of Television

Television has changed American politics more than any other invention. Most Americans watch some kind of television news every day. The average American watches television four and one-half hours a day, and most homes have more than two sets.[14] Television provides instant access to news from around the country and the globe, permitting citizens and leaders alike to observe firsthand the capture of Saddam Hussein, a kidnapping in Southern California, or a refugee crisis in Indonesia. This instant coverage increases the pressure on world leaders to respond quickly to crises, permits terrorists to gain widespread coverage of their actions, and elevates the role played by the president in both domestic and international politics.

The growth of around-the-clock cable news and information shows is one of the most important developments in recent years. Until the late 1980s, the network news programs on CBS, NBC, and ABC captured more than 90 percent of the audience for television news at set times in the morning and early evening hours. Owing to the rise of cable television and the advent of the Internet, the broadcast networks now attract only about 40 percent of the viewing public,[15] and half of the public are regular viewers of CNN, CNBC, MSNBC, or Fox News.[16]

Satellites, cable television, computers using Internet search engines like Google or Yahoo, and DVDs make vast amounts of political information available 24 hours a day. These technologies eliminate the obstacles of time and distance and increase the volume of information that can be stored, retrieved, and viewed. They have also reduced the impact of single sources of broadcast or cable news. Competition from cable stations for viewing has put pressure on broadcast networks to remain profitable, which has meant reduced budgets for news coverage and a tendency to look for ways of boosting the entertainment value of broadcast news.

One of the biggest changes in American electoral politics of the last half-century is that most voters now rely more on television commercials for information about candidates and issues and less on news coverage. Although debates and speeches by candidates generate coverage, the more pervasive battleground for votes is radio and TV ads. As a result, electoral campaigns now focus on image and slogans rather than on substance. Successful candidates must be able to communicate with voters through this medium. To get their message across to TV audiences, politicians increasingly rely on media advisers to define their opponent as well as themselves. These consultants also seek positive news coverage, but in many congressional campaigns, news coverage is fleeting.

Candidates are not the only ones who have used television and radio to communicate electioneering messages to voters. Political parties and interest groups in competitive elections between 1996 and 2002 have expended approximately as much as candidates in competitive races urging voters to reject one candidate or support another. The use of party soft money, which was unlimited, and "issue advocacy," which was not only unlimited but undisclosed, allowed noncandidate entities to become major factors in the most competitive contests for Congress and in presidential battleground states.[17] **Issue advocacy**, which was a way for individuals and groups to avoid contribution limitations and disclosure requirements, was curtailed somewhat by the campaign finance reforms that took effect in 2004, aimed at broadcast ads aired during the period before elections. To voters, the messages from the parties and interest groups were indistinguishable from the messages from the candidates,[18] except that the tone was generally more negative.[19]

Passage of the Bipartisan Campaign Reform Act (BCRA) in 2002 and the Supreme Court's subsequent upholding of the act substantially changed the way parties and interest groups behaved in 2004. BCRA banned soft-money-funded electioneering by

issue advocacy
Promoting a particular position or an issue paid for by interest groups or individuals but not candidates. Much issue advocacy is often electioneering for or against a candidate and, until 2004, had not been subject to any regulation.

parties, which had been the largest noncandidate source of broadcast and cable ads. BCRA also banned corporations and unions from using their general funds for election-eering communications, defined as "broadcast ads" that mention a federal candidate by name, occur within 30 days of a primary election and 60 days of a general election, and are targeted to a particular electorate (50,000 people or more in the district or state where the named candidates are running). Consistent with past Supreme Court decisions, BCRA exempted from this limitation nonprofit organizations that do not receive corporate or union funds. Examples of groups like this that were able to run ads within the 60 days before the 2004 election are the League of Conservation Voters and NARAL Pro-Choice America. While these groups were active in 2004, others were even more active, in part because the Federal Election Commission did not strictly define what constituted a political committee under BCRA. Examples of very active groups include the Media Fund, America Coming Together, Progress for America, and Swift Boat Veterans for Truth.

The amount of television news devoted to politics has been declining and now constitutes less than one minute per half-hour broadcast.[20] A major effort to get local television stations to devote a few minutes to candidate debate in their nightly local news ended up with stations averaging 45 seconds a night, or as one observer put it, just enough time to "let candidates clear their throats."[21] Stations also often ignored campaigns in 2002 with a majority (56 percent) of local news broadcasts airing in the weeks leading up to the election making no mention of the campaign.[22]

In large urban areas, it is rare for viewers to see stories about their member of Congress, in part because there are several congressional districts in that media market. Newspapers do a better job of covering politics and devote more attention to it than television stations. The decline in news coverage of elections and voting, especially on television, has only amplified the importance of political advertising on television, through the mail, and on the telephone.

In referendum elections, advertising is the most important source of information in voter decision making.[23] The campaign finance reforms enacted in 2002 will likely only increase the amount of issue advocacy, especially through the mail and on the telephone. As previously noted, BCRA bans issue advocacy on television or radio that mentions a candidate by name in the two months before a general election or one month before a primary election. But it does not limit what groups can do through the mail, on the phone, or in person. In 2004, a wide range of groups communicated directly with voters through the mail, on the phone, and in person. This "ground war" had been growing in importance before passage of BCRA but the reforms accelerated the groups' use of these techniques. In battleground states or districts, voters were often canvassed by groups and then received mail and phone calls reinforcing the message in the initial call. Even more effective are face-to-face conversations, especially with people the voter knows.

The Persistence of Radio

Television and the newer media have not displaced radio. On the contrary, radio continues to reach more American households than television does. Only one household in 100 does not have a radio, compared with four in 100 without a TV.[24] More than 9 out of 10 people listen to the radio every week, and 8 out of 10 do so every day.[25] Many Americans consider the radio an essential companion when driving. Americans get more than "the facts" from radio: They also get analysis and opinion from their favorite commentators and talk show hosts.

The Continuing Importance of Newspapers

Despite vigorous competition from radio and television, Americans still read newspapers. Daily newspaper circulation has been declining for the past 30 years to about 55 million nationwide—or just under one copy for every five people.[26] The circulation figures for newspapers reflect a troubling decline in readership among younger persons: About 30 percent fewer young people read newspapers on a regular basis.[27]

In addition to metropolitan and local newspapers, we now have national ones. Created in 1982 by the Gannett Corporation, *USA Today,* with a circulation of more than

Extensive use of computers by young children has left them vulnerable to sexual predators and commercial fraud, opening the issue of whether government regulation is needed. Parental supervision remains the best protection.

2.1 million, recently replaced *The Wall Street Journal* as America's top-circulating newspaper.[28] *The Wall Street Journal,* with a circulation of over 2 million, has long acted as a national newspaper specializing in business and finance. *The New York Times* has a national edition that is read by more than one million people.

The Internet

From its humble beginnings as a Pentagon research project in the 1960s,[29] the World Wide Web has blossomed into a global phenomenon. There are now more than one billion documents on the Web,[30] and more than 15 million unique domains have been registered worldwide. Many people mistakenly think the Internet and the World Wide Web are the same thing. The truth is that the Internet was the original "giant international plumbing system" for accessing information. It permits information to travel between computers. The World Wide Web is now the most popular way of using the Internet because it transmits pictures, data, and text. However, the WWW incorporates all of the Internet services and much more.

The Internet opens up resources for citizens in dramatic ways. One study found that nearly half of Americans go online to search for news on a particular topic; somewhat smaller proportions go online for updates on stock quotes and sports scores. For about 20 percent of people, the Internet is a primary source of news.[31] Internet users can also interact with other people or politicians about politics through electronic mail and chat rooms. Younger people, including teenagers, use the Internet extensively for schoolwork and nearly three in four prefer it to the library.[32]

Candidates are now using the Web for fund raising. Once a candidate gains recognition, as Howard Dean did, it is possible to raise money quickly and inexpensively via the Web. In fact, in the third quarter of 2003, Dean broke the record for money raised in a quarter by a Democratic presidential candidate, a record he would set again the following quarter. Internet fundraising was integral to his success; half of the estimated $40 million he raised in 2003 came through the Internet.[33] Ironically, Dean himself didn't use a computer until 1998 and had initially refused to have a government e-mail address.[34] John Kerry also found the Internet to be a boon to his fundraising in the general election campaign. The success of the parties and candidates in Internet fundraising may significantly change the way politics is financed. As people gained confidence in making credit card transactions via the Internet, it has opened up the possibility of people contributing to parties and candidates in this way.

The Web provides an inexpensive way to communicate with volunteers, contributors, and voters and promises to become an even larger component of campaigns in the future, as illustrated by several presidential and congressional campaigns in 2004. Candidates maintain home pages where voters can learn about office seekers or ballot referendums.

THE CHANGING ROLE OF THE AMERICAN NEWS MEDIA

The controversy over the 2004 Super Bowl half-time show discussed earlier in this chapter itself became a major media story. Media coverage of this incident demonstrates the public's tremendous appetite for instant news and analysis, at least when it comes to a crisis or major controversy. Americans spend on average an hour a day consuming news, and the older they are, the more time they devote to it.[35] Yet people are quick to criticize the media. Writes journalist James Fallows, "Americans have never been truly fond of their press. Through the last decade, however, their disdain for the media establishment has reached new levels. Americans believe that the news media have become too arrogant, cynical, scandal-minded, and destructive."[36]

How often have you or your friends blamed the media for being biased, criticized the frenzy that surrounds a particular story, or denounced the "if it bleeds, it leads" mentality of nightly television news? Yet the content and style of news coverage is driven by market research in which viewers and readers are asked what they want to see reported and how they want it presented. Advertising revenue is directly linked to the number of readers or viewers a media outlet has.

Media bashing has become something of a national pastime. Americans blame the media for everything from increased tension between the races, biased attacks on public officials, sleaze and sensationalism, increased violence in our society, and for being more interested in making money than in conveying information. Many in the media even agree with these charges.[37] But complaints about the media may simply be a case of criticizing the messenger in order to avoid dealing with the message. Comments like "It's the media's fault that we have lost our social values" or "The media's preoccupation with the private lives of politicians turns Americans off to politics" are overly broad assertions. Americans tend to blame far more problems on the media than are warranted.

There are also occasional examples of fabrication or plagiarism, as in the case of Jayson Blair of *The New York Times,* who plagiarized stories including the writing from a Texas newspaper about the family of Iraqi prisoner of war Jessica Lynch[38]; and Jack Kelley, a top reporter for *USA Today* who fabricated parts of numerous stories including one article that made him a Pulitzer Prize finalist.[39] Cases like these have prompted these newspapers and the media in general to evaluate editorial review and standards of integrity, but they also provoked criticism of the media.

The news media has changed dramatically over the course of U.S. history. At the time of the ratification of the Constitution, newspapers consisted of a single sheet, often printed irregularly by store owners to hawk their services or goods. Newspapers rarely stayed in business more than a year, due to delinquent subscribers and high costs.[40] But the framers understood the important role the press should play as a watchdog of politicians and government, and they included freedom of the press in the Bill of Rights.

Political Mouthpiece

The new nation's political leaders, including Alexander Hamilton and Thomas Jefferson, recognized the need to keep voters informed. Political parties as we know them did not exist, but the active role of the press in supporting the Revolution had fostered a growing awareness of the political potential of newspapers. Hamilton recruited staunch Federalist John Fenno to edit and publish a newspaper in the new national capital of Philadelphia. Jefferson responded by attracting Philip Freneau, a talented writer and editor and a loyal Republican, to do the same for the Republicans. (Jefferson's Republicans later became the Democratic party.) The two papers became the nucleus of a network of competing partisan newspapers throughout the nation.

Although the two newspapers competed in Philadelphia for only a few years, they served as a model for future partisan newspapers. The early American press served as a mouthpiece for political leaders. Its close connection with politicians and political parties offered the opportunity for financial stability—but at the cost of journalistic independence.

Financial Independence

During the Jacksonian era of the 1820s and 1830s, the right to vote was extended to all white adult males through the elimination of property qualifications. The press began to shift its appeal away from elite readers and toward large masses of less educated and less politically interested readers. The rising literacy rate reinforced this popularization of newspapers. These two forces—increased political participation by the common people and the rise of literacy among Americans—began to alter the relationship between politicians and the press.

Some newspaper publishers began to experiment with a new way to finance their newspapers. They charged a penny a paper, paid on delivery, instead of the traditional annual subscription fee of $8 to $10, which was beyond the ability of most readers to pay. The "penny press," as it was called, expanded circulation and put more emphasis on advertising, enabling newspapers to become financially independent of the political parties.

The New York World a day after

As the nineteenth century progressed, literacy grew among the U.S. masses and more people began to get their news from newspapers. The popularization of the print media forced politicians and public officials to devote growing attention to their relationship with the press.

The changing finances of newspapers also affected the definition of news. Before the penny press, all news was political—speeches, documents, editorials—directed at politically interested readers. The penny press reshaped the definition of news as it sought to appeal to less politically aware readers with human interest stories and reports on sports, crime, public trials, and social activities.

"Objective Journalism"

By the early decades of the twentieth century, many journalists began to argue that the press should be independent of the political parties. *New York Tribune* editor Whitelaw Reid eloquently expressed this sentiment: "Independent journalism! That is the watchword of the future in the profession. An end of concealments because it would hurt the party; an end of one-sided expositions . . .; an end of assaults that are not believed fully just but must be made because the exigency of party warfare demands them."[41]

Journalists began to view their work as a profession and established professional associations with journals and codes of ethics. This professionalization of journalism reinforced the notion that journalists should be independent of partisan politics. Further strengthening the trend toward objectivity was the rise of the wire services, such as the Associated Press and Reuters, which deliberately remained politically neutral so as to attract more customers.

The Impact of Broadcasting

Radio and television nationalized and personalized the news. People could follow events as they were happening and not have to wait for the publication of a newspaper. From the 1920s, when radio networks were formed, radio carried political speeches, campaign advertising, and coverage of political events such as national party conventions.[42] Radio provided a means to bypass the screening of editors and reporters, since politicians could now speak directly to listeners. It also increased interest in national and international news because events outside a listener's local area could be followed as if one were actually there.

President Franklin Roosevelt used radio with remarkable effectiveness. Before 1933, most radio speeches were formal orations, but Roosevelt spoke to his audience on a personal level, seemingly in one-on-one conversations. These "fireside chats" established a standard still followed today. When Roosevelt began speaking over the microphone, he would visualize a tiny group of average citizens in front of him. Roosevelt "would smile and light up as though he were actually sitting on the front porch or in the parlor with them."[43]

Television added a dramatic visual dimension, which contributed to rising audience interest in national events and permitted viewers to witness lunar landings and the aftermath of political assassinations, as well as more mundane news events. By 1963, the two largest networks at the time, CBS and NBC, had expanded their evening news programs from 15 to 30 minutes. Today news broadcasting has expanded to the point that many local stations provide 90 minutes of local news every evening as well as a half-hour in the morning and at noon. Programs such as *20/20* and other newsmagazine shows are among the most popular in the prime-time evening hours.

Cable television brought round-the-clock news coverage. During the Clinton impeachment hearings and the 2000 Florida ballot-counting controversy, American cable news was watched at home and around the world for its instantaneous coverage. C-SPAN now provides uninterrupted coverage of congressional deliberations, the courts, and state and local governments.

Investigatory Journalism

Contemporary news reporters do more than convey the news; they investigate it, and their investigations often have political consequences. Notable examples of influential investigatory reporters include Seymour Hersh of *The New York Times,* who exposed what became known as the *Pentagon Papers,* revealing how the United States became involved in the Vietnam War; Robert Woodward and Carl Bernstein of *The Washington Post,* who

Franklin D. Roosevelt was the first president to recognize the effectiveness of radio to reach the public. His fireside chats were the model for later presidents.

played an important role in uncovering the Watergate conspiracy; Nina Totenberg of National Public Radio, whose reporting on sexual harassment charges against Clarence Thomas helped force the Senate Judiciary Committee to extend the hearings on his confirmation to the U.S. Supreme Court; and Michael Isikoff of *Newsweek,* who broke the story of Bill Clinton's alleged perjury involving sexual misconduct with Monica Lewinsky.

Media Conglomerates

If a few owners corner the market on newspapers and television stations, is the free flow of information to the public endangered? As in other sectors of the economy, media companies have merged and created large conglomerates. When television was in its infancy, radio networks and newspapers were among the first to purchase television stations. These mergers established cross-ownership patterns that persist today. The Gannett Corporation, for example, owns 101 daily newspapers and 22 television stations and cable television systems—assets that provide news coverage to nearly 18 percent of the United States.[44] The *Chicago Tribune* substantially expanded its reach of newspapers and television stations by purchasing Times-Mirror, publisher of the *Los Angeles Times* and ten other newspapers, 22 TV stations, four radio stations, and a growing online business.[45]

Australian-born Rupert Murdoch owns the Fox network, dozens of U.S. television stations, magazines, publishing organizations, and movie studios.

Local firms used to own the local newspapers, radio, and television stations. Today large conglomerates, some of them foreign, have acquired ownership of many newspapers and broadcasting stations. Rupert Murdoch, founder of the Fox network, owns 35 television stations in the United States, 20th Century-Fox, HarperCollins publishers, and *TV Guide,* which has the largest magazine circulation in America. Murdoch's News Corporation recently purchased DirecTV and has moved its corporate headquarters to the United States.[46] The Federal Communications Commission (FCC) and the courts are reinforcing the trend toward media conglomeration by relaxing and striking down regulations that limit cable and television network ownership by the same company.[47] Congress responded by passing resolutions opposing the more lax FCC ownership limitations, prompting a compromise between the Bush administration and Congress increasing the maximum population reachable by conglomerates but not as much as the FCC had proposed.[48] An appeals court has ruled against even these modified relaxations, however, calling them "arbitrary and capricious."[49]

When reporting national news, local outlets depend heavily on news that is gathered, edited, and distributed by national organizations like the Associated Press. As a result, some people contend that information these days is more diluted, homogenized, and moderated than it would be if the newspapers and broadcast stations were locally owned and the news was gathered and edited locally.[50]

Regulation of the Media

Regulation of the broadcast media has existed in some form since their inception. Because of the limited number of television and radio frequencies, the national government oversees matters like licensing, financing, and even content. Once regulation required "fairness" in news programming.[51] As written into law and interpreted by the FCC, the **fairness doctrine** imposed an obligation on radio and television license holders to ensure that differing viewpoints were presented regarding controversial issues or persons. With the advent of cable television and the Reagan administration's antiregulatory campaign, much of the fairness doctrine was repealed in 1987, and the final remnants of it were repealed in 2000. Will broadcasters provide fair and balanced news coverage in the absence of regulation? Proponents of deregulation who pushed for repeal think so.[52]

MEDIATED POLITICS

When dramatic events like the terrorist attacks on the World Trade Center and the Pentagon on September 11, 2001, occur, we realize the power television has in bringing world events into our lives. Osama bin Laden, the purported mastermind behind the

fairness doctrine
Federal Communications Commission policy that required holders of radio and television licenses to ensure that different viewpoints were presented about controversial issues or persons; largely repealed in 1987.

IN COMPARATIVE PERSPECTIVE

A LESS THAN FREE PRESS IN RUSSIA

An example of a country struggling to establish a free press is Russia. After the fall of Communism and its state-controlled media, Russia saw multiple print and broadcast media take root. Over time these outlets have declined in number and in the ability to communicate. NTV, an independent television channel, had been critical of President Vladimir Putin, Boris Yeltsin, and the Russian war in Chechnya. Russian government officials, claiming the station was corrupt,[*] took over the channel in 2001. The government appointed Boris Jordan to head NTV after the takeover, only to fire him two years later after the channel had provided extensive coverage of a theater takeover by independence-seeking Chechen terrorists, with the Russian government's aggressive response and resulting loss of life. The moves by Putin's government against NTV have had a chilling impact on stations that are critical of the Putin government.[†] By June 2003, TVS, the last independent national network, went under, but more for financial than political reasons.[†] Harassment of the media has not been limited to television. The weekly paper *Versiya*, which had reported the death toll to be higher than government reports at the Chechen theater incident and that the gas used to suppress the terrorists had been military and not civilian gas, found its offices ransacked and its computers and servers taken.[§]

Muzzling the media or putting them out of business helped Putin's United Russia Party to monopolize media coverage in the 2003 and 2004 elections, giving Putin's party even more seats in Parliament and reelecting Putin to the presidency. Putin justifies his policies regarding the media as efforts to not allow media moguls to become "king makers."[‖] The difficulties Russia has had in maintaining a free press illustrate the difficulty new democracies encounter as they develop.

[*] "Media Muzzle," *The Economist*, April, 21, 2001.
[†] Erin E. Arvedlund, "News Corp. Said to Seek Russia Satellite T.V.," *The New York Times*, November 10, 2003, p. C2.
[†] "Unplugged," *The Economist*, U.S. Edition, June 28, 2003.
[§] Christian Caryl and Eve Conant, "The Dead and the Silent," *Newsweek*, November 11, 2002, p. 39.
[‖] "Russia—Looking East," *Campaign*, September 27, 2002, p. 16.

attacks, understood the power of the media both inside and outside the United States, as evidenced by his release of videotapes of himself through the Al-Jazeera network in the Middle East in the weeks and months after the attacks.

The pervasiveness of newspapers, magazines, radio, and television places the individuals who determine what we read, hear, and see in a position of great influence because they can reach so much of the American public so quickly. With a large population scattered over a continent, both the reach and the speed of the modern media elevate the importance of the people in charge of them. The main source of campaign news in 2004 for more than two-thirds of Americans was television (68 percent), a proportion that has held relatively constant since 1992. Newspapers were mentioned as the most important source by 15 percent. All other media trailed these two.[53]

Political parties and interest groups have long been political mediators that help organize the world of politics for the average citizen. Their role is less important today because the media now serve that function and political parties have largely lost control over the nominating process (see Chapters 7 and 9). Greater attention is now given to judging candidates not so much in terms of party affiliation and platform but in terms of character and competence. The press, not the parties, performs this evaluative function.

The news media have also assumed the role of "speaking for the people." Journalists report what "the people" want and think, and then they tell the people what politicians and policy makers are doing about it. Politicians realize how dependent they are on the media for getting their message out to voters, and they are well aware that a hostile press can hurt them. That explains why today's politicians spend so much of their time developing good relations with the press.

The Media and Public Opinion

The ability of television to present images and communicate events has influenced American public opinion. Television footage of the violence done to blacks during the civil rights revolution of the 1950s and 1960s made the issue more real and immediate.

News coverage of the war in Vietnam galvanized the antiwar movement in the United States because of the horrible images news shows brought into people's homes. The testimony of White House staff before the Senate Watergate and later House Judiciary committees intensified the crisis of confidence in the Nixon administration. The repeated television coverage of the terrorist attacks on the World Trade Center and Pentagon left an indelible impression on all who saw them.

For a long time, analysts tended to play down the influence wielded by the media in American politics relative to the influence wielded by political leaders. The impact of Franklin D. Roosevelt's fireside chats came to symbolize the power of the politician over that of the news editor. Roosevelt spoke directly to his listeners over the radio in a way and at a time of his own choosing, and no network official was able to block or influence that direct connection. President John Kennedy's use of the televised press conference represented a similar direct contact with the public. President Ronald Reagan was nicknamed the "Great Communicator" because of his ability to talk persuasively and often passionately about public policy issues with the people through television.

GLOBAL *Perceptions*

QUESTION: Is the influence of news organizations very good, somewhat good, somewhat bad, or very bad in your country?

How do people in other countries perceive the role of news organizations and the media? The Pew Global Attitudes Project asked people in many countries the question that begins this box. Africa is the region with the most positive assessment of the news media. In contrast, the Middle East is the region most likely to believe that the news media has a "very bad" influence on their countries. The proportion saying news organizations and the media have a very bad influence on their country ranged from a low of 2 percent in Asia and 3 percent in Africa to 10 percent in the Middle East. More than one in four Middle Easterners saw the news media as a very bad influence or somewhat bad influence.

Source: Pew Research Center for the People and the Press, "2002 Global Attitudes Survey: Final Top-line Results," p. T-34.

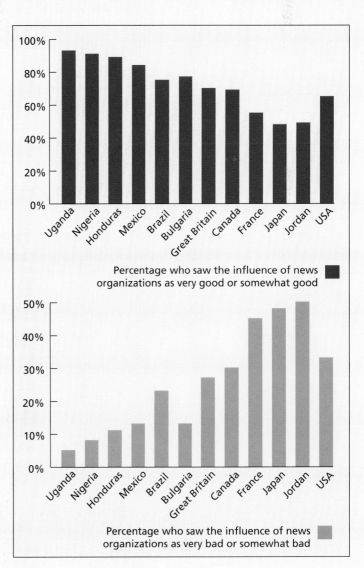

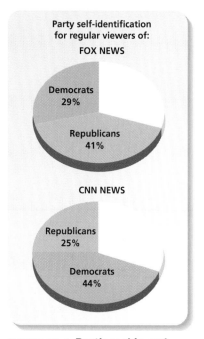

FIGURE 10–1 Partisanship and Preferred News Source.
Source: *The New York Times,* July 18, 2004.

However, broadcasters and journalists are now so important to the political process that elected officials and politicians spend considerable time trying to learn how to use them to their advantage. Presidential events and "photo opportunities" are planned with the evening news and its format in mind.[54] Members of Congress use Capitol Hill recording studios to tape messages for local television and radio stations. White House press briefings are frequently included in the evening news.

Factors That Limit Media Influence on Public Opinion

People are not just empty vessels into which politicians and journalists pour information and ideas. How people interpret political messages depends on a variety of factors: political socialization, selectivity, needs, and the individual's ability to recall and comprehend the message.

POLITICAL SOCIALIZATION   The media, particularly television, although not as important as family, play a role in socializing, influencing our values and attitudes.[55] The media shape public perceptions and knowledge. Television, with its concreteness and drama, has an emotional impact that print cannot hope to match.[56] Television cuts across age groups, educational levels, social classes, and races. Newspapers provide more detail about the news and often contain contrasting points of view, at least on the editorial pages, that help inform the public.

We develop our political attitudes, values, and beliefs through an education process that social scientists call **political socialization**.[57] (See Chapters 4 and 8 for more detail on this process.) Face-to-face contacts with friends and business associates (*peer pressure*) often have far more impact than the impersonal television or newspaper. Strong identification with a party also acts as a powerful filter.[58] A conservative Republican from Arizona might watch the "liberal eastern networks" and complain about their biased news coverage while sticking to her own opinions. A liberal from New York will often complain about right-wing talk radio, even if he listens to it some nights on the way home from work (see Figures 10–1 and 10–2).

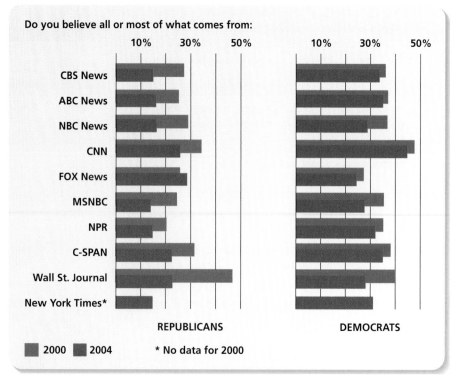

FIGURE 10–2 Partisanship and News Source Credibility.
Source: *The New York Times,* July 18, 2004.

political socialization
The process by which we develop our political attitudes, values, and beliefs.

SELECTIVITY   People practice **selective exposure**—screening out messages that do not conform to their own biases. They subscribe to newspapers or magazines that support their views. People also practice **selective perception**—perceiving what they want to in media messages.[59] One dramatic example was the differing reactions of Democrats and Republicans to reports of President Clinton's sexual misconduct with Monica Lewinsky, a former White House intern, and the possibility that he encouraged her to lie under oath. In the first weeks after the story broke, Republicans were four times more likely than Democrats to believe that Clinton had been sexually involved with Lewinsky.[60] More than two-thirds of Republicans and Democrats agreed that Clinton committed perjury before the grand jury, but they had dramatically different opinions on whether Clinton should remain in office. Nearly two-thirds of Republicans wanted Clinton out of office, while 63 percent of Independents and 87 percent of Democrats felt that Clinton should continue as president.[61]

NEEDS   People read newspapers, listen to the radio, or watch television for very different reasons, often out of habit or because they want information.[62] People who seek information and cultivate an interest in politics are affected by what they read and see differently from those who use media primarily for entertainment.[63] For those seeking entertainment, gossip about politicians' peccadilloes is more important than those politicians' opinions or voting patterns. Members of the broader audience are also more likely to pay attention to news that directly affects their lives, such as interest rate changes or the price of gasoline.[64]

RECALL AND COMPREHENSION   Still another limitation of media influence on public opinion is the extent to which the audience can recall the stories or comprehend their importance. Candidates and officials send out vast amounts of information designed to influence what people think and do, and especially how they vote, but people forget or fail to comprehend much of it.[65] The fragmentary and rapid mode of presentation of television news contributes to the problem. Most television news stories, for example, last less than 90 seconds.

Given the abundance of information available about politics and government, it is not surprising that most people pick and choose which media source—television, radio, newspapers, cable, the Web—they pay attention to and which news stories they consider important.[66] The best predictor of retention of news stories is political interest. People tend to fit today's news stories into their general assumptions or beliefs about government, politicians, or the media itself.

AUDIENCE FRAGMENTATION   With the growth of cable television and new media like the Web, the influence of any one media source is weakened. Because people are scattered across a larger number of press outlets and these outlets cover politics in varied ways, the impact of the press will be more disparate. People can now tailor their news to their preferred point of view. In a study of the 2004 election it was observed that "today's fractionalized media environment has taken the heaviest toll on local news, network news, and newspapers."[67] Fragmentation of the media audience tends to counteract the impact of media conglomeration. As media giants move to both cable and broadcast (NBC, CNBC, MSNBC, for example), the trends may converge.

Are the Media Biased?

Americans tend to blame the media for lots of things. Conservatives complain, "The media are too liberal." Radio talk show host Rush Limbaugh even once said, "They all just happen to believe the same way.... They are part of the same culture as Bill Clinton."[68] Extreme liberals contend that the ruling class controls the mainstream press, and they charge that government propaganda distorts the facts. Conservatives say the press is too liberal in its selection of news covered and the interpretation of events. Liberals point to newspaper endorsements of Republican presidential candidates to support their claim that newspapers are biased in favor of conservative policies and candidates.

"Hey, do you want to be on the news tonight or not? This is a sound bite, not the Gettysburg Address. Just say what you have to say, Senator, and get the hell off."

selective exposure
The process by which individuals screen out messages that do not conform to their own biases.

selective perception
The process by which individuals perceive what they want to in media messages.

Newspapers, magazines, and television stations are business corporations concerned about profits. They work to boost circulation and ratings and must please their advertisers, sponsors, and stockholders. Reporters and editors pride themselves on impartial reporting of the facts.[69] Yet some liberal critics contend that the media reflect a conservative bias not only in what they report but also in what they choose to ignore. Political scientist Michael Parenti states that journalists "rarely doubt their own objectivity even as they faithfully echo the established political vocabularies and the prevailing politico-economic orthodoxy."[70]

Newspapers and television management go to some lengths to insulate reporters from their advertising and business operations, in part to reduce criticism about favorable treatment of large advertisers or the corporate owners. When the management of the *Los Angeles Times* attempted to foster closer relations between the business and news divisions, it was criticized for insensitivity to this concern.[71] Another internal check on media bias is the fact that news coverage involves many reporters and a host of editors, all of whom have input into what is covered and how it is presented.

Some commentators have suggested that a possible bias flows from the fact that reporters and editors become too friendly with the people and organizations they write about. David Broder of *The Washington Post* voices his concern about the confusion of roles by journalists who have served in government. According to Broder, a line should divide objective journalism from partisan politics, but many members of the print and television media have crossed this line. Broder opposes the idea of journalists' becoming government officials and vice versa.[72] Others argue that journalists with previous government service have close working relationships with politicians and can give us a valuable perspective on government without losing their professional neutrality.

A frequent criticism is the media's alleged political bias, whether liberal or conservative (see Table 10–1). But to whom are these critics referring? To reporters, writers, editors, producers, or owners of TV stations and newspapers? Do they assume that a journalist's personal politics will be translated into biased reporting? And does the public think so? Journalists are usually more liberal than the population as a whole; editors tend to be a bit more conservative than their reporters are; and media owners are more conservative still. Elite journalists—those who work for national news media organizations—tend to share a similar culture: cosmopolitan, urban, upper-class. Their

TABLE 10–1 THE CHANGING FACE OF JOURNALISTS

	Journalists	Policy Makers	Public
Party Identification			
Democrat	27%	43%	34%
Republican	4	24	28
Independent	55	26	21
Other	5	5	12
Don't Know/Refused	9	2	2
Self-Described Ideology			
Liberal	25%	25%	21%
Moderate	59	52	37
Conservative	6	18	35
Don't Know/Refused	11	5	7

SOURCE: The Kaiser Foundation, *The Role of Polls in Policy Making*, Combined Topline Results, June 2001, p. 27. www.kff.org/kaiserpolls/loader.cfm?url=/commonspot/security/getfile.cfm&PageID=13842.

approach to the events and issues they cover is governed by their common worldview, which may be derived from their professional training.[73] The result, some critics contend, is that elite journalists give greater weight to the side of issues that corresponds to their own version of reality.[74]

One bias of the media that does not have a particular partisan or ideological slant is the bias toward sensationalism. Scandals of all types happen to liberals and conservatives, Republicans and Democrats. Once the province of tabloids like the *National Enquirer,* stories about scandal have recently become commonplace in the mainstream media. For years, the media have seemed to gravitate to stories involving celebrities, sex, or both. From the O. J. Simpson murder trial to the coverage of a missing intern who had been involved in an affair with a congressman, we have seen what some observers have called a media "feeding frenzy."[75] The intense and unrelenting focus on the scandal involving former President Bill Clinton and White House intern Monica Lewinsky is a clear example of the media's fondness for sensational coverage.

Newspapers and television news often set a tone of dissatisfaction with the performance of the national government and cynicism about politics and politicians. A critical tone may be an inevitable element of the mind-set of the press, but to whose benefit does that critical tone work? The media are accused of having an antireligion bias, a bias in favor of young viewers, and a bias fostering continuing crises.[76] The question is not whether the press is biased but whether a press bias—whatever the direction—seeps into the content of the news. The answer to that question is still not settled.

Public Opinion

Two important influences of print and broadcast media on public opinion are *agenda setting* and *issue framing*.

AGENDA SETTING[77] By calling public attention to certain issues, the media help determine what topics will become subjects of public debate and legislation.[78] However, the agenda-setting function of the media is not uniformly pervasive. The audience and the nature of the issue limit it.[79] According to former Vice President Walter Mondale, "If I had to give up . . . the opportunity to get on the evening news or the veto power, . . . I'd throw the veto power away. [Television news] is the President's most indispensable power."[80] Ronald Reagan, more than any president before him, effectively used the media to set the nation's agenda. Reagan and his advisers carefully crafted the images and scenes of his presidency to fit television. Thus television became an "electronic throne."

Communicating through the media works especially when it is natural and unscripted. When President Bush first visited the scene of the demolition of the World Trade Center in New York City, taking a bullhorn, he said, "I can hear you. The rest of the world hears you, and the people who knocked these buildings down will hear all of us soon."[81] This action projected leadership and empathy on the part of the president.

ISSUE FRAMING Politicians, like everybody else, try to frame issues to win arguments, and they try to influence the "spin" the media will give to their actions or issues. Examples abound. Opponents of U.S. intervention in Bosnia tried to portray such action as another Vietnam. Objectors to permanent normal trade relations with China framed the granting of that status as a human rights travesty. When Bill Clinton wanted to forestall a Republican tax cut, he decried the resulting need to dip into the budget surplus to "rescue Social Security." People who favor abortion define the issue as one of freedom of choice; those who oppose it define it as murder. In referendum campaigns, the side that wins the battle of interpreting what the referendum is about wins the election.[82]

In the 2004 election, voters indicated that the Iraq war and terrorism, the economy and jobs, and moral values were the most important issues. All of these issues had received a lot of attention in the media except "moral values," which prompted intense discussion after the election about what people meant by this response. The fact that gay marriage was on the ballot in eleven states and frequently mentioned in the campaign may help explain why moral values was mentioned by one in five voters.

FREE AIR TIME FOR CANDIDATES AND PARTIES?

Should television stations give free air time to candidates and parties during the election season?

An essential part of running for elective office today is purchasing television advertising. In the 2002 elections alone, candidates and political parties spent an estimated one billion dollars communicating with voters through radio and television advertising. Since broadcast stations have access to public airwaves at no fee, some have proposed that they be required to provide free air time to candidates and parties. What do you think? Should television stations be required to give free air time to candidates and parties?

THE MEDIA AND ELECTIONS

News coverage of campaigns and elections is greatest in presidential contests, less in statewide races for governor and U.S. senator, and least for other state and local races. Generally, the more news attention given the campaign, the less likely voters are to be swayed by any one source. Hence news coverage is likely to be more influential in a city council contest than in an election for president or the Senate. For most city elections, there are only one or two sources of information about what candidates say and stand for; for statewide and national contests, there are multiple sources.

Diversification of the news media lessens the ability of any one medium to influence the outcome of elections. Newspaper publishers who were once seen as key figures in state and local politics are now less important because politicians and their media advisers are no longer so dependent on newspapers and other news media to communicate their messages. Candidates can use ads on radio and television, direct mail, phone, the Web, and cable television to communicate with voters. In local contests, or even some larger settings like the Iowa caucuses or the New Hampshire primary, personal contact can also be very important.[83]

Choice of Candidates

The extensive use of television has made looking and sounding good on television much more important. It has also fostered growth in the political consulting industry and made visibility the watchword in politics. Television greatly affects the public's idea of what traits are important in a candidate. A century ago, successful candidates needed a strong pair of lungs; today it is a telegenic appearance, a pleasing voice, and no obvious physical impairments. Back in the 1930s, the press chose not to show Franklin Roosevelt in his wheelchair or using braces, whereas today the country knows every intimate detail of the president's health. The importance of the public's perception of these traits is evident in the ridicule often directed at candidates. In 2004, Kerry was described as "French-looking"[84] and flip-flopping on issues, and Bush as stubborn and frequently smirking as Kerry spoke in the televised debates.

Although the media insist that they pay attention to all candidates who have a chance to win, they also influence who gets such a chance. Consequently, candidates have to come up with creative ways to attract media attention. The late Paul Wellstone, in his 1996 Minnesota Senate campaign, said in his advertisements that he did not have much money to pay for ads, so he would have to talk fast to cram what he had to say into fewer commercials. His witty commercial became a news event itself—it got Wellstone additional coverage.

In another bid for media attention, some candidates in states bordering Canada have organized bus trips to Canada for people to purchase prescription drugs at Canadian prices, which were sharply lower than in the United States. Candidates in both parties have recently made hunting a pastime, in part to reassure voters that they support the Second Amendment. In 2004, John Kerry went duck hunting in camouflage attire one day during the final week of the campaign. House and Sentate candidates have also included in recent campaign literature photos of them shooting rifles.

Campaign Events

Candidates schedule events—press conferences, interviews, and "photo ops"—in settings that reinforce their verbal messages and public image. A much publicized example of such a staged event was President Bush landing on the aircraft carrier USS Lincoln to announce the end of "major combat operations" in Iraq. While the event provided a dramatic backdrop for the president in his flight jacket, a debate ensued about the cost of the carrier remaining at sea an extra day,[85] and, more fundamentally, as the resistance

"I'm still undecided—I like Leno's foreign policy, but Letterman makes a lot of sense on domestic issues."

to American forces in Iraq continued and intensified, Bush's declaration on the Lincoln seemed more and more premature. Many events organized by campaigns fail to receive attention from reporters because of competing news stories and a sense that the events were staged primarily to generate news coverage.

The parties' national conventions used to capture national attention. However, since candidates are now selected in party primaries, the conventions no longer provide much suspense or make news except perhaps over who will be the vice presidential nominee. This is one reason why the networks have dramatically cut back their coverage of presidential nominating conventions. In 1952, the average television set was tuned to the political conventions for 26 hours, or an average of more than three hours a night for the eight nights of convention coverage.[86] During the 2000 presidential conventions, by contrast, the major networks provided only one or two hours of prime-time coverage each evening. Political parties have sought, in vain, to regain audience interest by relying on "movie stars, entertainment routines, and professionally produced documentaries to spice up their conventions."[87]

Technology

Although the expense associated with television has contributed to the skyrocketing costs of campaigning, it has also made politics more accessible to more people. Thanks to satellites, candidates can conduct local television interviews without actually traveling to local studios. Specific voter groups can be targeted through cable television or low-power television stations that reach homogeneous neighborhoods and small towns. Videocassettes with messages from the candidates further extend the campaign's reach.[88] All serious candidates for Congress and governor in 2000 and 2002 made themselves and their positions available through a home page on the World Wide Web.

The Internet and e-mail have primarily been used to reinforce voter preferences or help answer questions more than to reach and persuade more passive citizens. But with the Web, citizens now have the opportunity to interact with each other on a wide range of political topics. In this sense, the Web is something like a town meeting, but without people leaving their homes or offices. In chat rooms on the Internet people express ideas and respond to each other's opinions. Examples of chat rooms include Abortion Chat, Democrat Chat, Environment Chat, Republican Chat, and Congress Chat. Most chat rooms offer group discussions in which anyone in the group can read and send messages, but some chat rooms also permit private messages to be sent. As discussed earlier, the Internet has also become a way for candidates and groups to raise funds.

Younger voters are much more likely to use the Internet to get campaign news than middle aged and older voters. In a study of the 2004 election, nearly three times as many 18- to 29-year-olds said they used the Internet for news (20 percent), compared with only 7 percent of those over age 50. Persons between 30 and 49 years of age were in between, with 16 percent citing the Internet as a source of campaign news. Younger voters also reported a much greater reliance on comedy TV shows as a source of campaign news.[89]

Image Making and Media Consultants

Candidates recognize that their messages about issues are often ignored. The press tends to emphasize goofs and gossip or tension among party leaders. Candidates in turn try to spin the news. Attempts to shape the news and to portray candidates in the best possible light are not new. Presidential campaign sloganeering such as "Tippecanoe and Tyler Too" in 1840, "Abe the Rail Splitter" in 1860, and "I Like Ike" in 1952 conveyed the candidate's image. Radio, television, and the Web have expanded the ability to project

★★ THINKING IT THROUGH

Proponents of free air time cite the fact that broadcast stations use public airwaves and that stations therefore have an obligation to provide free air time to candidates as a public service. Broadcasters, they argue, generate over $60 billion a year in advertising revenue.* Proponents of free air time also refer to studies that show how television stations charge candidates and politicians inflated rates to run advertisements in the days before an election. Finally, proponents point to the fact that television stations provide little news of federal elections, making advertising and free air time even more important.

Opponents of free air time argue that the media are already required to charge candidates the lowest rate for that time segment (i.e., prime time between 7 and 10 P.M.). They say the current system provides both sides equal access and forces the candidates and parties to have real support from voters and financial contributors. They argue that the media covers campaigns in sufficient depth and that requiring stations to provide free time will mean they lose viewers or listeners because people will switch stations because they are turned off to politics. Finally, they point out that broadcasters are being unfairly singled out from other means of communicating with voters. Businesses that produce mail, make phone calls, or even cable television would not be forced to provide access to resources for free.

* www.bettercampaign.org/freeairtime/factsheets/sweetheartdeal.pdf.

A candidate's image often takes precedence over that candidate's message in the mass media. This was as true in the mid-nineteenth century as it is today. This is why image makers and media consultants have been in such high demand for so long. On the top, we see a portrait of Abraham Lincoln as "Abe the Rail Splitter." On the bottom, we see George W. Bush riding a mountain bike.

horse race
A close contest; by extension, any contest in which the focus is on who is ahead and by how much rather than on substantive differences between the candidates.

images, and that expansion has in turn affected candidates' vote-getting strategies and their manner of communicating messages. Television is especially important because of the power of the visual image.

Television has contributed to the rise of new players in campaign politics: *media consultants,* campaign professionals who provide candidates with advice and services on media relations, advertising strategy, and opinion polling.[90] For example, candidates regularly receive consultants' advice on what colors work best for them, especially on television. Male U.S. Senators often appear in light blue shirts with red ties, sometimes called "power ties." A primary responsibility of a campaign media consultant is to present a positive image of the candidate and to reinforce negative images of the opponent.

Some media consultants have been credited with propelling candidates to success. Dick Morris was seen as important to Clinton's resurgence after the 1994 congressional election defeats, until he had to resign from the campaign following a personal scandal. Republican consultant Mark McKinnon produced ads for President Bush's 2000 and 2004 campaigns, and John Kerry's media was done by Bob Shrum and Jim Margolis. Both parties have scores of media consultants who have handled congressional and gubernatorial campaigns as well as campaigns over ballot questions. While sometimes credited with helping elect or defeat candidates and referendums, they have also been blamed for the negativity of recent campaigns.

Media consultants have taken over the role formerly played by party politicians. Before World War II, party professionals groomed candidates for office at all levels. Such leaders made judgments about possible candidates on the basis of their chances of victory and observation of the candidates' performance under fire, decisiveness, conviction, political skill, and other leadership qualities. Party professionals advised candidates which party and interest group leaders to placate, which issues to stress, and which topics to avoid.

Today consultants coach candidates about television technique, appearance, and subject matter. Consultants report the results of *focus groups* (small sample groups of people who are asked questions about candidates and issues in a discussion setting) and *public opinion polls,* which in turn determine what the candidate says and does. Some critics allege that political consultants have become a new "political elite" who can virtually choose candidates by determining in advance which men and women have the right images or at least images that can be restyled for the widest popularity.[91] But political consultants who specialize in media advertising and image making realize their own limitations in packaging candidates. As one media consultant put it, "It is a very hard job to turn a turkey into a movie star; you try instead to make people like the turkey."[92]

The Media and Voter Choice

As television has become increasingly important to politics, and as the political parties have been weakened with such reforms as primary elections, news coverage of candidates has taken on added significance. Although some critics think reporters pay too much attention to candidates' personality and background, others say character and personality are among the most important characteristics for readers and viewers to know about. What is not in dispute is the central role the news media play in our democratic process.

THE HORSE RACE　A common tendency in the media is to comment on a candidate's position in the polls compared with other candidates—what is sometimes called the **horse race**—than they are about policy issues.[93] "Many stories focus on who is ahead, who is behind, who is going to win, and who is going to lose, rather than examining how and why the race is as it is."[94] Reporters focus on the tactics and strategy of campaigns because they perceive that the public is interested and influenced by such coverage.[95]

The media's propensity to focus on the "game" of campaigns displaces coverage of issues.

NEGATIVE ADVERTISING Political advertising has always contained negative remarks about opponents, but recent campaigns have taken on an increasingly negative tone. A rule of thumb in the old politics was to ignore the charges of the opposition and thus to accord one's rival no importance or standing. That practice has changed as today's candidates trade charges and countercharges.

Voters say they are turned off by the attack style of politics, but the widespread perception among campaign consultants is that negative campaigning works. This seeming inconsistency may be explained by evidence suggesting that campaigns that foster negative impressions of the candidates contribute to lower turnout.[96] Negative advertising may thus discourage some voters who would be inclined to support a candidate (a phenomenon known as *vote suppression*) while reinforcing the inclination of committed supporters to come out to vote.

INFORMATION ABOUT ISSUES In recent elections, the media have experimented with a more issues-centered focus, what has been called *civic journalism*. With funding from charitable foundations, some newspapers have been identifying the concerns of community leaders and talking to ordinary voters and then writing campaign stories from their point of view.[97] Some newspaper editors and reporters disagree with this approach; they believe the media should stick to responding to newsworthy events. Advocates of civic journalism counter that important concerns of the community are often overshadowed by news events like murders and violence.

MAKING A DECISION Newspapers and television seem to have more influence in determining the outcome of primaries than of general elections,[98] probably because voters are less likely to know about the candidates and have fewer clues about how they stand in a primary. By the time of the November general election, however, party affiliation, incumbency, and other factors moderate the impact of media messages. The mass media are more likely to influence undecided voters who, in a close election, can determine who wins and who loses.

ELECTION NIGHT REPORTING Does TV coverage on election night affect the outcome of elections? Election returns from the East come in three hours before the polls close on the West Coast. Because major networks often project the presidential winner well ahead of poll closings in western states, some western voters have been discouraged from voting. As a result, voter turnout in congressional and local elections has been affected. In a close presidential election, however, such early reporting may well stimulate turnout because voters know their vote could determine the outcome. In short, it is only in elections in which one candidate appears to be winning by a large margin that television reporting makes voters believe their vote is meaningless.[99]

At 7:50 P.M. (EST) on election night, November 7, 2000, television networks projected Al Gore as the winner of Florida, but they soon had second thoughts and revoked their announcement. Hours later Fox News projected Bush as winning Florida. The truth was that the vote in Florida was by every measure too close to call, and no network should have called the race. In the days and weeks after the election, the Voter News Service admitted that its Florida sample was flawed, that it underestimated the Florida absentee vote, and that it relied on incomplete actual vote totals. The mistaken projections by the networks were embarrassing. Tom Brokaw of NBC said, "That's not 'an egg' on our faces; that's 'an omelet.' "[100]

In 2002, the media exit polls failed again. On election day, the networks that sponsor the Voter News Service (VNS), which conducts the media exit polling, announced that they would not be releasing exit poll numbers nor would they be projecting winners. Following the 2000 election and the controversy over the Florida exit polling,

VNS invested in new computers and software and developed new models to project winners. They gathered data on election day but did not have confidence in their ability to accurately predict contests. Viewers on election night 2002 thus got what many had wanted, a night with only local exit polling. The absence of exit polling data, however, meant it was hard to assess the national mood and which types of people actually voted.

THE MEDIA AND GOVERNANCE

The press rarely follows the policy process to its conclusion. Rather, it leaves the issue at the doorstep of public officials. By the time a political issue reaches the stages of policy formulation and implementation, the press has moved on to another issue. When policies are being formulated and implemented, decision makers are at their most impressionable, yet the press has little impact at this stage.[101]

Lack of press attention to policy implementation explains in part why we know less about how bureaucrats go about their business than we do about heated legislative debates or presidential scandals. Only in the case of a policy scandal, such as the lax security surrounding nuclear secrets at Los Alamos, does the press take notice. "Most executives would be satisfied with a press strategy of no surprises. All their press officers need do to be doing their job is provide a rudimentary early warning system [for crises] and issue routine announcements."[102]

Some media critics contend that the media's pressuring policy makers to provide immediate answers forces them to make untimely decisions. Foreign policy may be in particular danger from such quick responses:

> If an ominous foreign event is featured on TV news, the president and his advisers feel bound to make a response in time for the next evening news broadcast. . . . If he does not have a response ready by the late afternoon deadline, the evening news may report that the president's advisers are divided, that the president cannot make up his mind, or that while the president hesitates, his political opponents know exactly what to do.[103]

Political Institutions and the News Media

Presidents have become the stars of the media, particularly television, and have made the media their forum for setting the public agenda and achieving their legislative aims. Presidential news conferences command attention (see Table 10–2). Every public activity, both professional and personal, is potentially newsworthy; a presidential illness can become front-page news, as can presidential vacations and family pets.

A president attempts to manipulate news coverage to his benefit. Speeches are used to set the national agenda or spur congressional action. Travel to foreign countries usually boosts popular support at home, thanks to the largely favorable news coverage. Better yet for the president, most coverage of the president—either at home or abroad—is favorable to neutral.[104] President Clinton's trip to Israel during the height of the furor surrounding his impeachment may have helped distract attention from his domestic problems in both senses of that word.

Congress is a fragmented body usually unable to act quickly. It is also more likely to get negative coverage than either the White House or the Supreme Court. Unlike the executive branch, it lacks an ultimate spokesperson, a single individual who can speak for the whole institution.[105] Congress does not make it easy for the press to cover it. Whereas the White House engages in attentive care and feeding of the press corps, Congress does not arrange its schedule to accommodate the media; floor debates, for example, often compete with committee hearings and press conferences.[106] Singularly dramatic actions rarely occur in Congress; the press therefore turns to the president to describe federal government activity on a day-to-day basis and treats Congress largely as a foil to the president. Most coverage of Congress is of its reaction to the initiatives of the president.[107]

The federal judiciary is least dependent on the press. The Supreme Court does not rely on public communication for political support. Rather, it relies indirectly on public opinion for continued deference to or compliance with its decisions.[108] The Court does not allow television cameras to cover oral arguments, rarely allows audiotaping, and has no reporters present when it votes. The Court has strong incentives to avoid the perception of manipulating the press, so it retains an image of aloofness from politics and public opinion. The justices' manipulation of press coverage is far more subtle and complex than that of the other two institutions.[109] For example, the complexity of the Supreme Court's decision in 2000's Florida vote recount case, with multiple dissents and concurrences and no press release or executive summary, made broadcast reporting on the decision difficult.

The news media's most influential role may be at the local level.[110] Most of us have multiple sources for finding out what is happening in Washington that act as a check on the biases and limitations of reporters who cover national government and policy. But when it comes to finding out about the city council, the school board, or the local water district, most of us are dependent on the work of a single reporter. Consequently, the media's influence is much greater when there are fewer news sources.

Not all who think the media are powerful agree that their power is harmful. After all, they argue, the media perform a vital educational function. Almost 70 percent of the public thinks the press is a watchdog that keeps government leaders from doing bad things.[111] At the very least, the media have the power to mold the agenda of the day; at most, in the words of the late Theodore White, they have the power to "determine what people will talk and think about—an authority that in other nations is reserved for tyrants, priests, parties, and mandarins."[112]

TABLE 10–2 PRESIDENTIAL PRESS CONFERENCES: JOINT AND SOLO SESSIONS, 1913–2004

President	Total	Solo	Joint	Joint as Percentage of Total	Months in Office	Solo Sessions per Month	Solo Sessions per Year
Wilson	157	157	0	0	96	1.6	19.6
Harding	No Transcripts Available				29		
Coolidge	521	521	0	0	67	7.8	93.4
Hoover	268	267	1	0.4	48	5.6	66.8
Roosevelt	1020	984	33	3.2	145.5	6.8	81.1
Truman	324	311	13	4.0	94.5	3.3	39.5
Eisenhower	193	192	1	0.5	96	2.0	24.0
Kennedy	65	65	0	0	34	1.9	23.0
Johnson	135	118	16	11.9	62	1.9	22.8
Nixon	39	39	0	0	66	0.6	7.1
Ford	40	39	1	2.5	30	1.3	15.6
Carter	59	59	0	0	48	1.2	14.8
Reagan	46	46	0	0	96	0.5	5.8
G. H. W. Bush	143	84	59	41.3	48	1.8	21.0
Clinton	193	62	131	67.9	96	0.7	7.8
G. W. Bush	85	16	69	81.2	46	0.4	4.2

Note: A joint press conference is one where the president answers questions along with someone else, most often a foreign leader. In a solo session, only the president answers questions. There are three missing transcripts for Roosevelt and one for Johnson, which makes it impossible to determine whether those sessions were solo or joint ones.

Source: Chart from Martha Joynt Kumar, "Presidential Press Conferences: The Evolution of an Enduring Forum," *Presidential Studies Quarterly*, vol. 35, no. 1, March 2005.

S UMMARY

1. The news media include newspapers, magazines, radio, television, films, recordings, books, and electronic communications, in all their forms. These means of communication have been called the "fourth branch of government."

2. The news media are a pervasive feature of American politics and generally help define our culture. The rise of new communications technologies has made the media more influential throughout American society. The news media serve as a link between politicians and government officials and the public.

3. Our modern news media emerged from a more partisan and less professional past. Autonomy of the media from political parties is one of the important changes. Now journalists strive for objectivity and see themselves as important to the political process. They also engage in investigative journalism.

4. Broadcasting on radio and television has changed the news media, and most Americans use television and radio as primary news sources. The role of corporate ownership of media outlets, especially media conglomerates, raises questions about media competition and orientation.

5. The influence of the mass media over public opinion is significant but not overwhelming. People may not pay much attention to the media or may not believe everything they read or see or hear. They may be critical or suspicious of the media and hence resistant to it. People tend to filter the news through their political socialization, selectivity, needs, and ability to recall or comprehend the content of the news.

6. The media are criticized as biased both by conservatives (who charge that the media are too liberal) and by liberals (who claim that the media are captives of corporate interests and major advertisers). Little evidence exists of actual, deliberate bias in news reporting.

7. A major effect of mass media news is agenda setting—determining what problems will become salient issues for people to form opinions about and to discuss. The media are also influential in defining issues for the general public.

8. Presidential campaigns are dominated by media coverage both before and after the national convention. One effect of media influence is that most people seem more interested in the contest as a game or "horse race" than as an occasion for serious discussion of issues and candidates. Another effect has been the rise of image making and the media consultant.

9. The press serves as both observer and participant in politics, as a watchdog, agenda setter, and check on the abuse of power, but it rarely follows the policy process to its conclusion.

K EY T ERMS

mass media	**issue advocacy**	**political socialization**	**selective perception**
news media	**fairness doctrine**	**selective exposure**	**horse race**

F URTHER R EADING

STEPHEN ANSOLABEHERE AND SHANTO IYENGAR, *Going Negative: How Attack Ads Shrink and Polarize the Electorate* (Free Press, 1996).

BRUCE BIMBER AND RICHARD DAVIS, *Campaigning Online: The Internet in U.S. Elections* (Oxford University Press, 2003).

SIMONE CHAMBERS AND ANNE COSTAIN, EDS., *Deliberation, Democracy, and the Media* (Rowman & Littlefield, 2000).

TIMOTHY E. COOK, *Making Laws and Making News: Press Strategies in the U.S. House of Representatives* (Brookings Institution Press, 1990).

TIMOTHY E. COOK, *Governing with the News: The News Media as a Political Institution* (University of Chicago Press, 1998).

RICHARD DAVIS, *The American Press and American Politics: The New Mediator* (Prentice Hall, 2001).

ROBERT M. ENTMAN AND W. LANCE BENNETT, EDS., *Mediated Politics: Communication in the Future of Democracy* (Cambridge University Press, 2000).

JAMES FALLOWS, *Breaking the News: How the Media Undermine American Democracy* (Pantheon Books, 1996).

STEPHEN J. FARNSWORTH AND S. ROBERT LICHTER, *The Nightly News Nightmare: Network Television's Coverage of U.S. Presidential Elections, 1988–2000* (Rowman & Littlefield, 2003).

DORIS A. GRABER, *Mass Media and American Politics*, 6th ed. (CQ Press, 2002).

RODERICK P. HART, *Campaign Talk: Why Elections Are Good for Us* (Princeton University Press, 2000).

KATHLEEN H. JAMISON, *The Press Effect: Politicians, Journalists, and the Stories That Shape the Political World* (Oxford University Press, 2003).

PHYLISS KANISS, *Making Local News* (University of Chicago Press, 1991).

HOWARD KURTZ, *Spin Cycle: Inside the Clinton Propaganda Machine* (Free Press, 1998).

S. ROBERT LICHTER, STANLEY ROTHMAN, AND LINDA S. LICHTER, *The Media Elite* (Adler & Adler, 1986).

PIPPA NORRIS, *A Virtuous Circle: Political Communications in Post-Industrial Societies* (Cambridge University Press, 2000).

TOM ROSENSTEIL, *Strange Bedfellows: How Television and the Presidential Candidates Changed American Politics, 1992* (Hyperion, 1993).

MARK J. ROZELL, ED., *Media Power, Media Politics* (Rowman & Littefield, 2003).

JAMES A. THURBER, CANDICE J. NELSON, AND DAVID A. DULIO, EDS., *Crowded Airwaves: Campaign Advertising in Elections* (Brookings Institution Press, 2000).

DARRELL M. WEST, *Air Wars: Television Advertising in Election Campaigns, 1952–1992* (CQ Press, 1993).

CONGRESS
THE PEOPLE'S BRANCH

11

The United
States Congress is one of the world's greatest democratic institutions. Members fight hard on behalf of their states and districts, are free to introduce any legislation they wish, even if there is no chance of passage, have seemingly endless opportunities to voice their opinions on the issues of the day, and provide a constant stream of information back home.

This openness also makes Congress one of the world's most frustrating institutions. Senators are free to talk as long as they can stand; committee chairs can delay legislation for months and years; very few proposals ever receive a hearing, let alone a final vote, and the competition among members for media attention can make Congress look more like a three-ring circus than a deliberative body.

The tension between representation and action has existed from the very first Congress in 1789. Because Congress is divided into two houses, each with its own calendar, rules, and electoral base, action requires broad agreements both within anad across the institution as a whole. As a result, members of Congress often agree to disagree about major legislation, even when the public wants action.

Frustration has a purpose in the constitutional system. It forces majorities to make their case to the entire nation, not just to their passionate supporters, and gives opponents an opportunity to fight legislation they believe is wrong.

There is growing evidence, however, that Congress has become less able to reach consensus over the past half century as moderate Democrats and Republicans have been steadily replaced with more ideological members of their parties.[1] The trend is likely to continue in the future. In 2004, for example, five moderate Southern Democrats retired—

John Breaux of Louisana, John Edwards of North Carolina, Bob Graham of Florida, Ernest Hollings of South Carolina, and Zell Miller of Georgia. All five were replaced by much more conservative Republicans. The victories left just four of the south's 26 seats still in Democratic hands, two of which are at the fringe of the south in Arkansas. In 1970, Republicans held just seven of the 26.

The loss of moderate Democrats and Republicans increases the odds that Congress will be less able to act. Moderates are often key to finding compromises across the party lines, and frequently soften the intense arguments that arise between more ideological members of Congress. Thus, Breaux often joined with other moderates in both parties to find compromises on issues such as the Bush Administration's 2001 tax cut and the more recent legislation giving presciption drug coverage to senior citizens in 2003, while Miller and Hollings often provided needed votes for compromise on issues such as education reform and homeland security.

Congress can still pass legislation with sharp divisions between the two parties, as it did with the prescription drug bill in 2003. But the votes on such legislation are often close, and can involve intense conflict. The prescription bill only passed on a razor-thin 220 to 215 vote in the House and a 55 to 44 margin in the Senate.

In this chapter, we examine how Congress organizes itself to make laws and represent the people. We also look at how the framers designed the institution to work. We will ask how Congress can remain open and accessible, yet still make the deals needed to pass important legislation in the national interest. Before turning to these questions, however, it is first important to ask how members of Congress are elected to office and to consider the ways in which congressional elections often act to insulate individual members from their own constituents.

CONGRESSIONAL ELECTIONS

There is only one Congress described in the Constitution, but there are two very different electoral calendars for entering office. Each of the 435 members of the House of Representatives is elected to a two-year term in even-numbered years, while only a third of the Senate's 100 members are chosen for six-year terms every two years. The number of House members was finally capped at 435 when Congress ordered states to stop drawing new districts in 1910.

There are also somewhat different requirements for becoming members of the House and Senate. At minimum, members of the House must be 25 years old and have been citizens for seven years, whereas senators must be 30 years old and have been citizens for nine years. House and Senate candidates must be residents of the states from which they are elected.

By setting the Senate's requirements higher and giving its members a six-year term, the framers hoped the Senate would act as a check against what they saw as the less predictable House. Concerned about the "fickleness and passion" of the House of Representatives, James Madison in particular saw the Senate as "a necessary fence against this danger."[2]

The framers did not limit the number of terms a House member or senator could serve. The term limits imposed by the Articles of Confederation had forced several talented members out of office, leaving the Continental Congress less effective and souring the framers on the idea.[3]

Regardless of differences between the two houses of Congress, representatives and senators are all politicians who enter office by winning an election. Ironically, it is often good politics for them to deny that they are politicians and to lead the charge against the institution in which they serve. The willingness of "House members to stand and defend their own votes or voting record contrasts sharply with their disposition to run and hide when a defense of Congress might be called for," writes political scientist Richard F. Fenno Jr. "Members of Congress run *for* Congress by running *against* Congress. The strategy is ubiquitous, addictive, cost-free, and foolproof. . . . In the short run, everybody plays and nearly everybody wins. Yet the institution bleeds from 435 separate cuts."[4]

Who Elects the Congress?

Members of the House and Senate represent different populations. According to the Constitution, every state has two U.S. senators, each of whom represents the entire state.

Seats in the House of Representatives are distributed or apportioned among the states according to population. There are 435 House districts, each composed of about 650,000 people. No matter how small its population, every state is guaranteed at least one House member.

The exact apportionment among the states is determined by a national census of the population that is required by the Constitution every ten years. As a result of the 2000 census, Congress had to reallocate seats based on population shifts through a process called **reapportionment**. New York and Pennsylvania lost two House seats; Ohio, Indiana, Illinois, Wisconsin, and Michigan all lost one seat. Florida, Georgia, Texas, and Arizona gained two seats; Colorado, Nevada, North Carolina, and California gained one seat each.

While census figures dictate how House districts are apportioned across the nation, each state determines where those districts lie within its own boundaries. State legislatures nearly always control this **redistricting** process, subject to final approval by the governor or redistricting commissions in states such as Arizona and Iowa. By tradition, redistricting occurs in the state legislative session following the census.

When a single party controls both the legislative and executive branches in a state, it often draws the new map to increase the number of House districts that its own candidates are likely to win. In extreme cases, this process is known as **gerrymandering**, after Governor Elbridge Gerry who approved a Massachusetts redistricting plan that created a salamander-shaped district drawn for distinctly partisan purposes following the 1810 census.

Gerrymandering has become more sophisticated with the computer age. Both parties have developed redistricting software that allows majorities to "pack" and "crack" legislative districts to help their party. Packing is designed to concentrate a minority party's voters in the smallest number of districts possible, thereby weakening their influence in other races, while cracking is designed to disperse a party's voters into as many districts as possible, also weakening their influence.

As noted, redistricting has generally occurred in the state legislative session following the census. With a divided legislature in charge in 2001, Texas left the state congressional map mostly unchanged, yielding a 17 to 15 Democratic edge. But with a Republican legislature and a Republican governor in charge in 2003, Texas decided to redistrict the state again, hoping for a 22 to 10 Republican edge. When all the votes were counted, Republicans had defeated four sitting Democrats, producing a 21 to 11 Republican edge. In two districts, the 19th and the 32nd, Democratic incumbents lost their reelection bids to Republican incumbents who had been placed in the same district.

State legislatures may also draw districts in which a majority of voters are members of minority groups. Such racial gerrymandering is legal unless the legislature considered race and ignored traditional redistricting concerns, such as keeping communities together and reelecting incumbents.[5] Furthermore, a party attacking a majority-minority district must show that the legislature could have achieved the same political result with a significantly different racial balance. A challenge to a North Carolina congressional district failed because Republicans could not show that the district could include more white voters and still be drawn as favorably to Democratic interests.[6]

The principle of equal representation does not apply to the Senate. Because each state has two senators regardless of population, the Senate represents constituencies that are more rural, white, and conservative than would be the case if the one-person, one-vote norm applied to Senate elections.

The word "gerrymander" comes from the name of the governor of Massachusetts, Elbridge Gerry, and the salamander-shaped district that was created to favor his party in 1811.

reapportionment
The assigning by Congress of congressional seats after each census. State legislatures reapportion state legislative districts.

redistricting
The redrawing of congressional and other legislative district lines following the census, to accommodate population shifts and keep districts as equal as possible in population.

gerrymandering
The drawing of legislative district boundaries to benefit a party, group, or incumbent.

Betty Castor, the Democratic candidate for U.S. Senate in Florida, greets supporters on a campaign stop. State campaigns such as this are important as both parties struggle to gain control of the Senate. Castor lost her bid by less than 100,000 votes out of just over 7 million cast.

safe seat
An elected office that is predictably won by one party or the other, so the success of that party's candidate is almost taken for granted.

incumbents
The current holders of elected office.

Such disparities make the Senate the most malapportioned elected legislature in the democratic world, giving the advantage to residents of the smaller states. Frances Lee and Bruce Oppenheimer concluded that the size of a state's population affects senator-constituent relationships, fund raising and elections, strategic behavior within the Senate, and ultimately policy decisions.[7] The late Senator Daniel Patrick Moynihan (D.-N.Y.), who knew firsthand how citizens of larger states fared less well in U.S. Senate policy battles, predicted that "some time in the next century the United States is going to have to address the question of apportionment in the Senate,"[8] but the prospects for changing the two-senators-per-state constitutional rule are highly unlikely in the near future.

Predicting Congressional Elections

The outcome of any congressional election depends on many factors, including campaign financing, local and national policy issues, and each candidate's skills. But all congressional elections start with the nature of the seat at stake. Some House campaigns involve a **safe seat**—one that is predictably won by one party or the other. Others involve a competitive seat that draws strong candidates from both major parties, while still others involve an open seat that has been vacated by a sitting member who retires or runs for higher office.

Because only a third of Senate seats are up for election every two years, Senate elections tend to be highly competitive and better financed than House elections. They also tend to turn on national, not local, issues, particularly in states with substantial media coverage. Although contests in large states often involve the largest amounts of money, even small states such as South Dakota, where former Senate Majority Leader Tom Daschle lives, can play host to very expensive campaigns.

In contrast, House elections tend to be local affairs. Although current members of Congress are sometimes judged by what they do in Washington, particularly on nationally visible issues such as prescription drug coverage, the war in Iraq, or education, most citizens have a favorable view of their own member of Congress. They might not recognize their member on the street, but they will recognize their member's name on the ballot. Because **incumbents**, or sitting members of Congress, have such significant advantages in campaigns, they are almost always reelected if they decide to run. As a result, less than 10 percent of congressional districts are considered competitive in any given election.

In the Senate, incumbents also enjoy significant advantages, and the number of competitive contests has declined. But Senate elections can also turn into national contests depending upon the incumbent's visibility. Because there are fewer Senate contests in any given election year, money tends to concentrate on a relatively small number of competitive contests, which can draw the kind of national media attention to convert them into national, not local, contests.[9]

The last thing most candidates want to do is "nationalize" an election. They would much rather have the campaign be about how well they served the local community through constituent service.

The 2004 Congressional Elections

The 2004 congressional elections are best understood for what did not happen rather than for what did. Despite Democratic hopes for a surge in House seats and Republican hopes for a dramatic gain, the House campaigns produced a shift of only four seats for a balance of 232 to 202, with one independent reelected and the last two races decided in runoffs on December 4, 2004 (see table on page 277).

Also, despite Democratic hopes for a gain of enough Senate seats to recapture a majority and despite Republican hopes for a gain of enough seats to create the 60 votes needed to prevent filibusters, which are discussed later in this chapter, the Senate campaigns produced a net gain of four Republican seats for a balance of 55 to 44, with one independent who usually votes with the Democrats.

The elections were hardly uneventful, however, particularly in the Senate, where the Democrats had 19 seats to defend and the Republicans had 15. Republicans took six seats from the Democrats, including the seat held by Senate minority leader Tom Daschle (D.-S.D.), who was defeated by 8,000 votes in the most expensive Senate race in the nation, and the last five Southern seats still held by Democrats, four of which were vacated through Democratic retirements. In turn, Democrats took two seats from the Republicans, including the Illinois seat won by Barack Obama, who had established a national presence with his keynote address at the Democratic National Convention in July 2004, and the Colorado seat occupied by Native American Ben Nighthorse Campbell, who had entered the Senate a Democrat but who retired after having switched to the Republican party.

Freshmen House of Representatives of the 108th Congress, who took office in January 2003, on the steps of the U.S. Capitol for their "class" picture.

THE RESULTS   Beyond the Daschle upset and several tight contests in both chambers, the congressional elections produced little overall turnover. Voters reelected 18 of the 19 Senate incumbents who ran, and 394 of the 403 House incumbents who ran. Even including the Texas incumbents who lost, 98.2 percent of incumbents won reelection, marking the third highest rate in fifty years; without the Texans, the rate hit 99.2 percent.

Indeed, many Senators and Representatives faced token opposition at best. Even before the election, only 9 of the 33 Senate seats up for election were rated as competitive, six of which involved an open seat where an incumbent had retired; while 371 House districts were rated as "safe," including 28 Democrats and 34 Republicans who ran unopposed. "In more than half the states with Senate races, voters are being denied the experience of seeing their senators seriously tested on their records or their plans," Washington Post veteran columnist David Broder wrote just before election day, "The situation in the House of Representatives is similar—but worse." (See David Broder, "What Democracy Needs: Real Races," *The Washington Post,* October 31, 2004, p. B07.) As if to prove the point, four of the nine incumbents who were defeated came from Texas, where two of the losing Democratic incumbents were matched up against Republican incumbents in newly-created districts.

Much of the incumbency advantage involved campaign financing. According to the nonpartisan Campaign Finance Institute, candidates for the 435 House seats spent nearly $450 million in 2004, while candidates for the 33 Senate seats spent nearly $225 million. On average, the House campaigns cost more than $1 million per seat, up almost 20 percent from the winners in 2002, while the Senate campaigns cost more than $6.5 million, up nearly 50 percent from 2002 and almost 60 percent from 1998 when the same 33 seats were last up for election (see Campaign Finance Institute, "House Winners Average $1 Million for the First Time; Senate Winners Up 47%," news release, Washington, D.C., November 5, 2004).

More importantly, winners outspent their challengers by large margins. House incumbents who were reelected by 60 percent or more of the vote outspent their challengers by four to one, or $900,000 to $170,000; while Senate incumbents who won by similar margins outspent their challengers by a margin of five to one, or $4.9 million to $900,000. As of September 30, 2004, incumbent Senator George Voinovich (R.-Ohio) had $4.2 million in cash on hand against an opponent with just $93,000, while incumbent senator and future minority leader Harry Reid (D.-Nev.) had $3.3 million in hand against an opponent with just $15,000.

CONGRESSIONAL ELECTION RESULTS, 2004

SENATE

	2002	2004
Republican	51	55
Democrat	48	44
Independent	1	1

HOUSE

	2000	2004
Republican	229	232
Democrat	205	202
Independent	1	1

ADVANTAGES OF INCUMBENCY

- Incumbents are better known than their challengers, and to be known at all is generally to be known favorably.
- Except for the 90 days before an election, incumbents do not have to pay postage for mailings back home, and they are allowed to send bulk e-mails any time.*
- Incumbents have greater access to the media, especially on local or state issues.
- Incumbents can raise campaign money more easily than challengers—donors like to put their support behind winners.
- Incumbents usually have more campaign experience than their challengers, and they are usually better campaigners.
- Incumbents often help constituents solve problems with government, and they often take credit for federal spending in their districts or state.

*For a discussion of how members have evaded federal legislation against bulk e-mails, or spam, see Jennifer S. Lee, "We Hate Spam, Congress Says (Except When It's Sent by Us)," *The New York Times*, December 18, 2003, p. A1.

Given its national importance to both Democrats and Republicans, South Dakota had the most expensive Senate campaign at $33 million. But high spending was not always tied to competitiveness. Despite the lack of strong opposition, New York had the second most expensive Senate campaign at $28 million, followed by California at $23 million, and Pennsylvania at $20 million.

Texas had the most expensive House race at $8.4 million in a Dallas-Fort Worth contest between two incumbents, Democrat Martin Frost and Republican Pete Sessions, which Sessions won, while South Dakota came in with the second most expensive contest at almost $6 million as Democrat Stephanie Herseth outlasted Republican Larry Diedrich in a rematch of their special election battle only six months earlier.

Although incumbency and the campaign money that goes with it help explain the 2004 results, there were a number of unpredictable contests in which candidate conduct contributed to the uncertainty. In the Senate elections, Illinois Democrat Obama won his seat after the initial Republican candidate quit following reports that he had taken his wife to a sex club in Paris; Kentucky Republican incumbent and former major league Hall-of-Fame pitcher, Jim Bunning, survived despite having described his opponent as resembling one of Iraqi dictator Saddam Hussein's sons; Oklahoma Republican candidate Tom Colburn won his election after saying that physicians who perform abortions should be subject to the death penalty; and Alaska Republican Lisa Murkowski won her first election after having been appointed to her seat by her father, who was governor at the time. (For a complete summary of the 2004 congressional campaigns, see *Congressional Quarterly Weekly*, November 6, 2004.)

In the House, Illinois Democratic challenger Melissa Bean defeated the dean of the Republican majority, Philip Crane, who had been in the House since 1969 when she was just seven years old; while a Colorado Democrat and brother of the state's new senator won an open seat once held by a Republican.

If there was a single winner in the elections, it was House majority leader Tom DeLay, who designed the Texas redistricting strategy that gave the Republicans the four added seats. DeLay positioned himself as the heir-apparent when the current Speaker of the House, J. Dennis Hastert, retires. DeLay is not without enemies, however, and may yet face an indictment surrounding allegations that he directed corporate funding into the 2002 Texas state legislative campaigns that produced the new majority stemming from the redistricting.

GOVERNING IN THE NEW CONGRESS The Senate clearly emerged as the new battleground in governing. Several of the new Republican senators are deeply conservative and have promised to bring issues such as abortion and gay marriage to the floor for votes as soon as possible, while veterans in both chambers have already signaled their intention to press for Democratic concessions on social and economic issues. "I earned capital in the campaign, political capital, and now I intend to spend it," President Bush said in November 2004, and he clearly hopes that his dual majorities in Congress will do much of the spending.

However, as Democrats learned when they had similar majorities in both chambers, 55 votes in the Senate is still five votes shy of the 60 needed to shut down filibusters and 11 short of the number needed to ratify treaties.

THE STRUCTURE AND POWERS OF CONGRESS

The framers made two critical decisions about Congress early in the Constitutional Convention. First, they agreed to create a legislature as the first branch of government. Next, they divided that legislature into two chambers, the House of Representatives and the Senate. In doing so, the framers created one of the single most important obstacles to making laws. Worried about the tendency for the legislative branch to dominate government, they diluted the power of Congress by creating two chambers "as little connected with each other as the nature of their common functions and their common

Members of Congress are expected to fight for federal funding of projects in their district. Here Representative Nancy Pelosi (Democrat, 8th Congressional District in San Francisco) takes part in an official groundbreaking for the new Federal Building in San Francisco.

dependence on the society will admit."[10] Not only would Congress be balanced by the presidency and judiciary, but it would also be balanced against itself.

A Divided Branch

Bicameralism remains the most important organizational feature of the U.S. Congress. Each chamber meets in separate wings of the Capitol Building (see Figure 11–1); each has offices for its members on separate ends of Capitol Street; each has its own committee structure, its own rules for considering legislation, and its own record of proceedings (even though the records are published together as the *Congressional Record*); and each sets the rules governing its own members (each establishes its own legislative committees, for example).[11]

Bicameral legislatures were common in most of the colonies, and the framers believed that the arrangement was essential for preventing strong-willed majorities from oppressing individuals and minorities.[12] As James Madison explained in *The Federalist*, No. 51, "In order to control the legislative authority, you must divide it." (*The Federalist*, No. 51, is reprinted in the Appendix.) Although the Seventeenth Amendment to the Constitution (1913) provided for direct election of U.S. senators (senators were originally chosen by state legislatures), the two chambers remain very different (see Table 11–1).

Defenders of bicameralism point to its moderating influence on partisanship or possible errors in either chamber. This constitutionally mandated structure also guarantees that many votes will be taken before a policy is finally approved. The arrangement also provides more opportunities for bargaining and allows legislators with different policy goals a role in the shaping of national laws.

The Powers of Congress

The framers gave the longest list of **enumerated powers** to Congress. Because the Revolutionary War had been sparked by unfair taxation, the framers listed the power "to lay and collect Taxes" as the very first duty of Congress. They then gave Congress the power to borrow and coin money, regulate citizenship, build post offices and postal roads, and establish the lower courts of the federal judiciary, meaning every court below the Supreme Court. The framers also gave Congress the power to protect the nation against

bicameralism
The principle of a two-house legislature.

enumerated powers
The powers explicitly given to Congress in the Constitution.

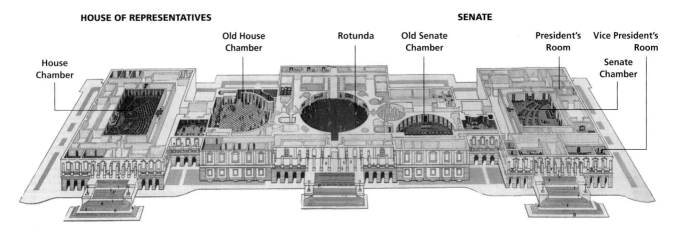

HOUSE OF REPRESENTATIVES   **SENATE**

House Chamber · Old House Chamber · Rotunda · Old Senate Chamber · President's Room · Vice President's Room · Senate Chamber

FIGURE 11–1 The Capitol Building.

foreign threats by declaring war, raising armies, and building navies; and the power to protect the nation from domestic threats by regulating commerce and immigration.

Just in case the list was not enough to allow Congress to do its job, the framers gave Congress the catchall power to "make all Laws which shall be necessary and proper for carrying into Execution the foregoing Powers, and all other Powers vested by this Constitution in the Government of the United States, or in any Department or Officer thereof." This clause is sometimes called the *elastic clause* because it stretches to cover much of what Congress might do. The Constitution also gave Congress complete authority to set its own rules for its proceedings.

Finally, the Constitution gave Congress several nonlegislative functions, such as participating in the process of constitutional amendment and impeachment (given to the House) and trying an impeached federal officer (given to the Senate). The Constitution stipulates that the grounds for impeachment that can lead to the removal from office of a president or vice president or other federal officers, including federal judges,

TABLE 11–1 DIFFERENCES BETWEEN THE HOUSE OF REPRESENTATIVES AND THE SENATE

House	Senate
Two-year term	Six-year term
435 members	100 members
Elected in districts	Elected by states
Fewer personal staff	More personal staff
Tighter rules	Looser rules
Decision to act made by majority	Decision to act made by unanimous consent
Tax bills must come from the House	Foreign treaties must be ratified by the Senate
Less media coverage	More media coverage
Less prestige	More prestige
More powerful committee leaders	More equal distribution of power
Nongermane amendments (riders) not allowed	Nongermane amendments (riders) not allowed
Rules Committee sets terms of debate	Senate as a whole sets terms of debate
Limited debate	Extended debate
Some bills permit no floor amendments (closed rule)	Amendments generally allowed
No filibuster allowed	Filibuster allowed

are the commission of "High Crimes and Misdemeanors" (never clearly defined). The House sits to determine whether or not an official's actions reach the level of impeachable offenses, and if so, it can impeach by a majority vote. The Senate sits as a court to decide if the impeached official should be convicted and whether the nature of the offense warrants removal from office. A two-thirds vote is needed to convict; thus a minority of just 34 senators can block the conviction of an impeached official.

As the impeachment power shows, the Constitution gives different duties to each chamber. The Senate has the power to confirm many presidential nominations. The Senate must also play a crucial "advise and consent" role in making treaties—formal agreements between the United States and other countries. All treaties must be approved by a two-thirds vote in the Senate before they can be ratified by the president.

The House has some of its own responsibilities, too, but they are not as important as those given to the Senate. For example, although all revenue bills must originate in the House, this practice does not give the House much advantage, because the Senate can freely amend spending bills even to the point of changing everything except the title.

Despite its position as the first branch of government and its substantial powers, Congress has difficulty keeping pace with its great rival, the presidency. The president's national security responsibilities, preparation of the budget, media visibility, and agenda-setting influence have all enhanced the position of the presidency relative to Congress.

MAKING CONGRESS WORK

Today's Congress bears the unmistakable imprint of the bicameralism created more than 200 years ago. The Senate prides itself on being an incubator of ideas, a place in which individual members can take the floor to defend an intense minority and delay action until at least 60 senators vote to end the debate; the House prides itself on being the voice of the people.

The two chambers are no more complex, however, than the society they have come to represent and the executive branch they must oversee. It was far easier to control the 59 House members and 22 senators who represented white male property owners in 1789 when the First Congress was gaveled to order than it is to control the 435 House members and 100 senators who represent the diverse United States today. It was far easier to write legislation for the small government in 1789 than for today's 15 departments

---

IN COMPARATIVE PERSPECTIVE

THE NIGERIAN ASSEMBLY

As one of the world's largest suppliers of oil, Nigeria has extraordinary wealth. It has also long been divided by political and ethnic conflict. Nigeria adopted a new constitution in 1999 after nearly 16 years of brutal military rule. Under its new constitution, Nigeria adopted a variation of America's divided government, opting for a separately elected president and a bicameral legislature. Both chambers of the National Assembly are elected by popular vote for four-year terms.

In its first four years in office, the Nigerian Assembly showed both strengths and weaknesses. It has been a reluctant participant in efforts to reduce the corruption and bribery that emerged after military rule, and it has been unable to control human rights abuses against civilians. The assembly has also shown little willingness to challenge the president.

Building an effective legislature takes time and experience, however. According to recent newspaper reports, the Nigerian Assembly is increasingly aware of its need for greater independence, especially in the wake of spring 2003 elections. As Representative Ganiyu Solomon argued in July 2003, "Nigerians should just give us time to settle down and pick up our work tools, then they will never regret they voted us as their representatives. It is just barely three months we got in here, so, we hardly could have done anything astonishing. . . . Ours will never be called a rubber stamp legislature, we will not drag our reputation and the trust of our people into the mud for compromise sake."[*]

[*] "Nigeria: What Role for the National Assembly," *Africa Today*, July 18, 2003, Nexis.com.

GLOBAL *Perceptions*

QUESTION: Some feel that we should rely on a democratic form of government to solve our country's problems. Others feel that we should rely on a leader with a strong hand to solve our country's problems. Which comes closer to your opinion?

When given a choice between the delays that sometimes come with democratic government and a strong leader who makes the key decisions, citizens around the world come to very different judgments.

SOURCE: The Pew Global Attitudes Project, June 2003, p. 87.

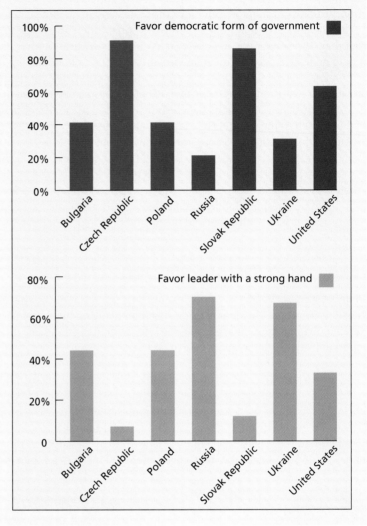

and 2.6 million employees. In the 1790s, a handful of permanent committees could handle the entire task of making the laws and checking government.

Leading the House of Representatives

The organization and procedures in the House are different from those in the Senate, largely because the House is more than four times larger than the Senate. A larger membership requires more rules, which means that *how* things are done affects *what* is done. The House assigns different types of bills to different calendars. For instance, financial measures—tax or appropriations bills—are put on a special calendar for quicker action.

The House has other ways to speed up lawmaking, including electronic voting. Ordinary rules may be suspended by a two-thirds vote, or immediate action may be taken by *unanimous consent* of the members on the floor. By acting as a *committee of the whole,* the House is able to operate more informally and more quickly than under its regular rules. A *quorum* in the committee of the whole requires only 100 members, rather than a majority of the whole chamber, and voting is quicker and simpler. Members are limited in how long they can speak, and debate may be cut off simply by majority vote.

These differences are based in part on how well each government has done in solving economic and social problems over the past decade. Russia and the Ukraine have been in nearly constant economic turmoil since the end of the Cold War, while the Czech Republic has made significant progress in strengthening its economy. Moreover, the Czech Republic was one of the leaders in the effort to overthrow communism in the late 1980s, which may help explains its support for democratic rule.

THE SPEAKER OF THE HOUSE   The **Speaker** is the presiding officer in the House of Representatives.[13] The Constitution mandates that the House of Representatives shall choose its Speaker, yet it does not say anything about the duties or powers of the office. The Speaker is formally elected by the entire House yet is actually selected by the majority party. As the highest-ranking officer in Congress, the Speaker represents the legislative branch on ceremonial occasions. The Speaker is second in the line of succession to the presidency (after the vice president) in case of the death, resignation, or impeachment of the president and must keep the White House informed about his or her whereabouts.

The Speaker has the power to recognize members who rise to speak, rule on questions of parliamentary procedure, and appoint members to temporary committees (but not the major committees that help make the laws). In a sentence, the Speaker directs business on the floor of the House. More significant, of course, is the Speaker's political and behind-the-scenes influence.

When the Republicans won control of the House in 1994, they elected Representative Newt Gingrich of Georgia as Speaker. As the first Republican Speaker in 40 years, he was a novelty in Washington. "I had set out to do a very unusual job," said Gingrich, as "part revolutionary, part national political figure, part Speaker, part intellectual."[14]

Gingrich established his authority—reorganizing House committees, naming committee chairs, bypassing the seniority rule to appoint his allies to leadership posts, reorganizing House committees, and reducing perks and committee staffs. He pushed through some of the legislation outlined in the long list of campaign promises called the "Contract with America." He delegated considerable power to fellow Republican leaders yet claimed for himself the main role as spokesperson for major policy initiatives. He published books detailing his ideas about government and his party, and he cheerfully took on the White House and the national press.[15]

After a long investigation into the Speaker's use of tax-exempt funds, the House Ethics Committee concluded that Gingrich had violated its standards of conduct. He insisted that there was little overlap between his political activities and his nonpartisan educational endeavors, but the committee recommended, and the House of Representatives quickly passed, a reprimand of Gingrich and imposed a fine of $300,000 for misusing charitable deductions for political purposes and for misleading the House Ethics Committee. This was an unprecedented rebuke for a Speaker.

Following his party's poor showing in the midterm election of 1998, Gingrich retired both as Speaker and as a member of Congress. Republicans soon selected Illinois Representative J. Dennis Hastert as Speaker. Hastert, a former high school teacher and wrestling coach, had served for six years in the Illinois state legislature and 12 years in the U.S. House of Representatives before becoming Speaker of the House. "It's a calling that I have not sought," said Hastert about the Speakership. "However, it is a duty that I cannot ignore."[16] Hastert displays a low-key, quiet self-confidence that has pleased most Republicans and has earned praise from Democrats.[17] He has been particularly effective in holding Republicans together on key party votes in the chamber while drawing extra votes from Democrats who belong to the "Blue Dog" coalition, a group of mostly southern conservatives.

OTHER HOUSE OFFICERS   The Speaker is assisted by the **majority leader**, who helps plan party strategy, confers with other party leaders, and tries to keep members of the party in line. The minority party elects the **minority leader**, who usually steps into the Speakership when his or her party gains a majority in the House. (These positions are also sometimes called majority and minority *floor leaders*.) Assisting each floor leader are the party **whips**. (The term comes from *whipper-in*, the huntsman who keeps the hounds

Republican Dennis Hastert, *Speaker of the House of Representatives.*

Speaker
The presiding officer in the House of Representatives, formally elected by the House but actually selected by the majority party.

majority leader
The legislative leader selected by the majority party who helps plan party strategy, confers with other party leaders, and tries to keep members of the party in line.

minority leader
The legislative leader selected by the minority party as spokesperson for the opposition.

whip
Party leader who is the liaison between the leadership and the rank-and-file in the legislature.

CHANGING FACE OF AMERICAN POLITICS

DIVERSITY IN CONGRESS

Although the Constitution does not mention race, gender, or wealth among the qualifications for office, the framers expected members of Congress to be white male property owners. After all, women and slaves could not vote, let alone hold office.

The framers would therefore be surprised at the face of Congress today. Recent Congresses have had record numbers of women and minorities. In 2004, Illinois voters elected only the third African American senator since the 1870s, Barack Obama, while Florida voters elected the first Cuban American, Mel Martinez, and Colorado voters elected the first Hispanic in thirty years, Ken Salazar. Voters also reelected all five women senators and added ten women and minority members to the list of U.S. representatives.

The changing face of Congress reflects the growing effectiveness of women and minority candidates in running for office, as well as increased participation by minority voters. The Voting Rights Act of 1965 allowed millions of African Americans to register and vote in the South. In Mississippi, for example, only 14 percent of African Americans were registered to vote in 1960. By 1968, the number had increased to 64 percent. As the number of African American voters increased, so did the number of African American legislators.

Congress is becoming more diverse by race and gender, but it still remains very different from the rest of America on income and occupation. Almost one-third of the senators who served in the 108th Congress were millionaires, and more than half were lawyers. Moreover, old customs die hard. Even with the Democratic senator from Washington, Patty Murray, sitting on his Appropriations Committee, Chairman Robert Byrd still addressed committee members as "Gentlemen." At the current rate of change in the number of women, for example, it

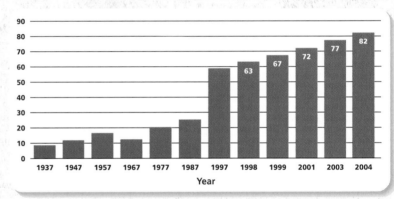

U.S. Senator Barbara Mikulsi (D-Md), shown at the podium, with the other female Democratic senators on stage at the 2004 Democratic National Convention in Boston.

Number of Women in U.S. Congress.
SOURCE: *Congressional Quarterly Weekly*, November 6, 2004, p. 263.

will take another 400 years before women constitute a majority in the House.[*]

[*]See the United States Capitol Historical Society, "Outstanding African-American Members of Congress" and "Women Members of Congress" at www.uschs.org/04_history/subs_articles/04e.html.

---

bunched in a pack during a fox hunt.) The whips serve as liaisons between the House leadership of each party and the rank-and-file. They inform members when important bills will come up for a vote, prepare summaries of the bills, do vote counts for the leadership, exert pressure (sometimes mild and sometimes heavy) on members to support the leadership, and try to ensure maximum attendance on the floor for critical votes.

At the beginning of the session and occasionally afterward, each party holds a **party caucus** of all its members (called a *conference* by the Republicans) to elect party officers, approve committee assignments, elect committee leaders, discuss important legislation, and perhaps try to agree on party policy.

THE HOUSE RULES COMMITTEE   The House has a powerful Rules Committee that regulates the time of floor debate for each bill and sets limitations on floor amendments.

party caucus
A meeting of the members of a party in a legislative chamber to select party leaders and to develop party policy. Called a *conference* by the Republicans.

By refusing to grant a *rule,* which describes the conditions of debate, the Rules Committee can delay consideration of a bill. A **closed rule** prohibits amendments altogether or provides that only members of the committee reporting the bill may offer amendments; closed rules are usually reserved for tax and spending bills. An **open rule** permits debate within the overall time allocated to the bill.

From the New Deal era in the mid-1930s until the mid-1960s, a coalition of Republicans and conservative Democrats used the Rules Committee to block significant legislation on civil rights, health care, and poverty. Liberals denounced it as unrepresentative, unfair, and dictatorial. More recently, the Rules Committee membership has come to reflect the views of the general makeup of the majority party. It has become much less an independent obstacle to legislation and more a place to design rules that help advance the general goals of the majority party.

Leading the Senate

The Senate has the same basic committee structure, elected party leadership, and decentralized power as the House, but because the Senate is a smaller body, its procedures are more informal, and it permits more time for debate. It is a more open, fluid, and decentralized body now than it was a generation or two ago. Indeed, it is often said that the Senate has 100 separate power centers and is so splintered that the party leaders have difficulty arranging the day-to-day schedule.[18]

The Senate is led by the Senate majority leader, who is elected by the majority party in the Senate. When the majority leader is from the president's party, the president is the party's most visible leader. However, when the majority leader and the president are from different parties, the majority leader is considered his or her party's national spokesperson.

As the Senate's power broker, the majority leader has the right to be the first senator heard on the floor. In consultation with the Senate minority leader, the majority leader controls the Senate's agenda and recommends committee assignments for members of the majority party. But the position confers less authority than the Speakership in the House, and its influence depends on the person's political and parliamentary skills and on the national political situation.[19] Senate majority leaders have to be persuaders and negotiators, not only working closely with the minority leader but also working with a number of powerful majority and minority senators and the White House.

Nevertheless, the majority leader does have substantial influence over the legislative agenda in the Senate. Senator Lott proved this point in the session of Congress immediately following the 2002 election. Although his party was not technically in the majority until the new Congress was sworn into office in January 2003, Lott worked with the president to make sure that the new Department of Homeland Security became law. (Chapter 13 provides more details on the new department.)

Lott was not to be majority leader for long, however. He soon became embroiled in a controversy surrounding remarks he made at the 100th birthday party for retiring South Carolina Senator Strom Thurmond. In congratulating Thurmond for his 48 years of Senate service, Lott remarked that the nation would have been better off had Thurmond won the presidency as the candidate of the Dixiecrat Party in 1948. The Dixiecrat Party was formed to oppose racial integration, and fought civil rights throughout the 1950s and into the 1960s. Lott was forced to resign his post on December 20, 2002, and was replaced by Tennessee Senator Bill Frist, a former heart surgeon who had been in the Senate for just eight years.

Party machinery in the Senate is similar to that in the House. There are party caucuses (conferences), majority and minority floor leaders, and party whips. Each party has a *policy committee,* composed of party leaders, which is theoretically responsible for the party's overall legislative program. In the Senate, the party policy committees assist the leadership in monitoring legislation and provide policy expertise. Unlike the House party committees, the Senate's party policy committees are formally provided for by law, and each has a regular staff and a budget. Although the Senate party policy committees have some influence on legislation, they have not asserted strong legislative leadership or managed to coordinate policy.

Senator Bill Frist of Tennessee, Republican majority leader, holds a sample drug discount card that will soon be available to Medicare recipients as a result of major changes in the Medicare program made late in 2003.

Former U.S. Senate minority leader Tom Daschle making a point on NBC's Meet the Press. Daschle was defeated for reelection in 2004, becoming the first senate leader of either party to lose his seat in over fifty years. Nevada's Harry Reid became the Senate Minority leader in January 2005.

closed rule
A procedural rule in the House of Representatives that prohibits any amendments to bills or provides that only members of the committee reporting the bill may offer amendments.

open rule
A procedural rule in the House of Representatives that permits floor amendments within the overall time allocated to the bill.

The president of the Senate (the vice president of the United States) also has little influence over Senate proceedings. A vice president can vote only in case of a tie. The Senate elects a **president pro tempore**, usually the most senior member from the majority party, who acts as chair in the absence of the vice president. Presiding over the Senate on most occasions is a thankless chore, so the president pro tempore regularly delegates this responsibility to junior members of the chamber's majority party.

Despite these various leaders and offices, the Senate is far less structured than the House. It has always operated under rules that vest great power in the individual senator. Extended debate allows senators to hold the floor as long as they wish unless a supermajority of 60 colleagues votes to end debate. Moreover, the Senate's rules allow individual senators to offer amendments on virtually any topic to a pending bill, allowing them to amend a bill to death.[20]

One relatively recent expression of this individualism is a practice called the **hold**. Holds were originally designed to give individual senators a short period to prepare for a debate or delay a vote for personal reasons. Over time, however, they have become a powerful device for blocking action on legislation and nominations.

Although successful Senate leadership still depends on personal relationships, individual members have become more partisan in recent decades. "Senators known for compromise, moderation and institutional loyalty," observe political scientists Nicol Rae and Colton Campbell, "have been replaced with more ideological and partisan members who see the chamber as a place to enhance their party fortunes."[21] Partisanship in the Senate was vehement during the Bill Clinton impeachment proceedings and to a lesser extent in the confirmation battle of George W. Bush's nominee, John Ashcroft, as his attorney general.

THE FILIBUSTER   Because of its smaller size and looser rules, debate is more open in the Senate. A senator who gains the floor may go on talking until he or she relinquishes the right to talk voluntarily or through exhaustion. This right to unlimited debate, known as the **filibuster**, may be used by a small group of senators to delay Senate proceedings by talking continuously so as to postpone or prevent a vote. At one time, the filibuster was a favorite weapon of southern senators intent on blocking civil rights legislation. More recently, the filibuster has been used for a wider range of issues, including efforts to stop judicial nominations and prevent passage of campaign finance reform.

A filibuster, or the threat of a filibuster, is typically most potent at the end of a congressional session, when a date has been fixed for adjournment, because it could mean that many bills that have otherwise made it through the legislative process will die for lack of a floor vote. The knowledge that a bill might be subject to a filibuster is often enough to force a compromise satisfactory to its opponents. Sometimes the leaders, knowing that a filibuster will tie up the Senate and keep it from enacting other needed legislation, do not bring a controversial bill to the floor.

A filibuster can be defeated. Until 1917, the Senate could terminate a filibuster only if every member agreed. That year, however, the Senate adopted its first debate-ending rule, or **cloture**. The rule specifies that the question of curtailing debate must be put to a vote two days after 16 senators sign a petition asking for cloture. If three-fifths of the total number of the Senate (60 of the 100 members) vote in favor of cloture, no senator may speak on the measure under consideration for more than one hour. Once invoked, cloture requires that the final vote on the measure be taken after no more than 30 hours of debate.

There has been an increase in the use and threat of filibusters in recent years, and these tactics have often been used for partisan and parochial purposes. Indeed, as noted, senators usually anticipate a filibuster on controversial measures, and the threat is often sufficient to force the majority to compromise and modify its position.[22] Both parties have learned to use the filibuster when they are in the minority. The Senate has averaged almost two dozen filibusters each year since 2001. Of the 45 cloture votes taken in 2001–2003, just 12 succeeded, 10 in 2001–2002, and two in 2003.[23]

THE POWER TO CONFIRM   The Constitution leaves the precise practices of the confirmation process somewhat ambiguous: "The President . . . shall nominate, and by and with the Advice and Consent of the Senate, shall appoint Ambassadors, other public

president pro tempore
Officer of the Senate selected by the majority party to act as chair in the absence of the vice president.

hold
A procedural practice in the Senate whereby a senator temporarily blocks the consideration of a bill or nomination.

filibuster
A procedural practice in the Senate whereby a senator refuses to relinguish the floor and thereby delays proceedings and prevents a vote on a controversial issue.

cloture
A procedure for terminating debate, especially filibusters, in the Senate.

Ministers and Consuls, Judges of the Supreme Court, all other officers of the United States." The framers of the Constitution regarded the confirmation process—the Senate's "advise and consent" power—as an important check on executive power. Alexander Hamilton viewed it as a way for the Senate to prevent the appointment of "unfit characters."

As with other legislative business, the confirmation process starts in committees, with the relevant committee that oversees the particular function or activity involved. For example, the Judiciary Committee considers federal judges and Supreme Court nominees; the Foreign Relations Committee considers ambassadorial appointments. Nominees appear before the committee to answer questions, and they typically meet individually with key senators before the hearing.

Presidents have never enjoyed exclusive control over hiring and firing in the executive branch. The Senate jealously guards its right to confirm or reject or even delay major appointments; during the period of strong Congresses after the Civil War, presidents had to struggle to keep their power to appoint and dismiss. But for most of the past century, presidents have gained a reasonable amount of control over top appointments, in part because a growing number of people in and out of Congress believe that chief executives without compatible cabinet-level appointees of their choice cannot be held accountable. The Senate's advise and consent powers sometimes force presidents to make compromises, plainly constraining their ability to use the presidential appointment power.

The Senate's role in the confirmation process was never intended to prevent a president from taking political considerations into account when appointments are made. Rather, the Senate was given the power to protect the judicial branch against weak or controversial nominees. During the Bush administration, conservatives complained that Senate Democrats were interfering with the executive power of the president by rejecting nominees because of their political beliefs. Only years before during the Clinton administration, however, liberals complained that Senate Republicans were doing the same thing.

In recent years, the Senate has taken a tough stand on some presidential appointments and spent more time evaluating and screening presidential nominations. The Senate rejected several nominees of Presidents Ronald Reagan and George Bush, and Presidents Bill Clinton and George W. Bush withdrew several nominees in the face of Senate opposition. In November, 2003, for example, Senate Republicans staged a 39-hour debate designed to break a Democratic filibuster of four controversial Bush administration judicial nominees. The debate began on a Wednesday night at 6 P.M. and continued until 9 A.M. Friday, but ended on 53 to 43 votes for all four nominees, seven votes short of the 60 needed to move ahead. During the debate, Democratic Senator Edward Kennedy (D.-Mass.) promised to "continue to resist any Neanderthal that is nominated by this president," while Republican Senator Orrin Hatch (R.-Utah) described the filibusters as "petty politics . . . cheap politics. . . ."[24]

There is an important distinction between *judicial* appointments, especially those to the Supreme Court, and *executive branch* or *administrative* appointments. For the most part, the Senate gives the president the benefit of the doubt in selecting executive appointees, but plays a greater role in judicial appointments because federal judges serve for life and constitute an independent check on both Congress and the executive branch.[25]

Even here, however, the Senate and the president often work closely to reach agreement, especially on district court judges. Under the tradition of **senatorial courtesy**, presidents confer with the senator or senators in their own political party from the state where a judge is to work, or "sit." Occasionally, a president has to take into account the views of a politically powerful senator in the opposition party. A nomination is less likely to secure Senate approval against the objection of these senators, especially if these senators are members of the president's party.

As part of her confirmation process, Labor Secretary Elaine Chao answered questions for congressional committee members on Capitol Hill.

Congressional Committees

It is sometimes said that Congress is a collection of committees that come together in a chamber every once in a while to approve one another's actions. Congress has long relied on committees to get its work done. Woodrow Wilson, a political science professor before he became president, expressed a similar thought: "Congress in session is

senatorial courtesy
Presidential custom of submitting the names of prospective appointees for approval to senators from the states in which the appointees are to work.

Members of the Senate Armed Services Committee hear testimony from Secretary of Defense Donald Rumsfeld on allegations of prisoner abuse in Iraq.

Congress on display. Congress in committee is Congress at work."[26] More precisely, Congress in subcommittee is Congress at work, because the initial struggle over legislation takes place in subcommittees.[27]

TYPES OF COMMITTEES   In theory, all congressional committees are created anew in each new Congress. In reality, however, most continue with little change from Congress to Congress. **Standing committees** are the most durable and are the sources of most bills, while **special or select committees** come together to address temporary priorities of Congress such as aging or taxes and rarely author legislation. **Joint committees** have members from both the House and the Senate and exist either to study an issue of interest to the entire Congress or to oversee congressional support agencies such as the Library of Congress or the U.S. Government Printing Office. Almost all standing committees have subcommittees that help handle the legislative workload.

Of the various types of committees, standing committees are the most important for making laws and representing constituents, and they fall into four types: authorizing, appropriations, rules, and revenue. There are more than three dozen standing committees in the House and Senate.

Authorizing committees   These committees pass the laws that tell government what to do. The House and Senate education and labor committees, for example, are responsible for setting the rules governing the Pell Grant student loan program, including who can apply, how much they can get, where the loans come from, and how defaults are handled. Simply stated, authorizing committees make the most basic decisions about who gets what, when, and how from government. In 1999–2000, there were 15 authorizing committees in the House and 17 in the Senate. The number of committees remained unchanged in 2003–2004.

Authorizing committees are also responsible for oversight of the federal bureaucracy. Some of this oversight is designed to ask whether programs are working well, and some is designed to reduce fraud, waste, or abuse in an agency of government. The amount of congressional oversight is increasing. Political scientist Joel Aberbach found, for example, that just 8 percent of all legislative hearings focused on oversight in 1961, compared to over 25 percent just two decades later.[28]

Appropriations committees   These committees make decisions about how much money government will spend on its programs and operations. Although there is just one appropriations committee in each chamber, each appropriations committee has one

standing committee
A permanent committee established in a legislature, usually focusing on a policy area.

special or select committee
A congressional committee created for a specific purpose, sometimes to conduct an investigation.

joint committee
A committee composed of members of both the House of Representatives and the Senate; such committees oversee the Library of Congress and conduct investigations.

subcommittee for each of the 13 appropriations bills that must be enacted each year to keep government running. Because they decide who gets how much from government, these subcommittees have great power to undo or limit decisions by the authorizing committees.

Rules and administration committees determine the basic operations of the two houses—for example, how many staffers individual members get. Again because of the number of members it must control, the House Rules Committee is more powerful than its twin in the Senate. As noted earlier, the House Rules Committee has special responsibility for giving each bill a rule, or ticket, to the floor of the House and determines what, if any, amendments to a bill will be permitted.

Revenue and budget committees   These committees deal with raising the money that appropriating committees spend while setting the broad targets that shape the federal budget. The House Ways and Means Committee is arguably the single most powerful committee in Congress, for it both raises and authorizes spending. As the only committee in either chamber that can originate tax and revenue legislation, it is also responsible for making basic decisions on the huge Social Security and Medicare programs.

CHOOSING COMMITTEE MEMBERS   The political parties control the selection of standing committee members. The chair and a majority of each standing committee come from the majority party. The minority party is represented on each committee roughly in proportion to its membership in the entire chamber, except on some powerful committees on which the majority may want to enhance its position.

Getting on a politically advantageous committee is important to members of Congress. A representative from Kansas, for example, would rather serve on the Agriculture Committee than on the Banking and Financial Services Committee. Members usually stay on the same committees from one Congress to the next, although junior members who have had less desirable assignments often seek better committees when places become available.

The House and Senate choose committee members in different ways, and actually rank committees in different ways. (See Table 11–2 for the differences.)

Republicans in the House choose committee members through their Committee on Committees, which is composed of one member from each state that has Republican representation in the House. Because each member has as many votes in the committee as there are Republicans in the delegation, the group is dominated by senior members from the large state delegations. Democrats in the House choose committee members through the Steering and Policy Committee of the Democratic caucus in negotiation with senior Democrats from the state delegations.

Veteran party members also dominate the Senate assignment process, where both parties have small Steering Committees that make committee assignments. In making assignments, leaders are guided by various considerations: how talented and cooperative a member is, whether his or her region is already well represented on a committee, and whether the assignment will aid in reelecting the member. Sometimes fierce battles erupt within these committees, reflecting ideological, geographical, and other differences.

One way Congress copes with its legislative workload is to organize its committees and subcommittees by subject matter. This specialization allows members to develop technical expertise in specific areas and to recruit skilled staffs. Thus Congress is often able to challenge experts from the bureaucracy. Interest groups and lobbyists realize the great power a specific committee has in certain areas and focus their attention on its members. Similarly, members of executive departments are careful to cultivate the committee and subcommittee chairs and members of "their" committees.

How each chamber in Congress uses committees is critical in its role as a partner in policy making, both with the other house and with the executive branch. In recent years, progress has been made in opening hearings to the public and improving the quality of committee staffs, but it is difficult to restructure committee jurisdictions so that they do not overlap. Consequently, a dozen different committees deal with energy, education, and the war on drugs. Efforts to make the committee system more efficient are often considered threats to the delicate balance of power within the chamber.

TABLE 11–2   RULES ON COMMITTEE SERVICE IN THE HOUSE AND SENATE

House	Senate
Exclusive Committees	**"A" Committees**
Members can usually serve on just one exclusive committee:	Members can usually serve on no more than two A committees:
Appropriations	Agriculture, Nutrition, and Forestry
Rules	Appropriations
Ways and Means	Banking, Housing, and Urban Affairs
Commerce	Commerce, Science, and Transportation
	Energy and Natural Resources
	Environment and Public Works
	Finance
	Foreign Relations
	Governmental Affairs
	Health, Education, Labor, and Pensions Judiciary
Nonexclusive Committees	**Super "A" Committees**
Members can usually serve on just two nonexclusive committees:	Members can serve on no more than one of the Super A Committees:
Agriculture	Appropriations
Armed Services	Armed Services
Banking and Financial Services	Finance
	Foreign Relations
Education and the Workforce	
International Relations	
Judiciary	
Resources	
Science	
Small Business	
Transportation and Infrastructure	
Veterans' Affairs	
Exempt Committees	**"B" Committees**
Members may serve on one exempt committee regardless of their other service:	Members may serve on one B Committee:
House Administration	Budget
Select Intelligence	Rules and Administration
Standards of Official	Small Business
	Veterans' Affairs
	Special Aging
	Select Intelligence
	Joint Economic Committee
	"C" Committees
	Members may serve on one or more C Committee:
	Select Ethics
	Indian Affairs
	Joint Taxation
	Joint Library
	Joint Printing

NOTE: Senate and House party rules have further restrictions on committee service that may affect these rules.

THE ROLE OF SENIORITY   Forty years ago, committee chairs determined the workload of committees, hired and fired staff, formed subcommittees, and assigned them jurisdictions, members, and aides. Chairs also managed the most important bills assigned to their committees. Since the mid-1970s, however, junior members have insisted on being given more authority. Subcommittee chairs have also become more independent. In recent years, there have also been moves to strengthen the powers of the party leaders and caucuses at the expense of committee chairs.

Most chairs are selected on the basis of the **seniority rule**; the member of the majority party with the longest continuous service on the committee becomes chair upon the retirement of the current chair or a change in the party in control of Congress. The seniority rule gives power to representatives who come from safe districts where one party is dominant and a member can build up years of continuous service. Conversely, the seniority rule lessens the influence of states or districts where the two parties are more evenly matched and where there is more turnover.

Although it is not uncommon for the party leadership to reward a junior member with a prestigious committee assignment, seniority has long been respected in Congress for several reasons: It encourages members to stay on a committee, it encourages specialization and expertise, and it reduces the interpersonal politics that would arise if several members of a committee sought to become chair. Under new rules adopted in the mid-1990s, however, both House and Senate Republicans agreed to limit committee chairs to serving no more than three consecutive terms.[29]

INVESTIGATIONS AND OVERSIGHT   Committees do more than produce legislation. They also have two additional roles in making government work.

The first is the power to *investigate*. Congress conducts investigations to determine if legislation is needed, to gather facts relevant to legislation, to assess the efficiency of executive agencies, to build public support, to expose corruption, and to enhance the image or reputation of its members.[30] Hearings by standing committees, their subcommittees, or special select committees are an important source of information and opinion. They provide an arena in which experts can submit their views.

The second is the *oversight* power—the responsibility to question executive branch officials to see whether their agencies are complying with the wishes of the Congress and conducting their programs efficiently. Authorization committees regularly hold oversight hearings, and appropriations committees, exercising "the congressional power of the purse," often use appropriations hearings to communicate committee members' views about how agency officials should conduct their business. Cabinet members and agency heads have been known to dread the loaded questions of hostile members of Congress and to hate having to watch themselves on the evening news trying to explain why their agency made some mistakes.

THE SPECIAL ROLE OF CONFERENCE COMMITTEES   Given the differences between the House and the Senate, it is not surprising that the version of a bill passed by one chamber may differ substantially from the version passed by the other. Only if both houses pass an absolutely identical measure can it become law. Most of the time, one house accepts the language of the other, but about 10 to 12 percent of all bills passed, usually major ones, must be referred to a **conference committee**—a special committee of members from each chamber that settles the differences between versions.[31] Both parties are represented, but the majority party has more members.

The proceedings of a conference committee are usually an elaborate bargaining process. When the revised bill is brought back to the two chambers, the conference report can be accepted or rejected (often with further negotiations ordered), but it cannot be amended. Conference members of each chamber must convince their colleagues that any concessions made to the other chamber were on unimportant points and that nothing basic to the original version of the bill was surrendered.

Conference committees have considerable leeway in reaching agreement, prompting President Ronald Reagan to note, "You know, if an orange and an apple went into conference consultations, it might come out a pear."[32] Ordinarily, members are expected to end up somewhere between the different versions. On matters for which there is no

Senator Orrin Hatch (R-Utah), shown on the right, left his post as Chair of the Senate Judiciary Committee at the end of his third term in 2005.

seniority rule
A legislative practice that assigns the chair of a committee or subcommittee to the member of the majority party with the longest continuous service on the committee.

conference committee
Committee appointed by the presiding officers of each chamber to adjust differences on a particular bill passed by each in different form.

clear middle ground, members are sometimes accused of exceeding their instructions and producing an entirely new bill. For this reason, the conference committee has been called a "third house" of Congress and one of the most significant congressional institutions.[33]

It is not clear whether the House or the Senate wins more often in conference committees. On the surface, it appears that the Senate's version wins more often, but this is partly because the Senate often acts on its legislation after the House. But by approving the initial bill first and thereby setting the agenda on an issue, the House often has more of an impact on the final outcome than the Senate.

CAUCUSES   In contrast to conference committees, which are appointed by the House and Senate leadership to perform a specific legislative role, caucuses are best defined as informal committees that allow individual members to promote shared legislative interests. There are caucuses for House members only, for senators only, and for members of both chambers together. By the 1990s, according to one count, House members actually served on more informal caucuses than on committees and subcommittees.[34]

The growing diversity of the caucuses parallels the rest of society. They include the Black Caucus, Hispanic Caucus, Women's Issues Caucus, Rural Health Caucus, Children's Caucus, Cuba Freedom Caucus, Pro-Life Caucus, Homelessness Task Force, Urban Caucus, and Ethiopian Jewry Caucus. The diversity also parallels the fragmentation of interest groups, with caucuses on nearly every business and public interest issue—including steel, beef, wheel bearings, the Internet, mushrooms, mining, gas, sweeteners, wine, footwear, soybeans, animal rights, Chesapeake Bay, clean water, drug enforcement, adoption, the arts, energy, military reform, AIDS, and antiterrorism. There are also caucuses composed of friends of the Caribbean Basin, animals, human rights monitors, and Ireland.

THE JOB OF THE LEGISLATOR

Membership in Congress was once a part-time job. Members came to Washington for a few terms, averaged less than five years of continuous service, and returned to their careers. Congressional pay was low, and Washington was no farther than a carriage ride from home.[35]

Congress started to meet more frequently in the late 1800s, pay increased, and being a member of Congress became increasingly attractive.[36] In the 1850s, roughly one-half of all House members retired or were defeated at each election; by 1900, the number who left at the end of each term had fallen to roughly one-quarter; by the 1970s, the number had fallen to barely a tenth. Even in the 1994 congressional elections, when Republicans won the House majority for the first time in 40 years, 90 percent of House incumbents who ran for reelection won.[37]

By the 1950s, being a member of Congress had become a full-time job and a long-term career. Members came to Washington to stay and began to exploit the natural advantages that come with running for reelection as an incumbent: name recognition, service to citizens back home, copious campaign funding, nearly unlimited access to the media, and free postage under the *franking privilege* for mailings back home. In 1954, for example, members of Congress sent 44 million pieces of mail back home. Fifty years later, the number will easily pass 500 million pieces. Include the amount of e-mail, and the average member of Congress is in touch with his or her district almost daily.[38]

The workday also got longer. According to a 1998 survey, most members reported that they worked more than 70 hours a week, dividing their time among committee and subcommittee hearings, floor debates, meetings with citizens and interest groups, and raising money for the next election. Members do not seem to think the job is too tough, at least not the 402 members who ran for reelection in 1998. Nor has job satisfaction declined: 96 percent of members reported that they were very or mostly satisfied with their jobs in 1998, and only 15 percent said the job had gotten less satisfying since they first entered Congress. There appears to be little softening of interest in holding these jobs, despite the high levels of public distrust in Congress as an institution.[39]

As members of Congress became attached to their careers, they began to abandon many of the norms that once guided their behavior in office.[40] The old norms were simple.

PEOPLE & POLITICS *Making a Difference* ★★★

GENERATION X IN CONGRESS (HAROLD FORD JR., AND ADAM PUTNAM)

As the two youngest members of Congress, Adam Putnam (R.-Fla.) and Harold Ford, Jr. (D.-Tenn.) care deeply about reengaging young Americans in politics. Both were elected in part on promises to give young Americans a stronger voice in debates about the future of programs such as Social Security, and both continue to work hard to connect with their generation on jobs and access to education.

Putnam was just 26 years old when he was elected to Congress in 2000. "I want to energize a whole new generation of young people to reengage in politics," Putnam says. You, know, Kennedy did it, Reagan did it, probably Clinton '92 did it. We've got to do a better job talking across generational lines."

Ford was just 26, too, when he was elected to Congress in 1996. Young people were a central part of his first campaign. He visited more than 100 schools and spoke to an estimated 40,000 to 50,000 high school students en route to a landslide victory. "We've grown up in a different world," his chief of staff explained to reporters when asked about Ford's view of politics. "We're more comfortable with diversity, with change, with new ideas and new attitudes."

Age does not create a shared agenda, however, Putnam opposes many of the issues that young Americans support, including abortion rights. He also rejected MTV's request to film his first campaign by saying he didn't want any "purple-hair yahoo" asking whether he wore "boxers or briefs." But he does support Social Security reform, which is a key issue for young Americans who do not believe the program will still be alive when they retire.

Putnam and Ford do believe they can make a difference in showing that age is no barrier to participation. "I'm not invited to a high school class to articulate

Adam Putnam

Harold Ford, Jr.

the merits of permanent normal trade relations with China," Putnam says. "I'm invited to classes to talk about why it's important for young people to get involved and how they can do it." Ford agrees. "Once you get young people to pay attention, you find that you've turned on a faucet that's hard to turn off." The fact that these two Gen X'ers are in Congress is no small part of showing young Americans that age is not a barrier to involvement at the very top of American politics.

Members were supposed to specialize in a small number of issues (the norm of specialization), defer to members with longer tenure in office (the norm of seniority), never criticize anyone personally (the norm of courtesy), and wait their turn to speak and introduce legislation (the norm of apprenticeship). As longtime House Speaker Sam Rayburn once said, new members were to go along in order to get along, and to be seen and not heard.

The new norms are equally simple. New members are no longer willing to wait their turn to speak or introduce legislation and now have enough staff to make their opinions known on just about any issue at just about any point in the legislative process. Although the norm of courtesy still lives on as members refer to each other with great respect, the new congressional career allows little time for the old norms of specialization, seniority, and apprenticeship. Members must take care of their electoral concerns first.

Legislators as Representatives

Congress has a split personality. On the one hand, it is a *lawmaking institution* that writes laws and makes policy for the entire nation. In this capacity, all the members are expected to set aside their personal ambitions and perhaps even the concerns of their own constituencies. Yet Congress is also a *representative assembly,* made up of 535 elected officials who serve as links between their constituents and the national government (see Table 11–3). The dual roles of making laws and responding to constituents' demands force members to balance national concerns against the specific interests of their states or districts.

TABLE 11–3　PROFILE OF THE 108TH CONGRESS, 2003–2005

	Senate (100)	House (435)
Party Affiliation		
Republican	51	229
Democratic	48	205
Independent	1	1
Sex		
Male	86	373
Female	14	62
Religion		
Catholic	25	124
Jewish	11	26
Protestant	63	278
Other	1	7
Average Age	60	54
Racial/Ethnic Minorities	3	64
Occupational Field		
Law	60	161
Education	12	88
Business, banking	25	165
Agriculture	5	26
Journalism	6	11
Engineering	1	8
Real estate	3	30

Source: *Congressional Quarterly Weekly,* January 25, 2003, pp. 190–193.

Individual members of Congress perceive their roles differently. Some believe they should serve as **delegates** from their districts. These legislators believe it is their duty to find out what "the folks back home" want and act accordingly. Other members see their role as that of **trustee**. Their constituents, they contend, did not send them to Congress to serve as mere robots or "errand runners." They act and vote according to their own view of what is best for their district or state as well as the nation.

Most legislators shift back and forth between the delegate and trustee roles, depending on their perception of the public interest, their standing in the last and next elections, and the pressures of the moment. Most also view themselves more as free agents than as instructed delegates for their districts. And recent research suggests that they often *are* free, since about 50 percent of citizens are unaware of how their representatives voted on major legislation and often believe their representative voted in accordance with constituent policy views. Still, nearly everyone in Congress spends a lot of time building constituency connections, mending political fences, reaching out to swing voters, and worrying about how a vote on a controversial issue will "play" back home.[41]

Legislators as Lawmakers

About 5,000 bills are introduced in the House every two years and as many as 3,000 in the Senate. Members of Congress cast as many as 1,000 votes each year.[42] When they vote, members of Congress are influenced by their own philosophy and values, their perceptions of their constituents' interests, the views of their trusted colleagues and staff, their partisan ties, and party leaders, lobbyists, and the president.

delegate
An official who is expected to represent the views of his or her constituents even when personally holding different views; one interpretation of the role of the legislator.

trustee
An official who is expected to vote independently based on his or her judgment of the circumstances; one interpretation of the role of the legislator.

CHANGING FACE OF AMERICAN POLITICS

COMPARING MEMBERS

The *National Journal* is not the only publication to rate individual members of Congress. Interest groups often publish scorecards on key votes on important issues to their constituents. Consider how the U.S. Chamber of Commerce (conservative), the American Federation of Labor (AFL-CIO) (liberal), the National Right to Life Committee (conservative), and the National Abortion and Reproductive Rights Action League (NARAL) (liberal) rated four members of Congress on votes taken leading up to the 2002 election:

	Senator Richard Lugar (R.-Ind.)	Senator Mark Dayton (D.-Minn.)	Representative David Dreier (R.-Calif.)	Representative Barney Frank (D.-Mass.)
Chamber of Commerce	95%	45%	100%	26%
AFL-CIO	31	100	11	100
National Right to Life	33	0	100	0
NARAL	0	100	0	100

Source: *Congressional Quarterly Weekly,* April 19, 2003, p. 925.

POLICY AND PHILOSOPHICAL CONVICTIONS Members are influenced by their ideological beliefs most of the time. Their experiences and their attitudes about the role of government shape their convictions and help explain a lot of the differences in voting patterns.[43] A liberal on social issues is also likely to be a liberal on tax and national security issues. On controversial issues such as Social Security reform, tax cuts, or defense spending, knowing the general philosophical leanings of individual members provides a helpful guide both to how they make up their minds and how they will vote.

In 2003, the widely respected weekly report *National Journal* rated Barbara Boxer (D.–Calif.) as the most liberal senator and Pat Roberts (R.–Kansas) as the most conservative and rated John Conyers (D.–Mich.) and Pete Stark (D.–Calif.) as the most liberal representatives, while 13 members of the House tied as the most conservative. Although Democrats are more likely to be liberals and Republicans more likely to be conservatives, there are centrists in both parties. Almost all of the most liberal Democrats in the House and Senate come from western states, while almost all of the most conservative Republicans come from southern states.

VOTERS Rarely does a legislator consistently and deliberately vote against the wishes of the people back home, but a paradox is evident here. Members of Congress sometimes think that what they do and how they vote make a lot of difference to voters back home, even though most voters do not follow Congress closely.[44] Aside from periodic polls, members hear most often from the **attentive public**—citizens who follow public affairs carefully—rather than the general public. Nearly 70 percent of constituents say they have not visited, faxed, phoned, e-mailed, or written their member of Congress in the past four years.[45] Still, members of Congress are generally concerned about how they will explain their votes, especially as election day approaches. Even if only a few voters are aware of their stand on a given issue, this group might make the difference between victory and defeat.

COLLEAGUES Legislators are often influenced by the advice of their close friends in Congress. Their busy schedules and the great number of votes force them to depend on the advice of like-minded colleagues. In particular, they look to respected members of the committee who worked on a bill.[46] Legislators find out how their friends stand on an issue, listen to the party leadership's advice, and take the various committee reports into account. Sometimes members are influenced to vote one way merely because they know

attentive public
Those citizens who follow public affairs carefully.

a colleague is on the other side of the issue. For some legislators, the state delegation (senators and representatives from their home state) reinforces a common identity.

A member may also vote with a colleague in the expectation that the colleague will later vote for a measure about which the member is concerned—called **logrolling**. Some vote trading takes place to build coalitions so that members can "bring home the bacon" to their constituents. Other vote trading reflects reciprocity in congressional relations or deference to colleagues' superior information or expertise.

CONGRESSIONAL STAFF   Representatives and senators used to be at a distinct disadvantage in dealing with the executive branch because they were overly dependent on information supplied by the White House or lobbyists. The complexity of the issues and increasingly demanding schedules created pressures for additional staff. Congress responded and gradually expanded its staffs, and this expansion has strengthened the role of Congress in the public policy process.

Because both chambers have roughly equal amounts of money for staff, Senate members and committees have much larger staffs than their House counterparts. About one-third of the House of Representatives staff and one-fourth of the Senate staff are based back home, where they help their bosses communicate with voters and provide constituency services and casework. (Helping people with a misplaced Social Security check or helping them qualify for veterans' benefits are examples of casework provided by congressional offices.) Much of the work done in district offices is akin to a continuous campaign effort: generating favorable publicity, arranging for local appearances and newspaper interviews, scheduling, and contacting important civic and business leaders in the region.

Members rely heavily on the advice of congressional staffers. Staff members draft bills, do research, and are often involved in negotiating and coalition building. Staff specialists in policy areas sometimes deal on a day-to-day basis with their counterparts in the executive branch departments and with interest groups. With their direct access to the members of Congress they serve, these staff aides are often among the most influential people in Washington.

PARTY   Members generally vote with their party. Whether as a result of party pressure or natural affinity, on major bills there is a tendency for most Democrats to be arrayed against most Republicans. Partisan voting has increased in the House since the early 1970s and has intensified even more since the 1994 elections. Indeed, party-line voting has been greater in recent years than at any time in recent decades. Party differences are stronger over domestic, regulatory, and welfare reform measures than over foreign policy or civil liberties issues. Ninety-eight percent of House Republicans, for example, voted to impeach Bill Clinton in a historic vote in late 1998; the same percentage of House Democrats voted *against* impeachment.

Congressional redistricting has helped increase partisanship in congressional voting. "Advances in computer-driven mapping capabilities have made an art form of the old-fashioned gerrymandering that occurs where congressional districts are redrawn after each decennial census." Party operatives in the states can with great precision draw district lines to create relatively safe Democratic or Republican districts, "increasing the number of secure members answerable to only their own party's primary votes."[47]

As redistricting has created more safe seats, the House of Representatives has become more polarized. House Republicans have become more politically conservative and House Democrats more liberal. The House is more politically partisan than the Senate not because of personalities but largely because of these constitutional-political procedures. As House districts have become more distinctly and safely Republican or Democratic, the incentives for compromise have declined.

Party leaders in both chambers do their best to get their members to vote together. Republican leaders claim that cohesive voting is the only way Republicans can implement their party platform and satisfy the majorities who elected them in recent years. Senators are usually more independent, so party leaders in the Senate have a harder time maintaining party discipline than leaders in the House do.

logrolling
Mutual aid and vote trading among legislators.

U.S. Senator James Jeffords of Vermont, on the steps of the Capitol with prominent Democrats the day before he left the Republican Party to become an Independent. Jeffords's decision gave the Democrats control of the Senate until 2003. He left the Republican Party because he believed it had grown too conservative and was putting undue pressure on him to vote the party line.

INTEREST GROUPS   Interest groups use Political Action Committees (PACs) to contribute campaign funds to congressional candidates. These PACs give disproportionately to incumbents; at least 70 percent of PAC contributions have gone to incumbents in recent years.[48] In addition to their role as financiers of elections, interest groups provide important information for making laws.

Interest groups not only watch and try to influence national legislators but also monitor one another. If a member of Congress tries to insert a "special interest" measure into an appropriations bill that is especially favorable to a particular interest, for example, opposing interest groups are almost certain to lobby for the measure's defeat. "The result," says Senator Joe Lieberman of Connecticut, "is that everyone on Capitol Hill is keeping a close eye on everyone else, creating a self-adjusting system of checks and balances."[49]

Interest groups can also be effective when they mobilize grassroots activists and rally various constituencies to lobby their home state members of Congress. For example, higher education lobbying groups have effectively mobilized students and educators to write and call members of Congress on behalf of student aid and related provisions in various measures before Congress.[50] And tobacco companies spent large sums to fight taxes on cigarettes. Although most members of Congress reject the popular perception that interest groups "buy" their votes, political contributions certainly do influence the parties and help provide access to members of Congress.

THE PRESIDENT   Through effective use of their constitutional and political powers, presidents are usually partners with Congress in the legislative process. In fact, the president is often the single most important (though not always decisive) force in determining the course of legislation.

Members of Congress, however, are invariably reluctant to admit that they are influenced by pressure from the White House. On domestic issues, legislators generally say they are more likely to be influenced by their own convictions or by their constituents than by what the White House wants. But presidents and their aides work hard to influence public opinion and to win members over to the president's point of view. For example, despite a Democratic majority in the Senate and a razor-thin Republican majority in the House, George W. Bush won an impressive 87 percent support from Congress on the 120 votes on which he took a clear position in 2001. That was the best success mark since 1965, when Lyndon Johnson won 93 percent of the key votes.[51]

Bush set the mark in part by taking fewer strong positions on legislation. Whereas Bill Clinton took a position on an average of 86 House votes a year during his eight years in office, Bush took a position on only 43 House bills in 2001. Moreover, when Bush did take a position, it was mostly in favor of bills that Congress was about to pass. Nevertheless, Bush's support scores remained high; in 2002, he won 88 percent of his votes, while in 2003, he won 78 percent.

For a variety of reasons, especially because of the tendency of the nation to rally around the president in time of foreign crisis, presidents have more influence on how members of Congress vote on foreign policy or national security issues than on domestic policy.[52] President George W. Bush benefited from a bipartisan coalition that passed the resolution authorizing the use of military force against terrorist forces in Afghanistan, for example.

THE LEGISLATIVE OBSTACLE COURSE

Congress operates under a system of multiple vetoes. The framers intentionally dispersed powers so that no would-be tyrant or majority could accumulate enough authority to oppress the nation. Follow a bill through the legislative process, and this dispersal of power is clear (see Figure 11–2). The procedures and rules of the Senate differ somewhat from those of the House, but in each chamber, power is fragmented and decentralized.

How Ideas Become Bills

Members introduce bills for different reasons. Although many bills are introduced to help win reelection or higher office, members of Congress do care about the national interest. As Democratic representative Tim Penny of Minnesota said of his decision to run for Congress, "I was young and idealistic. . . . I wanted to show people that government can work and that partisanship doesn't have to be the dominant force in politics, that interest groups don't have to be a deciding factor on every vote."[53]

Members also care about making a personal difference. "Politicians are human beings," said Massachusetts representative Joe Kennedy II, whose father was assassinated with a handgun during the 1968 presidential campaign and whose cousin suffered from bone cancer. "When there is a degree of very personal pain that one feels toward an issue—it might be gun control or my uncle's interest in fighting cancer—commitment level is higher and your willingness to compromise is lower."[54]

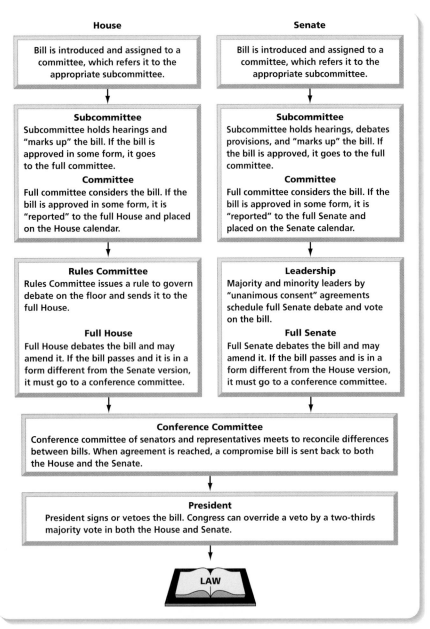

FIGURE 11–2 How a Bill Becomes a Law.

How Bills Become Laws

The odds against a bill's becoming a law are great, but Congress still produces an extraordinary amount of legislation. In 2003, a typical year, members of Congress introduced a total of 7,000 bills (4,600 in the House and 2,400 in the Senate). Of those, committees in one or the other chamber sent 727 bills to the floor for further consideration, of which the Senate passed 590 and the House passed 674; 174 of those were approved by both chambers and signed into law. Congress is obviously very selective about which bills survive.[55]

A bill must win many small contests on the way to final passage. There are four broad steps from beginning to end: (1) introduction, which involves putting a formal proposal before the House or the Senate; (2) committee review, which involves holding a hearing and "marking up" the bill; (3) floor debate and passage, which means getting on the legislative calendar, passing once in each chamber, surviving a conference to iron out any differences between the House and Senate versions, and passing once again in each chamber; and (4) presidential approval.

INTRODUCING A BILL   House members introduce a bill by placing it into a mahogany box (called the hopper) on a desk at the front of the House chamber; senators introduce a bill by either handing it to the clerk of the Senate or by presenting it to their colleagues in a floor speech. In the more informal Senate, members sometimes short-circuit the formalities by offering a bill as an amendment to pending legislation. A bill that comes from the House is always designated H.R. (House of Representatives) followed by its number, and a bill from the Senate is always designated S. (Senate) followed by its number. Although presidents often recommend legislation to Congress, all bills must be introduced by a member of the House or Senate.

COMMITTEE REVIEW   Once a bill is introduced in either chamber, it is "read" into the record as a formal proposal and referred to the appropriate committee—tax bills to Ways and Means or Finance; farm bills to Agriculture; technology bills to Science, Space, and Technology; small business to Small Business; and so forth. The parliamentarian in each chamber decides where to send each bill.

WHO CAN KILL A BILL

The complexity of the congressional system provides a tremendous built-in advantage for opponents of any measure. Multiple opportunities to kill a bill exist because of the dispersion of influence. At a dozen or more points, a bill may be stopped or allowed to die (inaction is the same as killing a bill). Sponsors of a bill must win at every step; opponents need to win only once. Whether good or bad, a proposal can be delayed or rejected by any one of the following:

1. The chair of the House subcommittee
2. The House subcommittee as a whole
3. The chair of the House standing committee
4. The House standing committee as a whole
5. The House Rules Committee
6. The majority of the House
7. The chair of the Senate subcommittee
8. The Senate subcommittee as a whole
9. The chair of the Senate standing committee
10. The Senate standing committee as a whole
11. A senator or senators who mount a filibuster
12. The majority of the Senate
13. The floor leaders in both chambers
14. The House-Senate conference committee, if the chambers disagree
15. The president (by veto)

BELOW THE BELTWAY

discharge petition
Petition that, if signed by a majority of the members of the House of Representatives, will pry a bill from committee and bring it to the floor for consideration.

rider
A provision attached to a bill—to which it may or may not be related—in order to secure its passage.

pocket veto
A veto exercised by the president after Congress has adjourned; if the president takes no action for ten days, the bill does not become law and is not returned to Congress for a possible override.

override
An action taken by Congress to reverse a presidential veto, requiring a two-thirds majority in each chamber.

The Referral Decision   Although most bills are referred to a single committee, particularly complex bills may be referred simultaneously or sequentially to multiple committees. President Bush's proposed department of homeland security bill was so complicated and touched so many agencies that it was managed by a temporary special committee in the House. The bill was referred to at least ten committees, including Judiciary, Ways and Means, and Government Reform, all of which held hearings on specific provisions of the largest government reorganization since the Department of Defense was created in 1947. The bill went into the House as a 35-page proposal and came out almost 500 pages long. Committees and their subcommittees are responsible for building a legislative record in support of a given bill. This *legislative record* also helps the president and federal courts interpret what Congress intended.

Markup   Once a committee or subcommittee decides to pass the bill, it "marks it up" to clean up the wording or amend its version of the bill. The term *markup* refers to the pencil marks that members make on the final version of the bill. Once markup is over, the bill must be passed by the committee or subcommittee and forwarded to the next step in the process. If it is passed by a subcommittee, for example, it is forwarded to the full committee; if it is passed by a full committee in the House, it is then forwarded to the House Rules Committee for a rule that will govern debate on the floor; if it is passed by a full committee in the Senate, it is forwarded to the full chamber.

Discharge   Although most bills die in committee without a hearing or further review, a bill can be forced to the floor of the House through a **discharge petition** signed by a majority of the membership. In 2002, for example, House members were able to collect enough signatures to discharge the Rules Committee on a campaign finance reform bill that had been stalled for six months. Because most members share a strong sense of reciprocity, or mutual respect, toward the work of other committees, few discharge petitions are successful. The Senate does not use discharge petitions.

FLOOR DEBATE AND PASSAGE   Once reported to the full chamber directly from committee in the Senate or through the Rules Committee in the House, a bill will either be scheduled for floor action or dropped entirely, depending on the party leadership and the amount of time left in the session. The busiest time of the year occurs just before the end of a session, usually in late September or early October, when bills must be passed or die.

In the Senate, it is not uncommon for members to propose **riders**, or amendments, that are unrelated to the bill on which they want to ride. Senators use riders to force the president to accept legislation attached to a bill that was otherwise popular, because the president has to either accept the *entire* bill or to veto it. The number of riders attached to appropriations bills has increased in recent years. Democrats and Republicans alike use riders to increase spending in their states and districts.[56]

Except for tax bills, the House and Senate discuss bills simultaneously rather than waiting for one to act first. If only one chamber passes a bill at the end of the two years that comprise each Congress, it is dead and must be reintroduced in the next Congress. If both houses pass bills on the same subject but there are differences between the bills—and there often are—the two versions must go to a conference committee for *reconciliation*. If a bill does not make it through both chambers in identical form in the same two-year Congress, it must begin the entire process again in the next Congress.

When a bill has passed both houses in identical form, it goes to the president, who may *sign* it into law or *veto* it. If Congress is in session and the president waits ten days (not counting Sundays), the bill becomes law *without* his signature. If Congress has adjourned and the president waits ten days without signing the bill, it is defeated by what is known as a **pocket veto**. After a pocket veto, the bill is dead. Otherwise, when a bill is vetoed, it is returned to the chamber of its origin by the president with a message explaining the reasons for the veto. Congress can vote to **override** the veto by a two-thirds vote in each chamber, but assembling such an extraordinary majority is often difficult.

The Importance of Compromise

Since it takes a majority vote in two chambers of Congress and the signature of the president before a bill becomes a law, sponsors of new legislation have to be willing to compromise. One tactical decision at the start is whether to push for action in the Senate first, in the House first, or in both simultaneously. For example, if it appears that the Senate is not likely to approve a bill, its sponsors may seek passage in the House and hope that a sizable victory there will spur the Senate into action. Another tactic concerns the committee that will consider a bill. Normally, referral to a committee is automatic, but sometimes sponsors have discretion. A bill that involves more than one jurisdiction can be written in such a way that it may go to a committee that will look on it more kindly.[57]

AN ASSESSMENT OF CONGRESS

More than two centuries after its creation, Congress is a larger, more vital, and very different kind of institution from the one the framers envisioned. Yet most of its major functions remain the same, and their effective exercise is crucial to the health of our constitutional democracy. Even in the twenty-first century, we still look to Congress to make laws, raise revenues, represent citizens, investigate abuses of power, and oversee the executive branch.

Although most incumbents are easily reelected, most campaign constantly to stay in office, creating what some observers have called the "permanent campaign." Members appear driven by their desire to win reelection, so that much of what takes place in Congress seems mainly designed to promote reelection. These efforts usually pay off for members of Congress: Members who seek reelection almost always win. At the same time, these efforts also pay off for our democracy. Members' concern with reelection fosters *accountability* and the desire to please the voters.

Yet, the permanent campaign clearly hinders legislative progress. In an institution where most members act as individual entrepreneurs and consider themselves leaders,

★★ THINKING IT THROUGH

The Constitution requires the Senate to give its advice and consent on nominations, but not a final vote. Senators argue that controversial nominees demand particularly close attention because of the potential harm they could do once in office, particularly if they hold lifetime appointments in the federal courts. Moreover, they argue that holds and filibusters do not prevent an up-or-down vote if the Senate can muster the 60 votes to remove a hold and end a filibuster. These ten extra votes are more difficult to find, especially when the Senate is closely divided between the two parties, but the process ensures that controversial nominees face an additional check before taking their posts.

On Tuesday, September 11, 2001, the leadership of the House of Representatives and the Senate gathered on the steps of the Capitol with other congressional members in a gesture of unity after the terrorist attacks.

RUNNING FOR CONGRESS

Deciding to run for Congress involves a variety of calculations. Potential candidates need to decide whether they want to take on an entrenched incumbent (difficult), run for an open seat (easier), or take on a vulnerable incumbent (easier still). They also need to ask whether they have enough funding, name recognition, and campaigning ability to mount a credible campaign, and whether their beliefs fit the prevailing opinions of their district. Once they have made the decision to run, candidates must also decide where to spend their money, how to spend their time, and what issues to emphasize. As the simulation on running for Congress shows, winning against incumbents is not easy, which helps explain why so many incumbents are reelected.

Go to Make It Real: Running for Congress.

the task of providing institutional leadership is increasingly difficult. With limited resources, and only sometimes aided by the president, congressional leaders are asked to bring together a diverse, fragmented, and independent institution. The congressional system acts only when majorities can be achieved. That the framers accomplished their original objective—creating a body that would not move with imprudent haste—has been generally well realized.

Newly elected presidents and members of Congress always arrive in Washington enthusiastically ready to enact the people's wishes. But they find that governing is invariably tougher and slower than they expected because government deals with complex issues about which there is often little consensus. Building policy majorities is hard because complex problems generate complex solutions, and the structure of Congress requires supermajorities to agree to serious changes. Thus the president's veto, the filibuster, and the use of holds and legislative riders all make consensus more difficult to find.

Criticism of Congress—its alleged incompetence, its overresponsiveness to organized interests, its inefficiencies, its partisan character—is difficult to separate from the context of policy preferences and democratic procedures. Sometimes criticism tells us more about the critic than it does about the effectiveness of Congress. Constitutional democracy is not the most efficient form of government. Congress was never intended to act swiftly; it was not created to be a rubber stamp or even a cooperative partner for presidents. Its greatest strengths—its diversity and deliberative character—also weaken its position in dealing with the more centralized executive branch.

The framers would not be troubled by the lack of action, however. By dividing power, they hoped to control it. The odds against action are high precisely because the framers did not want any one branch of the government to become a threat to individual liberty.

S U M M A R Y

1. Congress plays a crucial role in our system of shared powers, controlling key decisions and constraining presidents. Yet over time, Congress has lost some influence as the presidency has gained influence. In recent decades, however, Congress has become more capable as a policy-making competitor for presidents. Redistricting and reapportionment have shaped a Congress that somewhat more accurately reflects the population.

2. The most distinctive feature of Congress is its bicameralism, which the framers intended as a moderating influence on partisanship and possible error. Each chamber has a few distinctive functions. The organization and procedures of the two houses also differ slightly, as do their political environments.

3. Congress performs these functions: representation, lawmaking, consensus building, overseeing the bureaucracy, policy clarification, and investigating. The Senate also confirms or denies presidential appointments and participates in the ratification of treaties.

4. Congress manages its workload through a leadership system that is different in both chambers. The House is led by the Speaker, a majority and a minority leader, and whips in each party, while the Senate is led by a majority and a minority leader. The Senate is more difficult to lead because of its greater individualism, which is sometimes expressed through the use of holds and filibusters to control the legislative process.

5. Most of the work in Congress is done in committees and subcommittees. Congress has attempted in recent years to streamline its committee system and modify its methods of selecting committee chairs. Seniority practices are still generally followed. Subcommittees are important. They can prevent or delay legislation from being enacted. But there are numerous other stages where bills can be killed, making it easier to stop legislation than to enact it.

6. As a collective body, Congress must attempt to accomplish its tasks even as most of its members serve as delegates or trustees for their constituents. When they vote, members are influenced by their philosophy and values, their perceptions of constituents' interests, and the views of trusted colleagues and staff, partisan ties and party leaders, lobbyists, and the president.

7. The members of Congress do an excellent job of representing the values and views of most of their constituents. But they are cautious about enacting proposed measures by their own colleagues or the legislative agenda put forward by presidents. Most proposed legislation dies for lack of majority support.

8. Members of Congress are motivated by the desire to win reelection, and much of what Congress does is in response to this motive. Members work hard to get favors for their districts, to serve the needs of constituents, and to maintain a high visibility in their districts or states. Incumbents have advantages that help explain their success at reelection: They have greater name recognition, they have large staffs, they are much better able to raise campaign money, and they have greater access to the media.

9. A bill becomes a law through a process that involves many opportunities for defeat. Although all formal bills are referred to committees for consideration, very few receive a hearing, even fewer are marked up and sent to the floor, and fewer still are enacted by both chambers and signed into law by the president. In

addition, the legislative obstacle course sometimes involves filibusters, riders, holds, and the occasional override of a presidential veto.

10. Individual members of Congress are more popular than the institution. Congress is criticized for being inefficient, unrepresentative, unethical, and lacking in collective responsibility. Yet criticisms of Congress are difficult to separate from the context of policy preference and democratic procedures. Congress's greatest strengths—its diversity and its deliberative character—also contribute to its weaknesses.

KEY TERMS

reapportionment	majority leader	filibuster	delegate
redistricting	minority leader	cloture	trustee
gerrymandering	whip	senatorial courtesy	attentive public
safe seat	party caucus	standing committee	logrolling
incumbents	closed rule	special or select committee	discharge petition
bicameralism	open rule	joint committee	rider
enumerated powers	president pro tempore	seniority rule	pocket veto
Speaker	hold	conference committee	override

FURTHER READING

JOEL D. ABERBACH, *Keeping a Watchful Eye: The Politics of Congressional Oversight* (Brookings Institution Press, 1990).

E. SCOTT ADLER, *Why Congressional Reforms Fail: Reelection and the House Committee System* (University of Chicago Press, 2002).

SARAH A. BINDER AND STEVEN S. SMITH, *Politics or Principles? Filibustering in the United States Senate* (Brookings Institution Press, 1997).

SARAH A. BINDER, *Stalemate: Causes and Consequences of Legislative Gridlock* (Brookings Institution Press, 2003).

BILL BRADLEY, *Time Present, Time Past: A Memoir* (Knopf, 1996).

DAVID W. BRADY AND CRAIG VOLDEN, *Revolving Gridlock: Politics and Policy from Carter to Clinton* (Westview Press, 1998).

ADAM CLYMER, *Edward M. Kennedy: A Biography* (Morrow, 1999).

ROGER H. DAVIDSON AND WALTER J. OLESZEK, *Congress and Its Members*, 8th ed. (CQ Press, 2002).

CHRISTOPHER J. DEERING AND STEVEN S. SMITH, *Committees in Congress*, 3d ed. (CQ Press, 1997).

LAWRENCE C. DODD AND BRUCE J. OPPEN-HEIMER, EDS., *Congress Reconsidered*, 5th ed. (CQ Press, 1993).

RICHARD F. FENNO JR., *Home Style: House Members in Their Districts* (Little, Brown, 1978).

RICHARD F. FENNO JR., *Learning to Govern: An Institutional View of the 104th Congress* (Brookings Institution Press, 1997).

RICHARD F. FENNO JR., *Senators on the Campaign Trail: The Politics of Representation* (University of Oklahoma Press, 1996).

MORRIS P. FIORINA, *Congress: Keystone of the Washington Establishment*, 2d ed. (Yale University Press, 1989).

PAUL HERRNSON, *Congressional Elections*, 3d ed. (CQ Press, 2000).

JOHN R. HIBBING AND ELIZABETH THEISS-MORSE, *Congress as Public Enemy: Public Attitudes Toward American Political Institutions* (Cambridge University Press, 1995).

GODFREY HODGSON, *The Gentleman from New York: Daniel Patrick Moynihan* (Houghton Mifflin, 2000).

LINDA KILLIAN, *The Freshmen: What Happened to the Republican Revolution?* (Westview Press, 1998).

FRANCES E. LEE AND BRUCE I. OPPEN-HEIMER, *Sizing Up the Senate: The Unequal Consequences of Equal Representation* (University of Chicago Press, 1999).

JOSEPH I. LIEBERMAN, *In Praise of Public Life* (Simon & Schuster, 2000).

TOM LOFTUS, *The Art of Legislative Politics* (CQ Press, 1994).

JANET M. MARTIN, *Lessons from the Hill: The Legislative Journey of an Education Program* (St. Martin's Press, 1993).

DAVID R. MAYHEW, *America's Congress: Actions in the Public Sphere, James Madison Through Newt Gingrich* (Yale University Press, 2002).

BARBARA MIKULSKI ET AL., *Nine and Counting: The Women of the Senate* (Morrow, 2000).

WALTER J. OLESZEK, *Congressional Procedures and the Policy Process*, 4th ed. (CQ Press, 1995).

NORMAN J. ORNSTEIN, THOMAS MANN, AND MICHAEL MALBIN, *Vital Statistics on Congress, 2000–2002* (AEI Press, 2002).

RONALD M. PETERS JR., ED., *The Speaker: Leadership in the U.S. House of Representatives* (CQ Press, 1995).

DAVID E. PRICE, *The Congressional Experience: A View from the Hill* (Westview Press, 1993).

NICOL RAE AND COLTON CAMPBELL, EDS., *New Majority or Old Majority: The Impact of Republicans on Congress* (Rowman & Littlefield, 1999).

WARREN B. RUDMAN, *Combat: Twelve Years in the U.S. Senate* (Random House, 1996).

BARBARA SINCLAIR, *Unorthodox Lawmaking: New Legislative Processes in the U.S. Congress*, 2d ed. (CQ Press, 2000).

DARVELL M. WEST, *Patrick Kennedy: The Rise to Power* (Prentice Hall, 2001).

THE PRESIDENCY
THE LEADERSHIP BRANCH

12

The framers of the Constitution both admired and feared centralized leadership. Although they knew the country needed a more effective national government led by a single executive, they worried about the potential abuse of power if it were invested in a single executive. Having lived under the tyranny of the English monarchy, they had every right to worry. They wanted a president powerful enough to lead the nation during periods of domestic and international crisis, but they also wanted checks on his power.

Americans saw both sides of presidential power in the months and weeks leading up to the war with Iraq. President Bush began making the case for war in the summer of 2002 when he accused Saddam Hussein of hiding weapons of mass destruction that could be used against the United States. "If we wait for threats to fully materialize, we will have waited too long," Bush warned in a speech to graduates of West Point. "The war on terror will not be won on the defensive. We must take the battle to the enemy, disrupt his plans, and confront the worst threats before they emerge."

Congress eventually gave Bush authority to lauch a preemptive attack against Iraq. However, support was far from unanimous. Although Bush's request passed 296 to 133 in the House, and 77 to 23 in the Senate, many members of Congress urged the president to build the same broad multinational coalition of support that his father had rallied before the first Gulf War in 1991. Some also questioned the need for urgency, demanding hard evidence that the weapons of mass destruction, or WMD, actually existed.

TIME LINE

THE PRESIDENCY

1789	First president elected: George Washington, who was also the first to invoke executive privilege
1861	Lincoln suspends *Habeas corpus* for secessionists
1868	Johnson impeached but acquitted by one vote in the Senate
1901	McKinley assassinated by an anarchist
1932	FDR is elected to the first of a record four terms
1945	FDR casts the last of 635 vetoes—the most by any president
1963	JFK assassination shocks the nation
1970	OMB created to centralize presidential control over bureaucracy
1973	War Powers Act limits president's authority to commit troops without a declaration of war by Congress
1974	Nixon resigns before impeachment over Watergate scandal
1983	Supreme Court rules legislative vetoes unconstitutional
1986	Iran-Contra scandal exposes illegal diversion of secret funds
1998	Clinton impeached by House but acquitted by Senate
2000	Supreme Court rules that Florida can certify George W. Bush as the winner of the state's electoral votes, thereby securing his election as president

Americans were far from unanimous about the war, too. Although they initially gave the president strong support for action, their doubts increased as the nation moved closer to war. In August 2002, for example, 64 percent of Americans favored military action against Iraq, while only 21 percent were opposed; just before the war began in March 2003, 59 percent still favored action, while 30 percent were opposed. Moreover, of the 59 percent who favored war in March, more than a third supported action only if the United States had international support.[1]

Although Americans did rally behind the president when the war actually began, and rallied again after Saddam Hussein's capture the following December, they continued to worry about the cost of the war in both lives and money. So did Congress. Less than a year after the start of the war, Congress had launched a major investigation of the failure to find any weapons of mass destruction, asking hard questions about why the president and vice president could have been so sure Iraq actually posed an immediate threat to the United States.

These concerns clearly acted as a check on the Bush administration's plans. The administration accelerated its timetable for turning over power to the Iraqi people in response to public pressure, and it eventually created a national commission to investigate the questionable intelligence that had led to war. Thus, even though opponents of the war had been in the minority, they had been able to check the president's power, which is exactly how the framers intended the system to act.

This chapter will explore the presidential balancing act in more detail. We will start by reviewing the structure and powers of the presidency, then ask what Americans expect from the president, examine how presidents manage the presidency, outline the presidential job description, and conclude with a discussion of the ingredients of presidential greatness.

THE STRUCTURE AND POWERS OF THE PRESIDENCY

Just as the Constitution gives Congress the lawmaking power of the United States in the first sentence of Article I, it gives the president the executive power in the first sentence of Article II. The executive power includes everything from the president's role as commander in chief of the army and navy to broad responsibility for faithful execution of the nation's laws. It also provides the basic authority the president needs to oversee the federal bureaucracy, develop recommendations for spending money, and select the senior appointees of government.

Having given this executive responsibility to a single person, the framers insulated the presidency from public passions. To this day, for example, presidents are not elected by the public, but by electors who are selected in winner-take-all systems in all but two states, Maine and Nebraska. As a result, presidents often claim to speak for the entire nation, not a single district or state.

At the same time, the framers created a presidency of limited powers. They wanted a presidential office that would steer clear of parties and factions, enforce the laws passed by Congress, handle communications with foreign governments, and help states put down disorders. They wanted a presidency strong enough to match Congress yet not so strong that it would overpower Congress.

Separate Powers

The framers created a system of separate powers that prevents any one branch from controlling all of government. However, merely having three branches of national government—legislative, executive, and judicial—does not by itself create a pure system of separated powers; the United Kingdom also has legislative and executive branches, but both are automatically headed by the same political party.

In the United States, the legislative, executive, and judicial branches are all independent from one another. Although there are times when the legislative and executive branch are headed by the same political party, there is nothing automatic about unified government—it can exist only if voters in enough states and districts vote for the same party over enough elections to control the House, Senate, and presidency.

The United States is one of the few world powers that is neither a parliamentary democracy nor a wholly executive-dominated government. Our Constitution plainly invites both Congress and the president to set policy and govern the nation. Leadership and policy change are encouraged only when Congress and the president, and sometimes the courts along with them, concur on the desirability of new directions.

The president and Congress are legitimate participants in a whole range of policy activities. Triumphs for a president acting alone in a system of separated powers are rare. "Whenever powers are shared, attention must be devoted to the other decision makers," writes political scientist Charles O. Jones. "How do they view the problem? What are their present commitments? On what basis will they compromise? The test in a separated system is not simply one of presidential success. It is rather one of achievement by the system, with presidents and members of Congress inextricably bonded and similarly judged."[2]

Defining the Presidency

The framers' most important decision about the presidency was also their first. Meeting on June 1, 1787, the Constitutional Convention decided that there would be a single executive. Despite worries that a single president might lay the groundwork for a future monarchy, the framers also believed that the new government needed energy in the executive. They were willing to increase the risk of tyranny in return for some efficiency.

In Comparative Perspective

THE MEXICAN PRESIDENT

Mexican President Vicente Fox.

The Mexican president is one of the most powerful executives in the democratic world. Under the constitution of 1917, which was adopted after a decade of civil war, the president was given sweeping powers to run the country, including authority to hire and fire most government employees. Unlike the U.S. system, the Mexican legislature and judiciary have little power to check the presidency.

Elected by popular vote, the president holds the titles of chief of state, head of government, and commander in chief of the armed forces, and serves without a vice president. The president must be at least 35 years old on election day and cannot have been on active duty in the military during the six months preceding election. This latter provision was designed to prevent military officers from taking control of the government.

Because Mexican presidents can serve only for one six-year term, they have sometimes been called the most powerful "six-year monarchs" in the world. If the office becomes vacant during the first two years of a *sexenio*, or term, the congress appoints an interim president and holds a special election; if it becomes vacant in the final four years, the congress appoints a provisional president to serve out the term.

For 71 years from 1929 to 2000, the presidency was controlled by a single political party that the Mexican government created itself, the Institutional Revolutionary Party, or PRI. With party control ensured from term to term, presidents controlled the right to select their own successors through the *dedazo*, or tap. Although PRI candidates often faced opposition in the general election, the party earned a well-deserved reputation as the world's most efficient election machine.

Mexico took a dramatic step toward a more democratic system in 2000 when the nation elected Vicente Fox as president. A former Coca-Cola executive who ousted Pepsi as Mexico's favorite soft-drink, Fox drew upon his populist roots as a rancher from the rural state of Guanajuato, saying he was the only candidate who had ever milked a cow. But he also drew upon Mexico's desire for a change from one-party rule. "From today forward, we need to unite," he said at a victory rally in 2000. "Let's celebrate today, because beginning tomorrow there's a lot of work to do." Fox will have all the powers of the presidency to do so.

The Bush–Gore election in 2000 was so close that the role of the electoral college was brought into focus for the first time in years. On December 18, 2000, Alabama's nine Republican electors cast their votes for President-elect Bush.

Once past this first decision, the framers had to decide just how independent that executive would be from the rest of the national government, which in turn meant finding an appropriate method of selection or election. Had they wanted Congress to select the president from among its members, the framers would have created a **parliamentary system** of government that would look more like the English system.

The convention was initially divided on how the president would be selected. A small number of delegates favored direct election by the people, which Pennsylvania's James Wilson thought would ensure that the president was completely independent of Congress. Convinced that the nation was too diverse to handle direct election and afraid that states might join together to support regional candidates who would favor their part of the country, the delegates never seriously considered direct election. A larger number of delegates favored selection by Congress, tying the president more closely to the legislative branch.

Eventually, the framers compromised by creating an electoral college: Voters would cast their ballots for competing slates of electors, who would in turn cast their electoral votes for president. It might be called a form of indirect direct election. The framers also gave the executive a four-year term of office, further balancing the House (two-year term) and Senate (six-year term). Although they were silent on the number of terms a president could serve, the nation's first president, George Washington, quickly established a two-term precedent, which held until Franklin Roosevelt's historic four-term presidency from 1932 to 1945. The Twenty-Second Amendment to the Constitution, ratified in 1951, restored Washington's precedent by limiting presidents to two terms.

The framers also created the position of vice president just in case the president left office before the end of the term. With little debate, the founders decided to give the vice president the power to break tie votes in the Senate. Otherwise, the vice president has no constitutional duties but to wait for the president to be incapacitated or otherwise unable to discharge the powers and duties of the presidency.

The framers also established three simple qualifications for both offices. Under the Constitution, the president and vice president must be (1) at least thirty-five years old; (2) natural-born citizens of the United States, as opposed to immigrants who become

parliamentary system
A system of government in which the legislature selects the prime minister or president.

citizens by applying to the U.S. government for naturalization; and (3) residents of the United States for the previous fourteen years. The citizenship and residency requirements were designed to prevent a popular foreign-born citizen from capturing the office.

The Presidential Ticket

With this basic structure in place, the framers had to decide how the vice president would be selected. Once again, they created a remarkable electoral arrangement: The candidate who received the most electoral college votes would become president, and the candidate who came in second would become vice president.

It did not take long for the framers to discover the problem with this runner-up rule. The 1796 election produced Federalist President John Adams and Democratic-Republican Vice President Thomas Jefferson. Because the two disagreed so sharply about the future of the country, Jefferson was rendered virtually irrelevant to government.

This rule created a constitutional crisis in 1800. The election could not have been more important, for it occurred during a time of rising public anger about the nation's direction. With the Federalist party fading quickly in the wake of the Alien and Sedition Acts and growing anti-British sentiments, two Democratic-Republicans, Thomas Jefferson and Aaron Burr, emerged from the 1800 election with exactly 73 electoral votes each, leaving Federalist John Adams behind with just 63. With the election now thrown to the House of Representatives under the Constitution's tie-breaking rules, the nation teetered on the edge of a constitutional crisis for 36 ballots before Jefferson was finally elected. His vice president was none other than Aaron Burr, the candidate whom he had just defeated.

The problem was solved under the Twelfth Amendment, which was ratified in 1804. Under the new process, electors are allowed to cast two votes, one for president and one for vice president, thereby encouraging the two candidates to run together as a **presidential ticket.**

Presidential Powers

Article II of the Constitution begins even more simply than Article I: "The executive Power shall be vested in a President of the United States of America." Some experts argue that the executive power covers almost everything not granted to the legislature or judiciary, while others believe that the president's relatively short list of enumerated powers suggests that the framers wanted a more limited executive.[3] Although short, Article II does address foreign threats and the day-to-day operations of government, establishing the president's authority to play three central roles in the new government: (1) commander in chief, (2) diplomat in chief, and (3) administrator in chief.

COMMANDER IN CHIEF   The Constitution explicitly states that the president is to be commander in chief of the army and navy. It is a fundamental expression of the president's role in protecting the nation as a whole. The framers saw the president as the commander in chief but were divided over which branch would both declare and make war.[4]

The framers initially agreed that Congress would make war, raise armies, build and equip fleets, enforce treaties, and suppress and repel invasions, but eventually changed the phrase "make war" to "declare war." But they limited the presidential war power by giving to Congress as a whole the power to appropriate money for the purchase of arms and military pay, and to the Senate, responsibility to approve higher-level military promotion. Although they also gave Congress sole authority to declare war, recent presidents have used their power as commander in chief to order U.S. troops into battle without formal declarations dozens of times over the past century, including the recent wars in Afghanistan and Iraq.

DIPLOMAT IN CHIEF   Article II also makes the president negotiator in chief of treaties with foreign nations, which must be presented to the Senate and approved by a two-thirds vote. A **treaty** is a binding and public agreement between the United States and one or more nations that requires mutual action on the part of the signatories. Although

presidential ticket
The joint listing of the presidential and vice presidential candidates on the same ballot as required by the Twelfth Amendment.

treaty
A formal, public agreement between the United States and one or more nations that must be approved by two-thirds of the Senate.

President Bush meets with his national security advisors in the Situation Room of the White House soon after September 11, 2001.

presidents cannot make treaties without Senate approval, past presidents have argued that they have the power to terminate treaties without Senate consent.

Presidents can also make **executive agreements** with the leaders of foreign nations. Unlike treaties, which last beyond the end of any given administration and are between nations, executive agreements are generally between the chief executives of two or more nations, are sometimes secret, and can expire when one of the chief executives leaves office.

ADMINISTRATOR IN CHIEF   By giving the president the power to require the opinion of the principal officer in each of the executive departments "upon any subject relating to the duties of their respective offices," the Constitution puts the president in charge of the day-to-day operation of the federal bureaucracy. As we shall see, the president also has the responsibility to appoint ambassadors, judges, and all other officers of the United States, including the heads of executive departments, with the advice and consent of a majority of the Senate. Together, these powers give presidents the instruments needed to supervise and control the day-to-day operations of the federal bureaucracy.

ADDITIONAL EXECUTIVE POWERS   Alongside the specific powers associated with being commander, diplomat, and administrator in chief, the Constitution also gives the president five additional powers to lead government: (1) the power to appoint judges and officers of government; (2) the power to veto legislation, which serves as a check on Congress; (3) the power to grant pardons to individuals convicted of federal, but not state, crimes, thereby providing a check against the judiciary; (4) the power to take care that the laws are faithfully executed; and (5) the power to inform and convene Congress.

1. *The Appointment Power.* The Constitution gives the president authority to appoint judges, ambassadors, and other officers of the executive branch subject to the advice and consent of the Senate. Presidents choose appointees on the basis of party loyalty, interest group pressure, and management ability. Although the appointments process has become more controversial in recent years, the vast majority of judicial and executive appointees are easily confirmed—the Senate has rejected only eight nominations for cabinet positions since the first Congress, and just 29 out of 145 nominations to the Supreme Court.

Moreover, roughly 2,000 executive branch appointees serve entirely at the pleasure of the president, including the chiefs of staff to cabinet secretaries, who keep track of each department's political agenda. Because these jobs are not

executive agreement
A formal but often secret agreement between the U.S. president and the leaders of other nations that does not require Senate approval.

QUESTION: **Why do you have an unfavorable view of the United States? Is it mostly because of President George W. Bush, or is it a more general problem with America?**

Strong presidents often evoke strong views from citizens in other nations, especially when they take highly visible positions on world issues such as terrorism or international trade. Although many citizens around the world have a favorable view of the United States, citizens in the Middle East are sharply divided about both our nation and its president. Interviewed in 2002, 79 percent of Israelis said they were favorable toward the United States, compared to just 6 percent of citizens in the Palestinian Authority and 18 percent of Jordanians. When asked why they had an unfavorable view, citizens across the globe tended to blame George W. Bush more than the United States in general.

SOURCE: The Pew Global Attitudes Project, June 2003, pp. 134–135.

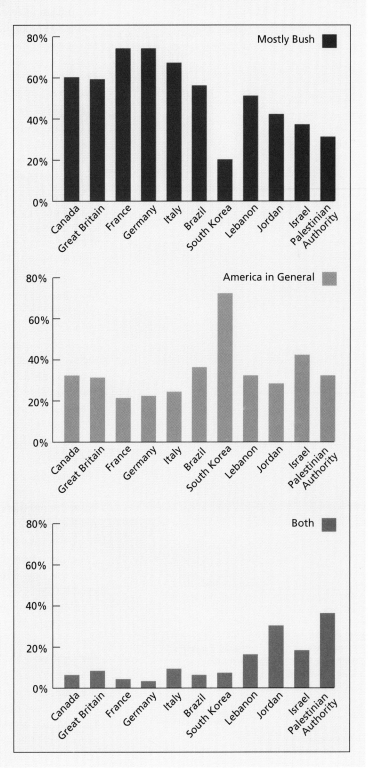

subject to Senate confirmation, they are often filled by campaign supporters, who act as the president's closest allies in the bureaucracy. All executive branch positions are considered "plums" for presidential friends, and are listed in a publication informally known as the "Plum Book." Because judges can serve for life, presidents view judicial appointments as a way to have influence far beyond the end of their term. Chief Justice Earl Warren was just such an influential figure. Nominated by President Dwight Eisenhower, Warren served for more than 15 years and presided over vast changes in civil rights and civil liberties. Presidents Clinton and Bush both nominated hundreds of federal judges who may have a similar impact, perhaps even as future Supreme Court justices.

2. *The Veto Power.* The Constitution provides that bills passed by the U.S. House of Representatives and Senate "shall be presented to the President of the United States," and the president can then approve the measure or issue a **veto**. If a bill is vetoed by a president, it can be enacted only if the veto is overridden, which requires a two-thirds vote in each chamber of Congress.

A variation of the veto is the **pocket veto**. In the ordinary course of events, if a president does not sign or veto a bill within ten days after receiving it (not counting Sundays), the bill becomes law without the president's signature. But if Congress adjourns within the ten days, the president, by taking no action, can kill the bill.

The power of a veto lies in the difficulty of overriding a president's decision. Recall that two-thirds of both houses must vote to overturn a veto. Historically, Congress has overridden fewer than 10 percent of presidents' regular vetoes. This requirement gives presidents a vital bargaining chip in the legislative process, where the mere threat of a veto, announced publicly or through legislative aides, can strengthen a president's hand in persuading Congress to accommodate his wishes. A president may also threaten to veto a bill that Congress wants unless action is taken on another bill that the president wants. Powerful though it is, the veto is essentially a negative weapon, more useful to presidents who want to block legislation than for those who seek programmatic changes.

Because the Constitution is straightforward about the veto power, its regular use by presidents stirs little controversy. Franklin Roosevelt holds the record with 635 vetoes, Ronald Reagan issued 78 vetoes in his two terms, and Bill Clinton vetoed only 37 times in his eight years. In late 1999, Clinton vetoed a Republican-backed appropriations bill and threatened to veto it again and again until Congress made major compromises with him. His use of the veto worked; Congress eventually went along on about two-thirds of the spending items that Clinton wanted.

3. *The Pardon Power.* The pardon power can be traced directly to the royal authority of the king of England, and is probably the most delicate power presidents exercise. The pardon power can be used to shorten prison sentences, correct judicial errors, and protect citizens from future prosecution. It can also be used to address national controversies. On his first full day in office in 1977, for example, President Jimmy Carter issued a pardon to any American who had avoided the draft during the Vietnam War by either not registering or leaving the country.

4. *The Take Care Power.* Presidents are also responsible to take care that the laws are faithfully exercised under the **take care clause**. Located near the end of Article II is the simple statement that the president "shall take Care that the Laws be faithfully executed." This clause makes the president responsible for implementing the laws that Congress enacts, even ones that are enacted through the override of a presidential veto.

Presidents sometimes use the take care clause to claim **inherent powers**, meaning powers they believe are essential to protecting the nation. Although Jefferson drew on this broad notion in making the Louisiana Purchase in 1804, Abraham Lincoln extended the concept early in the Civil War to suspend the rights of prisoners to seek judicial review of their cases, impose a blockade of Confederate shipping, and expand the size of the army beyond authorized

veto
A formal decision to reject a bill passed by Congress.

pocket veto
A formal decision to reject a bill passed by Congress after it adjourns—if Congress adjourns during the ten days that the president is allowed in order to sign or veto a law, the president can reject the law by taking no action at all.

take care clause
The constitutional requirement (in Article II, Section 3) that presidents take care that the laws are faithfully executed, even if they disagree with the purpose of those laws.

inherent powers
Powers that grow out of the very existence of government.

George W. Bush greets navy personnel after landing on the deck of the USS Abraham Lincoln in May 2003. Bush claimed inherent powers to justify the detention of Americans suspected of involvement with terrorism, arguing that they should be treated as a security threat to the nation.

    ceilings, all without prior congressional approval as required under the Constitution's lawmaking power.

5.   *The Power to Inform and Convene Congress.* Under Article II, presidents are required "from time to time [to] give to the Congress Information of the State of the Union, and recommend to their Consideration such Measures as he shall judge necessary." Over the years, the phrase "from time to time" has evolved to mean a constant stream of presidential messages, as well as the annual **State of the Union Address**. This power gives presidents a significant platform for presenting their legislative agenda to both Congress and the American people.

    The president also has the power to convene Congress in extraordinary circumstances and recommend "such Measures as he shall judge necessary and expedient." Those suggestions can range from simple ideas presented in a letter or news conference to the proposals President George W. Bush made in his speech before a joint session of Congress following September 11, 2001.

Presidential Succession

Having decided how a president would enter office, the framers also decided how a president would leave. In addition to impeachment, reelection defeat, retirement, resignation, or death, the Constitution now contains two other ways to remove a president from office. Under the Twenty-Second Amendment, presidents must leave office after completion of two elected terms in office.

    Under the Twenty-Fifth Amendment, presidents can also be forced from office temporarily if the vice president and a majority of either Congress or the president's own cabinet secretaries declares that the president is unable to discharge the powers and duties of the office. In such a case, the vice president becomes the acting president until the duly elected president returns to office. The amendment also allows a president to appoint a new vice president in the event of the vice president's own resignation, death, impeachment, or rise to the presidency.

    Under the Constitution, the vice president is the next in line if the president leaves office prematurely. Once past the vice president, Congress is responsible for determining the line of succession. Under current law, the Speaker of the House of Representatives would

State of the Union Address
The president's annual statement to Congress and the nation.

be next in line, followed by the Senate president pro tempore, the secretary of state, secretary of the treasury, secretary of defense, and on down through the list of 15 cabinet secretaries by the date each department was established. The framers gave Congress exclusive power to remove the president through the **impeachment** process. Under the process, the House drafts articles of impeachment that charge the president with treason, bribery, or other high crimes and misdemeanors. If the articles are approved by a majority vote, the Chief Justice of the Supreme Court oversees a trial before the entire Senate. If convicted by a two-thirds vote of the Senate, the president is removed immediately from office.

The impeachment process has been used only twice in history, first in 1868 against Andrew Johnson and second in 1998 against Bill Clinton. Both Senate trials resulted in acquittals. Richard Nixon resigned from office in 1974 before the House could finish drafting the articles of impeachment regarding his role in the Watergate cover-up. Nixon almost certainly would have been both impeached and convicted had he stayed in office.

CONTROVERSIES IN PRESIDENTIAL POWER

The Constitution is not always clear on which branch of government has what power, leading to a system of what political scientists often call separate institutions sharing power. Many of the ambiguities have provoked intense controversy in recent decades as Congress and the courts have tried to determine whether presidents actually have the powers they sometimes assert, particularly during periods of internal crisis.

The War Power

The Constitution divides the war power between the president and Congress. Article I states that Congress has the power to declare war, but Article II gives the president the power to wage war as commander in chief. The framers recognized that declaring war was both one of the most important powers of government and one of the most easily abused. Writing as a young member of Congress, Abraham Lincoln expressed the founders' intent as follows:

> The provision of the Constitution giving the war-making power to Congress was dictated, as I understand it, by the following reasons. Kings had always been involving and impoverishing their people in wars, pretending generally, if not always, that the good of the people was the object. This our convention understood to be the most oppressive of all kingly oppressions, and they resolved to so frame the Constitution that no one man should hold the power of bringing this oppression upon us.[5]

Over the past half century, U.S. presidents have ordered troops into battle in Korea, Vietnam, Grenada, Panama, Iraq (twice), Kosovo, and Afghanistan, all without asking Congress for a formal declaration of war. If they ask for congressional approval at all, they usually seek broad resolutions of support.

In 2002, for example, Bush merely asked Congress to give him authority to deploy U.S. forces as "he determines to be necessary and appropriate" to defend national security against the threat posed by Iraq. Even as he made the request, the White House also argued that the president already had the authority to act with or without congressional approval.[6]

Presidents defend such actions by arguing that they have better information, much of it secret, than Congress. They also argue that presidents need the flexibility and secrecy to respond quickly to military threats to the nation's security interests. One State Department official described the president's warmaking authority as follows: "The Constitution leaves to the President the judgment to determine whether the circumstances of a particular armed attack are so urgent and the potential consequences so threatening to the security of the U.S. that he should act without formally consulting the Congress."[7]

Presidents and some scholars also blame Congress for abdicating its constitutional authority to the presidency. Constitutional scholar Louis Fisher holds that Congress has repeatedly given up its fundamental war powers to the president. The framers knew what monarchy looked like and rejected it, writes Fisher. "Yet especially in matters of the

impeachment
Formal accusation against the president or other public official, the first step in removal from office.

war power, the United States is recreating a system of monarchy while it professes to champion democracy and the role of law abroad."[8] Fisher calls on members of Congress to reeducate themselves on their constitutional prerogatives.

Congress tried to reassert its role and authority in the use of military force at the end of the Vietnam War. In 1973, Congress enacted the War Power Resolution over Richard Nixon's veto. The law, which is still in place, declares that a president can commit the armed forces of the United States only (1) after a declaration of war by Congress, (2) by specific statutory authorization, or (3) in a national emergency created by an attack on the United States or its armed forces. After committing the armed forces under the third circumstance, the president is required to report to Congress within 48 hours. Unless Congress declares war, the troop commitment must be ended within 60 days.

This resolution signaled a new determination by Congress to take its prerogatives seriously, yet presidents have generally ignored it. And many leading scholars now believe that this earnest and well-intentioned effort by Congress to reclaim its proper role actually gave away more authority than previous practices had already done. They say it was ill conceived and badly written, full of tortured ambiguity and self-contradiction. As one critic has written, "The statute further subordinates Congress to presidential war initiatives and should be repealed in its entirety."[9]

Most observers believe the United States is best served when both president and Congress are fully engaged partners in foreign and defense policy making. Congressman Lee Hamilton sums up the virtues of joint action by these rival branches: "I believe that a partnership, characterized by creative tension between the president and the Congress, produces a foreign policy that better serves the American national interest—and better reflects the values of the American people—than policy produced by the president alone."[10]

Executive Privilege

The Constitution does not give presidents the explicit power to withhold information from Congress or the public. However, courts have recognized that presidents have the power, or **executive privilege**, to keep secrets, especially if doing so is essential to protect jeopardized national security.

Some experts argue that executive privilege has no constitutional basis.[11] Yet presidents have withheld documents from Congress at least as far back as 1792, when President George Washington temporarily refused to share sensitive documents with a House committee studying an Indian massacre of federal troops. Although he later shared the information with Congress, Washington set the precedent for the use of executive privilege. Thomas Jefferson and the primary author of the Constitution, James Madison, also withheld information during their presidencies.

Most scholars, the courts, and even members of Congress agree that a president does have the implicit, if not constitutionally explicit, right to withhold information that could harm national security. Presidents must keep secrets, and they often fight hard to do so. However, executive privilege cannot be asserted in either congressional or judicial proceedings when the issue is basically one of refusing to cooperate in investigations of personal wrongdoing.

Although the formal term "executive privilege" was first used in the 1950s during the Eisenhower administration, Richard Nixon created the controversy over the term.[12] In an effort to hide his own role in the Watergate scandal, President Nixon refused to release secret tapes of the Oval Office meetings that followed the failed burglary of Democratic party headquarters in the Watergate building. He and his lawyers went so far as to claim that the decision to invoke executive privilege was not subject to review by Congress or the courts.

In its complicated decision, the Supreme Court acknowledged for the first time that presidents do indeed have the power to claim executive privilege if the release of certain information would be damaging to the nation's security interests. At the same time, the Court held that such claims are not exempt from review by the courts, and that national security was not threatened in the Watergate case. And so the Court ordered that Nixon had to yield his tapes, effectively dooming his presidency.[13]

Twenty-five years later, Congress asked the Bush administration to disclose the names of energy industry executives who had met with Vice President Dick Cheney's

executive privilege
The right to keep executive communications confidential, especially if they relate to national security.

2001 energy task force. The White House refused, arguing that Congress has no constitutional right to investigate the process by which the president or his advisers make decisions about public issues. Although the White House never formally invoked executive privilege in the case, the refusal was clearly modeled on the notion that presidents have the right to keep secrets. Congress eventually sued Cheney for the information, but dropped the case in 2003 after losing the first round in a federal district court.

The president's right to keep secrets will be revisited in each administration and tested by presidents and by the legislative branch. On occasion, courts will try to settle the ongoing dispute about the limits and conditions under which a president can invoke this well-established, if sometimes abused, presidential practice.

Executive Orders

Presidents execute the laws and direct the federal bureaucracy in part through **executive orders**, which are formal directives to departments and agencies that are just as strong as laws and can be challenged in the courts.

Although executive orders are not mentioned in the Constitution, they are considered essential to the faithful execution of the laws. According to past Supreme Court decisions, executive orders are generally accepted as the supreme law of the land unless they are in conflict with the Constitution or a federal law.

Beginning with George Washington, presidents have issued more than 13,000 executive orders. These orders have been used to declare American neutrality in the war between France and England (1793), to intern Japanese Americans during World War II, and to protect large tracts of federal land as "national monuments" in Arizona, Colorado, Oregon, Utah, and Washington in the Clinton Administration. President George W. Bush has been just as active as recent presidents in using executive orders to manage government. He issued an order in October 2001 to create a White House Office of Homeland Security to coordinate the federal government's efforts to protect its borders, another in January 2003 to create a White House Council on Service and Civic Participation to encourage more Americans to volunteer, and still another in February 2004 to create a commission to investigate why the United States had been so wrong regarding Iraq's weapons of mass destruction. In his first four years Bush issued roughly 40 orders per year.[14]

The Budget and Spending Power

Battles over budgets and spending have been at the heart of national politics since the beginning of the Republic. The Constitution explicitly gives Congress the power to appropriate money; presidents are charged with implementing and administering the spending.

Congress dominated the budget-making process until 1921, when it approved the Budget and Accounting Act. That law required the president to submit annual budgets to Congress, and it established the Bureau of the Budget, which in 1970 became the Office of Management and Budget. Although the 1921 act also created the General Accounting Office as an auditing and oversight arm of Congress, presidents have played an increasingly powerful role in shaping the federal budget.

President Nixon, however, overplayed his hand when his White House developed legal theories that justified a bold change in the traditional definition of **impoundment**. Under the traditional definition, presidents were allowed to change the purpose of a spending bill to accommodate emergencies such as war or international crisis. Under the Nixon definition, impoundment was broadened to allow changes in a spending bill based on the president's ideology. Thus, if the president did not want appropriated funds to be spent for purposes he did not like, he could impound, or withhold, the money. In 1974, Congress approved the Congressional Budget and Impoundment Control Act, which sharply curtailed the president's use of impoundment. Enacted over Nixon's veto, the law gave Congress new powers to control its own budget process, created the Congressional Budget Office (CBO) to give the institution its own sources of economic and spending forecasts, and required the president to submit detailed requests to Congress for any proposed *recission* (cancellation) of congressional appropriations.

executive orders
A formal order issued by the president to direct action by the federal bureaucracy.

impoundment
A decision by the president not to spend money appropriated by Congress, now prohibited under federal law.

Every budget cycle witnesses a new round of clashes between the branches. In recent years, Congress has almost always failed to pass all of the appropriations bills by the beginning of the fiscal year. Instead, the two branches have relied on *continuing resolutions,* proclamations extending the authority for federal spending a few days, weeks, or months.

In an effort to control its own tendency to overspend, Congress in 1996 voted to give the president greater budget power through the **line item veto**. Presidents were allowed to strike out specific sections of an appropriations bill while signing the rest into law. Although many governors have the line item veto, the Supreme Court decided that the law had disturbed the "finely wrought" procedure for making the laws, and declared it unconstitutional in a 6 to 3 vote. If Congress wanted a new procedure for making the laws, Justice John Paul Stevens wrote for the majority, it would have to pursue a constitutional amendment.[15]

EVOLUTION OF THE PRESIDENCY

By and large, the history of presidential power is one of steady, if uneven, growth. Of the individuals who have filled the office, about one-third have enlarged its powers. Andrew Jackson, Abraham Lincoln, and both Roosevelts, for example, redefined both the institution and many of its powers by the way they set priorities and responded to crises.

Nevertheless, today's presidency reflects precedents established by the nation's very first chief executive, George Washington. The framers could not have anticipated the kinds of foreign and domestic threats that now preoccupy the office, but they would recognize the importance of the presidency in protecting the nation in times of trouble.

The First Presidency

The framers designed the presidency hoping that George Washington would be the first to occupy the post. Washington commanded the public's trust and respect and was unanimously elected as the first president of the new Republic in 1789. He understood that the people needed to have confidence in their fledgling government, a sense of continuity with the past, and a time of calm and stability free of emergencies and crises. He also knew that the new nation faced both domestic and foreign threats to its future.

Washington's presidency set important precedents for the future, not the least of which was how the president would be addressed in public. Vice President John Adams argued that the president should be called "His Highness the President of the United States and protector of Their Liberties," a title the popularly elected House immediately rejected. The president of the United States would be called "the President of the United States."[16]

Washington's presidency also produced a model against which to measure future presidents. Not only did he establish the legitimacy and basic authority of the office, Washington negotiated the new government's first treaty, appointed its first judges and department heads, received its first foreign ambassadors, vetoed its first legislation, and signed its first laws, thereby demonstrating just how future presidents should execute and influence the laws.

Washington also established a host of lesser precedents for running the presidency that still hold today. He started by assembling the first White House staff. It was hardly large, composed of just two clerks, but it was an office nonetheless. Indeed, it was so small that Washington paid for staff and office expenses from his own pocket. Washington also appointed the first department secretaries, appointing Thomas Jefferson as secretary of state and Alexander Hamilton as secretary of the treasury.

Washington may have set his most important precedent in establishing the president's sole authority for supervising the executive branch. He was absolutely clear about the division of executive and legislative powers. Congress could appropriate money, confirm appointees, conduct oversight hearings, and always change the laws, but it could not run the departments. That was to be the president's job.

Washington's final contribution to the presidency involved his retirement after serving two terms. Although he would have been easily reelected to a third term, Washington believed that two terms were enough and returned to his Mount Vernon estate in

line item veto
Presidential power to strike, or remove, specific items from a spending bill without vetoing the entire package, declared unconstitutional by the Supreme Court.

1796. It was a precedent that held until Roosevelt's four terms, and was finally enshrined in constitutional language under the Twenty-Second Amendment.

The First Modern Presidency

Designed in part to check what the founders thought would be a more powerful Congress, the presidency has evolved over the past two hundred years into a powerful institution in its own right. Thomas Jefferson, Abraham Lincoln, and Theodore and Franklin Roosevelt all extended the president's authority to meet foreign and domestic threats through the use of inherent powers.

However, the expansion of the presidency has involved more than inherent powers. It has also reflected a growing government role in regulating the U.S. economy and protecting national interests abroad, which has increased the size and mission of government, which in turn has increased the demand for presidential leadership.

Although the modern presidency was not formed by any single president, most historians and political scientists agree that Franklin Roosevelt was the first president to exploit the institution's inherent and enumerated powers to their fullest impact. Although conservatives do not always endorse the use of these powers to expand the federal bureaucracy, they agree with liberals that Roosevelt left an indelible mark on the institution of the presidency itself.

Over his 12 years in office, Roosevelt created an extraordinary record of achievement. He expanded the role of the president as commander, diplomat, and administrator in chief, while dominating Congress in both shaping and making the laws. Inaugurated for the first of four terms at the height of the nation's deepest economic crisis, Roosevelt's first one hundred days in office in 1933 still stand as the most significant moment of presidential leadership in modern history. Most of his New Deal agenda for helping working and poor Americans is still on the statute books today, including Social Security for the aged, unemployment insurance and a guaranteed minimum wage for workers, banking and stock market regulation for investors, price supports for farmers, and a host of federal agencies that continue to deliver everything from electric power to schoolbooks.

Roosevelt clearly moved the presidency to the center of the legislative process. He created a new clearance process for sending specific legislative proposals to Congress, and used the State of the Union to focus the nation's attention on a specific list of presidential priorities. Although previous presidents had expressed their opinions about pending legislation, Roosevelt created new lobbying techniques that are still used to this day, the most notable of which involved the use of media to build public support for his program.

Roosevelt's impact extended well beyond the legislative agenda, however. He also exploited the powers of the presidency to build a highly personal relationship with the American public, using his "fireside chats" on radio to calm the public during the darkest days of the economic depression, while calling the nation to action during the early days of World War II. In doing so, he became the nation's communicator-in-chief, starting each broadcast with the simple phrase "My friends."

Roosevelt also changed the president's relationship with the federal bureaucracy, which grew from 600,000 employees before the New Deal to well over 1 million just before World War II. Not only did the New Deal produce a host of new federal agencies, it also demanded a larger White House staff to oversee the implementation of the laws. By 1937, Roosevelt's small White House staff was so overwhelmed that a national study group opened a report on the need for a stronger White House staff with the words: "The President needs help."

The Presidency Today

The formal powers the U.S. Constitution vests in a president have not been changed for more than 200 years, but the influence of modern presidents is considerably greater today than it has ever been, particularly at this moment in world history.

But even before September 11, several factors had strengthened the presidency. The danger of war and the destructive potential of new weaponry plainly increased the president's influence. The cold war—with its enormous standing armies, nuclear weapons, and widespread intelligence and alliance operations—invited presidential leadership in national security matters.

The end of the cold war in 1989 did not reduce the need for presidential leadership, however. As the 2003 Iraq War and continuing unrest in the Middle East show, the world is just as dangerous as it was at the height of the cold war—perhaps even more so. As weapons of mass destruction become more easily available, the president's role in protecting the nation from terrorism has become more pronounced.

Increased federal involvement in economic and social issues and the rise of complex public issues such as genetic engineering, global warming, and international terrorism have all enhanced public demands for strong presidential leadership. Problems not easily delegated to any one department often get pulled into the White House. When new programs involve several federal agencies, someone near the president is often asked to reconcile conflicts and set a consistent policy. White House aides, with some justification, claim that the presidency is the only place in government where it is possible to establish and coordinate national priorities. Presidents set up central review and coordination units that help formulate new policies, settle jurisdictional disputes among departments, and provide access for the well-organized interest groups that want their views to be given weight in decision making.

Nevertheless, some experts believe that presidential influence has declined in recent years, in part because of political scandals such as Watergate (Nixon), Iran-Contra (Reagan), and Whitewater and Monica Lewinsky (Clinton). Richard Nixon's resignation clearly diminished public respect for the presidency, Bill Clinton's impeachment clearly distracted the nation from more pressing problems such as the rising tide of anti-American sentiment in the Middle East, and the controversy over the 2000 election raised questions about the legitimacy of the electoral process.

MANAGING THE PRESIDENCY

Without help, presidents could not manage crises, build morale, set priorities and agendas, build legislative and political coalitions, mold public opinion, lead their parties, and otherwise take care that the laws are faithfully executed. Although some of that help

President George W. Bush and former Presidents Bill Clinton, George Bush, Jimmy Carter, and Gerald Ford, along with their wives, attending the state funeral for former President Ronald Reagan. Also pictured here are Vice President Dick Cheney and his wife.

comes from their *inner circle,* which is composed of their closest advisers including the first lady, presidents could not do their job without a vast array of support that extends well beyond 1600 Pennsylvania Avenue to include the executive branch as a whole.

The White House Staff

Presidents have come to rely heavily on their personal staffs. Nowhere else—not in Congress, not in the cabinet, not in the party—can presidents find the loyalty and single-mindedness that often develops among their closest White House aides.[17] Cabinet heads are often perceived as staunch advocates of their departments and the constituencies their departments serve and so cannot be assumed to give objective advice. By contrast, presidents presume that their aides will provide them with sound and unbiased policy guidance. But there are sometimes substantial costs to listening only to one's closest associates.

THE WHITE HOUSE ORGANIZATION   The White House staff grew steadily from the early 1900s through the early 1990s, then stabilized at roughly 400 today. The staff is headed by the **chief of staff**, who is considered the president's most loyal assistant. The White House staff also includes the president's chief lawyer, speechwriters, legislative liaison staff, and press secretary. The chief of staff supervises all other White House staff and is considered a member of the president's inner circle.

Most of these advisers have offices in the West Wing of the White House or the Old Executive Office Building. Once used to house all the federal departments in the early 1800s, the Old Executive Office Building now holds mostly presidential and vice presidential staff.

White House staff members sometimes insist that they are simply the eyes and ears of the president, that they make few important decisions, and that they never intrude between the chief executive and the heads of departments. But the inevitable emergence of a few strong White House advisers such as Karl Rove and Karen Hughes in the Bush White House renders this traditional picture inaccurate.[18]

RUNNING THE WHITE HOUSE   Over the past three decades, presidents have used three very different models for running the White House staff: competitive, collegial, and hierarchical. Among modern presidents, Franklin Roosevelt and Lyndon Johnson both used the competitive approach, a "survival of the fittest" situation in which the president allows aides to fight each other for access to the Oval Office. Johnson sometimes gave different staffers the same assignment, hoping that the competition would produce a better final decision.

In contrast, John Kennedy, Jimmy Carter, and Bill Clinton all used the collegial approach, in which presidents encourage aides to work together toward a common position. It is a much friendlier way to work than the competitive approach but may have the serious drawback of producing what some social psychologists call *groupthink.* Groupthink is the tendency of small groups to stifle dissent in the search for common ground.[19]

Finally, Dwight Eisenhower, Richard Nixon, Ronald Reagan, and George H. W. Bush all used the hierarchical model, in which the president establishes tight control over who does what in making decisions. A hierarchy is a form of organization that looks very much like a pyramid: one leader at the top, two right underneath, three or more right underneath those two, and so on down the organization. The chief advantage of a hierarchy is that it reduces the number of people the leader has to deal with—the tighter the hierarchy, the fewer the contacts. Most hierarchies depend on a "gatekeeper" near the very top, usually the chief of staff, to enforce tight control over access to the leaders.

George W. Bush has used a hierarchical approach in organizing the White House. He has used clear lines of authority to minimize chaos and has expected his staff to be loyal above all else. Most decisions have been made through tightly controlled discussions led by the president, his top staff aides, or Vice President Cheney.

The Executive Office of the President

Created in 1939, the **Executive Office of the President** consists of the Office of Management and Budget, the Council of Economic Advisers, and several other staff units (see Figure 12–1). It also contains the White House staff.

chief of staff
The head of the White House staff.

Executive Office of the President
The cluster of presidential staff agencies that help the president carry out his responsibilities. Currently the office includes the Office of Management and Budget, the Council of Economic Advisers, and several other units.

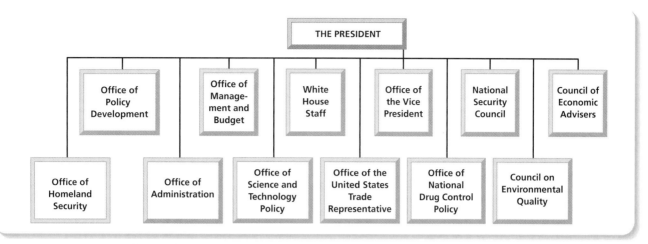

FIGURE 12–1 Executive Office of the President.
SOURCE: *United States Government Manual, 2000–2001* (Government Printing Office, 2000), p. 87.

The **Office of Management and Budget (OMB)** is the central presidential staff agency. Its director advises the president in detail about the hundreds of government agencies—how much money they should be allotted in the budget and what kind of job they are doing. OMB seeks to improve the planning, management, and statistical work of the agencies. It makes a special effort to see that each agency conforms to presidential policies in its dealings with Congress; each agency has to clear its policy recommendations to Congress through OMB first.[20]

Through the long budget-preparation process, presidents use OMB as a way of conserving and centralizing their own influence. A budget is more than just a financial plan because it reflects power struggles and indicates national priorities (and wishful thinking). To the president, the budget is a means of control over administrators who may be trying to join ranks with other politicians or interest groups to thwart presidential priorities.

The Cabinet

It is hard to find a more unusual institution than the president's **cabinet**. The cabinet is not specifically mentioned in the Constitution, yet since George Washington's administration, every president has had one. Washington's consisted of his secretaries of state, treasury, and war, plus his attorney general.

SELECTING THE CABINET   Selecting the cabinet today is the first major job for the president-elect. The cabinet consists of the president, the vice president, the heads of the 15 executive departments, and a few others a president considers cabinet-level officials. The cabinet has always been a loosely designated body, and it is not always clear who belongs in it. In recent years, certain executive branch administrators and White House counselors have been accorded cabinet rank. Nineteen officials have had cabinet status in the George W. Bush administration, including the 15 cabinet secretaries, the vice president, the chief of staff, and the director of Homeland Security.

CABINET GOVERNMENT   Cabinet government is generally defined as a system of advice in which the voice of individual cabinet members is of major importance. As such, cabinet government does not exist in the United States.[21] In fact, an American president is not required by the Constitution to form a cabinet or to hold regular meetings. Presidents John Kennedy, Lyndon Johnson, and Richard Nixon all preferred small conferences with individuals specifically involved in a problem and rarely held cabinet meetings. Kennedy saw no reason, for example, to discuss Defense Department matters with his secretaries of agriculture and labor, and he thought cabinet meetings wasted valuable time. Both Jimmy Carter and Ronald Reagan tried to revive the cabinet, and both met often with their cabinets during their first two years. But the longer they remained in office, the less frequently they met with their cabinets as a whole.

Office of Management and Budget (OMB)
Presidential staff agency that serves as a clearinghouse for budgetary requests and management improvements for government agencies.

cabinet
Advisory council for the president, consisting of the heads of the executive departments, the vice president, and a few other officials selected by the president.

President George W. Bush with his cabinet.

CHANGING FACE OF AMERICAN POLITICS

PRESIDENTIAL APPOINTEES

Presidents Bill Clinton and George W. Bush both promised to appoint administrations that were as diverse as the country. Although both presidents came surprisingly close on race, neither approached the 50 percent mark on gender. According to detailed analysis of every executive branch appointee nominated for Senate confirmation in the first year of the first term of both administrations, 30 percent of the appointees in Clinton's first year were women, compared to just 23 percent in Bush's first year.

Although the numbers seem disappointing given the changing face of the federal bureaucracy discussed in the next chapter, both administrations did much better than their predecessors—less than 15 percent of the appointees in Carter's first year (1977) were women, compared to just 8 percent in Reagan's first year (1981).* And the fact that both Clinton and Bush were both able to recruit many women and minority appointees at lower levels suggests that future administrations will be even more successful. Past research shows that the higher-level jobs almost always go to appointees with prior appointee service at lower levels. By increasing the numbers of women and minorities in the pipeline, the Clinton and Bush administrations increased the odds that there will be more women and minority candidates for the top jobs for future Democratic and Republican administrations alike.

*The Carter and Reagan numbers come from Gary King and Lynn Ragsdale, *The Elusive Executive: Discovering Elusive Statistical Patterns in the Presidency* (CQ Press, 1988), pp. 236–237.

	Clinton Administration, 1993	Bush Administration, 2001
Gender		
Women	30%	23%
Men	70	77
Race		
African American	14%	9%
Hispanic	6	8
Asian American	3	3
White	77	80

SOURCE: Data collected by the Presidential Appointee Initiative, analysis by authors.

Bill Clinton, like those he followed, seldom called for full cabinet meetings, holding just 18 such meetings in his first term and even fewer during his second.[22] George W. Bush has also shown limited interest in full cabinet meetings, preferring to assemble small groups of cabinet members on an as-needed basis.

Presidential advisers and the heads of various White House–based cabinet-level councils, such as the National Security Council and the Office of Management and Budget, have gained equal or even superior status to many cabinet secretaries. This shift occurred in part because these advisers are physically located in or next door to the White House (see Figure 12–2). Further, presidents are aware that some cabinet members adopt narrow "advocate" views: the Agriculture Department secretary is a strong advocate for farmers; the Housing and Urban Development Department secretary is an ambassador for the housing industry and, to some extent, also for big city mayors; and so on through much of the cabinet, especially in departments occupied primarily with domestic policy matters.

CABINET DIFFERENCES As the next chapter will discuss in more detail, cabinet departments vary by the number of employees (the Department of Defense has nearly a million employees, while the Department of Education has barely 5,000) and size of budget (the Department of Health and Human Services had a budget of well over $575 billion in 2005, while the Department of State barely hit $10 billion).

The departments also vary in their influence with the White House. Presidents tend to pay the greatest attention to the oldest and most visible of the departments: Defense, Justice, State, and Treasury. These four departments are often called the *inner cabinet* because they are so important to the president's foreign and domestic success. The economy (Treasury), crime (Justice), and international affairs (State and Defense) are rarely far from the top of the president's list of policy concerns. Presidents almost always appoint very close allies to the inner cabinet posts, even if those allies do not always have the best credentials for the jobs.

The other departments are generally called the *outer cabinet,* largely because they are more distant from the day-to-day worries that occupy the president and White House staff. The Department of Veterans Affairs, for example, is rarely in the headlines, even though its 250,000 full- and part-time employees make it the second-largest department in the federal bureaucracy.

The Vice Presidency

Despite Vice President Dick Cheney's visible role today, the vice presidency has not always been an important job. For most of American history, the vice president was at best seen as an insignificant officer and at worst a political rival who sometimes connived

In response to the terrorist attacks on September 11, 2001, President Bush used his presidential authority to appoint former Pennsylvania Governor Tom Ridge the director of Homeland Security. Ridge was later appointed as the first secretary of the Department of Homeland Security. In November 2004, Ridge announced that he would not continue as secretary of the Department of Homeland Security during President Bush's second term.

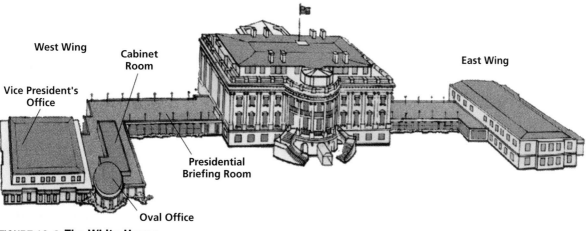

West Wing

Cabinet Room

East Wing

Vice President's Office

Presidential Briefing Room

Oval Office

FIGURE 12–2 The White House.

While the vice president's primary responsibility is to take the oath of office should the president become unable to carry out his or her term, some vice presidents have wielded more power and influence than others.

against the president. The office was often dismissed as a joke. One reason for the vice president's posture as an outsider was that presidential nominees usually chose running mates who were geographically, ideologically, demographically, and in other ways likely to "balance the ticket."

No matter how influential they become, vice presidents have only one major responsibility, to be ready to take the oath of office in case the president cannot. Vice presidents are not mere replacement parts, however. President Jimmy Carter included Walter Mondale in the daily processes of decision making in the White House; President Clinton used Al Gore as an important adviser and confidant on domestic as well as foreign policy matters and key appointments. Even when recent presidents have mostly ignored their vice presidents, as the first President Bush did with his vice president, Dan Quayle, vice presidents enter office with substantial access, including an office just down the hall from the president in the West Wing of the White House, a substantial staff of their own, and access to all of the information flowing into the Oval Office.

Vice President Dick Cheney had more than just access to the second President Bush, however. He also had considerable influence. As a former member of Congress and secretary of defense during the first Bush administration, Cheney brought significant credibility to the Bush–Cheney ticket, reassuring voters that the younger Bush was ready for the presidency, and was a trusted advisor to the Bush family. It is no surprise, therefore, that Cheney soon became one of the most influential, visible, and popular vice presidents in history.

But Cheney also became one of the administration's strongest advocates of war with Iraq. Although he shared the president's high public approval immediately after the war began, his approval fell much faster than the president's as the war lingered on and the search for weapons of mass destruction turned futile. By February 2004, Americans were evenly divided on whether Cheney should even remain on the presidential ticket—even 28 percent of Republicans said the president should make a change.[23] Cheney remained highly popular among social conservatives, however, and was reelected in November 2004.

Although the sorts of tensions between president and vice president that existed in the past rarely affected Clinton and Gore or Bush and Cheney, tension between a president and a vice president is natural. After all, except for the vice president, everybody who works closely with a president can be fired. It is almost certain that vice presidents will continue to have an undefined ad hoc set of assignments, subject more to the goodwill and mood of the president than to any fixed description.[24]

The First Lady

The president's inner circle of close advisers has always included the first lady. Eleanor Roosevelt was particularly visible as an advocate for a strong national government during the economic depression of the 1930s. In recent decades, however, the first lady has steadily become more prominent as a policy adviser to the president, in part because the media have become so aggressive in covering the White House. Lady Bird Johnson was a tireless and persuasive advocate for the beautification of America, Betty Ford for cancer research, Rosalyn Carter for the Equal Rights Amendment, Nancy Reagan for drug control, and Barbara Bush for literacy programs. Hillary Clinton clearly drew on these role models in setting her own White House course.

What made Hillary Clinton different from her predecessors was her highly visible role in actually shaping important presidential proposals. As head of the president's health care reform task force, she played a major role in designing a top legislative initiative and soon emerged as a key player on a host of other issues. She clearly had the experience and the credentials for the job: She attended Wellesley College, where she was elected president of the student body; graduated first in her class at Yale Law School, just ahead of the future president; and was headed for a career in law and public service long before her husband entered public life.

PEOPLE & POLITICS *Making a Difference*

CONDOLEEZZA RICE

As the president's national security advisor, Condoleezza Rice was a natural for one of the toughest foreign policy jobs in Washington. The national security advisors sit only a few doors away from the president and are always on call during crises. They must also resolve the often public disputes among the president's foreign policy team, which can involve a host of political heavyweights that include the vice president; the secretaries of commerce, defense, homeland security, state, and treasury; the attorney general; the director of Central Intelligence; the U.S. trade representative; and senior military officers.

Rice had a nearly perfect résumé for the job. She earned her bachelor's degree in political science from the University of Denver at 19 and received her Ph.D. from the Graduate School of International Studies at Denver seven years later. Already a full professor at Stanford University, she joined the first Bush administration in 1989 as the director, then senior director, of the Soviet and East European desk at the National Security Council, then returned to Stanford as provost, the second most im-

portant administrative post at the university.

That resume would have been more than enough to qualify her for almost any foreign policy job in the second Bush administration. She earned the White House job by almost never leaving the president's side as he crisscrossed the nation during the 2000 presidential campaign. By paying her dues on the campaign trail, she earned the president's trust. During the hours and days after the terrorist attacks, President Bush often asked her to remain silent at key meetings so she could later give him her private reading on the right course of action. Her service in this top job has not been without controversy. She came under fire for endorsing the claim that Saddam Hussein had tried to buy the ingredients for nuclear weapons, even though that claim had been discredited by the Central Intelligence Agency well before the president used it as part of his case for war. But the president never wavered from her side.

All this is by way of noting that her appointment had absolutely nothing to do with her being the first woman to serve as national security advisor. Nor did it

have anything to do with the fact that she is African American; the granddaughter of an Alabama sharecropper; that she was born in 1954, the year that the Supreme Court ruled that racial segregation of public schools was unconstitutional; that a nursery-school classmate was one of four girls killed by white extremists in a 1963 Birmingham church bombing; or that she has said she had to be "twice as good" to get ahead. Condoleezza Rice made it to the top by believing her parents when they told her that "you may not be able to have a hamburger at Woolworth's but you can be president of the United States."

Rice became secretary of state in 2005.

THE PRESIDENT'S JOB

Presidents are asked to perform roles not explicitly defined in the Constitution. Americans want the chief executive to be an international peacemaker as well as a national morale builder, a politician in chief as well as a commander in chief. They want the president to provide leadership on foreign, economic, and domestic policy. Americans also want presidents to be crisis managers and role models of a kind. They want them to be able to connect with ordinary Americans and be honest, yet be smarter, tougher, and more honest than the rest of us. (See Table 12–1 for what Americans say they care about most in picking a president.)

Presidents as Crisis Managers

The framers designed the president's job as commander in chief as a limited role. Congress, not the president, declares war, makes the rules for the army and navy, and controls the funding of wars. Yet the president is still in charge of the military as commander in chief.

The president's role is based on the principle of *civilian control over the military,* a central condition of a constitutional democracy.[25] Civilian control means that all soldiers

The first lady can be an important influence on a president. In recent decades, the first lady has evolved into a prominent policy adviser to the president as well as a champion of many important causes of her own choosing.

TABLE 12–1   WHAT AMERICANS WANT TO KNOW ABOUT THEIR CANDIDATES

Percentage of Americans who said it is very important to know the following about a presidential candidate:

	2000 Campaign	2004 Campaign
How well a candidate connects with average people	67%	71%
A candidate's voting record or policy positions he or she previously held	60	64
A candidate's reputation for honesty	84	88
A candidate's major campaign contributors	42	39
A candidate's military background	19	21
Whether a candidate is an active churchgoer	25	27

SOURCE: Pew Research Center for the People and the Press, "Democratic Primary Campaign Impresses Voters," February 19, 2004, p. 1.

and sailors, from the newest recruit to every general and admiral, take their orders from and owe their allegiance to the one person elected by all the people. The professional military, no matter what their own personal political views and values, take their military orders from the president and his chief civilian agent, the secretary of defense.

Presidents are expected to be crisis managers in the domestic sphere as well. Presidents or their surrogates in the cabinet are often the first on the scene in national disasters such as hurricanes and floods and are expected to play a significant role in reassuring the nation. In turn, the public often responds to presidential leadership with a temporary surge in support. These **rally points** are particularly strong when a military action, such as an invasion or a bombing, is both short and successful. Rally points do not necessarily last long, however. Although George W. Bush's ratings jumped dramatically following the capture of Saddam Hussein, they fell back quickly as questions emerged about the quality of the intelligence leading up to the war. (See Table 12–2 for examples of recent rally points.)

Not all rally points involve foreign crises, however. Clinton's approval rose after the Oklahoma City bombing in 1995 in large part because Americans turned to him for leadership in the crisis. Presidential approval can also rise during periods of great national pride. Reagan's public approval (and reelection chances) jumped during the 1984 Olympic Games as the United States won one gold medal after another, in part because the Soviet Union and its eastern European allies boycotted the event.

TABLE 12–2   RECENT RALLY POINTS

President and Event	Approval Before	Approval After	Change in Approval
George W. Bush			
Saddam Hussein's capture	50%	57%	+7%
Iraq War begins	55	67	+12
September 11 terrorist attacks	51	80	+29
Bill Clinton			
Oklahoma City bombing	46	51	+5
George H. W. Bush			
1991 Gulf War	59	79	+20

rally point
A rise in public approval of the president that follows a crisis as Americans "rally 'round the flag" and the chief executive.

Presidents as Morale Builders

As chief of state, the president must project a sense of national unity and authority as the country's chief ceremonial leader. The framers of the Constitution did not fully anticipate the symbolic and morale-building functions a president must perform. Certain magisterial functions, such as receiving ambassadors and granting pardons, were conferred. But over time, the presidency has acquired enormous symbolic significance.

Presidents are the nation's number one celebrities; almost anything they do is news. Presidents command attention merely by jogging, fishing, golfing, or going to church. By their actions, presidents can arouse a sense of hope or despair, honor or dishonor.

The morale-building job of the president involves much more than just ceremonial cheerleading or quasi-chaplain duties. Presidential leadership, at its finest, radiates national self-confidence and helps unlock the possibility for good that exists in the nation. Our best leaders have been able to provide this special and often intangible element. That is certainly what George W. Bush intended in the days and weeks that followed September 11, 2001. By his words and deeds, he sought to simultaneously calm the nation and warn the rest of the world that the United States would not tolerate further terrorist attacks.

Presidents as Agenda Setters

By custom and circumstance, presidents are now responsible for proposing initiatives in foreign policy and economic growth and stability. This was not always the case. But beginning with Woodrow Wilson, and especially since the New Deal, a president has been expected to propose reforms to ensure domestic progress. New ideas are seized on by a presidential candidate searching for campaign issues, and they are later refined and implemented by the executive office staff, by special presidential task forces, and by Congress.[26]

NATIONAL SECURITY POLICY The framers foresaw a special need for speed and unity in dealing with other nations. As a result, presidents generally have more leeway in foreign policy and military affairs than they have in domestic matters. The Constitution vests in the president command of the two major instruments of foreign policy—the diplomatic corps and the armed services. It also gives the president responsibility for negotiating treaties and commitments with other nations, although the Senate must consent to treaty ratifications, and almost all international agreements require congressional action for their implementation.

Congress has granted presidents discretion in initiating foreign policies, for diplomacy frequently requires quick action. The Supreme Court has upheld strong presidential authority in this area. In *United States* v. *Curtiss-Wright* (1936), the Court referred to the "exclusive power of the president as the sole organ of the federal government in the field of international relations—a power which does not require as a basis for its exercise an act of Congress, but which, of course, like every other governmental power, must be exercised in subordination to the applicable provisions of the Constitution."[27] These are sweeping and much-debated words.[28] Still, a determined Congress that knows what it wants does not lack power in foreign relations. Congress must authorize and appropriate the funds that back up the president's policies abroad.

ECONOMIC POLICY Ever since the New Deal, presidents have been expected to promote policies to keep unemployment low, fight inflation, keep taxes down, and promote economic growth and prosperity. The Constitution did not specify these duties for the executive, yet presidents know that when the nation is not prosperous and jobs are scarce, they may suffer the fate of Herbert Hoover, who was denounced for his inaction at the beginning of the Great Depression. The growth and complexity of economic problems since the Depression of the 1930s have placed more economic responsibility in the president's hands. The delicate balancing required to keep a modern economy operating means that presidents must make key fiscal and budgetary policy decisions.[29] The presidential elections in 1980 and 1992 turned largely on the economy, and the election of 2000 involved a debate about which candidate would be better able to keep the economic boom going. Although terrorism, social issues, and Iraq were top issues for Bush/Cheney supporters in 2004, economic issues were particularly inportant for Kerry/Edwards.

Although presidents sometimes get their economic advice elsewhere, their chief advisers on economic policy are the secretary of the treasury, the three members of the Council of Economic Advisers, and the director of the Office of Management and Budget. The chair of the Federal Reserve Board of Governors is also an influential, if independent, adviser on the economy.

DOMESTIC POLICY Some experts believe that a leader is one who knows where the followers are. Abraham Lincoln did not invent the antislavery movement. John Kennedy and Lyndon Johnson did not begin the civil rights movement. Bill Clinton was not the first leader to notice the unfairness of health care and welfare policies, nor was George W. Bush the first to note the skyrocketing price of prescription drugs. But they all, in their respective times, became embroiled in these controversies, for a president cannot long ignore what divides or inspires a nation.

At the same time, presidents sometimes take highly unpopular positions for the good of the country. The vast majority of Americans opposed Harry Truman's decision to integrate the armed services, and many southerners bolted the Democratic party when Lyndon Johnson demanded action on civil rights. Similarly, many Americans opposed George W. Bush's 2001 decision to limit fetal stem-cell research, which he believed might increase abortion.

Presidents as Persuaders

Presidents must build political coalitions if they are to have any chance of winning passage of their legislative programs. As candidates, they make promises to the people and assemble an electoral coalition of supporters. To get things done and to get reelected, however, they must work with interest groups and people who have differing loyalties and responsibilities. Inevitably, presidents become embroiled in legislative, bureaucratic, and lobbying politics, and their approval ratings often suffer as a consequence.

Despite their formal powers, presidents spend most of their time *persuading* people. As Richard Neustadt argues, the power to persuade is the president's chief resource, and that power comes through bargaining.[30] Bargaining, in turn, comes primarily through getting others to believe it is in their self-interest to cooperate. Presidents and their aides spend a lot of time dispensing favors to various members of Congress from whom they are seeking votes and political support. Hence the skill of a president in communicating and winning others over is the necessary energizing factor in moving the institutions of the national government to action.

Presidents have been communicating with the public from the very beginning of the Republic, using press conferences, speeches, and public events to maintain contact with the country. Although much of the communication is designed to support other presidential roles, today's presidents are making more prime-time television appearances, giving more speeches, and spending more time outside of Washington in efforts to influence the country. According to political scientist Samuel Kernell, the number of major and minor presidential addresses has grown from just a dozen or so in the first three years of the Hoover administration (1929–1931) to well over 100 in the first three years of the Bush presidency almost 60 years later. The greatest growth came in the number of minor addresses before specialized audiences—trade associations, college graduations, advocacy groups.[31]

At the same time, presidents have been spending less time holding press conferences. Whereas Franklin Roosevelt averaged almost seven press conferences a month during his dozen years in office, Reagan, Bush, and Clinton averaged barely one a month. Presidents would much rather be interviewed by local reporters outside Washington than by members of the experienced White House press corps, much rather give exclusive interviews to a sympathetic interviewer than face a roomful of unpredictable reporters, and much rather use live satellite feeds to remote stations to get their message across than deal with the *Washington Post, New York Times,* or *Wall Street Journal.*

(Presidential press conferences are covered in more detail in Chapter 10.) This strategy is often labeled as "going public."

Going public clearly fits with changes in the electoral process. Presidents now have the staff, the technology, and the public opinion research to tell them how to target their message and the nearly instant media access to go public easily. And as elections have become more image-oriented and candidate-centered, presidents have the incentive to use these tools to operate a permanent White House campaign. Presidents are still welcome to bargain and persuade, to focus congressional attention and twist arms, but members of Congress may pay attention only when pressure is coming from the voters back home. (See Figure 12–3 for presidential approval trends over the past half century). Bush became the first incumbent in modern history to win reelection despite starting his campaign with an approval rating below 50 percent.

ELECTION 2004: AN ANALYSIS

George W. Bush started the 2004 campaign with a long list of liabilities. His public approval rating was falling; the economy was still sluggish; the war in Iraq was anything but the "mission accomplished" that the president had celebrated the previous May; and Democrats were well-funded, highly motivated, and still angry about the 2000 election, which Bush had won in the courts, not in the popular vote count.

Yet, Bush also had significant assets. He was a likable wartime president with a stubborn commitment to the war in Iraq. Bush also had all the perquisites of the presidency, including Air Force One, a powerful political machine, some of the cleverest political strategists in the country, and a plainspoken persistence that just might appeal to undecided voters. If Bush could get all of his supporters to the polls, shift the public's focus from the economy to terrorism, and win enough of the swing voters who had voted for Vice President Al Gore in 2000, he just might be able to win.

Bush also needed the right opponent. If Democrats nominated someone with just enough inconsistency in his record, just enough of a Boston accent in his voice, and just enough mistakes in his strategy, the president might be able to argue that he was the safer choice in an uncertain world. If Bush could make the 2004 election a referendum on his opponent, not on his record, he might erase the doubts about his own record on jobs, the war in Iraq, and health care.

The Results

Remarkably, Bush did all of the above and more. Despite pink slips for workers in "battleground" states such as Ohio and Pennsylvania, rising Medicare premiums for the elderly, worries about a draft for the young, and rising casualties and a prison-abuse scandal in Iraq, Bush won both the electoral and popular vote on Tuesday, November 2, 2004. At 10:00 a.m. on Wednesday morning, Senator John Kerry called to concede the election—"We cannot win the election," he would tell supporters who had waited all night at Boston's Faneuil Hall. With Bush's 286–252 electoral margin, and a 4-million popular-vote cushion, there would be no repeat of the agonizing recount that had paralyzed the country in 2000 (see Adam Nagourney, "Bush Celebrates Victory," The New York Times, November 4, 2004, p. A1).

Yet, if Bush's victory was firm, it was also surprisingly familiar. Although Bush earned 9 million more votes in 2004 than 2000, only three states actually switched sides: New Hampshire "flipped" from the Republican to the Democratic column, while Iowa and New Mexico flipped from the Democratic column to the Republican. The other 47 states remained exactly where they had been four years earlier, with the Republican "red" states concentrated in the South and Midwest and most of the Democratic "blue" states in the Northeast and on the West Coast.

BUSH V. KERRY		
	Bush	*Kerry*
Men	55	44
Women	48	51
18–29 years old	45	54
30–44 years old	53	46
45–59 years old	51	48
60 years old or over	54	46
White	58	41
Black	11	88
Hispanic/Latino	44	53
Asian	44	56
Republican	93	6
Independent	48	49
Democratic	11	89
White evangelical or born again Christian	78	21
Gay, lesbian, or bisexual	23	77

SOURCE: "Survey of Voters: Who They Were . . . ," The New York Times, Novemeber 4, 2004, p. P4.

Moreover, Bush and Kerry did well in 2004 exactly where Bush and Vice President Al Gore had done well in 2000. Bush ran ahead of Kerry among men, older Americans, whites, Republicans, and white born-again Christians; while Kerry ran ahead of Bush among women, younger Americans, minority voters, Democrats, and gays.

The obvious question is what changed. Simply put, how did George W. Bush win?

A first answer is that Bush's supporters were more committed than Kerry's, in part because the Bush campaign was able to rally religious conservatives who had stayed home in 2000. Anti-gay-marriage initiatives were on the ballot in eleven states, including Ohio, which some pundits argue brought large numbers of passionate conservatives to the polls.

However, Bush's winning margin did not come from these groups alone. Indeed, of the 9 million votes that Bush gained between 2000 and 2004, the largest share came from two groups that were distinctly non-evangelical and not opponents of gay marriage. His share of the vote among white women surged from 49 percent in 2000 to 55 percent in 2004, and among Hispanic/Latino voters from 36 percent to 44 percent (see table on page 330). Put together, the gains produced exactly 3.5 percent of the popular vote, or roughly the 4 million votes that gave Bush the deciding margin.

A second answer is that Bush was a much better candidate than John Kerry, which helps explain at least some of his surge. He was always judged the more likeable candidate—although voters had significant concerns about his policies, particularly his management of the economy and the war in Iraq, they saw him as more approachable. Kerry never fully connected with the public as an individual—he was generally viewed as distant, even snobbish.

It is no surprise, for example, that Bush ran well among voters who said they cared most about each candidate's religious faith—Bush won 91 percent of that group. But Bush also won 70 percent of those who wanted an honest, trustworthy president; 87 percent of those who wanted a strong leader; and 79 percent of those who wanted a president who takes a clear stand on issues. Although Kerry ran well among those who wanted a president that cares about people, his greatest strength came from those who wanted an intelligent leader who would bring change to the country.

A third answer is simply that Bush ran a better campaign. In spite of all the bad news coming into the campaign from Iraq, including the last-second revelation that the U.S. military had somehow misplaced almost 400 tons of dangerous explosives that Iraqi dictator Saddam Hussein had stockpiled just outside Baghdad, the Bush campaign kept Kerry on the defensive. Bush operatives were particularly effective in exploiting Kerry's own statements and creating an image of him as a "flip flopper" who could not be trusted to run the nation during war. As a Bush aide said of Kerry's oft-quoted statement that he voted for an $87-billion bill to arm the troops in Iraq just before he voted against it, "As soon as we saw it, we knew that was exactly what we wanted to say, but he said it for us. That's something he couldn't undo."

A fourth and final answer involves issues. When asked what issue most influenced their vote, 22 percent of Americans referred to moral issues such as abortion and gay marriage, another 20 percent said the economy and jobs, 19 percent said terrorism, 15 percent said the war in Iraq, and 8 percent said health care. Bush won 80 percent of the votes among those who focused on moral issues and 86 percent of the votes among those who focused on terrorism, while Kerry did exceptionally well among the rest.

A Mandate to Govern?

No matter how close the actual results, Bush began preparing for his second term as if he had won a sweeping mandate. The fact that Republicans picked up seats in the Senate and House gave him additional ammunition for the case. After all, this was the first time since 1924 that an incumbent president won reelection and gained seats in both chambers.

But claiming a mandate and having one are two different things. Second-term presidents have very little time to set the legislative agenda, in part because the modern

President John F. Kennedy understood the importance of direct communication with the American people and often addressed the public with television broadcasts.

campaign system forces candidates in both parties to start planning for the next election early. Because Bush refused to pick an heir-apparent as his vice presidential running mate, Republicans were already lining up for the 2008 election even before the 2004 election was over.

CONGRESS AND THE PRESIDENCY

Tensions between Congress and presidents go back to the origins of American government. Alexander Hamilton, General George Washington's chief aide, complained about the political stalemate that faced the the Continental Congress more than 200 years ago.

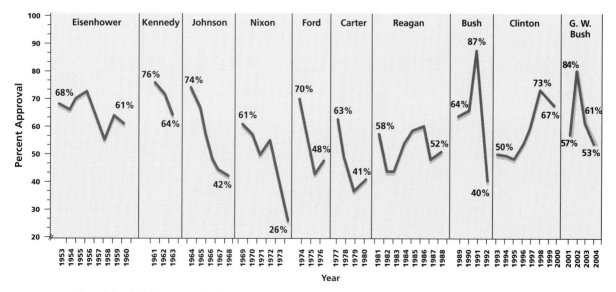

FIGURE 12–3 Presidential Approval Ratings, 1945–2004.
SOURCE: Gallup Organization, at www.gallup.com. Updated by the authors.

★ ★ **YOU DECIDE**

SHOULD PRESIDENTS BE LIMITED TO TWO TERMS IN OFFICE?

Before he left office, former President Ronald Reagan called for the repeal of the Twenty-Second Amendment to the Constitution, the one that limits a president to two terms. Why do you think he opposed the amendment? What additional reasons could be put forth to persuade people to repeal this relatively new (1951) provision in the Constitution? What are the best reasons for retaining the Twenty-Second Amendment?

Yet it was the intention of the framers of the U.S. Constitution to create a government of sharply limited powers and separated institutions that would both share and compete for power. The framers saw the separation of powers not necessarily as a weakness but as a source of strength and especially as a way to ensure deliberation and to prevent tyranny.

The Constitutional Framework

Article I of the Constitution grants Congress "all legislative Powers" but limits those powers to those "herein granted." It then sets forth in some detail the powers vested in Congress. In contrast, Article II vests in the president "the executive Power" without limiting it to such powers as are "herein granted" and then proceeds to describe those powers in very general terms.

Some scholars and most presidents have argued that Article II gives each president a general and undefined power to act to promote the well-being of the United States, subject only to precise constitutional limits. Therefore, they contend, a president is *not* limited to the specific powers spelled out in the Constitution, as Congress is, but has all the executive powers of the United States. Other scholars and many members of Congress contend that the president either has no such inherent power or has it only in extraordinary circumstances.[32]

Whatever the intent of the Constitution, the president has often exercised powers not expressly granted by it. These powers have been given a variety of names: *implied, inherent,* or *emergency powers.* For example, Bill Clinton found a way to lend Mexico billions of dollars in 1995 to stabilize its currency, even though Congress had essentially refused to do so. Similarly, George W. Bush ordered the armed services to start preparing for the war in Iraq well ahead of congressional authorization. Actions like these prompt many in Congress to criticize presidents, even if they believe that in certain emergencies a president must act promptly without clear constitutional or statutory support.

COMPETING CONSTITUENCIES The Constitution also guarantees that Congress and the president will represent different constituencies. Members of Congress represent state and local districts, and hence they reflect specific geographic, ethnic, and economic interests. James Madison and other framers of the Constitution anticipated that legislators would often be pressured by local and state interests to adopt a narrow or parochial view, as opposed to a national view, on certain policy issues, and presidents and their aides often think Madison was right. Members of Congress, of course, see sensitivity to state and local concerns as essential to their job as representatives and to their prospects for reelection. As a result, members of Congress—even those from the president's own party and own region—may look at problems and solutions somewhat differently from the way the president does. The president is expected to take a national perspective.

COMPETING CALENDARS The Constitution also ensures that Congress and the president will not share the same terms of office. Presidents serve for four years with a chance of reelection to a second term; senators have the luxury of six-year terms; members of the House of Representatives are elected to two-year terms. Different constituencies and lengths of service make these national officials responsive to different moods and points of view. Different electoral forces are at work in different election years. A majority of the voters can win control over only part of the national government at a time, and this arrangement, too, was by design.

Presidents often act quickly to shape national priorities in their first months following their electoral victory, to win support for their agendas before a possible decline in public approval. Congress, by contrast, usually moves more slowly "because it represents a vast array of local interests."[33] Another obvious difference in the speed of their two branches has to do with numbers: There is one president, but there are 435 members of the House and 100 senators.

COMPETING CAMPAIGNS Finally, the Constitution ensures that Congress and the president will run different kinds of election campaigns. Most members of Congress finance their election campaigns with only minimal assistance from their national political party.

They customarily respond to local conditions and run their campaigns independently of their party's presidential candidate or national platform. And changes in the electorate in recent years that enhance an incumbent's chances of reelection weaken the connection between the president and fellow partisans in Congress.

Members of the president's party have typically run well ahead of their president in elections in their home districts, and thus they are less fearful of punishment for ignoring occasional party appeals for loyalty. They are more likely to go along with the president when a measure converges with their own political philosophy and is in the interest of their home district or state. Although parties have become vigorously partisan within Congress, especially in the House of Representatives, there are always several independent thinkers who will at times—sometimes crucial times for the White House—go their own way rather than cooperate with the White House, even when the president is a member of the same party.[34]

Influencing Congress

Presidents are clearly much more than faithful executors of the laws passed by Congress. They have long had a substantial, if not always dominant, role in shaping what Congress does. Their primary vehicle for doing so is the president's agenda, which is an informal list of top legislative priorities. Whether through the State of the Union address or through other messages and signals, presidents make clear what they think Congress should do.[35]

It is one thing to proclaim a presidential priority, however, and quite another to actually influence congressional action. As Richard Neustadt argued in *Presidential Power,* a president's constitutional powers add up to little more than a job as America's most distinguished office clerk. It is a president's ability to persuade others that spells the difference between being a clerk and being a national leader.[36] This power to persuade rests in the resources a president brings to office and the skills that he or she uses in making the most of those resources. (Figure 12–4 compares recent presidents on their ability to influence Congress on key votes. Bush's support scores remained remarkably high through his first three years. His third year score, while lower than his first and second, showed surprising strength.

Although Bush lost a number of votes on his judicial nominees in the Senate and refused to bargain with Congress over post-war aid to Iraq, his third-year score reflects a sharp incrase in the number of votes on which he took a position. Whereas he took a position on 120 issues in 2001 and 98 in 2002, he took a position on 174 votes in 2003,

★★ THINKING IT THROUGH

Reagan felt that the people should be able to reelect a president as many times as they want, just as they now reelect House and Senate members. He also hinted that the Twenty-Second Amendment might weaken a president late in his second term by making him a lame duck, less powerful because everyone knows he will not be around in a year or so. Advocates of repeal also say we may sometimes need to keep a veteran president in office during a crisis period, much as we retained Franklin Roosevelt in 1940. Others say eight years may not be enough time to resolve certain major problems.

The Twenty-Second Amendment is not only a limit on the incumbent but also on the electorate, the first since the ratification of the Constitution to restrict the power of the electorate rather than expand it. It is based, advocates of repeal suggest, on the assumption that the voters cannot be trusted.

Advocates of the Twenty-Second Amendment argue that it acts as an additional check against presidential power by encouraging both parties to seek out effective candidates to take office, while discouraging dependence on a single ruler. In addition, few presidents are likely to have the health, the intellectual energy, and the new ideas needed to perform the demanding responsibilities of the presidency beyond eight years in office.

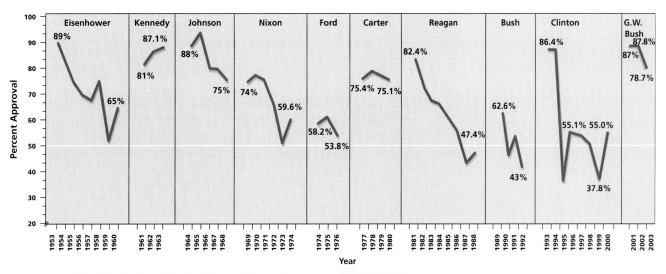

FIGURE 12–4 Presidential Legislative Support from Congress, 1953–2004.
SOURCE: *Congressional Quarterly Weekly,* January 12, 2002, p. 110. Updated by the authors.
NOTE: Percentages represent average scores for both chambers of Congress.

creating more opportunities for defeat. It was the largest numbr of votes since 1995. Bush's score was inflated somewhat by several issues that produced repeated victories for the president, including eight votes on legislation to prohibit federal funding for an abortion procedure called "partial-birth" abortion. The increase also reflected increased division between the two parties in the Senate, where the Republican majority sought party-line victories that could be used against the future Democratic presidential candidate, John Kerry.

Presidential Resources

There are two kinds of resources that shape both the size of a president's agenda and its ultimate impact on Congress. The first involves the political resources needed to convince Congress to support the president, while the second involves the decision-making resources that help presidents decide what they want.

POLITICAL RESOURCES A president's external influence comes from three sources: (1) the mandate provided by his election, (2) the level of public approval, and (3) the number of party seats in Congress. New presidents usually begin with at least some of each.

Presidents who enter office with a large electoral margin, high public approval, and a party majority in Congress often claim a **mandate** to govern. As noted in Chapter 9, the winner-take-all nature of the electoral college system tends to make the president's popular vote look larger than it truly is. In 1984, for example, Ronald Reagan set the modern record by winning every state but Massachusetts and the District of Columbia, rolling up 98 percent of the electoral votes with a popular total of 59 percent.

Mandates also reside in public approval for either the president or some policy issue. In 1993, for example, Clinton claimed a mandate for national health insurance, arguing that the issue was at the core of much of his public support. The claim would have been more plausible, however, had Clinton won with a popular vote larger than 43 percent. George W. Bush made a similar claim for a broad agenda in 2001, arguing that the American public wanted action in Washington. Again, the claim would have been more plausible had he won the popular vote.

PERSONAL RESOURCES Presidents can hardly claim mandates or invest their political resources if they do not have the time, energy, and information to actually set the agenda, or the political skills to focus congressional attention on their priorities. The first two of these personal resources, time and energy, run out over the course of the term and are difficult to replace. Presidents have only so much time to make their mark. Since they can only serve for two consecutive terms under the Twenty-Second Amendment, they must make every day count.

Presidents have only so much energy to give to the job. One need only compare pictures of presidents at the start and end of their terms to see the impact of the long hours and constant stress. As Gerald Ford once remarked, "It's a hard job being president. . . . Anybody who walks in there thinking he can punch a time clock at 9 in the morning and leave at 5 has got another think coming. We do not elect presidents who want that kind of a life."

The third personal resource, information, actually increases over time as presidents learn their jobs. In a sense, the presidency is the nation's most intense American government course. One way presidents can increase their learning is to take "prerequisites" before entering office—that is, by holding other executive offices, such as the vice presidency or a governorship, that are similar to the presidency or by studying issues as a senator or member of the House that are central to the president's constitutional duties.

The final personal resource is the president's skill at legislative timing and lobbying. Timing involves a president's ability to win congressional attention at key points in the legislative process, while lobbying involves the president's personal skill at persuading individual members of Congress.[37] Lobbying can involve everything from invitations to special White House events to giving members of Congress extra help with government projects back home.

mandate
A president's claim of broad public support.

JUDGING PRESIDENTS

Historians, political scientists, and the American public generally agree that Lincoln, Washington, Franklin Roosevelt, and Jefferson were the nation's greatest presidents. These four became great in part by expanding the presidency, while stretching the Constitution to address great crises and war. Sometimes this is called the "doctrine of necessity"—doing what needs to be done. These presidents often exercised powers that were thought to be solely or primarily congressional, and occasionally challenged Congress and the Supreme Court as well.

There are several sources of greatness. President Washington, more than any other person, converted the paper notions outlined in the Constitution into an enduring, practical governing process. With extraordinary character, he set the precedents that balanced self-government and leadership, chief of state and chief executive, constitutionalism and statesmanship.

Thomas Jefferson, a genius in his generation, was a skilled organizer and a resourceful party leader and chief executive. He made mistakes, yet he adapted the presidency to the new realities of his day. His expansions of territory with the Louisiana Purchase, his sponsorship of the Lewis and Clark expedition, and similar bold ventures ensure him a revered status among presidents. President Lincoln is remembered for saving the Union and is revered as the nation's foremost symbol of democracy and tenacious leadership in the nation's ultimate crisis. President Franklin Delano Roosevelt is viewed as guiding the nation through its worst economic crisis and for leading the "greatest generation" to victory in World War II. These presidential accomplishments are part of the legend of America. Yet this heroic view of presidents raises a good many questions. If presidents alone were responsible for these and similar feats, it is little wonder that our expectations are so high concerning what current and future presidents should accomplish. (See Table 12–3 for a comparison of two different ratings of presidents, one by the *New York Times/Chicago Sun Times* of leading presidential historians, who tend to be more liberal, and the other by the *Wall Street Journal* designed to include more conservative historians.)

In fact, a variety of people and institutions contributed to the achievements credited to past presidents. History seldom adequately honors the reformers and leaders who provided behind-the-scenes leadership. The best presidents surround themselves with talented advisers and administrators. Great leadership depends on situation, resources, opportunity, and teams of leaders. Being at the right place at the right time also helps.

PRESIDENTIAL GREATNESS: HOW DO WE JUDGE THEM?

Presidents rise and fall in the historical rankings based on a number of factors. Some rise because they led the nation through periods of intense domestic or international crisis; others rise because they had a distinctive vision of where the nation should go on issues such as civil rights, social policy, or the economy. Rankings also involve at least some assessment of how presidents did as political and moral leaders of the nation. Some fall because of political or personal scandal, others because they failed to grapple with a big issue such as national health insurance or economic crisis. In the end, rankings involve the overall measure of a president's impact in meeting the public's expectations.

Go to Make It Real "Presidential Greatness: How Do We Judge Them?"

TABLE 12–3   RANKING PRESIDENTS

	Ten Best		Ten Worst
New York Times/ Chicago Sun Times	**Wall Street Journal**	**New York Times/ Chicago Sun Times**	**Wall Street Journal**
1. Abraham Lincoln	1. George Washington	1. Warren Harding	1. James Buchanan
2. George Washington	2. Abraham Lincoln	2. James Buchanan	2. Warren Harding
3. Franklin Roosevelt	3. Franklin Roosevelt	3. Franklin Pierce	3. Franklin Pierce
4. Thomas Jefferson	4. Thomas Jefferson	4. Ulysses Grant	4. Andrew Johnson
5. Theodore Roosevelt	5. Theodore Roosevelt	5. Andrew Johnson	5. Millard Fillmore
6. Woodrow Wilson	6. Andrew Jackson	6. Millard Fillmore	6. John Tyler
7. Harry Truman	7. Harry Truman	7. Richard Nixon	7. Richard Nixon
8. Andrew Jackson	8. Ronald Reagan	8. John Tyler	8. Ulysses Grant
9. James Polk	9. Dwight Eisenhower	9. Calvin Coolidge	9. Zachary Taylor
10. Dwight Eisenhower	10. James Polk	10. Herbert Hoover	10. Jimmy Carter

Sources: Steve Neal, "Putting Presidents in Their Place," *Chicago Sun-Times*, November 19, 1995, pp. 30–31; Arthur M. Schlesinger Jr., "The Ultimate Approval Rating," *New York Times Magazine*, December 15, 1996, pp. 46–51; James Lindgren and Steven Calabresi, "Ranking the Presidents," *Wall Street Journal*, November 16, 2000, p. 13.

Many of the great presidents made mistakes, sometimes great mistakes. And the great presidents typically look better some years later than they did while they were at the helm. Harry Truman is a prime example of a presidential leader who was viewed in a lesser light while in office but was later recognized as great.

The nation can learn from those presidents judged as failures. Experts rank some presidents at or near the bottom because of political corruption while placing others near the bottom because they lacked a compelling program, vision, political skill, or integrity. Although Richard Nixon was respected for his foreign policy initiatives, especially for his recognition of the People's Republic of China, he is nonetheless viewed as one of the lesser presidents because he lied to the American public, plotted a cover-up of illegal and unconstitutional activities, resigned in disgrace, and, in the eyes of many, sullied the dignity of the Oval Office.

It is too early to guess where George W. Bush will be ranked by history. His early response to September 11 was steady and reassuring, and Americans rallied to his side in the early months of the war in Iraq. At the same time, soaring budget deficits and questions about the missing weapons of mass destruction undermined both his credibility and his public support.

Ultimately, a president's place in history is determined years, even decades, after the president has left office. By remembering that there is a future accounting, presidents can find some inspiration for making the hard and sometimes unpopular choices that have led to greatness among their predecessors. Thus the judgment of history may be one of the most important sources of accountability that the nation has on its presidents. Bush's reelection in 2004 provides four more years in which to shape that judgment, whether through Supreme Court appointments or through bold legislative reforms of national programs such as Social Security.

S U M M A R Y

1. The framers created a presidency with limited powers. To enact government business, the president must cooperate with Congress, but powers are divided among the branches, and the politics of shared power has often been stormy. In general, however, both the role and the influence of presidents have increased over the course of the nation's history.

2. The framers gave the president three central roles in the new government: commander in chief, diplomat in chief, and administrator in chief. Presidents have expanded their powers in several ways over the decades. Crises, both foreign and economic, have enlarged these powers. When there is a need for decisive action, presidents are asked to supply it. Congress, of course, is traditionally expected to share in the formulation of national policy. Every president must learn anew the need to work closely with the members of Congress.

3. The Constitution is not always clear on which branch has what powers, which creates controversies over the president's war power, authority to assert executive privilege, issue executive orders, and control the budget and spending process. Congress has made several attempts in recent decades to clarify the president's war and spending power.

4. Presidents manage the executive branch with the assistance of a White House staff composed of roughly 400 individuals and a cabinet of department secretaries that oversees the civil servants. The vice president is also involved in helping the president manage government.

5. The presidency has evolved over the past two centuries to become one of the world's most powerful institutions. This evolution began with George Washington, who set many of the precedents for presidential leadership that exist to this day. It continued with the first modern president, Franklin Roosevelt, who built the presidency into an instrument for sweeping national policy.

6. Americans expect a great deal from their presidents. They want them to be crisis managers, morale builders, and agenda setters, yet also want them to be able to connect with average Americans.

7. The president and Congress often have a tense relationship because of different constitutional expectations and party divisions. Presidents have a variety of tools for influencing Congress, however, and use their political and personal resources to gain support for their policy proposals.

8. Presidential greatness is hard to define. Historians, political scientists, and the American public consider Lincoln, Washington, Jefferson, and Franklin Roosevelt as their greatest presidents, and Harding and Buchanan as their worst. Greatness depends in part on how presidents deal with crisis and war.

KEY TERMS

parliamentary system	take care clause	executive orders	Office of Management and
presidential ticket	inherent powers	impoundment	Budget (OMB)
treaty	State of the Union address	line item veto	cabinet
executive agreement	impeachment	chief of staff	rally point
veto	executive privilege	Executive Office of the President	mandate
pocket veto			

FURTHER READING

DAVID GRAY ADLER AND LARRY N. GEORGE, EDS., *The Constitution and the Conduct of American Foreign Policy: Essays on Law and History* (University Press of Kansas, 1996).

PAUL BRACE AND BARBARA HINCKLEY, *Follow the Leader: Opinion Polls and the Modern Presidents* (Basic Books, 1992).

JOHN P. BURKE AND MICHAEL NELSON, *The Institutional Presidency: Organizing and Managing the White House from FDR to Clinton*, 2d ed. (Johns Hopkins University Press, 2000).

THOMAS E. CRONIN, ED., *Inventing the American Presidency* (University Press of Kansas, 1989).

THOMAS E. CRONIN AND MICHAEL A. GENOVESE, *The Paradoxes of the American Presidency*, 2d ed. (Oxford University Press, 2004).

TERRY EASTLAND, *Energy in the Executive* (Free Press, 1992).

MICHAEL A. GENOVESE, *The Power of the American Presidency, 1989–2000* (Oxford University Press, 2000).

DAVID GERGEN, *Eyewitness to Power: The Essence of Leadership, Nixon to Clinton* (Simon & Schuster, 2000).

STEPHEN HESS, *Organizing the Presidency*, 2d ed. (Brookings Institution Press, 2003).

FRED GREENSTEIN, *The Presidential Difference* (Free Press, 2000).

ERWIN C. HARGROVE, *The President as Leader: Appealing to the Better Angels of Our Nature* (University Press of Kansas, 1998).

CHARLES O. JONES, *Passages to the Presidency: From Campaigning to Governing* (Brookings Institution Press, 1998).

SAMUEL KERNELL, *Going Public: New Strategies of Presidential Leadership* (CQ Press, 1997).

GARY KING AND LYN RAGSDALE, *The Elusive Executive: Discovering Statistical Patterns in the Presidency*, 2d ed. (CQ Press, 2002).

MARK LANDY AND SIDNEY M. MILKIS, *Presidential Greatness* (University Press of Kansas, 2000).

LEONARD W. LEVY AND LOUIS FISHER, EDS., *Encyclopedia of the American Presidency* (Simon & Schuster, 1994).

JOHN A. MALTESE, *Spin Control: The White House Office of Communications and the Management of the Presidential News* (University of North Carolina Press, 1992).

SIDNEY M. MILKIS, *The President and the Parties: The Transformation of the American Party System Since the New Deal* (Oxford University Press, 1993).

SIDNEY M. MILKIS AND MICHAEL NELSON, *The American Presidency: Origins and Development, 1976–2000*, 4th ed. (CQ Press, 2003).

MICHAEL NELSON, ED., *The Presidency and the Political System*, 6th ed. (CQ Press, 2000).

RICHARD E. NEUSTADT, *Presidential Power and the Modern Presidents* (Free Press, 1991).

HUBERT S. PARMET, *George Bush: The Life of a Lone Star Yankee* (Scribner, 1998).

STEPHEN PONDER, *Managing the Press: Origins of the Media Presidency* (Palgrave, 2000).

BRADLEY H. PATTERSON, JR., *The White House Staff: Inside the West Wing and Beyond* (Brookings Institution Press, 2000).

JAMES P. PFIFFNER, *The Strategic Presidency: Hitting the Ground Running*, 2d ed. (University Press of Kansas, 1996).

GLENN A. PHELPS, *George Washington and American Constitutionalism* (University Press of Kansas, 1993).

LYN RAGSDALE, *Vital Statistics on the Presidency, rev. ed.* (CQ Press, 1998).

SHELLEY LYNNE TOMKINS, *Inside OMB: Politics and Process in the President's Budget Office* (Sharpe, 1998).

KENNETH T. WALSH, *Feeding the Beast: The White House Versus the Press* (Random House, 1996).

SHIRLEY ANNE WARSHAW, *Powersharing: White House–Cabinet Relations in the Modern Presidency* (State University of New York Press, 1996).

THE FEDERAL BUREAUCRACY
EXECUTING THE LAWS

13

Whether they know it or not, Americans interact with the federal bureaucracy every day. Their air and water is guarded by the Environmental Protection Agency and Department of Interior, their food is protected by the Food and Drug Administration and Department of Agriculture, threats to their health are being studied by the National Institutes of Health and Centers for Disease Control and Prevention, their college loans are either funded or insured by the Department of Education, at least part of their retirement income is being sheltered by the Social Security Administration, their workplaces are inspected by the Occupational Health and Safety Administration, and their roads are smoothed in part by the Department of Transportation.

Despite its reach, and perhaps because of it, Americans have a love-hate relationship with the federal bureaucracy. They want more of virtually everything government delivers, from health care to national parks, from faster drug approval to home loans, yet they often complain that government is too big and wasteful. A majority of Americans believe that the federal government creates more problems than it solves and that it controls too much of daily life.[1] In October 2003, for example, 93 percent of Americans said that the federal government wastes a great deal or fair amount of money.[2]

When problems arise, however, Americans often ask the federal government to respond. This is certainly what happened immediately after September 11, 2001. Confidence in the president and vice president rose dramatically in the days following the terrorist attacks on New York City and Washington, as did confidence in elected officials such as members of Congress. The number of Americans who said they trusted the federal government

TIME LINE
THE FEDERAL BUREAUCRACY

1776	Board of War and Ordnance created (becomes Secretary of War in 1781)
1781	Department of Foreign Affairs created (becomes Department of State in 1789)
1789	Departments of War, State, and Treasury created
1789	Office of the Attorney General created (becomes Department of Justice in 1870)
1849	Department of Interior created
1862	Department of Agriculture created
1862	Commission of Internal Revenue created
1865	United States Secret Service created
1867	Office of Education created (becomes part of the newly created Department of Health, Education, and Welfare in 1953; becomes Department of Education in 1979)
1914	Federal Trade Commission is created
1939	Hatch Act restricts political activity among federal employees
1958	NASA is created to compete with the Soviet space program
1966	Freedom of Information Act opens many government records to citizens
1970	Environmental Protection Agency created in response to demand for cleaner air, water, and land
1977	Department of Energy created in reaction to the energy crisis of the early 1970s
1989	Veterans Affairs elevated to a cabinet-level department
2003	Department of Homeland Security is created

to do the right thing almost always or most of the time jumped from 29 percent in July 2001 to 57 percent in October.

Yet, even as confidence went up, Americans remained skeptical about big government. Interviewed three weeks after the 2001 terrorist attacks, 70 percent of Americans assumed that most federal employees chose to work for the government because of the job security, and 68 percent cited the salary and benefits. Even at a time when Americans accepted the need for a strong federal government, they doubted the basic motivations of the people who work for it.[3]

Moreover, what goes up must eventually come down. As the intense emotions of September 11 faded, so did the newfound trust in government. By May 2002, the number of Americans who said they trusted the government in Washington to do the right thing just about always or most of the time had fallen to 40 percent, which is where it stood two years later in July 2004. Although trust was still above its pre-September 2001 levels, Americans still viewed the federal government as wasteful and its employees as more motivated by the pay, benefits, and job security than the chance to make a difference, serve the country, and pride. Americans also believe that the president's own appointees are driven more by interest in making connections and making money than serving the people.

In this chapter, we examine the origins, functions, and realities of our national public bureaucracy. We also explore how government agencies are held accountable to the president, Congress, and the American public, and ask how government might make public service more attractive to its most talented citizens.

UNDERSTANDING THE FEDERAL BUREAUCRACY

The framers believed that differences of opinion and what Alexander Hamilton called the "jarring of parties" were healthy for protecting the nation from "excesses in the majority." However, once the laws were made, the framers expected the disagreements to end. As Hamilton explained in *The Federalist*, No. 70, "a government ill executed, whatever it may be in theory, must be, in practice, a bad government."[4]

The Undefined Branch

The framers spent little time worrying about the administrative structure of government and left most of the details to the first Congress and president. They believed the first bureaucracy would be relatively small, and they expected Congress to establish the same departments that had existed under the Articles of Confederation.[5] They also expected George Washington to be the government's first chief executive and believed he would lead the new government with the same skill that he had led the Continental Army.

Nevertheless, the framers made two key decisions about who would be responsible for executing the laws.

First, they prohibited members of the House and Senate from holding executive branch positions. They drew a sharp line on the issue in Article I, Section 6, of the Constitution: "No Senator or Representative shall, during the Time for which he was elected, be appointed to any civil Office under the Authority of the United States, which shall have been created, or the Emoluments whereof shall have been increased during such time, and no Person holding any Office under the United States, shall be a Member of either House during his Continuance in Office."

This provision prevented members of Congress from creating jobs for themselves in the executive branch, a common form of corruption in England prior to the Revolutionary War.[6] The founders also worried that simultaneous service in both branches would weaken the separation of powers.

Second, the framers decided not to give Congress the power to appoint the treasurer of the United States (now called the secretary of the treasury). For much of the summer of 1787, appointing the treasurer was first on the list of the legislature's enumerated powers, reflecting the framers' concern about the financial stability of the new nation.

It was not until the third-to-last working day of the convention that the founders deleted the provision in an effort to reaffirm the president's authority to appoint and supervise the officers of government. Having already made the president commander in chief of the armed services, the founders reaffirmed the president's power to run the government as a whole. Under Article II, it is up to the president, not Congress or the judiciary, to require the opinion of the "principal officer" of each executive department. And it is up to the president, not Congress or the judiciary, to fill any vacancies in those jobs without Senate review when the Senate is in recess. Although Article I does give Congress the power to create the departments of government and the Senate the power to confirm presidential appointees by a two-thirds vote, the president emerged from the final days of the Constitutional Convention as the nation's administrator in chief.

These decisions did not give the president unlimited authority to execute the laws, however. The framers gave Congress, not the president, the power to create the departments and agencies of government in the first place, and the responsibility for appropriating the money to administer programs and hire government employees. They also gave the Senate the power to confirm presidential appointees and clearly expected both houses to monitor executive implementation.

The Federal Bureaucracy Today

More than two hundred years later, the federal bureaucracy is anything but small. Almost 2.7 million Americans work for the federal government today, whether in the 15 cabinet-level departments, the U.S. Postal Service, or in the more than 50 independent agencies. Another 1.4 million Americans serve in the armed forces.

The vast majority work in six agencies: the Departments of the Army, the Navy, and the Air Force (all three in the Department of Defense); the Department of Veterans Affairs; the Department of Homeland Security; and the U.S. Postal Service. Although most agencies are directly responsible to the president, some, like the Postal Service, are partly, or quasi-, independent. Moreover, all federal agencies are created by acts of Congress; Congress can abolish them either by passing a new law or by withholding funds.

The terms "bureaucrat" and "bureaucracy" date from the early nineteenth century. Originally, the word "bureau" referred to a cloth covering the desks of French government officials in the eighteenth century; eventually it came to be applied to the desk itself. The term was soon linked with the suffix "-ocracy" (as in "democracy" or "aristocracy") to describe government (essentially, "rule by people at desks").

At one time in history, the term **bureaucracy** actually mean fast, effective, and rational. In its ideal form, a bureaucracy made sure that every job was carefully designed to ensure faithful performance by well-trained, highly-motivated **bureaucrats**, or employees. Over time, however, the term came to mean slow, confusing, and self-serving. Although this chapter uses "bureaucracy" and "bureaucrats" in neutral terms, the terms are often invoked to criticize red tape and waste.

In theory, government bureaucracies are designed to hold every employee in the organization accountable to the president through a chain of command that describes who is responsible for every decision. Most jobs are highly specialized and are filled on the basis of merit, not political connections or favoritism.[7] Also in theory, bureaucracies are designed to increase efficiency and lower costs.

In reality, governmental bureaucracies are particularly difficult to manage because of their size, interest group connections, and political history. First, duplication and overlap across departments and agencies can create confusion about which agencies are responsible for a problem such as mad cow disease, which can be transmitted to human beings by eating diseased meat. The Department of Agriculture's Animal and Plant Health Inspection Service keeps diseased cattle out of the United States, which is the best way to prevent the disease; the Department of Health and Human Services' Food and Drug Administration is supposed to monitor cattle feed, which is another way to prevent

bureaucracy
A form of organization that operates through impersonal, uniform rules and procedures.

bureaucrat
A career government employee.

the disease, and the Department of Agriculture's Food Safety and Inspection Service inspects cattle as they go to slaughter, which is the last defense against letting diseased meat enter the food supply. All three may have failed in 2003 when the meat from a diseased cow entered the U.S. food supply.

Second, even within a single agency, bureaucracy often creates dense layers of management that keep information from moving up and down the organization quickly. Just consider the reporting relationships that lead down to the Food Safety and Inspection Service, which employs the 8,000 federal workers who actually inspect the cattle that go to slaughter. Each cattle inspector reports to (1) a local supervisor who reports to (2) a deputy district office director who reports to (3) the district office director who reports to (4) an executive assistant administrator for regulatory operations in Washington who reports to (5) the deputy assistant administrator for field operations who reports to (6) the assistant administrator for field operations who reports to (7) a deputy administrator who reports to (8) the administrator of the Food Safety Inspection Service who reports to (9) the deputy undersecretary and undersecretary for food safety who reports to (10) the deputy secretary of agriculture who reports to (11) the deputy chief of staff to the secretary who reports to (12) the chief of staff who reports to (13) the secretary of agriculture who reports to (14) the president. Like the childhood game of telephone in which messages are distorted as they are whispered from one child to another, there are many places in the food safety reporting chain where information can get lost or misunderstood.

These problems have led some advocates to call for the creation of a single food safety organization with the resources and authority to regulate and oversee all aspects of the food chain. Such a reorganization would not only give consumers and producers a single point of contact, it would allow a winnowing of the needless layers of management that get in the way of accountability, and a streamlining of responsibilities. Under current law, for example, the Food and Drug Administration is responsible for the safety of cheese pizzas, while the Department of Agriculture is responsible for meat pizzas.

How the Federal Government Is Organized

The federal bureaucracy contains a wide variety of organizations. Some, such as the Department of Defense, are collections of huge agencies in their own right, which can create duplication and overlap. The Defense Department and its 2 million employees contains the Departments of the Army, Navy, and Air Force, each with its own separate duties (as if to confirm how Congress sometimes divides responsibilities, the Army has its own air force, and the Navy has its own army called the Marine Corps). Others, such as the Department of Education and its 5,000 employees, are tiny by comparison, but they spend huge amounts of money through grants to students. Public management scholars classify the organizations of government into four broad categories: (1) *departments,* (2) *independent agencies,* (3) *independent regulatory commissions,* and (4) *government corporations.*

Departments tend to be the largest federal organizations of all and have the broadest missions. **Independent agencies** tend to be smaller and have more focused responsibilities. **Independent regulatory commissions** are similar to agencies but are designed to be free from direct presidential control. Finally, **government corporations** are designed to operate much like private businesses.

Departments Cabinet departments are the most visible organizations in the federal bureaucracy. Today's 15 departments of government employ more than 70 percent of all federal civil servants and spend 93 percent of all federal dollars—the rest is spent by the other kinds of agencies to be described. Fourteen of the departments are headed by secretaries; the fifteenth, the Justice Department, is headed by the attorney general. (See Figure 13–1 for the structure of the Department of Homeland Security, which was created in 2002 by merging 22 separate agencies.)

Measured by the total number of employees, the Defense Department is by far the largest department, followed by the Department of Veterans Affairs, which helps veterans return to civilian life after military service; the Department of Homeland Security, which was created to protect the nation from terrorism; the Department of the Treasury,

department
Usually the largest organization in government; also the highest rank in federal hierarchy.

independent agency
A government entity that is independent of the legislative, executive, and judicial branches.

independent regulatory commission
A government agency or commission with regulatory power whose independence is protected by Congress.

government corporation
A government agency that operates like a business corporation, created to secure greater freedom of action and flexibility for a particular program.

CHANGING FACE OF AMERICAN POLITICS

A REPRESENTATIVE BUREAUCRACY?

One way to make the federal bureaucracy more accountable to the public is to make it look more like the public. By creating a representative bureaucracy, at least in terms of race and gender, the federal government can strengthen its connection to the people it serves.

The federal government is clearly more representative of the public now than it was in the 1950s, when most of its employees were white and most women were clerk-typists. Women now occupy 45 percent of all federal jobs; minorities occupy nearly 30 percent.

Even though the number of women and minorities in the federal workforce is at an all-time high, they still face barriers in rising to the top. First, women and minorities are not equally represented in all departments and agencies. They tend to concentrate in departments with strong social service missions such as Education, Health and Human Services, Housing and Urban Development, and Veterans Affairs (which runs the VA hospital system, with its mostly female nursing corps), all of which have more than 50 percent female employees. Military and technical departments such as Defense, Energy, NASA, and Transportation have far fewer women. Health and Human Services has 65 percent women, while Transportation has just 25 percent; 50 percent of the Department of Education's employees are minorities, compared to just 16 percent of Agriculture's.

Second, women and minorities are not represented at all levels of the federal bureaucracy. In 2003, women held only 35 percent of the professional and administrative jobs, where the higher-paying management posts are, but 70 percent of the lower-paying technical and clerical positions. Minorities were also heavily represented in the lower-paying jobs. Together, women and minorities held almost half the jobs at the bottom level of the federal pay system in 2000 and just 10 percent of the posts at the top.

Education Department employee Claudia Gaines and Education Secretary Rod Paige work with a fourth grade student during National Volunteer Week.

The Face of the Federal Workforce, 2003

Gender	
Men	55%
Women	45

Race	
White	70
African American	17
Hispanic	7
Asian and Pacific Islander	5
American Indian	2

Education	
High school or some college	60
College graduate	40

SOURCE: Office of Personnel Management, *The Fact Book, 2003 Edition* (U.S. Government Printing Office, 2003).

which manages the economy and raises revenues through the Internal Revenue Service; and the Department of Justice, which enforces the laws through the federal courts and investigates crime through the Federal Bureau of Investigation.

Measured by budget, the Department of Health and Human Services comes first, followed by the Department of Defense. The Department of Health and Human Services provides health insurance to the elderly through the huge Medicare program, helps states cover health care for the poor through the Medicaid programs, covers the cost of health insurance for children through the Children's Health Insurance Program (CHIP), and administers a variety of programs to help poor Americans. It also contains the Food and Drug Administration, the National Institutes of Health, and the Centers for Disease Control and Prevention, all of which protect Americans from disease.

These 15 departments represent two very different approaches to department building. One approach is to create an umbrella department by combining a number of related programs. The Department of Homeland Security was created by combining elements of 22 separate agencies, including the Coast Guard, Immigration and Naturalization Service, Customs Service, Federal Emergency Management Agency, Secret Service, and the Animal and Plant Health Inspection Service. The Departments of Health and Human Services, Commerce, and Defense also reflect a conglomerate approach.

The other approach is to create a single-purpose department that owes much of its survival to the strength of a constituency group. Congress created the Department of Veterans Affairs in 1989 under pressure from veterans' groups such as the American Legion, who wanted their own advocate in the president's cabinet. It was hardly the first time that Congress yielded to such pressure. One can easily argue that the Departments of Agriculture, Commerce, Education, and Labor were all created in response to interest group pressure.

Creating a department does not necessarily guarantee greater performance. Three years after its creation, the Department of Homeland Security is still working to make the merger work. It took two years for the department to decide on a common uniform for customs agents, immigration inspectors, and passenger screeners, for example, and it is still looking for a permanent space for its Washington headquarters.

Independent Regulatory Commissions Size and age are not the only ways to compare units within the federal bureaucracy. Power, or impact on daily life, is also important. Indeed, when Americans complain about bureaucracy being on their backs, they

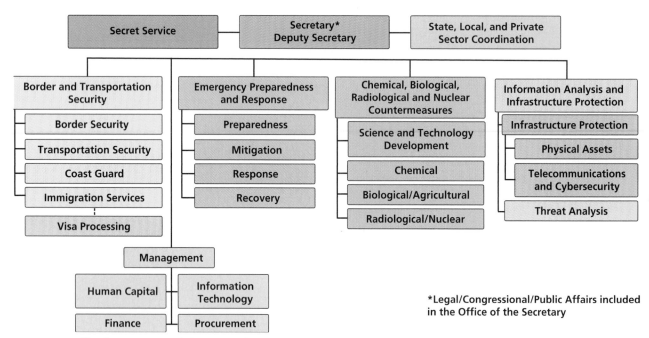

FIGURE 13–1 The Department of Homeland Security.

are often talking about the federal government's independent regulatory commissions.

Yet that is exactly why Congress and the president created the federal government's independent regulatory commissions. All were designed to "get on the backs" of people and corporations, whether to protect consumers (the Consumer Product Safety Commission), regulate stock markets (the Securities and Exchange Commission), oversee federal election laws (the Federal Election Commission), monitor television and radio (the Federal Communications Commission), regulate business (the Federal Trade Commission), control the supply of money (the Federal Reserve Board), or watch over nuclear power plants (Nuclear Regulatory Commission).

The commissions may be small in budget and employees (just $70 million and 1,200 employees for all the independent commissions combined), but their influence over American life is large. Many experts contend that the Federal Reserve Board chair is the second most influential person in making economic policy, and others would argue that the current chair, Alan Greenspan, is the most important leader in influencing public confidence about the economy.[8]

The Federal Reserve Board meets in Washington, D.C., under the seal of the U.S. Supreme Court.

Although independent regulatory commissions are part of the federal bureaucracy, they have a measure of independence from both Congress and the president through their leadership structure. By definition, these commissions are headed not by a single executive but by a small number of commissioners who are appointed by the president, with Senate confirmation, for fixed terms of office. Unlike other presidential appointees, commissioners cannot be removed from office without cause, which is defined by law to mean "inefficiency, neglect of duty, or malfeasance in office." As a result, independent regulatory commissions are less responsive to political pressure from either end of Pennsylvania Avenue.

Independent regulatory commissions are not completely independent, however. Their commissioners are appointed by the president and subject to Senate confirmation, their annual budgets must be approved by Congress, and their decisions are subject to judicial review. Nevertheless, most independent regulatory commissions operate with great freedom and public support. Any effort to reduce the independence of the Federal Reserve Board, Securities and Exchange Commission, or Federal Communications Commission would be seen as a threat to the economic vitality of the nation.

Moreover, the commissioners who lead these agencies often disagree on key issues, even to the point of being unable to reach majority decisions. Some have argued that the six-member Federal Election Commission was actually designed *not* to enforce the election laws. By law, three of its members are Democrats and three are Republicans, which often results in tie votes on key regulations.

Independent regulatory commissions tend to be much less visible than departments, at least until an issue such as corporate fraud becomes hot. The Securities and Exchange Commission was on the front pages for three years, for example, as one corporation after another disclosed accounting fraud in their annual reports to their investors. The SEC was created in the 1930s to restore investor confidence in the stock market, but it was accused of being negligent in monitoring accounting practices at big companies such as Enron and WorldCom in the early 2000s. It is currently rebuilding its staff and taking a much more aggressive stand on accounting standards.

Independent Agencies The word "independent" means at least two things in the federal bureaucracy. Applied to a regulatory commission, it means that the agency is outside the president's control. Applied to an agency or administration, it merely means "separate" or "standing alone." Whereas independent regulatory commissions do not report to the president, independent agencies do.

As a general rule, independent agencies are small federal bureaucracies that serve specific groups of Americans or work on specific problems. Becoming an agency is often the first step toward becoming a department. The Veterans Administration was created in 1930, but only became a department in 1988.

Independent agencies are usually headed by an administrator, which is the second most senior title in the federal bureaucracy behind secretary or attorney general. There are roughly 60 such agencies today, including the Environmental Protection Agency (EPA), the Central Intelligence Agency (CIA), the National Aeronautics and Space Administration (NASA), the National Security Agency (NSA), and the Small Business Administration (SBA).

Although independence increases each agency's ability to focus on its mission, independence also weakens its willingness to cooperate. The spread of independent agencies can also increase confusion about who is responsible for what in the federal government. Early in 2002, for example, White House homeland security "czar" and former Pennsylvania Governor, Tom Ridge, complained about the dozens of agencies involved in guarding the nation's borders:

"There is no line of accountability," he said. "As you take a look at twenty-first-century borders, you have got to have somebody in charge."[9] Congress eventually put Ridge in charge when it created the Department of Homeland Security.

Independent agencies come in many sizes, from small to very large. The National Aeronautics and Space Administration, for example, has an annual budget of over $11 billion and a workforce of more than 23,000 employees, not to mention several hundred thousand employees who work for the private companies that run the United Space Alliance, which is responsible for managing the space shuttle. NASA's budget ranks it ahead of four cabinet departments (Justice, Interior, State, and Commerce).

Moreover, independent agencies can be more important politically to the president than some cabinet departments. There are times, for example, when the director of the CIA or the administrator of the EPA gets a higher place on the president's agenda than the secretary of HUD or agriculture, particularly when an issue such as international spying or global warming is in the headlines.

The term "agency" does not just apply to independent agencies. Many highly visible agencies actually exist within departments, including the Forest Service (located in the Agriculture Department), the National Park Service (located in the Department of the Interior), the Occupational Safety and Health Administration (located in the Labor Department), and the Census Bureau (located in the Commerce Department). Unlike independent agencies, which report directly to the president, these agencies report to a department secretary, who, in turn, reports to the president.

Government Corporations Government corporations are perhaps the least understood organizations in the federal bureaucracy. Because they are intended to act more like businesses than like traditional government departments and agencies, they generally have more freedom from the rules that control traditional government agencies. They often have greater authority to hire and fire employees quickly, and are allowed to make money through the sale of services such as train tickets, stamps, or home loans.[10]

Ultimately, no two government corporations are alike. The term is so loosely used that no one knows exactly how many corporations the federal bureaucracy has. What experts do know is that the number is between 31 and 47, including the Corporation for Public Broadcasting (which runs PBS television), the U.S. Postal Service, the National Railroad Passenger Association (better known as Amtrak), and Americorps (which runs a national service program created by the Clinton administration), along with a host of financial enterprises that make loans of one kind or another.

Once again, the fact that these organizations are not departments does not mean they are small or insignificant. The U.S. Postal Service employs almost 800,000 people, making it the second-largest organization in the federal bureaucracy. It also lost $1.5

billion in 2002, bringing the amount of money it has borrowed from the federal government over the years to more than $12 billion. Unlike private firms such as United Parcel Service or FedEx, the Postal Service is required to deliver mail anywhere in the country, which means that it often loses money.

Leading the Bureaucracy

Every department and agency of the federal bureaucracy is headed by a presidential appointee, who is either subject to confirmation by the Senate or appointed on the sole authority of the president. As political officers, presidential appointees serve at the pleasure of the president and generally leave their posts at the end of that president's term in office. There are roughly 3,000 presidential appointees who run the federal government, including 600 administrative officers who are subject to Senate confirmation, and another 2,400 who serve entirely "at the pleasure of the president." The president also appoints roughly 1,000 U.S. marshals, U.S. attorneys, and ambassadors to foreign nations.

Becoming a Presidential Appointee Presidential appointees have some of the toughest jobs in the world. They work long hours, resolve complex disputes, and make important decisions about how the laws will be executed. Secretary of Defense Donald Rumsfeld made many of the key decisions about the war in Iraq, for example, including which military units would be assigned to the battle.

All presidential appointees who must be confirmed by the Senate are appointed through a four-step process, none of which is automatic (see Figure 13–2). The first step is to be selected as a candidate. Except for individuals who are extraordinarily close to the president, candidates are selected by the White House Office of Presidential Personnel, which often turns to senators and representatives for names. Although the Bush administration received more than 100,000 resumes by mail and through the Internet in 2001, almost all successful candidates had political connections of some kind. Not surprisingly, most presidential appointees are members of the president's party, and many contributed either time or money to the president's campaign.

The second step in becoming an appointee is to survive the White House clearance process, which is designed to ensure that candidates are legally qualified for office and pose no potential embarrassment to the president. All candidates receive a packet of

IN COMPARATIVE PERSPECTIVE

THE JAPANESE BUREAUCRACY

Until 2001, the Japanese bureaucracy was one of the strongest in the world. Created immediately after the Japanese surrendered at the end of World War II, the bureaucracy was given sweeping powers to run the country. The Japanese emperor became a ceremonial position, and the national parliament was given little authority to regulate the bureaucracy.

With no checks and balances, the bureaucracy made a series of disastrous economic decisions over the decades and failed to anticipate the economic downturn that fueled a financial crisis through Asia in the late 1990s. The bureaucracy also turned out to be riddled with corruption. Under Japanese custom, senior bureaucrats often negotiated high-paying jobs with large private corporations before they retired.

On January 1, 2001, the legislature finally acted to reform the bureaucracy. It cut government employment by 25 percent and reduced the number of departments and agencies almost in half, from 24 to 13. At the same time, it gave the prime minister and the ministers of departments new powers to control the bureaucracy. Although the reforms are still under way, the bureaucracy is no longer unchecked.

The bureaucracy is still considered a prestigious place to work, however. Many college students still think of the bureaucracy as the best place to start their careers, and they can qualify for jobs only through rigorous training and highly competitive exams.

forms that require detailed disclosure on every aspect of their personal and professional life, including job history, drug use, personal counseling, financial investments, and even traffic fines of more than $150. They must list every job they have held over the past 15 years, including the name of a supervisor, as well as every place of residence they have lived, including the names of neighbors who might remember them, and every school they have attended, including the name of a high-school classmate who can vouch for them. Some candidates withdraw from consideration at this stage, either because they see potential problems in their past or simply do not have the time to fill out the forms.

In turn, every answer is subject to further review by the White House, Federal Bureau of Investigation, Internal Revenue Service, Office of Government Ethics, and the Senate Committee that is responsible for confirming a given candidate.

The third step in the process is the simplest: The president submits the name of a nominee on parchment paper to the clerk of the Senate. The document is placed in a special envelope, sealed with wax, and hand-delivered to the Senate when it is actually in session.

The fourth step involves Senate confirmation. The Senate refers each nomination to the appropriate committee, which conducts its own review of each candidate. Depending on the position and nominee, the Senate may ask to review the entire file developed by the White House, including the FBI's investigation. Once the review is complete, the committee holds a hearing on the nomination and usually sends the

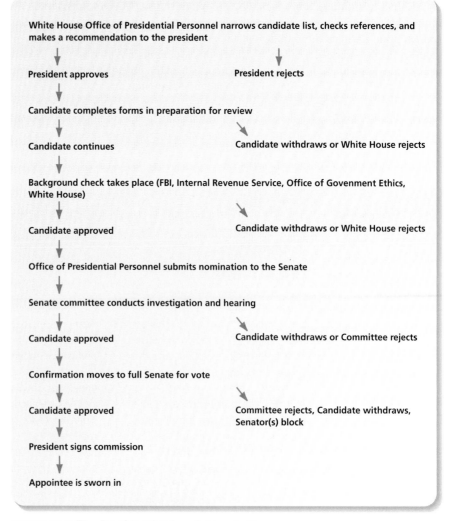

FIGURE 13–2 The Presidential Appointments Process.

nomination to the floor of the Senate with a favorable recommendation. In turn, most nominations are approved by the Senate on voice votes.

There are times, however, when the Senate uses nominations to send signals to the White House about political concerns. In late 2003, for example, Senator Hillary Clinton (D.-N.Y.) blocked the nomination of a new EPA admnistrator as a way to express her anger regarding air quality in New York City. Although she later withdrew her objections, she was able to delay the nomination long enough to force the Bush administration to make a promise to study air quality more closely in the future.

The Senior Leadership Corps Presidential appointees work closely with the 7,000 members of the **Senior Executive Service**, which includes roughly 6,400 career executives who are appointed through a rigorous review process, and another 600 political executives who are appointed by the president without Senate confirmation. Career senior executives continue in their posts regardless of who happens to be president and are selected on the basis of merit, not political history or campaign contributions.

Together with the president's political appointees, there are 10,000 senior executives who sit atop the federal bureaucracy. The number has grown dramatically over the past three decades as the federal government has "thickened" with more layers of leadership and more leaders at each layer.[11]

Some political scientists argue that Congress created the pressure for thickening by creating highly complex programs that demand close supervision, while others believe that thickening is driven in part by a competition for power among competing organizations. According to this *theory of public bureaucracy,* bureaucratic organizations constantly seek to enhance their power, whether by creating new titles, adding more staff, or increasing their budgets.[12]

How the Bureaucracy Evolved

As already noted, the federal bureaucracy started out small. As public administration scholar Leonard White once wrote, the entire federal bureaucracy of 1790 consisted of nothing more than a "foreign office with John Jay and a couple of clerks to deal with correspondence from John Adams in London and Thomas Jefferson in Paris; ... a Treasury Board with an empty treasury; ... a 'Secretary at War' with an authorized army of 840 men; ... [and] a dozen clerks whose pay was in arrears."[13] (See Table 13–1 for measures of the federal government's size since 1940.)

Creating the first departments was not easy, however. Congress fought to restrict the president's authority to fire appointees, and briefly considered creating a board to run

TYPES OF GOVERNMENT EMPLOYEES

1. Senior presidential appointees confirmed by the Senate: 550
2. Ambassadors, U.S. attorneys, and U.S. marshals also confirmed by the Senate: 600
3. Presidential appointees selected by the president and not confirmed by the Senate: 2,000
4. Senior career executives: 2,400
5. Middle-level managers and supervisors: 120,000
6. Middle-level employees: 600,000
7. Lower-level employees: 600,000
8. Postal Service employees: 850,000
9. Blue-collar employees: 250,000
10. Part-time/seasonal employees: 250,000
11. Military personnel: 1,400,000

In November 1995, the vast bureaucracy of the federal government shut down for lack of funds.

Senior Executive Service
Established by Congress in 1978 as a flexible, mobile corps of senior career executives who work closely with presidential appointees to manage government.

TABLE 13-1   MEASURING THE SIZE OF GOVERNMENT, 1940–2005

Year	Employment (in thousands)	Budget (in billions of current dollars)	Budget (in 1996 dollars)	Budget as a Percentage of Gross Domestic Product
1940	699	$ 9.5	$ 94.3	9.9%
1945	3,370	92.7	804.1	43.7
1950	1,439	42.6	312.5	16.0
1955	1,860	68.4	431.3	17.8
1960	1,808	92.2	493.0	18.3
1965	1,901	118.2	575.6	17.6
1970	2,203	195.6	761.6	19.9
1975	2,149	332.3	909.3	22.0
1980	2,161	590.9	1,092.5	22.3
1985	2,252	946.4	1,304.7	23.9
1990	2,250	1,253.2	1,483.6	21.9
1995	2,018	1,788.8	1,551.5	21.9
2000	1,784	1,788.8	1,659.5	18.2
2005	1,875	2,396.7	1,810.0	16.9

SOURCE: Office of Management and Budget, *Budget of the U.S. Government, Fiscal Year 2005, Historical Tables* (U.S. Government Printing Office, February 2004).

the new Department of the Treasury. President Washington won the arguments, however, and settled any remaining worries about his judgment by appointing Thomas Jefferson as Secretary of State, Alexander Hamilton as Secretary of the Treasury, and Henry Knox as Secretary of War. All three were easily confirmed and quickly went about the business of running their departments. At roughly the same time, Congress also created the Post Office Department and allowed for the appointment of a U.S. attorney general.

Even though the federal bureaucracy was but the tiniest fraction of its current size, it was not long before presidential candidates began promising smaller government. Indeed, Jefferson made waste in government a centerpiece of his first Inaugural Address in 1801, promising "a wise and frugal government, which shall restrain men from injuring one another, shall leave them otherwise free to regulate their own pursuits of industry and improvement, and shall not take from the mouth of labor what it has earned." Jefferson wanted a government that taxed lightly, paid its debts on time and in full, and sought "economy in the public expense." Jefferson set aside his promise long enough to make the Louisiana Purchase, which doubled the size of the nation and laid the groundwork for a vast expansion of America's economy.

Unfortunately, Jefferson's purchase also set off a wave of corruption at the federal government's General Land Office, where corrupt federal clerks reserved the best pieces of land to sell for themselves. The corruption eventually ignited the western anger that swept Andrew Jackson—and a new era in two-party competition—into office in 1828. Jackson soon introduced a **spoils system** into government—as in "to the victor belong the spoils."

Under Jackson's system, federal jobs were filled on the basis of political connections. Actual ability to do the work had almost nothing to do with obtaining an appointment. As such, the spoils system gave the president's party complete control over almost every government job, from cabinet secretaries all the way down to post office clerks. This political job system became known as *patronage*—individuals would patronize, or support, the president's party with money before an election, and get a job in government after.

The civil service was created in 1883 to end corruption in the spoils system. Indeed, it was a disappointed job seeker who started the federal bureaucracy down the road toward today's civil service system. Unfortunately for President James Garfield, that job seeker happened to be both disappointed and a good shot. Garfield's assassination

spoils system
A system of public employment based on rewarding party loyalists and friends.

prompted Congress to pass the Pendleton Act of 1883, which created an independent Civil Service Commission to assure that most federal jobs were awarded under a **merit system**, meaning on the basis of an individual's ability to do the work, not political connections. Federal service was placed under the control of a three-person bipartisan board called the Civil Service Commission, which functioned from 1883 to 1978.[14]

By the 1950s, coverage under the merit system had grown from 10 percent of all federal employees, when it was first established, to about 90 percent in 1950. In 1978, the Civil Service Reform Act abolished the Civil Service Commission and split its functions between two new agencies. This split was made to eliminate the possible conflict of interest in an agency that recruits, hires, and promotes employees and also passes judgment on employee grievances about fairness and discrimination.

Today, the **Office of Personnel Management (OPM)** administers civil service laws, rules, and regulations. The independent Merit Systems Protection Board is charged with protecting the integrity of the federal merit system and the rights of federal employees. It conducts studies of the merit system, hears and decides charges of wrongdoing, considers employee appeals against adverse agency actions, and orders corrective and disciplinary actions against an agency executive or employee when appropriate. (A sampling of current federal job offerings can be found at www.usajobs.opm.gov.)

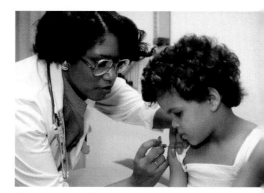

The Centers for Disease Control and Prevention (CDC) has been very successful in educating the public about the importance of immunization for children.

WORKING FOR GOVERNMENT

Americans believe a number of myths about the federal bureaucracy. Polls show that many of us think that most federal employees work in Washington, D.C., and that the federal government spends much more on welfare and assistance for the poor than it does on Social Security or defense.

The realities are much different:

- Only about 15 percent of the career civilian employees work in the Washington area. More federal employees work in California, Georgia, and Texas, for example, than in Washington.

- More than 25 percent of the civilian employees work for the Army, the Navy, the Air Force, or some other defense agency; another 30 percent work for the U.S. Postal Service.

- Welfare may consume a sizable portion of the U.S. budget, yet the federal bureaucracy that administers it is relatively small. Fewer than 10 percent of the bureaucrats work for welfare agencies such as the Social Security Administration or the Department of Veterans Affairs.

- Federal civilian servants are much more likely to look like the rest of the nation in terms of race, sex, religion, education, and disability than the political appointees or members of Congress who make the laws they execute.

- Although the civil service includes more than 450 different kinds of jobs, the vast majority of workers occupy white-collar jobs such as lawyers, contract managers, budget analysts, engineers, inspectors, and auditors.

Although the public believes most bureaucrats come to work for the security, paycheck, and benefits, most care deeply about making a difference for their country. According to surveys conducted in 2001 and 2002, the vast majority of federal employees say they contribute to their agency's mission, and half say their organizations are very good at helping people. Most federal employees also say the people they work with are open to new ideas, willing to help other employees learn new skills, and concerned about their organization's mission.[15]

Nevertheless, there are reasons to worry about the health of the federal civil service. Substantial minorities of federal employees say their organizations do not provide the information, technological equipment, and training to do their jobs well, and a majority believes their organizations do not have enough employees to succeed. In addition, many federal employees believe that their organizations do not do well at

merit system
A system of public employment in which selection and promotion depend on demonstrated performance rather than political patronage.

Office of Personnel Management (OPM)
Agency that administers civil service laws, rules, and regulations.

disciplining poor performers. They also describe the federal hiring process as slow and confusing, and often complain that their senior leaders are not qualified for their jobs.

The Hiring Process

Unlike presidential appointees who are selected by the president, the vast majority of federal employees are recruited through the civil service. The civil service system was designed to reduce political corruption by promoting merit in the hiring process. But hiring on the basis of merit is not the only way government seeks to reduce corruption. As we shall see, it also regulates the political activities of civil servants.

As already noted, the Office of Personnel Management sets the federal government's rules for recruiting, hiring, promoting, and disciplining civil servants. However, individual agencies have the actual responsibility for hiring new personnel, subject to agency standards. Individual agencies may promote people from within or transfer a civil servant from another agency in the government. If, however, they wish to consider an "outsider," they request that OPM certify possible candidates from its roster of applicants. OPM typically certifies the top three applicants for the opening, and the agency normally selects one of these. However, the agency can decide to make no appointment or to request other applicants if it thinks none of the three is suitable.

These procedures are intended to protect the merit principle and to meet agencies' needs for qualified personnel. In practice, the two objectives sometimes come into conflict. Trade-offs have to be made, particularly between central control by OPM and delegation of discretionary authority to the agencies. And sometimes the pursuit of both objectives is undermined by other goals, such as giving military veterans extra credit in the hiring process.

Regulating the Civil Service

In 1939, Congress passed the Act to Prevent Pernicious Political Activities, usually called the **Hatch Act** after its chief sponsor, Senator Carl Hatch of New Mexico. The act was designed to neutralize the danger of a federal civil service being able to shape, if not dictate, the election of presidents and members of Congress. In essence, the Hatch Act permitted federal employees to vote in government elections but not to take an active part in partisan politics. The Hatch Act also made it illegal to dismiss federal officials below cabinet and subcabinet rank for partisan reasons.[16]

In 1993, Congress, with the encouragement of the Clinton administration, overhauled the Hatch Act and made many forms of participation in partisan politics permissible. The revised Hatch Act still bars federal officials from running as candidates in partisan elections, but it does permit most federal civil servants to hold party positions and involve themselves in party fund raising and campaigning. This new law was welcomed by those who believed the old Hatch Act discouraged political participation by 3 million people who might otherwise be vigorous political activists.[17]

The new Hatch Act spells out many restrictions on federal bureaucrats; they cannot raise campaign funds in their agencies, and those who work in such highly sensitive federal agencies as the CIA, FBI, Secret Service, and certain divisions of the IRS are specifically barred from nearly all partisan activity. Those who work in the U.S. military have stricter rules regulating their political involvement. On the one hand, federal employees *may* register and vote as they choose; assist in voter registration; express opinions about candidates and issues; contribute money to political organizations; attend political fund-raising functions; wear or display political badges, buttons, or stickers; attend political rallies and meetings; and join political parties. On the other hand, they *may not* be candidates for public office in partisan elections, use their jobs or authority to interfere with or affect the results of an election, collect contributions or sell tickets to political fund-raising functions from subordinate employees, or solicit funds or discourage the political activity of any person who has business before the employee's office.

Hatch Act
Federal statute barring federal employees from active participation in certain kinds of politics and protecting them from being fired on partisan grounds.

The Role of Government Employee Unions

Since 1962, federal civilian employees have had the right to form unions or associations that represent them in seeking to improve government personnel policies, and about one-third of them have joined such unions. Some of the most important unions representing federal employees today are the American Federation of Government Employees, the National Treasury Employees Union, the National Association of Government Employees, and the National Federation of Federal Employees.

Unlike unions in the private sector, federal employee unions lack the right to strike and are not able to bargain over pay and benefits. But they can attempt to negotiate better personnel policies and practices for federal workers, they can represent federal bureaucrats at grievance and disciplinary proceedings, and they can lobby Congress on measures affecting personnel changes. They can also vote in elections. This is why members of Congress from districts that have large numbers of federal workers often sit on the House and Senate civil service subcommittees.

THE BUREAUCRACY'S JOB

Whatever their size or specialty, all federal organizations share one job: to faithfully execute, or implement, the laws. **Implementation** covers a broad range of bureaucratic activities, from writing checks at the Social Security Administration to inspecting job sites at the Occupational Health and Safety Administration, swearing in new citizens at the Immigration and Naturalization Service, or monitoring airline traffic at the Federal Aviation Administration. Some agencies implement the laws by spending money, others by raising revenues or by issuing rules that govern what private citizens and businesses do, and still others by collecting information or conducting research. Whatever tool government uses, implementation is the act of converting a law into action.

Because Congress and the president could never pass laws that are detailed enough to execute themselves, they give federal departments and agencies a certain amount of **administrative discretion** to implement the laws in the most efficient and effective manner possible. This freedom often varies from agency to agency, depending on both past performance and congressional politics. Political scientist Theodore Lowi believes that Congress often gives the federal bureaucracy vague directions because it is unable or unwilling to make the tough choices needed to resolve the conflicts that arise in the legislative process. Congress gets the credit for passing a law, while the federal bureaucracy gets the challenge of implementing an unclear law.[18]

Whether a law is clear or ambiguous, most agencies implement the law through two means: administrative *regulations,* which are formal instructions for either running an agency or for controlling the behavior of private citizens and organizations, or *spending,* which involves the transfer of money to and from government.

Making Regulations

Regulations, or rules, are designed to convert laws into action. They tell people what they can and cannot do, as well as what they must or must not do. It is an Agriculture Department rule that tells meat and poultry processors how to handle food, an Environmental Protection Agency rule that tells automobile makers how much gasoline mileage their cars must get, a Social Security Administration rule that tells Americans how long they must work before they are eligible for a federal retirement check, an Immigration and Naturalization Service rule that tells citizens of other nations how long they can stay on a student visa, and a Justice Department rule that tells states what they must do to ensure that every eligible citizen can vote. Although all these rules can be traced back to legislation, they provide the details that most laws leave out.

Rules are drafted and reviewed through a quasi-legislative **rule-making process** that is governed by the Administrative Procedure Act. Enacted in 1946 to make sure that all rules are made visible to the public, the act requires that all proposed rules be

implementation
The process of putting a law into practice through bureaucratic rules or spending.

administrative discretion
Authority given by Congress to the federal bureaucracy to use reasonable judgment in implementing the laws.

regulations
The formal instructions that government issues for implementing laws.

rule-making process
The formal process for making regulations.

published in the *Federal Register.* Publication in the federal government's newspaper marks the beginning of what is known as the "notice and comment" period in which all parties affected by the proposed regulation are encouraged to make their opinions known to the agency. Because rules have the force of law and can become the basis for legal challenges, the process can take years from start to finish and can involve thousands of pages of records. Some agencies even hold hearings and take testimony from witnesses in the effort to build a strong case for a particularly controversial rule.

The rule-making process does not end with final publication and enforcement. All rules are subject to the same judicial review that governs formal laws, thereby creating a check against potential abuse of power when agencies exceed their authority to faithfully execute the laws.

Moreover, rules, like laws, can be changed by future action. In late 2003, for example, the Bush administration anounced plans to change the rules governing coal-burning electric power plants. Under a Clinton administration rule, mercury had been declared extremely dangerous to public health. As a result of the ruling, power plants were about to be forced to install expensive new technology to reduce the amount of mercury released to the mimimum amount possible. Under the new rules, power plants would have more freedom to release larger amounts of mercury, and save billions. Environmentalists charged that the new EPA administrator, former Utah governor Mike Leavitt, had been forced by the White House to accept the change in policy. Although Leavitt admitted that the proposal had been discussed within the administration, he argued that "the rules are ultimately made and signed here."[19] It was a nearly perfect statement of just how important making the rules can be to society.

Spending Money

The federal bureaucracy also implements laws through spending, whether by writing checks to more than 35 million Social Security recipients a year, buying billions of dollars' worth of military equipment, or making grants to state governments and research universities. Viewed in relative terms as a percentage of gross domestic product (GDP), federal spending more than doubled over the past half-century but began to shrink with the end of the cold war in 1989. Viewed in constant dollars to adjust for inflation, however, federal spending continues to rise each year, driven in part by the cost of caring for a rapidly aging population.

Most of this spending goes to what political scientists and budget experts call **uncontrollable spending**, defined as spending for (1) **entitlement programs** that provide financial benefits for any American who is eligible, such as Social Security for older Americans, college loans for poor students, or help for the victims of natural disasters such as floods and hurricanes (in these programs, everyone who is eligible and applies automatically gets the help), and (2) programs that require more federal spending each year automatically through cost-of-living increases or interest on the national debt.

Uncontrollable spending sharply limits the amount of the federal budget that is actually subject to debate in any given year. Even funding for programs such as defense, which is technically subject to yearly control, is almost impossible to cut without controversy, especially during a time of high public concerns about terrorism.

The largest share of uncontrollable spending comes from Social Security and Medicare, which are guaranteed to any American who has paid taxes into the program for enough years. The aging of the American population means that more older people than ever will qualify for Social Security and Medicare, so uncontrollable spending will almost certainly rise over the next few decades. In total, uncontrollable spending accounted for more than $1.36 trillion in 2005, accounting for over half of the federal government's $2.4 trillion budget.

A much smaller share of the uncontrollable budget involves welfare for the poor, which is linked to economic performance. More unemployment, for example, means more federal unemployment insurance; more poverty means more food stamps, job training, temporary financial assistance, and other income support programs.

The uncontrollable budget is not growing just because more people are eligible for entitlements, however. Many of these entitlements are subject to **indexing**—that is, they

uncontrollable spending
The portion of the federal budget that is spent on programs, such as Social Security, that the president and Congress are unwilling to cut.

entitlement program
Programs such as unemployment insurance, disaster relief, or disability payments that provide benefits to all eligible citizens.

indexing
Providing automatic increases to compensate for inflation.

GLOBAL *Perceptions*

QUESTION: Please tell me if you completely agree, mostly agree, mostly disagree, or completely disagree with the following statements: When something is run by the government it is usually inefficient and wasteful. Generally government is run for the benefit of the people.

Americans are not the only citizens who believe their government is inefficient and wasteful. A majority of citizens in all but six of the 49 nations surveyed by the Pew Global Attitudes survey said government is usually inefficient and wasteful. At the same time, a majority of citizens in all but seven of the 49 nations also said that government is run for the benefit of all people. Government may be inefficient, but at least it is inefficient for the benefit of all.

In theory, governments that are viewed as both inefficient *and* run for the benefit of a few would be under the greatest pressure to change, which has been the case in Japan, Russia, and Brazil. Using these two measures, Uzbekistan has the most respected bureaucracy in the world: Just 32 percent of its citizens characterized it as wasteful and inefficient, while 85 percent said it was run for the benefit of all the people.

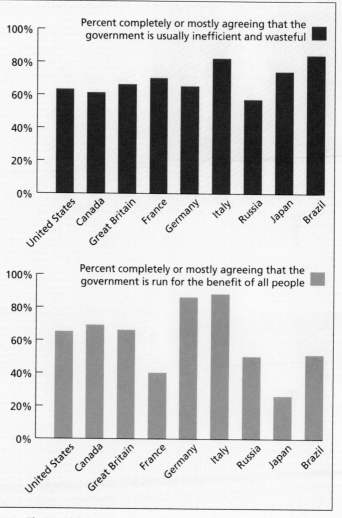

SOURCE: The Pew Global Attitudes Project, June, 2003, p. 109.

grow automatically with inflation, regardless of how the economy is doing. Indexing affects a growing list of federal programs, again leaving Congress and the president little control over year-to-year increases. The number of programs indexed to automatic cost-of-living adjustments (COLAs) grew from 17 in 1966 to almost 100 by 2004.[20]

HOLDING THE BUREAUCRACY ACCOUNTABLE

Every president enters office promising to make the federal bureaucracy work better. Indeed, Jimmy Carter, Ronald Reagan, Bill Clinton, and George W. Bush all made bureaucratic reform a central part of their presidential campaigns. Carter promised to create a government as good as the American people, Reagan promised to reduce waste in government, Clinton and Vice President Al Gore promised to reinvent government, and Bush promised to make government more friendly to citizens.

Yet presidents leave office frustrated by their lack of success. As political scientist James Q. Wilson noted, "Presidents see much of the bureaucracy as their natural enemy

Cabinet members, such as former Attorney General John Ashcroft, often have to answer questions Congress has regarding the bureaucratic and financial needs of their particular department. Ashcroft was one of the first Bush cabinet members to resign after the 2004 election.

and always are searching for ways to bring it to heel."[21] And presidents are not the only ones who want to control the bureaucracy. Congress, too, clearly worries about making bureaucracy work better. Together, both complain that the federal bureaucracy can be more accountable to interest groups and itself than either branch.

Accountability to the President

Modern presidents invariably contend that the president should be firmly in charge of the bureaucracy, for the chief executive is responsive to the broadest constituency. A president, it is argued, must see that popular needs and expectations are converted into administrative action. When the nation elects a conservative president who favors cutbacks in federal programs and less governmental intervention in the economy, for example, his policies must be carried out by the bureaucracy. The voters' wishes can be translated into action only if the bureaucrats support presidential policies.

Yet under the American system of checks and balances, the party winning the presidency does not acquire total control of the national government. Under our Constitution, the president is not even the undisputed master of the executive structure. Presidents come into an ongoing system over which they have little control and within which they have little leeway to make the bureaucracy responsive.

Still, the president has some control over the bureaucracy through the powers of appointment, reorganization, and budgeting. More specifically, a president can attempt to control the bureaucracy by appointing or promoting sympathetic personnel,

PEOPLE & POLITICS *Making a Difference* ★ ★ ★

DENISE JOHNSON

The federal government depends on talented employees like Denise Johnson to fulfill the promises Congress, presidents, and the judiciary make. As a senior executive at the U.S. Centers for Disease Control and Prevention in Atlanta, Georgia, Johnson is responsible for the U.S. part of the international effort to eliminate polio from the world.

The U.S. defeated polio in the 1950s and 1960s through an aggressive vaccination program funded by the federal government. Now it is trying to eliminate it around the world. Working through the United Nation's Children Fund, Johnson and her colleagues are part of the Global Polio Eradication Initiative, which seeks to educate foreign governments about the value of vaccination. In 2002 alone, Johnson traveled to India, where she helped India's eradication team organize a national immunization day, as well as to Ethiopia, Zimbabwe, and Nigeria.

Johnson has been at the Centers for Disease Control and Prevention for 25 years and has held assignments in Cincinnati; Kansas City; Baltimore; Harrisburg, Pennsylvania; New York; and most recently, Atlanta. Her career has spanned a long list of projects, including efforts to prevent sexually transmitted diseases, reduce domestic and sexual violence, and clean up toxic waste dumps. As deputy director of the Polio Eradication Branch of CDC, she has managed more than $300 million in grants to immunize more than 500 million children around the globe.

The international campaign against polio appears to be paying off. In 1988, polio still plagued 125 nations and infected more than 350,000 people a year. The rates are now falling so fast that polio may well be completely eradicated by 2008.

Johnson's commitment to making the world a safer place to live earned her a

2003 Service to America medal and $3,000 from *Government Executive Magazine*. When told of her award, Johnson refused to consider herself a hero: "I'm sitting here in my air-conditioned office. In India right now, there are people on the ground tromping through villages, going house to house, looking for kids to give them the vaccine. Those are real heroes."

mobilizing public opinion and congressional pressure, changing the administrative apparatus, influencing budget decisions, using extensive personal persuasion, and if all else fails, shifting a bureaucracy's assignment to another department or agency (although such a shift requires tacit if not explicit congressional approval).[22]

Recall that presidents appoint about 3,000 people to top positions within the executive branch, only a small number of which are subject to Senate confirmation. Some scholars suggest that presidents would be more effective chief executives if they were able to make many more appointments, while others argue that the large number of appointees, and the cumbersome appointments process that goes with it, weakens the president's ability to control the front lines of government.

Accountability to Congress

Congress has a number of ways to exercise control over the bureaucracy, whether by establishing agencies, formulating budgets, appropriating funds, confirming personnel, authorizing new programs or new shifts in direction, conducting investigations and hearings, or even terminating agencies.

Much of this authority is used to help constituents as they battle federal red tape. Members of Congress earn political credit by interceding in federal agencies on behalf of their constituents. Still, Congress deserves at least some of the blame for having created the red tape in the first place, whether by enacting pet programs, refusing to give federal agencies greater flexibility, delaying presidential appointments, or placing limits on bureaucratic discretion to protect some constituents but not others. Moreover, by demanding special attention for their constituents, members of Congress may undermine the fairness of the entire process. Like cutting into line at a movie theater, they slow the progress for everyone but the special few who get their attention.

The brutal fact is that only a small minority of our 535 members of Congress would trade the present bureaucratic structure for one that was an efficient, effective agent of the general interest—the political payoffs of the latter are lower than those of the former. Congressional talk of inefficient, irresponsible, out-of-control bureaucracy is typically just that—talk—and when it is not, it usually refers to agencies under the jurisdiction of other legislators' committees. Congress can abolish or reorganize an agency. Congress can limit or expand an agency's jurisdiction or allow its authority to lapse entirely. Congress can slash an agency's appropriations. Congress can investigate. Congress can do all these things, but individual members of Congress generally find reasons not to do so.[23]

It is not Congress as a whole that shares direction over the bureaucracy with the president. More accurately, individual members and committees specialize in the appropriations and oversight processes. They oversee policies of a particular cluster of agencies—often the agencies serving constituents in their own districts. Some legislators stake out a claim over specific areas. Members of Congress, who see presidents come and go, come to think they know more about particular agencies than the president does (and often they do). Some congressional leaders prefer to seal off "their" agencies from presidential direction and maintain their influence over public policy. Sometimes their power is institutionalized; the Army Corps of Engineers, for example, is given authority by law to plan public works and report to Congress without going through the president.

The Role of Oversight

Congress and the president spend a great deal of energy monitoring the federal bureaucracy. The hope is that **oversight**, the process of monitoring day-to-day activities, will somehow encourage agencies to perform better or at least deter them from worse performance.

Presidents have a number of tools for keeping a watchful eye. They can put loyal appointees, such as Attorney General John Ashcroft, into the top jobs at key agencies; they can direct White House aides, such as homeland security chief Tom Ridge or Vice

RECENT EFFORTS TO MAKE GOVERNMENT WORK

Since 1945, Congress has passed 177 major laws to make government work better. Some of these laws were designed to make government more efficient by combining independent agencies into new departments such as the Department of Health and Human Services or Homeland Security. Other laws were designed to make government more open to citizen review through freedom of information and other "sunshine in government" rules. Still other laws were designed to cut costs by reducing fraud, waste, and abuse.[*]

Patterns in the 177 laws show just how important the Watergate scandal was in changing political control of the bureaucracy. Prior to Watergate, Congress allowed the president to make most of the decisions about improving government. After Watergate, Congress became much more involved in drafting laws to improve how government works. Further review of the 177 laws reveals important patterns in how Congress, the president, and the judiciary have tried to improve government performance.

- The number of laws has increased over time, suggesting growing frustration with the inability to actually improve performance. One-third of the 177 laws were enacted before the Watergate scandal, two-thirds after.
- Congress has become more involved in shaping the laws, suggesting that it is less willing to let the president decide how to run the executive branch. Whereas 61 percent of pre-Watergate reforms originated in the White House, 82 percent of post-Watergate reforms originated in Congress.
- Finally, the laws have become less trusting toward federal employees. Whereas 56 percent of the pre-Watergate reforms had a trusting view of government employees, 81 percent of the post-Watergate reforms were distrusting.

[*]For an introduction to the laws, see Paul C. Light, *The Tides of Reform: Making Government Work, 1945–1995* (Yale University Press, 1998).

oversight
Legislative or executive review of a particular government program or organization. Can be in response to a crisis of some kind or part of routine review.

Among its proposed reforms of the bureaucracy in 1995, Congress wanted to end support of public broadcasting, claiming that programs like Sesame Street could support themselves on commercial television. The public, however, disagreed, and Big Bird, Oscar the Grouch, and other childhood favorites still receive government subsidies.

central clearance
Review of all executive branch testimony, reports, and draft legislation by the Office of Management and Budget to ensure that each communication to Congress is in accordance with the president's program.

President Dick Cheney, to oversee the work of certain agencies; and they can always call cabinet meetings to learn more about what is happening in the bureaucracy.

However, presidents tend to use the Office of Management and Budget for most routine oversight. Departments and agencies must get the president's approval before testifying before Congress on pending legislation, making legislative proposals, or answering congressional inquiries about their activities. Under this **central clearance** system, OMB forwards communications to Congress in three categories: "in accordance" with the president's program (reserved for the president's top priorities), "consistent with" the president's program (indicating the president's second-tier priorities), or "no objection." If the president objects to any communication, OMB simply does not forward the legislation to Congress. OMB also conducts oversight on all federal departments and agencies as it assembles the president's budget plan.

Congress also has a number of tools for overseeing the federal bureaucracy, not the least of which consists of the individual members of Congress themselves, who are free to ask agencies for detailed information on just about any issue. However, most members and committees tend to use the General Accounting Office or the Congressional Budget Office (both discussed in Chapter 11) to conduct a study or investigation of a particular program.

Congress uses these and other sources of information as a basis for committee and subcommittee hearings on specific agencies or programs. Today, Congress holds more oversight hearings than ever before. In the 1960s, for example, both chambers held a total of 157 days of oversight hearings per two-year Congress; by the early 1980s, the number had more than tripled, to 587 days. The greatest increase occurred in the 1970s, fueled in part by the increasing number of legislative committees and subcommittees. More committees and more staff meant more time and energy to hold oversight hearings.[24]

Together, Congress and the president conduct two basic types of oversight. One is what can be called "police patrol" oversight, in which the two branches watch the bureaucracy through a routine pattern. They read key reports, watch the budget, and generally pay attention to how the departments and agencies are running. If they happen to see a "crime" in progress, all the better. But the general goal of the patrol is to deter problems before they arise. The other can be called "fire alarm" oversight, in which the two branches wait for citizens, interest groups, or the press to find a major problem and pull the alarm. The media play a particularly important role in such oversight, often uncovering a scandal before a routine "police patrol" can spot it.[25]

The Problem of Self-Regulation

Career administrators are in a good position to know when a program is not operating properly and what action is needed. But many Americans believe that federal employees, whether selected on merit or not, fail to make things better. The problem is that many career employees act as if the expansion of their organization is vital to the public interest. They sometimes become more skillful at building political alliances to protect their own organization than at building political alliances to ensure their programs' effectiveness.

Career administrators usually try hard to be nonpartisan, yet they are inevitably involved in politics. Some of them have more bargaining and alliance-building skills than the elected and appointed officials to whom they report. In one sense, agency leaders are at the center of action in Washington. Over time, administrative agencies may come to resemble entrenched pressure groups in that they operate to advance their own interests. The growth of federal programs from the 1930s through the 1970s brought an increase in the number of policy aides on Capitol Hill, of Washington law firms that specialize in assisting clients who are interested in policy development, and of lobbyists (some say at least 40,000) who work with Congress and the federal bureaucracy to advance various economic and professional interests.

Special-interest groups that perceive real or potential harm to their interests cultivate the bureau chiefs and agency staffs who have jurisdiction over their programs. They also work closely with the committees and subcommittees of Congress that authorize, appropriate, and oversee programs run by these key bureaucracies. Recognizing the power of interest groups, bureau chiefs frequently recruit them as allies in pursuing common goals. What these bureau officials have in common with interest groups and their allies in Congress is a shared view that more money should be spent on federal programs run by the bureau in question. These alliances among bureaucrats, interest groups, and subcommittee members and their staffs on Capitol Hill are sometimes described as *iron triangles*, a topic discussed in Chapter 6.

GOVERNMENT'S ACHIEVEMENTS

Despite these and other flaws, Americans are reluctant to support cutbacks in what government does. To the contrary. The vast majority say the federal government's big problem is not the wrong priorities, but inefficiency, and few support a drastic reduction in federal responsibilities. Americans may complain about the red tape and waste in Washington, but the federal bureaucracy continues to make progress in solving some of the most difficult problems of modern society.

The federal government helped rebuild Europe after the devastation of World War II, won the cold war against communism, strengthened voting rights for all Americans, reduced workplace discrimination, ended racial segregation in public schools, and won the race to the moon. The list of objective success goes on and on:

- Poverty among older Americans has fallen to modern lows.
- Air and water quality have improved.
- More women are graduating from college and professional school, and more are competing in college sports.
- Food and drugs have become safer, the drug approval process has become faster, and older Americans will soon receive prescription drugs at reduced cost through Medicare.
- More poor children are getting a head start in preschool.
- More pregnant women are receiving proper medical care.
- Home ownership rates have risen to their highest levels ever.
- Americans are living longer with greater financial security and a new prescription drug benefit.
- Polio and tuberculosis have been virtually eliminated.
- The Internet (originally developed by the Defense Department) has revolutionized communications.
- Crime rates are much lower today than they were two decades ago.
- More Americans are completing high school and attending college.

Many of these achievements depend on making sure the federal government can recruit the next generation of civil servants. None of the laws on which these achievements are based can be faithfully executed without the help of talented public employees.

Moreover, not every federal endeavor has produced success. Too many American children still go to bed hungry, too many people are still homeless, too many workers are unable to make ends meet with minimum-wage jobs, and too many citizens have too little access to health care. But if the mark of a great society is what it asks its government to achieve, Americans can be proud of the federal bureaucracy today.

SUMMARY

1. The chief characteristics of bureaucracy are continuity, predictability, impartiality, standard operating procedures, and "red tape." Federal bureaucratic agencies reflect the ways in which the political system attempts to identify our most important national goals and how policies are implemented.

2. The framers made two key decisions about the structure of government. First, they prohibited members of Congress from serving in the executive branch, thereby guaranteeing some independence in executing the laws. Second, they gave the president the power to appoint the officers of government, albeit with the advice and consent of the Senate. These two decisions ensured that the president would be the nation's administrator in chief.

3. Most of the 2.7 million civilian employees of the federal government serve under a merit system that protects their independence of politics. They work in one of the 15 cabinet departments or elsewhere in a long list of government corporations, independent agencies, and independent regulatory boards or commissions. The bureaucracy is led by presidential appointees and senior career executives.

4. The federal government's Office of Personnel Management sets policy for recruiting and evaluating federal workers. Various restrictions on federal workers prevent them from running for political office or engaging in political fundraising activities. The federal bureaucracy generally prizes continuity, stability, and following the rules more than risk taking or innovation.

5. The bureaucracy generally uses regulations or spending to implement the laws. The rule-making process is governed by the Administration Procedure Act, while the spending process is governed by the federal budget. Most of the federal budget is uncontrollable, whether because of indexing to inflation or because Congress and the president are unwilling to cut highly popular programs such as Social Security.

6. The American bureaucracy has at least two immediate bosses: Congress and the president. It must pay considerable attention as well to the courts and their rulings and to well-organized interest groups and public opinion. In many ways, the bureaucracy is a semi-independent force—a fourth branch of government—in American politics.

7. Debates and controversy over big government and big bureaucracy, and over how to reorganize and eliminate waste in them, are never-ending. Compared with many other nations and their centralized bureaucracies, the hand of bureaucracy rests more gently and less oppressively on Americans than on citizens elsewhere.

KEY TERMS

bureaucracy	government corporation	Hatch Act	uncontrollable spending
bureaucrat	Senior Executive Service	implementation	entitlement programs
department	spoils system	administrative discretion	indexing
independent agency	merit system	regulations	oversight
independent regulatory commission	Office of Personnel Management (OPM)	rule-making process	central clearance

FURTHER READING

JOEL D. ABERBACH, *Keeping a Watchful Eye: The Politics of Congressional Oversight* (Brookings Institution Press, 1990).

DAN BAUM, *Smoke and Mirrors: The War on Drugs and the Politics of Failure* (Little, Brown, 1996).

ROBERT D. BEHN, *Rethinking Democratic Accountability* (Brookings Institution Press, 2001).

BARRY BOZEMAN, *Bureaucracy and Red Tape* (Prentice Hall, 2000).

COUNCIL FOR EXCELLENCE IN GOVERNMENT AND THE PRESIDENTIAL APPOINTEE INITIATIVE, *The Survivor's Guide for Presidential Nominees* (Brookings Institution Press, 2001).

SHELLEY L. DAVIS, *Unbridled Power: Inside the Secret Culture of the IRS* (HarperBusiness, 1997).

JOHN J. DIIULIO JR., ED., *Deregulating the Public Service: Can Government Be Improved?* (Brookings Institution Press, 1994).

JAMES W. FESLER AND DONALD F. KETTL, *The Politics of the Administrative Process* (Chatham House, 1991).

JANE E. FOUNTAIN, *Building the Virtual State: Information Technology and Institutional Change* (Brookings Institution Press, 2001).

CHARLES T. GOODSELL, *The Case for Bureaucracy*, 3d ed. (Chatham House, 1994).

AL GORE, *The Best Kept Secrets in Government: How the Clinton Administration Is Reinventing the Way Washington Works* (Random House, 1996).

AL GORE, *Creating a Government That Works Better and Costs Less: The Report of the National Performance Review* (Plume-Penguin, 1993).

PHILIP K. HOWARD, *The Death of Common Sense: How Law Is Suffocating America* (Random House, 1994).

RONALD N. JOHNSON AND GARY D. LIBECAP, *The Federal Civil Service System and the Problem of Bureaucracy* (University of Chicago Press, 1994).

HERBERT KAUFMAN, *The Administrative Behavior of Federal Bureau Chiefs* (Brookings Institution Press, 1981).

ANDREW KOHUT, ED., *Deconstructing Distrust: How Americans View Government* (Pew Research Center for the People and the Press, 1998).

PAUL C. LIGHT, *The New Public Service* (Brookings Institution Press, 1999).

PAUL C. LIGHT, *Thickening Government: Federal Hierarchy and the Diffusion of Accountability* (Brookings Institution Press, 1995).

PAUL C. LIGHT, *The Tides of Reform: Making Government Work, 1945–1995* (Yale University Press, 1997).

AREND LUPHART, *Patterns of Democracy: Government Forms and Performance in Thirty-Six Countries* (Yale University Press, 1999).

G. CALVIN MAKENZIE AND MICHAEL HAFKIN, *Scandal Proof: Do Ethics Laws Make Government Ethical?* (Brookings Institution Press, 2002).

DAVID OSBORNE AND TED GAEBLER, *Reinventing Government: How the Entrepreneurial Spirit Is Transforming the Public Sector* (Addison-Wesley, 1992).

DAVID OSBORNE AND PETER PLASTRIK, *Banishing Bureaucracy: The Five Strategies for Reinventing Government* (Addison-Wesley, 1997).

JAMES Q. WILSON, *Bureaucracy: What Government Agencies Do and Why They Do It* (Basic Books, 1989).

Four useful journals are the *Journal of Policy Analysis and Management, National Journal, Public Administration Review,* and *Government Executive.*

THE JUDICIARY
THE BALANCING BRANCH

14

Foreign visitors are often amazed at the power of American judges. They also marvel at the majesty of the Supreme Court building and other courthouses, compared with those in other countries. As French aristocrat Alexis de Tocqueville, after his visit to the United States in 1834, observed: "If I were asked where I place the American aristocracy, I should reply without hesitation . . . that it occupies the judicial bench and bar. . . . Scarcely any political question arises in the United States that is not resolved, sooner or later, into a judicial question."[1] A century later, British political scientist Harold J. Laski observed, "The respect in which federal courts and, above all, the Supreme Court are held is hardly surpassed by the influence they exert on the life of the United States."[2] Only in recent decades have national courts in Europe and elsewhere asserted their power in a similar way, and there is an emerging trend toward the "globalization of judicial power."[3]

Why do judges play such a central role in our political life? As discussed in Chapter 2, Chief Justice John Marshall in 1803 successfully claimed for judges the power of **judicial review**, that is, the power to authoritatively interpret the Constitution. Only a constitutional amendment or a later Supreme Court can modify the Court's doctrine. Justice Felix Frankfurter suggested tersely: "The Supreme Court is the Constitution."

Judges—and not just those on the Supreme Court—are also asked to resolve disputes involving billions of dollars, decide conflicts among competing interest groups, supervise the criminal justice system, and make rules affecting the lives of millions of people. They not only settle legal conflicts but in some cases have overseen the operation of schools,

TIME LINE

THE JUDICIARY

1789	John Jay becomes the first Chief Justice of the United States
1803	In *Marbury* v. *Madison*, the Supreme Court asserted the power of judicial review
1857	Chief Justice Roger Taney leads the Court in protecting slavery and states' rights in *Dred Scott* v. *Sanford*
1902	Oliver Wendell Holmes is appointed to the Court
1916	Louis D. Brandeis becomes the first Jewish member of the Supreme Court
1921	Former President Taft is appointed Chief Justice by political protégé Warren Harding
1932	Benjamin Cardozo becomes the second Jewish member of the Supreme Court
1953	Earl Warren is appointed Chief Justice—leads the Court in a liberal direction
1967	President Johnson appoints Thurgood Marshall as the first African American Justice
1972	William Rehnquist is appointed by President Richard M. Nixon
1981	Sandra Day O'Connor is appointed to the Court by President Ronald Reagan and becomes the first female justice
1991	Clarence Thomas becomes the second African American appointed to the Court
1993	Ruth Bader Ginsburg becomes the second female member of the Court

judicial review
The power of a court to refuse to enforce a law or government regulation that in the opinion of the judges conflicts with the U.S. Constitution or, in a state court, the state constitution.

adversary system
A judicial system in which the court of law is a neutral arena where two parties argue their differences.

justiciable dispute
A dispute growing out of an actual case or controversy and that is capable of settlement by legal methods.

class action suit
Lawsuit brought by an individual or a group of people on behalf of all those similarly situated.

prisons, mental hospitals, and complex businesses. Sometimes they decide the details of how these institutions should be run. Still, the scope and nature of judicial power limit the role of judges.

THE SCOPE OF JUDICIAL POWER

The American judicial process rests on an **adversary system**. A court of law is a neutral arena in which two parties argue their differences and present their points of view before an impartial arbiter. The adversary system is based on the *fight theory,* which holds that arguing over law and evidence, which may or may not arrive at the truth, guarantees fairness in the judicial system.[4] The adversary system thus imposes restraints on the exercise and scope of judicial power.

Judicial power is essentially *passive* and *reactive.* Judges cannot instigate cases. Moreover, not all disputes are within the scope of judicial power. Judges decide only **justiciable disputes**—lawsuits that grow out of actual controversies and are capable of judicial resolution. Judges do not use their power unless there is a real case or controversy. It is not enough for a judge merely to have a general interest in a subject or to believe that a law is unconstitutional.

The party bringing a lawsuit (the *plaintiff*) must have *standing to sue.* Plaintiffs must have sustained or be in immediate danger of sustaining a direct and personal injury. Plaintiffs may not raise hypothetical issues; they must have a real dispute and opposing interests with another party. Traditionally, individuals had to show an actual monetary damage in order to gain standing to sue. But in recent decades, the Supreme Court has granted standing to individuals who claim nonmonetary injuries that are shared by others. In a classic statement, the Court observed, "Aesthetic and environmental well-being, like economic well-being, are important ingredients of the quality of life in our society, and the fact that particular environmental interests are shared by the many rather than the few does not make them less deserving of legal protection through the judicial process."[5] Individuals still must claim a personal injury—the violation of a constitutional or other legal right—and show a "personal stake in the outcome." But they may now bring suits over environmental damages, defective consumer products, and other matters that affect interest groups and large numbers of people.[6]

A related and increasingly important development is the use of **class action suits**, in which a small number of persons represent all other people similarly situated—a suit on behalf of all students in a university, for example, or all persons who smoke a particular brand of cigarettes. "Would-be class action litigants must show that they are proper representatives for the class of persons they seek to champion [and] that the types of issues they wish to raise are common to the class, and they must be able to demonstrate how a remedy can be formed that will meet the needs of the class."[7] These lawsuits may force major changes in public policy—governing, for example, the operation of schools and prisons—and business practices, such as the marketing of defective or harmful products. In recent years, tobacco companies, drug manufacturers, and financial institutions have confronted a series of class action lawsuits and been ordered to pay damages.

When individuals sue each other over a traffic accident, for instance, they file suits under *civil law* and seek monetary awards for the injuries they suffered or the damages to their property. The government may also bring civil lawsuits against individuals and business. But only the government may prosecute individuals accused of crimes, such as carjacking and robbery, as defined in state and federal *criminal law.* As discussed further in Chapter 16, persons accused of crimes are guaranteed certain rights in the Bill of Rights and must be accorded the due process of law, but if convicted, they face imprisonment, and for murder, may be sentenced to death.

Judges decide cases; they do not prosecute persons for allegedly committing crimes. *Prosecutors* decide whether to charge an offense and which offense to charge. They have largely unreviewable discretion, so long as they have probable cause to believe that the accused has committed an offense.[8] Prosecutors negotiate with the lawyers for **defendants** (those accused of an offense) and often work out a **plea bargain**, whereby defendants agree to plead guilty to a lesser offense to avoid having to stand trial and face a sentence for a more serious offense. Prosecutors also make recommendations to judges about what sentences to impose.

On the federal level, the job of prosecution falls to the Department of Justice: the attorney general, the solicitor general, 94 U.S. attorneys, and some 1,200 assistant attorneys. The president, with the consent of the Senate, appoints a U.S. attorney for each district court. U.S. attorneys serve four-year terms but may be dismissed by the president at any time. These appointments are of great interest to senators, who exercise significant influence over the selection process. Because U.S. attorneys are almost always members of the president's political party, it is customary for them to resign if the opposition party wins the White House.

The attorney general, in consultation with the U.S. attorney in each district, appoints assistant attorneys. Some districts have only one; the largest, the Southern District of New York, has more than 65. These attorneys, working with the U.S. attorney and assisted by the Federal Bureau of Investigation and other federal law enforcement agencies, begin proceedings against those alleged to have broken federal laws. They also represent the United States in civil suits.

The state and federal governments provide lawyers for poor defendants in criminal trials. Traditionally, private attorneys have been appointed to provide assistance, but many state and federal courts employ a **public defender system**. Salaried public defenders operate in the federal courts under the general supervision of the Administrative Office of the United States Courts. The Judicial Conference of the United States, consisting of circuit and district court judges from around the country, has said that the most important problem confronting the public defender program is lack of money. The Legal Services Corporation also provides financial assistance to 323 organizations that assist the poor in noncriminal legal matters.

Courts cannot resolve all disputes. Some raise **political questions** that would require the use of methods not suitable for a court, for which there is no legal remedy, or which the Constitution explicitly assigns to Congress or the president to decide. Such is the case with many questions arising from the conduct of foreign affairs. Which of two competing state governments is the proper one? Which group of officials of a state or foreign nation should the United States recognize as the government?[9] When the president sends the military into international conflicts without congressional authorization, has the constitutional provision that only Congress may "declare war" been violated? These are political questions.

The political question doctrine is admittedly circular, and the Supreme Court ultimately decides what is and is not a "political question." In 2000, for instance, most observers thought that the Supreme Court would refuse to become involved in deciding which votes from Florida should be counted in the presidential election. There is hardly anything more political than this, and the Constitution specifically charges Congress with the responsibility for counting electoral votes. Nonetheless, the Supreme Court accepted the case in *Bush* v. *Gore*, deliberated promptly, and by a 5-to-4 majority stopped the recount of votes; the four dissenters contended that the matter should have been left to the political branches to decide.[10] In short, as political scientist John Roche observed, "Political questions are matters not soluble by the judicial process; matters not soluble by the judicial process are political questions. As an early dictionary explained, 'violins are small cellos, and cellos are large violins.' "[11]

Judicial Federalism: State and Federal Courts

Most countries have a single, unitary judiciary, but the United States has a dual judicial system of federal and state courts. Alongside the federal judiciary, each state maintains a judiciary of its own, and many large municipalities have judicial systems as complex as those of the states. Within both federal and state systems, judicial power is further

defendant
In a criminal action, the person or party accused of an offense.

plea bargain
Agreement between a prosecutor and a defendant that the defendant will plead guilty to a lesser offense to avoid having to stand trial for a more serious offense.

public defender system
Arrangement whereby public officials are hired to provide legal assistance to people accused of crimes who are unable to hire their own attorneys.

political question
A dispute that requires knowledge of a nonlegal character or the use of techniques not suitable for a court or explicitly assigned by the Constitution to Congress or the president; judges refuse to answer constitutional questions that they declare are political.

GLOBAL *Perceptions*

QUESTION: How important is it to you to live in a country where there is a judicial system that treats everyone the same? Is it very important?

In the United States, 89 percent of the public think that a fair judiciary is very important. That is one of the highest percentages around the world—on par with Bangladesh (89) and slightly above that in Kenya and Turkey (88); Germany (87); and Argentina, Brazil, and the Czech Republic (84). But independent courts are ranked even higher in Senegal (91). The countries with the lowest percentages include South Korea (57), Bolivia (56), Angola (51), and Jordan (33).

SOURCE: Pew Global Attitudes Survey, 2003, pp. T73–74.

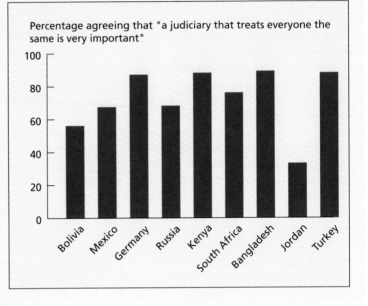

Percentage agreeing that "a judiciary that treats everyone the same is very important"

TYPES OF LAWS

Statutory Law

Law that comes from authoritative and specific lawmaking sources, primarily legislatures but also including treaties and executive orders.

Common Law

Judge-made law that originated in England in the twelfth century, when royal judges traveled around the country settling disputes in each locality according to prevailing custom. The common law continues to develop according to the rule of *stare decisis*, which means "let the decision stand." This is the rule of precedent, which implies that a rule established by a court is to be followed in all similar cases.

divided between trial courts (and other lesser courts such as traffic courts) and one or more levels of appellate courts, which hear appeals from the lower courts.

The federal and state court systems are related, but not in a superior-inferior hierarchy. State courts primarily interpret and apply their state constitutions and law. When their decisions are based solely on state law, their rulings may not be appealed to or reviewed by federal courts. Only decisions that raise a federal question, involving the application of the Bill of Rights or other federal law, are federal courts able to review. Federal courts have **writ of habeas corpus** jurisdiction (the power to release persons from custody if a judge determines that they are not being detained constitutionally) and may review criminal convictions in state courts for violations of the federal constitutional and legal rights of the accused. Except for habeas corpus jurisdiction, the Supreme Court is the only federal court that may review state court decisions, and only in cases involving a conflict with federal law. Other than the original jurisdiction the Constitution vests directly in the Supreme Court, no federal court has any jurisdiction except that granted to it by an act of Congress. Congress also determines whether the judicial power of the United States is exercised exclusively by federal courts or concurrently by both federal and state courts.

Most litigation occurs in state courts, which annually face about 90 million civil and criminal cases. The type of litigation in state courts also tends to differ from that in federal courts. Apart from criminal cases, the largest portion of state court cases involves economic issues—state regulation of public utilities, zoning and small business, labor relations, natural resources, energy, and the environment. Litigation varies from state to state as well, depending on the size of the population, urbanization, and the economy.[12] (For more information on state courts and links to state court Web sites, go to the site of the National Council of States Courts at www.ncsconline.org.)

THE FEDERAL JUDICIAL SYSTEM

writ of habeas corpus
A court order requiring explanation to a judge why a prisoner is being held in custody.

"The judicial Power of the United States," says Article III of the Constitution, "shall be vested in one supreme Court, and in such inferior courts as the Congress may from time to time ordain and establish." Courts created to carry out this judicial power are called

Article III or *constitutional courts.* Congress may also establish *Article I* or *legislative courts*—courts, for instance, to handle bankruptcies, claims involving property damage and contract disputes with the federal government, military appeals, and veterans' appeals—to carry out the legislative powers the Constitution has granted to it. The main difference between a legislative and a constitutional court is that the judges of a legislative court need not be appointed to "hold their Offices during good Behavior" and are appointed for fixed terms; they may be assigned other than purely judicial duties, such as supervising tax collections. Article III judges basically have lifetime appointments, subject only to removal by impeachment; only 11 federal judges have been impeached by the House of Representatives and seven convicted and removed by the Senate.[13]

The Constitution requires a Supreme Court. It is a necessity if the national government is to have the power to make and enforce laws that take precedence over those of the states. The lack of such a court to maintain national supremacy, ensure uniform interpretation of national legislation, and resolve conflicts among the states was one of the glaring defects of government under the Articles of Confederation.

Congress decides whether there will be other courts in addition to the Supreme Court. The First Congress divided the nation into circuits (geographical areas) and created lower courts for each. Today the hierarchy of federal courts of general jurisdiction consists of district courts, courts of appeals, and the Supreme Court (see Figure 14–1). In cases affecting ambassadors, other public ministers, and consuls, and in cases in which a state is a party, the Supreme Court has **original jurisdiction**, the authority of a court to hear a case "in the first instance." In all other cases, the Supreme Court has **appellate jurisdiction**—power to review decisions of other federal courts and agencies, as determined by Congress, and appeals from state supreme court decisions that raise questions of federal law. In general, federal courts may decide only cases or controversies arising under the Constitution, a federal law, a treaty, or admiralty and maritime law; cases brought by a foreign nation against a state or the federal government; and diversity suits—lawsuits between citizens of different states—if the amount of the controversy exceeds $50,000.

District Courts

Although the Supreme Court and its justices receive most of the attention, the workhorses of the federal judiciary are the district courts in the states, the District of Columbia, and U.S. territories. They hear more than 270,000 civil cases and 67,000 criminal cases annually.[14]

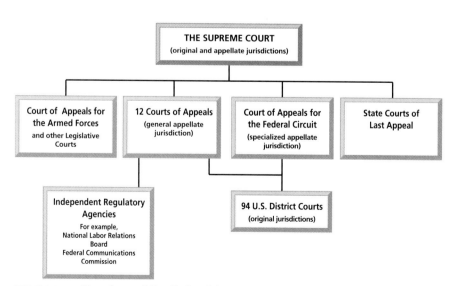

FIGURE 14–1 Structure of the Federal Courts.

original jurisdiction
The authority of a court to hear a case "in the first instance."

appellate jurisdiction
The authority of a court to review decisions made by lower courts.

IN COMPARATIVE PERSPECTIVE

CONSTITUTIONAL COURTS IN EUROPE

Historically, European countries rejected "American-style" judicial review. European courts remain subordinate to legislatures. After World War II, however, separate constitutional courts were created and set apart from national judiciaries in several countries in Western Europe. Austria was the first in 1945 and other constitutional courts were established in Italy (1948), the Federal Republic of Germany (1949), France (1958), Portugal (1976), Spain (1978), and Belgium (1985). Following the collapse of the former Soviet Union in 1989, constitutional courts were likewise established in the former communist countries of Central and Eastern Europe, including the Czech Republic, Hungary, Poland, Romania, Russia, Slovakia, the Baltics, and the countries of the former Yugoslavia.

A new European model of constitutional judicial review thus emerged. In contrast to the U.S. federal judiciary, which has general jurisdiction over issues of constitutional and statutory law, regular courts in Europe still have no jurisdiction over constitutional matters. Only constitutional courts may decide constitutional issues. That was an innovation,

but it is not all that separates the European model of judicial review from the American one.

In addition, unlike the U.S. federal judiciary's jurisdiction over only actual cases and controversies, European constitutional courts may exercise abstract and concrete review of legislation. Abstract constitutional review of legislation is initiated by elected officials or national and regional governmental bodies with respect to legislation that has been recently adopted but that either has not yet been put into force, as in France; or has not yet been enforced, or has been suspended, pending review by the constitutional court, as in Germany, Italy, and Spain. By contrast, concrete constitutional review arises from challenges to legislation in the courts when regular judges are uncertain about the constitutionality or the application of a statute or ordinance; they refer such cases to the national constitutional court for decision.

For further reading see Carlo Guarnieri and Patrizia Pederzoli, translated by C. A. Thomas, *The Power of Judges: A Comparative Study of Courts and Democracy* (Oxford University Press, 2002); and Ann-Marie Slaughter, Alec Stone Sweet, and J.H.H. Weiler, eds., *The European Court and National Courts—Doctrine and Jurisprudence* (Hart Publishing, 2000).

Each state has at least one federal district court. Larger states have as many as the demands of judicial business and the pressure of politics require, although no state has more than four. There are 665 judgeships in 94 district courts, located in each of the 50 states, the District of Columbia, and the Commonwealth of Puerto Rico. Each federal circuit has at least one district court judge but may have as many as 99.

District courts are the trial courts of original jurisdiction. They are the only federal courts that regularly employ **grand juries**, which are used to secure criminal indictments, and **petit juries**, used in trials. When cases tried before district judges involve citizens of different states, judges apply the appropriate state laws. Otherwise, district judges are concerned with federal laws. For example, they decide cases involving crimes against the United States—suits under the national revenue, postal, patent, copyright, trademark, bankruptcy, and civil rights laws.[15]

District judges normally sit separately and hold court by themselves; however, they sit in three-judge panels in cases involving reapportionment and voting rights. They are appointed by the president, subject to confirmation by the Senate, and hold office for life. District judges appoint and are assisted by clerks, bailiffs, stenographers, law clerks, court reporters, and probation officers.

District court judges also appoint **magistrate judges**, who are increasingly important because of rising caseloads. After being screened by panels composed of residents of the judicial districts, full-time magistrates are appointed for eight-year renewable terms and part-time magistrates for four-year renewable terms. There are 486 full-time and 51 part-time federal magistrate judges. Magistrates look and act like judges. Most wear robes and since 1990 are addressed as "Judge." They issue arrest warrants, hold hearings to determine whether arrested persons should be held for action by the grand jury, and if so, set bail. They hear motions subject to varying kinds of review by their district judges. They preside over civil trials—jury and nonjury—with the consent of both

grand jury
A jury of 12 to 23 persons who, in private, hear evidence presented by the government to determine whether persons shall be required to stand trial. If the jury believes there is sufficient evidence that a crime was committed, it issues an indictment.

petit jury
A jury of 6 to 12 persons who determine guilt or innocence in a civil or criminal action.

magistrate judge
An official who performs a variety of limited judicial duties.

parties and over nonjury trials for misdemeanors and petty offenses with the consent of the defendants. Under the supervision of the district judge, and with the consent of the accused, a magistrate may preside over preliminary hearings and the selection of a jury for a felony trial.[16]

Courts of Appeals

The decisions of federal district courts may be appealed and reviewed by federal **courts of appeals**, although reapportionment and voting rights cases decided by three-judge panels are taken directly to the Supreme Court. District judges are bound by the precedents of higher courts, but they have considerable discretion in applying them. Courts of appeals are located geographically in 11 *judicial circuits* that include all the states and U.S. territories (see Figure 14–2). A twelfth is located in the District of Columbia and hears the largest number of cases challenging federal statutes, regulations, and administrative decisions. The thirteenth appellate court is the Court of Appeals for the Federal Circuit, which is located in the District of Columbia and has national jurisdiction, though it deals primarily with appeals in patent, copyright, and international trade cases. The largest circuit is the ninth, with 28 circuit judges and 99 district judges. It is geographically the size of western Europe and contains 20 percent of the U.S. population.

Each circuit court of appeals consists of 6 to 28 permanent judgeships (179 in all). These courts normally hear cases in panels of three judges. But in especially important and controversial cases, all judges may be present; that is, they sit *en banc.* They annually hear about 57,000 appeals.

Although courts of appeals have only appellate jurisdiction, they are powerful policy makers. Fewer than 1 percent of their decisions are appealed to the Supreme Court. As the policy-making role of federal courts has become a prominent political issue, more attention has focused on these courts and the judges who serve on them.[17] One current controversy involves the growing failure of appellate courts to publish their opinions, due to their growing caseloads, and whether unpublished opinions are binding precedents.[18] Another controversy revolves around whether the number of judges should be increased to keep pace with rising caseloads. (For more information about the federal judiciary, go to the Web site of the Administrative Office of the U.S. Courts at www.uscourts.gov.)

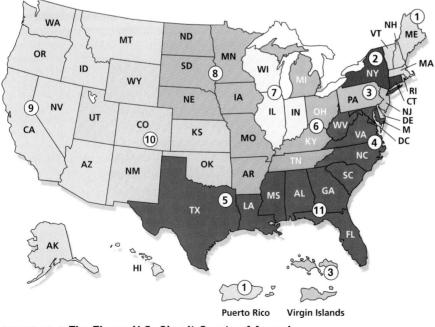

FIGURE 14–2 The Eleven U.S. Circuit Courts of Appeals.

court of appeals
A court with appellate jurisdiction that hears appeals from the decisions of lower courts.

THE POLITICS OF APPOINTING FEDERAL JUDGES

The selection of federal judges has always been a significant part of the political process. It makes a difference who serves on the federal courts. As the courts play an even more important role in the political process and as more and more interests—African Americans and women, for example—participate in that process, judicial selection politics has come front and center on the political stage.

Article II of the Constitution gives the president the power to appoint federal judges with the advice and consent of the Senate. Political reality imposes constraints on the president's discretion, so the selection of a federal judge is actually a complex bargaining process. The principal figures involved are the candidates, the president, and the "subpresidency for judicial selection,"[19] consisting of key members of the Department of Justice, U.S. senators, the American Bar Association, party leaders, and, increasingly, interest groups. In addition, recent presidents have inserted the White House much more directly into the process than their predecessors did.

Department of Justice officials and key White House staff meet often to review proposed candidates. Since the Reagan administration, the assistant attorney general in charge of the Office of Legal Policy in the Department of Justice oversees the screening of potential judicial nominees. After candidates' backgrounds and judicial philosophies have been checked, they are discussed by a White House working group that includes the legal counselor to the president and the attorney general. This group recommends to the president whom to nominate to the federal bench. (For more information about the Office of Legal Policy and current judicial nominations, go to its Web site at www.usdoj.gov/olp.)

In practice, before the White House submits names of nominees for the federal district and appeals courts, it observes the practice of **senatorial courtesy**—the custom of submitting the names of prospective appointees for approval to the senators from the states in which the appointees are to work. If negotiations are deadlocked between the senators or between the senators and the Department of Justice, a seat may stay vacant for years.[20] The custom of senatorial courtesy does not apply to Supreme Court appointments, since they have national jurisdiction; nevertheless, President Clinton consulted with Republican Senator Orrin Hatch, who at the time chaired the Senate Judiciary Committee because the Senate was controlled by Republicans, so as to avoid a confirmation battle over his nominees to the Supreme Court, Justices Ruth Bader Ginsburg in 1993 and Stephen Breyer in 1994.

In addition, liberal interest groups, such as People for the American Way and the Alliance for Justice, as well as conservative groups, such as the Heritage Foundation and a coalition of 260 conservative organizations called the Judicial Selection Monitoring Project, monitor potential judicial candidates. These organizations used to wait until after the president sent the name of a nominee to the Senate, but now they are active in the preliminaries, making known their views even before the names of nominees are released to the public or sent to the Senate Judiciary Committee.

The American Bar Association's Standing Committee on the Federal Judiciary once played a special role in evaluating candidates. Presidents were hesitant to submit for Senate confirmation a candidate rated "not qualified" by the ABA. In recent years, conservative groups mounted an attack on the ABA's role, contending that it reflects a liberal bias and has given low ratings to some conservative nominees. In response to this criticism, shortly after taking office, President George W. Bush announced in March 2001 that the ABA would no longer be asked to evaluate judicial candidates before nomination. But senators on the Judiciary Committee continue to receive the ABA's evaluations of judicial nominees.

Senate: Advice and Consent

The normal presumption is that the president should be allowed considerable discretion in the selection of federal judges. Despite this presumption, the Senate takes seriously its responsibility in confirming judicial nominations, especially when the party

senatorial courtesy
Presidential custom of submitting the names of prospective appointees for approval to senators from the states in which the appointees are to work.

controlling the Senate is different from that of the president, as has been the case in recent years.

When the Senate receives the name of a judicial nominee, it sends the nomination to the Judiciary Committee for consideration. Before the committee holds a hearing on the nominee, it sends to the senators of the nominee's home state a letter—called a "blue slip" because of its color—asking whether they approve. If one of the senators declines to return the slip, the nomination is dead, and no hearing will be held. During the last two years of Clinton's presidency, Republican senators delayed and defeated confirmation of many of his judicial nominees in this way. With Democrats in control of the Senate during his first two years, they retaliated and stalled the confirmation of a number of President George W. Bush's nominees. After Republicans regained control of the Senate following the 2002 midterm elections, Democrats continued to oppose some of Bush's most conservative nominees and in several cases held filibusters in order to prevent a Senate vote on their confirmation.[21] If both home-state senators approve of a nominee, the committee holds a hearing, votes on the nominee, and sends its recommendation to the full Senate for consideration and confirmation based on a majority vote.

Prior to 1955, the common practice was for the Senate to look into candidates' qualifications and background but not to interview the person. But since then, the committee has asked judicial nominees a wide range of questions, since their judicial and political philosophy is a major factor in determining how they might vote on particular cases and controversies. Except for Robert Bork, nominated by President Ronald Reagan in 1987, most judicial nominees have refused to answer questions that might reveal how they would decide a case. But Judge Bork had written so many articles, made so many speeches, and decided so many cases that he thought he had to clarify his constitutional views. His candor may well have contributed to the Senate's rejection of him, and that has made subsequent nominees even more reluctant to respond to similar questions.

Until recently, most judicial appointments, especially those for the lower federal courts, were processed without much controversy. However, "now that lower court judges are more commonly viewed as political actors, there is increasing Senate scrutiny of these nominees."[22] The battle over judicial confirmations ordinarily takes place before the Senate Judiciary Committee. The Senate usually goes along with the recommendations of its Judiciary Committee without much debate, although floor debates are not all that rare. Overall, the Senate has refused to confirm 29 of the 138 presidential nominations for Supreme Court justices.[23]

The Role of Party, Race, and Gender

Presidents so seldom nominate judges from the opposing party (around 90 percent of judicial appointments since the time of Franklin Roosevelt have gone to candidates from the president's party) that partisan considerations are taken for granted, and partisan affiliation is rarely mentioned. Today more attention is paid to other characteristics, such as ideology, race, and gender.[24]

President Jimmy Carter, who had no opportunity to make an appointment to the Supreme Court, selected more African Americans, Hispanics, and women for the lower federal courts than all other prior presidents combined—40 women, 37 African Americans, and 16 Hispanics. President Ronald Reagan, although the first to appoint a woman to the Supreme Court, appointed fewer minority members or women than Carter did, perhaps in part because fewer minorities and women could pass the Reagan administration's ideological screening.[25] Twenty percent of George H.W. Bush's appointees were women, 7 percent African Americans, and 4 percent Hispanics.[26]

Bill Clinton promised to appoint federal judges who would be more representative of the ethnic makeup of the United States. "We don't have litmus tests or judicial-philosophy tests," insisted Assistant Attorney General Eleanor Dean Acheson, who oversaw judicial selection during the Clinton administration, "but I do think we've put people on the bench who are interested in people and their problems"[27] and brought diversity to the federal bench. Clinton lived up to his pledge by naming more women and minorities to the bench than his predecessors had; 182 of his 367 appointees were women and minorities, 49 percent of his appointees.

George W. Bush appointed a number of women and minorities in his first year in office but fewer thereafter. About 37 percent of his judicial nominees were women and minorities; 41 women (20 percent), 14 African Americans (7 percent), 18 Hispanics (9 percent), one Arab American, and one Asian American were appointed.[28]

The Role of Ideology

Finding a party member is not enough; presidents want to pick the "right" kind of Republican or "our" kind of Democrat to serve as judges. By and large, they have been able to achieve this goal. Judges picked by Republican presidents tend to be judicial conservatives (with some notable exceptions, such as President Dwight Eisenhower's appointments of Chief Justice Earl Warren and Justice William J. Brennan Jr., President Gerald Ford's appointment of Justice John Paul Stevens, and President George H. W. Bush's appointment of Justice David H. Souter). Judges picked by Democratic presidents are more likely to be liberals. Both of these orientations are tempered by the fact that judges must go through a senatorial confirmation process that during recent administrations has been rigorous and driven by opposition to the White House.[29]

President Ronald Reagan's two terms made it possible for him to join Presidents Franklin D. Roosevelt and Dwight D. Eisenhower as the only presidents in the last century to appoint a majority of the federal bench. All told, Reagan appointed 368 lifetime judges. His administration acted carefully to nominate only those whose views about the role of the courts and constitutional issues were consistent with Reagan's own.[30] Not only were a large number of judicial conservatives appointed, but many of them—because they were comparatively young—will continue to have an effect on judicial policy well into the twenty-first century.

Because President George H. W. Bush was less committed to conservatism than Reagan, conservative organizations—the Heritage Foundation, the Pacific Legal Foun-

PEOPLE & POLITICS *Making a Difference* ★ ★ ★

JUSTICE SANDRA DAY O'CONNOR

Appointed to the Supreme Court by Republican President Ronald Reagan in 1981, Justice Sandra Day O'Connor is the first woman to serve on the high bench. After graduating at the top of her class from Stanford Law School, she found it difficult to find a job in her home state of Arizona. She eventually entered politics, serving first as assistant attorney general and then winning election to the Arizona state senate, where she served until her appointment to a state trial court and later to a state intermediate court of appeals.

On the Supreme Court, Justice O'Connor is conservative but less hardline than the other Reagan appointees. She casts the deciding vote on contro-versial issues such as abortion, affirmative action, minority-majority voting districts, and some disputes involving the separation of church and state.

Because Justice O'Connor is at the center of the Rehnquist Court and casts so many deciding votes, when she retires a controversy over the appointment of her successor may arise and the balance of power on the Court is certain to change.

Justice O'Connor and her brother, H. Alan Day, published a book on their growing up in rural Arizona in the early twentieth century, *Lazy B: Growing Up on a Cattle Ranch in the American Southwest* (Random House, 2002). More recently, Justice O'Connor published a book of es-

says on law and her approach to constitutional interpretation, *The Majesty of the Law: Reflections of a Supreme Court Justice* (New York: Random House, 2003).

CHANGING FACE OF AMERICAN POLITICS

DIVERSITY ON THE FEDERAL BENCH

The federal judiciary has long been dominated by white males. But diversity on the federal bench has been increasing during the last several decades, largely due to the judicial appointments of Democratic Presidents Jimmy Carter and Bill Clinton.

Although the number of women and minorities appointed to the federal courts has only recently increased significantly, the first woman, Judge Florence Allen, was appointed in 1934 by President Franklin D. Roosevelt. President Harry Truman named the first African American, Judge William Henry Hastie, in 1950. President John F. Kennedy appointed the first Hispanic, Judge Reynaldo G. Garza, in 1961, and President Richard M. Nixon in 1971 appointed the first Asian American, Judge Herbert Choy. The first Native American, Judge

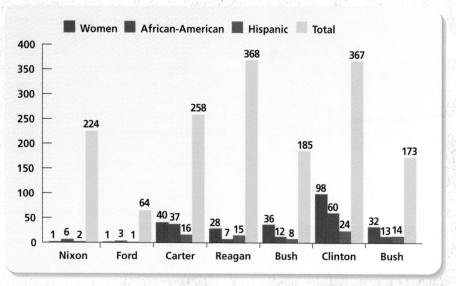

SOURCE: David M. O'Brien, "Ironies and Disappointments: Bush and Federal Judgeships," in Colin Campbell and Bert A. Rockman, eds., *The George W. Bush Presidency: Appraisals and Prospects* 147 (CQ Press, 2004); as updated through May 6, 2004, based on the data of the Federal Judicial Center at http://fcj.gov/newweb/ jnetweb.nsf/hisj.

Billy Michael Burrage, was appointed in 1994 by President Clinton.

dation, and the Federalist Society—focused more attention on his judicial nominees. Bush appointed 148 district judges, 37 appellate judges, and two Supreme Court justices—David Souter and Clarence Thomas. It turned out that his appointees, with the exception of Justice Souter, were among the most conservative in recent history.[31] His appointment of Justice Thomas helped consolidate the Court's "turn to the right."[32]

President Clinton gave Democratic senators "clear guidelines about the kind of judges he wants"[33]—competent professionals who would bring diversity to the bench. But after the Republicans took control of the Senate in 1994, Clinton instructed his advisers to consult closely with Republican Senator Orrin Hatch, chair of the Senate Judiciary Committee. Clinton abandoned or declined to nominate several judicial candidates opposed by conservative interest groups and had to reach compromises with Republican senators. In his second term, Clinton faced increasing opposition from the Republican-controlled Senate, which slowed down confirmations to such an extent that Chief Justice Rehnquist, in his annual reports on the federal judiciary, scolded the Senate for jeopardizing the ability of the federal courts to do their work. Despite the slowdown in Senate confirmations, by the time Clinton left office, he had named 367 of the 849 authorized federal judges and brought greater diversity to the federal bench.[34]

President George W. Bush likewise confronted increasing difficulties over his judicial nominees from the Democrats in the Senate. Democrats delayed Bush's most conservative nominees and held filibusters in order to prevent confirmation votes on ten appellate court nominees. In retaliation Bush bypassed the Senate by naming two— Judges Charles W. Pickering and William H. Pryor—to recess appointments, which they will hold until the next session of Congress in 2005; recess appointments, which go into

Justice David Souter was confirmed by an overwhelming vote in 1990, despite a dearth of information on his ideological orientation.

Justice Ruth Bader Ginsburg, a moderate nominated by President Clinton, was easily confirmed by the Senate in 1993.

Justice Stephen Breyer, another moderate Clinton nominee, was confirmed without fanfare in 1994.

judicial self-restraint
Philosophy proposing that judges should interpret the Constitution to reflect what the framers intended and what its words literally say.

judicial activism
Philosophy proposing that judges should interpret the Constitution to reflect current conditions and values.

effect without confirmation, have been made in only a handful of instances in the last 30 years.[35] Finally, five months before the 2004 presidential election the impasse was broken by a bipartisan deal. Democrats agreed to allow votes on the confirmation of 20 district court nominees and five appellate court nominees. In return, Bush agreed not to make any more recess appointments.[36]

The Role of Judicial Philosophy

What about a candidate's judicial philosophy? Does a candidate believe that judges should interpret the Constitution to reflect what the framers intended and what its words literally say; that is, does the candidate believe in **judicial self-restraint?** Or does the candidate believe that the Constitution should be adapted to reflect current conditions and philosophies; that is, does the candidate believe in **judicial activism?**

Throughout most of our history, federal courts have been more conservative than Congress, the White House, or state legislatures. Prior to 1937, judicial self-restraint was the battle cry of liberals who objected to judges' interpreting the due process clauses of the Fifth and Fourteenth Amendments to strike down many laws passed to protect labor and women and to keep the national and state governments from regulating the economy. These judges broadly construed the words of the Constitution to prevent what they thought to be unreasonable regulations of property.

With Presidents Richard Nixon, Ronald Reagan, George H. W. Bush, and George W. Bush, however, the judicial shoe was on the other foot, and it was conservatives who were advocates of judicial self-restraint. What is needed, they argued, are judges who will let Congress, the president, and the state legislatures regulate or forbid abortions, permit prayer in public schools, impose capital punishment, and not hinder law enforcement.

Still, it would be wrong to assume that judicial philosophy is nothing more than another way to argue about political ideology. Some conservatives, for example, favor judicial activism because they want current judges to reverse the last half-century of precedents on civil rights and to protect property rights from government regulation. The conservative majority on the Rehnquist Court has invited criticisms from liberals for its judicial activism in overturning precedents and striking down state and federal laws promoting affirmative action, for example, and invalidating congressional enactments for infringing on states' rights. In these areas, liberals favor judicial restraint because they believe that judges should defer to the democratic process and that democratic self-governance will flourish if judges stay out of such policy debates.

Hence the debate over the role of the Supreme Court and the federal judiciary today is less about activism and restraint than about competing conceptions of the proper balance between government authority and individual rights, between the power of democratically accountable legislatures and that of courts and unelected judges. The debate is also about whether and on what basis judges should make law.

Do Judges Make Law?

"Do judges make law? 'Course they do. Made some myself."[37] That was the candid response of New Hampshire Justice Jeremiah Smith. Most judges are less candid. Judges obviously make law, but to admit it is somehow disturbing. Such statements do not conform to popular notions of what judges do.

Why do people think judges should not make law? Many people equate a judge's role with that of a referee in a prizefight, because of their role in trials and the adversary system. We expect referees to be impartial and disinterested, treating both parties as equals. We expect them to apply rules, not make them. Laws are not made, however, in the same way as the rules of a sport, and therein lies the answer to our question. Not only *do* judges make law, but they *must*.

Legislatures make law by enacting statutes, but judges must apply the statutes to concrete situations. Statutes are drawn in broad terms: Drivers shall act with "reasonable care"; no one may make "excessive noise" in the vicinity of a hospital; employers must maintain "safe working conditions." Such broad terms must be used because legislators cannot know exactly what will happen in every circumstance. Courts must judge their application in concrete cases. In the words of Justice Felix Frankfurter, "Legislatures make law wholesale, judges retail."[38]

The problems of interpreting and applying law are intensified when judges are required—as American judges are—to apply our almost 220-year-old Constitution. The Constitution is full of generalizations: "due process of law," "equal protection of the laws," "unreasonable searches and seizures," "Commerce . . . among several States." Recourse to the intent of the framers or to the words of the Constitution may not help judges facing cases involving thermal imaging and other new forms of governmental surveillance, the Internet, reproductive rights, or same-sex marriages.

Adherence to Precedent

Just because judges make policy, they are not free to do whatever they wish. They are subject to a variety of limits on what they decide—some imposed by the political system of which they are a part and some imposed by higher courts and the legal profession. Among these constraints is the policy of **stare decisis**, the rule of precedent.

Stare decisis pervades our judicial system and promotes certainty, uniformity, and stability in the law. Judges are expected to abide by previous decisions of their own courts and by rulings of superior courts. Although adherence to precedent is the norm, the doctrine of *stare decisis* is not very restrictive.[39] Judges may distinguish between precedents because of differences in the context of cases, and many questions of law have conflicting precedents that can be used to support a decision for either party.

The doctrine of *stare decisis* is even less controlling in the field of constitutional law. Because the Constitution itself, rather than any one interpretation of it, is binding, the Court can *reverse* a previous decision it no longer wishes to follow, as it has done hundreds of times. Supreme Court justices are therefore not seriously restricted by *stare decisis*. Liberal Justice William O. Douglas, for one, maintained that *stare decisis* "was really no sure guideline because what did the judges who sat there in 1875 know about, say, electronic surveillance? They didn't know anything about it."[40] Chief Justice William H. Rehnquist is no less candid in holding that precedents dealing with civil rights that were handed down on a 5-to-4 vote should always be open for reconsideration, since they were decided by only a bare majority of the Court. Since 1789, the Supreme Court has reversed 218 of its own decisions and overturned more than 174 acts of Congress, more than 967 pieces of state legislation and state constitutional provisions, and more than 115 city ordinances.[41]

Judicial Longevity and Presidential Tenure

Ideology and judicial philosophy affect not only presidents' nominations for the federal courts but also when sitting judges choose to retire. Because federal judges serve for life, they may be able to schedule their retirement to allow a president whose views they approve to nominate their successors. Chief Justice Roger B. Taney stayed on the bench long after his health began to fail to prevent President Abraham Lincoln from nominating a Republican. In 1929, Chief Justice William Howard Taft wrote: "I am older and slower and less acute and more confused. However, as long as things continue as they are, and I am able to answer in my place, I must stay on the court in order to prevent the Bolsheviki [Herbert Hoover, a conservative Republican, was in the White House] from getting control."[42]

Although Chief Justice Warren Burger denied that he retired in 1986 in order to permit President Ronald Reagan to replace him with a conservative, his retirement gave Reagan an opportunity to rejuvenate the conservative wing of the Court by promoting William H. Rehnquist to the chief justiceship. Reagan then picked another conservative, Antonin Scalia, to take the seat vacated by Rehnquist. Liberal Supreme Court Justices William J. Brennan Jr. and Thurgood Marshall held on to their seats well into their eighties, and many assumed that they were doing so in the hope that they might be able to stay on the Court until a president more congenial to their views might be in the

stare decisis
The rule of precedent, whereby a rule or law contained in a judicial decision is commonly viewed as binding on judges whenever the same question is presented.

After a contentious confirmation process in 1987, the Senate rejected Judge Robert Bork by a vote of 58 to 42.

Despite extensive controversy surrounding his nomination, the Senate narrowly confirmed Justice Clarence Thomas in 1991.

White House. They did not make it. Republican President George H. W. Bush, rather than a Democrat, appointed their successors. It should be noted, however, that personal and institutional factors other than partisan concerns are the main reason justices retire.[43]

Reform of the Selection Process

The televised confirmation hearings of Robert Bork in 1987 and Clarence Thomas in 1991, which were lengthy and embattled, aroused considerable criticism from both liberals and conservatives and called forth widespread complaints that "something is wrong with the process." Subsequently, several task forces and studies recommended that attempts be made to constrain the partisan politics surrounding the confirmation process for Supreme Court justices and lower federal court judges. They proposed that "Supreme Court nominees should no longer be expected to appear as witnesses during the Senate Judiciary Committee's hearings on their confirmation" and that the Senate should return to the practice of judging nominees on their written record and on the testimony of legal experts.[44] A bipartisan commission on judicial selection from the Miller Center of Public Affairs at the University of Virginia recommended that the time between nominations and Senate confirmation be shortened.[45] But the problems of delaying and blocking confirmation of judicial nominees remain, as both Presidents Clinton and George W. Bush found, particularly when the Senate is controlled by the party in opposition to the president.[46]

The politics of judicial selection may shock those who like to think judges are picked strictly on the basis of legal merit and without regard for ideology, party, gender, or race. But as a former Justice Department official observed, "When courts cease being an instrument for political change, then maybe the judges will stop being politically selected."[47] Moreover, as another scholar put it, "Supreme Court Justices have always been appointed for political reasons by politicians, and their confirmation process has always been dictated by politicians for political purposes. . . . In fact," he concluded, "not despite the politicization of the appointment and confirmation process, but because of it, the Supreme Court has endured as a flexible, viable force in the American democracy for over 200 years."[48]

CHANGING THE NUMBERS One of the first actions a political party takes after gaining control of the White House and Congress is often to increase the number of federal judgeships. With divided government, however, when one party controls Congress and the other holds the White House, a stalemate is likely to occur, and relatively few new judicial positions will be created. During Andrew Johnson's administration, Congress went so far as to reduce the size of the Supreme Court to prevent the president from filling two vacancies. After Johnson left the White House, Congress returned the Court to its former size to permit Ulysses S. Grant to fill the vacancies.

In 1937, President Franklin Roosevelt proposed an increase in the size of the Supreme Court by one additional justice for every member of the Court over the age of 70, up to a total of 15 members. Ostensibly, the proposal was aimed at making the Court more efficient. In fact, Roosevelt and his advisers were frustrated because the Court had declared much of the early New Deal legislation unconstitutional. Despite Roosevelt's popularity, his "court-packing scheme" aroused intense opposition. Roosevelt's proposals to change the Court's size failed. He lost the battle but won the war, as the Court began to sustain some important New Deal legislation, and subsequent retirements from the bench enabled him to make eight appointments to the Court.

CHANGING THE JURISDICTION Congressional control over the structure and jurisdiction of federal courts has been used to influence the course of judicial policy making. Although unable to get rid of Federalist judges by impeachment, the Jeffersonians abolished the circuit courts created by the Federalist Congress just before they lost control. In 1869, radical Republicans in Congress altered the Supreme Court's appellate jurisdiction in order to snatch from the Court a case it was about to review involving the constitutionality of some Reconstruction legislation.[49]

Each year, a number of bills are introduced in Congress to eliminate the jurisdiction of federal courts over cases relating to abortion, school prayer, and school busing or to eliminate the appellate jurisdiction of the Supreme Court over such matters. These attacks on federal court jurisdiction spark debate about whether the Constitution gives Congress authority to take such actions. And Congress has not yet decided to do so, because it would amount to a fundamental shift in the relationship between Congress and the Supreme Court. As one scholar concluded, "History suggests the public has seen such attempts for precisely what they are, as attacks on judicial independence, and such attacks have been resisted."[50]

THE SUPREME COURT AND HOW IT OPERATES

The Supreme Court's term runs from the first Monday in October through the end of June. The justices listen to oral arguments for two weeks each month from October to April and then adjourn for two weeks to consider the cases and to write opinions. By agreement, six justices must participate in each decision. Cases are decided by a majority vote. In the event of a tie vote, the decision of the lower court is sustained, although on rare occasions the case may be reargued.

At 10:00 A.M. on the days when the Supreme Court sits, the eight associate justices and the chief justice, dressed in their robes (Chief Justice Rehnquist has four gold stripes on each sleeve of his robe), file into the courtroom. As they take their seats—arranged according to seniority, with the chief justice in the center—the clerk of the Court introduces them as the "Honorable Chief Justice and Associate Justices of the Supreme Court of the United States." Those present in the courtroom, asked to stand when the justices enter, are seated, and counsel take their places along tables in front of the bench. The attorneys for the Department of Justice are at the right. The other attorneys are dressed conservatively; sport coats are not considered proper. Dress and ceremony are all part of the high ritual of the Court (see Figure 14–3).

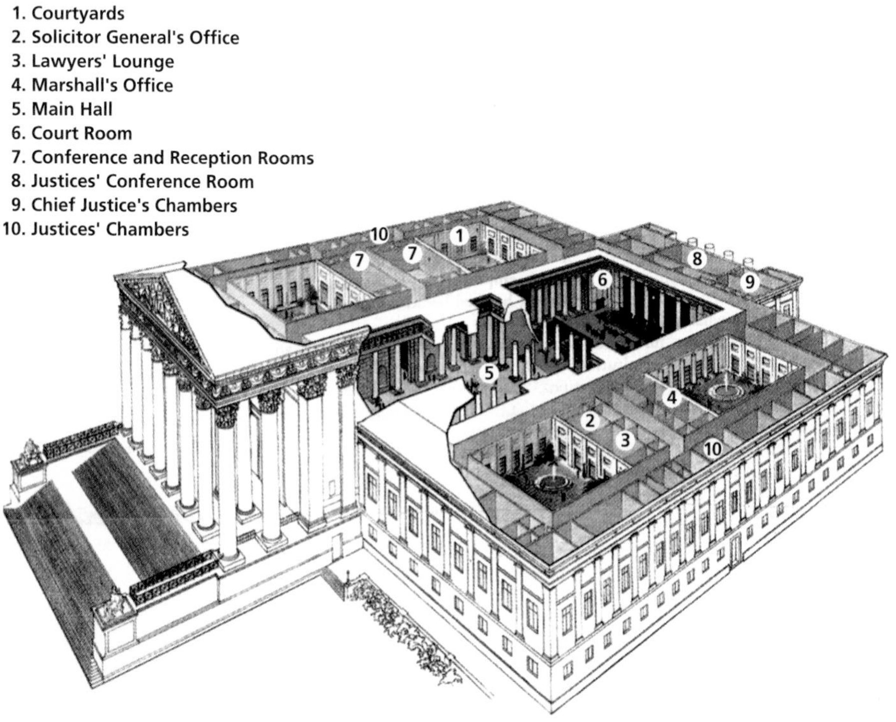

1. Courtyards
2. Solicitor General's Office
3. Lawyers' Lounge
4. Marshall's Office
5. Main Hall
6. Court Room
7. Conference and Reception Rooms
8. Justices' Conference Room
9. Chief Justice's Chambers
10. Justices' Chambers

FIGURE 14–3 The Supreme Court Building.

DOES THE NUMBER OF FEDERAL JUDGES NEED TO BE INCREASED IN ORDER TO ENSURE ACCESS TO JUSTICE?

The Committee on Long-Range Planning of the Judicial Conference of the United States has studied the increasing caseload of federal courts and projects a continued growth in cases and a need for more judges. In 1950 the federal judiciary handled a caseload of 93,835 cases with 289 judges. Thirty years later, in 1980, the case filings more than doubled to 219,957 cases and the number of judges had grown to 648. With continued growth in the size of the federal caseload, it is estimated that in 2010 the lower federal courts will face 814,100 cases and require 2,350 judges. By 2020, it is projected that federal district courts alone will confront over 1 million cases and require over 2,400 judges, while the appellate courts will require more than 1,500 judges in order to handle the projected 325,100 appeals.*

*Committee on Long-Range Planning, Judicial Conference of the United States, *Proposed Long-Range Plan for the Federal Courts* (Judicial Conference of the United States, 1995), pp. 14–15.

The Powers of the Chief Justice

The chief justice of the United States is appointed by the president upon confirmation by the Senate, like other federal judges. Yet the chief justice heads the entire federal judiciary; as a result, he (in our history, all have been men) has greater visibility than if selected by rotation of fellow justices, as is the practice in the state supreme courts, or by seniority, as is the practice in the federal courts of appeals. The chief justice has special administrative responsibilities in overseeing the operation of the judiciary, such as assigning judges to committees, responding to proposed legislation that affects the judiciary, and delivering the Annual Report on the State of the Judiciary.

But within the Supreme Court, the chief justice is only "first among equals," even though periods in Court history are often named after the chief justice. As Chief Justice Rehnquist said when he was still an associate justice, the chief deals not with "eight subordinates whom he may direct or instruct, but eight associates who, like him, have tenure during good behavior, and who are as independent as hogs on ice."[51] As political scientist David Danelski observed, "The Chief Justiceship does not guarantee leadership. It only offers its incumbent an opportunity to lead." Yet the chief justice "sets the tone, controls the conference, assigns the most opinions, and usually, takes the most important, nation-changing decisions for himself."[52]

The ability of the chief justice to influence the Court has varied considerably. Chief Justice Charles Evans Hughes ran the conferences like a stern schoolmaster, keeping the justices on the point, moving the discussion along, and doing his best to work out compromises in order to achieve unanimous decisions, which carry greater weight. By contrast, Chief Justice Harlan F. Stone encouraged justices to state their own points of view and let the discussions wander. Chief Justice Warren Burger was not very successful in leading conferences. He devoted much of his time to judicial reform, speaking to bar associations and trying to build political support for modernizing the judicial process.

William H. Rehnquist had 15 years of Court experience prior to his elevation to chief justice. Unlike his predecessor, he moves conferences along quickly with a dry sense of humor and concise statements of the cases. Moroever, as the Reagan–Bush justices became a majority, his constitutional views on federalism, crime control, and affirmative action, formerly expressed in his dissenting opinions, became the opinions of the Court.

Which Cases Reach the Supreme Court?

When citizens vow to take their cases to the highest court of the land even if it costs their last penny, they underestimate the difficulty of securing Supreme Court review and misunderstand the Court's role. The rules for appealing a case are established by the Supreme Court and Congress. Until 1988, when Congress enacted the Act to Improve the Administration of Justice, the Supreme Court was obliged by law to review a large number of appeals. Today, however, almost all appeals come to the Court by means of a discretionary **writ of certiorari**, a formal petition used to bring a case before the Court that may be denied. Since the Supreme Court's docket is now largely discretionary, it has the power to set its own agenda and to select which cases it wishes to review. As a result, the justices decide fewer than 100 of the over 9,000 cases appealed to them annually. That is half the number of cases decided annually two decades ago (see Figure 14–4).[53]

The crucial factor in determining whether the Supreme Court reviews a case is its importance to the operation of the governmental system as a whole. The Supreme Court will review a case only if the claim involves a substantial question of federal law that has broad public significance—what kinds of affirmative action programs are permissible, whether individuals have a right to doctor-assisted suicide, or under what conditions women may have abortions. The Court also tends to review cases in which rulings among the courts of appeals are in conflict, and by deciding a case, the Supreme Court establishes which ruling is to be followed. Or a case may raise a constitutional issue on which a state supreme court has presented an interpretation with which the Court disagrees.

writ of certiorari
A formal writ used to bring a case before the Supreme Court.

The Court grants cases based on the *rule of four.* If four justices are sufficiently interested in a petition for a *writ of certiorari,* it will be granted and the case brought up for review. The justices' law clerks read the petitions and write a memorandum on each, recommending whether a review should be granted. These memos circulate to all the justices except Justice John Paul Stevens, whose law clerks review the petitions for him, and he reads a few of them himself.[54]

Denial of a *writ of certiorari* does not mean that the justices agree with the decision of the lower court, nor does it establish precedent. Refusal to grant a review may indicate all kinds of possibilities. The justices may wish to avoid a political "hot potato," or the Court may be so divided on an issue that it is not yet prepared to take a stand, or it may want to let an issue "percolate" in the federal courts so that the Court may benefit from their rulings before it decides. The Court tends to take cases on which two or more appellate courts have rendered conflicting rulings on an issue, in order to resolve their conflict and to provide uniformity to the law.[55]

After a case is granted review, each side prepares written *briefs* presenting legal arguments, relevant precedents, and historical background for the justices and their law clerks to study and on the basis of which to render their decisions.

The Role of the Law Clerks

Beginning in the 1920s and 1930s, federal judges began hiring the best recent graduates of law schools to serve as clerks for a year or two. As the judicial workload increased, more law clerks have been appointed. Today each Supreme Court justice is entitled to four clerks. These are young people who have graduated from a leading law school and have previously clerked for a federal or state court.

Each justice picks his or her own clerks and works closely with them throughout the term. Clerks screen writs of certiorari and prepare draft opinions for the justices. Some observers and former law clerks claim that the justices now depend too much on their clerks and that the Court is "clerk-driven."[56] As the number of law clerks and computers has increased, so has the number of concurring and dissenting opinions. Today's opinions are longer and have more footnotes and elaborate citations of cases and law review articles. This is the result of the greater number of law clerks and that the justices' chambers operate like "nine little law firms," often practicing law against each other.[57]

The Solicitor General

Attorneys in the Department of Justice and from other federal agencies participate in more than half of the cases that the Supreme Court agrees to decide and therefore play a crucial role in setting its agenda. Of special importance is the *solicitor general* (SG), who represents the federal government before the Supreme Court and is sometimes called the "tenth justice."[58]

When the SG petitions the Supreme Court to review a decision of a lower court, the Court is likely to do so. That is in part because no appeal may be taken on behalf of the United States to any appellate court without the approval of the solicitor general. Hence the SG's office may pick which cases to appeal. Although an appointee of the president, the SG has considerable independence from the White House. The SG also relies on deputy attorneys general, who are experienced career attorneys and enjoy a reputation for the high quality of their work.

★★ THINKING IT THROUGH

Politicians and judges disagree over whether the number of judges should be increased. Some warn of the bureaucratization of the judiciary and the fragmentation of federal law. Others argue that if the number is not increased, citizens will confront lengthy delays and a denial of access to justice.

Second Circuit Judge Jon O. Newman argues that the number of judges should not rise above 1,000 because there would be a drop in the quality of judges, increased bureaucracy, inefficiency in large appellate courts, and a fragmentation of federal law. He and others recommend shifting to state courts cases involving routine traffic accidents, drug possession, tax, and other civil litigation.[†]

By contrast, Ninth Circuit Judge Stephen Reinhardt contends that freezing the size of the bench would be elitist. An increase in the number of judges would ensure access to justice for the poor, minorities, and other disadvantaged people. He maintains that large federal courts can and do work well.[†]

[†]Jon O. Newman, "1,000 Judges: The Limit for an Effective Judiciary," *Judicature* 76 (June–July 1993), p. 187.

[†]Stephen Reinhardt, "Whose Federal Judiciary Is It Anyway?" *Loyola of Los Angeles Law Review* 27 (1993), p. 1.

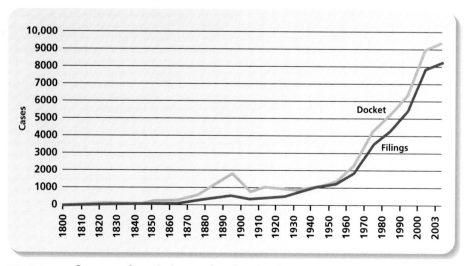

FIGURE 14–4 Supreme Court's Increasing Caseload.
SOURCE: David M. O'Brien, *Storm Center: The Supreme Court in American Politics,* 7th ed. (Norton, 2005).

The solicitor general also files ***amicus curiae*** (Latin for "friend of the court") **briefs** in cases in which the federal government is not a party. The practice of filing *amicus curiae* briefs guarantees that the Department of Justice is represented if a suit questions the constitutionality of an act of Congress or the executive branch. The solicitor general may also use these briefs to bring to the Court's attention the views of the current administration.[59] On occasion, though, solicitors general appear to compromise their independence, as during the administrations of Ronald Reagan and George H. W. Bush, in too aggressively asking the Court to overturn precedents.[60] Still, when the SG appears before the Supreme Court, only respectful formal attire is worn—dark vest, tails, and striped pants. (Briefs filed by the solicitor general may be found on the Web at www.usdoj.gov/osg.)

Amicus Curiae Briefs

Individuals, interest groups, and organizations may also file *amicus curiae* briefs if they claim to have an interest in the case and to have information of value to the Court.[61] An *amicus* brief may help the justices by presenting arguments or facts that the parties to the case have not raised. In recent decades, interest groups have increasingly filed such briefs in an effort to influence the Court and to counter the positions of the solicitor general and the government.

In *Webster* v. *Reproductive Health Services,* dealing with a Missouri law regulating abortions and asking the Court to reverse *Roe* v. *Wade,* 78 *amicus* briefs were filed.[62] In *United States* v. *Lopez,* which challenged congressional authority to ban guns in and around schools, more than 40 parties filed a dozen *amicus* briefs. Ohio, New York, and the District of Columbia argued in favor of federal power, as did associations of police and school officials. On the other side were some conservative public interest firms, the National Governors Association, and the National League of Cities.[63]

Interest groups once filed *amicus curiae* briefs before the Supreme Court granted a *writ of certiorari* in order to encourage the Supreme Court to review the case. Their doing so enhanced the probability that the Court would take the case for review but has almost no influence on how the case is decided.[64] More typically, these briefs are filed after the Court has granted a case review to urge the Court to reach a particular decision.

Oral Arguments

Once the justices receive printed briefs from each side, a case is set for oral arguments—usually in three to four months. Lengthy oratory before the Supreme Court, once lasting for several days, is a thing of the past. As a rule, counsel for each side is now allowed only 30 minutes. Lawyers use a lectern with two lights: A white light flashes five minutes before time is up. When the red light goes on, the lawyer must stop, even in the middle of a sentence.

The entire procedure is informally formal. Sometimes, to the annoyance of attorneys, justices talk among themselves or consult briefs or books during oral arguments. Other times, if justices find a presentation particularly bad, they will tell the attorneys so. Justices freely interrupt the lawyers to ask questions and request additional information. In recent years, "the justices seem barely able to contain themselves, often interrupting the answer to one question with another query."[65] Hence the 30-minute limit is problematic, especially when the solicitor general participates, since his 10 minutes come out of the time of the two parties before the Court.

If a lawyer is having a difficult time, the justices may try to help out with a question. Occasionally, justices bounce arguments off a hapless attorney and at one another. Justice Antonin Scalia is a harsh questioner. "When Scalia prepares to ask a question, he doesn't just adjust himself in his chair to get closer to the microphone like the others; he looks like a vulture, zooming in for the kill. He strains way forward, pinches his eyebrows, and poses the question, like '. . . do you want us to believe?' "[66] Justice Ruth Bader Ginsburg is a particularly persistent questioner, frequently rivaling Justice Scalia in asking the most questions.[67] Justice Clarence Thomas almost never asks a question. Justice David Souter has a thick New England accent. He once asked an attorney during oral arguments in an affirmative action case, "What's the floor?" The attorney hemmed and hawed until, with a smile, Souter explained he meant, "What's the flaw?"[68] (Oral

amicus curiae brief
Literally, a "friend of the court" brief, filed by an individual or organization to present arguments in addition to those presented by the immediate parties to a case.

arguments in landmark cases may be listened to on the Web by going to www.oyez.nwu.edu.)

Behind the Curtains: The Conference

On Wednesday afternoons and Fridays, the justices meet in private conference. They have heard the oral arguments and studied the briefs. Each brings to the meeting a book in which the cases and the votes of the justices are recorded. These conferences are held in secret. They are usually a collegial but vigorous give-and-take.

The chief justice presides, usually opening the discussion by stating the facts, summarizing the questions of law, and suggesting how to dispose of each case. Each justice, in order of seniority, then gives his or her views and conclusions. Chief Justice Rehnquist tries to see to it that "everybody [speaks] once before the vote is taken."[69] Recently, the justices have not bothered with casting formal votes because their votes are clear from their discussion of the case.[70]

Then it went to the U.S. Supreme Court.

Opinions

The Supreme Court announces and explains its decisions in **opinions of the Court**. Opinions generally state the facts, present the issues, and explain the reasoning of the Court. These opinions are the Court's principal method of expressing its views to the world. Their primary function is to instruct judges of state and federal courts how to decide similar cases in the future.

Opinions of the Court are delivered by a justice but do not reflect his or her thinking alone. They must explain the reasoning of the majority of the justices. Consequently, opinions of the Court are negotiated documents that require the author to compromise and at times bargain with other justices to attain agreement on an opinion.[71]

Judicial opinions may also be directed at Congress or at the president. If the Court regrets that "in the absence of action by Congress, we have no choice but to . . . ." or insists that "relief of the sort that petitioner demands can come only from the political branches of government," it is asking Congress to act.[72] Justices also use opinions to communicate with the public. A well-crafted opinion may increase support for a policy the Court favors.

ASSIGNING OPINIONS When voting with the majority, the chief justice decides who will draft the opinion of the Court. When the chief justice is in the minority, the senior justice among the majority makes the assignment. The justice assigned to write the opinion must give persuasive reasons for the outcome, for no vote in conference is final until the opinion of the Court has been agreed to. Justices are free to change their minds if not persuaded by draft opinions.

A justice is free to write a **dissenting opinion** if desired. Dissenting opinions are, in Chief Justice Charles Evans Hughes's words, "an appeal to the brooding spirit of the law, to the intelligence of a later day."[73] Dissenting opinions are quite common, as justices hope that someday these dissenting opinions will command a majority of the Court. If a justice agrees with the majority on how the case should be decided but differs on the reasoning, that justice may write a **concurring opinion**.

CIRCULATING DRAFTS Writing the opinion of the Court is an exacting task. The document must win the support of at least four—and more, if possible—intelligent, strong-willed persons. Assisted by the law clerks, the assigned justice writes a draft and sends it to colleagues for comments. If the justice is lucky, the majority will accept the draft, perhaps with only minor changes. If the draft is not satisfactory to the other justices, it must be redrafted and recirculated until a majority reaches agreement.

The two weapons justices can use against their colleagues are their votes and the threat of writing dissenting opinions attacking the majority's opinion. Especially if the Court is closely divided, one justice may be in a position to demand that a certain point or argument be included in, or removed from, the opinion of the Court as the price of his or her vote. Sometimes such bargaining occurs even though the Court is not closely

opinion of the court
An explanation of a decision of the Supreme Court or any other appellate court.

dissenting opinion
An opinion disagreeing with the majority in a Supreme Court ruling.

concurring opinion
An opinion that agrees with the majority in a Supreme Court ruling but differs on the reasoning.

divided. An opinion writer who anticipates that a decision will invite critical public reaction may want a unanimous Court and will therefore compromise to achieve unanimity. For this reason, the Court delayed declaring school segregation unconstitutional, in *Brown* v. *Board of Education,* until unanimity was secured.[74] The justices understood that any sign of dissension on the bench on this major social issue would be an invitation to evade the Court's ruling.

RELEASING OPINIONS TO THE PUBLIC   In the past, justices read their entire opinions from the bench on "opinion days." Now they give only brief summaries of the decision and their opinions. Copies are immediately made available to reporters and the public and published in the official *United States Supreme Court Reports.* Since April 2000, the Court has made its opinions immediately available on its Web site (www.supremecourtus.gov).

After the Court Decides

Victory in the Supreme Court does not necessarily mean that winning parties get what they want. The Court does not implement its own decision but *remands* the case, sending it back to the lower court with instructions to act in accordance with its opinion. The lower court often has considerable leeway in interpreting the Court's mandate as it disposes of the case.

Decisions whose enforcement requires only the action of a federal agency usually become effective immediately. Thus when the Supreme Court held that President Richard M. Nixon had to turn over confidential White House materials,[75] the president promptly complied.

The impact of a particular Supreme Court ruling on the behavior of individuals who are not immediate parties to a lawsuit is more uncertain. The most important rulings require a change in the behavior of thousands of administrative and elected officials. Sometimes Supreme Court pronouncements are simply ignored. For example, despite the Court's holding that it is unconstitutional for school boards to require students to pray within a school, some schools continue this practice.[76] And for years after the Supreme Court held public school segregation unconstitutional, many school districts remained segregated.[77]

The most difficult Supreme Court decisions to implement are those that require the cooperation of large numbers of officials. For example, a Supreme Court decision announcing a new standard for warrantless searches is not likely to have an impact on the way police make arrests for some time, since not many police officers subscribe to *United States Supreme Court Reports.* The process is more complex. Local prosecutors, state attorneys general, chiefs of police, and state and federal trial court judges must all participate to give meaning to Supreme Court decisions. The Constitution may be what the Supreme Court says it is, but a Supreme Court opinion, for the moment at least, is what a trial judge or police officer or prosecutor or school board or city council says it is.

JUDICIAL POWER IN A CONSTITUTIONAL DEMOCRACY

An independent judiciary is one of the hallmarks of a constitutional democracy and a free society. As impartial dispensers of equal justice under the law, judges should not be dependent on the executive, the legislature, parties to a case, or the electorate. But judicial independence, essential to protect judges in their role as legal umpire, encounters problems when a democratic society decides—as ours has—also to allow these same judges to make policy. Perhaps in no other society do the people resort to litigation as a means of making public policy as much as they do in the United States. For example, the National Association for the Advancement of Colored People (NAACP) turned to litigation to get relief from segregation practices in the 1930s, 1940s, and 1950s. More recently, an increasing number of women's organizations, environmental groups, and religious and conservative organizations have also turned to the courts.[78]

The involvement of courts in politics exposes the judiciary to political criticism. Throughout our history, the Supreme Court has been attacked for engaging in "judicial legislation." This is nothing new. Yet the active role of the federal courts on behalf of liberal causes since 1937 and Republican attacks on that role have returned these issues to the forefront of public debate.

Whereas in earlier times judges occasionally told public officials what they could *not* do, today they often tell them what they *must* do. For example, federal judges, responding to class action complaints, have told Congress, state legislatures, and local officials that they must provide attorneys for the poor, ensure adequate care for mental patients, modernize prisons, and even break up the telephone system. Often judges retain jurisdiction for years as they preside over the implementation of the decrees they have issued.[79] Judges have always been policy makers; that role is not a matter of choice but flows from the roles they play in deciding cases.

The Great Debate over the Proper Role of the Courts

Some people contend that the courts have a duty to protect the interests of the public. Defenders of this *activist* judicial role argue that if Congress, the White House, and the state legislatures are unwilling or unable to resolve pressing problems when people are denied justice and their constitutional rights, then the courts must address those problems. The Supreme Court, they say, should be "a leader in a vital national seminar that leads to the formulation of values for the American people."[80]

Critics of judicial activism contend that for the past half-century, the federal courts, in their zeal to protect people, have become unhinged from their political moorings in the political and constitutional system. Even if courts make the "right" decisions, these critics argue, it is still not right for them to take over the legislative function of elected representatives. Courts should exercise self-restraint and defer to elected representatives and the political process.

Others claim that the debate between those who favor judicial activism and those who favor judicial restraint oversimplifies the choices. Judges, they argue, should take a leadership role in some areas but a restrained role in others. They stand with Chief Justice Harlan F. Stone, who argued that courts have a special duty to intervene (1) whenever legislation restricts the political process by which decisions are made or (2) whenever legislation restricts the rights of "discrete and insular minorities" and (3) when guarantees of the Bill of Rights are violated. In all other areas, the political process should be allowed to work, and judges should not set aside legislation or interfere with administrative agencies merely because they would prefer some other policy or even some other interpretation of the Constitution.[81]

The People and the Court

Whether judges are liberal or conservative, defer to legislatures or not, try to apply the Constitution as they think the framers intended, or interpret it to conform to current values, there are linkages between what judges do and what the people want done. The linkages are not direct, and the people never speak with one mind, but these linkages are the heart of the matter.[82] In the first place, the president and the Senate are likely to appoint justices whose decisions reflect their values. Therefore, elections matter, because the perspectives of the people who nominate and confirm the judges are reflected in the composition of the courts. For instance, in 1992, the Supreme Court, by a 5-to-4 vote in *Planned Parenthood* v. *Casey,* refused to overturn *Roe* v. *Wade* and upheld its core holding—that the Constitution protects the right of a woman to an abortion—although upholding state regulations that do not "unduly burden" that right.[83] This close vote on abortion made it clear that presidential elections could determine whether that right would continue to be protected, depending on whether there are retirements from the bench and new appointments to the Court.

Scholars debate how public opinion influences what judges decide, whether it is direct or indirect through presidential selection and Senate confirmation of judges, but there is little question that there is a correlation between public opinion and judicial decisions.[84] Judicial opinions that reflect what the people want have the greatest survival value. When a new political coalition takes over the White House or Congress, the old regime may stay on in the federal courts. New electoral coalitions eventually take over

"Do you ever have one of those days when nothing seems constitutional?"

The Wall Street Journal, August 3, 1998. By permission of Cartoon Features Syndicate.

the federal courts, and before long, new interpretations of the Constitution reflect the dominant political ideology.[85]

Judges have neither armies nor police to execute their rulings. Although Congress cannot reverse Supreme Court decisions that relate to constitutional interpretations, and only six Supreme Court decisions have been reversed by formal constitutional amendment, the political system alters judicial policy in more subtle ways. Decisions are binding on the parties to a particular case, but the policies that result from judicial decisions are effective and durable only if they are supported by the electorate. To win a favorable Supreme Court decision is to win something of considerable political value.

"American courts are not all-powerful institutions."[86] If the Court's policies are too far out of step with the values of the country, the Court is likely to be reversed. In Chief Justice William H. Rehnquist's words, "No judge worthy of his salt would ever cast his vote in a particular case simply because he thought the majority of the public wanted him to vote that way, but that is quite a different thing from saying that no judge is ever influenced by the great tides of public opinion that run a country such as ours."[87]

"The people" speak in many ways and with many voices. The Supreme Court also hands down rulings on controversies—abortion, affirmative action, and the rights of homosexuals—on which the public is deeply divided. And the justices are often likewise split in deciding those cases. The Supreme Court—and the other courts—thus generally represent and reflect the competing values of the people. Whether they agree or disagree with particular rulings, the public generally holds the Supreme Court in high regard. Notably, the Court's public approval rating remained high and virtually unchanged after its controversial decision in *Bush* v. *Gore* (2000), contrary to predictions by the four dissenting justices and critics that the Court's reputation would be badly damaged by the bare majority's ruling assuring George W. Bush's election.[88]

Although the Court is not the defenseless institution portrayed by some commentators, and its decisions are as much shapers of public opinion as reflections of it, ultimately the power of the Supreme Court in a constitutional democracy rests on retaining the support of most of the people most of the time. The Court's power rests, as Chief Justice Edward White observed, "solely upon the approval of a free people."[89] No better standard for determining the legitimacy of a governmental institution has been discovered.

S U M M A R Y

1. The American judicial process is based on the adversary system. Judges in the United States play a more active role in the political process than they do in most other democracies. Unlike other countries, the United States has a dual judiciary—federal and state court systems. In both federal and state courts, individuals must have standing to sue and must assert a personal injury. Courts decide only justiciable disputes—actual cases or controversies—and not political questions.

2. Except for the Supreme Court, federal courts are established by and receive their jurisdiction directly from Congress, which must decide the constitutional division of responsibilities among federal and state courts. District courts are the trial courts of the federal judicial system, and their decisions may be reviewed by courts of appeals. Federal judges apply federal criminal and civil law but in doing so exercise discretion. Their decisions are subject to reversal by the Supreme Court, which resolves conflicts and tries to promote stability and uniformity in the law.

3. The Supreme Court has almost complete control over the cases it chooses to review as they come up from the state courts, the courts of appeals, and district courts. Law clerks and the solicitor general play important roles in determining the kinds of cases the Supreme Court agrees to decide. Its nine justices dispose of thousands of cases, but most of their time is concentrated on the fewer than 100 cases per year that they accept for review. The Court's decisions and opinions establish guidelines for lower courts and the country.

4. Partisanship and ideology are important factors in the selection of federal judges, and these factors ensure a linkage between the courts and the rest of the political system, so that the views of the people are reflected, even if indirectly, in the work of the courts. In recent decades, candidates for the presidency and the Senate have made judicial appointments an issue in their election campaigns.

5. The president's judicial nominees must be confirmed by the Senate, and the confirmation process tends to be stalled or to erupt into bitter political battles when the majority of the Senate and the president are from opposing political parties.

6. A continuing concern of major importance is the reconciliation of the role of judges—especially those on the Supreme Court—as independent and fair dispensers of justice with their vital role as interpreters of the Constitution. This is an especially complex problem in our democracy because of the power of judicial review and the significant role courts play in making public policy.

7. The debate about how judges should interpret the Constitution is almost as old as the Republic. Almost 220 years after the Constitution was adopted, the argument between those who contend that judges should interpret the document literally and those who believe they cannot and should not remains in the headlines. Both liberals and conservatives have attacked judicial activism and urged judicial self-restraint.

K E Y   T E R M S

judicial review
adversary system
justiciable dispute
class action suit
defendant
plea bargain

public defender system
political question
writ of habeas corpus
original jurisdiction
appellate jurisdiction
grand jury

petit jury
magistrate judge
court of appeals
senatorial courtesy
judicial self-restraint
judicial activism

stare decisis
writ of certiorari
amicus curiae brief
opinion of the court
dissenting opinion
concurring opinion

F U R T H E R   R E A D I N G

HENRY J. ABRAHAM, *Justices, Presidents, and Senators: A History of U.S. Supreme Court Appointments from Washington to Clinton* (Rowman & Littlefield, 1999).

ROBERT A. CARP AND RONALD STIDHAM, *The Federal Courts* (CQ Press, 2001).

CORNELL CLAYTON AND HOWARD GILMAN, EDS., *Supreme Court Decision Making: New Institutionalist Approaches* (University of Chicago Press, 1999).

CLARE CUSHMAN, *The Supreme Court Justices: Illustrated Biographies, 1789–1995,* 2d ed. (CQ Press, 1996).

DEL DICKSON, *The Supreme Court in Conference, 1940–1995* (Oxford University Press, 2001).

LEE A. EPSTEIN, JEFFREY A. SEGAL, HAROLD SPAETH, AND THOMAS WALKER, EDS., *The Supreme Court Compendium,* 2d ed. (CQ Press, 2001).

HOWARD GILLMAN, *The Votes That Counted: How the Court Decided the 2000 Presidential Election* (University of Chicago Press, 2001).

SHELDON GOLDMAN, *Picking Federal Judges: Lower Court Selection from Roosevelt Through Reagan* (Yale University Press, 1997).

KERMIT L. HALL, ED., *The Oxford Companion to the Supreme Court of the United States* (Oxford University Press, 1992).

PETER IRONS, *A People's History of the Supreme Court* (Viking, 1999).

RANDOLPH JONAKAIT, *The American Jury System* (Yale University Press, 2003).

DAVID KLEIN, *Making Law in the U.S. Courts of Appeals* (Cambridge University Press, 2002).

LISA KLOPPENBERG, *Playing It Safe: How the Supreme Court Sidesteps Hard Cases and Stunts the Development of the Law* (New York University Press, 2001).

ROBERT G. MCCLOSKEY, *The American Supreme Court,* 3d ed. (University of Chicago Press, 2001).

DAVID M. O'BRIEN, ED., *Judges on Judging: Views from the Bench,* 2d ed. (CQ Press, 2004).

DAVID M. O'BRIEN, *Storm Center: The Supreme Court in American Politics,* 7th ed. (Norton, 2005).

J. W. PELTASON, *Federal Courts in the Political Process* (Doubleday, 1955).

TERRI JENNINGS PERETTI, *In Defense of a Political Court* (Princeton University Press, 1999).

GERALD N. ROSENBERG, *The Hollow Hope: Can Courts Bring About Social Change?* (University of Chicago Press, 1991).

C. K. ROWLAND AND ROBERT A. CARP, *Politics and Judgment in Federal District Courts* (University Press of Kansas, 1996).

PETER RUSSELL AND DAVID M. O'BRIEN, EDS., *Judicial Independence in the Age of Democracy: Critical Perspectives from Around the World* (University Press of Virginia, 2001).

ELLIOT E. SLOTNICK, *Judicial Politics: Readings from Judicature,* 3d ed. (American Judicature Society, 2005).

DONALD R. SONGER AND SUSAN B. HAIRE, *Continuity and Change on the United States Courts of Appeals* (University of Michigan Press, 2000).

FIRST AMENDMENT FREEDOMS

15

The First Amendment declares, "Congress shall make no law respecting an establishment of religion, or prohibiting the free exercise thereof, or abridging the freedom of speech, or of the press, or the right of the people peaceably to assemble, and to petition the Government for a redress of grievances." In this one sentence, our Constitution lays down the fundamental principles of a free society: freedom of conscience and freedom of expression. These freedoms are essential to our individual self-determination and to our collective self-governance—to government by the people. Yet they are also vulnerable during times of war and now with recent security measures put into place to combat international terrorism.[1]

These freedoms were not constitutionally guaranteed, though, until the addition in 1791 of the first ten amendments, the Bill of Rights. For that reason, we begin this chapter by discussing the rights in the original Constitution and in the Bill of Rights as applied to both the national and state governments before turning to the "first freedoms" of religion, speech, press, and assembly. Before doing so, though, it may be helpful to clarify certain terms—*liberties, freedoms, rights,* and *privileges*—that are often used interchangeably in discussions of rights and freedoms. We offer these definitions. *Civil liberties* are the constitutionally protected freedoms of all persons against governmental restraint: the freedoms of conscience, religion, and expression, for example, which are secured by the First Amendment. These civil liberties are also protected by the due process and equal protection clauses of the Fifth and Fourteenth Amendments. *Civil rights* are the constitutional

TIME LINE ★★

FIRST AMENDMENT FREEDOMS

1798	Alien and Sedition Act imposes penalties for criticism of government
1918	World War I Sedition Act prohibits "disloyal speech"
1919	"Clear and Present Danger" doctrine set forth in *Schenck v. U.S.*
1925	*Gitlow v. New York* extends First Amendment freedoms of speech and press to states
1947	*Everson v. School Board of Education* applies the First Amendment provision for the separation of religion and government to the states
1964	*The New York Times v. Sullivan* holds that libel is not protected speech under the First Amendment
1973	*Miller v. California* establishes guidelines for pornography and obscenity decisions
1989	*Texas v. Johnson* ruling declares that flag-burning is symbolic expression protected by the First Amendment
1997	*Reno v. ACLU* strikes down regulations on indecent and obscene materials on the Internet
2002	*Zelman v. Simmons-Harris* holds that school vouchers may be used at private religious schools

writ of habeas corpus
Court order requiring explanation to a judge why a prisoner is being held in custody.

***ex post facto* law**
Retroactive criminal law that works to the disadvantage of an individual; forbidden in the Constitution.

bill of attainder
Legislative act inflicting punishment, including deprivation of property, without a trial, on named individuals or members of a specific group.

rights of all persons, not just citizens, to due process and the equal protection of the laws: the constitutional right not to be discriminated against by governments because of race, ethnic background, religion, or gender. These civil rights are protected by the due process and equal protection clauses of the Fifth and Fourteenth Amendments and by the civil rights laws of national and state governments; they are discussed further in Chapters 16 and 17. *Legal privileges* are granted by governments and they may be subject to conditions or restrictions, for example, the right to welfare benefits or to a driver's license.

RIGHTS IN THE ORIGINAL CONSTITUTION

Even though most of the framers did not think a bill of rights was necessary, they considered certain rights important enough to be spelled out in the Constitution. These rights included the writ of habeas corpus and protection against *ex post facto* laws and bills of attainder.

Foremost among constitutional rights is the **writ of habeas corpus**. Literally meaning "produce the body," this writ is a court order directing any official holding a person in custody to produce the prisoner in court and explain why the prisoner is being held. As originally used, the writ was merely a judicial inquiry to determine whether a person in custody was held as the result of the action of a court with proper jurisdiction. But over the years, it developed into a remedy for any illegal confinement. People who are incarcerated may appeal to a judge, usually through an attorney, stating why they believe they are held unlawfully and should be released. The judge then orders the jailer or a lower court to show cause of why the writ should not be issued. If a judge finds a petitioner is detained unlawfully, the judge may order the prisoner's immediate release. Although state judges lack jurisdiction to issue writs of habeas corpus to find out why federal authorities are holding persons, federal district judges may do so to find out if state and local officials are holding people in violation of the Constitution or national laws.

In recent years, the use of the writ of habeas corpus by federal courts to review convictions by state courts has been widely criticized. Some people believe the writ has been abused by state prisoners to get an endless and expensive round of reviews, which sometimes lead to convictions being set aside by a federal judge after the matter has been reviewed by two or more state courts. Partly because of concerns about maintaining the principles of federalism and partly because of the growing caseloads of federal courts, the Supreme Court and Congress have restricted the habeas corpus jurisdiction of federal judges. The Antiterrorism and Effective Death Penalty Act of 1996, for example, restricts the number of times a person may be granted a habeas corpus review, stops appeals for most habeas petitions at the level of the U.S. Court of Appeals, and calls for deference by federal judges to the decisions of state judges unless they are clearly "unreasonable."[2]

The Supreme Court nonetheless underscored the fundamental nature of the right to a writ of habeas corpus in two 2004 decisions rejecting the position of President George W. Bush's administration that it could hold indefinitely foreign nationals and U.S. citizens deemed "enemy combatants" in its war against terrorism. The Court held that detainees have a right to a review of the basis for their detention by an independent tribunal.[3]

An ***ex post facto law*** is a retroactive criminal law making a particular act a crime that was not a crime when an individual committed it, increasing punishment for a crime after the crime was committed, lessening the proof necessary to convict for a crime after it was committed, or permitting prosecutions from crimes that were previously barred by statutes of limitations.[4] This prohibition does not prevent the retroactive application of laws that work to the benefit of an accused person—a law decreasing punishment, for example—or prevent the retroactive application of civil law, such as an increase in income tax rates applied to income already earned.

Bills of attainder are legislative acts inflicting punishment, including deprivation of property, on named individuals or members of a specified group without a trial. For example, when Congress adopted a rider to an appropriations bill denying payment of the salaries of three federal employees for "disloyalty," the Supreme Court struck down the rider for being a bill of attainder.[5]

THE BILL OF RIGHTS AND THE STATES

Although it was the framers who wrote the Constitution, in a sense it was the American people who drafted our basic charter of rights. The Constitution drawn up in Philadelphia included guarantees of a few basic rights but lacked a specific bill of rights similar to those in most state constitutions. The Federalists argued that the Constitution established a limited government that would not threaten individual freedoms, and therefore a bill of rights was unnecessary. The Antifederalists were not persuaded, and the omission aroused widespread suspicion. As a result, to persuade delegates to the state ratification conventions to vote for the Constitution, the Federalists promised to correct this deficiency. In its first session, the Congress made good on that promise by proposing 12 amendments, ten of which were promptly ratified and became part of the Constitution.[6]

The guarantees of the Bill of Rights originally applied *only to the national government,* not state governments.[7] Why not the states? The framers were confident that citizens could control their own state officials, and most state constitutions already had bills of rights. It was the new and distant central government the people feared. As it turned out, those fears were largely misdirected. The national government has generally shown less tendency to curtail civil liberties than state and local governments have.

When the Fourteenth Amendment, which applies to the states, was adopted in 1868, supporters contended that its **due process clause**—which states that no person shall be deprived by a state of life, liberty, or property without due process of law—limits states in precisely the same way the Bill of Rights limits the national government. But for decades, the Supreme Court refused to interpret the Fourteenth Amendment in this way. Then in *Gitlow* v. *New York* (1925), the Court announced that it assumed "that freedom of speech and of the press—which are protected by the First Amendment from abridgment by Congress—are among the fundamental personal rights and 'liberties' protected by the due process clause of the Fourteenth Amendment from impairment by the States."[8]

Gitlow v. *New York* was a revolutionary decision. For the first time, the U.S. Constitution protected freedom of speech from abridgment by state and local governments. In the 1930s and continuing at an accelerated pace during the 1960s, through the **selective incorporation** of provision after provision of the Bill of Rights into the due process clause, the Supreme Court applied the most important of these rights to the states.[9] Today the Fourteenth Amendment imposes on the states all the provisions of the Bill of Rights except those of the Second and Third Amendments, the Fifth Amendment provision for indictment by a grand jury, the Seventh Amendment right to a jury trial in civil cases, and the Ninth and Tenth Amendments (see Table 15–1).

Selective incorporation of most provisions of the Bill of Rights into the Fourteenth Amendment is probably the most significant constitutional development since the writing of the Constitution. It has profoundly altered the relationship between the national government and the states. It made the federal courts, under the guidance of the Supreme Court of the United States, the most important protectors of our liberties.

Recently, however, there has been a renewal of interest in state constitutions as independent sources of additional protections for civil liberties and civil rights.[10] Advocates of what has come to be called the *new judicial federalism* contend that the U.S. Constitution should set minimum but not maximum standards for protecting our rights. State bills of rights sometimes provide more protection of rights—the rights to equal education and personal privacy, for instance—than the national Bill of Rights or the Supreme Court's rulings on its guarantees. Despite the revival of interest in state bills of rights, the U.S. Supreme Court and the national Bill of Rights remain the dominant protectors of civil liberties and civil rights.

due process clause
Clause in the Fifth Amendment limiting the power of the national government; similar clause in the Fourteenth Amendment prohibiting state governments from depriving any person of life, liberty, or property without due process of law.

selective incorporation
The process by which provisions of the Bill of Rights are brought within the scope of the Fourteenth Amendment and so applied to state and local governments.

TABLE 15–1 SELECTIVE INCORPORATION AND THE APPLICATION OF THE BILL OF RIGHTS TO THE STATES

Right	Amendment	Year
Public use and just compensation for the taking of private property by the government	5	1897
Freedom of speech	1	1925
Freedom of the press	1	1931
Fair trial	6	1932
Freedom of religion	1	1934
Freedom of assembly	1	1937
Free exercise of religion	1	1940
Separation of religion and government	1	1947
Right to a public trial	6	1948
Right against unreasonable searches and seizures	4	1949
Freedom of association	1	1958
Exclusionary rule	4	1961
Ban against cruel and unusual punishment	8	1962
Right to counsel in felony cases	6	1963
Right against self-incrimination	5	1964
Right to confront witness	6	1965
Right of privacy	1,3,4,5,9	1965
Right to an impartial jury	6	1966
Right to a speedy trial and compulsory process for obtaining witnesses	6	1967
Right to a jury trial in nonpetty cases	6	1968
Protection against double jeopardy	5	1969

FREEDOM OF RELIGION

The first words of the First Amendment are emphatic and brief: "Congress shall make no law respecting an establishment of religion, or prohibiting the free exercise thereof." Note that there are *two* religion clauses: the *establishment* clause and the *exercise* clause. The Supreme Court has struggled to reconcile these two clauses, both of which are cast in absolute terms, and either of which, if expanded to a logical extreme, would clash with the other. Does a state scholarship for blind students given to a college student who decides to attend a college to become a minister violate the establishment clause by indirectly aiding religion? Or would denying the scholarship violate the student's free exercise of religion? The Supreme Court has held that giving such benefits does not violate the establishment clause, but also that the free exercise clause does not entitle individuals to receive such benefits or compel states to make them available.[11]

The Establishment Clause

In writing what has come to be called the **establishment clause**, the framers were reacting to the English system, wherein the crown was the head not only of the government but also of the established church—the Church of England—and public officials were required to take an oath to support the established church as a condition of holding office. The establishment clause goes beyond merely separating government from religion by forbidding the establishment of a state religion. It is designed to prevent three evils: government sponsorship of religion, government financial support of religion, and government involvement in religious matters. However, the clause does not prevent governments from "accommodating" religious needs. To what extent and under

establishment clause
Clause in the First Amendment that states that Congress shall make no law respecting an establishment of religion. It has been interpreted by the Supreme Court as forbidding governmental support to any or all religions.

GLOBAL *Perceptions*

QUESTION: Does the statement "you can practice your religion freely" describe your country "very well"?

In spite of talk of "culture wars," most U.S. citizens (69 percent) believe very strongly that they may practice their religon freely. The only region of the world that compares as highly is Africa, where perceptions of religious freedom are higher than in the United States, except for Ghana (57), Nigeria (54), and Angola (52). Perceptions of the freedom of religious practice also rank higher in India (78). Public perceptions of the freedom of religion are lowest in Poland (39), Russia (35), and Bolivia and Turkey (29).

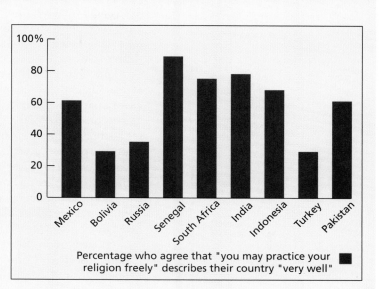

Percentage who agree that "you may practice your religion freely" describes their country "very well"

SOURCE: The Pew Global Attitudes Project, 2003, T-82–T83.

which conditions governments may accommodate these needs are at the heart of much of the debate in the Supreme Court and the country over interpreting the clause.

Controversies over the establishment clause are not easy to resolve. They stir deep feelings and frequently divide the justices among themselves. The prevailing interpretation stems from the decision in *Everson* v. *Board of Education of Ewing Township* (1947) that the establishment clause creates a "wall of separation" between church and state and prohibits any law or governmental action designed to specifically benefit any religion, even if all religions are treated the same.[12] That decision, though, was decided by a bare majority and upheld state support for transportation of children to private religious schools as a "child benefit."

The separation of church and state was further elaborated in *Lemon* v. *Kurtzman* (1971), which laid down a three-part test: (1) A law must have a secular legislative purpose, (2) it must neither advance nor inhibit religion, and (3) it must avoid "excessive government entanglement with religion."[13] This so-called *Lemon test* is often, but not always, used because the justices remain divided over how much separation between government and religion is required by the First Amendment.

Another test, championed by Justice Sandra Day O'Connor, is the *endorsement test.* Justice O'Connor believes that the establishment clause forbids governmental practices that a reasonable observer would view as endorsing religion, even if there is no coercion.[14] The endorsement test has been honed in a series of decisions as the Court struggled with the question of whether governments may allow religious symbols to be displayed on, in, or near public properties and in public places. For example, the Court concluded that when a nativity scene was displayed in a shopping district together with Santa's house and other secular and religious symbols of the Christmas season, there was little danger that a reasonable person would conclude that the city was endorsing religion.[15] But the Constitution does not permit a city government to display the nativity scene on the steps of the city hall, because in this context, the city gives the impression that it is endorsing the display's religious message.[16]

The Court's three most conservative justices—Chief Justice William Rehnquist and Justices Antonin Scalia and Clarence Thomas—support a *nonpreferentialist test.*[17] They believe the Constitution prohibits favoritism toward any particular religion but does not prohibit government aid to *all* religions. In their view, government may accommodate religious activities and even give nonpreferential support to religious organizations so long as individuals are not legally coerced into participating in religious activities and religious activities are not singled out for favorable treatment.[18]

By contrast, the more liberal justices—Justices David H. Souter, John Paul Stevens, Ruth Bader Ginsburg, and Stephen Breyer—usually maintain that there should be *strict separation* between religion and the state.[19] They generally hold that even indirect aid for religion, such as scholarships or teaching materials and aids for students attending private religious schools, crosses the line separating the government from religion.

Applying these generalizations, we find that the establishment clause forbids states—including state universities, colleges, and school districts—from introducing devotional exercises into the public school curriculum, including school graduations and events before football games.[20] However, the Supreme Court has not, as some people assume, entirely prohibited prayer in public schools. It is not unconstitutional for students to pray in a school building. What is unconstitutional is sponsorship or encouragement of prayer *by public school authorities*.[21] Devotional reading of the Bible, recitation of the Lord's Prayer, and posting of the Ten Commandments on the walls of classrooms in public schools have also been ruled to be unconstitutional. A state may not forbid the teaching of evolution or require the teaching of "creation science"—the belief that human life did not evolve but rather was created by a single act of God.[22]

Tax exemptions for church properties, similar to those granted to other nonprofit institutions, are constitutional. State legislatures and Congress may also hire chaplains to open each day's legislative session—a practice that has continued without interruption since the first session of Congress. But if done in a public school, this practice would be unconstitutional. Apparently, the difference is that legislators, as adults, are not "susceptible to religious indoctrination or peer pressure."[23] Also, as the joke goes, legislators need the prayer more.

A continuing controversy centers on whether requiring school children to recite the words "under God" in the Pledge of Allegiance violates the First Amendment. The Court avoided ruling on the issue in *Elk Grove Unified School District* v. *Newdow* (2004) by denying standing to Michael A. Newdow, an atheist, to sue on behalf of his daughter because he was not her legal guardian.[24] However, Chief Justice Rehnquist and Justices O'Connor and Thomas would have granted review and held that the Pledge does not violate the freedom of religion; Justice Scalia agrees with them but had to recuse himself because in an earlier speech he had criticized the lower court's ruling that the First Amendment was violated. Americans United for the Separation of Church and State and other supporters of Newdow plan other lawsuits; they also oppose the efforts of the American Family Association, an evangelical Christian group, to get states to require the display of the national motto, "In God We Trust," in public schools. The controversy over the Pledge and national motto is certain to continue in the courts and to return to the Supreme Court in another case.

Vouchers and State Aid for Religious Schools

Another troublesome area involving the separation of religion and government has revolved around states' providing financial assistance to parochial and other religious schools. The Supreme Court has tried to draw a line between permissible tax-provided aid to schoolchildren and impermissible aid to religion.

At the college level, the problems are relatively simple. Tax funds may be used to construct buildings and operate educational programs at church-related schools as long as the money is not spent directly on buildings used for religious purposes or on teaching religious subjects. Even if students choose to attend religious schools and become ministers, government aid to these students is permissible, because such aid has a secular purpose. Its effect on religion is the result of individual choice "and it does not confer any message of state endorsement of religion."[25]

At the level of elementary and secondary schools, however, the constitutional problems are more complicated. Here the secular and religious parts of institutions and instruction are much more closely interwoven. Also, students are younger and more susceptible to indoctrination, so the chances are greater that aid to church-operated schools aids religion in violation of the establishment clause.

Despite the constitutional obstacles, some states have provided tax credits or deductions for parents who send their children to private, largely religious-run schools. Such deductions or credits available *only* to parents of children attending nonpublic schools are unconstitutional, but allowing taxpaying parents to deduct or take a credit from their state income taxes for what they paid for tuition and other costs to send their children to school—public or private—is constitutional, even if most of the benefit goes to those sending their children to private religious schools.[26]

The Supreme Court has also approved using tax funds to provide students who attend primary and secondary church-operated schools (except those that deny admission because of race or religion) with textbooks, standardized tests, lunches, transportation to and from school, diagnostic services, sign language interpreters, and teachers for remedial and enrichment classes, as well as computers and software for both public and parochial schools.[27]

One hot controversy that the Supreme Court avoided for years involved whether states may also use tax money to give parents **vouchers** for the tuition of children to attend schools of their choice, including religious schools. Maine and Vermont have long had voucher programs for students living in rural areas. Cleveland, Milwaukee, and the state of Florida experimented with voucher programs, permitting the payment of tuition at religious schools, and faced challenges in the courts. Opponents argue that such programs violate the establishment clause, while supporters counter that they do not and argue that the denial of vouchers for attending religious schools violates the free exercise clause and denies parents the freedom of school choice in opting out of dysfunctional public schools.

The Supreme Court finally addressed the constitutionality of voucher programs in *Zelman* v. *Simmons-Harris* (2002),[28] and by a 5-to-4 vote found Ohio's program to be neutral and permissible. Ohio's law provides low-income families in Cleveland with vouchers of up to $2,250 per child to put toward the cost of their children's attending public or private schools outside of the failing inner-city school district, and 96 percent of the vouchers went to religious schools. As a result of this ruling, Congress authorized a $14 million voucher program for students of low-income families in the District of Columbia. In its first year of operation, however, there were not enough applications from public school students to fill all of the slots available. Officials with the Washington Scholarship Fund, a nonprofit organization that runs the program awarding grants of $7,500 per student, pushed to recruit more in the 2005–2006 academic year.[29] There may be increased pressure on state legislatures and school boards to adopt voucher programs.

The Free Exercise Clause

The right to hold any or no religious belief is one of our few absolute rights. The **free exercise clause** affirms that no government has authority to compel us to accept any creed or to deny us any right because of our beliefs or lack of them. Requiring religious oaths as a condition of public employment or as a prerequisite to running for public office is unconstitutional. In fact, the original Constitution states, "No religious Test shall ever be required as a Qualification to any Office or public Trust under the United States" (Article VI).

Although carefully protected, the right to practice a religion has had less protection than the right to hold particular beliefs. Prior to 1990, the Supreme Court carefully scrutinized laws allegedly infringing on religious practices and insisted that the government provide some compelling interest to justify actions that might infringe on somebody's religion. In other words, the First Amendment was thought to throw a "mantle of protection" around religious practices, and the burden was on the government to justify interfering with them in the least restrictive way.

Then, in *Employment Division* v. *Smith* (1990), the Rehnquist Court significantly altered the interpretation of the free exercise clause by discarding the compelling

vouchers
Money provided by the government to parents for payment of their children's tuition in a public or private school of their choice.

free exercise clause
Clause in the First Amendment that states that Congress shall make no law prohibiting the free exercise of religion.

CHANGING FACE OF AMERICAN POLITICS

GROWING RELIGIOUS INTENSITY AND POLARIZATION

The United States is an intensely religious country, and the trend during the last two decades has been toward stronger religious belief. According to a study by The Pew Research Center for the People and the Press, eight of ten (81%) say that prayer is an important part of their daily lives, and even more (87%) agree with the statement "I never doubt the existence of God."*

The growing religious intensity is evident in how citizens characterize their religious faith. In the late 1980s, 41% of Protestants and 24% of the population identified themselves as "born-again or evangelical" Christians, whereas today 54% of Protestants and 30% of the population descibe themselves in that way. The trend is especially marked with respect to African Americans; 50% now describe themselves that way, compared with 36% earlier. Fewer than one in ten (9%) report that they have no religion.

Moreover, recent generations are becoming more religious as they age. Almost two decades ago 61% of people in their late teens and twenties expressed deep religious faith, but 71% of people in these generations now in their thirties and forties do.

In addition, during the last two decades religion and religious faith have grown more aligned with partisan and ideological identification. Republicans and Democrats remain equally likely to express strong religious attitudes, but Republicans have become increasingly united in that belief, with a widening gap between the parties (78% versus 71% of Democrats). While religiosity and conservatism have always been correlated, that relationship has increased substantially among self-identified conservatives (81% today compared to 73% in the late 1980s), while liberals have become somewhat less religiously oriented (54% express strong religious belief today, compared to 59% in the late 1980s).

*The Pew Research Center for the People and the Press, *The 2004 Political Landscape: Evenly Divided and Increasingly Polarized* (November 3, 2003), at people-press.org/reports/display.php3?reported=196.

governmental interest test for overriding the interests of religious minorities.[30] As long as a law is generally applicable and does not single out and ban religious practices, the law may be applied to conduct even if it burdens a particular religious practice.[31]

The ruling in *Employment Division* v. *Smith* was controversial and led Congress to enact the Religious Freedom Restoration Act of 1993 (RFRA), which aimed to override the *Smith* decision and to restore the earlier test prohibiting the government—federal, state, or local—from limiting a person's exercise of religion unless the government demonstrates a compelling interest that is advanced by the least restrictive means. Congress asserted its power to pass the RFRA because the Fourteenth Amendment gives it the authority to enforce rights secured by that amendment, including the right to free exercise of religion.

However, when the Catholic archbishop of San Antonio was denied a building permit in 1997 to enlarge a church in Boerne, Texas, because the remodeling did not comply with the city's historical preservation plan, he claimed that the city's denial of a building permit interfered with religious freedom as protected by the Religious Freedom Restoration Act. The Supreme Court then ruled the RFRA to be unconstitutional because Congress was attempting to define, rather than enforce or remedy, constitutional rights and was thereby assuming the role of the courts, which contradicted "vital principles necessary to maintain separation of powers and the federal balance."[32]

Tensions between the establishment and free exercise clauses have recently become more prominent. On the one hand, the University of Virginia denied a Christian student group funds to pay for the printing of its newspaper, *Wide Awake,* because it interpreted the establishment clause to forbid allocating student fee money to a newspaper that "primarily promotes a belief in or about a deity." The students argued that the university deprived them of their freedom of speech, including religious speech, and the Supreme Court agreed with the students.[33] On the other hand, some Christian students at the University of Wisconsin objected to the use of mandatory student activity fees for funding groups they deemed offensive and contrary to their religious beliefs.

They argued that they should be exempt from paying that portion of their fees, but the Supreme Court rejected their claim.[34]

FREE SPEECH AND FREE PEOPLE

Government by the people is based on every person's right to speak freely, to organize in groups, to question the decisions of the government, and to campaign openly against them. Only through free and uncensored expression of opinion can government be kept responsive to the electorate and political power transferred peacefully. Elections, separation of powers, and constitutional guarantees are meaningless unless all persons have the right to speak frankly and to hear and judge for themselves the worth of what others have to say. As Justice Oliver Wendell Holmes observed, "The best test of truth is the power of the thought to get itself accepted in the competition of the market. . . . That at any rate is the theory of our Constitution. It is an experiment, as all life is an experiment."[35]

Free speech is not simply the personal right of individuals to have their say; it is also the right of the rest of us to hear them. John Stuart Mill, whose *Essay on Liberty* (1859) is the classic defense of free speech, put it this way: "The peculiar evil of silencing the expression of opinion, is that it is robbing the human race. . . . If the opinion is right, they are deprived of the opportunity of exchanging error for truth; if wrong, they lose what is almost as great a benefit, the clearer perception and livelier impression of truth, produced by its collision with error."[36]

Reverend Anthony Cummins, pastor of St. Peter the Apostle Church, in front of his church in Boerne, Texas, after a battle with city officials who denied the church permission to build an addition to the historic structure.

PEOPLE & POLITICS *Making a Difference* ★★★

ERNESTO PICHARDO

A Cuban-born immigrant, Ernesto Pichardo, cofounded with other family members the first church of the Santeria religion, the Church of the Lukumi Babalu Aye, in Hialeah, Florida. Slaves brought to Cuba in the eighteenth and nineteenth centuries worshipped African gods alongside Catholic saints, and their religion became known as Santeria—"the way of the saints." Followers of Santeria came to the United States in great numbers after Fidel Castro's rise to power in 1959 and again with the 1980 Mariel "boatlift" that followed Castro's deportation of some 125,000 Cubans.

The founding of the church created a major controversy. In Cuba, the practice of Santeria was illegal and done in secret. Pichardo wanted to give the religion legitimacy, to institutionalize it, and to publicly perform rituals, including ritual animal sacrifice. Not only did leaders of various religions in Hialeah oppose the church, but so did animal rights organizations.

Within weeks, the Hialeah city council passed ordinances making ritual animal sacrifice, except in slaughterhouses, a crime. The ordinances were defended as health and safety measures, as well as aimed at preventing animal cruelty. But Pichardo challenged them for violating the First Amendment free exercise clause. The ordinances specifically targeted a religious practice, and Hialeah did not criminalize hunting, fishing, and other kinds of killing of animals.

In *Church of the Lukumi Babalu Aye, Inc. and Ernesto Pichardo* v. *City of Hialeah,** the Court struck down Hialeah's ordinances banning ritual animal sacrifice. The Court unanimously held that the city had targeted and discriminated against a particular religion, thereby violating the First Amendment. Pichardo thus won an important victory

in the Court's reaffirming that government may not overtly discriminate against religious minorities.

*Church of the Lukumi Babalu Aye, Inc. and Ernesto Pichardo v. City of Hialeah, 508 U.S. 530 (1993); see also David M. O'Brien, Animal Sacrifice and Religious Freedom (University Press of Kansas, 2004); and more generally, Melvin Urofsky, ed., 100 Americans Making Constitutional History (CQ Press, 2004).

Police arrest Scott Tyler of Chicago after he set fire to an American flag on the steps of the Capitol building in Washington. The Supreme Court ruled that freedom of speech covers even "symbolic speech" like burning the U.S. flag.

Americans overwhelmingly support the principle of freedom of expression in general. Yet some who say they believe in free speech draw the line at ideas they consider dangerous or when speech attacks them or is critical of their race, religion, or ethnic origin. But what is a dangerous idea? Who decides? In the realm of political ideas, who can find an objective, eternally valid standard of right? The search for truth involves the possibility—even the inevitability—of error. The search cannot go on unless it proceeds freely in the minds and speech of all. This means, in the words of Justice Robert Jackson, that "freedom to differ is not limited to things that do not matter much. That would be a mere shadow of freedom. The test of its substance is the right to differ as to things that touch the heart of the existing order."[37]

Even though the First Amendment explicitly denies Congress the power to pass any law abridging freedom of speech, the amendment has never been interpreted in absolute terms. Like almost all rights, the freedoms of speech and of the press are limited. In discussing the constitutional power of government to regulate speech, it is useful to distinguish among *belief, speech,* and *action.*

At one extreme is the right to *believe* as we wish. Despite occasional deviations in practice, the traditional American view is that government should not punish a person for beliefs or interfere in any way with freedom of conscience. At the other extreme is *action,* which may be subject to governmental restraint. As has been said, "The right to swing your fist ends where my nose begins."

Speech stands somewhere between belief and action. It is not an absolute right, like belief, but neither is it as exposed to governmental restraint, like action. Some kinds of speech—libel, obscenity, fighting words, and commercial speech—are not entitled to constitutional protection. But many problems arise in distinguishing between what does and does not fit into the categories of nonprotected speech. People disagree, and it usually falls to the courts to decide and to defend the free speech of individual and minority dissenters.

Judging: Drawing the Line

Plainly, questions of free speech require that judges weigh a variety of factors: What was said? In what context? How was it said? Which level of government is attempting to regulate the speech—a city council speaking for a few people, or Congress, speaking for many? (The Supreme Court is much more deferential to acts of Congress than to those of a city council or state legislature.) How is the government attempting to regulate the speech—by prior restraint (censorship) or by punishment after the speech? Why is the government doing so—to preserve the public peace or to prevent criticism of the people in power? These and scores of other considerations are involved in the never-ending process of determining what the First Amendment permits and what it forbids.

Historical Constitutional Tests

It is useful to start with the three constitutional tests used in the first part of the twentieth century: the bad tendency test, the clear and present danger test, and the preferred position doctrine. Although they are no longer applied, they provide a background for the current judicial approach to governmental regulation of speech and to the courts' expanding protection for free speech.

THE BAD TENDENCY TEST   This test was rooted in English common law. According to the **bad tendency test**, judges presumed it was reasonable to forbid speech that has a tendency to corrupt society or cause people to engage in illegal acts. The test was abandoned because it swept too broadly and ran "contrary to the fundamental premises underlying the First Amendment as the guardian of our democracy."[38] Some legislators still appear to hold this position today, and it also seems to be the view of some college students, who want to see their institution punish student colleagues or faculty who express "hateful" or "offensive" ideas.

THE CLEAR AND PRESENT DANGER TEST   This is perhaps the most famous test. The **clear and present danger test** was formulated by Justice Oliver Wendell Holmes Jr. in *Schenck* v. *United States* (1919) as an alternative to the bad tendency test. In the words of

bad tendency test
Interpretation of the First Amendment that would permit legislatures to forbid speech encouraging people to engage in illegal action.

clear and present danger test
Interpretation of the First Amendment that holds that the government cannot interfere with speech unless the speech presents a clear and present danger that it will lead to evil or illegal acts. To shout "Fire!" falsely in a crowded theater is Justice Oliver Wendell Holmes's famous example.

Justice Holmes, "The question in every case is whether the words are used in circumstances and are of such a nature as to create a clear and present danger that they will bring about substantive evils that Congress has a right to prevent."[39] A government should not be allowed to interfere with speech unless it can prove, ultimately to a skeptical judiciary, that the particular speech in question presents an immediate danger—for example, speech leading to a riot, the destruction of property, or the corruption of an election.

Supporters of the clear and present danger test concede that speech is not an absolute right. Yet they believe free speech to be so fundamental to the operations of a constitutional democracy that no government should be allowed to restrict speech unless it can demonstrate a close connection between the speech and an imminent lawless action. To shout "Fire!" falsely in a crowded theater is the most famous example of unprotected speech.

THE PREFERRED POSITION DOCTRINE   This was advanced in the 1940s when the Court applied all of the guarantees of the First Amendment to the states. The **preferred position doctrine** came close to the position that freedom of expression—the use of words and pictures—should rarely, if ever, be curtailed. This interpretation of the First Amendment gives these freedoms, especially freedom of speech and of conscience, a preferred position in our constitutional hierarchy. Judges have a special duty to protect these freedoms and should be most skeptical about laws trespassing on them. Once that judicial responsibility was established, judges had to draw lines between nonprotected and protected speech, as well as between speech and nonspeech.

NONPROTECTED AND PROTECTED SPEECH

Today the Supreme Court holds that all speech is protected unless it falls into one of four narrow categories—*libel, obscenity, fighting words,* and *commercial speech.* Such **nonprotected speech** lacks social redeeming value and has been deemed not essential to democratic deliberations and self-governance.

Still, the fact that nonprotected speech does not receive First Amendment protection does not mean that the constitutional issues relating to these kinds of speech are simple. How we prove libel, how we define obscenity, how we determine which words are fighting words, and how much commercial speech may be regulated remain hotly contested issues.

Libel

At one time, newspaper publishers and editors had to take considerable care about what they wrote for fear they might be prosecuted for **libel**—published defamation or false statements—by the government or sued by individuals. Today, as a result of gradually rising constitutional standards, it has become more difficult to win a libel suit against a newspaper or magazine.

Seditious libel—defaming, criticizing, and advocating the overthrow of government—was once subject to criminal penalties but no longer is. Seditious libel was rooted in the common law of England, which has no First Amendment protections. In 1798, only seven years after the First Amendment had been ratified, Congress enacted the first national law against **sedition**, the Sedition Act of 1798. Those were perilous times for the young Republic, for war with France seemed imminent. The Federalists, in control of both Congress and the presidency, persuaded themselves that national safety required some suppression of speech. But popular reaction to the Sedition Act helped defeat the Federalists in the elections of 1800, and the Sedition Act expired in 1801. The Federalists had failed to grasp the democratic idea that a person may criticize the government, oppose its policies, and work for the removal of the individuals in power yet still be loyal to the nation. They also failed to grasp the distinction between *seditious speech* and *seditious action*—conspiring to commit and engaging in violence against the government, which can be prosecuted and punished.

preferred position doctrine
Interpretation of the First Amendment that holds that freedom of expression is so essential to democracy that governments should not punish persons for what they say, only for what they do.

nonprotected speech
Libel, obscenity, fighting words, and commercial speech, which are not entitled to constitutional protection in all circumstances.

libel
Written defamation of another person. Especially in the case of public officials and public figures, the constitutional tests designed to restrict libel actions are very rigid.

sedition
Attempting to overthrow the government by force or to interrupt its activities by violence.

Hustler *publisher Larry Flynt agrees to a plea bargain in which obscenity charges were dropped and a fine imposed if Flynt removed X-rated videos from a downtown store.*

obscenity
Quality or state of a work that taken as a whole appeals to a prurient interest in sex by depicting sexual conduct in a patently offensive way and that lacks serious literary, artistic, political, or scientific value.

Another attempt to limit political criticism of the government was the Smith Act of 1940. That law forbade advocating the overthrow of the government, distributing material advocating the overthrow of government by violence, and organizing any group having such purposes. In 1951, during the cold war, the Supreme Court agreed that the Smith Act could be applied to the leaders of the Communist party who had been charged with conspiring to advocate the violent overthrow of the government.[40]

Since then, however, the Court has substantially modified constitutional doctrine, giving all political speech First Amendment protection. In *New York Times* v. *Sullivan* (1964), seditious libel was declared unconstitutional.[41] Now neither Congress nor any government may outlaw mere advocacy of the abstract doctrine of violent overthrow of government: "The essential distinction is that those to whom the advocacy is addressed must be urged to do something now or in the future, rather than merely to believe in something."[42] Moreover, advocacy of the use of force may not be forbidden "except where such advocacy is directed to inciting or producing imminent lawless action and is likely to incite or produce such action."[43]

In the landmark ruling in *New York Times* v. *Sullivan* and subsequent cases, the Supreme Court established guidelines for libel cases and severely limited state power to award monetary damages in libel suits brought by public officials against critics of official conduct. Neither public officials nor public figures can collect damages for comments made about them unless they can prove with "convincing clarity" that the comments were made with "actual malice." *Actual malice* means not merely that the defendant made false statements but that the "statements were made with a knowing or reckless disregard for the truth."[44]

Public figures cannot collect damages even when subject to outrageous, clearly inaccurate parodies and cartoons. Such was the case when *Hustler* magazine printed a parody of the Reverend Jerry Falwell; the Court held that parodies and cartoons cannot reasonably be understood as describing actual facts or events.[45] Nor does the mere fact that a public figure is quoted as saying something that he or she did not say amount to a libel unless the alteration in what the person said was made deliberately, with knowledge of its falsity, and "results in material change" in the meaning of the quotation.[46]

Constitutional standards for libel charges brought by private persons are not as rigid as those for public officials and figures. State laws may permit private persons to collect damages without having to prove actual malice if they can prove the statements made about them are false and were negligently published.[47]

Obscenity and Pornography

Obscene publications are not entitled to constitutional protection, but members of the Supreme Court, like everybody else, have great difficulty in defining obscenity. As Justice Potter Stewart put it, "I know it when I see it."[48] Or, as the second Justice John Marshall Harlan explained, "One man's vulgarity is another man's lyric."[49]

In *Miller* v. *California* (1973), the Court finally agreed on a constitutional definition of **obscenity**. A work may be considered legally obscene if (1) the average person, applying contemporary standards of the particular community, would find that the work, taken as a whole, appeals to a prurient interest in sex; (2) the work depicts or describes in a patently offensive way sexual conduct specifically defined by the applicable law or authoritatively construed; and (3) the work, taken as a whole, lacks serious literary, artistic, political, or scientific value.[50]

Before *Miller,* the distinction between *pornography* and *obscenity* was not clear. The *Miller* standard clarified that only hard-core pornography is constitutionally unprotected. X-rated movies and adult theaters that fall short of the constitutional definition of obscenity are entitled to some constitutional protection, but less protection than political speech, and they are subject to greater government regulation. Cities may, as New York City has done, also regulate where adult theaters may be located by zoning laws,[51] and they may ban totally nude dancing in adult nightclubs.[52] Under narrowly drawn statutes, state and local governments can also ban the sale of "adult" magazines to minors, even if such materials would not be considered legally obscene if sold to adults.

The Court has also held that *child pornography*—sexually explicit materials either featuring minors or aimed at them—is not protected by the First Amendment.[53] Just as the government may protect minors, so apparently may it protect members of the armed forces. The Supreme Court left standing a ruling of a lower court upholding an act of Congress forbidding the sale or rental on military property of magazines or videos whose "dominant theme" is to portray nudity "in a lascivious way."[54]

Pressure for regulating pornography came primarily from political conservatives and religious fundamentalists concerned that it undermines moral standards. Some feminists have joined them, however, arguing that pornography is degrading and perpetuates sexual discrimination and violence. They argue that just as sexually explicit materials featuring minors are not entitled to First Amendment protection, so should there be no protection for pornographic materials. They contend that pornography promotes the sexual abuse of women and maintains the social subordination of women as a class. Some feminists define pornographic materials more broadly than the Court has and would include sexually explicit pictures or words that depict women as sexual objects enjoying pain and humiliation or that present abuse of women as a sexual stimulus for men.[55]

Not all feminists favor antipornography ordinances, yet those who do have joined social conservatives in a battle over regulating pornography. For this antipornography coalition to be successful, a substantial alteration in constitutional doctrine will be required. Unlike the Canadian Supreme Court, which redefined obscenity to include materials that degrade women,[56] the U.S. Supreme Court does not appear willing to substantially change current doctrine.

Fighting Words

Fighting words were held to be constitutionally unprotected because "their very utterance may inflict injury or tend to incite an immediate breach of peace."[57] That the words are abusive, offensive, and insulting or that they create anger, alarm, or resentment is not sufficient. Thus a four-letter word worn on a sweatshirt was not judged to be a fighting word in the constitutional sense, even though it was offensive and angered some people.[58] In recent years, the Court has overturned convictions for uttering fighting words and struck down laws that criminalized "hate speech"—insulting racial, ethnic, and gender slurs.[59] The Court, though, has indicated that cross-burning by the Klu Klux Klan may be punished because it has historically been associated with intimidation.[60]

Commercial Speech

Commercial speech—such as advertisements and commercials—used to be unprotected because it was deemed to have lesser value than political speech. But in recent years, the Court has reconsidered and extended more protection to commercial speech, as it has to fighting words. In *44 Liquormart, Inc.*, v. *Rhode Island* (1996), for instance, the Court struck down a law forbidding the advertising of the price of alcoholic drinks.[61] It now appears that states may forbid and punish only false and misleading advertising, along with advertising the sale of anything illegal—for example, narcotics. Although the Supreme Court has not specifically removed it from the nonprotected category, the Court has interpreted the First, Fifth, and Fourteenth Amendments so as to provide considerable constitutional protection for commercial speech.

Protected Speech

Apart from these four categories of nonprotected speech, all other expression is constitutionally protected, and courts strictly scrutinize government regulation of such speech. The Supreme Court uses the following doctrines to measure the limits of governmental power to regulate speech.

Virginia's Attorney General, Jerry Kilgore (right), speaks to reporters outside the U.S. Supreme Court building in Washington, D.C., where the justices heard a First Amendment challenge to Virginia's cross-burning law on December 11, 2002.

fighting words
Words that by their very nature inflict injury on those to whom they are addressed or incite them to acts of violence.

commercial speech
Advertisements and commercials for products and services; they receive less First Amendment protection, primarily to discourage false and misleading ads.

IN COMPARATIVE PERSPECTIVE

HATE SPEECH IN CANADA

Although the Supreme Court of Canada, in interpreting the nation's Charter of Rights, generally follows the rulings on freedom of speech of the Supreme Court of the United States, it refused to do so with respect to hate speech. Whereas the U.S. Supreme Court held that the First Amendment bars making hate speech a crime,* the Canadian Supreme Court upheld a law making it a crime to express "hatred against any identifiable group . . . distinguished by colour, race, religion, or ethnic origin."

James Keegstra, a high school teacher, was convicted of communicating anti-Semitic teachings to his students. His conviction, however, was overturned by an appeals court on the ground that the law punishing hate speech violated the Charter's guarantee of freedom of expression. In reversing the lower court and upholding Keegstra's conviction and Canada's hate speech law, the Supreme Court observed:

The international commitment to eradicate hate propaganda and, most importantly, the special role given equality and multiculturalism in the Canadian Constitution necessitate a departure from the view, reasonably prevalent in America at present, that the suppression of hate propaganda is incompatible with the guarantee of free expression. . . .

At the core of freedom of expression lies the need to ensure that truth and the common good are attained, whether in scientific and artistic endeavors or in the process of determining the best course to take in our political affairs. . . . Nevertheless, the argument from truth does not provide convincing support for the protection of hate propaganda. Taken to its extreme, this argument would require us to permit the communication of all expression, it being impossible to know with *absolute* certainty which factual statements are true, or which ideas obtain the greatest good. . . . There is very little chance that statements intended to promote hatred against an identifiable group are true, or that their vision of society will lead to a better world. To portray such statements as crucial to truth and the betterment of the political and social milieu is therefore misguided.[†]

*R.A.V. v. St. Paul, 505 U.S. 377 (1992).
[†]Regina v. Keegstra, 3 S.C.R. 697 (1990).

PRIOR RESTRAINT   Of all the forms of governmental interference with expression, judges are most suspicious of those that impose **prior restraint**—censorship before publication. Prior restraints include governmental review and approval before a speech can be made, before a motion picture can be shown, or before a newspaper can be published. Most prior restraints are unconstitutional, as the Court has said: "Any system of prior restraints of expression comes to this Court bearing a heavy presumption against its constitutional validity."[62] About the only prior restraints approved by the Court relate to military and national security matters—such as the disclosure of troop movements[63]—and to high school authorities' control over student newspapers.[64] Student newspapers at colleges and universities receive the same protections as other newspapers because they are independent and financially separate from the college or university.

VOID FOR VAGUENESS   Laws must not be so vague that people do not know whether their speech would violate the law and hence are afraid to exercise protected freedoms. Laws must not allow the authorities who administer them so much discretion that they may discriminate against people whose views they dislike. For these reasons, the Court strikes down laws using the void for vagueness doctrine.

prior restraint
Censorship imposed before a speech is made or a newspaper is published; usually presumed to be unconstitutional.

LEAST DRASTIC MEANS   Even for an important purpose, a legislature may not pass a law that impinges on First Amendment freedoms if other, less drastic means are available. To illustrate, a state may protect the public from unscrupulous lawyers, but it may not do so by forbidding attorneys from advertising their fees for simple services. The state could adopt other ways to protect the public from such lawyers that do not impinge on their freedom of speech; it could, for example, provide for the disbarment of lawyers who mislead their clients.

CONTENT AND VIEWPOINT NEUTRALITY   Laws concerning the time, place, or manner of speech that regulate some kinds of speech but not others or that regulate speech expressing some views but not others are much more likely to be struck down than those that are content-neutral or viewpoint-neutral, that is, laws that apply to *all* kinds of speech and to *all* views. For example, the Constitution does not prohibit laws forbidding the posting of handbills on telephone poles. Yet laws prohibiting only religious handbills or only handbills advocating racism or sexism would in all probability be declared unconstitutional because they would relate to the kinds of handbills or what is being said rather than to all handbills regardless of what they say.

The lack of viewpoint neutrality was the grounds for the Court's striking down a St. Paul, Minnesota, ordinance that prohibited the display of a symbol that would arouse anger on the basis of race, color, creed, religion, or gender. The ordinance was not considered viewpoint-neutral because it did not forbid displays that might arouse anger for other reasons, for example, because of political affiliation.[65]

FREEDOM OF THE PRESS

Courts have carefully protected the right to publish information, no matter how journalists get it. But some reporters, editors, and others argue that this is not enough. They insist that the First Amendment gives them the right to ignore legal requests and to withhold information. They also contend that the First Amendment gives them a *right of access,* a right to go wherever they need to go to get information.

Does the Press Have the Right to Withhold Information?

Although most reporters have challenged the right of public officials to withhold information, they claim the right to do so themselves, including the right to keep information from grand juries and legislative investigating committees. Without this right to withhold information, reporters insist, they cannot assure their sources of confidentiality, and they will not be able to get the information they need to keep the public informed.

The Supreme Court, however, has refused to acknowledge that reporters, and presumably scholars, have a constitutional right to ignore legal requests such as subpoenas and to withhold information from governmental bodies.[66] It is up to Congress and the states to provide such privileges for news reporters, and many states have passed *press shield laws* providing some protection for reporters from state court subpoenas.

Does the Press Have the Right to Know?

The press has argued that if reporters are excluded from places where public business is conducted or are denied access to information in government files, they are not able to perform their traditional function of keeping the public informed. In similar fashion, some reporters argue that they may enter facilities such as food markets, child care centers, and homes for the mentally ill, even using false identities, to expose racial discrimination, employment discrimination, and financial fraud. The Supreme Court, however, has refused to acknowledge a constitutional right of the press to know, although it did concede that there is a First Amendment right for the press, along with the public, to be present at criminal trials.[67]

Although they have no constitutional obligation to do so, many states have adopted *sunshine laws* requiring government agencies to open their meetings to the public and the press. Congress requires most federal executive agencies to open hearings and meetings of advisory groups to the public, and most congressional committee meetings are open to the public. Federal and state courtroom trials are also open, but judicial conferences, in which the judges discuss how to decide the cases, are not.

Congress has authorized the president to establish a classification system to keep some public documents and governmental files secret, and it is a crime for any person to divulge such classified information. So far, however, although they have been threatened, no newspapers have been prosecuted for doing so.

The Freedom of Information Act (FOIA) of 1966, since amended, liberalized access to nonclassified federal government records. This law makes the records of federal executive agencies available to the public, with certain exceptions, such as private financial transactions, personnel records, criminal investigation files, interoffice memorandums, and letters used in internal decision making. If federal agencies fail to act promptly on requests for information, applicants are entitled to speedy judicial hearings. The burden is on an agency to explain its refusal to supply material, and if the judge decides the government has improperly withheld information, the government has to pay the legal fees. Since the inception of FOIA, more than 250,000 people have requested information, and more than 90 percent of these requests have been granted.

President Bill Clinton issued an executive order requiring the automatic declassification of almost all government documents after 25 years. Any person who wants access to documents that are not declassified can appeal to an Interagency Security Classification Appeals panel, which has a record of ruling in favor of releasing documents. The Electronic Freedom of Information Act of 1996 requires most federal agencies to put their files online and to establish an index of all their records. The National Aeronautics and Space Administration (NASA) has done the most of the federal agencies (see www.nasa.gov). One of the most frequent requests to NASA's Electronic Reading Room is for documents relating to unidentified flying objects (UFOs).

Free Press Versus Fair Trials

When newspapers and television report in vivid detail the facts of a crime, interview prosecutors and police, question witnesses, and hold press conferences for defendants and their attorneys—as in the O. J. Simpson murder trial and Oklahoma City bombing cases—they may so inflame the public that finding a panel of impartial jurors and conducting a fair trial is difficult. In England, strict rules determine what the media may report, and judges do not hesitate to punish newspapers that comment on pending criminal proceedings. By contrast, in the United States free comment is protected. Yet the Supreme Court has not been indifferent to protecting persons on trial from inflammatory publicity. Judges may impose "gag orders" on lawyers and jurors, but not reporters, restraining them from talking about an ongoing trial, and new trials may be ordered as a remedy for prejudicial publicity. Trials may, on rare occasions, be closed to the press and the public. Although federal rules of criminal procedure forbid radio or photographic coverage of criminal cases in federal courts, most states permit televising courtroom proceedings, and court TV programs have become very popular.

OTHER MEDIA AND COMMUNICATIONS

When the First Amendment was written, freedom of "the press" referred to leaflets, newspapers, and books. Today the amendment protects other media as well—the mails, motion pictures, billboards, radio, television, cable, telephones, fax machines, and the Internet. Because each form of communication entails special problems, each needs a different degree of protection.

The Mails

More than 80 years ago, Justice Oliver Wendell Holmes Jr. wrote in dissent, "The United States may give up the Post Office when it sees fit, but while it carries it on, the use of the mails is almost as much a part of free speech as is the right to use our tongues."[68] In 1965, the Court adopted that view by striking down an act that had directed the postmaster general to detain foreign mailings of "communist political propaganda" and to deliver these materials only upon the addressee's request.[69] The Court has also set aside federal laws authorizing postal authorities to exclude from the mails materials they consider obscene.

Although government censorship of mail is unconstitutional, household censorship is not. The Court has sustained laws giving householders the right to ask the postmaster to order mailers to delete their names from certain mailing lists and to refrain from sending any advertisements that they believe to be "erotically arousing or sexually provocative."[70] Moreover, Congress may forbid—and has forbidden—the use of mailboxes for any materials except those sent through the United States mails.

Handbills, Sound Trucks, and Billboards

Religious and political pamphlets, leaflets, and handbills have been historic weapons in the defense of liberty, and their distribution is constitutionally protected. So, too, is the use of their contemporary counterparts, sound trucks and billboards. A state cannot restrain the distribution of leaflets merely to keep its streets clean,[71] but it may impose reasonable restrictions on their distribution so long as they are neutrally enforced, without regard to the content.

Motion Pictures and Plays

Prior censorship of films to prevent the showing of obscenity is not necessarily unconstitutional; however, laws calling for submission of films to a government review board are constitutional only if there is a prompt judicial hearing. The burden is on the government to prove to the court that the particular film in question is obscene. Prior censorship of films by review boards was once common, but no longer. Live performances, such as plays and revues, are also entitled to constitutional protection.[72]

Broadcast and Cable Communications

Television remains an important means of distributing news and appealing for votes, though the Internet has gained popularity. Yet of all the mass media, broadcasting receives the least First Amendment protection. Congress has established a system of commercial broadcasting, supplemented by the Corporation for Public Broadcasting, which provides funds for public radio and television. The Federal Communications Commission (FCC) regulates the entire system by granting licenses and making regulations for their use.

The First Amendment would prevent censorship if the FCC tried to impose it. The First Amendment does not, however, prevent the FCC from imposing sanctions on stations that broadcast indecent or filthy words, even if they are not legally obscene.[73] The FCC did precisely that when it fined Infinity Broadcasting for indecent remarks by "shock jock" Howard Stern. Nor does the First Amendment prevent the FCC from refusing to renew a license if, in its opinion, a broadcaster does not serve the public interest.

The Supreme Court allows more governmental regulation of broadcasters than of newspaper and magazine publishers because space on the airwaves was limited. However, technological advances such as cable television, videotapes, and satellite broadcasting have opened up new means of communication and brought competition to the electronic media. Recognizing these changes, Congress passed the Telecommunications Act of 1996, allowing telephone companies, broadcasters, and cable TV stations to compete with one another. In adopting the act, Congress did not abandon all government regulation of the airways. On the contrary, the act calls for many new regulations—for example, requiring that all new television sets sold in the United States be equipped with V-chips that allow viewers to block programs containing violent or sexual material.

The Court has upheld a congressional requirement that cable television stations must carry the signals of local broadcast television stations.[74] The Court has also held that Congress may authorize cable operators to refuse access to leased channels for "patently offensive" programs. The Court, however, struck down congressional requirements that if a cable operator allows such offensive programming, it must be blocked and unscrambled through special devices. In *United States* v. *Playboy Entertainment Group* (2000), the Court underscored the greater protection for cable than for broadcast television. Whereas broadcast television may be required to provide programming for

At a press conference, Howard Stern defends his use of raunchy language and subject matter that led to the FCC fining the Infinity Broadcasting network. Stern subsequently decided to leave the network to work on a satellite radio station.

children and not air violence at certain times, the Court held that such rules do not apply to cable television because unwanted programming can be blocked by homeowners.[75]

Telecommunications and the Internet

Millions of Americans log on to the Internet to buy books, clothing, jewelry, airplane tickets, stocks, and bonds. Because the Internet has become a commercial marketplace and a major channel for communication, Congress is struggling with issues raised by cyberspace communication. Although Congress has imposed a moratorium on state taxation of commercial transactions on the Internet, debate continues over whether the national government should preempt state taxation. How do existing laws against copyright piracy apply to the World Wide Web? Should there be national regulation of junk e-mail, or can state laws take care of the problem? In what ways may Congress regulate indecent and obscene communications on the Web? Should Congress try to protect the privacy of those who use the Web? (For more information about privacy and developments on the Web, go to the Electronic Privacy Information Center at www.epic.org.)

As Congress and the state legislatures begin to deal with these and other new problems, legislators and judges will have to apply traditional constitutional principles to new technologies and means of communication. The Court distinguishes between a limited ban on indecent messages on radio and broadcast television and those on telephones, cable television, and the Internet. Radio and broadcast messages are readily available to children and can intrude into the privacy of the home without prior warning. By contrast, telephone messages may be blocked, and access by minors is more readily restricted.[76]

In its first ruling on First Amendment protection for the Internet, *Reno* v. *American Civil Liberties Union* (1997), the Court struck down provisions of the Communications Decency Act of 1996 that had made it a crime to send obscene or indecent messages to anyone under 18 years of age. In doing so, the Court emphasized the unique character of the Internet, holding that it is less intrusive than radio and broadcast television.[77] In response to *Reno* v. *ACLU,* Congress passed the Child Online Protection Act of 1998 (COPA), which made it a crime for a commercial Web site to knowingly make available to anyone under the age of 17 sexually explicit material considered "harmful to minors" based on "community standards." But in 2004 the Supreme Court held that the law was unenforceable because imposing criminal penalties was not the least drastic means of achieving Congress's goals; Internet filters and adult checks could be used to block minors' access to sites with sexually explicit material.[78] In addition, the Court struck down the Child Pornography Prevention Act of 1996, which made it a federal crime to create or distribute "virtual child pornography" generated by computer images of young adults rather than actual children. The law went beyond punishing child pornography, which is a crime because actual children are involved, the Court ruled, and had the potential to chill clear artistic and literary expression.[79]

FREEDOM OF ASSEMBLY

In 1998, Khallid Abdul Muhammad, a known racist and anti-Semite, organized what he called a "Million Youth March" in New York City. Mayor Rudolph Giuliani denied a permit for the march on grounds that it would be a "hate march." A federal appeals court upheld a lower court ruling that denial of the permit was unconstitutional; however, the three-judge panel placed restrictions on the event, limiting its duration to four hours and scaling it back to a six-block area. The march proceeded, surrounded by police in riot gear who broke up the demonstration after Muhammad delivered a vitriolic speech against police, Jews, and city officials.[80]

It took judicial authorities to defend the rights of these unpopular speakers and marchers, but it is not always the "bad guys" whose rights have to be protected by the courts. It also took judicial intervention in the 1960s to preserve for Martin Luther King Jr. and those who marched with him the right to demonstrate in the streets of southern cities on behalf of civil rights for African Americans.

Although the First Amendment affirms the right of the people to peacefully assemble, demonstrations are often highly regulated affairs, involving an elaborate process on the part of organizers to obtain permits for rallies and marches and often resulting in a large, intimidating police presence at these events. Some cities even go so far as to establish "free speech zones," where protesters are forced to remain in designated areas surrounded by police barricades and even barbed wire.

Such incidents present a classic free speech problem. It is almost always easier, and certainly politically more prudent, to maintain order by curbing public demonstrations by unpopular groups. However, if police did not have the right to order groups to disperse, public order would be at the mercy of those who resort to street demonstrations to create tensions and provoke street battles.

A recent controversy surrounds Attorney General John Ashcroft's decision in 2002 to allow law enforcement agents to go undercover to monitor activities and assemblies in any public place—including mosques, churches, and chat rooms on the Internet—in combating international terrorism. He thereby abandoned the Department of Justice's guidelines adopted in 1976 after Congress discovered that FBI agents were conducting surveillance and had infiltrated the civil rights movement and other groups engaged in lawful activities, as well as closely monitored King and other leaders. In response to criticisms that the new guidelines infringed on the freedoms of assembly and association, Ashcroft stressed that FBI agents would be limited to investigating terrorist activities.

Public Forums and Time, Place, and Manner Regulations

The Constitution protects the right to speak, but it does not give people the right to communicate their views to everyone, in every place, at every time they wish. No one has the right to block traffic or to hold parades or make speeches in public streets or on public sidewalks whenever he or she wishes. Governments may not censor what can be said, but they can make "reasonable" *time, place,* and *manner* regulations for protests or parades. The Supreme Court has divided public property into three categories: public forums, limited public forums, and nonpublic forums. The extent to which governments may limit access depends on the kind of forum involved.

Public forums are public places historically associated with the free exercise of expressive activities, such as streets, sidewalks, and parks. Courts look closely at time, place, and manner regulations that apply to these traditional public forums to ensure that they are being applied evenhandedly and that action is not taken because of what is being said rather than how and where or by whom it is being said.

CIVIL LIBERTIES: THE GREAT BALANCING ACT

The war against international terrorism has highlighted the politics of rights in balancing freedom and security. In this simulation, you judge the constitutionality of state and local policies affecting civil rights and civil liberties and find out the political implications as well as how liberals, conservatives, and centrists would decide.

Go to Make It Real "Civil Liberties: The Great Balancing Act."

civil disobedience
Deliberate refusal to obey a law or comply with the orders of public officials as a means of expressing opposition.

Other kinds of public property, such as rooms in a city hall or in a school after hours, may be designated as *limited public forums*, available for assembly and speech for limited purposes, for a limited amount of time, and even for a limited class of speakers (such as only students, only teachers, or only employees), provided the distinctions between the people allowed access and those excluded are not biased.

Nonpublic forums include public facilities such as libraries, courthouses, prisons, schools, swimming pools, and government offices that are open to the public but are not public forums. As long as people use such facilities within the normal bounds of conduct, they may not be constitutionally restrained from doing so. However, people may be excluded from such places as a government office or a school if they engage in activities for which the facilities were not created. They have no right to interfere with programs or try to take over a building—especially facilities such as a university president's office—in order to stage a political protest.

Does the right of peaceful assembly include the right to violate a law nonviolently but deliberately? We have no precise answer, but in general, **civil disobedience**, even if peaceful, is not a protected right. When Martin Luther King Jr. and his followers refused to comply with a state court's injunction forbidding them to parade in Birmingham without first securing a permit, the Supreme Court sustained their conviction, even though there was serious doubt about the constitutionality of the injunction and the ordinance on which it was based.[81]

More recently, the First Amendment right of antiabortion protesters to picket in front of abortion clinics has come into conflict with a woman's right to go to an abortion clinic. Protesters have often massed in front of clinics, shouting at employees and patrons and blocking entrances to the clinic. The Supreme Court has struck down provisions that prohibit protesters from expressing their views. But the Court has upheld injunctions that keep antiabortion protesters outside of a buffer zone around abortion clinics and also upheld injunctions that were issued because of prior unlawful conduct by the protesters. The proper constitutional test for such injunctions is "whether the challenged provisions . . . burden no more speech than necessary to serve a significant government interest," such as public safety or the right of women to go into such a clinic.[82]

The combination of First Amendment guarantees for rights and freedoms and their judicial enforcement is one of the fundamental features of our government and political system. As Supreme Court Justice Robert H. Jackson wrote:

> The very purpose of [the] Bill of Rights was to withdraw certain subjects from the vicissitudes of political controversy, to place them beyond the reach of majorities and officials and to establish them as legal principles to be applied by the courts. One's right to life, liberty, and property, to free speech, a free press, freedom of worship and assembly, and other fundamental rights may not be submitted to vote: they depend on the outcome of no elections.[83]

The connection between constitutional limitations and judicial enforcement is an example of the "auxiliary precautions" James Madison believed were necessary to prevent arbitrary governmental action. Citizens in other free nations rely on elections and political checks to protect their rights; in the United States, we also appeal to judges when we fear our freedoms are in danger.

S U M M A R Y

1. The Constitution protects our right to seek a writ of habeas corpus and forbids *ex post facto* laws and bills of attainder.

2. First Amendment freedoms—freedom of religion, of speech, of the press, and of assembly and association—are at the heart of a healthy constitutional democracy.

3. Since World War I, the Supreme Court has become the primary branch of government for giving meaning to these constitutional restraints. And since 1925, these constitutional limits have been applied not only to Congress but to all governmental agencies—national, state, and local.

4. The First Amendment forbids the establishment of religion and also guarantees the free exercise of religion. These two freedoms, however, are often in conflict with each other and represent conflicting notions of what is in the public interest.

5. The Supreme Court holds that there are only four categories of nonprotected speech—libel, obscenity, fighting words, and commercial speech. All other speech is protected under the First Amendment, and government may regulate that speech only when it has a compelling reason and does so in a content-neutral way.

6. Over the years, the Supreme Court has taken a pragmatic approach to First Amendment freedoms. It has refused to make them absolute rights above any kind of governmental regulation, direct or indirect, or to say that they must be preserved at whatever price. But the justices have recognized that a constitu-

tional democracy tampers with these freedoms at great peril. They have insisted on compelling justification before permitting these rights to be limited. How compelling the justification is, in a free society, will always remain an open question, but is especially difficult during times of war.

K E Y T E R M S

writ of habeas corpus	establishment clause	preferred position doctrine	fighting words
ex post facto law	vouchers	nonprotected speech	commercial speech
bill of attainder	free exercise clause	libel	prior restraint
due process clause	bad tendency test	sedition	civil disobedience
selective incorporation	clear and present danger test	obscenity	

F U R T H E R R E A D I N G

STUART BIEGEL, *Beyond Our Control? Confronting the Limits of Our Legal System in the Age of Cyberspace* (MIT Press, 2001).

STEVEN P. BROWN, *Trumping Religion: The Christian Right, The Free Speech Clause, and the Courts* (University of Alabama Press, 2002).

JAMES MACGREGOR BURNS AND STEWART BURNS, *A People's Charter: The Pursuit of Rights in America* (Knopf, 1991).

JESSE CHOPER, *Securing Religious Liberty: Principles for Judicial Interpretation of Religion Clauses* (University of Chicago Press, 1995).

LOUIS FISHER, *Religious Liberty in America: Political Safeguards* (University Press of Kansas, 2002).

MIKE GODWIN, *Cyber Rights: Defending Free Speech in the Digital Age* (MIT Press, 2003).

ROBERT JUSTIN GOLDSTEIN, *Flag Burning and Free Speech: The Case of Texas* v. *Johnson* (University Press of Kansas, 2002).

NAT HENTOFF, *Living the Bill of Rights: How to Be an Authentic American* (Harper-Collins, 1998).

LAWRENCE LESSIG, *Code and Other Laws of Cyberspace* (Basic Books, 2000).

LEONARD W. LEVY, *Emergence of a Free Press* (Oxford University Press, 1985).

ANTHONY LEWIS, *Make No Law: The Sullivan Case and the First Amendment* (Random House, 1991).

CATHARINE A. MACKINNON, *Only Words* (Harvard University Press, 1993).

ALEXANDER MEIKLEJOHN, *Political Freedom: The Constitutional Powers of the People* (Harper & Row, 1965).

JOHN STUART MILL, *Essay on Liberty, in The English Philosophers from Bacon to Mill*, ed. Arthur Burtt (Random House, 1939), pp. 949–1041.

JOHN T. NOONAN JR., *The Lustre of Our Country: The American Experience of Religious Freedom* (University of California Press, 1998).

DAVID M. O'BRIEN, *Animal Sacrifice and Religious Freedom:* Church of the Lukumi Babalu Aye *v.* City of Hialeah (University Press of Kansas, 2004).

DAVID M. O'BRIEN, *Constitutional Law and Politics: Civil Rights and Civil Liberties*, 6th ed. (Norton, 2005).

SHAWN FRANCIS PETERS, *Judging Jehovah's Witnesses: Religious Persecution and the Dawn of the Right Revolution* (University Press of Kansas, 2002).

J. W. PELTASON AND SUE DAVIS, *Understanding the Constitution*, 16th ed. (Harcourt, 2004).

NADINE STROSSEN, *Defending Pornography: Free Speech, Sex, and the Fight for Women's Rights* (Scribner, 1995).

RIGHTS TO LIFE, LIBERTY, AND PROPERTY

16

We have had to rethink the balance between liberty and security since the terrorist attacks of September 2001. Neither is likely to be taken for granted again. We are all affected by measures to strengthen homeland security—whether in schools; at concerts; traveling in airports, on trains, or on public streets; or in our homes. Yet we are still the freest people in the world. And we need to remember how fortunate we are to live in a society that values *due process*—established rules and regulations that restrain persons in government who exercise power. Such procedures are not available to citizens in China, much of Africa and South America, and elsewhere in the world.

Public officials in the United States have great power. Under certain conditions, they can seize our property, put us in jail, and—in extreme circumstances—even take our lives. The framers of our Constitution recognized it is necessary—but dangerous—to give power to those who govern. It is so dangerous that we do not depend on the ballot box alone to keep our officials from becoming tyrants. Because political power may threaten our liberty, we parcel it out in small chunks and surround it with restraints. No single official can decide to take our lives, liberty, or property. Officials must act according to the rule of law. If they act outside the scope of their authority or contrary to law, they can be restrained, dismissed, or punished. These rights to due process are the precious rights of all who live under the American flag—rich or poor, young or old, man or woman, and regardless of race, religion, or color.

In this chapter, we look at the rights of all persons to due process, but before we do, let us look at the precious freedoms and rights that flow from citizenship.

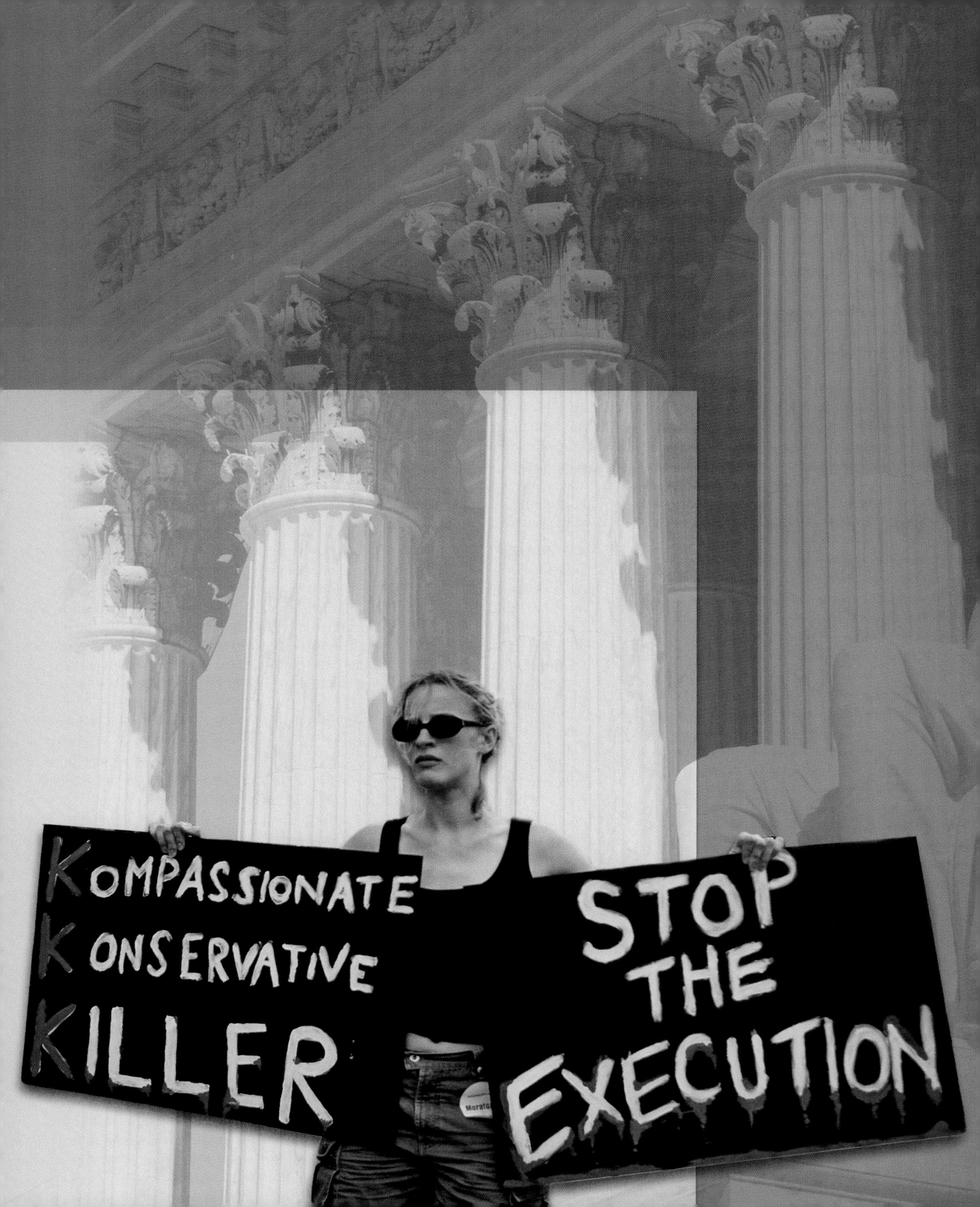

KOMPASSIONATE
KONSERVATIVE
KILLER
STOP
THE
EXECUTION

Proud naturalized citizens are sworn in at an emotional ceremony.

naturalization
A legal action conferring citizenship on an alien.

dual citizenship
Citizenship in more than one nation.

right of expatriation
The right to renounce one's citizenship.

CITIZENSHIP RIGHTS

Every nation has rules that determine nationality and define who is a member of, owes allegiance to, and is a subject of the nation. But in a constitutional democracy, citizenship is an *office,* and like other offices, it carries with it certain powers and responsibilities. How citizenship is acquired and retained is therefore a matter of considerable importance.

How Citizenship Is Acquired and Lost

The basic right of citizenship was not given constitutional protection until 1868, when the Fourteenth Amendment was adopted; prior to that, each state determined citizenship. The Fourteenth Amendment states, "All persons born or naturalized in the United States, and subject to the jurisdiction thereof, are citizens of the United States and of the State wherein they reside." This means that all persons born in the United States, except children born to foreign ambassadors and ministers, are citizens of this country regardless of the citizenship of their parents. (Congress has defined the United States for this purpose to include Puerto Rico, Guam, the Northern Marianas, and the Virgin Islands.) A child born to an American citizen living abroad or who has an American citizen as a grandparent is an American citizen if either the parent or grandparent has lived in the United States for at least five years, including two of which were after age 14. Although the Fourteenth Amendment does not make Native Americans citizens of the United States and of the states in which they live, Congress did so in 1924.

NATURALIZATION Citizenship may also be acquired by **naturalization**, a legal action conferring citizenship on an alien. Congress determines naturalization requirements. Today, with minor exceptions, nonenemy aliens over age 18 who have been lawfully admitted for permanent residence and who have resided in the United States for at least five years and in the state for at least six months are eligible for naturalization. Any state or federal court in the United States or the Immigration and Naturalization Service (INS) can grant citizenship. The INS, with the help of the Federal Bureau of Investigation (FBI), makes the necessary investigations.

Any person denied citizenship after a hearing before an immigration officer may appeal to a federal district judge. Citizenship is granted if the judge is satisfied that the applicant has met all the requirements after reviewing the FBI check that no disqualifying felony conviction has been found. The applicant renounces allegiance to his or her former country, swears to support and defend the Constitution and laws of the United States against all enemies, and promises to bear arms on behalf of the United States when required to do so by law. Those whose religious beliefs prevent them from bearing arms are allowed to take an oath swearing that if called to duty, they will serve in the armed forces as noncombatants or will perform work of national importance under civilian direction. The court or INS then grants a certificate of naturalization.

Naturalized citizenship may be revoked by court order if the government can prove that citizenship was secured by deception. But citizenship cannot be taken from people because of what they have done—for example, for committing certain crimes, voting in foreign elections, or serving in foreign armies. In addition, citizenship, however acquired, may be renounced voluntarily. Even so, the government must prove that the citizen "not only voluntarily committed the expatriating act prescribed in the statute, but also intended to relinquish his citizenship."[1]

DUAL CITIZENSHIP Because each nation has complete authority to decide for itself the definition of nationality, it is possible for a person to be considered a citizen by two or more nations. **Dual citizenship** is not unusual, especially for people from nations that do not recognize the right of individuals to renounce their citizenship, called the **right of expatriation**. (One of the issues of the War of 1812 was that England did not recognize sailors born in England as having abandoned their English citizenship on becoming naturalized American citizens.) Children born abroad to American citizens may also be citizens of the nation in which they were born. Children born in the United States of parents from a foreign nation may also be citizens of their parents' country.

Among the nations that allow dual citizenship are Canada, Mexico, France, and the United Kingdom. One expert estimates that based on the number of American children born to foreign-born parents, the number of Americans eligible to hold citizenship in another country grows by about 500,000 a year.[2] Moreover, with more than 7 million Mexican-born immigrants in the United States and their American-born children now becoming eligible to apply for Mexican citizenship, the number of dual citizens in the United States is on the rise. Dual citizenship carries negative as well as positive consequences; for example, a person with dual citizenship may be subject to national service obligations and taxes in both countries.

Rights of American Citizens

An American becomes a citizen of one of our states merely by residing in that state. *Residence* as understood in the Fourteenth Amendment means the place one calls home. The legal status of residence should not be confused with the fact of physical presence. A person may be living in Washington, D.C., but be a citizen of California—that is, consider California home and vote in that state.

Most of our most important rights flow from *state* citizenship. In the *Slaughter-House Cases* (1873), the Supreme Court carefully distinguished between the privileges of U.S. citizens and those of state citizens.[3] It held that the only privileges of national citizenship are those that "owe their existence to the Federal Government, its National Character, its Constitution, or its laws." These privileges have never been completely specified, but they include the right to use the navigable waters of the United States and to protection on the high seas, to assemble peacefully and petition for redress of grievances, to vote if qualified to do so under state laws and have one's vote counted properly, and to travel throughout the United States.

In times of war, the rights and liberties of citizenship are tested and have been curbed. Although the Supreme Court overruled President Abraham Lincoln's use of military courts to try civilians during the Civil War,[4] it upheld the World War II internment of Japanese Americans in "relocation camps" and never questioned their loyalty or the government's argument that they posed a threat to national security. The Supreme Court drew a distinction between the rights of citizenship during peacetime and wartime, observing that, "hardships are part of war, and war is an aggregation of hardships. All citizens alike, both in and out of uniform, feel the impact of war in greater or lesser measure. Citizenship has it responsibilities as well as its privileges, and in time of war the burden is always heavier."[5] The Supreme Court also approved the use of military tribunals to try captured foreign saboteurs[6] but held that citizens may not be subject to courts-martial or denied the guarantees of the Bill of Rights.[7] For that reason, John Walker Lindh, the young American captured fighting with the Taliban in Afghanistan, was accorded the assistance of counsel and tried in court. However, in his war against international terrorism, President George W. Bush issued orders declaring U.S. citizens "enemy combatants," for plotting with the Al-Qaeda network, and authorized their and other captured foreign nationals' detention in military compounds, without counsel or access to a court of law. His orders were controversial and the Supreme Court ruled in 2004 that U.S. citizens and foreign nationals may not be detained indefinitely without the opportunity to consult an attorney and to contest the basis for their detention before an independent tribunal.[8]

THE RIGHT TO LIVE AND TRAVEL IN THE UNITED STATES   This right, which is not subject to any congressional limitation, is perhaps the most precious aspect of American citizenship. Aliens have no such right. They may be stopped on the high seas or at the borders and turned away if they fail to meet the terms and conditions stipulated by Congress for admission. Today millions of people around the world yearn to come and live in the United States, but only American citizens have a constitutionally guaranteed right to do so.

REQUIREMENTS FOR NATURALIZATION

An applicant for naturalization must:

1. Be over age 18.
2. Be lawfully admitted to the United States for permanent residence and have resided in the United States for at least five years and in the state for at least six months.
3. File a petition of naturalization with a clerk of a court of record (federal or state) verified by two witnesses.
4. Be able to read, write, and speak English.
5. Possess a good moral character.
6. Understand and demonstrate an attachment to the history, principles, and form of government of the United States.
7. Demonstrate that he or she is well disposed toward the good order and happiness of the country.
8. Demonstrate that he or she does not now believe in, nor within the last ten years has ever believed in, advocated, or belonged to an organization that supports opposition to organized government, overthrow of government by violence, or the doctrines of world communism or any other form of totalitarianism.

For more information about immigration and naturalization, go to the Web site of the Federation for American Immigration Reform, at www.fairus.org.

THE RIGHT TO TRAVEL ABROAD   The right to international travel can be regulated within the bounds of due process. Under current law, it is unlawful for citizens to leave or enter the United States without a valid passport (except as otherwise provided by the president, as has been done for travel to Mexico, Canada, and parts of the Caribbean). Travel to Cuba is forbidden unless special permission is granted, as has increasingly been done for journalists, artists, scholars, and politicians; however, the Bush administration tightened restrictions on Cuban Americans who want to visit their families in Cuba.

Rights of Aliens

During periods of suspicion and hostility toward aliens, the protections of citizenship are even more precious. Congress enacted the Enemy Alien Act of 1798, which remains in effect, authorizing the president during wartime to detain and expel citizens of a country with which we are at war. Citizens may not be expelled from the country, but aliens may be expelled for even minor infractions.[9] The Supreme Court also upheld 1996 amendments to the Immigration and Naturalization Act that require mandatory detention during deportation hearings of aliens accused of certain crimes,[10] though they may not be held longer than six months.[11]

Still, the Constitution protects many rights of *all persons*, not just of American citizens. Only citizens may run for elective office and their right to vote may not be denied, but all other rights are not so literally restricted. Neither Congress nor the states can deny to aliens the right of freedom of religion or the right of freedom of speech. Nor can any government deprive any person of the due process of the law or equal protection under the laws.[12]

However, Congress and the states may deny or limit welfare and many other kinds of benefits to aliens. Congress has denied most federally assisted benefits to illegal immigrants and has permitted states to deny them many other benefits, making an exception only for emergency medical care, disaster relief, and some nutrition programs. The Court has also upheld laws barring the employment of aliens as police officers, schoolteachers, and probation officers.[13] While states have considerable discretion over what benefits they give to aliens, the Supreme Court has held that states cannot constitutionally exclude children of undocumented aliens from the public schools or charge their parents tuition.[14]

Admission to the United States

President Franklin Roosevelt, reminding us of our heritage as a haven for people fleeing religious and political persecution, opened his address to a convention of the Daughters of the American Revolution with the salutation, "Fellow immigrants and revolutionaries." Some Americans, however, are concerned that admitting so many people from abroad will dilute American traditions and values.[15] Throughout our history, debates have flared among those wishing to open our borders and those wishing to close them.

Aliens do not have a constitutional right to enter the United States. Congress has wide discretion in setting the numbers, terms, and conditions under which aliens can enter and stay in the United States. The Immigration Act of 1965, as amended in 1990 and 1996, sets an annual ceiling of 675,000 nonrefugee aliens allowed to come here as permanent residents, but when refugees and other exempt categories are added, about 800,000 people enter the United States each year. The law also sets an annual limit on immigrants from any single country. Preference is given for family reunification and to people who have special skills or who are needed to fill jobs for which U.S. workers are not available. Another provision allows for the admission of "millionaire immigrants" who are willing and able to invest a substantial sum to create or support a business in the United States that will provide jobs for Americans. There have been few takers for admission under this provision. There is also a "diversity" category to provide visas for 55,000 immigrants from 34 countries whether or not they have relatives living in the

Immigrants arriving at Ellis Island in 1900 came with high hopes but few material possessions.

United States. These visas are drawn annually by lottery from a pool of qualified applicants.

In addition to regularly admitted aliens, political refugees are admitted. In recent years, more than 100,000 were admitted annually, but the Bush administration decreased the number to 70,000.[16] *Political refugees* are people who have well-founded fears of persecution in their own countries based on their race, religion, nationality, social class, or political opinion. People admitted as political refugees can apply to become permanent residents after one year. The attorney general, acting through the Immigration and Naturalization Service, may also grant *asylum* to applicants who have well-founded fears of persecution in the country to which they would be returned, based on their race, religion, nationality, membership in a particular social group, or political opinion. It is not enough, however, that applicants face the same terrible conditions that all other citizens of their country face or that they wish to escape bad economic conditions. They must show specific danger of persecution.

The Immigration and Naturalization Service may turn back at the border persons seeking asylum if it considers their requests insubstantial; it may even hold them in detention camps. The president may order the Coast Guard—as Presidents George H. W. Bush and Bill Clinton did with respect to Haitian and Cuban refugees—to stop people on the high seas before they enter the territorial waters of the United States and return them to the country from which they have fled without determining whether they qualify as refugees.[17] Nonetheless, many people are still willing to risk great danger to get here and suffer detention once they arrive, just for the chance of being granted asylum. According to the 2000 census, an estimated 115,000 immigrants from the Middle East alone are here illegally.[18]

Once in the United States, aliens are subject to the full range of obligations, including the payment of taxes. Aliens are counted in the census for the purpose of apportioning seats in the U.S. House of Representatives. Legally admitted aliens may be detained and deported for a variety of reasons—for example, conviction of crimes involving immoral acts, turpitude, incitement of terrorist activity, illegal voting in elections, and conviction of domestic violence. In the months following the September 2001 terrorist attacks, over 1,100 people were detained for questioning and their identities not disclosed, and approximately 5,000 more people of Middle Eastern descent were questioned voluntarily.[19]

property rights
The rights of an individual to own, use, rent, invest in, buy, and sell property.

contract clause
Clause of the Constitution (Article I, Section 10) originally intended to prohibit state governments from modifying contracts made between individuals; for a while interpreted as prohibiting state governments from taking actions that adversely affect property rights; no longer interpreted so broadly and no longer constrains state governments from exercising their police powers.

police powers
Inherent powers of state governments to pass laws to protect the public health, safety, and welfare; the national government has no directly granted police powers but accomplishes the same goals through other delegated powers.

eminent domain
Power of a government to take private property for public use; the U.S. Constitution gives national and state governments this power and requires them to provide just compensation for property so taken.

regulatory taking
Government regulation of property so extensive that government is deemed to have taken the property by the power of eminent domain, for which it must compensate the property owners.

PROPERTY RIGHTS

Constitutional Protection of Property

Property does not have rights. People do. People have the right to own, use, rent, invest in, buy, and sell property. Historically, the close connection between liberty and ownership of property, between property and power, has been emphasized in American political thinking and American political institutions. A major purpose of the framers of the Constitution was to establish a government strong enough to protect people's rights to use and enjoy their property. At the same time, the framers wanted to limit government so it could not endanger that right. As a result, the framers included in the Constitution a variety of clauses protecting **property rights**.

Of special concern to the framers were the efforts of some state legislatures to protect debtors at the expense of their creditors by issuing paper currency and setting aside private contracts. To prevent these practices, the legal tender and contract clauses in the Constitution forbid states from making anything except gold or silver legal tender for the payment of debts and from passing any "Law impairing the Obligation of Contracts."

The **contract clause** (Article I, Section 10) was designed to prevent states from extending the period during which debtors could meet their payments or otherwise get out of contractual obligations. The framers had in mind an ordinary contract between private persons. However, beginning with Chief Justice John Marshall (1801–1835), the Supreme Court expanded the coverage of the clause to prevent states from taking away privileges previously conferred on corporations. In effect, the contract clause was used to protect property and to maintain the status quo at the expense of a state's power.

In the late nineteenth century, however, the Supreme Court gradually began to restrict the coverage of the contract clause and to subject contracts to what in constitutional law are known as **police powers**—the powers of states to protect the public health, safety, and welfare of their residents. By 1934, the Supreme Court actually held that even contracts between individuals—the very ones the contract clause was intended to protect—could be modified by state law to avert social and economic catastrophe.[20] Although the contract clause is still invoked occasionally to challenge state regulation of property, it is no longer a significant limitation on governmental power.

What Happens When the Government Takes Our Property?

Both the national and state governments have the power of **eminent domain**—the power to take private property for public use—but the owner must be fairly compensated. This limitation, contained in the Fifth Amendment, was the first provision of the Bill of Rights to be enforced as a limitation on state governments as well as on the national government.[21]

What constitutes a "taking" for purposes of eminent domain? Ordinarily, but not always, the taking must be direct, and a person must lose title and control over the property. Sometimes, especially in recent years, the courts have found that a governmental taking has gone "too far," and the government must pay compensation to its owners, even when title is left in the name of the owners.[22] These are called **regulatory takings**. Thus if a government creates landing and takeoff paths for airplanes over property adjacent to an airport, making the land completely unsuitable for its original use (say, raising chickens), compensation is warranted.[23] The government may, however, impose land use and environmental regulations, temporarily prohibiting the development of a property, without compensating the owners.[24]

"Just compensation" is not always easy to define. When there is a dispute over compensation, the courts make the final resolution based on the rule that "the owner is entitled to receive what a willing buyer would pay in cash to a willing seller at the time of the taking."[25] An owner is not entitled to compensation for the personal value of an old, broken-down house that is loved dearly—just the value of the old, broken-down house.

DUE PROCESS RIGHTS

Perhaps the most difficult parts of the Constitution to understand are the clauses in the Fifth and Fourteenth Amendments forbidding the national and state governments to deny any person life, liberty, or property without "due process of law." Cases involving these guarantees have resulted in hundreds of Supreme Court decisions. Even so, it is impossible to explain *due process* precisely. In fact, the Supreme Court has refused to give due process a precise definition and has emphasized that "due process, unlike some legal rules, is not a technical conception with a fixed content unrelated to time, place and circumstances."[26] We define **due process** as rules and regulations that restrain those in government who exercise power. There are, however, basically two kinds of due process: procedural and substantive.

Procedural Due Process

Traditionally, **procedural due process** refers not to the law itself but to the *way in which a law is applied.* To paraphrase Daniel Webster's famous definition, the due process of law requires a procedure that hears before it condemns, proceeds upon inquiry, and renders judgment only after a trial or some kind of hearing. Originally, procedural due process was limited to criminal prosecutions, but it now applies to most kinds of governmental proceedings. It is required, for instance, in juvenile hearings, disbarment proceedings, proceedings to determine eligibility for welfare payments, revocation of drivers' licenses, and disciplinary proceedings in state universities and public schools.

A law may also violate the procedural due process requirement if it is too vague or if it creates an improper presumption of guilt. A vague statute fails to provide adequate warning and does not contain sufficient guidelines for law enforcement officials, juries, and courts.

The liberty that is protected by due process includes "the right of the individual to contract, to engage in any of the common occupations of life, to acquire useful knowledge, to marry, to establish a home and bring up children, to worship God according to the dictates of his own conscience, and generally to enjoy those common law privileges long recognized as essential to the orderly pursuit of happiness by free men."[27] The property protected by due process includes a variety of rights that may be conferred by state law, such as certain kinds of licenses, protection from being fired from some jobs except for just cause (for example, incompetence) and according to certain procedures, and protection from deprivation of certain pension rights.

Substantive Due Process

Procedural due process places limits on *how* governmental power may be exercised; **substantive due process** places limits on *what* a government may do. Procedural due process mainly limits the executive and judicial branches because they apply the law and review its application; substantive due process mainly limits the legislative branch because it enacts laws. Substantive due process means that an "unreasonable" law, even if properly passed and properly applied, is unconstitutional. It means that there are certain things governments *should not be allowed to do.*

Before 1937, substantive due process was used primarily to protect the right of employers to make contracts with employees freely, without government interference.[28] During this period, the Supreme Court was dominated by conservative jurists who considered almost all social welfare legislation unreasonable. They used the due process clause to strike down laws setting maximum hours of labor, establishing minimum wages, regulating prices, and forbidding employers to fire workers because they joined a union.

Since 1937, the Supreme Court has largely refused to apply the doctrine of substantive due process in reviewing laws regulating business enterprises and economic

★ ★ THINKING IT THROUGH

The inability to keep illegal aliens out of the country is not a question of constitutional power, for Congress has complete power over the admission of aliens. Rather, the problems are political and practical. Although Congress has authorized an increase in the number of border patrol guards and funded additional fencing of the California–Mexico border, there are thousands of miles of borders. Moreover, it is difficult to track down undocumented aliens once inside the United States and then expel them in a fashion consistent with the practices and policies of a free society.

Congress faces conflicting pressures: from Hispanic groups concerned that making it illegal to hire undocumented workers will make employers hesitate to hire any Hispanics, from employers who do not want to keep costly records and investigate the legal status of everybody they hire, from employers of farm workers who want to be sure they will have enough laborers to pick seasonal crops, from American workers who do not want undocumented workers being used to keep wages low, and from city and local governmental officials who have to find the funds to provide social services for undocumented aliens.

The United States government tends to consider immigration policy a purely internal matter. In California and some other states, there are strong anti-immigration pressures. Immigration policy clearly affects our relations with other nations, especially with Mexico, as the lengthy negotiations over the North American Free Trade Agreement (NAFTA) demonstrated. Although we view immigration policy as a matter of national sovereignty, Mexicans see it as a matter that directly affects them and have advocated "open borders."

due process
Established rules and regulations that restrain people in government who exercise power.

procedural due process
Constitutional requirement that governments proceed by proper methods; places limits on how governmental power may be exercised.

substantive due process
Constitutional requirement that governments act reasonably and that the substance of the laws themselves be fair and reasonable; places limits on what a government may do.

The USA PATRIOT Act, passed in the wake of the September 11, 2001 attacks, removes those designated by the president as "enemy combatants" from many of the procedural due process protections that are the cornerstone of the U.S. legal system. Both U.S. citizens and noncitizens alike can be designated as "enemy combatants" at the president's discretion.

interests. The Court now believes that deciding what constitutes reasonable regulation of business and commercial life is a legislative, not a judicial, responsibility. As long as the justices find a conceivable connection between a law regulating business and the promotion of the public welfare, the Supreme Court will not interfere with laws passed by Congress or state legislatures.

This does not mean, however, that the Court has abandoned substantive due process. On the contrary, substantive due process has taken on new life as a protector of civil liberties, especially the right of privacy. Substantive due process has deep roots in concepts of natural law and a long history in the American constitutional tradition. For most Americans most of the time, it is not enough merely to say that a law reflects the wishes of the popular or legislative majority. We also want our laws to be just, and we continue to rely heavily on judges to decide what is just.

PRIVACY RIGHTS

The most important extension of substantive due process in recent decades has been its expansion to protect the right of privacy, especially marital privacy. Although there is no mention of the right of privacy in the Constitution, in *Griswold* v. *Connecticut* (1965), the Supreme Court pulled together elements of the First, Third, Fourth, Fifth, Ninth, and Fourteenth Amendments to recognize that personal privacy is one of the rights protected by the Constitution.[29]

There are three aspects of this right: (1) the right to be free from governmental surveillance and intrusion, especially with respect to intimate decisions on sexuality; (2) the right not to have private affairs made public by the government; and (3) the right to be free in thought and belief from governmental regulations.[30]

PEOPLE & POLITICS *Making a Difference* ★ ★ ★

ESTELLE GRISWOLD

Estelle Trébert Griswold was born in 1900 and, after working as a singer in France and, later, during World War II as a medical technologist in Washington, D.C., she became the executive director of the Planned Parenthood League of Connecticut (PPLC) in 1953. In that position, Griswold led a fight for the legalization of birth control in Connecticut that resulted in a landmark Supreme Court ruling on the right of privacy and the Constitution's protection for intimate decisions on human sexuality.

Connecticut had prohibited the use of contraceptives in an 1879 law and had also made it a crime to "assist, abet, or counsel" someone on birth control. By the 1950s, contraceptives were nonetheless widely sold in drug stores and the law was generally ignored. But Griswold and some doctors and advocates of women's rights contended that the law had a chilling effect. Griswold and the

PPLC lobbied the state legislature to repeal the law, but the legislation was repeatedly blocked by the Catholic-dominated Connecticut state senate. Attempts to have courts strike down the law also failed.

Griswold and Dr. Lee Buxton decided to open a birth control clinic and create a test case challenging Connecticut's law. After opening the clinic, they held a press conference and a few days later police arrived and, after receiving PPLC literature, they arrested Griswold and Buxton, who were tried, convicted, and fined $100 each for violating the law.

On appeal in *Griswold* v. *Connecticut* (1965),[*] the Supreme Court struck down Connecticut's law for violating a constitutionally-protected right of privacy. The decision remains controversial because a right of privacy is not specifically enumerated in the Bill of Rights. But the ruling laid the basis for other landmark

decisions on a woman's right to choose, in *Roe* v. *Wade* (1973),[†] and on constitutional protection for private consensual sexual activities in *Lawrence* v. *Texas* (2003),[‡] which struck down Texas's law making homosexual sodomy a crime.

[*] *Griswold* v. *Connecticut*, 381 U.S. 479 (1965).
[†] *Roe* v. *Wade*, 410 U.S. 113 (1973).
[‡] *Lawrence* v. *Texas*, 539 U.S. 558 (2003).

Abortion Rights

The most controversial aspect of constitutional protection of privacy relates to the extent of state power to regulate abortions. In *Roe* v. *Wade* (1973), the Supreme Court ruled that (1) during the first trimester of a woman's pregnancy, it is an unreasonable and therefore unconstitutional interference with her liberty and privacy rights for a state to set any limits on her choice to have an abortion or on her doctor's medical judgments about how to carry it out; (2) during the second trimester, the state's interest in protecting the health of women becomes compelling, and a state may make a reasonable regulation about how, where, and when abortions may be performed; and (3) during the third trimester, when the fetus becomes capable of surviving outside the womb, the state's interest in protecting the unborn child is so important that the state can prohibit abortions altogether, except when necessary to preserve the life or health of the mother.[31]

The *Roe* decision led to decades of heated public debate and attempts by Presidents Ronald Reagan and the first George Bush to select Supreme Court justices who might be expected to reverse it. Nonetheless, *Roe* v. *Wade* was reaffirmed in *Planned Parenthood* v. *Casey* (1992). A bitterly divided Rehnquist Court, by a five-person majority (O'Connor, Kennedy, Souter, Blackmun, and Stevens), upheld the view that the due process clause of the Constitution protects a woman's liberty to choose an abortion prior to viability. The Court, however, held that the right to have an abortion prior to viability may be subject to state regulation that does not "unduly burden" it. In other words, states may make "reasonable regulations" on how a woman exercises her right to an abortion so long as they do not prohibit any woman from making the ultimate decision on whether to terminate a pregnancy before viability.[32]

The battle over abortion has been fought in the courts and on the streets, and has been a key issue in recent presidential elections.

Applying the undue burden test, the Court has held, on the one hand, that states can prohibit the use of state funds and facilities for performing abortions; states may make a minor's right to an abortion conditional on her first notifying at least one parent or a judge; and states may require women to sign an informed consent form and to wait 24 hours before having an abortion. On the other hand, a state may not condition a woman's right to an abortion on her first notifying her husband. The Court also struck down Nebraska's ban on "partial birth" abortions in *Stenberg* v. *Carhart* (2000) because it completely forbade one kind of medical procedure and provided no exception for when a woman's life is at stake and thus imposed an "undue burden" on women.[33] Nonetheless, in 2003 Congress passed and President George W. Bush signed into federal law a similar ban on "partial birth" abortions that was immediately challenged in the courts, and which will be appealed to the Supreme Court.

Sexual Orientation Rights

Although there is general agreement on how much constitutional protection is provided for marital privacy, in *Bowers* v. *Hardwick* (1986), the Supreme Court refused to extend such protection to private relations between homosexuals[34]; a bare majority of the Court also held that homosexuals may be excluded from the Boy Scouts of America.[35] By a 5-to-4 vote in *Bowers,* the Court refused to declare unconstitutional a Georgia law that made consensual sodomy a crime. But a number of state supreme courts, including that in Georgia, later found greater privacy protection in their state constitutions than the U.S. Supreme Court found in the U.S. Constitution. Finally, in *Lawrence* v. *Texas* (2003),[36] the Court struck down Texas's law making homosexual sodomy a crime. Writing for the Court and noting the trend in state court decisions that did not follow *Bowers,* Justice Kennedy held the law to violate personal autonomy and the right of privacy. Dissenting Justice Scalia, along with Chief Justice Rehnquist and Justice Thomas, warned that the decision might lead to overturning laws barring same-sex marriages, as some state courts and Canadian courts had already done.

In addition, the U.S. Supreme Court, in *Romer* v. *Evans* (1996),[37] struck down an initiative amending the Colorado constitution that prohibited state and local governments from protecting homosexuals from discrimination. Although the Court did not rule on the basis of substantive due process, it held this provision to violate the equal protection clause because it lacked a rational basis and simply represented a prejudice toward a particular group of people.

Because of the strong emotions on both sides of this issue, the right of privacy as an element of substantive due process is one of the developing edges of constitutional law, one about which people both on and off the Court have strong disagreements. How the Supreme Court handles privacy issues has become front-page news.

RIGHTS OF PERSONS ACCUSED OF CRIMES

Despite what you sometimes see in television police dramas, law enforcement officers have no general right to break down doors and invade homes. They are not supposed to search people except under certain conditions, and they have no right to arrest them except under certain circumstances. They also may not compel confessions, and they must respect other procedural guarantees aimed at ensuring fairness and the rights of the accused. Persons accused of crimes are guaranteed these and other rights under the Fourth, Fifth, Sixth, Eighth, and Fourteenth Amendments.

Freedom from Unreasonable Searches and Seizures

According to the Fourth Amendment, "The right of the people to be secure in their persons, houses, papers, and effects, against unreasonable searches and seizures, shall not be violated, and no Warrants shall issue, but upon probable cause, supported by Oath or affirmation, and particularly describing the place to be searched, and the persons or things to be seized."

Protection from unreasonable searches and seizures requires police, if they have time, to obtain a valid **search warrant**, issued by a magistrate after the police indicate under oath that they have *probable cause* to justify its issuance. Magistrates must perform this function in a neutral and detached manner and not serve merely as rubber stamps for the police. The warrant must specify the place to be searched and the things to be seized. *General search warrants*—warrants that authorize police to search a particular place or person without limitation—are unconstitutional. A search warrant is usually needed to search a person in any place he or she has an "expectation of privacy that society is prepared to recognize as reasonable," for example, in a hotel room, a rented home, or a friend's apartment.[38] In short, the Fourth Amendment protects people, not places, from unreasonable governmental intrusions.[39]

Police may make reasonable *warrantless searches* in *public places* if the officers have probable cause, or at least a reasonable suspicion, that the persons in question have committed or are about to commit crimes. No later than two days after making such an arrest, the police must take the arrested person to a magistrate so that the magistrate—not just the police—can decide whether probable cause existed to justify the warrantless arrest.[40] Probable cause, however, does not, except in extreme emergencies, justify a warrantless arrest of people in their own homes.

Under the common law, police officers apprehending a fleeing suspected felon can use weapons that might result in the felon's serious injury or even death. But the Fourth Amendment places substantial limits on the use of what is called *deadly force*. It is unconstitutional to shoot at an apparently unarmed, fleeing suspected felon unless the officer has probable cause to believe that the suspect poses a significant threat of death or serious injury to the officer or others. Also, when feasible, the officer must first warn the suspect, "Halt or I'll shoot."

Not every time the police stop a person to ask questions or to seek that person's consent to a search is there a seizure or detention requiring probable cause or a warrant. If the police just ask questions or even seek consent to search an individual's person or possessions in a noncoercive atmosphere, there is no detention. "So long as a reasonable person would feel free 'to disregard the police and go about his business,' the encounter is consensual and no reasonable suspicion is required." But if the person refuses to answer questions or consent to a search, and the police, by either physical force or a show of authority, restrain the movement of the person, even though there is no arrest, the Fourth Amendment comes into play.[41] For example, if police approach people in airports and request identification, this act by itself does not constitute a detention. The same is true if police ask bus passengers for consent to search their luggage for drugs. But if the police do more, especially after consent is refused, then their actions require them to have some objective justification for the search beyond mere suspicion.[42]

The Supreme Court also upheld, in *Terry* v. *Ohio* (1968), a *stop and frisk* exception to searches of individuals when officers have reason to believe they are armed and dangerous or have committed or are about to commit a criminal offense. The *Terry* search is limited to a quick pat-down to check for weapons that might be used to assault the arresting officer, to check for contraband, to determine identity, or to maintain the status quo while obtaining more information.[43] If individuals who are stopped for questioning refuse to identify themselves, they may be arrested, though police must have a reasonable suspicion they are involved in criminal activities.[44] If an officer stops and frisks a suspect to look for weapons and finds criminal evidence that might justify an arrest, the officer can make a full search.[45] Police and border guards may also conduct *border* searches—searches of persons and the goods they bring with them at border crossings.[46] The border search exception also permits officials to open mail entering the country if they have "reasonable cause" to suspect it contains merchandise imported in violation of the law.[47]

There are several other exceptions to the general rule against warrantless searches and seizures of what is found by police and customs officials. The most important are the following:

1. *The Plain-View Exception.* The plain-view exception permits officers to seize evidence without a warrant if they are lawfully in a position from which the

Police may detain and search cars and their passengers if they have reasonable suspicion to believe the passengers may be involved in criminal activity.

search warrant
A writ issued by a magistrate that authorizes the police to search a particular place or person, specifying the place to be searched and the objects to be seized.

GLOBAL *Perceptions*

QUESTION: Do you think crime is a very big problem?

There is anxiety about crime in almost every country in the world. In virtually every region, except North America, majorities in nearly every country cite crime as a "very big problem." In the United States, only 48 percent of the public believe that crime is a very big problem, and only 26 percent in Canada. Some of the countries where public perceptions of crime as a big problem are the highest are Bangladesh and South Africa (96%), Guatemala and Honduras (93%), Argentina (88%), and India (86%). The lowest perceptions are in Jordan (22%), South Korea (35%), and Germany (45%). In most cases, though, crime is more of a *perceived* problem than an actual problem.

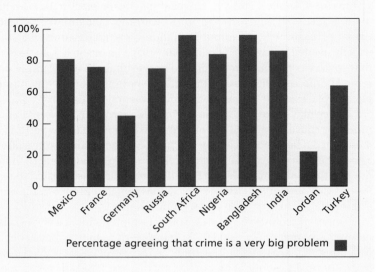

Percentage agreeing that crime is a very big problem ■

Source: The Pew Global Attitudes Project, *How Global Publics View Their Lives, Their Countries, the World, and America,* 2002, T-18.

evidence can be viewed, it is immediately apparent to them that the items they observe are evidence of a crime or are contraband, and they have probable cause to believe—a reasonable suspicion will not do—that the evidence uncovered is contraband or evidence of a crime.[48]

2. *Exigent Circumstances.* Searches are permissible when officers do not have time to secure a warrant before evidence is destroyed, when a criminal escapes capture, or when there is need "to protect or preserve life or avoid serious injury." An example is that firefighters and police may enter a burning building without a warrant and may remain there for a reasonable time to investigate the cause of the blaze after the fire has been extinguished. However, after the fire has been put out, the emergency is not to be used as an excuse to make an exhaustive, warrantless search for evidence.

3. *The Automobile Exception.* If officers have probable cause to believe that an automobile is being used to commit a crime, even a traffic offense, or that it contains persons who have committed crimes, or that it contains evidence of crimes, they may stop the automobile, detain the persons found therein, and search them and any containers or packages found inside the car.[49] Once an automobile has been lawfully detained, the police officers may order the driver and passengers to get out of the car without violating the Fourth Amendment[50]; if police arrest the driver, they may search the contents of the car.[51]

4. *Foreign Agents.* Although never directly sustained by the Supreme Court, Congress has endorsed the presidential claim that a president can authorize warrantless wiretaps and physical searches of agents of foreign countries. Congress created the Foreign Intelligence Surveillance Court to approve such requests; this court, consisting of federal district judges, meets in secret. The USA PATRIOT Act of 2001 expanded the size of this court and lowered the basis for its approval of warrants in cases involving terrorism and permits searches for intelligence and just evidence of terrorist activities.

In addition, various administrative searches by nonpolice government agents, such as teachers and health officials, do not require search warrants. Rules governing the conduct of such administrative searches are more lenient than those for searches by police investigating crimes. Administrative searches conducted without grounds for suspicion of particular individuals have been upheld in certain limited circumstances.[52]

One recent troublesome area relates to **racial profiling**—the police practice targeting members of certain racial groups for street questioning or traffic stops on the assumption that members of these groups are likely to be engaged in illegal activities. African Americans and civil rights organizations have complained for years about the practice because police do not need probable cause to stop someone and because it encourages racial discrimination.[53] In response, President George W. Bush issued guidelines governing 70 federal law enforcement agencies that bar the use of race and ethnicity in routine investigations; however, they may still be used to "identify terrorist threats and stop potential catastrophic attacks."[54]

Another controversial practice is the recent expansion of compulsory, random drug testing. The Supreme Court has upheld the constitutionality of blood and urine tests of rail employees involved in train accidents, of federal employees, and of high school students engaged in interscholastic athletic competitions. But it struck down a Georgia law requiring candidates for designated state offices to certify that they had taken and passed a drug test because Georgia failed to show why this invasion of personal privacy was necessary.[55] In 2002, however, the Court on a 5-to-4 vote held that schools may require students who participate in extracurricular activities of any kind to submit to random drug tests.[56]

Use of metal detectors and locker searches at schools does not require search warrants and other protections applied to police searches.

THE EXCLUSIONARY RULE   In *Mapp* v. *Ohio* (1961), the Supreme Court adopted a rule excluding from a criminal trial evidence that the police obtained unconstitutionally or illegally.[57] This **exclusionary rule** was adopted to prevent police misconduct. Critics of the exclusionary rule question why criminals should go free just because of police misconduct or ineptness,[58] but the Supreme Court has refused to abandon the rule. It has made some exceptions to it, however, such as cases in which police relied in "good faith" on a search warrant that subsequently turned out to be defective or granted improperly.[59]

THE RIGHT TO REMAIN SILENT   During the seventeenth century, certain special courts in England forced confessions from religious dissenters. The British privilege against self-incrimination developed in response to these practices. Because they were familiar with this history, the framers of our Bill of Rights included in the Fifth Amendment the provision that persons shall not be compelled to testify against themselves in criminal prosecutions. This protection against self-incrimination is designed to strengthen the fundamental principle that no person has an obligation to prove innocence. Rather, the burden is on the government to prove guilt.

The privilege against self-incrimination applies literally only in criminal prosecutions. But it has always been interpreted to protect any person subject to questioning by any agency of government, such as a congressional committee. It is not enough, however, to contend that answers might be embarrassing or might lead to loss of a job or even to civil suits; persons must have a reasonable fear that their answers might support a criminal prosecution against them.

Sometimes authorities would rather have information from witnesses than prosecute them. Congress has established procedures so that prosecutors and congressional committees may secure a grant of **immunity** for such a witness. When immunity has been granted, a witness no longer has a constitutional right to refuse to testify, and the government cannot use the information derived directly from the compelled testimony in any subsequent prosecution, though the witness may still be prosecuted for crimes on the basis of other evidence.

THE *MIRANDA* WARNING   Police questioning of suspects is a key procedure in solving crimes. Roughly 90 percent of all criminal convictions result from guilty pleas and never reach a full trial. Police questioning, however, can easily be abused. Police officers sometimes forget or ignore the constitutional rights of suspects, especially those who are frightened and ignorant. Unauthorized detention and lengthy interrogation to wring confessions from suspects, common practice in police states, were not unknown in the United States.

racial profiling
Police targeting of racial minorities as potential suspects of criminal activities.

exclusionary rule
Requirement that evidence unconstitutionally or illegally obtained be excluded from a criminal trial.

immunity
Exemption from prosecution for a particular crime in return for testimony pertaining to the case.

The Miranda warning is read to a suspect by a police officer to inform him of his rights, such as the right to remain silent and the right to have an attorney present.

Federal and state laws require police officers to take people they have arrested before a magistrate promptly so that the magistrate may inform them of their constitutional rights and allow them to get in touch with friends and seek legal advice. Despite these requirements, police were often tempted to quiz suspects first, trying to get them to confess before a magistrate informed them of their constitutional right to remain silent.

To put an end to such practices, the Supreme Court, in *Miranda* v. *Arizona* (1966), announced that no conviction could stand if evidence introduced at the trial had been obtained by the police during "custodial interrogation" unless suspects were notified that they have a right to remain silent and that anything they say can and will be used against them; to terminate questioning at any point; to have an attorney present during questioning by police; and to have a lawyer appointed to represent them if they cannot afford to hire their own attorney.[60] If suspects answer questions in the absence of an attorney, the burden is on prosecutors to demonstrate that suspects knowingly and intelligently gave up their right to remain silent. Failure to comply with these requirements leads to reversal of a conviction, even if other evidence is sufficient to establish guilt.

Critics of the *Miranda* decision believe that the Supreme Court severely limited the ability of the police to bring criminals to justice. Over the years, the Court has modified the original ruling by allowing evidence obtained contrary to the *Miranda* guidelines to be used to attack the credibility of defendants who offer testimony at their trial that conflicts with their statements to the police. Congress tried to get around *Miranda* in the Crime Control and Safe Streets Act of 1968 by allowing confessions made in violation of *Miranda* to be used as evidence in federal courts. But in *Dickerson* v. *United States* (2000), the Court reaffirmed the constitutionality of the *Miranda* doctrine. In an opinion by Chief Justice William H. Rehnquist, the Court held that the *Miranda* warning is not merely a rule of evidence to enforce the constitutional guarantee but is itself constitutionally required and applies in both state and federal courts.[61]

Fair Trial Procedures

Many people consider the rights of persons accused of a crime to be less important than other rights. But as Justice Felix Frankfurter observed, "The history of liberty has largely been the history of observance of procedural safeguards." Further, these safeguards have frequently "been forged in controversies involving not very nice people."[62] Nonetheless, they guarantee that all persons accused of crimes will have the right to representation by counsel and to a fair trial by an impartial jury.

THE RIGHT TO COUNSEL   If after questioning by police the suspect is arrested and charged with a crime, the Supreme Court has ruled that the accused has a constitutional right to counsel at every stage of the criminal proceedings—preliminary hearings, bail hearings, trial, sentencing, and first appeal. Communications between the accused and counsel are privileged. However, in cases of terrorism, under new guidelines issued by Attorney General John Ashcroft, police may listen in, undercover, on consultations between lawyers and detainees if "reasonable suspicion exists to believe that an inmate may use communications with attorneys or their agent to facilitate acts of terrorism."

INDICTMENT   Except for members of the armed forces and foreign terrorists, the national government cannot require anyone to stand trial for a serious crime except on the basis of a grand jury indictment or its equivalent; states are not required to use grand juries, and those that do not vest prosecutors with the power to seek indictments. A **grand jury** is concerned not with a person's guilt or innocence but merely with whether there is enough evidence to warrant a trial. The grand jury has wide-ranging investigatory powers and "is to inquire into all information that might bear on its investigations until it is satisfied that it has identified an offense or satisfied itself that none has occurred."[63] The strict rules that govern jury proceedings do not apply. The grand jury may admit hearsay evidence, and the exclusionary rule to enforce the Fourth Amendment does not apply. If a majority of the grand jurors agree that a trial is justified, they return what is known as a *true bill,* or **indictment**.

grand jury
A jury of 12 to 23 persons who, in private, hear evidence presented by the government to determine whether persons shall be required to stand trial. If the jury believes there is sufficient evidence that a crime was committed, it issues an indictment.

indictment
A formal written statement from a grand jury charging an individual with an offense; also called a *true bill.*

The Constitution guarantees the accused the right to be informed of the nature and cause of the accusation so that he or she can prepare a defense. After indictment for an offense, prosecutors and the attorney for the accused usually discuss the possibility of a **plea bargain** whereby the defendant pleads guilty to a lesser offense that carries a shorter prison sentence. Prosecutors, facing more cases than they can handle, like plea bargains because they save the expense and time of going to trial. Likewise, defendants are often willing to "cop a plea" for a lesser offense to avoid the risk of more serious punishment.

When defendants plead guilty, they are usually forever prevented from raising objections to their conviction. That is why, before accepting guilty pleas, the judge questions defendants to be sure their attorneys have explained the alternatives and they know what they are doing.

TRIAL After indictment and preliminary hearings that determine bail and what evidence will be used as evidence against the accused, the Constitution guarantees a *speedy and public trial.* Do not, however, take the word "speedy" too literally. Defendants are given time to prepare their defense and in fact often ask for delays because delays can work to their advantage. In contrast, if the government denies the accused a speedy trial, not only is the conviction reversed but the case must also be dismissed outright.

Under the Sixth Amendment, the accused has a right to trial before a **petit jury** selected from the state and district in which the alleged crime was committed. Although federal law requires juries of 12 members, the Supreme Court has held that states may try defendants before juries consisting of as few as six persons. Conviction in federal courts must be by unanimous vote, but the Court has ruled that state courts may render guilty verdicts by nonunanimous juries, provided that such juries consist of six or more persons.[64]

An *impartial jury,* one that meets the requirements of due process and equal protection, consists of persons who represent a fair cross section of the community. Although defendants are not entitled to juries on which there must be individuals of their own race, sex, religion, or national origin, government prosecutors cannot strike people from juries because of race or gender, and neither can defense attorneys use what are called *peremptory challenges* to keep people off juries because of race, ethnic origin, or sex.[65]

During the trial, the defendant has a right to obtain witnesses in his or her favor and to have the judge subpoena witnesses to appear at the trial and testify. Both the accused and witnesses may refuse to testify on the grounds that their testimony would tend to incriminate themselves. If they testify, the prosecution has the right to cross-examine them, just as the accused has the right to confront and to cross-examine witnesses.

Sentencing and Punishment

At the conclusion of the trial, the jury recommends a verdict of guilty or not guilty. If the accused is found guilty, the judge hands down the sentence. The Eighth Amendment forbids the levying of excessive fines and the inflicting of cruel and unusual punishment.

In federal courts, judges follow the sentencing guidelines set down by the United States Sentencing Commission. Such sentences are not considered cruel and unusual. Many states have also established guidelines for sentencing by state courts.

THREE STRIKES AND YOU'RE OUT Although the crime rate has actually been going down in the past few years, public concern about crime remains high. At the national and state level, presidents, governors, and legislators vie with one another to show their toughness on crime. California, Virginia, Washington, and a number of other states have "three strikes and you're out" laws, requiring a lifetime sentence without the possibility of parole for anyone convicted of a third felony, even though for a minor offense. In some states, the felonies must be for violent crimes; in others, any three felonies will do. Scholars are skeptical that "three strikes and you're out" laws reduce crime, and constructing

"The court finds itself on the horns of a dilemma. On the one hand, wiretap evidence is inadmissible, and on the other hand, I'm dying to hear it."

plea bargain
Agreement between a prosecutor and a defendant that the defendant will plead guilty to a lesser offense to avoid having to stand trial for a more serious offense.

petit jury
A jury of 6 to 12 persons that determines guilt or innocence in a civil or criminal action.

more jails to take care of aging felons requires great expenditures of public funds. California's tough law for committing three felonies was nonetheless upheld by the Supreme Court, and a 25-years-to-life sentence for stealing three golf clubs, each valued at $399, was held not to violate the prohibition against cruel and unusual punishment.[66]

APPEALS AND DOUBLE JEOPARDY   After trial, conviction, and sentencing, defendants may appeal their convictions if they claim they have been denied some constitutional right or denied the due process and equal protection of the law. The Fifth Amendment also provides that no person shall be "subject for the same offense to be twice put in jeopardy of life or limb." **Double jeopardy** does not prevent punishment by the national and the state governments for the same offense or for successive prosecutions for the same crime by two states. Nor does the double jeopardy clause forbid civil prosecutions, even after acquittal in a criminal trial for the same conduct.[67]

THE DEATH PENALTY   Capital punishment remains controversial. Japan and the United States are the only two industrialized countries to retain the death penalty. The 25 members of the European Union have outlawed capital punishment, and courts in South Africa and several central and eastern European countries have declared it unconstitutional and a denial of human dignity.

After a ten-year moratorium on executions in the late 1960s and early 1970s, the U.S. Supreme Court ruled that the death penalty is not necessarily cruel and unusual punishment if it is imposed for crimes that resulted in a victim's death, if the procedures used by the courts "ensure that death sentences are not meted out wantonly or freakishly," and if these processes "confer on the sentencer sufficient discretion to take account of the character and record of the individual offender and the circumstances of the particular offense to ensure that death is the appropriate punishment in a specific case."[68]

The Rehnquist Court has made it easier to impose death sentences, cut back on appeals, and carry out executions. More states have added the death penalty (there are now 38), and the national government has increased the number of crimes for which the death penalty may be imposed. As a result, the number of persons on death row has increased dramatically. Since capital punishment was reinstated in 1976, more than 600 people have been executed nationwide, and more than 3,500 are on death row. As the number of executions has increased, however, concerns have also grown about the fairness of how capital punishment is imposed. These concerns have been fueled by DNA tests that have established the innocence of a sizable number of those convicted of murder.[69]

The prohibition against cruel and unusual punishment also forbids punishments grossly disproportionate to the severity of the crime. In 2002, the Supreme Court overruled a prior ruling[70] and held that it is excessive and disproportionate to execute mentally retarded convicted murderers because they are not capable of understanding the seriousness of their offense. The Court noted that in recent years there has been a movement to bar executions of mentally retarded death-row inmates. And because 18 of the 38 states imposing capital punishment exempt the mentally retarded, the Court concluded that there was an emerging "national consensus" against executing mentally retarded inmates.[71]

HOW JUST IS OUR SYSTEM OF JUSTICE?

Because the American system of criminal justice contains many guarantees for protecting the rights of the accused, critics often argue that due to these protections, justice is not done. Among the other criticisms are that the system is inefficient, biased, and unfair.

Too Many Loopholes?

Some observers argue that by overprotecting criminals and placing too much of a burden on the criminal justice system not to make any mistakes, we delay justice, encourage disrespect for the law, and allow guilty persons to go unpunished. Justice should be swift and certain without being arbitrary. But under our procedures, criminals may go

double jeopardy
Trial or punishment for the same crime by the same government; forbidden by the Constitution.

IN COMPARATIVE PERSPECTIVE

THE DEATH PENALTY AROUND THE WORLD

The United States and Japan are the only two industrialized countries that retain the death penalty. Most of the 78 countries that still impose capital punishment are in Africa, the Middle East, the Carribean, and Central America.

According to Amnesty International, 117 countries have abolished capital punishment for all or most crimes. In the last 30 years 65 countries joined this group, most recently Bhutan and Samoa (2004), Armenia (2003), and Cyprus and Yugoslavia (2002).

Among the 79 countries that abolished capital punishment for all crimes are the 25 countries in the European Union, other Western and Eastern European countries, Cambodia,

and South Africa. Another 15 countries have abolished capital punishment for ordinary criminal offenses: Albania, Argentina, Armenia, Bolivia, Brazil, Chile, the Cook Islands, El Salvador, Fiji, Greece, Israel, Latvia, Mexico, Peru, and Turkey.

Another 23 countries retain the death penalty but have abolished it in practice by not carrying out executions in a decade or more. Among these countries are Algeria, Brunei, Congo, Kenya, the Russian Federation, Sri Lanka, and Tunisia.

Source: Amnesty International, "The Death Penalty" (as of May 1, 2004), at www.wen.amnesty.org/pages/deathpenalty-countries-eng.

---

unpunished because the police decide not to arrest them; the prosecutor decides not to prosecute them; the grand jury decides not to indict them; the judge decides not to hold them for trial; the jury decides not to convict them; the appeals court decides to reverse the conviction; the judge decides to release them on a writ of habeas corpus; or the president or governor decides to pardon, reprieve, or parole them if convicted. As a result, the public never knows whom to hold responsible when laws are not enforced. The police blame prosecutors, prosecutors blame the police, and they all blame the juries and judges.

Others take a different view and point out that there is more to justice than simply securing convictions. All the steps in the administration of criminal laws have been developed over centuries of trial and error, and each step has been constructed to protect ordinary persons from particular abuses by those in power. History warns against entrusting the instruments of criminal law enforcement to a single officer. For this reason, responsibility is vested in many officials.

Too Unreliable?

Critics who say that our system of justice is unreliable often point to trial by jury as the chief source of trouble. No other country relies as heavily on trial by jury as the United States. Jury trials are also time-consuming and costly. Trial by jury, critics argue, leads to a theatrical combat between lawyers who base their appeals on the prejudices and sentiments of the jurors. "Mr. Prejudice and Miss Sympathy are the names of witnesses whose testimony is never recorded, but must nevertheless be reckoned with in trials by jury."[72]

The jury system allows for what is called *jury nullification* when jurors ignore their instructions to consider only the evidence presented in court and vote for acquittal to express their displeasure with the law or the actions of prosecutors or police. Jury nullification has a long history. In colonial times, juries refused to convict colonists of political crimes against the king as a way to protest British rule. Before the Civil War, northern juries refused to convict people for helping runaway slaves. Before the 1970s, white southern juries sometimes refused to convict police for brutality against blacks.

Responding to growing public disenchantment with juries after a raft of unpopular verdicts, states have been rewriting the rules for the jury system. These changes include making it more difficult for people to be excused from jury service, allowing for nonunanimous decisions, limiting how long jurors can be sequestered, and exerting more control by judges over lawyers' statements to jurors in order to prevent appeals to jurors' emotions.

CHANGING FACE OF AMERICAN POLITICS

A RENEWED DEBATE OVER THE DEATH PENALTY

Although the number of individuals sentenced to death has grown in the last several decades, in recent years the number of death-row inmates and executions has declined (see below). While some groups, like the U.S. Conference of Catholic Bishops, oppose the death penalty on moral grounds, the renewed debate now focuses on the fairness of the entire process of administering capital punishment. The American Bar Association (ABA) has called for a halt to executions because the death penalty is administered in arbitrary and capricious ways that deny fundamental due process and the equal protection of the law. Prominent Republicans and Democrats also are questioning the system of imposing the death penalty.

The debate about the fairness of capital punishment was sparked by the increasing number of inmates who have been released because new DNA evidence proved their innocence—often after they had spent a decade or more on death row. Critics also point out the seeming randomness in imposing capital punishment. Public prosecutors seek the death penalty in less than 5 percent of all murder cases. Defendants often agree to plea bargains in return for life sentences. When murder trials are held, some juries refuse to impose the death sentence. And of the criminals sentenced to death, some receive clemency or are paroled. A study of more than 4,500 capital cases found that more than two-thirds of all death sentences are overturned. Why? The primary reasons are that defense lawyers were incompetent, important evidence was overlooked, witnesses lied, or prosecutors withheld evidence from the defense. In addition, racial discrimination in the imposition of capital punishment is a major concern. Blacks who murder whites are much more likely to receive death sentences than whites who murder blacks or blacks who kill blacks.

Persons Executed, 1930–2003

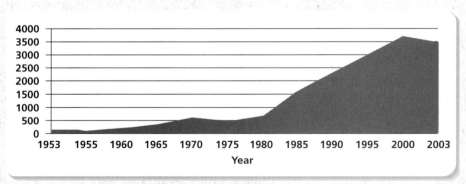

Number of Death Row Inmates, 1953–2003

SOURCE: Death Penalty Information Center. See also Hudo Bedau and Paul Cassell, eds., *Debating the Death Penalty* (Oxford University Press, 2004).

Defenders of the jury system reply that trial by jury provides a check by non-professionals on the actions of judges and prosecutors. There is no evidence that juries are unreliable; on the contrary, decisions of juries do not significantly differ from those of judges.[73] Moreover, the jury system helps educate citizens and enables them to participate in the application of their country's laws.

Too Discriminatory?

During the past several decades, the Supreme Court has worked particularly hard to enforce the ideal of equal justice under the law. Persons accused of crimes who cannot afford attorneys must be furnished them at government expense. If transcripts are required for appeals, such transcripts must be made available to those who cannot afford to purchase them. If appeals are permitted, the government must provide attorneys for at least one appeal of the decision of the trial court. Poor people cannot be imprisoned because of the inability to pay a fine. Nor, once sentenced, can poor people be kept in jail beyond the term of the sentence because they cannot afford to pay a fine. Even for civil proceedings—divorce proceedings, for example—fees cannot be imposed that deny poor people their fundamental rights, such as the right to obtain a divorce.

Tribune Media Services.

Unfair to Minorities?

One of the acute problems of our society is the tension between the police and the African American, Hispanic, and Middle Eastern communities congregated in inner cities. Many members of minorities believe they do not have equal protection under the law and that they are targeted by law enforcement officers. "Whether the stated belief is well founded or not," one political scientist observed, "is at least partly beside the point. The existence of the belief is damaging enough."[74]

Some blacks consider the police to be enforcers of white law. Studies proving prejudice on the part of some white police officers and examples of rough, even brutal, police treatment of blacks are ample evidence to support this viewpoint. One study in California found that "the rate of unfounded arrest was four times higher for African Americans than Anglos. Latino rates were double those of Anglos."[75] Police use of racial profiling, already a concern of blacks and Hispanics, has also became a concern of Muslims and whites.[76]

In recent decades, action has been taken to recruit more African Americans, Hispanics, and women as police officers, including appointment to command posts. In larger cities, there are now oversight boards including civilians to which complaints about police misconduct can be brought. **Community policing** is also being substituted in some cities for traditional police procedures. Police departments work with churches and other local community groups and take police out of patrol cars to walk the beat and work in neighborhoods. Community policing, when combined with working with community organizations to sponsor crime prevention programs, appears not only to reduce crime but also to improve minorities' confidence in the police.[77]

THE SUPREME COURT AND CIVIL LIBERTIES

Judges play a major role in enforcing constitutional guarantees. Such reliance on judicial protection of our civil liberties focuses public attention on the Supreme Court. Yet only a small number of controversies are actually carried to the Supreme Court, and a Supreme Court decision is not the end of the judicial process. Lower court judges as well as police, superintendents of schools, local prosecutors, school boards, state legislatures, and thousands of others clarify the Court's doctrines.

Moreover, the Supreme Court can do little unless its decisions over time reflect a national consensus. As Supreme Court Justice Robert H. Jackson observed, "The attitude of a society and of its organized political forces, rather than its legal machinery, is the controlling force in the character of free institutions. Any court that undertakes by its

community policing
Assigning police to neighborhoods where they walk the beat and work with churches and other community groups to reduce crime and improve relations with minorities.

legal processes to enforce civil liberties needs the support of an enlightened and vigorous public opinion."[78] Thus the Bill of Rights—and the other procedural and substantive liberties of our Constitution—cannot rest on a foundation merely of tradition. The preservation of these rights depends on wide, continuing, and knowledgeable public support.

Summary

1. One of the basic distinctions between a free society and a police state is that in a free society, there are effective restraints on the way public officials, especially law enforcement officials, perform their duties. In the United States, the courts enforce these constitutional restraints.

2. The Constitution protects the acquisition and retention of citizenship. It protects the basic liberties of citizens as well as aliens, although in times of war, foreign saboteurs and terrorists may be detained and tried without the rights accorded citizens and other aliens.

3. The Constitution protects our property from arbitrary governmental interference, although debates about which interferences are reasonable and which are arbitrary are not easily settled. If private property is taken or rendered worthless by the government, just compensation must be paid to the owner.

4. The Constitution imposes limits not only on the procedures government must follow but also on the ends it may pursue. Some actions are out of bounds no matter what procedures are followed. Legislatures have the primary role in determining what is reasonable and what is unreasonable. However, the Supreme Court continues to exercise its own independent and final review of legislative determinations of reasonableness, especially on matters affecting civil liberties and civil rights.

5. The Supreme Court has pulled together elements from the First, Fourth, Fifth, Ninth, and Fourteenth Amendments to recognize a constitutionally protected right to personal privacy, especially with regard to marital privacy, including the right of a woman to choose an abortion.

6. The framers knew from their own experiences that in their zeal to maintain power and to enforce the laws, especially in wartime, public officials are often tempted to infringe on the rights of persons accused of crimes. To prevent such abuse, the Bill of Rights requires federal officials to follow detailed procedures in making searches and arrests and in bringing people to trial.

7. The Supreme Court continues to play a prominent role in developing public policy to protect the rights of the accused, to ensure that the innocent are not punished, and to guarantee that the public is protected against those who break the laws. The Court's decisions influence what the public believes and how police officers and others involved in the administration of justice behave. But the Court alone cannot guarantee fairness in the administration of justice.

Key Terms

naturalization
dual citizenship
right of expatriation
property rights
contract clause
police powers

eminent domain
regulatory taking
due process
procedural due process
substantive due process
search warrant

racial profiling
exclusionary rule
immunity
grand jury
indictment
plea bargain

petit jury
double jeopardy
community policing

Further Reading

JEFFREY ABRAMSON, *We, the Jury: The Jury System and the Ideal of Democracy* (Harvard University Press, 2000).

LIVA BAKER, *Miranda: Crime, Law and Politics* (Atheneum, 1983).

STUART BANNER, *The Death Penalty: An American History* (Harvard University Press, 2002).

ROBERT P. BURNS, *A Theory of the Trial* (Princeton University Press, 1999).

DAVID COLE, *Enemy Aliens: Double Standards and Constitutional Freedoms in the War on Terrorism* (The New Press, 2003).

JOHN DENVIR, *Democracy's Constitution: Claiming the Privileges of American Citizenship* (University of Illinois Press, 2001).

LOUIS FISHER, *Nazi Saboteurs on Trial: A Military Tribunal and American Law* (University Press of Kansas, 2003).

GEORGE P. FLETCHER, *Basic Concepts of Criminal Law* (Oxford University Press, 1998).

DAVID J. GARROW, *Liberty and Sexuality: The Right to Privacy and the Making of* Roe v. Wade (Macmillan, 1994).

ROGER HOOD, *The Death Penalty: A Worldwide Perspective,* 3d ed. (Oxford University Press, 2002).

RANDALL KENNEDY, *Race, Crime, and the Law* (Pantheon, 1997).

ANTHONY LEWIS, *Gideon's Trumpet* (Random House, 1964).

JOHN R. LOTT JR., *More Guns, Less Crime: Understanding Crime and Gun Control Laws* (University of Chicago Press, 2000).

DAVID M. O'BRIEN, *Constitutional Law and Politics: Vol. 2, Civil Rights and Civil Liberties,* 6th ed. (Norton, 2005).

J. W. PELTASON AND SUE DAVIS, *Understanding the Constitution,* 15th ed. (Harcourt, 2001).

WILLIAM H. REHNQUIST, *All the Laws but One: Civil Liberties in Wartime* (Knopf, 1998).

BARRY SCHECK, PETER NEUFELD, AND JIM DWYER, *Actual Innocence: Five Days to Execution, and Other Dispatches from the Wrongly Convicted* (Doubleday, 2000).

MARY E. VOGEL, *Coercion to Compromise: Plea Bargaining, the Courts, and the Making of Political Authority* (Oxford University Press, 2001).

WELSH S. WHITE, *Miranda's Waning Protections: Police Interrogation Practices After Dickerson* (University of Michigan Press, 2001).

EQUAL RIGHTS UNDER THE LAW

17

The Declaration of Independence proclaims the precious rights of *equality* and *liberty:* "We hold these truths to be self-evident, that all men are created equal, that they are endowed by their Creator with certain unalienable Rights, that among these are Life, Liberty, and the pursuit of Happiness." Although the Declaration does not specify equality of white, Christian, or Anglo-Saxon men (at that time "all men" meant white, property-owning Anglo-Saxon men), it took almost 200 years for that definition to be expanded to include all races, all religions, and all women as well as men. This creed of individual dignity and equality is nonetheless older than our Declaration of Independence; its roots go back into the teachings of Judaism and Christianity.

The Constitution, however, does not make any reference to "equality" (the word never appears in the Constitution or in the Bill of Rights). But we know the framers believed that all men—at least all white adult men—were equally entitled to life, liberty, and the pursuit of happiness. But like the Declaration, the Constitution refers only to "person," "people, "citizens," and "he," but not to women, and none of its lofty sentiments applied to slaves, who enjoyed neither liberty nor equality.

The framers resolved their ambiguity about what kind of equality and for whom by creating a system of government designed to protect what they called *natural rights.* (Today we speak of *human rights,* but the idea is basically the same.) By **natural rights** the framers meant that every person has an equal right to protection against arbitrary treatment and an equal right to the liberties guaranteed by the Bill of Rights. These rights

TIME LINE

EQUAL RIGHTS UNDER THE LAW

1865–1868	Reconstruction Era leads to freedom for former slaves
1896	*Plessy* v. *Ferguson* upholds "separate but equal" doctrine
1942	FDR orders internment of Japanese Americans in internment camps
1948	Truman desegregates the military
1954	*Brown* v. *Board of Education* declares school segregation unconstitutional
1963	March on Washington held to demand equal rights for African Americans
1964	Civil Rights Act forbids racial discrimination in public accomodations
1967	Age Discrimination Act creates the first legal protections based on age
1972	Title IX prohibits sex discrimination in education
1978	*University of California Regents* v. *Bakke* upholds affirmative action programs in higher education aimed at achieving diverse student bodies
1991	Americans with Disabilities Act is the first expansion of civil rights since the 1970s
2003	*Grutter* v. *Bollinger* reaffirms *Bakke* on the permissibility of affirmative action programs

natural rights
The rights of all people to dignity and worth; also called *human rights*.

affirmative action
Remedial action designed to overcome the effects of past discrimination against minorities and women.

do not depend on citizenship; they are not granted by governments. They are the rights of *all people*.

The terms *civil liberties* and *civil rights* are often used interchangeably to refer to rights that are protected by constitutional democracies. *Civil liberties* is sometimes used more narrowly to refer to freedom of conscience, religion, and expression. *Civil rights* is used to refer to the right not to be discriminated against because of race, religion, gender, or ethnic origin. Our Constitution provides two ways of protecting civil rights. First, it ensures that government officials do not discriminate against us; second, it grants national and state governments the power to protect these civil rights against interference by private individuals.

This chapter is concerned with both the protection of our rights from abuse *by government* and the protection *through government* of our right to be free from abuse by our *fellow citizens*. Here, we focus on the struggles of African Americans, women, Hispanics, Asian Americans, and Native Americans to secure the basic civil rights to the vote, to an education, to a job, and to a place to live on equal terms with their fellow citizens.

EQUALITY AND EQUAL RIGHTS

Americans are committed to equality. "Equality," however, is an elusive term. The concept for which there is the greatest consensus and that is most clearly written into the Constitution is that everybody should have *equality of opportunity* regardless of race, ethnic origin, religion, and, in recent years, gender and sexual orientation. Advancing the equality of opportunity has led to the historic struggles for civil rights.

A variation of the concept of equal opportunity is *equality of starting conditions*. There is not much equal opportunity if one person is born into a well-to-do family, lives in a safe suburb, and receives a good education, while another is born into a poor, broken family, lives in an inner-city neighborhood, and attends inferior schools. Thus, it is argued, if we are to have equality of opportunity in a meaningful sense, special opportunities must be provided for the disadvantaged through federal programs such as Head Start, which provides children from poor families with preschool experiences that prepare them for elementary school.

Traditionally, we have emphasized *individual* achievement, but in recent decades, some politicians and civil rights leaders have focused attention on the concept of *equality between groups*. When large disparities in wealth and advantage exist between groups—as between blacks and whites or between women and men—equality becomes a highly divisive political issue. Those who are disadvantaged tend to emphasize economic and social factors that exclude them from the mainstream. They champion programs like **affirmative action** that are designed to provide special help to people who have been disadvantaged due to their group memberships. Those who are advantaged, however, often act to maintain the status quo and downplay socioeconomic disparities. As a result, whether such programs promote or deny equality remains one of the most controversial current debates.

Finally, equality can also mean *equality of results*. A perennial debate, especially among college students, is whether social justice and genuine equality can exist in a nation in which people of one class have so much and others have so little and where the gap between them grows ever wider.[1] There is considerable support for guaranteeing a minimum floor—a "safety net"—below which no one should be allowed to fall. Yet Americans generally do not support an equality of results—that everybody should have the same amount of material goods—but instead tend to take the view that regardless of current economic status, a person should be able to expect that things will get better and that hard work and an entrepreneurial spirit will be rewarded.

THE QUEST FOR EQUAL JUSTICE

To gain some perspective on the court decisions, laws, and other governmental actions relating to civil rights for women and minorities, we review here the political history and social contexts in which these constitutional issues arise. These issues involve not only court decisions, laws, and constitutional amendments, however. They encompass the entire social, economic, and political system. And although the struggles of all groups are interwoven, they are not identical, so we deal briefly and separately with each.

Racial Equality

Americans had a painful confrontation with the problem of race before, during, and after the Civil War (1861–1865). As a result of the northern victory, the Thirteenth, Fourteenth, and Fifteenth Amendments became part of the Constitution. During Reconstruction, Congress passed a series of civil rights laws to implement these amendments and established programs to provide educational and social services for the freed slaves. But the Supreme Court struck down many of these laws, and it was not until the 1960s that progress was again made toward ensuring African Americans their civil rights.

"When my distinguished colleague refers to the will of the 'people,' does he mean his 'people' or my 'people'?"

SEGREGATION AND WHITE SUPREMACY   Before Reconstruction programs had any significant effect, the white southern political leadership was restored to power, and by 1877, Reconstruction was ended. Northern political leaders abandoned African Americans to their fate at the hands of their former white masters; presidents no longer concerned themselves with the enforcement of civil rights laws, and Congress enacted no new ones. The Supreme Court either declared old laws unconstitutional or interpreted them so narrowly that they were ineffective. The Court also gave such a limited construction to the Thirteenth, Fourteenth, and Fifteenth Amendments that they failed to accomplish their intended purpose of protecting the rights of African Americans.[2]

White supremacy went unchallenged in the South, where most African Americans lived. They were kept from voting; they were forced to accept menial jobs; they were denied educational opportunities; they were segregated in public facilities.[3] African Americans were lynched on an average of one every four days, and few whites raised a voice in protest.

During World War I, African Americans began to migrate to northern cities to seek jobs in war factories. Their relocation was accelerated in the 1930s by the Great Depression and in the 1940s by World War II. Although discrimination continued, more jobs became available, and social gains resulted. As migration of African Americans out of the rural South into southern and northern cities shifted the racial composition of cities, the African American vote became important in national elections. These changes created an African American middle class opposed to segregation as a symbol of servitude and a cause of inequality. By the middle of the twentieth century, urban African Americans were active and politically powerful citizens. There was a growing demand for the abolition of color barriers.

SLOW GOVERNMENT RESPONSE   By the 1930s, African Americans were resorting to lawsuits to challenge the doctrine of segregation. And after World War II, this civil rights litigation began to have a major impact. In the years that followed, the Supreme Court, beginning with the landmark 1954 ruling in *Brown* v. *Board of Education,* outlawed racially segregated public schools[4] and subsequently struck down most of the devices that had been used by state and local authorities to keep African Americans from voting.[5]

Presidents Harry S Truman and Dwight D. Eisenhower used their executive authority to fight segregation in the armed services and the federal bureaucracy. They directed the Department of Justice to enforce whatever civil rights laws were on the books, but Congress still held back. In the late 1950s, an emerging national consensus in favor of governmental action to protect civil rights plus the political clout of African Americans in the northern states began to have some influence on Congress. In 1957, Congress

Rosa Parks decision not to give up her seat on the bus in Montgomery, Alabama, sparked a boycott by African Americans who, for more than a year, refused to ride the segregated city buses.

overrode a southern filibuster in the Senate and enacted the first federal civil rights laws since Reconstruction.

A TURNING POINT Even after the Supreme Court declared racially segregated public schools unconstitutional, most African Americans still went to segregated schools, and there was widespread resistance to integration in the South. Many legal barriers in the path of equal rights had fallen, yet most African Americans still could not buy houses where they wanted, secure the jobs they needed, find educational opportunities for their children, or eat in a restaurant or walk freely on the streets of "white neighborhoods."

But times were changing. What had once been deemed a "southern problem" was finally recognized as a national challenge. A massive social, economic, and political movement began to supplement the struggles in the courtrooms. It began in Montgomery, Alabama, on December 1, 1955, when Rosa Parks refused to give up her seat to a white man in the front of a bus and as required by law was removed from the bus. The black community responded by boycotting city buses.

The boycott worked. It also produced a charismatic national civil rights leader, the Reverend Martin Luther King Jr. Through his doctrine of nonviolent resistance, King gave a new dimension to the struggle. By the early 1960s, new organizational resources came into existence in almost every city to support and sponsor "sit-ins," "freedom rides," "live-ins," and other nonviolent demonstrations. These measures were often met with violence, and some state and local governments failed to protect the victims or to prosecute the parties responsible for the violence.[6]

The simmering forces of social discontent boiled over in the summer of 1963. A peaceful demonstration in Birmingham, Alabama, was countered with fire hoses, police dogs, and mass arrests. More than a quarter of a million people converged on Washington, D.C., to hear King and other civil rights leaders speak while countless millions more watched them on television. By the time the summer was over, there was hardly a city, North or South, that had not had demonstrations, protests, or sit-ins; some also had violence.

This direct action had some effect. Many cities enacted civil rights ordinances, more schools were desegregated, and President John F. Kennedy urged Congress to enact a comprehensive civil rights bill. Late in 1963, the nation's grief over the assassination of President Kennedy, who had become identified with civil rights goals, added political fuel to the drive for decisive federal action to protect civil rights.[7] President Lyndon B. Johnson made civil rights legislation his highest priority, and on July 2, 1964, after months of

Firefighters in Birmingham, Alabama, turned their hoses full blast on civil rights demonstrators in the 1960s. At times the water came with such force, even on children, that it literally tore the bark off fully-grown trees.

debate, he signed into law the Civil Rights Act of 1964, forbidding discrimination on the basis of race, color, religion, sex, or nationality.[8]

RIOTS AND REACTION   By the early 1970s, the legal phase of the civil rights movement had largely come to a close, but as things got better, discontent grew. Millions of impoverished African Americans demonstrated growing impatience with the discrimination that remained. This volatile situation gave way to racial violence and disorders. In 1965, a brutal riot took place in Watts, a section of Los Angeles. In 1966 and 1967, the disorders spread in scope and intensity. The Detroit riot in July 1967, the worst such disturbance up to that time in modern American history, made clear the deep divisions between the races and the urgency of taking corrective action.[9]

President Johnson appointed the special Advisory Commission on Civil Disorders in 1967 to investigate the origins of the riots and to recommend measures to prevent such disasters in the future. When the commission (called the Kerner Commission after its chair, Illinois Governor Otto Kerner) issued its report, it said in stark, clear language: "What white Americans have never fully understood—but what the Negro can never forget—is that white society is deeply implicated in the ghetto. White institutions created it, white institutions maintain it, and white society condones it." The basic conclusion of the commission was this: "Our nation is moving toward two societies, one black, one white—separate and unequal" and that "only a commitment to national action on an unprecedented scale" could change this trend.[10]

The commission made sweeping recommendations on jobs, education, housing, and the welfare system. But other events diverted attention from these recommenda-

PEOPLE & POLITICS   *Making a Difference* ★ ★ ★

MARTIN LUTHER KING, JR.

Martin Luther King, Jr., a Baptist minister and civil rights leader, was born January 25, 1929, in Atlanta, Georgia. After graduating from high school, he entered Morehouse College in 1944 and majored in sociology, but in his junior year he decided to enter the ministry. After Morehouse, King entered the Crozer Theological Seminary in Pennsylvania and there he became a follower of Indian pacifist Mohandas Gandhi. Following graduation, King earned a doctorate from Boston University in 1955. He then became pastor of the Dexter Avenue Baptist Church in Montgomery, Alabama.

In 1957, King and Ralph Abernathy founded the Southern Christian Leadership Conference in order to advance the cause of civil rights. In that year, King's home and church were bombed and violence against black protesters began to escalate. In March 1963, King was jailed in Birmingham, Alabama, for leading a protest parade without a permit. Subsequently, he led the March on Washington, on August 28, 1963, at which hundreds of thousands of civil rights activists demonstrated and focused national attention on the racial problems in the country. The March contributed to building support for the passage of the Civil Rights Act of 1964.

Speaking at the March from the steps of the Lincoln Memorial, King delivered his famous "I Have A Dream" speech, in which he said he dreamed of the day when "my four little children . . . will not be judged by the color of their skin but by the content of their character," and concluded with the memorable line, "Free at last! Thank God Almighty, we are free at last!"

In 1963 King became *Time* magazine's Man of the Year, and in 1964 he was awarded the Nobel Peace Prize for his leadership in the civil rights movement and advocacy of nonviolent protest.

King was assassinated on April 4, 1968, outside his Memphis, Tennessee, motel room.

Susan B. Anthony and Elizabeth Cady Stanton were the two most influential leaders of the women's suffrage movement in the nineteenth century.

tions: the Vietnam War; Watergate; the elections of Ronald Reagan and George H. W. Bush, who were reluctant to take governmental actions to enforce civil rights; and a growing skepticism about the effectiveness of governmental action generally.

The Clinton administration was more sympathetic toward the use of governmental power to deal with issues of inequality than its immediate predecessors, but because of budgetary constraints and Republican opposition to "big government" programs, it was largely unable to promote any major initiatives directly aimed at the problems of the inner cities. The administration of George W. Bush pursued more race-neutral policies like the No Child Left Behind program aimed at raising educational standards across the nation. Still, civil rights leaders like the Reverend Jesse Jackson continue efforts to eliminate the vestiges of past racial discrimination through boycotts and lawsuits aimed at persuading businesses and corporations to reach out and hire and promote more African Americans.

Women's Rights

The struggle for equal rights for women was intertwined with the battle to secure equal rights for African Americans. The Seneca Falls Women's Rights Convention (1848), which launched the women's movement, involved men and women who actively campaigned to abolish slavery and to secure the rights of African Americans and women. But as the Civil War approached, women were urged to abandon their cause and devote their energies to getting rid of slavery.[11] The Civil War brought the women's movement to a halt, and the temperance movement to prohibit the sale of liquor diverted attention away from women's rights as well. The Fourteenth and Fifteenth Amendments did not advance voting rights for women, even as they guaranteed that right to freed male slaves.

By the turn of the twentieth century, however, a vigorous campaign was under way for **women's suffrage**—the right to vote. The first victories came in western states, where Wyoming led the way. As a territory, Wyoming had given women the right to vote. When members of Congress in Washington grumbled about this "petticoat provision," the Wyoming legislators replied they would stay out of the Union 100 years rather than come in without women's suffrage. Congress gave in and admitted Wyoming to the Union. By the end of World War I, more than half the states had granted women the right to vote in some or all elections.

To many suffrists, this state-by-state approach seemed slow and uncertain. They wanted a decisive victory—a constitutional amendment that would force all states to allow qualified women to vote. Finally, in 1919, Congress proposed the Nineteenth Amendment. Opposition to granting voting rights to women was intertwined with opposition to granting voting rights to African Americans. Many southerners opposed the amendment because it gave Congress enforcement power, which might bring federal officials to investigate elections to ensure that the amendment was being obeyed—an interference that might call attention to how blacks were being kept from voting.

With the ratification of the Nineteenth Amendment in 1920, women won the right to vote, but they were still denied equal pay and equal rights, and they suffered numerous legal disabilities imposed by both national and state laws. In the 1970s and 1980s, the unsuccessful struggle to secure the adoption of the Equal Rights Amendment occupied much of the attention of the women's movement. But there are now other goals, and the political clout of women is mobilized behind issues that range from equal pay to world peace, sexual harassment, abortion rights, and election to office.[12]

Since the late 1980s, the Supreme Court has been reluctant to expand the Fourteenth Amendment's protection against gender discrimination, though it did hold that Virginia could not create a separate military academy for women instead of admitting them into the all-male Virginia Military Institute, a 150-year-old state-run institution.[13]

The courts, however, have increasingly enforced the prohibition against sex discrimination in the 1964 Civil Rights Act and expanded it to forbid sexual harassment in the workplace. Ironically, that prohibition was put into the act in an effort by members of the House of Representatives to defeat passage of the legislation, which aimed primarily at ending racial discrimination.[14] As a result, it was initially not taken very seriously, and not until the 1980s did it apply to "quid pro quo" sexual harassment, in which an employer makes a person provide sexual favors as a condition of employment (in

women's suffrage
The right of women to vote.

hiring, promotions, and firing).[15] Sexual harassment was then brought to national attention in 1991 by accusations made against Justice Clarence Thomas by Anita Hill, a law professor and former colleague, at the time of his Senate confirmation. Subsequently, the Supreme Court ruled that the law also applies to situations in which employees experience discrimination because they are forced to work in a "hostile environment." A hostile environment is defined as a workplace "permeated" with intimidation, ridicule, and insult that is severe and pervasive, and this includes same-sex harassment.[16]

Some women still complain of a "glass ceiling" in large corporations, preventing their advancement. But there is no denying that major progress has been made, with more and more women going to college and professional schools and into the media and business. Indeed, during the past three decades, the percentage of women graduating from colleges and universities has outpaced that of men (see Figure 17–1).

Hispanics

The struggle for civil rights has not been limited to women and African Americans. Each new wave of immigrants has been considered suspect by those who arrived earlier—all the more so if its members were not white or English-speaking. Formal barriers of law and informal barriers of custom combined to deny equal rights. But as groups established themselves—first economically and then politically—most of these barriers were swept away, and constitutionally guaranteed rights were asserted.

As we discussed in Chapter 5, most Hispanics—many of whose ancestors have been Americans for generations—are bilingual, speaking English as well as Spanish. However, because English may not be their first language, it has been difficult for some Hispanics to establish themselves educationally or to advance into the ranks of executives and professionals. Although not as visible as African Americans, Hispanics have suffered the same kinds of discrimination in employment, education, and accommodations.

Hispanic political clout has been unrealized because of internal political differences and because many Hispanics are not citizens or registered to vote. However, after California adopted Proposition 187 in 1994, which denied medical, educational, and social services to illegal immigrants, and Congress amended the federal welfare laws to curtail benefits to noncitizens, many immigrants rushed to become naturalized. Half of all Hispanic Americans live in two states: in 2001, California became the first big state in which whites are in the minority; Texas, the second most populous state, became the second majority-minority state in 2004.[17]

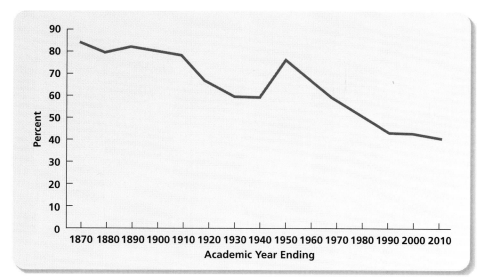

FIGURE 17–1 Percentage of Bachelor's Degrees Awarded to Men.
*Percentage for 2010 is projected by the Pell Institute for the Study of Opportunity in Higher Education, National Center for Education Statistics.
SOURCE: Michael A. Fletcher, "Degrees of Separation," *The Washington Post*, June 25, 2002, p. A1.

Asian Americans

The term "Asian American" describes approximately 10 million individuals from many different countries and many different ethnic backgrounds. Most do not think of themselves as Asians but as Americans of Chinese, Japanese, Indian, Vietnamese, Cambodian, Korean, or other specific ancestry. They live chiefly in the western states, but their number has been increasing rapidly in New York and Texas.

Although Asian Americans are often considered a "model minority" because of their general success in education and business, the U.S. Civil Rights Commission found that "Asian-Americans do face widespread prejudice, discrimination and barriers to equal opportunity" and that racially motivated violence against them "occurs with disturbing frequency."[18]

CHINESE AMERICANS The Chinese were the first Asians to come to the United States. Beginning in 1847, when young male peasants came here to get away from poverty and to work in mines, on railroads, and on farms, the Chinese encountered economic and cultural fears of the white majority, who did not understand them or their culture. In response, the Chinese seldom tried to assimilate but instead gravitated to "Chinatowns." Discriminatory immigration and naturalization restrictions, imposed beginning in 1882, were strengthened in later years and were not removed until the end of World War II.

Since that time, the Chinese have moved into the mainstream of American society, and they are beginning to run for and win local political offices. Gary Locke, a Democrat and a graduate of Yale and Boston University Law School, was elected in 1996 and re-elected in 2000 governor of Washington, the first Chinese American to become governor of a continental state.

JAPANESE AMERICANS The Japanese first migrated to Hawaii in the 1860s and then to California in the 1880s. Most Japanese immigrants remained in the West Coast states. By the beginning of the twentieth century, they faced overt hostility. In 1905, labor leaders organized the Japanese and Korean Exclusion League, and in 1906, the San Francisco Board of Education excluded all Chinese, Japanese, and Korean children from neighborhood schools. Some western states passed laws denying the right to own land to aliens who were ineligible to become citizens—meaning aliens of Asian ancestry.

During World War II, anti-Japanese hysteria provoked the internment of West Coast Japanese—most of whom were loyal American citizens guilty of no crimes—in prison camps in California, Colorado, and some other states. During this time, the property of

In the war hysteria following the outbreak of World War II, Japanese Americans were rounded up and transported to internment camps.

Japanese Americans was often sold at confiscatory rates, and many lost their businesses, jobs, and incomes. Following the war, the exclusionary acts were repealed. In 1988, President Ronald Reagan signed a law providing $20,000 restitution to each of the approximately 60,000 surviving World War II internees.

OTHER ASIAN AMERICANS Like other Asian Americans, Koreans faced overt discrimination in jobs and housing, but a Korean middle class has been growing, with many Korean Americans becoming teachers, doctors, and lawyers. Others operate small family businesses such as dry cleaners, florist shops, service stations, and small grocery stores, often in inner cities.[19]

When Filipinos first came to the United States in the early part of the twentieth century, they were considered American nationals because the Philippine Islands were an American possession. Nonetheless, they were denied rights to full citizenship and faced discrimination and even violence, including anti-Filipino riots in the state of Washington in 1928 and later in California, where nearly one-third of the over 1.5 million Filipinos live.[20] Their economic status has improved, but their influence in politics remains as small as their numbers.

The newest Asian arrivals consist of more than a million refugees from Vietnam, Laos, and Cambodia, who first came to the United States in 1975 and settled mostly in California. Although this group included middle-class people who left during the fall of Saigon following the end of the Vietnam War, it also consisted of large numbers of "boat people" who came to our shores without any financial resources. In a relatively short time, most established themselves economically. Although they are starting to have political influence, some remain socially and economically segregated.

Native Americans

Almost half of the more than 2 million Native Americans live on or near a *reservation*—a tract of land given to the tribal nations by treaty—and are enrolled as members of one of the 550 federally recognized tribes, including 226 groups in Alaska.[21] About 200 different Native American languages are spoken.

Native Americans speak of their tribes as "nations," yet they are not possessed of the full attributes of sovereignty. Rather, they are a separate people with power to regulate their own internal affairs, subject to congressional supervision. States are precluded from regulating or taxing the tribes or extending the jurisdiction of their courts over the tribes unless authorized to do so by Congress.[22] In recent years, Congress has stepped in to mediate growing tensions between Indian tribes who have used their sovereignty over reservations to operate gambling casinos and the states in which these reservations are located.

By acts of Congress, Native Americans are citizens of the United States and of the states in which they live. They have the right to vote. Native Americans living off reservations and working in the general community pay taxes just like everybody else; off reservations they have the same rights as any other Americans. If they are enrolled members of a recognized tribe, they are entitled to certain benefits created by law and by treaty. The Bureau of Indian Affairs of the Department of the Interior administers these benefits.

During the period of assimilation that began in 1887 and lasted until 1934, tribal governments were weak, some reservations were dissolved, and more than 100 tribes had their relationship with the federal government severed.[23] The civil rights movement of the 1960s created a more favorable climate for the concerns of Native Americans. Their goals were to reassert treaty rights and secure greater autonomy for the tribes. Under the leadership of the Native American Rights Fund (NARF), more Indian law cases were brought in the past several decades than at any time in our history.[24]

As a result of the efforts of Native American leaders and a greater national consciousness of the concerns of minorities, most Americans are now aware that many Native Americans live in poverty. Native Americans "are in far worse health than the rest of the population, dying earlier and suffering disproportionately from alcoholism, accidents, diabetes, and pneumonia."[25] Although in recent years the rest of the United States has enjoyed about 4 percent unemployment, many reservations continue to experience 50 to 60 percent unemployment. Some reservations lack adequate health care facilities,

MAJOR CIVIL RIGHTS LAWS

- **Civil Rights Act, 1957** Makes it a federal crime to prevent persons from voting in federal elections.
- **Civil Rights Act, 1964** Bars discrimination in employment or in public accommodations on the basis of race, color, religion, sex, or national origin; created the Equal Employment Opportunity Commission.
- **Voting Rights Act, 1965** Authorizes the appointment of federal examiners to register voters in areas that have been discriminating.
- **Age Discrimination in Employment Act, 1967** Prohibits job discrimination against workers or job applicants aged 40 through 65 and prohibits mandatory retirement.
- **Fair Housing Act, 1968** Prohibits discrimination on the basis of race, color, religion, or national origin in the sale or rental of most housing.
- **Title IX, Education Amendment of 1972** Prohibits discrimination on the basis of sex in any education program receiving federal financial assistance.
- **Rehabilitation Act, 1973** Requires that recipients of federal grants greater than $2,500 hire and promote qualified handicapped individuals.
- **Fair Housing Act Amendments, 1988** Gave the Department of Housing and Urban Development authority to prohibit housing bias against the handicapped and families with children.
- **Americans with Disabilities Act, 1991** Prohibits discrimination based on disability and requires that facilities be made accessible to those with disabilities.
- **Civil Rights Act, 1991** Requires that employers justify practices that negatively affect women and minorities as job-related or show that no alternative practices would have a lesser impact. Also established a commission to examine the "glass ceiling" that keeps women from becoming executives and make recommendations on how to increase promotion of women and minorities to management positions.

CHANGING FACE OF AMERICAN POLITICS

RACIAL AND ETHNIC IDENTIFICATION

Since 1860, the U.S. census has changed its classifications of race and ethnicity in light of the nation's growing diversity and political developments. The classifications have changed several times and continue to provoke controversy. The classification "Hispanic," for example, was picked by an ad hoc government committee over "Latino" in 1975 to identify Spanish-speaking and Spanish-surnamed individuals. The term was chosen because it connotes the cultural diasporas of centuries-old conquests by Spain. But some prefer "Latino" because it refers to the Latin-based Romance languages of

1860	1870	1880	1890	1900	1910	1920	1930	1940	1950
White	White	White	White	White	White	White	White	White	White
Black	Black	Black	Black	Black	Black	Black	Black	Black	Negro
Mulatto	Mulatto	Mulatto	Mulatto		Mulatto	Mulatto			
	Chinese	Chinese	Chinese	Chinese	Chinese	Chinese	Chinese	Chinese	Chinese
	Indian	Indian	Indian	Indian	Indian	Indian	Indian	Indian	American Indian
			Quadroon						
			Octoroon						
			Japanese	Japanese	Japanese	Japanese	Japanese	Japanese	Japanese
						Filipino	Filipino	Filipino	Filipino
						Hindu	Hindu	Hindu	
						Korean	Korean	Korean	
							Mexican		
					Other	**Other**	**Other**	**Other**	**Other**

Tiger Woods, the prize-winning golfer, is proud of his diverse heritage. He is both African American and Asian (Thai). He feels that ethnic background should not make a difference. It doesn't to him. As Woods says, "I am an American and proud of it."

equal protection clause
Clause in the Fourteenth Amendment that forbids any state to deny to any person within its jurisdiction the equal protection of the laws. By interpretation, the Fifth Amendment imposes the same limitation on the national government. This clause is the major constitutional restraint on the power of governments to discriminate against persons because of race, national origin, or sex.

educational opportunities, decent housing, and jobs. Congress has started to compensate Native Americans for past injustices and to provide more opportunities for the development of tribal economic independence, and judges are showing greater vigilance in the enforcement of Indian treaty rights.

In 1986, Ben Nighthorse Campbell became the first Native American to be elected to Congress. He was elected as a Democrat from Colorado but became a Republican after being elected to the Senate in 1992, and then was reelected in 1998; he retired in 2005.

Spain, France, Italy, and Portugal, as well as Portuguese-speaking Brazilians. In recent years "Latino" has become a more popular term, but many still prefer "Hispanic" because it connotes a history of imperialism and does not include the French and Italians.*

Below are the categories used in the decennial counts from 1860 to 2000. Each new category is boldfaced at its first inclusion. For more information, see AmeriStat's Web site, at www.ameristat.org.

1960	1970	1980	1990	2000
White	**White**	**White**	**White**	**White**
Negro	**Negro/Black**	**Black/Negro**	**Black/Negro**	**Black/African American/Negro**
Chinese	Chinese	Chinese	Chinese	Chinese
American Indian	American Indian	Indian	Indian	American Indian or Alaska Native
Japanese	Japanese	Japanese	Japanese	Japanese
Filipino	Filipino	Filipino	Filipino	Filipino
		Asian Indian	Asian Indian	Asian Indian
	Korean	Korean	Korean	Korean
Aleut		Aleut	Aleut	
Eskimo		Eskimo	Eskimo	
Hawaiian	Hawaiian	Hawaiian	Hawaiian	Native Hawaiian
Part Hawaiian				
		Vietnamese	Vietnamese	Vietnamese
		Guamanian	Guamanian	Guamanian or Chamorro
		Samoan	Samoan	Samoan
			Other Asian	**Other Asian**
			Pacific Islander	**Pacific Islander**
Other	**Other**	**Other**	**Other race**	**Some other race**
E T H N I C I T Y	Mexican	Mexican American	Mexican/Mexican American	Mexican/Mexican American
		Chicano	Chicano	Chicano
	Puerto Rican	Puerto Rican	Puerto Rican	Puerto Rican
	Central/South American			
	Cuban	Cuban	Cuban	Cuban
	Other Spanish	Other Spanish/Hispanic	Other Spanish/Hispanic	Other Spanish/Hispanic/Latino
	(None of these)	Not Spanish/Hispanic	Not Spanish/Hispanic	Not Spanish/Hispanic/Latino

* Darryl Fears, "The Roots of 'Hispanic'," *The Washington Post*, October 15, 2003, p. A21.

EQUAL PROTECTION OF THE LAWS: WHAT DOES IT MEAN?

The **equal protection clause** of the Fourteenth Amendment declares that no state (including any subdivision thereof) shall "deny to any person within its jurisdiction the equal protection of the laws." Although there is no parallel clause explicitly limiting the national government, the Fifth Amendment's **due process clause**, which states that no person shall "be deprived of life, liberty, or property, without due process of law," has

due process clause
Clause in the Fifth Amendment limiting the power of the national government; similar clause in the Fourteenth Amendment prohibiting state governments from depriving any person of life, liberty, or property without due process of law.

been interpreted to impose the same restraints on the national government as the equal protection clause imposes on the states.

The equal protection clause applies only to the actions of *governments,* not to those of private individuals. If a discriminatory action is performed by a private person, it does not violate the Constitution, although it may violate federal and state laws. The equal protection clause does not, however, prevent governments from creating various classifications of people in its laws. What the Constitution forbids is *unreasonable* classifications. In general, a classification is unreasonable when there is no relation between the classes it creates and permissible governmental goals. A law prohibiting redheads from voting, for example, would be unreasonable. In contrast, laws denying persons under 18 the right to vote, to marry without the permission of their parents, or to apply for a license to drive a car appear to be reasonable (at least to most persons over 18).

Constitutional Classifications and Tests

One of the most troublesome constitutional questions is how to distinguish between constitutional and unconstitutional classifications. The Supreme Court uses three tests for this purpose: the *rational basis* test, the *strict scrutiny* test, and the *heightened scrutiny* test.

THE RATIONAL BASIS TEST   The traditional test to determine whether a law complies with the equal protection requirement places the burden of proof on the parties attacking the law. They must show that the law has no rational or legitimate governmental goals. Traditionally the rational basis test applied only to legislation affecting economic interests and, with two exceptions in the last 70 years,[26] the Court upheld the legislation and deferred to legislative judgments. But recently the Court has applied the test to challenges to legislation affecting noneconomic interests.[27] Notably, in *Roemer* v. *Evans* (1996) the Court struck down an amendment to Colorado's constitution that barred local governments from adopting laws that forbid discrimination against homosexuals.[28] The Court held that the law lacked a rational basis and was based on animus and bias against gays and lesbians.

GLOBAL *Perceptions*

QUESTION: Do you agree that "homosexuality is a way of life that should be accepted by society"?

Public perceptions of homosexuals vary widely around the world. In the United States a bare majority (51%) think homosexuality should be accepted, a smaller percentage than in Canada (69%) and West European countries, such as Germany (83%), France (77%), Great Britain (74%), and Italy (74%). The lowest public acceptance appears in African countries, with the exception of South Africa (33%); and in Middle Eastern countries; as well as most Asian countries, with the exception of Japan (54%) and the Philippines (64%).

SOURCE: The Pew Global Attitudes Project, 2003, p. T-65.

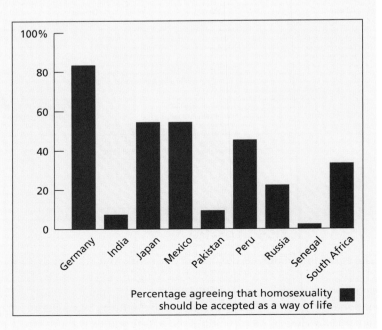

Percentage agreeing that homosexuality should be accepted as a way of life

SUSPECT CLASSIFICATIONS AND STRICT SCRUTINY   When a law is subject to strict scrutiny, the courts must be persuaded that there is both a "compelling governmental interest" to justify such a classification and no less restrictive way to accomplish this compelling purpose. The Court applies the strict scrutiny test to suspect classifications. A *suspect classification* is a class of people deliberately subjected to such unequal treatment in the past or relegated by society to a position of such political powerlessness as to require extraordinary judicial protection.[29]

Classifications based on race or national origin are always suspect. It does not make any difference if the laws are designed for supposedly benign purposes—that is, to help persons of a particular race or national origin. For example, the Supreme Court has held that laws that give preference for public employment based on race are subject to strict scrutiny.

QUASI-SUSPECT CLASSIFICATIONS AND HEIGHTENED SCRUTINY   To sustain a law under this test, the burden is on the government to show that its classification serves "important governmental objectives." Classifications based on gender are subject to heightened scrutiny. Not until 1971 was any classification based on gender declared unconstitutional. Before that time, many laws provided special protection for women—such as a Michigan law forbidding any woman other than the wife or daughter of a tavern owner to serve as a barmaid. As Justice William J. Brennan Jr. wrote for the Court, "There can be no doubt that our nation has had a long and unfortunate history of sex discrimination. Traditionally such discrimination was rationalized by an attitude of 'romantic paternalism' which in practical effect put women, not on a pedestal, but in a cage."[30]

Today the Court's view is that treating women differently from men (or vice versa) is forbidden when supported by no more substantial justification than "the role-typing society has long imposed upon women."[31] If the government's objective is "to protect members of one sex because they are presumed to suffer from an inherent handicap or to be innately inferior," that objective is illegitimate, and the government must have "an exceedingly persuasive justification" for discriminating between men and women.[32] In recent years, the Supreme Court has struck down most laws brought before it that were

IN COMPARATIVE PERSPECTIVE

CANADIAN COURTS FORBID DISCRIMINATION AGAINST HOMOSEXUALS

Within months of the Massachusetts state supreme court's ruling that its state constitution forbids discrimination against same-sex marriages and the U.S. Supreme Court's decision striking down laws making homosexual sodomy a crime,[*] the Ontario High Court ruled that the government had to recognize same-sex marriages. In doing so the court extended a series of rulings barring discrimination against homosexuals in Canada.

The Supreme Court of Canada in 1995 held that sexual orientation was embraced by the equality guarantee of Section 15(1) of Canada's Charter of Rights and Freedom, which provides: "Every individual is equal before and under the law and has the right to the equal protection and equal benefit of the law without discrimination and, in particular, without discrimination based on race, national or ethnic origin, colour, religion, sex, age or mental or physical disability."[†]

Subsequent decisions further expanded protection for gays and lesbians in holding, for example, that they may not be discriminated against in employment.[‡] On the basis of those rulings, courts in Quebec and British Columbia invalidated prohibitions against same-sex marriages. And in *Halpern* v. *Attorney General of Canada* (2003), the Court of Appeal for Ontario held that Canada's Charter of Rights and Freedoms bars discrimination against same-sex marriages. The high court rejected the government's arguments that it had compelling interests in barring same-sex marriages. Specifically, the court ruled that interests in uniting the opposite sexes, encouraging the birth and rearing of children of the marriage, and promoting companionship, were not compelling justifications for discrimination against homosexuals and same-sex marriages.

The full text of the opinion in *Halpern* v. *Attorney General of Canada* is available on the Web site of the Court of Appeal of Ontario at www.ontariocourts.on.ca/decisions.

[*]*Lawrence* v. *Texas*, 539 U.S. 558 (2003).
[†]*Egan* v. *Canada*, 2 S.C.R. 513 (1995).
[‡]*Vriend* v. *Albert*, 1 S.C.R. 493 (1998); and *M.* v. *H.*, 2 S.C.R. 3 (1999).

alleged to discriminate against women but has tended to do so on the basis of federal statutes like the 1964 Civil Rights Act.

POVERTY AND AGE   Just as racial minorities and women are entitled to special constitutional protection, it is argued, so should the poor and the elderly be protected. But the Supreme Court rejected the argument "that financial need alone identifies a suspect class for purposes of equal protection analysis."[33] However, state supreme courts in Texas, Ohio, and elsewhere have ruled that unequal funding for public schools as a result of "rich" districts spending more per pupil than "poor" districts violates their state constitutional provisions for free and equal education.[34]

Age is not a suspect class. Many laws commonly make distinctions based on age: to obtain a driver's license, to marry without parental consent, to attend schools, to buy alcohol, and so on. Many governmental institutions have age-specific programs: for senior citizens, for adult students, for midcareer persons. The Supreme Court has repeatedly refused to make age a suspect classification requiring extra judicial protection. As Justice Sandra Day O'Connor observed, "States may discriminate on the basis of age without offending the Fourteenth Amendment if the age classification in question is rationally related to a legitimate state interest."[35]

Congress, however, responding to "gray power," frequently treats age as a protected category. Congress has made it illegal for most employers to discriminate on the basis of advancing age. Except for a few exempt occupations, employers may not impose mandatory retirement requirements. Congress also attempted to extend the protections against age discrimination to cover state employees, but the Supreme Court ruled that Congress lacks the constitutional authority to open the federal courts to suits by state employees for alleged age discrimination. State employees are limited to recovering monetary damages under state laws in state courts.[36]

FUNDAMENTAL RIGHTS AND STRICT SCRUTINY   The Court also strictly scrutinizes laws impinging on *fundamental rights*. What makes a right fundamental in the constitutional sense? It is not the importance or the significance of the right that makes it fundamental but whether it is explicitly or implicitly *guaranteed by the Constitution*. Under this test, the rights to travel and to vote have been held to be fundamental, as well as First Amendment rights such as the right to associate for the advancement of political beliefs. Rights to an education, to housing, or to welfare benefits have not been deemed fundamental.

There is a continuing legal debate on whether or not schools in poorer districts deny the right to equal education because these districts are not able to fund their public schools as successfully as wealthier districts.

Important as these rights may be, there are no constitutional provisions specifically protecting them from governmental regulation.

Proving Discrimination

Does the fact that a law or a regulation has a differential effect—what has come to be known as *disparate impact*—on persons of a different race or sex by itself establish that the law is unconstitutional? In one of its most important decisions, *Washington* v. *Davis* (1976), the Supreme Court said no.[37] "An unwavering line of cases" from the Supreme Court "hold that a violation of the Equal Protection Clause requires state action motivated by discriminatory intent; the disproportionate effects of state action are not sufficient to establish such a violation."[38] Or, as the Court said in another case, "the Fourteenth Amendment guarantees equal laws, not equal results."[39]

What do these rulings on disparate impact mean in practical terms? They mean, for example, that even when city ordinances permit only single-family residences and thus make low-cost housing projects impossible, they are not unconstitutional—even if their effect is to keep minorities from moving into the city—unless it can be shown that they were adopted with the *intent* to discriminate against minorities. For another example, preference for veterans in public employment does not violate the equal protection clause, even though its effect is to keep many women from getting jobs; the distinction between veterans and nonveterans was not adopted deliberately to create a sex barrier.

What is constitutional can nonetheless be illegal. For example, state laws creating legislative districts with no intent to discriminate against African Americans that in effect dilute their voting power are not unconstitutional. But in the Voting Rights Act of 1965, Congress made such laws illegal if the result is to dilute the voting power of African Americans, regardless of the laws' intent. The Voting Rights Act of 1965 tests the legality of state voting laws and practices by their *effects* rather than by the *intentions* of the legislatures that passed them.

VOTING RIGHTS

Under our Constitution, it is the states, not the federal government, that regulate elections and voting qualifications. However, Article I, Section 4, gives Congress the power to supersede state regulations as to the "Times, Places and Manner" of elections for representatives and senators. Congress has used this authority, along with its authority under Article II, Section 2, to set the date for selection of electors, to set age qualifications and residency requirements to vote in national elections, to establish a uniform day for all states to hold elections for members of Congress and presidential electors, and to give American citizens who reside outside the United States the right to vote for members of Congress and presidential electors in the states in which they previously lived.

Limitations on the states' power to set voting qualifications are contained in the Fourteenth Amendment (forbidding qualifications that have no reasonable relation to the ability to vote), the Fifteenth Amendment (forbidding qualifications based on race), the Nineteenth Amendment (forbidding qualifications based on sex), and the Twenty-Sixth Amendment (forbidding states to deny citizens 18 years of age or older the right to vote on account of age). These amendments also empower Congress to enact the laws necessary to enforce their provisions.

Protecting Voting Rights

In the 1940s, the Supreme Court began to strike down one after another of the devices that had been used to keep African Americans from voting. In the one-party South of the early decades of the twentieth century, the Democratic party would hold whites-only primaries, effectively disenfranchising black voters. In *Smith* v. *Allwright* (1944), the Court declared the **white primary** unconstitutional.[40] In 1960, the Court held that **racial gerrymandering**—the drawing of election districts to ensure that African Americans would be a minority in all districts—was contrary to the Fifteenth Amendment.[41] In 1964, the

white primary
Primary operated by the Democratic party in southern states that, before Republicans gained strength in the "one-party South," essentially constituted an election; ruled unconstitutional in *Smith* v. *Allwright* (1944).

racial gerrymandering
The drawing of election districts so as to ensure that members of a certain race are a minority in the district; ruled unconstitutional in *Gomillion* v. *Lightfoot* (1960).

Twenty-Fourth Amendment eliminated the **poll tax**—payment required as a condition for voting—in presidential and congressional elections. In 1966, the Court held that the Fourteenth Amendment forbade the poll tax as a condition in any election.[42]

Officials seeking to deny African Americans the right to vote were forced to rely on registration requirements. On the surface, such requirements appeared to be perfectly proper, but it was the way they were administered that kept blacks from the polls. White election officers confronted African Americans trying to register while white police stood guard; white judges heard appeals of decisions made by registration officials. Officials often seized on the smallest error on an application form as an excuse to disqualify a black voter. In one parish in Louisiana, after four white voters challenged the registration of some black voters on the grounds that those voters had made an "error in spilling" [*sic*] in their applications, registration officials struck 1,300 out of approximately 1,500 black voters from the rolls.[43]

In many southern areas, **literacy tests** were used to discriminate against African Americans. Some states required applicants to demonstrate that they understood the national and state constitutions and that they were persons of good character. Although poor whites often avoided registering out of fear of embarrassment from failing a literacy test, the tests were more often used to discriminate against African Americans.[44] Whites were often asked simple questions; blacks were asked questions that would baffle a Supreme Court justice. "In the 1960s southern registrars were observed testing black applicants on such matters as the number of bubbles in a soap bar, the news contained in a copy of the *Peking Daily,* the meaning of obscure passages in state constitutions, and the definition of terms such as *habeas corpus.*"[45] In Louisiana, 49,603 illiterate white voters were able to persuade election officials they could understand the Constitution, but only two illiterate black voters were able to do so.

The Voting Rights Act of 1965

For two decades after World War II, under the leadership of the Supreme Court, many limitations on voting were declared unconstitutional, but this approach still did not open the voting booth to African Americans. Finally Congress acted. The Civil Rights Act of 1964 had hardly become law when events in Selma, Alabama, dramatized the inadequacy of depending on the courts to prevent racial barriers in polling places. Led by Martin Luther King Jr., a voter registration drive in Selma sparked arrests, marches on the state capital, and the murder of two civil rights workers. Still there was no dent in the color bar at the polls. Responding to events in Selma, President Lyndon Johnson made a dramatic address to Congress and the nation calling for federal action to ensure that no person would be deprived of the right to vote in any election for any office because of color or race. Congress responded with the Voting Rights Act of 1965.

Section 2 of the Voting Rights Act prohibits voting qualifications or standards that result in a denial of the right of any citizen to vote on account of race and color. Section 5 requires that states with a history of denying African Americans or Hispanic citizens the right to vote must clear with the Department of Justice changes in voting practice or laws that might dilute the voting power of these groups.[46] What precisely constitutes "dilution" and how it is to be measured are the subject of much litigation. Examples include changes in the location of polling places, changes in candidacy requirements and qualifications, changes in filing deadlines, changes from ward to at-large elections, changes in boundary lines of voting districts, and changes that affect the creation or abolition of an elective office and imposition by state political parties of fees for delegates to nominating conventions.[47]

Following the 1990 census, the Department of Justice pressured southern state legislatures to draw as many districts as possible in which minorities would constitute a majority of the electorate. Most of these districts tended to be Democratic, leaving the other congressional districts in these states heavily white and Republican. The lower federal courts sustained the Department of Justice's interpretation. As a result, there was a considerable increase in the number of congressional districts represented by minorities and Republicans.

poll tax
Payment required as a condition for voting; prohibited for national elections by the Twenty-Fourth Amendment (1964) and ruled unconstitutional for all elections in *Harper* v. *Virginia Board of Elections* (1966).

literacy test
Literacy requirement imposed by some states as a condition of voting, generally used to disqualify blacks from voting in the South; now illegal.

The Supreme Court, however, in a series of cases beginning with *Shaw* v. *Reno* (1993), announced that although it was a legitimate goal for state legislatures to take race into account when they drew electoral districts in order to increase the voting strength of minorities, they could not make race the sole or predominant reason for drawing district lines. The Department of Justice, said the Supreme Court, was wrong in forcing states to create as many **majority-minority districts** as possible. A test case involved the North Carolina legislature's creation of a majority-minority district 160 miles long and in some places only an interstate highway wide. "If you drove down the interstate," said one legislator about this district, "with both car doors open, you'd kill most of the people in the district." North Carolina's reapportionment scheme, the Supreme Court declared, was so "irrational on its face that it can be understood only as an effort to segregate voters into separate voting districts because of their race." To comply with the Voting Rights Act, the Supreme Court explained, states must provide for districts roughly proportional to the minority voters' respective shares in the voting-age population.[48]

Since then the Court has expanded *Shaw* by clarifying that it was not meant to suggest that a "district must be bizarre on its face before there is a constitutional violation." Legislatures may take racial considerations into account when they draw district lines, but when race becomes the overriding motive, the state violates the equal protection clause.[49] Even though many southern states had to redraw legislative districts, when African American incumbents ran in the newly drawn districts, with majority white electors, they were reelected.[50]

Problems with voting irregularities remain. After the 2000 presidential election, some black voters in several counties in Florida complained that they were discouraged from voting or that their votes were not counted. Also, in some states, like Florida, felons are denied the right to vote but in not in other states. In the 2004 presidential election, both parties, as well as international observers, monitored and contested processes for violations of voting procedures.

EDUCATION RIGHTS

Until the Supreme Court struck down such laws in the 1950s, southern states had made it illegal for whites and blacks to ride in the same train cars, attend the same theaters, go to the same schools, be born in the same hospitals, or be buried in the same cemeteries. **Jim Crow laws**, as they came to be called, blanketed southern life. How could these laws stand in the face of the equal protection clause? This was the question raised in *Plessy* v. *Ferguson* (1896).

In the *Plessy* decision, the Supreme Court endorsed the view that governmentally imposed racial segregation in public transportation, and presumably in public education, did not necessarily constitute discrimination if "equal" accommodations were provided for the members of both races.[51] But the "equal" part of the formula was meaningless. African Americans were segregated in unequal facilities and lacked the political power to protest effectively. The passage of time did not lessen the inequalities. Beginning in the late 1930s, African Americans started to file lawsuits challenging the doctrine. They cited facts to show that in practice "separate but equal" was not equal and always resulted in discrimination against African Americans.

The End of "Separate but Equal": *Brown* v. *Board of Education*

At first, the Supreme Court was not willing to upset the separate but equal doctrine, but in *Brown* v. *Board of Education of Topeka* (1954), the Court finally reversed the *Plessy* doctrine as it applied to public schools by holding that "separate but equal" is a contradiction in terms. *Segregation is itself discrimination.*[52] A year later, the Court ordered school boards to proceed with "all deliberate speed to desegregate public schools at the earliest practical date."[53]

But many school districts moved very slowly, and in the 1960s, Congress and the president joined even more directly in the battle against school segregation. Title VI of the Civil Rights Act of 1964, as subsequently amended, stipulated that federal dollars under any

majority-minority district
A congressional district created to include a majority of minority voters; ruled constitutional so long as race is not the main factor in redistricting.

Jim Crow laws
State laws formerly pervasive throughout the South requiring public facilities and accommodations to be segregated by race; ruled unconstitutional.

Thurgood Marshall (center), George C.E. Hayes (left), and James Nabrit Jr. (right) argued and won Brown v. Board of Education of Topeka *before the Supreme Court in 1954.*

grant program or project must be withdrawn from an entire school or institution of higher education that discriminates "on the ground of race, color, or national origin," gender, age, or disability, in "any program or activity receiving federal financial assistance."

From Segregation to Desegregation—but Not Yet Integration

School districts that had operated two kinds of schools, one for whites and one for blacks, now had an obligation to develop plans and programs to move from segregation to integration. For such school districts, desegregation would not be enough; they would have a duty to bring about integration. If they failed to do so on their own initiative, federal judges would supervise the school districts to ensure that they were doing what was necessary and proper to overcome the evils of segregation.

But since most whites and most African Americans continued to live in separate neighborhoods, merely removing legal barriers to school integration did not by itself integrate the schools. To overcome this residential clustering by race, some federal courts mandated busing across neighborhoods, moving white students to once predominantly black schools and vice versa. Busing students was not popular and triggered protests in many cities.

The Supreme Court sustained busing only if it was to remedy the consequences of *officially* sanctioned segregation, **de jure segregation**. The Court refused to permit federal judges to order busing to overcome the effects of **de facto segregation**, segregation that arises as a result of social and economic conditions such as housing patterns.

Following *Brown* v. *Board of Education,* the federal government intervened in more than 500 school desegregation cases. As a result, many southern cities now have more integrated schools than large northern cities do. However, in both North and South, many school districts in central cities today are predominantly African American or

de jure segregation
Segregation imposed by law.

de facto segregation
Segregation resulting from economic or social conditions or personal choice.

Hispanic. This segregated pattern of schools is partly the result of "white flight" to the suburbs in the 1970s and 1980s and the transfer of white students to private schools to escape court-ordered busing. In more recent years, it is also due to higher birthrates and immigration among African Americans and Hispanics.

After a period of vigorous federal court supervision of school desegregation programs, the Supreme Court in the 1990s restricted the role of federal judges.[54] It instructed some of them to restore control of a school system to the state and local authorities and to release districts from any busing obligations once a judge concludes that the authorities "have done everything practicable to overcome the past consequences of segregation."[55]

Political support for busing and for other efforts to integrate the schools also faded.[56] Many school districts eliminated mandatory busing, with the result that *Brown*'s era of court-ordered desegregation drew to a close. The percentage of southern blacks attending white-majority schools fell from over 40 percent to 30 percent, or about the level in 1969.[57] Some African American leaders, while still supporting desegregation efforts, are now more concerned about improving the quality of inner-city schools than desegregating them. They are turning to state courts and state constitutions, which mandate equal public education, in order to force increases in public school financing and to make adequate educational resources available to all on equal terms.[58]

RIGHTS OF ASSOCIATION, ACCOMMODATIONS, JOBS, AND HOMES

Association

As we have noted, the Fifth and Fourteenth Amendments apply only to governmental action, not to private discriminatory conduct. As Justice William O. Douglas said, our Constitution creates "a zone of privacy which precludes government from interfering

Residents of the Charlestown section of Boston took part in a "March Against Forced Busing" in May 1976.

with private clubs or groups. The associational rights which our system honors permit all-white, all-black, all-brown, and all-yellow clubs to be established. They also permit all-Catholic, all-Jewish, or all-agnostic clubs.... Government may not tell a man or a woman who his or her associates must be. The individual may be as selective as he desires."[59]

Families, churches, or private groups organized for political, religious, cultural, or social purposes are constitutionally different from large associations organized along other lines. For example, the Supreme Court has upheld the application of laws forbidding sex or racial discrimination by organizations such as the Jaycees, the Rotary Club, and large (in this case, more than 400 members) private eating clubs. Such associations and clubs are not small, intimate groups. Nor were they able to demonstrate that allowing women or minorities to become members would change the content or impact of their purposes.[60] In *Boy Scouts of America* v. *Dale* (2000), however, the Court held that the Boy Scouts may exclude homosexuals because it is a private association and because of its overall mission.[61]

Accommodations

In 1883, the Supreme Court had declared unconstitutional an act of Congress that made it a federal offense for any operator of a public conveyance, hotel, or theater to deny accommodations to any person because of race or color on the grounds that the Fourteenth Amendment does not give Congress such authority.[62] Since the 1960s, however, the constitutional authority of Congress to legislate against discrimination by private individuals is no longer an issue because the Court has broadly construed the **commerce clause**—which gives Congress the power to regulate interstate and foreign commerce—to justify action against discriminatory conduct by individuals. Congress has also used its power to tax and spend to prevent not only racial discrimination but also discrimination based on ethnic origin, sex, disability, and age.

TITLE II: PLACES OF PUBLIC ACCOMMODATION For the first time since Reconstruction, the Civil Rights Act of 1964 authorized the massive use of federal authority to combat privately imposed racial discrimination. Title II makes it a federal offense to discriminate against any customer or patron in a place of public accommodation because of race, color, religion, or national origin. It applies to any inn, hotel, motel, or lodging establishment (except establishments with fewer than five rooms and occupied by the proprietor—in other words, small boardinghouses); to any restaurant or gasoline station that serves interstate travelers or serves food or products that have moved in interstate commerce; and to any movie house, theater, concert hall, sports arena, or other place of entertainment that customarily hosts films, performances, athletic teams, or other sources of entertainment that are moved in interstate commerce. Within a few months after its adoption, the Supreme Court sustained the constitutionality of Title II.[63] As a result, public establishments, including those in the South, opened their doors to all customers.

TITLE VII: EMPLOYMENT Title VII of the 1964 Civil Rights Act made it illegal for any employer or trade union in any industry affecting interstate commerce and employing 15 or more people (and, since 1972, any state or local agency such as a school or university) to discriminate in employment practices against any person because of race, color, national origin, religion, or sex. Employers have an obligation to create workplaces that avoid abusive environments. Related legislation made it illegal to discriminate against persons with physical handicaps, veterans, or persons over 40.

There are a few exceptions. Religious institutions such as parochial schools may use religious standards. Age, sex, or handicap may be considered where occupational qualifications are absolutely necessary to the normal operation of a particular business or enterprise—for example, hiring only women to work in women's locker rooms.

The Equal Employment Opportunity Commission (EEOC) was created to enforce Title VII. The commission works together with state authorities to try to bring about compliance with the act and may seek judicial enforcement of complaints against private employers. The attorney general prosecutes Title VII violations by public agencies. Not only do aggrieved persons have a right to sue for damages for themselves, but they can also do so for other persons similarly situated in a **class action suit**. The vigor with

commerce clause
The clause of the Constitution (Article I, Section 8, Clause 3) that gives Congress the power to regulate all business activities that cross state lines or affect more than one state or other nations.

class action suit
Lawsuit brought by an individual or a group of people on behalf of all those similarly situated.

which the EEOC and the attorney general have acted has varied over the years, depending on the commitment of the president in office and the willingness of Congress to provide an adequate budget for the EEOC.[64]

Title VII was supplemented by a 1965 presidential executive order requiring all contractors doing work for the federal government, including universities, to adopt and implement affirmative action programs to correct "underutilization" of women and minorities. Such programs may not establish racial or ethnic quotas for minorities or women, but they may require contractors to establish timetables and goals; to follow open recruitment procedures; to keep records of applicants by race, sex, and national origin; and to explain why their labor force does not reflect the same proportion of persons in the appropriate labor market pools. Failure of contractors to file and implement an approved affirmative action plan may lead to loss of federal contracts or grants.

THE FAIR HOUSING ACT AND AMENDMENTS   Housing is the last frontier of the civil rights crusade, the area in which progress is slowest and genuine change most remote.

> Segregated housing contributes mightily to a vicious circle that also includes educational and employment discrimination. . . . Because of poor schools for many minorities, they cannot find well-paying jobs. Without such jobs, they often cannot afford to live in nicer neighborhoods with decent housing. And because of their location in less desirable communities, good educational systems are less likely to be available.[65]

In 1948, the Supreme Court made racial or religious **restrictive covenants** (a provision in a deed to real property restricting its sale) legally unenforceable.[66] The 1968 Fair Housing Act forbids discrimination in housing, excluding from its protection what it called "Mrs. Murphy boardinghouses," housing owned by private individuals who own no more than three houses; dwellings that have no more than four separate living units in which the owner maintains a residence; and religious organizations and private clubs housing their own members on a noncommercial basis. For all other housing, the act forbids owners to refuse to sell or rent to any person because of race, color, religion, national origin, sex, or physical handicap or because a person has children. Discrimination in housing also covers efforts to deny loans to minorities.

The Department of Justice has filed hundreds of cases, especially those involving large apartment complexes, yet African Americans and Hispanics continue to face discrimination in housing. Some real estate agents continue to steer African Americans and Hispanics toward neighborhoods that are not predominantly white and to require larger rental deposits from minorities than from whites. Yet less than 1 percent of these discriminatory actions are complained about because they are so subtle that victims are often unaware that they are being discriminated against. However, the number of discrimination complaints received by the Department of Housing and Urban Development and local and state agencies has been increasing as the result of more aggressive enforcement.

Voluntary segregation obviously exists. "It's a fact of life that blacks like to live in black neighborhoods and whites like to live in white neighborhoods," according to Daniel Mitchell, who added, "Real estate agents generally like to bring customers to places they will like and where the agent can make a sale."[67] Whatever the reasons, housing segregation persists.

THE AFFIRMATIVE ACTION CONTROVERSY

When white majorities were using governmental power to discriminate against African Americans, civil rights advocates cited with approval the famous words of the first Justice John Marshall Harlan: "Our Constitution is color-blind and neither knows nor tolerates class among citizens."[68] But by the 1960s, there was a new set of constitutional and national policy debates. Many people began to assert that government neutrality is not enough. If governments, universities, and employers stopped discriminating but changed nothing else, individuals previously discriminated against would still be kept from equal participation in American life. Because they had been so disadvantaged by past discrimination,

restrictive covenant
A provision in a deed to real property prohibiting its sale to a person of a particular race or religion. Judicial enforcement of such deeds is unconstitutional.

they suffered disabilities not shared by white males in the competition for openings in medical schools, for skilled jobs, or for their share of government grants and contracts.

Remedies to overcome the consequences of past discrimination against African Americans, Hispanics, Native Americans, and women are known as *affirmative action* by supporters but as *reverse discrimination* by opponents. The Supreme Court's first major statement on the constitutionality of affirmative action programs came in a celebrated case relating to university admissions. Allan Bakke—a white male and a top student at Minnesota and Stanford universities, as well as a Vietnam War veteran—applied in 1973 and again in 1974 to the medical school of the University of California at Davis. In each of those years, the school admitted 100 new students, 84 in a general admissions program and 16 in a special admissions program created for minorities who had previously been underrepresented. Bakke's application was rejected each year while students with lower grade-point averages, test scores, and interview ratings were admitted under the special admissions program. After his second rejection, Bakke brought suit in federal court claiming he had been excluded because of his race, contrary to requirements of the Constitution and Title VI of the Civil Rights Act of 1964.

In *University of California Regents* v. *Bakke* (1978), the Supreme Court ruled the California plan unconstitutional.[69] The problem with the California plan was it created a *quota*—a set number of admissions from which whites were excluded solely because of race. But the Court also declared that affirmative action programs are not necessarily unconstitutional. A state university may properly take race and ethnic background into account as "a plus," as one of several factors in choosing students in order to achieve a diverse student body.

After *Bakke:* Refinements and Uncertainty

Following *Bakke,* the Court dealt with a variety of affirmative action programs in public and private employment, sustaining most but not all of them. As the justices continued to disagree on the application of the equal protection clause, opposition to such programs became more heated.

Many Americans believe that affirmative action is the best way to address the issue of past racial and ethnic quotas.

In *Richmond* v. *Croson* (1989), the Rehnquist Court struck down a regulation by the city of Richmond requiring nonminority city contractors to subcontract at least 30 percent of the dollar amount of their contracts to one or more minority business enterprises. Writing for the Court, Justice Sandra Day O'Connor called into question the validity of most government affirmative action plans and stated, "Race-sensitive remedial measures are to be justified only after a strong basis in evidence has established that remedial action is necessary to overcome the consequences of past discriminatory action."[70]

Since *Croson*, a bare majority of the Court has rejected the view that racial classifications, whether benign or hostile, should ever be subject to less than strict scrutiny by either the national or state and local governments.[71] And as we have noted, the Rehnquist Court is similarly opposed to the use of race as the sole criterion in the drawing of electoral district lines.[72] The only permissible programs in government employment and contracting are those that are narrowly tailored remedies for past discrimination.

California's Proposition 209 and Other Plans

In 1995, the Regents of the University of California voted to eliminate race or gender as factors in employment, purchasing, contracting, or admissions. The following year, Californians voted overwhelmingly for Proposition 209 to amend the state constitution to forbid state agencies—including schools, colleges, and universities—to discriminate against or grant preferential treatment to any individual or group on the basis of race, sex, color, ethnicity, or national origin in public employment, public education, or public contracting, except where necessary to comply with a federal requirement.

Although Proposition 209 clearly forbids universities and other state agencies to take race and gender into account, it did not make unconstitutional state-supported outreach programs designed to recruit more women and minorities to become scientists and engineers, nor does it prevent state universities from continuing outreach programs aimed at schools with large minority enrollments. Due to such outreach programs the percentage of students admitted to the University of California from "underrepresented groups"—African Americans, Native Americans, and Hispanics—gradually rebounded.[73] The University of California's board of regents also shifted policy to take into account the economic backgrounds and personal achievements, not just grades and SAT scores, of students applying for admission. As a result, the percentage of racial and ethnic minorities moved back to previous levels, though still low at Berkeley, where Asian Americans make up more than 40 percent of the student body.[74]

Opponents of affirmative action had hoped that the adoption of Proposition 209 in California would start a national movement to restrict or eliminate affirmative action programs, and some federal programs designed to give women- and minority-owned businesses greater access to federal contracts were cut back. Under pressure from the Office of Civil Rights, some universities stopped offering scholarships based solely on race or ethnicity. But Congress has not moved to limit other federal affirmative action programs.

California and six other states (Texas, Louisiana, Mississippi, Georgia, Florida, and Washington) abandoned affirmative action programs—some like California and Washington because of voter opposition and others like Texas and Georgia because federal courts held that they were unconstitutional.[75] They adopted the strategy of automatic admissions for a certain percentage of all high school graduates as a means of maintaining diversity in colleges and expanding educational opportunities for minorities. California offers admission to the top 4 percent of high school graduates, Texas offers admission to the top 10 percent, and Florida to the top 20 percent of every high school graduating class.

These programs, though, have been sharply criticized for taking students from poor inner-city and rural schools who are not prepared to compete effectively in college with students from wealthier and more advantaged school districts. Critics also complain that under the program some students from the top high schools are denied admission to state flagship universities. Texas Republican Governor Rick Perry and others argue that too many graduates of the most demanding high schools are leaving the state when they do not get into the University of Texas at Austin. In 2005, the Texas legislature will

★★ YOU DECIDE

Are affirmative action programs aimed at promoting diversity in education and employment legitimate and worthwhile?

The Supreme Court in *Grutter* v. *Bollinger* (2003) by a five-to-four vote upheld law schools' admissions policies aimed at achieving diverse student bodies through "special efforts" to recruit, but not fixed quotas for, students from groups that have historically been discriminated against, like African Americans, Hispanics, and Native Americans. Do you think affirmative-action programs aimed at promoting diversity in education and employment are legitimate and worthwhile?

consider modifying the program to give universities and colleges more discretion in admissions.[76]

Reaffirming the Importance of Diversity

The controversy and the conflicting lower court decisions on the permissibility of affirmative action in higher education resulted in confusion and uncertainty about the holding in *University of California Regents* v. *Bakke* that colleges and universities may pursue diverse student bodies. Finally, the Supreme Court clarified the matter in 2003, reaffirming *Bakke* in two companion cases challenging the admission policies of the University of Michigan undergraduate college and law school. Both sought to achieve diverse student bodies, but with different kinds of programs.

Jennifer Gratz, a white high school student with a 3.8 GPA, was denied admission to the undergraduate college. She challenged its admissions policy based on a "selection index" that ranked on a 150-point scale applicants' test scores and grades for up to 100 points, and allocated 40 points for other factors, including 4 points for children of alumni, 16 points for residents of rural areas, and 20 points for students from underrepresented minority groups or from socioeconomically disadvantaged families. Writing for the Court in *Gratz* v. *Bollinger* (2003) over the dissent of Justices Stevens, Souter, and Ginsburg, Chief Justice Rehnquist struck down

Jennifer Gratz, (right) is the successful plaintiff in Gratz v. Bollinger, *a case that struck down the University of Michigan's undergraduate admissions policy that awarded points to applicants based on various factors including racial and ethnic background. Barbara Grutter (left) is the unsuccessful plaintiff in* Grutter v. Bollinger, *a case that challenged the admissions policy of the University of Michigan's law school. Unlike the undergraduate admissions policy, the law school took an applicant's racial and ethnic background into account when considering that applicant's qualifications but did not award points based on this information.*

the policy as too mechanical and not narrowly tailored to giving applicants "individualized consideration" as *Bakke* required.[77]

In *Grutter* v. *Bollinger* (2003), however, a bare majority upheld the law school's affirmative-action policy that made "special efforts" to achieve racial and ethnic diversity.[78] Unlike the undergraduate program, the law school did not use a point system based in part on race. Writing for the Court, Justice O'Connor held that law school admissions were based on a "highly individualized, holistic review of each applicant's file" and did not use race as a factor in a "mechanical way." For that reason, it was consistent with *Bakke*'s holding that race may be used as a "plus factor" in achieving a diverse student body.

Justice O'Connor reaffirmed the importance of diversity, observing: "In order to cultivate a set of leaders with legitimacy in the eyes of the citizenry, it is necessary that the path to leadership be visibly open to talented and qualified individuals of every race and ethnicity." But she also added that, "We expect 25 years from now, the use of racial preferences will no longer be necessary." Chief Justice Rehnquist and Justices Scalia, Kennedy, and Thomas dissented, maintaining that race may never be used as a consideration in college admissions.

The Court thus reaffirmed the importance of diversity in education and employment. Public support for affirmative action as measured in public opinion polls varies by race, social class, education, and life experience, but close inspection suggests that "whites and blacks are not separated by unbridgeable gaps on affirmative action issues, at least not insofar as college admissions decisions are concerned."[79] People's responses seem to depend to a significant degree on how the survey question is put. If the question asked is something like "Are you in favor of abolishing preferences in hiring or college admissions based on race or gender?" most people say yes. But if the question is something like "Do you favor affirmative action programs to increase the number of minorities in colleges or in jobs?" there is general support for such programs.

EQUAL RIGHTS TODAY

Today, legal barriers have been lowered, if not removed, by civil rights legislation, executive orders, and judicial decisions. Important as these victories are, according to civil rights leader James Farmer, "They were victories largely for the middle class—those who could travel, entertain in restaurants, and stay in hotels. Those victories did not change life conditions for the mass of blacks who are still poor."[80]

As prosperous middle-class African Americans have moved out of inner cities, the remaining *underclass,* as they are coming to be called, has become even more isolated from the rest of the nation.[81] There are similar trends in Hispanic communities in Los Angeles, Dallas, and Houston.[82] Children are growing up on streets where drug abuse and crime are everyday events. They live in "separate and deteriorating societies, with separate economies, diverging family structures and basic institutions, and even growing linguistic separation within the core ghettos. The scale of their isolation by race, class, and economic situation is much greater than it was in the 1960s, with impoverishment, joblessness, educational inequality, and housing insufficiency even more severe."[83]

One of the difficulties is that as conditions have become better for many African Americans and Hispanics, the less fortunate see themselves as getting worse off, while most Americans see conditions for minorities as improving. "Both perceptions will be correct. And the fact that both are correct in arriving at opposite perceptions of what is going on will itself lead to further misunderstanding."[84]

> Despite the lack of improvement in social conditions, the push for integration has lessened: In fact, power on both sides of the color line is based to some extent on acceptance of segregation. On the black side of the color line, it is advantageous to keep African Americans within black electoral areas and keep black-controlled resources within black institutions; integrationist policies are often viewed as posing larger

threats than they actually do. On the white side of the line, . . . some residents in outlying suburbs see critical advantages in their almost all-white and all middle-class status.[85]

Some contend that attention should be paid to the plight of the underclass and that instead of focusing on issues of race, what is needed is a focus on class differences and policies that provide jobs and improve education.[86] Others say there has to be a revival of the civil rights crusade, a restoration of vigorous civil rights enforcement, job training, and, above all, an attack on residential segregation.[87] In any event, it is clear that questions as to how best to provide equal opportunities for all citizens remain high on the national agenda.

S U M M A R Y

1. Americans are committed to "equality," an elusive term, with most support for equality of opportunity, some for equality of starting conditions, and some for equality of results.

2. Progress in securing civil rights for African Americans was a long time coming. After the Civil War, the national government briefly tried to secure some measure of protection for the freed slaves and to enforce the Thirteenth, Fourteenth, and Fifteenth Amendments and the civil rights laws passed to implement them. But when federal troops withdrew from the South in 1877, the national government withdrew from the field, and blacks were left to their own resources. Not for nearly a century did the national government take action to prevent racial segregation and discrimination against blacks.

3. The crusade for women's rights was born partly out of the struggle to abolish slavery. Similarly, the modern women's movement learned and gained power from the civil rights movements of the 1950s and early 1960s. The fate of these two social movements has long been intertwined. Women secured the right to vote in the Nineteenth Amendment.

4. Concern for equal rights under the law continues today for African Americans and women. Hispanics, Asian Americans, and Native Americans have also experienced discrimination.

5. The Supreme Court uses a three-tiered approach to evaluate the constitutionality of laws challenged as violating the equal protection clause. Laws touching economic concerns are sustained if they are rationally related to the accomplishment of a legitimate government goal. Laws that classify people because of gender or sexual orientation are subject by the courts to heightened scrutiny and are sustained only if they serve important governmental objectives. Strict scrutiny is used to review laws that touch fundamental rights or classify people because of race or ethnic origin. Such laws will be sustained only if the government can show a compelling public purpose.

6. A series of constitutional amendments, Supreme Court decisions, and laws passed by Congress have now secured the right to vote to all Americans aged 18 and over. Following the Voting Rights Act of 1965, the Justice Department can oversee practices in locales with a history of discrimination. Recent Supreme Court decisions have refined the lengths to which legislatures can go, or are obliged to go, in creating minority-majority districts.

7. *Brown v. Board of Education of Topeka* (1954) struck down the "separate but equal" doctrine that had justified segregated schools in the South, but school districts responded slowly. The Supreme Court demanded compliance, and some federal courts mandated busing children across neighborhoods to comply. Still, full integration has proved elusive, as "white flight" has left many inner cities, and their schools, predominantly black or Hispanic.

8. Discrimination in public accommodations was outlawed by the Civil Rights Act of 1964. This act also provided for equal employment opportunity. The Fair Housing Act of 1968 and its 1988 amendments prohibited discrimination in housing.

9. The desirability and constitutionality of affirmative action programs that provide special benefits to members of groups subjected to past discrimination divide the nation and the Supreme Court. Remedial programs tailored to overcome specific instances of past discrimination are likely to pass the Supreme Court's suspicion of classifications based on race, national origin, and gender. The Court has also reaffirmed the importance of achieving diversity in education and employment.

K E Y   T E R M S

natural rights
affirmative action
women's suffrage
equal protection clause

due process clause
white primary
racial gerrymandering
poll tax

literacy test
majority-minority district
Jim Crow laws
de jure segregation

de facto segregation
commerce clause
class action suit
restrictive covenant

FURTHER READING

TAYLOR BRANCH, *Parting the Waters: America in the King Years, 1954–1963* (Simon & Schuster, 1988).

TAYLOR BRANCH, *Pillar of Fire: America in the King Years, 1963–65* (Simon & Schuster, 1998).

GORDON H. CHANG, ED., *Asian Americans and Politics* (Stanford University Press, 2001).

IRIS CHANG, *The Chinese in America: A Narrative History* (Viking, 2003).

CLARE CUSHMAN, ED., *Supreme Court Decisions and Women's Rights* (CQ Press, 2000).

ARLENE M. DAVILA, *Latinos, Inc.: The Marketing and Making of a People* (University of California Press, 2001).

DAVID DENT, *In Search of Black America: Discovering the African American Dream* (Simon & Schuster, 2000).

JANET DEWART, ED., *The State of Black America* (National Urban League, published annually).

WILLIAM N. ESKRIDGE JR., *Gaylaw: Challenging the Apartheid of the Closet* (Harvard University Press, 2000).

JONATHAN GOLDBERG-HILLER, *The Limits to Union: Same-Sex Marriage and the Politics of Civil Rights* (University of Michigan Press, 2002).

ANDREW HACKER, *Two Nations: Black and White, Separate, Hostile, Unequal* (Scribner, 1992).

RANDALL KENNEDY, *Race, Crime, and the Law* (Pantheon, 1997).

PHILIP A. KLINKER AND ROGER M. SMITH, *The Unsteady March: The Rise and Decline of Racial Equality in America* (University of Chicago Press, 2000).

RICHARD KLUGER, *Simple Justice: The History of Brown v. Board of Education* (Knopf, 1976).

DAVID M. O'BRIEN, *Constitutional Law and Politics: Civil Rights and Civil Liberties*, 6th ed. (Norton, 2005).

GARY ORFIELD, AND CHUNGMEI LEE, *Brown at 50: King's Dream or Plessy's Nightmare* (The Civil Rights Project, Harvard University, 2004).

J. W. PELTASON, *Fifty-Eight Lonely Men: Southern Federal Judges and School Desegregation* (University of Illinois Press, 1971).

RUTH ROSEN, *The World Split Open: How the Modern Women's Movement Changed America* (Viking, 2000).

JOHN DAVID SKRENTNY, ED., *Color Lines: Affirmative Action, Immigration, and Civil Rights Options for America* (University of Chicago Press, 2001).

GIRARDEAU A. SPANN, *The Law of Affirmative Action: Twenty-Five Years of Supreme Court Decisions on Race and Remedies* (New York University Press, 1999).

PHILIPPA STRUM, *Women in the Barracks: The VMI Case and Equal Rights* (University Press of Kansas, 2002).

ROBERTO SURO, *Strangers Among Us: How Latino Immigration Is Transforming America* (Knopf, 1998).

SUSAN F. VAN BURKLEO, *"Belonging to the World": Women's Rights and Constitutional Culture* (Oxford University Press, 2001).

MAKING ECONOMIC AND REGULATORY POLICY

18

Congress and the president received some stunning news in the summer of 1999: For the first time in two decades, the federal government's budget was balanced. Although Congress and the president had set the process in motion with budget agreements in 1990, 1993, and 1997, the news came nearly three years ahead of schedule and showed a much larger surplus in the future than anyone had predicted. Suddenly, the federal government was looking at almost $6 trillion in surpluses over the next ten years.

The balanced budget and projected surplus was the product of three events. Defense spending fell dramatically with the end of the cold war, spending for domestic programs did not rise as fast, largely because the economy was growing, and tax revenues increased more than expected. Practically everything that could go right did go right, and the budget forecast became brighter with each passing month.

Just as surprisingly, perhaps, the budget surplus was gone within three years, in part because just about everything that could go wrong with the economy and the world did go wrong, and in part because Congress and the new Bush administration decided to give $1.3 trillion of the projected surpluses back to the American public in the 2001 tax cuts, subtracted another $300 billion for further tax cuts in 2003 and $400 billion for a new prescription drug plan for the elderly in 2004, and allocated $200 billion for the wars in Afghanistan and Iraq. Suddenly, the $6 trillion in projected surpluses became $3 trillion in projected deficits.

The disappearing surplus shows just how sensitive federal budgets are to unexpected events such as wars and economic downturns, as well as legislative decisions.

TIME LINE
MAKING ECONOMIC AND REGULATORY POLICY

1890	Sherman Antitrust Act seeks to control monopolies
1906	Congress enacts the Pure Food and Drug Act establishing the first regulations of food and drug safety
1913	Federal Reserve Board created
1913	Sixteenth Amendment allows federal income tax
1921	Budget and Accounting Act
1938	Fair Labor Standards Act establishes a 40-hour work week
1947	World Trade Organization is created to facilitate free trade among nations
1967	Clean Air Act begins decades of improving air quality
1970	Occupational Safety and Health Administration regulates safety in the workplace
1974	Congressional Budget Office is created to provide budgetary expertise to Congress
1987	Alan Greenspan is selected as chair of the Federal Reserve
1999	First balanced budget in 30 years

Having worked for twenty years to get the budget balanced, Congress and the president subtracted much of the money away over a three-month span, leading some critics to argue that Republicans were hoping to "strangle the beast" of big government by denying it the money to create new programs such as national health insurance.

Although there may be some truth to the charge, Congress and the president did not stop spending. Moreover, as the budget deficit increases, so does the national debt and the interest payments the federal government must make to its lenders. Like credit-card debt for individuals, the federal government must pay interest on its bills, too. In 2005, for example, the federal government will spend almost $170 billion in interest, or almost five times as much as aid to college students and their schools.

The preceding chapters concentrated on the structure of our federal system and how government institutions are organized and operate. In this chapter and the two that follow, we focus on what the national government *does*—how voters, interest groups, and institutions (Congress, the White House, the executive branch, the courts) interact to promote the general welfare and provide for the common defense. We will be talking about making and implementing three different kinds of *public policy:* economic, social, and foreign policy.

MAKING PUBLIC POLICY

When government decides to act, it mostly does so through a **public policy**, which is a specific course of action that government takes to address a problem such as the federal budget deficit. A public policy can be conveyed to the public in the laws passed by Congress and signed by the president, opinions issued by the Supreme Court, and/or rules written by the executive branch. But whatever form it takes, a public policy tells the public who is about to get what, when, and how from government.

The Policy Making Process

Every policy reflects a series of separate decisions leading to final implementation and action. The process involves six steps: (1) making assumptions about the world, (2) identifying the problem to be solved, (3) deciding whether to act at all, (4) deciding how much to do, (5) choosing a tool for solving the problem, and (6) making rules for implementation.

The process does not always follow these seven steps in order. Making public policy is an often unpredictable process in which problems and solutions are loosely connected. It can start anywhere in the circle and skip back and forth at will. The result is a policy-making process that is often unpredictable and almost always in flux.[1]

1. *Making Assumptions about the World.* Every government decision involves assumptions about the future. Is the economy going to get stronger? If so, perhaps employment will go up and the costs of supporting the unemployed will go down. Is teenage pregnancy going to increase? If so, perhaps childhood poverty, which increases as more single teenagers have children, will also increase. Is world terrorism going to increase? If so, perhaps the United States needs to strengthen its border security or build an antimissile defense.

    Because there is no sure way to choose among competing assumptions about such a distant future, policy makers often make choices that help sell their particular views of the world. They are often pessimistic about the future when they define problems, but optimistic when they announce specific proposals to fix the problems. The result is that problems may look much worse than they truly are, while solutions may seem likely to work better than they possibly could.

2. *Picking the Problem.* Choosing the problem to be solved is the essential decision in setting the **policy agenda**. The policy agenda, as John Kingdon defines

---

public policy
A specific course of action taken by government to achieve a public goal.

policy agenda
The informal list of issues that Congress and the president consider most important for action.

Antitax protests erupted all over the country after Californians passed Proposition 13 in 1978, which placed strict limitations on state government revenues. California voters later enacted limits on state spending.

it, "is the list of subjects or problems to which governmental officials, and people outside of government closely associated with those officials, are paying some serious attention at any given time."[2]

Problems reach the list of possible agenda items from a variety of sources. Some arise from events such as the September 11 terrorist attacks; others because of newspaper or television stories about a controversial issue such as gay marriage; and still others because of interest group pressure. The government monitors a battery of assumptions on the state of the economy, for example, that can show the beginnings of an economic slowdown through the number of jobless claims, the rise of inflation through the consumer price index, or problems in credit through rising or falling interest rates. Readers need only visit www.fedstats.gov to see the range of information government provides to policy makers in search of problems.

3. *Deciding Whether to Act at All.* The fact that a problem exists does not automatically mean Congress and the president will try to solve it. Nothing forces presidents, members of Congress, or judges to act unless doing so will further some goal that they value such as reelection or a place in history. Some problems help policy makers achieve their personal or political goals, in which case they will decide to act, while others do not, in which case they pick other problems to solve.

    Policy makers clearly understand that public pressure for action ebbs and flows over time. In fact, writes political scientist Anthony Downs, "American public attention rarely remains sharply focused upon any one domestic issue for very long—even if it involves a continuing problem of crucial importance to society." According to Downs, attention to problems follows an issue-attention cycle in which each problem "suddenly leaps into prominence, remains there for a short time, and then—though still largely unresolved—gradually fades from the center of public attention."[3]

4. *Deciding How Much to Do.* Once the federal government decides that it wants to do something about a problem, one of its most difficult decisions is how much to do. It can launch a comprehensive program such as Social Security or Medicare, or an incremental program that can be expanded bit by bit over time.

RAISING REVENUE

In the federal budget for fiscal year 2005 (see Figure 18-1), federal receipts include six basic sources of revenue:

1. *Individual income taxes.* Taxes on individual Americans account for more than 40 percent of the federal government's tax revenue. Over the years, the income tax has grown increasingly complex as Congress responded to claims for differing kinds of exemptions and rates. Some members of Congress have advocated simplification or even elimination of the income tax in favor of a national sales tax.

2. *Corporate income taxes.* These taxes account for just under 10 percent of the national government's tax revenues. As late as 1943, revenue from corporate income taxes exceeded that from individual income taxes.

3. *Payroll receipts.* Payroll taxes are the second-largest and most rapidly rising source of federal revenue, accounting for 33.2 percent of all federal revenue, not including borrowing. Most people pay more in Social Security taxes than in federal income taxes. These are highly **regressive taxes**, meaning that low-income people generally pay larger fractions of their income than high-income people do.

4. *Excise taxes.* These taxes on liquor, tobacco, gasoline, telephones, air travel, and other so-called "luxury items" account for roughly 4 percent of federal revenue.

5. *Customs duties and tariffs.* Although no longer the main source of federal income, in recent years these taxes provided an annual yield of almost $20 billion.

6. *Borrowing.* Since World War II, the government has regularly resorted to borrowing money through the sale of federal securities such as savings bonds and treasury bills to private investors, many of whom are located in other nations. The government must pay interest rates on the money it borrows, which in turn becomes a significant cost in the annual federal budget.

distributive policy
A type of policy that provides benefits to all Americans.

redistributive policy
A type of policy that takes benefits (usually through taxes) from one group of Americans and gives them to another (usually through spending).

regressive tax
A tax whereby people with lower incomes pay a higher fraction of their income than people with higher incomes.

The first involves the size of the proposed solution. Will it be an incremental proposal or a major policy reform? Will it involve a slight change in existing regulations or a new federal program? Although major policy reforms are generally much more difficult to pass, in part because they involve more federal spending and/or produce greater regulation, such initiatives allow Congress and the president to claim much greater credit for solving a problem.

The second decision involves the way in which government benefits are to be distributed across the various groups in society. Federal programs that offer new benefits to all groups in society and are funded by all citizens equally are usually described as **distributive policy**. National parks, air traffic control, the interstate highway system, education funding, national defense, and Social Security are all defined as distributive in nature.

In contrast, federal programs that take resources (usually through taxes) from one or more groups in society so that another group can benefit (usually in the form of an entitlement program) are described as **redistributive policy**. Such programs tend to provide benefits to the less fortunate in society, often provoking conflict between the haves and have nots. Welfare, poverty programs, Head Start for poor preschool children, and special programs to help minority groups are often characterized as redistributive. Some political scientists call these programs zero-sum games, meaning that one group's gain (the program's benefits) is another's loss (the program's cost in taxes).

5. *Choosing a Tool.* Public policy scholars generally argue that the federal government has four basic tools available to solve most public problems: (1) spending money, (2) providing goods or services directly, (3) providing protection against risk, and (4) enforcing restrictions and penalties.[4]

   Outright money payments are made either directly to individuals or to agencies that provide services to them. Social Security is a direct payment to individuals; Head Start, which provides early-childhood education for disadvantaged children, is funded by the federal government and delivered by local agencies.

   Goods and services are provided either completely free to the public or for a price. National parks such as Yosemite and the Grand Canyon generally charge an admission fee; the National Air and Space Museum on the Washington Mall is open to the public for free; and Americans do not pay anything directly for national defense. Ultimately, of course, nothing the government does is completely free—the National Air and Space Museum is supported by general taxes, as is defense.

   Protections against risk involve a range of devices to encourage activities where the private sector might otherwise not go. The most familiar protections are federal loan guarantees, under which the government promises to cover the losses in the event that a student, farmer, small business, or other borrower fails to repay a debt. The federal government also provides protection against risk in the form of special exemptions from certain laws. Major league baseball, for example, is exempted from federal antitrust law. The exemption was designed to encourage the expansion of the national pastime, but was never given to professional football, hockey, or basketball.

   Restrictions and penalties are designed to encourage or discourage certain behaviors. The list of laws and regulations that limit what individual citizens, associations, and businesses can do is seemingly endless, and includes everything from criminal laws to requirements that all cigarette packages carry the surgeon general's warning that smoking can be dangerous to your health. The violation of a particular law usually results in a government sanction of some kind, usually a fine or imprisonment.

6. *Making Rules for Implementation.* As we shall see later in this chapter, almost everything the federal government does involves a rule. Technically, a government **rule** is a precise legal statement that implements a law. It is issued through a

formal process that tells the public exactly who will get what, when, and how from government, whether, for example, by specifying the amount of sulfur dioxide that can be released from a smokestack, the required height of a wheelchair ramp in a private building, or the number of life jackets that must be on a ferryboat. As such, rules are essential for turning even the most detailed legislation into action, and rule making is the central device used to execute the laws.

Technically, rule making comes at the very end of the policy-making process and is almost invisible to most Americans. Nevertheless, it is the essential step in converting the abstract ideas and language of laws, presidential orders, and court rulings into precise rules governing what individual members of the public, companies, or agencies can or must do.

Policy Making Alliances

Although formal decisions about public policy are made by Congress, the president, and/or the courts, most decisions involve collections of political leaders and interest groups that join together on behalf of a specific cause. Some of these collections exist for decades, while others come together for a specific cause, then disband. The former are often called **iron triangles**, while the latter are labeled **issue networks**.

IRON TRIANGLES By definition, an iron triangle has three sides that hold together over long periods of time: (1) a federal department or agency, (2) a set of loyal interest groups, and (3) a House and/or Senate authorizing committee. Each side supports the other two. Congress gives money to the agency, for example, and gets campaign money and endorsements from the interest groups in return; the interest groups give money and endorsements to Congress and gets special services from the agency in return; the agency gives special services to the interest groups and gets money from Congress in return.

ISSUE NETWORKS As the number of interest groups has increased, iron triangles have been replaced by much looser collections of participants. As political scientist Hugh Heclo has argued, the notion that iron triangles make all policy was "not so much wrong as it was disastrously incomplete" in today's complicated policy environment.[5] Although iron triangles can exist for decades, even centuries, the increasing number of small, highly specialized interest groups makes an iron triangle almost impossible to create, if only because Congress and federal agencies can no longer identify a steady occupant for the third corner of the triangle. They have to find temporary allies, depending on the issue. There is nothing "iron" about such coalitions of smaller groups: They last only as long as a given issue is hot.

Issue networks tend to concentrate power in the relatively small number of individuals that organize and maintain the networks. Like the promoters of rock concerts, these individuals make the key decisions about who participates and what they say. As such, some political scientists refer to the rise of well-financed issue networks such as the ones used to promote prescription drugs for older Americans or tax cuts for business as a form of elitism, not pluralism, in which a very small number of leaders gain significant influence from delaying action as a way to maintain power.

ECONOMIC POLICY

The federal government has been involved in economic policy since the end of the Revolutionary War. The framers wanted a government strong enough to promote free trade, protect patents and trademarks, and enforce contracts between individuals and businesses. And they wanted a government with enough funding so that it could build the postal roads, bridges, railroads, and canals that would allow the young economy to grow.

Much as they worried about the state of the economy, the framers did not concentrate economic policy in any branch. Instead, they divided economic policy-making control between the the legislative and executive branches and between the House and the Senate. Article I, Section 8, of the Constitution gives Congress the power to borrow, coin, and print money yet requires that all bills for raising revenue originate in the House, while Article

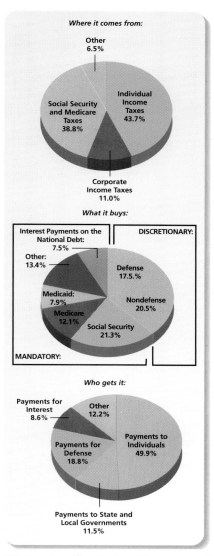

FIGURE 18–1 The Federal Government Dollar, 2005.
SOURCE: Summary Tables, *Budget of the United States, Fiscal Year 2005*, Washington: D.C., U.S. Government Printing Office, February, 2004

rule
A precise legal definition of how government will implement a policy.

iron triangle
A policy making alliance that involves very strong ties among a congressional committee, an interest group, and a federal department or agency.

issue network
A policy making alliance among loosely connected participants that comes together on a particular issue, then disbands.

II, Section 2, gives the president the power to appoint the officers of government who would actually do the borrowing, coining, spending, and taxing yet requires that all officers be confirmed by the Senate. In a similar vein, Article I gives Congress the power to regulate commerce with foreign nations, among the states, and with Native American tribes, while Article II gives the president authority to negotiate the treaties and enforce the laws. Finally, Article I gives Congress the power to establish post offices and build postal roads, which were as important to the free movement of commerce in the 1700s as the highways, rails, and Internet are today, yet Article II gives the president the power to appoint executive officials such as the postmaster general of the United States.

By creating a national government of limited powers and providing constitutional guarantees to protect property from excessive regulation, the framers succeeded in protecting capitalism. More than two centuries later, the U.S. economy is the strongest in the world, and the federal government continues to safeguard the basic conditions needed for capitalism to thrive. Part of the government's role is to stay out of the way as individuals and businesses create wealth through new ideas and hard work, but part is to promote the national welfare through **fiscal policy**, which uses federal spending and taxation to stimulate or slow the economy, and **monetary policy**, which manipulates the supply of money that individuals and businesses have in their hands to keep the economy from swinging wildly from boom to bust. In addition, the federal government promotes economic growth and trade and controls many economic decisions through regulations against certain kinds of business, labor, and environmental practices.

These tools are designed to smooth the ups and downs of the normal *business cycle*. Economists tend to focus on four discrete stages of the cycle: (1) expansion, in which the economy produces new jobs and growth; (2) contraction, as the economy starts to slow down; (3) recession, in which the economy reaches a trough of low growth; and (4) recovery, in which the economy rebounds. The goal of effective economic policy today is to make sure the peaks are not too high and the troughs are not too low. In general, **inflation** is considered the primary policy problem during expansion and recovery, while **unemployment** is considered the greatest problem during contraction and recession.

Inflation is usually measured by the Consumer Price Index (CPI), which shows how much more or less consumers are paying for the same "basket of goods" over time. The major components of the CPI are food, shelter, fuel, clothing, transportation, and medical care. In turn, unemployment is measured simply by the percentage of able-bodied workers who are looking for jobs but cannot find them. It does not measure the number of able-bodied workers who have given up looking for work or who have taken jobs below their skill levels with lower pay.

The federal government exercises less control over the national economy than it does over social or foreign policy. Nevertheless, it keeps a firm hand on many of the gears and levers that guide not only the economy's general direction but the rate at which it moves. These controls are taxes, spending, and borrowing.

FISCAL POLICY

Congress and the president make fiscal policy by taxing, borrowing, and spending money. Nothing reflects the growth of federal programs and the rise of big government more clearly than the increased spending by the national government. In 1933, the federal government spent only $4 billion, about $30 per capita. In 2005, the figure was $2.4 trillion, or more than $8,000 per person.

The Federal Budget

Today federal, state, and local governments spend an amount equal to about one-third of the income of all Americans. The national government is the biggest spender of all—it spends more than all state and local governments combined. Annual spending by the national government accounts for some 23 percent of the gross domestic product (GDP), or nearly one dollar out of every four spent in the U.S. economy. The national debt is approaching $7 trillion, and the United States paid almost $180 billion in 2005 in interest payments on that debt.

---

fiscal policy
Government policy that attempts to manage the economy by controlling taxing and spending.

monetary policy
Government policy that attempts to manage the economy by controlling the money supply and thus interest rates.

inflation
A rise in the general price level (and decrease in dollar value) owing to an increase in the volume of money and credit in relation to available goods.

unemployment
The number of Americans who are out of work but actively looking for a job. The number does not usually include those who are not looking.

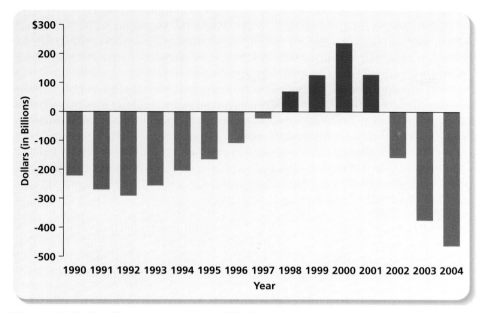

Figure 18–2 The Disappearing Federal Budget Deficit

SOURCE: *Congressional Quarterly Weekly,* January 17, 2004, p. 172.

WHERE THE MONEY COMES FROM   "In this world," Benjamin Franklin once said, "nothing is certain but death and taxes." Tax collecting is one of the oldest activities of government. Today the federal government gets most of its funds from payroll taxes for Social Security and Medicare, personal and corporate income taxes, admission fees to federal parks, import taxes, fines, and revenues from the sale of federal products such as maps and data (see Figure 18–1 on page 463).

Putting power over taxation into the hands of the people was a major achievement in the development of self-government. "No taxation without representation" has been a battle cry the world over. The Constitution clearly provided that Congress "shall have Power to lay and collect Taxes, Duties, Imposts, and Excises." **Tariffs** (import duties) and **excise taxes** (consumer taxes on specific kinds of merchandise) have to be levied uniformly throughout the United States.

Raising money is only one objective of taxation. Regulation and, more recently, promoting economic growth are other objectives. In a broad sense, all taxation regulates human behavior. For example, a **progressive tax**—under which people with high incomes pay larger fractions of their incomes than people with low incomes—has a leveling tendency on people's wealth.

Ordinary people borrow money when they face emergency expenses. The same is true of governments. The **deficit** is the difference between the annual revenues raised and the expenditures of government, including the interest on past borrowing. Deficits and surpluses affect the **national debt**, which is the cumulative total of all deficits, minus surpluses, over the years.[6] The debt began growing again in 2002 as revenues fell because of an economic slowdown and tax cuts, while spending increased dramatically with the September 11 relief effort and new measures for homeland security, followed by the wars in Afghanistan and Iraq and their aftermath, and later with prescription drug coverage for the elderly (see Figure 18–2).[7]

Borrowing costs money. The federal government borrows from investors who buy Treasury notes, Treasury bills, and U.S. savings bonds. These investors include individuals (foreign and domestic), U.S. government accounts, banks, and other institutions.

Americans might not be as troubled by the size of the debt if they understood two characteristics of federal borrowing. First, the government owes roughly 90 percent of the money to its own citizens rather than to foreign governments or investors, although the amount owed to foreigners is growing. Second, the economic strength and resources of the country are more significant than the size of the debt.

tariff
Tax levied on imports to help protect a nation's industries, labor, or farmers from foreign competition. It can also be used to raise additional revenue.

excise tax
Consumer tax on a specific kind of merchandise, such as tobacco.

progressive tax
A tax graduated so that people with higher incomes pay a larger fraction of their income than people with lower incomes.

deficit
The difference between the revenues raised annually from sources of income other than borrowing and the expenditures of government, including paying the interest on past borrowing.

national debt
The total amount of money the federal government has borrowed to finance deficit spending over the years.

WHERE THE MONEY GOES   Much of the money the federal government takes in is spent on benefit payments to individuals and national defense. Measured in absolute dollars spent in 2005, almost half of federal spending went to required benefit payments for individuals such as Social Security, Medicare, Medicaid, and other major social programs (again, see Figure 18–1 on page 463).

The proportions do not change when spending is measured as a percentage of the nation's **gross domestic product (GDP)**, which is an estimate of the total output of all U.S. economic activity. Spending on domestic **entitlement** programs, such as Social Security, Medicare, and unemployment insurance, to which qualified citizens are "entitled" by national legislation runs at about 11 percent of the GDP. Spending for defense is a little more than 3 percent of GDP, payments on the deficit make up another 3 percent of GDP, and nondefense discretionary spending comes to just over 3 percent.

Years ago, revenues and outlays were so small that federal tax and spending decisions had little impact on the overall economy. In today's $2.4 trillion federal budget, even small changes in taxes and spending can alter the direction of the economy. However, because many federal programs are open to all eligible citizens, much of the federal budget is "uncontrollable." The most uncontrollable parts of the budget are Social Security, Medicare, unemployment benefits, health benefits for the poor through Medicaid, and interest on the national debt.

The Budget Process

Before Congress enacted the Budget and Accounting Act of 1921, each executive agency dealt with Congress on its own, requesting that Congress appropriate funds for its activities with little or no presidential coordination. In 1921, the Bureau of the Budget (changed to the Office of Management and Budget in 1970) was created in the Treasury Department, and for the first time, the executive branch presented one budget to Congress.

THE EXECUTIVE BRANCH   The federal government's fiscal year begins on October 1. The budget process begins nearly two years in advance, when the various departments and agencies estimate their needs and propose their budgets to the president.[8] While Congress is debating the budget for the coming fiscal year, the agencies are making estimates for the year after that (see Table 18–1). Agency officials take into account not only their needs as they see them but also the overall presidential program and the probable reactions of Congress. Departmental budgets are detailed; they include estimates of expected needs for personnel, supplies, office space, and the like.

The **Office of Management and Budget (OMB)**, a staff agency of the president, handles the next phase. OMB budget examiners review each agency's budget and reconcile

gross domestic product (GDP)
The total output of all economic activity in the nation, including goods and services.

entitlements
Government programs, such as unemployment insurance, disaster relief, and disability payments, that provide benefits to all eligible citizens.

Office of Management and Budget (OMB)
Presidential staff agency that serves as a clearinghouse for budgetary requests and management improvements for government agencies.

TABLE 18–1 STEPS IN THE BUDGET PROCESS, FISCAL YEAR 2006	
February–December 2004	Executive branch agencies develop requests for funds, which are reviewed by the Office of Management and Budget and forwarded to the president for final decision.
December 2004	The formal budget documents are prepared.
January–February 2005	The budget is transmitted to Congress as a formal message from the president.
March–September 2005	Congress reviews the president's proposed budget, develops its own budget, and approves spending and revenue bills.
October 1, 2005	Fiscal year 2006 begins.
October 1, 2005–September 30, 2006	Executive branch agencies execute the budget provided in law.
October–November 2006	Data on actual spending and receipts for the completed fiscal year become available.

White House budget director Josh Bolton discussing President Bush's 2005 budget proposal. The proposed budget called for an increase in spending on the military and on homeland security and cuts in spending on domestic programs.

it with the president's overall plans. OMB then holds informal hearings with every department and agency to give each one a chance to clarify and defend its estimates.

Once this give-and-take is over, the OMB director gives the president a single, consolidated set of estimates of both revenue and expenditures—the product of perhaps a year's work. The president takes several days to review these figures and make adjustments. The budget director also helps the president prepare a budget message that will stress key aspects of the budget and tie it to broad national goals. The president must submit the budget recommendations and accompanying message to Congress between the first Monday in January and the first Monday in February. The president's budget recommendations cover thousands of pages.

THE LEGISLATIVE BRANCH Presidential submission of a budget proposal is only the beginning. Under our Constitution, Congress must appropriate the funds and raise the taxes. But the president also plays a role, since all appropriations and tax proposals are subject to a presidential veto. Thus the White House is an active participant in the congressional budget battles. When Congress acts on the budget, it does so by first approving the overall budget resolution. Then the actual appropriation of funds is detailed in 13 different bills, each of which is presented to the president for approval.

Congress adopted the Budget and Impoundment Control Act of 1974 to enhance its role in the budget process. This act specifies that the president must include proposed changes in tax laws, estimates of amounts of revenue lost through existing preferential tax treatments, and five-year estimates of the costs of new and continuing federal programs. The act also calls on the president to seek authorizing legislation for a program a year before asking Congress to fund it.

The 1974 Budget Act also created the **Congressional Budget Office (CBO)**, which gave Congress its own independent agency to prepare budget data and analyze budgetary issues. By February 15 of each year, CBO furnishes its analysis of the presidential recommendations to the House and Senate budget committees. CBO also provides Congress with biannual forecasts of the economy, analyzes alternative fiscal policies, prepares five-year cost estimates for bills proposed by congressional committees, and undertakes studies requested by committees. CBO also monitors the results of congressional action on individual appropriations and revenues against the targets or ceilings specified by legislation.

Such budget reform efforts did not by themselves balance the budget, but they did set in place a discipline and a mind-set that moved toward balancing the budget. Equally

Congressional Budget Office (CBO)
An agency of Congress that analyzes presidential budget recommendations and estimates the costs of proposed legislation.

In Comparative Perspective

TAXING POLICY IN THE UNITED STATES AND DENMARK

One way to compare nations is to ask how much citizens pay in income taxes. The higher the amount paid, the larger the national government is likely to be. Because income taxes are progressive in nature, they allow for the redistribution of income from wealthier households to low-income households.

Much as Congress and the president complain that Americans are overtaxed, the United States actually ranks well down the list of Western democracies in its income tax rates. Although it makes up the difference through an across-the-board Social Security and Medicare tax on all workers, as well as state and local sales taxes, its overall tax rate is roughly half as high as that in Denmark and other Scandinavian countries.

The difference is in what Denmark provides in government services. Whereas the United States provides help for needy and older Americans on a more selective basis, Denmark has a universal system of support that covers every citizen regardless of their income. The Danish government provides free health care, retirement pensions, and free college education, including some living expenses, for all of its citizens. It also provides child care, paid maternity leave, and unemployment support and welfare for those who qualify. Families also receive a government allowance for each child under the age of 18.

The Danish government also runs nursing homes, homeless shelters, children's homes, and alcohol and drug treatment centers, which are often provided in the United States through charitable institutions. These benefits are not only guaranteed for Danish citizens, they are often provided in government-run facilities such as hospitals and clinics.

Although the United States provides health coverage to older Americans and poor families and children, its coverage is less generous and often requires co-payments by participants. Moreover, the United States generally gives its citizens cash assistance to purchase health care and other services from private, not government, providers and sets time limits on how long needy Americans can receive services. In general, Denmark imposes few, if any, time limits.

As a result, Denmark's government spends more money on each citizen and must raise more money through taxes, hence the significant difference between what U.S. and Danish citizens pay each year to their governments.

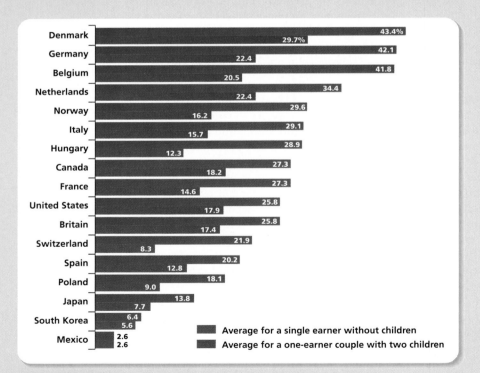

Percentage of Wages Full-Time Workers Pay in Income Taxes in Selected Countries.

NOTE: The rates include contributions to social insurance and retirement funds, less cash benefits paid, such as child allowances.

SOURCE: "Tax Burdens," *The Washington Post*, September 30, 2000, p. A14.

if not more important was the economic boom of the 1990s, which generated huge tax revenues that helped achieve the first budget surpluses in 30 years.

The Politics of Taxing and Spending

In addition to raising funds to run the government, taxes also promote economic growth and reward certain types of behavior, such as owning a home, contributing to charities, and investing in high-risk but desirable (from a national standpoint) energy or housing ventures. Cynics suggest, too, that from a member of Congress's point of view, tax legislation has the additional and important function of raising campaign funds. As long as tax legislation is under consideration, lobbyists will be more inclined to contribute.[9]

Among people outside government, no one likes taxes, but nearly everyone realizes how necessary they are. There is considerable disagreement about the best type of tax. Some say a *progressive income tax* (also called a *graduated income tax*) is best because it is relatively easy to collect, hits hardest those who are most able to pay, and hardly touches those at the bottom of the income ladder. Others argue that *excise taxes* are the fairest because they are paid by people who spend money for luxury goods and thus obviously have money to spare. In addition, by discouraging people from buying expensive goods, excise taxes occasionally have a deflationary effect when prices are on the rise. However, excise taxes are more expensive to collect than income taxes. In some cases, such as the tax on tobacco, they may hit the poor the hardest. Excise taxes also face strong resistance from affected industries—tobacco, liquor, and airlines, for example.

The most controversial tax is a general **sales tax**, which is levied by all but a few states on the sale of most goods, sometimes exempting food and drugs. Labor and liberal organizations see sales taxes as *regressive:* Because a sales tax is the same for all persons, these taxes are not related to a taxpayer's ability to pay, and poor persons pay a higher percentage of their income in sales taxes for the goods and services they buy than rich people do. Proponents of a national sales tax stress its potential anti-inflationary effect and point to its successful use in a number of states.

The sales tax is exclusively a state and local tax in the United States, but in Europe a similar tax, a **value-added tax (VAT)**, is used to raise revenues for central governments. The VAT differs from a sales tax in that it collects a tax on the increased value of a product *at each stage of production and distribution* rather than just at the point of sale, as with a sales tax. A loaf of bread would thus have value added several times: The farmer would pay a value-added tax on the grain before selling to the miller, who would be taxed before selling to the baker, and so forth. The value-added tax is seen by some as a way to infuse a large amount of new revenue into the federal government. Opponents of the tax see it as regressive and increasing the tax burden. States see a federal VAT as invading their turf. Since it taxes consumption and not savings, a VAT could encourage savings and investment, both of which are vital to economic growth.

Tax Expenditures

Tax expenditures are a final type of fiscal policy that uses the tax code to provide special tax incentives or benefits to individuals and businesses for economic goals such as home ownership, retirement savings, and college education. These benefits, which now total more than $400 billion each year, come from special exclusions, exemptions, or reductions from gross income or from special credits, preferential tax rates, or deferrals of tax liability.

Tax expenditures are one means by which the national government carries out public policy objectives. For example, the government encourages investment in research and development by allowing such costs to be deducted from a company's taxes. Federal grants could also achieve this objective.

Critics assert that the rich get their "welfare" through such loopholes. This form of "welfare" does not require a visible appropriation of money plainly identified in the budget. However meritorious the objectives of tax expenditures are—encouraging home ownership, research and development, retirement savings—these tax benefits do not benefit all levels of society. In many instances, they lead investors to put their money into low-yield investments to obtain large tax benefits, which in turn pulls money out of more productive parts of the economy.

sales tax
General tax on sales transactions, sometimes exempting food and drugs.

value-added tax (VAT)
A tax on increased value of a product at each stage of production and distribution rather than just at the point of sale.

tax expenditure
Loss of tax revenue due to federal laws that provide special tax incentives or benefits to individuals or businesses.

MONETARY POLICY

Monetary policy is the second way the national government manages the economy. The core element of **monetarism** is the idea that prices, incomes, and economic stability reflect growth in the amount of money that circulates through the economy at any one time. Monetarists contend that money supply is the key factor affecting the economy's performance and that restrained yet steady growth in the money supply will encourage solid economic growth but not inflation.

The Federal Reserve System

Monetary policy is not made by either Congress or the president but by the Board of Governors of the **Federal Reserve System** (often simply called "the Fed"), specifically its Federal Open Market Committee. The members of the committee, some of the most powerful people in the United States, have a lot to say about how much interest you pay on the car you are buying and whether you refinance your home because of lower interest rates. They can stimulate the economy so that it could be easier for you to find a job or slow it down so that it could be harder. Who are these people with so much power, and how do they influence economic policy?

The Fed's Board of Governors consists of a chair and six other members who are appointed by the president with the consent of the Senate to 14-year terms, with one member's term expiring every two years. These long, staggered terms are intended to insulate members from politics as much as possible. They supervise 12 regional Federal Reserve banks, each headed by a president and governed by a nine-member board of directors chosen from the private banking business in that region.

The 12 members of the Fed's Open Market Committee are all professional economists or bankers. Though their names are unfamiliar to most people, this group, which meets every six to eight weeks, decides how much money will be allowed to enter the economy, manages foreign currency operations, and regulates banks. It does this by buying and selling government securities, which can encourage either lower or higher interest rates. Other lenders closely watch the decisions of the Fed and typically make their interest rates consistent with Fed decisions. Because lenders make it either more or less expensive to borrow money, they influence a wide range of economic activity.

The chair of the Board of Governors, by tradition an economist, is appointed by the president to a four-year term. The current chair, Alan Greenspan, is one of the most influential national public policy officials. Greenspan was first appointed by President Ronald Reagan in 1987 and reappointed by Presidents George H. W. Bush and Bill Clinton. Greenspan's leadership had helped foster economic growth and was widely respected by financial leaders, factors that influenced Clinton's decision to reappoint him. The staff of the Fed reports directly to the chair, not to the board, and the chair is the one who appears before Congress and the country to explain the policies of the Federal Reserve System. The chair heads the Federal Open Market Committee and is credited or blamed for the decisions made by the Fed.

The Fed has three basic tools for influencing the economy. First, it can change the discount rate that determines how much banks must pay for borrowing money. Raising rates slows down the economy by increasing costs for money and credit; lowering rates stimulates the economy by making money more easily available for investment and growth.

Second, the Fed buys and sells federal debt. Selling federal debt to the public tends to slow down the economy by taking dollars out of circulation that could have been used for investment or growth, while buying federal debt back from the public tends to free up money that can be used for new activities, thereby stimulating the economy.

Third, the Fed determines how much money nationally chartered banks must keep in their reserves. Raising the requirement tends to slow down the economy by reducing the funds banks have available to lend to the public for investment and growth, while decreasing the requirement injects more money into the economy.

monetarism
A theory that government should control the money supply to encourage economic growth and restrain inflation.

Federal Reserve System
The system created by Congress in 1913 to establish banking practices and regulate currency in circulation and the amount of credit available. It consists of 12 regional banks supervised by the Board of Governors. Often called simply *the Fed.*

PEOPLE & POLITICS *Making a Difference* ★ ★ ★

ALAN GREENSPAN, INFLATION BUSTER

Already regarded as one of the most important economic policy makers of the late twentieth century, Federal Reserve Board chair Alan Greenspan may well be remembered more for stopping inflation than promoting growth. Appointed to his post in 1987 by Ronald Reagan, Greenspan is best described as a monetarist who used the Fed to promote his view that the economy can only grow so fast before it ignites inflation.

Greenspan is best known for using interest rates to either stimulate or slow down the economy. As the economy worsened in late 2000 and early 2001, for example, the Fed began cutting interest rates to stimulate demand. In all, the Fed cut its federal funds rate 11 times in 2001, dropping the amount banks charge each other to borrow money from 6.5 percent in January to just 1.75 by December. When the economy did not respond, the Fed lowered the rate again to 1.25 percent in Novem-

ber 2002, and to just 1.0 pecent in June 2003, where it remained through most of 2004. Worried about inflation, the Fed raised the rate to 1.25 in June 2004, 1.50 in August 2004, 1.75 in September 2004, 2.0 in November 2004, and 2.25 in December 2004.

Whether as an inflation fighter or a recession breaker, Greenspan is now one of the world's most watched economic leaders. Although he once joked that he had learned "to mumble with great incoherence" early on at the Fed, he also knew the power of words to slow the economy. In December 1996, for example, he wondered out loud whether the stock market was suffering from what he called "irrational exuberance," which prompted an immediate 145-point drop in the Dow Jones Industrial Average, the most widely followed stock indicator.

Greenspan finished his doctorate in economics in 1977, after leaving the Ford

administration. He starts each day with a 2½-hour hot bath to soothe his ailing back. It is time he uses to read memos and analyze the latest economic data. "The unsung hero at the Fed is the assistant who has to read his waterlogged scribblings," says his wife, Andrea Mitchell, an NBC News correspondent. How interesting to think that the major architect of contemporary economic policy makes some of his toughest choices in the bathtub.

Government and Economic Policy

Depression is a hard teacher, and the 1930s had a tremendous impact on American thinking about the role of government in the economy. The Great Depression that began in 1929 brought mass misery. "One vivid, gruesome moment of those dark days we shall never forget," wrote one observer. "We saw a crowd of some fifty men fighting over a barrel of garbage which had been set outside the back door of a restaurant. American citizens fighting for scraps of food like animals!"[10]

The Depression continued despite Franklin D. Roosevelt's New Deal economic agenda, which pumped new money into the economy, created hundreds of thousands of federally subsidized jobs, and established new regulations governing the financial markets. Faint signs of recovery could be seen in the mid-1930s, but a new recession in 1937 and 1938 indicated that the country was by no means out of the woods. Between 8 and 9 million people were jobless in 1939. Then came World War II, and unemployment seemed cured. Millions of people had more income, more security, and higher standards of living. Lord Beveridge in England posed a question that bothered many thoughtful Americans: "Unemployment has been practically abolished twice in the lives of most of us—in the last war and in this war. Why does war solve the problem of unemployment which is so insoluble in peace?"[11]

There were several theories about what the federal government could do to stimulate the economy at the time. Some economists urged the government to reduce spending, lower taxes, curb the power of labor, and generally leave business and the economy alone. This first theory is called **laissez-faire economics**.

laissez-faire economics
Theory that opposes governmental interference in economic affairs beyond what is necessary to protect life and property.

GLOBAL *Perceptions*

QUESTION: Does the phrase "there is economic prosperity" describe your country very well, somewhat well, not too well, or not well at all?

conomic prosperity is a very important goal for citizens around the world, but many countries are far from the goal. But whether the citizens of a country believe their nation is actually prosperous varies in part by the degree to which their economies are getting better in a relative sense. Thus, even though their nations are poor by comparison with the United States, the citizens of Honduras, Vietnam, Pakistan, and Uzbekistan are actually the most likely to say their countries are the most prosperous. In turn, some of the world's most prosperous nations have the least satisfied citizens, in part because they have come to expect better economic performance.

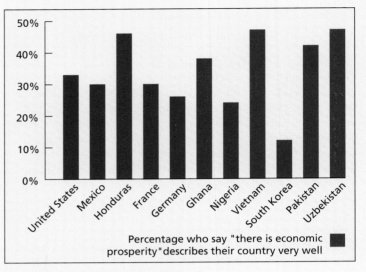

Percentage who say "there is economic prosperity" describes their country very well

SOURCE: Pew Global Attitudes Project, 2003, p. 81.

Another group, deeply influenced by the work of English economist John Maynard Keynes,[12] recommended that when consumer spending and investment decline, government spending and investing should increase. Government must do the spending and investing during a recession because private enterprise will not or cannot. This second theory is called **Keynesian economics**. Roosevelt embraced Keynesian economics and pushed for much greater spending by the federal government as the answer to continued hard times.

Keynesian economics influences government management of the economy to this day. Yet politically, Keynesian economics presents a problem. It is much easier to increase spending and government programs than it is to curb them. As a result, deficit spending became a habit in this country for 50 years. To stimulate demand, the government spent more money than it took in. For many years, this policy was thought to be beneficial to the economy. It was also convenient politically. However, when the national debt soared, both Congress and the president searched for ways to balance the budget.

PROMOTING ECONOMIC GROWTH

Federal economic policy involves more than the effort to smooth the ups and downs of the business cycle. It also involves efforts to promote economic growth, often measured by the number of new jobs or businesses created. In doing so, it helps create jobs for individual Americans, which in turn produces higher revenues, which in turn produces either greater savings or more federal spending.

Promoting Business

The national government promotes a prosperous economy through its monetary and fiscal policies. It also provides various services to business and industry through an economic development infrastructure composed of several dozen departments and agencies, including the Departments of Agriculture and Commerce and the Small Business Administration.

The Department of Commerce is the most visible business promoter within the federal bureaucracy and is sometimes known as the nation's "service center for business." Its cabinet secretary, usually a person with an extensive business background, is

Keynesian economics
Economic theory based on the principles of John Maynard Keynes stating that government spending should increase during business slumps and be curbed during booms.

a spokesperson for business interests. Historically, the department has been at the center of the government's efforts to promote economic growth and encourage business research and development.

The Department of Commerce also encourages innovation through the protection of intellectual property. Its Patent and Trademark Office (PTO) administers the patent system that Congress established "to promote the Progress of Science and useful Arts" under Article I of the Constitution. Each year, the PTO issues more than 100,000 patents to cover new and useful inventions that provide their owners certain exclusive rights for 17 years. The number of patents issued annually almost doubled during the economic expansion of the 1990s, but fell back during the 2001–2002 economic downturn.

The Department of Agriculture continues to provide ample support for farmers, including federal subsidies for corn, barley, oats, wheat, soybeans, cotton, and rice. Under a mix of programs that cost more than $15 billion in 2005 alone, the federal government either guarantees farmers a minimum price for their crops or pays a fee for not planting their fields. The department also provides a host of services to farmers, from education on how to generate higher yields to research on everything from blueberries to forest management. Although these payments were originally designed to help small family farmers, research by the Environmental Working Group, a Washington, D.C., advocacy group, showed that two-thirds of all payments from 1996 to 2000 went to just 10 percent of farmers, most of whom owned large tracts of land.[13]

Speaking at the Chinese University of Finance and Economics in Beijing, U.S. Trade Representative Robert Zoellick makes a point while answering a student's question.

Promoting International Trade

The United States experienced its first **trade deficit** in in more than a century when the amount of imports exceeded the value of exports in 1971. Since then, the nation has had trade deficits in the billions of dollars every year. Congress and the president are under continuing pressure from industry, unions, and regional political leaders to protect American jobs, companies, and communities from foreign competition. These pressures come not only from the textile and auto industries but also from glass, steel, shoes, lumber, electronics, book publishing, aluminum, farming, and domestic wine and spirit coalitions, to name just a few. These leaders claim that the trade deficit justifies the imposition of trade sanctions.

The problem, however, is not that the United States is importing too much but that it is exporting too little. German cars, Japanese technology, and Indonesian textiles are fine products; if other countries produce better cars or shoes at a lower price, free traders argue, the United States should buy from them and direct our labor and capital to areas in which it can do better.

The question is also whether U.S. products are given fair treatment by other nations. American agricultural products are denied entry into some countries and are subject to high tariffs in others. American automobile manufacturers complain of unfair restrictions imposed by the Japanese on our cars. Finally, some countries exploit the U.S. advantage in technology by slavishly copying our products and then selling them back to us or to other countries at a profit.

Another unfair trade practice is *dumping*—selling products below the cost of manufacturing or below their domestic price with the intention of driving other producers out of the market and then raising prices to profitable levels. Another practice is government *subsidizing* of certain industries. Some countries, for example, subsidize steel for export. Others require lengthy inspection procedures for imported goods. Japan has protected several of its industries—producers of automobiles, baseball bats, and even chopsticks, for example—by setting standards that are virtually impossible for U.S. manufacturers to meet. Japan also sets limits on rice imports.

In 1947, a group of countries formed a trade organization to negotiate free trade by lowering tariffs (taxes on imports that raise their price) and quotas (limits on the quantity of a particular product that may be imported) and other disadvantages countries face when trading. Today the **World Trade Organization (WTO)**, based on the **General Agreement on Tariffs and Trade (GATT)**, includes more than 130 countries, and its membership accounts for four-fifths of the world's trade. The WTO has negotiated agreements through eight rounds of trade negotiations (the most recent was called the Uruguay Round, named after the site of the initial conference).

trade deficit
An imbalance in international trade in which the value of imports exceeds the value of exports.

World Trade Organization (WTO)
International organization derived from the General Agreement on Tariffs and Trade (GATT) that promotes free trade around the world.

General Agreement on Tariffs and Trade (GATT)
An international trade organization with more than 130 members, including the United States and the People's Republic of China, that seeks to encourage free trade by lowering tariffs and other trade restrictions.

SHOULD THE UNITED STATES PROHIBIT OUTSOURCING?

Free trade has many economic benefits, not the least of which is access to inexpensive goods made in other countries. But it also carries costs, most notably in the loss of jobs in the United States. Between 2004 and 2015, the United States will export, or outsource, more than 3.3 million jobs to other nations, including hundreds of thousands of computer programming, accounting, data entry, and customer service jobs that used to be held by American workers. Concerns about the job losses have led some labor leaders to call for penalties on companies that convert higher-paying U.S. jobs into much lower-paying jobs abroad.

The United States has tried to focus WTO and GATT negotiations on trade in agricultural items, foreign investment, and protection of technological innovations and intellectual property. Although U.S. imports and those of other countries still face many trade restrictions, the WTO and GATT have greatly helped lower tariffs and quotas and increase fair trade throughout the world. Many analysts maintain that GATT is one of the most successful innovations in the history of international relations and one of the contributing factors to the United States' economic success since the end of the cold war.[14]

Not everyone believes that free trade should be unlimited, however. Labor unions, environmentalists, and human rights advocates argue that U.S. trade policies spur the creation of low-wage jobs abroad and encourage child labor, pollution, and worker abuse.

THE NORTH AMERICAN FREE TRADE AGREEMENT In 1992, the United States, Canada, and Mexico signed the **North American Free Trade Agreement (NAFTA)**, which formed the largest geographical free trade zone in the world, even surpassing the European Community's 15-country conglomerate. Although President George Bush signed NAFTA near the end of his presidency, the agreement could not become law until ratified by Congress. President Bill Clinton promoted NAFTA, even though many members of his own party were its most vigorous opponents. Congress passed NAFTA by a thin margin in a bipartisan vote in which the Democrats were the minority.

Though trade among the United States, Canada, and Mexico is not absolutely "free" or unimpeded, the agreement has had a tremendous impact on the economies of all three countries. Today Mexico is the United States' third most important trading partner, and the United States is Mexico's most important trading partner. Critics of NAFTA remain concerned because Mexican antipollution laws are significantly less stringent than those in the United States, and Mexican workers work for considerably lower wages. Both of these factors make relocation to Mexico attractive to many U.S. companies seeking to lower labor and pollution control costs.

Recent reports suggest that many of those lower-paid jobs in Mexico have moved to China. Hourly wages in Tijuana, Mexico, range from $1.50 to $2.00, well below the U.S. minimum wage of $5.15 per hour but well above the 25 cents per hour paid in China. More than 500 low-wage assembly line factories in Mexico closed between 2000 and 2002, due largely to the migration of jobs in the global economy to Asia.[15]

REMOVING BARRIERS TO FREE TRADE Worries about the migration of jobs often leads to calls for **protectionism**, which can take the form of special taxes, or tariffs, placed on imported goods. Most economists oppose protectionism because it prevents efficient use of resources and because consumers pay much more for protected products than they otherwise would in the world economy. Tariffs merely divert attention from real solutions like increased productivity and capital investments and inevitably invite retaliation from foreign countries.

In the 1930s, many nations experienced high unemployment, low production, and general economic misery. The United States was no exception. In an effort to aid ailing American industries, Congress passed the Smoot-Hawley tariff, the highest general tariff the United States had ever had. Supporters hoped high tariffs on imported goods would increase the demand for goods produced in the United States and thus help get the country out of the Great Depression. The exact opposite occurred. Other nations retaliated with high tariffs on American goods. Demand fell, intensifying the Depression.

Later, Congress gave the president power to negotiate mutual tariff reductions with other nations, subject to certain restrictions, and by the early 1970s, tariffs on industrial products had been substantially reduced. Trade barriers are less severe today than they were back in the 1930s. But restrictions still exist. Certain tariffs, quotas on imported goods, and import regulations limit American consumption of foreign products. Most exist to protect American farmers, businesses, or workers in certain industries. Thus we have restrictions on clothing and textile imports, and these restrictions cost U.S. consumers a lot more than they benefit workers' wages.

The United States has generally supported increased trade and fewer trade barriers, yet many Americans worry that globalization will hurt the country. Free trade and

North American Free Trade Agreement (NAFTA)
Agreement signed by the United States, Canada, and Mexico in 1992 to form the largest free trade zone in the world.

protectionism
Policy of erecting trade barriers to protect domestic industry.

globalization policies do not confer equal benefits on everyone. Inevitably, some workers will be worse off as a result of a freer international flow of goods and capital. All told, trade barriers cost U.S. consumers approximately $80 billion a year—equal to more than $1,200 per family.[16] At least some of these barriers helped save U.S. jobs, however, while protecting the environment and promoting human rights abroad.

U.S. economic policy in the future will probably be a combination of free trade and selective protectionism. Though protectionism shields highly visible industries from competition at home or abroad, such measures often constitute a kind of subsidy that protects one industry at the expense of another—and always at high cost to American consumers.

Even free trade advocates can occasionally find a reason, often political, for protectionism. In March 2002, for example, President George W. Bush imposed 30 percent tariffs on a range of products made with imported steel in an effort to protect the ailing U.S. steel industry. In doing so, he honored a campaign promise he had made in Ohio, Pennsylvania, and West Virginia, which were key battleground states in his 2000 campaign.

There is no question that steel imports hurt the U.S. industry. Nearly 50,000 jobs were lost between 1997 and 2002 because of bankruptcies and factory closings, and more than 300,000 jobs were at risk. As European steel makers complained to the World Trade Organization, however, the international economy was merely working its will by rewarding more efficient foreign steelmakers with a bigger market. The WTO agreed that the U.S. tariffs violated free trade rules, forcing the United States to drop the tariffs or face international retaliation on a range of products from Florida oranges to North Carolina tobacco. In December 2003, the Bush administration dropped the tariffs.

REGULATING THE ECONOMY

The Constitution explicitly authorizes Congress to regulate commerce among the states and with foreign nations. In our earliest years, Congress used this regulatory power to impose or suspend tariffs on imports from other nations. In the nineteenth century, the federal government created a number of agencies to regulate the conduct of citizens and commercial enterprises with an eye toward promoting economic development. Among these were the Army Corps of Engineers (1824), the Patent and Trademark Office

★★ THINKING IT THROUGH

Although outsourcing clearly hurts U.S. workers in the short term, most economists agree that efforts to stop the movement would hurt the economy in the longer term. "Protectionism will do little to create jobs," Federal Reserve Board Chairman Alan Greenspan said in 2004, "and if foreigners retailiate, we will surely lose jobs. We need to discover the means to enhance the skills of our work force and to further open markets here and abroad." Liberals tend to agree, but argue that the federal government should provide greater help for workers who lose their jobs to foreign nations. "The answer is not to try to stop outsourcing," says former Clinton administration Secretary of Labor Robert Reich, "but we do have to get serious about job retraining, lifetime learning, extended unemployment insurance, and wage insurance."

Outsourcing may make perfect economic sense in the long term, but has very harsh consequences in the short term. Workers whose jobs move abroad often face years of unemployment, which is why the issue became so central early in the 2004 campaign.

SOURCE: Jyoti Thottam, "Is Your Job Going Abroad?" *Time*, March 1, 2004, pp. 26–30.

United Steelworkers of America President Leo Gerard addresses steelworkers who came to Washington, D.C., to protest the problems globalization and free trade have created in their industry.

(1836), the Steamboat Inspecting Service (1837), and the Copyright Office of the Library of Congress (1870). In 1887, Congress created the Interstate Commerce Commission to deal with the widespread dissatisfaction over the practices of railroads.

Additional regulations were created to break up monopolies, to clean up meat-packing conditions such as those exposed in Upton Sinclair's *Jungle* (1906), to prevent the kind of pesticide contamination described in Rachel Carson's *Silent Spring* (1962), to correct the lack of auto safety documented in Ralph Nader's *Unsafe at Any Speed* (1965), and to prevent employment discrimination on the basis of race, color, national origin, religion, sex, and age. More recently, government has created regulations to protect citizens from raw sewage in rivers; lead in paint and gasoline; toxins in the air; radon gas in homes; and asbestos, cotton dust, and hazardous products in the environment. Federal regulations for environmental, health, and safety are estimated at about $200 billion in higher product cost.[17]

The Role of Regulation

In a broad sense, *regulation* is any attempt by the government to control the behavior of corporations, other governments, or citizens. **Regulation** is commonly defined as any method the government uses to alter the natural workings of the open market to achieve some desired goal. Regulation by government interjects political goals and values into the economy in the form of rules that direct behavior in the marketplace. These rules have the force of law and are backed by the government's police powers. (See the discussion of rules earlier in this chapter.)

There are no unregulated economies in the world. The United States operates in a competitive market economy in which wages, prices, the allocation of goods and services, and the employment of resources are generally regulated by the laws of supply and demand. The nation relies on private enterprise and market incentives to carry out most of our production and distribution.

Nevertheless, market economies have imperfections. Even opponents of regulation recognize that the market does not always solve every problem. Consider pollution. For a long time, no price was imposed on a business for using air and water to discharge toxic wastes. Therefore, market forces did not consider the social costs of its air and water pollution. When the market fails to set appropriate costs and benefits, pressures develop for the government to step in. The government can, for example, create regulations imposing penalties for air pollution. Market forces also do not encourage taking a bus instead of a car to work. If government enacted higher taxes on gasoline, our fuel costs would be brought more in line with Europe's. Such a policy would also reduce our dependence on Middle East oil and promote domestic energy production.

In 1935, there were 4,000 pages of regulations in the *Code of Federal Regulations,* which lists all federal rules; today, there are more than 70,000 pages of regulations.[18] Both political parties say regulatory overkill threatens to overwhelm entrepreneurs and divert them from building vital, innovative companies. Although some economists estimate that regulations can add as much as $3,000 to the cost of a new car, the regulations also purchase important benefits such as cleaner air and safer cars, which, in turn, reduce accidents and improve the overall quality of life.[19] The question is not whether there are both costs and benefits from regulation but whether the balance is right. Conservatives tend to overstate the costs of many regulations and understate the benefits, while liberals tend to overstate the benefits and understate the costs.

Types of Regulation

There are two general categories of regulation: economic and social regulation.

Economic regulation generally refers to government controls on the behavior of businesses in the marketplace: the entry of individual firms into particular lines of business, the prices that firms may charge, and the standards of service they must offer.

Although the national government has been regulating interstate commerce since 1789, it was generally reluctant to regulate private businesses until the industrial revolution of the late 1800s. As the U.S. economy grew, so did the need for rules governing business and labor. Congress created the Interstate Commerce Commission in 1887

Regulation
Efforts by government to alter the free operation of the market to achieve social goals such as protecting workers and the environment.

as the first of what would become many independent regulatory commissions. The ICC was established to regulate the railroads and other transporation industries, but was abolished in the late 1970s as part of the deregulation movement discussed later in this chapter (see Table 18–2 for a list of key government regulatory agencies).

The second type of regulation, *social regulation,* refers to government attempts to correct a wide variety of side effects, usually unintended, brought about by economic activity. Concern for worker health and safety and for environmental hazards has led to much social regulation. Social regulation also includes efforts by government to ensure equal rights in employment, education, and housing. Whereas economic regulation is usually organized along industry lines, social regulation cuts across these lines.

The Environmental Protection Agency, the Consumer Product Safety Commission, and the Occupational Safety and Health Administration are regulatory agencies engaged in social regulation. In economic terms, producers regulated by social regulation must now pay for external costs that once were free, such as using rivers, landfills, or the atmosphere for waste disposal. These costs, however, are then passed along to the consumer, so the true cost of the product is more accurately reflected in its price. Some goods subsequently become too costly, and demand drops. Others become more popular (for instance, safe toys), and demand increases. The final goal of social regulation is the socially beneficial allocation of resources.

Congress has created two types of regulatory agencies: those within the executive branch and those that have a degree of independence from Congress and the president. Members of executive branch agencies serve at the pleasure of the president. Executive

TABLE 18–2 KEY REGULATORY AGENCIES AND THEIR MISSIONS

Agency	Year Established	Primary Functions
Federal Trade Commission (FTC)	1914	Administers certain antitrust laws concerning advertising, labeling, and packaging to protect consumers from unfair business practices
Food and Drug Administration (FDA)	1931	Establishes regulations concerning purity, safety, and labeling accuracy of certain foods and drugs; issues licenses for manufacturing and distribution
Securities and Exchange Commission (SEC)	1934	Oversees the activities of the stock markets and assures that all publicly-reported information is honest
National Labor Relations Board (NLRB)	1935	Guarantees the right of employees to organize and oversees complaints about unfair practices by employers and unions
Federal Communications Commission (FCC)	1934	Licenses civilian radio and television communication; licenses and sets rates for interstate and international communication
Animal and Plant Health Inspection Service	1953	Sets standards; inspects and enforces laws relating to meat, poultry, and plant safety
Environmental Protection Agency (EPA)	1970	Develops environmental quality standards; approves state environmental plans
Occupational Safety and Health Administration (OSHA)	1970	Develops and enforces worker safety and health regulations
Bureau of Alcohol, Tobacco and Firearms (ATF)	1972	Enforces laws and regulates legal flow of these materials
Consumer Product Safety Commission (CPSC)	1972	Establishes mandatory product safety standards and bans sales of products that do not comply
Nuclear Regulatory Commission (NRC)	1974	Licenses the construction and operation of nuclear reactors and similar facilities and regulates nuclear materials; licenses the export of nuclear reactors and the export and import of uranium and plutonium
National Nuclear Security Administration	2000	Monitors the nation's nuclear bomb-building laboratories; oversees the military's stockpile of nuclear weapons; protects the secrecy of U.S. weapons research
Transportation Security Administration (TSA)	2001	Controls passenger and baggage screening; regulates what passengers can carry; requires airlines to check bags through electronic screens; oversees all airport, land, and maritime security

CHANGING FACE OF AMERICAN POLITICS

WOMEN AND MINORITIES IN THE BOARDROOM

Boards of directors wield great power in directing the activities of their companies—they oversee executive salaries and compensation, approve major decisions such as mergers and acquisitions of other companies, and are responsible for the honesty of corporate financial reports.

Although women and minorities now constitute a significant percentage of the U.S. workforce, they occupy relatively few of the seats on the boards of America's largest corporations. As of 2003, just 10.6 percent of board members at the nation's 1,500 largest companies were women, and 9.5 percent were minorities. These percentages have grown slightly over the past decade, but they still remain well below the representation of women and minorities in the workforce and among mangers and executives.

These percentages may increase in coming years as corporations seek to add more board members under new federal rules adopted in the wake of the accounting scandals at Enron, WorldCom, and other leading corporations. The problem is not a lack of names for nomination—in May 2002, for example, the New American Alliance, a nonprofit association of Latino business leaders, and the Hispanic Association for Corporate Responsibility joined together to create a database of more than 1,000 Hispanic candidates for board openings. If the numbers do not grow, advocacy groups have promised to pressure the Securities and Exchange Commission for a rule requiring greater diversity.

Percentage of Women and Minorities in the Workforce and Board Room, 2003

	Percent Women	Percent Racial Minorities
U.S. Workforce	47.2%	29.7%
Executives and Managers	34.2	14.9
Seats on the Boards of the 1,500 Largest Companies	10.6	9.5

SOURCE: Data from Susan Williams, "Board Diversity," Investment Responsibility Resource Center, Background Report A, February 9, 2004.

branch regulatory agencies include the Food and Drug Administration, the Office of Surface Mining, and the National Highway Traffic Safety Administration. Commissioners of independent regulatory agencies are appointed by the president and confirmed by the Senate, and they cannot be removed by a president except for cause. Independent agencies, usually headed by a board composed of seven members, include the Federal Communications Commission, the Equal Employment Opportunity Commission, and the Nuclear Regulatory Commission.

Regulating Business

During most of the nineteenth century, our national policy was to leave business pretty much alone. However, four major waves of regulatory legislation occurred in the twentieth century: at its start, in the 1910s, in the 1930s, and in the late 1960s through 1980. In each case, changing circumstances gave rise to the legislation.

Perhaps the number one responsibility of government regulation in our free market system is to maintain competition. When one company gains a **monopoly**, or several create an *oligopoly*, the market system operates ineffectively. The aim of **antitrust legislation** is to prevent monopolies, break up those that exist, and ensure competition. In the past, so-called natural monopolies, such as electric utilities and telephone companies, were protected by the government because it was assumed that in these fields competition would be grossly inefficient.

In the late nineteenth century, social critics and populist reformers believed that consumers were being cheated, especially in the oil, sugar, whiskey, and steel industries, where large monopolies, called **trusts**, stifled competition. People began to have mixed feelings about big business. Americans, who have often been impressed by bigness—the tallest skyscraper, the largest football stadium, the biggest steel mill—and the efficiency that often goes with bigness, became skeptical about giant enterprises.

In 1890, Congress responded by passing the Sherman Antitrust Act, which was designed "to protect trade and commerce against unlawful restraints and monopolies."

monopoly
Domination of an industry by a single company; also the company that dominates the industry.

antitrust legislation
Federal laws (starting with the Sherman Antitrust Act of 1890) that try to prevent a monopoly from dominating an industry and restraining trade.

trust
A monopoly that controls goods and services, often in combinations that reduce competition.

Henceforth, persons making contracts, combinations, or conspiracies in restraint of trade in interstate and foreign commerce could be sued for damages, required to stop their illegal practices, and subjected to criminal penalties. However, the Sherman Antitrust Act had little immediate impact; presidents made few attempts to enforce it, and the Supreme Court's early interpretation of the act limited its scope.[20]

Congress added the Clayton Act to the antitrust arsenal in 1914. This act outlawed such specific abuses as charging different prices to different buyers in order to destroy a weaker competitor, granting rebates, making false statements about competitors and their products, buying up supplies to suppress competition, and bribing competitors' employees. In addition, *interlocking directorates* (having an officer or director in one corporation serve on the board of a competitor) were banned, and corporations were prohibited from acquiring stock in competing concerns if such acquisitions substantially lessened interstate competition. That same year, Congress established the Federal Trade Commission (FTC), run by a five-person board, to enforce the Clayton Act and prevent unfair competitive practices. The FTC was to be the "traffic cop" for competition.[21]

Regulating Labor

Government regulation of business is essentially restrictive. Most laws and rules curb business practices and steer private enterprise into socially useful channels. But regulation cuts two ways. In the case of American workers, most laws in recent decades have tended not to restrict labor but to confer rights and opportunities on it. Actually, many labor laws do not touch labor directly; instead they regulate relations with employers.

Federal regulations protect workers in the following important areas, among others:

1. *Public contracts.* The Walsh-Healy Act of 1936, as amended, requires that no worker employed under contracts with the national government in excess of $10,000 be paid less than the prevailing wage and that he or she be paid overtime for all work in excess of eight hours per day or 40 hours per week.

2. *Wages and hours.* The Fair Labor Standards Act of 1938 set a maximum workweek of 40 hours for all employees engaged in interstate commerce or in the production of goods for interstate commerce (with certain exemptions). Work beyond that amount must be paid for at 1½ times the regular rate.

3. *Child labor.* The Fair Labor Standards Act of 1938 prohibits child labor (under 16 years of age, or under 18 in hazardous occupations) in industries that engage in or produce goods for interstate commerce.

4. *Industrial safety and occupational health.* The Occupational Safety and Health Act of 1970 created the first comprehensive federal industrial safety program. It gave the secretary of labor broad authority to set safety and health standards for companies engaged in interstate commerce.

Federal regulations also protect employee rights to organize unions. Under the 1935 National Labor Relations Act (usually called the Wagner Act), for example, the federal government gave workers significant new rights to organize unions, while prohibiting businesses from discriminating against union members or refusing to bargain in good faith with union representatives.

Congress passed a major modification of the labor laws in 1947, the Labor-Management Relations Act, commonly called the Taft-Hartley Act. The act outlawed the **closed shop** (a company that requires an employer to hire and retain only union members in good standing) and permits the **union shop** (a company in which new employees are obligated to join the union within a stated period of time), prohibits employers from refusing to bargain with employees, allows courts to issue **labor injunctions** forbidding specific individuals or groups to perform acts considered harmful to the rights or property of an employer or community, and structures the process of **collective bargaining** between unions and employers to set wages, benefits, and working conditions.

closed shop
A company with a labor agreement under which union membership is a condition of employment.

union shop
A company in which new employees must join a union within a stated time period.

labor injunction
A court order forbidding specific individuals or groups from performing certain acts (such as striking) that the court considers harmful to the rights and property of an employer or a community.

collective bargaining
Method whereby representatives of the union and employer determine wages, hours, and other conditions of employment through direct negotiation.

Martha Stewart was tried and convicted in 2004 for misleading federal investigators about why she sold her stock in a drug company called ImClone Systems. Her decision to sell was based on inside information she received about a failed cancer drug trial before this information was made public.

Regulating Markets

The stock market crash of 1929 did more than devastate the American economy and usher in the Great Depression. It also revealed deep problems in how stocks were sold to investors. Millions of new investors entered the stock market in the 1920s only to find out that the companies in which they had invested were virtually worthless.

Prior to 1934, when the Securities and Exchange Commission (SEC) was created, investors had to determine whether a company was telling the truth about its stock. Since 1934, that responsibility has fallen to the SEC. Under the Securities Exchange Act of 1934 and a long list of later laws, companies that offer their stock for sale to the public must tell the truth about their businesses, which means full disclosure of all financial statements, as well as the stocks they are selling and the risks involved in investing.

At the same time, the act also required that anyone in the business of selling stocks, including brokers, dealers, and stock exchanges such as the New York Stock Exchange and NASDAQ, must treat investors fairly and honestly, putting investors' interests first. That means, for example, that individuals who know about a new stock offering in advance or have other inside information on events that might increase or decrease the value of a given stock are prohibited from using that information to benefit themselves.

Congress added to the long inventory of other laws to protect investors when it passed a corporate reform bill in 2002. The law was designed to prevent the kind of deceptive accounting games that led to the Enron collapse earlier in the year. The law strengthened the SEC, created a new oversight board to monitor accounting practices, and set new disclosure requirements on how corporations treat certain expenditures. Despite the public's concern about Enron, the bill was stalled in the Senate until the WorldCom scandal broke in June. The bill passed the Senate almost immediately after by a 97-to-0 vote.

Regulating and Protecting the Environment

Air and water pollution vividly illustrates the regulatory dilemma. Critics of strict controls on air, water, and noise pollution say the pursuit of a clean environment increases the costs of products and causes unemployment. They call attention, for example, to the disastrous economic consequences of the shutdown of companies for pollution violations. Until relatively recently, governments at all levels did little to protect the environment, and what little was done was by state and local governments. In recent decades, however, the national government has taken on new responsibilities, primarily because local governments failed to act.

The fall of Enron, the nation's largest energy trading company, caused thousands of employees to lose their jobs as well as their pensions.

Perhaps the most controversial environmental regulation involves **environmental impact statements**, which are used to assess the potential effects of new construction or development on the environment. Most projects using federal funds must file such statements. Since 1970, thousands of statements have been filed. Supporters contend that such statements point out major flaws in projects and can lead to cost savings along with greater environmental awareness. Critics claim that environmental impact reviews simply represent more government interference, paperwork, and delays in the public and private sectors.

Environmental impact statements are only one form of environmental regulation, however. The 1990 Clean Air Act was designed to tighten controls on automobiles and the fuel they use. Building on regulations established under the 1967, 1970, and 1977 acts of the same name, the 1990 act required automakers to install pollution controls to reduce emissions of hydrocarbons and nitrogen oxides and set stiff standards for the kinds of gasoline that can be sold. The 1990 act also required power companies to cut pollution from coal-burning power plants, phased out the use of certain chemicals that harm the earth's protective ozone layer and may contribute to global warming, and set new limits on a long list of cancer-causing pollutants.

The act also promoted further use of the profit motive to encourage self-regulation by private business. Under new rules issued by the Environmental Protection Agency, businesses are allowed to generate a certain amount of pollution. If they cut the amount of pollution below their allotment, they can sell the balance to other companies that are polluting more. By setting overall caps for certain regions of the country, this "cap-and-trade" system encourages individual companies to reduce the total amount of pollution they would have produced under traditional regulations. Initial efforts along these lines have been successful, while saving billions.

Protecting the Global Environment

As globalization has expanded, so have the environmental challenges and hazards associated with that growth. Global temperatures are on the rise, suggesting the possibility that economic development and the burning of carbon-based fuels that goes with it may have created a blanket of carbon dioxide "greenhouse gases" that traps heat in the earth's atmosphere.

Concerns about the consequences of global warming led to negotiation of the Kyoto Protocol in 1997. Named for the Japanese city in which it was negotiated, this treaty

environmental impact statement
A statement required by federal law from all agencies for any project using federal funds to assess the potential effect of the new construction or development on the environment.

required participating countries to make substantial cuts in greenhouse gas emissions year by year until 2012. Because not all nations participated in the negotiations and because the effort to control carbon-based fuels would slow the growth of less developed nations, the Kyoto Protocol immediately divided the world between North (developed countries) and South (less developed countries). Moreover, because the United States would be required to spend billions of dollars reducing the greenhouse gases from its cars and coal-fired electric plants, the Senate signaled its reluctance to participate, too. As of 2005, the Kyoto Protocol has yet to be fully embraced by the world, while nations in both North and South continue to pump carbon dioxide into their skies.

Global warming is only one of several environmental problems the world faces, however. Greenhouse gases may be on the rise, but the world's ozone layer, which protects humans from cancer-causing ultraviolet radiation, is thinning. Unlike global warming, the world has made considerable progress in limiting the major chemicals that have contributed to the "ozone hole" in the atmosphere.

THE DEREGULATION MOVEMENT

One solution to criticisms of government regulation has been **deregulation**, the reduction or complete abolition of federal regulation in a particular sector of the economy. Deregulation began in 1977 with the airline, trucking, and railroad industries, and has continued with banking and telecommunications.

At the same time the federal government has been working to deregulate certain industries, it has also created new procedures to limit the amount of regulation the federal government can impose. In 1993, for example, President Bill Clinton issued an executive order prohibiting agencies from issuing regulations unless the benefits of the regulations (in lives saved, for example) outweighed the costs. In 2001, President George W. Bush followed suit by imposing a 60-day hold on all regulations published by the Clinton administration until his administration could ensure that the regulations met the benefit/cost test.

Deregulating Transportation

No industry has undergone more extensive deregulation than the transportation industry. Over the past generation, airlines, trucking, and railroads have been granted considerable freedom in conducting their operations. No deregulation effort was more visible to individual consumers than airline deregulation.

deregulation
A policy promoting cutbacks in the amount of federal regulation in specific areas of economic activity.

Meeting of the United Nations Global Warming Conference in Kyoto, Japan, in December 1997, which constructed the treaty known as the Kyoto Protocol.

The federal government began regulating aviation when the Civil Aeronautics Board (CAB) was established by the federal government in 1938 to protect airlines from unreasonable competition by controlling rates and fares. Critics charged that airlines competed only in the frequency of flights and in the services they offered, forcing consumers to pay higher fares than needed.

After years of debate, Congress abolished the CAB in 1978, allowing the market to set fares through competition. Although many fares fell, some medium-sized cities lost service because carriers found it more profitable to use their aircraft in busier markets. Airlines were raising fares on routes over which they had monopolies in order to subsidize lower fares on more competitive routes. Critics charged that safety precautions and maintenance suffered as a result of cutthroat competition and the ease with which new airlines could enter the market.

Although problems have been associated with airline deregulation, it has resulted in generally lower fares, greater choice of routes and fares in most markets, and more efficient use of assets by the industry.[22] Some airlines have been driven into bankruptcy and others have merged, but deregulation of the airlines has been judged a success by the surviving airlines and most observers of the industry. If an airline is overcharging passengers, a competitor will eventually steal those travelers away. Southwest Airlines is an example of a discount airline that took advantage of deregulation to take on larger airlines.[23] Deregulation has strengthened the industry by forcing companies to streamline their operations in order to survive in a competitive market. But recent mergers of major airlines have worsened the problems caused by deregulation and cancellation of service to rural and medium-sized cities in parts of states in the West, while the post–September 11 collapse in travel has pushed several airlines toward bankruptcy, which in turn prompted Congress to provide loans to many airlines to help them through the crisis.

Deregulating Telecommunications

Airline deregulation may have been the most visible to consumers, but the deregulation of telecommunications may eventually have a greater impact on how Americans live, whether in the form of lower phone bills, easier access to the Internet, or better cellular technology. Unlike the deregulation of transportation, which came in a number of steps over time, deregulation of telecommunications came in a single, massive bill called the Telecommunications Act of 1996.

The act opened up large areas of telecommunications to companies that once were regulated both in the services they could provide and the prices they could charge. The main objective of the new law was to increase competition among phone, cable, and other communications companies. Telephone companies that were once divided into seven local "baby Bells" were allowed to offer services outside their defined regions. Local telephone companies won the freedom to provide long-distance service, manufacture communications equipment, and offer video service in competition with cable television.

At the same time, local telephone companies opened their networks to competition for local telephone service from cable television and long-distance companies. In short, restrictions were removed so that cable television and local and long-distance telephone companies could effectively compete with one another.

The Telecommunications Act also contained two highly controversial provisions: new regulation on Internet content and a requirement that all television makers install a "V-chip" to allow parents to block out television shows with objectionable content. However, the Supreme Court struck down the provisions making it a crime for any person knowingly to make indecent material accessible to minors on the Internet. The Court found the provision too vague and held that the Internet receives full protection under the First Amendment.[24] Although the debate continues on who will decide what is deemed violent or offensive, most surveys suggest that parents are unwilling or unable to use the V-chip to control their family viewing habits.[25]

MAKE IT *REAL* ✓

BALANCING THE NATION'S BUDGET: WHAT CAN YOU GET FOR $4 TRILLION?

Imagine for a moment that you are the director of the Office of Management and Budget and have been directed to recommend budget cuts that are equal to the amount of revenue lost through the president's tax cuts. Each budget cut carries more than a dollar cost, of course. Each has some political impact on the president's approval and reelection. If the damage is too high, you will be out of a job long before the next election.

Go to Make It Real "Balancing the Nation's Budget: What Can You Get for $4 Trillion?"

The Cost of Regulation

Although the need for regulation, especially in areas affecting health and safety, is widely accepted, there are concerns about the negative consequences of regulation. A marked decrease in lead paint poisonings, the use of childproof bottle tops, and the banning of many cancer-producing pesticides are all positive outcomes. On the negative side, regulations generally increase the cost of products and may hamper some industries:

- *Regulation disrupts the operation of the market.* Some governmental intervention upsets the normal adjustment processes of the market and thus encourages higher prices, misallocation of resources, and inefficiency.

- *Regulation may discourage competition.* Some forms of regulation (often the kind desired by industry) actually have the reverse of their desired effect. This is especially true when the government grants operating licenses and charters to maintain a certain level of quality or stability in the market. Regulatory red tape has also been charged with discouraging entry into industries and driving small businesses out.

- *Regulation may discourage technological development.* If the reward for innovation is a new set of rules and a struggle for permission to use a new product, business may not find it worth the effort to innovate.

- *Regulation increases costs to industry and consumers.* Some critics estimate that government regulations cost every U.S. household $8,000 to $10,000 annually, while advocates argue that regulations return even more in health and safety.

The mere fact that the national government stops regulating an industry does not mean that the industry will be unregulated, however. Sometimes the states take over, making it even more difficult for an industry to operate on a large scale. California, for example, has much tougher automobile emission rules than the national government. Variations in state regulations are the reason businesspeople themselves sometimes call for more, not less, national regulation; they would prefer one set of national guidelines to 50 different state ones.

In sum, the federal government is heavily involved in making economic and regulatory policies. It collects taxes, regulates the money supply, tries to prevent monopolies that would hurt consumers, and seeks to promote free trade. It does all this while trying to let the market, not government bureaucrats, shape the demand and price of products and services. Most Americans want their government to play only a limited role in the economy, but competing values such as fairness, equality, protecting the environment, and encouraging healthy competition inevitably encourage elected officials to take on certain balancing or referee responsibilities in order to promote the common good.

S U M M A R Y

1. The policy-making process involves a variety of choices made by Congress, the president, and the courts, including (1) making assumptions about the world, (2) identifying the problem to be solved, (3) deciding whether to act at all, (4) deciding how much to do, (5) choosing a tool for solving the problem, and (6) making rules for implementation.

2. The national government influences how wealth is produced and distributed primarily via fiscal policy (taxing and spending), monetary policy (control of the money supply), and regulatory policy.

3. Fiscal policy is implemented by the federal budget, which is annually negotiated between the president and Congress. Monetary policy is primarily under the control of the Federal Reserve System, which has considerable independence from both Congress and the president as it works to supply sufficient amounts of money and credit so that the economy will grow but not so much that it will lead to inflation.

4. Government's role in promoting growth and jobs is not new. It is as old as the Republic itself. The federal government has long been involved in promoting agriculture and concerned about the health of producers and consumers of farm commodities. Working through the Department of Commerce, it also promotes business. The national government is also involved in promoting trade and commerce with other nations. Our ability to buy from other nations and sell them our goods and services has much to do with the health of our economy.

5. Regulation, now a major activity of government, involves altering the natural workings of the open market to achieve some desired goal. Economic regulation aims to control the behavior of business in the marketplace. Social regulation aims to correct the unintended side effects of economic activity and to ensure

equal rights in employment, education, and housing.

6. Regulation is a means of eliminating some of the abuses and problems generated by the private economy while avoiding government ownership and the risks of too much centralization. Regulation is an inevitable byproduct of a complex, industrialized, high-technology society.

7. The federal government regulates the economy in five ways. It maintains competition by preventing monopoly and oligopoly. It regulates labor to give workers the right to organize into unions. It regulates markets to protect investors. It regulates the environment to protect the public. And it is increasingly involved in regulating the global environment. A deregulation movement designed to get the government out of the regulation of certain businesses has taken form over the past 30 years. Liberals sometimes favor deregulation if they believe it will foster more competition. Conservatives generally favor deregulation that will get federal regulators off their backs in areas such as safety, health, and environmental and consumer protection standards.

K E Y   T E R M S

public policy
policy agenda
distributive policy
redistributive policy
rule
iron triangle
issue network
fiscal policy
monetary policy
inflation
unemployment
tariff
excise tax

progressive tax
regressive tax
deficit
national debt
gross domestic product (GDP)
entitlements
Office of Management and Budget (OMB)
Congressional Budget Office (CBO)
sales tax
value-added tax (VAT)

tax expenditure
monetarism
Federal Reserve System
laissez-faire economics
Keynesian economics
trade deficit
World Trade Organization (WTO)
General Agreement on Tariffs and Trade (GATT)
North American Free Trade Agreement (NAFTA)

protectionism
regulation
monopoly
antitrust legislation
trust
closed shop
union shop
labor injunction
collective bargaining
environmental impact statement
deregulation

F U R T H E R   R E A D I N G

JEFFREY H. BIRNBAUM AND ALAN S. MURRAY, *Showdown at Gucci Gulch: Lawmakers, Lobbyists, and the Unlikely Triumph of Tax Reform* (Vintage, 1988).

STEPHEN G. BREYER, *Breaking the Vicious Circle: Toward Effective Risk Regulation* (Harvard University Press, 1993).

GARY BRYNER, *Blue Skies, Green Politics: The Clean Air Act of 1990 and Its Interpretation*, 2d ed. (CQ Press, 1995).

GARY BURTLESS, ROBERT J. LAWRENCE, ROBERT E. LITAN, AND ROBERT J. SHAPIRO, *Globaphobia: Confronting Fears About Open Trade* (Brookings Institution Press, 1998).

THOMAS W. CHURCH AND ROBERT T. NAKAMURA, *Cleaning Up the Mess: Implementation Strategies in Superfund* (Brookings Institution Press, 1993).

ROBERT W. CRANDALL AND HAROLD FURCHTGOTT-ROTH, *Cable TV: Regulation or Competition?* (Brookings Institution Press, 1996).

ROBERT W. CRANDALL AND LEONARD WAVERMAN, *Who Pays for Universal Service? When Telephone Subsidies Become Transparent* (Brookings Institution Press, 2000).

ROBERT W. CRANDALL ET AL., *An Agenda for Federal Regulatory Reform* (American Enterprise Institute/Brookings Institution, 1997).

ROBERT M. ENTMAN, *Competition, Innovation, and Investment in Telecommunications* (Aspen Institute, 1998).

THOMAS L. FRIEDMAN, *The Lexus and the Olive Tree: Understanding Globalization* (Anchor Books, 2000).

AL GORE, *Earth in the Balance: Ecology and the Human Spirit* (Houghton Mifflin, 1992).

WILLIAM GREIDER, *Secrets of the Temple: How the Federal Reserve Runs the Country* (Simon & Schuster, 1987).

PHILIP K. HOWARD, *The Death of Common Sense: How Law Is Suffocating America* (Random House, 1994).

CORNELIUS M. KERWIN, *Rulemaking: How Government Agencies Write Law and Make Policy*, 2d ed. (CQ, 1998).

ROBERT KUTTNER, *Everything for Sale: The Virtues and Limits of Markets* (Knopf, 1997).

LAWRENCE LESSIG, *Code and Other Laws of Cyberspace* (Basic Books, 2000).

CALVIN MACKENZIE AND SARANNA THORTON, *Bucking the Deficit: Economic Policy-Making in America* (Westview Press, 1996).

STEVEN A. MORRISON AND CLIFFORD WINSTON, *The Evolution of the Airline Industry* (Brookings Institution Press, 1995).

PETER G. PETERSON, *Facing Up: Paying Our Nation's Debt and Saving Our Children's Future* (Simon & Schuster, 1994).

ALLEN SCHICK, *The Federal Budget: Politics, Policy, Process*, rev. ed. (Brookings Institution Press, 2000).

JOSEPH E. STIGLITZ, *Globlization and Its Discontents* (Norton, 2002).

JOHN WARGO, *Our Children's Toxic Legacy: How Science and Law Fail to Protect Us from Pesticides* (Yale University Press, 1997).

BOB WOODWARD, *Maestro: Greenspan's Fed and the American Boom* (Simon & Schuster, 2000).

JEFFREY WORSHAW, *Other People's Money: Policy Changes, Congress, and Bank Regulation* (Westview Press, 1997).

DANIEL YERGIN AND JOSEPH STANISLAW, *The Commanding Heights: The Battle Between Government and the Marketplace That Is Remaking the Modern World* (Simon & Schuster, 1998).

A lthough the Preamble to the Constitution promises that the federal government will promote the general welfare, liberals and conservatives often differ sharply on just what the promise means. Liberals tend to believe that the federal government should take the lead in helping needy Americans, while conservatives tend to believe that the free market and state and local governments should be the source of support for those in need.

These differences came to a head at 3 A.M. early Saturday morning, November 22, 2003, when the House held its final vote on prescription drug coverage for older Americans. Although most members of Congress wanted to add drug coverage to the 1965 Medicare program, Democrats and Republicans disagreed sharply on how much the government should provide and who should deliver the coverage. Democrats wanted the federal government to provide more coverage and run the program, while Republicans wanted to provide limited coverage and allow private insurance companies to compete against each other to run the program.

But Republicans controlled a majority in the House, and neither party was sure how conservative members would vote on the $400 billion bill. If enough conservative Republicans voted to defeat their party's proposal, Democrats might have a chance to offer their own version of prescription drug coverage.

With members eager to adjourn for the Thanksgiving recess, most House members hurried to the floor to cast their votes and leave town. With all but one member voting and constrained by the customary 15-minute period, Democrats and a handful of conservative Republicans defeated the bill, 216 to 219. All that remained was the bang of the gavel bringing the vote to a close.

MAKING SOCIAL POLICY

19

TIME LINE ★★

MAKING SOCIAL POLICY

1862	Morrill Land Grant Act helps create state universities
1933	FDR's New Deal creates dozens of federal agencies that employ many people during the Great Depression
1935	Social Security system is created
1935	Aid to Families with Dependent Children nationalizes welfare
1944	GI Bill allows World War II vets to attend college
1946	School Lunch Act finances school lunches for children around the country
1964	Food Stamp Act is the first federal program to provide food directly
1965	Medicare and Medicaid are created to provide health care for the elderly and disabled
1966	Department of Housing and Urban Development is created to promote urban renewal

Orphanages run by religious orders provided for needy children. These orphans attended the Sisters of Charity of the Incarnate World Orphanage in Galveston, Texas, in the late 1890s.

Unfortunately for the Democrats, the Speaker of the House, J. Dennis Hastert, refused to let the gavel drop at the 15-minute deadline. Instead, he kept the vote open for another 158 minutes as the Republican leadership lobbied members to change their votes on the biggest vote of Hastert's career. With his whips working the aisles and President Bush working the phones, Hastert concentrated his fire on the six conservative Republicans who had voted against the bill.

Just before 6:00 A.M., C. L. "Butch" Otter of Idaho and Trent Franks of Arizona switched their votes from nay to aye, turning the 216 to 219 defeat into what would become a 220 to 215 victory as a handful of other members switched from one side to the other, too. Although Democrats complained bitterly about the outcome, the extended vote was perfectly legal under House rules, which only *recommend* a 15-minute limit. "A vote is a pressure cooker sometimes," Hastert said later. "It just took that amount of time to get people to change their minds.[1]

With the victory in hand, the bill moved quickly through the legislative process and to the president's desk on December 8 for a signature. In return for a $35 monthly premium, the federal government will cover 75 percent of all yearly drug costs between $250 and $2,250, thereby helping all participants regardless of need. In addition, the federal government will cover 95 percent of all drug costs above $3,600, thereby protecting participants who face extremely high, or catastrophic, drug costs.

Athough the new program will certainly help older Americans, it did nothing to help the 60 million Americans who have no health insurance at all in any given year, let alone those who have no prescription drug coverage. Moreover, it did not address rising drug costs for Americans of any age. The faster drug costs rise, the less valuable will be the new Medicare benefit for older Americans, and the more all Americans will need help.

More important perhaps, Congress and the president did nothing to address the long-term financial problems facing Medicare. According to the latest projections, the Medicare program will start to run a deficit in 2019, which means that the federal government will have to either raise taxes or cut benefits to cover the total cost. Unless something is done soon to control costs, Congress may yet have another tight vote to cut the prescription drug program it just enacted.

This chapter will explore how the federal government promotes the general welfare today, how that promise has expanded over the past century, and what remains to be done to protect the needy. It will also examine three areas of social policy that are likely to be active over the next few years: health, education, and crime control.

THE ROLE OF GOVERNMENT IN SOCIAL POLICY

The nation has been debating the federal government's role in promoting the general welfare from the beginning of the Republic. Some Americans ask whether government should be involved at all in social policies such as child care, help for the needy, and job training, all of which were once thought of as purely private, religious, or charitable responsibilities. Others ask which level of government should be involved in specific issues such as education, welfare distribution, and crime control, all of which were once thought to be solely state and local responsibilities. Today, these responsibilities are a large part of the agenda of our national government.

Who Is Responsible for the Needy?

Americans are sharply divided on whether and how much the government at all levels should do to care for the less fortunate. Conservative Americans believe that people are responsible for their own lot in life even if that means they must live in poverty. They doubt government's ability to provide effective, efficient protection against misfortune and put their faith in the free market instead. They believe that the economy will provide opportunities for those who are willing to work hard. Many also believe that charities and religious institutions, not government, should help the less fortunate.

Liberal Americans believe that government must step in to help the needy through social programs such as job training, child care assistance, public housing, and other forms of aid. Although they too may doubt the efficiency of public solutions, they believe that the free market is often unfair, leaving some Americans behind because of their race, sex, lack of access to education, and so forth. They believe that government should provide a safety net against poverty, joblessness, and prejudice.

The two political parties tend to divide sharply in this debate along these ideological lines. Republicans believe that the national government is part of the problem, not the solution, to poverty and other social ills because it gets in the way of the free market. They tend to favor programs that create incentives for people to pull themselves out of poverty through hard work.

In contrast, Democrats are more likely to believe that only the national government has the resources and jurisdiction to provide adequate Social Security, help local governments improve the quality of education, and ensure that all Americans, rich and poor, have access to proper medical attention. They tend to favor programs that make sure all Americans are protected from the occasional failures of the free market system. They believe that the national government must provide a safety net for individuals and a minimum standard of living—a job, an education, health care, housing, and basic nutrition—for all citizens.

These differences are clear in recent public opinion surveys. Just 20 percent of Republicans interviewed in 2003 mostly or completely agreed that success in life is pretty much determined by forces outside our control, compared to 36 percent of Democrats. Similarly, just 46 percent of Republicans mostly or completely agreed that government should guarantee every citizen enough to eat and a place to sleep, compared to 81 percent of Democrats.[2]

Which Level of Government Should Take Care of the Needy?

Americans also disagree on whether the federal government should care for the needy. Some Americans argue that state and local governments should solve social policy problems such as poverty, in part because states and localities know more about the specific needs in their communities. Others believe that only the national government can ensure that every American is protected against misfortune, in part because poor states and localities do not have the resources to provide as much help as their richer neighbors.

In recent years, Democrats and Republicans have resolved the debate in part by setting national standards that require all states and localities to provide minimum levels of help. In turn, state governors have been increasingly critical of *unfunded mandates* such as the annual student testing required under the No Child Left Behind Act of 2002 that require state action with little or no federal funding for implementation. The tendency of Congress to impose unfunded mandates forces state governments to raise taxes or reduce funding for other state programs. Governors argue that if Congress inaugurates a new program requiring states to take action, Congress should provide the federal funds to help pay for the state's costs to administer that program.

THE EARLY HISTORY OF SOCIAL POLICY IN THE UNITED STATES

Most Western governments expanded their social programs long before the United States did. Americans generally believed that people who could not succeed in a nation as big, rich, and open as the United States simply were not working hard enough. This commitment to *rugged individualism* meant that government, be it local, state, or national, played only a limited role in people's lives. Rather grudgingly, state governments in the early twentieth century extended relief to needy groups, especially the old, the blind, and the orphaned. But government aid was limited, and much reliance was placed on private charity.[3]

This is not to suggest that the national government ignored domestic policy, however. From its founding, the national government took care of its military veterans. Indeed, with the Revolutionary War barely over, the Continental Congress established the nation's first programs to help soldiers who had been disabled in battle, as well as

GLOBAL *Perceptions*

Citizens around the world differ greatly on who is responsible for individual success. Americans tend to believe that success is determined more by the individual, while citizens in countries with relatively weak economies tend to blame forces beyond their control. Only 32 percent of Americans completely or mostly agree that success in life is pretty much determined by events outside our control, compared with 55 percent of Brazilians, 56 percent of Polish, 58 percent of the citizens of India, 63 percent of South Africans, 71 percent of Kenyans, 76 percent of the Turkish, and 75 percent of South Koreans. The Japanese and Canadians come closest to the U.S. view at 43 and 35 percent, respectively.

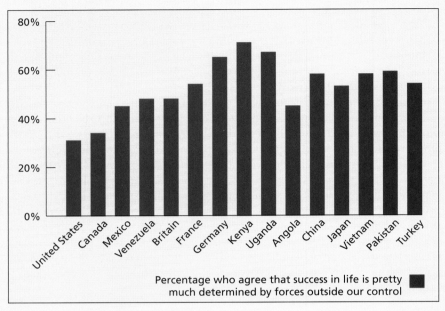

Percentage who agree that success in life is pretty much determined by forces outside our control

SOURCE: Pew Global Attitudes Project, 2003, p. T7.

general retirement pensions for officers. Thus, contrary to those who argue that government did little to care for older Americans until it created the Social Security system in 1935, the Continental Congress actually provided care for older veterans well before the new government was even created.

Once established in the 1780s, the financial security system for veterans expanded slowly but steadily as the soldiers aged into disability and poverty. Americans could not stand to see their veterans in tattered clothing and felt obliged to provide support for the less fortunate. In 1818, for example, Congress expanded retirement benefits to cover all veterans of the Revolutionary War, whether officers or not, and created the first old soldiers' homes for poor veterans. In 1840, Congress expanded the veterans program again to provide financial relief to the widows of soldiers killed in battle.[4]

These early programs set two important precedents for contemporary domestic policy. First, they established the notion that some Americans would be automatically entitled to certain government benefits on the basis of an eligibility requirement such as service in the nation's armed forces. Thus veterans' relief was the nation's first **entitlement**, under which the government provides benefits to any citizen who is eligible. In the original program, only military officers met the eligibility requirement.

Second, these early programs also established government's right to restrict some benefits only to those citizens who could actually prove their need for help. Thus veterans' programs were early examples of what are now called **means-tested entitlements**, under which citizens must prove they are poor enough to deserve the government's help. In the original program, only poor veterans could go to old soldiers' homes.

Veterans' benefits are also important because they eventually came to cover huge numbers of Americans. As political scientist Theda Skocpol has noted, the Civil War triggered a massive expansion in veterans' benefits. The war involved 2.2 million Union

entitlements
Programs such as unemployment insurance, disaster relief, or disability payments that provide benefits to all eligible citizens.

means-tested entitlements
Programs such as Medicaid and welfare under which applicants must meet eligibility requirements based on need.

On July 4, 1932, over 20,000 war veterans marched to the Capitol in Washington, D.C. to demand the passage of the Bonus Bill, which allowed the immediate payment of the Soldiers' Bonus.

soldiers who would later qualify for veterans' benefits. "By 1910, about 28 percent of all American men aged 65 or more, more than half a million of them, received federal benefits averaging $189 a year," writes Skocpol. "Over three hundred thousand widows, orphans, and other dependents were also receiving payments from the federal treasury."[5]

Because so many men served in the Civil War and because veterans' benefits were even more generous toward Spanish-American War and World War I veterans, veterans' benefits accounted for one-quarter of all federal spending by 1932. The numbers would have been even higher if Confederate soldiers had been entitled to benefits. However, Congress decided to leave their care to the former Confederate states.

TYPES OF SOCIAL POLICY

Having entered the twentieth century with only a handful of federal domestic programs, most of which were built around helping veterans, the federal government left the century with a deep inventory of domestic programs. According to the *Catalog of Federal Domestic Assistance,* which lists every one of the federal government's 1,425 domestic funding programs in a searchable database (at www.cfda.gov), there are at least 38 separate programs for farmers, another 142 for colleges and their students, 148 for women, and 257 for children.

The Goals of Social Policy

Because most of these programs are restricted to one group of citizens only, they are often described as *categorical* aid. One only needs to type in a search term on the Internet such as "students," "elderly," "children," "disabled," "workers," "farmers," "women," or "veterans" to see just how much help the federal government provides in each category. But regardless of category, federal domestic policy focuses on two broad goals.

The first goal is to protect citizens against poverty and personal misfortune, whether by providing relief for unemployed workers, health care for the elderly, emergency shelter for the homeless, or school lunches for poor children, almost all of which are available to citizens only on the basis of a means test. Although almost all Americans are covered by federal unemployment insurance through a payroll tax, only workers who have been laid off from their jobs through no fault of their own can qualify for benefits, and only then for a relatively brief period of time. (For an inventory of federal programs for helping workers, visit the Department of Labor Web site at www.workers.gov.)

The second goal of federal domestic policy is to raise the quality of life for all Americans, whether by improving air and water quality, building roads and bridges, regulating air traffic, fighting crime, or strengthening local schools through federal aid, almost all of which are available to all communities regardless of need. Almost all federal aid to the states is distributed on the basis of formula grants that allocate money on the basis of population, not need.

Most scholars trace the federal government's effort to protect citizens against economic and personal hard times to the Great Depression and the Social Security Act of 1935. Although there is no question that Franklin Roosevelt's New Deal agenda stimulated a remarkable expansion in the federal government's domestic policy role, there is also no question that federal, state, and local governments were helping citizens long before the Depression began.

Until about a century ago, the poor were divided into two groups: the worthy poor, meaning people who were in poverty through no fault of their own, and the unworthy poor, meaning people who were in poverty because of idleness or the unwillingness to work, which was deemed the source of most unemployment at the time. As historian Joel Handler writes, this categorization emerged in the early 1800s as states began to place the worthy poor into separate government institutions such as schools for the blind and disabled. This movement was driven by a clear recognition that "those who were dependent by misfortune did not deserve the stigma of the unworthy poor."[6]

Types of Protection

By the early 1900s, however, public attitudes toward the poor had begun to change. Although the nation continued to distinguish between the worthy and unworthy poor, Congress and the president soon invented two very different types of federal programs to protect Americans against hardship, both of which continue to exist today.

The first type of help for the less fortunate is called **public assistance**, a term that is often used interchangeably with the word "welfare" to label government aid for the poor. The first public assistance programs were actually created in the late 1800s when states established aid programs to help single, poor mothers and their children. Although these programs were often described as "mothers' pensions" to create the impression that the beneficiaries had earned the benefits through some contribution, they created a precedent for many of the federal government's later antipoverty programs.

Most of this assistance flows through noncontributory programs, meaning that recipients do not have to pay anything in advance to receive benefits. Most federal assistance programs also impose a means test on all applicants. As noted earlier, these tests require applicants to disclose all financial assets and income to prove that they fall below the poverty line, which is generally calculated as three times the amount of money an individual or family needs to purchase the food for a nutritious diet. Defined as such, the poverty level changes with the size of the family. The poverty line for participation in federal assistance programs is set by the Department of Health and Human Services. In 2004, the line was drawn at $9,310 of pretax income for an individual, while the level for a four-person family was set at $18,850.[7]

The U.S. Bureau of the Census uses a somewhat different measure of income to determine how many Americans are poor at any given time. According to its measure, which runs a year or two behind the Department of Health and Human Services, 12 percent, or 35 million Americans were poor in 2002. The poverty rate was 16.7 percent among children, 10.3 among Asian Americans, 24.1 percent among African Americans, and 21.8 percent among Hispanics.[8]

Public assistance in the United States today incorporates elements of job training, transportation subsidies, housing subsidies, free school lunches, food aid for poor families and pregnant mothers with young children, and tax credits for low-income people. The national government also provides what some opponents label as "corporate welfare" to favored industries such as agriculture and steel, as well as "middle-class welfare" to college students, home buyers, and the citizenry as a whole in the form of college loans, tax deductions for home mortgages, and access to national parks and forests

public assistance
Aid to the poor; "welfare."

(supported by taxpayers but rarely used by poor people). However, the term "welfare" is generally used for public assistance to the needy, including the following forms:

■ Direct payments to single parents with young children, the unemployed, and the disabled

■ Vouchers that can be exchanged for food

■ Low-cost and/or public housing

■ Reduced cost or free access to public transportation, higher education, or job training

■ Free or low-cost medical care

In absolute numbers, most poor people are white. As a percentage within their own population, however, a larger proportion of African Americans and Hispanics are poor. Moreover, in both absolute and proportional terms, more women than men are poor. Indeed, some scholars refer to the relatively recent rise in poverty among women as the "feminization of poverty."[9] Although women tend to take jobs in lower-paying occupations than men, they earn less than men even when they are in the same jobs. They also save money over their lifetimes less than men, in part because they often take time off from their careers to care for their children and parents.

The second type of protection against hardship is called **social insurance**, a term that refers to government programs that provide benefits to anyone who is eligible either because of past service (veterans, miners, merchant marines) or payments of some kind (payroll taxes for Social Security and Medicare, insurance premiums). Some social insurance programs, such as unemployment and disability insurance, provide benefits only to those in need, thereby acting like private automobile and life insurance, which pay off only when an accident or death occurs. Other social insurance programs, such as Social Security and Medicare, pay benefits regardless of wealth, thereby acting more like a private savings program or annuity, which pays off at a set point in time.

Many federal assistance programs involve partnerships with state governments. There are two reasons for the connection. First, except for veterans' policy, states have been responsible for protecting their citizens against hardship since the United States was formed. Second, states and local governments have the administrative agencies to stay in touch with recipients of aid, whether to make sure they are actually eligible for support or to provide services such as job training or school lunches.

Because states vary greatly in their generosity, most federal assistance is designed to set a minimum floor of support that individual states can raise on their own. The most generous states in the country tend to be located in the Northeast and West, where living costs tend to be higher and legislatures more liberal, while the least generous tend to be found in the South. In this way, states act as a check on the federal government's ability to raise benefits too far, frustrating those who believe that the federal government should set a uniform level of benefits for all citizens while ensuring the consent of the governed for helping those in need. (Table 19–1 shows the amount of federal payments to individuals in 2005.)

THE EXPANSION OF SOCIAL POLICY IN THE TWENTIETH CENTURY

The federal government's commitment to helping the poor and improving the quality of life expanded rapidly during the Great Depression that followed the stock market crash of 1929. The "social safety net" built by state and local governments and private charities simply could not meet the needs of the huge increase in the homeless, unemployed, and poor.

TABLE 19–1 FEDERAL PAYMENTS TO INDIVIDUALS, 2005

Major Public Assistance Programs

Medicaid	$182 billion
State Children's Health Insurance	5.2 billion
Supplemental Security Income	35.5 billion
Food stamps	30.7 billion
Child nutrition	11.6 billion
Family support payments to states	22.6 billion
Low Income Tax Credit	33.7 billion

Social Insurance Funding

Social Security	$428 billion
Medicare	325 billion
Disability insurance	82 billion
Unemployment insurance	41 billion

SOURCE: Summary Tables, *Budget of the United States, Fiscal Year 2005*, Washington, D.C., U.S. Government Printing Office, February 2004.

social insurance
Programs in which eligibility is based on prior contributions to government, usually in the form of payroll taxes.

The WPA, part of President Roosevelt's New Deal, created jobs for thousands of workers during the Great Depression of the 1930s.

The New Deal

The most significant expansion of federal social policy occurred in the five years that followed Franklin Roosevelt's inauguration in 1933. That year, as part of Roosevelt's New Deal agenda, the federal government began making loans to states and localities to help the poor, and soon it launched a long list of programs to help older Americans (Social Security), the jobless (unemployment insurance), and the poor (Aid to Families with Dependent Children).

THE FIRST 100 DAYS   Before creating these signature New Deal programs, however, the Roosevelt administration moved quickly to help the needy. The first 100 days of the administration produced the most significant list of legislation ever passed in American history, including the Federal Emergency Relief Administration (FERA), established in May 1933 to give unemployed workers cash grants to get them through the summer, and the Civil Works Administration (CWA), created in November 1933 to provide millions of public jobs to help many of those same workers make it through the winter.

The list of "alphabet agencies" grew longer as the administration created a host of new programs to help the poor, including the Works Progress Administration (WPA), which was created in 1935 to provide work for millions of unemployed Americans, and the Civilian Conservation Corps (CCC), which put millions of young Americans to work clearing trails and building roads in the national forests and parks. Between 1933 and 1945, for example, the WPA put 8.5 million Americans to work at a cost of $10 billion. All told, the WPA built 650,000 miles of roads, 125,000 public buildings, 8,200 parks, and 850 airports. The wages were hardly generous, however. The average WPA worker received just $55 a month, far below the $100 the federal government deemed a subsistence wage. The WPA was abolished during World War II when the economy finally rebounded.

Together, these and other New Deal programs created a national safety net to catch those in need. It is little wonder, therefore, that scholars would describe the New Deal as the "big bang" of domestic policy.[10] Although the distinction between the worthy and unworthy poor still remained, joblessness was no longer defined as merely a problem of individual idleness or the unwillingness to work.

HELP FOR OLDER AMERICANS   Once past the immediate crisis, the Roosevelt administration began designing the flagship programs of the New Deal. First on the list was **Social Security**, which was enacted in 1935 and stands today as the federal government's most popular social program. Social Security was designed to meet two goals: (1) to provide a minimum income floor for poor beneficiaries and (2) to ensure that benefits bear a relationship to the amount of payroll taxes a beneficiary actually paid. Supported by equal contributions from employers and employees, the program now covers more than 90 percent of the American work force.[11] The universal nature of Social Security is one reason it is politically so popular: Everyone benefits, regardless of need. In 2004, the Social Security Administration issued checks to almost 50 million Americans every month, and three times that many working people contribute to the fund.

Social Security was expanded in 1939 to include financial support for survivors of workers covered by Social Security when the retired worker died, and in 1954, the program was again expanded to include support for disabled workers and the children of deceased or disabled workers. Benefit levels were raised repeatedly during the first 40 years of the program, often just before an election. The increases became so frequent and so costly that Congress finally indexed benefits to rise with inflation in 1975. Under legislation enacted in 1983, the Social Security retirement age started to rise in 2003 and will reach 67 years of age by the year 2027. In 2005, for example, workers who retire at age 65 years and 6 months are eligible for full benefits, while workers who retire early at age 62 are eligible for a reduced amount. The average benefit in 2004 was $922, while the maximum benefit for a worker retiring at full retirement age was $1,850.[12]

Until the 1970s, growth in Social Security benefits was relatively uncontroversial, largely because "the costs were initially deceptively low," while the benefits increased steadily, making the system politically painless.[13] Since Social Security began, the program has experienced steady growth and is now the world's largest insurance program for retirees, survivors, and people with disabilities. In 2005, Social Security and Medicare expenditures totaled nearly $753 billion.

Social Security, unlike many welfare programs, is financed not from general taxes but from a trust fund into which taxes on employees and employers are paid under the Federal Insurance Contribution Act, commonly known as FICA. Over the years, Congress added benefits to the Social Security system without adding enough money to the trust fund to cover the added expense. In 1983, Congress tried to solve the problem by raising the retirement age at which one qualifies for Social Security benefits, increasing Social Security taxes, imposing the first-ever tax on the Social Security payments of

The Gray Panthers, an activist group made up of elderly Americans, often marches in support of numerous social issues, not only those causes that relate specifically to their needs.

Social Security
A combination of entitlement programs, paid for by employer and employee taxes, that includes retirement benefits, health insurance, and support for disabled workers and the children of deceased or disabled workers.

upper-income individuals, and imposing a one-time cut in the annual cost-of-living increase in benefits.

Social Security taxes are now the largest tax paid by most Americans, and for three-quarters of Americans, their Social Security tax now exceeds their income tax. Employees paid a 6.2 percent FICA tax on all wages up to $87,900 in 2004, and an additional 1.45 percent on all wages up to any amount for Medicare. All employee taxes are matched dollar for dollar by employers, meaning that self-employed Americans must pay 15.3 percent total.

Although Social Security has been enormously successful in lowering the poverty rate among older Americans, it is under increasing pressure as Americans get older. In 1990, for example, the average American was 33 years old; by 2020, the average age will be 38 years. The average age is rising in part because Americans are having fewer children, and in part because of medical advances that have increased the lifespan. Medical advances have been particularly important in increasing the number of very old Americans—the number of Americans over the age of 85 is expected to grow from roughly 3 million in 2000 to 17 million in 2050, which means increased Social Security and Medicare costs.

These increases would not be a problem if the payroll taxes coming into Social Security and Medicare from today's workers were put away for their eventual retirement.

PEOPLE & POLITICS *Making a Difference* ★★★

LUCILLE ROYBAL-ALLARD

Having served Los Angeles's Hispanic community in the California legislature for six years, Lucille Roybal-Allard entered the U.S. Congress in 1992 as the first Mexican-American woman elected to the House. Six years later, she became the first Mexican-American woman to head the Hispanic Congressional Caucus, which had been founded by her father and two other Hispanic House members in 1976. In 1998, she was elected chair of the entire California congressional delegation, another first for a Mexican-American woman.

Although Roybal-Allard is proud of her father's work, she represents a new generation of Hispanic Caucus members who are trying to broaden the debate about Hispanic issues. "People need to understand that Latino issues are American issues and American issues are Latino issues," she says. "We all care about the same thing."*

As the number of Hispanic Americans has grown steadily over the past three decades, Roybal-Allard and other leaders have worked hard to educate the rest of the country that the term "Hispanic" cov-

ers a wide range of groups such as Mexicans, Cubans, Puerto Ricans, and Central and South Americans who care just as much about jobs, education, and health care as the rest of the nation.

Indeed, Roybal-Allard is careful to note that she was not the first Hispanic woman elected to Congress. That honor belongs to Ileana Ros-Lehtinen, who was born in Havana, Cuba, in 1952, immigrated to the United States in 1959, and was elected to Congress in 1988.

Whatever their country of origin, many of today's Hispanic members of Congress have a broader agenda than their predecessors. "The era that my father grew up in, in which his principles and values were formed, was totally different than my own," says San Antonio Democratic Representative Charles Gonzalez, who replaced his father, Henry B. Gonzalez, in Congress in 1999. "He was a product of a time when discrimination was open and obvious. We are products of a different process."†

New Jersey Representative Bob Menendez agrees. A Cuban-American who has served as vice-chair of the entire

House Democratic Caucus, Menendez says that "I'd like to think that we as Latinos are just as interested in health care, retirement security and our place in the world as any other American. We should be going beyond the issues we're forced to deal with by necessity, and into other issues where we can make a difference. We are coming into our own."

*Roxanne Roberts, Janelle Erlichman, "Politics with a Latin Beat: Hispanic Caucus Celebrates a Major Minority," *The Washington Post,* September 21, 2000, p. C-1.
†Gregory Rodriguez, "From Minority to Mainstream: Latinos Find Their Voice," *The Washington Post,* January 24, 1999, p. B1.

But much of the revenue actually goes to payments for today's retirees. Social Security is thus a "pay-as-you-go" system, in which today's young workers finance the retirement of today's elderly. At some point in the not-too-distant future, there will not be enough workers paying into the two programs to cover all the benefits. Under current projections, Medicare is expected to start running deficits in 2019, and Social Security in 2029. Sooner or later, Congress will have to decide whether to raise taxes on workers, cut benefits for older Americans, increase the retirement age, or some combination of all three.

The Social Security system is still running a surplus, meaning that the amount of revenue collected through Social Security taxes is still greater than the amount of money going out in benefits. The surpluses are invested in Treasury bonds, with the promise that they will be repaid with interest later. As the baby boomers retire and begin to collect Social Security, however, the bonds must be redeemed to pay benefits, and the program will start running annual deficits. Experts differ on when the next Social Security funding crisis will come, but there is little disagreement that something will have to be done to ensure the viability of Social Security for young people now paying into the system.[14]

HELP FOR THE UNEMPLOYED Social Security was not the only strand of economic protection woven during the New Deal. The New Deal also produced the federal government's first unemployment insurance program, which was enacted as part of the 1935 Social Security Act. Under the program, which is administered by state governments but funded in part with federal unemployment taxes, eligible workers can receive benefits for up to 26 weeks in most states. In periods of high unemployment, the federal government also provides funds for extended benefits for a maximum of 39 weeks in most states.

HELP FOR THE POOR The federal government became involved in protecting women and children against poverty when Congress passed the Infancy and Maternity Protection Act of 1921. Supported by many of the same women's groups that had just won ratification of the Nineteenth Amendment, which gave women the right to vote, the act gave the newly created federal Children's Bureau funds to encourage states to create new maternal, infant, and early childhood health programs. Although the act was allowed to expire in 1929, it set a precedent for future federal involvement in protecting families against poverty.

Congress also established the school lunch program during the New Deal as both a way to help feed the hungry and to strengthen the ailing farm economy. The Federal Surplus Relief Corporation began purchasing surplus agriculture products for needy families in 1935 and launched the nation's first school lunch programs for poor children shortly thereafter. By 1941, more than 5 million children were receiving free school lunches, consuming more than 450 million pounds of surplus pork, dairy products, and bread. Although the program was disbanded during World War II because of food shortages, it was restored under the 1946 National School Lunch Act. As President Harry Truman said at the signing ceremony, "No nation is any healthier than its children." He could have added that many draftees had been rejected for service in World War II because of malnutrition.

Congress moved even further to help the needy when it passed the Aid to Families with Dependent Children (AFDC) program in 1935.[15] By its very name, AFDC tried to shift the focus away from what the mother had or had not done to deserve poverty and onto the children who suffered whatever the cause, thereby reducing public opposition to expanded benefits. Under the program, states were given federal money to establish cash grants for poor families under two conditions: (1) States had to match the federal funds with some contribution of their own, and (2) states had to establish a means test for all families receiving benefits. AFDC was abolished in 1996 when Congress and the president created an entirely new program that required states to set time limits on public assistance, thereby creating a greater incentive for welfare recipients to find work.

The Great Society

The second major expansion of social policy came in the 1960s with what became known as the Great Society. At a commencement speech at the University of Michigan in May 1964, President Lyndon Johnson described his vision of the Great Society:

THE FEDERAL GOVERNMENT'S SAFETY NET FOR OLDER AMERICANS

Social Security and Disability— established 1935

Provides *retirement* benefits starting at age 65 and 4 months in 2004 (with reduced benefits available as early as age 62), and *disability* benefits payable at any age to people with a severe physical or mental impairment that prevents them from doing "substantial" work for a year or more or who have a condition that is expected to result in death. Other members of the family of persons eligible for retirement or disability benefits may be entitled to *family* benefits. The Old Age, Survivors, and Disability Insurance Trust Fund (OASDI) also provides *survivors'* benefits for certain family members of deceased persons who earned enough Social Security credits while working.

Medicare—established 1965

Provides hospital insurance (Part A) and medical insurance (Part B) to individuals who are also entitled to Social Security. Part A is funded by a portion of the Social Security taxes paid by people still working and pays for inpatient hospital care, skilled nursing care, and other services. Part B is funded by monthly premiums paid by enrollees and from general revenues and pays for a portion of doctors' fees, outpatient hospital visits, and other medical services and supplies.

Supplemental Security Income (SSI)—established 1972

Provides monthly payments to disabled persons or those over age 65 who meet an income test. Levels of SSI support vary by state to reflect cost-of-living differences. SSI recipients also qualify for Medicaid, food stamps, and other assistance. SSI benefits are financed by general tax revenues.

SOURCE: Social Security Administration, at www.ssa.gov/pubs/10006.html.

President Lyndon Johnson's vision of a Great Society relied on the principle of government action to solve economic and social problems.

The Great Society rests on abundance and liberty for all. It demands an end to poverty and racial injustice. . . . But that is just the beginning. The Great Society is a place where every child can find knowledge to enrich his mind and to enlarge his talents. . . . It is a challenge constantly renewed, beckoning us toward a destiny where the meaning of our lives matches the marvelous products of our labors.[16]

Johnson's agenda was as broad as his rhetoric, and Congress enacted much of it in a fairly short period of time. Great Society programs dramatically increased the role of the federal government in education through a number of programs that exist today:

- *Food stamps.* The food stamp program gives poor families coupons that can be used to purchase the basics of a healthy, nutritious diet. The average benefit is about $75 per person per month.

- *Head Start.* Head Start is a preschool program designed to help poor children get ready for kindergarten. The program serves more than 900,000 children each year at a cost of roughly $7,000 per child. Almost 30 percent of Head Start teachers and staff are parents of Head Start children or were Head Start children themselves.

- *Medicaid.* **Medicaid** was created in 1965 to provide basic health services for poor families. The program is administered by state governments, which are responsible for determining eligibility, and covers everything from hospital care to family planning.

- *Supplemental Security Income.* The SSI program was created in 1972, to provide an extra measure of support for the elderly poor and the blind or disabled. The program provides monthly benefit checks ranging from just $1 to roughly $800 and is administered by the Social Security Administration.

- *Housing assistance.* The Department of Housing and Urban Development, which was created in 1965, administers a number of programs designed to help low-income families find affordable, safe housing, in part by giving property owners subsidies to make up the difference between what tenants can pay and what the local housing market will bear.

The Great Society also produced a vast new social insurance program to cover all hospital and most other health care costs for older Americans. Under the **Medicare** program, the federal government pays all of the reasonable costs of all inpatient hospital care, including drugs, surgery, and postoperative care, regardless of the beneficiary's personal wealth. Like Social Security, this insurance is "purchased" through payroll taxes, which are set aside solely for Medicare expenditures. Medicare beneficiaries are also entitled to purchase additional federal health insurance to cover the costs of outpatient care, physician visits, and laboratory fees, but not prescription drugs.[17] Medicare beneficiaries must also pay a deductible on all hospital stays and a monthly premium for the additional insurance.

The Great Society also produced a long list of important changes in other social policies, including the following:

- *Civil Rights Act of 1964*—set forth the most comprehensive civil rights protections since Reconstruction

- *Food Stamp Act of 1965*—expanded the New Deal program to improve nutrition among the poor

- *Elementary and Secondary Education Act of 1965*—established federal funding and programs in public education for disadvantaged children

- *Higher Education Act of 1965*—established federal funding for colleges and college students

- *Department of Housing and Urban Development Act of 1965*—created a new department with responsibility for low-rent housing and urban renewal programs

- *Child Nutrition Act of 1966*—expanded federal programs to reduce childhood hunger

Medicaid
Federal program that provides medical benefits for low-income persons.

Medicare
National health insurance program for the elderly and disabled.

■ *Fair Packaging and Labeling Act of 1966*—expanded federal oversight of consumer labeling

■ *Age Discrimination Act of 1967*—prohibited discrimination based on age

■ *Housing and Urban Development Act of 1968*—expanded federal housing and urban development programs

■ *Open Housing Act of 1968*—prohibited discrimination in housing

■ *Omnibus Crime Control and Safe Streets Act of 1968*—provided federal aid for local law enforcement, crime prevention, and corrections programs

Although Great Society programs such as Medicare, Head Start, and food stamps remain essential threads in the social safety net today, they were enacted during a period of enormous domestic unrest over race relations and the Vietnam War. Unable to win public support for his "guns and butter" agenda, and unsure that he could even win his own party's presidential nomination, Johnson eventually decided not to seek reelection in 1968.

Reforming Welfare

Republicans have not been the only critics of the New Deal and Great Society welfare programs. President Bill Clinton made welfare reform a centerpiece of his reelection agenda in 1996, having promised to "end welfare as we know it."[18]

Working with the new Republican congressional majority, Clinton won passage of the Personal Responsibility and Work Opportunity Reconciliation Act in 1996, which replaced AFDC with Temporary Assistance for Needy Families (TANF). Its name captures two themes of the new act—individuals should take more responsibility for themselves, and work, not welfare, is the goal of public assistance.

The burden of administering the new program was shifted entirely to the states. The federal government now gives *block grants* of money to the states and generally requires that the states match those funds. Under the new rules, federally funded public assistance is limited to five years over a person's lifetime, and all recipients must enter some kind of work training program within two months of receiving initial benefits. Although states can exempt up to 20 percent of cases from the work requirements and lifetime limits—an exemption intended for blind and disabled persons, the message to recipients is clear: find work soon.

The law originally excluded legal immigrants from many welfare programs, but at the strong urging of the governors, most welfare benefits were later restored to legal immigrants. To discourage persons on welfare from moving to states with more generous assistance payments, the law gave states the option of limiting welfare to newcomers from other states. This provision was declared unconstitutional by a federal district court judge, who said it "denies 'equal protection of the laws' to indigent families moving from one state to another."[19]

There are several ways to measure the success of the 1996 welfare reform. One is simply to ask whether the number of welfare recipients has declined. By 2002, the number of welfare recipients was lower than it had been in more than three decades. As the authors of a 2002 study of welfare reform argue, "The welfare rolls have declined greatly, more mothers than ever are working, the average income of female-headed families is increasing, and poverty has dropped substantially."[20] The number continued to fall in 2003 despite the economic downturn. As of March 2003, the total number of Americans who received federal welfare benefits had fallen to 4.9 million, 60 percent fewer than in August 1996 when the reforms were enacted.

Yet merely reducing the number of welfare recipients is no guarantee that they either have good-paying jobs or are moving out of poverty. It is one thing to remove a recipient from the welfare rolls and quite another to get the person into a good job with decent benefits. Research suggests that most mothers who leave welfare make $7 to 8 per hour, well above the minimum wage. However, most mothers who leave welfare have other expenses, such as transportation and child care, that may or may not be covered

Although the 1996 welfare reform focused most on replacing welfare with work, it also ordered the federal government to promote marriage. Advocates argue that marriage improves the lives of both children and parents. Married adults, whether women or men, are happier, healthier, and wealthier than their unmarried peers and are more likely to give their children a healthier start. Some advocates even argue that more marriages would reduce health costs by reducing depression and crime. None of these advocates supports same-sex marriage, however.

The federal government can promote marriage in two ways. First, it can reduce the penalties it imposes on welfare recipients who get married. Under current law, for example, a single mother working full time at a minimum-wage job who marries stands to lose as much as $8,000 a year in cash and noncash benefits. Second, it can promote marriage through advertising, counseling, or even providing cash grants for getting married to be paid out over a period of years.

by state or local assistance, and many who go to work lose their food stamps and Medicaid, which means they are more dependent on food banks and have to go without preventive health care.

Besides confirming the fundamental American belief in rugged individualism, the 1996 welfare bill has significant ramifications for our federal system. This *devolution* of power to the states in the area of welfare is seen as a testing ground for other transfers of responsibility to the states with and without federal funding.

SOCIAL POLICY CHALLENGES FOR THE FUTURE: HEALTH, EDUCATION, AND SAFETY

Even if states take on a greater social policy role, the federal government is sure to remain the greatest source of funding for the safety net. As Table 19–2 shows, human resource spending for programs such as Social Security, Medicare, Medicaid, and child nutrition has more than doubled since 1950. Spending is almost certain to rise in coming years as the baby boom generation enters retirement and starts to draw down the Social Security surplus and use Medicare. Moreover, the federal social policy agenda will almost certainly expand as Congress and the president respond to public pressure for action on health care, education, and crime control.

The Federal Role in Health Care

Medicare is just one of the federal government's many health programs. It has been involved in reducing disease since 1887, when the federal government opened a one-room laboratory on Staten Island, New York, to study infectious diseases carried to the United States on passenger ships. In time, that one-room laboratory expanded into the National Institutes of Health (NIH), a conglomeration of 37 separate institutes on a 300-acre campus in Bethesda, Maryland.

The surgeon general of the United States is arguably the most visible health care official in government. As head of the Public Health Service (PHS), the surgeon general works closely with the NIH. Researchers in these institutes, working closely with experts in private laboratories, study causes and seek cures for serious diseases. Fellowships for health research are granted to able scientists and physicians. The NIH administers billions of dollars in grants each year to support the research of university and other scientists and physicians. The PHS also administers grants to states and local communities to help improve public health. Another federal agency promoting health is the Food and Drug Administration (FDA).

There are dozens of other federal agencies that work to improve public health. The Centers for Disease Control and Prevention (CDC) in Atlanta is also intimately involved in preventing disease. The CDC and its 7,800 "disease detectives" have been at the forefront of identifying a host of mystery illnesses, including the respiratory disease that attacked attendees at an American Legion convention in 1976 (Legionnaire's disease), toxic shock syndrome in 1980, and hepatitis C in 1989, while tracking down the causes of major health disasters, including the outbreak of the SARS upper-respiratory virus in 2003 and 2004.

TABLE 19–2   CHANGING PRIORITIES IN THE FEDERAL BUDGET

Function	1950	1960	1970	1980	1990	2000	2005
National defense	32%	52%	42%	23%	24%	15%	19%
Human resources	33	28	39	53	49	64	65
Physical resources	7	9	8	11	10	5	5
Interest on the debt	11	8	8	10	15	13	7

SOURCE: Summary Tables, *Budget of the United States, Fiscal Year 2005*, Washington, D.C., U.S. Government Printing Office, February 2004.

Despite its success in improving the nation's health, the federal government faces two major health care challenges in the future: containing costs and expanding coverage.

THE RISING COST OF HEALTH CARE   Health care costs in the United States have nearly quadrupled, after controlling for inflation, since 1970.[21] Although they slowed with the rest of the economy in 2001, costs are expected to escalate rapidly as the nation ages over the next two decades.

All Americans pay for the increasing costs (see Figure 19–1). Employers directly pay a large share of the costs of health insurance; about 6 percent of employee compensation is the cost of health care.[22] Consumers also pay more for health care, whether through increased private insurance premiums, deductibles, or copayments for services. Finally, taxpayers pay for the increases through federal dollars that might otherwise go to other programs such as homeland security, college loans, or highway construction.

The good news is that costs have risen in part because people live longer. Life expectancy increased by more than five years between 1970 and 1995. Most experts believe it will rise another year by 2015, in part because of advanced treatments, including new drugs for battling HIV-AIDS.[23] In 1900, only one out of every 25 Americans was over the age of 65. By 1950, the number was one in 12 and by 1985, one in nine. According to experts, the number will rise to one in five by 2030. In 1900, the average American lived to age 47; by 2000, the average had increased to 79. Again according to experts, the number will rise into the mid-80s by 2030.

As people live longer, of course, they place greater demands on the health care system, as well as on the Social Security program. New and advanced medical technology—life-support systems, ultrasound, sophisticated x-ray equipment, and genetic counseling—have all increased the costs of health care. They also place greater demands on other social policies.

The bad news is that some costs have nothing to do with saving lives or preventing disease. Some physicians claim that they have to perform procedures that may be medically unnecessary but are legally essential to reduce the risk of being sued by patients. These procedures are alleged to add up to billions in unnecessary costs, but they do not necessarily improve the quality of care provided to patients.[24] Physicians also complain about the high cost of malpractice insurance, nine times more costly in the United States than in Canada. Malpractice insurance costs for all physicians have more than doubled in a decade. A physician's insurance coverage routinely costs as much as $60,000 a year.[25] For specialists like obstetricians, premiums are 400 percent higher than for internists.[26]

Trial lawyers who represent people whose health was damaged or families of those whose lives were lost due to medical malpractice defend the huge punitive awards. They argue that physicians, like all professionals, have a responsibility to exercise sound professional judgment in their jobs, and when they do not, they should provide restitution to their victims.

Moreover, at least part of the cost crisis is avoidable. Medicare alone spends billions of dollars each year treating smoking-related diseases, and over the next 20 years the costs to treat such diseases will continue to rise.[27] Other illnesses at least partly related to lifestyle include heart disease, liver disease, HIV/AIDS, and the epidemic of health disorders created by obesity.

COVERING THE UNINSURED   Despite passage of the Medicare program, the nation has yet to develop a comprehensive insurance program for the approximately 60 million Americans who are uninsured at some point in any given year.[28] Although some rely on public clinics, emergency room care, or charity, many people go without any health or dental care.[29] Many of the uninsured have jobs, but their employers do not provide health insurance, and because their incomes are above the poverty line, they do not qualify for Medicaid. Uninsured individuals usually seek care in hospital emergency rooms only when their illness has reached a critical stage. Postponing medical care drives up costs because critical care is much more expensive than preventive medicine or early treatment.

★★ THINKING IT THROUGH

Although the federal government has long engaged in activities designed to promote good social behavior, such as early childhood vaccinations, campaigns against smoking, the use of seat belts, and the 55-mile-an-hour speed limit, not all Americans believe that marriage is the answer to welfare. They note that domestic violence and child abuse occur almost as frequently in married as in unmarried households. They also worry that government grants for marriage would promote a rash of false marriages designed to get the cash.

Most important, opponents believe that the best way to encourage marriage among welfare recipients is to find them good-paying jobs. They look to states such as Minnesota that have created strong welfare-to-work programs that do not punish married women for getting a job. Married women who entered Minnesota's Family Investment Program were a third more likely to still be married three years later than married women who stayed in the old welfare system. In theory, good-paying jobs lead to higher self-esteem, which leads to a sustainable marriage.

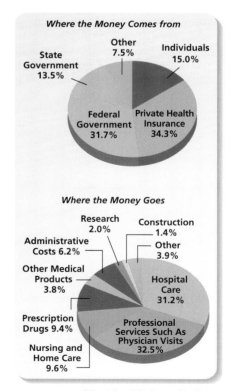

FIGURE 19–1 The Health Care Dollar, 2000.
Source: Centers for Medicare and Medicaid Services, at www.cms.bhs.gov/statistics/nhe.

IN COMPARATIVE PERSPECTIVE

HEALTH CARE IN THE UNITED STATES AND CANADA

Advanced industrial democracies like Canada, Germany, Japan, the Netherlands, and the United Kingdom provide health care for their entire population either through national health insurance or a national health service. Although the United States outspends all these countries in terms of health expenditures as a percentage of gross domestic product (see chart), this high level of spending on health care does not mean that the United States has a healthier population. The nation's infant mortality rates, for instance, are among the worst of all industrialized countries, and the United States ranks below average for industrialized nations in male and female life expectancy at birth.

The United States also differs from other countries in the extent to which health care costs are paid by public funds. Central or local governments fund approximately three-quarters of the cost of health care in most advanced industrial democracies.

In Canada, about 9 percent of the nation's GDP is devoted to health care spending, and all Canadians are covered by provincial health insurance. Canada's administration of health care is based on a publicly funded system, whereas the program in the United States is divided among public and private insurers. Canada's administrative costs per patient are only one-fourth the size of ours, and companies in the United States often pay three to five times more than Canadian companies to fund employee health and social benefits, including taxes collected by governments to pay for some of these benefits.

The Canadian health care system is not without its faults. Canadians are taxed at a much higher rate than Americans, in part to pay for the publicly funded system. In addition, patients may face delays in receiving services, especially for routine health problems and elective surgery. Doctors and nurses are also paid less in Canada, and thousands of them have moved to the United States, where salaries are much higher. Costs for health care are also increasing faster than the rate of inflation, and the Canadian federal and provincial governments have begun to cut back on funding certain services. Nevertheless, most Canadians express satisfaction with their health care system, and Canada manages to insure all of its people while spending far less per capita than the United States.

United States	14.6%
Switzerland	11.2%
Germany	10.9%
France	9.7%
Canada	9.6%
Japan	7.8%
United Kingdom	7.7%

Total Health Care Expenditures as a Share of Gross Domestic Product, 2002.
SOURCE: Organization for Economic Cooperation and Development, Health Data, 2004.

But it is not just the poor who are uninsured. People who change jobs may often go without coverage for several months before their new insurance takes effect. And people with serious medical conditions may find the insurance company unwilling to cover their expenses, claiming that the illness is a "preexisting condition." Some insurance companies set caps on their coverage, meaning that families coping with very expensive illnesses end up essentially uninsured.

Although there are many different proposals for health care reform, the essential approaches include a single-payer system, prepaid health plans, employer-mandated coverage, spending caps, individual responsibility, and medical savings accounts.

Single Payer.   Under a single-payer system, the national government, using broad-based taxes, covers the costs of health care and hospitalization and sets the rates. Like the system in Canada, such a plan would provide universal coverage and benefits to *all* Americans. No longer would people need to worry about the costs of catastrophic illnesses or a change in jobs that would exclude them from coverage. Proponents claim that the single-payer system would save billions of dollars in administrative expenses by reducing the number of insurers from about 1,200 to 1. Opponents of the single-payer system claim it would lead to a bureaucratic mess, with little incentive for innovation, cost control, or diversity of coverage. They further claim that the government would be put in the position of deciding which procedures to pay for and how to ration access to these procedures. As a result, they contend, Americans would lose not only quality in their health care but their freedom of choice as well.

It takes banks of computers for HMO employees to organize and run the bureaucracy of managed health care.

Business leaders generally oppose single-payer coverage out of concern for costs and what the program would do to taxes and the federal budget. The American Medical Association, U.S. Chamber of Commerce, Health Insurance Association of America, and other interest groups representing health care providers oppose the single-payer system. Labor unions, some senior citizens groups, and most consumer groups advocate this type of plan.

Prepaid Health Plans.   Cost containment has been a frequent refrain of large corporations and consumer groups. In the 1970s and 1980s, business owners reduced benefits, increased payments by employees, and encouraged employees to join managed care plans called **health maintenance organizations (HMOs)** in which individuals or their employees pay a set amount for each person covered each year in return for health care and hospital coverage. During the 1980s and 1990s, HMO enrollment increased fourfold, from just under 10 million in 1980 to almost 80 million Americans in 2004. Most HMOs guarantee access, but many do not guarantee that a patient can see the same physician.

Because there are no national standards of heath care quality, consumer groups are pressing HMOs to improve treatment of specific conditions and are urging Congress and the president to enter the battle.[30] HMOs counter that they provide adequate care at reasonable costs and that national standards would drive up costs. Consumers want the reduced costs associated with HMOs but do not like the limitations on choice of physicians and the right to sue health plans or the lack of coverage for some procedures.[31]

The quality of HMO care and limitations on patient choice became political issues in the 2000 elections. Both parties endorsed competing variations of what they call a "patient's bill of rights." Such a bill of rights would permit a woman to see a gynecologist as her primary care physician, allow for review of the need for medical procedures, leave it to the doctor to determine the length of stay in the hospital, require coverage of emergency care a "prudent layperson" would deem necessary, and remove rules that deny doctors permission to talk to patients. George W. Bush called for granting HMO patients the right to appeal denials of care to an independent review panel, providing report cards on HMOs, giving women direct access to their obstetrician-gynecologist, and in some cases being able to sue HMOs. Even though both presidential nominees called for expanded rights for HMO consumers, legislation on this matter after the election consistently stalled in both houses, due in part to an aggressive advertising campaign against the reforms that was funded by insurance companies and HMOs.

health maintenance organization (HMO)
Alternative means of health care in which people or their employers are charged a set amount and the HMO provides health care and covers hospital costs.

Employer-Mandated Coverage. Currently more than 161 million Americans get some form of medical insurance from their employers.[32] But many small businesses contend that they cannot afford to provide this benefit and stay in business. Some have estimated that the costs of health care for small businesses may be 10 to 40 percent higher than for large businesses. In businesses with fewer than 25 employees, only about one-third of the workers receive coverage directly from their employer.[33] Mandating coverage does not solve this problem, nor does it take care of individuals who do not have jobs.

Proponents counter that the negative consequences can be mitigated through tax credits and government subsidies. They also point out that if all small businesses provide health insurance, none of them will be put at a disadvantage compared to other small businesses. As noted, the federal government allows businesses to deduct what they pay in health benefits to employees as a business expense and gives tax credits to low-income families to purchase coverage for their children.

Spending Caps. Because the cost of providing health care each year consumes a larger and larger share of our gross domestic product, some have proposed that the national government impose an overall expenditure cap on health care that applies not only to public expenditures but to private ones as well. Supporters of a cap include some prominent Democrats. The American Hospital Association, American Medical Association, and Pharmaceutical Manufacturers Association vigorously oppose the idea. They argue that spending caps would limit research and development in medicine and deter talented young people from pursuing medical careers. However, the costs associated with an ever-older population may yet lead to some form of spending caps and the health rationing that would clearly go with them.

Individual Responsibility for Coverage. Another reform proposal is to apply a free market approach to health care by abolishing *all* employer-provided benefits and encouraging individuals to buy health insurance on their own, in much the same way that individuals are responsible for purchasing their own automobile insurance. Those with low incomes, including people not now insured, would have tax credits or vouchers to assist in the purchase of insurance.

Advocates of such a market solution say that if individuals purchased their own insurance, they might pay more attention to costs and more closely monitor doctor and hospital fees. When higher wages are combined with tax credits, some individuals could end up with improved benefits tailored to their individual needs. Such a plan would also eliminate the need to impose price controls or pay for a large health care bureaucracy. It is unlikely, however, that employees would recover all they now spend on health care from their employers, so costs to individual consumers might increase. It is also unlikely that all uninsured persons who need government assistance could be taken care of without a tax increase to pay for it. Perhaps most important, such a proposal would run into so much political opposition that it presents an unlikely alternative.

Medical Savings Accounts. In 1996, Congress authorized an experiment with **medical savings accounts**. As of 2004, individuals may make tax-deductible contributions of roughly $2,600 a year ($5,150 for a family) to a special medical savings account that can be used to pay medical expenses not covered by insurance or government.[34] Withdrawals for other purposes are taxable and subject to an early withdrawal penalty.

Supporters of medical savings accounts say that they will eventually lower health care costs by giving people the incentive to spend their own money more carefully. They also allow people to go to a doctor of their own choosing without prior approval from their insurance company. Opponents of medical savings accounts say that they amount to nothing more than a tax break for the wealthy and the healthy. Because of high deductibles, people may decide not to seek needed services and preventive care. Opponents also argue that because healthier people are more likely to sign up for medical savings accounts, sicker people pay higher insurance premiums. Older and less wealthy people will not be able to afford to invest in medical savings accounts, critics charge, and will be forced to depend on more expensive insurance.

medical savings account
Alternative means of health care in which individuals make tax-deductible contributions to a special account that can be used to pay medical expenses.

The Federal Role in Education

The federal government has been involved with education at least since the Northwest Ordinance of 1785, in which Congress set aside one section in each township for support of a public school. In 1862, the Morrill Land Grant Act provided grants of land to states for universities specializing in the mechanical or agricultural arts. The U.S. Office of Education was established in 1867 to oversee these programs, but the scope of federal involvement was modest by today's standards. Even the G.I. Bill, which helped provide a college education for approximately 20 million World War II veterans, was seen more as an employment program than educational one.

During the cold war, however, education became one part of the national defense. When the Soviet Union launched *Sputnik*—the first man-made satellite to orbit the earth—in 1957, Congress responded in 1958 by passing the National Defense Education Act to upgrade science, language, and mathematics courses.

ELEMENTARY AND SECONDARY EDUCATION Kindergarten through high school education is generally seen as a state and local responsibility. Most children go to public schools run by local school boards and funded, at least partly, by property taxes. Because school districts vary greatly in the wealth of their residents, children from poor districts are much more likely to have lower-quality public schools than those from wealthier districts. As a result, public schools vary in the quality of teacher preparation, student performance, dropout rates, and educational opportunities provided to minority students.

Although the federal government has been reluctant to make direct investments in poor school districts, it has tried to help the children those districts serve. In 1964, for example, Congress created the Head Start program for preschool children. Under the program, needy children get help learning to read and understand numbers. Head Start centers also provide healthy meals and snacks and monitor child health care. Many also work with parents to encourage greater involvement and literacy.

Recent evaluations of the program suggests that Head Start increases learning, but they have also revealed the need for improvement. In 2004, Head Start provided funding to 19,000 child-care centers with almost 50,000 classrooms, some of which reported chronic shortages of well-trained teachers. In addition, the student–teacher ratio varied significantly across the centers. Moreover, the program is not an entitlement, meaning that funding only covers roughly a third of all eligible children. When the dollars run out, Head Start centers stop enrolling participants.

Head Start is not the federal government's only education program, however. In 1965, Congress passed the Elementary and Secondary Education Act (ESEA), which supplied educational materials for underprivileged public school students and provided funding for research on how to assist children from disadvantaged backgrounds. Over the years, the act was amended to provide federal support for special education, as well as additional funding for textbooks, teacher training, and other support for poor schools. In 2005, the federal government spent $38 billion on local education, or barely 9 percent of total school spending.

As concerns about the quality of public education increased during the 1990s, however, the federal government became more involved in local education, first by setting national goals for student achievement, then by passing the No Child Left Behind Act in 2001. In return for federal funding, states were required to annually test at least 95 percent of all third and eighth graders in reading and math. In addition, states were required to grade schools as passing or failing, set higher standards for teachers, and give students in failing schools the option to move to higher-performing schools. Schools must either improve test scores each year or risk being labeled "in need of improvement." Under the act, all students are supposed to be proficient in reading and math by 2014.

Although the new law set higher standards, it increased federal spending for education by only a tiny percentage. By 2005, many states were complaining that they did not have enough funding to test every student every year, nor enough to meet the law's requirement for teacher training and certification. In addition, schools with many disabled or special-needs-type students can be unfairly categorized as "failing" because they cannot meet the test-score requirement.

Americans ask more of their schools than just to educate their children. Schools have become one-stop social policy centers and are now a major means by which basic nutrition is provided to millions of poor children. Schools screen at-risk children and attempt to get them medical and psychological assistance; they seek to socialize students into acceptable behaviors, often in the face of increasing violence in the surrounding neighborhoods; and they often reach out to families to provide basic help in parenting.

HIGHER EDUCATION The federal government also provides help to college and universities. In 2005, the federal government provided roughly 70 percent, or $23 billion, of the financial aid that college students receive. Pell grants for low-income students and low-interest guaranteed student loans continue to be the most available and most used subsidies for college expenses. In 1998, Congress added three new programs to improve the odds that needy children will make it to college. GEAR-UP, which supports early interventions to help students complete high school, the Learning Anytime Anywhere Partnerships (LAAP), which provide federal funding for distance-learning through the Internet, and a new initiative designed to improve teacher quality in primary and elementary schools. Although the three programs account for less than 1 percent of federal spending for education, they acknowledge the link between the quality of primary and elementary education and college success, as well as the need to act early to increase the odds of success for needy students.

CHANGING FACE OF AMERICAN POLITICS

ACCESS TO COLLEGE

Federal aid to education has increased access to college for all Americans, but it has had a particularly significant effect on women and students of color. The effect has been pronounced at both the community college and four-year college levels, where women now earn the majority of associate and bachelor degrees, and where students of color have more than doubled over the decades. Under the 1998 Higher Education Act, the number of students of color should increase even faster as the federal government puts more dollars into preparing students for college.

	1976–77	2000–01
Associate Degrees		
Men	51.8%	40.0%
Women	48.2	60.0
White	84.5	71.0
Black, non-Hispanic	8.2	11.0
Hispanic	4.1	9.9
Asian/Pacific Islander	1.7	4.9
American Indian/Alaska Native	0.6	1.1
Nonresident alien	0.8	2.0
Bachelor's Degrees		
Men	53.8%	42.7%
Women	46.2	57.3
White	88.0	73.8
Black, non-Hispanic	6.4	10.3
Hispanic	2.0	6.5
Asian/Pacific Islander	1.5	6.0
American Indian/Alaska Native	0.4	0.7
Nonresident alien	1.7	2.6

SOURCE: U.S. Department of Education, National Center for Education Statistics: *Postsecondary Institutions in the United States: Fall 2001 Degrees and Other Awards Conferred: 2000–01* (Washington, D.C., 2003), accessed at nces.edu.gov/fastfacts.

The Federal Role in Crime Control

Controlling crime is also considered primarily a state and local matter. The federal government usually acts more as a banker than a police officer, providing grants to states and local governments to hire their own police officers, build more prisons, improve drug enforcement, and prosecute organized crime.

Crime is hardly unimportant to national politics, however. The federal government must enforce its own laws against everything from counterfeiting to pollution while protecting its borders and preventing drugs from flowing into the country.

Congress has intervened on such matters as gun control. Because guns are manufactured and transported across state lines, Congress has the power to regulate sales under the Constitution's commerce clause and has used it to ban the sale and ownership of semiautomatic weapons and assault rifles and set age minimums for the purchase of handguns (21 years of age) and long guns such as rifles and shotguns (18 years of age).

In 1993, for example, Congress passed landmark legislation imposing a waiting period on the purchase of handguns. Under the Brady Handgun Violence Prevention Act, federally licensed firearms dealers have five days to check with local law enforcement officials regarding the background of a potential purchaser. If local law enforcement officials fail to respond within five business days, the handgun can be sold. The National Rifle Association has been powerful enough to stop most other antigun legislation, even though such legislation has had the support of most police chiefs and most of the general public. The debate over gun control at the local, state, and national levels remains intense.

In 1994, Congress passed an omnibus anticrime bill that authorized over $30 billion in spending on federal crime initiatives. The money funded the hiring of as many as 100,000 new police officers and the construction of new prisons and "boot camps" for juvenile offenders. The bill also added new assault rifle restrictions, made a long list of federal offenses punishable by death, imposed federal penalties and programs aimed at curbing domestic violence, and, with its "three strikes and you're out" provision, mandated life imprisonment upon conviction for a third violent felony.

The federal government enforces its laws primarily through the Department of Justice, which contains the Federal Bureau of Investigation (FBI). The FBI was created in 1908 and charged with gathering and reporting evidence in matters relating to federal criminal laws. In addition, the FBI provides investigative services on a cooperative basis to local law enforcement in fingerprint identification and laboratory services. Other law enforcement agencies of the federal government include the Drug Enforcement Agency

Sarah Brady campaigned tirelessly to win passage of the Brady Handgun Violence Prevention Act. She became a vocal advocate for gun control after her husband, James Brady, President Ronald Reagan's White House Press Secretary, was shot on March 30, 1981. Brady was shot by John Hinckley Jr. during his failed assassination attempt on President Reagan.

Legislation has been proposed to require purchasers of guns at gun shows to undergo an identity check on whether they have a record of criminal activity.

(DEA), which is responsible for preventing the flow of illegal narcotics into the United States, patrolling U.S. borders, and conducting joint operations with countries where drugs are produced, and the Bureau of Alcohol, Tobacco and Firearms, which monitors the sale of destructive weapons and guns inside the United States, regulates alcoholic beverage production, and oversees the collection of taxes on alcohol and tobacco.

Although the number of violent crimes decreased through the 1990s, it began rising in 2001, reinforcing the widespread perception that crime and violence are increasing and the federal government needs to step in. As a result, Congress has made more and more crimes federal ones and increased the severity of punishments for them. As more people are put in prisons, the costs for building and running them has increased dramatically.

Terrorism is clearly the federal government's top crime priority today. Only weeks after the September 11, 2001, terrorist attacks on New York City and Washington, D.C., Congress passed a massive antiterrorism law in October 2001 and created the new Department of Homeland Security the following summer. For his part, the president created the Office of Homeland Security within the White House in October and ordered a complete reorganization of the Federal Bureau of Investigation in early 2002 to create a stronger focus on preventing terrorism. Under the USA PATRIOT Act of 2001 (the letters stand for Uniting and Strengthening America by Providing Appropriate Tools Required to Intercept and Obstruct Terrorism), for example, the federal government was given sweeping authority to conduct secret investigations of suspected terrorists, use "roving wiretaps" to intercept conversations on any phones that a suspect might use, and detain any noncitizens believed to be a national security risk for up to seven days without being charged with a crime.

Although the USA PATRIOT Act is not scheduled to expire until December 31, 2005, the Bush administration made its renewal a centerpiece of the president's 2004 State of the Union Address. "Key provisions of the Patriot Act are set to expire next year," the president told Congress. "The terrorist threat will not expire on that schedule. Our law enforcement needs this vital legislation to protect our citizens." The administration also asked Congress to expand authority to investigate what it called "lone-wolf' terrorists who are not affiliated with a foreign government or known terrorist organization such as Al-Qaeda, which planned the September 11 attacks.[35]

THE POLITICS OF SOCIAL POLICY

Despite the nation's current focus on terrorism and homeland security, social policy still dominates the agenda of American politics. Welfare, health care, education, and crime—and their costs—are today's political battleground between the parties and between contending interest groups. Education reform was at the forefront of the 2000 presidential election, while the war on terrorism was part of the 2004 campaign.

The nation long ago answered questions about whether the national government has a role in providing decent housing, adequate health care, and a solid education for all of its citizens. The question is not whether the nation will provide a safety net for its needy citizens, but how strong the net will be and who will be responsible for providing it. Although the vast majority of Americans support Social Security and Medicare, for example, they are sharply divided over how much the nation should do for its poorest citizens. They are also increasingly divided about reforms such as the No Child Left Behind Act and its mandatory testing.

Nevertheless, social policy will be part of the federal agenda far into the future. Although Presidents and Congress cannot always know what Americans will support and how much they are willing to pay, they can be sure that most Americans want government to take care of citizens who are needy through no fault of their own.

SUMMARY

1. Conservatives advocate private solutions for most social problems, while liberals argue that it is the responsibility of government to provide a minimum standard of living—including a job, an education, health care, housing, and nutrition—for all citizens. Since the New Deal, some national government involvement in social programs has been widely accepted, although the extent of involvement has waxed and waned. Conservatives generally prefer state and local government action over federal programs.

2. Social Security, inaugurated in 1935 as part of the New Deal, is perhaps the most significant social legislation in U.S. history. Through a system of employee and employer taxes, retired workers and disabled individuals receive monthly payments and health benefits. With the country's aging population, strains on the system are likely to increase.

3. Welfare takes many forms, including direct payments to the poor, the unemployed, and the disabled; food stamps; job training; housing subsidies; free school lunches; tax credits; and subsidized medical care. Public assistance programs began with the New Deal and have grown ever since.

4. Welfare has long been criticized as creating disincentives to work, and many proposals have been put forward to make programs more effective and efficient. The most recent welfare reform, which became law in August 1996, transferred the administrative burden to the states, giving them more discretion over recipients and benefits while helping to fund welfare programs through block grants of federal money.

5. The federal government supports medical research and has increased its role in health care cost control and access as the country's mostly private health care system is beset by rising costs, increasing numbers of uninsured Americans, unnecessary procedures, endless paperwork, high litigation costs, avoidable illnesses, and limited access. A variety of proposals for reform are under consideration, including a single-payer system, prepaid health plans, employer-mandated coverage, spending caps, individual responsibility for coverage, and medical savings accounts.

6. Education continues to be primarily a state and local government function in the United States. The federal government plays an important role in funding public schools and pushing national goals for better education, and is also heavily involved in helping finance college and university education.

7. Crime control has been part of the national agenda for decades, especially related to drugs, but has become much more visible as part of the war on terrorism.

KEY TERMS

entitlements
means-tested entitlements
public assistance

social insurance
Social Security
Medicaid

Medicare
health maintenance
   organization (HMO)

medical savings account

FURTHER READING

ANNE MARIE CAMMISA, *From Rhetoric to Reform? Welfare Policy in American Politics* (Westview Press, 1998).

BARBARA EHRENREICH, *Nickled and Dimed: On (Not) Getting By in America* (Metropolitan Books, 2001).

FRANK FISCHER, *Evaluating Public Policy* (Nelson-Hall, 1995).

LAURENE A. GRAIG, *Health of Nations: An International Perspective on U.S. Health Care Reform* (CQ Press, 1993).

CHRISTOPHER JENCKS, *The Homeless* (Harvard University Press, 1994).

PAUL C. LIGHT, *Still Artful Work: The Continuing Politics of Social Security Reform* (McGraw-Hill, 1995).

THOMAS E. MANN AND NORMAN J. ORNSTEIN, EDS., *Intensive Care: How Congress Shapes Health Policy* (Brookings Institution Press, 1995).

DANIEL PATRICK MOYNIHAN, *Miles to Go: A Personal History of Social Policy* (Harvard University Press, 1996).

CHARLES MURRAY, *Losing Ground: American Social Policy, 1950–80* (Basic Books, 1984).

B. GUY PETERS, *American Public Policy: Promise and Performance*, 4th ed. (Chatham House, 1996).

PAUL E. PETERSON AND MARTIN R. WEST, EDS., *No Child Left Behind: The Politics and Practice of School Accountability* (Brookings Institution Press, 2004).

FRANCES FOX PIVEN AND RICHARD A. CLOWARD, *Regulating the Poor: The Functions of Public Welfare* (Vintage, 1993).

THEDA SKOCPOL, *Social Policy in the United States: Future Possibilities in Historical Perspective* (Princeton University Press, 1995).

R. KENT WEAVER, *Ending Welfare as We Know It* (Brookings Institution Press, 2001).

MARGARET WEIR, ED., *The Social Divide: Political Parties and the Future of Activist Government* (Brookings Institution Press, 1998).

BOB WOODWARD, *Agenda: Inside the Clinton White House* (Simon & Schuster, 1994).

MAKING FOREIGN AND DEFENSE POLICY

20

The Bush administration entered office facing a long list of foreign policy challenges. North Korea and Iran were continuing to develop nuclear weapons, Israel and the Palestinians were embroiled in violence, the global economy was entering a deep downturn, HIV-AIDS was spreading rapidly through Africa and Asia, and terrorism was on the rise.

Iraq and its brutal dictator, Saddam Hussein, were also on the foreign policy agenda. "From the very beginning, there was a conviction, that Saddam Hussein was a bad person and that he needed to go," Bush's former Treasury Secretary Paul O'Neill told CBS News in 2004. "From the very first instance, it was about Iraq. It was about what we can do to change this regime. Day one, these things were laid and sealed." No one ever questioned the basic assumption that Hussein had to go. "It was all about finding a way to do it," O'Neill recalled. "That was the tone of it. The president saying 'Go find me a way to do this.'"[1]

The Bush administration was particularly concerned about Iraq's interest in developing **weapons of mass destruction** (WMD)—a term that refers to chemical, biological, and/or nuclear weapons that can be used to inflict massive casualties on an enemy. Hussein had used chemical weapons against his own citizens in the 1980s, but he had promised to destroy his inventory of biological and chemical agents at the end of the Gulf War in 1991, which followed Iraq's invasion of its oil-rich neighbor, Kuwait. As President Bush warned in his first press conference in mid-February 2001, "the primary goal is to make it clear to Saddam that we expect him to be a peaceful neighbor in the region and we expect him not to develop weapons of mass destruction. And if we find him doing so, there will be a consequence."

Despite these concerns, Iraq was hardly the top foreign policy issue early in the Bush administration. The president did not mention Iraq once when he outlined his domestic

TIME LINE
MAKING FOREIGN AND DEFENSE POLICY

1862	First military draft provokes riots
1917	United States enters World War I
1941	Pearl Harbor bombed, United States enters World War II
1945	Nuclear bombing of Hiroshima and Nagasaki ends World War II
1945	United Nations Charter signed in San Francisco
1947	National Security Agency and CIA created
1949	North Atlantic Treaty Organization created
1950	Start of the Korean War
1961	Kennedy seeks to motivate idealist youth through the Peace Corps
1964	Gulf of Tonkin resolution authorizes expansion of war in Vietnam
1972	Biological and Chemical Weapons treaty
1975	End of Vietnam War
1989	Cold war ends with the collapse of the Soviet Union
1993	World Trade Center is bombed but survives
2001	Attacks on World Trade Center and Pentagon

weapons of mass destruction
Biological, chemical, and nuclear weapons that can inflict massive casualties in a single event.

and foreign policy agenda before Congress in late February 2001, for example, nor did he ask for any new authority to remove Hussein from power.

Iraq moved rapidly up the list of priorities in the days and weeks following the terrorist attacks on New York City and Washington, D.C., on September 11 of that year, however. The war on terrorism was now the nation's top priority, and Iraq a potent enemy. Convinced that Iraq was ready and willing to use weapons of mass destruction against the United States, Bush ordered the military to start planning for a possible invasion on September 17, only six days after the terrorist attacks.[2] He also began building the case for action with the American public, arguing in his 2002 State of the Union Address that Iraq was part of an "axis of evil" that threatened the peace of the world.

On September 12, 2002, one year and one day after the terrorist attacks, Bush took the case to the United Nations. Iraq was not only "expanding and improving facilities that were used for the production of biological weapons," he said, it also had made several attempts to buy the equipment required to enrich uranium for a nuclear weapon. Bush also made the case for removing Hussein from power: "The United States has no quarrel with the Iraqi people; they've suffered too long in silent captivity. Liberty for the Iraqi people is a great moral cause, and a great strategic goal. The people of Iraq deserve it; the security of all nations requires it. Free societies do not intimidate through cruelty and conquest, and open societies do not threaten the world with mass murder. The United States supports political and economic liberty in a unified Iraq."

Three weeks later, on October 1, the Central Intelligence Agency gave members of Congress its 90-page National Intelligence Estimate on Iraq, which provided the evidence for war and formed the backbone of the president's October 7 address to the nation making the case for war. Three days later, on October 10, the House voted 296 to 133 in favor of a joint resolution authorizing the use of force in Iraq; the next day, the Senate voted 77 to 23 for the same resolution. The votes clearly indicated bipartisan, if not unified, support for action. Future Democratic presidential candidate John Kerry (D.-Mass.) voted in favor of the resolution, as did his running mate, John Edwards (D.-N.C.), and Senators Joseph Biden (D.-Del.), Hillary Clinton (D.-N.Y.), and Joseph Lieberman (D.-Conn.).

Meanwhile, the U.S. military continued planning for a possible war, moving thousands of troops and supplies into position in the Persian Gulf region. On March 20, 2003, the war began. U.S. troops reached the outskirts of Baghdad on April 6, secured the city over the next two days, and helped topple Hussein's statue at the center of the city on April 9. On May 1, President Bush stood on the deck of the USS *Abraham Lincoln* underneath a banner that read "MISSION ACCOMPLISHED" and told the nation that "Major combat operations in Iraq have ended."

Unfortunately, many of the assumptions on which the war was fought turned out to be wrong. Planners assumed, for example, that the Iraqi people would greet U.S. troops as liberators and accept a long, quiet occupation as the country returned to normalcy. Instead, the streets were soon filled with looting, followed by armed conflict between U.S. troops and religious militias. Having disarmed the Iraqi army and disbanded the local police, U.S. troops found themselves in charge of everything from directing traffic to protecting supply convoys.

Planners also assumed the Iraqi economy would make a quick recovery based on revenues from its oil fields, which in turn would help pay for the reconstruction of hospitals, schools, and other civic institutions. Instead, the Iraqi economy was on the verge of complete collapse. Although the oil fields emerged from the war intact, pipelines were damaged, roads and bridges were destroyed, sewer and water systems had collapsed, and few Iraqis were willing to risk their lives to help in the rebuilding.

Finally, planners assumed that U.S. troops would quickly find the weapons of mass destruction that had been so important to the case for war. Eighteen months after entering Baghdad, no such weapons had been found. As the Senate Select Committee on Intelligence reported in July 2004, most of the key judgments embedded in warnings about Iraq's weapons of mass destruction were "either overstated, or were not supported by, the underlying intelligence reporting."[3] Moreover, the highly critical Senate report concluded that the intelligence community "did not accurately or adequately explain to policy makers the uncertainties behind the judgments" that underpinned the conclusion that Iraq still had an active weapons program.

As these and other assumptions failed, and casualties mounted, public support for the war declined. The number of Americans who approved of the president's handling of the situation in Iraq fell from 73 percent just after the fall of Baghdad in April 2003 to just 42 percent by mid-June 2004, while the number who said the war was going "not too well" or "not well at all" rose from just 6 percent to 39 percent during the same period.[4] Although the United States did transfer some control to an interim government in late June 2004, it was clearly preparing for a long stay as the president entered the fall election campaign. Serious fighting continued.

This chapter will ask how choices are made in planning and executing foreign policy. We will first examine the foreign policy challenges before the nation today, including the new war against terrorism, then turn to the key actors in making foreign and defense policy, appraise the politics of making foreign and defense policy, and inventory the range of foreign and defense policy options. We will conclude with a more detailed assessment of defense policy.

VITAL INTERESTS IN THE TWENTY-FIRST CENTURY

The framers of the U.S. Constitution did not have a grand strategy for using the basic tools of foreign and defense policy to preserve the nation and protect U.S. interests across the globe. Rather, they worried first about protecting the nation long enough to survive. Although the framers generally believed in free trade and hoped to protect their young nation from foreign threats, their general focus was on keeping the nation out of harm's way in Europe as it addressed its economic and domestic problems.

Toward these ends, the framers made three basic decisions that guide foreign policy to this day. First, they declared that foreign policy was a national, not state, responsibility. Even as the Constitution divided power between the president and Congress, Article I, Section 10 declares that no state shall enter into a treaty, alliance, or confederation with another nation, meaning that only the national government can conduct foreign policy.

Second, the framers concentrated the authority to make foreign and defense policy in the presidency. They gave the president sole authority to command the army and navy, make treaties, appoint ambassadors, and oversee the departments of government, thereby making the president both commander and diplomat in chief. The framers recognized that foreign policy could not be conducted by a collection of interests. The nation needed a single point of contact for representing what was then a very clearly defined national interest: survival.

Finally, having given the president authority to implement policy, the framers checked that power by giving Congress as a whole the power to declare war, raise an army and a navy, and make the rules of war and by giving the Senate the power to ratify all treaties by a two-thirds vote and confirm all ambassadors by a majority vote. Even as they made sure the national government could protect the United States against foreign threats through the use of armed force, they worried that a president might exploit that power to deny basic liberties. As John Jay argued in *The Federalist,* No. 4, "Absolute monarchs will often make war when their nations are to get nothing by it, but for purposes and objects merely personal, such as, a thirst for military glory."

Defining Vital U.S. Interests

In the broadest sense, the primary goal of U.S. foreign and defense policy is to protect the nation from harm, whether from other nations or individual terrorists, nuclear missiles, or suicide bombings. Over the past several generations, the United States has become involved in world affairs to a degree unprecedented in its history. Although much of this activity was due to the cold war against communism from 1945 to 1990, the

President Bush on the deck of the USS Abraham Lincoln *on May 1, 2003, declares an end to major combat operations in Iraq. Since that time, thousands of injuries and deaths have occurred on both sides of the conflict.*

sheer size and wealth of the United States makes it both a natural world leader and a target for criticism. There are other reasons as well. U.S. security and economic interests are inevitably tied to what happens in the rest of the world. Whether Americans like it or not, events far from home affect their life, liberty, and pursuit of happiness.

Balancing political, economic, and social values is critical in defining vital U.S. interests. Americans want peace, but not if it means that they must give up basic freedoms. Americans favor human rights, but not if it means less trade and fewer jobs. Americans support the general concept of a United Nations that represents all the nations of the world, but not if the United States must give up command of its own troops in U.N. missions. They want the United States to protect weaker nations against aggression, as long as not too many U.S. soldiers are put in harm's way. Where possible, they want to improve the standard of living in less-developed nations and protect the global environment, but they also want new markets for U.S. products, inexpensive imports, and adequate supplies of energy. The task of defining our interests requires extensive balancing of sometimes competing goals.

This balancing continues to involve a mix of long-standing goals such as stopping the spread of HIV-AIDS, enhancing human rights, addressing global warming and other environmental threats, reducing hunger and illiteracy, finding a lasting peace in the Middle East, and closing the gap between rich and poor nations. But it has also expanded in recent years to include the war on terrorism and a much more aggressive effort to control the spread of weapons of mass destruction.

The War on Terrorism

September 11 clearly changed the U.S. foreign policy agenda radically. As the 9/11 Commission argues, the foreign policy agenda used to be determined by national boundaries, industrial strength, and military strength. "Threats emerged slowly, often visibly, as weapons were forged, armies conscripted, and units trained and moved into place."[5] (See Table 20–1 for examples of how public opinion changed after September 11.)

Today's threats know no borders—they emerge quickly and without respect for power, prestige, or military might. Driven by their hatred of America and its allies such as Spain, terrorists do not distinguish between politics and religion, nor between governments and civilians. "It is not a position with which Americans can bargain or negotiate," the Commission argues. "With it there is no common ground—not even respect for life—on which to begin a dialogue."

EARLY WARNINGS The 9/11 Commission also notes that the September 11 attacks were a shock, but should not have been a surprise to the U.S. government. After all, terrorist activity increased dramatically during the 1990s. Terrorists had tried and failed to destroy the World Trade Center in New York City with a truck bomb in 1993; planned but failed to destroy a dozen U.S. airliners over the Pacific in 1995; killed 19 U.S. soldiers and wounded hundreds in Saudi Arabia with a truck bomb in 1996; killed 224 people, including 12 Americans, in truck bomb attacks on U.S. embassies in Nairobi, Kenya, and Dar es Salaam, Tanzania, in 1998; planned, but failed, to bomb Los Angeles International Airport on New Year's Eve, 1999; and killed 17 U.S. sailors on the USS *Cole* in 2000.

Yet, the U.S. government was still unprepared for September 11, in part because the nation's intelligence agencies missed a number of key warning signs, and in part because this attack involved such a massive loss of human life. As the 9/11 Commission reported, the most important failure leading to the tragedy was one of imagination: Americans and their leaders never thought it could happen here.

THE WAR IN AFGHANISTAN Days after the September 11 attacks, the United States put the international community on notice that it would pursue terrorists wherever they found comfort. Speaking before a joint session of Congress on September 20, 2001, President Bush announced, "From this day forward, any nation that continues to harbor or support terrorism will be regarded by the United States as a hostile regime. Every nation in every region now has a decision to make. Either you are with us, or you are with the terrorists."

The war in Afghanistan was the first major action against a nation that clearly harbored terrorism. The United States quickly linked the attacks to Osama bin Laden and his Al-Qaeda terrorist network, and Bin Laden to Afghanistan's extremist Taliban government. "The Taliban must act and act immediately," Bush told Congress. "They will hand over the terrorists or they will share in their fate." Two weeks later, Bush demanded bin Laden's arrest again, warning the Taliban that "Full warning has been given. For those nations that stand with the terrorists, there will be a heavy price."

The war began the next morning, October 7, and was effectively over on December 7 when Taliban forces withdrew from the southern city of Kandahar. Afghan's interim leader, Hamid Karzai, took control of the new government two weeks later.

Although the war was quick, and U.S. casualties were light, the Afghan government is still unstable, the economy weak, and drug trafficking still robust. Moreover, as the 9/11 Commission warned, Taliban and Al-Qaeda fighters have regrouped in the south, warlords control much of the country, relief workers refuse to operate in many regions, and guns and ammunition are easily available.

TABLE 20–1 CHANGING FOREIGN POLICY GOALS BEFORE AND AFTER SEPTEMBER 11, 2001			
	Before	*After*	*Change*
Reduce spread of AIDS	73%	59%	−14%
Deal with world hunger	47	34	−13
Combat drug trafficking	64	55	−9
Promote U.S. business interests	37	30	−7
Ensure adequate energy supplies	74	69	−5
Promote democracy	29	24	−5
Help reduce world poverty	25	20	−5

SOURCE: Pew Research Center for the People and the Press, *Public Opinion in a Year for the Books* (Pew Research Center, 2002), p. 12.

Still, there is at least some cause for hope. More than 90 percent of the Afghanistan public registered for the nation's first democratic elections in October, 2004, 40 percent of whom were women. Moreover, the current government appeared to be initially tolerant of competition—two dozen candidates announced their intention to enter the presidential campaign, for example, which required copies of at least 10,000 voter registration cards from supporters. The election was held on October 9, 2004, with reports of heavy turnout despite threats of violence. Interim President Hamid Karzai emerged with 55 percent of the votes among a field of candidates.

PREVENTING FUTURE ATTACKS   The war in Afghanistan was the first phase of what will be a very long war against terrorism. In many ways, terrorists have the advantage in an open society such as the United States. Short of curbing basic freedoms, there is only so much the nation can do to tighten its borders, police its streets, and prevent attacks. Even in Afghanistan, where the United States secured a quick victory in overthrowing the fundamentalist Taliban government that had provided a safe haven for Al Qaeda, the United States could not be sure that it destroyed even a fraction of the network that planned the attacks on New York City and Washington, D.C.

Unlike a traditional war, in which great armies mass against each other in battle, the war on terrorism must be fought against a highly agile adversary that will use all means at its disposal, including suicide bombings, to create terror. Doing so involves more than hunting down terrorists before they strike, however. "The U.S. government must define what the message is, what it stands for," the 9/11 Commission argues. "We should offer an example of moral leadership in the world, committed to treat people humanely, abide by the rule of law, and be generous and caring to our neighbors. . . . To Muslim parents, terrorists like bin Laden have nothing to offer their children but visions of violence and death. America and its friends have a crucial advantage—we can offer these parents a vision that might given their children a better future."[6]

Unfortunately, the 2004 reports of Iraqi prisoner abuse by U.S. military police did little to reinforce America's reputation for treating people humanely. As of July 2004, the Army had identified 94 cases of abuse, including 40 deaths, in the 16 prisons it has used to detain suspected terrorists and prisoners of war. (See the People and Politics: Making a Difference box later in this chapter for a profile of the army general who led the first investigation of abuse.)

Weapons of Mass Destruction

The international community has been working to reduce the threat of biological, chemical, and nuclear war for decades, starting with the nuclear disarmament talks between the United States and the Soviet Union in the 1970s. With the cold war over in 1989, the United States and Russia began to look for new ways of reducing their nuclear arsenals and agreed in 2002 to reduce the number of nuclear warheads dramatically.

Indian and Pakistani troops patrol the border in escalating numbers as religious and territorial differences over ownership of Kashmir bring the two countries closer to war. Tensions were reduced in part due to interventions by U.S. corporations that are dependent on India's high-tech workforce.

The world is still threatened by weapons of mass destruction, however. A handful of nations continue to maintain biological weapons, and at least nine have declared that they have developed chemical weapons, including Russia, China, Ethiopia, India, Iran, Pakistan, South Korea, and Vietnam. Still others may have biological and chemical weapons programs that they have not declared. Moreover, several other nations have or intend to develop nuclear weapons, including India, Iran, North Korea, and Pakistan. Israel is said to have nuclear weapons as well.

THE BUSH DOCTRINE   Increased worries about the use of weapons of mass destruction against the United States following September 11 led to the **Bush Doctrine**, which the president announced at the U.S. Military Academy at West Point in June 2002. "If we wait for threats to materialize," Bush told the class of '02, "we will have waited too long."[7]

Under the doctrine, the United States reserves the right to attack any nation or group that threatens to use weapons of mass destruction against the United States and its interests. The doctrine supports the use of **preemption**, under which the United States promises to take action *before* an adversary could use its weapons.

The Bush Doctrine was central to the administration's case for war in Iraq. As already noted in the introduction to this chapter, the administration had discussed the need to remove Saddam Hussein from power at the very first meeting of the National Security Council on January 30.

The discussions became much more serious after September 11. The president reportedly asked the White House's senior counterterrorism officer, Richard Clarke, to investigate the possibility that Iraq had been involved in the terrorist attacks. "Go back over everything, everything," Bush allegedly told Clarke. "See if Saddam did this." When Clarke answered, "But Mr. President, Al-Qaeda did this," Bush reportedly replied, "I know, I know, but . . . see if Saddam was involved. Just look. I want to know any shred." Although Clarke insisted that the CIA, FBI, and White House had already concluded that there were no such links, the president nevertheless insisted that Clarke "Look into Iraq, Saddam."[8]

THE CASE FOR WAR   Convinced that Iraq continued to be a great threat to U.S. security regardless of its role in September 11, the Bush administration decided to force Iraq to disarm, while making the argument for war if Iraq refused. Despite cautions from U.N. inspectors who argued that Iraq had dismantled its biological and chemical weapons program and abandoned its quest for nuclear weapons after the war in 1991, the Bush administration was convinced that the weapons not only existed, but constituted a clear and present danger to the United States.

The administration was sharply divided on how to disarm Iraq, however. The president's national security adviser, Condoleezza Rice, argued that the United States had a moral obligation to remove Hussein from power, even if doing so meant war. "This is an evil man who, left to his own devices, will wreak havoc again on his own population, his neighbors, and, if he gets weapons of mass destruction and the means to deliver them, on all of us," Rice told the British Broadcasting Corporation in August 2002. "There is a very powerful moral case for regime change. We certainly do not have the luxury of doing nothing."[9] Her position was strongly supported by Secretary of Defense Donald Rumsfeld and Vice President Dick Cheney.

In contrast, Secretary of State Colin Powell argued that the United States needed to consider the impact of such an attack on other foreign and defense policy goals, as well as on the war on terrorism itself. Although he also believed the world would be better off without Hussein in power, he worried about both the cost and impact of war. Having overseen the first war with Iraq as the U.S. Army's most senior officer in 1991, Powell knew that U.S. military power would win any war against Iraq, but he also believed that a prolonged war in Iraq, especially one waged with minimal international support, might increase hostility toward the United States, while giving terrorist organizations more targets for violence.

THE WAR IN IRAQ   On September 20, 2002, the Bush administration resolved the debate by asking Congress for the authorization to use armed force to defend the United States from the Iraqi threat and enforce the terms of all past U.N. resolutions regarding disarmament and ongoing inspections. As noted at the start of this chapter, Congress granted the authority on October 10.

Bush Doctrine
A policy adopted by the Bush administration in 2001 that asserts America's right to attack any nation that has weapons of mass destruction that might be used against U.S. interests at home or abroad.

preemption
Associated with the Bush Doctrine, a belief that a nation is justified in attacking another nation to prevent possible attacks on itself.

After six more months of international negotiation and further preparation for war, the Bush administration used the authority. With Britain as its only major military ally, the United States launched a massive bombing campaign on March 20, 2003, followed by a ground assault through southern Iraq on March 21. With the Air Force in close support using precision-guided bombs, the Army and Marine Corps moved quickly up the road to Baghdad. One hundred thirty-nine soldiers had been killed in combat as of May 1 when the president announced an end to the war.

The battle for Iraq was only beginning, however. Another 613 soldiers died during the year that followed, including 150 at the height of the internal uprising against the U.S. military in April 2004. The mounting death toll has led some analysts to ask whether there are enough troops in Iraq to provide needed security. According to one estimate by the RAND Corporation, a Santa Monica, California, think tank, winning the peace in Iraq would take roughly 500,000 troops at any one time, or more than three times the number of foreign troops assigned to the effort in 2004. Assuming a 24-month rotation cycle, the world would need to draw upon a force of 2.5 million troops, or almost double the total number of troops now in the U.S. military alone.[10]

Terrorism has also increased as opponents of the U.S. engagement have turned to kidnapping, beheadings, and suicide bombings against governments and private companies that are involved in the campaign. Both Spain and the Philippines withdrew their troops from Iraq following terrorist attacks on their citizens. Spain removed its 1,300 troops after 200 citizens were killed in a series of Madrid train bombings just days before national elections.

As the war continued to take its toll on U.S. forces, the Bush administration finally returned to the United Nations in the spring of 2004 to ask for help in rebuilding Iraq. In June 2004, the United Nations helped select an interim Iraqi government headed by Prime Minister Iyad Allawi, but has been unwilling to commit a peacekeeping force until Iraq becomes less dangerous. Despite hopes to the contrary, the war continued to intensify even after the United States transferred authority to the new Iraqi government two days ahead of schedule on June 30, 2004. By the end of September 2004, more than 1,000 U.S. troops had been killed in battle and the number continued to rise through October and November.

More importantly, violence against both the United States and the new Iraqi government escalated dramatically. On October 25, 2004, for example, 49 newly-trained Iraqi troops were executed; on October 28, another 11 were executed; and on October 30, just three days before the presidential election, nine U.S. Marines were killed in a suicide attack on their convoy, marking the worst day in the war in six months.

THE MISSING WEAPONS OF MASS DESTRUCTION   Although the case for war was based almost entirely on allegations that Iraq was ready to use weapons of mass destruction against the United States., the weapons have never been found. According to a U.S. Intelligence Committee report released in July 2004, most of the key judgments in the intelligence community's assessment of Iraq's weapons programs were "either overstated, or were not supported by, the underlying intelligence reporting."[11]

Equally important for making foreign policy, the intelligence community "did not accurately or adequately explain to policy makers the uncertainties behind the judgments" contained in a key October 2002 assessment that the Central Intelligence Director, George Tenet, had called a "slam dunk case" that Iraq had the weapons.[12] Tenet resigned three weeks before the report was released and was replaced by a former CIA intelligence officer and member of Congress, Porter Goss (R.-Fla.) three months later.

Continued Priorities

Although the war on terrorism has occupied the headlines since September 11, the United States still has a deep inventory of other foreign policy goals that require ongoing attention, including efforts to promote democracy around the world; prevent the spread of infectious diseases such as HIV-AIDS, tuberculosis, and polio; address global climate change; and provide humanitarian aid. The United States has also pursued three other priorities we will discuss next: (1) finding a Middle East peace, (2) promoting free trade, and (3) encouraging international understanding.

President Bush addresses the General Assembly at the United Nations on September 12, 2002, seeking approval for military action against Iraq. The U.N. Security Council ultimately did not grant its approval and in 2004, U.N. Secretary General Kofi Annan (left) charged that the U.S. war against Iraq was in violation of international law because it did not have the backing of the U.N. Security Council.

The U.S. war against Iraq began on March 20, 2003, with a bombing campaign designed to produce "shock and awe" within Iraq and thereby assure the collapse of military resistance.

An increase in suicide bombings by Palestinians is a violent indication of the distance Palestine and Israel still have to travel to find a lasting peace. Israel responded with its own attack on terrorist bases in Palestine.

MIDDLE EAST PEACE   Progress toward a lasting Middle East peace is particularly important in reducing international terrorism. However, despite decades of U.S. effort, the region remains locked in a violent struggle between Israel and the Palestinians who live in occupied territory called the West Bank. Although the United States has made some progress in designing a road map to peace, much of the past progress toward that goal was lost in the wave of suicide bombings that began on Passover in October 2001, and Israel's subsequent decision to build a 225-mile wall separating itself from Palestine.

The rising tide of attack and counterattack put the United States in an extraordinarily difficult position. As a longtime ally of Israel, the United States supported Israel's use of force against the camps that sheltered the militants. Moreover, Israel Prime Minister Ariel Sharon used the language of the Bush Doctrine to justify his actions. However, the United States could not condone a renewed Israeli occupation of the Palestinian territories without weakening support for the war on terrorism among key Arab nations. The United States eventually resolved its dilemma by calling for Israel to withdraw while encouraging the Palestinian people to remove their leader, Yasser Arafat, from power, but found itself no closer to resolving the Palestinian question.

INTERNATIONAL TRADE   Even as the world has become more dangerous, it has become more interdependent and competitive economically. The United States has generally responded to this globalization with a basic policy of free trade, meaning a commitment to the free movement of goods across international borders. It does not allow the export of technologies that can be used to build nuclear weapons, however, and has long protected certain defense industries that would be essential should it ever be forced into another world war. It has also used trade as a tool to promote human rights and democratic reform.

The United States pursued a mix of goals in the battle over free trade with mainland China. On the one hand, China has a long history of violating basic human and democratic rights. On the other hand, China has one of the fastest-growing economies in the world. U.S. exports to China have tripled over the past decade, and imports from China have grown rapidly. This balancing effort reached a crescendo over President Clinton's request for **permanent normal trade relations (PNTR) status** for China, granting China the same favorable trade concessions and tariffs that its best trading partners receive.

The debate over China trade was so controversial that Congress refused to give President Clinton an extension of past "fast-track," or accelerated congressional action on trade agreements. Under fast-track authority, which had been given to every president since Nixon but expired in 1994, Congress limited its own debate about trade agreements to a simple yes-or-no vote with no amendments. In 1998, however, Congress finally granted PNTR status to China. Four years later, it restored fast-track authority under the Trade Act of 2002, giving the Bush administration the opportunity to open new rounds of trade talks with Chile, Singapore, and South Africa.

ECONOMIC DEVELOPMENT AND INTERNATIONAL UNDERSTANDING   The United States has long promoted these twin goals through foreign aid, which is discussed later in this chapter, and programs such as the Peace Corps, which was established in 1961 as one of the top priorities of the Kennedy administration.

Advertised on its Web site as "the toughest job you'll ever love," Peace Corps volunteers are expected to serve in another nation for two years and become part of the community they are serving. Volunteers work on a variety of projects, such as teaching math and science, doing community development work, and improving water and sanitation systems. Most volunteers either have a college degree, specific international experience, or a combination of both. About 10 percent of the 7,300 current volunteers are over 50 years old. The Peace Corps picks up the expenses and typically trains each volunteer in language and job skills for about three months prior to service abroad.[13]

The Peace Corps operates in about 80 nations and has had funding of about $260 million a year. More than 170,000 Americans have been Peace Corps volunteers. Eight Peace Corps alumni have served in Congress. The Peace Corps is wholly separate from the State and Defense Departments and the intelligence agencies.

permanent normal trade relations (PNTR) status

Trade status granted as part of an international trade policy that gives a nation the same favorable trade concessions and tariffs that the best trading partners receive.

THE FOREIGN AND DEFENSE POLICY BUREAUCRACY

Even in troubled times, the president does not have absolute authority to act. Congress has the power to declare war, to appropriate funds for the armed forces, and to make rules that govern the armed forces. But the president is commander in chief of the armed forces and is authorized to negotiate treaties and receive and send ambassadors—that is, to recognize or refuse to recognize other governments. The Senate confirms U.S. ambassadorial appointments and gives consent (by a two-thirds vote) to treaty ratification. The courts have the power to interpret treaties, but by and large they have ruled that relations with other nations are matters for the executive to decide. The primacy of the executive in foreign policy is a fact of political life of all nations, including constitutional democracies.

Officially, the president's principal foreign policy adviser is the secretary of state, although others, such as the national security adviser or the vice president, are sometimes equally influential. The secretary of state administers the State Department, receives visits from foreign diplomats, attends international conferences, and usually heads the U.S. delegation in the General Assembly of the United Nations. The secretary also serves as the administration's chief coordinator of all governmental actions that affect our relations with other nations. In practice, the secretary of state delegates the day-to-day responsibilities for running the State Department and spends most of the time negotiating with the leaders of other countries.

The interdependence of foreign, economic, and domestic policies requires more than just one or two advisers. The conduct of foreign affairs is now the business of several major departments and agencies, including State, Defense, Treasury, Agriculture, Commerce, Labor, Energy, the Central Intelligence Agency (CIA), and the new Department of Homeland Security. The need for immediate reaction and full preparedness has transferred many responsibilities directly to the president and to a great extent to the senior White House aides who assist in coordinating information and advice. Yet no matter what the system for advice and coordination, there are always overlaps of responsibilities, redundancy, and competition among agencies.

The National Security Council

The key coordinating agency for the president is the National Security Council (NSC). Created by Congress in 1947, it is intended to help presidents integrate foreign, military, and economic policies that affect national security. The NSC serves directly under the president. By law, it consists of the president, vice president, secretary of state, and secretary of defense. Recent presidents have sometimes included the director of the CIA, the White House chief of staff, and the national security adviser as nonstatutory members of the NSC.

The national security adviser, appointed by the president, has emerged as one of the most influential foreign policy makers, sometimes rivaling the secretary of state in influence. Presidents come to rely on these White House aides both because of their proximity (down the hall in the West Wing of the White House) and because they owe their primary loyalties to the president, not to any department or program. Each president has shaped the NSC structure and adapted its staff procedures to suit his personal preferences, but over the years, the NSC, as both a committee and a staff, has taken on a major role in making and implementing foreign policy. For her part, Condoleezza Rice has generally sided with the Bush administration's neoconservatives against the State Department and Colin Powell. In doing so, she has followed a time-honored path in which the NSC adviser can be more of an adversary of the State Department than an ally.

The State Department

The State Department is responsible for the diplomatic realm of foreign and defense policy. The department is organized around a series of "desks" representing different parts of the world and foreign policy missions. The State Department is also responsible for negotiating treaties with other nations and international organizations, protecting U.S. citizens abroad, promoting U.S. commercial interests in other nations, and granting visas to foreign visitors.

National Security Advisor Condoleezza Rice meets with President George W. Bush at the presidential retreat at Camp David. President Bush chose Rice to be secretary of state during his second term.

The State Department also plays a significant role in homeland security. Many of the September 2001 attackers had entered the United States on student visas granted by the State Department's Bureau of Consular Affairs. Although their movements once in the United States were supposed to be monitored by the Justice Department's Immigration and Naturalization Service, the State Department was criticized for being too lax in granting visas to almost anyone with enough income to purchase an airline ticket.

The State Department's budget of about $6 billion (not counting foreign aid) is the lowest of all the cabinet departments—only a fraction of the Department of Defense's much larger budget.[14] Considering the State Department's role and prestige, its staff of 25,000 worldwide is small, especially compared with the more than 2 million civilian and military personnel in the Department of Defense.

Its role is particularly impressive given recent cutbacks. The United States has closed at least 30 consulates and embassies over the past two decades, and many operate with obsolete technology and in antiquated and unsafe buildings. These cutbacks help explain the breakdowns in the visa issuance process. The State Department simply did not have enough employees to interview every applicant for a visa.

STAFFING THE DIPLOMATIC SYSTEM   American embassies are staffed largely by members of the U.S. Foreign Service. Although part of the State Department, the service represents the entire government and performs jobs for many other agencies. Its main duties are to carry out foreign policy as expressed in the directives of the secretary of state; gather political, economic, and intelligence data for American policy makers; protect Americans and American interests in foreign countries; and cultivate friendly relations with host governments and foreign peoples.

The Foreign Service is composed of highly-trained civil servants who are comparable to army officers in the military. They are a select, specially trained group expected to take assignments anyplace in the world on short notice. There are approximately 4,000 such officers; in recent years, fewer than 225 junior officers have won appointment each year. Approximately two-thirds of our U.S. ambassadors to about 160 nations come from the ranks of the Foreign Service. The others are usually political appointees, large donors, or friends of the president.

The Foreign Service is one of the most prestigious yet most criticized career services of the national government. Criticism sometimes comes as much from within as from outside. Critics claim that the organizational culture of the Foreign Service stifles creativity; attracts officers who are, or at least become, more concerned about their status than their responsibilities; and requires new recruits to wait 15 years or more before being considered for positions of responsibility. Like other federal agencies, most notably the Central Intelligence Agency and the Federal Bureau of Investigation, the Foreign Service has had great difficulty recruiting officers with significant Arabic-language skills, which clearly weakens the ability to interpret, let alone collect, intelligence on the terrorist networks that have emerged in the Middle East and central Asia.

Perhaps the greatest challenge for Foreign Service diplomats is how to function effectively in a high-tech world. Some have even suggested that diplomats posted in foreign countries are no longer needed to gather intelligence or to speak for the United States and that they should be replaced altogether and most of their work be conducted by e-mail, fax, and videoconferencing from Washington. Yet having a diplomat on the scene in Iran or Saudi Arabia who speaks Farsi and Arabic and who knows a country's major leaders personally is often a better method than relying on even the most sophisticated technologies, especially when making subtle judgments about a nation's political, economic, and military policies.[15]

The Central Intelligence Agency and the Intelligence Community

As the Senate Intelligence Committee and 9/11 Commission both noted, effective foreign policy is dependent on accurate, timely information. Before our foreign policy makers can act on important issues, they have to know as much as possible about other countries: their possible reactions to a particular policy, their strengths and weaknesses, the character of their leaders, and, if possible, their strategic plans and intentions. The people who gather and analyze intelligence data are therefore among the most important advisers to policy makers.[16]

The Central Intelligence Agency, an outgrowth of the World War II Office of Strategic Services, was created in 1947 to coordinate the gathering and analysis of information that flows into various parts of the U.S. government from all over the world. In recent years, the CIA has had about 20,000 employees, who both collect information and shape the intelligence estimates that policy makers use to set priorities.

Although most of the information the CIA gathers comes from open sources, the term "intelligence" conjures up visions of spies and undercover agents. Secret intelligence occasionally does supply crucial data. But it is not all glamour; much is routine. Intelligence work involves three basic operations: reporting, research, and dissemination. *Reporting* is based on the close and rigorous observation of developments around the world; *research* is the attempt to detect meaningful patterns out of what was observed in the past and to understand what appears to be going on now; *dissemination* means getting the right information to the right people at the right time.

The CIA is only one of 15 intelligence agencies in the federal government, including the State Department's Bureau of Intelligence and Research; the Defense Department's Defense Intelligence Agency (which combines the intelligence operations of the Army, Navy, Air Force, and Marine Corps); the Federal Bureau of Investigation; the Treasury Department's Office of Terrorism and Finance Intelligence; the Energy Department's Office of Intelligence; the Homeland Security Department's Directorate of Information Analysis and Infrastructure Protection and Directorate of Coast Guard Intelligence; and the National Security Agency (which specializes in electronic reconnaissance and code breaking), National Reconnaissance Office (which runs the U.S. satellite surveillance programs), and National Geospatial-Intelligence Agency (which collects and analyzes photographic imagery). Together, the 15 agencies constitute the *intelligence community.*

Because each of these agencies was created to collect unique information (imagery, electronic intelligence, and so forth) for a unique client (the president, the secretary of defense, or others), they rarely share information with each other. The lack of cooperation clearly affected the government's ability to prevent the September 11 attacks. "Many dedicated officers worked day and night for years to piece together the growing body of evidence on Al Qaeda and to understand the threats," the 9/11 Commission concluded. "Yet, while there were many reports on bin Laden and his growing Al-Qaeda organization, there was no comprehensive review of what the intelligence community knew and what it did not know, and what that meant."[17] Although the Commission noted merit in keeping the agencies separate, not the least of which is the need for competing sources of information, it did recommend the creation of a single cabinet-level National Intelligence Director, or czar, to oversee the community. Congress was unable to reach agreement on how much power to give the czar. The legislation stalled before the 2004 presidential election.

The Department of Defense

The president, Congress, the National Security Council, the State Department, and the Defense Department all make overall defense policy and attempt to integrate U.S. national security programs, but the day-to-day work of organizing for defense is the job of the Defense Department. Its headquarters, the Pentagon, houses within its 17.5 miles of corridors 23,000 top military and civilian personnel. The offices of several hundred generals and admirals are there, as is the office of the secretary of defense, who provides civilian control of the armed services.

Although the Department of Defense has existed for more than half a century, its leaders are still working to ensure both strategic vision and practical coordination among the military services. Prior to 1947, there were two separate

FBI Agent Coleen Rowley's testimony before the Senate Judiciary Committee on June 6, 2002, exposed communication problems between FBI field offices and FBI headquarters in Washington, D.C. Agent Rowley outlined how the FBI headquarters hindered the field office in Minneapolis in its investigation of a suspected terrorist before September 11, 2001.

The Pentagon, headquarters for the Defense Department, is the world's largest building. It has 17.5 miles of corridors and houses nearly 23,000 workers, who tell time by 4,200 clocks, consume 30,000 cups of coffee daily, and place 200,000 calls a day on 87,000 phones connected by 100,000 miles of cable.

Its significance as the center of U.S. defense policy made the Pentagon a prime target in the attacks on September 11, 2001. More than 150 civilian and military personnel were killed in the early morning attack.

military departments—War and Navy. The difficulty of coordinating them during World War II led to demands for unification. In 1947, the Air Force, already an autonomous unit within the War Department, was made an independent department, and all three military departments—Army, Navy, and Air Force— were placed under the general supervision of the secretary of defense. The Unification Act of 1947 was a bundle of compromises between the Army, which favored a tightly integrated department, and the Navy, which wanted a loosely federated structure, but the act at least brought the military services onto a common organizational chart.

The committee known as the Joint Chiefs of Staff serves as the principal military adviser to the president, the National Security Council, and the secretary of defense. It includes the heads of the three armed services, plus the commandant of the Marine Corps, and the chair and vice chair of the Joint Chiefs. The president, with the consent of the Senate, appoints all the service chiefs to four-year nonrenewable terms. Note that the twice-renewable two-year term of the chair of the Joint Chiefs is part of the process of ensuring civilian control over the military.

Before 1986, the members of the Joint Chiefs of Staff were, collectively, very powerful. They advised the president and the secretary of defense. Because they functioned as a committee and could not act until unanimous agreement was reached, however, they often produced overly broad decisions. Critics therefore viewed much of the work of the Joint Chiefs as wasteful and even dangerous.

The Department of Defense Reorganization Act of 1986 shifted considerable power to the chair. Reporting through the secretary of defense, the chair now advises the president on military matters, exercises authority over the forces in the field, and is responsible for overall military planning. In theory, the chair of the Joint Chiefs can even make a military decision that the chiefs of the other services oppose. On paper at least, these other chiefs now serve the chair merely as advisers, and even the chair's deputy, the vice chair, outranks the other service chiefs. The chair has a mandate to encourage "jointness" in military education and in other spheres to integrate the

GLOBAL *Perceptions*

QUESTION: How important is it to you to live in a country where the military is under the control of civilian leaders?

Civilian control of the military is considered essential for preventing tyranny. Although the U.S. military has always been under the control of elected, civilian leaders, many nations are led by military officers who stay in power solely through the threat of force. Citizens in nations that have recently broken free of military control were particularly likely to say it is very important to have civilian control of the military. Thus, 58 percent of Nigerians, 55 percent of Ugandans, and 48 percent of Argentineans say it is very important to maintain civilian control.

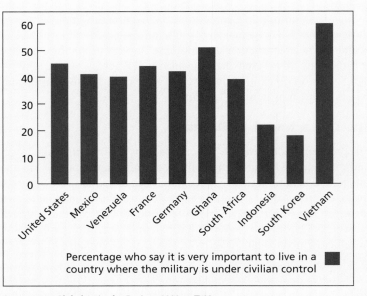

Percentage who say it is very important to live in a country where the military is under civilian control

SOURCE: Pew Global Attitudes Project, 2003, p. T-69.

services for maximum effectiveness. The chair of the Joint Chiefs today is the most powerful peacetime military officer in U.S. history. These changes clearly contributed to military success in the Afghanistan and Iraq wars, where special operations forces and U.S. Marines worked closely with Navy and Air Force pilots to target precision-guided weapons on enemy positions.

It is crucial to recognize, however, that the chair of the Joint Chiefs is *not* the head of the military. The chair and the Joint Chiefs are advisers to the secretary of defense and the president, but the president can, and on occasion has, disregarded their advice. A president must weigh military action or inaction against the larger foreign and security interests of the nation.

UNDERSTANDING THE DEFENSE BUREAUCRACY   The defense bureaucracy is best understood—as is any bureaucracy—as something less than a monolith. Insiders often stress that this policy-making structure is best thought of as a *confederation* or a bargaining arena rather than a tight chain-of-command hierarchy. In fact, in recent years, strong sentiment has emerged for more centralized control and direction of the nation's defense bureaucracy.

CHANGING FACE OF AMERICAN POLITICS

DIVERSITY IN THE MILITARY

The U.S. military has become much more diverse over the past three decades, in part due to much more aggressive recruiting of women and minorities. In 1973, for example, just 2 percent of all recruits were women, while 23 percent were people of color. By 2002, 17 percent were women, and 35 percent were people of color.

Year	Percentage of White Recruits	Percentage of Women Recruits
1973	77%	2%
1983	76	12
1993	73	24
2002	67	17

SOURCE: Department of Defense, *Population Characteristics in the Military Services, 2002,* U.S. Government Printing Office, 2003, Appendix D.

Former Secretary of State Colin Powell.

The four armed services—Army, Navy, Marine Corps, and Air Force—vary greatly in terms of diversity, however. As of 2004, roughly 42 percent of the Army, 37 percent of the Navy, 32 percent of the Marine Corps, and 26 percent of the Air Force were African American, Hispanic, Asian American, or another minority group. At the same time, 19 percent of the Air Force, 16 percent of the Army, 14 percent of the Navy, and just 6 percent of the Marine Corps were women.

There are several reasons why the armed forces have done better recruiting people of color than recruiting women. First, the military has worked hard to improve its reputation as an equal opportunity employer. Colin Powell's rise to the highest post in the armed services has often been used to show recruits of color that anything is possible in the military. Powell entered the military as a second lieutenant in 1958, served two tours of duty in Vietnam, and eventually became the first African American officer to chair the Joint Chiefs of Staff.

Second, the military has long focused on recruiting high school graduates who are not college-bound, which is a group that contains more people of color. The military has also developed several new programs that set aside substantial amounts of funding for future college tuition, which has also been effective in recruiting people of color.

Disputes among the military services involve more than professional jealousies. The technological revolution in warfare has rendered obsolete many concepts about military missions, thereby threatening the traditional roles of some of the services. In the past, it made sense to divide command among land, sea, and air forces. Today, defense research and development are constantly altering formerly established roles and missions, yet the individual services are reluctant to give up their traditional functions or to serve each other's crucial needs. The Navy, for example, is interested in waging sea warfare, not in running a freight service for the Army. Interservice rivalries erupt when the Army and Air Force quarrel over who should provide air support for ground troops. Each branch also supports weapons that bring it prestige. The Air Force and Navy dispute, for example, the effectiveness of land-based versus sea-based missiles.[18]

Whether strategic policies are worked out by the Defense Department, the White House, or Congress, the decisions result from a political process in which some measure of consensus is essential. The Joint Chiefs engage in the same type of vote trading used in Congress. On budget issues, the chiefs often endorse all the programs desired by each service. When forced to choose on an issue of policy, the chiefs have traditionally compromised among the different service positions rather than attempt to develop a position based on a unified military point of view.

The Department of Homeland Security

The new Department of Homeland Security plays a small but important role in foreign policy by policing U.S. borders. Created in late 2002, the department is composed of 22 agencies and a work force of 170,000 full-time civil servants. It includes the Border Patrol, the Coast Guard, the Customs Service, the Secret Service, the Immigration Service, and the Transportation Security Administration.

The department has three basic goals: to prevent the entry of terrorists into the country, reduce the chances of a terrorist attack, and help the nation recover from an attack if and when it occurs. Toward these goals, it is responsible for screening all passengers and baggage on U.S. domestic flights (Transportation Security Administration), checking all cargo (Customs Service, Coast Guard) and visitors entering the United States (Immigration Service), patrolling the borders (Border Patrol, Coast Guard), and providing aid and assistance to communities affected by human and natural disasters (Federal Emergency Management Administration). Although the Bureau of Consular Affairs remains in the State Department, the secretary of homeland security now has primary responsibility for making sure that visas are not issued to potential terrorists.

Despite making significant progress toward tighter airport security over its first three years, it still needs time to develop similar programs for the nation's seaports and so-called "soft targets" such as nuclear power plants, chemical factories, sports facilities, and shopping malls. The 9/11 Commission recommended that the department move as quickly as possible to create a biometric screening system that uses fingerprints and digital photographs to identify U.S. citizens and visitors alike.

PARTICIPANTS IN FOREIGN AND DEFENSE POLICY

Foreign policy flows through the same institutional and constitutional structures as domestic policy. Public opinion, interest groups, foreign countries, political parties, and Congress all affect the making of foreign policy. Yet these structures operate somewhat differently from the way they do in domestic affairs.

The Public

In crisis situations such as the new war against terrorism, presidents and their military and intelligence advisers make the key decisions, often operating from a high-tech operations center in the basement of the White House. Yet even in these situations, presidents and their advisers know that their decisions will ultimately require support from the public and from Congress.

At first glance, many Americans appear indifferent or uninformed about foreign and defense policy. Foreign affairs issues are more remote than domestic issues. Most Americans have a poor sense of world geography and an even weaker grasp of geopolitics. However, Figure 20–1 shows that many Americans, whether ill-informed or not, have strong opinions about which nations are vital to U.S. interests. They also had strong reactions to the September 11 terrorist attacks. Three months before the attacks, for example, 64 percent of Americans said that international terrorism was a "major threat" to the well-being of the United States; one month before the attacks, 53 percent said the world was a "more dangerous place" than it had been a decade earlier.[19]

Americans also had clear preferences for action. Interviewed only days after the attacks, 77 percent said the United States should go to war with Afghanistan even if it meant taking heavy casualties, and 44 percent said military action to attack terrorism abroad was a wiser investment than building up the nation's defenses at home. As for the aims of military intervention, 57 percent said the United States should use military force to prevent terrorism. As Table 20–2 shows, Americans became much more concerned about making foreign policy with the nation's allies in mind, in making sure the United States was in charge, and increasing defense spending.

Individual Americans have also been deeply involved in the war on terrorism, whether by attending rallies and protests for and against the Iraq war, donating blood and money to the victims of the September 11 attacks, or writing letters to their members of Congress or the president. Many Americans have also joined together to create new organizations such as MoveOn.org, which opposes the Iraq war, while the families

Sergeant First Class Nathan Ross Chapman, 31, was the first American casualty in Afghanistan after the start of the war on terrorism. Deaths, such as Chapman's, affect the general public more than specific foreign policy issues.

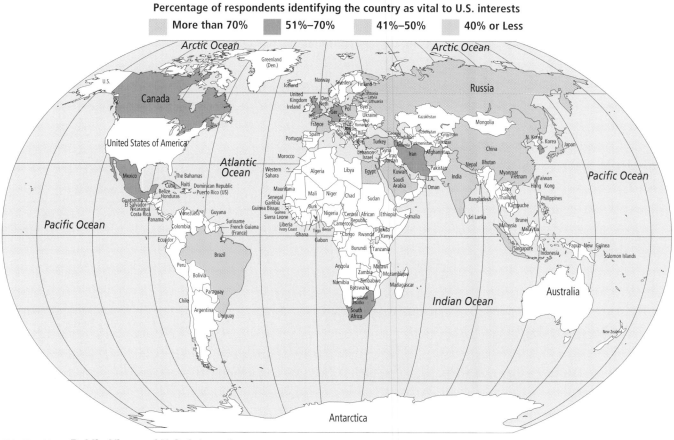

FIGURE 20–1 Public Views of U.S. Interests.
SOURCE: John E. Reilly, ed., *American Public Opinion and U.S. Foreign Policy, 1999* (Chicago Council on Foreign Relations, 1999), p. 13.

★★ You Decide

SHOULD THE UNITED STATES BUILD A MISSILE SHIELD?

The United States has been trying to design a missile shield for more than 20 years. First proposed by President Ronald Reagan, the goal of his "Star Wars" system was simple: identify, intercept, and destroy incoming ballistic missiles before they enter the atmosphere above the United States. The idea mostly languished after the end of the cold war but regained momentum with the possibility that China, North Korea, and Iran were all developing long-range missiles capable of reaching the United States.

The idea also gained added support following the terrorist attacks on New York City and Washington, D.C. According to the Pew Research Center for the People and the Press, 35 percent of Americans favored a missile defense system before the attacks, compared with 49 percent after.

of the September 11 victims also created a charitable organization to put pressure on Congress to create the 9/11 Commission and have remained a powerful voice in demanding implementation of the Commission's report.

Interest Groups

It is difficult to generalize about the impact of interest groups on American foreign policy. At times of international crisis, the president is usually able to mobilize public support so that interest groups find it difficult to exert much influence. As a general rule, special-interest groups with other than major economic interests rarely have a decisive role in the formulation of foreign policy.

Ethnic interest groups, however, sometimes play an important role in foreign and defense policy decisions. As a nation of immigrants and the children and grandchildren of immigrants, our citizens often retain a special bond with their country of origin. Thus Irish Americans, Jewish Americans, Cuban Americans, African Americans, Asian Americans, Polish Americans, Greek Americans, Arab Americans, and Mexican Americans take a keen interest in decisions affecting Ireland, Israel, Cuba, South Africa, China, Japan, Vietnam, the Philippines, South Korea and other Pacific Rim nations, Poland, Greece, the Middle East, and Mexico. Such groups sometimes exert great pressures on policy makers to support (or in the case of Cuba, contest) the country to which they are emotionally linked.

Business groups also play a role in foreign and defense policy decisions. Defense contractors are heavily involved in decisions about defense spending and contribute large amounts of campaign money to presidential and congressional candidates. They also lobby hard on behalf of their projects before Congress and the executive branch, which can and does raise questions of conflicts of interest and special favors.

In July 2004, for example, executives of Houston-based Halliburton, Inc., were called before Congress to address allegations of waste and abuse in administering more than $8 billion in defense contracts that had been awarded without competition from other potential contractors. The charges were particularly visible because the company had been led by Vice President Dick Cheney during the 1990s, which created the appearance of favoritism in the contracting process.

TABLE 20–2 VIEWS OF FOREIGN POLICY BEFORE AND AFTER SEPTEMBER 11, 2001

	Before	After
The United States should formulate foreign policy based on		
Mostly U.S. interests	38%	30%
Interests of allies	48	59
Neither or both	8	7
The U.S. leadership role should be		
Single leader or first among equals	38	45
Just one of leading nations	50	46
No leadership role	8	3
National defense spending should be		
Increased	32	50
Kept the same	44	41
Cut back	20	7

Source: Pew Research Center for the People and the Press, *Public Opinion in a Year for the Books* (Pew Research Center, 2002), p. 12.

Defense contractors are not the only business interests involved in foreign and defense policy. Agricultural interests have lobbied successfully for expanded grain and food exports, the steel industry has lobbied successfully for import quotas on foreign steel, the entertainment industry has campaigned against piracy of music and film abroad, and the high-tech industry has pressed Congress to allow the immigration of more computer programmers.

Businesses may even have their own foreign policies. *New York Times* reporter Thomas L. Friedman wrote in August 2002 that General Electric played a major role in reducing the nuclear tension between Pakistan and India over the disputed Kashmir region. According to Friedman, the U.S. high-tech economy has become dependent on millions of English-speaking, low-wage workers in India for everything from computer programming to troubleshooting. Not surprisingly, U.S. companies were angered when the State Department urged U.S. citizens to leave India because of the nuclear tension. They warned India that they would move their operations to other countries if the nation continued to threaten nuclear war. As Friedman wrote, "This was a real education for India's leaders in New Delhi, but, officials conceded, they got the message: loose talk about war or nukes could be disastrous for India. This was reinforced by another new lobby: the information technology ministers who now exist in every Indian state to drum up business."[20]

Foreign Nations

Most countries have embassies that lobby for their interests in Washington. In addition, some countries like Japan have built up a powerful network of lawyers, lobbyists, and Washington-based publicists who are retained by Japanese companies and trade associations, as well as by the Japanese government, to defend their extensive economic interests in the United States.[21] Lobbyists representing industrialized countries like South Korea, Taiwan, Singapore, Brazil, and Mexico have also expanded their Washington lobbying efforts to fight U.S. protectionism and import quotas on textiles, shoes, and other products. Such lobbying is legal, provided that the lobbyists register and report their activities to Congress.

Foreign nations have occasionally tried to influence U.S. policy through less visible means. In 1996, for example, the fact that China and Indonesia had made large contributions to the Clinton–Gore reelection campaign came to light. Although the president vigorously denied any connection between the contributions and administration policy, the Democratic National Committee returned the money. George W. Bush's inaugural committee returned a $100,000 gift in early 2001 to a donor who had questionable ties to foreign leaders.[22]

Political Parties

Political parties do not usually play a major role in shaping foreign and defense policy, for two reasons: (1) Many Americans still prefer to keep partisan politics out of foreign policy, and (2) parties usually take less clear and candid stands on foreign policy than they do on domestic policy. Party platforms often obscure the issues instead of highlighting them, and many members of Congress fail to follow any strict party line when it comes to foreign policy.

At the end of World War II, sentiment grew strong for a bipartisan approach to foreign policy. An ambiguous concept, **bipartisanship** in foreign affairs generally means (1) collaboration between the executive and the congressional leaders of both parties, (2) support of presidential foreign policies by both parties in Congress, and (3) downplaying major foreign policy differences in national elections and in presidential debates. Overall, bipartisanship is an attempt to remove the issues of foreign policy from partisan politics.

Not everybody agrees that bipartisanship is desirable. There is virtue, critics say, in debating contending ideas—such as foreign aid or the missile shield.

★ ★ THINKING IT THROUGH

There are three potential problems with a missile shield. First, it would be extremely expensive to build. Some experts predict that an effective shield would cost $100 billion or more to design, test, and implement. Second, experts argue that a shield could be easily defeated by launching thousands of decoys, all of which would have to be identified or destroyed to find the real missiles. Third, a missile shield could undermine the nuclear stability created by the concept of mutual assured destruction. Finally, a shield does nothing to protect the United States against the kind of low-tech terrorist attacks that have become so frequent around the world. Some advocates of the shield have responded to these concerns by supporting a limited shield that could be used to destroy enemy missiles immediately after launch.

---

bipartisanship
A policy that emphasizes a united front and cooperation between the major political parties, especially on sensitive foreign policy issues.

The spirit of bipartisanship is reflected in the report of the 9/11 Commission, issued on July 22, 2004. The commission was made up of both Democrats and Republicans who managed to put their ideological differences aside and to ultimately issue a report that is critical of both the Clinton and Bush administrations in their handling of terrorism. Shown here are 9/11 Commission Chairman Thomas Kean and Vice Chairman Lee Hamilton.

Congress

Although Congress seldom initiates foreign policy on its own, it has taken the lead on some trade and economic assistance questions and, of course, controls the power of the purse. In addition, Congress is authorized to define the limits of presidential war powers.[23]

Congress is a crucial link between policy makers and the public. Regardless of their party, members of Congress want a voice in foreign policy, or at least what some members call "meaningful consulation." After all, they represent the constituents who must fight the wars, pay the taxes, and bear the burdens of wartime. Congress also represents a check on presidential power through its spending and oversight power.

To date, however, Congress has not been a significant check in the Iraq War. With U.S. troops at risk, Congress has approved the president's requests for additional spending, including an additional $25 billion in 2004 on top of the $65 billion already approved and spent on the wars in Afghanistan and Iraq.

Making Foreign Policy in a Democracy

A democratic foreign policy is presumably one in which policy makers are known and are held accountable to the people. This is a tough test for any policy, yet it is especially tough for foreign policy because of the frequent need to act with speed and sometimes with secrecy, the generally low level of information among the general public, the anonymity of most foreign policy leaders, and the complexity of most international issues and strategic policy options. Still, the American public wants to be consulted and informed, and it wants its leaders held accountable.[24]

A constitutional democracy may not be able to keep leaders from making mistakes, but it can make sure that policy mistakes eventually become public. It is then that the safeguarding agencies of democracy—the opposition party, the press, and public opinion—play a crucial role in demanding accountability. The public's opposition to the Vietnam War eventually forced the United States to withdraw, for example, and its outrage over the genocide in Kosovo eventually forced the United States to intervene.

The temptation during times of crisis is to rally around the president and the flag in support of the country. But as noted elsewhere in this book, dissent is an essential element of maintaining accountability during such moments.

FOREIGN AND DEFENSE POLICY OPTIONS

The United States has a number of tools for achieving foreign policy success, not the least of which is military might. But military might is no longer enough to ensure success, or even deter foreign threats. Absent conventional diplomacy to send its message clearly, foreign aid to help nations in need, economic sanctions to isolate its adversaries, and public diplomacy to help other nations understand its agenda, no amount of military might will succeed.

Conventional Diplomacy

Much of U.S. foreign policy is conducted by the Foreign Service and ambassadors in face-to-face discussions in Washington and other capitals, at the United Nations in New York and Geneva, at North Atlantic Treaty Organization or World Trade Organization meetings, and elsewhere around the world in regional or international organizations and world conferences. International summit meetings, with their high-profile pomp and drama, are another form of conventional diplomacy. Even though traditional diplomacy appears more subdued and somewhat less vital in this era of personal leader-to-leader communication by telephone, fax, and teleconferencing, it is still an important, if slow, process by which nations can gain information, talk about mutual interests, and try to resolve disputes.

Much of the conventional diplomacy carried out by the State Department may not produce important breakthroughs, yet it is difficult to measure the value of diplomatic representation. No price tag can be placed on close personal relations with foreign

The inability of both the Israelis and the Palestinians to reach an agreement on Israeli settlements in the West Bank by means of conventional diplomacy has led to the use of violence on both sides of the issue and ultimately to Israel's construction of a "separation wall" that it believes will protect Israeli settlers from further violence.

officials or on information gathered and arguments made to promote American interests around the world. Surely the closing of one embassy or the withdrawal from an international organization is unlikely to cause major setbacks for the United States, yet a less active diplomatic corps could mean a less effective foreign policy.

When relations between nations become strained, diplomatic relations are sometimes broken as a means of political coercion. When the United States breaks diplomatic ties, the consequences are more than merely symbolic. Doing so greatly restricts tourist and business travel to a country and in effect curbs economic as well as political relations with the nation.

Breaking diplomatic relations, however, is a next-to-last resort (force is the last resort), for such action undermines the ability to reason with a nation's leaders or to use other diplomatic strategies to resolve conflicts. The act also undermines our ability to get valuable information about what is going on in a nation and to have a presence there.

THE ROLE OF THE UNITED NATIONS The United Nations is one of the most important arenas for traditional diplomacy. Established in 1945 by the victors of World War II, the United Nations now has 189 nation members.

Despite its promise as a forum for world peace, the United Nations was mostly ineffective during its first 45 years. Critics contend that it either ducked crucial global issues or was politically unable to tackle them. During much of that time, the U.N. General Assembly, dominated by a combination of Third World and communist nations, was hostile to many U.S. interests. The General Assembly often became a talk shop, passing vague resolutions. More recently, the five permanent members of the U.N. Security Council—the United States, China, Russia (which replaced the Soviet Union), Britain, and France—have usually worked in harmony. Moreover, the United Nations' assumption of responsibilities in the Persian Gulf War and its extensive peacekeeping missions in Cyprus and Lebanon won it respect. U.N. efforts in Cambodia and Somalia were less successful.

In addition, several of the specialized agencies of the United Nations—including the World Health Organization, the United Nations High Commission for Refugees, and the World Food Program—are considered major successes. But the review is much more mixed with respect to the United Nations' peacekeeping efforts, of which it has conducted more than 50. Such a review suggests that these operations are plagued by inadequate and often under-prepared personnel. "First-world countries with first-rate armies are usually unwilling to put their troops at risk," writes former United States Ambassador Dennis Jett. "Thus these operations are often left to third-world countries, and the United Nations sends some of the worst soldiers in the world off to situations where it can only hope they are not called on to actually do anything."[25]

Kofi Annan, secretary general of the United Nations. Annan came under intense criticism in late 2004 for his role in managing the Iraqi oil accounts during the 1900s when Iraq was allowed to sell oil to purchase medical supplies and food.

Foreign Aid

The United States offers aid to more than 100 countries directly and to other nations through contributions to various U.N. development funds. Since 1945, the United States has provided about $400 billion in economic assistance to foreign countries. In recent years, however, foreign aid spending has amounted to around $15 billion per year, or less than 50 percent of what it spent in inflation-adjusted dollars back in 1985.[26]

Most foreign aid goes to a few countries that the United States deems to be of strategic importance to our national security: Israel, Egypt, Ukraine, Jordan, India, Russia, South Africa, and Haiti. That list is sure to change in the future as the nation reallocates its budget to nations central to the war on terrorism. However, regardless of which nation receives the aid, most foreign aid is actually spent in the United States, where it pays for the purchase of American services and products being sent to those countries. It thus amounts to a hefty subsidy for American companies and their employees.

Many Americans and members of Congress oppose foreign aid. A recent poll of American citizens found that only 9 percent supported increasing foreign aid, while 47 percent favored reducing it. Another 40 percent would keep it pretty much at the same level.[27] Few powerful interest groups or constituencies back foreign aid initiatives. State Department officials are invariably the biggest advocates of foreign aid. Presidents also recognize the vital role foreign aid plays in advancing U.S. interests. Successive presidents have all wanted to maintain the leverage with key countries that economic and military assistance provides. One of the major debates today is how much debt relief to provide for the world's poorest nations, some of which spend up to 50 percent of their budgets to service debt on old loans. The problem is particularly severe in Central and South America, where international debt has brought high inflation, unemployment, and civil unrest.

Despite these arguments, Congress invariably trims the foreign aid budget, responding in part to polls that show most Americans believe the United States spends more on foreign aid than it does on Medicare and other domestic priorities. Members of Congress often criticize foreign aid as a "Ghana versus Grandma" case. How, they say, can you give away taxpayers' money to some foreign country when we have poor older people who can't afford their prescription drugs and decent medical help?[28]

Critics also note that U.S. foreign aid has subsidized the most autocratic and most corrupt of dictators. And there are plenty of instances in which foreign aid money has been stolen or misspent. Defenders counter that some corruption is inevitable. "You can't engage in bone-poor countries that lack laws and independent journalists and elections, and expect American standards of transparency," writes *Washington Post* editorial writer Sebastian Mallaby. "Yes, many aid programs fail and will continue to do so. But you don't give up trying to educate and house people just because it's hard. And you don't give up on international engagement just because it's as daunting as it is important."[29]

Economic Sanctions

The United States has frequently applied economic pressure in response to a nation's unwillingness to abide by what we perceive to be international law or proper relations. Indeed, the United States has employed economic sanctions more than any other nation—over 100 times in the past 50 years. **Economic sanctions** entail a denial of export, import, or financial relations with a target country in an effort to change that country's policies. Economic sanctions imposed on South Africa doubtless helped end apartheid and encourage democracy in that nation, while sanctions on Libya helped end its nuclear weapons program. But sanctions imposed on Cuba have not had much effect in dislodging that nations' dictatorial regime. The United States imposed sanctions on India and Pakistan in 1998 when both nations began a round of nuclear testing, but because of economic distress both in Pakistan and among U.S. wheat growers, Congress and the president lifted most of the sanctions within months of imposing them.

The popularity of economic sanctions has risen and fallen over the years. They are especially unpopular among farmers and corporations that have to sacrifice part of their overseas markets to comply with government controls, and they rarely work as effectively as intended. Brookings Institution scholar Richard Haass claims, "Sanctions have caused humanitarian suffering (Haiti), weakened friendly governments (Bosnia), bolstered tyrants (Cuba), and left countries with little choice but to develop nuclear weapons (Pakistan)."[30] They can also be costly to U.S. businesses and workers while intensifying anti-American sentiment.

Senator Richard Lugar believes that sanctions seldom work unless they are multilateral rather than imposed by the United States alone.[31] Scholars suggest that when dealing with authoritarian regimes, the United States should direct sanctions at rulers, not the populace at large. "Iraqis are not our enemies. Nor are the Cubans," writes Gary Hufbauer. "Where the president imposes comprehensive sanctions on an authoritarian regime, he should view those sanctions as a prelude to the exercise of military force, not as a substitute for force. Unless we are prepared to remove bad governments with military force, we have no business heaping prolonged punishment on innocent people."[32]

Military Intervention

War is not merely an extension of diplomacy but rather the complete and total breakdown of diplomatic efforts. The United States has used military force in other nations on the average of almost once a year since 1789, although usually in short-term initiatives

economic sanctions
Denial of export, import, or financial relations with a target country in an effort to change that nation's policies.

In Comparative Perspective

FOREIGN AID IN THE NETHERLANDS

Wealthy nations can do many things to help other countries around the world, not the least of which is provide direct foreign aid. According to the Organization for Economic Cooperation and Development, which monitors international governance, the United States was the largest foreign aid contributor in the world in 2003, giving $15 billion to a variety of projects around the globe. The United States is far from the most generous, however. Although the Netherlands gives less foreign aid in absolute dollars, it contributes a much greater amount measured against its gross national income. By that measure, it is nearly six times more generous than the United States.

The Netherlands is more generous than the United States and most other nations in other ways, too. According to the Center for Global Development, a nonpartisan Washington, D.C., think tank, the Netherlands is also open to free trade with other nations, willing to invest its own money in less-developed economies, welcoming to immigrants, helpful in improving environmental protection and technological innovation in less-developed economies, and ready to contribute troops in peacekeeping missions. When all its contributions are added up into a single index of commitment to helping poorer nations, the Netherlands emerges as the most committed nation in the world, followed by Denmark, Portugal, New Zealand, and Switzerland.* By these same measures, the U.S. ends up number 20 on the list of the world's 21 richest nations.

Foreign Aid Spending, 2003

Nation	Total Spending (billions of U.S. dollars)	Percentage of Gross National Income
Norway	$2.04	0.92%
Denmark	1.24	0.84
Netherlands	4.07	0.81
Sweden	2.10	0.70
France	7.34	0.41
Switzerland	1.23	0.38
United Kingdom	6.17	0.34
Germany	6.7	0.28
Canada	2.21	0.26
Spain	2.03	0.25
Japan	8.91	0.20
Italy	2.39	0.16
United States	15.79	0.14

Source: Organization for Economic Cooperation and Development, 2003.
*The rankings come from the Center for Global Development, www.cgd.org.

such as NATO's military activities in Bosnia and Kosovo. Although presidential candidate John Kerry argued that the Iraq war was the first time in history that the United States had gone to war because it chose to, not because it had to, it has actually sent forces into combat many times without a clear threat. It did not have to go to war against Spain in 1898 or send troops to Cuba, Haiti, the Dominican Republic, Lebanon, Mexico, Nicaragua, Somalia, South Vietnam, or even Europe in World War I.[33] (See Table 20–3 for the number of Americans killed in the nation's major wars.)

Experts tend to agree that the use of force is most successful when it is used in small and even medium-sized countries for short engagements (Grenada, Panama, Kuwait, Kosovo, and Afghanistan). They also agree that it "often proves ineffective in the context of national civil wars (the United States in Vietnam; Israel in Lebanon)."[34] Lessons from past interventions are one reason Americans were reluctant to support, if not opposed to, U.S. military intervention in Haiti, Bosnia, and Kosovo. It also helps explain the public's weakening support for the Iraq war.

U.S. military efforts with its NATO allies in Kosovo sought to put an end to "ethnic cleansing" in that area. After an extensive air campaign, ground troops were able to force the withdrawal of Serbian military and police, permit the safe return of refugees, and secure stability in the province. President Clinton had been hesitant to use the military in a decisive way in Kosovo in large part because of the apparent opposition of the American people and Congress. And many in the military were also reluctant to commit forces to what they viewed as primarily a humanitarian initiative rather than a defense of America's vital national security interests. These opposing views prompted renewed debates about the conditions under which the United States should resort to military intervention.[35]

TABLE 20–3 THE COSTS OF WAR	
Number killed	
Revolutionary War	4,435
War of 1812	2,260
Civil War	214,939
Spanish-American War	385
World War I	53,402
World War II	291,557
Korean War	35,516
Vietnam War	58,516
Persian Gulf War	382
Afghanistan War	74*
Iraq war	937*

SOURCE: *The Washington Post*, May 26, 2003; figures updated by authors.

*Figures as of July 25, 2004.

Not all military action is visible to the public or even the intended target. Covert activities are planned and executed to conceal the identity of the sponsor. The United States repeatedly engaged in covert operations during the cold war, including early intervention in Vietnam and Central America, as well as in Afghanistan, where it supported rebels fighting the Soviet invasion. But covert activities in Cuba, Chile, and elsewhere have backfired, and support for this strategy has cooled in the post–cold war era.[36] Ironically, U.S. covert aid to the Afghan rebels eventually led to the Soviet withdrawal, which in turn led to the establishment of the Taliban, which allowed Osama bin Laden and his followers to establish training bases in its territory.

Public Diplomacy

In July 2002, President George W. Bush created the White House Office of Global Communications to address the question he asked before a joint session of Congress only a week after the terrorist attacks on New York City and Washington, D.C.: "Why do they hate us?" The office is designed to enhance America's image abroad, thereby countering the image of the United States as the "Great Satan," as some of its enemies describe it.[37]

Bush was not the first president to worry about the U.S. image abroad. President Franklin Roosevelt created the Office of War Information early in World War II, which in turn established the Voice of America program to broadcast pro-American information into Nazi Germany. President Harry Truman followed suit early in the cold war with the Soviet Union by launching the Campaign of Truth, which eventually led to the creation of the United States Information Agency under President Dwight Eisenhower. Both agencies exist today and are being strengthened as part of the "new public diplomacy." In this case, the word "public" refers to citizens of other nations, not the United States.

Public diplomacy is a blend of age-old propaganda techniques and modern information warfare. It has three basic goals: (1) to cast the enemy in a less favorable light among its supporters, (2) to mold the image of a conflict such as the war in Afghanistan, and (3) to clarify the ultimate goals of U.S. foreign policy. The United States has tried to convince the people of Afghanistan that Osama bin Laden is the true enemy of the people, the war is not between Muslims and Western democracies, and the war is about preventing the deaths of innocent women and children in both Afghanistan and the United States. Public diplomacy is not a substitute for traditional information warfare such as jamming enemy radio broadcasts, destroying radio and television towers, and disseminating misleading information about the enemy. But it does strike at the heart of the hate that fuels terrorism.

SPECIAL PROBLEMS IN DEFENSE POLICY

The United States has a long history of military involvement in world affairs. Since 1945, more than 100,000 U.S. military personnel have died in undeclared wars; more than 400,000 have suffered battle injuries.[38] But Congress has formally declared war on only a few occasions. The war in Afghanistan was never formally declared, nor was the air war over Kosovo or the Iraq war. Although Congress passed joint resolutions supporting both engagements, the president moved military forces into position well before passage.

Americans believe that the United States should use its military power carefully. As noted earlier in this chapter, almost three out of five Americans said the United States should use military force to prevent future terrorism, compared to just one out of five who said it should use force to punish the terrorists. Even after the events of September 11, 2001, substantial numbers of Americans continued to believe that the United States should not send forces into regional conflicts when other means are available to achieve our objectives. Many also continued to believe that the United States should not intervene in conflicts without a broad public consensus at home and an alliance of nations abroad.

These views eventually led to the Powell Doctrine, formulated by General Colin Powell, the future secretary of state, when he served as chair of the Joint Chiefs of Staff in the late 1980s. The Powell Doctrine reflects the concerns of both average Americans and

In the first major offensive of the war on terrorism, American troops invaded Afghanistan.

many senior military leaders. "When the United States goes to war," he said, "it should be for a clear purpose, only when our vital national security interests are threatened, and our goal should be overwhelming victory." Powell pointed out that "halfhearted warfare for half-baked reasons" is misguided defense policy.[39] As one analyst explained Powell's reasoning: "He argues that the people he calls 'K-mart parents'—working class Americans who tend to be the parents of soldiers—should understand why their children are being put at risk and should never doubt that the country will back them to the hilt."[40]

This doctrine involves far more than a simple contest between internationalism and isolationism; it raises issues about human rights and moral leadership as well as about military effectiveness. The Powell Doctrine has widespread support. Still, most Americans believe it would be a mistake to forsake our unique leadership position and abandon responsibilities to encourage peace and human rights at this time of incredible global change.[41]

The All-Volunteer Force

The Constitution authorizes Congress to do what is "necessary and proper" in order to "raise and support Armies," "to provide and maintain a Navy," and "to provide for calling forth the Militia." The problem is that the role of the United States in the world has changed dramatically since 1789, as have the nation's military needs. Although our boundaries once defined our major national interest, U.S. interests now reach around the globe.

Military conscription (the draft) was first instituted in 1862, during the Civil War. It was used during World War I, when Congress passed the Selective Service Act. This act called for a draft of males between the ages of 21 and 30, with exemptions for certain public officials and for clergy. In both instances, conscription ended when the conflicts ended. The first peacetime draft began in 1940, with the Selective Service and Training Act. By the time of Pearl Harbor, in late 1941, men between the ages of 18 and 35 were eligible for the draft. When World War II ended, however, the draft continued, in various forms, for almost three decades.

Shortly before the Vietnam War ended, Congress replaced the draft with an *all-volunteer force*, which is composed entirely of citizens who choose to serve. The armed services offer a variety of benefits to make sure they meet their annual recruiting targets, including college loans, signing bonuses, special training, and even job placement with private employers after tours of duty are completed. The all-volunteer concept has worked well during peacetime, particularly when the quality of recruits is measured by the educational achievement and performance on standardized intelligence tests.

However, it is not yet clear that the all-volunteer force will able to recruit enough Army troops to fight the wars in Afghanistan and Iraq. "I worry about this every single day—recruiting and retention," said the Army's top personnel officer in July 2004. "We are recruiting a volunteer force during a time of war. We've never done that before."[42] Although the Air Force and Navy continue to meet their annual recruiting targets, the Army failed to meet its targets in the spring of 2004, in part because of the increased death toll in Iraq, and in part because of the prison abuse scandal.

The Army is far from a crisis point, however, and expects to meet its targets by increasing recruitment and retention bonuses—soldiers now receive a one-time $10,000 bonus for reenlisting at the end of their two-year tour. But the Army could easily use a draft if necessary. Because males must register with the Selective Service at age 18, the list of potential draftees is already on file.

Women in Combat

As the number of women in the armed forces has increased, so has the number of women who serve in combat zones. Whereas women constituted 6 percent of U.S. forces in the first war in Iraq in 1991, they constituted 14 percent of forces in the second war in 2002–2004, during which they protected supply convoys, flown transport and supply aircraft, medical helicopters, fired Patriot antimissile systems, and worked as tank mechanics and military police guarding Iraqi prisoners of war. They have also borne the ultimate sacrifice of

PEOPLE & POLITICS *Making a Difference* ★ ★ ★

GEN. ANTONIO TAGUBA

In March 2004, Americans were shocked to read that some U.S. military police had abused Iraqi prisoners held in Baghdad's notorious Abu Ghraib prison, which had once been used by Saddam Hussein's secret police. Much of the information involved an internal Army report by Major General Antonio M. Taguba, who cited "egregious acts and grave breaches of international law" by prison guards, including sleep deprivation, intimidation by military guard dogs, and sexual humiliation.

Taguba is the son of a Philippine resistance fighter in World War II, who was captured by the Japanese in 1943 and escaped from the Bataan Death March. Born in Manila in 1950, Taguba moved to the United States with his family when he was 11 years old. Taguba later worked his way up through the Army to become

the second highest ranking Filipino-American in uniform.

Taguba was assigned to the Abu Ghraib investigation in January 2004 to conduct an "informal investigation" into allegations of mistreatment raised by military officers and the International Red Cross. Taguba earned the assignment because of his reputation for absolute integrity. "If you want the truth, he's going to tell you the truth," said one Army general who was quoted in a *New York Times* profile of Taguba. "He's not bullied; he's a stand up guy."*

Taguba brought a deep love of country to the difficult task, which exposed the Army to intense criticism and further investigation. "I am proud to serve in the world's best Army," he once said. But "if we are to remain the best, the well-being of its soldiers and families must be its principal focus." It was not until 1999,

he remembers, that the Army finally recognized the service of his father with a Bronze star and a letter of recognition. "It took over 54 years to gain my parents their due recognition. They sought not to be recognized, only to be appreciated."

*Douglas Jehl, "Head of Inquiry on Iraq Now in Spotlight," *The New York Times*, May 11, 2004, p. A1.

Women now make up approximately 14 percent of the total enlistment in the U.S. armed forces.

service—22 women were killed in the line of duty between March 2003 and July 2004, starting with Army private Lori Piestewa, a member of the Hopi Indian Tribe, who was killed in the same ambush in which private Jessica Lynch was captured.

Federal law already allows women to fly Air Force and Navy combat aircraft, and the Pentagon has now opened thousands of combat-related positions in the military services to women. The military is redesigning its assignments to ensure that equal opportunity exists within its ranks but has yet to assign women to specific combat roles.

Despite their accomplishments in battlefield support positions, women have faced significant barriers to advancement in the armed services, most notably sexual harassment.[43] In March 2003, for example, the Air Force removed the senior leadership at the Air Force Academy in Colorado Springs following repeated allegations of sexual abuse. Further congressional investigation found 142 specific complaints of verbal and physical abuse between 1993 and 2003, many of which had been received with indifference or retribution. Most of the Academy's senior leadership was removed in the wake of the scandal, including the superintendent, commandant and vice commandant of cadets, and dean of the faculty.

The Politics of Defense Spending

The U.S. defense budget reached more than $440 billion in 2005, a figure that covers everything from weapons and ammunition to salaries for soldiers, sailors, pilots, and civil servants, and pensions for more than 1.5 million retired Defense Department personnel. The defense budget also includes more than $12 billion dedicated to nuclear weapons research and maintenance and environmental cleanup projects that are actually run by the Department of Energy.[44]

Defense spending fell dramatically at the end of the cold war as weapons systems were canceled or postponed, bases closed, ships retired, and large numbers of troops brought home from Germany, the Philippines, and elsewhere. The Army was cut by over 30 percent, and the National Guard and the military reserve were cut back about 25 percent. As a result, defense spending has also fallen, dropping from 25 percent at the height of the cold war in the mid-1980s to 15 percent in 2000.

The defense budget has been rising ever since, however, and will hit 19 percent of the budget in 2005. Most of the increase involves the purchase of new equipment such as the Joint Strike Fighter, which will serve the Air Force, Navy, and Army, and will be used for the wars in Afghanistan and Iraq.[45] The budget also included the combined costs of the wars in Afghanistan and Iraq, which are expected to hit a $90 billion total by 2005.

Even as defense spending rises, some experts argue that the nation needs a much lighter, highly mobile force to combat terrorism and that further spending on "cold war legacy" systems such as nuclear attack submarines and heavy tanks is wasteful.[46] They argue that the United States cannot have it all—meaning old cold war systems, high-tech space defenses, decent military pay, and the kind of expensive precision weaponry used in Afghanistan. Nor do they believe that the United States should continue spending money on weapons systems, such as the Comanche helicopter or V-22 tilt-rotor aircraft, that simply fail to perform as promised.

Despite the logic, Congress can rarely muster the will to kill a weapons system. Cutting defense spending means cutting jobs, and cutting jobs, especially those in the home districts of powerful members of Congress, is politically painful.[47]

The B-2 Stealth bomber is often used as a notable example. The Pentagon has not asked for more of these billion-dollar planes, yet Congress often approves funds for them because cuts in weapons systems and plant closings mean not only that people in the Defense Department and on bases lose their jobs but also that local shopkeepers, bankers, lawyers, doctors, contractors, housekeepers, baby-sitters—the list goes on and on—are put out of work.

Weapons are, in fact, a major American industry, one that members of Congress work hard to promote and protect. As former World War II hero Dwight Eisenhower warned in his presidential Farewell Address in 1960, the United States must be wary of the *military-industrial complex* that supports increased defense spending as a way to protect jobs. Eisenhower's words are well-worth rereading today:

> This conjunction of an immense military establishment and a large arms industry is new in the American experience. The total influence—economic, political, even spiritual—is felt in every city, every State house, every office of the Federal government. We recognize the imperative need for this development. Yet we must not fail to comprehend its gave implications. Our toil, resources and livelihood are all involved; so is the very structure of our society.
>
> In the councils of government, we must guard against the acquisition of unwarranted influence, whether sought or unsought, by the military industrial complex. The potential for the disastrous rise of misplaced power exists and will persist.[48]

The military-industrial complex has become even more significant as the U.S. military has privatized many of the jobs that are essential for war. Private contractors were responsible for building the bases and feeding U.S. troops in Iraq, for example, as well as maintaining and repairing military equipment, providing security for foreign diplomats, and even interrogating prisoners. As of August 1, 2004, at least 110 contractors had been killed in the Iraq war.[49]

The military is also dealing with the dramatic number of mergers and acquisitions in the defense industry. In the 1950s, for example, 11 different companies were building fighter aircraft; by 2004, just three companies remained: Boeing, Lockheed-Martin, and Northrop Grumman. As the consolidation has increased, the amount of competition between firms has declined, while making the U.S. more dependent on a handful of firms to build the next generation of weapons.[50]

FIGURE 20–2 Defense Expenditures, 2003.
Source: Michael O'Hanlon, "Protecting the American Homeland," *Brookings Review* 20 (Summer, 2002), p. 15.

Although Secretary of Defense Donald Rumsfeld asked Congress to cancel the Crusader mobile cannon in the spring of 2002, members of Congress were able to salvage funding for continued development.

THE IMPACT OF FOREIGN AID

U.S. policy makers have at least three choices to make in giving foreign aid to a country. First, they must decide whether to give any funding at all. The decision depends in part on the strategic value of the recipient nation to U.S. foreign policy goals such as fighting the war on terrorism or reducing the flow of illegal drugs. Second, they must decide what kind of aid to give. Third, they must decide how much to give. Because the foreign aid budget is limited, these decisions determine which nations will be helped or hurt, which in turn determines whether the United States is able to achieve its policy goals. This simulation challenges readers to make the key decisions in distributing a fixed foreign aid budget. Where should the money go, and in what form?

Go to make it Real "The Impact of Foreign Aid."

PROSPECTS FOR THE FUTURE

The world has become a much more uncertain place since the end of the cold war. The Internet has rendered borders virtually meaningless for controlling the flow of information; the global economy has increased the number and size of multinational corporations; and terrorism appears to be spreading rapidly.

The United States is clearly struggling to address this uncertainty without frustrating the public or compromising basic democratic principles. On the one hand, for example, Americans favor open borders, easy movement of imports and exports, short lines at airports, quick access to information, and protection of their privacy. On the other hand, they want government to monitor terrorists, detect dangerous cargo, ensure airport security, keep secrets from the enemy, and make sure that no one slips through the border to bring harm to the nation.

Although the goals are not necessarily contradictory, they do require a careful balance of individual liberty and national interest. They also involve an effort to prevent the spread of terrorism by promoting global peace and understanding. The war on terrorism will not be won in a single battle with a single adversary, nor will weapons of mass destruction disappear without a broad international commitment to action. As the United States has learned over the hard months of combat in Iraq, coalition building may be difficult, frustrating, and most certainly time-consuming, but, ultimately, it may be the only option available.

S U M M A R Y

1. The United States has adopted many, sometimes competing foreign policy goals over the years, from promoting peace in the Middle East to addressing the spread of HIV-AIDS. It is putting its greatest emphasis today on three primary goals: winning the war on terrorism, controlling weapons of mass destruction, and promoting U.S. trade in an increasingly competitive global economy.

2. The president has the primary responsibility to shape foreign and defense policy. The principal foreign policy adviser is the secretary of state, although other cabinet secretaries, including the secretary of defense, are also influential. The National Security Council and the intelligence agencies also play key roles. Public opinion, interest groups, foreign countries, political parties, and Congress also affect the making of foreign policy.

3. Presidents, Congress, and the American people all become involved in defining our vital national security interests, but they often have contradictory views. Presidents must sometimes act swiftly and decisively. Plainly, the role of the president in foreign affairs was strengthened during the cold war years as the United States developed an enormous standing military capability and an extensive intelligence network. Presidents are often in a good position to see the nation's long-term interests above the tugging of bureaucratic and special interests. But in our constitutional democracy, presidents and their advisers must consult with Congress and inform the American people. The media and special interests also play a role.

4. U.S. foreign policy interests are advanced by one or a combination of the following strategies: diplomacy, foreign aid, eco-

nomic sanctions, political coercion (including the breaking off of diplomatic relations), covert action, and military intervention. Traditional diplomacy is often augmented by the U.S. role in the United Nations.

5. The U.S. military is an all-volunteer force. Although the military does provide enormous opportunities for women and minorities, women have yet to play a significant role in combat.

6. Although the past decade witnessed major reductions in the size of the military and major cuts in military spending, some critics say the defense budget can be cut much further. Critics on the right, however, claim that we have weakened our defense preparedness. The nature of warfare and the preventing of wars are changing in ways that are hard to predict.

K E Y T E R M S

weapons of mass destruction
Bush Doctrine
preemption

permanent normal trade relations (PNTR) status

bipartisanship

economic sanctions

Further Reading

GEORGE H. W. BUSH AND BRENT SCOWCROFT, *A World Transformed* (Knopf, 1998).

WARREN CRISTOPHER, *In the Stream of History: Shaping Foreign Policy for a New Era* (Stanford University Press, 1998).

IVO H. DAALDER AND MICHAEL E. O'HANLON, *Winning Ugly: NATO's War to Save Kosovo* (Brookings Institution Press, 2000).

JOSEPH G. DAWSON III, ED., *Commanders-in-Chief: Presidential Leadership in Modern Wars* (University Press of Kansas, 1993).

LOUIS FISHER, *Presidential War Power* 2nd ed. (University Press of Kansas, 2004).

JOHN LEWIS GADDIS, *The United States and the End of the Cold War* (Oxford University Press, 1992).

RICHARD N. HAASS, *The Reluctant Sheriff: The United States After the Cold War* (Council on Foreign Relations, 1997).

RICHARD N. HAASS AND MEGHAN L. O'SULLIVAN, EDS., *Honey and Vinegar: Incentives, Sanctions, and Foreign Policy* (Brookings Institution Press, 2000).

OLE HOLSTI, *Public Opinion and American Foreign Policy* (University of Michigan Press, 1996).

SAMUEL HUNTINGTON, *The Clash of Civilization and the Remaking of World Order* (Simon & Schuster, 1996).

LOCH K. JOHNSON, *Secret Agencies: U.S. Intelligence in a Hostile World* (Yale University Press, 1996).

HAROLD HONGJU KOH, *The National Security Constitution: Sharing Power After the Iran-Contra Affair* (Yale University Press, 1990).

STEVEN KULL AND I. M. DESTLER, *Misreading the Public: The Myth of a New Isolationism* (Brookings Institution Press, 1999).

THOMAS W. LIPPMAN, *Madeleine Albright and the New American Diplomacy* (Westview Press, 2000).

ROBERT LITAN, *Globalphobia* (Brookings Institution Press, 2002).

ROBERT S. LITWAK, *Rogue States and U.S. Foreign Policy: Containment After the Cold War* (Johns Hopkins University Press, 2000).

NATIONAL COMMISSION ON TERRORIST ATTACKS ON THE UNITED STATES, *The 9/11 Commission Report* (W.W. Norton, 2004).

MICHAEL E. O'HANLON, *How to Be a Cheap Defense Hawk* (Brookings Institution Press, 2002).

WILLIAM PERRY, *Preventive Defense: A New Security Strategy for America* (Brookings Institution Press, 1999).

JOHN PRADOS, *Keepers of the Keys: A History of the National Security Council from Truman to Bush* (Morrow, 1991).

ROSEMARY RIGHTER, *Utopia Lost: The United Nations and World Order* (Twentieth Century Fund, 1995).

JOSEPH ROMM, *Defining National Security: The Nonmilitary Aspect* (Council on Foreign Relations, 1993).

GEORGE SHULTZ, *Turmoil and Triumph: My Years as Secretary of State* (Scribner, 1993).

RONALD STEEL, *Temptations of a Superpower* (Harvard University Press, 1995).

STEPHEN R. WEISSMAN, *A Culture of Deference: Congress's Failure of Leadership in Foreign Affairs* (Basic Books, 1995).

GEORGE C. WILSON, *This War Really Matters: Inside the Fight for Defense Dollars* (CQ Press, 2000).

BOB WOODWARD, *Plan of Attack* (Simon & Schuster, 2004).

THE SOCIAL AND ECONOMIC MILIEU OF TEXAS POLITICS

21

DECADES OF CHANGE AND CHALLENGE

Texas entered the twenty-first century with considerable optimism. The state's economy appeared to be in overdrive, continuing to outpace the nation's economy as it had done throughout the 1990s. Unemployment was low, and many individuals were working who previously had difficulty finding jobs. With increased revenues, governments across the state were able to hold the line on taxes and increase services.

Deregulation of the energy industry was touted as a solution to high energy costs and a guarantee of adequate supplies of power. Commercial and residential construction expanded dramatically, and increased exports, particularly to Mexico, clearly demonstrated the state's links to the global economy. Many of the historic political conflicts seemed to be moving toward resolution, and the president of the United States—George W. Bush—was one of Texas's own.

But this exuberance was soon jolted by a number of events that will shape the politics of the state for years. Excesses in the stock market resulted in reversals of dramatic proportions. Corporations and individuals lost huge amounts of money, and many of the baby boomers who had assumed that they were adequately prepared for retirement awoke to the reality of evaporating wealth. Enron Corporation, a Houston firm and major player in energy deregulation, engaged in predatory policies and fraudulent accounting that raised questions about financial practices throughout the country when Enron imploded. Recession set in with the loss of jobs and revenues, and governments across the state found themselves facing deficits that required reductions in services and employment. Illegal immigration from Mexico continued at a rapid pace despite increased efforts to regain control of the border. And finally, the terrorist attacks on the World Trade Center and the

TIME LINE

THE SOCIAL AND ECONOMIC MILIEU OF TEXAS

1830s	Beginning of policies that virtually eliminated the Native American population
1836	Texans win war of independence and establish Republic of Texas
1846	Slavery is legalized under the Constitution of 1845
1950	First census in which a majority of Texans are identified as living in urban areas
1993	North American Free Trade Agreement, which established closer economic ties to Mexico
2000	Texas is second largest state, with a population of 20,851,820
2000	Minorities comprise 47 percent of state's population
2002	Texas exports $41.6 billion in goods and services to Mexico
2003	State's gross domestic product is $827 billion

Pentagon on September 11, 2001, challenged our long-held assumptions about the basic security of our country and state.

Increasingly, the politics and economy of Texas, often described in terms of the state's uniqueness, are now challenged by global trends. The state's population has been, and will continue to be, transformed by immigration into Texas and changing demographic patterns. The frontier, rural society, characterized by the cowboy, is long gone. The "Oil Patch," where wildcatters and roughnecks once prevailed, has been replaced by what one author dubbed the "Silicon Prairie, . . . where venture capitalists and software engineers roam."[1]

But Texas still has a rugged, bigger-than-life mystique that annoys or amuses many non-Texans. In many obvious and not-so-obvious ways, Texans continue to manifest this historical legacy of the frontier in their speech, their "can-do" attitude, their celebration of their "Texan-ness," and their actions (see *FYI:* "Perpetuating an Image: The Cowboy President and the 'Killer Ds'"). In what other state do you find the pervasive display of the state's flag or the pilgrimage of so many to the state's "holy shrine"—the Alamo? Behaviors and language with which others take umbrage and often misunderstand are viewed by most Texans to be simply part of the rich culture and legacy of the state.

Texas and Texans are not immune from the host of nagging, down-to-earth problems that confront most states in these early years of the twenty-first century. Despite the sense of size and wide open spaces, Texans are only now coming to understand that their state is urban, with more than 80 percent of the population living in urbanized areas. Three of the ten largest cities in the United States—Houston, Dallas, and San Antonio—are in Texas. Texans now confront many of the problems that other states have faced for decades, but a legacy of individualism and limited government make it difficult to adjust to these new realities of a changing economy, a changing society, and a changing political landscape.

Citizens across our country are woefully ignorant of their state and local governments. Texans are no different. Government is seen by many to be something in Austin or the courthouse, where people do things to us, not for us. It's often described in terms of red tape, inefficiency, and anonymous or rude bureaucrats. Political campaigns are perceived as a form of organized mud wrestling in which candidates characterize each other as despicable, immoral, incompetent, or whatever, and this perception results in large numbers of Texans tuning out politics. Many distrust government—a traditionally strong sentiment in Texas—and hope it interferes with their lives as little as possible. Most Texans don't vote in elections, leaving the selection of public leaders to others. Texans expect a wide variety of public services, but they are ill disposed to paying for them with increased taxes.

Our past, which has been marked by good times as well as bad, is a prelude to our future, and decisions that we make about our politics, governments and public policies will determine how we can adapt to inevitable changes.

Challenges of the 21st Century

Sustained population growth; the continued transformation of the state's economy; environmental, transportation, and water problems; and increased demands for governmental services pose tremendous challenges to the resources, capabilities, and the very structure of Texas government. Federal mandates and reductions in federal funds have forced state and local governments to scramble to develop more effective and efficient means of assisting low-income people. Public officials are also challenged by a regressive and outdated tax system, high rates of unemployment and underemployment in various areas of the state, the influx of immigrants from Mexico and other countries, an aging population that requires long-term nursing care, large numbers of people who have no health insurance, and changes in welfare law. Inequities in public education persist in posing a challenge for developing a workforce that can compete in the global economy. Finally, the state's growth has aggravated environmental problems, including water use, that affect the health and well-being of everyone.

These problems and issues are the ingredients of contemporary Texas politics. They reflect the fundamental conflicts between competing interests and the way Texans decide who gets "what, when, and how."[2] Unfortunately, only a small part of the population is involved in developing solutions. The only time many people get excited or concerned about government is when it fails to meet their demands or expectations. Such indifference and ignorance are harmful to the public interest as Texas faces critical changes.

As we begin our analysis of Texas government and politics, we ask why Texans and their public officials make the political choices they do. Why, for example, do expenditures for public education rank low in comparison to other states? How do we account for Texas's highly regressive tax system, which requires low-income citizens to pay a higher proportion of their income in state and local taxes than do the wealthy? Why are Texans so willing to fund the construction of highways and roads while letting their state rank near the bottom of all the states in expenditures for public welfare?[3]

These policy issues are directly linked to a variety of other questions about governmental institutions and the political system. Why are Texans content to live under a state constitution that most scholars regard as obsolete? Why, until recently, was Texas a one-party Democratic state? Why are state politics now dominated by Republicans? Does a small group of powerful individuals make the primary policy decisions for the state, or are there various competitive centers of power? Have bitter, mudslinging political campaigns contributed to the public's loss of confidence in government and elected officials? Do Texans feel they are paying more but getting less for their tax dollars?

Most of these issues affect Texans personally. They pay the costs, even though they may not receive the benefits of every policy decision. The actions and decisions of governmental leaders can have an immediate and direct effect on people's lives, and, from time to time, those holding positions of power have made decisions that have cost Texans dearly. For example, the Enron debacle and the manipulation of energy markets were the result, in large part, of the failure of state and federal governments to regulate the energy industry adequately. And major cuts in governmental services in 2003 were the direct result of the Texas legislature's refusal to increase taxes to offset the loss of revenue caused by the downturn in the state's economy.

The fundamental changes in the social, economic, and political structure of the state have required new solutions. Funding public education in the days of the one-room schoolhouse was one thing. Funding today's educational system in a way that provides equity among the state's 1,000-plus school districts is much more complex.

The demographics, or population characteristics, of the state have changed dramatically since the 1940s, when Texas was still predominantly rural. Texas is now an urban state with urban problems. With more than 22 million residents, Texas now is second only to California in population. Its ethnic and racial composition has changed, and it is now also home to a large number of individuals who were born and reared in other parts of the United States or outside the country—people who have a limited sense of Texas history and politics. Although oil and natural gas are still important to the state's economy, economic diversification is the dominant theme promoted by business leaders, government officials, and economists.

Change places heavy demands on the state's basic governmental institutions, and there is increasing evidence that many of these institutions are incapable of responding adequately. As Texans face the accelerating rate of change in the twenty-first century, they will need to give increased attention to modernizing and adapting government to these new realities.

This chapter will introduce you to the people of Texas, the views they have of themselves, the state's political subcultures and economy, and the increased interdependence of Texas and Mexico. We refer to these factors generally as the *political environment*, a concept developed by political scientist David Easton to describe the milieu or context in which political institutions function.[4]

PERPETUATING AN IMAGE: THE COWBOY PRESIDENT AND THE "KILLER Ds"

As the nation pursued the war on terrorism, President George W. Bush, who has been described by some as the "cowboy president," used a number of allusions to the frontier culture. He branded former Iraqi leader Saddam Hussein an "outlaw" and declared that he wanted terrorist Osama bin Laden "dead or alive." At a conference in Aqaba on the Red Sea, Bush said that he was going to appoint a coordinator to "ride herd" on Middle East leaders along the peace trail. Many in his audience had no idea what he was talking about, but the characterization of Bush in cartoons and articles as a cowboy continues to feed the perceptions others have of the frontier culture of Texas and its style of politics.

The distorted images that other Americans have of Texans and the state were further reinforced during the 2003 legislative sessions, when House Democrats—characterized as the "Killer Ds"—fled to Ardmore, Oklahoma, and later Senate Democrats flew to Albuquerque, New Mexico, to delay Republican efforts to redraw congressional districts to favor GOP candidates. The national and world press attempted to sort out these theatrics in light of the state's political culture. Needless to say, the cartoonists had a field day in their caricatures of Texas politicians.

SOURCE: *BBC News,* June 6, 2003.

The dime novel helped create the myth of Texas individualism by popularizing and exaggerating the image of the cowboy.

The Texas Rangers played an important (but sometimes controversial) role in the taming of the Texas frontier.

TEXAS MYTHS

Although most Texans have only a cursory knowledge of the state's governmental institutions, political history, and contemporary public policy, they do have views—often ill-defined—of the state, its people, and its culture. Key elements of these views, shared by millions of Texans, are described by some scholars as *political myths.*

In recent years, serious scholarship has focused on myths as ways to assess the views people have of their common historical and cultural experiences. A myth can be regarded as a "mode of truth . . . that codifies and preserves moral and spiritual values" for a particular culture or society.[5] Myths are stories or narratives that are used to describe past events, explain their significance to successive generations, and provide an interpretive overview and understanding of a society. Myths provide a world picture or, in our case, a picture of the state of Texas. The relevance of a myth depends, in part, on the degree to which it approximates the event it is describing and its pervasiveness in the literature and popular culture of the state.

Texas has produced its own *myth of origin,* which continues to be a powerful statement about the political system and the social order on which it is based.[6] For many Texans, the battle of the Alamo clearly serves to identify the common experiences of independence and the creation of a separate, unique political order. No other state was a **republic** prior to joining the Union, and several scholars argue that independence and "going at it alone" from 1836 to 1845 resulted in a cultural experience that distinguishes the Texas political system from that of other states. The state's motto— the Lone Star State—is a constant reminder of this unique history. A whole set of heroes came out of the formative period of Texas history, including many who fought and died at the Alamo or secured Texas independence on the San Jacinto battlefield. Texas school children are introduced to these heroes at a very early age with field trips or "pilgrimages" to the Alamo in San Antonio and visits to the San Jacinto monument in Houston.

The Texas mythology also includes the Texas Ranger and the cowboy. There is considerable lore of the invincible, enduring ranger defeating overwhelming odds. Newspapers and dime novels in the nineteenth century introduced readers throughout the United States to the cowboy, who often was portrayed as an honest, hardworking individual wrestling with the harsh Texas environment. The cowboy's rugged **individualism,** with strong connotations of self-help, symbolizes a political culture in Texas that does not like to look to government as a solution to many problems.[7] It is the kind of individualism that continues to be exploited by political candidates in campaign ads and public rhetoric and by the state legislature in limited appropriations for welfare, health care, and other public assistance programs.

The frontier to which the Texas Ranger and the cowboy belong is part of a cultural myth of limited government and unlimited personal opportunity. The frontier in the Texas experience also perpetuates the myths of "land as wilderness and land as garden."[8] Space, distance, and size are pervasive in a great deal of literature on the state, reinforcing perceptions of the "wide open spaces" that shape Texans' views of their autonomy and independence.

The Texas myths, however, have been primarily the myths of the white (Anglo) population and have limited relevance to the cultural and historical experiences of many African American and Hispanic Texans. From the 1840s to the mid-1960s, these latter groups were excluded from full participation in Texas politics and the state's economic and social life. To many Hispanics, for example, the Texas Ranger is not a hero but a symbol of ruthless suppression.

Over the past thirty years, African Americans and Hispanics have made significant political and economic gains. Their share of the population has been increasing as well, and they are expected to constitute a majority of the state's population during the first quarter of the twenty-first century.

As this shift occurs, Hispanic and African American historical experiences are likely to be incorporated into the mythology of the state, and some components of the

republic
Form of government in which representatives of the people, rather than the people themselves, govern.

individualism
Attitude, rooted in classical liberal theory and reinforced by the frontier tradition, that citizens are capable of taking care of themselves with minimal governmental assistance.

One of many activities celebrating Martin Luther King, Jr.'s birthday, which is now a national and state holiday, was held outside the Texas state capitol.

contemporary mythology will be redefined. These revisions may already be under way, as demonstrated by the recent heated debates over what actually took place during the battle of the Alamo. According to recently published accounts, some of the Alamo's heroes surrendered to Mexican soldiers and were executed, rather than fighting to the death. African Americans in Texas have been successful, after several years of trying, in getting the legislature to make Martin Luther King, Jr.'s birthday a state holiday. And for Hispanics, the *Cinco de Mayo* holiday speaks to common cultural and historical experiences.

Throughout Texas, Cinco de Mayo is celebrated by Hispanics in commemoration of Mexico's defeat of French troops at Puebla, Mexico, in 1862.

THE POLITICAL CULTURE OF TEXAS

Texas shares the common institutional and legal arrangements that have developed in all fifty states, including a commitment to personal liberties, equality, justice, the rule of law, and popular sovereignty with its limitations on government. But there are differences among the states and even among regions within individual states. Texas is a highly diverse state, with racial and ethnic differences from one region to another and divergences in political attitudes and behavior that are reflected in the state's politics and public policies.

The concept of political culture helps us compare some of these differences. **Political culture** has been defined as "the set of attitudes, beliefs, and sentiments which give order and meaning to a political process and which provide the underlying assumptions and rules that govern behavior in the political system."[9] The political culture of the state includes fundamental beliefs about the proper role of government, the relationship of the government to its citizens, and who should govern.[10] These complex attitudes and behaviors are rooted in the historical experience of the nation, shaped by the groups that immigrated to the United States, and carried across the continent to Texas.

One authority on American political culture, Daniel Elazar, believes that three political subcultures have emerged over time in the United States: the individualistic, the moralistic, and the traditionalistic. While all three draw from the common historical legacy of the nation, they have produced regional political differences. Sometimes they complement each other; at other times they produce conflict.[11]

The Individualistic Subculture

The political view of the **individualistic subculture** holds that politics and government function as a marketplace. Government does not have to be concerned with creating a good or moral society but exists for strictly "utilitarian reasons, to handle those functions demanded by the people it is created to serve."[12] Government should be limited, and its intervention in the private activities of its citizens kept to a minimum. The primary function of government is to assure the stability of a society so that individuals can pursue their own interests.

In this view, politics is not a high calling or noble pursuit but is like any other business venture in which skill and talent prevail and the individual can anticipate economic and social benefits. Politics is often perceived by the general public to be a dirty business that should be left to those willing to soil their hands. This tradition may well contribute to political corruption, and members of the electorate who share this view may not be concerned when governmental corruption is revealed. New policies are more likely to be initiated by interest groups or private individuals than by public officials.

The Moralistic Subculture

The **moralistic subculture** regards politics as one of the "great activities of man in his search for the good society."[13] Politics, it maintains, is the pursuit of the common good. Unlike the attitude expressed in the individualistic subculture that governments are to be limited, the moralistic subculture considers government a positive instrument with a responsibility to promote the general welfare. Politics, therefore, is not to be left to the few but is a responsibility of every individual. Politics is a duty and possibly a high calling. This cultural tradition has a strong sense of service. It requires a high standard for those holding public office and believes public office is not to be used for personal gain. Politics may be organized around political parties, but this tradition has produced nonpartisanship, in which party labels and organizations are eliminated or play a reduced role. This tradition produces a large number of "amateur" or "nonprofessional" political activists and officeholders and has little toleration for political corruption. From the moralistic perspective, governments should actively intervene to enhance the social and economic lives of their citizens. Public policy initiatives can come from officeholders as well as from those outside the formal governmental structure.

political culture
Widely shared set of views, attitudes, beliefs, and customs of a people as to how their government should be organized and run.

individualistic subculture
View that government should interfere as little as possible in the private activities of its citizens while assuring that adequate public facilities and a favorable business climate are available to permit individuals to pursue their self-interests.

moralistic subculture
View that government's primary responsibility is to promote the public welfare and that it should actively use its authority and power to improve the social and economic well-being of its citizens.

The Traditionalistic Subculture

The **traditionalistic** political subculture holds the political view that there is a hierarchical arrangement to the political order. This hierarchy serves to limit the power and influence of the general public, while allocating authority to a few individuals who constitute a self-perpetuating **elite.** The elite may enact policies that benefit the general public, but that is secondary to its interests and objectives. Public policy reflects the interests of those who exercise influence and control, and the benefits of public policy go disproportionately to the elite.

Family and social relationships form the basis for maintaining this elite structure, rather than mass political participation. In fact, in many regions of the country where traditionalistic patterns existed, there were systematic efforts to reduce or eliminate the participation of the general public. Although political parties may exist in such a subculture, they have only minimal importance. Many of the states characterized by the traditionalistic subculture were southern states in which two-party politics was replaced by factionalism within the Democratic party.[14]

Historical Origins of Political Subcultures

The historical origins of these three subcultures can be explained, in part, by the early settlement patterns of the United States and by the cultural differences among the groups of people who initially settled the eastern seaboard. In very general terms, the New England colonists, influenced by Puritan and congregational religious groups, spawned the moralistic subculture. Settlers with entrepreneurial concerns and individualistic attitudes tended to locate in the mid-Atlantic states, while the initial settlement of the South was dominated by elites who aspired, in part, to recreate a semi-feudal society.

As expansion toward the frontiers progressed, there were identifiable migration patterns from the initial three settlement regions. Texas was settled primarily by people holding the individualistic and traditionalistic views of a political system. The blending of these two views, along with the historical experience of the Republic and the frontier, contributed to the distinct characteristics of Texas's political culture.[15]

These two political subcultures have merged to shape Texans' general views of what governments should do, who should govern, and what constitutes good public policy. Given the characteristics of these two traditions, one might well conclude, as have many scholars, that the Texas political culture is conservative. Politics in Texas is designed to minimize the role of government, is hostile toward taxes—especially those that are allocated toward social services—and is potentially manipulated by the few for their narrow advantages.

Some scholars have reservations about the concept of political subcultures because the theory is difficult to test. Their reservations are legitimate, but we know of no other single theory that presents such a rich historical perspective on the relationship of settlement patterns in the state and the evolution of political attitudes and behavior.

THE PEOPLE OF TEXAS

The politics and government of Texas can be understood, in part, from the perspective of the people living in the state. What follows is a descriptive analysis of a select number of demographic characteristics of Texans. In subsequent chapters, we examine the relationship of race, ethnicity, and other demographic characteristics to partisan behavior, public opinion, institutional power, and public policy.

Native Americans

There are only three small Native American groups (Alabama-Coushatta, Tigua, and Kickapoo) living on reservations in Texas, and the Native American population is less than one-half of 1 percent of the state's total population.[16] Unlike Native American populations in Oklahoma, New Mexico, and Arizona, those in Texas have little influence on governmental institutions, politics, or public policy.

A Tigua father prepares a meal for his children. The Tiguas are one of only three Native American groups with reservations in Texas.

traditionalistic subculture
View that political power should be concentrated in the hands of a few elite citizens who belong to established families or influential social groups. Public policy basically serves the interests of this small group.

elite
Small group of people who exercise disproportionate power and influence in the policy-making processes.

WHAT'S IN A NAME?

The Native American legacy of Texas remains in the state's name. The word "Texas" came from *Tejas*, which means "friends" or "allies." As Spanish explorers and missionaries moved across Texas, they confronted a Native American confederacy, the Hasinai. It was to this particular group that they applied the term, and eventually the Anglo form of the name became the permanent name of the region and then the state.

In 1989, the Texas Department of Transportation proposed changing the state's vehicle license plates to include the phrase "The Friendship State." The proposal was dropped, however, because of a generally hostile public reaction. Some Texans apparently found the phrase incompatible with the state's rugged frontier image. The irony is that the state's very name, which means friendship, is used almost every day by these same people.

SOURCE: Rupert N. Richardson, Ernest Wallace, and Adrian N. Anderson, *Texas: The Lone Star State*, 6th ed. (Prentice Hall, 1993), p. 1.

In the early nineteenth century, there were at least twenty-three different Native American groups residing in Texas (see *FYI:* "What's in a Name?"). During the period of the Republic (1836–1845), President Sam Houston attempted to follow a policy of "peace and friendship" with the Native Americans, but he was followed by President Mirabeau B. Lamar, who set out to "expel, defeat or exterminate" them. As the European populations expanded to lands traditionally claimed by various Native American groups, conflict ensued, and most of the Native American population was eventually eliminated or displaced to other states.[17]

In recent years, the Native American tribes have been involved with state officials over the operation of gambling casinos on tribal reservations. Such casinos are allowed under federal law, but they conflict with state law prohibiting casino gambling. Some Native American leaders consider casinos a major source of revenue, jobs, and economic development for their people.

Hispanics

In the eighteenth and nineteenth centuries, neither Spain nor Mexico was very successful in convincing Hispanics to settle in the Tejas territory of Mexico. The Spanish regarded it as a border province with relatively little value except as a strategic buffer between Spanish colonies and those held by the British and the French. By the time Mexico declared its independence from Spain in 1821, the total Texas population under Spanish control was estimated to be approximately 5,000. With the rapid expansion of Anglo American immigration to Texas in the 1820s and 1830s, Hispanics became a small minority of the population.[18]

Some Hispanics were part of the Texas independence movement from Mexico, and after independence in 1836, men such as José Antonio Navarro and Juan Seguin were part of the Republic's political establishment. But the Anglo migration rapidly overwhelmed the Hispanic population and greatly reduced its political and economic power. There was even an effort at the Constitutional Convention of 1845 to strip Hispanics of the right to vote. The attempt failed, but it was an early indication of Anglo hostility toward the Hispanic population.[19]

By 1887, the Hispanic population had declined to approximately 4 percent of the state's total. In 1930, it was 12 percent and was concentrated in the border counties from Brownsville to El Paso (see Figure 21–1). There were modest increases in the Hispanic population until it reached 18 percent of the state's population in 1970, after which it grew at a more rapid rate. By 1990, it had reached 25 percent, spurred by immigration from Mexico and other Latin American countries as well as by higher birth rates among Hispanic women. These growth patterns continued in the 1990s, and by 2000, Hispanics were approximately 32 percent of the state's population.[20] In addition to their traditional concentrations in the Rio Grande Valley and South-Central Texas, large Hispanic populations are found in most metropolitan areas. Except for the Asian population, which is still considerably smaller, the Hispanic population is growing at a significantly higher rate than other populations in Texas.

Hispanics will continue to increase at a higher rate than most other populations, and by 2010, the Hispanic population is likely to exceed 39 percent of the state's total; by 2020, this figure may grow to 46 percent (see *Changing Face of Texas Politics:* "Hispanics Become a Majority in 2040").[21] This growth already has produced significant political power and influence. Five Hispanics have been elected to statewide office. And after successful redistricting and legal challenges to city, county, school board, and state legislative districts, Hispanics in 2003 held some 1,965 elected positions in Texas, the highest number of any state.[22]

The regions of the state where Hispanics were concentrated (South Texas and along the Mexican border) before their more widespread migration to cities were areas heavily influenced by the traditionalistic subculture. Extreme poverty, low levels of education, and local economies based on agriculture contributed to the development of political systems dominated by a few Anglos, who often considered Hispanics second-class citizens. Hispanics' increasing political clout, however, has produced major political and governmental changes in those regions.

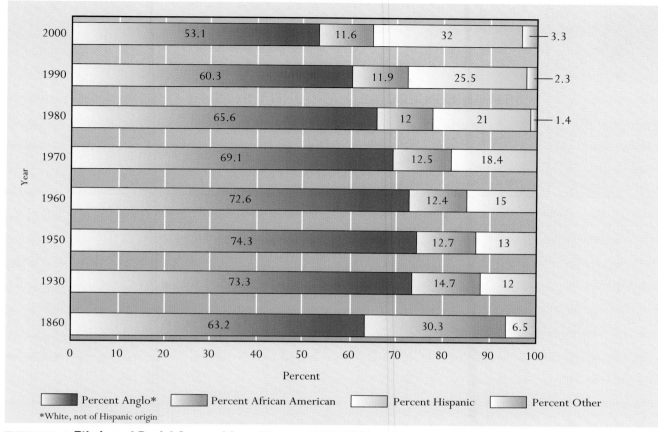

FIGURE 21–1 Ethnic and Racial Composition of Texas, 1860–2000.

Note: Data for Asian and other populations not tabulated by the Bureau of the Census prior to 1980. Spanish total for 1970 based on "Persons of Spanish language or surname."

*White, not of Hispanic origin.

SOURCE: Terry G. Jordan with John L. Bean Jr., and William M. Holmes, *Texas: A Geography* (Westview Press, 1984), pp. 81, 83; U.S. Censuses 1860–2000; Texas State Data Center.

African Americans

Some African Americans lived in Texas during the colonization period, but the modern story of African American settlement did not begin until after independence in 1836. When Texas was part of Mexico, Mexican law restricted slavery within the territory. During the period of the Republic and early statehood prior to the U.S. Civil War, there was a significant increase in the African American population as Americans settling in Texas brought cotton cultivation and the slavery system with them. At the time of the Civil War, 30 percent of the state's residents were African American, but that percentage declined after the war. By 1960, it had leveled off to 12 percent, about the same level counted in the 2000 census (see Figure 21–1). African Americans are expected to represent between 11 percent and 12 percent of the state's population during the next 25 years.

There is a large concentration of African Americans in East Texas, where white southerners and their slaves originally settled. African Americans are also concentrated in the urban areas of Dallas, Fort Worth, Austin, and Houston. Relatively few African Americans live in the western counties or in the counties along the border with Mexico. The increased number of African American state legislators, city council members, county commissioners, and school board trustees representing urban communities is an indication of the political power of the African American population in selected areas. In 2001, the most recent year for which data were available, there were 460 African American elected officials in Texas. Four African Americans have been elected to statewide office.[23]

The slaveholding whites who migrated to Texas from the lower southern states brought with them the dominant values of the traditionalistic political subculture.

CHANGING FACE OF TEXAS POLITICS

HISPANICS BECOME A MAJORITY IN 2040

According to projections of the Office of the State Demographer, in 2040 Hispanics will be the majority of the population of Texas. This change over the next several decades will change the landscape of Texas politics.

Projected Population 2000–2040 by Race/Ethnicity

Year	Total	Anglo	Black	Hispanic	Other
2000	20,851,820	11,074,716	2,421,653	6,669,666	685,785
2005	22,556,027	11,327,876	2,588,603	7,820,842	818,706
2010	24,330,643	11,533,980	2,754,737	9,080,466	961,460
2015	26,156,761	11,694,534	2,913,059	10,436,556	1,112,612
2020	28,005,792	11,796,479	3,052,412	11,882,993	1,273,908
2025	29,897,444	11,830,586	3,170,981	13,448,477	1,447,400
2030	31,830,579	11,789,292	3,268,611	15,140,088	1,632,588
2035	33,789,670	11,682,021	3,345,693	16,934,443	1,827,513
2040	35,761,159	11,525,083	3,403,176	18,804,297	2,028,603

SOURCE: Office of the State Demographer, Texas State Data Center, *Population 2000 and Projected Population 2005–2040 by Race/Ethnicity and Migration Scenario for State of Texas,* 2004 (Institute of Demographic and Socioeconomic Research, College of Business, University of Texas at San Antonio).

Although slaves were freed after the Civil War, continued political and economic discrimination against African Americans was commonplace in the eastern part of Texas into the 1960s. As in South Texas, the politics of East Texas served the interests of the white elites by reducing or eliminating African American participation in the political process through election laws and outright physical intimidation.

Anglos

In the vernacular of Texas politics, the white population is referred to as "Anglos," although there is no census designation by that name. The term includes Jews, Irish, Poles, and just about any other individual who is designated by the U.S. Bureau of the Census as "non-Hispanic white."

Scholars have identified two distinct early patterns of Anglo migration into Texas from other states. These patterns, as well as population movements through much of the late nineteenth and early twentieth centuries, largely explain the regional locations of the state's two dominant political subcultures.

In the early nineteenth century, the first Anglos moving to Texas were from the upper South—Tennessee, Kentucky, Arkansas, and North Carolina—a region significantly influenced by the individualistic subculture of limited government. The earliest settlements were primarily in what is now Northeast Texas in the Red River Valley. After Mexican independence from Spain, there was a second wave of immigration from the upper South. Few of the early colonists were plantation slaveholders from the lower South.

After Texas became independent, slavery was legalized, and settlers from the lower South began arriving. By the outbreak of the Civil War, Anglos who had moved to Texas from the lower South were roughly equal in number to those from the upper South. Arrivals from the slaveholding lower South initially settled in southeastern Texas near Louisiana, but soon they began to move northward and westward.

A line between Texarkana and San Antonio in effect divides Texas subcultures. Most of those Anglos who settled north and west of this line were from the upper South and heavily influenced by the individualistic subculture, which favors limited government. Anglos who settled south and east of the line were by and large from the lower South and shaped by its traditionalistic subculture.

This pattern of immigration and settlement continued after the Civil War. It was primarily those populations from the upper South who pushed westward to the Panhandle and West Texas. This expansion introduced into the western part of the state the cultural experience of those who resisted the notion that government existed to solve society's ills. To this day, West Texas is still one of the most politically conservative areas of the state.[24]

In 1860, Anglos constituted approximately 63 percent of Texas' population (see Figure 21–1). The Anglo population increased until it reached 74 percent in 1950. But by 1990 the stabilization of the African American population and the increase in the Hispanic population had reduced the Anglo proportion to 60 percent. Anglos accounted for only 53.1 percent of Texas's population by the year 2000 and were expected to continue to decline as a percentage of the total population through the first three decades of the twenty-first century.

The Anglo population is diverse, as exhibits in the Institute of Texan Cultures in San Antonio remind us. Towns throughout Texas are identified with immigrants of national origin other than Anglo-Saxon, and these national groups brought with them a rich heritage. Castroville, for example, is identified with the Alsatians; New Braunfels and Fredericksburg, the Germans; Panna Maria, the Poles; West and Hallettsville, the Czechs.

The Asian American Population

In 1980, Asian Americans accounted for 0.8 percent of Texas's population, but by 1990 the figure had grown to 1.9 percent. It had grown to approximately 2.7 percent of the state total by 2000 and was projected to increase to 4.2 percent by 2020. This rapid increase parallels national trends. Changes in immigration policy and the dislocation of Asians due to war and political persecution have resulted in larger numbers of Asian immigrants entering the United States and Texas since the 1970s.

The largest concentration of Asian Americans in Texas is in Houston, where several Asian Americans have been elected to major public offices. Among them, community activist Martha Wong was elected to the Houston City Council in 1993 and then to the Texas House of Representatives in 2002. Wong apparently was the second Asian American to serve in the Texas House of Representatives. Tom Lee of San Antonio, who served in the 1960s, was believed to be the first. Another Houstonian, Robert Gee, became one of the first Asian Americans to hold a state office when Governor Ann Richards appointed him to the Public Utility Commission in 1991. Asian Americans hold or have held public offices in several other Texas cities as well.

POLITICS, RACE, AND ETHNICITY

Today few Texans go running around the state wearing Ku Klux Klan robes, burning crosses, or marching in support of white supremacy, but there still are occasions of extreme racial violence and cruelty, such as the murder of James Byrd, Jr., who was dragged to death in early 1999 near Jasper in East Texas. A state law barring African Americans from voting in party primaries was declared unconstitutional in the 1940s, and many other laws intended to reduce the political participation of African Americans and Hispanics have been eliminated. The federal Voting Rights Act, which was enacted in 1965 and extended to Texas in 1975, has also helped open up state and local electoral systems to minorities. There is still evidence of employment and housing discrimination, and opposition to the desegregation of a public housing project in Vidor received national publicity in 1993. But restrictive codes prohibiting specific groups of people from buying residential property have been declared unconstitutional, and federal and state laws have given minorities greater access to jobs.

Nonetheless, race and ethnicity are implicit in many contemporary political and policy issues. Throughout the debate on restructuring the school finance system, the protagonists were identified as the "rich" and "poor" school districts of the state. But in large part, these were alternative terms for "non-minority" and "minority" school systems. There have been bitter debates about redistricting of political districts to increase Hispanic and African American representation on city councils, school boards, and special districts, and in the state legislature and the U.S. Congress. And although many poor Anglos live in Texas, the disproportionately high poverty rates among minority groups often influence discussions about social services.

The budget crisis of 2003 produced a particularly contentious session, when funding was reduced for many of the state's health and social programs. Many state and local elections show evidence of polarized voting along ethnic lines. Race and ethnicity also emerge in jury selection, employment patterns, contracts with state and local governments, and expenditures for public health and social service programs. Admissions policies of Texas colleges and universities resulted in a succession of legal challenges that centered on affirmative action and reverse discrimination.

More than forty years ago, V.O. Key, a Texan scholar of American politics, concluded that Texas politics was moving from issues of race to issues of class and economics. He argued that voters in Texas "divide along class lines in accord with their class interests as related to liberal and conservative candidates."[25] In part, he was correct, in that unabashed racial bigotry and public demagoguery are no longer acceptable. In part, though, he was incorrect and much too optimistic. If the state divides on economic issues, this division puts the majority of Anglos on one side and the majority of Hispanics and African Americans on the other.[26]

THE POLITICAL IMPLICATIONS OF DEMOGRAPHICS

Population Increase

Over the past fifty years, the population of Texas has increased much faster than the national average. According to the 2000 census, the state's population was 20,851,820, an increase of approximately 4 million people in ten years. In the last decade of the

State troopers separate members of the Ku Klux Klan and crowd at a rally in Jasper, Texas, where James Byrd, Jr., an African American, was dragged to his death by three whites.

twentieth century, the state's population grew by 22.8 percent, significantly higher than the national growth rate of 13.2 percent.[27] Texas is now the second most populous state.

High birth rates explain part of the population increase, but migration from other states has also been a significant factor. In recent decades, demographers (those who study populations) have described a nationwide shift in population from the Northeast and Midwest to the South and West. For each of the censuses from 1940 to 1970, in-migration accounted for less than 10 percent of Texas's growth. But in-migration jumped to 58.5 percent of the total growth between 1970 and 1980. Between 1980 and 1990, it contributed 34.4 percent.[28]

In-migration slowed down somewhat between 1990 and 2000, but at the beginning of this decade, approximately 23 percent of Texas residents reported other states as their place of birth.

Although it is expected to become less significant in the future, in-migration from other states has already contributed to the restructuring of Texas's traditional one-party, Democratic political system into a Republican-dominated system. Many new residents came from states with strong Republican party traditions and brought their party affiliation with them. In the long run, in-migration may affect additional elements of the state's political culture.

Texas also attracts individuals from other countries. Approximately 2.9 million, or 14 percent of Texas residents, were identified as foreign-born in the 2000 census. Between 1990 and 2000, approximately 1.4 million, or 6.4 percent, of the state's population arrived from other countries. More than 70 percent of Texans born in other countries come from Latin America. Approximately ten percent of all Texas residents are not U.S. citizens, a fact that has several implications.[29]

Citizenship is directly related to political participation, and noncitizens, while counted in the census for reapportionment of congressional seats, cannot vote. The overwhelming majority of noncitizens are Hispanic, thus reducing the number of eligible Hispanic voters in the state.

Under current federal policy, noncitizens have been denied access to some public social services that are funded in whole or in part by the national government. Needy immigrants are especially affected by such policies, and in some instances, the state has found it necessary to use its own funds to provide services.

Some 6 million Texans over the age of five speak languages other than English at home, and close to half of these individuals report that they don't speak English well.[30] Some states have adopted English as their state language, but there has not been a significant English language movement in Texas. Nonetheless, language is a policy issue for Texas in terms of bilingual education, official documents and publications, translators for court proceedings, and a host of related language issues in the workplace.

The increase in population places demands on all levels of government, and many local governments throughout Texas are hard pressed to provide adequate services. Many Texas cities, for example, are running out of landfill space. Environmental laws make it difficult to obtain new licenses for garbage and waste disposal, and without these additional facilities, new population growth cannot be serviced. The increased population has also raised questions about the adequacy of water supplies throughout the state with different cities, regions, and industries competing intensely for the resources now available. While the state has been engaged in a massive road construction program, streets and highways in urban and suburban areas are clogged with traffic. A driving survey, released in the fall of 2003, indicated significant increases in daily commute time in metropolitan areas. This means additional gasoline consumption, pollution, and costs of time.[31]

The Aging Population

Texans, along with other Americans, are aging. In 2000, the median age of the state's population was 32.3 years as compared to 35.3 for the entire country. Approximately 10 percent of the state's population was older than sixty-five in 2000, and that group was expected to increase to 17 percent by 2030.[32] This aging population will place unprecedented demands on the public and private sectors for goods and services, including expanded health care and long-term care. In recent years, increasing state expenditures under the Medicaid programs for long-term nursing care have strained the state's budget and forced the state to shift priorities in public programs.

Urbanization

Although Texas was a rural state during the first one hundred years of its history, 83 percent of the state's population in 2000 resided in areas classified by the Bureau of the Census as urban (Table 21–1). **Urbanization** and suburban sprawl now characterize Texas's settlement patterns, and many urban corridors and suburban areas cross county boundaries. Residents of these areas often encounter problems that cut across political jurisdictions, and local governments sometimes find it difficult to resolve them.

The dramatic growth of Texas's largest cities is shown in Table 21–2. From 1960 to 2000, the population of Houston and El Paso more than doubled. Dallas increased by approximately 74 percent and San Antonio, 94 percent. Arlington had a population of only 44,775 in 1960, but in 2000 its population was 332,969, an increase of 744 percent. During this forty-year period, Austin's population increased by 352 percent.

Three of the ten largest cities in the United States are in Texas, and, like urban areas throughout the country, Texas's largest cities are increasingly populated by minority and low-income populations. This trend results from higher birth rates among minority populations, urban migration patterns, and what is often referred to as "white flight" from the cities to suburban areas. Minority groups now account for the majority of the population in five of Texas's ten largest cities (Houston, San Antonio, Dallas, El Paso, and Corpus Christi). These minority residents include Hispanics, African Americans, and Asian Americans—groups that do not always constitute a cohesive bloc of interests. As minority growth continues, areas of potential conflict will emerge among these groups.

Population Density

Population density refers to the number of people per square mile in a specific political jurisdiction, and it provides another measure of urbanization. As people crowd into smaller areas, living in close proximity to each other, problems are inevitable. Noise,

urbanization
Process by which a predominantly rural society or area becomes urban.

population density
Number of residents living within the boundaries of a city, county, or state in relationship to the land area. Population density is a significant factor in determining the level of local public services.

TABLE 21–1   URBAN–RURAL POPULATION OF TEXAS

Year	Urban		Rural		Total
	Percentage	Population	Percentage	Population	
1850	4	7,665	96	204,927	212,592
1860	4	26,615	96	577,600	604,215
1870	7	54,521	93	764,058	818,579
1880	9	146,795	91	1,444,954	1,591,749
1890	16	359,511	84	1,886,016	2,245,527
1900	17	520,759	83	2,527,951	3,048,710
1910	24	938,104	76	2,958,438	3,896,542
1920	32	1,512,689	68	3,150,539	4,663,228
1930	41	2,389,148	59	3,435,367	5,824,715
1940	45	2,911,389	55	3,503,435	6,414,824
1950	63	4,838,050	37	2,873,134	7,711,194
1960	75	7,187,470	25	2,392,207	9,579,677
1970	80	8,922,211	20	2,274,519	11,196,730
1980	80	11,333,017	20	2,836,174	14,229,191
1990	80	13,634,517	20	3,351,993	16,986,510
2000	83	17,204,073	17	3,647,747	20,851,820.00

Source: U.S. Bureau of the Census, U.S. Censuses 1850–2000.

TABLE 21–2 TEN LARGEST CITIES, 1900–2000

City	1900	1920	1940	1960	1980	1990	2000
Houston	44,633	138,276	384,514	838,219	1,595,138	1,630,553	1,953,631
Dallas	42,638	158,976	294,734	679,684	904,078	1,006,877	1,188,580
San Antonio	53,321	161,379	253,854	587,718	785,880	935,933	1,144,646
Austin	22,258	34,876	87,960	186,545	345,496	465,622	656,562
El Paso	15,906	77,560	96,810	276,687	425,259	515,342	563,662
Fort Worth	26,688	106,482	177,662	356,268	385,164	447,619	534,694
Arlington	1,079	3,031	4,240	44,775	160,113	261,721	332,969
Corpus Christi	4,703	10,522	57,301	167,690	231,999	257,453	277,454
Plano	1,304	1,715	1,582	3,695	72,331	128,713	222,030
Garland	819	1,421	2,233	38,501	132,857	180,650	215,768

SOURCE: U.S. Censuses, 1900–2000.

land use, property maintenance, traffic patterns, and a whole host of other issues must be addressed (see *FYI:* "Do Size and Geography Shape Texas Politics?").

There are marked differences in the population and density of Texas's 254 counties. Loving County in West Texas has a population of about 67 persons living in an area of 677 square miles. The most populous county is Harris County (Houston), with more than 3.4 million people living in 1,777 square miles.[33] Clearly the problems and issues that Loving County faces are significantly different from those faced by Harris County, yet both counties function with the same form of government created by the Texas Constitution of 1876.

Conflict in Texas politics has often divided along urban–rural lines, and in recent years, suburban areas of the state have taken on more importance, further compounding conflict along the rural–urban dimension. Redistricting battles and a host of other public policy issues are evidence of that. Until recently, the Texas legislature was dominated by rural lawmakers, many of whom were often insensitive to urban needs. To make matters more difficult, suburban legislators with a different constituency base and interests often pursue policies in conflict with both the central city and rural legislators. Moreover, many of urban Texas's problems are aggravated by constitutional restrictions written when Texas was still a rural state.

Wealth and Income Distribution

There is a wide disparity in the distribution of income and wealth across the state. In 1999, the median household income in Texas was $39,927, and the median family income was $45,861, both below national income levels (see Table 21–3). Thirty-one

TABLE 21–3 U.S AND TEXAS INCOME FIGURES

	U.S.	Texas					
	All Persons	All Persons	Anglos	Hispanics	African American	Native American	Asian American
Median income*							
Household	$41,494	$39,927	$47,162	$29,873	$29,305	$34,926	$50,049
Families	50,046	45,861	57,194	30,840	33,276	37,503	57,103
Per capita income*	21,690	19,617	26,197	16,770	14,253	15,899	20,956
Percent of persons below poverty level	12.4%	15.4%	7.8%	25.4%	23.4%	19.3%	11.9%

*1999 dollars.

SOURCE: Bureau of the Census, 2000 *Census of Population*.

DO SIZE AND GEOGRAPHY SHAPE TEXAS POLITICS?

Texas is a big state. Covering 267,339 square miles, it is second only to Alaska in land mass. Texans appear to have adjusted to long distances but many visitors from out of state are overwhelmed by Texas's size and diversity. The distance from Texarkana in Northeast Texas to El Paso in far West Texas is about 800 miles, and a person living in Texarkana is closer to Chicago than to El Paso. Brownsville in far South Texas is closer to Mexico City than it is to Texline in the Texas Panhandle.

It is argued by some that the state's size has helped shape political attitudes and perceptions of public needs and policy. Roads and highways, for example, have historically received a significant—and some would argue a disproportionate—share of the state's budget. Economic development in such a large, diverse state required a commitment to highway construction, and roads were regarded as essential to the development of an integrated economy.

One scholar argued that the great distances in Texas were politically important because they made it difficult for a politician to develop a personal following, such as could be cultivated in many southern states. Size and distance deterred the development of a statewide political machine similar to those that developed in Virginia and Louisiana in the 1920s and 1930s. Although there have been regional or local political machines, such as the now-defunct Parr machine in South Texas, none extended statewide.

Size also contributes to the high cost of political campaigns. Candidates in the 2002 gubernatorial race spent more than $100 million to communicate with and mobilize Texas voters. There are twenty separate media markets in the state, and the cost of communicating with the voters is likely to increase.

Geography shaped historical migration and land use in Texas, and, although we are capable of partially compensating for climate and geography through modern technology, geography continues to shape the economies and population patterns of the state.

SOURCE: *Terry G. Jordan with John L. Bean, Jr., and William M. Holmes, *Texas: A Geography:* (Westview Press, 1984), p. 7.

percent of Texas households reported incomes less than $25,000 per year. These data obscure the fact that there are Texans who made millions of dollars in 1999 and had assets in the hundreds of millions or several billions of dollars. *Forbes* magazine conducts an annual survey of the 400 richest Americans. Thirty-six Texans made the list in 2003, including 26 billionaires with a reported worth ranging from $1.1 billion to $20.5 billion.[34]

The vast majority of Texans have incomes or assets that come nowhere near those of the super wealthy, but what is particularly distressing to many observers is that there are significant income differences among most Texans and areas of the state where poverty is very high (see *In Comparative Perspective:* "Texas and Other States").

On all measures of income, Hispanics and African Americans fall significantly below the Anglo population. According to the 2000 census, 32 percent of Hispanic households and 35 percent of African American households in Texas reported incomes below $20,000, but only 21 percent of Anglo households and a similar portion of the Asian American population reported incomes below that level. By contrast, 43 percent of Anglo households but only 25 percent of Hispanic households and 27 percent of African American households reported incomes above $50,000.[35]

Many Texans live in severe poverty. Some of the nation's poorest counties are in Texas. These are border counties (Dimmit, Hidalgo, Maverick, Starr, Willacy, Zapata, and Zavala) with large Hispanic populations and unemployment rates that are twice the state average. The per capita income (total state income divided by the population) for Texas was $19,617 in 1999. For the Anglo population, it was significantly higher, $26,197, but for African Americans, the figure was $14,253, and for Hispanics, $16,770.

In 2002, the poverty level guidelines used in Texas to establish eligibility for many federal and state programs were $18,244 for a family of four and $9,359 for one person. According to the U.S. Bureau of the Census, 15.3 percent of the state's population, or 3.3 million people, fell below the poverty level. Nationally, 12.1 percent or 34.6 million persons fell below the poverty level in 2002. The impact of poverty was felt disproportionately by children, particularly those living in one-parent households, Hispanics, and African Americans.[36]

While the state's economic growth over the last decade has reduced some poverty, scholars who look at demographic trends express concerns that it is likely to worsen in Texas if several policy issues are not addressed. Without significant changes in educational levels and expanded economic opportunities, it is possible that approximately 20 percent of the state's households will fall below the poverty level by 2030, and income disparity will be especially problematic for minorities.[37]

Financial resources can be translated into political power and influence through campaign contributions, funding one's own campaign for public office, access to the mass media, and active support for policy think tanks, interest groups, and lobbying activities. Wealth is not the only dimension of political power, but some Texans obviously have the potential for much greater clout than others.

Education and Literacy

Public education has been a dominant issue in state politics for many years now. Litigation has forced the legislature to struggle with changes in the funding of public schools, and education will be a primary factor in determining whether Texas can successfully compete in a new global economy.

Over the next decade, a large proportion of the new jobs created in Texas will be in service industries. Most of these jobs will require increased reading, writing, and math skills, and high school dropouts will find fewer and fewer employment opportunities for decent paying jobs. Some experts predict that 50 percent of the jobs that will be created in the United States in the next decade will require a college education, compared to only 22 percent in the mid-1990s.[38] Texas faces a crisis in public education, and the state's ability to resolve it will directly affect the financial well-being of many Texans.

According to the 2000 census, 75.7 percent of Texans age twenty-five and older had completed high school, and 23.8 percent had completed college (Table 21–4). Educational attainment improved between 1990 and 2000, and positive changes were reported for all racial or ethnic groups in the state.[39] But there continued to be wide disparities in the

IN COMPARATIVE PERSPECTIVE

TEXAS AND OTHER STATES

If you compare Texas to other states, it ranks:

#1 in percentage of nonelderly population without health insurance in 2001 (25.9%)

#2 in total resident population in 2002 (21,779,893)
in youngest median age in 2000 (32.3)

#3 in gross state product in 2002 ($791.3 billion in current dollars)
in Hispanic population in 2000 (32%)

#4 in percentage of resident population under 18 in 2000 (28.2%)

#5 in lowest voter turnout in November 2002 (33.1%)

#6 in percentage change in food stamp participation from 1997 to 2001 (-32.8%)

#7 in crime rate in 2001 (5,153 crimes per 100,000 inhabitants)

#8 in percentage change in population, 1990–2000 (22.8%)
in lowest cost of living in 2002

#9 in poverty rate in 2001 (14.9%)
in sales taxes per capita in 2000 ($1,275)

#10 in percentage of households headed by married couples in 2000 (54%)
in rate of children in poverty in 2001 (21.1%)

#11 in percentage of public elementary and secondary students eligible for free or reduced-price lunch in 2000 (44.7%)

#12 in marriage rate in 2000 (9.4 per 1,000 population)

#13 in age-adjusted death rate by AIDS in 1999 (5.4 deaths per 100,000 population)
in violent crime rate in 2001 (572.8 per 100,000 population)

#14 in per capita state government general sales tax revenue in 2001 ($690)

#15 in per capita state and local government expenditures for elementary and secondary education in 1999 ($1,267)
in average annual pay in 2001 ($36,039)

#16 in per capita state and local government property taxes in 1999 ($938)

#17 in rape rate in 1999 (38 rapes per 1,000 population)

#18 in per capita gross state product in 2000 ($35,598)
in percentage change in state and local taxes from 1994 to 1999 (32.2%)

#19 in abortions in 1998 (239 per 1,000 births)
in percentage of population subscribing to wireless telephone service in 2002 (45.7%)

#20 in per capita local government revenue from federal government in 1999 ($101)

SOURCE: Texas Comptroller of Public Accounts, June 2003, Window on State Government; Hovey, *Congressional Quarterly's State Fact Finder 2003* (CQ Press, 2003).

TABLE 21–4   TEXAS AND UNITED STATES EDUCATIONAL ATTAINMENT BY RACE AND ETHNICITY 2000 (for POPULATION 25 AND OLDER)

	United States		Texas	
	High School Degree	College Degree	High School Degree	College Degree
Anglo*	85.4%	27.0%	87.2%	30.0%
Hispanic	52.4	10.5	49.3	8.9
African American	72.3	14.3	75.8	15.4
Native American	71.0	11.5	71.6	15.7
Asian	80.4	44.1	80.7	47.8
All Persons	80.4	24.4	75.7	23.8

*White, not of Hispanic origin.

SOURCE: U.S. Bureau of the Census, *2000 Census of the Population.*

educational levels of the three major ethnic–racial groups. In 2000, 87 percent of the Anglo population reported that they had completed high school, and 30 percent had college degrees. By contrast, 49 percent of the Hispanic population had high school degrees but only 8.9 percent reported that they had a college degree. Some 76 percent of African Americans graduated from high school, with 15 percent indicating they had college degrees. What is particularly compelling in the 2000 census data is the level of education reported for the Asian American population. Approximately 48 percent reported college degrees.

Education not only helps determine a person's employment and income potential but also affects his or her participation in politics. Individuals with high educational levels are much more likely to believe they can influence the actions of policy makers, be informed about politics, and participate in the political process than those who are less educated.

THE ECONOMY OF TEXAS

Politics, government, and economics are inextricably linked. An economy that is robust and expanding provides far more options to government policy makers than an economy in recession. A healthy tax base is dependent on an expanding economy, and when the economy goes through periods of recession, state and local governments are confronted with the harsh realities of having to increase taxes or cut back on public services, usually at a time when more people are in need of governmental assistance.

At the beginning of the 1980s, Texas had experienced a sustained period of growth, and state government adopted new policies and expanded existing services with only minimal tax increases. But by 1991, the state had experienced a decade of economic boom and bust with two severe recessions, and the legislature had been forced to tighten up on public services and impose a series of significant tax increases.

For much of the twentieth century, oil played a dominant role in the Texas economy, as the derricks in this photo of the town of Kilgore in the 1930s reflect. But with increased U.S. reliance on imported oil and the subsequent decline in Texas oil exploration and production, the Texas economy has become more diversified, reducing its reliance on oil and natural gas.

Historically, the health of the Texas economy had been linked to oil and natural gas. In 1981, for example, 27 percent of the state's economy was tied to energy-related industries. The decade started with rapid increases in the world price of oil, and there was an economic boom throughout the financial, construction, and manufacturing sectors of the state's economy.[40]

But a series of national and international events soon produced major problems. World oil prices began to drop in 1981, resulting in serious unemployment problems in the Gulf Coast and Plains regions of the state. There was a disastrous decline in the value of the Mexican peso, which had a negative impact on the economies of border cities and counties, and in 1983, a harsh freeze in South Texas and a severe drought in West Texas had serious adverse effects on the agricultural sector. Some regions of the state were insulated from these conditions, but other areas experienced a significant economic downturn.[41]

Economic disaster struck again in 1986, with a 60 percent drop in the price of oil and corresponding reductions in the price of natural gas. Drilling activity in the state plummeted and was followed by a loss of 84,000 energy-related jobs. The problem was compounded by a worldwide slump in the electronics industry. These events hurt the construction and real estate sectors of the economy and, in turn, manufacturing and retail trade. For sixteen straight months in 1986 and 1987, the state's employment rate dropped, with a loss of an estimated 233,000 jobs.[42]

These economic reversals had a disastrous effect on Texas's banks and savings and loan institutions. "In 1987 and 1988, more Texas financial institutions failed than at any other time since the Great Depression," the state comptroller's office reported. And the pattern of bank failures continued through 1990. The federal government developed a plan to bail out institutions that were covered by federal deposit insurance. But as the magnitude of the problem became clearer, there was a bitter debate over its causes, including the deregulation of the savings and loan and banking industries, inadequate government scrutiny of banking practices, a frenzy of speculation with questionable or unsecured loans, and outright fraud and malfeasance.[43]

State and local governments consequently suffered declines in revenues. With falling property values, local governments that depended on the property tax were particularly vulnerable. The legislature convened in special session in 1986 to pass an $875 million tax bill and cut the state budget by about $580 million in an attempt to "patch up" the widening holes in projected state revenues. In 1987, the legislature, mandated by the state constitution to a "pay as you go" system of government and denied the option of deficit financing, enacted a $5.6 billion tax bill, including an increase in the sales tax, a **regressive tax** that most adversely affects low-income people.[44]

By 1988, the economy was recovering, with slow, modest growth in most of the state. Oil and natural gas, while still important to the economy, were being replaced as the driving force in economic expansion. Increased manufacturing and the expansion of service industries, in particular, were responsible for the incremental recovery the state experienced through 1990. The state's growth rate declined slightly in 1991, reflecting broad recessionary patterns of the national economy. But beginning in 1992 and continuing through the end of the decade, there was robust growth in the state's economy that outpaced the national economy at rather significant rates. Unemployment dropped throughout the state, and business expanded across most sectors of the economy. Texas created more jobs than any other state, and personal and family income increased. New industries came to the state, and foreign exports rose. Government revenues also increased, and the state and local governments were able to expand services without significant tax increases.

But in early 2001, recessionary pressures returned with a significant decline in the state's rate of growth. Unemployment inched up, and business activity slowed down in many sectors of the economy. By late 2003, many economists argued that the recession was over, but few predicted that the recovery would be anything like the robust growth of the late 1990s. When the Texas legislature convened in early 2003, state government faced a large revenue shortfall. Lawmakers, led by a new Republican majority, made major reductions in state services to balance a new budget without

regressive tax
Tax that imposes a disproportionately heavier burden on low-income people than on the more affluent.

raising state taxes. The spending cuts affected virtually every local government across the state.

In 2003, Texas had a gross state product of $739 billion in 1996 dollars (or $827 billion in current dollars). By comparison, the gross domestic product of the United States that year was $9.7 trillion in 1996 dollars. The Texas economy was the third largest among the states, following California and New York. If Texas were a nation, its economy would rank eleventh in the world.[45]

Several lessons can be drawn from the state's economic history. Because of the significant economic changes, a number of experts believe that the state is now less vulnerable to the volatility of the energy industry. Oil and gas production has declined in the last two decades, and now only 10 percent of the state's economy is tied to oil- and gas-related industries.[46] **Economic diversification** has made the state less reliant on one dominant industry. So now, even in recessionary periods, not all sectors of the state's economy are affected the same way.

The state has created a significant number of jobs for its expanding economy. Some 2.35 million new jobs were created in Texas, more than in any other state, during the 1990s. More than half of those were linked to services and trade. Construction and government employment also expanded during this period.[47] And a restructured financial industry experienced a noticeable recovery by 1993.

Another dimension of the state's economic success has been an ever-increasing shift to high-tech industries. Many economic and political leaders believe that the state's future must be directly tied to these developing industries, and the state and many cities have developed aggressive recruitment programs that include economic development bonds and tax abatements for high-tech companies.

The term *high-tech* is generally used to describe business activities that produce new technology based on highly sophisticated scientific research and computer applications. Companies that make semiconductors, microprocessors, and computer hardware and software clearly fall into this category, as do companies that produce telecommunications devices, fiber optics, aerospace guidance systems, and some medical instruments.[48] These industries have been joined by new biotechnology industries involved in producing new medicines, vaccines, and genetic engineering of plants and animals. Houston and Dallas have emerged as centers for biotechnology, with some development also occurring in San Antonio, Austin, and Fort Worth.[49] With the cooperation and support of state universities and two major research consortia in the area, Austin also has attracted a significant number of computer-related industries.

Texas and the United States also are contributing to what is often referred to as the **globalization of the economy.** Throughout the 1980s, as world oil prices directly affected the state's economy, Texans were made keenly aware of their increased dependence on the world economy. Foreign investment in Texas business has become increasingly common. Moreover, Texas exported $95 billion in goods and services in 2001 with approximately 44 percent going to Mexico.[50] The North American Free Trade Agreement among the United States, Mexico, and Canada, which will be discussed later in this chapter, has already produced changes in the economic relationships among these countries, and more economic interdependence for North America is anticipated.

ECONOMIC REGIONS OF TEXAS

The economic diversity of Texas can be described in terms of thirteen distinct economic regions (see Figure 21–2). There are marked differences among these areas.[51] One may be undergoing rapid growth, while another may be experiencing a recession. Regions vary in population, economic infrastructures, economic performance, and rates of growth. One region's economy may be heavily dependent on only two or three industries. If one or two of those industries suffers an economic downturn, that region may have a more severe recession than the state overall. There are also marked differences in

economic diversification
Development of new and varied business activities. New businesses were encouraged to relocate or expand in Texas after the oil and gas industry, which had been the base of the state's economy, suffered a major recession in the 1980s.

globalization of the economy
Increased interdependence in trade, manufacturing, and commerce as well as most other business activities between the United States and other countries.

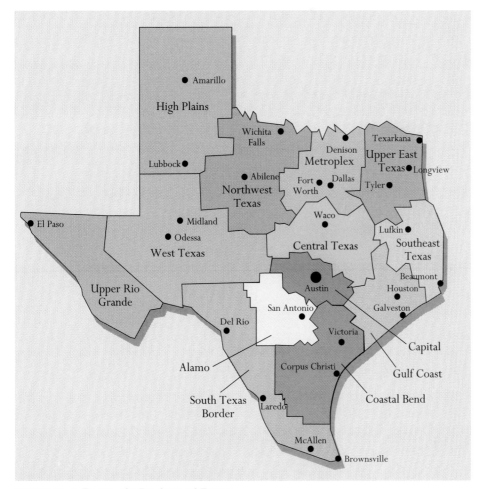

FIGURE 21–2 Economic Regions of Texas.
Source: Texas Comptroller of Public Accounts.

personal income, poverty levels, and geography among the regions. All regions, meanwhile, share in one economic sector—fairly significant levels of government employment.

Houston, linked to the Gulf Coast by a ship channel, is the second largest port city in the nation. Dallas is a major transportation hub thanks to Interstate 35, a primary north–south highway that runs from Laredo to Duluth, Minnesota. Dallas and other cities along this route have benefited from increased trade between the U.S. and Mexico.

The economic factors at play in a region help shape the priorities of local governments and the priorities of state legislators elected from that area. The following descriptions of four of the thirteen regions offer a sampling of the economic differences encountered throughout Texas (see Table 21–5).

The *High Plains Region* is made up of 41 counties and includes Amarillo, Lubbock, the XIT Ranch, and Palo Duro Canyon. Agricultural production, whose major source of water is the Ogallala Aquifer, is a dominant industry. Related businesses include agricultural services, food processing, and the manufacturing of feed, fertilizers, and farm machinery and equipment. Oil and gas production also is still an important component of the region's economy, but employment in the energy industry has declined from earlier periods. The region's population grew by only 13 percent from 1970 to 2000—to 753,000 people. Its per capita income was higher than the state average, but it is projected to produce only 20,000 new jobs in the next few years. This region had a gross regional product of $19.8 billion in 2000, which grew at an annual rate of 3.3 percent from 1970 to 2000.

TABLE 21–5 CHARACTERISTICS OF THE COMPTROLLER'S THIRTEEN ECONOMIC DISTRICTS

Economic Region of the State	Number of Counties	1970 Population	2000 Population	Percent Population Change, 1970–2000	1970 Per Capita Real Income*	2000 Per Capita Real Income*	Projected Employment 2005	Projected Average Yearly Increase in Jobs	1970 Gross Regional Product in Billions	2000 Gross Regional Product in Billions	Annual Growth Rate 1970–2000
Alamo	12	1,012,300	1,805,200	78	$11,200	$20,200	1,126,600	23,100	$15.6	$44.1	3.5
Capital	10	450,000	1,291,600	187	11,500	23,700	972,000	19,200	6.7	45.7	6.6
Central Texas	20	564,300	916,300	62	11,050	19,400	572,100	9,900	7.9	21.8	3.4
Coastal Bend	19	564,400	749,900	33	10,600	19,000	426,500	5,600	9.1	17.5	3.2
Gulf Coast	13	2,320,000	4,730,000	103	12,400	23,600	3,147,700	68,600	47.8	159.6	4.1
High Plains	41	665,900	753,400	13	13,000	21,800	505,000	6,900	10.4	19.8	3.3
Metroplex	19	2,649,900	5,284,500	99	12,600	23,800	3,961,600	97,300	49.3	193.2	4.7
Northwest Texas	30	485,700	530,700	9	12,000	21,600	338,900	4,800	7.5	12.8	1.8
South Texas Border	16	535,000	1,300,000	143	7,400	13,000	612,900	13,000	5.3	20.3	4.6
Southeast Texas	15	564,400	731,600	30	10,800	19,000	385,600	4,500	8.7	16.1	3.2
Upper East Texas	23	640,900	987,200	54	11,000	20,100	573,300	11,400	8.6	23.8	3.5
Upper Rio Grande	6	380,400	745,700	96	9,600	14,770	365,500	8,900	5.5	15.4	3.5
West Texas	30	415,900	524,100	26	12,100	20,500	325,000	4,500	9.3	14.9	1.6

*Based on 1992 dollars.

SOURCE: Texas Comptroller of Public Accounts, *Texas Regional Outlook*, 2002.

The *Metroplex Region* includes nineteen counties and, with the cities of Dallas, Fort Worth, Plano, Garland, and Arlington, has the greatest concentration of large and middle-sized cities in the state. The area is a major financial center, with regional offices of the Federal Reserve Bank and the Federal Home Loan Bank. It also has the Dallas Market Center (the world's largest trade complex) and the Dallas–Fort Worth International Airport. This region's manufacturing base is the most diversified in the state. The area is also home to growing and highly specialized electronics and communications industries. The region had a total population of 5.3 million people in 2000, doubling in numbers since 1970. Its gross regional product was approximately $193 billion in 2000, and it will generate approximately 100,000 new jobs annually over the next few years.

The *South Texas Border Region* includes the Lower Rio Grande Valley and runs to Val Verde County. This region includes some of the poorest counties in the United States and has high unemployment rates. Agriculture, livestock, and food processing are major industries in this region. This area has received a boost from the construction of the manufacturing plants in Mexico and trading benefits from the North American Free Trade Agreement (NAFTA). Laredo is the region's primary point of imports from Mexico. The population in this region, which is overwhelmingly Hispanic, increased by 143 percent over the past 30 years. Its per capita income—$13,000 in 1999—was the lowest in the state. It is projected to generate an additional 13,000 jobs annually over the next few years, and its gross regional product was $20 billion in 2000.

The six-county *Upper Rio Grande Region* is located in the Chihuahuan Desert and includes El Paso (the oldest city in Texas) and Big Bend National Park. This area has close economic ties to Mexico. Rapid industrialization has produced impressive job gains, particularly in manufacturing, since the late 1980s. NAFTA has further stimulated economic growth in this region because Juarez, a major center of manufacturing in Mexico, is just across the border. Economic and population growth on both sides of the border have increased concerns about clean air and water. The region's economy grew 3.5 percent annually over the past thirty years to produce a gross regional product of $15.4 billion in 2000. It had a population of approximately 750,000 and a per capita income of approximately $14,800 in 2000.

TRANSNATIONAL REGIONALISM

Texas shares a 1,248 mile border with Mexico, and common problems and interests that bond the two neighbors, called **transnational regionalism,** have taken on increased importance since the mid-1980s.

Historically, relations between the United States and Mexico were often strained. The United States fought a war against Mexico in 1846–48, and on subsequent occasions, American troops entered Mexican territory, ostensibly to protect United States economic and national security interests. Apprehension about U.S. objectives resulted in Mexican policies on trade, commerce, and foreign ownership of property that were designed to insulate the country from excessive foreign influence and domination. Nevertheless, the interests of the two countries have long been bound by geopolitical factors, economics, and demographics. One Mexican author has compared the interdependence of the two countries to Siamese twins, warning that "if one becomes gangrenous, the other twin will also be afflicted."[52]

Maquiladoras

Changes in the economic relationships between Mexico and the United States began with the **maquiladora program,** an initiative under Mexico's Border Industrialization Program in 1964 to boost employment, foreign exchange, and industrial development. It was also designed to transfer technology to Mexico, help train workers, and develop managerial skills among Mexican nationals.[53]

transnational regionalism
Expanding economic and social interdependence of South Texas and Mexico.

maquiladora program
Policies initiated by Mexico in 1964 to stimulate economic growth along the U.S.–Mexico border.

The concept was to develop twin plants, one in the United States and one in Mexico, under a single management. The plant in the United States would manufacture parts, and its Mexican counterpart would assemble them into a product, which, in turn, would be sent back to the United States for further processing or for shipping to customers.[54] Parts shipped into Mexico would not be subject to the normal tariffs, and the tax imposed on the assembled product would be minimal. In 1984, Mexico changed its laws to permit the United States and other foreign countries to establish these relationships throughout Mexico, rather than just on the border, and to permit 100 percent foreign ownership of the assembly plants in Mexico. The latter step was a radical departure from previous Mexican law, which prohibited such foreign ownership.[55]

The maquiladora program has not resulted in the construction of a significant number of manufacturing plants on the Texas side of the border because American companies have used existing plants throughout the United States to produce parts to be assembled in Mexico. Nevertheless, Texas's border counties have benefited through the creation of thousands of support jobs in transportation, warehousing, and services.[56] Some 3,300 maquiladora plants were in operation in 2002, providing hundreds of thousands of jobs but also contributing to increased population density on the Mexican side of the border.

With Mexico's membership (since 1986) in the international General Agreement on Tariffs and Trade (GATT)—which later became the World Trade Organization—and the implementation of the North American Free Trade Agreement, the maquiladora program continues to play a major role in transnational economic development. American organized labor opposes the program, arguing that the maquiladoras drain jobs from the United States. But the program provides a source of inexpensive labor for American businesses, which have complained for years that they cannot compete against cheap foreign labor costs.

The North American Free Trade Agreement (NAFTA)

Negotiations on a free trade agreement in 1991 marked a significant change in the relationship between Mexico and the United States. The negotiations were precipitated, in part, by world economics and the emergence of regional trading zones. But the administration of Mexican President Carlos Salinas de Gortari also was reacting to the failure of Mexico's economic policies of the 1980s and a fear of economic isolation. The end of the Cold War, a reduction in Central American conflicts, and internal population pressures were additional factors.[57]

The convergence of interests of the United States, Mexico, and Canada produced the **North American Free Trade Agreement (NAFTA)** to reduce tariffs and increase trade among the three countries. It created the world's largest trading bloc, with a combined population of approximately 400 million and a combined gross national product of more than $8 trillion in 1997.[58] Approved by the U.S. Congress in late 1993, the agreement had the strong support of the Texas business community, Governor Ann Richards, both U.S. senators from Texas, and 24 of the state's 30 members of the U.S. House of Representatives.

The treaty has increased trade among the three countries, strengthening previous economic ties and creating new ones. Texas has experienced significant economic changes from these new relationships, but the benefits have not been uniformly distributed throughout the state. The regions expected to benefit most in terms of new manufacturing jobs are the Dallas–Fort Worth area and Houston because of their concentrations of chemical and electronics industries.[59]

NAFTA'S INFRASTRUCTURE The Free Trade Commission, based in Mexico City, is the central agency responsible for implementing NAFTA. Assisted by twenty-one committees, subcommittees, and advisory groups, it is charged with resolving disputes and developing and administering procedures, measures, and standards authorized by the agreement.[60]

North American Free Trade Agreement (NAFTA)
Treaty among the United States, Canada, and Mexico that created the world's largest trading bloc. Approved by the U.S. Congress in 1993, the treaty is designed to reduce tariffs and increase trade among the three countries.

Three agencies were created under side agreements to NAFTA to help address common problems arising under the treaty. The Border Environmental Cooperation Commission (BECC) is responsible for tackling international environmental issues that face the three nations. Working with states and local communities along the U.S.–Mexican border, the agency is charged with developing plans to improve such things as water supplies, wastewater treatment, and waste disposal. It is responsible for certifying infrastructure projects for funding by the North American Development Bank, or NADBank, or other financial institutions. By the fall of 2003, it had certified 91 projects with a total cost of $1.9 billion.[61]

The North American Development Bank, which is located in San Antonio, was created by the United States and Mexico to fund infrastructure and environmental projects along the U.S.–Mexico border.[62]

The Commission for Labor Cooperation is charged with improving working conditions and living standards and strengthening the enforcement of domestic labor laws with trade sanctions and other penalties. It takes complaints from interested parties and conducts quasi-judicial proceedings with recommendations based on the labor laws of the three treaty participants.[63] The Working Group on Emergency Action addresses import surges that may adversely affect industries in the three countries.

CONTINUED CONCERNS ABOUT NAFTA AND MEXICO   Some people on both sides of the U.S.–Mexico border fear that NAFTA is harming their respective countries. Labor unions in the United States are particularly concerned that lower labor costs in Mexico have moved jobs from the United States. Mexican critics declaim the low wage scales of Mexican laborers. Some manufacturers argue that labor and capital costs in Mexico threaten their American markets. Some Texas officials and many Texas residents fear that opening up the state's highways to Mexican trucks will create safety problems, and American trucking interests, including owners and drivers, opposed the added competition. By 2004, Mexican trucks still were not allowed unlimited movement in all fifty states, despite treaty provisions to the contrary. The Bush administration was prepared to carry out the free access provisions, but opponents continued to fight by forcing Mexican trucks and drivers to comply with U.S. standards. In Mexico, there is concern that American corporations will dominate and reduce Mexico's control over its own economy since more than 80 percent of Mexico's exports are going to the United States. And, finally, environmentalists have argued that increased commerce will compound air and water pollution problems on both sides of the border.

A number of American critics of NAFTA also have raised questions about Mexican political corruption, the stability of the country, increased drug smuggling into the United States, human rights violations, and the longtime domination of Mexican politics by the Institutional Revolutionary Party (PRI).

Drug-related violence and alleged collusion between high-ranking Mexican officials and drug smugglers have raised questions about Mexico's ability to fight the drug problem. In recent years, there has been considerable violence among the competing drug cartels in Mexico, and several Mexican government officials responsible for enforcing drug laws have been murdered.

Efforts to control drug smuggling along the border have had only limited success because the border is simply too long and cross-border traffic too heavy. Thousands of trucks cross from Mexico into the United States each day. The flood of illegal immigration into the United States from Mexico also is an issue, which will be discussed in more detail later in this chapter.

The potential for political instability in Mexico surfaced dramatically with the uprising on January 1, 1994, of the Zapatistas, a peasant-based guerrilla movement centered in Chiapas. Although some efforts were made to address the Zapatistas' grievances, the massacre of 45 people in late December of 1997 by gunmen with alleged links to the ruling party cast more shadows on Mexico's political system.

Presidential candidate Luis Donaldo Colosio was assassinated in March of 1994, and José Francisco Ruiz Massieu, secretary general of the ruling party, was murdered in September of that year. There are still widespread suspicions in the United States and Mexico that officials of the ruling party were involved in these murders.

With the devaluation of the peso in late 1994 and the beginning of a serious Mexican recession in 1995, there was further concern about the instability of the Mexican economy and its potential for destabilizing the Mexican political system. The Clinton Administration responded with an economic rescue plan for Mexico. President Clinton maintained that the collapse of the Mexican economy threatened to weaken the U.S. dollar, hurt exports, and generate disruption in other Latin American countries. It also was feared that social unrest could spill over into the United States, with an increase in illegal immigration.[64] The Mexican government responded with austere economic measures and repaid its guaranteed loans before they were due. By early 1997, there were signs that the Mexican economy was slowly improving, but concerns about corruption and social unrest continued.

For more than 70 years, Mexico operated with a one-party system dominated by the Institutional Revolutionary Party (PRI), a situation which many argue contributed to widespread corruption. When Vicente Fox Quesada, a candidate of the largest opposition party, the National Action Party (PAN), captured the presidency in 2000, there was hope that he would initiate widespread reforms in the economy, the bureaucracy, the military, and law enforcement. Some changes have occurred, but the task he faced was daunting, with formidable entrenched opposition.

President Fox and President Bush had developed a cooperative relationship when they served as governors of their respective states, and most observers assumed that this cooperation would extend into their presidencies. Initially, it did, but their relationship soured in 2003 when Mexico, along with most other members of the United Nations, refused to endorse America's military action against Iraq. Relations between the two countries further eroded because of a dispute over water allocations from the Rio Grande under a 1944 treaty and the perception that the Bush administration was giving little attention to the interests of Mexico and other Latin American countries.

TABLE 21–6   TEXAS AND U.S. EXPORTS TO MEXICO, 1993–2002

Year	Texas Exports to Mexico	U.S. Exports to Mexico	Texas as a Percent of U.S.
1993	$20,379,583,586	$41,581,100,000	49.01%
1994	$23,849,512,126	$50,843,500,000	46.91
1995	$21,863,455,716	$46,292,100,000	47.23
1996	$27,036,930,968	$56,791,500,000	47.61
1997	$31,172,597,636	$71,388,400,000	43.67
1998	$36,328,363,149	$78,772,500,000	46.12
1999*	$37,860,871,019	$87,044,038,183	43.50
2000	$47,761,021,704	$111,720,877,976	42.75
2001	$41,647,797,064	$101,503,075,013	41.03
2002	$41,647,027,169	$97,530,612,979	42.70
% Change, 1993–2002		104.36%	134.56%

*Note: The Massachusetts Institute for Social and Economic Research applied a more advanced algorithm to data beginning in 1999. Thus, the post-1998 export figures more accurately account for unreported exports by states and therefore more accurately reflect actual export revenue than do pre-1999 figures.

SOURCE: Massachusetts Institute for Social and Economic Research and the U.S. Census Bureau (based on "origin of movement to port" state-level data series); Texas Department of Economic Development, April 2000.

Trade Patterns between Texas and Mexico

The United States and Texas clearly profit from Mexico's prosperity. U.S. exports to Mexico were $12.4 billion in 1986 and $97.5 billion in 2002 (see Table 21–6). Imports from Mexico, now the United States's second largest trading partner, were $134 billion in 2002.[65] Texas exported more than $41 billion worth of goods, comprising close to six percent of the state's gross economy, to Mexico in 2002. Texas's exports to Mexico had increased dramatically from the $8.8 billion exported in 1987. These exports create hundreds of thousands of jobs in Texas.

The sheer volume of the movement of goods, services, and people is obvious on the highways leading into Mexico and the long lines of autos and trucks at border crossings in Brownsville, Laredo, and El Paso. There are an estimated 100 million legal border crossings into Texas from Mexico each year. More than 10,000 trucks cross the border each day at Laredo, the nation's largest inland port, and this number will continue to increase. Billions of dollars are required to upgrade and expand the roads, highways, bridges, water and sanitation systems, and other facilities on both sides of the border. Some initiatives have been taken by both countries, but many of the facilities will not be completed for years, contributing to delays and gridlock in both countries. As noted earlier, the North American Development Bank was established, in part, to address these needs.

The U.S. government's response to the terrorist attacks of September 11, 2001, will further compound the congestion on the border. New border security procedures imposed by the United States may impede the flow of goods, cost individuals an untold amount of time waiting in long lines, and generate hostility from Mexican citizens because the same criteria are not applied to visitors from other countries.[66]

Common Borders, Common Problems

To anyone living on the border, the economic interdependence of the United States and Mexico is evident every day. Thousands of pedestrians, cars, and trucks move across the international bridges, to and from the commercial centers on both sides of the Rio Grande. When the Mexican economy suffered a precipitous decline in 1982, the peso devaluation severely disrupted the Texas border economy, causing unemployment to skyrocket and a considerable number of U.S. businesses to fail.

While much of the effort toward improving relations between the United States and Mexico has focused on potential economic benefits, other complex problems confronting both countries also merit attention.

One is health care. On both sides of the border, many children have not been immunized against basic childhood diseases. On the Texas side are more than 1,200 *colonias*—rural, unincorporated slums that have substandard housing, roads, and drainage and, in many cases, lack water and sewage systems. These conditions have contributed to severe health problems, including hepatitis, dysentery, and tuberculosis. Higher than normal numbers of both Texan and Mexican children along the border also have been born with serious birth defects. Public health facilities in Texas report that Mexican women come across the border to give birth to their children in American facilities. This practice, which has the effect of creating "binational families," increases the burden on public hospitals—and taxpayers—in Texas. Children born in the United States are U.S. citizens and are entitled to various public services.[67]

Industrial development and population growth along the border also increase environmental problems. U.S. antipollution laws have been more stringent than those of Mexico, but air and water pollution generated in Mexico does not stop at the border. The side agreements to NAFTA provide a basic framework for addressing these problems, but some have argued that a country such as Mexico, under enormous pressure to industrialize rapidly, is less likely to be concerned with environmental issues. In addition, U.S. efforts to impose its environmental standards on Mexico could be interpreted as another American effort to dominate the country.[68] In June 1994, several maquiladora plants in Matamoras, across the border from Brownsville, settled lawsuits alleging that

★★ You Decide

DO WELFARE REFORMS DETER ILLEGAL IMMIGRATION?

Illegal immigration continues to be a major problem in Texas. Along with provisions for amnesty and temporary status for agricultural workers, Congress enacted in 1986 penalties that imposed fines and potential jail sentences on employers who knowingly hired illegal aliens. Despite these changes in the immigration laws, the flow of illegal immigrants continued. Congress looked for additional deterrents to illegal immigration and enacted major changes in welfare laws in 1996, cutting off most public assistance to both legal and illegal immigrants in the United States.

pollution caused rare birth defects in children born in Texas. There have been numerous initiatives by both governments and private groups to deal with these common health and environmental problems, but it will take years to see widespread improvements.

Regional interdependence, while perhaps not recognized by most people on both sides of the border, has taken on greater importance in the press and in the academic, business, and labor communities in the United States. Transnational public policies are emerging, creating legal issues in product liability, insurance, copyrights, and patents that must still be resolved. The governors of Mexican and U.S. border states have their own association, the Border Governors Conference, which meets regularly to discuss such issues as free trade, the environment, education, and tourism.

Recent Texas governors have supported efforts to improve relations with Mexico, and Texas state agencies have been given increased authority to work in cooperative efforts with Mexican officials.[69] Private groups have also organized to address transnational issues and pressure governments on both sides of the border to develop policies and allocate resources to resolve common problems.

Illegal Immigration

Population growth in Texas has always been affected by migration from other states and foreign countries. But the proximity of Texas to Mexico has put the state in the center of a long-running dispute over the illegal immigration of large numbers of Mexicans and other Latin Americans. In 2002, there were an estimated 7.9 million people, mostly from Mexico and Central America, living in the United States illegally.[70] Many enter through Texas and continue on to other areas of the country, but others remain in the state. The actual number of illegal immigrants in Texas will never be known because they don't participate in studies or report their status, but the most recent estimates are 600,000 to one million.[71]

The failure of the Mexican economy and the attraction of employment opportunities north of the border have been major reasons for this migration, although political instability and persecutions in Central America have also been significant factors. Large portions of the Texas and American economies were built on the availability of cheap,

A U.S. Border Patrol officer keeps watch along the U.S.–Mexico border.

low-skilled Mexican labor.[72] If arrested, illegal workers are returned to Mexico, but, until recently, it was not illegal for American employers to hire them.[73]

In 1986, the U.S. Congress enacted the Immigration Reform and Control Act, which imposed fines on employers who hired illegal aliens and provided jail sentences for flagrant violators (see You Decide *Thinking It Through* "Do Welfare Reforms Deter Immigration?"). Potential employees had to provide documentation, and employers had to verify their employees' citizenship or residency status. The new law also provided a means for giving legal status, or amnesty, to hundreds of thousands of illegal immigrants who had moved to the United States prior to January 1, 1982. It also provided for temporary status for agricultural workers who could satisfy specific residency requirements.[74]

Additional legislation was passed in 1996 to increase funds for border guards and inspectors, to increase penalties for smuggling people into the United States and using fraudulent documents, to construct fences along the border, and to make it easier to detain and deport illegal immigrants.[75] But by 2004, it was clear that these laws had not stemmed the tide of illegal immigration, because Mexicans and other nationalities were still drawn to the economic opportunities available in the United States. Throughout the Southwest, hundreds of thousands of illegal aliens were still being arrested and detained before being returned home, and the movement of Mexican workers into Texas and the rest of the United States remained a controversial political issue.

Children of illegal immigrants can represent a heavy financial burden for many school districts and taxpayers along the border. Undocumented workers also increase demands on public health care programs. Some citizens, particularly unskilled workers, view the illegal arrivals as a threat to their jobs and standard of living.[76]

There is a widespread complaint in Texas that the state's citizens carry the burden for the failure of the federal government to develop policies to stem the illegal flow. In 1994, Texas joined several other states in filing lawsuits seeking reimbursement from the federal government for billions of dollars in state and local expenditures attributed to illegal immigration.

One of the unspoken realities of illegal immigration in Texas is that many native Texans have no desire to curtail the flow of people from the south. Within blocks of where one of the authors works, there are household domestics, nannies, and yardmen who are "illegals," and neighbors know their status. Numerous businesses throughout the state hire illegal immigrants for low-wage labor, despite the legal and financial risks. Good, law-abiding citizens have hired undocumented workers for temporary, contract jobs and never asked their status, as required by law. There are so many "illegals" in Texas that the responsible federal agencies simply cannot always enforce the law. As a source of cheap labor, the illegal immigrant is, in effect, subsidizing business interests and others throughout the state. State funds that are spent for social services for the immigrants also are a subsidy.

★★ THINKING IT THROUGH

Critics of the previous welfare system had argued that the accessibility of public funds and services was a strong attraction to immigrants. They argued that American taxpayers had no obligation to support anyone who entered the country illegally or even legal immigrants who couldn't support themselves.

With some exceptions for medical emergencies, the 1996 welfare law barred illegal immigrants from receiving benefits provided by a federal agency or by federal funds, including welfare, retirement, health, disability, food assistance, or unemployment benefits. States are also prohibited from providing state or local benefits to illegal immigrants unless state officials pass specific laws making immigrants eligible for aid from state or local funds.

These welfare changes were designed to discourage persons who are unable to support themselves and perceive the possibility of easy access to public assistance from immigrating to the United States.

But do these changes deter immigrants who come to the United States to escape desperate economic, political, or social conditions in their own countries?

Several years have now passed, and there is considerable evidence that welfare restrictions are not deterring legal or illegal immigration.

After a few years, there appeared to be a decline in the use of the welfare system by immigrants. But by 2002 participation rates in welfare programs just about matched the figures for 1996, the year the law was enacted. There were reductions in the use of Temporary Assistance to Needy Families and food stamp funds, but they were offset by a dramatic increase in participation in Medicaid. Based on a national study completed in 2001, the average support for low-income immigrant households was approximately $2,000. For the illegal immigrant household, the figure was $1,000.

Source: Jeffrey L. Katz, "Welfare Overhaul Law," *Congressional Quarterly Weekly Report*, 54 (September 21, 1996), pp. 2696–2705; Stephen A. Camarota, "Back Where We Started: An Examination of Trends in Immigrant Welfare Use Since Welfare Reform," Center for Immigration Studies, March, 2003; *San Antonio Express News*, September 4, 2001.

S U M M A R Y

1. Texas has experienced significant demographic, social, and economic changes over the past four decades that have transformed state politics, governmental institutions, and public policy.

2. Political myths provide Texans with generalized views of the state, its common historical experience, its people, and its institutions.

3. The conservative politics of the state are rooted in its individualistic and traditionalistic political subcultures. The beliefs Texans hold about what government should do, who should govern, and what constitutes good public policy are rooted in these cultural patterns.

4. Demographically, Texans are diverse. The population continues to increase at a rapid pace, with the most significant increases among Hispanics and Asian Americans. The state will have a "major-

ity minority" population in the first quarter of the twenty-first century.

5. Race and economics have historically shaped Texas's politics. Largely excluded from participation in the past, racial and ethnic groups are quickly acquiring political influence and power that will continue to increase in the future.

6. The rural frontier has passed. Texas is an urban state, with more than eight out of ten Texans living in urban areas.

7. The disparities in wealth and income levels among Texans point to the political influence of class as well as of race and ethnicity.

8. The educational disparities among Texans follow race, ethnicity, and economics. With the exception of Asian Americans, minorities in Texas report lower levels of educational attainment than the Anglo population. Improved literacy and the development of a technologically competent work force are essential to the state's ability to compete in the global economy.

9. Over the past thirty years, Texas has experienced the normal business cycles of "booms and busts." But the state's economy has diversified giving the state greater flexibility in dealing with economic downturns.

10. The economy of Texas is the third largest in the nation, and it is helpful to view it in terms of thirteen distinct economic regions in Texas, with significant variations in population, basic industries, growth rates, and overall productivity. Periods of economic downturn and recovery are not felt uniformly across the state.

11. The Texas economy is bound to the economy of Mexico. This development has occurred rapidly over the past twenty years, stimulated, in part, by Mexico's maquiladora program, the North American Free Trade Agreement, Mexico's membership in the World Trade Organization, and the globalization of the state's economy.

12. Texas shares a 1,200-mile border with Mexico. The two countries also share many common problems, including illegal immigration, drug smuggling, and environmental concerns. Transnational regionalism speaks to the increased interdependence of the two countries and the necessity for governments on both sides of the Rio Grande to collaborate on solutions.

KEY TERMS

republic
individualism
political culture
individualistic subculture

moralistic subculture
traditionalistic subculture
elite
urbanization

population density
regressive tax
economic diversification
globalization of the economy

transnational regionalism
maquiladora program
North American Free Trade
 Agreement (NAFTA)

FURTHER READING

BUENGER, WALTER L., AND ROBERT A. CALVERT, EDS. *Texas through Time: Evolving Interpretations* (Texas A&M University Press, 1991). An analysis of Texas myths, emphasizing potential distortions of the state's history and the need to utilize critical historical analysis to provide a more accurate understanding of Texans and their historical experiences.

CHAMPAGNE, ANTHONY AND EDWARD J. HARPHAM. "The Changing Political Economy of Texas," in *Texas Politics: A Reader,* eds. Anthony Champagne and Edward J. Harpham (W.W. Norton, 1997), pp. 3–15. An analysis of economic changes in Texas that shape contemporary politics.

ELAZAR, DANIEL. *American Federalism: A View from the States.* (Thomas Y. Crowell, 1966). A ground-breaking analysis of American federalism focusing on the collaborative aspects of state–federal relationships with emphasis on the political culture of states.

FEHRENBACH, T. R. *Lone Star: A History of Texas and the Texans* (Macmillan, 1968). One of the most comprehensive histories of Texas. A must for the serious student of Texas history and politics.

HILL, KIM QUAILE. *Democracy in the Fifty States* (University of Nebraska Press, 1994). A provocative "comprehensive, empirical, theory-based analysis of the extent to which the governments of the fifty states can be judged to be democratic and of the policy consequences of the degree to which they are democratic."

JORDAN, TERRY G., WITH JOHN L. BEAN JR. AND WILLIAM M. HOLMES. *Texas: A Geography* (Westview Press, 1984). An excellent introduction to the physical, demographic, economic, and cultural geography of Texas.

LANGLEY, LESTER D. *MexAmerica: Two Countries, One Future* (Crown, 1988). A highly readable perspective on the impact of Mexican immigration on the politics, economy, policies, and culture of the United States.

McCOMB, DAVID G. *Texas: A Modern History* (University of Texas Press, 1989). A brief narrative history that provides a quick introduction to Texans, their culture, and their experiences.

METZ, LEON C. *Border: The U.S.–Mexico Line* (Mangan Books, 1989). A chronicle of the nearly 2,000-mile U.S.–Mexican border through "the eyes and experiences of government agents, politicians, soldiers, revolutionaries, outlaws, Indians, developers, illegal aliens, business people, and people looking for work."

MURDOCK, STEVE H., MD. NAZRUL HOQUE, MARTHA MICHAEL, STEVE WHITE, AND BEVERLY PECOTTE. *The Texas Challenge: Population Change and the Future of Texas* (Texas A&M University Press, 1997). Using extensive demographic data, the authors point to future problems for the state if significant educational and economic disparities among racial, ethnic and economic groups are not addressed.

O'CONNOR, ROBERT F., ED. *Texas Myths* (Texas A&M University Press, 1986). Utilizing the general concept of myth, these fourteen essays address various aspects of the state's history and political culture.

RICHARDSON, RUPERT N., ERNEST WALLACE, AND ADRIAN N. ANDERSON. *Texas: The Lone Star State*, 7th ed. (Prentice Hall, 1997). A comprehensive text on the history of Texas.

WRIGHT, BILL. *The Tigua: Pueblo Indians of Texas* (Texas Western Press, 1993). A pictorial history of the Tiguas.

ZAMORA, EMILIO. *The World of the Mexican Worker in Texas* (Texas A&M University Press, 1993). A history of Mexican labor in the early part of the twentieth century.

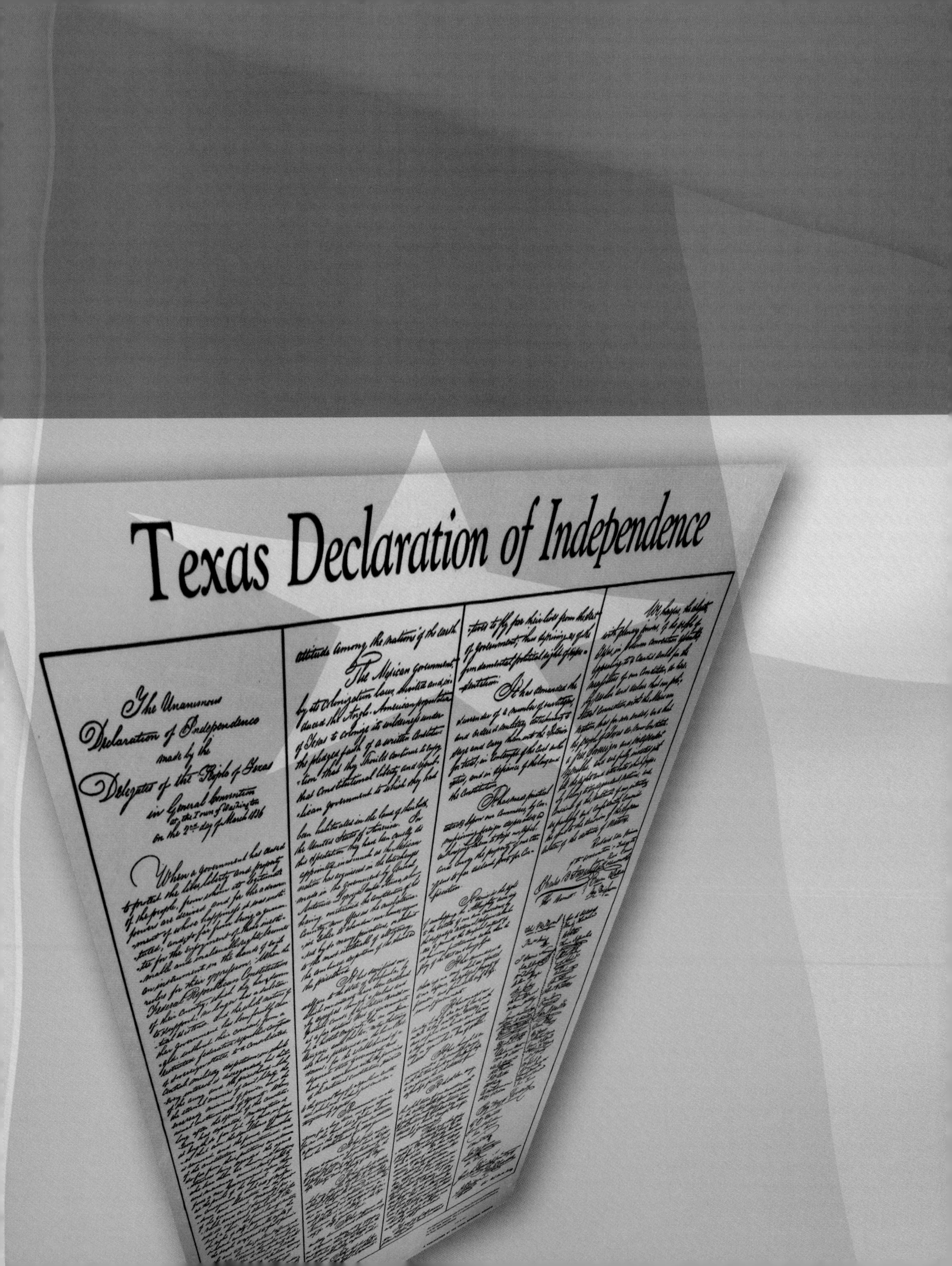

Texas Declaration of Independence

The Unanimous
Declaration of Independence
made by the
Delegates of the People of Texas
in General Convention
at the Town of Washington
on the 2nd day of March 1836

THE TEXAS CONSTITUTION

22

THE CONSTITUTIONAL LEGACY

The year was 1874, and unusual events marked the end of the darkest chapter in Texas history—the Reconstruction era and the military occupation that followed the Civil War. Texans, still smarting from some of the most oppressive laws ever imposed on American citizens, had overwhelmingly voted their governor out of office, but he refused to leave the Capitol and hand over his duties to his elected successor. For several tense days, the city of Austin was divided into two armed camps of people—those supporting the deposed governor, Edmund J. Davis, and those supporting the man who defeated him at the polls, Richard Coke. Davis finally gave up only after the Texas militia turned against him and marched on the Capitol.

That long-ago period bears little resemblance to modern Texas, but the experience still casts a long shadow over state government. The state constitution written by Texans at the close of Reconstruction was designed to put strong restraints on government to guard against future abuses, and most of those restraints remain in place today. The Texas Constitution, adopted in 1876 and amended many times since, is so restrictive that many scholars and politicians believe it is counterproductive to effective modern governance. They believe the document, which is bogged down with statutory detail, is a textbook example of what a constitution should *not* be. State government functions despite its constitutional shackles: a weak chief executive, an outdated and part-time legislature, a poorly organized judiciary, and dedicated funds that limit the state's budgetary options. But a total rewriting of the Constitution has been elusive, thanks to numerous special interests that find security in the present document—from holders of obsolete offices to beneficiaries of dedicated funds and bureaucrats who fear change. Public ignorance and indifference to the

TIME LINE

THE TEXAS CONSTITUTION

1821	Mexico wins its independence
1827	Constitution of the state of Coahuila y Tejas
1836	Texans win war of independence and create the Republic of Texas
1845	Texas adopts a state constitution and is annexed by the United States in 1846
1861	Texas secedes from the Union, joins the Confederacy, and rewrites its constitution
1865	End of Civil War but state is administered by a military government
1866	Adoption of new short-lived constitution with military government soon reinstated
1869	New post-Civil War constitution adopted to meet demands of U.S. government
1875	Constitutional Convention enacts a highly restrictive constitution that is implemented in 1876
1919	Voters reject a proposal for a constitutional convention
1967	Voters reject a proposal for a constitutional convention
1974	Constitutional convention fails to adopt a new constitution
2003	Texas has one of the longest state constitutions, with more than 100,000 words

constitution
Legal structure of a political system, establishing governmental bodies and defining their powers.

statutory law
Law enacted by a legislative body.

problems created by the restrictive constitutional provisions also thwart an overhaul of the document.

It is our opinion, shared by others who study state governments, that one cannot develop a clear understanding of Texas government or its politics without some familiarity and understanding of the Texas constitution.[1] Constitutions are more than the formal frameworks that define the structure, authority, and responsibilities of governmental institutions. They also reflect fundamental political, economic, and power relationships as determined by the culture, values, and interests of the people who create them and the events of the period in which they were written.[2]

The constitution of Texas is not an easy read, and one can quickly get bogged down in details that make little sense to the casual reader. But a careful study of the document will provide insights into the distribution of power among competing groups and regions within the state. The constitution outlines the powers of the state and local governments, and it defines the limitations imposed on these governments. The constitution also speaks to "the relation of the state to economic activity, including both the extent of direct governmental support for enterprise and the appropriate balance between promotion and regulation of economic development."[3]

Texas has had seven constitutions, and understanding that legacy is critical to understanding contemporary Texas politics and public policy (see Table 22–1). The first constitution was adopted in 1827, when the state was still part of Mexico. The second was drafted when Texas declared its independence from Mexico in 1836 and became a republic, and the third was adopted in 1845, when the state joined the Union. The fourth constitution was written when Texas joined the Confederacy in 1861, and the fifth was adopted when the state rejoined the Union in 1866. The sixth constitution was adopted in 1869 to satisfy the Radical Reconstructionists' opposition to the 1866 constitution, and the seventh constitution was adopted in 1876 after the termination of Reconstruction policies. Each of Texas's seven constitutions was written in a distinct historical setting. And although there are significant differences among these documents, each contributed to the state and local governments that exist in Texas today.

The Texas Constitution in a Comparative Perspective

The formal legal language of a **constitution** often obscures the general objectives of the document and its relevance to contemporary issues of political power and public policy. Scholars believe, first, that constitutions should be brief and should include general principles rather than specific legislative provisions. In other words, constitutions should provide a basic framework for government and leave the details to be developed in **statutory law.** Second, these experts say, constitutions should make direct grants of authority to specific institutions, so as to increase the responsiveness and the accountability of individuals elected or appointed to public office. Scholars also believe that constitutions should provide for orderly change but should not be written in such a restrictive fashion that they require continual modifications to meet contemporary needs.[4]

Amended only twenty-seven times since its ratification in 1788, the U.S. Constitution is a concise 7,000-word document that outlines broad basic principles of authority and governance. No one would argue that the government of the 2000s is comparable to that of the 1790s, yet the flexibility of the U.S. Constitution makes it as relevant now as it was in the eighteenth century. It is often spoken of as "a living charter or document" that does not have to be continually amended to meet society's ever-changing needs and conditions. Its reinterpretations by the courts, the Congress, and the president have produced an expansion of powers and responsibilities within the framework of the original language of the document.

By contrast, the Texas constitution—like those of many other states—is an unwieldy, restrictive document (see Table 22–2). With more than 100,000 words, it has been on a life-support system—the piecemeal amendment process—for most of its existence. It is less a set of basic governmental principles than a compilation of detailed statutory

TABLE 22–1   THE SEVEN TEXAS CONSTITUTIONS

1827: Constitution of Coahuila y Tejas

The first Texas constitution, adopted in 1827. It recognized Texas as a Mexican state with Coahuila.

1836: Constitution of the Republic

The constitution, adopted March 16, 1836, by Texas colonists declaring independence from Mexico. Under this constitution, Texas functioned as an independent republic for nine years.

1845: Constitution of 1845

The constitution under which Texas was admitted to the United States.

1861: Civil War Constitution

The constitution adopted by Texans after the state seceded from the Union and joined the Confederacy in 1861.

1866: Constitution of 1866

The short-lived constitution under which Texas sought to be readmitted to the Union after the Civil War and before the Radical Reconstructionists took control of the U.S. Congress.

1869: Reconstruction Constitution

The constitution centralizing power in state government and weakening local governments. It reflected the sentiments of Radical Reconstructionists, not of most Texans.

1876: Texas Constitution

The constitution adopted at the end of Reconstruction, amended many times since, and still in effect. Highly restrictive and antigovernment, this constitution places strict limitations on the powers of the governor, the legislature, and other state officials.

language reflecting the distrust of government that was widespread in Texas when it was written. In effect, it attempts to diffuse political power among many different institutions. As drafted in 1875, it also included restrictions on elections and civil rights that were later invalidated by the U.S. Supreme Court. Those early provisions were efforts to limit the power of minority groups to fully participate in state government.[5]

The historical constitutional experiences of Texas parallel those of many southern states that have had multiple constitutions in the post–Civil War era. The southern states, Texas included, are the only states whose constitutions formally acknowledge the supremacy of the U.S. Constitution, a provision required by the Radical Reconstructionists for readmission of the former Confederate states to the Union.

The Constitution of Coahuila y Tejas, 1827

Sparsely populated Texas was part of Mexico when that country secured its independence from Spain in 1821, about the same time that Stephen F. Austin and others initiated Anglo colonization of Texas. Initially, Anglo Texans appeared to be willing to be incorporated into the Mexican political system as long as there was limited intrusion by the Mexican government into their daily affairs. In 1824 the new Republic of Mexico adopted a constitution for a federal system of government that recognized as a single state Texas and Coahuila, its neighbor south of the Rio Grande. Saltillo, Mexico, was the state capital.

The Constitution of Coahuila y Tejas, completed in 1827, provided for a **unicameral** legislature of twelve deputies, including two from Texas, elected by the people. Most of the legislators were from the more populous, Spanish-speaking Coahuila, and the laws were published in Spanish, which few Texas colonists understood. The executive department included a governor and a vice-governor. The governor enforced the law, led the state militia, and granted pardons. The constitution made Catholicism the state religion, although that requirement was not enforced among Texas's Anglo settlers. Additionally, Anglo Texans were not subject to military service, taxes, or custom duties. In effect, Texas served as a buffer between Mexico and various Native American peoples and the United States.

unicameral
A legislature consisting of a single chamber.

TABLE 22–2   TEN SHORTEST AND TEN LONGEST STATE CONSTITUTIONS (AS OF JANUARY 1, 2003)

State	Number of Constitutions	Effective Date of Current Constitution	Estimated Number of Words	Amendments Submitted to voters	Amendments Adopted
Ten Shortest State Constitutions					
New Hampshire	2	1784	9,200	283	143
Vermont	3	1793	10,286	211	53
Indiana	2	1851	10,315	75	43
Rhode Island	3	1843	10,908	105	59
North Carolina	3	1971	11,000	39	31
Utah	1	1896	11,000	154	103
Minnesota	1	1858	11,547	213	118
Kansas	1	1861	12,246	122	92
Iowa	2	1857	12,616	57	52
Montana	2	1973	13,145	49	27
Ten Longest State Constitutions					
New York	4	1895	51,700	288	215
Florida	6	1969	52,421	127	96
Louisiana	11	1975	54,112	169	113
California	2	1879	54,645	846	507
Colorado	1	1876	56,944	297	143
Arkansas	5	1874	59,500	186	89
Oregon	1	1859	63,372	468	234
Oklahoma	1	1907	74,075	329	165
Texas	7	1876	100,000	605	432
Alabama	6	1901	340,136	1,024	743

But with increased Anglo immigration and the perceived threat of U.S. imperial or expansionary policies, Mexico soon attempted to extend its control over Texas. This effort reinforced cultural differences between the Anglo and Spanish populations and would eventually lead to revolution by Anglo Texans.[6]

This formative period produced some enduring contributions to the Texas constitutional tradition. Elements of the Mexican legal system are still found in property and land laws, water laws and water rights, and community property laws. One justification for the Revolution of 1836 was the failure of the Mexican government to provide sufficient funding for public education. But while there were expectations of funding by the central government, a "concept of local control over school development was firmly established."[7] This paradox has raised a continuing constitutional question and is central to the current issue of funding public education.

The Constitution of the Republic of Texas, 1836

During the late 1820s and the early 1830s, increased immigration from the United States into the territory of Texas heightened tensions between the Anglo settlers and the Mexican government. Mexico's efforts to enforce its laws within Texas produced conflicts between cultures, legal traditions, and economic interests that resulted in open rebellion by the colonists.

At the same time, Mexico was embroiled in its own internal dissension. It struggled to stabilize its political system but did not have the legacy or social and political institutions to ensure a successful democratic system. In many respects, the events in Texas were a footnote to the power politics in Mexico. Had the autonomy of Texas that was provided for under the Mexican Constitution of 1824 been maintained, the history of this region might well have been different.

Increased internal conflict among competing Mexican interests resulted in the seizure of power by the popular general Antonio López de Santa Anna Perez de Lebron. Santa Anna began to systematically suspend the powers of the Mexican Congress and local governments, and in October 1835, the national Constitution of 1824 was voided. Mexico adopted a new constitution providing for a **unitary system** with power centralized in the national Congress and the presidency. The principle of **federalism,** which divided power and authority between the national government and the states, was repudiated. This major change intensified conflict between the national government and the Mexican states. Texas was not the only area of Mexico where the principles of federalism were highly regarded, and although Texas was eventually successful in establishing its autonomy, several other rebellious Mexican states were subjected to harsh military retaliation.

As the Mexican government under Santa Anna attempted to regain control over Texas, colonists who initially supported the national government and those who expressed ambivalence were slowly converted to the cause of independence. Stephen F. Austin had consistently supported the position that Texas was a Mexican state, and he represented the views of a large part of the Anglo population living in Texas. But when Mexican troops moved across the Rio Grande into Texas in the autumn of 1835, Austin sent out a call for resistance.

The numerous special interests that later were to obstruct the course of constitutional development in Texas were missing at the small settlement of Washington-on-the-Brazos in 1836. The 59 male colonists who convened to declare Texas's independence from Mexico on March 2 and to adopt a constitution for the new republic two weeks later had two overriding interests: the preservation of their fledgling nation and the preservation of their own lives. By the time they had completed their work, the Alamo—only 150 miles away—had fallen to a large Mexican army under Santa Anna, and a second Mexican force had arrived north of the Rio Grande. Accordingly, the constitution writers wasted little time on speech making.

Consequently, the Constitution of the Republic, adopted on March 16, 1836, was not cluttered with the details that weaken the present Texas constitution. It drew heavily on the U.S. Constitution, and since 44 of the 59 delegates were from the South, from the constitutions of several southern states. The document created an elected **bicameral** Congress and provided for an elected president. Members of the clergy were prohibited from serving as president or in Congress, and there was no official, state-preferred religion. Slavery was legal, but importation of slaves from any country other than the United States was illegal. Free African Americans had to have Congress's permission to leave Texas.

Approximately six weeks after the disastrous defeat at the Alamo, the Texas army, under Sam Houston, defeated Santa Anna's army at the battle of San Jacinto on April 21, 1836. The war of independence had been relatively short and involved limited casualties, but the problems of creating a stable political system under the new constitution were formidable. There was no viable government in place, no money for paying the costs of government, and no party system. And although defeated, Mexico did not relinquish its claim to Texas and was to demonstrate in subsequent actions that it wanted to regain this lost territory. Nevertheless, the "transition from colony to constitutional republic was accomplished quickly and with a minimum of disorganization."[8]

Independence and national autonomy from 1836 to 1845 contributed significantly to the development of a sense of historical uniqueness among Texans. While the effects on the state's political psyche may be difficult to measure, the "Lone Star" experience has been kept alive through school history texts, the celebration of key events, and the development of a mythology of the independence period.

The Constitution of 1845

During the independence movement and immediately thereafter, some Texans made overtures to the United States to annex Texas, but they were initially blocked by the issue of slavery and its relationship to economic and regional influence in U.S. politics. Increased immigration to Texas in the late 1830s and early 1840s, more interest among Texans in joining the Union, and expansionist policies of the U.S. government stepped

unitary system
Constitutional arrangement whereby authority rests with the national government; subnational governments have only those powers given them by the national government.

federalism
Constitutional arrangement in which power is formally divided between national and subnational governments.

bicameral
A legislature consisting of two chambers.

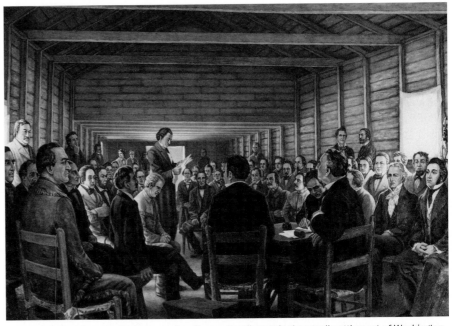

Faced with the advancing Mexican armies, Texans hastily met in the small settlement of Washington-on-the-Brazos, declared their independence on March 2, 1836, and wrote the Constitution of the Republic, which was adopted on March 16, 1836.

up pressures for annexation. It was a major issue in the U.S. presidential campaign of 1844, and the election of James K. Polk accelerated the move toward Texas's admission to the United States in 1845.

The annexation bill approved by the U.S. Congress included a compromise that allowed slavery to continue in Texas.[9] Racial issues that emerged from this period continue to shape contemporary politics and public policy in the state. Texas still struggles with voting rights issues, inequities in funding of education, and the maldistribution of economic resources that directly affect the quality of life of many minorities.

The terms of Texas's admission into the Union also provided that Texas could divide itself into as many as five states, a provision largely forgotten until State Representative David Swinford, a Republican from Dumas, made such a proposal in 1991. The idea attracted some newspaper headlines and some interest in the Panhandle, which is geographically isolated from most of Texas, but was not given serious consideration by Swinford's colleagues.

The state constitution drafted to allow Texas's annexation was about twice as long as the constitution of 1836. It borrowed not only from its predecessor but also from the constitutions of other southern states, particularly Louisiana.

The constitution of 1845 created an elected legislature that met biennially and included a house of representatives and a senate. It provided for an elected governor and an elected lieutenant governor, and it empowered the governor to appoint a secretary of state, attorney general, and state judges, subject to senate confirmation. The legislature chose a comptroller, treasurer, and land commissioner. But in 1850, Texas voters amended the constitution to make most state offices elective. In this respect, Texas was following a national pattern of fragmenting the powers of the executive branch of state government. Today Texas still has a plural executive system under which practically all statewide officeholders are elected independently of the governor, a system that contrasts sharply with the appointive cabinet system of executive government enjoyed by the president of the United States.

The constitution of 1845 protected private homesteads from foreclosure, guaranteed separate property rights for married women, and established a permanent fund for the support of public schools—provisions also found in the present constitution. The 1845 charter also recognized slavery, prohibited anyone who had ever participated in a duel from holding public office, and prohibited state-chartered banks. This constitution "worked so well that after several intervening constitutions, the people of Texas recopied it almost in toto as the Constitution of 1876."[10]

The Civil War Constitution, 1861

When Texas seceded from the Union in 1861, just before the outbreak of the Civil War, the state constitution was again revised. Although most of the provisions of the 1845 document were retained, significant changes were made in line with Texas's new membership in the Confederacy. Public officials were required to pledge their support of the Confederate constitution, greater protection was given to slavery, and the freeing of slaves was prohibited.

Any semblance of a two-party system had been destroyed by the issues of slavery and secession during the 1850s, and state politics was dominated by personalities and factions. Factionalism within the Democratic party persisted for more than 100 years, until the emergence of a two-party system in the 1980s.

The Civil War era also contributed to a legacy of states' rights, which was to persist well into the next century and spark an extended struggle for desegregation. Theoretically, the constitutional issue of the Civil War was whether a state, once having joined the Union, could leave it. The southern states subscribed to a view of the national government as a **confederacy,** and it was their position that a state could withdraw, or secede. Although the northern victory dispelled this interpretation, Texas, along with other southern states, found ways to thwart national policy through the 1960s. Their efforts were based, in part, on their continued arguments for states' rights.

The Constitution of 1866

After the Civil War, Texas was subject to national control through, first, a military government, then a provisional government headed by A. J. Hamilton, a former U.S. congressman who had remained loyal to the Union. These were dark days for Texans. Although the state had experienced relatively few battles and had not suffered from the scorched-earth tactics used by Union generals elsewhere, the economy was in disarray. Many Texas families had also lost loved ones, and many surviving Confederate veterans had been wounded physically or psychologically. Although the national government developed policies to assist the newly freed slaves, these policies were never fully funded and were halfheartedly—and often dishonestly—carried out. And the presence of an occupation army heightened tension and shaped subsequent political attitudes.

The reconstruction plan initiated by President Abraham Lincoln but never fully implemented envisioned a rapid return to civilian government for the southern states and their quick reintegration as equals into the national political system. Requirements were modest: the abolition of slavery, the repudiation of the Secession Ordinance of 1861, and the repudiation of all debts and obligations incurred under the Confederacy.[11]

Texas voters revived the Constitution of 1845 and amended it to include the stipulations required by the national government. Although slavery was eliminated and the freed slaves were given the right to hold property and were accorded legal rights before a jury, black people could not testify in any court case involving whites. And African Americans were denied the right to vote. The new constitution was adopted in June 1866, a new government was elected, and on August 20, 1866, President Andrew Johnson "declared the rebellion in Texas at an end."[12]

In short order, however, the mild reconstruction policies of Johnson were replaced by the severe policies of the **Radical Reconstructionists** who captured control of Congress in 1866. The new Texas constitution was invalidated by Congress, which passed, over the president's veto, the Reconstruction Acts that established military governments throughout the South. The civilian government initiated by the state constitution of 1866 was short-lived, and Texas functioned for two years under a reinstituted military government.

This period had an enduring impact on Texas constitutional law and politics. In a broad sense, it prolonged the full reintegration of Texas into the national political system,

confederacy
National government created by states that relies on the states for its authority.

Radical Reconstructionists
The group of Republicans who took control of the U.S. Congress in 1866 and imposed hated military governments on the former Confederate states after the Civil War.

A Union general and later governor of Texas (1870–74), Edmund J. Davis conducted one of the most oppressive administrations in U.S. history. Texas reacted to such practices with restrictions built into the constitution of 1876.

and, in specific terms, it transformed the constitutional tradition of Texas into one of hostility and suspicion toward government.

The Reconstruction Constitution, 1869

The Reconstruction Acts required a Texas constitution that would grant African Americans the right to vote and include other provisions acceptable to the U.S. Congress. A Republican slate of delegates to a new state constitutional convention produced a new charter that was published in 1869. It did not reflect the majority Texas sentiment of the time, but it conformed to Republican wishes. Centralizing more powers in state government while weakening local government, it gave the governor a four-year term and the power to appoint other top state officials, including members of the judiciary. It provided for annual legislative sessions, gave African Americans the right to vote, and, for the first time, provided for a centralized, statewide system of public schools. Texans were unhappy enough with their new constitution, but the widespread abuses of the document that followed under the oppressive and corrupt administration of Radical Republican Governor Edmund J. Davis paved the way for the shackles on state government that are still in place today.

In the 1869 election, the first under the new constitution, the military governor certified that Davis, a former Union Army officer, beat conservative Republican A. J. Hamilton by 39,901 to 39,092 votes. This outcome was allowed despite widespread, flagrant incidents of voter fraud, which were also ignored by President Ulysses S. Grant and the U.S. Congress. A radical majority in the new Texas legislature then approved a series of authoritarian—and, in some respects, unconstitutional—laws proposed by Davis. They gave the governor the power to declare martial law and suspend the laws in any county and created a state police force under the governor's control that could deprive citizens of constitutional protections. The governor also was empowered to appoint mayors, district attorneys, and hundreds of other local officials. Another law that designated newspapers as official printers of state documents in effect put much of the press under government control.

Davis exercised some of the most repressive powers ever imposed on United States citizens. And Texans responded. First, in 1872, they elected a Democratic majority to the legislature, which abolished the state police and repealed other oppressive laws. Then, in 1873, they elected a Confederate veteran, Democrat Richard Coke, governor by more than a 2-to-1 margin over Davis. Like the Radical Republicans in the previous gubernatorial election, the Democrats were not above abusing the democratic process, and, once again, voting fraud was rampant.

As was described earlier in the chapter, Davis initially refused to leave office and appealed to President Grant for federal troops to help him retain power. Grant refused, and Davis finally gave up after the Texas militia turned against him and marched on the Capitol in January 1874. Bloodshed was avoided, Reconstruction was ending, and the constitution of 1869 was doomed.

The Constitution of 1876: Retrenchment and Reform

The restored Democratic majority promptly took steps to write a new constitution. A new constitutional convention convened in Austin on September 6, 1875. The delegates were all men. Most were products of a rural and frontier South, and still smarting from Reconstruction abuses, they considered government a necessary evil that had to be heavily restricted. Many, however, had previous governmental experience. Initially, 75 Democrats and 15 Republicans were elected delegates, but one Republican resigned after only limited service and was replaced by a Democrat.[13]

The vast majority of the delegates were white, and some disagreement remains over how many African Americans served in the convention. Some historians say there were six. According to one account, however, six African Americans were elected but one resigned after only one day of service and was replaced in a special election by a white delegate. All of the African American delegates were Republicans.[14]

Only four of the delegates were native Texans. Most had immigrated to Texas from other southern states, including nineteen—the largest single group—from Tennessee, which one author called the "breeding ground" of Texas delegates. Their average age was 45. The oldest was 68; the youngest was 23.[15] Eleven of the delegates had been members of previous constitutional conventions in Texas, but there is disagreement over whether any had participated in drafting the Reconstruction Constitution of 1869. In any event, the influences of the 1869 Constitution were negative, not positive.

At least thirty of the delegates had served in the Texas legislature, two others had served in the Tennessee and Mississippi legislatures, two had represented Texas in the U.S. Congress, and two had represented Texas in the Confederate Congress. Delegates also included a former attorney general, a former lieutenant governor, and a former secretary of state of Texas; at least eight delegates had judicial experience. Many delegates had been high-ranking Confederate military officers. One, John H. Reagan, had been postmaster general of the Confederacy.[16] Reagan later would become a U.S. senator from Texas and would serve as the first chair of the Texas Railroad Commission.

Another delegate who epitomized the independent, frontier spirit of the time was John S. "Rip" Ford, a native of South Carolina who had come to Texas in 1836 as a physician. He later became a lawyer, journalist, state senator, mayor of Austin, and Texas Ranger captain. In 1874, he was a leader of the militia that marched on the Capitol and forced Edmund J. Davis to relinquish the governor's office to his elected successor. Ford had been a secessionist delegate to the 1861 convention, which voted for secession and drafted a constitution. During the Civil War he had commanded a makeshift cavalry regiment that fought Union soldiers along the Texas–Mexico border.[17]

According to one account, delegates to the 1875 convention included 33 lawyers, 28 farmers, three physicians, three merchants, two teachers, two editors, and one minister. At least eleven other delegates were part-time farmers who also pursued other occupations.[18] Other historians have come up with slightly different breakdowns, but all agree that the influence of agricultural interests was substantial in the writing of the new Texas charter.

About half the delegates were members of the Society of the Patrons of Husbandry, or the **Grange.** An organization formed to improve the lot of farmers, the Grange became politically active in the wake of national scandals involving abuses by big business and government. The Grange started organizing in Texas in 1873, and its influence was felt directly in constitutional provisions limiting taxes and governmental expenditures and restricting banks, railroads, and other corporations.

The delegates did not try to produce a document that would be lauded as a model of constitutional perfection or mistaken for a literary classic. They faced the reality of addressing serious, pressing problems—an immediate crisis that did not encourage debate over the finer points of academic or political theory or produce any prophetic visions of the next century.

The Civil War and Reconstruction had plunged the state into economic ruin and state government into deep debt, despite the heavy taxation of Texas citizens, particularly property owners. The bottom had fallen out of land prices, a disaster for what was still an agricultural state. Governmental corruption had been pervasive under the Davis administration, and the dictatorial powers that Davis had exercised, particularly the abuses of his hated state police, had left deep scars. Moreover, the national political scene under President Grant's two administrations (1869–77) had also been plagued by corruption and scandal.

The framers of the Texas Constitution of 1876 reacted accordingly. In seeking to restore control of their state government to the people and reestablish economic stability, they fashioned what was essentially an antigovernment charter. Centralization was replaced with more local control, strict limits were placed on taxation, and short leashes were put on the legislature, the courts, and, especially, the governor.[19]

Texas's traditional agricultural interests, which had been called upon to finance industrial development and new social services during the Reconstruction era, were once again protected from onerous governmental intrusion and taxation. The retrenchment

Grange
Organization formed in the late nineteenth century to improve the lot of farmers. The Grange influenced provisions in the Texas constitution of 1876 limiting taxes and government spending and restricting big business, including banks and railroads.

Ninety delegates, including six recently emancipated African Americans, were elected to the 1875 Constitutional Convention.

and reform embodied in the new charter would soon hamper the state's commercial and economic development. But post-Reconstruction Texans applauded the multitude of restrictive details that the new constitution carried. They ratified the document in February 1876 by a vote of 136,606 to 56,052.

GENERAL PRINCIPLES OF THE TEXAS CONSTITUTION

The Texas constitution of 1876 draws from the national constitutional tradition discussed earlier and embodies four dominant principles: popular sovereignty, compact theory, limited government, and separation of powers (see Table 22–3).

A relatively short Preamble and the first two sections of the Bill of Rights express the document's underlying principle. It is a social compact, formed by free men (no women participated in its drafting), in which "all political power is inherent in the people, . . . founded on their authority, and instituted for their benefit." These brief sections are based on the principles of **popular sovereignty** and compact theory, both of which were part of a legacy of constitutional law in the United States. Although the language articulates the noble aspirations of a free and just society, it was limited in scope and application. Women and minorities were initially denied full citizenship rights. And although women gained the right to vote by amendment to the U.S. Constitution in 1920, it has

TABLE 22–3 COMPARISON OF THE TEXAS CONSTITUTION AND THE U.S. CONSTITUTION

	U.S. Constitution	Texas Constitution
General principles	Popular sovereignty	Popular sovereignty
	Limited government	Limited government
	Representative government	Representative government
	Compact theory	Compact theory
	Separation of powers	Separation of powers
Context of adoption	Reaction to weakness of Articles of Confederation—strengthened national powers significantly	Post-Reconstruction—designed to limit powers of government
Style	General principles stated in broad terms	Detailed provisions
Length	7,000 words	100,000 words
Date of implementation	1789	1876
Amendments	27	432
Amendment process	Difficult	Relatively easy
Adaptation to change	Moderately easy through interpretation	Difficult; often requires constitutional amendments
Bill of Rights	Amendments to the Constitution—adopted in 1791	Article 1 of the constitution of 1876
Structure of government	Separation of powers, with a unified executive based on provisions of Articles I, II, III	Separation of powers with plural executive defined by Article 2
Legislature	Bicameral	Bicameral
Judiciary	Creation of one Supreme Court and other courts to be created by the Congress	Detailed provisions creating two appellate courts and other state courts
Distribution of powers	Federal	Unitary
Public policy	Little reference to policy	Detailed policy provisions

popular sovereignty
Constitutional principle of self-government; belief that the people control their government and governments are subject to limitations and constraints.

taken years for African Americans and Hispanics to receive the full protections implicit in these statements.

A third major principle is **limited government.** The Texas Bill of Rights and other provisions throughout the constitution place limits on governmental authority and power. The constitution spells out the traditional rights of religious freedom, procedural due process of law, and other rights of the citizen in relation to the government.

A fourth major principle is **separation of powers.** Unlike the U.S. Constitution, in which this principle emerges through powers defined in the three articles related to the Congress, the president, and the judiciary, Article 2 of the Texas constitution specifically provides for it.

The constitution of 1876 created three branches of government—legislative, executive and judicial—and provided for a system of checks and balances that assured that no single branch would dominate the others. This principle originated with the U.S. Constitution, whose drafters were concerned about the so-called "mischief of factions." They feared that groups or special interests would be able to capture governmental institutions and pursue policies that were not in the national interest. So institutional power was fragmented to guard against that potential problem. In some respects, this was an issue of even greater concern to the framers of the Texas constitution. Reacting to the highly centralized authority and abuses of the Davis administration, they took the separation of powers principle to its extreme.

Lawmaking authority is vested in an elected legislature that includes a 150-member House of Representatives and a 31-member Senate. The Texas legislature meets in regular sessions in odd-numbered years and in special sessions of limited scope and duration when called by the governor. The 65 sections of Article 3 spell out in detail the powers granted to and the restrictions imposed on the legislature.

An elected governor shares authority over the executive branch with several other independently elected, statewide officeholders. The governor, who has limited constitutional powers, can veto bills approved by the legislature and can call and set the agendas for special legislative sessions. A gubernatorial veto can be overridden only by a two-thirds vote of the House and the Senate.

Also elected are members of the judiciary—from justices of the peace, with limited jurisdiction at the county level, to judges on the highest statewide appellate courts. This provision reflects the strong sentiment of post-Reconstruction Texans for an independent judiciary and is a major difference from the federal government, in which judges are appointed by the president. Also unlike the federal system, in which the U.S. Supreme Court is the court of last resort in both civil and criminal appeals, Texas has two courts of last resort. The Texas Supreme Court has final jurisdiction over civil matters, and the Texas Court of Criminal Appeals has final review of criminal cases.

WEAKNESSES AND CRITICISMS OF THE CONSTITUTION OF 1876

Executive Branch

Many experts believe that the Texas constitution excessively fragments governmental authority and responsibility, particularly in the executive branch. Although there is a natural disposition for the public to look to the governor to establish policy priorities, the governor does not have control over other elected state executives but rather shares both authority and responsibility for policy with them. This situation can be problematic, as when former Republican Governor Bill Clements, for example, shared executive responsibilities with Democrats who sharply disagreed with his priorities. Even when the governor and other elected officials are of the same party, differences in personality, political philosophy, and policy objectives can produce tension and sometimes deadlock.

The governor's power has been further diffused by the creation over the years of numerous boards and commissions that set policy for executive agencies not headed by elected officials. Although the governor appoints most of those board members, they

limited government
Constitutional principle restricting governmental authority and spelling out personal rights.

separation of powers
Division of powers among three distinct branches of government—the legislative, the executive, and the judicial—which serve as checks and balances on each other's actions.

serve staggered six-year terms, which are longer than a governor's term. A newly elected governor—who cannot fire a predecessor's appointees—usually has to wait through most of his or her first term to gain a majority of appointees to most boards.

Fragmented authority and responsibility are also found in county governments, which are administrative agents of the state (see Chapter 27). Various elected county officials often clash over public policy, producing inefficiencies or failing to meet public needs. And just as voters are faced with a long ballot for statewide offices, they must also choose among a long, often confusing list of county officers. Because a long ballot discourages many people from voting, this obstacle reduces public accountability, an end result that the framers of the Constitution of 1876 certainly never intended.

Legislative Branch

The constitution created a low-paid, part-time legislature to ensure the election of citizen-lawmakers who would be sensitive to the needs of their constituents, not of professional politicians who would live off the taxpayers. Unwittingly, however, the constitution writers also produced a lawmaking body easily influenced by special interest groups. And the strict limitations placed on the legislature's operations and powers slow its ability to meet the increasingly complex needs of a growing, modern Texas.

In 1972, voters approved a constitutional change to lengthen the terms of the governor and other executive officeholders from two to four years. This change gives the governor more time to develop public policies with the prospect of seeing those policies implemented. But voters have repeatedly rejected proposals to provide for regular, annual legislative sessions, and legislative pay remains among the lowest in the country.

Judicial Branch

The Texas constitution also created numerous locally elected judicial offices, including justice of the peace and county and district courts. Although there are appeal procedures, these judges have a great deal of autonomy, power, and influence through their local constituencies.

Education

Another example of decentralization is the public school system. The centralized school system authorized under the Reconstruction constitution of 1869 was abolished, and local authorities were given primary responsibility for supervising public education. The concept of "local control" over their schools is important to many Texans, but decentralization and wide disparities in local tax bases have produced an inequitable public education system.

Budgeting and Finances

The Texas constitution, including key amendments adopted after 1876, requires a balanced state budget but also heavily restricts the legislature's choices over state spending. The dedication of large amounts of revenue to specific purposes has made it increasingly difficult for lawmakers to address changing state needs (see *You Decide/Thinking It Through:* "Budget Restrictions").

Individual Rights

Although articulating a general commitment to democracy and individual rights, the constitution initially retarded democratic development in Texas. Like many other southern states, Texas had restrictive laws on voter participation. It levied a poll tax, which reduced the voting of minorities and poor whites until 1966, when an amendment to the U.S. Constitution and a decision by the U.S. Supreme Court outlawed it. Federal courts also struck down a Texas election system that excluded African Americans from voting in the Democratic primary, which was where elections were decided when Texas was a one-party, Democratic state. The elimination of significant numbers of people from participating in elections helped perpetuate the one-party political system for approximately 100 years.[20]

Consequence of Details

The Texas constitution is burdened with excessive detail. Although few individuals are disposed to read the 100,000-plus-word document, a person casually perusing it can find language, for example, governing the operation of hospital districts in Ochiltree, Castro, Hansford, and Hopkins counties. There also is a provision dealing with expenditures for relocation or replacement of sanitary sewer laterals on private property. Whereas the 7,000-word U.S. Constitution leaves the details of implementation to congressional legislation, the Texas constitution often spells out the authority and power of a governmental agency in specific detail. Most experts agree that many constitutional articles are of a legislative nature and have no business in a constitution.[21] The excessive detail limits the adaptability of the constitution to changing circumstances and places undue restrictions on state and local governments.

Consequently, there are obsolete and contradictory provisions in the constitution. Subsequent state and federal constitutional amendments have superseded some of these provisions, but much obsolete language remains. Periodically, state constitutional amendments have been approved to "clean up" such deadwood, but the problem persists.[22]

Another important criticism of the Texas constitution focuses on the amendments and the amendment process. Alabama has had more constitutional amendments than any other state, but Texas ranked fourth, with 432 amendments from 1876 through 2003 (see *In Comparative Perspective:* "States Frequently Amend Their Constitutions"). In contrast, the U.S. Constitution has been amended only 27 times since 1789, and ten of those amendments were adopted as the Bill of Rights immediately after the government organized. The numerous restrictions and prohibitions in the Texas constitution require excessive amendments to enable state government to adapt to social, economic, and political changes.

Minority participation in Texas politics has increased significantly since the 1960s as a result of the Voting Rights Act and of federal court decisions that overturned restrictive state laws that kept minorities from registering and voting. Democratic gubernatorial nominee Tony Sanchez is shown campaigning in 2002.

CONSTITUTIONAL CHANGE AND ADAPTATION

Amendment

Although the drafters filled the Texas constitution with a multitude of restrictive provisions, they also provided a relatively easy method of amending it. This piecemeal amendment process has enabled state government to meet some changing needs, but it also has added thousands of words to the document.

Proposed constitutional amendments can be submitted only by the legislature. Approval by two-thirds of the House and the Senate puts them on the ballot, where adoption requires a majority vote. Although voters had approved 432 amendments through 2003, they had rejected 173 others. Since the present charter was ratified in 1876, there have been only a few years in which voters have not been asked to change it. The first amendment was adopted on September 2, 1879. A record 25 amendments were on the November 3, 1987, ballot. Seventeen were adopted, and eight were defeated.

Some amendments are of major statewide importance, but many have affected only a single county or a handful of counties or have been offered simply to rid the constitution of obsolete language (see *FYI:* "A Lot of Trouble for a Minor Office"). One amendment approved by voters in 1993 affected only about 140 families, two church congregations, and one school district in Fort Bend and Austin counties. It cleared up a title defect to their land.

Unlike voters in many other states, Texas citizens cannot force the placement of constitutional amendments on the ballot because Texas does not have the **initiative** or **referendum** on a statewide level. On taking office in January 1979 as Texas's first Republican governor since Reconstruction, Bill Clements made adoption of the initiative and referendum a priority. But these innovations could not take effect without a constitutional amendment, and the legislature—which did not want to give up such a significant policy prerogative to the electorate—ignored Clements.

In recent years, however, the legislature has demonstrated a tendency to seek political cover by selectively letting the voters decide some particularly controversial issues, such as a binding referendum in 1987 on the legalization of parimutuel betting on horse and dog racing. In 1993 the legislature proposed a constitutional amendment, which voters overwhelmingly endorsed, to prohibit a personal income tax in Texas without voter approval.

Constitutional Convention

The constitution also provides for revision by constitutional convention, which the legislature can call with the approval of the voters. Convention delegates have to be elected, and their terms also are subject to voter approval. In 1919, voters overwhelmingly rejected a proposal for a constitutional convention. Subsequent efforts, including an attempt by Governor John Connally in 1967, to initiate reforms using a constitutional convention were also defeated.[23] Connally's efforts did, however, result in adoption of a "cleanup" amendment in 1969 that removed many obsolete provisions from the constitution, and they laid the groundwork for a constitutional convention in 1974.

Constitutional Reform Efforts of 1971–1975

The 1974 convention, the only one ever held under the present 1876 charter, ended in failure. Its delegates were the 181 members of the legislature. The constitutional convention of 1974 had its beginning in 1971, when State Representative Nelson Wolff of San Antonio and several other first-term legislators won the leadership's backing for a full-scale revision effort. In 1972 voters approved the necessary constitutional amendment

---

★★★ THINKING IT THROUGH

Like most other states and unlike the federal government, Texas—thanks to a constitutional requirement—operates on a pay-as-you-go basis that prohibits deficit financing. The comptroller must certify that each budget can be paid for with anticipated revenue from taxes, fees, and other sources. Although that provision is designed to protect taxpayers and keep state government solvent, other sections of the constitution make it more difficult for the legislature to meet the state's budgetary needs adequately and fairly.

One handicap is the two-year budget period, necessitated by the fact that the legislature meets in regular session only every other year. Critics, including many legislators and state agency directors, say two-year budgets require too much guesswork and cause inadequate funding of some programs and wasteful spending in other areas. Voters in 1985 approved a constitutional amendment to allow the governor and legislative leaders to transfer funds between programs or agencies to meet emergencies when the legislature is not in session. But that provision only partially addressed the problem.

The legislature's control over the budget-setting process is further restricted by constitutional requirements that dedicate significant portions of state revenue to specific purposes. Three-fourths of the revenue from the motor fuels tax is automatically set aside for highways and the remaining one-fourth for public education. The Permanent School Fund and the Permanent University Fund are land- and mineral-rich endowments that help support the public schools and boost funding for the University of Texas and Texas A&M University systems.

The legislature can bend the pay-as-you-go requirement by issuing general obligation bonds, serviced by future tax revenues, to build prisons and other public facilities. Such bonds require voter approval in the form of constitutional amendments, several of which, totaling more than $3 billion, have been approved in recent years to build new prisons. That debt will have to be paid off with tax dollars over the next generation.

initiative
Procedure by which voters propose constitutional amendments or other laws through petitions subject to adoption by a popular vote.

referendum
Vote by the general electorate on a public policy issue, such as a constitutional amendment or statute.

IN COMPARATIVE PERSPECTIVE

STATES FREQUENTLY AMEND THEIR CONSTITUTIONS

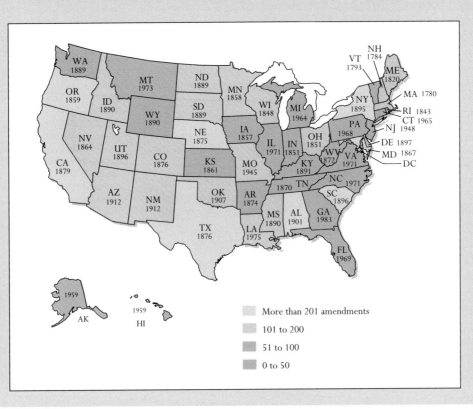

NH 1784
VT 1793
ME 1820
MA 1780
RI 1843
CT 1965
NJ 1948
DE 1897
MD 1867
DC

WA 1889
OR 1859
ID 1890
MT 1973
ND 1889
MN 1858
WI 1848
MI 1964
NY 1895
PA 1968
OH 1851
WV 1872
VA 1971
NV 1864
UT 1896
WY 1890
SD 1889
NE 1875
IA 1857
IL 1971
IN 1851
KY 1891
CA 1879
CO 1876
KS 1861
MO 1945
TN 1870
NC 1971
AZ 1912
NM 1912
OK 1907
AR 1874
SC 1896
TX 1876
MS 1890
AL 1901
GA 1983
LA 1975
FL 1969

1959 AK
1959 HI

More than 201 amendments
101 to 200
51 to 100
0 to 50

that specified that the convention would comprise house members and senators elected the same year.

In 1973 the legislature created a 37-member Constitutional Revision Commission to hold public hearings around the state and make recommendations to the convention. Members of the commission, chaired by former Texas Supreme Court Chief Justice Robert W. Calvert, were appointed by Governor Dolph Briscoe and other top state officials.

The constitutional convention, or "con-con," as it came to be called by legislators and members of the media, convened on January 8, 1974. House Speaker Price Daniel, Jr., was elected president, and Lieutenant Governor Bill Hobby, in an address to delegates, offered a prophetic warning: "The special interests of today will be replaced by new and different special interests tomorrow, and any attempt to draft a constitution to serve such interests would be futile and also dishonorable."[24]

Hobby's plea was ignored. Special interests dominated the convention, which finally adjourned in bitter failure on July 30, failing by three votes to get the two-thirds vote necessary to send a new constitution to Texas voters for ratification. The crucial fight was over a business-backed attempt to lock the state's right-to-work law into the constitution. The **right-to-work law** prohibits union membership as a condition of employment, so the effort was bitterly fought by organized labor. Then as now, business was politically stronger than labor in Texas, but the two-thirds vote necessary to put a new constitution on the ballot was too great an obstacle.

The gallery in the house of representatives chamber, which served as the convention hall, was packed with labor representatives and other spectators when the final vote was taken, about a half-hour before the convention's midnight adjournment

right-to-work law
Law prohibiting the requirement of union membership in order to hold or get a job.

After three years of preparation and deliberations, the proposed constitution of 1974 failed by three votes in the final hectic session of the constitutional convention, when the gallery was filled with interested onlookers, including many representatives of labor.

deadline. Daniel held the electronic voting board open for 28 minutes, hoping three delegates could be persuaded to switch their votes, but time ran out. Tension and emotions were running so high that, at one point, state Representative Jim Mattox of Dallas, who would later become attorney general, challenged Daniel's delay in announcing the vote and publicly called the convention president a liar.[25]

Although the right-to-work dispute took the brunt of the blame, other factors also worked against the revision effort (see *You Decide:* "Do Most Voters Really Care?"). One was Governor Briscoe's refusal to exercise any significant leadership on behalf of a new state charter. Except for opposing proposals that he thought would further weaken the authority of the governor, he provided little input to the convention and did not attempt to twist delegates' arms to get enough votes to send the document to the electorate. Louisiana voters approved a new state constitution in 1974, and Governor Edwin Edwards's strong support was considered instrumental. Gubernatorial leadership in other states also appears to have been critical to successful constitutional conventions.

Another major obstacle was the convention's makeup. Texas, unlike most other states, chose to use the 181 members of the legislature as its constitutional convention. Soon after the convention began its work, many of them were facing reelection campaigns in the party primaries, which diverted their attention from the business of the convention.

Additionally, a minority of legislators—dubbed "cockroaches" by President Daniel—did not want a new constitution and attempted to delay or obstruct the convention's work at every opportunity. Most legislators, even those who wanted a new constitution, reacted to their own political fears and ambitions. They were very susceptible to the influence of special interests, far more susceptible than most private-citizen delegates would likely have been. And special interests were legion at the convention. In addition to various business and professional groups and organized labor, many county officeholders whose jobs—protected by the constitution of 1876—were suddenly in jeopardy put pressure on the delegates.

Some county judges lobbied against a proposal to streamline the judiciary because they feared it would relieve them of judicial duties. Under the present constitution, county judges are primarily administrative officers and do not have to be lawyers, but they do have limited judicial responsibilities. So persistent was their lobbying that Daniel referred to some of them as a "wrecking crew." Representative DeWitt Hale of Corpus

A LOT OF TROUBLE FOR A MINOR OFFICE

Roberts County Judge Vernon H. Cook was convinced that his rural county near the top of the Texas Panhandle did not need a constable. He believed the sheriff provided enough law enforcement for the county's 1,500 residents. For years, the county had not had a constable, but the office, which was created in the Texas constitution, remained on the books. Unexpectedly, in 1992 a write-in candidate ran for constable and was elected. The office then became an extra expense for county taxpayers, as county commissioners felt obliged to pay the new officeholder a $600-a-month salary plus a $200-a-month car allowance and health insurance benefits.

Convinced they were not getting their money's worth—"As near as we can tell, he served two official papers in his first year in office," Cook complained—commissioners later reduced his salary, and the constable left town. To avoid a recurrence of the problem, commissioners had to ask the state legislature to put a constitutional amendment abolishing the Roberts County constable's office on a statewide ballot. Thus voters in Houston—600 miles away—would have a greater say on abolishing the office than Roberts County's own taxpayers, because Houston's 1.6 million residents cast many more votes. Although that may not seem fair—Houston taxpayers, after all, did not pay the Roberts County constable's salary—it is just one of many obstacles and inconveniences imposed on modern government by a nineteenth-century constitution. Most amendments abolishing obsolete county offices are approved by Texas voters, including amendments abolishing the constables' offices in Roberts County and two other rural counties in 1995.

SOURCE: *Houston Chronicle,* November 6, 1995.

During the 1999 legislative session, Senator Bill Ratliff, R-Mount Pleasant, left, and Representative Rob Junell, D-San Angelo, chairmen of their respective budget committees, proposed rewriting the constitution of 1876.

★★ **YOU DECIDE**

DO MOST VOTERS REALLY CARE?

Do most voters know enough about the Texas constitution to have an opinion as to whether the state should adopt a new constitution? Do they even care about a general overhaul of the 100,000-word document? Would a new constitution make any difference in the overall effectiveness of state government?

Christi, chair of the Committee on the Judiciary, was "disgusted because a handful of judges could be so disruptive to the convention."[26]

Influential regents, lobbyists, and alumni of the University of Texas and Texas A&M University systems guarded the Permanent University Fund, their rich constitutional endowment. Further, highway lobbyists, backed by thousands of contractors and businesspeople from throughout the state, fought any attempt to raid the highway trust fund, the constitutional provision that dedicates three-fourths of the revenue from the state motor fuels tax to highway projects.

Delegates tried to walk a tightrope over the emotionally charged issue of gambling. They yielded to the wishes of charitable and fraternal organizations and tentatively approved a provision to allow bingo and raffles to be conducted for charity, receiving some public ridicule for giving constitutional status to a game of chance. But delegates voted to retain the general constitutional prohibition against lotteries. In a letter to Robert W. Calvert, the chair of the Constitutional Revision Commission, Baylor University President Abner McCall had warned of considerable public opposition to any new constitution that legalized gambling: "The commission may adopt proposals to make the machinery of Texas government more efficient, but

HIGH STAKES OVER LAWSUITS

Supporters said Proposition 12 was a cure for high medical malpractice insurance premiums that were forcing some doctors, particularly in rural areas, to close their practices. Opponents argued that medical malpractice coverage was high because state regulators weren't effectively clamping down on bad doctors. They warned that Proposition 12 was instead an effort by business and insurance interests to further restrict access to the courts for injured or aggrieved consumers. In any event, Texas voters narrowly approved the constitutional amendment in 2003 after a multimillion-dollar advertising war. Doctors, hospitals, nursing homes, and other business interests primarily financed the campaign promoting the amendment. Plaintiffs' lawyers, who make their living suing doctors, hospitals, and businesses on behalf of injured consumers, picked up most of the tab for the media campaign against it, although numerous consumer advocacy groups also opposed the proposal.

The amendment did two things. First, it ratified a 2003 law enacted by the legislature to put new limits on noneconomic damages—money awarded for such things as pain, suffering, and disfigurement—in medical malpractice suits. Such damages, which are in addition to medical costs and other actual economic losses that could be awarded a patient who suffered from a botched medical procedure, were capped at $750,000 for each case. Of that amount, only $250,000 can be recovered from physicians or other medical personnel. The remainder would come from hospitals, nursing homes, or other health care facilities that may be involved. Additionally—and potentially more far-reaching—Proposition 12 included language clearing the way for future sessions of the legislature to enact new limits on damages in other civil lawsuits.

Legislative sponsors of Proposition 12 also were accused of trying to sneak the proposal past the voters by scheduling the constitutional amendments election for September 13, rather than November 4, the general election date on which constitutional amendments were traditionally set for voter review. Supporters of the amendment said it was important to win voter approval earlier than normal to remove any legal uncertainty over the new malpractice limits. But opponents argued that the early election, with no other issues to attract voters, was designed to avoid the higher voter turnout that would be generated by a hotly contested mayoral race in Houston on November 4. Voters in Houston, the state's largest city, usually are a major factor in determining state elections, and a high voter turnout there could prove to be pivotal in determining the fate of Proposition 12. According to this argument, the higher the voter turnout in Houston, the greater the likelihood that the amendment would be defeated, because Democrats and plaintiffs lawyers still had some clout over elections in that city. Opponents of Proposition 12, as it turned out, had reason to fear the early election date. The proposal narrowly passed statewide, but 58 percent of Houston voters—turning out in far fewer numbers than would vote two months later in the mayor's race—cast ballots against it. "It (the statewide result) would have been a real horse race if it had been held in conjunction with the Houston mayor's race," said University of Houston political scientist Richard Murray.

SOURCE: *Houston Chronicle*, September 16, 2003, p. 13A.

many of us will not trade a little more efficiency for a greater danger of corruption of government by state sponsored gambling."[27] The ban on lotteries was to remain in the constitution for another seventeen years until Governor Ann Richards successfully promoted the creation of a state lottery as a new revenue source for state government in 1991.

During its next regular session, in 1975, the legislature, with the strong support of House Speaker Bill Clayton and Lieutenant Governor Bill Hobby, resurrected the constitutional revision effort. Lawmakers voted to present to Texans the basic document that the convention had barely rejected the previous summer in the form of eight separate constitutional amendments. The first three articles dealing with the separation of powers and the legislative and executive branches were combined into one ballot proposition. Each of the remaining seven propositions was a separate article, each to be independently approved or rejected by the voters. The most controversial issues that the 1974 convention had debated, such as right-to-work, were excluded. The streamlined amendments would have considerably shortened the constitution and provided some major changes, including annual legislative sessions, a unified judicial system, and more flexibility in county government. It would have been a much more flexible, modern constitution than the 1876 document and had cost several million tax dollars and countless hours to produce. But voters rejected all eight propositions on November 4, 1975, some by margins of more than 2 to 1.

A stock fraud scandal in the legislature in 1971 (see Chapter 24) and the Watergate scandal that forced the resignation of President Richard Nixon in 1974 raised Texans' distrust of government, and the proposed new constitution had been drafted by state officials, not by private citizens.

Efforts to enact these proposals were further thwarted by Governor Briscoe. Although he had never taken an active role in the revision effort, three weeks before the 1975 election, he openly opposed the eight propositions and suggested that the existing constitution had served the state well and would continue to be adequate for the future.[28]

Further Piecemeal Reforms

So it was back to piecemeal constitutional changes. Between 1975 and 2003, 212 amendments were approved by Texas voters and 37 were rejected. Besides the lottery, amendments winning approval included the 1993 amendment to ban a personal income tax without voter approval and a series of propositions authorizing $3 billion in tax-backed bonds for a huge prison expansion program. In 1985, voters approved an amendment to give the governor and legislative leaders authority to deal with budgetary emergencies between legislative sessions. Martha Whitehead, the state's last treasurer, ran on a promise in 1994 to seek the elimination of the office on the grounds that it was obsolete. In 1995, voters approved an amendment to abolish the state treasurer's office and transfer its duties to the comptroller. And in 1997, Texas voters by a wide margin approved a constitutional amendment to increase homeowners' $5,000 exemptions from school property taxes to $15,000. The measure, part of a property tax relief effort promoted by Governor George W. Bush, saved the average homeowner about $140 a year in local school taxes. In 1999, voters approved an amendment—prompted by Governor Bush's presidential campaign—to make it clear that a lieutenant governor who was promoted to fill out an elected governor's unexpired term would have to give up the lieutenant governor's job to take the higher office. During its 1999 session, the legislature rejected a proposal—the first of its kind in more than twenty years—to rewrite the constitution. But legislators approved an amendment, which voters also approved, to remove more obsolete language from the document. One of the more controversial amendments in recent years, Proposition 12, ratified new limits on some monetary damages in medical malpractice lawsuits. It was narrowly approved by voters in 2003 (see *FYI:* "High Stakes Over Lawsuits").

★★ THINKING IT THROUGH

State Senator Bill Ratliff, R-Mount Pleasant, believed that many Texans were so tired of being asked to vote on constitutional amendments that they would support an effort to shorten the document. So Ratliff and State Representative Rob Junell, D-San Angelo, proposed a shorter, more modern constitution for the Texas legislature to consider during its 1999 session. As chairmen that year of the legislature's key budget-writing committees, Ratliff and Junell usually had enough clout to get their legislative priorities passed. But they didn't have enough influence to remove the public apathy that greeted their constitutional revision effort. Legislative committees held public hearings on the proposal, but lawmakers did not feel an urgency to write a new constitution because the idea aroused no interest among their constituents. Halfway through the session, for example, Lieutenant Governor Rick Perry, the state Senate's presiding officer, had received only two letters on the proposed new constitution, compared to thousands of letters and electronic messages on other issues. The Ratliff–Junell proposal also included some controversial features, including more powers for the governor and term limits for legislators, which most lawmakers were in no hurry to address. Governor George W. Bush, who was anticipating a race for president, was also cool toward the new document. "Can this Legislature tackle a matter of the gravity of the constitution in the absence of a crisis?"[*] Ratliff asked.

Apparently it couldn't. But the legislature approved 17 more constitutional amendments—including an amendment to remove obsolete language—to put on the November 1999 ballot. Voters approved 13 of the amendments, including the "cleanup" measure, and rejected four. Turnout was extremely low. Less than 10 percent of registered voters cast ballots on the amendments.[†]

[*]*Houston Chronicle,* March 14, 1999.

[†]*Houston Chronicle,* November 4, 1999.

ADDING A LITTLE FLAVOR TO THE CONSTITUTION

Many people may enjoy a cup of coffee with a chocolate dessert. But do such treats belong in the state constitution? Most Texas voters said they did. One of 19 propositions approved on the 2001 constitutional amendments ballot exempted raw coffee beans and cocoa imported through the Port of Houston from property taxes. The proposal was promoted by business people seeking to increase imports of those commodities through Houston. More imports, they hoped, would increase the need for more warehouses, create more jobs, and boost business profits. The tax exemption met a condition necessary for the New York Board of Trade to award "exchange port" status to the Port of Houston, a key requirement for import growth.

There was no organized opposition to the amendment, which also was endorsed by city and county officials in Houston, who believed it offered a potential boost to the area's overall economy. But the proposal was approved by a relatively close margin—52 percent—perhaps because many non-Houstonians viewed it as a special-interest favor for the state's largest city and didn't like the way it tasted.

Constitutional Provisions, Interest Groups, and Elites

Only a small percentage of registered voters–often less than 10 percent—participate in elections when constitutional amendments are the only issues on the ballot (see Figure 22–1). When amendments are submitted to the voters during gubernatorial or presidential elections, the turnout is much higher. But in many instances, a relative handful of Texans ultimately decides on fundamental changes in government, which enhances their influence over the constitutional revision process.

Interest groups, which historically have been strong in Texas, work diligently to protect their concerns and objectives. They develop strategies to get provisions into the constitution that would benefit them and to keep provisions out of the constitution that they fear would hurt them. Because most amendments represent nonpartisan issues, a well-financed public relations campaign is likely to produce public support for an amendment.[29]

Interest groups are able to kill many proposed constitutional changes in the legislature, where the two-thirds vote requirement works to their advantage. Only a small fraction of constitutional amendments proposed by legislators get put on the ballot. Those that do usually have the support of one or more special interest groups, which often finance publicity campaigns to promote the propositions to the voters. Few amendments attract organized opposition after being put on the ballot, but there have been exceptions. In 2003, doctors, insurance companies, and business interests heavily promoted Proposition 12, the ratification of new medical malpractice limits. They were successful, despite a media campaign against the amendment financed primarily by plaintiffs' lawyers.

Many recent constitutional changes have reflected a pro-industry and economic development push that contrasts sharply with the anti-business sentiment of the original constitutional framers (see *FYI:* "Adding a Little Flavor to the Constitution"). Recent amendments also have helped build up a public bonded indebtedness that the nineteenth-century constitution writers would have been unable to comprehend. Texas was rural then. It is now largely urban and is working to diversify and expand its economy as well as provide the infrastructure required to support the large increases in its population. Business has repeatedly turned to state government for tax breaks and other economic incentives and has found receptive ears in the legislature and the governor's office.

Nine of the record 25 amendments on the November 1987 ballot were actively promoted as an economic development package by the Build Texas Committee, a bipartisan group of business and civic leaders. Voters approved most of the amendments, including bonds for new water projects and prisons.

Industry, with the unusual support of organized labor and environmentalists, won a major tax break through a constitutional amendment approved by Texas voters in 1993. It requires local governments to grant property tax exemptions for expensive pollution control equipment that businesses are required by state or federal law to install in their plants and other facilities. The business community supported the amendment because it represented untold millions of dollars in potential tax savings. Labor supported it because money not spent on taxes could mean more money spent on jobs. And environmentalists viewed it as an antipollution measure. Some local officials were fearful of the potential loss of large amounts of revenue to counties, school districts,

Type of Election	Number of Elections	Percent of Registered Voters	Percent of Voting Age Population
Special *	15	12.7	8.5
General (Gubernatorial)	9	43.7	28.4
General (Presidential)	8	66.9	45.2

* Only constitutional amendments on the ballot

FIGURE 22–1 Turnout for Constitutional Amendments, 1970–2003.
Source: Texas Secretary of State, Elections Division.

and other local governments, but they were clearly overpowered. Sometimes, however, relief can turn into heartburn, as it did in 2001, when lawmakers and Texas voters accidentally put a new tax into the constitution when they thought they were repealing one (See *FYI:* "Oops! How Did That Happen?").

It has been argued that the Texas Constitution serves the interests of a small number of **elites**—those individuals who control businesses and other dominant institutions in the state. This argument suggests that the severe constraints built into the constitution limit the policy options of state government and have historically thwarted the efforts of larger public-interest groups to restructure or improve the tax system, education policy, social services, health care, and other policies and programs that would benefit low- and middle-income Texans. Power is so fragmented that these groups have had to turn to the courts to force change. This same argument, incidentally, has often been made about the U.S. Constitution.

If this interpretation is accurate, it is ironic that those who framed the Texas constitution of 1876 directed much of their wrath against railroads, banks, and other institutions that are today considered elitist. The tumultuous last quarter of the nineteenth century witnessed high levels of class and economic conflict, with the emergence of the Greenback and Populist political parties, which articulated the interests of lower-income groups. But monied business interests eventually were able to use the state constitution and subsequent legislation to reestablish their dominance over Texas government. Although the elite structure of the state has changed since 1876, some scholars argue that there has been a gradual transfer of power and control to new elites, who continue to exercise enormous influence over public policy.

Change Through Court Interpretation

Some evidence indicates that Texas courts are now prepared to play a more expansive role in the interpretation of the constitution and, in turn, effect major changes in state policy. The best-known example is the Edgewood school finance case, in which the courts invalidated the system of funding public education and ordered the legislature to provide more equity in tax resources among the state's more than 1,000 school districts. Wide disparities in spending on students between rich and poor districts—the result of wide disparities in local property values—violated the state constitution's requirement for an "efficient" system of public schools, the Texas Supreme Court ruled.

CONSTITUTIONAL RESTRAINTS AND THE ABILITY TO GOVERN

The nonpartisan League of Women Voters of Texas has been a long-suffering advocate of a total rewrite of the state constitution. Nevertheless, before each constitutional amendments election, it normally announces which propositions it endorses for the sake of good government and which it opposes. But league leaders lost their patience in 1987 with the placement of a record 25 amendments on the same ballot. They announced they would neither support nor oppose any amendment that year. Instead, they urged voters to examine the propositions carefully and complain to their legislators about the length of the ballot. "Enough is enough. Let us work together to halt this ridiculous system of running the government by means of the constitution," the league said. But without a new constitution, the only way state government can prepare for the challenges of the twenty-first century under a highly restrictive constitution written in the nineteenth is to continue this pattern of "amendomania."[30]

Prospects for Future Change

Experts can point out the many flaws of the Texas constitution, but attempts at wholesale revision have not been successful. Numerous piecemeal changes have been made, but they have not addressed the fundamental criticisms of the charter. What is to be made of all this?

OOPS! HOW DID THAT HAPPEN?

People who have any doubts that an election ballot loaded with constitutional amendments is an accident waiting to happen need only consider Proposition 14, one of nineteen amendments on the November 2001 ballot, all of which were approved by voters. The proposal was promoted as a means of allowing local governments, except for school districts, to exempt registered, non-income-producing travel trailers from local property taxes. Supporters said the tax break was needed to encourage the so-called "winter Texans" to continue making their seasonal homes in the Rio Grande Valley. These people, who travel south to escape the cold winters up north, have become an important part of the South Texas economy and represent an important financial boost to some of Texas's poorest counties. Many of the winter visitors are senior citizens who live in recreational vehicles.

Everybody was sure the amendment did what it was intended to do. No one—legislative sponsors, legislative analysts, local officials, the media—noticed a problem, until after the amendment was approved and then became part of the constitution. Only then did someone discover that the amendment had inadvertently imposed a new tax on travel trailers, rather than removed one. The new provision labeled trailers as taxable, while the constitution previously had said nothing about them. And because the exemption didn't apply to school districts, legal experts believed that travel trailers had been made subject to school taxes.

The goof prompted Governor Rick Perry and legislative sponsors to start scrambling. Perry asked school districts to refrain from taxing travel trailers until the legislature had a chance to correct the mistake, which it did in 2003.

"I guess it moved through the process and went and went and went," the amendment's sponsor, State Representative Kino Flores of Mission, said of the blunder.

SOURCE: Associated Press, March 8, 2002.

elites
Small groups of people who exercise disproportionate power and influence in the policymaking processes.

First, Texas has a long history of suspicion of government, and this tradition continues. Most people fear governmental abuses and excesses more than they worry about government's inability to respond quickly and efficiently to the needs of its citizens. In the vernacular of the layperson, "If it ain't broke, don't fix it." And it is not clear that the layperson regards the constitution as "broke."

Second, many groups and interests benefit from the existing constitution, and they have demonstrated a collective resolve to minimize change.

Finally, most Texans give little thought to changing the constitution because they are ill-prepared to deal with the complexities of the document. Enormous problems must be overcome if citizens are to be educated and motivated to press for constitutional revision.

S U M M A R Y

1. Texas, like most other states, has functioned under a series of constitutions, each of which has contributed to the state's constitutional legacy. Each is appropriately understood from the perspective of the period in which it was adopted.

2. Texas currently operates under a constitution that was adopted following the Civil War and the Radical Reconstruction era, and the events of that period left an enduring legacy of suspicion of government, limited government, and fragmented governmental institutions. The 1876 constitution was predicated on the theory that governmental excesses could be minimized by carefully defining what governments could and could not do.

3. The framers failed to anticipate that the limitations they imposed on governmental institutions would ultimately allow major economic interests within the state to dominate the policy-making process, often to the detriment of the lower socioeconomic groups.

4. What the delegates to the Constitutional Convention of 1875 regarded as the strengths of the constitution—fragmented authority, detailed limitations on the power of governmental institutions, and decentralization—have served to limit the ability of state and local governments to adapt effectively to economic and demographic changes. The perceived solutions to many of the problems of 1875 have compounded the problems of state and local governments in the 2000s.

5. Efforts to overhaul the Texas constitution have failed. Consequently, the state has been forced to amend the document continually on a piecemeal basis. This process has produced some success in modernizing the charter, but many structural problems of state government require major institutional changes that cannot be resolved through this amendment process.

6. In many ways, the Texas constitution reflects the values of the state's conservative political culture, which continues to be suspicious of far-reaching constitutional changes. Moreover, constitutions and the debates that surround them are complex, and most people give little attention to these issues. Consequently, it is much easier to mobilize public opinion against rather than for wholesale change.

7. Over the years, numerous groups have attempted to protect their interests through constitutional amendments. But the same groups usually oppose any proposed changes that threaten their influence, power, or benefits. Consequently, the interests of small segments of the state's population often prevail over the interests of the majority.

K E Y   T E R M S

constitution
statutory law
unicameral
unitary system

federalism
bicameral
confederacy
Radical Reconstructionists

Grange
popular sovereignty
limited government
separation of powers

initiative
referendum
right-to-work law
elites

F U R T H E R   R E A D I N G

BRADEN, GEORGE D., ET AL. *The Constitution of the State of Texas: An Annotated and Comparative Analysis.* 2 vols. (Texas Advisory Commission on Intergovernmental Relations, 1977). Originally designed as a research tool for delegates to the 1974 Constitutional Convention, this work provides an explanation of the historical development of the Texas constitution and a comparative perspective on other state constitutions.

BRUFF, HAROLD H. "Separation of Powers Under the Texas Constitution," *Texas Law Review* 68 (June 1990), pp. 1337–1367. Summarizes leading state court cases pertaining to the separation of powers clause of the Texas constitution and addresses issue of judicial review.

CNUDDE, CHARLES F., AND ROBERT E. CREW JR. *Constitutional Democracy in Texas* (West, 1989). A constitutional perspective on Texas government and politics.

LUTZ, DONALD S. "The Texas Constitution," *in Perspectives on American and Texas Politics: A Collection of Essays,* ed. Donald S. Lutz and Kent L. Tedin (Kendall/Hunt, 1987). pp. 193–211. An analysis of the 1876 Texas constitution that argues the document reflects the dominant sub-cultures of the state with a tilt toward individualism.

MAUER, JOHN WALKER. *"State Constitutions in a Time of Crisis: The Case of the Texas Constitution of 1876,"* *Texas Law Review* 68 (June 1990, pp. 1615–1647. Focuses on the enactment of post-Reconstruction constitutions in Texas and the South, arguing that the constitutional framers of 1875 were reacting not only to Republican Reconstruction but the recently elected Democratic administration.

MAY, JANICE C. *The Texas Constitution Revision Experience in the '70s.* (Sterling Swift, 1975). Written by an expert on state constitutions, this work provides a historical perspective on the efforts to rewrite the Texas constitution in the 1970s.

McKAY, SETH SHEPARD. *Seven Decades of the Texas Constitution of 1876.* (Texas Technical College, 1943). A historical perspective on the impact of the 1876 constitution.

TARR, ALAN, *Understanding State Constitutions.* (Princeton University Press, 1998). An introduction to state constitutional theory that addresses a series of issues, including the differences among state constitutions and between federal and state constitutions and state constitutions within the federal context.

WOLFF, NELSON. *Challenge of Change.* (Naylor, 1975). Written by a delegate to the 1974 Constitutional Convention, this book discusses divisive issues and provides an abbreviated history of the convention proceedings.

INTEREST GROUPS, POLITICAL PARTIES, AND ELECTIONS IN TEXAS

23

THE POWER OF INTEREST GROUPS

The business community, through endorsements and political contributions, was influential in Republicans capturing a majority of Texas House of Representatives seats in 2002, giving the GOP control of that body for the first time since Reconstruction and leading to the election of the first Republican House speaker of modern times. The Texas Association of Business, or TAB, an umbrella group representing many businesses, was one of the most visible backers of Republican candidates who supported business priorities, including more restrictions on civil lawsuits, fewer governmental regulations and holding the line on state taxes. In pursuit of its policy agenda, TAB took the unusual—and controversial—step of spending $2 million in corporate contributions on political advertising in 24 legislative races. Most of the candidates supported by TAB won, but the tactic prompted a criminal investigation of the business group and precipitated a debate over free speech versus undue corporate influence over elections.

State law allows officers and employees of corporations to make personal contributions to political candidates or to contribute through political action committees established for that purpose. But it is illegal for corporate funds to be given directly to a candidate, and soon after the election, Travis County District Attorney Ronnie Earle began investigating the Texas Association of Business's contributions. TAB argued that the corporate donations were legal because they weren't given directly to candidates but were used to purchase advertising that educated voters on issues important to the group. The ads didn't directly advocate the election or defeat of any candidates, although they obviously influenced election results. More than a year after it had begun, the investigation was still incomplete, because TAB fought it with a series of legal maneuvers, arguing that the

TIME LINE

INTEREST GROUPS, POLITICAL PARTIES, AND ELECTIONS IN TEXAS

1865	Republicans dominate state politics immediately after the Civil War
1874	Beginning of one-party Democratic politics that lasts until the 1970s
1904	Poll tax implemented
1920	Women gain the right to vote
1930s	Great Depression dominates state's politics, producing sharp political divisions
1944	White primary declared unconstitutional by U.S. Supreme Court
1952	Democratic Governor Allan Shivers leads many conservative Democrats to vote for Republican presidential nominee Dwight D. Eisenhower
1961	Senator John Tower is the first Republican elected to statewide office in Texas since Reconstruction
1964	Poll tax is declared unconstitutional
1973	Lobbyists required by law to register with Secretary of State
1975	Texas included under the provisions of the Voting Rights Act
1978	Bill Clements elected first Republican governor since Reconstruction, leading the way for the transformation of the state's party system
1991	Creation of Ethics Commission
1994	Republican George W. Bush elected governor
1994	Religious Right instrumental in a takeover of the Republican Party by social conservatives
1998	Republicans control all statewide offices and capture control of the Texas Senate
2002	Republicans gain control of Texas House

interest group
Organization seeking to influence government policy.

pluralism
Political system in which power is distributed among multiple groups.

lobbyists
Individuals who attempt, directly or indirectly, to shape and influence the decisions of policy makers.

ads amounted to constitutionally protected free speech. National business groups also rallied to TAB's defense, claiming that Earle, a Democrat, was letting politics influence his investigation. But Earle argued that he was merely investigating "allegations of crime."[1]

The Texas Association of Business's ad campaign was one of the more visible examples of an interest group's influence in Austin in recent years. But under both Democratic and Republican statehouse control, interest groups have long dominated Texas's policy-making process and most likely will continue to do so.

Interest groups have priorities that usually cross partisan lines. Their organizational strengths and initiatives are reflected in public policy, and those segments of Texas society that are unorganized are likely to have little, if any, impact on governmental decisions. Many interest groups that function on the state and local level are linked to some extent to the national system.

Just as they do at the national level, interest groups in Texas spend millions of dollars a year trying to elect favored candidates or to influence the outcome of governmental decisions through a number of direct and indirect lobbying activities. Campaign contributions have always raised ethical questions of undue influence on policy makers and are a continuing source of controversy, as the Texas Association of Business's involvement demonstrates. Moreover, aggressive and often heavy-handed lobbying efforts contribute to the view that state and local governments are dominated by a few big interests looking out for themselves (see *You Decide/Thinking It Through:* "Do We Need to Regulate the Type and Number of Conferences Legislators Attend?").

Two studies, conducted more than forty years apart, placed Texas among states with strong interest-group systems.[2] Powerful pressure groups usually evolve in states with weak political parties, a condition that characterized Texas during most of the twentieth century.[3] During the many years that Texas was a one-party, Democratic state, the Republican party posed no serious challenge to the Democratic monopoly, and the Democratic party was marked by intense factionalism. Although the conservative Democratic wing dominated state politics through the 1970s, interest groups often played a greater role in the policy-making process. Subsequent Republican growth has changed Texas's party system, but interest groups remain strong and, more often than not, still have a greater impact on the policy-making process than the political parties.

PLURALISM OR ELITISM?

There are thousands of interest groups at the state and local level in Texas. Some have long histories and a durable presence in the policy process, while others are formed to address a specific need and disappear after a relatively short period. Although most groups have the potential to participate in policy making, many will not.

One can find evidence in Texas to support the pluralist view of power. **Pluralism** holds that significant numbers of diverse and competing interest groups serve to limit the power of any single group. Although most people do not actively participate in the policy-making process, they have access to the process through their group leaders. Pluralists believe that there are numerous leadership opportunities within groups for people who want active roles.

The number of **lobbyists** has grown significantly over the past three decades, and the hundreds now registered in Austin represent a wide assortment of economic, social, civic, and cultural organizations. Supporters of the pluralist view say this growth proves that the political system is open and accessible to new organizations. They argue that public officeholders are responsive to the needs and interests of a greater diversity of Texans than ever before.

Lobbyists and visitors, who are denied access to the floor of the senate chamber while it is in session, are seen mingling outside the chamber during a tax debate.

Others insist that pluralist theories simply do not describe the realities of power and policy making in Texas. Convinced of the persuasiveness of **elitism**, they contend that the ability to influence the most important policy decisions is monopolized by a few individuals who derive power from their leadership positions in organizations or institutions with great financial resources. In one view, from 1938 to 1957 Texas was "governed by conservatives, collectively dubbed **The Establishment**." This was a "loosely knit plutocracy comprised mostly of Anglo businessmen, oilmen, bankers and lawyers" that emerged in the late 1930s, in part, as a response to the liberal policies of the New Deal. They were extremely conservative, producing a "virulent" strain of conservatism marked by "Texanism" and "super-Americanism."[4]

The "traditionalistic-individualistic" political culture described in Chapter 21 was especially conducive to the dominance of the conservative establishment, which had little interest in the needs of the lower socioeconomic groups and minorities within the state. The exclusion of minorities from participation in elections and the low rates of voter turnout, particularly among the lower socioeconomic groups, resulted in the election of public officials who were sympathetic to the views of the conservative elites. In addition, public opinion was manipulated by "unprincipled public relations men" and "the rise of reactionary newspapers."[5]

A more recent study of Texas politics argues that there is a group of Texans—extraordinarily wealthy or linked to large corporations—who constitute "an upper class in the precise meaning of the term: a social group whose common background and effective control of wealth bring them together politically."[6] While warning against the hasty conclusion that this upper class is a ruling class, the study describes their shared values, group cohesiveness, and interlocking relationships.[7] The upper class has enormous political power. When united on specific policy objectives, its members have usually prevailed against "their liberal enemies concentrated in the working class."[8] Moreover, the institutional arrangements of the state's economic and political structure work to produce upper-class unity that contributes to their successes in public policy.[9]

These sharply contrasting views of political power in Texas have produced an ongoing debate. To a large extent, the issue of who really controls Texas politics has not been resolved because of insufficient data to support one position over the other. There also is evidence that power relationships have changed over time. Historically, Texas

elitism
Political system in which power is concentrated in the hands of a relatively small group of individuals or institutions.

"The Establishment"
In the days of one-party Democratic politics in Texas, the Establishment was a loosely knit coalition of Anglo business and oil company executives, bankers, and lawyers who controlled state policy making through the dominant conservative wing of the Democratic party.

government and public policy were dominated by an "upper class" or a "conservative establishment." But with the enormous social and economic changes that have taken place over the past twenty years, Texans may well be moving from an elitist system to some variation of pluralism.

DOMINANT INTEREST GROUPS IN TEXAS

Throughout much of the twentieth century, state government was dominated by large corporations, banks, oil companies, and agricultural interests that backed the conservative Democratic officeholders who had a stranglehold on the legislature, the courts, and the executive branch. Big business still carries a lot of weight in Austin and can purchase a lot of influence through major political contributions.

State officials who want to build public support for new policy proposals usually solicit the support of the business community first.

But beginning in the 1970s, influence began to be more diffused. **Single-member districts** increased the numbers of minorities, Republicans, and liberal Democrats elected to the legislature (see Chapter 24). Consumer, environmental, and other public advocacy groups emerged. Organized labor, which had been shut out by the corporate establishment, found some common interests with the trial lawyers, who earn fees suing businesses on behalf of consumers and other plaintiffs claiming damages or injuries caused by various companies or products. The decline of oil and gas production and the emergence of high-tech manufacturing and service industries also helped diffuse the business lobby into more competing factions.

Business Groups

The diverse business interests in Texas organize in several ways to influence the policy-making process. First, broad-based associations, including the Texas Association of Business and the Texas Taxpayers and Research Association, represent business and industry in general. Their overall goal is to maintain and improve upon a favorable business climate.

The business community also organizes through trade associations, such as the Texas Bankers Association, the Texas Automobile Dealers Association, the Texas Independent Producers & Royalty Owners Association, the Wholesale Beer Distributors of Texas, and the Texas Chemical Council. These groups represent and seek to advance the interests of specific industries.

Finally, many individual companies retain their own lobbyists to represent them before the legislature and administrative agencies. Some wealthy individuals, such as computer magnate Ross Perot of Dallas, even hire their own lobbyists.

Although most business groups band together against organized labor, consumer advocates, and trial lawyers on major political and philosophical issues, the business lobby is far from monolithic (see *You Decide/Thinking It Through:* "Do Lobbyists Represent You—the Average Citizen?"). There are numerous issues, including tax policy and utility regulation, on which companies or trade associations differ.

Professional Groups

A number of professional groups have played dominant roles in Texas politics and the policy-making process. One of the best known is the Texas Medical Association (TMA), which in recent years has joined forces with business against the trial lawyers in support of laws putting limits on malpractice suits and other damage claims against physicians and the business community. The TMA's political action committee is a major contributor of campaign dollars to candidates for the legislature and other state offices.

Litigation over medical malpractice, product liability, and workers' compensation has also expanded the influence of trial lawyers, who make their living representing injured persons. Individually and through their **political action committee**, trial lawyers have contributed millions of dollars to judicial, legislative, and other selected candidates since the 1970s. In the early 1980s, they succeeded in electing several Texas

single-member district
Election system in which one person is elected to represent the people living within one geographic district.

political action committee
Committee organized by a corporation, labor union, trade association, ideological or issue-oriented group, cooperative, or nonprofit corporation for the purpose of collecting campaign contributions and distributing the money to political candidates.

Supreme Court justices who shared their viewpoint, and the court issued major, precedent-setting opinions making it easier for plaintiffs to win large damage awards from businesses, doctors, and insurance companies. The business and medical communities retaliated by boosting their own political contributions and lobbying efforts and, by 1990, had succeeded in tipping the Supreme Court's philosophical scale back to its traditional business-oriented viewpoint.

But the war over **tort** law, as these types of damage suits are called, continued to rage before the judiciary and in the legislature. In 1995 and 2003, the legislature enacted several laws putting significant restrictions on damage lawsuits.

Education Groups

In the past several years, educational interests have been very visible in the policy-making process in Austin, and higher education lobbying has been particularly effective. The changing global economy has enhanced the role of higher education in developing the state's future, and there is widespread public support for expanded access to higher education.

Most university regents, chancellors, and presidents are well connected politically. Universities also are capable—through the use of donations and other nontax funds—of hiring a well-paid cadre of lobbyists. Another effective lobbying source for universities, particularly the larger ones, are the armies of alumni—many of them politically influential—who are ready to make phone calls, send e-mails, or write letters on behalf of their alma mater when the need arises. The business community is also a strong supporter of higher education. The influence of the University of Texas System, in particular, was instrumental in the legislature's enactment of a law in 2003 giving university governing boards the authority, for the first time in Texas, to raise student tuition independently of legislative control.

The struggle for equity and quality in public elementary and secondary education in Texas, a major issue since the 1940s, has been complicated by more than two dozen groups representing various—and often conflicting—interests within the educational community. There are at least four different teachers' groups, one for school boards, one for school administrators, and still others for elementary school principals and secondary school principals. Separate groups have also been formed for urban school districts, suburban districts, rural districts, and districts with large numbers of special needs students. Virtually all these groups employ paid lobbyists, and while all claim to support educational quality, their primary goals are to protect the specific interests of their members.

Public Interest Groups

Most of the public interest groups represented in Austin are concerned with protecting consumers and the environment from big business, promoting stronger ethical standards for public officials, and increasing funding for health and human services programs for the poor, the elderly, the young, and the disabled. Many have full-time lobbyists, but these groups are seldom able to match the financial resources of business and professional organizations. Grassroots volunteer efforts and the adroit use of the mass media are crucial to their success. Among the most active are Common Cause, the Sierra Club, Consumers Union, Texas Citizen Action, Texas Watch, the Gray Panthers, Americans Disabled for Attendant Programs Today (ADAPT), and Public Citizen, a Texas affiliate of the national public interest group founded by consumer advocate Ralph Nader.

Minority Interest Groups

The advent of single-member, urban legislative districts in the 1970s significantly increased the number of African American and Hispanic lawmakers and strengthened the influence of minority interest groups. These groups have often found that the

---

★★ THINKING IT THROUGH

Special interest groups and lobbyists legally spend money to influence Texas legislators during legislative sessions as well as at summer conferences. Some argue that these summer conferences are nothing more than vacations for the legislators. The special interests pay for the conference, food, liquor, and entertainment such as golf. The taxpayers pay for the transportation for the conferences. Legislators argue that this is an opportunity to network with legislators from other states and interact with experts on issues facing the state.

Arguments for Change

1. These conferences are nothing more than lobbyists buying influence.
2. Legislators should rely on interaction with voters to shape their policy-making responsibility.
3. This sort of interaction with well-financed interests leads to corruption.

Arguments Against Change

1. A good legislator is well informed. These conferences are a valuable tool in gaining information.
2. Legislators can learn from the success and failures of other states before enacting new programs in Texas.
3. Legislators work long hours, are paid little and thus deserve these vacation conferences.

---

tort
A wrongful act or injury for which a damage lawsuit can be brought.

★★ YOU DECIDE

DO LOBBYISTS REPRESENT YOU—THE AVERAGE CITIZEN?

Do lobbyists represent you? Should lobbyists be restricted in their activities? Should former members of the legislature be restricted from lobbying? How could legislation be enacted that would not violate First Amendment rights?

courthouse is a shorter route to success than the statehouse, but the legislature has become increasingly attentive to their voices.

The League of United Latin American Citizens (LULAC) and the Mexican American Legal Defense and Educational Fund (MALDEF) are two of the better-known Hispanic organizations. LULAC, founded in 1929, is the oldest and largest Hispanic organization in the United States and continues to be particularly influential in causes such as education and election reform in Texas. MALDEF, formed in San Antonio in 1968, fights in the courtroom for the civil rights of Hispanics. It has been successful in numerous battles over the drawing of political boundaries for governmental bodies in Texas and in lengthy litigation over public school finance. MALDEF represented the property-poor school districts that won a unanimous landmark Texas Supreme Court order in 1989 (*Edgewood* v. *Kirby*) for a more equitable distribution of education aid between rich and poor school districts. The victory led to major legislative changes in the school finance system.

The National Association for the Advancement of Colored People (NAACP) is a leader in promoting and protecting the interests of African Americans. The NAACP initiated many of the early court attacks on educational inequality and the disfranchisement of minorities. More recently, this group has worked hard to increase employment opportunities for African Americans in state agencies, particularly in higher-paying administrative jobs.

In recent years, the Industrial Areas Foundation, a collection of well-organized, church-supported community groups, has become a strong and effective voice for low-income minorities. Member groups include Valley Interfaith in South Texas, Communities Organized for Public Service (COPS) in San Antonio, The Metropolitan Organization (TMO) in Houston, and the El Paso Interreligious Sponsoring Organization (EPISO).

Organized Labor Groups

Organized labor has traditionally taken a back seat to business in Texas, a strong right-to-work state in which union membership cannot be required as a condition of employment. Antilabor sentiment ran particularly high in the 1940s and 1950s, at the height of the conservative Democratic establishment's control of Texas politics. Labor-baiting campaigns in which unions were portrayed as evil communist sympathizers were not uncommon then.[10]

Today, about 500,000 Texans are members of labor unions. Among the largest unions in the state are the Communications Workers of America, the International Brotherhood of Electrical Workers, the International Association of Machinists and Aerospace Workers, the United Food and Commercial Workers International Union, and the American Federation of State, County and Municipal Employees.

Unions can provide strong grassroots support for political candidates through the distribution of campaign literature endorsing specific candidates, the use of union phone banks, and other get-out-the-vote efforts. Such union support has historically gone to Democratic candidates. Labor generally sides with the trial lawyers on such issues as workers' compensation, worker safety, and business liability for faulty products.

Government Lobbyists

Local governments are significantly affected by state laws and budgetary decisions. The stakes are particularly high now because most governments are finding revenue harder to raise—especially with the federal government passing the cost of numerous programs on to the state, and the state issuing similar mandates to local governments. As a result, counties, cities, prosecutors, metropolitan transit authorities, and various special districts are represented by lobbyists in Austin.

Many local governments belong to umbrella organizations, such as the Texas Municipal League, the Texas Association of Counties, and the Texas District and County Attorneys Association, which have full-time lobbyists. Several of the larger cities and counties also retain their own lobbyists. Mayors, city council members, and county judges also frequently travel to Austin to visit with legislators and testify for or against bills.

Agriculture Groups

Although Texas is now predominantly urban, agriculture is still an important part of the state's economy, and a number of agriculture groups are represented in Austin. Their influence is obviously strongest among rural legislators. But the Texas Farm Bureau—the largest such group and probably the most conservative—was instrumental in the 1990 defeat of liberal Democratic Agriculture Commissioner Jim Hightower, who had angered many agricultural producers and the chemical industry with tough stands on farm worker rights and pesticide regulation.

Other producer groups include the Texas and Southwestern Cattle Raisers Association, the Texas Poultry Federation, and the Texas Corn Producers Board.

Religious Groups

Many people, influenced in part by their views on separation of church and state, think religious groups have little or no legitimate role in the political process. Nevertheless, religious groups have helped influence policy in Texas, and the abortion issue and other social and economic issues have increased the presence of religious groups in Austin.

A number of religious groups emerged in the 1940s with an identifiable right-wing orientation. These groups, predecessors to what is now known as the **Religious Right**, combined Christian rhetoric and symbols with anticommunist, antilabor, anti–civil rights, antiliberal, or anti–New Deal themes. Although these groups were often very small, they were linked to the extreme right wing of the Texas establishment, and they were the precursors of many of the conservative ideological groups that have emerged in American politics in the past twenty years.[11] Many of these organizations have gravitated toward the Republican party[12] (see *FYI:* "The Religious Right and Republican Growth"). With a strong organizational effort, religious conservatives were influential in a right-wing takeover of leadership positions in the Texas Republican party in 1994.

Many religious denominations have boards or commissions responsible for monitoring governmental action. Although staff members or volunteers serving in this capacity may not register as lobbyists, they function much like lobbyists.

Churches across the state have formed community-based organizations to address the social and economic needs of the poor. In many regards, this is a redefinition of the Social Gospel, a church-based social movement of the late nineteenth and early twentieth centuries.

THE DEVELOPMENT OF A TWO-PARTY SYSTEM IN TEXAS

The Texas party system has been restructured by the social and economic changes that the state has experienced over the past thirty years. Texas now has a strong Republican Party and a competitive **two-party system**, but for more than a century, Texas was a **one-party** Democratic state. There was no organized opposition party to mobilize those who felt excluded from the Democratic Party. Electoral politics were based on factions and personalities; the interests of the lower socioeconomic classes—especially minorities—were blatantly neglected.

One-Party Democratic Politics

Texas's long domination by the Democratic party can be traced to the period immediately after the Civil War, when the Republican party was able to capture control of Texas government for a short period. Strong anti-Republican feelings were generated by the

Religious Right
Political movement, based primarily in evangelical Protestant churches, that has played an increasingly prominent role in Texas and national politics.

two-party system
Political system that has two dominant parties, such as that of the United States.

one-party system
Domination of elections and governmental processes by a single party, which may be split into different ideological, economic, or regional factions. In Texas, the phrase is used to describe the period from the late 1870s to the late 1970s, when the Democratic party claimed virtually all elected, partisan offices.

THE RELIGIOUS RIGHT AND REPUBLICAN GROWTH

As the Republican party expanded its support in Texas, it experienced sharp, often bitter, philosophical and ideological differences among its members. Overwhelmingly conservative, Republicans were split along the lines of economic conservatism and the "lifestyle" conservatism advocated by the Religious Right.

The Religious Right has long been part of the Texas political landscape.* While its influence was occasionally manifested in conservative Democratic politics, it found far greater potential in the Republican party for shaping electoral politics. It has strong religious overtones and draws considerable support from evangelical groups across the state. Some scholars attribute much of its success to its ability to mobilize voters who were traditionally inactive and bring them into the Republican party. The Republicans' difficulty in attracting minority groups also gave the social conservative wing greater influence in the party.

In 1990, one scholar concluded that the Religious Right had not taken over the Republican party, "but its influence is significant and gives the Texas Republicans their particular stridency and, at times, their appearance of a Know-Nothing movement."[†] In 1994, however, the Religious Right was instrumental in a takeover by social conservatives of the Republican state convention and the party leadership.

Low voter turnout in the Republican primary enabled well-organized social conservatives to gain control of the party's precinct conventions and elect a majority of delegates to the June state convention. Sensing defeat, Fred Meyer, a traditional Republican who had guided the state party for six years during a period of growth and electoral success, stepped down and was replaced by Tom Pauken, a Dallas lawyer and former Reagan administration official who courted Christian activists. Delegates also elected a new party vice chair, Christian activist Susan Weddington of San Antonio, and put other members of the Religious Right on the State Republican Executive Committee.

The Religious Right also was instrumental in the election of Republican George W. Bush over Democrat Ann Richards in the 1994 gubernatorial race. According to a survey of voters as they left the polls, 20 percent of the 4.4 million Texans who voted in that election identified themselves as white Christian fundamentalists. Of those, 84 percent said they voted for Bush. They also voted heavily for other Republican candidates.[†]

Social and religious conservatives also took control of the 1996 Republican state convention and dominated the Texas delegation to the Republican National Convention. Some social conservatives, insisting the party retain its strong anti-abortion policy, tried to deny U.S. Senator Kay Bailey Hutchison a delegate's slot to the national convention because she favored abortion rights with some restrictions. Such a move would have been an unheard-of snub for a high-ranking officeholder from the party. Hutchison finally got on the delegate list with the help of Governor Bush, U.S. Senator Phil Gramm, and Republican presidential nominee Bob Dole.

The State Republican Executive Committee elected Susan Weddington state party chair after Pauken resigned in 1997 to seek the Republican nomination for state attorney general. Weddington served in that post and was an outspoken advocate for social conservative causes until 2003, when she resigned to take a job directing a new state charitable foundation. The State Republican Executive Committee elected party activist Tina Benkiser, an attorney from Houston, to succeed her.

---

*George Norris Green, *The Establishment in Texas Politics, 1938–1957* (Greenwood Press, 1979), chap. 15.
[†]Chandler Davidson, *Race and Class in Texas Politics* (Princeton University Press, 1990), p. 206.
[‡]*Dallas Morning News,* November 11, 1994.

Reconstruction administration of Radical Republican Governor Edmund J. Davis, and the Republican party was perceived by most Texans of that era to be the party of conquest and occupation. By the time the Constitution of 1876 was implemented, the Republican party's influence in state politics was negligible. From 1874 to 1961, no Republican won a statewide office in Texas, and Republicans were elected to local offices in a few scattered districts.

The anti-Republicanism that evolved from the Civil War and Reconstruction, however, is only a partial explanation for the Democratic Party's longtime control of Texas politics. One classic study presents the provocative thesis that Texas politics might be better understood in terms of "modified class politics."[13]

As Texas's conservative agricultural leaders attempted to regain control over the state's political system after Reconstruction, the postwar economic devastation was dividing Texans along class lines. Small farmers, African Americans, and an emerging urban labor class suffered disproportionately from the economic depression of this period. They turned their discontent into support for agrarian third parties, particularly the Populist party, which began to threaten the monopoly of the traditional Texas power structure.

To protect their political power, the established agricultural leaders moved to divide the lower social groups by directing the discontent of lower-income whites against blacks. The rural elites, who manifested traditionalistic political values and wanted to consolidate power in the hands of the privileged few, also created alliances with the mercantile, banking, and emerging industrial leaders, who reflected the individualistic view of a limited government that served to protect their interests. Over the years, these two dominant forces consolidated political power and merged the politics of race with the politics of economics.

The elites were able to institutionalize their control through the adoption of constitutional restrictions and segregation legislation, called **Jim Crow laws**, designed to reduce the size of the electorate and the potential of a popular challenge to the establishment's political monopoly.[14]

The Texas Democratic party, however, was not homogeneous. There were factions, regional differences, and personal political rivalries. Initially, there were no sustained, identifiable factions, as voting coalitions changed from election to election through much of the first third of the twentieth century. But the onset of the Great Depression in 1929, the election of President Franklin D. Roosevelt in 1932, and the policies of the New Deal reshaped Texas politics in the 1930s.

Factionalism in the Democratic Party

Franklin Roosevelt's administrations (1933–1945) articulated and developed a policy agenda radically different from that of the Republican party, which had dominated national politics from 1860 to 1932. Government was to become a buffer against economic downturns as well as a positive force for change. Under Roosevelt, the regulatory function of the federal government was expanded to exercise control and authority over much of the nation's economy. The federal government also enacted programs such as Social Security, public housing, and labor legislation to benefit lower socioeconomic groups.

These national policies produced an active philosophical split within the Texas Democratic party that was to characterize Texas politics for the next two generations. A majority of Texas voters supported Roosevelt in his four elections, and the Democratic party maintained its monopoly over Texas politics. But competing economic interests clearly—and often bitterly—divided Texas Democrats along liberal and conservative lines.

A strong Republican Party did not emerge at this time in Texas or any other southern state because "southern conservative Democratic politicians, who would have been expected to lead such a realignment, or any politicians for that matter, did not relish jumping from a majority-status party to one in the minority."[15]

Despite some liberal successes under Governor James Allred, who was elected in 1934 and again in 1936, the conservative wing of the Democratic Party prevailed in state elections from the 1940s to the late 1970s. Democratic presidential candidates carried Texas in 1944, 1948, 1960, 1964, 1968, and 1976, even though some of them were too liberal to suit the tastes of the state's conservative Democratic establishment.

At first glance, it might appear that the **bifactionalism** in the Democratic Party partially compensated for the lack of a competitive two-party system, but one scholar argued against that perception, concluding that factionalism resulted in "no-party politics." Factionalism results in discontinuity in leadership and group support, and the voter has no permanent reference point from which to judge the performance of the party or selected candidates. Since there are no clear distinctions between who holds power and who does not, the influence of pressure groups increases.[16] In one-party Democratic Texas, as noted, state government and public policy were susceptible to control by wealthy and corporate interests.

Jim Crow laws
Legislation enacted by many states after the Civil War to limit the rights and power of African Americans.

bifactionalism
Presence of two dominant factions organized around regional, economic, or ideological differences within a single political party. For much of the twentieth century, Texas functioned as a one-party system with two dominant factions.

John Tower's surprise election to the U.S. Senate in 1961 was the first statewide victory by a Republican in Texas since Reconstruction.

realignment
Major shift in political party support or identification that usually occurs around a critical election. In Texas, realignment took place as a gradual transformation from a one-party system dominated by Democrats to a two-party system in which Republicans became competitive in elections.

gerrymandering
Drawing the boundaries of legislative districts in such a way as to increase the power of one group over another.

Voting Rights Act
Federal law designed to protect the voting rights of minorities by requiring the Justice Department's approval of changes in political districts and certain other electoral procedures. The 1965 act, as amended, has eliminated most of the restrictive practices that limited minority political participation.

This bifactional pattern of state Democratic politics was tested by a number of factors, including the national party's increased commitment after 1948 to civil rights legislation. That development alienated segments of the white population and prompted many voters eventually to leave the Democratic party and align with the Republicans.

Efforts by Texas oil interests to reestablish state control over the oil-rich tidelands also played a key role in the demise of one-party politics and the development of a two-party system. President Harry Truman, concerned about national security and federal access to these offshore oil resources, refused to accede to state demands and vetoed legislation favorable to Texas oil interests in 1952. That veto prompted a series of maneuvers orchestrated by Democratic Governor Allan Shivers to take the support of conservative Democrats to the Republican party.

The "Shivercrats," as they were called, were successful in carrying Texas for the 1952 Republican presidential nominee, Dwight D. Eisenhower. This election helped establish a pattern of Texas's retaining its Democratic leanings in state and local elections but voting Republican in many presidential elections. Moreover, this election marked a shift in the state leadership of the Republican party and led to efforts to create a party capable of winning local and statewide elections.[17]

In 1960, Democrat Lyndon B. Johnson ran both for election as vice president and for reelection as U.S. senator from Texas—a dual candidacy permitted under state law—and won both offices. His Republican opponent in the Senate race was John Tower, a relatively unknown college professor from Wichita Falls, who received 41 percent of the vote. After Johnson won the vice presidency and resigned from the Senate, a special election to fill the Senate seat was called in 1961. It attracted 71 candidates, including Tower, who defeated conservative Democrat William Blakely with 50.6 percent of the vote in a runoff.[18] Some evidence indicates that liberal Democrats, in retaliation for having been locked out of the power centers of their party and in anticipation of an ideological realignment of the party system, supported Tower in this election. The *Texas Observer*, an influential liberal publication, endorsed Tower with an argument for a two-party system. "How many liberals voted for Tower will never be known, nor will it be known how many 'went fishing,'" wrote a Republican campaign consultant.[19] Tower was reelected in 1966, 1972, and 1978, but no other Texas Republican won a statewide office until 1978, when Bill Clements was elected governor. Nevertheless, many students of Texas politics regard Tower's election in 1961 as a key factor in the development of the state's two-party system.[20]

Although Republicans made some gains in suburban congressional districts and local elections in the 1960s—including the election to Congress of a Houston Republican named George Herbert Walker Bush—the numbers were inconsequential. Most significant election battles continued to take place for a while longer within the Democratic party, where the conservative wing generally prevailed until 1978.

Two-Party Politics in Texas

On the national level, **realignment** of political parties is often associated with a critical election in which economic or social issues cut across existing party allegiances and produce a permanent shift in party support and identification.[21] What apparently has happened in Texas is that the state party system has been integrated into the national party system and now more closely approximates the political divisions that exist in states outside the South. Rather than occurring in a single election, this process has occurred over many years.

A major contributor to change was the civil rights movement. African Americans and Hispanics went to federal court to attack state laws requiring segregation and restricting minority voting rights. Successful lawsuits were brought against the white primary, the preprimary endorsement, the poll tax (all discussed later in this chapter), and racial **gerrymandering** of political districts. Then minorities turned to the U.S. Congress for civil rights legislation, a process that produced the 1965 **Voting Rights Act**, which Congress extended to cover Texas after 1975.

Economic factors have also shaped minority political support and, in turn, have contributed to two-party development. African Americans and Hispanics are disproportionately low-income populations and generally support such governmental services as public housing, public health care, day care, and income support. These policies are associated with the liberal wing of the Democratic party.

Minority organizations have made concerted efforts to register, educate, and mobilize the people in their communities. As the numerical strength of minorities increased, conservative Anglo Democrats found their position within the party threatened and began to look to the Republican party as an alternative.

The large number of people who migrated to Texas from other states, particularly when the Sunbelt economy of the 1970s and early 1980s was booming and many northern industrial states were struggling, also contributed to two-party development in Texas. Many of these new arrivals were Republicans from states with strong Republican parties, and many of them settled in high-income, suburban, Anglo areas in Texas. Other significant factors were Presidents Ronald Reagan's and George Bush's popularity in the 1980s and the 1978 election of Republican Governor Bill Clements, who encouraged many conservative Democratic officeholders to switch parties.

Other events of the 1970s and the 1980s demonstrated that the transformation of the Texas party system was well on its way. After a major stock fraud scandal, the Texas House elected a liberal Democrat, Price Daniel Jr. as Speaker in 1973. Three other moderate-to-liberal Democrats were also elected to statewide office in the early 1970s—Bob Armstrong as land commissioner in 1970, John Hill as attorney general in 1972, and Bob Bullock as comptroller in 1974.

In 1978, John Hill defeated Governor Dolph Briscoe, a conservative, in the Democratic primary and was subsequently defeated by Republican Bill Clements, then a political unknown, in the general election by a narrow margin of 17,000 votes. Four years later, Clements lost to Democratic Attorney General Mark White, but in 1986 he returned to defeat White in an expensive, bitter campaign. In the 1982 election, Democratic candidates who were considered liberal won additional statewide offices: Ann Richards was elected state treasurer; Jim Mattox, attorney general; Jim Hightower, agriculture commissioner; and Garry Mauro, land commissioner.

The 1990 election further demonstrated how far the realignment process had gone. Democratic gubernatorial nominee Ann Richards defeated conservative business executive Clayton Williams, who had spent $6 million of his own money to win the Republican primary. But Republican Kay Bailey Hutchison was elected state treasurer, and Republican Rick Perry unseated liberal Democrat Jim Hightower to become agriculture commissioner. Republicans also retained one of the U.S. Senate seats from Texas when Phil Gramm easily won reelection to the seat once held by John Tower, and the GOP claimed 8 of the 27 congressional seats that Texas then had in Congress.

In a special election in 1993 to fill the U.S. Senate seat vacated by Democrat Lloyd Bentsen when he was appointed secretary of the treasury by President Bill Clinton, Kay Bailey Hutchison defeated Democrat Bob Krueger, thus giving the Republicans both U.S. Senate seats from Texas. Hutchison easily won reelection in 1994, despite a political and legal controversy over her administration of the state treasurer's office.

Also in 1994, Democratic Governor Ann Richards was unseated by Republican nominee George W. Bush, the son of former President George Bush and a future president himself. Republicans that year also captured four other statewide offices that had been held by Democrats, marking the most statewide gains by Republicans in any single election since Reconstruction.

Party realignment was also reflected in the Texas legislature. In 1971, Republicans held only 12 of the 181 legislative seats. But by 2004, Republicans held 88 of the 150 House seats and 19 of the 31 Senate seats.

Toward Republican Dominance

The political transformation of Texas accelerated even more in 1996, when Republicans swept all statewide offices on the general election ballot and captured a majority of the state Senate for the first time since Reconstruction. Republican presidential nominee Bob Dole also carried the Lone Star State, despite a poor national showing against

LA RAZA UNIDA

La Raza Unida, led by Jose Angel Gutierrez and Mario Compean, began in 1969 to organize in Crystal City in Zavala County and then extended its influence to Dimmit, La Salle, and Hidalgo counties.* Overwhelmingly Hispanic and poor, these counties were characteristic of many South Texas counties where the Anglo minority controlled both the political and economic institutions, and there was little sensitivity to the needs of low-income residents. In 1972, Ramsey Muniz ran as the party's gubernatorial candidate. During the general election campaign, there was considerable speculation in the press and apprehension among conservative Democrats that La Raza would drain a sufficient number of votes away from Dolph Briscoe, the Democratic nominee, to give Henry "Hank" Grover, a right-wing Republican, the governorship. Briscoe won the election, but without a majority of the votes. The subsequent growth of liberal and minority influence within the Democratic Party, internal dissension within La Raza Unida, and legal problems encountered by Muniz contributed to the demise of this third party after 1978.

*Juan Gomez Quinones, *Chicano Politics* (University of New Mexico Press, 1990), pp. 128–31.

President Clinton. Republicans also increased their numbers in the Texas House and in the Texas congressional delegation. When the electoral dust had cleared, Republicans held 20 of Texas's 29 statewide elected offices, including the top three. That number increased to 21 in 1997, when Presiding Judge Michael McCormick of the Texas Court of Criminal Appeals switched from the Democratic to the Republican party.

Lieutenant Governor Bob Bullock and Attorney General Dan Morales, both Democrats, chose not to seek reelection or any other office in 1998, and Republicans cashed in on the opportunity. With Governor Bush winning reelection in a landslide, Republicans again swept all statewide offices on the ballot. And a few weeks after the 1998 election, the GOP secured all statewide offices in Texas for the first time since Reconstruction when Texas Supreme Court Justice Raul A. Gonzalez, a Democrat, retired in midterm and was replaced by a Republican appointee of Bush. Republicans did not capture control of the Texas House but picked up four seats to narrow the Democratic margin to six seats. In the governor's race, Bush carried 69 percent of the vote against Democratic challenger Garry Mauro, the longtime land commissioner.

Democrats fielded candidates for only three of the nine statewide offices up for election in 2000. One Democrat filed for each of two seats on the Texas Court of Criminal Appeals, and five Democrats, all minor candidates with little financial support, filed for Republican Kay Bailey Hutchison's U.S. Senate seat. Democrats lost all their statewide races in 2000 but held their ground in legislative races.

Republicans also swept all statewide races in 2002, including Governor Rick Perry's victory over Democratic nominee Tony Sanchez and former Texas Attorney General John Cornyn's victory over former Dallas Mayor Ron Kirk in a race to succeed retiring U.S. Senator Phil Gramm. Republicans also finally gained control of the Texas House of Representatives in 2002, capturing 88 of the 150 seats after the Legislative Redistricting Board in 2001 had drawn new districts that favored Republicans (see Chapter 24). Additionally, the GOP increased its margin in the state Senate by winning 19 of the 31 seats. All statewide elected officials remained Republican.

The statewide losses in 2002 were particularly disappointing for Democratic leaders, who had carefully assembled a racially diverse ticket with an eye toward increasing minority turnout. Kirk, the U.S. Senate candidate, was African American, and Sanchez, a wealthy businessman from Laredo, was Hispanic. The Democratic nominee for lieutenant governor, John Sharp, a former state comptroller, was Anglo. Sanchez was unexpectedly challenged in the Democratic primary by former Texas Attorney General Dan Morales. The race was historic because it was the first gubernatorial contest in Texas between two Hispanics, and it was extremely contentious. Sanchez was supported by most party leaders because the party was banking on his wealth to help finance the Democrats' general election campaign.

Republicans achieved still another long-sought goal in 2004—a majority of Texas's congressional delegation—after the legislature, in a bitter partisan fight in 2003, had redrawn congressional district boundaries to favor GOP candidates (see Chapter 24).

The GOP also has made significant gains across Texas at the county level. In 1974, Republicans held 53 county offices but had claimed 1,443 by 2003, paralleling the dramatic statewide realignment that was occurring. Democrats still held most county offices, but Republicans were battling for dominance as local voting patterns began to reflect those for statewide offices (see Table 23–1).

Third Parties

There has been a tradition of third parties in Texas, including Grangers, Populists, Progressives, Socialists, Dixiecrats, the American Independent party, Libertarians, and La Raza Unida (see *FYI:* "La Raza Unida"). None has had statewide electoral success, a situation that can be explained in part by the cultural consensus supporting the two-party and winner-take-all election systems. Most Americans do not have highly cohesive political views, which are part of the appeal of many third parties.

The most successful third party in Texas in recent years has been the Libertarian party. Libertarians have qualified for a place on the ballot in every Texas general election

TABLE 23–1		GROWTH OF REPUBLICAN OFFICEHOLDERS IN TEXAS, 1974–2002					
Year	U.S. Senate	Other Statewide	U.S. Congress	Texas Senate	Texas House	County Offices	Total
1974	1	0	2	3	16	53	75
1976	1	0	2	3	19	67	92
1978	1	1	4	4	22	87	119
1980	1	1	5	7	35	166	215
1982	1	0	5	5	36	191	238
1984	1	0	10	6	52	287	356
1986	1	1	10	6	56	410	484
1988	1	5	8	8	57	485	564
1990	1	6	8	8	57	547	627
1992	1	8	9	13	58	634	723
1994	2	13	11	14	61	734	835
1996	2	18	13	17	68	938	1056
1998	2	27	13	16	72	1108	1238
2000	2	27	13	16	72	1299	1429
2002	2	27	15	19	88	1443	1594

SOURCE: Republican party of Texas.

since 1986 because the party has succeeded in winning at least 5 percent of the vote in at least one statewide race during each election year. But the party has never won an elected office in Texas. Another minor party, the Green party, which puts a high priority on environmental protection, also qualified for the Texas ballot in 2002.

In addition to statewide third parties, local political organizations connected to neither the Democratic nor the Republican party have been influential in some cities. Elections for city offices are nonpartisan, and most are held during odd-numbered years, when there are no state offices on the ballot. Cities such as San Antonio and Dallas developed citizens' associations, which controlled city governments for decades and maintained a virtual monopoly over city elections. But these local political parties have disappeared in recent years.

CHANGING PATTERNS OF PARTY SUPPORT AND IDENTIFICATION

The changes in party affiliations over the past forty years reinforce the argument that Texas is now a two-party state. In 1952, 66 percent of Texans called themselves Democrats, and only 6 percent claimed to be Republicans,[22] a pattern that changed little from 1952 to 1964. During the next decade, however, Republican party identification increased to 16 percent, and Democratic party identification declined to 59 percent (see Figure 23–1).

Between 1975 and 1984, there was a dramatic decline in voter identification with the Democratic Party and a significant increase in Republican party identification (see *FYI:* "Where Have All the Yellow Dogs Gone?"). By 2004, approximately 35 percent of Texas voters called themselves Republicans, and 27 percent identified as Democrats. The remainder called themselves independents (24 percent), third-party affiliates or undecided (14 percent). This shift in party identification is further proof that Texas is now a Republican-dominant state. (see Figure 23–2).

As noted above, a large number of voters identify themselves as independents. Independents don't have their own party, and their choices in most elections are limited

WHERE HAVE ALL THE YELLOW DOGS GONE?

For a longtime Democrat (who is a person 50 or older), there is a bit of nostalgia when someone asks, "Where have all the yellow dogs gone?" To a newcomer to the state, this probably conjures up an image of a mangy, brownish-yellow mutt that is used for coon hunting or running the dogs at night while his keeper drinks hard liquor with friends around the campfire. But to a real Democrat, it is a code term for those Democrats, often white conservatives, who swore by the phrase, "I'd vote for a yellow dog if he ran on the Democratic ticket." Moreover, those "yellow dogs" also would encourage voters to "pull one lever"—that is, vote straight Democratic.

The yellow-dog, one-party voters are a dying breed. Historically, there were counties in Texas that, until recently, had never elected a Republican to local office. Some never had a Republican party organization or had seen a Republican challenge a Democrat in a local election. With the transformation of the state to Republican dominance, there are fewer and fewer yellow dogs. Franklin County, which is in deep East Texas, didn't elect a member of the GOP from 1875 to 2000. But in 2002, three Republicans won election to local offices.

So, where have all the yellow dogs gone? The answer is clear. Many of them have died and passed over. Many others have converted to the Republican party and are now voting the straight GOP ticket. Some of those yellow dogs have become pedigreed Republicans.

SOURCE: John Williams, *Houston Chronicle*, November 17, 2002.

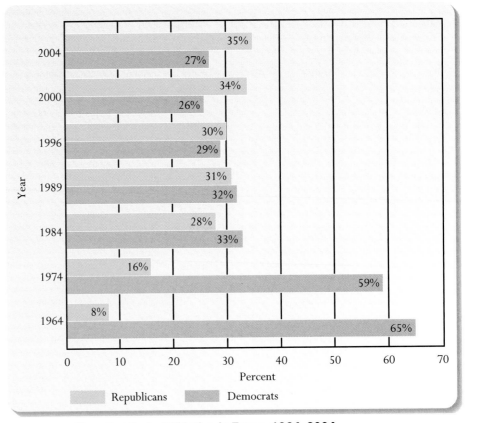

FIGURE 23–1 Changing Party Affiliation in Texas, 1964–2004.
SOURCE: *Texas Poll,* Summer 1993, Fall 1993, Winter 1996, Spring 1996, Fall 1996, Spring 1999, Summer 1999, Fall 1999, Winter 2000, Summer 2003, Fall 2003, Winter 2004, Spring 2004.

to candidates from the two major parties. Further survey research, moreover, suggests that most self-proclaimed independents vote consistently for Republican candidates.

Ticket splitting, a practice associated with the realignment process, has been common in recent Texas elections. It explains, in part, why Democrats have still been able to keep most local offices despite Republican sweeps statewide. Many Texans cast their votes selectively as they go down the general election ballot. Ticket splitting, however, is likely to decrease in the future as the new patterns of party affiliation solidify with a further increase of elected Republican officials and a reduction in the number of Democratic candidates in areas where Republicans dominate.

The *Texas Poll* and other studies indicate marked differences in the social and economic characteristics of party identifiers. From these data, analysts have made the following generalizations:

1. The Republican party is composed disproportionately of voters who fall into one or more of the following categories:
    - College educated
    - Newcomers to Texas
    - Anglos
    - Large metropolitan area residents
    - Earning higher incomes
    - Middle aged

2. Democrats are strongly represented among:
    - Minorities
    - Older residents
    - Native Texans
    - Those with lower income levels
    - Those with less education[23]

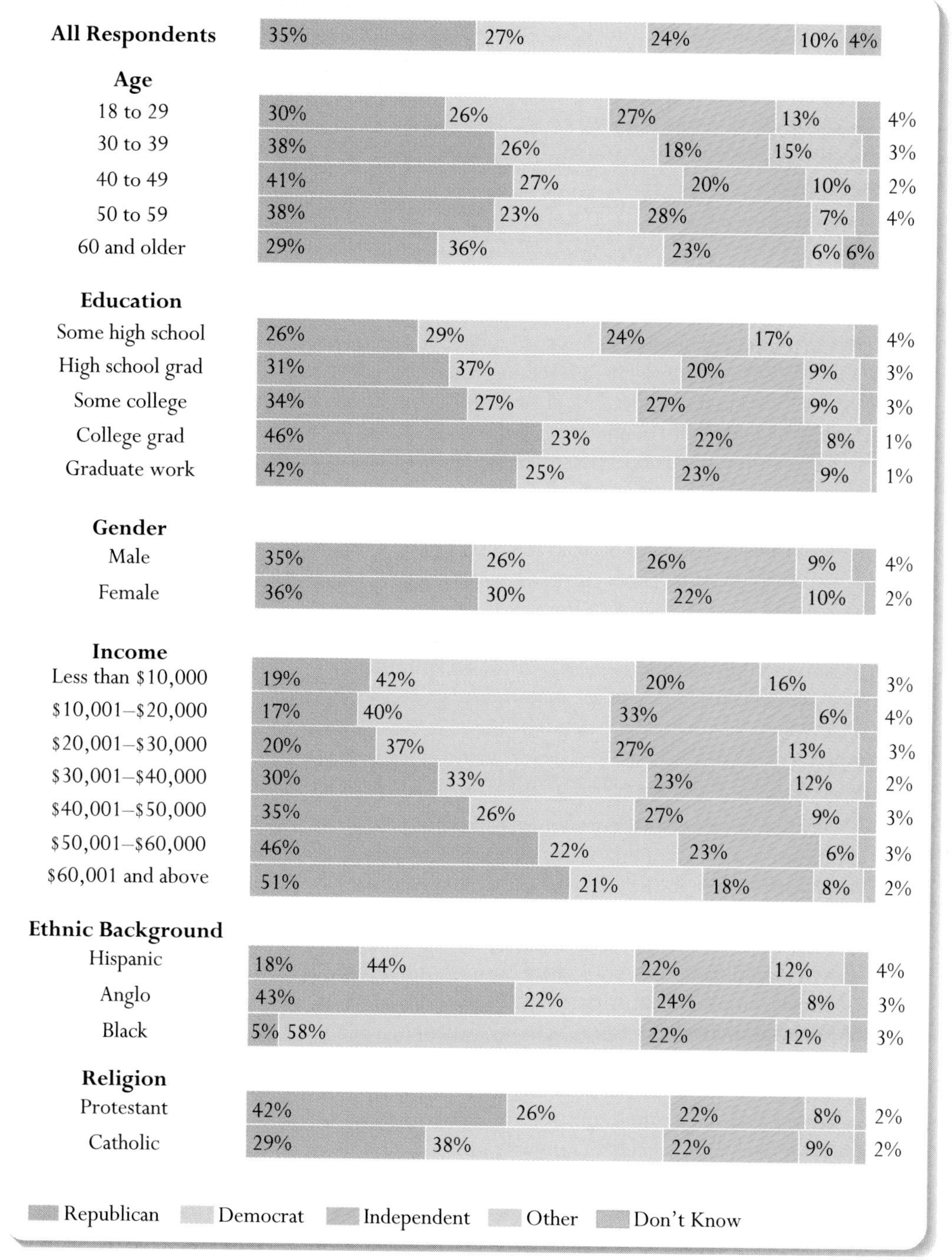

All Respondents	35%	27%	24%	10%	4%

Age

18 to 29	30%	26%	27%	13%	4%
30 to 39	38%	26%	18%	15%	3%
40 to 49	41%	27%	20%	10%	2%
50 to 59	38%	23%	28%	7%	4%
60 and older	29%	36%	23%	6%	6%

Education

Some high school	26%	29%	24%	17%	4%
High school grad	31%	37%	20%	9%	3%
Some college	34%	27%	27%	9%	3%
College grad	46%	23%	22%	8%	1%
Graduate work	42%	25%	23%	9%	1%

Gender

Male	35%	26%	26%	9%	4%
Female	36%	30%	22%	10%	2%

Income

Less than $10,000	19%	42%	20%	16%	3%
$10,001–$20,000	17%	40%	33%	6%	4%
$20,001–$30,000	20%	37%	27%	13%	3%
$30,001–$40,000	30%	33%	23%	12%	2%
$40,001–$50,000	35%	26%	27%	9%	3%
$50,001–$60,000	46%	22%	23%	6%	3%
$60,001 and above	51%	21%	18%	8%	2%

Ethnic Background

Hispanic	18%	44%	22%	12%	4%
Anglo	43%	22%	24%	8%	3%
Black	5%	58%	22%	12%	3%

Religion

Protestant	42%	26%	22%	8%	2%
Catholic	29%	38%	22%	9%	2%

■ Republican   ■ Democrat   ■ Independent   ■ Other   ■ Don't Know

FIGURE 23–2 Party Identification of Texas Voters by Social Groups, 2004.
SOURCE: Scripps Howard, *Texas Poll*, Summer 2003, Fall 2003, Winter 2004, Spring 2004. A total of 4,000 Texans were surveyed in these polls.

Seeking to expand the Republican party's base, Governor George W. Bush made a strong appeal to Hispanics during his 1998 reelection campaign and was rewarded with about 40 percent of the Hispanic vote. Republicans in 2000 and 2002 also used campaign strategies aimed at peeling off Hispanic voters from the Democratic party. Some Republican strategists have been arguing for years that the GOP must strengthen its appeal to the growing Hispanic population—and chip away at Hispanics' traditional support for the Democratic party—if the GOP is to maintain its control over state politics. Anglo Protestants, who form the core of the Republican party, are declining in proportion to the increased number of Hispanics in Texas. To maintain dominance, it has been argued, Republicans must embrace issues, such as improved health care and educational opportunities, which are central to Hispanic voting interests. It is premature to conclude that there will be an erosion of Hispanic support from the Democratic party, but both parties will be battling for the Hispanic vote over the next two decades. Republicans also have spoken about the need to appeal to African American Texans who share their core values, but the GOP has had little success attracting African Americans from the Democratic Party.

THE PARTY ORGANIZATION

To carry out their functions, the two major parties in Texas have developed permanent and temporary organizations, structured by state law, state and national party rules and a series of court decisions protecting voters' rights.

Party organizations are built around geographic election districts, starting with the precinct. There is, however, no hierarchical arrangement to party organization. The party structure has been described as a "system of layers of organization," with each level—county, state, and federal—concentrating on the elections within its jurisdiction.[24]

There are no membership requirements for either the Democratic or the Republican party. Party members do not have to pay dues, attend meetings, campaign for candidates, or make contributions. When people register to vote in Texas, they are not required to state their party preference. The right to participate in a party's electoral and nominating activities is based simply on voting in that party's primary election. When a person votes in one of the major party primaries, his or her voter registration card is stamped "Democrat" or "Republican."

The Permanent Organization

Election **precincts**—there were an estimated 8,500 in Texas in 2002—are created by the county commissioners of each of the 254 counties. Voters in each precinct elect a **precinct chair** in the party primary (see Figure 23–3). Any eligible voter within the precinct can file for this position, or the names of write-in candidates can be added to the ballot. The chair calls to order the precinct convention (discussed later) and serves as a member of the county executive committee. Many people do nothing with the position, but others contribute a great deal of time and energy to deliver the precinct's votes for their party's candidates in the general election.

The second level of the party organization is the **county executive committee**, which includes each precinct chair and the **county chair**, who is elected to a two-year term by primary voters countywide. A major responsibility of the county chair and the executive committee is the organization and management of the primary election in their county. The county executive committee accepts filings by candidates and is also responsible for planning the county or district conventions. Funds for the management of primary elections are provided to the county party by the state through the secretary of state's office.

County committees may be well organized and may actively work to carry out a wide range of organizational and electoral activities, or they may meet irregularly and have difficulty getting a quorum of members to attend. The county chair is an unpaid position. But party organizations in some counties have successful ongoing fund-raising operations, and they support a party headquarters, retain professional staff, and are engaged in various party activities between elections.

At the state level, a party's permanent organization is the **state executive committee**, which is composed of 64 members, including the party's state chair and vice chair. When the parties meet in their biennial state conventions, two committee members—a man and a woman—are selected by delegation caucuses from each of the 31 state senatorial districts. The **state chair** and the **vice chair**, one of whom must be a woman, also are selected by the convention. The two top state party leaders and other executive committee members serve two-year terms and are unpaid.

precincts
Specific local voting areas created by county commissioners courts. The state election code provides detailed requirements for drawing up these election units.

precinct chair
Local officer in a political party who presides over the precinct convention and serves on the party's county executive committee. Voters in each precinct elect a chair in the party's primary election.

county executive committee
Panel responsible on the local level for the organization and management of a political party's primary election. It includes the party's county chair and each precinct chair.

county chair
Presiding officer of a political party's county executive committee. He or she is elected countywide by voters in the party primary.

state executive committee
Statewide governing board of a political party. It includes a man and a woman from each of the 31 state senatorial districts and the state chair and vice chair, who are selected by delegates to the party's biennial state convention.

state chair and **vice chair**
Two top state leaders of a political party, one of whom must be a woman. They are selected every two years by delegates to the party's state convention.

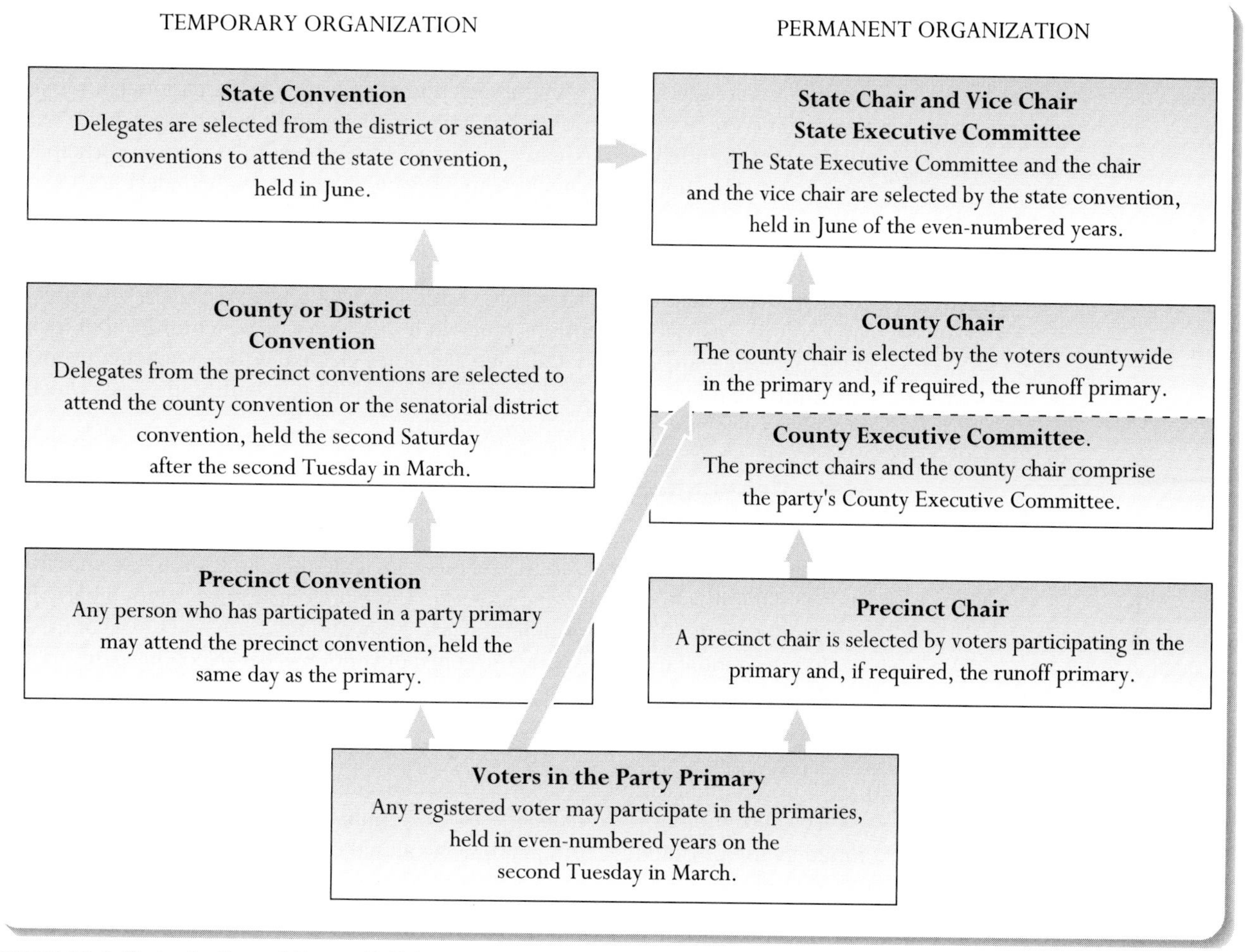

TEMPORARY ORGANIZATION   PERMANENT ORGANIZATION

State Convention
Delegates are selected from the district or senatorial conventions to attend the state convention, held in June.

State Chair and Vice Chair
State Executive Committee
The State Executive Committee and the chair and the vice chair are selected by the state convention, held in June of the even-numbered years.

County or District Convention
Delegates from the precinct conventions are selected to attend the county convention or the senatorial district convention, held the second Saturday after the second Tuesday in March.

County Chair
The county chair is elected by the voters countywide in the primary and, if required, the runoff primary.

County Executive Committee.
The precinct chairs and the county chair comprise the party's County Executive Committee.

Precinct Convention
Any person who has participated in a party primary may attend the precinct convention, held the same day as the primary.

Precinct Chair
A precinct chair is selected by voters participating in the primary and, if required, the runoff primary.

Voters in the Party Primary
Any registered voter may participate in the primaries, held in even-numbered years on the second Tuesday in March.

FIGURE 23–3 Organization of Texas Political Parties.

Statewide candidates file for office with the executive committee, which is also responsible for planning and organizing the party's state convention and helps raise funds for the ongoing operations of the party. The committee serves to establish party policy, but day-to-day party operations are entrusted to the party's executive director and professional staff. The Texas Democratic party and the Texas Republican party have permanent staffs and headquarters in Austin.

Temporary Organizations

The temporary organizations of the political parties are the series of conventions that are held every two years, beginning on the day of the party primaries. They are particularly significant in presidential election years because they help select the state's delegates to the national party conventions. The convention system also helps organize the permanent party structure and brings party activists together to share common political concerns and shape party policies. Most Texans, however, have little knowledge of the convention system, and few participate in it.

Precinct Conventions

Anyone who votes in a party primary, held on the second Tuesday in March of even-numbered years, is eligible to participate in that party's **precinct convention**, normally held in the same place as the primary after voting stops at 7 P.M. The main business of the convention is the selection of delegates and alternate delegates to the county or senatorial district convention. Since 1972, the Democrats have used complex procedures designed to assure broad-based delegate representation by ethnicity, gender, and

precinct convention
Meeting held by a political party in each precinct on the same day as the party primary. In presidential election years, the precinct conventions and the primaries are the first steps in the selection of delegates to the major parties' national nominating conventions.

age. A precinct convention can also adopt resolutions to be submitted at the county or district conventions for possible inclusion in the party's platform.

In presidential election years, the presidential preference primary and the precinct conventions are the first steps in the selection of delegates to the national nominating conventions. Precinct conventions held in nonpresidential election years, however, are often poorly attended, and in many precincts no one shows up. Such low participation rates are cited by those who conclude that the political parties are in decline.

County or Senatorial District Conventions

County or state senatorial district conventions are held two weeks after the precinct conventions. District conventions are held in the larger urban counties that include more than one state senatorial district. Delegates elected at the precinct conventions constitute the membership of this second level of the convention process, which, in turn, elects delegates to the state convention.

State Conventions

The two major parties hold their **state conventions** in June of even-numbered years. Convention delegates certify to the secretary of state the names of those individuals who were nominated to statewide offices in the March primaries, adopt a party platform, and elect the state party chair, the vice chair, and the state executive committee.

In presidential election years, the state conventions also select delegates to their respective parties' national nominating conventions, elect members to their parties' national committees, and choose presidential electors. Electors from the party that carries Texas in the presidential race will formally cast the state's electoral votes for that party's presidential candidate in December after the general election.

The allocation of Texas delegates to the Republican national convention is determined by the presidential primary, but the actual delegates are selected at the state convention.

Texas delegates to the Democratic National Convention are determined through a more complicated process based both on the primary vote and on candidate support from attendees at the series of party conventions, beginning at the precinct level.

PARTIES AND GOVERNMENT

Political parties in Texas do not produce cohesive, policy-oriented coalitions in government, and they have been unable to hold their elected officials accountable or responsive to those supporting the party. Under ideal circumstances, some students of government believe, the two major parties would articulate clearly defined political philosophies and policies they would pursue if their candidates were elected. Once elected, persons supported by the party would be committed to these programs, giving the voters a clear standard by which to evaluate their performances in office. This perspective is often referred to as the *responsible party model.*

There are several reasons why Texas parties are incapable of functioning in this manner, none of which lessens the disenchantment and disgust that many voters feel toward political parties and politicians. First, the political parties in Texas are highly decentralized and unable to discipline members who pursue goals that conflict with the party's stated objectives. The large number of elected officials at both the state and the local level serves to diffuse party leadership. Furthermore, most of these elected officials rely primarily on their own fund-raising skills and receive very limited direct financial support through the parties.

Moreover, the coalitions that parties form with groups harboring different objectives, interests, and agendas make it next to impossible to develop clearly stated positions that would always differentiate one party from another. Philosophical, ideological, and programmatic differences among members and supporters of the same party result, for example, in ideological voting patterns in the legislature that cross party lines.

state convention
Meeting held in June of even-numbered years by each of the two major political parties. Delegates to this convention elect the party's state leadership and adopt a party platform. In presidential election years, the state convention selects the delegates to the party's national nominating convention.

Another explanation for the lack of partisan accountability is the long-standing antiparty tradition of American politics. Many voters are ambivalent—even outright hostile—toward political parties, and the parties make only limited efforts to include a large number of individuals in their organizational activities.

MINORITIES AND POLITICAL PARTICIPATION

At a time when millions of people around the world have eliminated authoritarian political systems and made great sacrifices to win free and open elections, Texans congratulate themselves if one-third of the eligible population votes. Such a poor turnout cannot be blamed on a lack of opportunity. After decades of denying voting rights to large parts of the population, Texas now has one of the most progressive voter registration laws in the United States. Contemporary political campaigns, especially those for national and statewide offices, have high media visibility. People are bombarded by sophisticated television advertising campaigns, direct mail, phone bank solicitations for candidates, and daily news coverage. Yet something fundamental is disturbing Texas voters as well as voters across the nation. Statewide turnout rates in Texas are consistently low, and turnout rates in many local elections are downright appalling.

Texas has had a dark history of voter disfranchisement. The systematic exclusion of African Americans, Hispanics, and low-income whites was clearly undemocratic and created a political system in which the interests of a few could prevail over the interests of the majority.

Texas enacted a **poll tax** in 1902. Although not a large sum of money by today's standards, the $1.50 to $1.75 people had to pay in order to vote eliminated large numbers of people, especially those who were likely to support liberal social and economic policies and undermine the political establishment.[25] The poll tax was in effect for more than sixty years in Texas. It was outlawed for federal elections by the Twenty-Fourth Amendment to the U.S. Constitution, adopted in 1964, but Texas retained it for state and local elections until November 1966.

In 1923, the Texas legislature enacted a law that denied African Americans the right to vote in the Democratic primary. After a series of challenges in the U.S. Supreme Court, the so-called **white primary** was finally eliminated in 1944 as a result of the court's decision in *Smith* v. *Allwright.*[26] But those who were intent on keeping African Americans from voting began to utilize a restrictive preprimary selection process to pick candidates, who then would be formally nominated in the Democratic primary and subsequently elected in the general election. Finally, in 1953, the Supreme Court also declared this arrangement unconstitutional.[27]

Until 1971, Texas had one of the most restrictive voter registration systems in the nation. Voters had to register annually between October 1 and January 31. Voters who did not register in person at the county courthouse could be registered by deputy registrars. But deputy registrars could not mail a large number of registrations together; they were required to deliver or mail in only one registration form at a time. This requirement thwarted coordinated voter registration drives that targeted minorities and low-income populations.[28]

Court action eliminated this system, and the legislature—pressured by Common Cause, the League of Women Voters, and minority groups—enacted one of the most progressive voter registration systems in the country.[29] Permanent registration was implemented, and citizens could register by mail or in person up to thirty days prior to an election. The law also made it easier to organize large voter registration drives. In 1993, the U.S. Congress enacted "motor-voter registration," which requires states to provide facilities for voter registration where a person obtains a driver's license.

Women were not given the right to vote until the adoption of the Nineteenth Amendment to the U.S. Constitution in 1920, and the adoption of the Twenty-Sixth Amendment lowered the voting age from 21 to 18 in 1971. Until the 1970s, property qualifications were used to exclude many voters from voting in local bond elections.

President Johnson, in a White House ceremony in 1964, signs the Twenty-Fourth Amendment to the Constitution barring the levying of a poll tax in federal elections. Texas soon followed with the elimination of the poll tax in state elections.

poll tax
Tax that Texas and some other states required before people were allowed to vote. The purpose was to discourage minorities and poor whites from participating in the political process. The tax was declared unconstitutional in the 1960s.

white primary
Series of state laws and party rules that denied African Americans the right to vote in the Democratic primary in Texas in the first half of the twentieth century.

Even after the most obvious discriminatory practices against minorities were eliminated, there were more subtle, but just as pervasive, techniques for reducing the political power and influence of these same groups.

One technique is racial gerrymandering of political boundaries. State legislators and many city council members are elected from single-member districts, each of which represents a specific number of people in a designated area. To minimize the possibilities of minority candidates being elected, policy makers could divide minority communities and attach them to predominantly nonminority communities. This tactic is called cracking. Or, the minority communities could be consolidated into one district, a tactic called packing, with an 80 to 90 percent minority population, which would reduce the number of other districts in which minorities might have a chance of winning office.

At-large elections also have been used to reduce minority representation. At one time, members of the Texas House from urban counties were elected in multimember districts, which required candidates to win election in countywide races, a very difficult prospect for most minority candidates. The practice was eliminated in legislative races in the 1970s as a result of federal lawsuits. But until recently, many cities, school districts, and special districts across Texas with significant minority populations continued to use at-large elections requiring candidates to run for office citywide or districtwide. The system dilutes minority representation in most communities in which it is used because of the higher costs of campaigning and the prevalence of polarized voting, in which minorities vote for minority candidates and Anglo voters, the majority, vote for white candidates.

POLITICAL GAINS BY MINORITIES AND WOMEN

Over the past thirty years, nevertheless, minorities have made substantial gains in the electoral process. Elimination of restrictive voting laws and adoption of a liberal voter registration system have contributed to an increase in minority voters across the state, as have voter registration and mobilization drives coordinated by groups such as the National Association for the Advancement of Colored People and the Southwest Voter Registration Education Project. The federal Voting Rights Act, which was passed by the U.S. Congress in 1965 and extended to Texas 10 years later, also has played a key role. Minority groups have used the Voting Rights Act to challenge discriminatory state and local election systems in the federal courts. An election system that dilutes minority voting strength is illegal, and the Voting Rights Act requires changes in the election systems of state or local governments, including redistricting plans, to be reviewed and precleared by the U.S. Justice Department or approved by the U.S. District Court in Washington, D.C. This law has been used with considerable success to eliminate at-large elections and attack racial gerrymandering of political districts. These changes enhanced election opportunities for African Americans and Hispanics, but the fight continued.

By the mid-1990s, the Voting Rights Act was under attack by conservatives. And the U.S. Supreme Court, in "reverse-discrimination" cases from Texas and Georgia, ruled that some congressional districts had been illegally gerrymandered to elect minority candidates.[30] In the Texas case, three federal judges held that the Texas legislature had violated the U.S. Constitution by designing two districts in Houston and one in the Dallas area to favor the election of African American or Hispanic candidates. The court redrew 13 congressional districts in Texas—the three minority districts and 10 districts adjoining them—and ordered special elections to fill the seats. Despite the redrawn boundaries, two incumbent African American congresswomen in the affected districts were reelected.

Hispanics

According to the 2000 census, Hispanics made up 32 percent of Texas's population. But the Hispanic population is younger than the Anglo and African American populations, and Hispanics accounted for only 28.6 percent of Texans of voting age (Figure 23–4).

Hispanics also include a significant number of immigrants (an estimated one out of seven) not eligible to vote, thus reducing eligible Hispanic voters to approximately 25 percent of adult citizens. Approximately 17 percent, or 2,121,962 of the 12,455,503 Texas

	Total Population	Percent of Total	Population of Voting Age	Percent of Total
Hispanic/Latino (any race)	6,669,666	32%	4,282,901	28.6%
White	10,933,313	52.4%	8,426,166	56.3%
African American	2,364,255	11.3%	1,631,448	10.9%
Other	884,586	4.2%	624,546	4.2%
Total	20,851,820		14,965,061	

FIGURE 23–4 2000 Population and Voting Age Population.
SOURCE: U.S. Census, 2000; Texas State Data Center.

voters registered in February 2002 had Hispanic surnames. (These figures underrepresent Hispanic registered voters because Hispanic women married to non-Hispanics cannot be identified with methods used by the secretary of state). But in recent general elections, Hispanics were only 12 to 15 percent of Texas voters participating.[31] Voter turnout rates among Hispanics are lower, in part, because of the lower education and income levels of many Hispanics.

Approximately 29 percent of Hispanic adults interviewed in the 2003–2004 *Texas Polls* said they identified with the Democratic Party (see Figure 21–2), but this percentage tells only part of the story. Until Governor George W. Bush made substantial inroads into the Hispanic vote in 1998, Democratic candidates for president and governor consistently received more than 70 percent of the Hispanic vote in Texas.[32]

Hispanic voters dominated the 2002 Democratic primary, which for the first time featured two Hispanic gubernatorial candidates, Laredo businessman Tony Sanchez and former Attorney General Dan Morales. One of three major candidates for the party's U.S. Senate nomination also was Hispanic—Victor Morales, a schoolteacher who had shocked party leaders by winning the 1996 nomination. The William C. Velasquez Institute, which specializes in Hispanic-related voting activity, reported that preliminary figures indicated that Hispanics cast a record 33 percent of the 2002 Democratic primary votes.[33] Spending heavily from his wealth on television advertising, Sanchez easily defeated Dan Morales for the gubernatorial nomination. Tapping into the Hispanic vote, Victor Morales got into a runoff for the Senate nomination with former Dallas Mayor Ron Kirk, an African American. Each received about one-third of the vote. But Kirk, who was supported by most party leaders and swamped Victor Morales in fundraising, won the Senate runoff, when Hispanic voter turnout had fallen off. Both Sanchez and Kirk later lost their general election races to Republicans.

The increased electoral strength of the Hispanic population is borne out in Table 23–2, which compares the number of Hispanic elected officials in Texas in 1974 to those holding office in 2003. Some 540 Hispanics held elected office in 1974. By 2003, there were 1,965 Hispanic elected officials, the highest in any state. The marked increase can be attributed to a more equitable apportionment of city, county, and school district political boundaries (see Chapter 24); the growth of the Hispanic population; and increased organizational efforts among Hispanics.

By 2004, only four Hispanics—Texas Supreme Court Justices Raul A. Gonzalez and Alberto R. Gonzales, Attorney General Dan Morales, and Texas Railroad Commissioner Tony Garza—had been elected to statewide office in Texas. Victor Morales, a Hispanic schoolteacher from Crandall, a small town in north Texas, generated some excitement and received national publicity when he ran for the U.S. Senate in 1996. Operating on a shoestring budget in the primary, Morales campaigned across Texas in a white pickup truck that became a symbol of his longshot effort. To the surprise of most political observers, he defeated two incumbent congressmen and a politically experienced lawyer to win the Democratic nomination. But this David-versus-Goliath challenge of Republican Senator Phil Gramm fell short in the general election campaign. Gramm outspent his Democratic challenger 6 to 1 and easily won reelection. As noted above, Victor Morales also ran for the Democratic Senate nomination in 2002 but lost a runoff that year.

TABLE 23–2 LATINO ELECTED OFFICIALS IN TEXAS, 1974–2003

	1974	*1996*	*2001*	*2003*
Federal	2	5	6	6
State	13	35	36	38
County	102	203	213	236
Municipal	251	536	555	565
Judicial/Law Enforcement	172	323	280	338
School Board	—	536	701	736
Special District	—	51	37	46
Total	540	1,689	1,828	1,965

SOURCE: Juan A. Sepulveda, Jr., *The Question of Representative Responsiveness for Hispanics* (Harvard College, honors thesis, March 1985; National Association of Latino Elected and Appointed Officials, *National Roster of Hispanic Elected Officials*, 1996, 2001, 2003).

African Americans

African Americans constitute approximately 11.3 percent of the state's population, 11 percent of the voting-age population, and 9 to 10 percent of those who vote. Approximately 61 percent of Texas African Americans call themselves Democrats, but 80 to 90 percent of the African American vote is normally cast for Democratic candidates. Voting cohesively as a group, African Americans, like Hispanics, have considerable potential to influence the outcome of both primaries and general elections.

The increased political clout of the African American population is also manifested in the number of African American elected officials (Table 23–3). In 1970, there were only 29 African Americans elected to public office in Texas. The number increased to 196 in 1980 and to 475 in 2000. Only two African Americans, former Texas Court of Criminal Appeals Judge Morris Overstreet, a Democrat, and Railroad Commissioner Michael Williams, a Republican, had been elected to statewide office before 2002. Two other African Americans—Republicans Wallace Jefferson and Dale Wainwright—won statewide races for the Texas Supreme Court in 2002. As noted earlier, former Dallas Mayor Ron Kirk, an African American, won the Democratic nomination for the U.S. Senate that year but lost to Republican John Cornyn in the general election.

Women

Historically, the world of Texas politics has been dominated by men. Prior to Ann Richards's election as state treasurer in 1982, only two other women had been elected to statewide office. Richards was elected governor in 1990, and Kay Bailey Hutchison, who had succeeded Richards as state treasurer, was elected to the U.S. Senate in 1993. As governor, Richards also appointed more women to key positions on state boards and commissions than her predecessors.

By 2003, nine women were holding statewide offices in Texas, including Hutchison, who was still in the U.S. Senate; state Comptroller Carole Keeton Strayhorn; state Agriculture Commissioner Susan Combs; two members of the Texas Supreme Court, and four members of the Texas Court of Criminal Appeals. That same year, there were four women in the state Senate and 31 in the Texas House, a significant increase over 1981, when the legislature included only one woman in the Senate and 11 in the House.

Women are playing an increased role in local government as well, and this pattern can be expected to continue. Over the past three decades, the state's three largest cities—Houston, Dallas, and San Antonio—had women mayors. A 2004 survey by the Texas Municipal League counted 204 women mayors (or 17 percent) in the state's 1,211 cities. The 5,971 council members in the cities included 1,535 women, or 26 percent of the total. Of the 254 county judges in 2002, 26 (or 10 percent) were women, and women held 67 (or 6.6 percent) of 1,016 county commissioner posts.[34]

TABLE 23–3 AFRICAN AMERICAN ELECTED OFFICIALS IN TEXAS, 1970–2001

	1970	*1980*	*2001*
Federal	—	1	2
State	3	14	17
County	—	5	20
Municipal	16	75	282
Judicial/Law Enforcement	—	21	44
School Board	10	78	95
Special District	—	2	—
Total	29	196	460

SOURCE: Metropolitan Applied Research Center, Inc. and Voter Regional Council, Inc., *National Roster of Black Elected Officials*; Joint Center for Political Studies, *National Roster of Black Elected Officials*, 1980, 1998, 2001.

There has been little increase in the number of African American elected officials over the past few years, but there has been an increase in the number of African American women elected to public office. Of the 460 black elected officials in 2001, 30 percent were women.[35]

ELECTIONS IN TEXAS

Texans have numerous opportunities to vote, often as many as three or four times a year. While there are various rationales for this election scheduling by the legislature, there is evidence that it contributes to "voter fatigue," reduced voter turnout, and the disproportionate influence of a few individuals in many local and special elections where voter turnout is usually the lowest. Turnout and interest are highest in the general election in presidential election years but can be abysmally low in elections for school boards and the governing bodies of other single-purpose districts, such as hospital and water districts.

Primary Elections

Texas uses the **direct primary election**, adopted in 1903, to nominate major party candidates for public office. Administered by the political parties, primaries are held on the second Tuesday in March in even-numbered years. If no candidate receives a majority, the two top vote-getters must face each other in a runoff election. For practical purposes, Texas utilizes an **open primary** where voters do not register by party. People who vote in one party's primary, however, cannot vote in the other party's runoff election.

Voter turnout in the primary is traditionally lower than in the general election, but the emergence of a two-party system in Texas is producing appreciable changes in participation patterns in the Democratic and Republican primaries (Table 23–4).

During the period of one-party, Democratic politics, the candidate who won the Democratic primary usually won the general election. From the 1920s through 1970, the rate of turnout for the Democratic primary never exceeded 35 percent of the voting-age population. Over the past 30 years, it has eroded further, reflecting the realignment of the state's party system. About 28 percent of the voting-age population (persons 18 or older) voted in the hotly contested Democratic gubernatorial primary in 1972. Since then, turnout in Democratic primaries has fallen below 20 percent.[36] Less than 7 percent of the voting-age population voted in the 2002 Democratic gubernatorial primary and less than 5.2 percent in the 2004 presidential primary.[37]

Prior to 1980, participation in the Republican primaries in Texas never exceeded 5 percent of the voting-age population.[38] That rate has increased somewhat since then, but the percentage of Texans voting in a Republican primary has never reached the level of participation that the Democratic party experienced when it dominated state politics. One million voters, or 8.3 percent of voting-age Texans, cast ballots in the 1988 Republican presidential primary, when Texan George Bush was on the ballot. That is the highest turnout percentage in a Republican primary in Texas so far. Only 4 percent of Texans old enough to vote participated in the 2002 Republican gubernatorial primary, when incumbent Governor Rick Perry had only minor opposition. Approximately 688,000 voters cast ballots in the 2004 Republican presidential primary, when George W. Bush sought a second term, but they accounted for only 4.3 percent of the voting-age population.[39]

The above data mean that a smaller percentage of the population is now involved in selecting political nominees throughout the state. And those who participate in party primaries tend to be more ideological in their political orientation than the general population.

General Elections

General elections for state and federal offices are held on the first Tuesday after the first Monday in November in even-numbered years. The names of the candidates nominated in the primaries by the two major parties are placed on a ballot, along with the names of Libertarian and Green party candidates and other third party candidates who

direct primary election
Selection of candidates for government office through direct election by the voters of a political party.

open primary
Primary election in which a voter may cast a ballot in either party's primary election.

TABLE 23–4 DEMOCRATIC AND REPUBLICAN PRIMARY TURNOUT, 1972–2002

Year	Race	Republican Primary Vote	Democratic Primary Vote
1972	President/Governor	114,007	2,192,903
1974	Governor	69,101	1,521,306
1976	President	356,307	1,529,168
1978	Governor	158,403	1,812,896
1980	President	526,769	1,377,767
1982	Governor	265,794	1,318,663
1984	President	336,814	1,463,449
1986	Governor	544,719	1,096,552
1988	President	1,014,956	1,767,045
1990	Governor	855,231	1,487,260
1992	President	797,146	1,482,075
1994	Governor	557,340	1,036,944
1996	President	1,019,803	921,256
1998	Governor	596,839	664,532
2000	President	1,159,645	793,825
2002	Governor	622,423	1,024,814
2004	President	687,615	839,231

Source: Secretary of State, Election Division.

have submitted petitions bearing the names of eligible registered voters equal to 1 percent of the vote in the last gubernatorial election.

In the 1896 presidential election, the turnout rate was more than 80 percent of the eligible voting-age population, but in 1908, four years after the effective date of the poll tax, turnout had fallen to approximately 35 percent. During much of the period from 1910 to 1958, turnout rates in nonpresidential elections were less than 20 percent. Presidential elections generated a somewhat higher turnout, but in very few instances did the turnout rate exceed 40 percent of eligible voters.

Forty-seven percent of Texas's voting-age population cast general-election ballots in the 1984 presidential race, 44 percent in the 1988 presidential election, approximately 50 percent in the spirited three-way presidential election of 1992, 41 percent in 1996, and 44 percent in 2000. But only 29 percent of the voting-age population cast general-election ballots in the 1986 gubernatorial race, 31 percent in the 1990 race, 34 percent in the 1994 gubernatorial election, 27 percent in 1998 and 29 percent in 2002.[40]

City, School Board, and Single-Purpose District Elections

Most local elections, which are nonpartisan, are held in May in odd-numbered years to minimize the convergence of issues in state and local races. Across the state, there are wide variations in the competitiveness of these elections, campaign costs, and turnout. But turnout rates rarely match those in the general election and are often abysmally low.

Special Elections

The legislature can submit constitutional amendments to the voters in a general election or schedule them in a special statewide election. Local governments also conduct special elections for bond issues, local initiatives and referenda, and the recall of public officials. Although these elections occasionally arouse high interest, turnout rates tend to be extremely low. The governor also can call special elections to fill vacancies in certain offices, including legislative and congressional seats.

Extended Absentee Balloting

In 1988 Texas made a major change in the requirements for **absentee (or early) voting** to permit any voter to cast a ballot from the twentieth day to the fourth day prior to an election. Special early voting areas are established—including many at shopping malls and other convenient locations—and voters do not have to provide an excuse for casting their ballots early. Consequently, there has been a notable increase in the number of early votes—20 percent to 30 percent of all votes in some areas. Extended early voting has forced candidates to identify two different sets of voters and develop strategies that require campaigns to "peak" twice. Several other states have followed Texas's lead in eliminating another barrier to political participation.

CAMPAIGN FINANCES

Campaign Costs

No one knows precisely how much is spent on political campaigns in Texas because there is no single place where all this information is collected. Candidates for state office file campaign finance reports with the state Ethics Commission, but candidates for city councils, county offices, and school boards file reports with the jurisdictions in which they are running. Costs vary across the more than 2,000 governmental units, but modern campaign technology and paid media are extremely expensive, even on the local level. A few recent examples of campaign costs in selected races are illuminating.

City council races in major cities such as San Antonio, Houston, Fort Worth, and Dallas can easily cost $50,000 to $100,000. Bob Lanier spent $3 million getting elected mayor of Houston in 1991, and eight candidates spent more than $6.6 million in the 1997 race to succeed him. The 1997 winner, Lee Brown, spent more than $2.1 million alone, and the second place finisher, businessman Rob Mosbacher, spent more than $3.5 million.[41] Those earlier figures, however, paled in comparison to the nearly $9 million that businessman Bill White spent to win the 2003 Houston mayor's race.[42] There have been reports of candidates for county commissioner spending $100,000 and of district judges in metropolitan counties spending more than $150,000. Historically, school board elections have been low budget, but it is not uncommon for slates of candidates in large urban school districts to spend $10,000 to $15,000 in low-turnout elections.

Many people believe that campaign expenditures in statewide races in Texas, particularly gubernatorial races, are excessive. But fueled by the rising costs of television advertising and other modern campaign techniques—and two-party competition—expenditures continue to increase (see *People and Politics: Making a Difference:* "Karl Rove: An Adviser in High Places"). Republican Rick Perry and Democrat Tony Sanchez spent almost $100 million in the 2002 governor's race. Sanchez's expenditures included more than $50 million from his own pocket. He won a hard-fought victory over former Attorney General Dan Morales in the Democratic primary before losing to Perry in the general election (Table 23–5).

Candidates for lieutenant governor in 2002 raised more than $25 million. Republican David Dewhurst, the victor, raised $16.3 million, including $11.3 million of his own money. Candidates for other statewide executive offices that year raised $24.1 million combined, with Republican candidates raising much more than Democrats.[43] Winning candidates in state Senate races in 2002 raised an average of $587,000, and winners of races for the Texas House raised an average of $165,000.

Fund Raising

Soaring campaign costs have raised considerable concern about campaign fund raising and contributions in Texas, as they have also nationally. There is concern that elections are being bought and that major campaign contributors are purchasing influence in

absentee (or **early**) **voting**
Period before the regularly scheduled election date, during which voters are allowed to cast ballots. With recent changes in election law, a person does not have to offer a reason for voting absentee.

PEOPLE & POLITICS *Making a Difference* ★★★

KARL ROVE: AN ADVISER IN HIGH PLACES

Probably the best-known Republican consultant from Texas is Karl Rove, a strategist and direct-mail specialist who worked for most major GOP officeholders in Texas in the 1980s and 1990s and, in the process, hitched his career to a future president. Rove first met George W. Bush in 1973 and supervised his first political campaign, an unsuccessful race for Congress in West Texas in 1978. Rove later managed Bush's successful races for governor in 1994 and 1998 and was a key adviser in his presidential campaign in 2000. In the White House, Rove re-mained Bush's chief political adviser, working out of an office in the West Wing.

Rove is a master of details and a consummate "spinner" of the political views he and Bush espouse. Rove's career hasn't been without controversy, mainly because he developed a reputation, early on, for winning at any cost. But the personal, as well as professional, bond between the president and his long-time adviser remained strong through Bush's governorship and his early months in the Oval Office.

"Rove is, quite simply, the most influential presidential aide in two decades," correspondent Howard Fineman wrote in *Newsweek* magazine in 2001. "He's in charge of legislative AND political strategy, and outreach to citizen groups. He doesn't decide whether to fire on a Chinese fighter jet, but he does figure out how Bush's decision will 'play' in the country," Fineman added.

SOURCE: "Political Soul Mates Since 1973," *Newsweek,* April 18, 2001.

the policy-making process. Some critics of contemporary campaigns have argued that current practices are a form of legalized bribery, implying that public officials are available to the highest bidder.

Unlike the federal government, Texas places no limits on the amount of money a single individual or political action committee can contribute to most political candidates. The only exceptions in Texas are campaign contribution limits in judicial races, which were imposed by the legislature in 1995. There are no limits on how much a candidate in any race can contribute to his or her own campaign. Large contributions have long played a role in Texas politics, and, over the years, most large contributions have gone to the conservative candidates, both Democratic and Republican.

TABLE 23–5   CONTRIBUTIONS BY TYPE OF STATE OFFICE, 2001–2002

Office	Totals for Winner in General Election	Totals for Loser in General Election	Totals for Primary Losers
Governor	$20,469,556	$62,373,012	$132,797
Lt. Governor	16,347,728	8,703,573	—
Comptroller	4,996,428	825,059	—
Attorney General	7,803,818	5,250,157	—
Land Commissioner	1,399,122	1,308,427	—
Railroad Commissioner	1,198,258	202,742	671,375
Agriculture Commissioner	1,744,202	233,249	—
Supreme Court	3,229,026	1,866,737	1,657,643
Court of Criminal Appeals	13,103	5,450	110,321
House	24,664,676	5,504,926	2,914,705
Senate	17,735,122	1,886,165	1,845,598
Totals	**$99,587,936**	**$88,159,496**	**$7,332,439**

SOURCE: From *Money in Politex: A Guide to Money in the 2002 Texas Elections,* November 2003. Copyright © 2003 by Texans for Public Justice. Reprinted by permission of Texans for Public Justice.

Political Action Committees and Fat Cats

Just as they have on the national level, political action committees (PACs) have increased their importance at the state and local level by bringing sophisticated fund-raising skills to political campaigns. Representing special interest groups or individual companies, PACs collect money from their members and are a ready source of campaign dollars. They are in the business of influencing elections.

PACs and business-connected donors gave more than $50 million to candidates during the 2002 campaign season in Texas. One of the biggest contributors was Texans for Lawsuit Reform, which gave almost $2 million and played a leading role in a successful lobbying effort in 2003 that produced more restrictions on damage lawsuits against doctors and businesses. Other major contributors included the Texas Association of Realtors, the Texas Trial Lawyers Association, the Texas Medical Association, the Texas Dental Association and the Texas State Teachers Association. Forty-one individuals, often referred to as "fat cats," made contributions to candidates and PACs of $200,000 or more during the 2002 election cycle. The 50 top individual contributors to candidates gave $14.3 million, or 11 percent of the total contributions[44] (see *People and Politics: Making a Difference:* "Bob Perry: Homebuilder and Big Contributor").

Attempts at Reform

On the heels of the Sharpstown scandal, in which high-ranking state officials were given preferential treatment in the purchase of stock in an insurance company (see Chapter 24), the legislature enacted a major campaign finance disclosure law in 1973 that, with some changes, is now administered by the state Ethics Commission. Although it did not limit the size of political contributions, for the first time it required candidates to list the addresses as well as the names of donors and the amounts and dates of contributions. It also required political action committees contributing to candidates or officeholders to report the sources of their donations, which in the past had usually been hidden. Also for the first time, officeholders were required to file annual reports of their political contributions and expenditures—even during years when they were not seeking reelection—and candidates were required to report contributions and other financial activity that occurred after an election. A candidate also had to formally designate a campaign treasurer before he or she could legally accept political contributions. Campaign finance reform, however, remains a difficult and seemingly endless struggle.

PEOPLE & POLITICS *Making a Difference* ★ ★ ★

BOB PERRY: HOMEBUILDER AND BIG CONTRIBUTOR

Houston homebuilder Bob Perry tries to maintain a low public profile, but in recent years he has received significant publicity for emerging as one of Texas's most generous political contributors. In 2002, he was the biggest donor to state political candidates and causes, contributing at least $3.8 million during that election cycle, mostly to Republicans. Texas Land Commissioner Jerry Patterson, a former state senator and one of many candidates backed by Perry, said the homebuilder had never asked for favors. "He's a reserved, serious and principled guy who has never tried to influence my vote. He truly is a philosophical contributor, who wants to improve the Republican party," Patterson said.[*]

But Perry's voice obviously is heard. He was believed to be influential in the legislature's creation in 2003 of a new state agency, the Residential Construction Commission, to develop performance standards for builders and discourage lawsuits against builders by unhappy homebuyers. Governor Rick Perry (who isn't related to the homebuilder) appointed an executive of Bob Perry's company to the new agency's board, less than one month after the governor had received a $100,000 contribution from Bob Perry. The homebuilder had contributed more than half a million dollars to Rick Perry since 1997. The governor's office said the appointment wasn't influenced by the contributions, but by the appointee's experience in the homebuilding industry.[†]

[*]*Houston Chronicle,* December 22, 2002, p. 1A.
[†]*Houston Chronicle,* September 30, 2003, p. 1A.

Summary

1. Political power in Texas is related to the resources available to groups and organizations actively engaged in the political process. The great disparity in the distribution of resources raises fundamental questions about equity in access to policy makers and the decision-making process.

2. Pluralist theorists argue that political power in Texas is distributed among a wide range of groups and interests, none of which has a monopoly on the institutions of government. While there are marked differences in the resources of groups, there is sufficient competition and interaction among groups to achieve the goals of a democratic society. Public policy, in this view, reflects the compromise of competing interests.

3. Advocates of elitist theory argue that political power in Texas is concentrated in the hands of a relatively small number of individuals who derive their resources from powerful institutional bases. These institutions are tied together with complex interlocking relationships, and access to their leadership positions is limited. Called the "Texas Establishment," those who monopolized power in the past were predominantly white males from the higher socioeconomic groups. Although there is some competition among these elites, there also is a great deal of consensus. Historically, the establishment has expressed indifference, if not hostility, toward the interests of labor, minorities, and the lower socioeconomic groups.

4. The interest group system in Texas was historically dominated by oil and gas, agriculture, and financial institutions. But dramatic changes in the state's economy, the political mobilization of minorities, and the development of public interest groups have produced considerable change. Not only are more groups now participating in the policy arena, but some of the traditionally dominant groups apparently have experienced a dilution of their power. Policies directed to the interests of the lower socioeconomic groups are modest indications of these changes.

5. For much of its political history, Texas had a one-party, Democratic system, characterized by two dominant factions. This weak party system, based in part on the systematic exclusion of many citizens through discriminatory election laws, contributed to a powerful interest group system. In Austin, as well as at the local level, the raw power of interest groups is seen in most aspects of the decision-making process, often to the detriment of the general public.

6. Over the past thirty years, there have been significant changes in the state's party structure. One-party Democratic control has been transformed by complex economic, social, and political changes, and Texas is now a two-party state dominated by the Republican Party. Texas voters are divided among Democrats, Republicans, and independents, but the GOP has an edge.

7. Historically, politics in Texas was configured around class and race, and these two factors are still primary dimensions of partisan alliances.

8. Parties have rarely functioned as highly cohesive, disciplined organizations, either in the electorate or in government. With candidate-centered campaigns, many elected officials act as free agents, aligning with other groups and having little fear of recrimination from the political party.

9. One of the most disturbing aspects of the contemporary Texas political system is the low voter turnout in most elections, despite the elimination of discriminatory election laws, the creation of an extended voting period, and easy voter registration.

10. Although most discriminatory election barriers have been eliminated, racial gerrymandering and at-large election systems continue to generate controversy.

11. Over the past thirty years, Hispanics and African Americans have realized substantial gains in the electoral process and increased success in winning election to public office. There has also been a dramatic increase in the number of women elected to public office.

12. With varied election cycles for multiple levels of government, Texans are subjected to a continuous election process, contributing to "voter fatigue" and indifference.

13. The costs of statewide campaigns, as well as many regional and local campaigns, have escalated over the past three decades. While money may not buy public officials, it certainly buys access to them, and it creates the impression that well-organized interests, corporations, and wealthy individuals have a disproportionate influence on policy makers.

14. Despite changes in the partisan lineup, Texans have not expressed a significant shift in their philosophical orientations over the past twenty years. Most Texans still classify themselves as moderate to conservative.

Key Terms

interest group
pluralism
lobbyists
elitism
"The Establishment"
single-member district
political action committee
tort

Religious Right
two-party system
one-party system
Jim Crow laws
bifactionalism
realignment
gerrymandering
Voting Rights Act

precincts
precinct chair
county executive committee
county chair
state executive committee
state chair and vice chair
precinct convention
state convention

poll tax
white primary
direct primary election
open primary
absentee (or early) voting

FURTHER READING

ANDERS, EVAN. *Boss Rule in South Texas: The Progressive Era.* (University of Texas Press, 1982). Utilizing recent perspectives on political machines, the author provides a comprehensive analysis of political bosses in South Texas counties during the Progressive Era.

BLACK, EARL, AND MERLE BLACK. *The Rise of Southern Republicanism.* (Belknap Press, 2002). A comprehensive assessment of Republican realignment in the southern states.

DAVIDSON, CHANDLER. *Race and Class in Texas Politics.* (Princeton University Press, 1990). An adaptation of V.O. Key's earlier analysis to contemporary Texas politics, this work assesses the dimensions of race and class and addresses the issue of a governing elite.

DYER, JAMES A., JAN E. LEIGHLEY, AND ARNOLD VEDLITZ. "Party Identification and Public Opinion in Texas, 1984–1994: Establishing a Competitive Two-Party System," in *Texas Politics,* ed. Anthony Champagne and Edward J. Harpham (W.W. Norton, 1997). A pre-2000 analysis of party realignment in Texas, offering various scenarios for the configuration of party politics in the state.

ELLIOTT, CHARLES P. "The Texas Trial Lawyers Association: Interest Group Under Siege," in *Texas Politics,* ed. Anthony Champagne and Edward J. Harpham (W.W. Norton, 1997). Examines the activities of the Texas Trial Lawyers Association, the organization's relationships with like-minded interest groups, and the problems faced battling the dominant business interests in the state

GARCIA, IGNACIO. *United We Win: The Rise and Fall of La Raza Unida Party.* (Mexican American Studies and Research Center at the University of Arizona, 1989). Written from the perspective of an activist, this book is an "interpretive essay" tracing the development of La Raza Unida with the formation of MAYO (Mexican-American Youth Organization) to its demise in the early 1980s.

GREEN, GEORGE NORRIS. *The Establishment in Texas Politics: 1938–1957.* (Greenwood Press, 1979). A historical perspective that concludes Texas politics were controlled by corporate elites who, in their reaction to the New Deal, developed and fostered a form of reactionary conservatism permitting predatory interest groups to dominate the electoral and policy processes.

HREBENAR, ROBERT J., AND CLIVE S. THOMAS, EDS. *Interest Group Politics in Southern States.* (University of Alabama Press, 1992). A twelve-state study of interest groups in which the authors conclude that interest groups in Texas have moved from personalized lobbying to information-based communications.

KEY, V. O. *Southern Politics.* (Vintage Books, 1949). This classic study of southern politics details the politics in each of the states of the Confederacy and provides a historical framework for understanding contemporary political changes in the region.

KNAGGS, JOHN R. *Two-Party Texas: The John Tower Era, 1961–1984.* (Eakin Press, 1986). An assessment of the early development of the modern Republican party in Texas.

LENCHNER, PAUL. "The Party System in Texas," in *Texas Politics,* eds. Anthony Champagne and Edward J. Harpham (W.W. Norton, 1997). In addition to a brief overview of Republican successes since the 1960s, this article raises the issue of the potential of Texas becoming a one-party Republican state.

NAVARRO, ARMANDO. *La Raza Unida Party: A Chicano Challenge to the U.S. Two-Party Dictatorship.* (Temple University Press, 2000). An assessment of the La Raza Unida party grounded in third-party literature.

SAN MIGUEL, GUADALUPE, JR. *Let Them Take Heed: Mexican Americans and the Campaign for Educational Equality in Texas, 1910–1981.* (University of Texas Press, 1987). Describes Mexican American organizational efforts to promote educational equality over a seventy-year period.

THE TEXAS LEGISLATURE

24

THE TEXAS LEGISLATURE: A TIME OF CHANGE

The Republican takeover of the Texas House of Representatives in 2003 was a watershed event in state politics. It marked the first GOP majority of that body since the 1870s and assured Tom Craddick's election as the first Republican House speaker since Reconstruction. Moreover, it gave Republicans control of all major power points in the statehouse because they also maintained their majority in the state Senate and their hold on the governor's office. The conservative GOP agenda dominated legislative deliberations, including the crucial balancing of a new state budget. Despite a $10 billion revenue shortfall, Republican leaders held the line against higher state taxes, drawing applause from many middle-income and wealthy Texans. But lawmakers imposed spending cuts that reduced the availability of health care and other services for low-income and disadvantaged Texans and further widened the divide between the privileged and the unfortunate.

Legislative partisanship also increased in 2003, thanks primarily to a bitter fight over congressional redistricting that took the regular session and three special sessions to resolve. The effort was orchestrated by U.S. House Majority Leader Tom DeLay of Texas to give Republicans a majority of the Texas congressional delegation and help the GOP maintain control of the U.S. Congress. Until that point, Democrats had held a 17 to 15 majority of the congressional seats from Texas, despite widespread Republican gains in other state offices. The battle to redraw the district lines to favor more Republican candidates focused national attention on the legislature when Democratic lawmakers, on two separate occasions, fled to neighboring states to block action on redistricting bills. More than 50 Democrats fled to Ardmore, Oklahoma, for four days that spring to deprive the House of a quorum and kill a redistricting bill in the regular session. And 11 Democratic state senators spent

TIME LINE

THE TEXAS LEGISLATURE

1876	New constitution imposes strict limits on the power of state lawmakers
1888	Completion of state Capitol
1971	Sharpstown stock fraud scandal
1973	Lobbyists required to register with Secretary of State
1975	Provisions of the Voting Rights Act apply to legislative redistricting
1987	Increased partisanship in the Texas House
1990	Capitol Restoration Project
1991	Creation of Ethics Commission
1996	Republicans gain control of Texas senate
2002	Republicans gain control of both houses of the Texas legislature

more than a month in Albuquerque, New Mexico, to shut down the Senate for an entire special session that summer. Eventually, the Republicans prevailed, but the experience left behind a bitter, partisan taste in Austin that could affect future legislative deliberations.

The legislative experiences of 2003 reflected some of the enormous social, political, and economic changes that have occurred in Texas during the past generation. Forty years ago, a rural-dominated legislature showed little concern for the problems of urban areas and minority groups. Operating within the context of one-party Democratic control and an interest group system dominated by oil, finance, and agriculture, legislative leaders tied to conservative factions in the Democratic party pursued selected policies that benefited those sectors of the Texas economy.

Today, Texas is the country's second most populous state and is more than 80 percent urban. The ethnic and racial characteristics of its population have changed, and still more changes are projected in its social composition. Texas is now dominated by the Republican party, its economy is diversifying, and there are more demands today on the legislature than in the past. The issues and policy questions that confront lawmakers are more complex, and the special interests demanding attention are more numerous and diverse.

Despite these major demographic and political changes, however, lawmakers still have to operate under outdated constitutional restrictions—including strict limits on when they can meet—that were written for a rural state in a bygone era.

LEGISLATIVE FUNCTIONS

The legislature, whose members are elected from districts throughout Texas, is the chief policy-making branch of state government. Its basic role is similar to that of Congress at the federal level, although there are major differences between the two institutions. The Texas legislature performs a variety of functions, but its primary task is to decide how conflicts between competing groups and interests are to be resolved—that is, who gets what, when, and how. Although often taken for granted, this orderly, institutionalized process of conflict management and resolution is critical to a stable political system.[1]

Enacting Laws

Every two years, the legislature enacts several hundred laws governing our behavior; allocating resources, benefits and costs; and defining the duties of those institutions and bureaucrats responsible for putting these laws into effect. From local legislation that affects only a city or county, to general statewide policies and proposals for constitutional amendments, there are literally thousands of ideas advanced for new laws every legislative session. The legislative arena includes a wide range of players in addition to legislators, and lawmaking requires compromise and accommodation of competing ideas and interests.

Budgets and Taxes

The legislature establishes programs providing a variety of public services and sets priorities through the budgetary process. It sets the budgets for the governor, the bureaucracy, and the state courts. It decides whether state taxes should be increased, how high they should be increased, and how the tax burden should be distributed. Indirectly, its actions affect local tax rates as well.

Overseeing State Agencies

Hundreds of laws are passed each legislative session, and the legislature assigns to specific state agencies and local governments the responsibility of carrying out the laws on a day-to-day basis. It is ultimately the legislature's responsibility to make sure agencies and bureaucrats are doing what they are charged with by law, and this review, or "oversight," process is achieved through legislative budget hearings, other committee investigations, and program audits. The Senate further influences policy by confirming or rejecting the governor's appointees to hundreds of state boards and commissions that administer public programs.

Educating the Public

The 181 members of the Texas legislature certainly do not speak with one voice, and on major policy issues it is inevitable that there will be a variety of opinions and proposed solutions. Individual lawmakers try to inform the public about their own actions and the collective actions of the legislature. They use speeches, letters to constituents, news releases, telephone calls, newsletters, Web sites, e-mails, and other techniques to explain the legislative process, substantive policy issues, and their views on issues.

Representing the Public

The legislature is a representative body whose members are chosen in free elections. This process provides legitimacy to legislative actions and decisions. People may disagree over how "representative" the legislature is in terms of race, ethnicity, gender, or class. And many Texans may be indifferent toward or ignorant about public policy. But successful lawmakers must demonstrate concern for the attitudes and demands of their constituents. Legislators use many methods to learn how their constituents feel, including public opinion polls, questionnaires, phone calls, town hall meetings, and personal visits with constituents.

INSTITUTIONALIZATION OF THE TEXAS LEGISLATURE

As noted at the beginning of this chapter, the Texas legislature has undergone significant institutional changes over the past 130 years. Some changes have been due to external factors, such as the development of a two-party system within the electorate, changes in the state's interest group system, and complex social and economic problems. Other changes were internal. They included the increased tenure of the membership, changing career and leadership patterns, expanded workload, the development and enforcement of complex rules and procedures, and the emergence of partisan divisions. Political scientists describe these developments as **institutionalization**.[2]

Institutionalization varies throughout the fifty states. Some state legislatures are highly professional; others are not. In some states, salaries are high, turnover is limited, and legislators think in terms of legislative careers. Similarly, some legislatures have developed sophisticated staff and support services. By contrast, in other legislatures, members are poorly paid, turnover is high, legislative service is regarded as a part-time activity, and support services are limited. The Texas legislature falls somewhere between those legislatures that can be classified as highly professional and those that can be classified as amateur or citizen lawmaking bodies.[3] The institutionalization process has produced a more professional legislature in Texas, and this development is likely to continue in the future.

THE ORGANIZATION AND COMPOSITION OF THE TEXAS LEGISLATURE

Following the oppressive efforts of Governor Edmund J. Davis and the Reconstruction Republicans to centralize power (see Chapter 22), the delegates to the constitutional convention in 1875 were distrustful, even fearful, of the excesses and abuses of big government. They created a part-time, **bicameral legislature** that included a 31-member

Institutionalization
In the context of political science, the development of a legislative body into a formally structured system with stable membership, complex rules, expanded internal operations, and the delineation of staff functions.

bicameral legislature
Lawmaking body, such as the Texas legislature, that includes two chambers.

Senate and a 150-member House of Representatives, and they placed strong restrictions on it. All other states also have bicameral legislatures except Nebraska, which has only one lawmaking body with 49 members. The sizes of other state senates range from 20 in Alaska to 67 in Minnesota, while houses of representatives vary in size from 40 in Alaska to 400 in New Hampshire.[4]

Legislative Sessions

To curb lawmakers' power, the Texas constitutional framers limited **regular sessions** of the legislature to a maximum of 140 days every two years but gave the governor the authority to call **special sessions** when necessary. Lawmakers convene in regular session on the second Tuesday of January in odd-numbered years. Special sessions are limited to 30 days each and to subjects submitted by the governor, but there is no limit on the number of special sessions a governor can call.

There have been periods of frequent special sessions. From midsummer of 1986 through midsummer of 1987, for example, during a lingering budgetary crisis spawned by a depressed oil industry, the legislature convened for its regular 140-day session plus four special sessions, two of which lasted the maximum 30 days. The seventy-first legislature in 1989–90 held six special sessions to deal with equalization of school funding and the provision of medical expenses and other compensation for workers injured on the job. The seventy-second legislature had two special sessions in the summer of 1991 to write a new budget, pass a tax bill, make major changes in the criminal justice system, and redraw the boundaries of congressional districts. And, as noted earlier, the seventy-eighth legislature had three special sessions in the summer and early fall of 2003 in a protracted, partisan fight over congressional redistricting. The governor called a special session to deal with financing public education, but the session adjourned without action being taken.

Some state officials and government experts believe that the Texas legislature should have annual regular sessions, at least for budgetary purposes. Only six other state legislatures do not. But the change would require a constitutional amendment.

Terms of Office and Qualifications

Article III of the Texas constitution contains the constitutional provisions pertaining to the structure, membership, and selection of the Texas legislature. Representatives serve two-year terms, and senators are elected to four-year, staggered terms. A senator has to be a qualified voter, at least 26 years old, a resident of Texas for five years preceding his or her election, and a resident of the district from which elected for at least one year. A representative must be a qualified voter, at least 21 years old, a Texas resident for two years, and a resident of the district represented for one year. There is no limit on the number of terms an individual can serve in the legislature.

Pay and Compensation

Members of both the house and the senate and their presiding officers have a base pay of $7,200 per year. This figure is set by the state constitution and can be raised only with voter approval. This is one of the lowest legislative pay levels in the country and was last increased in 1975 by a constitutional amendment that also set lawmakers' per diem, or personal expense allowance, at $30 a day while they were in session. The house and the senate authorize additional expense allowances for members to cover staff salaries and other costs of operating legislative offices.

In 1991, Texas voters approved a constitutional amendment creating a state Ethics Commission that could recommend legislative pay raises to the voters and change legislative per diem on its own. The commission set per diem at $125 per day for the 2003 legislative sessions.

By 2002, only Texas, Alabama, New Hampshire, and Rhode Island had limits on legislative pay that could be changed only by constitutional amendment. Compensation commissions now recommend legislative pay levels in some states, while legislatures in other states set their own salaries, often with the approval of voters. In 2000, legislative pay ranged from a high of $99,000 a year in California, where lawmakers set their own

regular session
140-day period in the odd-numbered years in which the legislature meets and can consider and pass laws on any issue or subject.

special session
Legislative session that can be called at any time by the governor. This session is limited to thirty days and to issues or subjects designated by the governor.

salaries and are considered a full-time legislature, to a low of $100 a year in New Hampshire, which has annual sessions but a constitutional limit on salaries[5] (see *You Decide/Thinking It Through:* "What Should a Legislator Be Paid?").

Physical Facilities

The house chamber and representatives' offices have traditionally been located in the west wing of the state Capitol, and the senate chamber and senators' offices in the east wing (see Figure 24–1). The pink granite building was completed in 1888, but the growth of state government and periodic renovations created a hodgepodge of cramped legislative offices. After one visitor died in a fire behind the senate chamber in 1983, it also became obvious that the building had become a firetrap. So in 1990 the state launched a $187 million Capitol restoration and expansion project that included a four-story underground addition to the building. Legislative committee hearing rooms and many lawmakers' offices were relocated from the main building to the underground extension, which is connected to the original Capitol and nearby office buildings by tunnels.

When the legislature is in session, access to the floor of each chamber on the second floor of the Capitol is restricted to lawmakers, certain state officials, some staff members, and accredited media representatives. The galleries, to which the public is admitted, overlook the chambers from the third floor of the Capitol. In both the house and senate chambers, members have desks facing the presiding officer's podium, which, in turn, is flanked by desks of the clerical staff. Unlike the U.S. Congress, where seating is arranged by party affiliation, seats are assigned to state legislators by seniority.

Membership and Careers

In 1971, the Texas legislature was overwhelmingly white, male, and Democratic. There were two African Americans in the 150-member house and one in the 31-member senate. The one African American senator was also the only woman in the senate. She was Barbara Jordan of Houston, who two years later would begin a distinguished career in the U.S. Congress. Frances Farenthold of Corpus Christi was the only woman in the house. She was a reform-minded lawmaker who was often referred to as "the Den Mother of the Dirty Thirty," a coalition of liberal Democrats and conservative Republicans who challenged the power of Speaker Gus Mutscher while a major political scandal in which he was involved was unfolding. In 1972, Farenthold ran a strong race for governor in the Democratic primary but lost a runoff election to Uvalde rancher Dolph Briscoe. There were eleven Hispanic members of the house and only one Hispanic senator in 1971. Only twelve legislators were Republicans—ten in the house and two in the senate.

By 2003, changing political patterns and attitudes, redrawn political boundaries, and court-ordered single-member districts for urban house members had significantly altered the composition of the legislature (see Table 24–1). During the regular session and special sessions that year, Republicans had a 19 to 12 majority in the senate. The senate also had two African American members, seven Hispanics and four women (see *Changing Face of Texas Politics:* "Women of the Texas Legislature 1923–2005"). The house in 2003 had an 88 to 62 Republican majority, its first Republican majority of modern times. The 150 house members included 14 African Americans, 30 Hispanics, one Asian American, and 31 women. Representation from the urban and suburban areas of the state had grown, reflecting the population shifts accommodated by redistricting.

Business has been the dominant occupation of legislators serving in recent years, followed by law. Most of the 31 senators and more than 60 of the 150 house members in 2003 had a business background. Eight senators and 47 house members were attorneys, although not all of them made their living practicing law. The house included one chiropractor, one pharmacist, one automobile dealer, a drive-in restaurant owner, and a flight instructor. Two senators were physicians, one was a consulting engineer, and one was a retired firefighter.

★★ THINKING IT THROUGH

House and senate members are paid $7,200 per year. Legislators also receive a per diem of $125 per day while in session. This per diem is an expense allowance that covers the cost of the legislator staying in Austin. The two houses also provide allowances for offices and salaries of staff. In addition, members of the legislature receive retirement benefits computed on the basis of state district judges' salaries. Most members have law practices or businesses that allow them to be away on state business. Additionally, legislators make lucrative business and professional contacts while in the legislature.

Arguments for Increasing Legislative Salary

1. Most citizens would not be able to live on a salary of $7,200 per year. A higher salary would encourage more citizens to run for office.
2. Legislators serve on committees and do constituent work when the legislature is not in session.
3. A higher salary would undermine the temptation of corruption.

Arguments Against Increasing Legislative Salary

1. Legislators meet in Austin for a relatively short regular session every two years and for special sessions. It is a part-time job.
2. A higher salary would create professional politicians rather than representatives motivated by civic duty.
3. Legislators have created a lucrative pension plan for themselves and receive a per diem for their time when the legislature is in session.

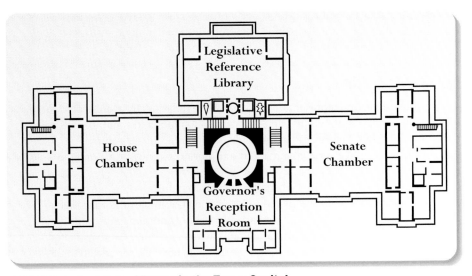

FIGURE 24–1 Corridors of Power in the Texas Capitol.
The second floor of the Texas Capitol, shown here, houses the senate and house chambers, the Legislative Reference Library, and the Governor's Reception Room.

Senators' ages ranged from 39 to 68, with an average age of 54. The age range for members of the house was 24 to 78, with an average age of 49.

Various career patterns lead to election to the legislature.[6] Lawmakers include former members of city councils and school boards, former prosecutors, former legislative aides, and longtime Democratic and Republican party activists. Twenty of the 31 senators in 2003 had previously served in the house. Many first-term legislators, however, arrive in Austin with relatively little political experience.

Legislative Turnover

Compared to other states, turnover in the Texas legislature is moderate. Relatively few individuals who serve can be considered career legislators. Only four senators and ten house members entered the 2003 regular session with twenty or more years of legislative service. The average legislative experience in the senate was thirteen years; house

Completed in 1888 and recently renovated, the Texas Capitol in downtown Austin houses the governor's office and meeting chambers for the house of representatives and the senate.

CHANGING FACE OF TEXAS POLITICS

WOMEN MEMBERS OF THE TEXAS LEGISLATURE, 1923–2005

Over the last eight decades, women in the legislature have grown from a small token number to one-fifth of the House of representatives, while less than one-eighth of the senate are women.

Legislative Term	House	Senate
2003–2005	31	4
2001–2003	31	4
1999–2001	30	4
1997–1999	31	3
1995–1997	33	4
1993–1995	27	4
1991–1993	21	4
1989–1991	16	3
1987–1989	15	3
1985–1987	15	1
1983–1985	14	0
1981–1983	11	1
1979–1981	11	1
1977–1979	12	1
1975–1977	8	1
1973–1975	5	1
1971–1973	1	1
1969–1971	1	1
1967–1969	1	1
1965–1967	1	1
1963–1965	1	1

Legislative Term	House	Senate
1961–1963	3	1
1959–1961	2	1
1957–1959	2	1
1955–1957	2	1
1953–1955	4	1
1951–1953	2	1
1949–1951	2	1
1947–1949	3	1
1945–1947	4	0
1943–1945	4	0
1941–1943	2	0
1939–1941	2	0
1937–1939	0	0
1935–1937	2	0
1933–1935	1	0
1931–1933	4	1
1929–1931	2	1
1927–1929	0	1
1925–1927	0	0
1923–1925	1	0

No women were elected prior to 1923.

SOURCE: Legislative Reference Library of Texas.

TABLE 24–1 COMPARATIVE PROFILE OF TEXAS LEGISLATORS, 1971–2003

	House			Senate		
	1971	1981	2003	1971	1981	2003
Democrats	140	112	88	29	24	12
Republicans	10	38	62	2	7	19
Males	149	139	119	30	30	27
Females	1	11	31	1	1	4
Hispanics	11	17	30	1	4	7
African Americans	2	13	14	1	0	2
Anglos	137	120	105	29	27	22

SOURCE: Texas house and senate rosters, 1971, 1981, 2003.

members had served an average of seven years. In addition to the effects of redistricting of legislative seats every ten years, turnover is due to the low pay and the personal costs involved in running for public office. While in session, many legislators lose income from their regular sources of employment. Political ambition is also a factor. Many lawmakers who want to move up the political ladder serve only a few terms in the Texas house before running for the Texas senate, the U.S. Congress, or other state or local offices. Other legislators quit after a few sessions to become lobbyists.

Redistricting and voluntary retirements took a toll on legislative experience after the 2001 session. Several veteran lawmakers didn't seek reelection in 2002, including the two most senior members of the senate, Senators Carlos Truan, D-Corpus Christi, and J. E. "Buster" Brown, R-Lake Jackson. Truan had served twenty-four years in the senate and eight in the house. Brown had been in the senate for twenty years. Representative Rob Junell, D-San Angelo, longtime chairman of the budget-writing House Appropriations Committee, also called it quits.

REPRESENTATION AND REDISTRICTING

Many European legislatures use a system called *proportional representation,* in which legislative seats are allocated on the basis of each party's percentage of the total vote in an election. By contrast, the Texas legislature and most other American legislatures allocate seats geographically on the basis of **single-member districts**. The long legal and political battles over apportionment and redistricting address some of the fundamental questions of who should be represented and how they should be represented.

The Texas Constitution of 1876 provided that the legislature redraw state representative and senatorial districts every ten years, "at its first session after the publication of each United States decennial census," to reflect changing population patterns. But members of earlier rural-dominated legislatures were reluctant to apportion the legislative seats equitably to reflect the increased urbanization of the state, and inequities grew. In 1948, Texas voters approved a constitutional amendment creating the **Legislative Redistricting Board** to carry out redistricting responsibilities if the legislature failed to do so during the required session. The board includes the lieutenant governor, the speaker of the house, the attorney general, the comptroller, and the land commissioner.

But for many more years, the urban areas of the state were still denied equality in representation. After the 1960 census, it was possible for approximately 33 percent of the state's population to elect a majority of both the Texas house and the senate. And rural legislators tended to neglect urban problems.

Equality in redistricting finally came to Texas as a result of federal court intervention. In 1962, the U.S. Supreme Court, in the case of *Baker* v. *Carr,* applied the principle of equality to congressional districts. Then, in the case of *Reynolds* v. *Sims* (1964), the court held that state legislative districts had to be apportioned on the "one person, one vote" principle. Litigation in 1965 (*Kilgarlin* v. *Martin*) extended this ruling to Texas, and the "reapportionment revolution" was to produce dramatic changes in the composition and structure of the Texas legislature.[7] To a large degree, the increased representation of minorities and Republicans in Texas's lawmaking body is a result of the legal and political redistricting battles.

The Texas senate has always been elected by single-member districts, and after the 1970 census, the application of the "equality principle" to the senate resulted in districts that were comparable in size. The issues of racial and partisan gerrymandering—the practice of drawing lines to favor a particular individual or group (see Chapter 23)— were still to be resolved through subsequent litigation and federal legislation.

Rural members of the Texas house were also elected from single-member districts, but in the urban counties that had been allocated more than one representative, the elections were held in multimember districts. Each candidate for a house seat in an urban area had to run for election countywide, a practice that put ethnic and political minorities at a disadvantage because their votes were diluted by the dominant Anglo and Democratic populations.

single-member district
System in which a legislator, city council member, or other public official is elected from a specific geographic area.

Legislative Redistricting Board
A board created by constitutional amendment charged to redistrict the Texas legislature if it is not accomplished in the regular session following the release of the census.

In 1972, a three-judge federal court ruled that multimember districts in Dallas and Bexar counties were unconstitutional because they diluted the voting strength of African Americans in Dallas and Hispanics in Bexar. Coincidentally, the **at-large districts** diluted the voting strength of Republicans in both counties.

Despite the fact that 50 percent of Bexar County's population was Hispanic, under the at-large election system only one Hispanic from Bexar had served in the Texas house in 1971. Dallas County, which had a large African American population, had only one African American house member. Single-member districts in Harris County had been drawn by the Legislative Redistricting Board in 1971, and after the U.S. Supreme Court upheld the lower court's decision regarding Dallas and Bexar counties, multimember legislative districts were soon eliminated in all other urban counties. After 1975, the U.S. Congress put Texas under the provisions of the federal Voting Rights Act, which prohibits the dilution of minority voting strength, requires clearance in advance of redistricting plans by the Department of Justice, and gives African Americans and Hispanics an effective weapon to use in challenging a redistricting plan in court.

At the beginning of the twenty-first century, however, minorities believed their fight for equal representation was still far from over. The Voting Rights Act was under attack by conservatives. The U.S. Supreme Court, in "reverse discrimination" cases from Texas and Georgia, ruled that some congressional districts had been illegally gerrymandered to elect minority candidates. And in another case from Georgia, the high court held in 2003 that states have the right to determine how best to draw legislative and congressional districts to protect minority voters.[8]

Texas Republicans scored huge redistricting victories in 2001, after the legislature failed to redraw its own districts during that year's regular session. Under the state constitution, the task then fell to the five statewide elected officials, four of whom were Republicans, on the Legislative Redistricting Board. The panel drew new legislative maps that helped increase Republican strength in the 31-member senate to 19 GOP senators. It also enabled Republicans to capture their first majority of modern times in the 150-member house. With legislative candidates running under the new plan in the 2002 elections, the GOP increased its strength in the house from 72 seats to 88 seats, a margin that cleared the way for state Representative Tom Craddick of Midland, a Republican, to be elected speaker after the regular session convened in 2003. The GOP takeover of the Texas House also gave Republicans the opportunity to redraw the boundaries for Texas's congressional districts later that year. Republicans prevailed after a bitter partisan fight that included two walkouts by Democratic legislators. The new congressional map was expected to give Republicans a strong majority among members of the U.S. Congress elected from Texas (See *Changing Face of Texas Politics:* "Partisanship in the 2003 Redistricting Battles").

Speaker Tom Craddick presides over the House of Representatives.

LEGISLATIVE LEADERSHIP

The highly institutionalized leadership structure found in the U.S. Congress is only now beginning to emerge in the Texas legislature—and to only a limited extent. Until recent years, the Texas legislature was dominated by a small group of Democratic lawmakers. With no significant party opposition or minority representation for much of the state's history, legislative leadership was highly personal and dependent on the political relationships between the presiding officers and key legislators. Recent Republican growth in the statehouse, however, is beginning to force changes.

House Leadership

The presiding officer of the house of representatives is the **speaker**, who is elected by the house from among its membership. With the long tenures of Gib Lewis and his immediate predecessor in the speaker's office, Bill Clayton, there was not a contested speaker's race between 1975 and 1991. Lewis's decision not to seek reelection in 1992 prompted several house members to announce their candidacy for the post. But veteran

at-large district
Legislative or other political district, sometimes called a multimember district because two or more officials are elected from it, that includes an entire county, city, or other political subdivision.

speaker
Presiding officer of the house of representatives.

Democratic Representative James E. "Pete" Laney, a farmer-businessman from Hale Center, secured the support of the necessary majority of house members several weeks before the 1993 legislature convened, and his election on the opening day of the session was unopposed.

Laney served five terms as speaker and, although he was a Democrat, enjoyed the support of many Republican house members. Continuing a bipartisan tradition, he appointed several Republicans to chair house committees. But Republicans, after winning a strong majority of house seats in the 2002 elections, elected state Representative Tom Craddick, a Republican from Midland, to succeed Laney as presiding officer in 2003. Laney, who had won reelection to his West Texas district in 2002, remained in the house, becoming the first former speaker in years to return to a seat on the house floor after having been presiding officer.

It is illegal for a speaker candidate to make outright promises in return for members' support. But, continuing a tradition, Craddick gave his key supporters choice leadership positions when the new speaker exercised one of his most significant, formal powers and made his committee assignments. Legislators know that the earlier they hop onto a winning bandwagon in a speaker's race, the better chance they will have of getting their preferred committee assignments or the opportunity to advance their legislative programs. Sometimes, however, choosing the winning candidate is difficult because the campaigning is conducted largely behind the scenes, with candidates making personal pleas to individual house members.

Until the 1950s, it was unusual for a speaker to serve more than one two-year term (see Table 24–2). The position was circulated among a small group of legislators who dominated the house. Clayton, a lawmaker from Springlake in West Texas, set a record by serving four consecutive terms before retiring in 1983. Lewis of Fort Worth and Laney each surpassed Clayton's record by serving five terms.

Unlike most of their predecessors, Clayton, Lewis, Laney, and Craddick devoted long hours to the job and kept large full-time staffs. With the complexities of a growing state putting more demands on the legislative leadership, recent senate leaders (lieutenant governors) have also made their jobs virtually full-time and, like the speaker, have hired large staffs of specialists to research issues and help develop legislation. The presiding officers also depend on key committee chairs to take the lead in pushing their legislative priorities.

During Laney's speakership, the state completed a multibillion-dollar expansion of its prison system, overhauled criminal justice laws, and enacted a school finance law that addressed a Texas Supreme Court order for more equity in education spending. In a bipartisan endeavor, Laney actively supported then-Governor George W. Bush's unsuccessful effort to replace a large chunk of local school property taxes with higher state taxes in 1997. He also encouraged opposing sides to find common ground on other major issues, but one of his own priorities was to improve the way the house conducted its business. Laney won significant changes in house rules that produced, in the view of many house members, a more democratic lawmaking process than under previous speakers.

Backed by a Republican majority, Craddick was a key figure in the legislature's tight-fisted approach to drafting the new state budget in 2003, which cut spending in many areas to bridge a $10 billion revenue shortfall. He was a strong opponent of raising state taxes, although he insisted the legislature enact a separate law allowing university governing boards to raise college tuition. Craddick also was a key figure in the legislature's enactment of the redistricting bill to increase the number of Republicans elected to Congress from Texas. He was a consistently tough negotiator. "He's the toughest, hardest trader I've ever met. When you start trading with the speaker, it's tough trading," said state Senator Steve Ogden, a Republican from Bryan and a longtime friend of Craddick's.[9]

The speaker appoints a speaker pro tempore, or assistant presiding officer, who is usually a close ally. In 1981, Speaker Clayton named the first African American, Representative Craig Washington of Houston, to the post. Although Clayton was a rural conservative and Washington was an urban liberal, Washington proved to be a critical member of the speaker's team. He also exercised considerable influence in the house on

CHANGING FACE OF TEXAS POLITICS

PARTISANSHIP IN THE 2003 REDISTRICTING BATTLES

The contentious, nationally publicized fight over congressional redistricting in 2003 was not the Texas Legislature's finest hour. But the drama of Democratic lawmakers fleeing across state lines to shut down legislative business in Austin, the bitter partisan rhetoric, and the persistence of the eventual Republican victors vividly illustrated the huge political stakes that were involved.

The Republican takeover of the Texas house in 2003 gave the GOP control of state government, but Democrats still held a 17 to 15 edge among members of the U.S. Congress elected from Texas. The lines for congressional districts had been redrawn to reflect new census data in 2001 by a federal court, not by the legislature, because the Texas house, which still had a Democratic majority in 2001, couldn't agree on a new map with the Republican-dominated senate. Once Republicans had control of both legislative chambers, the Republican leader of the U.S. House, Congressman Tom DeLay, began urging Texas Republican leaders to redraw the congressional lines to favor more Republican candidates and help their party maintain its narrow majority of the U.S. House. But a redistricting bill died late in the regular legislative session that spring when more than fifty Democratic members of the Texas House fled to Ardmore, Oklahoma, to break a house quorum and prevent the body from conducting business for four days—long enough to miss a deadline for action on the redistricting measure. The Democrats, outnumbered 88 to 62, didn't have enough votes in the house to defeat the bill outright, but they had enough members to shut down work, because a quorum required two-thirds of the members to be present. The Democrats left the state in order to avoid being arrested by state troopers and forced to return to the Capitol. In their absence, Speaker Tom Craddick and the remaining members had placed a "call" on the house, authorizing the sergeant-at-arms to enlist the aid of law enforcement officers to round up the missing members.

Republican leaders, most notably DeLay and Governor Rick Perry, didn't give up. Perry called the legislature back into a thirty-day special session in June to tackle redistricting again. This time, Democrats didn't bolt, and the house easily approved the bill. But the measure died in the senate, where Democratic senators used the "two-thirds rule" to block action on it. That traditional procedure required two-thirds of the senators to approve debate on any legislation, and Republicans, although they were in the majority, didn't constitute two-thirds of the body. At the end of the first special session, Lieutenant Governor David Dewhurst, a Republican who earlier had been reluctant to force a vote on redistricting, announced that he would bypass the two-thirds requirement during a second special session. That prompted eleven Democratic senators to fly to Albuquerque, New Mexico, breaking a senate quorum, only minutes before

Perry issued a proclamation calling the second special session. The Democrats remained holed up in New Mexico for more than a month, outlasting the entire second session. The only Democratic senator who didn't flee was Ken Armbrister of Victoria, who represented a strongly Republican district.

While the national media listened and watched, the Democrats in Albuquerque and the Republicans in Austin exchanged a barrage of partisan charges and countercharges. The dissident Democrats—who included nine minorities and two Anglos who represented predominantly minority districts—accused the Republicans of trying to redraw congressional districts to dilute the voting strength of Hispanics and African Americans. "This is a shameful return to the days of the Jim Crow laws designed to prevent electoral participation of minorities in the South," said state Senator Leticia Van de Putte of San Antonio, chair of the Senate Democratic Caucus. Dewhurst and the Republican senators denied the charges. They said redistricting would enhance minority voting strength. And they argued that Republicans, who had a majority in Texas, were entitled to a majority of congressional seats from the state. Republican senators also took the unusual step of imposing sanctions—including thousands of dollars in fines—on the absentees.

The stalemate finally ended when one of the Democrats, state Senator John Whitmire of Houston, returned to Texas, announcing that he would continue the fight on the senate floor. Because Whitmire's return restored the senate's two-thirds quorum, the remaining dissidents returned as well. Perry called a third special session in September, and Republican majorities in the house and the senate approved different versions of a redistricting map. Final approval was delayed for several days because house and senate Republicans, ironically, continued to fight among themselves over a handful of districts. The main hangup was over West Texas, where Speaker Craddick insisted that his hometown, Midland, get a congressional district it could dominate. In the end, Craddick got his wish, but not before DeLay visited Austin to personally help negotiate between house and senate members of the conference committee that drew the final map.

The third special session ended on October 12, and Perry quickly signed the new redistricting plan, which was expected to give Republicans as many as twenty-two of Texas's thirty-two congressional seats. Democrats filed suit in federal court to block the plan, but a three-judge federal panel approved it in time for the 2004 elections. Republican state senators, meanwhile, didn't enforce the fines they had imposed on the dissident Democrats.

SOURCE: *Houston Chronicle,* August 14, 2003, p. 25A.

TABLE 24–2   RECENT PRESIDING OFFICERS

Lieutenant Governors	When Served	Home
Ben Ramsey	1951–1961*	San Augustine
Preston Smith	1963–1969	Lubbock
Ben Barnes	1969–1973	DeLeon
Bill Hobby, Jr.	1973–1991	Houston
Bob Bullock	1991–1999	Hillsboro
Rick Perry	1999–2000	Haskell
Bill Ratliff	2000–2003	Mt. Pleasant
David Dewhurst	2003–	Houston

Speakers	When Served	Home
Reuben Senterfitt	1951–1955	San Saba
Jim T. Lindsey	1955–1957	Texarkana
Waggoner Carr	1957–1961	Lubbock
James A. Turman	1961–1963	Gober
Byron M. Tunnell	1963–1965	Tyler
Ben Barnes	1965–1969	DeLeon
Gus Mutscher	1969–1972	Brenham
Rayford Price	1972–1973	Palestine
Price Daniel, Jr.	1973–1975	Liberty
Bill Clayton	1975–1983	Springlake
Gib Lewis	1983–1993	Fort Worth
James E. "Pete" Laney	1993–2003	Hale Center
Tom Craddick	2003–	Midland

*Ben Ramsey resigned as lieutenant governor on September 18, 1961, upon his appointment to the Railroad Commission. The office was vacant until Preston Smith took office in 1963.

SOURCE: Texas Legislative Council, *Presiding Officers of the Texas Legislature, 1846–1982* (Texas Legislative Council, 1982); Texas Legislature Online.

a wide range of issues of importance to minorities. Ten years later, Gib Lewis named another African American legislator, Representative Wilhelmina Delco of Austin, as the first woman speaker pro tempore.

The membership of most house committees is determined partly by seniority. The speaker has total discretion, however, in naming committee chairs and vice chairs and in appointing all the members of procedural committees, including the influential Calendars Committee, which will be described in more detail later in this chapter. Under a rules change in 2003, Craddick also had total discretion—without regard for seniority—in appointing the budget-writing House Appropriations Committee. The new speaker bumped some senior Democratic members from the panel.

Senate Leadership

The **lieutenant governor** is chosen by the voters in a statewide election to serve a four-year term as presiding officer of the senate. Unlike the vice president of the United States—the counterpart in the federal government, who has only limited legislative functions—the lieutenant governor has traditionally been the senate's legislative leader. This office, which is elected independently of the governor, has often been called the most powerful office in state government because of the lieutenant governor's opportunity to merge a statewide electoral base into a dominant legislative role.[10] Lieutenant governors, however, get most of their power from rules set by the senators, not from the constitution.

lieutenant governor
Presiding officer of the senate. This officeholder would become governor if the governor were to die, be incapacitated, or removed from office.

The lieutenant governor's power is based in part on the same coalitional strategies that are used by the speaker through committee assignments and relationships with interest groups. But the lieutenant governor has traditionally had more direct control over the senate's agenda than the speaker has over the house's agenda. Under long-standing senate rules, the lieutenant governor has determined when—and if—a committee-approved bill will be brought up for a vote by the full senate. In the house, the order of floor debate is determined by the Calendars Committee. Although that key panel is appointed by the speaker and is sensitive to the speaker's wishes, it represents an intermediate step that the lieutenant governor does not have to encounter.

The lieutenant governor also has had more formal control over the membership of senate committees than the speaker has over house panels. Under its rules, the senate traditionally has allowed the lieutenant governor to appoint members of all standing committees without regard to seniority or any other restrictions.

The senate has a president pro tempore, who is chosen by senators from among their membership. This position is rotated among the senators on a seniority basis. It is held for a limited period, and the holder of the position is third in line of succession to the governorship. There is a tradition that the governor and the lieutenant governor both allegedly "leave" the state on the same day so that the president pro tempore can serve as "governor for a day" at one point during his or her term.

Bill Hobby, a quiet-spoken media executive who served a record eighteen years as lieutenant governor before voluntarily leaving the office in January 1991, patiently sought consensus among senators on most major issues and rarely took the lead in promoting specific legislative proposals. One notable exception occurred in 1979, when Hobby, a Democrat, tried to force senate approval of a presidential primary bill opposed by most Democratic senators. After Hobby served notice that he would alter the senate's traditional operating procedure to give the bill special consideration, twelve Democratic senators, dubbed the "Killer Bees," hid out for several days to break a **quorum** and keep the senate from conducting business. They succeeded in killing the primary bill and reminding Hobby that the senators set the rules.

Hobby's successor, Bob Bullock, had demonstrated strong leadership and a mercurial temperament during sixteen years as state comptroller. Upon taking office as lieutenant governor, he had major policy and structural changes in mind for state government and was impatient to see them carried out by the legislature. Unlike Hobby, Bullock took the lead in making proposals and then actively lobbying for them. During his first session in 1991, he reportedly had shouting matches with some lawmakers behind closed doors and one day abruptly and angrily adjourned the senate when not enough members were present for a quorum at the scheduled starting time. But his experience and knowledge of state government and his tireless work habits won the respect of most senators and their support for most of his proposals.

Bullock, a Democrat, strengthened his leadership role during the 1993 and 1995 sessions and was actively involved in every major issue that the senate addressed. Recognizing that increases in Republican strength after the 1992 and 1994 elections made the senate more conservative than it had been in several years, and eager to strengthen his support in the business community, Bullock saw to it that compromises on major issues—including some long sought by business—were reached behind closed doors before they were made public. This approach kept controversy to a minimum and defused partisanship, but it distressed consumer advocates and environmentalists, who felt excluded from the process. It also prompted remarks that the senate had abandoned democracy. There were so many unanimous or near-unanimous votes in the senate in 1993 that some house members joked that senators who wanted to show dissent voted aye with their eyes closed.[11]

Bullock played a less active role during the 1997 session, after Republicans, for the first time this century, had won a majority of senate seats. He was strongly supportive of some key legislation, including a statewide water conservation and management plan, but he did little to promote a property tax relief effort that Governor Bush had made his highest priority for the session. One key element of Bush's proposal, an increase in state taxes as a partial trade-off for lower school district taxes, died primarily because of strong senate opposition, which Bullock did not try to defuse.

quorum
Required number of the members of a governing body who must be present so that official business, such as voting, can be conducted. In Texas, a quorum of the house and the senate is two-thirds of the membership. For committees, it is a majority of the members.

Former Lieutenant Governor Bob Bullock, who retired in 1999 and died later that year, was one of the more influential senate leaders in the modern era.

A few days after the 1997 session ended, Bullock surprised the Texas political community by announcing that he would not seek reelection in 1998. The former state leader, who had a history of health problems, was later diagnosed with lung cancer, and he died in June 1999.

After defeating Democrat John Sharp in a hard-fought race in 1998, former Agriculture Commissioner Rick Perry became Texas's first Republican lieutenant governor of modern times in 1999. Perry not only had to follow in Bullock's legendary footsteps, he also had to preside over the senate during a session overshadowed by Governor George W. Bush's anticipated presidential race. The new lieutenant governor had the advantage, though, of entering the 1999 session with a $6 billion state surplus and a rare absence of emergencies. Perry lost one of his biggest priorities, a pilot project to allow students in low-performing public schools to use state-paid vouchers to transfer to private schools. But he generally received high marks for his performance during the session from both Democrats and Republicans. As one senator observed, "He might not have used the Bullock style of cracking heads or the woodshed" to force legislative solutions. "He did effectively bring people together and kept us from having any meltdowns."[12] Perry was more low key than Bullock, perhaps choosing to learn more about the senate and its members before plunging into potential controversies. Nevertheless, he was credited with helping Republican and Democratic lawmakers negotiate a compromise on one of the key legislative packages of the session—a series of tax cuts, teacher pay raises, and other increased education spending.

Perry was elected to a lieutenant governor's term that wasn't to expire until January 2003. But in anticipation of Governor Bush's presidential race, the legislature in 1999 approved a constitutional amendment—which Texas voters later endorsed—to make it clear that Perry would have to give up the lieutenant governor's job in midterm if he were promoted to fill a vacancy in the governor's office. After Bush resigned the governorship in December 2000 to become president, Perry was promoted to governor. And, acting under the new constitutional amendment, senators elected state Senator Bill Ratliff, R-Mount Pleasant, to serve as lieutenant governor during the 2001 session.

Ratliff, a former chairman of the senate Education and Finance committees, was businesslike in his role as presiding officer, and he generally received favorable reviews. He appointed the first African American, state Senator Rodney Ellis, D-Houston, to chair the budget-writing Finance Committee. He also parted ways with most Republican senators and supported Ellis's bill to strengthen the state law against hate crimes, which passed that session. And Ratliff blocked a bill that would have removed state legal restrictions against Native Americans operating casinos on their reservations in Texas. At the end of the 2001 session, Ratliff announced that he would seek election to the lieutenant governor's post in 2002. But several days later, admitting he didn't have the stomach for the compromises often involved in a statewide race, he announced that he had changed his mind and would seek reelection to his senate seat instead. "I do love policymaking, but I do not love politics," he said.[13] After winning reelection to the senate in 2002 and serving during the regular and special sessions in 2003, Ratliff resigned in early 2004, expressing weariness after 15 years in the legislative arena.

Republican David Dewhurst won the 2002 lieutenant governor's race over Democrat John Sharp, who had narrowly lost the same office to Rick Perry in 1998. A wealthy businessman, Dewhurst had no legislative experience when he became the senate's presiding officer in January 2003. His only experience in elected office had been his four previous years as state land commissioner, but he moved quickly to establish credibility as a leader. He appointed respected legislative insiders to key staff positions and spent many hours studying issues and meeting with individual senators. Although Republicans held a 19 to 12 senate majority, he continued the tradition of appointing both Republicans and Democrats to leadership positions. Dewhurst agreed with Governor Rick Perry and Speaker Tom Craddick that the legislature would close a $10 billion revenue shortfall and write a new state budget without increasing state taxes. But he and the senate helped to minimize some of the spending cuts by insisting that lawmakers tap into nontax revenue, such as the state's Rainy Day savings account. On such budgetary details and other matters, including how quickly the legislature should move to improve the school finance system, Dewhurst sometimes differed with Perry and Craddick. Their differences stemmed partly from Dewhurst's independent nature, which was bolstered by the fact that he—not special interest groups—had largely funded his election to the state's number two office. The senate's rules and traditions also required the lieutenant governor to seek more consensus among senators than the speaker normally has to do in the house. Legislation traditionally wasn't approved without the consent of two-thirds of the senators, which meant that the twelve Democratic senators had enough clout to force some budgetary concessions.

Dewhurst orchestrated the senate's biggest show of independence during the 2003 regular session by hammering out in a series of private meetings a new public education funding plan that would have raised the state sales tax in exchange for sharp reductions in local property taxes, which were increasingly under fire, particularly in many suburban and heavily Republican school districts. Dewhurst won unanimous senate approval of the proposal, but the house never acted on it. Craddick and Perry insisted instead that lawmakers conduct another study of school finance, which had already been studied several times in recent years, and attempt to tackle the issue later.

Senate unanimity disappeared—and Dewhurst's leadership was severely challenged—during the bitter partisan fight over congressional redistricting that took three special sessions in the summer and fall of 2003 to resolve. Democratic senators blocked a house-passed redistricting bill during the first special session by using a senate tradition that required two-thirds of the senators to approve debate on any legislation. After Dewhurst announced that he would bypass that procedure—known as the "two-thirds rule"—to allow a redistricting bill to be passed on a simple majority vote during the second special session, eleven of the senate's twelve Democrats fled to Albuquerque, New Mexico, where they remained for more than a month. Their flight, which received national media coverage, deprived the senate of a quorum and the ability to conduct any business during the entire, 30-day second special session. It also severely damaged the senate's tradition of personal and partisan cooperation as Democratic and Republican senators exchanged verbal attacks across state lines. The boycotting senators eventually returned to Austin, and the legislature approved a congressional redistricting bill favoring Republicans during a third special session. Dewhurst immediately began working behind the scenes to restore the senate's ability to conduct business in a civil, bipartisan fashion.

David Dewhurst (seated, left) was elected lieutenant governor in 2002 after serving as land commissioner.

Influence and Control over the Legislative Process

The power of each presiding officer to appoint committees and determine which committee will have jurisdiction over a specific bill gives the speaker and the lieutenant governor tremendous influence over the lawmaking process.

The speaker and the lieutenant governor control the legislative process through the application of the rules, including those set in the state constitution and those adopted by the house and the senate. Each presiding officer is advised on procedures by a parliamentarian. The speaker and the lieutenant governor do not participate in house or senate debate on bills and usually attempt to present an image of neutral presiding officers. Their formal powers, however, are further strengthened by their informal relationships with their committee leaders and interest groups. And, with the notable exceptions of the separate walkouts by house and senate Democrats during the 2003 redistricting battle, the speaker and the lieutenant governor rarely lose control of the process.

In the senate, the lieutenant governor can vote only to break a tie. The speaker can vote on any issue in the house but normally abstains from voting except to break a tie or to send a signal to encourage reluctant or wavering house members to vote a particular way on an issue.

Leadership Teams

Traditionally, there has been no formal division along party lines or a formal system of floor leaders in either the Texas house or the senate. The longtime, Democrat-dominated legislative system with the speaker's and lieutenant governor's control of committee appointments did not produce a leadership structure comparable to that of the U.S. Congress. The committee chairs constitute the speaker's and lieutenant governor's teams and usually act as their unofficial floor leaders in developing and building support for the leadership's legislative priorities. Most chairs are philosophically, if not always politically, aligned with the presiding officers.

THE COMMITTEE SYSTEM

The committee system is the backbone of the legislative process, and it is molded by the lieutenant governor and the speaker.[14] It is a screening process that decides the fate of most legislation.

The **committee** is where technical drafting errors and oversights in bills can be corrected and where compromise can begin to work for those bills that do eventually become law. Only 1,405 of the 5,753 bills and constitutional amendments introduced in the 2003 regular session won final legislative approval. Most of those that did not make it died in a senate or a house committee, many without ever being heard. Rarely does a committee kill a bill on an outright vote, because there are much easier, less obvious ways to scuttle legislation. A bill can be gutted, or so drastically amended or weakened, that even its sponsor can hardly recognize it. Or it can be simply ignored.

Committee chairs have considerable power over legislation that comes to their committees. They may kill bills by simply refusing to schedule them for a hearing. Or, after a hearing, a chair may send a bill to a subcommittee that he or she stacks with members opposed to the legislation, thus allowing the bill to die slowly and quietly in the legislative deep freeze. Even if a majority of committee members want to approve a bill, the chair can simply refuse to recognize such a motion. Most chairs, however, are sensitive to the wishes of the presiding officers. If the speaker or the lieutenant governor wants a bill to win committee approval or wants another measure to die in committee, the chair will usually comply.

Referral to a **subcommittee** does not always mean the death of a bill. Subcommittees also help committees distribute the workload. They work out compromises, correct technical problems in bills, or draft substitute legislation to accommodate competing interest groups.

committee
In the legislature, a group of lawmakers who review and hold public hearings on issues or bills they are assigned by the presiding officer. Committees that specialize in bills by subject matter are designated as standing committees. A bill has to win committee approval before it can be considered by the full house or senate. Most bills die in committees, which perform as a legislative screening process.

subcommittee
A few members of a larger committee appointed to review a particular bill and make recommendations on its disposition to the full committee.

Standing Committees

The number and names of committees are periodically revised under house and senate rules, but there have been relatively few major changes in the basic committee structure in recent years. During the 2003 sessions, the senate had sixteen **standing committees**, including the Committee of the Whole, varying in membership from five to thirty-one.

There were forty-three standing committees in the house, with memberships ranging from five to twenty nine (Table 24–3). Most of these committees are substantive; that is, they hold public hearings and evaluate bills related to their areas, such as higher education, natural resources, or public health. A few committees are *procedural,* such as the Rules and Resolutions Committee, which handles many routine congratulatory resolutions, and the **Calendars Committee**, which schedules bills for debate by the full house.

Some committees play more dominant roles in the lawmaking process than others, particularly in the house. The house State Affairs Committee, for example, handles many more major statewide bills than the Committee on State Cultural and Recreational Resources or the Committee on Agriculture and Livestock. The house Urban Affairs and County Affairs committees handle several hundred bills of importance to local governments each session. The importance of a committee is determined by the area of public policy over which it has jurisdiction or by its role in the house's operating procedure.

The house Calendars Committee historically has had more life and death power over legislation than any other committee because it sets the order of debate on the house floor. During each regular session, it kills hundreds of bills that have been approved by various substantive committees by refusing to schedule them for debate by the full house or scheduling them so late in the session they don't have time to win senate approval. This committee traditionally works closely with the speaker and is one means by which the speaker and the speaker's team control the house. Although many legislators complain about the committee killing their priority bills, some lawmakers defend the panel as a means of keeping controversial legislation—on which many members would rather not have to cast votes—from reaching the house floor.

The state budget is the single most important bill enacted by the legislature because, through it, lawmakers determine how much money is spent on the state's public programs and services. In the house, the Appropriations Committee takes the lead in drafting state budgets, while the house Ways and Means Committee normally is responsible for producing any tax or revenue measures necessary to balance the budget. The two most important committees in the senate are the Finance Committee, which handles the budget and, usually, tax bills, and the State Affairs Committee, which, like its house counterpart, handles a variety of legislation of major, statewide importance.

Although committees have general subject areas of responsibility, legislative rules allow the lieutenant governor and the speaker some latitude in assigning bills. The presiding officer can ensure the death of a bill by sending it to a committee known to oppose it or can guarantee quick action on a measure by referring it to a receptive, or friendly, panel.

Standing Subcommittees

The formal, standing subcommittee structure of the U.S. Congress has only begun to develop in the Texas legislature, where committee chairs traditionally appointed subcommittees as needed to handle specific bills.

Conference Committees

Legislation must be passed in exactly the same form by the house and the senate. If one chamber refuses to accept the other's version of a bill, a **conference committee** can try to resolve the differences. Conference committees of five senators and five representatives are appointed by the presiding officers. A compromise bill has to be approved by at least three senators and three house members who serve on the conference committee before it is sent back to the full house and the full senate for subsequent approval

standing committee
Committee that is created by house or senate rules to consider legislation or perform a procedural role in the lawmaking process.

Calendars Committee
Special procedural committee that schedules bills that already have been approved by other committees for floor debate in the house.

conference committee
Panel of house members and senators appointed to work out a compromise on a bill if different versions of the legislation were passed by the house and the senate.

TABLE 24–3 SENATE AND HOUSE STANDING COMMITTEES, 78TH LEGISLATURE, 2003

Senate Committee	Number of Members	Bills Referred to Committee in the Regular Session	Bills Out of Committee
Administration	7	106	86
Business & Commerce	9	277	159
Committee of the Whole Senate*	31	3	3
Criminal Justice	7	287	179
Education	9	331	168
Finance	15	175	67
Government Organization	7	118	75
Health and Human Services	9	262	168
Infrastructure Development and Security	9	242	111
Intergovernmental Relations	5	356	252
International Relations and Trade	7	37	29
Jurisprudence	7	256	146
Natural Resources	11	349	246
Nominations	7	0	0
State Affairs	9	365	208
Veteran Affairs and Military Installations	5	58	49

House Committee	Number of Members	Bills Referred to Committee in the Regular Session	Bills Out of Committee
Agriculture and Livestock	7	49	37
Appropriations	29	39	21
Border and International Affairs	7	48	36
Business and Industry	9	122	62
Calendars	11	0	0
Civil Practices	9	108	31
Corrections	7	87	38
County Affairs	9	165	115
Criminal Jurisprudence	9	277	107
Defense Affairs and State–Federal Relations	9	90	68
Economic Development	7	89	43
Elections	7	114	60
Energy Resources	7	33	22
Environmental Regulation	7	86	44
Ethics, Select	7	2	1
Financial Institutions	7	77	43
General Investigating	5	0	0
Government Reform	7	90	30
Higher Education	9	157	79
House Administration	11	12	6
Human Services	9	111	69
Insurance	9	217	70
Judicial Affairs	9	183	112

(continued)

TABLE 24–3   SENATE AND HOUSE STANDING COMMITTEES, 78TH LEGISLATURE, 2003 (CONTINUED)

House Committee	Number of Members	Bills Referred to Committee in the Regular Session	Bills Out of Committee
Juvenile Justice and Family Issues	9	132	74
Land and Resource Management	9	97	46
Law Enforcement	7	180	91
Licensing and Administrative Procedures	9	159	84
Local and Consent Calendars	11	0	0
Local Government Ways and Means	7	181	102
Natural Resources	9	195	149
Pensions and Investments	7	65	29
Public Education	9	342	145
Public Health	9	260	161
Public School Finance, Select	29	0	0
Redistricting	15	4	2
Regulated Industries	7	64	23
Rules and Resolutions	11	1254	1229
State Affairs	9	222	116
State Cultural and Recreational Resources	7	77	49
State Health Care Expenditures, Select	11	67	33
Transportation	9	244	156
Urban Affairs	7	127	69
Ways and Means	9	115	21

SOURCE: Texas Legislature Online, Legislative Reports for the 78th Legislature.

or rejection. Over the years, conference committees have drafted legislation in forms dramatically different from earlier versions approved by the house or senate. But because a conference committee is supposed to do no more than adjust the differences between the house and the senate versions of a bill, both chambers have to pass a concurrent resolution to allow a conference committee to add significant new language.

Special Committees

Special, or **select, committees** are occasionally appointed by the governor, the lieutenant governor, and the speaker to study major policy issues, such as tax equity or school finance. These panels usually include private citizens as well as legislators, and they usually recommend legislation. Standing legislative committees also study issues in their assigned areas during the **interims** between sessions, and the presiding officers can ask committees to conduct special investigations or inquiries pertaining to governmental matters.

RULES AND PROCEDURES

Laws are made in Texas according to the same basic process followed by the U.S. Congress and other state legislatures.[15] But as the discussion of the committee system already has indicated, legislative rules are complex and are loaded with traps where legislation can be killed. One often hears the remark around the capitol that "there are a lot more ways to kill a bill than to pass one." Legislators and lobbyists who master the rules can

special, or **select, committees**
Special panels appointed to study major policy issues.

interims
Periods between legislative sessions.

wield a tremendous amount of influence over the lawmaking process. Both the house and the senate have detailed rules governing the disposition of legislation, and each has a parliamentarian to help interpret them.

How a Bill Becomes a Law

The simplified outline of the process by which a bill becomes a law (Figure 24–2) starts with the introduction of a bill in the house or the senate and its referral to a committee by the presiding officer, which constitutes **first reading**. That is the only reading most bills ever get.

A bill that wins committee approval can be considered on **second reading** by the full house or senate, where it is debated and often amended. Some amendments are designed to improve a bill, but others are designed to kill it by loading it down with controversial or objectionable provisions. Amendments that may be punitive toward particular individuals or groups are also sometimes offered. Such an amendment, which may be temporarily added to a bill only to be removed before the measure becomes law, is designed to give a group or perhaps a local official a message that the sponsoring legislator expects his or her wishes to be heeded on a particular issue. Lawmakers also may offer amendments that they know have little chance of being approved merely to make favorable political points with constituents or special interest groups.

If a bill is approved on second reading, it has to win one more vote on **third reading** before it goes to the other chamber for the same process. If the second chamber approves the bill without any changes, or amendments, it then goes to the governor for signature into law or for **veto**. The governor also can allow a bill to become law without his or her signature. This procedure is just the opposite of the pocket veto power afforded the president of the United States. If the president does not sign a bill approved by Congress by a certain deadline, it is automatically vetoed. If the governor of Texas does not sign or veto a bill by a certain deadline, it becomes law. A veto can be overridden and the bill allowed to become law by a two-thirds vote of both houses, although this process is rarely attempted.

The governor must accept or reject a bill in its entirety except for the general **appropriations bill**, or state budget, from which the governor can delete specific spending proposals while approving others. This power is called a **line item veto**. The budget or any other bill approved by the legislature that appropriates money has to be certified by the comptroller before it is sent to the governor. Texas has a **pay-as-you-go** government, and the comptroller has to certify that there will be enough revenue available to fund the bill.

If the second chamber amends the bill, the originating chamber must approve the change or request a conference committee. Any compromise worked out by a conference committee has to be approved by both houses, without further changes, before it is sent to the governor.

All bills except revenue-raising measures can originate in either the house or the senate. Tax bills must originate in the house, although the legislative leadership severely bent that rule to win approval, in a special session in 1991, of a tax bill necessary to balance a new state budget. After the house had dismantled a $3.3 billion revenue bill recommended by its Ways and Means Committee and sent the senate nothing but a $30 million shell, Lieutenant Governor Bob Bullock and the senate, in consultation with lobbyists, took over the writing of a new tax bill, which the house later approved.

Procedural Obstacles to Legislation

Pieces of legislation also encounter other significant procedural obstacles. In the house, there is the Calendars Committee, discussed earlier in this chapter. In the senate, there is the so-called "**two-thirds rule**."

The two-thirds requirement for debating bills on the senate floor is a strong obstacle to controversial bills because it means that only eleven senators, if they are determined enough and one is not absent at the wrong time, can keep any measure from

first reading
Introduction of a bill in the house or the senate and its referral to a committee by the presiding officer.

second reading
Initial debate by the full house or senate on a bill that has been approved by a committee.

third reading
Final presentation of a bill before the full house or senate.

veto
Power of the governor to reject, or kill, a bill passed by the legislature.

appropriations bill
Bill that authorizes the expenditure of money for a public program or purpose. In Texas, the general appropriations bill approved by the legislature every two years is the state budget.

line item veto
Power of the Texas governor to reject certain parts of the general appropriations, or spending, bill without killing the entire measure.

pay-as-you-go
Constitutional requirement that prohibits the legislature from borrowing money for the state's operating expenses.

two-thirds rule
Procedure under which the Texas senate has traditionally operated that requires approval of at least two-thirds of senators before a bill can be debated on the senate floor. It allows a minority of senators to block controversial legislation.

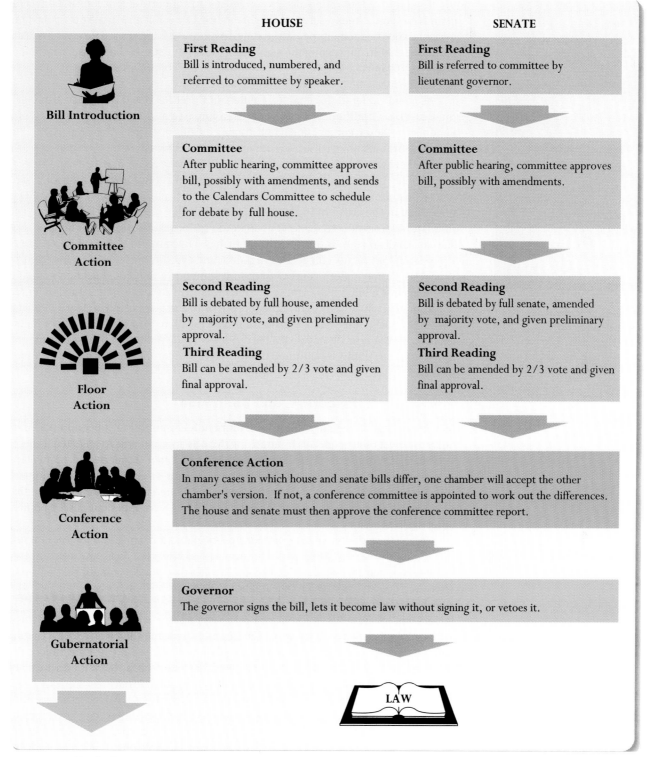

HOUSE

First Reading
Bill is introduced, numbered, and referred to committee by speaker.

Committee
After public hearing, committee approves bill, possibly with amendments, and sends to the Calendars Committee to schedule for debate by full house.

Second Reading
Bill is debated by full house, amended by majority vote, and given preliminary approval.

Third Reading
Bill can be amended by 2/3 vote and given final approval.

SENATE

First Reading
Bill is referred to committee by lieutenant governor.

Committee
After public hearing, committee approves bill, possibly with amendments.

Second Reading
Bill is debated by full senate, amended by majority vote, and given preliminary approval.

Third Reading
Bill can be amended by 2/3 vote and given final approval.

Conference Action
In many cases in which house and senate bills differ, one chamber will accept the other chamber's version. If not, a conference committee is appointed to work out the differences. The house and senate must then approve the conference committee report.

Governor
The governor signs the bill, lets it become law without signing it, or vetoes it.

LAW

Bill Introduction

Committee Action

Floor Action

Conference Action

Gubernatorial Action

FIGURE 24–2 Basic Steps in the Texas Legislative Process.

becoming law. This tradition also has been a source of the lieutenant governor's power. After a bill is approved by a committee, its sponsor can have it placed on the daily **intent calendar**. If the sponsor is recognized by the lieutenant governor, he or she will seek senate permission to consider the bill. A sponsor can have majority senate support for a measure but will watch it die if he or she cannot convince two-thirds of the senators to let the body formally debate it.

intent calendar
Daily list of bills eligible for debate on the floor of the Texas senate, if the sponsor is recognized by the lieutenant governor.

State Senator Gonzalo Barrientos of Austin puts on comfortable shoes in anticipation of a lengthy filibuster.

The two-thirds tradition also gives a senator the opportunity to vote on both sides of an issue. Sometimes a senator will vote to bring up a bill and then vote against the measure when it is actually passed, as only a majority vote is required for approval. This procedure enables the senator to please the bill's supporters, give the sponsor a favor that can be repaid later, and, at the same time, tell the bill's opponents that he or she voted against the measure.

As noted earlier in this chapter, Lieutenant Governor David Dewhurst suspended the two-thirds tradition to break a partisan impasse and win senate approval of a Republican-backed congressional redistricting bill during a special session in 2003. But the procedure still enjoyed strong support among senators.

The senate rules also provide for tags and filibusters, both of which can be effective in killing bills near the end of a legislative session. A **tag** allows an individual senator to postpone a committee hearing on any bill for at least 48 hours, a delay that is often fatal in the crush of unfinished business during a session's closing days. The **filibuster**, a procedure that allows a senator to speak against a bill for as long as he or she can stand and talk, is usually little more than a nuisance to a bill's supporters early in a session, but it, too, can become a potent and ever-present threat against controversial legislation near the end of a session. Sometimes the mere likelihood of a filibuster against a bill is sufficient to kill the measure. Late in a session, the lieutenant governor may refuse to recognize the sponsor of a controversial bill for fear a filibuster will fatally delay other major legislative proposals. State Senator Bill Meier of Euless spoke for 43 hours in 1977 against a bill dealing with the public reporting of on-the-job accidents. In so doing, he captured the world's record for the longest filibuster, which he held for years.

Shortcuts, Obfuscation, and Confusion

Sponsors of legislation languishing in an unfriendly committee or subcommittee often try to resurrect their proposals by attaching them as amendments to related bills being debated on the house or senate floor. Such maneuvers often are successful, particularly if opponents are absent or if the sponsor succeeds in "mumbling" the amendment through without challenge. But the speaker or the lieutenant governor must find that such amendments are germane to the pending bill if an alert opponent raises a point of order against them.

To facilitate the passage of noncontroversial and local pieces of legislation, the house and the senate have periodic local and consent or local and uncontested **calendars**, which are conducted under special rules that enable scores of bills to be routinely and quickly approved by the full house or senate without debate. Bills of major statewide significance, even controversial measures, sometimes get placed on these calendars, but it takes only one senator or three representatives to have any bill struck. Legislators will sometimes knowingly let a controversial bill slip by on a local calendar without moving to strike it so as not to offend the sponsor or the presiding officer. But to protect themselves politically, should the bill become an issue later, they will quietly register a vote against the measure in the house or senate journal.

As noted earlier in this chapter, compromises on controversial legislation are often worked out behind closed doors long before a bill is debated on the house or senate floor or even afforded a public hearing. It can be argued that this approach to consensus building is an efficient, businesslike way to enact legislation, but it also serves to discourage the free and open debate that is so important to the democratic process.

Recent speakers have also discouraged the taking of **record votes** during house floor debate on most bills. Many important issues are decided with **division votes**, which are taken on the computerized voting boards but leave no formal record once the boards are cleared. This approach saves the taxpayers some printing costs and can give lawmakers some respite from lobby pressure. But it also serves to keep the public in the dark about significant decisions made by their elected representatives. The fewer record votes legislators have to make, the more easily they can dodge accountability to their constituents.

tag
Rule that allows an individual senator to postpone a committee hearing on any bill for at least 48 hours, a delay that can be fatal to a bill during the closing days of a legislative session.

filibuster
Procedure that allows a senator to speak against a bill for as long as he or she can stand and talk. A filibuster can become a formidable obstacle or threat against controversial bills near the end of a legislative session.

calendar
Agenda or the list of bills to be considered by the house or the senate on a given day.

record vote
Vote taken in the house or the senate of which a permanent record is kept, listing how individual legislators voted.

division votes
Votes taken on the computerized voting boards in the Texas house but erased without being permanently recorded.

Often, legislators have made up their minds on an issue before the matter is debated on the floor. But when they are not familiar with a bill and have no political interest in it, they may simply vote the way the sponsor votes or the way the house or senate leadership wants them to vote. Despite what tourists in the gallery may think, legislators who raise their fingers above their heads when a vote is taken are not asking the presiding officer for a rest break. They are signaling the way they are voting and encouraging other lawmakers to vote the same way. One finger means yes; two fingers mean no.

When record votes are taken, house rules prohibit members from punching the voting buttons on other members' desks, but the practice occurs regularly. Sometimes members instruct a deskmate or another legislator to cast a specific vote for them if they expect to be off the floor when the vote is called for. Other legislators make a habit of punching the voting buttons at all the empty desks within reach. This practice is normally challenged only in cases of close votes, when members of the losing side request a roll-call verification of the computerized vote and the votes of members who do not answer the roll call are struck. The house was embarrassed in 1991 when a dead lawmaker was recorded as answering the daily roll call and voting on several record votes. The legislator had died in his Austin apartment, but his body was not discovered for several hours. Meanwhile, colleagues had been pushing his voting button. This practice is not a problem in the senate, where the secretary of the senate orally calls the roll on record votes.

Partly because of the rules under which the legislature operates, partly because of the heavy volume of legislation, and partly because of political maneuvering, the closing weeks of a regular session are hectic. Legislators in both houses are asked to vote on dozens of conference committee reports they do not have time to read. With hundreds of bills being rushed through the legislature to the governor's desk, mistakes occur. And deliberate attempts are made—often successfully—to slip major changes in law through the confusion. For every surprise bill or special interest amendment that is caught, dozens slip through and become law.

Senate committees often meet in the senate chamber when large numbers of people are expected to attend.

THE EMERGING PARTY SYSTEM

Unlike the U.S. Congress, the Texas legislature is not organized along party lines, with rules automatically giving leadership positions to members of the majority party. The arrangement in Texas is due primarily to the absence of Republican legislators for many years and the more recent practice—before Republicans gained a house majority in 2003—of rural Democrats aligning themselves with Republicans to produce a conservative coalition. As recently as 1971, the year before a federal court declared urban, countywide house districts unconstitutional, there were only ten Republicans in the house and two in the senate. As Republicans increased their numbers, they aligned themselves with conservative Democrats to attempt to control the policy-setting process, particularly in the house. This ideological coalition became increasingly important as single-member districts boosted not only the number of Republican lawmakers but also the number of moderate and liberal Democratic legislators elected from urban areas. The coalition became a means of maintaining some legislative control for conservative Democrats as the base of power shifted in their own party.

Republicans and conservative Democrats formally organized the Texas Conservative Coalition in the house in the 1980s. The coalition remained a strong force in the 1990s, chaired for several years by Representative Warren Chisum of Pampa, who switched from the Democratic to the Republican party in 1995. Chisum's mastery of the rules blocked many pieces of legislation on technicalities.

On occasion, liberal Democrats and conservative Republicans have formed "unholy alliances," but these coalitions were usually short-lived. During the controversy over the Sharpstown stock fraud scandal in 1971, liberal Democrats and Republicans formed a loose coalition called the "Dirty Thirty" that continually harassed Speaker Gus Mutscher, who not only was a key figure in the scandal but also epitomized the rural conservative Democratic tradition of the statehouse.

The Growth of Partisanship

With the growth of the Republican Party in Texas in the 1980s, Speaker Gib Lewis, a conservative urban Democrat, appointed Republicans to major committee chairs in the house. But partisan divisions increased in 1987 when Lewis, Democratic Lieutenant Governor Bill Hobby, and Republican Governor Bill Clements fought over a new state budget in the face of a huge revenue shortfall. On one side of the debate were moderate and liberal Democratic legislators, including inner-city and South Texas minorities whose constituents had the most to gain from a tax increase and the most to lose from deep cuts in spending on human services and educational programs. On the other side were a handful of conservative, primarily rural Democrats and Republicans with middle- and upper-middle-class suburban constituents who insisted on fiscal restraint. Clements eventually gave in and supported a tax increase, but most of the house Republicans continued to fight the measure until it was approved in a summer special session.

In 1989, Republicans formed their first caucus in the house, and soon both parties had active caucuses in both the house and the senate, which began to play key roles in marshaling legislative support on selected issues. They also became active in legislative races as Republicans began to mount aggressive, well-financed challenges of Democratic incumbents.

During the 1995 legislative session, when Democrats still held a majority of house and senate seats, Lieutenant Governor Bob Bullock and Speaker Pete Laney, both Democrats, continued the practice of naming Republicans, as well as Democrats, to committee chairs. Bullock and Laney also were strongly supportive of Republican Governor George W. Bush's legislative priorities. All three leaders cooperated in making major changes in public education and juvenile justice and setting limits on civil liability lawsuits.

After many bitterly contested legislative races, Republicans won their first majority of the senate in modern times during the 1996 elections and gained four seats in the house to narrow the Democratic majority in that body to 82 to 68. Bipartisanship, however, still prevailed for the most part in the 1997 session. Bullock, the Democratic lieutenant governor, gave Republicans some new leadership positions in the senate but named Democrats to chair most committees. The senate, which had a 17 to 14 Republican majority, slammed the door on an attempt by Bush to trade higher state taxes for major cuts in local school taxes, and opposition came from both Democratic and Republican senators. Special interests that did not want to pay the higher state taxes were a more significant factor than partisanship in the death of the tax bill. The house had approved the tax trade off, with Bush persuading many Republicans in the house to vote for the measure. But legislative fights with strong partisan overtones increased in 1997 and subsequent sessions over such issues as abortion, gay rights, and whether tax dollars should be spent on private school tuition for some students (see *People and Politics: Making a Difference:* "Arlene Wohlgemuth's 'Memorial Day Massacre'").

Another partisan-charged issue in 1999 and 2001 was an attempt by some Democrats to strengthen the state law against hate crimes, after three white men in East Texas were accused—and later convicted—of dragging an African American man, James Byrd Jr., to death behind a pickup truck. Most of the Republican opposition to the bill was because it increased penalties for crimes motivated by prejudice against homosexuals as well as prejudice over race or religion. That provision was opposed by social conservatives, and in 1999 Governor Bush—who did not want to anger conservatives on the eve of his race for the Republican presidential nomination—called the bill unnecessary. The measure, which sponsors named for Byrd, died in the senate in 1999 but was passed in 2001.

Republicans Take Control

Aided by the redrawn legislative districts discussed earlier in this chapter, Republicans made major gains in the 2002 elections. They increased their majority in the state senate to 19 to 12, captured an 88 to 62 majority in the Texas house, their first since

PEOPLE & POLITICS *Making a Difference* ★★★

ARLENE WOHLGEMUTH'S "MEMORIAL DAY MASSACRE"

Partisan differences, which were building in the years leading up to the Republican takeover of the Texas house in 2003, erupted on Memorial Day in 1997, one week before the regular legislative session ended. They were ignited by fights over a bill to require parents to be notified before their minor daughters could receive abortions and a measure that would have prohibited the recognition of gay marriages in Texas. Both measures were to be approved in later years, but they died in 1997, despite the strong support of social conservatives, who formed a significant bloc among Republicans in the house.

After abortion rights supporters and other Democratic house members used parliamentary maneuvers to block debate on both bills, Representative Arlene Wohlgemuth, a Republican from Burleson, used a technical procedural point to block consideration of 52 other bills remaining on the house's Memorial Day calendar. Wohlgemuth's move effectively killed most of the bills because that day was the deadline for the house to consider them on second reading. Sponsors managed to save only a few of the measures, including an education bill strongly supported by then-Governor George W. Bush, by tagging them on as amendments to related bills that had already won house approval.

Wohlgemuth said she was simply retaliating against House members who killed the bills on abortion restrictions and same-sex marriages, which social conservatives believed would have passed had they been able to vote on them. "I think that a statement needs to be made about why measures that are important to families, important to the people of this state, have not been heard, have not been voted on," she said.

Wohlgemuth's action wasn't entirely partisan because some of the bills that she killed or jeopardized, including Bush's education priority, were sponsored by other Republican legislators. But the action had strong partisan overtones and was a preview of future legislative sessions.

Representative Kent Grusendorf of Arlington, an outspoken Republican critic of then-Democratic Speaker Pete Laney, supported Wohlgemuth. He said committees controlled by Democrats had stalled bills that were important to Republicans and that had majority support in the house.

But longtime Democratic Representative Dan Kubiak of Rockdale, in a speech on the house floor, strongly criticized Wohlgemuth's tactic. Kubiak said the incident—which he dubbed the "Memorial Day Massacre"—"was only the latest outbreak of the cancer that threatens not only this body, but the democratic process itself."

Kubiak died the next year, and the voters in his central Texas district replaced him with a Republican. Partisanship remained a threat in the statehouse.

SOURCE: *Dallas Morning News,* May 28, 1997.

Reconstruction, and elected Republican Tom Craddick of Midland as speaker. Those victories, plus the elections of Governor Rick Perry and Lieutenant Governor David Dewhurst, gave Republicans control of all the points of power in the statehouse. They controlled the budget-setting process in 2003, making significant cuts in services to close a $10 billion revenue shortfall, enacted significant new restrictions on civil lawsuits, and won the fight over congressional redistricting. Throughout the year, partisanship was stronger than it had been since the GOP became a competitive party in Texas.

Craddick and Dewhurst appointed Democrats, as well as Republicans, to chair committees and serve in other leadership positions. Democrats chaired six of the senate's 16 standing committees and thirteen of the 43 committees in the house. Craddick also appointed a Democrat, state Representative Sylvester Turner of Houston, as speaker pro tempore. But Craddick stacked the key chairmanships and the membership of the budget-writing house Appropriations Committee with Republicans who clearly reflected his conservative viewpoint. After winning a change in house rules that removed seniority as a factor in appropriations appointments, the new speaker bumped from the panel three outspoken Democrats who opposed budget cuts.

Partisanship will remain part of the legislative process for the foreseeable future. Before too many more years, the legislature may even organize itself along the same partisan lines as the U.S. Congress—with distinct party positions, such as floor leaders, caucus leaders, and whips. If this were to happen, the legislative rules and powers of the presiding officers discussed earlier in this chapter would be significantly changed.

PEOPLE & POLITICS *Making a Difference* ★ ★ ★

GREGORY LUNA AND IRMA RANGEL, CHAMPIONS OF EDUCATION

Gregory Luna and Irma Rangel made important contributions to young people, particularly minorities, in the legislature and other public forums.

Luna, whose father died when he was an infant, knew firsthand the difficulties that many Texas children faced in securing an education and a chance at a better life. He was only 11 when he got his first job as a busboy in a restaurant. After working as a police officer to help put himself through college and law school, Luna then devoted much of his adult life to improving civil rights and educational opportunities for Hispanics and all Texans.

As an attorney in San Antonio in 1968, Luna helped found the Mexican American Legal Defense and Educational Fund (MALDEF), which has waged successful courtroom fights for civil rights. MALDEF has forced school boards and other governments to redraw political boundaries to assure minority representation on governing bodies. And in the 1980s, MALDEF filed a landmark lawsuit against the state that forced the Texas legislature to more equitably distribute state education dollars among wealthy and poor school districts.

Luna served in the Texas House from 1985 to 1992 and in the state Senate from 1993 until illness forced his resignation in September 1999. He died a few weeks later of complications related to diabetes. He was 66.

Luna was chair of the Senate Hispanic Caucus and vice chair of the Senate Education Committee, and throughout his legislative career he fought for improvements in school funding and for better educational opportunities. His legislative style was usually low key, but he was effective. He knew what he had to do to accomplish a goal and quietly went about doing it.

"He was a monument of many, many people who were able to benefit from his efforts for a better education system for everyone," said the Rev. Virgil Elizondo. "He was in the ministry of public service."*

Rangel, a Democrat from Kingsville, was a schoolteacher and a prosecutor before becoming, in 1976, the first Hispanic woman elected to the Texas House. She chaired the House Higher Education Committee for several years and sponsored a state law to boost affirmative action by requiring Texas colleges and universities to automatically admit students who graduated in the top 10 percent of their high school classes. She also was instrumental in boosting state funding for higher education institutions along the border with Mexico.

Rangel was still a member of the House—its fifth most senior member—when she died of cancer in March 2003 at age 71. State Representative Pete Gallego, D-Alpine, chairman of the Mexican American Legislative Caucus, called Rangel's life a "testament to everything that is good about public service."[†]

*The Associated Press, as published in the *Houston Chronicle,* November 10, 1999.
[†]*Houston Chronicle,* March 19, 2003, p. 25A.

But this development will depend on how long Republicans continue to dominate the statehouse, on how Democrats continue to react, and on the future leadership personalities that emerge in both parties. Another factor will be how well the two factions in the Republican party—the traditional, fiscal conservatives and the social conservatives—are able to accommodate each other's interests.

OTHER LEGISLATIVE CAUCUSES

Hispanic and African American house members formed their own caucuses as their numbers began to increase in the 1970s in the wake of redistricting and the creation of urban single-member districts. Their cohesive **blocs** of votes have proved influential in speaker elections and the resolution of major statewide issues, such as health care for the poor, public school finance, and taxation. Their ability to broker votes has won committee chairs and other concessions they may not otherwise have received (see *People and Politics: Making a Difference:* "Gregory Luna and Irma Rangel, Champions of Education").

Some urban delegations, such as the group of legislators representing Harris County, the state's most populous county, have formed their own caucuses to discuss and seek consensus on issues of local importance. In Harris County's case, consensus is often

bloc
Group of legislators who act together for a common goal regardless of party affiliation.

difficult to achieve on local controversies because of the political, ethnic, and urban-suburban diversity within the delegation. Twenty-five house members—one-sixth of the body's membership—represent various parts of Houston and Harris County, and seven senators have districts that are wholly within or include part of the county.

LEGISLATORS AND THEIR CONSTITUENTS

Although representative government is an essential component of American society, there are continued debates as to how people elected to public office should identify the interests and preferences of the people they represent.[16] Political theorists as well as legislators struggle with the problem of translating the will of the people into public policy. Most legislators represent diverse groups and interests in their districts. During a normal legislative session, there are thousands of proposed laws to consider, and legislators must constantly make decisions that will benefit or harm specific constituents.

Except for an occasional emotional issue—such as whether motorcycle riders should have to wear safety helmets or whether private citizens should be allowed to carry pistols—most Texans pay little attention to what the legislature is doing. That is why they are often surprised to discover they have to pay a few extra dollars to register their cars or learn that the fee for camping in a state park has suddenly been increased. Very few Texans can identify their state representatives or senators by name, and far fewer can tell you what their legislators have voted for or against. This public inattention gives a legislator great latitude when voting on public policies. It also is a major reason that most incumbent lawmakers who seek reelection are successful. Most legislative turnover is the result of voluntary retirements, not voter retribution. Several Democratic incumbents, however, fell victim to redistricting that favored Republican challengers in 2002. Some were unseated at the polls, and others didn't seek reelection because of the redrawn district lines.

Media coverage of the legislature is uneven. The large daily newspapers with reporters in Austin make commendable efforts to cover the major legislative issues and players and provide both spot news accounts and in-depth interpretation of the legislature's actions. All too frequently, however, they are limited by insufficient space and rarely publish individual voting records or attempt to evaluate the performance of individual legislators. Most television and radio news shows provide only cursory legislative coverage.

Although legislators are aware of latent public opinion, they tend to be more responsive to the interest groups, or attentive publics, that operate in their individual districts or statewide.[17] People who are well informed and attentive to public policy issues are a relatively small portion of the total population, but they can be mobilized for or against an individual legislator. In some instances, they are community opinion leaders who, directly or indirectly, are able to communicate information to other individuals about a legislator's performance. Or they may belong to public interest and special interest groups that compile legislative voting records on selected issues of importance to their memberships. Although these records are only sporadically disseminated by the news media to the general public, they are mailed or e-mailed to the sponsoring groups' members.

Many special interest groups contribute thousands of dollars to a legislator's reelection campaign or to the campaign of an opponent. But politically astute legislators duly take note of all the letters, phone calls, e-mail messages, petitions, and visits by their constituents—plus media coverage—lest they lose touch with a significant number of voters with different views on the issues and become politically vulnerable.

A favorite voter-contact tool of many legislators is an occasional newsletter, which they can mail to households in their districts at state expense. These mailings usually include photos of the lawmaker plus articles summarizing, in the best possible light, his or her accomplishments in Austin. Sometimes legislators also include a public opinion survey seeking constituent responses on a number of issues.

LEGISLATIVE DECISION MAKING

In addition to the formal rules of each legislative body, there are unwritten rules, or norms, that shape the behavior of legislators and other actors in the lawmaking process. The legislature is like most other social institutions in that its members have perceptions of the institution and the process as well as the way they are expected to behave or carry out their responsibilities. Other participants also impose their views and expectations on lawmakers.[18]

The legislative process is designed to institutionalize conflict, and the rules and norms of the legislature are designed to give this conflict an element of civility. Debate is often intense and vigorous, and it may be difficult for some lawmakers to separate attacks on their positions from attacks on their personalities. But most legislators have learned the necessity of decorum and courtesy. Even if lawmakers believe some of their opponents in the house and senate are deceitful, personal attacks on other legislators are considered unacceptable. Personal attacks, even to the point of fistfights, occasionally occur, but they are rare.

With about 5,700 pieces of legislation introduced during a regular session—the level reached in 2003—no legislator could possibly read and understand each bill, much less the hundreds of amendments offered during floor debate. And while there are moments of high drama when issues of major statewide importance are being debated, most of the legislative workload is tedious and dull and produces little direct political benefit for most senators and representatives. But many of those bills contain hidden traps and potential controversies that can haunt a legislator later, often during a reelection campaign. So legislators use numerous information sources and rely on the norms of the process to assist them in decision making.

To make the process work, legislators must accommodate the competing interests they represent and achieve considerable reciprocity among themselves. An individual legislator will usually have no direct political or personal interest in most bills because much legislation is local in nature and affects only a limited number of lawmakers and constituents. A legislator accumulates obligations as he or she supports another lawmaker's bill, with the full expectation that the action will be returned in kind.

A number of factors, however, help shape lawmakers' decisions on major legislation.[19] The wishes of constituents will be considered, particularly if there is a groundswell of dominant opinion coming from a legislator's district. Legislators also exchange information with other lawmakers, particularly with members of the same caucus, members who share the same political philosophy, and colleagues from the same counties or regions of the state. Lawmakers often take their cues from bill sponsors or the speaker's and lieutenant governor's leadership teams. Identifiable patterns of giving and taking cues also are emerging along party lines, particularly on budgetary, taxation, and redistricting issues.

A legislator's staff also assists in the decision-making process, not only by evaluating the substantive merits of legislation but also by assessing the political implications of a lawmaker's decisions. The Legislative Budget Board and the Legislative Council provide technical information and expertise that can also be weighed by legislators.

Interest groups are major sources of information and influence. Although an individual legislator will occasionally rail against a specific group, most lawmakers consider interest groups absolutely essential to the legislative process. Through their lobbyists, interest groups provide a vast amount of technical information and can signal the level of constituency interest, support, or opposition to proposed laws. A senator or representative can use interest groups to establish coalitions of support for a bill, and some legislators become closely identified with powerful interest groups because they almost always support a particular lobby's position.

The governor can also influence the legislature in several ways. He or she can raise the public's consciousness of an issue or need and can promote solutions through speeches and through the media. The governor can communicate indirectly to individual lawmakers through the governor's staff, party leaders, and influential persons in a lawmaker's district. The governor can also personally appeal to lawmakers in direct

Governor Rick Perry "works the floor" of the Texas house of representatives during the 2003 legislative session.

one-on-one meetings or in meetings with groups of legislators. At the beginning of each regular session, the governor outlines his or her legislative priorities in a State of the State address to a joint session of the house and the senate, and the governor usually has frequent meetings with the lieutenant governor and the speaker throughout a session.

The governor may also visit the house or senate chamber in a personal show of support when legislation that he or she strongly advocates is being debated. Unlike most recent governors, Governor Ann Richards personally testified before legislative committees on several of her priorities, including ethics reform and government reorganization, during her first year in office. The severity of a governor's arm-twisting is often in the eye of the beholder, but it can include appeals to a lawmaker's reason or conscience, threats of retaliation, appeals for party support, and promises of a quid pro quo. The greatest threat that a governor can hang over a legislator is the possible veto of legislation or a budget item of importance to the lawmaker. In special sessions, the governor also can negotiate with a lawmaker over whether to add a bill that is important to the legislator to the special session's agenda, which is controlled by the governor.

Legislators also get information and support from other elected statewide office-holders, such as the attorney general, the comptroller, or the land commissioner. These officials and lawmakers can assist each other in achieving political agendas.

The news media provide information and perspective on issues in broader political terms. In part, the policy agenda is established by those issues the media perceive to be important.

The relative importance of any groups or actors on decision making is difficult to measure and varies from lawmaker to lawmaker and from issue to issue. Outside influences can also be tempered by a legislator's own attitude and opinion. On many issues, legislators get competing advice and pressure. As much as a lawmaker may like to be all things to all people, that cannot be. She cannot please a chemical lobbyist, who is seeking a tax break for a new plant on the Gulf Coast and also happens to be a large campaign contributor, and environmentalists, who fear the facility would spoil a nearby wildlife habitat. He cannot please the governor, who is promoting a lottery as a new state revenue source, and most of the voters in his district, who have consistently voted against gambling. The ultimate decision and its eventual political consequences are the legislator's.

Should lawmakers cast particular votes on the basis of the specific concerns of their districts, their personal convictions, the position of their political party, or the wishes of the special interest groups that helped fund their campaigns? These issues reflect complex relationships between the legislator and the people represented. And since the overriding consideration for most lawmakers is to get reelected, the legislator must balance them carefully (see *FYI:* "Legislative Reputations, Power, and Influence").

THE DEVELOPMENT OF LEGISLATIVE STAFF

The quality of a legislator's staff can help determine his or her success, and both the quality and quantity of legislative staffs have been significantly enhanced since the early 1970s.[20] This growth reflects an emerging professional approach to lawmaking and meeting the needs of an increasingly complex urban state. During recent regular sessions, the house has had about 900 employees, including part-time workers, and the senate about 800. These figures included Capitol and district office staff for individual senators and representatives, committee staffs, assistants to the lieutenant governor and the speaker, and other support staff hired directly by the house and the senate.

Additionally, there are permanent staff members assigned to the Legislative Budget Board, the legislature's financial research arm; the Legislative Council, which researches issues and drafts bills and resolutions for introduction by legislators; and the Legislative Reference Library, which provides resource materials for lawmakers, their staffs, and the general public. Other support staff is assigned to the Sunset Advisory Commission, which assists the legislature in periodic reviews of state agencies, and the state auditor, who is chosen by and reports to the legislative leadership.

LEGISLATIVE REPUTATIONS, POWER, AND INFLUENCE

Some legislators become known for their commitment to producing good legislation. They spend endless hours developing programs and are repeatedly turned to by presiding officers to handle tough policy issues. Other lawmakers tend to look to their leadership for direction and cues, giving them considerable influence and power. And they are also essential to a productive legislative session.

Other legislators earn reputations as grandstanders. Almost every legislator has shown off for the media or the spectators in the gallery at one time or another, but a number have developed a distinct reputation for this style of behavior. They appear to be more interested in scoring political points with their constituents or interest groups—with the objective of being reelected or seeking higher office—than with mastering the substance of legislation. Many of these lawmakers are lightweights who contribute little to the legislature's product. And while they may introduce many bills during a session, they are not interested in the details of the lawmaking process and are unable to influence other legislators to support their legislation.

The legislature also has a number of opportunists, including members who pursue issues to produce personal or political benefits for themselves. They may sponsor legislation or take a position on an issue to curry favor with a special interest group or benefit their personal businesses or professions. Legislative rules prohibit legislators from voting on issues in which they have a personal monetary interest, but individual lawmakers can interpret that prohibition as they see fit. Many lawmakers will try to cash in on their legislative experience by becoming lobbyists after they leave office at considerably higher pay than they received as legislators.

Still other legislators appear to be little more than spectators. They enjoy the receptions and the other perks of the office much more than the drudgery of the committee hearings, research, and floor debates. Some quickly become weary of the legislative process and, after a few sessions, decide against seeking reelection.[*]

---

[*]These legislative styles are similar to those developed by James David Barber, *The Lawmakers* (Yale University Press, 1965), chap. 2–5.

State Senator Ken Armbrister of Victoria talking with staff.

Legislative staffers range from part-time secretaries and clerks to lawyers and professionals who draft bills and direct research that result in major state laws. There are limits on the number of staff members and funds allocated for legislators' personal staffs. As a general rule, senators have larger staffs than house members. Staffing levels are usually reduced between sessions, and some members shut down their capitol offices entirely. Most lawmakers, however, maintain offices both in Austin and in their districts, even if staffs function only to answer the phone.

A key support group in the house is the House Research Organization, which was organized as the House Study Group in the 1970s by a handful of primarily liberal lawmakers. The group's name was later changed, and its structure was reorganized to represent the entire house, but it still fills a strong research role. It is supported by funds from the house budget and is governed by a steering committee that represents a cross section of Democratic and Republican house members. During legislative sessions, its staff provides detailed analyses, including pro and con arguments, of many bills on the daily house calendar. During interims between sessions, it provides periodic analyses of proposed constitutional amendments and other issues. The senate formed a similar organization, the Senate Research Center, in 1991.

The quality of other resources available to lawmakers has also improved in recent years. Legislators and their staffs can routinely check the status or texts of bills online, and so can the public. The Legislative Council maintains a Web site on the Internet that includes committee schedules, bill texts and analyses, and other legislative information. Private citizens also can use the Web site to identify their state representatives and senators.

LEGISLATIVE ETHICS AND REFORMS

The vast majority of legislators are honest, hardworking individuals. But the weaknesses of a few and the millions of dollars spent by special interests to influence the lawmaking process undermine Texans' confidence in their legislature and their entire state government. Although legislators cannot pass laws guaranteeing ethical behavior, they can set strong standards for themselves, other public officials, and lobbyists; and they can institute stiff penalties for those who fail to comply. Such reform efforts are periodically attempted, but, unfortunately, they usually are the result of scandals and fall short of creating an ideal ethical climate.

Fallout from the Sharpstown stock scandal helped an outsider, Uvalde rancher Dolph Briscoe, win the 1972 gubernatorial race and helped produce a large turnover in legislative elections (see *FYI:* "The Sharpstown Stock Fraud Scandal"). In 1973, the legislature responded with a series of ethics reform laws, including requirements that lobbyists register with the secretary of state and report their expenditures. State officials were required to file public reports identifying their sources of income, although not specific amounts.

Weaknesses in those laws, however, were vividly demonstrated in 1989, when wealthy East Texas poultry producer Lonnie "Bo" Pilgrim distributed $10,000 checks to several senators in the Capitol while lobbying them on workers' compensation reform, and the Travis County district attorney could find no law under which to prosecute him. There also were published reports that lobbyists had spent nearly $2 million entertaining lawmakers during the 1989 regular session without having to specify which legislators received the "freebies," thanks to a large loophole in the lobby registration law. The revelations—including frequent news stories about lobbyists treating lawmakers to golf tournaments, ski trips, a junket to Las Vegas for a boxing match, and limousine service to a Cher concert—created an uproar.

Some senators had angrily rejected Pilgrim's checks on the spot, while others returned them after the media pounced on the story. But the very next year, Pilgrim—a longtime political contributor—again contributed thousands of dollars to several statewide officeholders and candidates. This time the checks were not offered under the Capitol dome but were more traditionally sent through the mail, and they were gratefully accepted. Only one officeholder, who was passed over by Pilgrim in favor of his opponent, tried to make a campaign issue of the new contributions.

Despite all the headlines over ethical problems, legislative turnover was minimal in 1990. But in early December, about a month after the general election, a Travis County grand jury began investigating Speaker Gib Lewis's ties to a San Antonio law firm, Heard Goggan Blair and Williams. The firm had made large profits collecting delinquent taxes for local governments throughout Texas under a law that allowed it to collect an extra 15 percent from the taxpayers as its fee. For several years, it had successfully defeated legislation that would have hurt its business. The *Fort Worth Star-Telegram* reported that Heard Goggan had paid about half of a $10,000 tax bill owed to Tarrant County by a business that Lewis partly owned.[21] And the *Houston Chronicle* reported that the grand jury was also looking into a trip that Lewis had taken to a Mexican resort during the 1987 legislative session with four Heard Goggan partners and a lobbyist (all males) and six women (including a waitress from a topless nightclub in Houston).[22] The trip had been taken while a bill opposed by Heard Goggan was dying in a house committee.

On December 28, only twelve days before the 1991 regular legislative session was to convene and Lewis was to be reelected to a fifth term as the house's presiding officer, grand jurors indicted him on two misdemeanor ethics charges. He was accused of soliciting, accepting, and failing to report an illegal gift from Heard Goggan—the partial payment of the tax bill. Lewis insisted he was innocent and vowed to fight the charges. He said the tax payment was the settlement of a legal dispute, and he angrily accused Travis County District Attorney Ronnie Earle, who headed the prosecution and had been publicly advocating stronger ethics laws, of using the grand jury to "influence the speaker's election." Lewis said that Earle was guilty of "unethical and reprehensible behavior."[23]

Lewis won a postponement of his trial under a law that automatically grants continuances to legislators when they are in session. The grand jury investigation, which prosecutors said would include other legislators or former legislators, continued for several more weeks, but no more indictments were issued.

Meanwhile, attention was focused on an ethics reform bill. Governor Ann Richards, who had campaigned for reform, testified before house and senate committees for tougher ethical requirements for state officials and lobbyists. The senate approved an ethics bill fairly early in the session, but the house did not act on its version of the bill until late in the session. The final bill was produced by a conference committee on the last night of the regular session in a private meeting and was approved by the house and the senate only a few minutes before the legislature adjourned at midnight. There was no time to print and distribute copies, and very few legislators knew for sure what was in the bill.

This performance and the bill itself left a bad taste all around. Despite complaints that the measure was not strong enough and the controversy over the secretive way in which the final compromise had been written, Richards signed the bill. But she did so in the privacy of her office, not in the public ceremony that governors usually hold for their priority pieces of legislation. Ronnie Earle, the Travis County district attorney, was among those displeased with the legislation, but Richards called the new law a "very strong step in the direction of openness and ethics reform in this state."[24]

The new law required additional reporting of lobby expenditures and conflicts of interest between lobbyists and state officials, prohibited special interests from treating legislators to pleasure trips, prohibited lawmakers from accepting fees for speaking before special interest groups, and created a new state Ethics Commission to review complaints about public officials.

But the measure did not put any limits on financial contributions to political campaigns, nor did it prohibit legislator-attorneys from representing clients before state agencies for pay. Moreover, it authorized the Ethics Commission to slap a bigger fine ($10,000) on someone who filed a frivolous complaint against a public official than the maximum fine ($5,000) that could be levied on an officeholder for violating the ethics law. That latter provision was viewed by many critics as an unreasonable effort to discourage citizen complaints. The new law also provided that complaints filed with the Ethics Commission would remain confidential unless the commission took action, a provision that would allow the commission to dismiss or sit on legitimate complaints without any public accounting.

THE SHARPSTOWN STOCK FRAUD SCANDAL

The Sharpstown stock fraud scandal rocked the state Capitol in 1971 and 1972 and helped produce some far-reaching legislative and political changes. The scandal involved banking legislation sought by Houston banker-developer Frank Sharp and approved by the legislature in a special session in 1969, only to be vetoed by Governor Preston Smith. A civil lawsuit filed by the federal Securities and Exchange Commission broke the news that Smith, House Speaker Gus Mutscher, Representative Tommy Shannon of Fort Worth (who had sponsored the bills) and other individuals had profited from stock deals involving Sharp's National Bankers Life Insurance Company. Much of their stock was purchased with unsecured loans from Sharp's Sharpstown State Bank. Mutscher, Shannon, and an aide to the speaker were later convicted of conspiracy to accept bribes. Mutscher, who had consolidated power in the house and was often regarded as ironhanded and arbitrary, was forced to resign. Later the house moved to limit the speaker's power through a modified seniority system for committee appointments. Subsequent speakers still exercised a great deal of power, but it was checked by expectations that the speaker would be more responsive to the membership. The media also started giving greater scrutiny and coverage to the activities of the speaker.

Source: Richard Morehead, *50 Years in Texas Politics* (Eakin Press, 1982), pp. 236–237.

In January 1992, Lewis announced that he would not seek reelection to another term in the house. In a plea bargain later the same month, prosecutors dropped the two ethics indictments against him in return for the speaker's "no contest" plea to two minor, unrelated charges. Lewis paid a $2,000 fine for failing to publicly disclose a business holding in 1988 and 1989, for which he had already paid a minor civil penalty to the secretary of state.

Lewis's decision to retire set off the first speaker's race in the house since 1975, and many house members, including most of the first-term legislators, used the campaign to bargain for reforms in the way the house conducted its business. As noted earlier, some of those reforms were adopted in 1993 with the support of the new speaker, Pete Laney, who, ironically, had been a long-time member of Lewis's team. The first-term legislators, in particular, had complained in 1991 that the house rules had been used to create an undemocratic process that catered to special interests and favored an inner circle of legislators close to the speaker.

The legislature enacted other significant changes in ethics laws in 2003. The new provisions required officeholders and candidates to identify the occupations and employers of people who contribute more than $500, required financial reports to be filed with the Ethics Commission electronically, increased penalties for people who filed their reports late, and required—for the first time—officeholders and candidates for municipal offices in the large cities to file personal financial disclosure statements, similar to those already filed by state officeholders.

Also in 2003, Travis County District Attorney Ronnie Earle began a lengthy investigation of how corporate contributions were used to affect several legislative elections in the Republican takeover of the house (see Chapter 23). Republicans accused Earle, a Democrat, of playing politics, but Earle said that he was investigating the possibility that corporate funds had been illegally spent on political activity.

SUMMARY

1. Texas, the nation's second most populous state, has a part-time legislature that operates under detailed antigovernment restrictions drafted by nineteenth-century Texans in the wake of the repressive Reconstruction era. It is a lawmaking body that is not structured to respond readily to twenty-first century needs and crises. Emergencies often require special legislative sessions and increase financial and personal pressures on lawmakers, who are among the lowest-paid state legislators in the country. Legislative turnover in Texas is moderate.

2. As recently as 1971, there was only a handful of African Americans, Hispanics, Republicans, and women in the 150-member house of representatives and the 31-member senate. But political realignment and federal court intervention in redistricting—particularly the ordering of single-member House districts for urban counties in 1972—have significantly increased the number of women, ethnic minorities, and Republicans in the legislature. Republicans now have a majority of both legislative bodies.

3. Unlike the U.S. Congress, the Texas legislature is not organized along party lines and has only the tentative beginnings of an institutionalized leadership structure. The presiding officer of the house is the speaker, who is elected by the other house members. The presiding officer of the senate is the lieutenant governor, who is elected by the voters statewide.

4. The most significant powers of the speaker and the lieutenant governor are the appointment of house and senate committees, which screen and draft legislation, and the assignment of bills to committees. The fate of most legislation is decided at the committee level. While most house committees are partially appointed on the basis of seniority, the lieutenant governor has absolute control over the composition of senate committees. The presiding officers also play key roles in the development of major legislative proposals and, to a great extent, depend on their handpicked committee chairs to sell their legislative programs to house and senate colleagues.

5. Traditionally, the powers of the presiding officers have been enhanced by the Calendars Committee in the house and the "two-thirds rule" in the senate. The Calendars Committee, composed entirely of speaker appointees, sets the schedule for floor debate in the house. The "two-thirds rule" provides that two-thirds of the senate must approve before any bill can be debated on the floor of that body. That means that eleven senators can block, or kill, any piece of legislation that has majority support. The lieutenant governor decides which senate sponsors are recognized for consideration of specific bills.

6. To be sent to the governor for signature into law, a bill must be approved after three readings in both the house and the senate. Referral to committee is the first reading, which is as far as most bills progress. Many are never scheduled for a public hearing by the chairs of the committees to which they are assigned. Many others die in subcommittees to which they are sent after being heard by the full committee. And others do not survive the Calendars Committee in the house or the two-thirds requirement in the senate. Those that do win committee approval are often amended, or changed.

7. For those bills that survive the committee process, second reading is a crucial step. That is where most floor debate on legislation occurs and where many bills are further amended. If a bill is approved on second reading, it advances to a third reading and then to the other legislative chamber, where it is referred to a committee and has to repeat the process.

8. A bill must be approved in exactly the same form by both chambers. If the senate, for example, approves a house bill after making some changes in it, the house will have to concur in—or accept—the senate version, or a conference committee of house and senate members will have to be appointed to try to work out a compromise.

9. The governor can sign a bill, veto it, or let it become law without his or her signature. The governor can use the line-item veto to delete specific spending provisions from the general appropriations bill, or state budget. All other bills have to be accepted or rejected in their entirety.

10. Tax bills have to originate in the house. All other bills can originate in either chamber.

11. The legislative rules and heavy volume of bills considered sometimes enable lawmakers to sneak major, controversial proposals into law by adding little-noticed amendments to other bills.

12. The growth of Republican strength has increased partisan activity in the legislature and fueled speculation that, sooner or later, attempts may be made to organize the legislature along the partisan lines of the U.S. Congress. Both major parties already have active legislative caucuses.

13. Legislators' decisions are influenced by a number of factors, including constituents, interest groups, colleagues, staff, the governor, and the media.

14. Legislators have increasingly come to rely on their staffs to develop legislation, perform constituent services, and act as liaisons to interest groups.

15. Although most legislators are honest, hardworking individuals, the weaknesses of a few and the millions of dollars spent by special interests to influence the lawmaking process have undermined Texans' confidence in state government. Lawmakers make periodic efforts to strengthen their ethical standards, but usually only after well-publicized scandals.

KEY TERMS

institutionalization	lieutenant governor	interims	two-thirds rule
bicameral legislature	quorum	first reading	intent calendar
regular session	committee	second reading	tag
special session	subcommittee	third reading	filibuster
single-member district	standing committee	veto	calendar
Legislative Redistricting Board	Calendars Committee	appropriations bill	record vote
at-large district	conference committee	line item veto	division votes
speaker	special, or select, committees	pay-as-you-go	bloc

FURTHER READING

BICKERSTAFF, STEVE. "State Legislative and Congressional Reapportionment in Texas: A Historical Perspective," *Public Affairs Comment* 37 (Winter 1991), pp. 1–13. An excellent overview of three decades of reapportionment litigation in Texas.

BOULARD, GARRY. "Lobbyists as Outlaws," *State Legislatures* 22 (January 1996), pp. 20–25. A short essay focusing on issues facing state legislatures in the regulation of lobbyists.

BURKA, PAUL. "Bob Bullock: The Man Who Runs Texas Politics," *Texas Monthly* (September 1994), pp. 100, 162–163. An informative essay on the leadership style of the late Bob Bullock.

DEATON, CHARLES. *The Year They Threw the Rascals Out.* (Shoal Creek Press, 1973). A detailed account of the 1971 Sharpstown Bank scandal.

HAMM, ROBERT, AND ROBERT HARMEL. "Legislative Party Development and the Speaker System: The Case of the Texas House," *Journal of Politics* 55 (November 1993), pp. 1140–1151. Traces the development of the Republican party in the Texas house, emphasizing the potential for the reduction of the power of the speaker.

JEWELL, MALCOLM E., AND MARCIA LYNN WHICKER. *Legislative Leadership in the American States.* (University of Michigan Press, 1994). A comparative study of state legislative leadership focusing on leaders' goals, leadership styles, and efforts to be more effective.

JONES, NANCY BAKER, AND RUTHIE WINEGARTEN. *Capitol Women: Texas Female Legislators, 1923–1999.* (University of Texas Press, 2000). A compilation of biographies and biographical sketches of the 86 females who served in the Texas legislature from 1923 to 1999, with a focus on their impact on the legislative process and public policy.

MONCRIEF, GARY F., JOEL A. THOMPSON, AND KARL T. KURTZ. "The Old Statehouse, It Ain't What It Used to Be," *Legislative Studies Quarterly* 21 (February 1996), pp. 57–72. A comparative study based on a survey of 330 veteran state legislators summarizing their perceptions of changes in state legislatures.

MOONEY, CHRISTOPHER Z. "Citizens, Structures and Sister States: Influences on State Legislative Professionalism," *Legislative Studies Quarterly* 20 (February 1995), pp. 47–67. Discusses from a comparative perspective the development of "legislative professionalism in terms of a state's population, its governance structures, and the level of professionalism in its peer group states."

TEXAS LEGISLATIVE COUNCIL. *Presiding Officers of the Texas Legislature, 1846–1995.* (Texas Legislative Council, 1995). Brief biographic sketches of presiding officers.

THORBURN, WAYNE. "The Growth of Republican Representation in the Texas Legislature: Coattails, Incumbency, Special Elections, and Urbanization," *Texas Journal of Political Studies* 11 (Spring/Summer 1989), pp. 16–28. An early study of the gains made by Republicans in the Texas legislature.

THE TEXAS EXECUTIVE AND BUREAUCRACY

25

A FRAGMENTED GOVERNMENT

"One thing Texans have today is a state government that doesn't work very well," the state comptroller concluded after an exhaustive study of state agencies and programs. "It is time to rethink Texas government and how it provides basic services to the state's citizens."[1]

When that study was conducted in 1991, Texas had already been operating under an inefficient, fragmented government for more than a century. Yet no changes in what could be considered the root of the problem—the basic governmental structure—have been made since.

For starters, in Texas no single, elected official is ultimately responsible for the executive branch of state government—for the quality of public services performed by hundreds of thousands of state workers. Despite public perception to the contrary, Texas has one of the weaker governors in the country. Unlike the president of the United States, the governor of Texas has no formal appointive cabinet through which to impose policy on the governmental bureaucracy. Several major state agencies are headed by independently elected officeholders who don't answer to the governor and sometimes don't even belong to the same political party. Approximately 250 other state agencies and universities are headed by boards and commissions appointed by the governor, but the governor has only indirect—and often spotty—influence over them.

The office of governor is not without prestige and leadership opportunities. Candidates spend millions of dollars and countless hours campaigning for the job. Clearly, it is the most visible state office. But it is institutionally weak, thanks to constitutional restrictions ensuring that no governor repeat the oppressive abuses of Governor Edmund J. Davis and his Reconstruction administration.[2]

TIME LINE

THE TEXAS EXECUTIVE AND BUREAUCRACY

1876	Constitution creates a plural executive of seven elected offices which severely limits the power of the governor
1917	James "Pa" Ferguson impeached and removed from office
1925	Miriam "Ma" Ferguson is the first woman elected governor
1974	Governor's term increased to four years
1977	Sunset legislation enacted to review state agencies
1978	Bill Clements is the first Republican elected governor since Reconstruction
1980	Governor given limited removal power
1995	Voters abolish the office of State Treasurer
1990	Dan Morales, the first Hispanic to win statewide office in Texas, is elected attorney general
1994	George W. Bush is elected governor—his first elected office
1996	All members of the executive branch are Republicans
2000	Rick Perry assumes the governorship after the election of George W. Bush to the presidency
2002	Republicans win control of all state wide elected offices and both houses of the Texas legislature

plural executive
A fragmented system of authority under which most statewide executive officeholders are elected independently of the governor.

Over the years, the governor's lot has improved somewhat. By constitutional amendment, voters empowered the legislature to raise the governor's salary, and the terms of office for the governor and most other statewide executive officeholders were lengthened from two to four years. In 1980, the governor was given the power, with the approval of the Texas Senate, to remove board members he or she had personally appointed.[3] Nevertheless, these changes have not significantly enhanced the governor's authority. When Governor Ann Richards in 1991 tried to revive interest in giving the governor cabinet-style appointment powers over major state agencies, she had only limited success.

The governor can veto legislation and has the exclusive authority to schedule special sessions of the legislature and set their agendas. And, despite its limitations, the appointment power offers the governor an opportunity to make a strong mark on state government. The high visibility of the office also offers a ready-made public forum. Although the Texas constitution limits the formal powers of the office, a governor's influence is shaped by his or her personality, political adroitness, staff appointments, and ability to define and sell an agenda that addresses broad needs and interests.

THE STRUCTURE OF THE PLURAL EXECUTIVE

Article IV, Section 1, of the 1876 Constitution created a **plural executive** branch, which "shall consist of a Governor, who shall be the Chief Executive Officer of the State, a Lieutenant Governor, Secretary of State, Comptroller of Public Accounts, Treasurer, Commissioner of the General Land Office, and Attorney General." Elected officials added later to the executive branch were the agriculture commissioner, the three-member Railroad Commission, and the fifteen-member State Board of Education. The office of treasurer was eliminated by constitutional amendment in 1995. Only the secretary of state is appointed by the governor. Members of the education board are elected from districts, while the other officeholders are elected statewide (see Figure 25–1). Article IV, Section 4, of the Texas Constitution requires most of these officials to be at least thirty years old and a resident of Texas for at least five years.

Agencies headed by these elected officials are autonomous and, except for limited budgetary review, independent of the governor. In a confrontation with the governor over policy, agency heads can claim their own electoral mandates. For many years, there were only "scattered incidents of hostility within the executive branch," and elected officials generally "cooperated remarkably well with their chief executives"[4]—at least while Texas was a one-party Democratic state. During that period, party politics was dominated by conservatives, whose interests were generally served by state officials who believed it was in their own best political interests to cooperate with one another.

But the potential for conflict between the governor and other executive officials increased as Texas became a two-party state, and conflict is likely to become more common in the future, even among officials from the same party. During Republican Governor Bill Clements's first term (1979–83), the other elected officers in the executive branch were Democrats, including Attorney General Mark White, who frequently feuded with the governor. White jockeyed for the political advantage that allowed him to unseat Clements in 1982.

In 2003, budgetary differences erupted between Republican Comptroller Carole Keeton Strayhorn and other Republican officeholders, including Governor Rick Perry. They resulted in the legislature's approval of a bill, signed by Perry, that transferred two key programs from the comptroller's office to the Legislative Budget Board. The political animosity between Strayhorn and Perry, meanwhile, intensified. (This dispute will be discussed in more detail in the section on the comptroller of public accounts later in this chapter.)

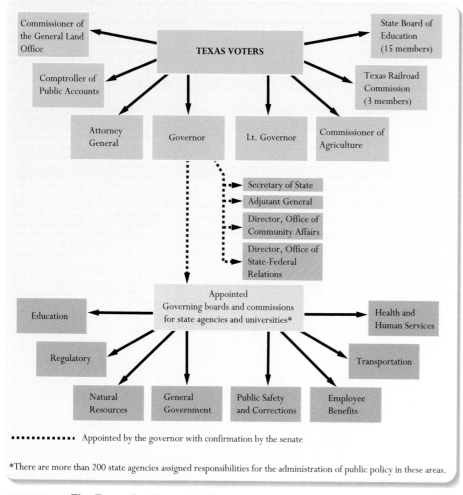

FIGURE 25–1 The Executive Branch in Texas.
The executive branch in Texas is a combination of elected and appointed officials who administer more than two hundred state agencies.
SOURCE: Comptroller of Public Accounts, *Breaking the Mold: A Report of the Texas Performance Review*, vol. 1, p. 13.

When those holding office in a plural executive system have sharply different or competing agendas, it is difficult to develop coordinated policies. The governor, in an effort to avoid conflict, may pursue policies that are not likely to be disruptive, innovative, or responsive to pressing issues. But proponents of the plural executive contend that it does what it was intended to do: control and constrain the governor. Although collegial or collective decision making is often inefficient and can lead to deadlock, the advocates of the plural executive contend that democracy, in most instances, is to be preferred over efficiency.

THE GOVERNOR

Gubernatorial leadership styles have been as varied as the personalities that the chief executives have brought to their jobs. Some governors come to the office with well-defined policy agendas and attempt to exploit every resource available to achieve them. Other governors take a more limited view of the office. They adopt an administrative or managerial posture while leaving policy initiatives to other institutions or elected officials. Such governors tend to pursue new programs, especially those with far-reaching tax or social implications, with considerable caution.

Some governors thrive on the constant attention and political and social interactions that go with the office. They work long hours and continually engage in public

Governor James E. "Pa" Ferguson was the only governor to be removed from office through the impeachment process. Ferguson was impeached and convicted in 1917 during a controversy over his efforts to remove five University of Texas faculty members.

Miriam A. "Ma" Ferguson was the first woman to serve as governor of Texas (1925–1927 and 1933–1935).

impeachment
A procedure by which the legislature can remove a governor or certain other public officials from office for misconduct.

relations and coalition building. Strange as it may seem, however, there have also been governors who were introverted, even shy, and apparently found many aspects of the office distasteful. They often insulated themselves from the public and other political officials and seemed detached from the activities necessary to influence public policy.[5]

Backgrounds and Requirements for Governorship

The Texas constitution has few requirements for a person who desires to run for governor. A governor must be at least thirty years old, a U.S. citizen, and a resident of Texas for at least five years. There also is a vague requirement that no individual can be excluded from office for religious beliefs, "provided he acknowledges the existence of a Supreme Being" (Article I, Section 4). The constitution, however, does not spell out all the roadblocks to winning the office.

Until the election of Republican Bill Clements in 1978, every governor since 1874 had been a Democrat. Clements served two terms (1979–83 and 1987–91). Republican George W. Bush was elected to the office in 1994 and again in 1998, and Republican Rick Perry was elected in 2002, as Republican strength increased in Texas.

Most governors have been well-educated, middle-aged, and affluent white Protestant males. In many cases, their families also were active in public life and helped shape their careers. No minorities and only two women have been elected to the office. Miriam A. "Ma" Ferguson, whose husband, James E. "Pa" Ferguson, had earlier been governor, served two terms (1925–27 and 1933–35), and Ann Richards served one term (1991–95). By the time Richards became governor, only three women had ever been elected to any other statewide executive office in Texas. Richards, a Democrat, served two terms as state treasurer before being elected governor, and she was succeeded as treasurer by Republican Kay Bailey Hutchison. From 1919 to 1923, Annie Webb Blanton was state superintendent of schools, an elective office that no longer exists.

With the rising costs of statewide political campaigns, a candidate's personal wealth or ability to raise large sums of money has taken on increased importance. Otherwise qualified individuals are dissuaded from running for governor and other offices because of the difficult burden of fund raising. Former Governor Bill Clements and fellow Republican Clayton Williams, a Midland business executive who lost the 1990 gubernatorial race to Richards, spent millions of dollars out of their own pockets on gubernatorial races that were their first bids for elective office (see *People and Politics: Making a Difference:* "Governor Bill Clements"). Similarly, Democrat Tony Sanchez, a wealthy Laredo businessman, spent more than $60 million of his personal fortune in an unsuccessful race for governor in 2002. Their experience raises the possibility that personal wealth and the willingness to spend it on one's own election campaign will take on more importance in future races.

Previous public service has provided gubernatorial aspirants with public recognition and ties to party leaders, interest groups, and public officials around the state. Texas governors have previously served in local and statewide offices, the legislature, and Congress. Preston Smith (1969–73) was a legislator and lieutenant governor before being elected governor. Dolph Briscoe (1973–79) also served in the legislature. Mark White (1983–87) served as secretary of state and then as attorney general. Ann Richards was a county commissioner and then state treasurer. Although he had never previously held elective office, Clements was a deputy U.S. secretary of defense prior to winning his first gubernatorial race. George W. Bush was elected governor in 1994 without any previous formal government experience. He had been an unofficial adviser to his father, former President George Bush. Rick Perry was a state representative, agriculture commissioner and lieutenant governor before becoming governor. Table 25–1 lists the governors of Texas from 1870 to the present.

Impeachment and Incapacitation

A governor can be removed from office through **impeachment** proceedings initiated in the house of representatives and conviction by the senate in a trial on the impeachment charges. Texas is one of only a few states that have removed a governor with this

GOVERNOR BILL CLEMENTS

Bill Clements, a self-made multimillionaire who had founded an international oil drilling firm, personally funded much of his first campaign for governor in 1978. The man who shocked the Democratic establishment by defeating John Hill by 17,000 votes had held no previous elected office. His only governmental experience had been as deputy secretary of defense under Presidents Richard Nixon and Gerald Ford. Clements was an outsider, a Republican, a highly opinionated and blunt person, but he had a reputation for solid management skills. All the other elected statewide officials were Democrats, as were most legislators, although many lawmakers shared Clements's conservative views.

Upon arriving in Austin, Clements did not understand the limitations on the powers of the governor. In his election campaign, he had tapped a rather widely held view that state government was wasteful by proposing that 25,000 state jobs be eliminated. He also appealed to the popular notion of limited government and proposed that the Texas constitution be amended to allow private citizens to propose laws through a statewide initiative and referendum process. But he gradually learned that he could not run the statehouse and the bureaucracy single-handedly the way he had run the corporate boardroom, and he did not accomplish either of these goals.

In an interview years later, Clements admitted that he did not fully understood how state government worked when he first took office:

> Until I came to Austin and until I actually was in office and everything, I really didn't understand the detailed nuances of how the state government really functioned. I'd say it took me at least through that first legislative session. And by the time that was over, well, I began to understand exactly how the state government works.[*]

Clements eagerly exercised his veto power. During his first legislative session in 1979, he vetoed 51 bills. He also struck $252 million from the $20.7 billion state budget for 1980–81.

Clements generally received high marks for the quality of his staff and board appointments during his first term. He naturally appointed many fellow Republicans, who for years had been shut out of appointments to boards and commissions, and he also appointed many conservative Democrats. In part, his appointment strategies were designed to convert conservative Democrats to the Republican Party, thus extending and consolidating Republican gains across the state.

But Clements never developed effective ways of communicating with the legislature, the news media, and the general public, and he often found himself at odds with other elected officials and interest groups, primarily because of his outspokenness. He was often portrayed as insensitive, as someone inclined to "shoot from the lip" and worry about the consequences later.

By the end of his first term in 1982, Clements's job performance rating had dropped, his image had suffered, and the Texas economy had begun to show signs of weakness. A revitalized Democratic statewide political effort helped Mark White unseat Clements in a bitterly fought campaign.

In 1986 Clements became only the second person in Texas history to regain the governor's office after losing it. He spent his first six months back in Austin battling Lieutenant Governor Bill Hobby and Democratic legislators over the state budget. The problem was critical because revenue from existing taxes had fallen in the midst of a recession. Clements insisted on deep service cuts that would have enabled him to keep a 1986 campaign promise not to raise taxes, but he finally gave in during a summer special session in 1987 and signed a record $5.6 billion tax increase. The public's

opinion of Clements, meanwhile, was plummeting. Two-thirds of the respondents to the *Texas Poll* that summer said they disapproved of the governor's job performance. And Clements's negative ratings remained high throughout the remainder of his term. By the time he left the governor's office the second time, in 1991, he was widely viewed more as an obstructionist who would rather fight the Democratic majority in the legislature than as a leader who was ready to seek solutions to significant state problems.

Clements's two terms coincided with the emergence of a two-party system in Texas, and his candidacy and elections contributed significantly to this historic development. By proving that a Republican could win the governorship, Clements made the Republican Party attractive to many conservative Democrats, and many switched to the GOP.

In an interview shortly before leaving office for the last time, Clements assessed his contribution to the development of a two-party system:

> The electorate out there breaks down into about one-third Democrats, one-third Republicans, and one-third independents. Well, that is a significant change in the political profile of Texas. That's a historic change, and I guess I'd like to say that I put a brick in place to bring that about.[†]

[*]*Houston Chronicle,* December 2, 1990.
[†]Quoted in *Houston Chronicle,* December 2, 1990.

TABLE 25–1 GOVERNORS OF TEXAS SINCE 1870

Edmund J. Davis	1870–1874
Richard Coke	1874–1876
Richard B. Hubbard	1876–1879
Oran M. Roberts	1879–1883
John Ireland	1883–1887
Lawrence Sullivan Ross	1887–1891
James Stephen Hogg	1891–1895
Charles A. Culberson	1895–1899
Joseph D. Sayers	1899–1903
Samuel W.T. Lanham	1903–1907
Thomas Mitchell Campbell	1907–1911
Oscar Branch Colquitt	1911–1915
James E. Ferguson[*]	1915–1917
William Pettus Hobby	1917–1921
Pat Morris Neff	1921–1925
Miriam A. Ferguson	1925–1927
Dan Moody	1927–1931
Ross S. Sterling	1931–1933
Miriam A. Ferguson	1933–1935
James V. Allred	1935–1939
W. Lee O'Daniel	1939–1941
Coke R. Stevenson	1941–1947
Beauford H. Jester	1947–1949
Allan Shivers	1949–1957
Price Daniel	1957–1963
John Connally	1963–1969
Preston Smith	1969–1973
Dolph Briscoe, Jr.[†]	1973–1979
Williams P. Clements, Jr.	1979–1983
Mark White	1983–1987
William P. Clements, Jr.	1987–1991
Ann Richards	1991–1995
George W. Bush	1995–2000
Rick Perry	2000–

[*] Only governor of Texas to be impeached and convicted.

[†]Prior to 1974, governors were elected for two-year terms of office.

SOURCE: *Texas Almanac, 1996–1997* (The Dallas Morning News, Inc., 1995).

special session
A legislative session that can be called at any time by the governor. This session is limited to thirty days and to issues or subjects designated by the governor.

procedure. In 1917 a controversy erupted over Governor James E. "Pa" Ferguson's efforts to remove five University of Texas faculty members. The governor vetoed the UT appropriations, and when he called a special legislative session to consider other funding, he was immediately faced with articles of impeachment based primarily on the misuse of public funds. He was ultimately convicted and removed from office, a landmark in the two decades of controversy that surrounded the husband-and-wife team of Pa and Ma Ferguson.[6]

If the governor dies, is incapacitated, is impeached and convicted, or leaves office for another reason in midterm, the lieutenant governor replaces the governor until the next general election. When the governor leaves the state, the lieutenant governor serves as acting governor.

Some other states, such as California, can remove a governor through recall, as well as impeachment. Through a process that begins with petitions signed by a defined number of voters, a special election can be held on the question of removing the governor from office. If the governor is removed by popular vote, a new governor is then elected. This occurred in California in late 2003, when Democrat Gray Davis was recalled as governor, and voters in the same election chose movie star Arnold Schwarzenegger, a Republican, to replace him. Texas doesn't have the recall process for the governor or other statewide officeholders.

Salary and Perks of the Office

In 2004, the governor of Texas was paid $115,345. The state also provides the governor with a mansion and a staff to maintain it, a security detail, travel expenses, and access to state-owned planes and cars.

Legislative Powers of the Governor

Governors have the opportunity to outline their legislative priorities at the beginning of each regular biennial session through the traditional State of the State Address to the legislature. The governor can also communicate with lawmakers—collectively or individually—throughout the session. In this fashion, the governor can establish a policy agenda, recommend specific legislation, and set the stage for negotiations with legislative leaders, other state officials, and interest groups. The governor's addresses and other formal messages to the legislature are well covered by the media. They give governors the opportunity to mobilize the public support that may be essential to the success of their initiatives.

The governor's effectiveness can be enhanced by the office's two major constitutional powers over the legislature: the veto and the authority to call and set the agenda for special legislative sessions.

The governor can call any number of **special sessions**, which can last as long as thirty days each, and designate the issues to be considered during each one. Sometimes the mere threat of a special session can be enough to convince reluctant lawmakers to approve a priority program of the governor or reach an acceptable compromise during a regular session. Most legislators, who are paid only part-time salaries by the state, dread special sessions because they interfere with their regular occupations and disrupt their personal lives. Governor Bill Clements, who called two special sessions on workers' compensation reform in 1989, used the threat of a third to convince a handful of senators to break a year-long impasse and approve legislation backed by the governor, a majority of the house, and the business community. Governor Rick Perry called three special sessions in 2003 to win approval of a congressional redistricting bill that favored Republican candidates. The bill wouldn't have passed without Perry's persistence (see Chapter 24).

There also are risks in calling special sessions. The governor's influence and reputation are on the line, and further inaction by the legislature can become a political liability or embarrassment. In some instances, the legislative leadership has liberally interpreted the subject matter of a governor's special session proclamation and considered bills not sought by the governor. Because the speaker and the lieutenant governor make the parliamentary rulings that determine whether a specific piece of legislation falls within the governor's call, the governor has to draft proclamations setting special session agendas very carefully. Once a special session is called, the governor can increase his or her bargaining power by adding legislators' pet bills to the agenda in exchange for the lawmakers' support of the governor's program.

The governor of Texas has one of the strongest **veto** powers of any governor. While the legislature is in session, the governor has ten days to veto a bill or let it become law without his or her signature. A veto can be overridden by a two-thirds vote of both the house and the senate. During the past fifty years, Governor Clements was the only governor to have a veto overridden. It was a local bill related to game management that the Democrat-dominated legislature voted to override during the Republican governor's first term. The governor has twenty days after the legislature adjourns to veto bills passed in the closing days of a session. Such vetoes are absolute because the only way the legislature can respond is to have the bill reintroduced in the next session.

The governor also has **line item veto** authority over the state budget: that is, the governor can strike specific spending items without vetoing the entire bill. All other bills have to be accepted or rejected in their entirety.

A governor may veto a bill for a number of reasons, including doubts about its constitutionality, objections to its wording, concerns that it duplicates existing law, or substantive differences with its policy. A governor's threat of a veto is often as effective as an actual veto because such threats can prompt legislators to make changes in their bills to meet the governor's objections.

Historic records on gubernatorial vetoes are not complete, but Governor Rick Perry is believed to have set a single-year record by vetoing 82 bills at the end of the 2001 legislative session. His vetoes also sparked a lot of anger from doctors, criminal justice reformers, state employees, advocates for the poor, and others. One veto, the striking down of a bill that would have banned execution of mentally retarded convicts in Texas, received international attention. And although that veto was sharply criticized by death penalty opponents, it drew praise from crime victims' advocates. Perry attempted to milk the most favorable publicity that he could from the event by inviting more than a dozen relatives of people murdered by mentally retarded convicts to join him at a state Capitol news conference to announce the veto. Despite his veto, however, the U.S. Supreme Court later had the final say on the issue when it ruled the execution of mentally retarded convicts was unconstitutional. Perry vetoed 48 bills after the 2003 regular session.

Governor Dan Moody also was a frequent veto user. He vetoed 117 bills and resolutions between 1927 and 1931. Governor Ann Richards vetoed 36 bills and resolutions in one regular and two special sessions in 1991 and allowed 228 bills to become law without her signature.

Budgetary Powers of the Governor

The governor of Texas has weaker budgetary authority than the governors of most states and the president of the United States. These budgetary constraints limit the governor's ability to develop a comprehensive legislative program. The legislature has the lead in budget setting, with a major role played by the **Legislative Budget Board** (LBB), a ten-member panel that includes the lieutenant governor, the speaker, and eight key lawmakers.

To meet emergencies between legislative sessions, the governor can propose the transfer of funds between programs or agencies, with the approval of the LBB. Or the LBB can recommend a funds transfer, subject to the governor's approval.

Appointive and Removal Powers of the Governor

Much of the state bureaucracy falls under more than 200 boards and commissions that oversee various agencies created by state law. Most of these are part-time, unpaid positions whose occupants are heavily dependent on agency staffs and constituents for

veto
The power of the governor to reject, or kill, a bill passed by the legislature.

line item veto
The power of the governor to reject certain parts of an appropriations, of spending, bill without killing the entire measure.

Legislative Budget Board
The panel that makes budgetary recommendations to the full legislature. It is chaired by the lieutenant governor and includes the speaker of the house and eight other key lawmakers.

guidance. Although members of these boards are appointed by the governor and confirmed by the senate, the structure creates the potential for boards and commissions to become captives of the narrow constituencies they are serving or regulating and reduces their accountability to both the governor and the legislature.

Most board members serve six-year **staggered terms**, an arrangement under which the terms of one-third of a board's membership expire every two years. That means it takes new governors at least two years to get majorities favoring their policies on most boards. Resignations or deaths of board members may speed up the process, but a governor cannot remove a predecessor's appointees. Governors, with the approval of two-thirds of the senate, can fire only their own appointees.

During her first year in office in 1991, Governor Ann Richards asked the legislature to give her the power to appoint the executive directors of state agencies directly. These officials historically had been hired by the various boards and commissions. In reorganizing a handful of agencies, the legislature gave the governor a small taste of the cabinet-style authority she had sought, but it hardly changed the system. The governor was given the authority to appoint a new commissioner to oversee several health and human services agencies, the executive director of the Department of Commerce, and the executive director of a new Department of Housing and Community Affairs. The governor retained her previous authority to appoint the secretary of state, the adjutant general, and the director of the Office of State–Federal Relations (see *People and Politics: Making a Difference:* "Governor Ann Richards").

The governor appoints individuals to boards and commissions with the approval of two-thirds of the senate. **Senatorial courtesy**, an unwritten norm of the senate, permits a senator to block the governor's nomination of a person who lives in that senator's district. The governor and staff members involved in appointments spend considerable time clearing potential nominees with senators because political considerations are as important in the confirmation process as a nominee's qualifications.

Individuals seek gubernatorial appointments for a variety of reasons, and the appointments process can be hectic, particularly at the beginning of a new governor's administration. Potential nominees are screened by the governor's staff to determine their availability, competence, political acceptability, and support by key interest groups. And although most governors would deny it, campaign contributions are a significant factor. A number of Governor Clements's appointees had made substantial contributions to his campaign.[7] Governors Richards, Bush, and Perry also appointed major contributors to important posts. Governor Perry made the most controversial appointment of his first year in office, former Enron Corporation executive Max Yzaguirre as chairman of the Public Utility Commission, one day before receiving a $25,000 political donation from then–Enron Chairman Ken Lay in 2001. Perry insisted the timing was coincidental, but it generated much controversy after Enron filed for bankruptcy a few months later, prompting Yzaguirre's resignation from the post. Then, in 2003, less than one month after receiving a $100,000 contribution from homebuilder Bob Perry of Houston, Governor Perry appointed a top executive of the homebuilder's company to a new state commission charged with developing building performance standards. The commission had been created by the legislature to reduce consumer lawsuits against builders. Since June 1997, Bob Perry, who wasn't related to the governor, had contributed $580,000 to Rick Perry[8] (see *People and Politics: Making a Difference:* Governor Rick Perry).

The governor appoints individuals to fill vacancies on all courts at the district level or higher. If a U.S. senator dies or resigns, the governor appoints a replacement. When a vacancy occurs in another statewide office, except for the lieutenant governor, the governor also appoints a replacement. All of these appointees must later win election to keep their seats.

Governor Richards was particularly sensitive to constituencies that had historically been excluded from full participation in the governmental process and appointed a record number of women and minorities to state posts. About 45 percent of Richards's appointees during her four-year term were women, and about 35 percent were

staggered terms
Terms that begin on different dates, a requirement for members of state boards and commissions appointed by the governor.

senatorial courtesy
An unwritten practice that permits a senator to block the confirmation of a gubernatorial appointee who lives in the senator's district.

minorities. Her successor, Governor Bush, appointed women to 37 percent and minorities to 22 percent of the posts he filled during his first five years in office. Bush appointed the first African American, Michael Williams, to the Texas Railroad Commission, and, at different times during his administration, appointed two Hispanics—Tony Garza and Alberto R. Gonzales—secretary of state. Bush later appointed Gonzales to fill a vacancy on the Texas Supreme Court and, after becoming president, appointed Gonzales to the important White House counsel post. Governor Perry appointed the first African American, Wallace Jefferson of San Antonio, to the Texas Supreme Court.

Judicial Powers of the Governor

Texas has a seven-member Board of Pardons and Paroles appointed by the governor. This panel, which was reduced from 18 members by a 2003 law, decides when prisoners can be released early, and its decisions do not require action by the governor. The governor, however, can influence the board's overall approach to paroles. The governor has the authority to grant executive clemency—acts of leniency or mercy—toward convicted criminals. One is a thirty-day stay of execution for a condemned murderer, which a governor can grant without a recommendation of the parole board. The governor, on recommendation of the board, can grant a full pardon to a criminal, a conditional pardon, or the commutation of a death sentence to life imprisonment.

If a person flees a state to avoid prosecution or a prison term, the U.S. Constitution, under the **extradition** clause, requires that person, upon arrest in another state, to be returned to the state from which he or she fled. The governor is legally responsible for ordering state officials to carry out such extradition requests.[9]

Military Powers of the Governor

The Texas constitution authorizes the governor to function as the "commander-in-chief of the military force of the state, except when they are called into actual service of the United States" (Article IV, Section 7). The governor appoints the adjutant general to carry out this duty. Texas cannot declare war on another country, and the president of the United States has the primary responsibility for national defense. But when riots or natural disasters occur within the state, the governor can mobilize the Texas National Guard to protect lives and property and keep the peace. Should the United States go to war, the National Guard can be mobilized by the president as part of the national military forces. After the September 11, 2001, terrorist attacks on the World Trade Center and the Pentagon, some National Guard members from Texas were activated to temporarily bolster security at airports. Others went overseas to participate in the military operations in Afghanistan and Iraq.

Informal Resources of the Governor

Governors can compensate for the constitutional limitations on their office with their articulation of problems and issues, leadership capabilities, personalities, work habits, and administrative styles. Some governors relish being involved in the minutiae of building policy coalitions and devote much of their personal time to bringing about compromises and agreements. Other governors find such hands-on involvement distasteful, inefficient, and time consuming, and leave such detail work to subordinates.

As the most visible state official, the governor sometimes gets credit that belongs to others but can just as readily be blamed for problems beyond his or her control. For example, falling oil prices that had devastated the state's economy were a major factor in Mark White's loss of his 1986 reelection bid. White had no choice but to call a special legislative session only a few months before the November election and, under the circumstances, probably exercised the best leadership that he could in convincing lawmakers to cut the budget and raise taxes. But it was not the type of leadership appreciated by most voters.

extradition
A process by which a person in one state is returned to another state to face criminal charges.

PEOPLE & POLITICS *Making a Difference* ★ ★ ★ ★ ★

GOVERNOR ANN RICHARDS

Taking her oath in January 1991, Ann Richards attempted to convince the public that her election marked the emergence of a "New Texas." She invited supporters to join her in a march up Congress Avenue to symbolically retake the Capitol for "the people." And, hitting on the progressive Democratic themes of her campaign, she promised in her inaugural address a user-friendly, compassionate state government that would expand opportunities for everyone, particularly minorities and women. But the euphoria of the day was tempered by the reality of a $4 billion-plus potential deficit, a court order for school finance reform that could make the shortfall even greater, and a grand jury investigation into legislative behavior that had eroded public confidence in state government.

Richards moved quickly to establish herself as an activist governor. The day after her inauguration, she continued a campaign assault on high insurance rates by marching over to a meeting of the State Board of Insurance to speak publicly against a proposed increase in auto insurance premiums. Unlike her recent predecessors, she also testified for her priorities before house and senate committees and used the media to attack the state bureaucracy.

Richards also quickly fulfilled a campaign promise to appoint more women and minorities to key positions in state government. She appointed the first African American to the University of Texas System Board of Regents, the first African American woman to the Texas A&M University governing board, and the first Hispanic to the Texas Court of Criminal appeals. Some 25 percent of her appointees during her first three months in office were Hispanic, 21 percent were African American, and 49 percent were women. Richards also named a disabled person to the Board of Human Services and a crime victim to the Board of Criminal Justice.*

With the state facing a revenue crunch, Richards took the lead in lobbying legislators for a constitutional amendment to create a state lottery. The lottery was a relatively safe issue on which to stake a leadership claim because polls indicated it had the strong support of most Texans as a new source of revenue for state government.

Most other major issues before the legislature during Richards's first year in office, however, were not so simple, and the new governor was less willing to strike specific policy positions on them. She preferred to support the initiatives

of Democratic legislative leaders—or take the best bill they were willing to give her—rather than demand that legislators enact a specific plan. Detractors would say Richards's leadership wilted in the heat of legislative battle. Supporters would say she was a pragmatist who knew the limits of her office and recognized the necessity of political compromise.

The progressive goals that Richards had outlined in her campaign were also tempered by the reality that Texas was a predominantly conservative state. Despite promoting a vision of a "New Texas" that offered more compassion for the poor, improved health care for the sick, and greater educational opportunity for all, Richards took pains to establish credentials for fiscal restraint. She opposed a proposal for a personal income tax, even though it could have provided funds for a big boost in spending on health and human services programs and education. And she eagerly embraced a thorough review of state spending practices that helped reduce the size of the revenue and tax bill she eventually signed during her first year in office.

Although Richards entered the 1993 legislative session with one of the highest public approval ratings of any

The Governor's Staff

Nineteenth-century governors had only three or four individuals to assist them, but staffs have grown with the increased complexity of state government and greater demands on the governor's time. By 1963, under John Connally, the governor's staff had grown to 68 full-time and 12 part-time employees.[10] Under the administration of Dolph Briscoe in the 1970s, the staff had further expanded to more than 300, but staff sizes were smaller in most subsequent administrations. At one point in her term, Ann Richards had almost 300 people on her staff. The number decreased to about 200 under George W. Bush, but Bush approved higher salaries for some of his key staffers. In 2002, Governor Perry had approximately 200 employees (see Figure 25–2).

The critical question involving staff is whether the governor has access to sufficient information on which to make decisions that produce good public policy and minimize the potential for controversy, conflict, and embarrassment. Under ideal circumstances, governor in Texas history, she remained cautious during the entire session, apparently to save political capital for a 1994 reelection race. She joined Lieutenant Governor Bob Bullock and Pete Laney, the new house speaker, in insisting that a new state budget be written without an increase in state taxes. There was no tax bill, but the new budget did not enable the legislature to give teachers a pay raise, which had been another Richards priority, and it did not keep up with growing caseloads in health and human services programs.

In one of the most emotional issues of the session, Richards sided with police chiefs, mayors, physicians, and members of the clergy—and against a majority of the legislature—in killing a proposal to allow private citizens to carry handguns. (It was revived and approved under Governor George W. Bush two years later.) She successfully advocated an immunization program for children and actively promoted the legislature's efforts to comply with a Texas Supreme Court order for a constitutional school finance system but did not propose a plan of her own.

Richards staked out a strong anticrime position early in her term. In 1991 she ordered her appointees to the Board of Pardons and Paroles to sharply curtail a high rate of releases from state prisons, and she supported a huge prison expansion program. Richards also made economic development a major goal. She actively recruited companies to locate or expand in Texas and was instrumental in lobbying the U.S. Congress for approval of the North American Free Trade Agreement (NAFTA), even though NAFTA was bitterly opposed by organized labor, one of her key longtime supporters.

Richards was a national figure who was readily welcomed on Wall Street, at Hollywood parties, and in corporate boardrooms throughout the country. Many analysts believed her role as Texas's chief salesperson, or ambassador, was her greatest contribution to the state, along with the appointments that opened up the state policy-making process to a record number of women, Hispanics, and African Americans.

Richards, who had no legislative experience, did not seem to relish the often bloody give-and-take of the legislative process, but she obviously enjoyed her celebrity role as governor. During the 1993 session, Richards told reporters that she was not the kind of leader who could force results. Instead, she said, she tried to contribute to "an atmos-

phere in which good things can happen."[†]

Although Richards was unseated by Republican George W. Bush in 1994, polls indicated she remained personally popular with her constituents. But most conservative, independent voters had never been comfortable with Richards politically. Her defeat coincided with voter discontent with the Democratic party that swept the country that year. A number of other Democratic governors were also defeated, and Republicans captured control of both houses of the U.S. Congress. Richards's opposition to the handgun bill during the 1993 legislative session was another factor, particularly in key conservative areas of the state.

Texas Government Newsletter, February 25, 1991.
[†]Quoted in *Houston Chronicle,* June 2, 1993.

the staff enhances the governor's political, administrative, and policy-making capabilities. There have been instances, however, when governors have permitted staff to insulate them by denying access to persons with significant information or recommendations.

Governors generally choose staffers who are loyal and share their basic political attitudes. Because communication with the governor's various constituencies is fundamental to success, some staffers are chosen for their skills in mass communications and public relations. Others are hired for their expertise in specific policy areas. In many respects, staff members function as the governor's surrogates. Thus if one makes a mistake—particularly a serious mistake—the public perceives it as the governor's error.

The staff collects, organizes, and screens information, helps decide who sees the governor, and otherwise schedules the governor's time. Staffers also work on strategies to garner support for the governor's proposals from legislators, agencies, and interest groups. Because the governor often lacks the time to conduct discussions and

PEOPLE & POLITICS *Making a Difference* ★ ★ ★ ★ ★

GOVERNOR RICK PERRY

Republican Rick Perry came to the governor's office with much more governmental experience than his immediate and more famous predecessor, George W. Bush. He had served six years as a state representative, eight years as state agriculture commissioner and almost two years as lieutenant governor before succeeding Bush as governor in December 2000, after Bush had resigned to become president. But Perry wasn't blessed with Bush's politically powerful name or his popularity, and he hadn't been elected governor. He had inherited the job. Moreover, the 2001 legislative session, with which Perry immediately had to deal, promised to be contentious because of political redistricting and a worrisome budgetary outlook.

Perry, however, survived his first session mostly unscarred. He didn't have to sign or veto any redistricting bills because Republicans and Democrats in the legislature were unable to agree on new political boundaries for themselves or for Texas's congressional delegation. The legislative impasse put legislative redistricting in the hands of the Legislative Redistricting Board and deferred congressional redistricting—for the time being, anyway—to a federal court. Lawmakers wrote a new state budget without having to raise taxes and, at Perry's urging, even found enough money to triple funding for a grant program to help thousands of young Texans from low-income families attend college.

The legislature enacted one of Perry's criminal justice priorities, a law to give inmates the ability to obtain court-ordered DNA testing if they could demonstrate that there was a substantial possibility that the results would prove them innocent. But the governor didn't get his way on another criminal justice issue with significant political overtones. In one of the

most emotional and partisan issues of the session, the legislature approved a bill, backed by most Democrats and opposed by most Republicans, to strengthen penalties for crimes motivated by hate or prejudice. It was a fight that had begun in earnest two years earlier, after three white assailants had dragged an African American, James Byrd Jr., to death behind a pickup in east Texas. At one point, Perry convinced a Republican senator to help delay action on the bill because he opposed a provision that listed protected classes of people, including homosexuals, which was strongly opposed by social conservatives in the Republican Party. But after the measure won final legislative approval, Perry signed it within a few hours after it reached his desk. He said he still had doubts about it. "But I also believe that as governor, and as a Texan, I have an obligation to see issues from another person's perspective, to walk in another person's shoes," he said.*

Some legislators criticized Perry's mostly low-key style during the 2001 session and complained that he didn't let them know early enough and clearly enough what he wanted. Shortly after the legislative session had ended, however, Perry flexed his muscles and vetoed a record 82 bills, including a measure that would have banned the execution of mentally retarded convicts in Texas. Aware that international attention was focused on his decision, Perry invited relatives of murder victims to join him at a state capitol news conference announcing the veto. Crime victims' advocates praised the veto, but death penalty opponents criticized it. A year later, the U.S. Supreme Court, acting in a case from another state, would prohibit the execution of mentally retarded inmates throughout the country.

Other vetoes drew sharp criticism from a range of people. Among the loudest complaints came from doctors over the governor's veto of a bill that would have required insurance companies to promptly pay health care providers for their services. Physicians and hospitals complained that health maintenance organizations and other insurers were dragging their feet in paying valid claims, often creating financial hardships for providers. Perry vetoed the bill at the urging of business groups that argued that it would have removed arbitration as an option for settling health insurance claims and would have encouraged lawsuits. A similar prompt-pay bill was enacted by the legislature in 2003—without the provision that offended the business groups—and Perry signed it.

During his first year as governor, Perry also had to dodge political fallout from the spectacular collapse of Enron Corp., the Houston-based energy-trading giant, which had been a major source of political donations during his public career. Soon after Enron filed for bankruptcy in late 2001, throwing thousands of employees out of work and costing investors and retirees millions of dollars, controversy erupted over Perry's appointment of a former Enron executive, Max Yzaguirre, to chair the Texas Public Utility Commission. Perry had appointed Yzaguirre in June 2001, several months before most people even suspected that Enron was in financial trouble. But after the Enron story exploded, Democrats started questioning Yzaguirre's eligibility for the regulatory post and the timing of his appointment. Perry had received a $25,000 political donation from then–Enron Chairman Ken Lay the day after appointing Yzaguirre. Perry insisted Yzaguirre was legally qualified and that the timing of the contribution was coincidental. But after the controversy had raged for several weeks, Yzaguirre resigned. It wasn't clear whether he chose to step down on his own or was quietly encouraged to do so by the governor.

Despite his rural roots—Perry grew up in Paint Creek, a tiny town in northwest Texas—the governor was acutely aware of the clogged freeways that plagued the daily lives of urban and suburban Texans and, early on, sought to make improved transportation a signature issue of his administration. He actively campaigned for a constitutional amendment, which voters approved in November 2001, creating the Texas Mobility Fund, a revolving fund against which bonds could be pledged for highway construction. It was a significant departure from the state's traditional pay-as-you-go method of paying for highways. Then, in early 2002, Perry proposed a massive, $175 billion transportation network for Texas, which would include toll roads, railroads, and underground utility tunnels grouped in corridors stretching across the state. The plan, which Perry called the Trans Texas Corridor, would take an estimated fifty years to complete.

Perry defeated Democratic nominee Tony Sanchez, a multimillionaire Laredo businessman, in a bruising campaign to win a full term in the governor's office in 2002. Perry's victory and the first Republican takeover of the Texas house in modern times put the GOP in undisputed control of state government, and Perry acted accordingly. The governor joined Republican legislative leaders in demanding that a $10 billion revenue shortfall be closed by cutting spending, not raising taxes, and Republicans prevailed. Advocates of health care programs and other services protested the spending reductions, and many of the state's daily newspapers editorialized for limited tax increases to help minimize the cuts in services. The legislature raised some state fees and enacted legislation to allow university governing boards to increase tuition, but Perry refused to budge on taxes, apparently convinced that most middle-class Texans agreed with him. He also argued that the state's relatively low tax burden had to be protected to keep the state attractive to businesses looking for places to expand. Perry also won from the legislature a special economic development fund that could be used to provide economic incentives for business recruitment.

The governor also advocated and won significant new restrictions on medical malpractice claims and other civil lawsuits. He said the so-called tort reform changes were essential to easing a crisis in health care, particularly in rural areas, and improving the state's business climate, although opponents argued that they put unnecessary, new restrictions on consumers' access to the courts.

As was more fully discussed in Chapter 24, Perry also played a dominant role in a bitter, partisan fight over congressional redistricting in 2003. Perry fully supported an effort, initiated by U.S. House Majority Leader Tom DeLay of Sugar Land, to increase the number of Republicans elected to the U.S. House from Texas. Under a 2001 redistricting plan drawn by a federal court, Democrats still held a 17 to 15 majority in the Texas congressional delegation, despite recent Republican sweeps of all statewide offices and Republican majorities in both the Texas house and the state senate. DeLay, Perry, and other GOP leaders argued that the congressional delegation should more accurately reflect the state's Republican strength. A bill that would have redrawn congressional districts to favor more Republican candidates died during the 2003 regular session after more than fifty Democratic members of the Texas house fled to Ardmore, Oklahoma, to break a quorum and keep the house from acting on the measure. Using one of his strongest constitutional powers, Perry then called the legislature back into special session that summer to try again. Eventually, it took three special sessions to complete the task, but Perry was persistent. He even waited out a second Democratic boycott, when eleven Democratic senators flew to Albuquerque, New Mexico, to hold out for more than a month and shut down the senate during the entire second special session. A redistricting bill that the Republican-dominated legislature finally passed during the third special session—and which survived an initial court challenge—was expected to increase the number of Republicans elected to Congress from Texas by as many as seven, all at the expense of incumbent Democrats.

For a while, at least, the redistricting dispute may have put a dent in Perry's popularity. A Scripps Howard *Texas Poll* taken at the height of the controversy in August 2003, while the Democratic senators were still in New Mexico, indicated that Perry's job approval rating was at its lowest, 44 percent, since he had become governor. It had fallen 6 percentage points since June. The same poll showed that Texans by a narrow margin (46 percent to 40 percent) opposed congressional redistricting but strongly disagreed (62 percent to 29 percent) with the Democratic walkout. Perry said he wasn't worried. "I get up every day and try to do what's right for the people of Texas," he said. "I don't wake up and fret about what a particular poll at a particular point in time says."

Houston Chronicle, August 27, 2003, p. 23A.

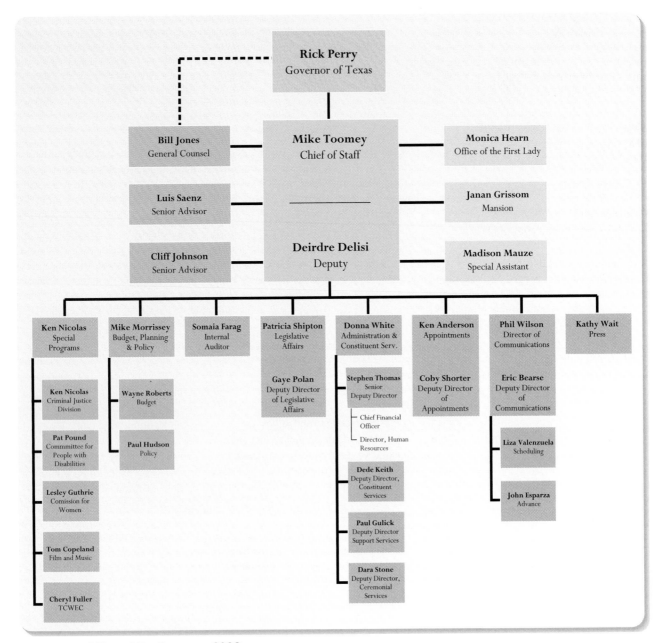

FIGURE 25–2 Office of the Governor, 2003.

negotiations, key staff members represent the governor in such meetings and in personal lobbying of lawmakers. Sometimes governors get involved personally, particularly if their participation is needed to break an impasse and bring about a solution.[11]

The Governor and the Mass Media

The mass media help shape the political and policy options of the governor. Governors who have failed to understand the impact of the media have often courted disaster. A governor who is readily accessible to reporters and understands the constraints under which the media operate is likely to develop a good working relationship with the press. But success with the media involves more than being accessible and friendly.

Governors call press conferences to announce new policies or to explain their positions on pending issues. They stage pseudo "news events," such as visits to classrooms to emphasize concern for educational quality or appearances at high-tech facilities to demonstrate a commitment to economic development. They or their staffers sometimes leak information to selected reporters to embarrass the opposition, put an action of the administration in the best possible light, or float a trial balloon to gauge legislative or public reaction to a proposal. Some governors have spent political funds to purchase radio or television time in an attempt to mobilize public opinion in support of pet proposals before the legislature. Overall, the timely use of the media can contribute significantly to the power and influence of a governor.

The Governor and the Political Party

Historically, the political factions within one-party Democratic Texas were somewhat ill defined. Factionalism was often described in terms of liberal or conservative, but there also were complex urban–rural, regional, and economic differences. Democratic governors built policy coalitions around these factions, but there was little stability or continuity, and most governors derived only limited power from their position as party leader.

Under the two-party system, however, the political party is taking on more importance and may provide greater resources to the governor (see In *Comparative Perspective:* "Party Control of the Governor's Office, 2004"). During his second term in the late 1980s, Bill Clements often had enough Republican votes in the house to thwart the will of the Democratic majority. After Republicans had gained legislative control, Rick Perry

IN COMPARATIVE PERSPECTIVE

PARTY CONTROL OF THE GOVERNOR'S OFFICE, 2004

PEOPLE & POLITICS *Making a Difference* ★ ★ ★ ★

GOVERNOR GEORGE W. BUSH

George W. Bush, son of former President George Bush, had never held public office before being elected governor, but he had gained valuable political experience campaigning for and serving as an unofficial advisor to his father. The younger Bush became Texas's second Republican governor in modern times by conducting an effective campaign for improvements in the public schools, tougher penalties for juvenile offenders, and reform of the welfare and civil justice systems. He succeeded in winning approval for legislation addressing all four priorities during the 1995 legislative session, the first of his term.

Bush's public style was low key. He seemed to go out of his way to avoid controversy during his first year in office. But he remained focused on his four primary goals, and he was assisted by conservative Democratic legislative leaders, who shared his views and sensed that public sentiment was on the governor's side. Although Democrats had majorities in both the house and the senate in 1995, the Texas legislature was dominated by conservatives of both parties, and some of the reforms the new governor wanted already had been initiated by Democratic officials.

Bush actively worked with legislators behind the scenes, making minor compromises, when necessary, on his policy priorities. The governor had frequent private meetings with house and senate members, sometimes even dropping by their Capitol offices unannounced. He had weekly breakfast meetings with Lieutenant Governor Bob Bullock and Speaker Pete Laney, two Democrats whose work was crucial to the governor's program. "We disagree, but you'll never read about it," Bush said of his meetings with the two legislative leaders. "The way to forge good public policy amongst the leadership of the legislative branch and executive branch is to air our differences in private meetings that happen all the time. The way to ruin a relationship is to leak things [to the media] and to be disrespectful of meeting in private."*

Bush also believed his decisive victory in the 1994 election had helped his cause in the legislature. "I won by 352,000 votes," he told reporters the day after the legislature adjourned. "And when you stand up in front of the legislature and outline a legislative agenda that was endorsed by the will of the people, that helps remind people that this is what Texans want."†

Unlike Governors Mark White, Bill Clements, and Ann Richards before him, Bush did not face budgetary problems in state government that could have distracted lawmakers' attention from his priorities. And unlike Richards, Bush supported legislation that gave adult Texans the right to carry concealed handguns. The gun bill was not one of Bush's major priorities, but it had been an issue in his victory over Richards. Bush signed the gun measure approved by lawmakers in 1995.

Bush faced a tougher challenge during the 1997 legislative session, when he made school property tax relief a major goal. He proposed that state government assume a larger share of the cost of funding the public schools by lowering local school taxes by about $3 billion a year. To replace the lost revenue, he proposed an increase in the state sales tax, the enactment of a new business tax, and the transfer of $1 billion in state budgetary savings to the public schools. The house rejected most of Bush's proposal and approved a controversial tax trade-off that would have increased numerous state taxes in exchange for major cuts in local school taxes. Bush lobbied Republican legislators for the house plan and helped convince about half of the 68 Republicans in the house to vote for it. Assured that Bush was actively backing the plan, Speaker Laney helped persuade a large

had strong support from Republican lawmakers and party officials during the budgetary and redistricting battles of 2003 (see Chapter 24).

Upon taking office in 1995, Republican Governor George W. Bush enjoyed the support of party leaders for his own priorities—efforts to improve education, restrict civil lawsuits, reform juvenile justice, and change the welfare system. Initially, he kept his distance from much of the agenda advocated by the social conservatives who had taken control of leadership positions in the Texas Republican party in 1994. But in 1999, when he was preparing for a presidential race, Bush strengthened his antiabortion credentials with social conservatives by convincing the legislature to enact one of their major priorities—a law requiring parents to be notified before their minor daughters could have abortions (see *People and Politics: Making a Difference:* "Governor George W. Bush").

number of Democratic house members to vote for it. The bipartisan balancing act was necessary because many Republican legislators had campaigned against higher taxes of any kind and many Democratic lawmakers had previously been targeted by Republicans over the tax issue.

Despite the success in the house, the senate, which had a Republican majority in 1997, refused to approve a large increase in state taxes. Bush remained mostly in the background while the senate debated the issue. After it became obvious the house and the senate were in a stalemate, legislative negotiators requested the governor's active participation once again. But Bush was unable to forge any compromise that raised state taxes. The governor managed to salvage only a modest amount of property tax relief—about $140 a year for the average homeowner—by convincing the legislature to increase homestead exemptions, a form of tax break that homeowners get on their school taxes. The legislature used $1 billion in state budgetary savings to repay school districts for the revenue they lost from the higher exemptions.

In failing to win more substantial property tax relief, Bush was stymied by two major obstacles. One was strong opposition from business lobbyists to the proposed state tax increases. The other was the absence of a state budgetary crisis that would have forced the legislature to increase taxes.

Bush said he wanted to lower property taxes because they had become so high they were making home ownership difficult for many Texans. Some Democrats said Bush had failed as a leader because he had been unable to convince the legislature to enact a more substantial property tax cut package, but the governor dismissed the criticism. "I think people are going to say this is a man who set a very bold agenda and acted boldly," he said.[†] He said the higher homestead exemption that the legislature did pass was important.

Bush easily won reelection over Democratic challenger Garry Mauro in 1998 and entered the 1999 legislative session amid widespread speculation that he was preparing for a presidential race. With his pending White House campaign obviously on his mind, he convinced the legislature to enact some additional tax cuts and increase education spending. And he accepted a priority of Democratic lawmakers to give school teachers a $3,000-a-year pay raise. Bush's biggest legislative defeat in 1999 was the rejection of a pilot program to allow students from

low-performing public schools to use tax-backed vouchers to attend private schools. But, in an effort to shore up support among religious and social conservatives in the Republican party, Bush won approval of a law to require parents to be notified before their minor, unmarried daughters could receive abortions. It was the most significant piece of abortion-control legislation to be passed by Texas lawmakers since the U.S. Supreme Court had legalized abortion 26 years earlier.

Bush officially launched a campaign for the 2000 Republican presidential nomination in June 1999. He was elected President in the 2000 election and resigned as governor in December.

*Quoted in *Houston Chronicle,* April 15, 1995.
†Quoted in *Houston Chronicle,* May 31, 1995.
‡Quoted in *Dallas Morning News,* June 4, 1997.

The Governor and Interest Groups

Successful governors must be consummate political animals who continually nurture relationships throughout the political system. A gubernatorial candidate aggressively solicits the endorsements and contributions of various groups. These groups, in turn, develop stakes in gubernatorial elections and usually assume that the candidates they support will be responsive to their interests. A governor's policy initiatives often include legislation of benefit to key support groups, which maintain active roles throughout the policy process. Business groups, for example, were major contributors to Governor Rick Perry's successful election race in 2002, and the governor strongly supported their priorities, including additional limits on civil lawsuits, during the 2003 regular legislative session.

Former Texas Supreme Court justice Greg Abbott, a Republican, was elected attorney general in 2002.

OTHER OFFICES OF THE EXECUTIVE BRANCH

Lieutenant Governor

The **lieutenant governor** is the second highest-ranking official in the state, but the executive powers of this office are limited. Were the governor to die, be incapacitated, be removed from office, or voluntarily leave office in midterm, the lieutenant governor would become governor. That eventuality has occurred only four times. In 1917, William P. Hobby replaced James E. Ferguson, who was impeached. Governor W. Lee O'Daniel resigned in 1941 to enter the U.S. Senate and was succeeded by Coke Stevenson. Governor Beauford Jester died in office in 1949 and was replaced by Allan Shivers. And George W. Bush resigned in December 2000 after being elected president and was succeeded by Rick Perry.

In Texas, the office of lieutenant governor is primarily a legislative office. Many experts consider this position, because of its key legislative role and statewide constituency, the most powerful office in state government. The lieutenant governor, who need not belong to the same party as the governor and is elected independently of the governor, presides over the senate and has traditionally been given enormous power over the legislative process by the senate rules. The legislative powers and prerogatives far exceed those of the vice president on the federal level. The lieutenant governor also chairs the Legislative Budget Board, which plays a key role in the state budgetary process.

Democrat Bill Hobby, son of the former governor, served a record eighteen years as lieutenant governor before retiring in 1991. He was succeeded by Democrat Bob Bullock, a former state comptroller and one of the most influential state officials in recent history (see Chapter 24). Bullock, who chose not to seek reelection in 1998 and died the next year, was succeeded by Republican Rick Perry, a former state agriculture commissioner.

Perry generally received high marks from senators for his work as presiding officer, but he presided over the senate for only one session before succeeding Bush as governor after the 2000 presidential election. State senators then elected Senator Bill Ratliff (R-Mt. Pleasant) to complete Perry's term as lieutenant governor and preside over the senate during the 2001 session. Republican David Dewhurst was elected lieutenant governor in 2002. The former land commissioner had no legislative experience but made a quick, yet thorough, study of major issues and legislative procedures (see Chapter 24).

Attorney General

As the state's chief legal officer, the **attorney general** is called upon to defend state laws enacted by the legislature and orders adopted by regulatory agencies. The office also enforces the state's antitrust and consumer protection laws and helps collect child support payments from delinquent noncustodial parents. Recent attorneys general have been kept busy defending the state or negotiating settlements in lawsuits challenging the constitutionality of state prisons, the public school finance system, the method of selecting state judges, and other major policies.

Unlike counterparts in the federal government and some other states, the Texas attorney general is primarily a civil lawyer. Except for representing the state in the appeals of death penalty cases and assisting local prosecutors, the attorney general has relatively little responsibility for criminal law enforcement. Many candidates for the office campaign on tough law and order platforms, but responsibilities for criminal prosecution are vested in locally elected county and district attorneys. The attorney general also gives opinions on the legality of actions of other state and local officials and is at the center of the policy-making process.[12]

Dan Morales, a former Democratic state representative from San Antonio, was elected attorney general in 1990, becoming the second Hispanic elected to statewide office in Texas. He won reelection in 1994 but choose not to run for a third term in 1998. He was succeeded by former Texas Supreme Court Justice John Cornyn, Texas's first

---

lieutenant governor
The presiding officer of the senate. This officeholder would become governor if the governor were to die, be incapacitated, be removed from office, or leave office voluntarily in midterm.

attorney general
The state's chief legal officer, who represents Texas in lawsuits and is responsible for enforcing the state's antitrust, consumer protection, and other civil laws.

PEOPLE & POLITICS *Making a Difference* ★★★

ATTORNEY GENERAL DAN MORALES

Dan Morales was one of state government's biggest vote-getters during two terms as attorney general and, as only the second Hispanic ever elected to statewide office in Texas, was considered a rising star of the Democratic party. He chose not to seek reelection in 1998. But before leaving office, he sued the tobacco industry over smoking-related health care costs and won a $17.3 billion settlement for the state from cigarette manufacturers. The settlement, to be paid out over many years, would generate huge amounts of revenue for health care or any other programs the legislature chose.

The settlement was clearly the highlight of Morales's political career, but, ironically, it also contributed to his eventual downfall. The settlement sparked much controversy over $3.3 billion in legal fees awarded to five private lawyers whom Morales had hired under a contingency contract to represent the state in the litigation. Although tobacco companies agreed to pay the lawyers' fees, Attorney General John Cornyn, Morales's Republican successor, called the payments excessive. He also questioned the legality of the outside lawyers' agreement with Morales and spent much of his first year in office investigating the lawyers' work. The legal fees also were attacked by business groups seeking limits on civil court judgments and lawyers' payments. These same groups—so-called tort reformers—had contributed heavily to Cornyn's election campaign.

Neither Cornyn nor federal prosecutors found any illegalities in Morales's dealings with the five lawyers or in the outside lawyers' work for the state. But Morales's attempt to steer as much as $520 million in legal fees to a sixth lawyer, Marc Murr of Houston, resulted in a lengthy federal investigation. Morales said Murr, a personal friend, was an important part of his antitobacco legal team, but other lawyers said Murr did little, if any, work on the case.

While the investigation, which stretched over four years, was still pending, Morales attempted a political comeback by running for governor in the 2002 Democratic primary. He lost to Laredo businessman Tony Sanchez and later crossed party lines to endorse Republican Governor Rick Perry, who defeated Sanchez in the general election.

Finally, in March 2003, a federal grand jury indicted Morales, accusing him of trying to improperly steer millions of dollars in legal fees from the tobacco settlement to Murr. The indictment also charged the former attorney general with misappropriating campaign money to make a downpayment on a $775,000 house while he was still in office, lying on a loan application for a $600,000 mortgage and filing a false income tax return for 1998, his last year in office. Seven months later, Morales was sentenced to four years in federal prison after pleading guilty to mail fraud and filing a false income tax return. He admitted backdating a government contract and forging government records related to the tobacco suit. In a separate deal with prosecutors, Murr pleaded guilty to one count of mail fraud.

Morales expressed "sincere regret and remorse" at his sentencing before U.S. District Judge Sam Sparks of Austin. But he said that the "vast majority of misdeeds" he had been accused of were untrue. Most political observers were left scratching their heads.

Source: *Houston Chronicle,* November 1, 2003, p. 29A.

Republican attorney general in modern times. Cornyn was elected to the U.S. Senate in 2002 and was succeeded by Republican Greg Abbott, another former Texas Supreme Court justice.

In a major policy decision made independently of the governor, the legislature, and other state officials, Morales in 1996 filed a multibillion-dollar damage suit against tobacco companies, seeking reimbursement for public health care costs associated with smoking. Some state officials supported Morales's decision, although others had reservations about the state jumping into the tobacco controversy. But Morales acted within his authority as the state's chief legal officer. The decision was his alone to make, and it resulted in a $17.3 billion settlement for the state. The tobacco suit also sparked a controversy over legal fees that, several years after Morales had left office, resulted in his being sentenced to federal prison for four years for mail fraud and filing a false income tax return (see *People and Politics: Making a Difference:* Attorney General "Dan Morales").

Carole Keeton Strayhorn, the first Republican comptroller of modern times, won a second term in 2002.

Comptroller of Public Accounts

The **comptroller** is the state's primary tax administrator, accounting officer, and revenue estimator. Texas functions under a **pay-as-you-go principle**, which means that the state cannot adopt an operating budget that exceeds anticipated revenue. The comptroller is responsible for providing the revenue estimates on which biennial state budgets are drafted by the legislature. A budget cannot become law without the comptroller's certification that it falls within the official revenue projection. The comptroller's office produces a revenue estimate of all projected state income for the two-year budget period by using sophisticated models of the state's economy.[13]

The comptroller's powerful role in budgetary affairs was enhanced by the legislature in 1990 with the additional authority to conduct management audits of local school districts, and again in 1991 with similar oversight authority over other state agencies. Through this process, Comptroller John Sharp, a Democrat, and his successor, Republican Carole Keeton Strayhorn, identified billions of dollars' worth of potential savings for legislative budget writers and local school boards (see *People and Politics: Making a Difference:* "Texas Comptroller Carole Keeton Strayhorn").

Strayhorn, who changed her name from Rylander after marrying in early 2003, was a strong supporter of—and reaped favorable publicity from—the management audits. But the legislature, in a 2003 special session, transferred those programs to the Legislative Budget Board after the comptroller had become involved in a series of budgetary disputes with legislators and other Republican leaders. Always outspoken and widely viewed as politically ambitious, Strayhorn had surprised the governor and the legislature with a larger-than-anticipated revenue shortfall of $10 billion at the beginning of the 2003 regular session. Strayhorn later threatened—but only briefly—not to certify the new state budget drafted by lawmakers. And, finally, to make matters worse, she announced that the no-new-taxes budget about which the governor and Republican lawmakers had bragged actually included $2.7 billion in higher fees to be paid by millions of Texans. Strayhorn blamed Governor Rick Perry for the decision to strip the manage-

comptroller
The state's primary tax administrator, accounting officer, and revenue estimator.

pay-as-you-go principle
A principle written into the Texas Constitution prohibiting state government from borrowing money to meet its operating budget.

PEOPLE & POLITICS *Making a Difference* ★★★

MARTHA WHITEHEAD: SHE CAMPAIGNED TO END HER OWN JOB

State Treasurer Martha Whitehead was a rarity in politics—an office-holder who campaigned to abolish her own job. The treasurer's post was created by the constitution of 1876 to manage the state's money, but by the 1990s, it had become a relatively minor office overshadowed by the much larger fiscal operations of the state comptroller. It nevertheless still offered some political benefits for its occupants. Democrat Ann Richards, who was state treasurer for eight years, used the office to launch a successful race for governor. Republican Kay Bailey Hutchison, the next treasurer, made it a springboard to the U.S. Senate. But Whitehead, a Democrat appointed by Richards in 1993 to complete Hutchison's term when Hutchison was elected to the U.S. Senate, held the office for only a few months before deciding it was wasting taxpayers' money and needed to be abolished.

Pledging to lead a campaign to wipe the office off the books, Whitehead was elected to a new term in 1994 over a Republican opponent. Austin banker David Hartman, who argued that the treasurer's office should remain an independent agency to assure adequate checks and balances on state finances. The legislature placed a constitutional amendment on the November 1995 ballot to abolish the office and transfer its duties to the comptroller. The amendment was opposed by the State Republican Executive Committee but was overwhelmingly approved by voters. The comptroller's office estimated that taxpayers would save about $20 million during the first five years after the change. The elimination of the elected treasurer's post was effective on September 1, 1996. Some of the agency's 200 employees were transferred to the comptroller's office, but officials estimated that about 160 jobs would soon be phased out.

Whitehead's successful initiative to eliminate the treasurer's office and the subsequent reassignment of its functions reinforce arguments made by critics of the Texas constitution. There are state and county constitutional offices, created in an earlier political context, that may no longer have significant functions or responsibilities. They are costly and perform overlapping or redundant functions. Some segments of the population may have a vested interest in maintaining these offices but they do little to serve the public interest. In some cases, necessary functions can be assigned to other agencies. The sunset laws apply to non-constitutional agencies of the state, but they do not apply to the offices created by the Texas constitution. There is no provision to review the functions and effectiveness of constitutional offices. So it takes a somewhat unusual political effort to review, modify, or eliminate a constitutional agency. Whitehead's efforts demonstrate that for the foreseeable future, constitutional changes will occur on a piecemeal basis.

ment audit programs from her agency. The governor's office denied the allegation, but Perry had signed the bill. Strayhorn was so angry that she strongly hinted that she might challenge Perry in the 2006 Republican gubernatorial primary. And, over the next several months, she delivered a series of public speeches criticizing the governor's budgetary priorities.

Commissioner of the General Land Office

Texas retains ownership, including the mineral rights, to approximately 22 million acres of public lands, which are managed by the state **land commissioner**. Revenues generated by mineral leases and other land uses are earmarked for education through the Permanent University Fund and the Permanent School Fund. This agency is also responsible for the Veterans Land Program, which provides low-interest loans to veterans for the purchase of land and houses.

During sixteen years in office, Land Commissioner Garry Mauro, a Democrat, developed several environmental initiatives, including beach cleanup efforts and a program for cleaning up oil spills off the Texas coast. Mauro also took the lead in developing a coastal zone management plan to coordinate environmental protection efforts along

land commissioner
The elected official who manages the state's public lands and administers the Veterans Land Program, which provides low-interest loans to veterans for the purchase of land and houses.

Republican Jerry Patterson, a former state senator, was elected land commissioner in 2002.

the coast. After Mauro unsuccessfully ran for governor in 1998, the next land commissioner, Republican David Dewhurst, a businessman from Houston, continued the beach cleanup efforts. Dewhurst also won legislative approval of a program to replenish beaches and protect them from erosion. Dewhurst was elected lieutenant governor in 2002 and was succeeded as land commissioner by Jerry Patterson, a former state senator from Harris County. Patterson's priorities included development of new nursing homes for veterans and new veterans' cemeteries.

Commissioner of Agriculture

The **agriculture commissioner** is responsible for carrying out laws regulating and benefiting the agricultural sector of the state's economy. In addition to providing support for agricultural research and education, the agency is responsible for the administration of consumer protection laws in the areas of weights and measures, packaging and labeling, and marketing. Republican Rick Perry aggressively promoted Texas agricultural products during two terms as commissioner. Republican Susan Combs, a former state representative from Austin, was elected to the office in 1998 after Perry ran for lieutenant governor. She also urged Texans to buy more produce grown in the Lone Star State and, concerned about obesity among Texas children, she led a campaign to reduce the sales of soft drinks and junk foods in the public schools.

Secretary of State

The **secretary of state**, the only constitutional official appointed by the governor, has a variety of duties, including granting charters to corporations and processing the extradition of prisoners to other states. The primary function of this office, however, is to administer state election laws. That responsibility includes reviewing county and local election procedures, developing statewide policy for voter registration, and receiving and tabulating election returns.

State Treasurer

The constitution of 1876 created a **state treasurer** to be the custodian of state funds. Shortly after taking office in 1993, however, Treasurer Martha Whitehead came to believe the office was no longer needed. She convinced the legislature and the voters to abolish it with a constitutional amendment, which was adopted in 1995. The agency's duties were transferred to the comptroller's office.

ELECTED BOARDS AND COMMISSIONS

Only two of the more than 200 boards and commissions that head most state agencies are elected. They are the Texas Railroad Commission and the State Board of Education.

Texas Railroad Commission

The **Railroad Commission** was originally designed to regulate intrastate (within Texas) operations of railroads. It also regulated intrastate trucking for many years. But it lost its trucking responsibilities and most of its railroad regulation to the federal government. It still has some oversight over rail safety and regulates oil and natural gas production and lignite mining in Texas.

The commission includes three elected members who serve six-year staggered terms and rotate the position of chair among themselves. The oil and gas industry has historically focused much attention on this agency and made large campaign contributions to commission members. Many critics claim the commission is a prime example of a regulatory body that has been co-opted by those interests it was created to regulate. And, in recent years, it has become a staging area for opportunistic politicians

agriculture commissioner
The elected official responsible for administering laws and programs that benefit agriculture.

secretary of state
The official who administers state election laws, grants charters to corporations, and processes the extradition of prisoners to other states. This officeholder is appointed by the governor.

state treasurer
This elective office was created by the Constitution of 1876 to manage state funds. It was abolished by the voters in 1995, and its duties were transferred to the comptroller's office.

Railroad Commission
A three-member, elected body that has some oversight over rail safety but now primarily regulates oil and natural gas production in Texas.

who seek election to the commission primarily as a stepping-stone to higher office. A commissioner doesn't have to resign in the middle of his or her six-year term to seek another office and, as an incumbent regulator, has little trouble collecting large contributions from the oil and gas industry that can be used to further political ambitions. Both Democrat John Sharp and Republican Carole Keeton Strayhorn used seats on the commission to strengthen their political bases for successful races for state comptroller in 1990 and 1998, respectively. Other recent commission members haven't been as successful, but not because they didn't try. Between 1980 and 2002, fifteen people served on the commission, and only four actually completed a full six-year term. One recent commissioner, Tony Garza, resigned in midterm to accept President George W. Bush's appointment as ambassador to Mexico.

The game of musical chairs has prompted calls in recent years for the commission to be abolished and its duties transferred to other agencies appointed by the governor, including the Public Utility Commission, which already has oversight over electric utilities, and the Texas Commission on Environmental Quality, the state's main environmental protection agency. Democrat Hector Uribe, a former state senator, ran for the commission in 1996, promising to work to abolish it. But Strayhorn, his Republican opponent, argued that the agency was important and needed to be retained. Strayhorn defeated Uribe for a six-year term on the commission, but two years later she ran for and won election to the comptroller's office.

State Board of Education

Prior to educational reforms enacted in 1984, the **State Board of Education** was made up of 27 members elected from congressional districts across the state. At the urging of reformers dissatisfied with student performance, the legislature provided for a new education board of fifteen members to be appointed by the governor and confirmed by the senate. The idea was to reduce the board's independence while new education reforms ordered by the legislature were being carried out. But the law also mandated that the board once again become an elected body within a few years. Some state leaders later proposed that the board remain appointive and put the question to the voters, who opted for an elected board in 1986. The present board has fifteen members elected from districts established by the legislature.

Philosophical and partisan bickering on the board in recent years prompted the legislature to reduce its powers. The panel's main remaining duties include investment of education dollars in the Permanent School Fund and some oversight over textbook selection and curriculum standards.

But the day-to-day administration of the Texas Education Agency, the agency responsible for public education, is under the direction of the commissioner of education, who is appointed by the governor.

THE TEXAS BUREAUCRACY

A loosely connected, highly fragmented, and often confusing network of approximately 250 state agencies and universities with more than 300,000 full- and part-time employees is responsible for carrying out programs and policies approved and funded by the legislature and the governor. In addition, more than 950,000 other full- and part-time workers are employed by school districts, cities, counties, and special districts in Texas.

This **bureaucracy** is often on the receiving end when someone complains about government. But without it, government would come to a grinding halt. The bureaucracy issues drivers' licenses, builds highways, distributes welfare benefits, and performs myriad other public services. On an individual basis, the bureaucracy is the clerk, the inspector, the highway patrol officer, the computer programmer, the engineer, or one of hundreds of other occupational specialists delivering state services on a daily basis. On a larger scale, it is an assortment of agencies, some employing thousands of individuals, with designated responsibilities for specific public programs and services.

State Board of Education
An elected panel that oversees the administration of public education in Texas.

bureaucracy
The agencies of government and their employees responsible for carrying out policies and providing public services approved by elected officials.

Although it is overstating the case to say that the bureaucracy runs state government, its role is enhanced in Texas because the legislature meets in regular session only five months every other year and the governor has only limited powers over the executive branch. The part-time boards and commissions that oversee most state agencies can exercise considerable independence in interpreting policies and determining the character and the quality of public services. Many boards depend heavily on the guidance of veteran administrators and career bureaucrats within their agencies.

THE GROWTH OF GOVERNMENT IN TEXAS

In 1967, there were 388,000 full-time state and local government employees in Texas. Thirty years later, there were almost three times that many (Table 25–2). By 1997, the latest year for which we have comprehensive data, Texas had 582 full-time state and local government employees per 10,000 residents, making it eleventh highest in that category among the 50 states. Texas had only 137 state employees per 10,000 population, forty-fourth among the states. But its 447 local government workers per 10,000 population ranked sixth highest.[14] The number of employees has increased along with the state's population since the 1997 Census of Governments, but the rankings have remained much the same. Many services performed by local governments—including education, fire and police protection, and sanitation services—require large numbers of professionals and other workers.

There has been a substantial expansion of programs at all levels of government in recent years. State spending during the 1982–83 biennium was $25.6 billion, and only 22 years later, the legislature appropriated $118 billion for the 2004–2005 biennium. Nevertheless, Texas still ranks low in per capita expenditures. Texas was fiftieth among the states in per capita spending by state government alone—$2,611 per person—in 2000. When combined state and local spending was compared, Texas rose to forty-fifth, thanks partly to the large share of public school costs borne by local taxpayers. In such key areas as per capita state spending on public health, education, and welfare, Texas ranked below many other states.[15]

Efforts to curtail government growth and spending have met with only marginal success. Texas citizens have come to expect a wide range of public services, and these expectations increase as the population grows. The federal government also has imposed mandates on state and local governments that require additional expenditures and personnel. Moreover, the success of interest groups in winning approval of new programs adds to the growth of public employment. The legislature reduced spending on many programs to help bridge a $10 billion revenue shortfall in 2003. And that same

TABLE 25–2 EMPLOYMENT BY TYPE OF GOVERNMENT, 1967–1997

Unit of Government	Full-Time Equivalent Employees			
	1967	*1977*	*1987*	*1997*
State	88,734	163,870	198,769	261,975
Total Local	299,578	477,177	646,913	850,380
Counties	32,978	60,287	77,851	103,481
Municipalities	75,168	115,481	139,340	160,574
School Districts	177,734	282,492	400,035	539,530
Special Districts	13,698	18,917	29,687	46,794
Total Texas	**388,312**	**641,047**	**845,682**	**1,112,355**

Source: U.S. Department of Commerce, Bureau of the Census, *Census of Governments, 1967*, vol. 3, no. 2, table 15; *Census of Governments, 1977*, vol. 3, no. 2, table 13; *Census of Governments, 1987*, vol. 3, no. 2, table 14; *Census of Governments, 1997*, vol. 1, table 12.

year, it ordered a major reorganization of health and human services agencies, with an eye toward privatizing some services. But it remained to be seen how those budget cuts and changes would affect overall state government employment.

Some 80 percent of state government employees work in three areas: higher education, public safety and corrections, and social services (which include public welfare and health care). Most employees of county governments work in social services, public safety and corrections, and general governmental administration (Table 25–3). More than one-third of city employees are engaged in fire and police protection, and another 30 percent work for city utilities and in housing, sewerage, sanitation, parks and recreation, and natural resources departments. Elementary and secondary schoolteachers are employees of local school districts.

BUREAUCRATS AND PUBLIC POLICY

The bureaucracy does more than carry out the policies set by the legislature. It is involved in virtually every stage of the policy-making process. The legislature usually broadly defines a program and gives the affected agency the responsibility for filling in the details.[16] Administrative agencies can sometimes interpret a vaguely worded law differently from its original legislative purpose. Although the legislature can use oversight committees and the budgetary process to control the bureaucracy, agencies often have resources and political influence that protect their prerogatives. Many appointed agency heads have political ties to interest groups affected by the work of their agencies, and these officials help develop policy alternatives and laws because legislators depend on their technical expertise.

Policy Implementation

Although one state agency may be primarily responsible for translating legislative intent into a specific program, other governmental bodies are also involved. The courts, for example, shape the actions of bureaucrats through their interpretation of statutes and administrative rules. And there may be jurisdictional and political battles between different agencies over program objectives.

In some cases, a new agency may have to be organized and staffed to carry out the goals of a new law. More often, however, the new responsibilities are assigned by the legislature to an existing agency, which develops the necessary rules, procedures, and

---

TABLE 25–3 STATE AND LOCAL EMPLOYMENT BY GENERAL FUNCTIONS, 1997

	State	Counties	Cities/Towns	School Districts	Special Districts
Education	32.7%	0.8%	2.7%	100.0%	-
Social services*	30.1	28.0	7.5	—	52.8
Public safety and corrections	17.7	33.6	35.6	—	0.2
Transportation	5.4	8.2	8.6	—	1.7
Government administration	6.5	22.5	9.4	—	-
Environment housing	5.1	2.4	18.5	—	15.6
Utilities	—	0.1	11.8	—	28.1
All other	2.6	4.4	5.9	—	1.5
Total Employees	**261,975**	**103,481**	**160,574**	**539,530**	**46,794**

*Includes income maintenance.

SOURCE: U.S. Department of Commerce, Bureau of the Census, *1997 Census of Governments*, vol. 1, table 13.

guidelines for operating the new program. Additional employees are hired if the legislature provides the necessary funding. If not, responsibilities are reassigned among existing personnel. Sometimes tasks are coordinated with other agencies. Ultimately, all this activity translates into hundreds of thousands of daily transactions between governmental employees and the public.

Almost everyone has heard horror stories about persons who have suffered abuse or neglect at the hands of public employees and agencies. Whether they involve an indigent family that fell through the cracks of the welfare system or a county jail prisoner who was lost in the administrative process of the judicial system, these stories tend to reinforce the suspicion and hostility that many people have toward bureaucracies and public employees. Unquestionably, such abuses deserve attention and demand correction, yet thousands of governmental programs are successfully carried out with little or no fanfare and are fully consistent with the purpose of the authorizing legislation.

Most public employees take pride in what they do and attempt to be conscientious in translating policy objectives into workable public services. They are citizens and taxpayers who also receive services from other state and local agencies. A complex, interdependent state that is home to more than 22 million people depends on the effectiveness and efficiency of governmental agencies. That activity appears, on the whole, to be mutually satisfactory or beneficial to most parties.

Obstacles to Policy Implementation

When things go wrong in state government and problems go unresolved, there is a tendency to blame the bureaucrats for excessive red tape, inefficiency, mismanagement, or incompetence. "Bureaucrat bashing" plays well politically, and many candidates for public office run on such campaigns. But in many cases they are unfairly blaming government employees for complex problems that policy makers have been unable, or unwilling, to resolve. One high-profile issue is the perennial struggle to improve the quality of the public education system. Some of the criticism directed at educational bureaucrats has been justified, but the legislature and the governor are ultimately responsible for the enactment of sound educational policies—and the development of a sufficient and equitable system of paying for them.

Some legislative policies may be misdirected, with little potential for producing the intended results. Or economic and social conditions may change, making programs inappropriate. In hindsight, administrators may also find that approaches different from those outlined by the legislature would have worked better. The legislature also frequently fails to fund programs adequately. In some cases, those charged with carrying out a new policy may not have the know-how or the resources to make it work. And, finally, programs often produce unanticipated results.

The accountability and responsiveness of state and local agencies are also affected by other factors, including the influence of special interests. Thanks to the clout of special interest lobbyists with the legislature, regulatory agencies are often headed by boards with a majority of members from the professions or industries they are supposed to regulate. Many taxpayers may feel this system is merely a legalized way of letting the foxes guard the henhouse. It is an extension of the **iron triangle** concept, whereby special interests seek to influence not only the legislators responsible for enacting laws but the agencies responsible for enforcing them.

Business and professional groups argue that their professions can be regulated effectively only by individuals knowledgeable in their fields. Although that argument has some validity, it also increases the potential for incestuous relationships that mock the regulatory process. There is always the possibility—and often the likelihood—that industry representatives serving on boards, commissions, or in agencies will be inclined to protect their industries against the best interests of consumers. This pattern of influence and control is often referred to as *cooptation*, underscoring the possibility that agencies may be captured by the industries they are supposed to regulate. Licensing agencies may also seek to adopt unfair regulations designed to restrict new competitors from entering an industry.

iron triangle
Mutually supportive interrelationships among the interest groups, administrative agencies, and legislative committees involved in drafting the laws and regulations affecting a particular area of the economy or a specific segment of the population.

Historically, many nine-member state regulatory boards included only industry representatives. But under the sunset review process, discussed in more detail later in this chapter, laws have gradually been changed to turn over some positions on most of those boards to members of the public. The Sunset Advisory Commission has concluded:

> Boards consisting only of members from a regulated profession or group affected by the activities of an agency may not respond adequately to broad public interests. This potential problem can be addressed by giving the general public a direct voice in the activities of the agency through representation on the board.[17]

The "fox and the henhouse" approach to state regulation was highlighted when Governor Ann Richards demanded that the Texas Department of Health crack down on deplorable conditions in some nursing homes. It was revealed that state inspectors had repeatedly found unsanitary conditions in three nursing homes partly owned by a member of the Texas Board of Health. The board member, an appointee of former Governor Bill Clements, denied any allegations of improper care but resigned after moving to another state.[18] Texas law in effect then required that one member of the eighteen-member health board be involved in the nursing home industry and the other members represent other health care professions. The board has since been restructured.

STRATEGIES FOR CONTROLLING THE BUREAUCRACY

Elected policy makers can use several strategies to control bureaucracies and help ensure that policies are implemented as intended:

- Change the law or make legislation detailed enough to reduce or eliminate the discretionary authority of an agency.

- Overrule the bureaucracy and reverse or rescind an action or decision of an agency. With the independence of many agencies, boards, and commissions at the state level, the governor can reverse few agency decisions. Consequently, this step often requires legislative action.

- Transfer the responsibility for a program to another agency through administrative reorganization.

- Replace an agency head who refuses to or is incapable of carrying out program objectives. But there are only a few agencies over which the governor can directly exercise such authority in Texas.

- Cut or threaten to reduce the budget of an agency to force compliance with policy objectives.

- Abolish an agency or program through sunset legislation.

- Pressure the bureaucracy to change with legislative hearings and public disclosures of agency neglect or inadequacies.

- Protect public employees who reveal incompetence, mismanagement, and corruption through **whistleblower** legislation (see *FYI:* "Should Texas Toughen Its Whistleblower Laws to Protect Public Employees?").

- Enact **revolving door** restrictions to reduce or eliminate the movement of former state employees to industries over which they had regulatory authority.[19]

The Revolving Door

Over the years—at least until 1991—many regulatory agencies had become training grounds for young attorneys and other professionals taking their first jobs out of college or law school. They would work for state agencies for a few years for relatively low pay while gaining valuable experience in a particular regulatory area and making influential

whistleblower
A public employee who reports illegal activities or "blows the whistle" on agency wrongdoing.

revolving door
A term describing the practice of former members of state boards and commissions or key employees of agencies leaving state government for more lucrative jobs with the industries they used to regulate.

contacts in the state bureaucracy. Then they would leave state employment for higher-paying jobs in the industries they used to regulate and would represent their new employers before the state boards and commissions for which they had once worked—or they would become consultants or join law firms representing regulatory clients. Former gubernatorial appointees to boards and commissions—not just hired staffers—also participated in this revolving door phenomenon, which raised ethical questions about possible insider advantages.

An early step in restricting the revolving door was part of the Public Utility Regulatory Act (PURA) of 1975 that created the Public Utility Commission (PUC); this law prohibited PUC members and key staffers from going to work for regulated utilities immediately after leaving the agency. The ethics reform law of 1991 expanded the restrictions to other agencies.

Legislative Budgetary Control

Every two years, the legislature sets the budgets for state agencies but subsequently provides little oversight as to how effectively the money is spent, unless there is a financial crisis requiring a special legislative session or an emergency transfer of funds by the governor and the Legislative Budget Board. Perhaps the most control that lawmakers exercise over agency spending, besides setting the bottom line, is their approval of a number of line items in agency budgets that restrict portions of the funds to specific programs.

Sunset Legislation

Although Texas has been slow to modernize its budgetary process and other key functions of state government, it was one of the first states to require formal, exhaustive reviews of how effectively agencies are doing their jobs. The **sunset** law enacted in 1977 was so named because most agencies have to be periodically recreated by the legislature or automatically go out of business. Relatively few agencies—except for a number of inactive ones like the Pink Bollworm Commission and the Stonewall Jackson Memorial Board—have been abolished. But the obligatory review has produced some significant structural and policy changes in the state bureaucracy that the legislature may not have otherwise ordered. It also has expanded employment opportunities for lobbyists, because special interest groups have much to win or lose in the sunset process. In many cases, special interests have succeeded in protecting the status quo.

Each agency is usually up for review every twelve years, under a rotating order set out in the sunset law. The review begins with the Sunset Advisory Commission, which includes four state representatives appointed by the speaker of the house, four senators appointed by the lieutenant governor, and two public members, one named by the speaker and the other by the lieutenant governor. The commission employs a staff that studies each agency up for review during the next regular, biennial legislative session and reports its findings to the panel, which makes recommendations to the legislature.

In a few cases, the commission proposes that an agency—usually a minor one—be terminated or consolidated with another agency. In most cases, however, the commission recommends the continuation of an agency but outlines suggested changes in its organizational structure and/or operations. The future of the agency is then debated by the full legislature. If lawmakers fail to approve a sunset bill for any agency by September 1 of the year the agency is scheduled for review, the agency will be phased out of existence over the next year, or it will be terminated abruptly on September 1 if the legislature also refuses to approve a new budget for the agency. In recent years, however, the legislature has postponed controversial sunset decisions by passing special laws to allow some agencies to stay open past their review dates.

The Texas Higher Education Coordinating Board is subject to sunset review, but individual universities are not. Also exempted from sunset review are the courts and state agencies created by the constitution, such as the governor's office, the attorney general, the comptroller, and the General Land Office.

The sunset process has not reduced the size of the bureaucracy. By 2001, there were more than 277,000 full-time state employees, compared to about 164,000 in 1977, the

sunset
The process under which most state agencies have to be periodically reviewed and recreated by the legislature or go out of business.

WHAT CAN HAPPEN TO A WHISTLEBLOWER?

Governmental agencies make mistakes that can be very costly to the public in terms of financial waste or neglect. Texas has a whistleblower protection law, which is designed to protect public employees who report wrongdoing within their agencies to their supervisors. If an employee is subjected to retaliation after having come forward, the law permits the worker to file a lawsuit against the offending agency.

A major test of the effectiveness of the law was brought by George Green, an architect for the Texas Department of Human Services (DHS). Green complained of shoddy construction on agency facilities, kickbacks, and noncompliance with contracts. He said his supervisors refused to take action against the offending contractors. After he went public with his charges, Green was fired by the agency for allegedly abusing sick leave time and making one unauthorized call on his state telephone—a 13-cent call to his father. Criminal charges were brought against him, and, although they were eventually dropped, he had spent $130,000 in legal fees, could not find a new job, and had depleted many of his personal assets.

Green sued the state and won a $13.6 million judgment from a Travis County jury in 1991. The amount included $3.6 million in actual damages that Green had suffered and $10 million in punitive damages to punish the state for the way he had been treated. The state appealed, dragging out a resolution of the case, until the judgment was upheld by the Texas Supreme Court in 1994. But the legislature was not in session that year, and state leaders said there was no money in the state budget to pay Green. So the whistleblower had to wait for the legislature to convene in 1995. Green, meanwhile, was still unemployed and living off the generosity of friends and family and a personal loan he had made against a portion of his judgment.

By the time the legislature convened in January 1995, Green's judgment, with interest, had grown to almost $20 million, and interest continued to grow at the rate of more than $4,500 a day. The whistleblower's case also was receiving considerable media attention, nationally as well as in Texas. But many legislators, particularly in the house, did not want to pay him the full amount, which they considered excessive. They particularly objected to the $10 million the jury had awarded as punitive damages and pointed out that taxpayers would ultimately have to pick up the tab.

Green refused to accept an amount smaller than the judgment and interest, and the 1995 session ended in late May without Green receiving any payment. Legislators, however, took steps to ensure that such a large whistleblower judgment would never be awarded again. They changed the law to limit whistleblower suit damages against the state to $250,000. Critics of the change warned it would seriously curtail whistleblower suits—and damage an important taxpayer protection— because the best lawyers, whose fees are based on the size of a judgment, would no longer accept whistleblower cases.

Finally, in November 1995, Green reached a compromise with legislative leaders. The Legislative Budget Board (LBB), which can transfer funds when the full legislature is not in session, approved a $13.8 million settlement, which Green accepted. Part of the money went to lawyers and a lobbyist who had helped Green collect payment, and $1 million went to an investor who had loaned Green money during his battle. Lieutenant Governor Bob Bullock, who chaired the LBB, apologized to Green and called his ordeal a "black mark on the history of Texas."*

Even then, Green's story continued. A former consultant sued Green for allegedly failing to pay him for helping Green collect the judgment from the state. In December 1996 another Travis County jury awarded the former consultant more than $600,000 in actual and punitive damages against Green.

Green's experience speaks to a major problem. Few public employees can afford to be subjected to this type of retaliation, and few have the resources to fight state government. Although the original intent of the law was to protect whistleblowers and to encourage their coming forward with inside information, most state and local employees may have received a different message from the Green case and the legislature's decision to weaken the law.

*Quoted in *Houston Chronicle*, November 16, 1995.

year the sunset law was approved. Although more than 45 agencies had been terminated or merged, others had been created (see Table 25–4). But Bill Wells, the Sunset Advisory Commission's former executive director, said the statistics did not tell the full story. He believed the sunset process had served to slow down the creation of new agencies. "You can't say how many [new agencies] would have been created if sunset hadn't heightened the awareness of the fact that we've got maybe too many agencies now," he said. "There is a heightened awareness of the fact that you need to go a little slower and you need to really have a problem before you create an agency."[20]

TABLE 25–4   SUNSET ACTION FROM 1979 TO 2003, 66TH TO 78TH LEGISLATIVE SESSIONS

Actions Taken	Total	Percent
Agencies reviewed	346*	
Agencies continued	282	81%
Agencies abolished outright	31	9
Agencies abolished and functions transferred	16	5
Agencies combined	11	3
Agencies separated	2	1

*Some agencies reviewed were not subject to continuation or abolishment.

SOURCE: Texas Sunset Advisory Commission.

The sunset review process has helped rid state government of some deadwood, modernized some state laws and bureaucratic procedures, and made some agencies more responsive and accountable to the public. Under a sunset policy discussed earlier in this chapter, public members have been added to the boards of regulatory agencies that previously had included only representatives of the professions or industries that they regulated.

The largest agencies and those with influential constituencies are usually the most difficult to change because special interests are working overtime and making large political contributions to protect their turf. In 1993, for example, the insurance lobby succeeded in weakening some regulatory reforms in the Department of Insurance sunset bill. In another case, there was such a high-stakes battle involving telephone companies, newspaper publishers, electric utilities, and consumers over the Public Utility Commission sunset bill that the legislature postponed action for two years. The lobby's influence over the 1993 sunset bills prompted Governor Ann Richards and some legislative leaders to suggest that the sunset process should be changed or repealed because it was being abused by special interests. But consumer advocates, who value the sunset process, blamed the problem on legislators who had difficulty saying "no" to special interest lobbyists.

Performance Reviews

Facing a large revenue shortfall in 1991, the legislature directed Comptroller John Sharp to conduct unprecedented performance reviews of all state agencies to determine ways to eliminate mismanagement and inefficiency and to save tax dollars. Sharp recommended $4 billion in spending cuts, agency and funds consolidations, accounting changes, some minor tax increases, and increases in various state fees to reflect more accurately the costs of providing services. Pressure from special interests killed many of the recommendations, but the legislature adopted about $2.4 billion of them. Sharp produced follow-up reports in 1993, 1995, and 1997, and his successor, Carole Keeton Strayhorn, continued the performance reviews after she took office. At the beginning of the 2003 regular legislative session, Strayhorn made 64 recommendations for further restructuring of state agencies and their operations, some of which were adopted by lawmakers. The comptroller also has similarly reviewed the operations of a number of local school districts.

The performance reviews generally have been considered instrumental in improving administrative practices. But as discussed earlier in this chapter, the legislature, with Governor Rick Perry's approval, transferred the work from the comptroller's office to the Legislative Budget Board after a series of budgetary disputes with Strayhorn in 2003. The move was criticized by those who believed the reviews should have remained under the oversight of an independently elected officeholder, but it remained to be seen what the ultimate effect of the transfer would be.

One of Sharp's proposals adopted by the legislature in 1993 created the Council on Competitive Government, which was designed to give Texas businesses more opportunities to bid on state contracts and provide some state services more efficiently. It also enabled state agencies to bid on services performed by other state agencies if the bidding agencies thought they could do the work more efficiently. The council, which evaluates the proposals, includes the governor, the lieutenant governor, the comptroller, the chair of the General Services Commission, and the employee representative on the Texas Workforce Commission.[21]

Some state government functions had been privatized before the council was created. One of the best known was the state lottery, which was administered from the beginning by a private company under a state contract.

Merit Systems and Professional Management

One hundred years ago, public employees in Texas were hired on the basis of **political patronage**, or the personal relationships they had with elected or appointed officials. Little consideration was given to their skills, competence, or expertise. Few rules dictated terms of employment, advancement, or the rights or conduct of public employees, and wages and salaries varied widely from agency to agency. There also were high rates of employee turnover.

To serve the public and state workers more effectively, some reform advocates pushed for a **merit system** based, in part, on the Civil Service Commission created by the federal government for its workers in 1883. Although some other states have developed comprehensive statewide employment or personnel systems administered by a single agency, the reform movement in Texas has not been as successful. Improvements have been made, but state government here continues to function under a decentralized personnel system, in part because the various elected executive officeholders have jealously guarded their prerogatives to hire and fire the people who work for them.

Texas's personnel "system" is not a merit system but a highly fragmented arrangement with different agencies assigned various personnel responsibilities. Ultimately, the legislature has the legal authority to define personnel practices, and the biennial budget is the major tool used by legislators to establish some 1,300 job classifications and corresponding salary schedules. The legislature also establishes policies on vacations, holidays, and retirement. But the primary responsibility for carrying out personnel policies is still delegated to the various state agencies. An administrator can develop specific policies for an agency as long as the agency works within the general framework defined by the legislature.

All state job openings are required to be listed with the Texas Workforce Commission. Agencies also advertise for workers through the mass media and college placement centers. But many jobs still are filled as a result of friendships, other personal contacts, and the influence of key political players.

Higher and public education employees are subject to different employment policies, which are determined by individual university governing boards and local school districts. Unlike state government, many cities across Texas have adopted centrally administered merit systems organized around the accepted principles of modern personnel management.

political patronage
The hiring of government employees on the basis of personal friendships or favors rather than ability or merit.

merit system
A personnel system in which public employees are selected for government jobs through competitive examinations and are systematically evaluated after being hired.

S U M M A R Y

1. Although it is the most visible office in state government and the public believes it has considerable power, the office of governor is weak in formal powers.

2. Unlike the president of the United States, governors of Texas have no formal cabinet that serves at their pleasure. Texas has a "plural executive," which includes several other statewide officeholders elected independently of the governor. This diffusion of power was a reaction to the abuses of the Davis administration during the Reconstruction era, but reform advocates argue that this structure diminishes the capacity of the executive branch to respond to the state's modern problems.

3. Other elected officeholders in the executive branch are the lieutenant governor, the attorney general, the comptroller, the land commissioner, the agriculture commissioner, and members of the Texas Railroad Commission and the Texas State Board of Education. The top appointed official in the executive branch is the secretary of state. Although the lieutenant governor is part of the executive branch, the duties of that office are primarily legislative.

4. Administrative responsibilities are further fragmented through approximately 250 boards and commissions authorized by statutory law. Although the governor appoints individuals to these boards, the governor's control is diluted by board members' staggered terms, the need for

senatorial approval of the governor's appointments, and legal requirements relating to the composition of these boards.

5. Besides appointments, the governor's main formal powers are the veto of legislation, line-item veto authority over the budget, and the authority to call and set the agenda for special sessions of the legislature.

6. As part of the judicial powers, a governor can stay executions and, with the recommendation of the Board of Pardons and Paroles, grant full or conditional pardons or commute a death sentence to life imprisonment. The governor is the commander-in-chief of the state's military force and is responsible for maintaining order within the state and responding to various disasters by mobilizing the National Guard.

7. Potentially, the governor also has a number of informal resources that can be used to shape public policy and the administrative process. Governors have used their staffs, their access to the mass media, their party roles, and their relationships to key interest groups to bring pressure to bear on legislators and other elected officials.

8. More than one million Texans are employed by state and local governments. Collectively, we refer to them and the agencies for which they work as the bureaucracy. The bureaucracy has the primary responsibility of carrying out public policies adopted by the legislature and local governing bodies. But administrative agencies also are involved in virtually every stage of the policy-making process. Legislators depend on administrative agencies for counsel and advice when they draft public policies, and they rely on them to help assess the success or failure of policies.

9. When things go wrong and problems go unresolved, there is a tendency to blame bureaucrats. But often government employees are unfairly blamed for complex problems that elected policy makers have been unwilling or unable to resolve. The fragmented structure of the executive branch of state government is, in itself, a major obstacle to the efficient, responsive delivery of public services. There also is the potential for agencies

headed by appointed, part-time boards to become unaccountable to the electorate and susceptible to the influence of special interest groups.

10. Through sunset legislation, Texas became one of the first states to require formal reviews of how effectively state agencies are doing their jobs. Most state agencies are subject to periodic review and reauthorization by the legislature. The process has not reduced the size of the bureaucracy, but it has helped rid state government of obsolete agencies and produced greater accountability. Texas also has adopted revolving door restrictions. Former board members and key employees of regulatory agencies are prohibited from going to work for regulated companies within a certain period after leaving their state posts.

11. Although many local governments have adopted merit employment systems, state government functions under a decentralized personnel system. It is highly fragmented, with each agency largely free to set its own personnel policies.

K E Y   T E R M S

plural executive	senatorial courtesy	agriculture commissioner	whistleblower
impeachment	extradition	secretary of state	revolving door
special session	lieutenant governor	state treasurer	sunset
veto	attorney general	Railroad Commission	political patronage
line item veto	comptroller	State Board of Education	merit system
Legislative Budget Board	pay-as-you-go principle	bureaucracy	
staggered terms	land commissioner	iron triangle	

F U R T H E R   R E A D I N G

BARTA, CAROLYN. *Bill Clements: Texian to His Toenails.* (Eakin Press, 1996). A detailed account of Bill Clements's three campaigns for governor and his two terms in office.

BEYLE, THAD. "Governors: The Middlemen and Women in Our Political System." In *Politics in the American States: A Comparative Analysis,* 6th ed., ed. Virginia Gray and Herbert Jacob. (CQ Press, 1996). A comparative analysis of the formal and informal powers of U.S. governors.

FREDERICK, DOUGLAS W. "Reexamining the Texas Railroad Commission." In *Texas Pol-*

itics: A Reader, ed. Anthony Champagne and Edward J. Harpham (New York: W.W. Norton, 1997). Using theories of capture, authors address the issue of the Railroad Commission's domination by the oil and gas industries which it regulates.

GANTT, FRED, JR. *The Chief Executive in Texas: A Study in Gubernatorial Leadership.* (University of Texas Press, 1964). An extensive analysis of the governorship of Texas, including the development of the office and roles played by governors in the administrative and policy processes.

HENDRICKSON, KENNETH E. *Chief Executives of Texas: From Stephen F. Austin to John B. Connally, Jr.* (Texas A & M University Press, 1995). Brief biographic sketches of the political careers of 43 individuals who have held the office of governor or president of the Republic.

MORRIS, CELIA. *Storming the Statehouse: Running for Governor with Ann Richards and Dianne Feinstein.* (Scribner's Sons, 1992). An analysis of the hotly contested 1990 governor's race.

PRINDLE, DAVID. *Petroleum Politics and the Texas Railroad Commission.* (University of Texas Press, 1981). An assessment of energy policy in Texas and the role of the Railroad Commission in policy development and industry regulation.

TEXAS GENERAL LAND OFFICE. *The Land Commissioners of Texas.* (Texas General Land Office, 1986). Brief biographical sketches of past land commissioners.

TOLLESON-RINEHART, SUE. *Claytie and the Lady: Ann Richards, Gender and Politics in Texas.* (University of Texas Press, 1994).

THE TEXAS JUDICIARY

26

THE POWER OF THE COURTS IN TEXAS

Although most people would like to think that justice in Texas is blind, it is not. Most judges try to be fair, but, even so, their decisions are molded by their political and ideological views, life experiences, ethnicity and gender. In recent years, moreover, Texas courts have been beset by a series of controversies that also have severely strained the popular notion that the scales of justice are balanced in an atmosphere that is above reproach. Instead, large campaign contributions to elected state judges from lawyers who practice before them and from other special interests have fueled a high-stakes war for philosophical and political control of the judiciary. The practice has drawn frequent criticism and even raised questions in the national media about whether Texas courtrooms are "for sale."

Women and minorities, meanwhile, remain grossly underrepresented among the ranks of Texas judges. And the basic structure of the judicial system—an assortment of about 2,600 courts of various, often overlapping jurisdictions—is so outdated that many experts believe it should be overhauled. But change doesn't come easily.

State courts resolve civil disputes over property rights and personal injuries. They also determine guilt or innocence and set punishment in criminal cases involving offenses against people, their property, and public institutions. And, to a more limited extent than the federal judiciary, they help set public policy by reviewing the actions of the executive and legislative branches of government. A civil dispute may stem from something as simple as a tenant's breaking an apartment lease to something as complex and potentially expensive as a manufacturer's liability for defective tires that contribute to the deaths or injuries of dozens of motorists. Criminal cases range from traffic offenses, punishable by fines, to capital murder, for which the death penalty can be imposed.

1876	Establishment of the current court structure
1891	Creation of the Court of Criminal Appeals to hear appeals of criminal cases
1935	Sarah Hughes is the first woman to serve as a state district judge
1977	Legislature enacts law providing for execution by lethal injection
1982	First execution under new law
1989	Lawsuit tried in federal court to address minority under-representation on state courts
1993	Fifth Court of Appeals ruled present system of judicial selection constitutional
1995	Modest limits imposed on campaign contributions to judges and judicial candidates
1995	Major changes in state's tort laws
1999	All nine justices of the Supreme Court and nine judges of the Court of Criminal Appeals are Republicans
2003	Renewed legal attacks on school finance
2003	Additional tort reforms

penal code
Body of law that defines most criminal offenses and sets a range of punishments that can be assessed.

felony
Serious criminal offense that can be punished by imprisonment and/or a fine.

misdemeanor
Minor criminal offense punishable by a fine and/or a short sentence in the county jail.

civil lawsuit
Noncriminal legal dispute between two or more individuals, businesses, governments, or other entities.

statutes
Laws enacted by a legislative body.

plaintiff
Individual or party who initiates a lawsuit.

Some streamlining of Texas's judicial processes, especially at the appellate level, was accomplished in 1981. But the Texas judiciary, particularly in urban areas, has become overloaded by criminal cases and an increasingly litigious approach to civil disputes. It can take months to get a civil or a criminal case—one that is not settled out of court or in a plea bargain with prosecutors—to trial.

The State Courts in the Federal System

Like people in every state, Texans are subject to the jurisdiction of both state and federal courts. The federal judiciary has jurisdiction over violations of federal laws, including criminal offenses that occur across state lines, and over banking, securities, and other activities regulated by the federal government. Federal courts have also had major effects on state government policies and Texas's criminal justice system through interpretations and applications of the U.S. Constitution and federal laws, including the Bill of Rights.

Although Texas has a bill of rights in its constitution, the federal courts have taken the lead in protecting many civil and political rights, as when the U.S. Supreme Court declared the white primary election unconstitutional in *Smith* v. *Allwright* in 1944 (see Chapter 23).[1] Federal court intervention continues in the redistricting of legislative and congressional district lines. The federal judiciary also has ordered far-reaching improvements in the state prison system. And when police officers read criminal suspects their rights, the officers are complying with constitutional requirements determined by the U.S. Supreme Court in the *Miranda* case.[2]

Nevertheless, it is estimated that more than 97 percent of all litigation is based on state laws or local ordinances. Thus anyone involved in litigation is likely to be found in a state rather than a federal court.

The Legal Framework of the Judicial System

The United States and Texas constitutions form the basic legal framework of the Texas court system. Building on that framework, the Texas legislature has enacted codes of criminal and civil procedure to govern conduct in the courtroom and statutory laws for the courts to apply. Most criminal activities are defined and their punishments established in the Texas **penal code**. In criminal cases, the state—often based on charges made by another individual—initiates action against a person accused of a crime. The most serious criminal offenses, for which prison sentences can be imposed, are called **felonies**. More minor offenses, punishable by fines or short sentences in county jails, are called **misdemeanors**. Many property crimes and drug offenses are classified as state jail felonies and are punishable by community service work or time in a state jail, a prison-like facility operated by the state.

Civil lawsuits, which can be brought under numerous **statutes**, involve conflicts between two or more parties—individuals, corporations, governments, or other entities. Civil law governs contracts and property rights between private citizens, affords individuals an avenue for relief against corporate abuses, and determines liability for personal injuries. Administrative law includes enforcement powers over many aspects of the state's economy.

An individual with a grievance to be addressed has to take the initiative of going to court. A person can experience problems with a landlord who refuses to return a deposit, a dry cleaner that lost a suit, or a friend who borrowed and wrecked a car. But in a civil dispute, there is no legal issue to be resolved unless a lawsuit is filed. An injured person filing a lawsuit is a **plaintiff**. Because even the most minor disputes in the lowest courts can require professional assistance from a lawyer, a person will soon discover that the pursuit of justice can be very costly and time consuming.

Statutes and constitutional laws are subject to change through legislative action and popular consent of the electorate, and over the years there have been significant changes in what is legal and illegal, permissible and impermissible. At one time, for example, state law provided for a potential life prison sentence for the possession of a few ounces of marijuana. Small amounts are now considered a misdemeanor punishable by a fine. The legal drinking age was lowered to eighteen for a few years but was reestablished at 21 after parents and school officials convinced the legislature that the younger age had helped increase alcohol abuse among teenagers.

THE STRUCTURE OF THE TEXAS COURT SYSTEM

There are five levels of Texas courts, but some courts at different levels have overlapping authority and jurisdiction (see Figure 26–1). Some courts have only **original jurisdiction**; that is, they try or resolve only those cases being heard for the first time. They weigh the facts presented as evidence and apply the law in reaching a decision or verdict. Other courts have only **appellate jurisdiction**. They review the decisions of lower courts to determine if constitutional and statutory principles and procedures were correctly interpreted and followed. Appellate courts are empowered to reverse the judgments of the lower courts and to order cases to be retried if constitutional or procedural mistakes were made. Still other courts have both original and appellate jurisdiction.

At the highest appellate level, Texas has a **bifurcated court system**, with the nine-member Texas Supreme Court serving as the court of last resort in civil cases and the nine-member Texas Court of Criminal Appeals functioning as the court of last resort in criminal cases. Only one other state, Oklahoma, has a similar structure.[3]

Unlike federal judges, who are appointed by the president to lifetime terms, state judges, except for those on municipal courts, are elected to limited terms in partisan elections. Midterm vacancies, however, are filled by appointment. Vacancies on the justice of the peace and county courts are filled by county commissioners courts, while vacancies on the district and appellate benches are filled by the governor.

Courts of Limited Jurisdiction

The lowest-ranking courts in Texas are municipal courts and justice of the peace courts. You or someone you know has probably appeared before a judge in one of these courts because both handle a large volume of traffic tickets. Some of these courts are big revenue raisers for local governments, and they are often accused of subordinating justice and fairness to financial considerations.[4]

Some 882 **municipal courts** are established under state law, including some with multiple judges. The qualifications, terms of office, and methods of selecting municipal judges are determined by the individual cities, but they are generally appointed by the city council. Municipal courts have original and exclusive jurisdiction over city **ordinances**, but most of these courts are not courts of record, where a word-for-word transcript is made of trial proceedings. Only very rudimentary information is officially recorded in most of these courts, and any appeal from them is heard **de novo** by the higher court; that is, the second court has to conduct a new trial and hear the same witnesses and evidence all over again because no official record of the original proceedings was kept. The informality of these proceedings and the absence of a record add to the confusion and cost of using the system.[5] In response to these problems, the legislature in recent years has created municipal courts of record for some cities.

Each county in Texas is required to provide for one **justice of the peace court**, and each county government in the larger metropolitan areas may create sixteen (see Chapter 27). There are 835 of these courts in Texas. Justices of the peace are elected to four-year terms from precincts, or subdivisions of the county drawn by the commissioners court, which also sets their salaries. Justices of the peace are not required to be licensed attorneys, a situation that has generated much criticism of these courts.

original jurisdiction
Authority of a court to try or resolve a civil lawsuit or a criminal prosecution being heard for the first time.

appellate jurisdiction
Authority of a court to review the decisions of lower courts to determine if the law was correctly interpreted and legal procedures were correctly followed.

bifurcated court system
Existence of two courts at the highest level of the state judiciary. The Texas Supreme Court is the court of last resort in civil cases, and the Texas Court of Criminal Appeals has the final authority to review criminal cases.

municipal court
Court of limited jurisdiction that hears cases involving city ordinances and primarily handles traffic tickets.

ordinances
Local laws enacted by a city council.

de novo
In a civil lawsuit or criminal trial, evidence is presented again before an appellate court because no record was kept of the evidence presented to the trial court.

justice of the peace court
Low-ranking court with jurisdiction over minor civil disputes and criminal cases.

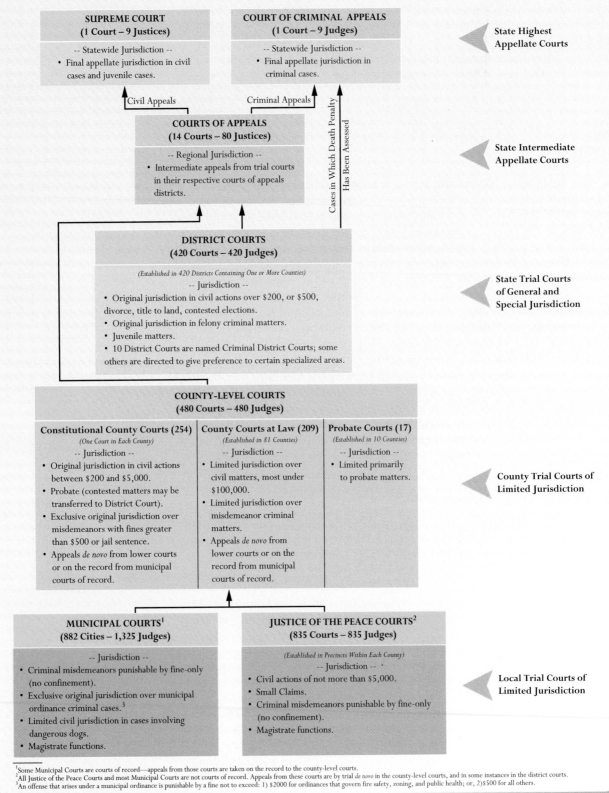

FIGURE 26–1 Court Structure of Texas.
SOURCE: Office of Court Administration, September 2003.

Associate Judge Peter Sakai is seen presiding over the Child Abuse and Neglect Court in San Antonio.

Although their duties vary from county to county, justice of the peace courts, with certain restrictions, have original jurisdiction in civil cases when the amount in dispute is $5,000 or less and have original jurisdiction over criminal offenses that are punishable by fines only. In some areas of criminal law, they have overlapping jurisdiction with municipal courts. Justices of the peace also sit as judges of small-claims courts, and in many rural counties they serve as coroners. They also function as state magistrates with the authority to hold preliminary hearings to determine if there is probable cause to hold a criminal defendant.

These are not courts of record, and cases appealed from these courts are tried de novo in county courts, county courts-at-law, or district courts. Each justice court has an elected constable to serve warrants and perform other duties for the court.

County Courts

If there is confusion about the authority and jurisdiction of municipal and justice of the peace courts, it is compounded by the county courts. They were created by the Texas constitution to serve the needs of the sparsely populated, rural society that existed when the charter was written in 1875. But population growth and urbanization have placed enormous demands on the judicial system, and rather than modernize the system, the state has added courts while making only minor changes in the structure and jurisdiction of the older courts.

Each county has a **constitutional county court**. The holder of this office, the county judge, is elected countywide to a four-year term. This individual is the chief executive officer of the county and presides over the county commissioners court, the policy-making body of county government (see Chapter 27). Most urban county judges do not perform judicial duties, but county judges in many rural counties perform both executive and judicial functions, a dual responsibility that some experts believe is inconsistent with the Texas constitution's separation-of-powers doctrine. Although a large number of county judges are lawyers, they are not required to be. They are required only to be "well informed in the law" and to take appropriate courses in evidence and legal procedures.

The constitutional county court shares some original civil jurisdiction with both the justice of the peace and the district court. It has original criminal jurisdiction over misdemeanors punishable by fines of more than $500 and jail sentences of one year or less. These courts also probate wills and have appellate jurisdiction over cases tried originally in justice of the peace and municipal courts.

Over the years, the legislature also has created 226 **statutory county courts**, or county courts-at-law, in more than 70 counties. Some specialize in probate cases and are called probate courts. These courts were designed to deal with specific local problems

constitutional county court
County court created by the Texas Constitution, presided over by the county judge.

statutory county court
Court that exercises limited jurisdiction over criminal and/or civil cases. The jurisdiction of these courts varies from county to county.

JUSTICE DELAYED, JUSTICE DENIED?

Trial delays are bad enough for prosecutors and taxpayers. But they can be a nightmare for criminal defendants innocent of the charges against them, especially if they have to spend months in jail awaiting trial. In one case, a 23-year-old construction worker from Mexico spent 575 days—more than a year and a half—in the Tarrant County jail awaiting trial on charges of fondling a five-year-old girl.* When his case finally reached the courtroom, it took a jury 42 minutes to find him innocent and free him. His room and board in jail had cost Tarrant County taxpayers $23,000. But his ordeal had cost him much more, and his case should make all of us ask how long justice can be delayed before it is justice denied.

Fort Worth Star-Telegram, April 25, 1993.

---

district court
Primary trial court in Texas. It has jurisdiction over criminal felony cases and civil disputes.

plea bargaining
Procedure that allows a person charged with a crime to negotiate a guilty plea with prosecutors in exchange for a lighter sentence than he or she would expect to receive if convicted in a trial.

and, consequently, have inconsistent jurisdictions. Judges on these courts are elected countywide and have to be lawyers, but the authority of a particular court is defined by the legislation creating it. Some cannot hear civil disputes involving more than $2,500, while others can hear disputes involving as much as $100,000. Drunken driving cases are the primary criminal cases tried before these courts. Some of these courts also hear appeals de novo from lower courts.

County courts across the state disposed of more than 137,000 civil cases during the 2003 fiscal year but saw more than 148,000 cases added to their dockets. Approximately 553,000 criminal cases were disposed of, but an additional 550,000 cases were added. At the end of the year, more than 790,000 cases were pending before the county courts.[6]

Courts of General Jurisdiction

The primary trial court in Texas is the **district court**. Although there is some overlapping jurisdiction with county courts, the district courts have original jurisdiction over civil cases involving $200 or more in damages, divorce cases, contested elections, suits over land titles and liens, suits for slander or defamation, all criminal felony cases, and misdemeanors involving official misconduct. In recent years, the legislature has created district courts with specialized jurisdictions over criminal or civil law or over such specialties as family law—divorces and child custody cases. In some large metropolitan counties that have numerous district courts, the jurisdictions of the respective courts are determined by informal agreements among the judges. District court judges are elected to four-year terms, must be at least twenty-five years old, and must have practiced law or served as a judge of another court for four years prior to taking office.

The Texas Constitution gives the legislature the responsibility to define judicial districts, and as the expanding population produced greater caseloads, new districts were created. In 1981, there were 328 district courts. In 2003, there were 420. A single county may be allocated more than one district court with overlapping geographical jurisdiction. Harris County, the state's most populous county, has fifty-nine district courts, each covering the entire county. By contrast, one rural district court may include several counties. As these courts evolved, there was little systematic consideration of the respective workloads of individual courts, and there are now great disparities in the number of people that district courts serve.

Many urban counties suffer from a heavy backlog of cases that can delay a trial date in civil lawsuits and even some criminal cases for months or years. The district courts disposed of 513,000 civil cases and 241,000 criminal cases during the 2003 fiscal year, but new cases were added, and the courts began the 2004 fiscal year with 846,000 pending cases[7] (see *FYI:* "Justice Delayed, Justice Denied?").

Delays in criminal cases have prompted a widespread use of plea bargains. In **plea bargaining**, a criminal defendant, through a lawyer, negotiates with prosecutors a guilty plea that will get a lesser sentence than he or she could expect to receive if convicted in a trial. The process saves the state the time-consuming expense of a full-blown trial and has become an essential tool in clearing urban court dockets.

Former District Attorney John B. Holmes Jr., estimated that 90 percent of the thousands of felony cases filed in Harris County (Houston) each year were disposed of through plea bargains. Without plea bargains, the caseload would simply overwhelm the twenty-two Harris County district courts that handle criminal cases.

Harris County's civil district courts disposed of more than 84,000 lawsuits—divorces, personal injuries, tax disputes, and others—in fiscal year 2003 but left more than 101,000 other cases pending.[8] Many civil lawsuits are resolved through negotiations between the opposing parties, but those that are tried and appealed can take several years to be resolved.

The wide disparities in populations and caseloads served by the various district courts prompted the adoption of a constitutional amendment in 1985 that created the Judicial Districts Board. That panel was responsible for redrawing judicial districts with an eye toward a more equitable distribution of the workload. But in 1994, yielding to pressure from incumbent judges who did not want to lose their offices, it issued recommendations that primarily preserved the status quo. Extensive changes by the legislature were considered unlikely.

Although the district court is the state's primary trial court and the state pays the district judges' base salaries, the counties pick up virtually all other district court expenses. The counties provide courtrooms, pay the courts' operating expenses, and supplement the judges' state pay.

Intermediate Courts of Appeals

Fourteen intermediate **courts of appeals** cover thirteen multicounty regions that hear appeals of both civil and criminal cases from the district courts. Two courts, the First Court of Appeals and the Fourteenth Court of Appeals, are based in Houston and cover the same area. The Texas constitution provides that each court shall have a chief justice and at least two other justices, but the legislature can add to that number and has done so for most courts. Each Houston court has nine judges, and the Fifth Court of Appeals, in Dallas, has thirteen judges. Five of these intermediate courts, however, have only three members. Appellate judges are elected to six-year terms. They must be at least thirty-five years old and have at least ten years of experience as an attorney or a judge on a court of record.

Although the appellate courts disposed of more than 12,000 civil and criminal cases during fiscal 2003, they left almost 8,000 other cases pending on their dockets at the end of the year, with criminal cases accounting for more than half of the unfinished business.[9] But there are wide disparities in the caseloads between individual courts, with those in Houston and Dallas handling the lion's share. The Texas Supreme Court partially balances the load by transferring cases among courts. The courts of appeals normally decide cases in panels of three judges, but an entire court can hear some appeals en banc.

The Highest Appellate Courts

The creation of separate courts of last resort for civil and criminal cases was part of the effort by the constitutional framers of 1875 to fragment political power and decentralize the structure of state and local government. It was also based on the rationale that criminal cases should be tried more expeditiously, and the way to accomplish this was through a separate appellate court.

Although it decides only civil appeals, the **Texas Supreme Court** is probably viewed by most Texans as the titular head of the state judiciary, and it has been given some authority to coordinate the state judicial system.[10] The Supreme Court is charged with developing administrative procedures for the state courts and rules of civil procedure. It appoints the Board of Law Examiners, which is responsible for licensing attorneys, and has oversight of the state bar, the professional organization to which all lawyers in Texas must belong. The Supreme Court also has disciplinary authority over state judges through recommendations of the State Commission on Judicial Conduct.

The Texas Supreme Court includes a chief justice and eight justices who serve staggered six-year terms. Three members are up for election every two years on a statewide ballot. Members must be at least thirty-five years old and must have been a practicing attorney, a judge of a court of record, or a combination of both for at least ten years.

The **Texas Court of Criminal Appeals**, which hears only criminal cases on appeal, includes a presiding judge and eight other judges elected statewide to staggered six-year terms. The qualifications for members of this court are the same as those for the Texas Supreme Court.

Under the federal system, some decisions of the Texas Supreme Court and the Texas Court of Criminal Appeals can be appealed to the U.S. Supreme Court. Those cases have to involve a federal question or a right assured under the U.S. Constitution.

Texas Judges

In 2002, the last year for which extensive data were available, about one-half of the members of the intermediate and highest appellate courts had come to the bench from private law practice. About one-third had previously served on lower courts. Most

court of appeals
Intermediate-level court that reviews civil and criminal cases from the district courts.

Texas Supreme Court
Nine-member court with final appellate jurisdiction over civil lawsuits.

Texas Court of Criminal Appeals
Nine-member court with final appellate jurisdiction over criminal cases.

district judges had come to their offices from private law practice or from a prosecutor's office.

The development of a two-party system in Texas has affected the partisan affiliation of state judges. Republicans have seen election gains and more appointments to judicial vacancies. A number of judges also have switched from the Democratic party. By 2003, almost two-thirds of the judges at the district court level and higher were Republicans, including all nine members of the Texas Supreme Court and all nine members of the Texas Court of Criminal Appeals.

Most Texas judges are white males. With increasing frequency, women, Hispanics, and African Americans are entering the legal profession and running for judicial offices, but they are still proportionately underrepresented in the judiciary. As will be discussed later in this chapter, minorities have pressed for changes in the judicial selection process to enhance their chances to serve on the bench.

Judicial elections have been diluted by a large number of appointments to judicial vacancies. The governor appoints judges to fill midterm vacancies on the district and appellate courts. County commissioners courts fill midterm vacancies on county court-at-law and justice of the peace courts. Appointees are required to run for office in the next general election to keep their seats, but their incumbency can enhance their election chances.

Other Participants in the State Judiciary

County and district clerks, both elected offices, are custodians of court records. Bailiffs are peace officers assigned to the courts to help maintain order and protect judges and other parties from physical attacks. Other law enforcement officers play critical roles in the arrest, detention, and investigation of persons accused of crimes.

County attorneys and district attorneys are responsible for prosecuting criminal cases. Both positions are elected. Some counties do not have a county attorney. In those that do, the county attorney is the chief legal adviser to the commissioners court, represents the county in civil lawsuits, and may prosecute misdemeanors. The district attorney prosecutes felonies and, in some counties, also handles misdemeanors. The district attorney represents one county in metropolitan areas and several counties in less populated areas of the state (see Chapter 27).

Other important players in the judicial process are the private citizens who serve on juries. Although there is some debate about the competency of a jury of ordinary citizens to make reasonable decisions on complex and technical civil and criminal matters, no acceptable alternatives have been found.

Efforts to Reform the Judicial System

Judicial reform has been a recurring issue in Texas politics. Small, incremental changes have been made since the 1970s, but many jurists and scholars continue to push for an overhaul of the state courts. In September 1989, Texas Supreme Court Chief Justice Thomas R. Phillips requested an in-depth study of the Texas judiciary by the Texas Research League, a privately financed, nonprofit group specializing in studies of state government.

The League concluded that the court system was fundamentally flawed and sorely in need of an overhaul. It made 27 recommendations, including one that the legislature rewrite the judiciary article of the Texas constitution to provide a fundamental framework for a unified court system.[11]

Despite a series of similar studies and reports, however, reform of Texas courts has been difficult. The public may have a lot to gain from judicial restructuring, but the primary stakeholders—the judges, the attorneys, the court administrative personnel, and litigants who benefit from delays, confusion, and inefficiency—have resisted change. Unless there is a popular demand for reform, there will be few structural changes in the judiciary until some or all of these participants perceive some advantages from reform.

THE JURY SYSTEM

The Grand Jury

Citizens serve on two kinds of juries—grand juries and trial, or petit, juries. The **grand jury** functions, in theory, to ensure that the government has sufficient reason to proceed with a criminal **prosecution** against an individual. It includes twelve persons selected by a district judge from a list proposed by a jury commission appointed by the local district judge or judges. Although the grand jury evolved to protect the individual against arbitrary and capricious behavior by governmental officials, a district attorney can exercise great control over a grand jury through deciding what evidence and which witnesses jurors will hear. There also have been allegations over the years that grand juries overrepresent the interests of upper social and economic groups and underrepresent minorities. Grand jury meetings and deliberations are conducted in private, and the accused is not allowed to have an attorney present during grand jury questioning.

A grand jury usually meets on specified days of the week and serves for the duration of the district court's term, usually from three to six months. If at least nine grand jurors believe there is enough evidence to warrant a trial in a case under investigation, they will issue an **indictment**, or a "true bill"—a written statement charging a person or persons with a crime. A grand jury investigation also may result in no indictment, or a "no bill."

In some cases—especially when an investigation fails to produce a strong enough case for a felony indictment—grand juries issue indictments alleging misdemeanors. Most misdemeanors, however, are not handled by grand juries. They are handled by the district or county attorney, who prepares an **information**—a document formally charging an individual with a misdemeanor—on the basis of a complaint filed by a private citizen.

The Petit Jury

The jury on which most people are likely to be called to serve is the trial jury, or **petit jury**. Citizens who are at least eighteen years old and meet other minimal requirements are eligible for jury duty, and anyone refusing to comply with a jury summons can be fined for contempt of court (see *FYI:* "Is This Any Way to Round Up a Jury?"). Persons older than seventy, individuals with legal custody of young children, and full-time students are exempted from jury duty. The legislature in 1991 increased the likelihood of an individual's being called to jury duty by providing that county and district clerks prepare jury summonses from lists of those Texans who have drivers' licenses or hold Department of Public Safety identification cards. Previously, prospective jurors were chosen from voter registration lists, and it was believed that some Texans had not been registering to vote in order to avoid jury duty.

Six persons make up a jury in a justice of the peace or county court, and twelve in a district court. Attorneys for both sides in a criminal or civil case screen the prospective jurors, known as **veniremen,** before a jury is seated. In major felony cases, such as capital murder, prosecutors and defense attorneys may take several days to select a jury from among hundreds of prospects.

Attorneys for each side in a criminal case are permitted a certain number of peremptory challenges, which allow them to dismiss a prospective juror without having to explain the reason, and an unlimited number of challenges for cause. In the latter case, the lawyer has to state why he or she believes a particular venireman would not be able to evaluate the evidence in the case impartially. The judge decides whether to grant each challenge for cause but can rule against a peremptory challenge only if he or she believes a prosecutor is trying to exclude prospective jurors because of their race, such as keeping African Americans off a jury that is to try an African American defendant. If that happens, the defendant is entitled to a new group, or panel, of prospective jurors.

In civil cases, attorneys for both sides determine whether any persons on the jury panel should be disqualified because they are related to one of the parties, have some other personal or business connection, or could otherwise be prejudiced. For example, a lawyer defending a doctor in a malpractice suit probably would not want to seat a

grand jury
Panel that reviews evidence submitted by prosecutors to determine whether to indict, or charge, an individual with a criminal offense.

prosecution
Conduct of legal proceedings against an individual charged with a crime.

indictment
Written statement issued by a grand jury charging a person with a punishable offense.

information
Document formally charging a person with a misdemeanor.

petit jury
Panel of citizens that hears evidence in a civil lawsuit or a criminal prosecution and decides the outcome by issuing a verdict.

veniremen
Members of a panel from which a petit, or trial, jury is chosen.

IS THIS ANY WAY TO ROUND UP A JURY?

Some people called it "street justice." Others said it was bad public relations. It was probably both, and it was certainly unusual.

Justice of the Peace Mark Fury had scheduled a night jury trial for a minor traffic case in his southwest Houston courtroom but, at the last minute, discovered he didn't have enough jurors. So he issued a writ, ordering deputy constables to go across the street and round up some shoppers in a grocery store parking lot.

Nineteen people soon found themselves unexpectedly pressed into jury duty. Not all were chosen for the jury, but all had to report to the courtroom and had their evening plans disrupted. Several weren't too happy about it.

"It just seemed everybody was a little crusty toward everybody. They were just all mad," one draftee said.

Lisa Sedgwick, who had planned to go to a soccer game that night, ended up being the jury foreman instead.

The jury roundup, although rare, was legal. But people caught in the judge's net couldn't understand why he didn't just simply postpone the trial of such a minor case.

Fury said he believed the jurors had "a positive experience."

"I thought it went very smoothly. I expected there to be a larger number of acrimonious people," he said.

The jury convicted the defendant, a teenager, of speeding.

SOURCE: *Houston Chronicle*, August 22, 1997.

petition for review
Petition to the Texas Supreme Court claiming that legal or procedural mistakes were made in the lower court.

prospective juror who had been dissatisfied with his own medical treatment. Such potential conflicts are discovered by attorneys' careful screening and questioning of veniremen.

Unanimous jury verdicts are required to convict a defendant in a criminal case. In a criminal case, jurors have to be convinced "beyond a reasonable doubt" that a defendant is guilty before returning a guilty verdict. In contrast, agreement of only ten of the twelve members of a district court jury and five of the six on a county court jury are sufficient to reach a verdict in a civil suit.

JUDICIAL PROCEDURES AND DECISION MAKING

Civil litigants and criminal defendants (except those charged with capital murder) can waive their right to a jury trial if they believe it would be to their advantage to have their cases decided by a judge. Following established procedures, which differ between civil and criminal cases and are enforced by the judge, the trial moves through the presentation of opening arguments by the opposing attorneys, examination and cross-examination of witnesses, presentation of evidence, rebuttal, and summation. Some trials can be completed in a few hours, but the trial of a complex civil lawsuit or a sensational criminal case can take weeks or months. Convicted criminal defendants or parties dissatisfied with a judge or jury's verdict in a civil lawsuit can then appeal their case to higher courts.

The procedure in appellate courts is markedly different from that in trial courts. There is no jury at the appellate level to rehear evidence. Instead, judges review the decisions and the procedures of the lower court for conformance to constitutional and statutory requirements. The record of the trial court proceedings and legal briefs filed by the attorneys are available for appellate judges to review.

Most civil and criminal appeals are initially made to one of the fourteen intermediate courts of appeals. Parties dissatisfied with decisions of the courts of appeals can appeal to the Texas Supreme Court or the Texas Court of Criminal Appeals.

Cases reach the Texas Supreme Court primarily on **petitions for review**, usually filed by the losing parties, claiming that legal or procedural mistakes were made in the lower courts. These petitions are distributed among the nine Supreme Court justices. The justices and their briefing attorneys then prepare memoranda on their assigned cases

An attorney addressing a jury in a state court in Dallas.

for circulation among the other court members. Meeting in private conference, the court decides which applications to reject outright—thus upholding the lower court decisions—and which to schedule for attorneys' oral arguments. A case will not be heard without the approval of at least four of the nine justices.

Oral arguments, in which the lawyers present their perspectives on the legal points that are at issue in their case and answer questions from the justices, are presented in open court. Most hearings are held in the Supreme Court chambers in Austin, but since 1998 the court, in an effort to try to educate more people about its work, has been holding occasional hearings in other Texas cities. The responsibility for writing the majority opinions that state the court's decisions is determined by lot among the justices. It often takes several months after oral arguments before a decision is issued. Legal points and judicial philosophies are debated among the justices behind the closed doors of their conference room. But differences sometimes spill out for public view through split decisions and strongly worded dissenting opinions.

Most cases taken to the Texas Supreme Court on appeal are from one of the courts of appeals, but occasionally the Supreme Court receives a direct appeal from a district court. In recent years, the court has been hearing about 10 percent of the petitions for review it receives.

The Texas Supreme Court also acts on petitions for **writs of mandamus**, or orders directing a lower court or another public official to take a certain action. Many involve disputes over procedure or evidence in cases still pending in trial courts.

The Texas Court of Criminal Appeals has appellate jurisdiction in criminal cases that originate in the district and county courts. Death penalty cases are appealed directly to the Court of Criminal Appeals. Other criminal cases are appealed first to the intermediate courts of appeals. Either the defendant or the prosecution can appeal the courts of appeals' decisions to the Court of Criminal Appeals by filing petitions for discretionary review, which the high court may grant if at least four judges agree. The court sets one day a week aside for lawyers' oral arguments in the cases it agrees to review. The task of writing majority opinions is rotated among the nine judges.

JUDICIAL CONCERNS AND CONTROVERSIES

For more than twenty years, Texas courts have been at the center of conflict and controversy. Large campaign contributions from lawyers and other special interests to judges and judicial candidates have raised allegations that Texas has the best justice that money can buy. With billions of dollars at stake in crucial legal decisions, the Texas Supreme Court has been a philosophical and political battleground. Meanwhile, minorities— who hold a disproportionately small number of judicial offices—continue to press for greater influence in electing judges. Lengthy ballots, particularly in urban areas, make it increasingly difficult for most voters to choose intelligently among judicial candidates (see *People and Politics: Making a Difference:* Steve Mansfield, an Election Day Surprise). Although these issues and concerns may seem unrelated, they all share one important characteristic: they cast a cloud over the Texas judiciary. Each, in its own way, undermines public confidence in the state courts and makes many Texans question how just their system of justice is.

Judicial Activism

In earlier chapters, we noted the historical domination of Texas politics and policies by the conservative, business-oriented establishment. For decades, that domination also applied to the judiciary, as insurance companies, banks, utilities, and other large corporate entities became accustomed to favorable rulings from a Democratic, but conservative, Texas Supreme Court.

Establishment-oriented justices, usually elected with the support of the state's largest law firms, tended to view their role as strict constructionists. The legislature had the authority to enact public policy; the responsibility of the courts, they believed, was

writ of mandamus
Court order directing a lower court or another public official to take a certain action.

PEOPLE & POLITICS *Making a Difference* ★ ★ ★

STEVE MANSFIELD, AN ELECTION DAY SURPRISE

Like most other candidates for the Texas Court of Criminal Appeals, Houston attorney Steve Mansfield received little publicity when he began a campaign in 1994 to unseat Democratic Judge Charles Campbell, a twelve-year incumbent. Running as a crime victims' advocate, he defeated an equally unknown attorney for the Republican nomination and then got more publicity than he wanted—all of it negative. In the middle of his campaign, it was revealed that Mansfield had lied about his personal and political background and had exaggerated his legal experience. He was primarily an insurance lawyer with little experience in criminal law. But he unseated Campbell, thanks to heavy straight-ticket Republican voting in a GOP landslide.

Bad publicity continued to dog Mansfield even after he took office. Texas Republican party officials shunned him at a party fund-raiser, and the Board of Law Examiners investigated the circumstances under which he had obtained a Texas law license, which he had to have to serve on the court. But at his swearing-in ceremony in January 1995, Mansfield promised to be a hardworking judge, and he spent his first year in office living up to his promise by authoring 33 opinions, slightly more than the court average. It was unknown how much of the actual research and writing could be credited to Mansfield and how much to the experienced staff he inherited from Campbell and was wise enough to retain. But, as he had promised during his campaign, Mansfield usually sided with the prosecution.

Several months after Mansfield took office, the state bar publicly reprimanded him for his campaign lies. But the Board of Law Examiners did not challenge his law license, which cleared the way for him to remain on the court. Many judges, prosecutors, and other state officials considered Mansfield's election an embarrassment and a good argument for appointing, rather than electing, judges. But despite the controversy, Mansfield said he enjoyed his new job. "It's certainly been the greatest challenge I've ever faced. I've worked very hard to live up to the trust the people of Texas put in me," he said.*

Mansfield didn't seek reelection in 2000 and left the court after six years. Attempting a comeback, he ran for another Court of Criminal Appeals seat in the 2002 Republican primary but lost.

Unfortunately, Mansfield was not the first candidate of questionable qualifications to win election to a statewide court in Texas. The most infamous example was Donald B. Yarbrough. Yarbrough, also an unknown attorney from Houston, claimed that God had told him to run for the Texas Supreme Court. Thanks to his familiar name, he upset a much more qualified candidate, Appellate Judge Charles Barrow, for a seat on the high court in 1976. Yarbrough's name was

similar to that of Don Yarborough, who had run unsuccessfully for governor two times in the 1960s, and that of former U.S. Senator Ralph Yarborough. Yarbrough spent approximately $350 campaigning, while Barrow had the endorsement of the legal establishment.

Yarbrough, a Democrat, served about six months on the Supreme Court, then became the target of a criminal investigation and resigned as the legislature was preparing to remove him. After he left the court, he was convicted of lying to a grand jury investigating allegations that he plotted to have a banker killed. Yarbrough was sentenced to five years in prison. While free on bond during an appeal, he left the country to attend medical school in Grenada and refused to return when his appeal was denied. He finally was apprehended in the Caribbean, sentenced to two additional years for bond jumping, and imprisoned.

*Quoted in *Houston Chronicle*, June 28, 1995.

to narrowly interpret and apply the law. Judges were not to engage in setting policy but were to honor legal precedent and prior case law, which had generally favored the interests of corporations over those of consumers, laborers, and the lower social classes.

The establishment began to feel the first tremors of a philosophical earthquake in the 1970s. The Texas Trial Lawyers Association, whose members represent consumers in lawsuits against businesses, doctors, and insurance companies, increased its political activity. And in 1973, the legislature, with increased minority and female membership from single-member House districts ordered by the federal courts (see Chapter 24), enacted the Deceptive Trade Practices–Consumer Protection Act, which encouraged plaintiffs, or injured parties, to take their grievances to court. Among other things, the new law allowed plaintiffs to sue for attorneys' fees as well as compensatory and punitive damages.

Trial, or plaintiffs', attorneys, who usually receive a healthy percentage of monetary damages awarded their clients, began contributing millions of dollars to successful Texas Supreme Court candidates, and judicial precedents started falling. A revamped court issued significant decisions that made it easier for consumers to win large judgments for medical malpractice, faulty products, and other complaints against businesses and their insurers. The new activist, liberal interpretation of the law contrasted sharply with the traditional record of the court. "All of a sudden, we have a magnificent Supreme Court, which is not controlled by a sinister, rich, opulent elite," trial attorney Pat Maloney of San Antonio, a major contributor to Supreme Court candidates, said in a 1983 interview with the *Fort Worth Star-Telegram*.[12]

The business community and defense lawyers accused the new court majority of exceeding its constitutional authority by trying to write its own laws. Some business leaders contended that the court's activism endangered the state's economy by discouraging new businesses from moving to Texas, a fear that was soon to be put to partisan advantage by Republican leaders.

Judicial Impropriety

Controversy over the Texas Supreme Court escalated into a full-blown storm in 1986 when the Judicial Affairs Committee of the Texas House investigated two justices, Democrats C. L. Ray and William Kilgarlin, for alleged improper contact with attorneys practicing before the court. The two justices denied the allegations, made largely by former briefing attorneys, but never testified before the legislative panel. Both justices had consistently sided with plaintiffs' lawyers and had received considerable campaign support from them, and they contended the investigation was politically motivated and orchestrated by defense lawyers and corporate interests opposed to their judicial activism.

Chief Justice John L. Hill voluntarily testified before the committee and said he suspected but could not prove that information about the Supreme Court's deliberations on some cases had been improperly leaked to outsiders. Hill urged the committee to let the State Commission on Judicial Conduct, a state agency charged with investigating complaints of ethical violations by state judges, look into the allegations and "let the chips fall where they may."[13] The committee eventually concluded its investigation without recommending any action against the justices.

But in June 1987, the State Commission on Judicial Conduct issued public sanctions against both. Ray was reprimanded for seven violations of the Code of Judicial Conduct, including the acceptance of free airplane rides from attorneys practicing before the court and improper communication with lawyers about pending cases. Kilgarlin received a milder admonishment because two of his law clerks had accepted a weekend trip to Las Vegas from a law firm with cases pending before the court. Both justices were cited for soliciting funds from attorneys to help pay for litigation the justices had brought against the House Judicial Affairs Committee and a former briefing attorney who testified against them.

Later in 1987, the Texas judiciary, particularly the Texas Supreme Court, received negative publicity on a national scale when the high court upheld a record $11 billion judgment awarded Pennzoil Company in a dispute with Texaco, Inc. Several members of the Supreme Court were even featured on a network television program that questioned whether justice was "for sale" in Texas. The record judgment was awarded to Pennzoil after a state district court jury in Houston had determined that Texaco had wrongfully interfered in Pennzoil's attempt to acquire Getty Oil Company in 1984. Texaco, which sought protection under federal bankruptcy laws, later reached a settlement with Pennzoil, but it also waged a massive public relations campaign against the Texas judiciary.

In a segment on CBS-TV's *60 Minutes,* correspondent Mike Wallace pointed out that plaintiffs' attorney Joe Jamail of Houston, who represented Pennzoil, had contributed $10,000 to the original trial judge in the case and thousands of dollars more to

Texas Supreme Court justices. The program also generally criticized the elective system that allowed Texas judges legally to accept large campaign contributions from lawyers who practiced before them. The program presented what had already been reported in the Texas media, but after the national exposure, Governor Bill Clements and other Republicans renewed attacks on the activist, Democratic justices. And some Texas newspapers published editorials calling for changes in the judicial selection process.

Campaign Contributions and Republican Gains

Chief Justice Hill, a former attorney general who had narrowly lost a gubernatorial race to Clements in 1978, had been a strong supporter of electing state judges and had spent more than $1 million winning the chief justice's seat in 1984. As did his colleagues on the court, he accepted many campaign contributions from lawyers. But in 1986, Hill announced that the "recent trend toward excessive political contributions in judicial races" had prompted him to change his mind.[14] He now advocated a so-called **merit selection** plan of gubernatorial appointments and periodic retention elections. But the other eight Supreme Court justices—like Hill, all Democrats—still favored the elective system, and the legislature ignored pleas for change.

Hill resigned from the court on January 1, 1988, to return to private law practice and lobby as a private citizen for changing the judicial selection method. His resignation and the midterm resignations of two other Democratic justices before the 1988 elections gave Republicans a golden opportunity to make historic inroads on the high court. And they helped the business community regain control of the court from plaintiffs' attorneys.

Party realignment, including midterm judicial appointments by Clements, had already increased the number of Republican judges across the state, particularly on district court benches in urban areas. But only one Republican had ever served on the Supreme Court in modern times. Will Garwood was appointed by Clements in 1979 to fill a vacancy on the court but was defeated by Democrat C. L. Ray in the 1980 election. GOP leaders already had been planning to recruit a Republican slate of candidates for the three Supreme Court seats that normally would have been on the ballot in 1988. Now, six seats were contested, including those held by three new Republican justices appointed by Clements to fill the unexpected vacancies. Even though a full Texas Supreme Court term is six years, the governor's judicial appointees have to run in the next election to keep their seats. Clements appointed Thomas R. Phillips, a state district judge from Houston, to succeed Hill and become the first Republican chief justice since Reconstruction.

The competing legal and financial interests in Texas also understood that the six Texas Supreme Court races on the 1988 ballot would help set the philosophy of the court for years to come. Consequently, these were the most expensive court races Texas had ever experienced, with the twelve Republican and Democratic nominees raising $10 million in direct campaign contributions. Contributions to the winners averaged $836,347. Phillips, one of three Republican winners, spent $2 million, the most by a winning candidate. Some individual donations to other candidates were as large as $65,000.[15] Reformers argued that such large contributions created an appearance of impropriety and eroded public confidence in the judiciary's independence.

But the successes of Republicans and conservative Democrats in the 1988 races probably hindered, more than helped, the cause of reforming the judicial selection process. The business and medical communities, which had considerable success fighting the plaintiffs' lawyers under the existing rules—with large campaign contributions of their own—were pleased with the election results. "I'm a happy camper today," said one lobbyist for the Texas Medical Association, whose political action committee had supported two conservative Democratic winners and the three Republican victors.[16]

In several key liability cases over the next few years, the Supreme Court began to demonstrate a rediscovered philosophy favoring business defendants over plaintiffs.[17]

Republicans won a fourth seat on the court in 1990 and a fifth in 1994, to give the GOP a majority for the first time since Reconstruction. Republican challengers in 1994 also unseated nineteen incumbent Democratic district judges in Harris County in strong straight-party voting. Republicans picked up a sixth and a seventh seat on the Supreme

merit selection
Proposal under which the governor would appoint state judges from lists of potential nominees recommended by committees of experts. Appointed judges would have to run later in retention elections to keep their seats but would not have opponents on the ballot. Voters would simply decide whether a judge should remain in office or be replaced by another gubernatorial appointee.

Court after two Democratic justices resigned in midterm in 1995 and were replaced with Republican appointees of Governor George W. Bush. Republicans completed their sweep of the high court in 1998 when Justice Rose Spector, one of two remaining Democratic justices, was unseated by Republican Harriet O'Neill and Democrat Raul A. Gonzalez retired in midterm and was replaced by Bush appointee Alberto R. Gonzales. No Democratic challengers filed for the three Supreme Court seats that were on the 2000 ballot. Democrats ran for all five seats on the 2002 ballot but lost all five races.

Phillips, the chief justice, was reelected over minor opposition in 2002 and accepted no campaign contributions that year. He resigned in midterm in 2004 to become a visiting professor at the South Texas College of Law in Houston. Phillips believed the court's reputation had been enhanced during his tenure, but, as his predecessor had done on stepping down 16 years earlier, he criticized the money-driven, partisan election system for judges. He said it "creates great instability in the judiciary and erodes public confidence in the fairness of our decisions."[18]

Legislative Reaction to Judicial Activism

The business community had also moved its war against the trial lawyers to the legislature, which in 1987 enacted a so-called **tort reform** package that attempted to put some limits on personal-injury lawsuits and damage judgments entered by the courts. (A tort is a wrongful act over which a lawsuit can be brought.) Insurance companies, which had been lobbying nationwide for states to set limits on jury awards in personal injury cases, were major proponents of the legislation. They were joined by the Texas Civil Justice League, an organization of trade and professional associations, cities, and businesses formed in 1986 to seek similar changes in Texas tort law. The high-stakes campaign for change was enthusiastically supported by Governor Bill Clements but was opposed by consumer groups and plaintiffs' lawyers, who had been making millions of dollars from the judiciary's new liberalism.

Cities, businesses, doctors, and even charitable organizations had been hit with tremendous increases in insurance premiums, which they blamed on greedy trial lawyers and large court awards in malpractice and personal-injury lawsuits. Trial lawyers blamed the insurance industry, which, they said, had started raising premiums to recoup losses in investment income after interest rates had fallen.

Among other things, the 1987 tort-reform laws limited governmental liability, attempted to discourage frivolous lawsuits, and limited the ability of claimants to collect damages for injuries that were largely their own fault. They also set limits on punitive damages, which are designed to punish whoever caused an accident or an injury and are often awarded in addition to an injured party's compensation for actual losses.

Other limits on lawsuits were enacted in later legislative sessions, including 1995 and 2003. The 1995 changes, major priorities of then-Governor George W. Bush, imposed even stricter limits on punitive damages and limited the liability of a party who is only partially responsible for an injury. The 2003 legislation, actively sought by Governor Rick Perry and a new Republican majority in the Texas house, set new restrictions on class action lawsuits—which are brought on behalf of large groups of people—and imposed new limits on money that could be awarded for noneconomic damages—such as pain, suffering, or disfigurement—in medical malpractice cases. Lawsuits, or the threat of lawsuits, had been blamed for rising premiums for medical malpractice insurance, which some doctors and other advocates of civil justice changes had characterized as a "crisis" in health care in Texas.

A leading proponent for the civil justice restrictions in 2003 was Texans for Lawsuit Reform, a Houston-based business group whose political action committee gave more than $1 million to successful legislative candidates during the 2002 campaigns.[19]

Winners and Losers

In a study released in 1999, Texas Watch, a consumer advocacy group, said that doctors, hospitals, and other business-related litigants had been big winners before the Texas Supreme Court during the previous four years and that consumers had fared poorly.

tort reform
Changes in state law to put limits on personal injury lawsuits and damage judgments entered by the courts.

The group studied more than 625 cases in which the court had written opinions between January 1, 1995, and April 14, 1999. That was a period during which most court members had received substantial campaign funding from doctors, insurers, and other business interests. The opinions also were issued after the Texas legislature had begun enacting tort reform laws setting limits on civil lawsuits. The study determined that physicians and hospitals had won 86 percent of their appeals, most of which involved medical malpractice claims brought by injured patients or their families. Other consistent winners were insurance companies (73 percent), manufacturers (72 percent), banks (67 percent), utilities (65 percent), and other businesses (68 percent). Insurance policyholders, injured workers, injured patients, and other individual litigants won only 36 percent of the time.[20] The report covered only cases in which the Supreme Court had written opinions. Hundreds of other cases in which the high court upheld lower courts without issuing its own opinions weren't studied. "Individuals are the lowest link in the legal food chain that ends in the Texas Supreme Court," said Walt Borges, who directed the study. "The study raises a question about the fairness of the Texas Supreme Court and state law," he added.[21]

CBS-TV's *60 Minutes,* which had turned the national spotlight on plaintiffs' lawyers and their political contributions to Texas judges in 1987, revisited the Texas judiciary in a follow-up program in 1998. Noting that the partisan system of electing judges had remained unchanged, the new *60 Minutes* segment suggested that justice may still be for sale in Texas, but with different people—the business community—now wielding the influence. The Texas legislature in 1995 had imposed modest limits on campaign contributions to judges and judicial candidates and restricted the periods during which judges and their challengers could raise funds. But a judge could still receive as much as $30,000 from members of the same law firm and as much as $300,000 in total contributions from special interests through political action committees. The 1996 races for the Texas Supreme Court—the first conducted under the new law—demonstrated how weak the new reforms were. Four Republican incumbents, including Chief Justice Thomas R. Phillips, still raised a combined $4 million, easily swamping fund-raising efforts by their unsuccessful challengers.

Texas Watch, the consumer advocacy group, issued a follow-up report on the Supreme Court's 2000–2001 term, which found that consumers were beginning to fare better in some court decisions. But the group determined that businesses, insurance companies and other defendants still won 52 percent of cases pitting consumers against businesses. Consumers won 41 percent of the cases, and the remaining decisions were split, according to the new study.[22] Some observers attributed the moderating influence to appointees whom then-Governor George W. Bush had made to midterm vacancies on the court in the late 1990s. As some of those justices began to leave the court, however, consumer advocates complained of another philosophical shift against plaintiffs. Texas Watch issued still another report in September 2002, noting that the Supreme Court had ruled for business defendants and against workers and other consumers in about two-thirds of the cases it had decided during the previous 12 months.[23]

Minorities and the Judicial System

As the high-stakes battles were being waged over the Texas Supreme Court's philosophical and political makeup, minorities were actively seeking more representation in the Texas judiciary. But instead of pouring millions of dollars into judicial races, Hispanics and African Americans filed lawsuits to try to force change through the federal courts.

Throughout Texas history, Hispanics and African Americans have had difficulty winning election to state courts. The high cost of judicial campaigns, polarized voting along ethnic lines in the statewide or countywide races that are required of most judges, and low rates of minority participation in elections have minimized their electoral successes. The first Hispanic was seated on the Texas Supreme Court in 1984 and on the Court of Criminal Appeals in 1991. The first African American was seated on the Texas Court of Criminal Appeals in 1990 and on the Texas Supreme Court in 2001.

Another factor limiting the number of minority judges is a proportional shortage of minority attorneys, from whose ranks judges are drawn. State leaders' efforts to increase the number of minority lawyers were thwarted for several years by an anti–affirmative action federal court ruling in 1996 and a related state attorney general's opinion, which prohibited Texas law schools and universities from giving preferential treatment to minorities in admissions, student aid, and other programs. Those restrictions were eased in 2003, when the U.S. Supreme Court ruled that college admissions policies could include race as a factor, provided racial quotas weren't established (see *FYI:* Should Colleges and Universities in Texas Use Some Form of Affirmative Action to Increase Minority Enrollments?)

As of February 1989, a few months before a major lawsuit went to trial over the issue, only 35 of 375 state district judges were Hispanic, and only 7 were African American. Only 3 Hispanics and no African Americans were among the 80 judges on the 14 intermediate courts of appeals. Although they constituted at least one-third of the Texas population, African Americans and Hispanics held only 11.2 percent of the district judgeships and less than 4 percent of the intermediate appellate seats.[24] African Americans sat on only 3 of the 59 district court benches in Harris County (Houston), although they accounted for 20 percent of that county's population. African Americans held only 2 of 36 district judgeships in Dallas County, where they made up 18 percent of the population. Hispanics held 3 district court seats in Houston and 1 in Dallas.

Three African American judges in Dallas, who had been appointed by Governor Mark White to fill judicial vacancies, had been unseated in countywide elections. One was Jesse Oliver, a former legislator who had won election to the Texas House from a subdistrict within Dallas County but could not win a 1988 judicial race countywide. Oliver, a Democrat, had overwhelming African American support but lost about 90 percent of Dallas's white precincts.[25]

In a lawsuit tried in September 1989 in federal district court in Midland, attorneys for the League of United Latin American Citizens (LULAC) and other minority plaintiffs argued that the countywide system of electing state district judges violated the Voting Rights Act by diluting the voting strength of minorities. That federal law allows a federal court to strike down an electoral system that denies a protected class of voters an equal opportunity to elect officeholders of their choice. This case, *League of United Latin American Citizens et al.* v. *Mattox et al.,* took almost five years and two appeals to the U.S. Supreme Court to resolve. It did not change Texas's judicial selection system, but a summary of the case and its bumpy journey through the judicial process highlights the political stakes involved in the issue.

In November 1989, U.S. District Judge Lucius Bunton ruled that the countywide system was illegal in nine of the state's largest counties—Harris, Dallas, Tarrant, Bexar, Travis, Jefferson, Lubbock, Ector, and Midland. Those counties elected 172 district judges, almost half of the state's total, but had only a handful of minorities serving on the district courts. Bunton did not order an immediate remedy but strongly urged the legislature to address the issue. After the legislature failed to act, Bunton the next year ordered judges in the nine counties to run for election from districts in nonpartisan elections. But the state won a stay of Bunton's order from the Fifth U.S. Circuit Court of Appeals, and partisan, countywide judicial elections were held as scheduled in 1990.

Ironically, one minority judge was outspoken in his opposition to district elections. State District Judge Felix Salazar of Houston did not seek reelection in 1990, at least in part because he disliked the prospect of having to run from a district rather than countywide. A Democrat, Salazar lived in a predominantly non-Hispanic white Houston neighborhood and in previous elections had been endorsed by a diversity of groups. He claimed that small districts could work against the interests of minorities because a judge from a conservative Anglo district could feel political pressure to sentence minority criminal defendants more harshly than whites. "The judge will have to espouse the feeling of the community. His district may think that's all right, and it will be hell unseating him," he told the *Houston Chronicle.*[26]

Other opponents of district elections argued that districts could also put undue pressure from minority communities on judges. But Jesse Oliver, the former African

American legislator and judge who had been unseated in a countywide race in Dallas, did not agree that judicial districts would distort the administration of justice any more than countywide elections. "For one thing, if the community does exert pressure, then the white community is exerting all the pressure now because they are electing the judges in Dallas County," he said.[27]

Ruling in the Texas case and one from Louisiana in June 1991, the U.S. Supreme Court held that the Voting Rights Act applied to elections for the judiciary. But the high court did not strike down the at-large election system. "We believe that the state's interest in maintaining an electoral system—in this case, Texas's interest in maintaining the link between a district judge's (countywide) jurisdiction and the area of residency of his or her voters—is a legitimate factor to be considered" in determining whether the Voting Rights Act has been violated, the court wrote. But it also emphasized that the state's interest was only one factor to be considered and did not automatically outweigh proof of diluting minority votes.[28]

The U.S. Supreme Court returned the Texas lawsuit to the Fifth U.S. Circuit Court of Appeals for more deliberations, and, in January 1993, a three-judge panel of the Fifth Circuit ruled 2 to 1 that countywide elections illegally diluted the voting strength of minorities in eight counties—Harris, Dallas, Bexar, Tarrant, Jefferson, Lubbock, Ector, and Midland. Under pressure from minority legislators, Attorney General Dan Morales agreed to a settlement with the plaintiffs that would have required district elections for most of the judges in those counties and a ninth, Travis County. The settlement was endorsed by Governor Ann Richards, Democratic legislative leaders, and Democratic majorities in the Texas House and Senate. But it was opposed by Texas Supreme Court Chief Justice Thomas R. Phillips and state District Judges Sharolyn Wood of Houston and Harold Entz of Dallas, Republican defendants in the lawsuit.

The full Fifth Circuit rejected the settlement on a 9-to-4 vote in August 1993, holding that the "evidence of any dilution of minority voting power [in countywide judicial elections] is marginal at best."[29] The Fifth Circuit said partisan affiliation was a more significant factor than ethnicity in judicial elections. Then in January 1994, the U.S. Supreme Court brought the lawsuit to an end by upholding the Fifth Circuit's opinion. That left the issue of judicial selection in the hands of the Texas legislature, which for years had refused to change the elective system. State Senator Rodney Ellis, a Houston Democrat and a leading proponent of district elections, called the decision "devastating" and said it amounted to a "wholesale assault on civil rights." State District Judge Sharolyn Wood, a Houston Republican who had fought district elections, had a different reaction. "Hooray for Texas!" she said.[30]

By 1998, according to the most recent, complete data available, only 8 percent of the state judges at the county court level and higher were Hispanic and 2.5 percent were African American.[31]

Minority Judicial Appointments

Democratic Governor Mark White appointed the first Hispanic, Raul A. Gonzalez, the son of migrant workers, to the Texas Supreme Court in 1984 to fill a vacancy created by a resignation. Gonzalez made history a second time in 1986 by winning election to the seat and becoming the first Hispanic to win a statewide election in Texas. A native of Weslaco in the Rio Grande Valley, Gonzalez had been a state district judge in Brownsville and had been appointed to the Thirteenth Court of Appeals in Corpus Christi by Republican Governor Bill Clements in 1981.

Despite his background, Gonzalez, a Democrat, was one of the most conservative members of the Supreme Court during his tenure. Consequently, he came under frequent attack from plaintiffs' lawyers and, ironically, from many of the constituent groups within his own party who advocated increasing the number of minority judges. Gonzalez's reelection race in 1994, one of the most bitterly contested Supreme Court races in recent memory, proved that ethnicity can quickly take a backseat to judicial philosophy and partisanship.

Raul A. Gonzalez, now retired, was the first Hispanic to serve on the Texas Supreme Court and the first Hispanic to win election to a statewide office in Texas.

AN ATTACK ON AFFIRMATIVE ACTION

The power of the federal courts over state policy was clearly demonstrated by a reverse discrimination lawsuit filed by four white students who had been denied admission to the University of Texas School of Law. For a few years, it thwarted efforts to promote racial and ethnic diversity in some of Texas's colleges and universities. Ruling in the so-called *Hopwood* case, the Fifth U.S. Circuit Court of Appeals in 1996 said a law school admissions policy that had given preferences to minority applicants was unconstitutional. The decision later was upheld by the U.S. Supreme Court.* The nation's high court, however, did not reverse its earlier, landmark opinion in the *Bakke* case from California, which had held that race could be a factor in university admissions policies,† thus allowing other states to continue using affirmative action programs.

In a related legal opinion in 1997, Texas Attorney General Dan Morales held that the *Hopwood* restrictions applied to admissions, student aid, and all other student policies at all colleges and universities in Texas. Morales's opinion was attacked as overly broad by many civil rights leaders and minority legislators, but it had the force of law. The Texas legislature, which met in 1997, attempted to soften the blow to affirmative action by enacting a new law that guaranteed automatic admissions to state universities for high school graduates who finished in the top 10 percent of their classes, regardless of their scores on college entrance examinations. The law was designed to give the best students from poor and predominantly minority school districts an equal footing in university admissions with better-prepared graduates of wealthier school districts. The new law also allowed university officials to consider other admissions criteria, including a student's family income and parents' education level.

There was little change in minority enrollments at many Texas universities after the *Hopwood* decision because many universities hadn't used race as a factor in admissions anyway. But the two largest—the University of Texas at Austin and Texas A & M University—did. The drop-off in minority enrollment was particularly troubling at the UT law school the first year after the *Hopwood* restrictions went into effect. The first-year law class of almost 500 students in the fall of 1997 included only four African Americans and 25 Hispanics. There had been 31 African Americans and 42 Hispanics in the previous year's entering class. And the more flexible admissions standards set by the legislature applied only to entering undergraduate students, not to those seeking admission to law school and other professional schools.

Many higher education administrators and civil rights leaders said it was wrong to dismantle affirmative action programs that had been designed to improve the educational and professional opportunities of minorities, who had historically suffered from segregation and were still overrepresented among the nation's poor. They said it was particularly shortsighted to de-emphasize minority recruitment efforts at a time when Hispanics and African Americans were only a few years away from making up a majority of the Texas population.

But Morales urged university officials to redouble their efforts to recruit disadvantaged students of all races. "We must express to young Texans the reality that in this country one is capable of rising as high as his or her individual talents, ability and hard work will allow," he said.†

The U.S. Supreme Court refused to hear two appeals by Texas of the *Hopwood* decision. But ruling in a separate case from Michigan in 2003, the high court held that college admissions policies could include race as a factor, provided the policies didn't set racial quotas. University officials in Texas then began revising admissions policies to once again include affirmative action.

**Hopwood v. *Texas,* 135 L.Ed. 1095 (1996).
†*University of California Regents* v. *Bakke,* 438 U.S. 265 (1978).
‡Quoted in *Houston Chronicle,* February 7, 1997.

Gonzalez defeated a strong challenge in the Democratic primary from Corpus Christi attorney Rene Haas, who was supported by trial lawyers, women's groups, consumer advocates, several key Democratic legislators, and a number of African American and Hispanic leaders in the Democratic party. Gonzalez drew heavy financial support from business interests, insurance companies, and defense attorneys. He had angered many Democrats by siding with the Republican justices in a 5 to 4 decision upholding a state senate redistricting plan that favored Republicans in the 1992 legislative elections. And he angered many women, as well as trial lawyers, by voting with the court majority in two cases overturning damages awarded women who had complained of being emotionally and physically abused by men.

Raul Gonzalez resigned from the Supreme Court in midterm in late 1998 and was replaced by Alberto R. Gonzalez, an appointee of Governor George W. Bush and only the second Hispanic to serve on the high court. As had Raul Gonzalez, Alberto Gonzales

Morris Overstreet of Amarillo became the first African American to win a statewide election in Texas when be won a seat on the Court of Criminal Appeals in 1990. He served on the court until 1998, when, instead of seeking reelection, be lost a race for the Democratic nomination for Texas attorney general.

came from a modest background. His parents were migrant workers when he was born in San Antonio, but they soon moved to Houston, where his father became a construction worker. The young Gonzales, one of eight children, joined the Air Force after graduating from high school, attended the Air Force Academy, and earned degrees from Rice University and Harvard Law School. He had never been a judge before Governor Bush named him to the Supreme Court. But he had been a partner in one of Houston's largest law firms, had been Bush's top staff lawyer, and had served under Bush as Texas secretary of state.

Alberto Gonzales' appointment came at a time when Governor Bush was actively trying to increase the Republican party's appeal to Hispanics, and Bush acknowledged that it was important to him that Gonzales was Hispanic. "Of course, it mattered what his ethnicity is, but first and foremost what mattered is, I've got great confidence in Al. I know him well. He's a good friend. He'll do a fine job," Bush said.[32] Bush's confidence in Gonzales continued after Bush became president in 2001. He appointed Gonzales White House counsel and later U.S. attorney general. There also was speculation that Bush was grooming Gonzales for an appointment to the U.S. Supreme Court, if a vacancy occurred during the Bush administration.

On succeeding Bush, Republican Governor Rick Perry named minorities to the first two vacancies he had the opportunity to fill on the Texas Supreme Court in 2001. One was Wallace Jefferson, an appellate lawyer from San Antonio who became the first African American to serve on the high court. Perry named Jefferson to succeed Alberto Gonzales, who had resigned to take the White House job. Jefferson, a Republican, was the great-great-great-grandson of a slave. Later the same year, Perry appointed Xavier Rodriguez, a San Antonio labor lawyer, to the Supreme Court to succeed former Justice Greg Abbott, who had resigned to run for Texas attorney general. Rodriguez became the third Hispanic to serve on the court, but he was unseated in the 2002 Republican primary by Austin lawyer Steven Wayne Smith, an Anglo. Jefferson was elected in 2002 to keep his seat on the high court, and a second African American, Republican Dale Wainwright, a state district judge from Houston, was elected to an open Supreme Court seat the same year.

Governor Ann Richards appointed the first Hispanic, Fortunato P. Benavides, to the Texas Court of Criminal Appeals in 1991 to fill a vacancy. Benavides had been a justice on the Thirteenth Court of Appeals and a district judge and a county court-at-law judge in Hidalgo County. But his tenure on the statewide court was short-lived. He was narrowly unseated in 1992 by Republican Lawrence Meyers of Fort Worth, an Anglo, who became the first Republican elected to the criminal court. Benavides later was appointed by President Bill Clinton to the Fifth U.S. Circuit Court of Appeals.

Governor Bill Clements appointed the first African American, Louis Sturns, a Republican state district judge from Fort Worth, to the Texas Court of Criminal Appeals on March 16, 1990. Because the vacancy that Sturns filled had occurred after the 1990 party primaries, the State Republican Executive Committee put Sturns on the general election ballot as the GOP nominee for the seat. The State Democratic Executive Committee nominated another African American, Morris Overstreet, a county court-at-law judge from Amarillo. Overstreet narrowly defeated Sturns in the November general election to become the first African American elected to a statewide office in Texas. Overstreet served on the court until 1998, when, instead of seeking reelection, he lost a race for the Democratic nomination for Texas attorney general.

Women in the Judiciary

The first woman to serve as a state district judge in Texas was Sarah T. Hughes of Dallas, who was appointed to the bench in 1935 by Governor James V. Allred and served until 1961, when she resigned to accept an appointment by President John F. Kennedy to the federal district bench. Ironically, Hughes is best known for swearing a grim-faced Lyndon B. Johnson into office aboard *Air Force One* on November 22, 1963, following Kennedy's assassination in Dallas.

Ruby Sondock of Houston was the first woman to serve on the Texas Supreme Court. She had been a state district judge before Governor Bill Clements named her to the high court on June 25, 1982, to fill a vacancy temporarily. Sondock chose not to seek election to the seat and served only a few months. She later returned to the district bench.

Democrat Rose Spector, a state district judge from San Antonio, became the first woman elected to the Supreme Court when she defeated Republican Justice Eugene Cook in 1992. In 2004, there were two women on the Supreme Court, including Justice Harriet O'Neill, who had unseated Spector in 1998.

In 1994, Republican Sharon Keller, a former Dallas County prosecutor, became the first woman elected to the Texas Court of Criminal Appeals. She was elected presiding judge in 2000. Four women, including Keller, were serving on the nine-member court in 2004. By that year, more than 160 women were judges at the county court level or higher in Texas.[33]

The Search for Solutions

The debates and lawsuits over judicial elections and representation in Texas emphasize the significant role of the courts in policy making as well as day-to-day litigation. The composition of the courts makes a difference. Although some may argue that the role of a judge is simply to apply the law to the facts and issues of a specific case, judges bring to the courts their own values, philosophical views, and life experiences, and these factors serve to filter their interpretations of the law and determine the shape of justice for millions of people.

There is no one simple solution to all the problems and inequities outlined above. Strict limits on the amount of campaign funds that judges and judicial candidates could raise from lawyers and other special interests, for example, could reduce the appearance of influence peddling in the judiciary and temper the high-stakes war between the trial lawyers and the business community for philosophical control of the courts. Campaign finance reform could also help build or restore public confidence in the impartiality of the judiciary. Such reform, however, may not improve opportunities for minorities to win election to the bench. Nor would it shorten the long election ballots that discourage Texans from casting informed votes in judicial races.

The same shortcomings could be anticipated with nonpartisan judicial elections or a merit selection system—two frequently mentioned alternatives to Texas's system of partisan judicial elections. In nonpartisan elections, judges and judicial candidates would not run under Democratic, Republican, or other party labels. This arrangement would guard against partisan bickering on the multimember appellate courts and eliminate the possibility that a poorly qualified candidate could be swept into office by one-party, straight-ticket voting.

Under the merit selection plan (sometimes referred to as the Missouri Plan), the governor would appoint judges from lists of nominees recommended by nominating commissions. The appointed judges would have to run later in **retention elections** to keep their seats, but they would not have opponents on the ballot. Voters would simply decide whether a judge should remain in office or be removed, to be replaced by another gubernatorial appointee.

Texas was one of only eight states in 1998 with a partisan election system for judges. Fourteen states had nonpartisan judicial elections, while thirty-nine used some form of judicial nominating commission, usually in conjunction with a gubernatorial appointment. Only sixteen states, however, combined the use of nominating commissions with retention elections, as provided for in the Missouri Plan. Each alternative has its advantages, but none would necessarily eliminate undue political influence on the judiciary.

Under a merit selection system, interest groups could still apply pressure on the governor and the members of the committees making recommendations for appointments. Although a merit selection plan could be written to require the nominating panels to make ethnically diverse recommendations to the governor, that would not answer the question of how to structure the retention elections. Minority appointees could still be at a disadvantage in retention elections if they have to run countywide, rather than in smaller geographic districts. Despite their popularity among minority leaders, district

Sarah T. Hughes (center), the first woman to serve as a district judge in Texas, in 1961 was appointed a federal district court judge and in 1963 swore in Lyndon Johnson as president after John F. Kennedy was assassinated in Dallas.

retention elections
Elections in which judges run on their own records rather than against other candidates. Voters cast their ballots on the question of whether the incumbent judge should stay in office.

elections for judges are still viewed by many decision makers as a form of **ward politics** that may be appropriate or desirable for legislative seats but not for judges. Judges, they argue, do not represent a particular constituency.

Attempts were made to overhaul the judicial selection process during recent legislative sessions, but they failed. In 1995, as discussed earlier in this chapter, lawmakers set modest limits on campaign contributions to judges and judicial candidates and restricted the periods during which judges and judicial candidates could accept political donations.

CRIME AND PUNISHMENT

Under both the U.S. Constitution and the Texas constitution, a person charged with a crime is presumed innocent until the state can prove guilt beyond a reasonable doubt to a judge or a jury. The state also has the burden to prosecute fairly—to follow principles of procedural due process outlined in constitutional and statutory law and interpreted by the courts. Even persons charged with the most heinous crimes retain these fundamental rights, and although there is often a public outcry about "coddling criminals," the process is designed to protect an individual from governmental abuses, to lessen the chance that an innocent person will be wrongly convicted of a crime.

In Texas, as well as in other states, these rights have sometimes been violated (see *FYI:* "A Huge Injustice in Tulia.") But over the years, the federal courts, in particular, have strengthened their enforcement. Through a case-by-case process, the U.S. Supreme Court has applied the Bill of Rights to the states by way of the Due Process and the Equal Protection Clauses of the Fourteenth Amendment to the U.S. Constitution. The failure of police or prosecutors to comply with specific procedures for handling a person accused of a crime may result in charges against an individual being dropped or a conviction reversed on appeal.

Arrested suspects must be taken before a magistrate—usually a justice of the peace or a municipal court judge—to be formally informed of the offense or offenses with which they are charged and to be told their legal rights. Depending on the charges, a bond may be set to allow them to get out of jail and remain free pending their trials. They have the right to remain silent, to consult with an attorney and have an attorney present during questioning by law enforcement officers or prosecutors, and to be warned that any statement they make can be used against them in a trial. Defendants who cannot afford to hire a lawyer must be provided with court-appointed attorneys at taxpayer expense. Many of these protections were extended to the states by the U.S. Supreme Court in the landmark *Miranda* **ruling** in 1966.[34]

All criminal defendants have the right to a trial by jury but, except in capital murder cases, may waive a jury trial and have their cases decided by a judge. Defendants may plead guilty, not guilty, or **nolo contendere** (no contest). Prosecutors and defense attorneys settle many cases through plea bargaining, a process described earlier in this chapter. The trial judge does not have to accept a plea bargain but usually does. When defendants choose to have their guilt or innocence determined by the judge, the judge also determines the punishment if they are convicted. A jury can return a guilty verdict only if all jurors agree that the defendant is guilty beyond a reasonable doubt. If a jury cannot reach a unanimous verdict, even after lengthy negotiations and prodding from the judge, the judge must declare a mistrial. In that case, the prosecution has to seek a new trial with another jury or drop the charges. In a jury trial, a defendant may choose to have the punishment also set by the jury. If not, it is determined by the judge.

In 1991, the Texas Court of Criminal Appeals took the major step of ordering, for the first time, an official definition of "reasonable doubt" that was to be submitted to every jury deciding a criminal case. According to the definition, evidence against a criminal defendant had to be so convincing that jurors would be willing to rely upon it "without hesitation" in the most important events in their own lives.[35] But, reflecting a change in philosophy, a more conservative Court of Criminal Appeals eliminated that definition in 2000, to the dismay of some criminal defense lawyers. "We find the better practice is

ward politics
Term, often with negative connotations, that refers to partisan politics linked to political favoritism.

Miranda ruling
Far-reaching decision of the U.S. Supreme Court that requires law enforcement officers to warn a criminal suspect of his or her right to remain silent and have an attorney present before questioning.

nolo contendere
Plea of "no contest" to a criminal charge.

A HUGE INJUSTICE IN TULIA

What began as a drug sting in Tulia, a small town in the Texas Panhandle, quickly escalated into one of the biggest miscarriages of justice in recent Texas history. After belated, but intense, media coverage, help finally arrived for 35 victims, but not before they had paid a high price.

In July 1999, 46 Tulia residents, including thirty-nine African Americans, were arrested on drug charges. 38 of the defendants were later convicted, all on the testimony of Tom Coleman, an undercover officer and the only prosecution witness against them. After the *Texas Observer* newspaper, followed by other media, focused attention on the arrests and raised questions about whether they were racially motivated, special evidentiary hearings into the drug sting were convened in March 2003. Retired state District Judge Ron Chapman of Dallas presided over the hearings, during which Coleman's testimony was discredited. Chapman recommended that the Texas Court of Criminal Appeals overturn all 38 convictions. In a separate proceeding, Coleman was later indicted on three counts of perjury stemming from his testimony before Chapman.

The Texas legislature then stepped in, passing a law that allowed fourteen Tulia defendants who were still in prison to be released on bond while the Court of Criminal Appeals considered their cases. And, finally, Governor Rick Perry pardoned thirty-five of the defendants in August 2003, more than four years after their arrests. "Questions surrounding testimony from the key witnesses in these cases, coupled with recommendations from the Board of Pardons and Paroles, weighed heavily in my final decision," the governor said. "Texans demand a system that is tough but fair. I believe my decision to grant pardons in these cases is both appropriate and just," he added. Perry's office said three of the Tulia defendants weren't eligible for pardons.

Jeff Blackburn of Amarillo, an attorney for the Tulia defendants, also filed a civil lawsuit in federal court, seeking damages against a regional drug task force and several local government officials in Swisher County, where Tulia is located. Will Harrell, executive director for Texas of the American Civil Liberties Union, said systemic flaws in the criminal justice system, such as police misconduct, abuse of authority, and inadequate legal representation of the poor, still needed to be addressed.

SOURCE: *Houston Chronicle,* August 23, 2003, p. 1A.

---

to give no definition of reasonable doubt at all to the jury," said the new opinion written by Judge Mike Keasler.[36]

Jury trials are required in **capital murder** cases, which are punishable by death or life in prison. Executions in Texas used to be carried out by electrocution at the state prison unit in downtown Huntsville. Some 361 individuals were executed in Texas from 1924 to 1964, when executions were suspended because of legal challenges.

In 1972, the U.S. Supreme Court halted executions in all the states by striking down all the death penalty laws then on the books as unconstitutional. The high court held that capital punishment, as then practiced, violated the constitutional prohibition against "cruel and unusual punishment" because it could be applied in a discriminatory fashion.[37] Not only could virtually any act of murder be punished by death under the old Texas law, but so could rape and certain other crimes.

In 1973, the Texas legislature rewrote the death penalty statute to try to meet the Supreme Court's standards by defining capital crimes as murder committed under specific circumstances. The list was expanded later and now includes the murder of a law enforcement officer or firefighter who is on duty, murder committed during the course of committing certain other major crimes, murder for hire, murdering more than one person, murder of a prison guard or employee, murder committed while escaping or attempting to escape from a penal institution, or murder of a child younger than six.

A jury that has found a person guilty of capital murder must answer certain questions about the defendant before choosing between death or life imprisonment, the only punishments available. Jurors are required to consider whether a convicted murderer will be a continuing danger to society as well as mitigating circumstances, including evidence of mental retardation, before deciding punishment.[38]

The first execution under the 1973 Texas law was carried out in 1982. By then the legislature, acting in 1977, had changed the method of execution from the electric chair to

capital murder
Murder committed under certain circumstances for which the death penalty or life in prison must be imposed.

the intravenous injection of a lethal substance. By 2004, more than 300 men and two women had been executed in Texas by lethal injection. Karla Faye Tucker, the first woman executed in Texas since the Civil War, was put to death in 1998 for killing two people with a pickax almost fifteen years earlier. The second woman was executed in early 2000 for the murder of her husband.

After considerable controversy in Texas and other states, the U.S. Supreme Court in June 2002 banned the execution of mentally retarded convicts. Death penalty opponents had argued that before the high court ruling Texas had executed at least six inmates who were demonstrably retarded. The Texas legislature, in its first session after the Supreme Court ban, failed to revise its death penalty statute to comply with the court's order, requiring defense attorneys to continue the battle, case by case. Some feared that, without new state guidelines for evaluating and trying convicts, additional mentally retarded persons would be executed in Texas, despite the Supreme Court's ban.[39]

After capital murder, the most serious criminal offense is a first-degree felony—for example, aggravated sexual assault and noncapital murder—punishable by a prison sentence of five to 99 years or life. Second-degree felonies, such as burglary of someone's home and bribery, are punishable by two to twenty years in prison. Third-degree felonies—including intentional bodily injury to a child and theft of trade secrets—are punishable by two to ten years in prison. State jail felonies—which include many property crimes, such as burglary of an office building, and minor drug offenses—are punishable by up to two years in a state-run jail or time in a community corrections program, each of which is supposed to emphasize rehabilitation as well as punishment.

The most minor crimes are classified as Class A, B, or C misdemeanors. Crimes such as public lewdness and harboring a runaway child are examples of Class A misdemeanors and are punishable by a maximum $4,000 fine and/or one year in a county jail. The unauthorized use of television cable decoding equipment or falsely claiming to be a police officer are examples of Class B misdemeanors and carry a maximum sentence of 180 days in a county jail and a $2,000 fine. Class C misdemeanors include illegal gambling and the issuance of a bad check. They are punishable by a maximum $500 fine.

People convicted of crimes can be sentenced to **probation** (also called community supervision): they are not sent to prison but must meet certain conditions, such as restrictions on where they travel and with whom they associate. Except for those under the death penalty, convicted felons sentenced to prison can become eligible for **parole**—or early release under supervisory restrictions—after serving a portion of their sentence.

Death penalty protesters outside the Huntsville prison on the occasion of the execution of Karla Faye Tucker, the first woman to be put to death in Texas since the Civil War.

probation
Procedure under which a convicted criminal is not sent to prison if he or she meets certain conditions, such as restrictions on travel and associates.

parole
Early release of an inmate from prison, subject to certain conditions.

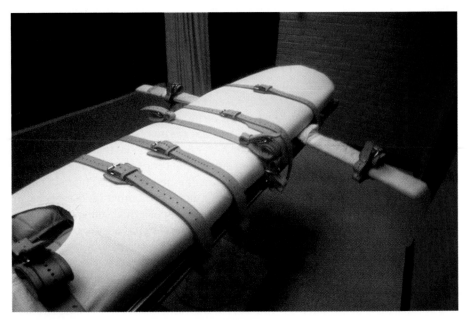

Texas now executes capital murderers by lethal injection.

Capital murderers sentenced to life in prison can be considered for parole after serving forty years. Parole decisions are made by the Board of Pardons and Paroles, which is appointed by the governor.

A landmark federal court order in 1980 forced the state to spend billions of dollars expanding and improving its prison system and forced the legislature to reevaluate the punishment of some criminals (see *FYI:* "Criminal Justice, an Expensive Headache").

THE POLITICS OF CRIMINAL JUSTICE

The Texas Court of Criminal Appeals must try to balance the constitutional rights of convicts against the public welfare, a role that puts the court at the center of major philosophical and political battles.

The combatants on one side of the debate include the prosecutors—the elected district and county attorneys—who do not like to see the convictions they have won reversed, partly because too many reversals could cost them reelection. Judges of the trial courts, who also periodically face the voters, are sensitive to reversals, too. So are the police and sheriffs' departments that arrest the defendants and provide the evidence on which criminal convictions are based.

On the other side of the debate are defense attorneys, who have an obligation to protect the rights and interests of their clients and who in their appeals often attack procedures used by police, prosecutors, and trial judges. Also on this side are civil libertarians, who insist that a criminal defendant's every right—even the most technical—be protected, and minority groups, who have challenged the conduct of trials when minorities have been excluded from juries weighing the fate of minority defendants. (see *FYI:* "More Is Involved than Technicalities").

Throughout much of its early history, the Texas Court of Criminal Appeals was accused of excessive concern with legal technicalities that benefited convicted criminals.[40] The court reversed 42 percent of the cases appealed to it during the first quarter of the twentieth century, when Texas and many other states had a harsh system of criminal justice that often reflected class and racial bias at the trial level. By 1966, the reversal rate had dropped to 3 percent. But changes in the court's makeup and changes in political attitudes produced fluctuations in that record in subsequent years.

The court signaled a shift toward a conservative philosophy after the 1994 elections of Judges Sharon Keller and Steve Mansfield had increased the number of Republicans on the court to three. During the first thirteen months the new judges were in office, for example, the court ordered the reinstatement of two death sentences it had reversed before Keller's and Mansfield's arrival. The court's conservatism was solidified with a Republican sweep of all three court seats on the 1996 ballot. A 6-to-3 Democratic majority had become a 6-to-3 Republican majority, the first GOP majority on the court since Reconstruction. Republicans increased their majority to 7 to 2 in 1997, when longtime Presiding Judge Mike McCormick, one of the court's most conservative members, switched from the Democratic to the Republican party. The Republican takeover of the court was completed in 1998, when Democrats lost their last two seats on the panel. McCormick did not seek reelection in 2000 and was replaced as presiding judge by Sharon Keller, a former prosecutor.

After the GOP takeover, the Court of Criminal Appeals quickly began compiling a strong, pro-prosecutorial record, particularly in death penalty cases. The court upheld a number of death sentences that later were overturned by federal courts. In one case, later reversed by a federal court, it affirmed a capital conviction even though the defendant's attorney had slept through part of his trial (see *FYI:* "Can Justice Afford a Nap?"). In another case, it upheld a death sentence despite the fact that a prosecution witness had argued improperly that the defendant was a future danger to society partly because he was Hispanic. That ruling prompted then–Texas Attorney General John Cornyn, a Republican and strong law-and-order advocate, to admit to the U.S. Supreme Court that the prosecution had committed reversible error in the case. Such rulings prompted defense lawyers and civil libertarians to heap much criticism upon the court. "They're

CRIMINAL JUSTICE, AN EXPENSIVE HEADACHE

An overcrowded and inadequately staffed prison system prompted U.S. District Judge William Wayne Justice of Tyler to declare Texas's prisons unconstitutional in 1980 in a landmark lawsuit brought by inmates (*Ruiz v. Estelle*). Among other things, the court ordered the population of prison units limited to 95 percent of capacity. That limit and an increase in the violent crime rate in the 1980s helped produce a criminal justice crisis that saw hundreds of dangerous convicts released from prison early and thousands of other criminals backlogged in overcrowded county jails.

The *Ruiz* lawsuit was settled in 1992, with the state promising to maintain constitutional prisons. In 1993 the legislature enacted a major package of criminal justice reforms. The minimum time that violent criminals would have to serve in prison before being eligible for parole was doubled—from one-fourth to one-half of their sentences. To make sure there was enough room to keep the most dangerous felons in prison longer, thousands of property and drug offenders were to be diverted into community corrections programs or a new system of state jails, where education, drug abuse treatment, and other rehabilitation programs were to be emphasized.

Financed by bond issues totaling $3 billion, a huge prison expansion program was completed in the mid-1990s. With more than 140,000 spaces, Texas finally had enough room for all its prisoners in its corrections system. Some counties had sufficient jail space to permit them to lease space to house convicts from other states. But criminal justice experts warned that the relief was only temporary, and before long, lower parole rates and long prison sentences were once again taking their toll on the state's resources.

MORE IS INVOLVED THAN TECHNICALITIES

Randall Dale Adams and Clarence Lee Brandley owe their lives to the appellate process. Both men came perilously close to being executed for murders they apparently did not commit. Adams spent more than a decade behind bars before he was released in 1989, after a documentary film indicated he had been wrongfully convicted of the murder of a Dallas police officer. The Texas Court of Criminal Appeals ordered a new trial, but the Dallas County district attorney chose not to retry him.

Brandley, an African American janitor at Conroe High School, was convicted by an all-white jury of the rape and murder of a sixteen-year-old girl, but the Court of Criminal Appeals reversed the conviction after being presented with evidence that Brandley had not received a fair trial and had been a victim of racial prejudice. Neither man would have lived long enough to win freedom had not the appellate process, which many prosecutors attack as too time consuming and too "technical," worked to delay their scheduled executions.

CAN JUSTICE AFFORD A NAP?

Justice is supposed to be blind, but it isn't supposed to be asleep. At least that was the conclusion of one of the more controversial death penalty convictions to emerge from Texas in recent years. Calvin Burdine was convicted and sentenced to death for the 1983 murder of his roommate, W. T. "Dub" Wise. His conviction was upheld by the Texas Court of Criminal Appeals, and he spent eighteen years on death row before the Fifth U.S. Circuit Court of Appeals overturned the sentence because Burdine's defense attorney had slept through portions of his trial. In a plea bargain with prosecutors, Burdine then was sentenced to life in prison.

SOURCE: *Houston Chronicle,* June 20, 2003, p. 29A.

so far gone they're barely even a court anymore," lawyer Jeff Blackburn of Amarillo said in an interview with the *Houston Chronicle.*[41]

INCREASED POLICY ROLE OF THE STATE COURTS

The federal judiciary has traditionally had more influence than the state courts in molding public policy. Over the years, it has been at the center of political debate over the proper role of the judiciary in the policy-making process.

Much of the Texas Supreme Court's time is spent refereeing disputes between trial lawyers and insurance companies. But in recent years this court has sometimes played an active role in shaping broader public policies and addressing significant constitutional issues (see *FYI:* "The Constitution Is for Everybody").

The Courts and Education

In one of its most significant and best-known rulings, the Texas Supreme Court in the Edgewood school finance case in 1989 unanimously ordered major, basic changes in the financing of public education to provide more equity between rich and poor school districts.[42] The lawsuit was brought against the state by poor districts after years of legislative inaction against a property tax–based finance system that had produced huge disparities in local education resources and in the quality of local schools.

The unanimity of the opinion, written by Justice Oscar Mauzy, a Democrat, surprised many legislators and school officials because two of the three Republican justices on the court at that time had initially been appointed by Governor Bill Clements, who had insisted that the courts had no business trying to tell the legislature what to do about school finance. The decision, which held that the school finance law violated a constitutional requirement for an efficient education system, was obviously the product of considerable compromise among the nine justices. Their deliberations were secret, but Justice Franklin Spears, a Democrat, told the *Fort Worth Star-Telegram:* "We wanted to speak with one voice. The opinion is a composite of many ideas, much brainstorming, much compromising." Mark Yudof, then dean of the University of Texas School of Law, said the court may have been determined to offer a united front because it attached as much importance to the school finance case as a united U.S. Supreme Court had to the landmark *Brown* v. *Board of Education of Topeka* desegregation case in the 1950s.[43]

Compliance with the school finance order did not come easily, however. A 1990 school finance law failed to meet the court's standards, so the court issued another order in 1991 and a third order in 1992 after the legislature again came up short. The court lost its unanimity on the third order, which struck down a 1991 law that had established special county education districts with a minimum property tax. In a challenge brought this time by wealthy school districts, a 7 to 2 court majority ruled that the tax was a statewide property tax prohibited by the Texas Constitution. Mauzy and fellow Democratic Justice Lloyd Doggett sharply dissented.

The legislature responded with still another school finance law in 1993. This law gave wealthy school districts several options for sharing revenue with poor districts, and it was challenged by both rich and poor districts. The rich districts objected to sharing their property wealth, while the poor districts argued that the new law was inadequately funded and did not sufficiently reduce the funding gap between rich and poor districts. The Texas Supreme Court upheld the law in a 5 to 4 decision in January 1995. By that time, a majority of the court's members were Republicans. In the majority opinion, Justice John Cornyn, a Republican, wrote:

> Children who live in property-poor districts and children who live in property-rich districts now have substantially equal access to the funds necessary for a general

diffusion of knowledge. It is apparent from the court's opinions that we have recognized that an efficient system does not require equality of access to revenue at all levels.[44]

But Republican Justice Craig Enoch, who dissented, wrote that the state had failed to adequately provide for the public schools. He said the new law contributed to further "constitutional tensions" by promoting continued use of local property taxes.[45]

By 2003, the school finance law was under attack again, this time from school districts contending that the "Robin Hood" share-the-wealth requirement and inadequate state aid were forcing many districts to raise local school maintenance tax rates to the maximum $1.50 per $100 valuation. They argued that amounted to an unconstitutional statewide property tax.

In 1992, a state district judge in Brownsville ruled that the state's system of funding higher education also was unconstitutional because it shortchanged Hispanics in South Texas. But the Texas Supreme Court reversed that decision and upheld the higher education system.[46]

In another education case with major implications, the Texas Supreme Court in 1994 upheld the right of Texas parents to educate their own children. Ending a ten-year legal battle, the court overturned a Texas Education Agency ruling that home schools were illegal. The court held that a home school was legitimate if parents used books, workbooks, or other written materials and met "basic education goals" by teaching basic subjects.[47]

The Courts and Abortion Rights

In 1998, the Texas Supreme Court upheld $1.2 million in damages against anti-abortion protesters who had staged massive demonstrations at Houston abortion clinics during the 1992 Republican National Convention. Some clinics had been vandalized and patients harassed. The high court also upheld most of the restrictions a lower court had set on protests near the clinics and the homes of several doctors who performed abortions. The court said it was trying to balance free speech rights with the rights of the clinics to conduct business, the rights of women to have access to pregnancy counseling and abortion services, and privacy rights of physicians. The court prohibited demonstrators from blocking access to clinics, intimidating patients, and engaging in other forms of aggressive behavior.[48] In a case from Florida, the U.S. Supreme Court had ruled in 1994 that judges could limit protests near abortion clinics but that restrictions had to be strictly limited.[49]

The Texas Supreme Court became embroiled in the abortion issue again in 2000 after a state law went into effect requiring parents to be notified by the doctors before their minor daughters could have abortions. The law included a "judicial bypass" provision, giving a young woman who didn't want her parents to be told an opportunity to convince a judge that she was mature and well-informed enough to make an abortion decision by herself or that notifying her parents would be harmful. Acting on several early cases, the Texas Supreme Court set guidelines for district judges to follow in making bypass decisions.

In another abortion case, decided in 2002, the Texas Supreme Court held that the state's refusal to pay for medically necessary abortions for poor women didn't violate the Texas constitution. The court ruled that the restriction on funding abortions for women on Medicaid didn't discriminate by gender and advanced a legitimate governmental interest of favoring childbirth over abortion.

The Courts and Gay Rights

Deciding still another controversial issue, the Texas Supreme Court in 1996 ruled against the Log Cabin Republicans, a gay GOP group that had been denied a booth at the Republican State Convention in San Antonio. The court said the group had no grounds to sue the Republican party for deprivation of rights under the Texas constitution because the party was not a governmental agency.[50]

THE CONSTITUTION IS FOR EVERYBODY

The Texas Supreme Court ruled in 1994 that a Ku Klux Klan leader had a constitutional right to keep Klan membership lists secret. The high court held that a state district judge had illegally jailed Michael Lowe for refusing to turn over the membership lists to state officials investigating the harassment and intimidation of African Americans attempting to desegregate a public housing project in Vidor. "The rights to form, discuss and express unpopular views are protected fundamental rights," the court said. "Where the organization advocates views which might subject members to ridicule . . . from the mere fact of membership, First Amendment associational rights are the basis for a qualified privilege against disclosure of membership lists."*

In an unusual twist, the white supremacist was represented by an African American civil liberties lawyer, Anthony Griffin of Galveston. Griffin, who took the case at the request of the American Civil Liberties Union, said he was "ecstatic" about the court's ruling. "I think it's a wonderful opinion for the state supreme court to reaffirm the virtue of the First Amendment," he said.[†]

Ex Parte Lowe, 887 S.W.2d 1 (1994).
[†]Quoted in *Houston Chronicle,* June 9, 1994, p. 1A.

SUMMARY

1. Texas has a confusing array of courts, many with overlapping jurisdictions. It is one of only two states with a bifurcated court system at the highest appellate level. The Texas Supreme Court is the court of last resort in civil cases and the Texas Court of Criminal Appeals in criminal cases.

2. The judicial system is particularly inadequate in urban counties, where thousands of criminal cases each year are disposed of through plea bargains negotiated by prosecutors and defendants and where it can take years to resolve civil disputes that are not settled out of court.

3. State judges, except those on municipal court benches, are elected in partisan elections. But there has been increasing political and legal pressure to change the selection process. Possible alternatives are nonpartisan elections, elections from geographic districts, or a merit selection plan under which the governor would appoint judges from lists of nominees recommended by experts. The latter plan would require the appointed judges to run later in retention elections to keep their seats, but they would not have opponents on the ballot.

4. Grand juries are supposed to ensure that the government has sufficient evidence to proceed with a criminal prosecution against an individual. Petit, or trial, juries hear evidence and render verdicts in cases involving both civil and criminal matters.

5. Litigants in civil cases and most criminal cases can waive a jury trial and have their cases decided by a judge. Trials move through opening statements, examination and cross-examination of witnesses, presentation of evidence, rebuttal, summation, and verdict.

6. Cases can be appealed to appellate courts, where there are no juries. Appellate courts review the decisions and procedures of lower courts for conformity to constitutional and statutory requirements.

7. Judges who espouse strict construction believe their role to be one of narrowly interpreting and applying the law while leaving public policy initiatives to the legislature. Judicial activists believe their role to be one of taking a more expansive view of the law by reading broad policy implications into their decisions.

8. The Texas Supreme Court became a battleground in the 1980s between trial attorneys who represent injured parties, or plaintiffs, in damage lawsuits and the businesses, doctors, and insurance companies they sue. After trial lawyers began contributing millions of dollars to successful Supreme Court candidates, longtime judicial precedents that had favored the corporate establishment began to fall, and it became easier for plaintiffs to win huge damage awards.

9. The business and medical communities retaliated by winning some legislative changes in the procedures under which lawsuits are tried and by increasing their political contributions in judicial races.

10. Party realignment, including appointments by Governor Bill Clements to fill midterm vacancies, increased the number of Republican judges on trial courts in the 1980s. The philosophical confrontation gave Republicans, with support from the business and medical communities, their first majority on the Texas Supreme Court in modern times.

11. Only a handful of women and minorities have ever served on the state's highest appellate courts, and historically they have been underrepresented on the lower-court benches as well. In a lawsuit by minority plaintiffs, U.S. District Judge Lucius Bunton of Midland ruled in 1989 that the countywide system of electing district, or trial, judges in nine of the state's largest counties violated the federal Voting Rights Act by diluting the voting strength of minorities. But that ruling was reversed by the U.S. Supreme Court in 1994.

12. The Texas Court of Criminal Appeals is at the center of philosophical and political disputes as it weighs the constitutional rights of convicted criminals against public concern about crime.

13. The federal judiciary has traditionally had more influence than the state courts in molding public policy. But in recent years the Texas Supreme Court has sometimes played an active role in addressing significant constitutional issues.

KEY TERMS

penal code	ordinances	**Texas Court of Criminal Appeals**	merit selection
felony	de novo	grand jury	tort reform
misdemeanor	justice of the peace court	prosecution	retention elections
civil lawsuit	constitutional county court	indictment	ward politics
statutes	statutory county court	information	*Miranda* ruling
plaintiff	district court	petit jury	nolo contendere
original jurisdiction	plea bargaining	veniremen	capital murder
appellate jurisdiction	court of appeals	petition for review	probation
bifurcated court system	Texas Supreme Court	writ of mandamus	parole
municipal court			

FURTHER READING

BAUM, LAWRENCE. "Supreme Courts in the Policy Process." *In The State of the States,* ed. Carl E. Van Horn (CQ Press, 1996), pp. 143–160. Recent state court decisions indicate increased judicial activism producing a counterreaction by those adversely affected by the actions of the courts.

CHAMPAGNE, ANTHONY. "Judicial Selection in Texas: Democracy's Deadlock." In *Texas Politics: A Reader,* eds. Anthony

Champagne and Edward J. Harpham (W.W. Norton, 1997), pp. 97–110. Addresses issues and problems related to the partisan selection of Texas state judges.

HILL, JOHN. "Taking Texas Judges Out of Politics: An Argument for Merit Election." *Baylor Law Review 40* (Summer 1988), pp. 340–366. A former chief justice of the Texas Supreme Court argues for nonpartisan elections of state judges.

JACOB, HERBERT, "Courts: The Invisible Branch." In *Politics in the American States: A Comparative Analysis,* 6th ed. Ed. Virginia Gray and Herbert Jacob. (CQ Press, 1996), pp. 253–285. A comparative analysis of state court systems.

TEXAS JUDICIAL COUNCIL, OFFICE OF COURT ADMINISTRATION. *Texas Judicial System, 75th Annual Report.* (Texas Judicial Council, 2003). Annual compilation of data on the activities of state courts.

TEXAS RESEARCH LEAGUE. *The Texas Judiciary: A Structural-Functional Overview,* Report 1. (Texas Research League, 1990). Describes the court structure of Texas with a focus on its primary weaknesses.

TEXAS RESEARCH LEAGUE. *Texas Courts: A Proposal for Structural-Functional Reform,* Report 2. (Texas Research League, 1991). Recommendations for a major overhaul of the state's court system.

LOCAL GOVERNMENT IN TEXAS
CITIES, TOWNS, COUNTIES, AND SPECIAL DISTRICTS

27

THE LEGACY OF LOCAL GOVERNMENT

Texans have an affinity for local government. There are more than 4,700 local governments, of all sizes, across the state. Some operate with a handful of employees and budgets of one or two hundred thousand dollars a year, while others have tens of thousands of employees with billion dollar-plus budgets. Their governmental structures range from the simple to the complex. Some special districts perform one basic function, while large cities perform any number of services that are limited only by budgetary and legal restraints. Some counties have fewer than 1,000 people, and others have more than two million residents. One school district in West Texas has only twenty students, while the Houston Independent School District has more than 200,000. Three of the ten largest cities in the United States are in Texas, but many cities across the state have fewer than 1,000 residents.

The key to understanding local governments in Texas is to understand what responsibilities have been assigned to them by the Texas constitution and statutory law. Once the institutional structures and functions of local governments have been studied, attention will be directed to a number of core problems confronting them and their political capacities to address these issues. Throughout this analysis will be two underlying themes—what changes can make local governments more effective, and is it possible or desirable to reduce the fragmentation in local governments?

A tradition of localism is rooted in the fabric of our political history. Since the founding of the nation, Americans have expressed a strong belief in the right to local self-government.[1] In many areas of the young country, local governments existed long before there was a viable state or federal government. Early communities had to fend for themselves

TIME LINE

LOCAL GOVERNMENT IN TEXAS

1900	Galveston Hurricane kills 6,000 people, resulting in the development of the commission form of government
1912	Cities granted home rule authority
1913	Amarillo and Terrell adopt council-manager government
1921	Texas has 254 counties with the creation of Kenedy County
1933	Counties given home rule powers; authority never used and repealed in 1969
1963	Cities given expanded annexation powers
1965	Creation of Councils of Governments
1971	Interlocal contracting among local governments authorized
1975	Voting Rights Act covers Texas, resulting in concerted legal attacks on election systems of local governments
1981	San Antonio elects the first Hispanic mayor, Henry Cisneros
1995	Election of the first black mayor, Ron Kirk, in Dallas
1997	Election of the first black mayor, Lee Brown, in Houston
2000	Eighty-three percent of the state's population lives in urbanized areas

unitary system
Constitutional arrangement whereby authority rests with the central government; regional governments have only those powers given them by the central government.

Dillon rule
Principle holding that local governments are creations of state government and that their powers and responsibilities are defined by the state.

and had limited expectations of services or protections to be provided by state or federal governments.

This history of local self-help has led to the popular notion that local governments have fundamental rights based on the concept of local sovereignty, or ultimate power. Thomas Jefferson, for example, developed a theory of local government, designed in part to strengthen the powers of the states, in which local sovereignty was rooted in the sovereignty of the individual.[2] Some scholars suggest that this cultural legacy persists in grass-roots politics, the flight to suburbia, and the creation of neighborhood organizations. Today it is common to hear the argument that local government is closest to the people and best represents their interests and desires.[3]

Although this view is widely held, the prevailing constitutional theory on the relationship of local governments to the state is the **unitary system**. Simply stated, this theory holds that local governments are the creations of the state. The powers, functions, and responsibilities that they exercise have been delegated or granted them by the state government, and no local government has sovereign powers. There have been numerous court cases enunciating this principle, which is referred to as the **Dillon rule**, but the best summary is derived from an Iowa case in which a court held the following:

> The true view is this: Municipal corporations owe their origin to, and derive their powers and rights wholly from, the legislature. It breathes into them the breath of life, without which they cannot exist. As it creates, so it may destroy. If it may destroy, it may abridge and control. Unless there is some constitutional limitation on the right, the legislature might by a single act sweep from its existence all of the municipal corporations in the State, and the corporations could not prevent it. We know of no limitation on this right so far as the corporations are concerned.[4]

The Dillon rule is now the prevailing theory defining the relationships of states and local governments, and it is applicable to local governments in Texas.

LOCAL GOVERNMENTS IN THE TEXAS POLITICAL SYSTEM

Local governments—counties, cities, school districts, and special districts—are created by the state and operate under limits set by the Texas constitution and the legislature. They have found their capabilities and resources increasingly burdened by the pressing needs of a growing, urban state. Some of this pressure has come from the state and federal governments ordering or mandating significant improvements in environmental, educational, health, and other programs but letting cities, counties, and school districts pick up much of the tab. Prior to the state's commitment to an extensive prison construction program in the 1990s, for example, the Texas government forced counties to spend millions of local taxpayer dollars to house state prisoners in county jails because it had failed to adequately address a criminal justice crisis. Local school districts and their property taxpayers also are at the mercy of the legislature, which has ordered expensive educational programs and has raised classroom standards without fully paying for them. Cities, too, find their budgetary problems exacerbated by state mandates. Local governments are the governments closest to the people, but they have to shoulder much of the responsibility—and often take much of the public outrage—for policy decisions made in Austin and Washington.

Although the legal position expressed by the Dillon rule subordinates local governments to the state, there are practical and political limitations on what the state can do with local governments. More importantly, the state relies on local governments to carry out many of its responsibilities.[5]

Texas granted cities home rule authority in 1912. Home rule cities, discussed in more detail below, have considerable authority and discretion over their own local policies, but within limits set by state law. Texas voters approved a constitutional amendment in

TABLE 27–1 GOVERNMENTS IN THE UNITED STATES AND TEXAS, 2002

	U.S.	Texas
U.S. government	1	—
State government	50	1
Counties	3,034	254
Municipalities	19,429	1,196
Townships and towns	16,504	—
School districts	13,506	1,089
Special districts	35,052	2,245
Total	87,576	4,785

Source: U.S. Department of Commerce, Bureau of the Census, *2002 Census of Governments: Government Organizations*, vol. 1, table 3.

1933 that also gave counties home rule authority, but no county established home rule government before the amendment was repealed in 1969.[6] County home rule provisions were again introduced in the 1997 and 1999 legislative sessions by several urban legislators but were defeated because of opposition from a variety of state and local interests.

In a 1980 study, the Advisory Commission on Intergovernmental Relations ranked the states according to the discretionary authority they granted to their local governments. Texas ranked eleventh in a composite ranking that included all local subdivisions—cities, counties, school districts, and other special districts. But Texas ranked forty-third, or near the bottom, in the discretionary authority given to its counties alone, while ranking first in the discretionary authority given to its cities.[7]

The states vary considerably in the major responsibilities assigned to different levels of government. Texas, like most other states, assigns the primary responsibility for public education to local school districts while retaining the primary responsibility for highways, public welfare, and public health at the state level. Police and fire protection, water and sanitation services, parks, recreation, and libraries are the primary responsibility of city governments. Public hospitals are a shared function of the state, county, and special districts.[8] Texas counties share with the state a primary responsibility for the court and criminal justice system. Altogether, there are some 4,700 local governments in Texas (see Table 27–1).

TABLE 27–2 SELECT CHARACTERISTICS FOR THE TEN LARGEST CITIES IN TEXAS, 2000

City	Population	% over 65	% under 18	Median Age	% African American	% Hispanic	Persons per Square Mile
Houston	1,953,631	8.4	27.5	30.9	25.3	37.4	3,372
Dallas	1,188,580	8.6	26.6	30.5	26.0	35.6	3,470
San Antonio	1,144,646	10.4	28.5	31.7	6.8	58.7	2,808
Austin	656,562	6.7	22.5	29.6	10.2	30.6	2,611
El Paso	563,662	10.7	31.0	31.1	3.0	76.6	2,263
Fort Worth	534,694	9.6	28.3	30.9	20.4	29.8	1,828
Arlington	332,969	6.1	28.3	30.7	14.1	18.3	3,476
Corpus Christi	277,454	11.1	28.1	33.2	4.7	54.3	1,795
Plano	222,030	4.9	28.7	31.1	5.2	10.1	3,101
Garland	215,768	7.1	29.8	31.7	12.1	25.6	3,779

Source: Texas State Data Center; U.S. Census 2000.

Bill White was elected mayor of Houston in 2003.

MUNICIPAL GOVERNMENT IN TEXAS

Despite popular images of wide open spaces dotted with cattle and oil wells, Texas is an urban state. Some areas, particularly in West Texas, still offer a good deal of room to roam, but most Texans live in cities. First-time visitors to the state often express surprise at the size and diversity of Houston and Dallas and the more relaxed charm of San Antonio, whose Riverwalk reminds many tourists of some European cities. Austin, the seat of state government and location of a world-class university, is highly attractive to young professionals and high-technology businesses.

When the Texas constitution was adopted in 1876, the state was rural and agrarian; less than 10 percent of the population lived in cities. According to the 1880 census, Galveston was the largest city, with a population of 22,248, followed by San Antonio with 20,550. Dallas, a relatively new settlement, had 10,358 residents, and Houston had 16,513. For most of the period from 1880 to 1920, San Antonio was Texas's largest city, but since the 1930 census, Houston has held that distinction.[9] In 1940, only 45 percent of Texans lived in urban areas, but by 1950, 60 percent of the population resided in cities. Since the 1970 census, eight of every ten Texans have been living in cities.

Houston, Dallas, and San Antonio are among the ten largest cities in the United States. According to the 2000 census, Houston had a population of 1.95 million; Dallas, 1.19 million; and San Antonio, 1.14 million. Five additional Texas cities—El Paso, Austin, Fort Worth, Corpus Christi, and Arlington—each had more than 250,000. Five of Texas's ten largest cities—Houston, Dallas, San Antonio, El Paso, and Corpus Christi—have minority populations exceeding 50 percent (see Table 27–2).

The more than 1,200 incorporated municipalities in Texas are diverse, and urban life, politics, and government have developed different styles across the state. The basic forms of city government are defined by statutory and constitutional law, but cities vary in their demographic makeup, their economies, the historical experiences that shaped their development, and their quality of life. There are local differences in economic stability, public safety, public education, health and environmental quality, housing, transportation, culture, recreation, and politics.[10]

General Law and Home Rule Cities

The Texas constitution provides for two general categories of cities: general law and home rule. **General law cities** have fewer than 5,000 residents and have more restrictions in organizing their governments, setting taxes, and annexing territory than do home rule cities. They are allowed only those powers specifically granted to them by the legislature. Most Texas cities—approximately 885—are general law cities.[11]

A city with more than 5,000 inhabitants can adopt any form of government its residents choose, provided it does not conflict with the state constitution (Article XI, Sections 4, 5) or statutes. This option is called **home rule** and is formalized through the voters' adoption of a **charter**, which is the fundamental document—something like a constitution—under which a city operates. A charter establishes a city's governing body, the organization of its administrative agencies and municipal courts, its taxing authority, and procedures for conducting elections, annexing additional territory, and revising the charter (see *FYI:* "Is This Any Way to Change a City Charter?"). As of 2002, there were 318 home rule cities in Texas.[12]

FORMS OF CITY GOVERNMENT IN TEXAS

Texas cities have experimented with three forms of government: the mayor-council, the commission, and the council-manager (see *You Decide/Thinking It Through:* "Does the Form of Government under Which a City Operates Make Any Significant Differences?"). According to the Texas Municipal League, there were 1,208 municipal governments in Texas in 2004. Over 900 cities operated with some variation of the mayor-council form; approximately 280 used some form of council-manager or commission-manager government; and only a handful used the commission form of government.[13]

general law cities
City allowed to exercise only those powers specifically granted to it by the legislature. General law cities have fewer than 5,000 residents.

home rule
City with a population of more than 5,000, which can adopt any form of government residents choose, provided it does not conflict with the state constitution or statutes.

charter
Document based on state authorization, which defines the structure, powers, and responsibilities of a city government.

Mayor-Council

The **mayor-council**, the most common form of municipal government in Texas, was derived from the English model of city government. The legislative function of the city is vested in the city council, and the executive function is assigned to the mayor. This type of government is based on the separation of powers principle, which also characterizes the state and federal governments.

In theory, the mayor, who is elected citywide, is the chief executive officer. In terms of power, however, there are two distinguishable forms of mayor—the **weak mayor** and the **strong mayor**—and in most Texas cities, the mayor is weak.

The city charter determines a mayor's strength. The weak mayor has little control over policy initiation or implementation. The mayor's powers may be constrained by one or more of the following: limited or no appointment or removal power over city offices, limited budgetary authority, and the election of other city administrators independently of the mayor (Figure 27–1). Under these circumstances, the mayor shares power with the city council over city administration and policy implementation and "is the chief executive in name only."[14] These restrictions limit both the political and the administrative leadership of the mayor. Although it is possible for a mayor to use informal or noninstitutional resources to influence the city council and other administrators and to provide energetic leadership, there are formidable obstacles to overcome.[15]

A strong mayor has real power and authority, including appointive and removal powers over city agency heads (see Figure 27–2). Such appointments often require city council approval, but the appointees are responsible to the mayor and serve at mayoral discretion. The mayor has control over budget preparation and exercises some veto authority over city council actions. This form of city government clearly distinguishes between executive and legislative functions.

The strong mayor form of government is found in many of the larger American cities, but it is now used by only one major city in Texas—Houston. El Paso functioned under this form of government until 2004, when the city changed to council-manager government. The form may be unpopular in the state because the strong mayor often was associated with urban political machines, ward politics, and political corruption. Moreover, the fragmentation of authority and responsibility in local government parallels that found in state government and is another reminder of the deep distrust of government that Reconstruction produced in Texas. Finally, the state's individualistic and traditionalistic subcultures (see Chapter 21) reinforce hostile attitudes toward governmental institutions that are potentially more responsive to lower socioeconomic groups.

As might be expected, the salaries of the mayors and council members of cities with the strong mayor system are generally higher than under other forms of city government. In many cities, mayors and council members receive no pay or only modest reimbursement for services. The mayor of Houston earned $165,817 in 2002, and council members, $44,218. El Paso's mayor earned $28,944, and council members, $17,364.[16]

City Commission

The commission and council-manager forms of government are products of the twentieth century. Both reflect, in part, efforts to reform city governments through administrative efficiency, the reduction of partisan conflict, and the adaptation of a business-like approach to running city government.

The origin of the **city commission** is usually traced to the Texas island city of Galveston. After a hurricane and subsequent flooding devastated most of the city in 1900, the government then in office proved incompetent and incapable of responding. That crisis prompted a group of citizens to win the legislature's approval of a new form of government designed to be more responsive by combining the city's legislative and administrative functions in the offices of five city commissioners. City commissions were soon adopted by other major Texas cities, including Dallas, Houston, and San Antonio. But with the subsequent development of council-manager government as an alternative, there has been a marked decline in the city commission's popularity. It has

IS THIS ANY WAY TO CHANGE A CITY CHARTER?

Boerne, Texas, which is just northwest of San Antonio, held a special election in May 2002 to amend its charter to bring it in line with a law recently enacted by the Texas legislature. The new law permits local governments to purchase items valued at $25,000 or less without seeking bids. Prior to its enactment, the limit was $15,000, and the charter of Boerne included this figure. To permit the city to follow the state law and to anticipate future increases in the cap, a charter amendment would have permitted the city council to change spending caps each year as allowed by state law.

In a cliff-hanger election in which only 57 of 4,836 registered voters participated, the charter amendment was defeated, 29 to 28. The election occurred when there were no city or school board elections to draw voters to the polls. Few voters apparently were even aware the issue was on the ballot, and some just didn't care or believe the issue was important to them.

What happened in Boerne occurs throughout the state in charter elections. Just as is true for changes to the state constitution, all too often a small minority of a city's voters decide on changes in its fundamental law. While we have no empirical evidence, it might be argued that most changes are well-intentioned and necessary. But it is evident that a few individuals can use charter elections for their own self-interest.

SOURCE: "Boerne Rejects Charter Change," *San Antonio Express-News,* May 7, 2002.

mayor-council
Form of city government in which the legislative function is vested in the city council and the executive function in the mayor.

weak mayor
Form of city government in which the mayor shares authority with the city council and other elected officials but has little independent control over city policy or administration.

strong mayor
Form of city government that gives the mayor considerable power, including budgetary control and appointment and removal authority over city department heads.

city commission
Form of city government in which elected commissioners collectively serve as a city's policy-making body and individually serve as administrative heads of different city departments.

DOES THE FORM OF GOVERNMENT UNDER WHICH A CITY OPERATES MAKE ANY SIGNIFICANT DIFFERENCES?

Most major Texas cities have functioned under more than one form of government. Both Houston and San Antonio have functioned under all three primary forms described in this chapter. Changes in city charters often follow periods of intense political conflict, inertia, or an inability to respond to long-term problems. Proposed changes in governmental structures and election systems often threaten groups and interests that have a stake in the way business is currently being conducted, and charter revisions have a tendency to polarize a community.

council-manager
Form of city government in which policy is set by an elected city council, which hires a professional city manager to head the daily administration of city government.

been replaced in Houston, Dallas, and San Antonio, and only a few cities in Texas still have this form of government (see Figure 27–3).

Initially, the commission was supported as a businesslike approach to running city government. By eliminating partisan elections and combining the executive, administrative, and legislative functions, it was argued, cities could provide services more efficiently. But critics have identified several problems. The commission minimizes the potential for effective political leadership because no single individual can be identified as the person in charge. Moreover, there is minimal oversight and review of policies and budgets. Commissioners are elected primarily as policy makers, not administrators, and there are downsides to electing amateurs to administer increasingly technical and complex city programs.

The few cities in Texas that use the pure form of commission government generally have three members—a mayor and two commissioners—who are assigned responsibilities for specific city functions, such as water, sanitation, and public safety. Several of the commission cities now use a city administrator or manager, hired by the commission, to run the daily affairs of the city.

Council-Manager

After enthusiasm for the city commission waned, urban reformers, both in Texas and nationally, looked to the **council-manager** form of government. Its specific origins are disputed, but it was influenced by the same reform principals on which the city commission was based. The first cities in Texas to use council-manager government were Amarillo and Terrell in 1913, and it soon became popular among home rule cities. Dallas and San Antonio have been the largest cities in the state to adopt it (see Figure 27–4). Its principal characteristics are professional city management, nonpartisan city elections, and a clear distinction between policy making and administration. But in recent years, it has become evident that this policy–administration distinction has been modified by the increased roles of mayors and council members in the day-to-day operations of city government.

In some council-manager cities, the mayor is chosen by the city council from among its membership to preside over council meetings and fulfill a primarily symbolic role. But in other cities, the mayor is elected citywide, an arrangement that enhances the political

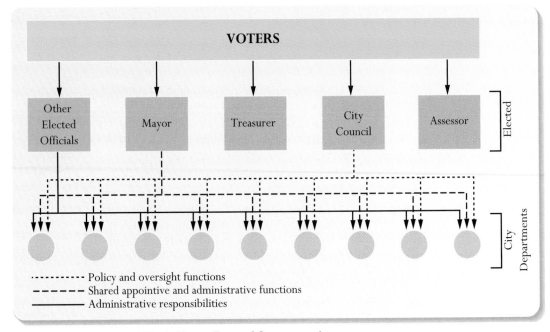

FIGURE 27–1 Example of Weak Mayor Form of Government.

position of the office without necessarily vesting it with formal legal authority. The mayor is usually a voting member of the city council but has few other institutional powers in a council-manager government. The mayor does, however, have the opportunity to become a visible spokesperson for the city and has a forum from which to promote ideas and programs (see *People and Politics: Making a Difference:* Ron Kirk and Lee Brown, History-Making Mayors).

The city council is primarily responsible for developing public policy (see *FYI:* "The Job of the City Council Member"). It creates, organizes, and restructures city departments, approves the city budget, establishes the tax rate, authorizes the issuance of bonds (subject to voter approval), enacts local laws (ordinances), and conducts inquiries and investigations into the operations and functions of city agencies.[17]

The council hires a full-time city manager, who is responsible for administering city government on a day-to-day basis. The manager hires and fires assistants and department heads, supervises their activities, and translates the policy directives of the city council into concrete action by city employees. The city manager is also responsible for developing a city budget for council approval and then supervising its implementation. Professionalism is one of the key attributes of the council-manager form of government. Initially, many city managers were engineers, but in recent years there has been a tendency for managers to be generalists with solid skills in public finance. City managers are fairly well paid. In 2002 the salary of the city manager of Dallas was $263,000. The San Antonio city manager was paid $200,000, and the city manager of even a small city such as Seguin received $111,580.[18]

At one time in the not too distant past, the salaries of mayors and council members serving in council-manager cities were very low, but there has been a trend in recent years to increase salaries in response to the expanded workload. Salaries of the mayor and city council members in Austin are $53,000 and $45,000, respectively. Until recently, the mayor and council members in Dallas received $50 per meeting, but voters approved a charter amendment in 2001 to raise the mayor's pay to $60,000 a year and council members to $37,500. By contrast, San Antonio's council members earn $20 per meeting and the mayor, $50 per meeting.

There is a delicate line between policy making and administration, and a city manager is, in principle, supposed to be politically neutral. The overall effectiveness of city managers depends on three main factors: their relationships with their city councils; their ability to develop support for their recommendations within the council and the community at large without appearing to have gone beyond the scope of their authority; and the overall perception of their financial and managerial skills. In the real world of municipal government, city managers play a central role in setting policy as well as carrying it out. Managers' adroit use of their resources and sensitivity to political factions and the personal agendas of elected officials are key to determining their success.

★★ THINKING IT THROUGH

Does the form of government under which a city operates make any significant difference? Political scientists have spent a lot of time trying to answer that question, and while there is some consensus on the general weaknesses of the city commission, opinions are divided on the other forms of local government. The general public appears to pay little attention to city charters or governmental structures, but elected officials and other city leaders, public employees, special interest groups, minority leaders, and some reform-minded citizens consider the structure of city government a crucial issue.

A city charter spells out how a city will run its affairs and helps determine which citizens will have access to policy making. In part, a charter is an expression of a city's social, economic, and political structure. Some scholars have concluded that the urban reform movements advocating nonpartisan at-large elections, which often were tied to council-manager government, were advancing middle- and upper-middle-class views and interests. The original intent of these changes may have been to encourage managerial efficiencies, but many urban governments became less responsive to the needs and interests of lower-income groups and minority populations.

SOURCE: William Lyons, "Reform and Response in American Cities: Structure and Policy Reconsidered," *Social Science Quarterly* 59 (June 1978), p. 130; Robert Lineberry and Edmund Fowler, "Reformism and Public Policies in American Cities," *American Political Science Review* 61 (September 1967), pp. 701–717; Willis D. Hawley, *Nonpartisan Elections and the Case for Party Politics* (John Wiley and Sons, 1973).

MUNICIPAL ELECTION SYSTEMS

Nonpartisan City Elections

Virtually every city in Texas elects its council members in **nonpartisan elections**. Claiming that there was no Democratic or Republican way to pave a street, city reformers who were part of the nonpartisan movement (1920s to 1950s) expressed a strong aversion to political parties and particularly to the urban political machines (see *You Decide/Thinking It Through:* "What Type of Electoral System Produces the Most Responsive City Council?"). To enforce separation of city elections from party politics, most municipal elections are held at times other than the party primaries or the general election.

The nonpartisan ballot—combined with at-large, citywide elections—has historically benefited higher social and economic groups. Parties and party labels normally

nonpartisan elections
Elections in which candidates do not represent a political party.

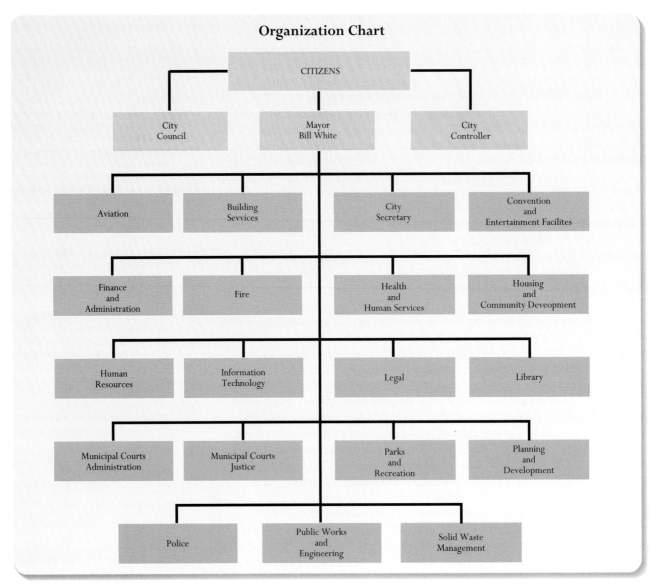

FIGURE 27–2 Example of Strong Mayor Form of Government, city of Houston.

SOURCE: Office of the Mayor, city of Houston, 2004.

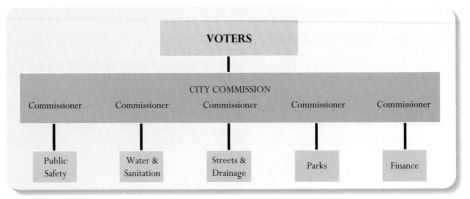

FIGURE 27–3 Example of a City Commission Form of Government.

CITY OF SAN ANTONIO

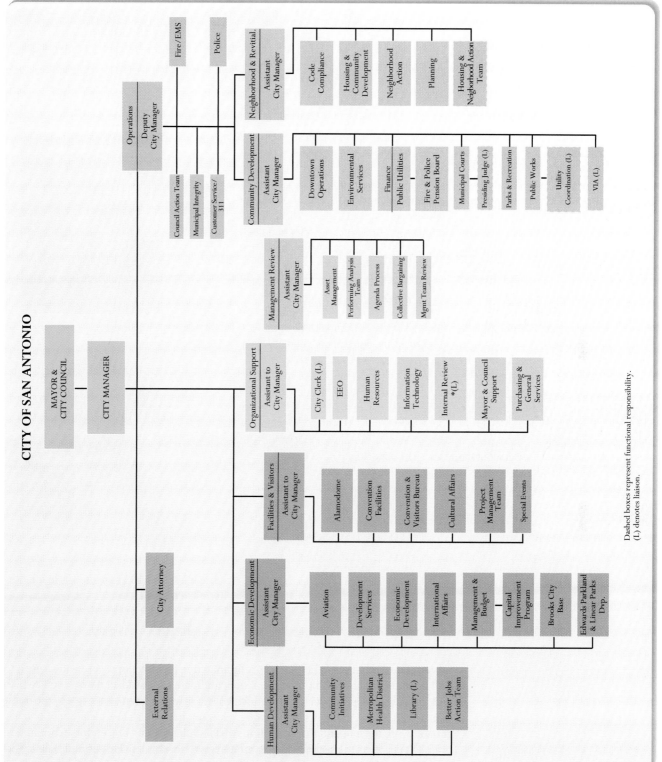

Dashed boxes represent functional responsibility.
(L) denotes liaison.

FIGURE 27–4 Example of a Council-Manager Government.

PEOPLE & POLITICS *Making a Difference* ★★★

RON KIRK AND LEE BROWN, HISTORY-MAKING MAYORS

In one key respect, Ron Kirk's election as mayor of Dallas in 1995 wasn't all that unusual. He had the strong support of the city's business leaders, who liked his campaign pledge for more aggressive economic development. Kirk's election, however, made history. He was Dallas's first African American mayor. In a city well known for its conservatism and recent racial divisions, Kirk attracted a broad base of support that included both establishment whites and African Americans who had long been unhappy with the city's power structure.

A former Texas secretary of state under Governor Ann Richards, Kirk was elected to head a city council that included four other African Americans, two Hispanics, and eight whites. Dallas has a council-manager form of government, and its mayor's office is weak in terms of formal powers. But the high-profile post offered Kirk the opportunity to use the skills of salesmanship and persuasion that had served him so well during his campaign. Successful economic development, which he viewed as essential to the city's future, would improve racial harmony in Dallas, he predicted. "It doesn't matter whether your ancestors came over on the *Mayflower,* or on a slave ship," he said, "we're all in the same boat now."* Kirk was reelected to a second

four-year term in 1999 but resigned in late 2001 to make an unsuccessful run for the U.S. Senate.

In 1997, Lee Brown scored a similar historical victory in Houston, when he was elected that city's first African American mayor. Brown, who earlier had been Houston's first African American police chief and had been drug policy director under President Bill Clinton, campaigned as a "mayor for all of Houston." Unlike Dallas, Houston has a strong mayoral office, giving Brown appointment powers over most city department heads and significant influence over city policies.

After taking 53 percent of the vote in a runoff against white businessman Rob Mosbacher, he told supporters at a victory celebration, "Another great barrier has fallen in the city of Houston—the doors of opportunity have opened wider for all of Houston's children."†

Brown received virtually all the African American vote and almost 30 percent of the white vote in the runoff. He and Mosbacher split the Hispanic vote.

Brown was easily reelected to a second two-year term in 1999 and won a third term in 2001 after a hard-fought runoff against Houston City Council Member Orlando Sanchez. Brown had to give up the mayor's office after his third

Ron Kirk

Lee Brown

term ended in 2003 because of Houston term limitations.

* Quoted in *Governing,* July 1995, p. 108.
† Quoted in *Houston Chronicle,* December 8, 1997.

serve as cues for voters. When they are eliminated in city elections, voters are forced to find different sources of information about candidates. Many local newspapers, which endorse candidates and decide how much coverage to give them, have ties to the dominant urban elites. Candidates from lower socioeconomic groups historically have had few contacts with the influential organizations that recruit, support, and endorse candidates. Although no longer in existence, San Antonio's Good Government League and Dallas's Citizens Charter Association controlled the recruitment and election of candidates in those two cities for several decades. Both organizations drew members from the Democratic and the Republican parties, but they reflected and pursued the interests of higher socioeconomic groups, often to the detriment of lower-income and minority populations.

At-Large Elections

at-large elections
Election systems under which officeholders are elected by voters in the entire city, school district, or single-purpose district.

Another notable feature of city politics in Texas is the general use of citywide or **at-large elections**. In 1992, the latest year for which U.S. census data were available, there were 6,409 individuals elected to the governing bodies of 1,171 cities and towns in Texas.

THE JOB OF THE CITY COUNCIL MEMBER

Regardless of the form of government, most city councils in Texas are small, with five to fifteen members elected for two-year terms. Most council seats are elected at-large, or citywide, and council elections are nonpartisan. Council members in most cities can serve for an unlimited number of terms. Recent referenda on term limitations, however, have been held in several Texas cities, including San Antonio and Houston, which imposed a two-term limitation on council members in 1991.

In most cities, a council office is part-time with little or no compensation, and while some large cities—such as Houston, Austin and Dallas—have recently increased salaries significantly, many council members do not consider their pay to be commensurate with the time spent on the job. Council members in San Antonio are still paid $20 per meeting. Low salaries were part of the early urban reform tradition. The idea was that people would run for office out of a sense of civic duty rather than to advance themselves financially.

The frequency of council meetings varies. In many small towns, councils may meet for only a few hours each month, but councils in large cities meet much more frequently, usually weekly, with meetings lasting several hours. Cities are dealing with a wider range of complex issues than ever before, and demands on a council member's time are great. In addition to their policy-making roles, council members in large cities are faced with increased demands for constituent services. Many council members are finding that public service is extremely costly in terms of time lost from their families and the jobs or professions that provide their livelihoods.

Council members often complain that they had no idea how much time the public would demand of them and their families. The following commandments for surviving have been offered by Hal Conklin, a former mayor of Santa Barbara:

1. Make an honest inventory of the hours that your political commitment will take.
2. Establish a contract with your employer for the hours that you are going to spend in your political commitment.
3. Set office hours and stick to them.
4. Delegate and hold accountable staff members and volunteers.
5. Put unmonitored phone lines on answering machines, especially at home.
6. Distinguish between home hours and work hours.
7. Make a date with your spouse (or significant other) for the same time each week.
8. Exercise regularly each day; eat a healthy diet.
9. Start and end your day with activities that soothe the soul.
10. Keep your sense of humor.*

---

* Hal Conklin, "Ten Commandments for Surviving as a City Council Member," *Texas Town and City* 83 (June 1995), pp. 12, 19.

Former journalist Laura Miller was elected mayor of Dallas in 2002.

Some 5,649, or 88 percent, were elected at large. Only 12 percent were elected from single-member districts, discussed in the following section.[19] Of the 1,204 Texas cities in 2002, some 207, or 14 percent, had single-member districts.[20]

In an at-large election, all of a city's voters participate in the selection of all members of the city council. In a pure at-large system, every candidate runs against every other candidate. If there are eight candidates running for five positions on the city council, the candidates with the five highest vote totals are the winners. Many of these election systems have been struck down by the federal courts or by the U.S. Justice Department under the Voting Rights Act as discriminatory against minorities.

A variation of the at-large system is the **place system**. Candidates file for a specific council seat and run citywide for places, or positions. Cities using the place system may require that the winning candidate receive a simple plurality of votes (more votes than any other candidate running for the same position) or an absolute majority of votes (more than half the votes cast.) If a city requires the latter and there are more than two persons in a race, **runoff elections** between the two highest vote-getters are often required.

Single-Member Districts

An alternative to at-large elections is the **single-member district**, or ward. Under this system, a city is divided into separate geographic districts, each represented by a different council member. A candidate must live in and run for election from a specific district,

place system
Form of at-large election in which candidates run for specific positions, or places, on a city council or other governing body.

runoff elections
Elections that are required if no candidate receives an absolute majority of the votes cast in a city council, school district, or party primary race. The runoff is between the two top vote-getters.

single-member district
System in which city council members, legislators, or other public officials are elected from specific geographical areas.

WHAT TYPE OF ELECTORAL SYSTEM PRODUCES THE MOST RESPONSIVE CITY COUNCIL?

There has been a great deal of debate over the most desirable form of city election system. There are those who argue that partisan elections with single-member districts produce greater access and accountability to elected officials. Others argue that nonpartisan, at-large elections produce a more effective city council. Others argue for nonpartisan elections with single-member districts. Is there any evidence that one system should be preferred over another?

and voters can cast a ballot only in the race for the council seat that represents their district. A person elected from a single-member district can, depending on the city's charter, be elected by a plurality or an absolute majority of votes.

Legal Attacks on At-Large Elections

Hispanics and African Americans, through various advocacy groups such as the National Association for the Advancement of Colored People, the Mexican American Legal Defense and Educational Fund, Texas Rural Legal Aid, and the Southwest Voter Registration and Education Project, have challenged in federal courts the election systems used by numerous Texas cities. From the small East Texas town of Jefferson to El Paso, Houston, and Dallas, minority groups have, with considerable success, challenged the inequities of at-large elections and forced city governments to adopt electoral plans that give minorities a better chance of electing candidates to city councils. The ethnic and racial composition of city councils has changed dramatically over the past twenty years, with a marked increase in the number of Hispanics and African Americans elected to these governing bodies (see Chapter 23).

CITY REVENUES AND EXPENDITURES

Despite a growing number of expensive needs that they are expected to address, Texas cities have limited financial options. Unlike counties and school districts, they receive no state appropriations for any purpose. City governments are disproportionately dependent on **regressive taxes**, such as property taxes and fees for services. Moreover, the state limits the property tax rate that a city can impose and permits citizens to petition their city council for a **rollback election** to nullify any tax increase of more than 8 percent in a given year. Although there have been few rollback elections in recent years, the potential for such citizen initiatives serves to constrain policy makers.

When the Texas economy went sour in 1985 and 1986, cities experienced revenue shortfalls from a decline in sales tax revenues, reductions in the assessed value of property, and the elimination of many federal assistance programs. By 1993, the financial positions of most cities improved as a result of a rebound in the real estate market and the overall improvement of the state's economy. Municipal financial conditions improved dramatically by 1995, and for the remainder of the decade, municipal revenues continued to increase due to the robust expansion of the real estate market and the overall economy.

The financial downturns that were experienced in the last half of 2001 once again imposed financial pressures on Texas cities. The sluggish economy and the decline in the state sales tax forced cities through 2003 to scramble to maintain services and minimize tax increases. A survey of Texas cities by the Texas Municipal League in early 2003 led to the conclusion that fiscal conditions facing cities were worse than they had been in the past twelve years.[21] More than 23 percent of the cities responding to the survey anticipated lower tax revenues in 2003, but few city financial officers projected additional revenue declines in 2004. Property taxes were increased in 46 percent of the cities. Approximately 43 percent of the responding cities raised one or more fees on such services as water, wastewater, and solid waste disposal. Cities also used other cost reduction strategies such as hiring freezes, wage freezes, and employment layoffs. A significant number of Texas cities postponed capital spending as a major part of their efforts to balance their budgets.[22]

Although cities are required by law to balance their operating budgets, many municipal construction projects are financed by loans through the issuance of **general obligation bonds**, which are subject to voter approval. These bonds are secured by the city's taxing power. The city pledges its full faith and credit to the lender and, over a number of years, repays the bonds with tax revenue. Cities also fund various projects through **revenue bonds** that are payable solely from the revenues derived from an income-producing facility.[23] The poor economy of the late 1980s made it more difficult for cities to borrow money. And with a pent-up demand for improving **infrastructure**

regressive taxes
Taxes that impose a disproportionately heavier burden on low-income people than on the more affluent.

rollback election
Election in which local voters can nullify a property tax increase that exceeds 8 percent in a given year.

general obligation bonds
Method of borrowing money to pay for new construction projects, such as prisons, mental hospitals, or school facilities. The bonds, which require voter approval, are repaid with tax revenue.

revenue bonds
Bonds that are used to finance construction of a public facility and are repaid with income produced by the facility.

infrastructure
Streets, waste disposal systems, libraries, and other public facilities built and operated by governments.

(streets, waste disposal systems, libraries, and other facilities), cities have entered an era of bond financing that has been radically altered by the performance of Wall Street and changes in state and federal tax laws.[24] Although city finances had improved as the state entered the twenty-first century, cities continued to postpone capital spending for streets, roads, water systems, and a variety of other capital improvements.[25]

URBAN PROBLEMS IN TEXAS

During the 1970s and through the early 1980s, Texas cities were key participants in the dramatic economic growth of the state. Many older cities across the country—particularly in the East and the Midwest—"looked at their Texas counterparts and envied their capacity to attract population and business."[26] Texas cities had low taxes, a pro-business tradition, few labor unions with significant economic clout, an abundant workforce, proximity to natural resources, and governing bodies that favored economic growth and development. At the beginning of the twenty-first century, however, many Texas cities were confronted with many of the problems associated with older urban areas outside of Texas.

The Graying of Texas Cities

The Texas population is aging, or graying. Americans are living longer, and older age groups are among the fastest growing segments of the population. As the population ages, additional pressures are placed on city governments for public services. The local property tax, a major source of revenue for city governments as well as other local governments, is stretched almost to its limits in many communities. Moreover, many Texas cities have granted, in addition to the standard **homestead exemption**, additional property tax exemptions for individuals older than sixty-five. As more and more people become old enough to claim these exemptions, younger taxpayers will be called upon to shoulder the burden through higher tax rates. There is also the looming possibility that older citizens on fixed incomes will be much more reluctant to support bond issues if they result in significant property tax increases.

"White Flight"

The population characteristics of Texas cities change over time, and major metropolitan areas have experienced "white flight" to the suburbs, a dramatic increase in the growth rate of minority populations, and small growth rates among Anglos in the central cities. Income levels for most minority Texans have always been lower than those of Anglos, and a larger proportion of the minority population falls below the poverty level (see Chapter 21). The increased concentration of lower-income people in the central cities increases pressure for more public services, while a declining proportion of affluent property owners weakens the local tax bases that pay for the services.

Declining Infrastructures

There has been much concern across Texas and the United States about the declining infrastructures of local governments. Streets, bridges, water and sewer systems, libraries, and other facilities must be continually maintained or expanded to support a growing population. Moreover, many Texas cities are out of compliance with federal standards for treating water and sewage and disposing of solid waste and must spend millions of dollars on physical improvements to avoid or reduce fines. Some capital improvements are paid for out of current operating budgets, but a more common practice is for cities to borrow money to improve roads, streets, water systems, and the like. These bonds are repaid from taxes on property. When property values decline—as they did in the late

homestead exemption
Reduction in property taxes that some local governments grant on a taxpayer's residence.

Poor neighborhoods stand in sharp contrast to the nearby high-rise office buildings of downtown Houston.

1980s—cities are restrained by the constitution and statutes as to the indebtedness they can incur to support improvements.

By the end of the 1990s, property values were increasing across most areas of the state, and cities had more opportunities to borrow money for capital improvements. Nevertheless, most cities have a large backlog of proposed projects and are often forced to put off or defer needed construction.

Crime and Urban Violence

Crime is a major problem facing Texas cities and counties, just as it is in many other parts of the country. Although crime rates in most offense categories declined in the 1990s, many Texans continued to believe that crime was on the rise. Much of the problem is related to drug abuse, gang violence, and juvenile crime. Expanded law enforcement patrols are proposed by political candidates and elected officials, but many city and county budgets cannot absorb the costs.

State- and Federally Mandated Programs

Both federal and state governments have increasingly used mandates to implement public policy in recent years. A **mandate** is a law or regulation enacted by a higher level of government that compels a lower level of government to carry out a specific action. In simpler terms, it is a form of "passing the buck." Federal mandates, along with pre-emptions, cover a wide range of governmental functions, including transportation, education for the disabled, water and air quality, and voter registration. States, meanwhile, have shifted much of the cost of public education to local governments.

Despite a decrease in federal funding for many urban problems during the 1980s, there has been an increase in federal mandates on the states, counties, and cities and an increase in state mandates on local governments, often with no financial support. In some cases, the state simply passes on the responsibility for—and the costs of—carrying out federal mandates to local governments. Congress enacted a law in 1995 to restrict unfunded mandates, but the law applied only to future, not existing, mandates. And such restrictions can still be circumvented if Congress chooses.

Although this practice may seem unfair and illogical, it is politically attractive to policy makers because they can "appease a large and vocal interest group that demands an extensive program without incurring the wrath of their constituents." They get the

mandate
Law or regulation enacted by a higher level of government that compels a lower level of government to carry out a specific function.

credit for such programs, but they do not get the blame for their costs.[27] Cities and other local governments across Texas claim that these unfunded requirements are excessively expensive, force them to rearrange their priorities, and limit local initiatives dealing with their most pressing issues. If local governments do not comply with mandates, they will be subject to litigation and face the prospect of losing federal or state funds. If they comply with mandates, they are then likely to reduce other services or seek alternative sources of funding now denied them.

COUNTY GOVERNMENT IN TEXAS

Texas has 254 counties, more than any other state. Counties are administrative subunits of the state that were developed initially to serve a predominantly rural population. Created primarily to administer state law, they possess powers delegated to them by the state, but they have relatively few implied powers. Unlike home rule cities, counties lack the basic legislative power of enacting ordinances. They can carry out only those administrative functions granted them by the state. Counties administer and collect some state taxes and enforce a variety of state laws and regulations. They also build roads and bridges, administer local welfare programs, aid in fire protection, and perform other functions primarily local in nature.[28] All counties function under the same constitutional restrictions and basic organizational structure despite wide variations in population, local characteristics, and public needs.

According to the 2000 census, Loving County, the state's least populous, had only 67 residents, compared to 3,400,578 in Harris County, the most populous (see Table 27–3). Rockwall County includes only 147 square miles, while Brewster County covers 6,204 square miles. Some 56 percent of the state's population lives in the ten most populous counties.

TABLE 27–3   TEN LARGEST AND TEN SMALLEST TEXAS COUNTIES, 1980–2000

	1980 Population	1990 Population	2000 Population
Harris	2,409,547	2,818,199	3,400,578
Dallas	1,556,390	1,852,810	2,218,899
Tarrant	860,880	1,170,103	1,446,219
Bexar	988,800	1,185,394	1,392,391
Travis	419,573	576,407	812,280
El Paso	479,899	591,610	679,622
Hidalgo	283,229	383,545	569,463
Collin	144,576	264,036	491,675
Denton	143,126	273,525	432,976
Fort Bend	130,846	225,421	354,452
Glasscock	1,304	1,447	1,406
Sterling	1,206	1,438	1,393
Terrell	1,595	1,410	1,081
Kent	1,145	1,010	859
Roberts	1,187	1,025	887
McMullen	789	817	851
Borden	859	799	729
Kenedy	543	460	414
King	425	354	356
Loving	91	107	67

Source: U.S. Censuses, 1980, 1990, 2000.

Motley County with a population of about 1,400 had a 2003 budget of $666,747 and paid its county judge $14,501 and its commissioners $11,786. Dallas County had a $678 million budget and paid its county judge $130,262 and its commissioners $107,358 a year. Harris County's 2003 budget was $1.39 billion. Its county judge was paid $133,000, and each of its commissioners received $126,000.[29] Although there is an obvious relationship between the population of a county and salaries paid to its officials, the county's tax base is also a significant factor.

Structure of County Government

The organizational structure of county government is highly fragmented, reflecting the principles of Jacksonian democracy and the reaction of late-nineteenth-century Texans to Radical Reconstruction. The governing body of a county is the **commissioners court**, but it shares administrative functions with other independently elected officials (see Figure 27–5). Moreover, the name "commissioners court" is somewhat misleading because that body has no judicial functions.

The Commissioners Court and County Judge

The commissioners court comprises a county judge, who is elected countywide, and four county commissioners, who are elected from a county's four commissioners precincts. Like other elected county officials, the judge and the commissioners serve four-year terms and are elected in partisan elections.

Until recent years, there were gross inequities in the population distributions among commissioners precincts in most counties. This issue of malapportionment came to a head in the 1968 case of *Avery* v. *Midland County,* in which the U.S. Supreme Court applied the "one person, one vote" principle to the counties and required districts to be equally apportioned.[30] Subsequently, Congress forced Texas to comply with the Voting Rights Act in 1975, and counties were required to consider the interests of minority populations in drawing up the boundaries for commissioners precincts. African Americans and Hispanics across the state have challenged county electoral systems and have increased minority representation on county commissioners courts. After the 2000 census, most Texas counties quickly redistricted their commissioner precincts in compliance with state and federal law.

The **county judge** presides over commissioners court, participates in the court's deliberations, and votes on issues before it. If there is a vacancy among the commissioners, the county judge appoints a replacement. If the county judge vacates the office, the commissioners choose a replacement.

The Texas constitution also gives the county judge some judicial responsibilities but does not require the officeholder to be a lawyer. Most urban counties have county courts-at-law that relieve the county judge of judicial duties. However, county judges in some rural counties perform a judicial as well as an executive role, combining two sets of duties in one office.

The commissioners court fills midterm vacancies in other county offices. It also has authority over the county budget, which permits the court to exercise some influence, if not control, over other officeholders.[31] The court sets the annual tax rate, which is limited by the Texas constitution, approves the tax roll, and supervises all expenditures of county money. Other county officials must obtain the court's authorization for personnel positions, salaries, and office expenses. Consequently, the budgetary process often sparks political disputes and other conflicts.

Historically, county road construction and maintenance were primary functions of commissioners court. The Optional Road Law of 1947 gave counties the authority to create a consolidated road system under the supervision of a county engineer, who relieved commissioners of road maintenance and construction headaches. But the importance of roads to the commissioners and their constituents still generates political disputes.

commissioners court
Principal policy-making body for county government. It sets the county tax rate and supervises expenditures.

county judge
Presiding officer of a county commissioners court. This office also has some judicial authority, which is assumed by separate county courts-at-law in most urban counties.

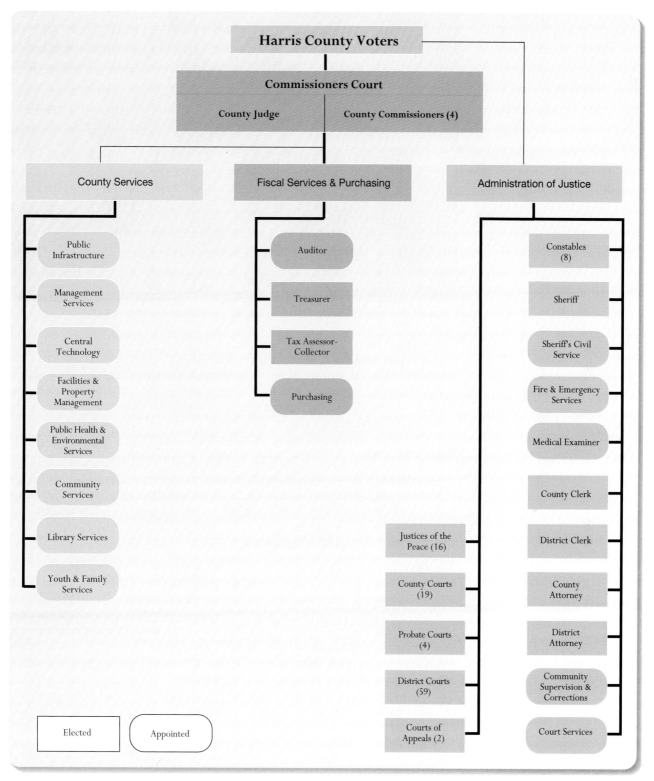

FIGURE 27–5 Harris County Organizational Chart.

County Clerk

The Texas constitution provides for an elected **county clerk** to serve as the clerk of the commissioners court, the clerk of the county courts, and (in the smaller counties) the clerk of the district court. Over the years, the legislature has enacted hundreds of statutory provisions defining specific responsibilities of the office, prompting one writer to describe the office as the "dumping ground for miscellaneous functions of the county."[32]

county clerk
Chief record-keeping officer of a county.

The Crockett County Courthouse, located in Ozona, was completed in 1902.

The office is the depository of a county's vital statistics, such as birth and death records, and documents related to real estate transactions. It issues marriage licenses and various other licenses required by state law.[33] The county clerk also serves as a county's chief elections administrator if the commissioners court has not created a separate elections administrator's office.[34]

District Clerk

The **district clerk**, also elected countywide, assists the district court by maintaining custody of court documents and records.[35] In small counties, the county clerk is authorized to double as the district clerk, and 53 counties combined these two offices in 2003.[36]

County and District Attorneys

The state's legal interests in both civil and criminal matters are represented at the local level by one of three officers—the **county attorney**, the **district attorney**, or the criminal district attorney. The legislature has enacted numerous provisions for legal departments that vary from county to county. Some counties have no county attorney but have a criminal district attorney. Under state law, others are authorized both a county attorney and a district attorney. District attorneys prosecute more serious cases, usually felonies, in the district courts, while the county attorneys usually prosecute lesser offenses, primarily misdemeanors, in the county courts.[37]

These officers can also provide legal advice and opinions to other county officials and give legal counsel to public officials or employees who have been sued for acts committed in carrying out their official duties (see *People and Politics: Making a Difference:* "Ronnie Earle: Corruption Fighter or Vindictive Politician?"). Upon request of the commissioners court, the district attorney or county attorney may initiate lawsuits on behalf of the county. Various other laws charge these attorneys with protecting the public health, assisting the state attorney general in cases involving deceptive trade practices, enforcing the state's election laws, collecting delinquent taxes, and even enforcing the Texas Communist Control Act of 1951.[38]

Tax Assessor-Collector

The property tax is the primary source of revenue for counties. Although the commissioners court sets property tax rates, the **tax assessor-collector**, another elected county officer, has the task of ascertaining who owns what property, determining how much tax

district clerk
Elected county official who maintains custody of state district court records.

county attorney
Elected official who is the chief legal officer of some counties. He or she also prosecutes lesser criminal offenses, primarily misdemeanors, in county courts.

district attorney
Elected official who prosecutes more serious criminal offenses, usually felonies, before state district courts.

tax assessor-collector
Elected official who determines how much property tax is owed on the different pieces of property within a county and then collects the tax.

County Judge Nelson Wolff presiding over a meeting of the Bexar County Commissioners Court.

PEOPLE & POLITICS *Making a Difference* ★★★

RONNIE EARLE: CORRUPTION FIGHTER OR VINDICTIVE POLITICIAN?

Few would argue that the Republican party has come to be the dominant political party in Texas today. Over the past decade Democrats have become extinct in statewide elected offices, decimated in the legislature, and redistricted out of congressional seats. The most powerful Democrat left in the State of Texas may be the district attorney of Travis County, Ronnie Earle.

State law gives the Travis County district attorney the authority to investigate corruption and crime in state government. This Public Integrity Unit is funded with $1 million per biennium.* Earle, born in Fort Worth and a graduate of the University of Texas, served briefly in the Texas legislature and then was elected Travis County district attorney in 1976. Serving in that position for over 27 years, Earle has investigated and prosecuted prominent Texas politicians, including a Texas Supreme Court justice, a United States senator, a state treasurer, the state attorney general, and various members of the legislature. In 1983, Earle even filed misdemeanor charges against himself for failure to file campaign finance reports and paid a $200 fine. Earle has prosecuted eleven Democratic and four Republican elected officials. These officials from both parties have ac-

cused Earle of everything from being on a witch hunt to playing politics and being mean and vindictive.

In 2003, the Travis County district attorney began an investigation into the successful efforts of U.S. Representative Tom DeLay, House Speaker Tom Craddick, Governor Perry's chief of staff, and the Texas Association of Business to gain control of the Texas house of representatives for the Republican party. Earle's investigation alleges individuals and corporations used huge amounts of money to control elections in violation of a 1905 Texas law.[†] In 2004, Mr. Earle extended the life of the grand jury investigating the alleged misconduct and successfully waged court battles to gain the release of documents.[‡]

As in previous cases investigated by Earle, targets of this probe have been unsettled about being under the microscope of the law. Texas Association of Business attorney Andy Taylor asserts that he is fighting to protect First Amendment rights and to restore his client's good name. Taylor accused Earle of political grandstanding.[§] Republican party of Texas Chairman Tina Benkiser announced in March 2004 that she would submit a resolution to the State Republican Executive Committee calling on the legislature to

transfer funding and authority of the Public Integrity Unit from the Travis County district attorney's office to the office of attorney general. "It makes absolutely no sense for a local District Attorney to have such far-reaching authority, especially since it can clearly be abused for partisan purposes," said Benkiser. "No other district attorney in the state is given such broad powers, and geography should not arbitrarily entitle one liberal prosecutor to a platform for launching vicious, partisan attacks."[∥] Earle has been relentless in his pursuits. In the current investigation, Earle warns that World War II Italian dictator Mussolini defined fascism as the merger of state and corporate power and asserts that the Texas Association of Businesses would contribute to a similar merger in Texas.[¶]

Until retirement, defeat in an election, or the removal of funding from his office by the legislature, Travis County District Attorney Ronnie Earle will continue to be the watchdog of state government.

* *The Houston Chronicle*, March 4, 2004.
† Jay Root, *The Fort Worth Star Telegram*, March 1, 2004.
‡ *The Austin American Statesman*, June 27, 2004.
§ *The Austin Chronicle*, April 11, 2003.
∥ The Republican Party of Texas, Press Release, March 1, 2004.
¶ *The Austin Chronicle* April 11, 2003.

is owed on that property, then collecting the tax. In counties with fewer than 10,000 people, these responsibilities are assigned to the sheriff, unless voters decide to create a separate tax assessor-collector's office. Seventeen counties, mainly those below 5,000 in population, continue to let the sheriff handle the job.

Prior to reforms enacted in the 1970s, the tax assessor-collector also was responsible for appraising property or determining its value. This process was often steeped in politics because the higher the value of a piece of property, the more taxes its owner has to pay. Lowering property values for select friends or supporters gave people holding this office considerable power, which often was abused. In an effort to move toward greater consistency across the state and to enhance the professionalism of tax appraisals, the legislature now requires each county to create an appraisal district separate from the tax office.[39] Property tax appraisals are now conducted countywide by an **appraisal district** whose members represent other governmental units in the county. The district also certifies the tax rolls, and other governmental units are required by law to use its appraisals.[40]

County Law Enforcement

Sheriffs and **constables**, a county's law enforcement officers, are part of an old tradition under the Anglo-Saxon legal system. Each county has one sheriff with countywide jurisdiction, but the number of constables can vary. In counties with fewer than 18,000 residents, the commissioners court can designate the entire county as a single justice of the peace precinct or can create as many as four precincts, with each precinct assigned one constable. In the large counties, as many as eight justice of the peace precincts can be created, with a constable assigned to each. Most counties have four constables.[41]

In a small rural county, the sheriff is the primary law enforcement officer for the entire county. But in urban counties, city police departments generally assume exclusive jurisdiction in the incorporated municipal areas, leaving the sheriff jurisdiction over the unincorporated areas. Most sheriffs have considerable discretion in the hiring, promotion, and firing of deputies and other employees, although some counties have adopted a merit employment system for the sheriff's office. The sheriff also serves as the administrative officer for the district and county courts.

Constables are authorized to patrol their precincts, make arrests, and conduct criminal investigations, but their primary function is to serve as administrative officers of the justice of the peace courts. They are responsible for serving **subpoenas**, executing judgments of the court, and delivering other legal documents.[42]

County governments are responsible for constructing and staffing county jails, which are managed in most counties by the sheriff and in some counties by a jail administrator. During the late 1980s and early 1990s, counties across the state pursued an aggressive policy of jail construction in response to court decisions, increased crime rates, and a shortage of state prison space. Jail construction was a "growth" industry during this period, but by the mid-1990s, some counties found that they had overextended their finances to construct these jails. They also were left with excess jail capacity after an increase in state-built prison facilities. To compensate for these problems, several counties contracted with other states to house their prisoners in Texas jails.

All counties are authorized to create an office of **medical examiner**. This individual is appointed by the commissioners court and determines the cause of death of murder victims or others who die under suspicious or unusual circumstances. In counties that do not have a medical examiner, the justice of the peace is charged with conducting an **inquest** to determine if there are conditions to merit an autopsy.

Counties, either individually or as part of multicounty judicial districts, are required to provide facilities for a criminal probation office. Funded by the state, the chief adult probation officer of a county is chosen by the district judges, who supervise the office.

County Auditor

All counties with 10,000 or more people are required to have a **county auditor**, and smaller counties may have one if the commissioners court chooses. Two counties with fewer than 25,000 residents may jointly agree to hire an auditor to serve both counties.

---

appraisal district
Local agency that determines the value of pieces of property in a county. All local governments are required to use its evaluations, or appraisals, for tax purposes.

sheriff
Elected official who is the chief law enforcement officer of a county.

constable
Elected law enforcement officer who is primarily responsible for executing court judgments, serving subpoenas, and delivering other legal documents.

subpoenas
Court orders requiring people to testify in court or before grand juries or to produce certain documents.

medical examiner
Appointed official who is responsible for determining the cause of death of murder victims or others who die under suspicious or unusual circumstances.

inquest
Examination by a justice of the peace or a medical examiner of unusual circumstances under which someone has died.

county auditor
Appointed officer who is primarily responsible for reviewing every bill and expenditure of a county to assure it is correct and legal.

The county auditor is appointed by the district judges of the county for a two-year term. He or she is primarily responsible for reviewing every bill and expenditure of a county to assure its correctness and legality. Such oversight can, in effect, impose budgetary restrictions on the commissioners court and produce political conflict with other county officers.

The role of the auditor varies from county to county. In counties with more than 225,000 people, the auditor is the budget officer and prepares the county budget for submission to commissioners court, unless an alternative has been authorized by the legislature.[43] In smaller counties, the commissioners court prepares the budget, based on estimates provided by the auditor.

County Treasurer

The **county treasurer** is responsible for receiving and disbursing county funds. Although this office has existed since 1846, its primary functions are now carried out by the county auditor, and constitutional amendments have eliminated the office in a number of counties.

CRITICISMS OF COUNTY GOVERNMENT

The structure of county government in Texas, designed for a rural state, has inhibited efforts of urban counties to respond to growing needs for public services. The state experimented with county home rule years ago, but the provisions were so poorly written, confusing, and contradictory that local self-rule at the county level was never given a real chance. Efforts were made in the 1997 and 1999 sessions of the legislature to amend the constitution to once again allow counties to adopt home rule, but there was limited statewide support for this change.

Even though the county functions primarily as an extension, or administrative subdivision, of state government, there is limited supervision of the counties by the state and a wide disparity in the way counties interpret and administer their functions. Some counties do a very good job, while others have a dismal record. The fragmentation represented by several independently elected officers always poses a danger of jurisdictional conflict, administrative inefficiency, and even government deadlock.

Like other local governments in Texas, counties rely heavily on the property tax for revenue but cannot exceed tax rate limits set by the state constitution. Those limits reflected a general apprehension about government when they were initially set in 1876. They now further restrict the counties' ability to provide services.

Historically, county courthouses have been associated with political patronage and the **spoils system**. Victorious candidates have claimed the right to appoint personal and political friends to work for them, and state courts have held that elected county officials have wide discretion in the selection of their employees. Reformers have advocated a **civil service system** for county employees based on merit and competitive examinations and offering job security from one election to the next. A 1971 law allows counties with more than 200,000 residents to create a civil service system, but it excludes several county offices, including the district attorney. An elected public official retains considerable control over the initial hiring of employees through a probationary period of six months.[44]

SPECIAL DISTRICTS IN TEXAS

Every day, Texans use the services of municipal utility districts (MUDs), water conservation and improvement districts (WCIDs), hospital districts, and a host of other local governments, which have been deemed by some as the "invisible governments" of the state.[45] There are approximately 3,300 such governmental units across Texas classified as **special-purpose districts,** and almost every year additional ones are created. These include drainage districts, navigation districts, fresh water supply districts, river

county treasurer
Elected officer who is responsible for receiving and disbursing county funds.

spoils system
System of filling public jobs by hiring friends and other politically connected applicants, regardless of their abilities.

civil service system
System under which public employees are hired and promoted on their abilities. It features competitive examinations and offers job security from one election to another.

special-purpose districts
Units of local government created by the state to perform specific functions not met by cities or counties, including the provision of public services to unincorporated areas.

authorities, underground water districts, sanitation districts, housing authorities, soil conservation districts, MUDs, and WCIDs. School districts are also considered a form of special purpose district.

Functions and Structures

Special districts are units of local government created by the state to perform specific functions. Wide variations in their functions, taxing and borrowing authority, governance, and performance limit generalizations about them. Most special districts are authorized to perform a single function and are designated single-purpose districts. But some are multipurpose districts because the laws creating them permit them to provide more than one service to constituents. For example, in addition to providing water to people in their service areas, MUDs may assume responsibility for drainage, solid waste collection, firefighting, and parks and other recreational facilities.[46] Some districts, such as hospital districts, normally cover an entire county. Others, such as MUDs, cover part of one county, while still others, such as river authorities, cover a number of counties.

A special district is governed by a board either appointed by other governmental units or elected in nonpartisan elections. The board members of hospital districts are appointed by county commissioners courts; city housing authority boards are appointed by mayors or city councils. Many of these districts have taxing and borrowing authority, but others have no taxing powers and are supported by user fees or funds dedicated to them by other governmental agencies. Many special districts are eligible for federal grants-in-aid.

Special districts exist for a variety of reasons. Independent school districts were created, in part, to depoliticize education and remove the responsibility for it from county and city governments. In some cases, existing governments are unwilling or unable—because of state restrictions on their tax, debt, or jurisdictional authority—to provide essential services to developing communities. So special districts were created to fill the gap.

The cost of providing a particular governmental service is another reason for the growth of special districts. By creating a special district that includes a number of governmental units and a larger population and tax base, the costs can be spread over a wider area. Special districts often are promoted by individuals, groups, or corporations for selfish gains. Builders, for example, sometimes develop plans for large tracts of land in the unincorporated areas of a county and then get local governments or the legislature to create municipal utility or water districts to provide water and sewer services.

Some special districts have been designed to serve specific geographical areas. River basins that extend for thousands of square miles and cover ten or twenty counties have presented a particular problem. Because no existing governments had jurisdiction over the use of water resources in these basins, river authorities with multicounty jurisdictions were created.[47]

Consequences of Single-Purpose Districts

From one perspective, special districts compensate for the fragmentation of local government that exists throughout Texas. But, ironically, these districts contribute to further fragmentation and delay the more difficult development of comprehensive, multipurpose governmental units that could more efficiently provide public services. A special district has been called a "halfway house between cityhood and noncityhood, between incorporation and nonincorporation."[48] Residents of a developing community or subdivision may not want to create a new city or become part of a nearby existing city, but they need certain fundamental services, such as water, electricity, and fire protection, some of which can be provided through the creation of special districts.

Many special districts are small operations with limited financial resources and few employees. Salaries often are low, and some districts have difficulty retaining the licensed technical people required to perform daily operations. In some cases, record-keeping and management operations are shoddy and amateurish, and the costs of providing services by many of these operations may actually be higher than what similar services cost in larger governmental systems. Special districts may also use outside legal and professional assistance, which can be very costly, and many districts lack the expertise to maximize their investments or borrowing potential.[49]

Some special districts expand their functions beyond the purpose for which they were created. The metropolitan transit authority in San Antonio, for example, authorized under state law to impose a 1 percent sales tax for public transportation, became involved in building the Alamodome, a multipurpose convention and sports facility. As governments expand their functions, there is a greater potential for intergovernmental rivalry, conflict, deadlock, and duplication of costs.

Except for the 1,000-plus independent school districts and a small number of other highly visible districts, such as river authorities, most special districts operate in anonymity. The public has only limited knowledge of their jurisdiction, management, operations, or performance. Many taxpayers may not even be aware they are paying taxes to some of these entities. There is little media coverage of their work, few individuals attend their board meetings, and turnout for their elections is extremely low. In the case of the governing boards that are appointed by other governmental agencies, the appointment process is often dominated by a small number of individuals or groups who also dominate the activities of the special district. This domination is probably the most damning indictment of special districts.

INDEPENDENT SCHOOL DISTRICTS

The **independent school district**, currently the basic organizational structure for public education in Texas, had its origins in the constitution of 1876. Cities and towns were allowed to create independent school districts and to impose a tax to support them. Initially, the city government served as the school board, but in 1879, school districts were permitted to organize independently of the city or town, elect their own boards of trustees, and impose their own school tax. But residents of rural areas, where most nineteenth-century Texans lived, were denied these powers and only had the option of forming community schools. So, in effect, Texas operated under a dual school system, with the majority of students subject to the discretionary and often arbitrary powers of county governments.

Inequities in the Public Education System

From the very beginning, the inequities in the school system were clear to many parents, elected officials, and educators, and there were early efforts to reform and modernize public schools. Most were linked to national education reform movements. For example, the Peabody Education Board, a national organization, provided financial aid and technical support to the leaders of the state reform movement during the early part of the twentieth century. More recently, national attention was directed to the problems of public education through widely publicized studies such as *A Nation at Risk: The Imperative for Educational Reform* (1983), which was conducted by the National Commission on Excellence in Education. Many national, state, and local organizations have attempted to identify the most serious problems in public education, develop alternatives for resolving these problems, and initiate related litigation or legislative and administrative initiatives. Although education is primarily a local responsibility, three recent presidents have made educational policy one of their top priorities.

Reformers have focused much of their attention on compulsory education laws, adequacy and equity in school funding, quality curricula, and teacher preparation. Some reform efforts also have been directed at the structure and governance of local school districts. The diverse and fragmented structure of Texas schools has been modified over the years through consolidation, greater uniformity in the organization of school

independent school district
Specific form of special district that administers the public schools in a designated area.

The Board of Trustees of the San Antonio Independent School District comprises seven members elected from single-member districts. This body has the primary responsibility for setting school district policies.

districts, and the extension of the independent school district to virtually every community in the state.

Local School Governance

Although regulation and coordination are provided on a statewide level through the State Board of Education and the Texas Education Agency (TEA), public education is now administered through more than 1,000 local school districts. In 2002, the smallest districts, the Divide Independent School District in Kerr County and the San Vicente ISD in far West Texas, each had twenty students. The largest, the Houston Independent School District, had 210,670 students. The thirteen largest districts—with more than 50,000 students each—enrolled more than one million of the 4.1 million students attending prekindergarten through grade 12 in Texas public schools during the 2001–2002 school year. By contrast, 502 districts had fewer than 500 students each, serving a total of only 115,000 students. By 2002, students from minority ethnic or racial groups constituted 59 percent of the public school population in Texas, and their numbers are projected to increase.[50]

School districts are governed by **school boards**, ranging in size from three to nine members; most have seven. Trustees are elected in nonpartisan elections for terms that vary from two to six years, with most serving three-year terms. In 2003, 176 of the 1,000-plus school districts elected their boards from single-member districts.[51] School districts with significant minority populations have shifted from at-large elections to single-member districting, primarily as a consequence of lawsuits or the threats of lawsuits by minority plaintiffs under the Voting Rights Act.

Most school board elections are held on the first Saturday in May, the same day most cities hold their elections. School board election turnouts are low, usually less than 10 percent of registered voters. But turnout increases when there are highly visible issues, such as the firing of a superintendent or a dramatic increase in taxes.

Recruiting qualified candidates for school boards is often difficult, and many times elections are uncontested. Individuals are encouraged to run by the superintendent, other members of the board, or key community leaders, many of whom point out that it is difficult to find people who are willing to give the required time and energy. Individuals often have little knowledge of what school board members do, and because many trustees serve for only one term, some boards have high turnover rates. Moreover, there is no way for a potential trustee to anticipate the amount of time it will take for

school board
Governing body of a school district. Its responsibilities include the development or approval of educational policies, approval of the budget, hiring of the superintendent, and other personnel matters.

briefings by the superintendent and staff, preparing for and participating in board meetings, and taking phone calls from parents and taxpayers. A board member must also deal with the political aspects of the job, including attendance at community functions and major school programs and meeting with teachers and taxpayer groups. Board members receive no salaries but are reimbursed for travel related to board business.

The most important decision that a school board makes is the hiring of a **school superintendent**. In organization and management structure, the school district is similar to the council-manager form of government. The board hires a superintendent, who is in charge of the district's day-to-day operations. Although the board has the primary policy-making responsibility for a district, part-time board members are often dominated by the superintendent and the superintendent's staff. School trustees and superintendents tend to talk about "keeping politics out of education," and superintendents often attempt to convey the impression that they serve simply to carry out the will of their boards. In most instances, however, a school board's agenda is established by the superintendent, and the board members depend on the superintendent and other professional staff members for information and policy recommendations. Very few board members have much time to give to the district, and most have only limited knowledge of the laws affecting education. State law, in fact, restricts the intrusion of board members into the daily management and administration of a district. An excessively politicized school board that becomes involved in day-to-day administration can be called to task by the Texas Education Agency. In an extreme case, the TEA can even take over the management of a school district.

COUNCILS OF GOVERNMENT

Local issues or problems do not start or stop at the boundaries of local governments. Water issues, for example, are usually of a regional nature and transcend the boundaries of cities and counties. Land use, crime and transportation issues similarly affect multiple governments, and, in fact, there are relatively few policy issues that do not impact more than one government. Under the complex system of local government that has evolved in Texas and throughout the United States, it has long been argued by policy makers and students of government that greater coordination and collaboration is imperative if sound public policy is to be developed in response to these mutual issues.

Councils of government (COGs), or regional planning commissions, were created under the Texas Regional Planning Act of 1965 (see Figure 27–6). That law was enacted, in part, to comply with federal regulations requiring local planning and review procedures.[52] These organizations evolved over the years to take on additional duties, including comprehensive planning and service responsibilities for employment and job training, criminal justice, economic development, health, aging, early childhood development, alcoholism, drug abuse, transportation, land resource management, environmental quality, and rural development.[53]

Although councils of government are "defined by law as political subdivisions of the state, they have no regulatory power or other authority possessed by cities, counties, or other local governments."[54] Stated another way, they do not have jurisdictional authority with police and taxing powers. They cannot enact local legislation, nor do they have the power to force compliance. Decisions of the COGs are not binding on their members.[55]

The councils, instead, are support agencies designed to promote voluntary collaboration and coordination of public services among local governments. Their effectiveness varies across the state and appears to be partially related to the willingness of their members to engage in serious intergovernmental policy planning and implementation, the technical expertise of their staffs, and the political effectiveness of their leaders.

Twenty-four regional councils of government in Texas each serve a specific geographic area. Membership is voluntary; in 2002, more than 2,000 counties, cities, school districts, and other special districts were members of COGs.[56] Each COG decides the

school superintendent
Top administrator of a school district. He or she is hired by the elected school board to direct the district's daily operations.

council of government (COG)
Council comprised of representatives of other governments in a defined region of the state.

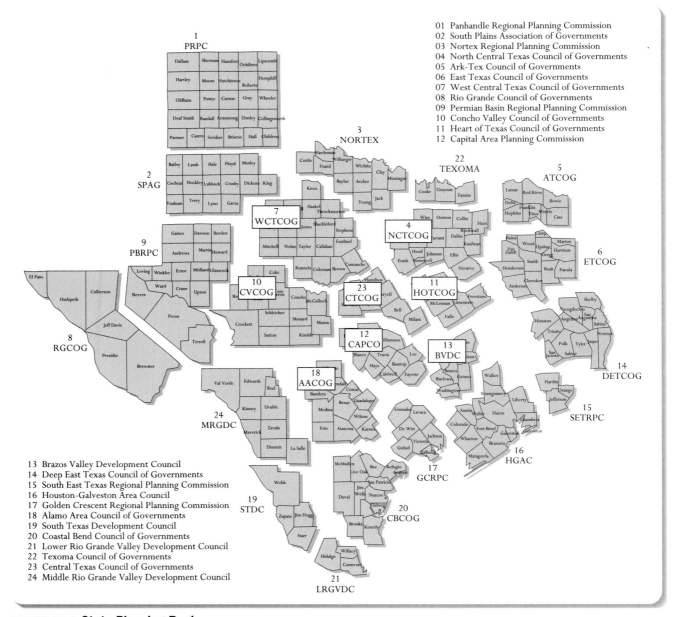

FIGURE 27–6 State Planning Regions.
SOURCE: Office of the Governor.

01 Panhandle Regional Planning Commission
02 South Plains Association of Governments
03 Nortex Regional Planning Commission
04 North Central Texas Council of Governments
05 Ark-Tex Council of Governments
06 East Texas Council of Governments
07 West Central Texas Council of Governments
08 Rio Grande Council of Governments
09 Permian Basin Regional Planning Commission
10 Concho Valley Council of Governments
11 Heart of Texas Council of Governments
12 Capital Area Planning Commission

13 Brazos Valley Development Council
14 Deep East Texas Council of Governments
15 South East Texas Regional Planning Commission
16 Houston-Galveston Area Council
17 Golden Crescent Regional Planning Commission
18 Alamo Area Council of Governments
19 South Texas Development Council
20 Coastal Bend Council of Governments
21 Lower Rio Grande Valley Development Council
22 Texoma Council of Governments
23 Central Texas Council of Governments
24 Middle Rio Grande Valley Development Council

composition and structure of its governing body, so long as two-thirds of its members are elected officials from counties or cities.

Member governments pay dues, but the primary sources of funding for COGs have been the state and federal governments. The state pays a regional council a flat fee for each county that is a member and provides a per capita payment for each person residing in the COG. At one time, the regional councils relied extensively on federal grants-in-aid, but there was a 70 percent decrease in direct federal funding of COGs during the 1980s. Indirect federal pass-through funds administered by state agencies also provide funds for the COGs.[57] Several COGs have expanded their technical support and some management services to offset these lost revenues.[58] At the end of 2003, COGs were reviewing the impact of budget cuts and administrative reorganization on their functions, programs, and staffs.

SOLUTIONS TO THE PROBLEMS OF LOCAL GOVERNMENT

Privatization of Functions

As local governments have juggled their financial problems with increased demands for public services, they have tended to contract out some services to private companies. Many governments believe **privatization** can reduce costs through businesslike efficiency, and they consider it an attractive alternative in the face of voter hostility toward higher taxes. Cities, for example, are contracting for garbage pickup, waste disposal, towing, food services, security, and a variety of other services. Privatization also provides a way for cities that have reached their limit on bonded indebtedness to make new capital improvements by leasing a facility from a private contractor. A civic center or school facility can be constructed by a private contractor and leased back to the government for an extended period.

Annexation and Extraterritorial Jurisdiction

Population growth in the areas surrounding most large Texas cities has forced municipalities and counties to wrestle with urban sprawl. El Paso covered 26 square miles in 1950 but had expanded to 250 square miles by 2000. Houston grew from 160 square miles in 1950 to 579 square miles in 2000, and similar expansions have occurred in most of the state's other metropolitan areas.

The cities' ability to expand their boundaries beyond suburban development derives from their **annexation powers** and **extraterritorial jurisdiction** over neighboring areas. With the Municipal Annexation Act of 1963, the legislature granted cities considerable discretionary authority over nearby unincorporated areas. Specific annexation powers and extraterritorial jurisdiction vary with the size and charter of a city. Generally, cities have extraterritorial jurisdiction over unincorporated areas within one-half mile to five miles of the city limits, making development in those areas subject to the city's building codes, zoning and land use restrictions, utility easement requirements, and road and street specifications. This authority restricts the use of unincorporated land and requires those building outside the city to build according to at least minimal standards. Later, when those areas are annexed by the city, they are less likely to degenerate quickly into suburban slums that will require a high infusion of city dollars for basic services.

Cities can annex areas equivalent to 10 percent of their existing territory in a given year, and if this authority is not exercised in one year, it can be carried over to subsequent years. Annexation usually does not require a vote of those people who are to be incorporated into the city (see *You Decide/Thinking It Through:* "Should the Annexation Powers of Texas Home Rule Cities Be Limited?"). However, within two and one-half years, a city is required to provide annexed areas with services comparable to those provided in its older neighborhoods. Otherwise, individuals living in these newly annexed areas can exercise an option to be deannexed, a situation that rarely occurs.

Aggressive use of annexation has permitted several large cities to expand geographically with population growth, thus often limiting the development of small suburban towns that would potentially limit future expansion. Cities have even annexed thin strips of land, miles from urban development, along major roads and highways leading into them. Since a city's extraterritorial jurisdiction extended as far as five miles on either side of the strip that was annexed, this practice has enabled a city to control future development in a large area. In San Antonio, these annexation policies have often been referred to as "spoke annexation," and it has taken more than thirty years for much of the territory brought under the city's jurisdiction to be developed and annexed by the city.[59]

In recent legislative sessions, many lawmakers have demonstrated an anticity sentiment with proposals that would have eroded municipal authority, reduced municipal revenues, and imposed costly new mandates. Of particular concern to cities were attacks on annexation powers. The legislature in 1999 enacted a major overhaul of annexation authority, including a provision that requires cities to outline their annexation

privatization
Contracting by government with private companies to provide some public services.

annexation powers
Authority of cities to add territory, subject to restrictions set by state law.

extraterritorial jurisdiction
Power of an incorporated city to control development within nearby unincorporated areas.

★★ **YOU DECIDE**

**SHOULD THE ANNEXATION POWERS
OF TEXAS HOME RULE CITIES
BE LIMITED?**

For years, developers building subdivisions on
the scenic western outskirts of Austin have
been fighting environmentalists and Austin city
officials over environmental restrictions. That
war reached new intensity in 1995, when
the developer of Circle C Ranch, a planned
community in southwest Travis County, went
to the Texas legislature to win unprecedented
independence for his subdivision.

Texas home rule cities have rather expansive
annexation powers, but there are occasions when
these powers come into conflict with developers
and builders, smaller cities in proximity to the
home rule city, and private citizens who live
outside of the city. Should these annexation
powers be limited?

Houses in the Circle C Ranch development.

tax abatements
Exemptions from property taxes granted to
certain businesses, usually to encourage
them to move to or expand their operations
in a city or county. The exemptions are
granted for specific periods.

metro government
Local government in which city and county
governments consolidate to avoid duplication of public services.

public improvement district
Specific area of a city in which property
owners pay special taxes in return for improvements to streets and other public facilities in their neighborhood.

plans three years in advance. But cities felt, through their lobbying efforts, that
they were able to obtain a relatively "well-balanced" law.[60] The legislature in 2001
continued to reflect growing suburban–rural hostility toward the cities. It enacted
a law that modified the extraterritorial jurisdiction of cities by requiring city–
county agreements on the regulation of subdivisions.[61]

Modernization of County Government

City governments provide most basic public services in urban areas, and as cities
expand to county boundaries and beyond, there is increased overlapping jurisdiction of county and city governments and a reduction of county services in the
annexed areas. Counties, nevertheless, still play an important role in Texas. Rural
Texans, in particular, continue to rely on counties to provide a number of services, and demands on many counties will increase. Recommendations to modernize county government include further attempts at county home rule, granting
counties some legislative or ordinance-making authority, and creating an office
of county administrator, appointed by the commissioners court to run the departments now assigned to commissioners. Another recommendation is to extend the civil service system to smaller counties and to all county employees.[62]

Economic Development

Historically, cities have collaborated with the private sector to stimulate local
economies. Private sector initiatives have come from chambers of commerce or economic development foundations, and local governments have participated. Cities also
are using a variety of new financing techniques to assist in economic development, including development impact taxes and fees, user charges, creation of special-district
assessments, tax increment financing, and privatization of governmental functions.[63] A
state law was enacted in 1989 to permit cities, with the approval of local voters, to impose a 0.5 percent sales tax for local economic development. By 1995, voters in 229 Texas
cities had approved this tax option.[64]

Texas cities, as well as some counties, aggressively court American and foreign companies to relocate or develop new plants or operations in their communities. Cities and
local chambers of commerce sponsor public relations campaigns touting local benefits and attractions. Local governments offer **tax abatements**—exemptions from property taxes on a business for a specified period—to encourage a company to locate or
expand in a community. (See *FYI:* "Abatements—Expensive Tax Breaks"). Other financial incentives to companies being courted include lowered utility bills and assistance
in obtaining housing for employees.

The legislature has permitted counties to form industrial development corporations or enterprise zones and to relax state regulatory policies to encourage the rede-
velopment of depressed areas. Portions of a county may be designated as reinvestment
zones, in which tax abatements can be offered to attract new businesses. Counties also
can create county boards of development, civic centers, foreign trade zones, and research and development authorities.[65]

Interlocal Contracting

Because many small governments have limited tax bases and staffs, they enter into
contracts with larger governments for various public services. In 1971, the legislature,
following a constitutional amendment, enacted the Interlocal Cooperation Act, which
gave cities, counties, and other political subdivisions rather broad authority for such
contracts.[66] The law has been amended several times to expand the scope of these
agreements, and local governments are now contracting with each other for services in
25 functional areas, ranging from aviation to water and wastewater management.[67]
Contracting is not an alternative to consolidation of local governments, but it does
hold out some promise for improving the quality of local services and reducing their
costs.

Metro Government and Consolidation

In the metropolitan areas of Houston, Dallas, and San Antonio, there are literally hundreds of cities and special districts providing public services. In Harris County (Houston) alone, there are 498 separate governmental units (see Table 27–4). Legislators, scholars, and reform groups have extensively studied the duplication and other problems produced by such proliferation and fragmentation and have made numerous recommendations over the years. One proposed solution is a consolidation of city and county governments known as **metro government**, which has been tried in a dozen or so areas outside Texas. Efforts initiated by San Antonio and Bexar County to obtain constitutional authority to propose city-county consolidation to voters in the county failed in the 1997 legislative session. Other metropolitan areas joined Bexar County and San Antonio in an expanded effort to obtain this authority from the legislature in 1999, but again it failed. Without such authority, county–city collaboration is more likely to take the form of increased intergovernmental contracting and the informal cooperation that local governments develop out of necessity and mutual self-interest.[68]

Public Improvement Districts

Under one state law, property owners in a specific area of a city or its extraterritorial jurisdiction can petition the city to create a special **public improvement district.** These districts can undertake a wide range of improvements—landscaping, lighting, signs, sidewalks, streets, pedestrian malls, libraries, parking, and water, wastewater, and drainage facilities. Public improvement districts do

TABLE 27–4 LOCAL GOVERNMENTS IN THE TEN LARGEST AND THE TEN SMALLEST TEXAS COUNTIES, 1997

County	Total	County	Municipal	School Districts	Special Districts
County	**4,700**	**254**	**1,177**	**1,087**	**2,182**
Harris	498	1	28	24	445
Dallas	64	1	25	16	22
Tarrant	68	1	34	17	16
Bexar	51	1	22	16	12
Travis	94	1	14	8	71
El Paso	36	1	6	10	19
Hidalgo	77	1	21	16	39
Collin	50	1	24	15	10
Denton	62	1	33	11	17
Fort Bend	132	1	15	5	111
Motley	6	1	2	1	2
Glasscock	4	1		1	2
Terrell	4	1		1	2
Kent	5	1	1	1	2
Roberts	4	1	1	1	1
McMullen	5	1		1	3
Borden	2	1		1	
Kenedy	2	1		1	
King	3	1		1	1
Loving	2	1			1

ABATEMENTS—EXPENSIVE TAX BREAKS

As the Texas economy was diversifying in the 1990s, economic development was very important to many communities. Texas towns and cities competed with each other and with cities in other states for industries that would provide jobs and help their communities grow. They offered incentives for companies to build new plants or expand existing facilities. One popular incentive was a form of tax break called a tax abatement: Companies receiving tax abatements from local governments did not have to pay property taxes on their new facilities for a designated number of years. Proponents defended such breaks as an important economic development tool and argued that abatements eventually paid for themselves in the form of an expanded tax base. But some legislators and other critics believed school districts and other local governments were giving away too much potential tax revenue. There also was fear that a company could go out of business or move its operations out of a community before it had paid any taxes or hired the projected number of people it claimed it would employ.

According to a staff report prepared for the Senate Economic Development Committee in 1996, 186 of the state's 1,050 school districts had given tax abatements since 1985. The state comptroller's office said those abatements had cost $480 million in lost property tax revenue. "Our children's future should not be traded for new jobs now," said state Senator David Sibley of Waco, the committee chairman.* The lost money, he said, could have been spent on supplies, teacher salaries, and other educational needs. The legislature, however, let tax abatements continue.

*Quoted in *Austin American-Statesman,* October 31, 1996.

not have the same autonomy as other special districts. They are created solely through the discretionary powers of a city and are funded by assessments on property within their boundaries.[69] Although their budgets and assessments must be approved by the city, they can be operated and managed by private management companies or by the citizens themselves. Fort Worth created a public improvement district for its downtown area in 1986, and other cities have considered the option.

S U M M A R Y

1. Local governments in Texas are the creations of the state and have only those powers granted to them by the Texas Constitution and statutes. With limited discretionary authority but with a great deal of responsibility, local governments often find it difficult to respond effectively to the needs of their citizens.

2. More than 80 percent of the state's population lives in urban areas. Texas cities have highly diverse social structures, economies, and historical traditions, and, subsequently, there are marked differences in urban politics across the state. Five of the ten largest cities have more than 50 percent minority populations, contributing to longstanding controversies over urban electoral systems.

3. Texas cities with fewer than 5,000 people are designated general law cities and are limited as to the form of government they can use. Cities with more than 5,000 residents can function as home rule cities, choosing a form of government

that satisfies community needs as long as it does not conflict with the state constitution or statutes.

4. Texas cities have experimented with three forms of government—mayor-council, city commission, and council-manager.

5. A notable feature of city politics in Texas is the widespread use of nonpartisan, at-large elections. Prompted by legal attacks on at-large elections under the Voting Rights Act, many cities, as well as special purpose districts, have adopted single-member districts, thus increasing minority representation on local governing bodies.

6. County governments, initially created to serve a rural population, function primarily as administrative subdivisions of the state. Much like state government, county government is highly fragmented, with administrative powers shared by a variety of elected officials.

7. Hundreds of special purpose districts provide numerous public services and add to the fragmentation of local government. Most people know little about their jurisdiction, structure, functions, and leadership, making them the "invisible governments" of Texas. Texas has approximately 1,050 independent school districts, which are working to improve the quality of education against a backdrop of social, cultural, and financial problems.

8. Texas cities are now experiencing many of the same problems as the older cities of the East and Midwest. Populations are aging, and there is evidence of white flight from the core urban centers. A disproportionately larger share of the population in the central cities is low income and least able to pay taxes to support municipal services. Crime rates are high, and cities are faced with significant problems of deteriorating infrastructures. Federal and state governments have

imposed additional requirements, or mandates, on the cities that are increasingly difficult to meet.

9. Local governments are experimenting with a variety of techniques to deal with their problems. Cities have used their annexation powers and extraterritorial jurisdiction to expand their tax bases and exercise limited controls over development in adjacent areas. Cities are also using public improvement districts to permit targeted areas to impose additional taxes for needed services. Both counties and cities are privatizing governmental functions to decrease costs and increase efficiency. Interlocal contracting permits governments to provide services to each other on a contractual basis, and many counties and cities are engaged in aggressive economic development programs. Some people advocate governmental consolidation, but there is limited support for this alternative in Texas.

K E Y   T E R M S

unitary system	runoff elections	county attorney	special-purpose districts
Dillon rule	single-member district	district attorney	independent school district
general law cities	regressive taxes	tax assessor-collector	school board
home rule	rollback election	appraisal district	school superintendent
charter	general obligation bonds	sheriff	council of government (COG)
mayor-council	revenue bonds	constable	privatization
weak mayor	infrastructure	subpoenas	annexation powers
strong mayor	homestead exemption	medical examiner	extraterritorial jurisdiction
city commission	mandate	inquest	tax abatements
council-manager	commissioners court	county auditor	metro government
nonpartisan elections	county judge	county treasurer	public improvement district
at-large elections	county clerk	spoils system	
place system	district clerk	civil service system	

F U R T H E R   R E A D I N G

BRIDGES, AMY. *Morning Glories: Municipal Reform in the Southwest.* (Princeton University Press, 1997). Traces the development and successes of urban reformers in the southwest.

BROOKS, DAVID B. *Texas Practice: County and Special District Law,* vols. 35 and 36. (West, 1989). The definitive legal analysis of county and local governments in Texas.

BURNS, NANCY. *The Formation of American Local Governments: Private Values in Public Institutions.* (Oxford University Press, 1994). A study of the political and economic reasons citizens create local governments.

FEAGIN, JOE R. *Free Enterprise City: Houston in Political-Economic Perspective.* (Rutgers University Press, 1988). History of the economic development of Houston and its politics.

JOHNSON, DAVID R., JOHN A. BOOTH, AND RICHARD J. HARRIS, EDS. *The Politics of San Antonio: Community, Progress, and Power.* (University of Nebraska Press, 1983). Essays written to assess changes in San Antonio based on concepts of political community, power, and progress.

MILLER, CHAR, AND HEYWOOD T. SANDERS, EDS. *Urban Texas.* (Texas A & M University Press, 1990). Essays provide multiple perspectives on the development of urban Texas.

NORWOOD, ROBERT E., AND SABRINA STRAWN. *Texas County Government: Let the People Choose,* 2nd ed. (Texas Research League, 1984). A summary of the structure, powers, and duties of Texas county governments.

ORUM, ANTHONY M. *Power, Money and the People: The Making of Modern Austin.* (Texas Monthly Press, 1987). A study of the dramatic growth of Austin, providing reasons for expansion and development, an analysis of political events linked to this period of growth, and an assessment of the "episodic struggles" between the business community and proponents of controlled growth and more inclusive politics.

PERRENOD, VIRGINIA MARION. *Special Districts, Special Purposes: Fringe Governments and Urban Problems in the Houston Area.* (Texas A & M University Press, 1984). Focuses on Harris County but provides generalizations about the development of special districts, their benefits, and their weaknesses.

SUSTAINING CONSTITUTIONAL DEMOCRACY

America's founding generation fought an eight-year revolution to secure its rights and liberty. First at the Constitutional Convention in 1787 and later in the first Congress, they confronted the challenges of creating a government, writing a Constitution, and drafting a Bill of Rights that would protect rights to life, liberty, and self-government for themselves and subsequent generations. But they knew, as we also know, that passive allegiance to ideals and rights is never enough. Every generation must see itself as responsible for nurturing these ideals by actively renewing the community and nation of which it is a part.

The framers knew about the rise and decline of ancient Athens. They were familiar with Pericles's funeral oration, which states that the person who takes no part in public affairs is a useless person, a good-for-nothing.[1] According to Pericles and many Athenians, the city's business was everyone's business. Athens had flourished as an example of what a civilized city might be, but it collapsed when greed, self-centeredness, and complacency set in. As time went on, the Athenians wanted security more than they wanted liberty, comfort more than freedom. In the end they lost it all—security, comfort, and freedom. "Responsibility was the price every man must pay for freedom. It was to be had on no other terms."[2]

If we are to be responsible citizens of the United States in the truest meaning of the term, our dreams must transcend personal ambition and the accumulation of material goods. Our responsibilities as citizens include speaking up for what we believe, such as support for or opposition to particular policies like the War in Iraq, same-sex unions, health care reform, or less regulation of the economy. Such a discourse of opinion helps produce more representative policy and informed citizens. Our country needs citizens who understand that our well-being is tied to the well-being of our neighbors, community, and country. This spirit was evident in the days and weeks following the September 11, 2001, terrorist attacks on New York City and Washington, D.C. All across the country, people contributed to relief efforts. In an address to the nation in the evening of the day of the attacks, President Bush said, "Terrorist attacks can shake the foundations of our biggest buildings, but they cannot touch the foundation of America. These acts shatter steel, but they cannot dent the steel of American resolve."[3] As the war on terrorism was waged, what also became clear was the tremendous contrast between the freedom of citizens in the United States and the repression that had been part of the Taliban regime in Afghanistan and the reign of Saddam Hussein in Iraq.

More people today live under conditions of political freedom than under authoritarian governments than at any previous time. The transition from living under authoritarian rule to political freedom is often difficult, as evidenced by the efforts to form democratic governments in Afghanistan and Iraq. Throughout history, most people have lived in societies in which a small group at the top imposed its will on others. Authoritarian governments justify their actions by saying that people are too weak to govern themselves; they need to be ruled. Thus neither in Castro's Cuba nor in the military regime of North Korea, neither in the People's Republic of China nor in Saudi Arabia, do ordinary people have a voice in the type of decisions we Americans routinely make: Who should be admitted into college or serve in the military? Who should be allowed to immigrate into the country? How much money should be spent for schools, economic development initiatives, health care, or environmental protection? In America, we take the freedom to make such decisions for granted.

The theme in this epilogue is simple: elected leadership and constitutional structures and protections are important, but an active, committed citizenry is equally important. Freedom and obligation go together. Liberty and duty go together. The answer to a nation's problems lies not in producing a perfect constitution or a few larger-than-life leaders. The answer lies in encouraging a nation of attentive and active citizens who will, above and beyond their professional and private ambitions, care about the common concerns of the Republic and strive to make democracy work.

THE CASE FOR GOVERNMENT BY THE PEOPLE

The essence of our Constitution is that it both grants power to government and withholds power from it. Fearing a weak national government and popular disorder, the framers wanted to strengthen the powers of the national government so that it could carry out its responsibilities, such as ensuring domestic order and maintaining national defense. They also wanted to limit state governments in order to keep them from interfering with interstate commerce and property rights. Valuing above all the principle of individual liberty, the framers wanted to protect the people from too much government. They wanted a limited government—yet one that would work. The solution was to divide up the power of the national government, to make it ultimately responsive, if only indirectly, to the voters.

Most Americans want a government that is efficient and effective but that also promotes social justice. We want to maintain our commitment to liberty and freedom. We want a government that acts for the majority yet also protects minorities. We want to safeguard our nation and our streets in a world full of change and violence. We want to protect the rights of the poor, the elderly, and minorities. Do we expect too much from our elected officials and public servants? Of course we do!

Constitutional democracy is a system of checks and balances. It balances values against competing values. Government must balance individual liberties against the collective security and needs of society. The question always is, which rights of which people are to be protected by what means and at what price to individuals and to the whole society? These questions arose again and again in the war on terrorism following the terrorist attacks of September 2001. Following these attacks, the USA PATRIOT Act became law, allowing greater government surveillance. Both conservatives and liberals have criticized the USA PATRIOT

GLOBAL *Perceptions*

QUESTION: Please indicate if you have a very favorable, somewhat favorable, somewhat unfavorable, or very unfavorable opinion of the United States?

American's like to think of their country as leading the free world and point to our long history of constitutional democracy. Over our history we have attempted to export our views of good government to other countries, or to "make the world safe for democracy." How realistic are these self-assessments? How does the rest of the world view the United States?

The Pew Global Attitudes Project asked random samples of adults all over the world about their views of the United States. In both surveys, majorities in most countries had a favorable view of the United States with a range from 10 percent favorable (Pakistan in 2002) to a high of 94 percent (Kenya in 1999/2000). In most countries public opinion was less favorable toward the United States in 2002 than in 1999/2000.

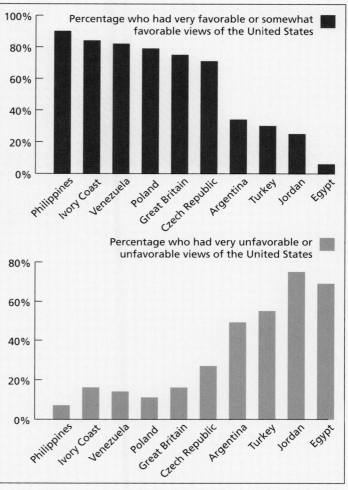

SOURCE: Pew Global Attitudes Project, *What the World Thinks in 2002* (Washington, D.C.: The Pew Research Center for the People and the Press, 2002), pp. 4, T-45.

Act. The Supreme Court also rebuffed the Bush administration's position that it could hold "enemy combatants" indefinitely and without access to the courts.

PARTICIPATION AND REPRESENTATION

No political problem is more complicated than working out the proper relationship between voters and elected officials. It is not just a simple issue of being sure that elected officials do what the voters want them to do. Every individual has a host of conflicting desires, fears, hopes, and expectations, and no government can represent them all. But even if millions of voters could be represented in their many interests, the question of how they would be represented would remain. Through direct representation, such as a traditional New England town meeting or ballot initiatives and referendums? Through economic or professional associations, such as labor unions or political action committees? Through a coalition of minority groups? All of these and other alternatives can be defended as proper forms of representation in a constitutional democracy. Yet all also have limitations.

These participants in a voter's rally urge citizens to accept responsibility for perpetuating democracy.

Some propose to bypass this thorny problem of representation by vastly increasing the role of direct popular participation in decision making.[4] An example of an expanded direct popular participation in governmental decision making is the recall, a process that removes office holders from office based on a petiton process and election. The 2003 recall of California Governor Gray Davis and election of Arnold Schwarzenegger is an example of the recall in action. The use of the recall has been relatively rare at the statewide level, but the process has the potential to alter the relationship between voters and representatives. If the process were to become a means for people who disagree with policy positons of office holders to remove those persons from office between elections, representatives might hesitate to say or do much.

What many people regard as the most perfect form of democracy would exist when every person has a full and equal opportunity to participate in all decisions and in all processes of influence, persuasion, and discussion that bear on those decisions. Direct participation in decision making, its advocates contend, will serve two major purposes. First, it will enhance the dignity, self-respect, and understanding of individuals by giving them responsibility for the decisions that shape their lives. Second, direct participation will act as a safeguard against undemocratic and antidemocratic forms of government and prevent the replacement of democracy by dictatorship or tyranny. This idea rests on a theory of self-protection that says interests can be represented, furthered, and defended best by the people they concern directly.

New technologies as well as new uses of old technologies present ways in which governments can appeal directly to voters and voters can speak directly to public officials. We now have voting by mail in Oregon and other places, and some people advocate voting on the Internet. Digital town halls may be next. Some applaud these developments; others are appalled by them.

But we still need institutions such as elected legislatures, which can take the time to digest complicated information and conduct impartial hearings to air competing points of view. The average citizen rarely has the time or experience to evaluate all the available information. Experience with many forms of participatory democracy also suggests its limitations as a form of decision making. In an age of rapidly growing population, increasingly complex economic and social systems, and enormously wide-ranging decision-making units of government, direct participation works best in small communities or at the neighborhood level. As a practical matter, people simply cannot spend endless hours taking part in every decision that affects their lives.

Participatory democracy can still play an important role in smaller units—in neighborhood associations, local party committees, and the like. But much of the work of government at all levels requires elected representatives. Since we must have representatives, who shall represent whom? By electing representatives in a multitude of districts, it is possible to build into representative institutions—the U.S. Congress, for example—most minority interests and attitudes. In the United States, we generally have election processes in which only the candidate receiving the greatest number of votes wins. But there are other ways. For example, one way widely used in European nations like Austria and Denmark is proportional representation—a system in which each party running receives the proportion of legislative seats corresponding to its proportion of votes.[5]

Representation can also be influenced by whether there is only one party, two, or several. Ours is generally a strong two-party system that knits local constituencies into coalitions that can elect and sustain national majorities. A major factor in maintaining our two-party system is that single-member legislative districts such as those for the U.S. Congress and state legislatures tend to lead to two-party systems. This regularity, called *Duverger's law,* is generally seen as helping moderate our politics.[6] In contrast, when countries adopt proportional representation, minor parties have greater influence.

Which is better, elected officials who represent coalitions of minorities or officials who represent a relatively clear-cut majority and have little or no obligation to the minority? The answer depends on what you expect from government. A system that represents coalitions of minorities usually reflects the trading, competition, and compromising that must take place in order to reach agreement among the various groups. Such a government has been called *broker rule:* Elected officials act essentially as a go-between or mediator among organized groups that have definite policy goals. Under broker rule, leaders cannot get too far ahead of the groups; they must talk back and forth, shifting in response to changing group pressures. Instead of acting for a united popular majority with a fairly definite program, either liberal or conservative, the government tries to satisfy all major interests by giving them a voice in decisions and sometimes a veto over actions. In the pushing and hauling of political groups, the government is continually involved in delicate balancing acts, and no one wins all the time.

Some critics argue that fair representation has not been achieved in the American system. In the U.S. Congress and many state legislatures, for example, we still have relatively few women and minorities. Critics also point to the extent of nonvoting and other forms of nonparticipation in politics; the fact that low-income persons are less well organized than upper-income persons; the bias of strong organized groups toward the status quo; the domination of television and the press by a few corporations; and the virtual monopoly of party politics by the two major parties, which do not always offer the voters meaningful alternatives. Critics are concerned that our system of government builds in procedures designed to curtail legislative majorities—for example, the filibuster in the Senate or the power of the Supreme Court to declare laws unconstitutional. The use of the filibuster to block judicial nominees from President George W. Bush is an example of the filibuster curtailing legislative majorities. The Supreme Court overturns laws enacted by Congress or state legislatures, as it did when it declared the Texas sodomy law unconstitutional in *Lawrence* v. *Texas.*[7]

Such charges may be exaggerated, but they cannot be denied. Those who believe that governments should be more directly responsive to political majorities can point to steady improvement in recent years. Election laws have been changed to simplify voter registration, expand and improve voting procedures, and enforce one-person, one-vote standards. Efforts to limit the ability of rich people and well-financed interests to influence elections were cited by Congress as a motivation for passage of campaign finance reform in 2002 and by the Supreme Court in upholding that legislation in 2003.[8] Pressure has also been building to streamline voting systems and simplify voter registraton processes.

Over the course of U.S. history, there has been a shift toward greater direct democracy, and this trend is likely to continue. The founders designed a system with direct representation limited to the House of Representatives. Today both the House and Senate are directly elected. Moreover, with the advent of direct primaries, voters decide the nominees for federal office. The initiative and referendum process provides a direct way for citizens to enact or overturn laws, or even recall those in government. Who may vote in our elections has also been dramatically expanded from white male property owners to all citizens over 18 years of age.

In the age of the Internet, pressures to expand the role of citizens in making laws and voting on candidates or recalling officeholders via petition are examples of how direct democracy may be further expanded. Some states in recent elections have allowed voters to cast their ballots via the Internet. Arizona did so in the 2000 Democratic presidential primary and Michigan did the same in 2004. In the 2004 general election the Pentagon will use an internet voting program for overseas voters. The Internet also has become a means to help organize and inform volunteers, raise funds, and learn about current events.[9]

By this point, you undoubtedly appreciate that democracy has to mean much more than popular government and unchecked majority rule. A democracy needs competing politicians with differing views about the public interest. A vital democracy, living and growing, places its faith in the participation of citizens as voters, faith that they will elect not just people who will mirror their views but leaders who will exercise their best judgment—"faith that the people will not condemn those whose devotion to principle leads them to unpopular courses, but will reward courage, respect honor, and ultimately recognize right."[10]

The Role of the Politician

Americans today have decidedly mixed views about elected officials. They realize that at their best, politicians are skillful at compromising, mediating, negotiating, and brokering—and that governing often requires these qualities. But they also suspect politicians of being ambitious, conniving, unprincipled, opportunistic, and corrupt. Americans hold politicians in low esteem compared with people in other professions.

Still, we often find that individual officeholders are bright, hardworking, and friendly (even though we may suspect they are simply trying to win our vote). And our liking sometimes turns into reverence after these same politicians die. George Washington, Abraham Lincoln, Dwight D. Eisenhower, and John F. Kennedy are acclaimed today. Harry Truman liked to joke that "a statesman is a politician who has been dead for about ten or fifteen years."[11] Of course, we must put the problem in perspective. In all democracies, the public probably expects too much from politicians. Further, people naturally distrust those who wield power. Public officeholders, after all, tax us, regulate us, and conscript us. We dislike political compromisers and ambitious opportunists—even though we may need such people to get things done.[12]

Yet as we have demonstrated with numerous examples in this book, individuals can and do make a difference in public life. Individuals can make a difference in shaping policy on the local, state, national, and international levels, whether the policy be drunk driving, early childhood medical care, land mines, or using the courts to influence a policy agenda.

Politics is a necessity. Politics is a vital and at times a noble leadership activity. Politicians are essential for running the American Republic, whose fragmented powers require them to mediate among factions, build coalitions, and compromise among and within branches of government to produce policy and action.

Leadership in a Constitutional Democracy

While the need for leadership in government is easily recognized, defining what leadership is and how it operates in a constitutional democracy is more challenging. Leadership can be understood only in the context of both leaders and followers. A leader without followers is a contradiction in terms. Leadership is also situational and contextual; a person is often effective in only one kind of situation. Leadership is not necessarily transferable. James Madison, for example, was a brilliant political and constitutional theorist; he was also a superb politician. Yet he was not a brilliant president.[13] The leadership required to lead a marine platoon up a hill in battle is different from the leadership needed to change racist or sexist attitudes in city governments. The leadership required of a campaign manager differs from that required of a candidate.

Although leaders are often skilled managers, they need more than just managerial skills. Managers are concerned with doing things the right way; leaders are concerned with doing the right thing. Managers are concerned with efficiency and process, especially routines and standard operating procedures. Leaders, by contrast, concentrate on goals, purposes, and a vision of the future. Some leaders have indispensable qualities of contagious self-confidence, unwarranted optimism, and dogged idealism that attract and mobilize others to undertake tasks they never dreamed they could accomplish. In short, they empower others and enable many of their followers to become leaders in their own right. Most of the significant breakthroughs in our nation, as well as in our communities, have been made or shaped by people who, while seeing all the complexities and obstacles ahead of them, believed in themselves and in their purposes so much that they refused to be overwhelmed and paralyzed by self-doubts. They were willing to gamble, to take risks, to look at things in a fresh way, and often to invent new rules.

Must a politician gain public office by denouncing the profession of politics? From the tone of many recent congressional and presidential races, it would appear that this may be so. Presidential candidates who have denounced Washington politics include Jimmy Carter, Ronald Reagan, Bill Clinton, and Howard Dean. In 2004 Dean said that if he was elected, members of Congress were "going to be scurrying for shelter, just like a giant flashlight on a bunch of cockroaches."[14] Political Scientist Richard Fenno's landmark study of congressional candidates found that incumbents often run against Washington in general and Congress in particular when at home in their districts.[15] Journalist Charles McDowell of the *Richmond Times-Dispatch* noted this trend on the PBS series *The Lawmakers* and suggested that such a tactic "demeans an honorable and essential profession—that of the politician." McDowell proposed that every member of Congress be required to take the following oath:

> I affirm that I am a politician. That I am willing to associate with other known politicians. That I have no moral reservations about committing acts of politics. Under the Constitution, I insist that politicians have as much right to indulge in politics as preachers, single-issue zealots, generals, bird-watchers, labor leaders, big business lobbyists, and all other truth-givers.
>
> I confess that, as a politician, I participate in negotiation, compromise, and trade-offs in order to achieve something that seems reasonable to a majority. And although I try to be guided by principle, I confess that I often find people of principle on the other side, too.
>
> So help me God.

Politics and politicians, including those who work in Washington, are necessary and important to our freedom, security, and prosperity. While people will disagree about particular policies and processes, there is no disputing the need for government. It is also the case that the vast majority of politicians are smart, honorable, and deserve our respect and admiration. Political leaders recognize the fundamental—unexpressed as well as expressed—wants and needs of potential followers. By bringing followers to a fuller consciousness of their needs, they help convert their hopes and aspirations into practical demands on other leaders, especially leaders in government. A leader in a democracy consults and listens while educating followers and attempting to renew the goals of an organization.

RECONCILING DEMOCRACY AND LEADERSHIP

Americans are fond of saying, "It is all politics, you know." This greatly oversimplified insight is offered as profound. More important, it is intended as a negative judgment, as if things somehow would be improved if we did not have politics and politicians.

But politics is the lifeblood of democracy, and without politics, there is no freedom. To conclude that politicians are interested in winning elections is about as profound as to conclude that businesspeople are interested in profits. Of course they are! We do not expect our economy to operate because the shoe store owner is motivated only by a desire to see that people have dry, warm feet. Rather, we harness the store owner's desire to make a living as a way to see to it that the largest number of people get the shoes they want at the lowest possible price. Similarly, we harness the elected official's desire for re-election as the way to ensure that elected officials do what most of the voters want them to do. It is the politician's need to serve and please the voters that is the indispensable link in making democracy work.[16]

One of our major political challenges is to reconcile democracy and leadership. In the past, we often have held a view of leaders as all-powerful. Yet a nation of subservient followers can never be a democratic one. A democratic nation requires educated, skeptical, caring, engaged, and conscientious citizens. It also requires citizens who will recognize when change is needed and have the courage to bring about necessary reforms and progress.[17] Such citizens provide the leaders that enable constitutional democracy to survive and thrive. Constitutional democracy requires citizens who are willing to run for office and then serve with integrity. It is understandable that good people shy away from seeking office, with the ensuing loss of privacy and other burdens of public office. But no matter how brilliant our Constitution or strong our economy, ultimately our system depends on individuals willing to compete for office.

Experience teaches that power wielded justly today may be wielded corruptly tomorrow. It is right and necessary to protest when a policy is wrong or when the rights of other citizens are diminished. Democracy rests solidly on a realistic view of human nature. Criticism of official error is not unpatriotic. Our capacity for justice, as theologian and philosopher Reinhold Niebuhr observed, makes democracy possible. But our "inclination to injustice makes democracy necessary."[18] Democratic politics is the forum where, by acting together, citizens become and remain free.[19]

Leadership thought of as an engagement among equals can empower people and enlarge their opinions, choices, and freedoms. The answer for our republic lies not in producing a handful of great, charismatic, Mount Rushmore-type leaders but in educating a citizenry who can boast that we are no longer in need of superheroes because we have become a nation of citizens who believe that each of us can make a difference and that all of us should regularly try to do so.[20]

Leaders will always be needed. However, our system of government is, in many ways, designed to prevent strong and decisive action, lest too much political power be placed in the hands of too few people. Thus, although we have emphasized the role of leadership in constitutional democracies in these last few pages, the potential for abuse is checked not only by an involved citizenry but also by the very structure of our constitutional system—separation of powers, checks and balances, federalism, bicameral legislatures, and the rule of law.

The ultimate test of a democratic system is the legal existence of an officially recognized opposition. A cardinal characteristic of a constitutional democracy is that it not only recognizes the need for the free organization of opposing views but also positively encourages this organization. Freedom for political expression and dissent is basic— even freedom for nonsense to be spoken so that good sense not yet recognized gets a chance to be heard.[21]

THE DEMOCRATIC FAITH

Crucial to the democratic faith is the belief that a constitutional democracy cherishes the free play of ideas. Only where the safety valve of public discussion is available and where almost any policy is subject to perpetual questioning and challenge can there be the assurance that both minority and majority rights will be served. To be afraid of public debate is to be afraid of self-government. "Rulers always have and always will find it dangerous to their security to permit people to think, believe, talk, write, assemble, and

Louisiana Governor Kathleen Babineaux Blanco at her inauguration on January 12, 2004. The peaceful transfer of power is a sign of a mature and successful democracy.

particularly to criticize the government as they please," said former Supreme Court Justice William J. Brennan, "but the language of the First Amendment indicates the framers weighed the risk involved in such freedoms and deliberately chose to stake this government's security and life upon preserving liberty to discuss public affairs intact and untouched by government."[22]

Thomas Jefferson once said, "Were it left to me to decide whether we should have a government without newspapers or newspapers without a government, I should not hesitate for a moment to prefer the latter." This is reflective of the high importance he placed on informing the citizenry. Jefferson also had boundless faith in education. He believed that people are rationally endowed by nature with an innate sense of justice; the average person has only to be informed to act wisely. In the long run, said Jefferson, only an educated and enlightened democracy can hope to endure.

Education is one of the best predictors of voting, participation in politics, and knowledge of public affairs. People may not be equally involved or equally willing to invest in democracy, but the attentive public—frequently people like yourself who have gone to college—has the willingness and self-confidence to see government and politics as necessary and important. An educated public has an understanding of how government works, how individuals can influence decision makers, and how to elect like-minded people.

As college students who are studying American government, you have knowledge of ways to influence public policy and the political process. You have gained an appreciation for the ways individuals and groups can both push and block an agenda. You also know that many people choose not to participate in elections or politics, enhancing the power of those who do. Finally, you should also have an appreciation that when knowledge is combined with political activity, the influence of the individual participant is expanded.

Does political participation by committed individuals bring about constructive change? It is important to recall that in the last half-century, restaurants, motels, and landlords once openly discriminated against individuals on the basis of race. Racial segregation in education was commonplace in several states; segregated neighborhoods were a fact of life in others and in some places remains so. Finally, in some sections of the country, discriminatory practices denied blacks and poor whites access to voting. Women were discriminated against in the workplace and in government. The significant changes toward more freedom and equality that have resulted from civil rights legislation and court cases are remarkable. This is not to say that we have erased the legacies

Education fosters self-confidence in dealing with bureaucracy, is a strong predictor of voting, and provides a knowledge base important to political influence.

of racism and other kinds of discrimination from our national life. But as historian Arthur M. Schlesinger Jr. writes, "The genius of America lies in its capacity to forge a single nation from peoples of remarkably diverse racial, religious, and ethnic origins." Schlesinger acknowledges that our government and society have been more open to some than to others, "but it is more open to all today than it was yesterday and it is likely to be even more open tomorrow than today."[23]

We are a restless, dissatisfied, and searching people. We are often our own toughest critics. Our political system is far from perfect, but it still is an open system and one that has become more and more democratic over time. People *can* fight city hall. People who disagree with policies in the nation can band together and be heard. We know only too well that the American dream is never fully attained. It must always be pursued.

Millions of Americans visit the great monuments in our nation's capital each year. They are always impressed by the memorials to Washington, Jefferson, Lincoln, Franklin D. Roosevelt, and the Vietnam, Korean, and World War II veterans. They are awed by the beauty of the Capitol, the Supreme Court, and the White House. The strength of the nation, however, resides not in these official buildings and monuments but in the hearts, minds, and behavior of citizens. If we lose faith, stop caring, stop participating, and stop believing in the possibilities of self-government, the monuments "will be meaningless piles of stone, and the venture that began with the Declaration of Independence, the venture familiarly known as America will be as lifeless as the stone."[24]

The future of democracy in America will be shaped by citizens who care about preserving and extending our political rights and freedoms. Our individual liberties will never be ensured unless there are people willing to take responsibility for the progress of the whole community, people willing to exercise their determination and democratic faith. Carved in granite on one of the long corridors in a building on the Harvard University campus are these words of American poet Archibald MacLeish: "How shall freedom be defended? By arms when it is attacked by arms, by truth when it is attacked by lies, by democratic faith when it is attacked by authoritarian dogma. Always, in the final act, by determination and faith."

FURTHER READING

DEREK BOK, *The Trouble with Government* (Harvard University Press, 2001).

RICHARD D. BROWN, *The Strength of a People: The Idea of an Informed Citizenry in America, 1650–1870* (University of North Carolina Press, 1996).

JAMES MACGREGOR BURNS, *Leadership* (Harper & Row, 1978).

ROBERT COLES, *Lives of Moral Leadership: Men and Women Who Have Made a Difference* (Random House, 2000).

AMY GUTMANN AND DENNIS THOMSON, *Democracy and Discontent: Why Moral Conflict Cannot Be Avoided in Politics, and What Should Be Done About It* (Belknap Press, 1996).

APPENDIX

The Declaration of Independence

Drafted mainly by Thomas Jefferson, this document adopted by the Second Continental Congress, and signed by John Hancock and fifty-five others, outlined the rights of man and the rights to rebellion and self-government. It declared the independence of the colonies from Great Britain, justified rebellion, and listed the grievances against George the III and his government. What is memorable about this famous document is not only that it declared the birth of a new nation, but that it set forth, with eloquence, our basic philosophy of liberty and representative democracy.

IN CONGRESS, JULY 4, 1776
(The unanimous Declaration of the Thirteen United States of America)

PREAMBLE

When, in the course of human events, it becomes necessary for one people to dissolve the political bands which have connected them with another, and to assume, among the powers of the earth, the separate and equal station to which the laws of nature and of nature's God entitle them, a decent respect to the opinions of mankind requires that they should declare the causes which impel them to the separation.

New Principles of Government

We hold these truths to be self-evident; that all men are created equal, that they are endowed by their Creator with certain unalienable rights, that among these are life, liberty, and the pursuit of happiness.

That, to secure these rights, governments are instituted among men, deriving their just powers from the consent of the governed.

That whenever any form of government becomes destructive of these ends, it is the right of the people to alter or to abolish it, and to institute new government, laying its foundation on such principles, and organizing its powers in such form, as to them shall seem most likely to effect their safety and happiness. Prudence, indeed will dictate that governments long established should not be changed for light and transient causes; and accordingly all experience hath shown that mankind are more disposed to suffer while evils are sufferable, than to right themselves by abolishing the forms to which they are accustomed. But when a long train of abuses and usurpations, pursuing invariably the same object, evinces a design to reduce them under absolute despotism, it is their right, it is their duty, to throw off such government, and to provide new guards for their future security.

Reasons for Separation

Such has been the patient sufferance of these colonies; and such is now the necessity which constrains them to alter their former systems of government. The history of the present king of Great Britain is a history of repeated injuries and usurpations, all having in direct object the establishment of an absolute tyranny over these states. To prove this, let facts be submitted to a candid world.

He has refused his assent to laws, the most wholesome and necessary for the public good.

He has forbidden his governors to pass laws of immediate and pressing importance unless suspended in their operation till his assent should be obtained; and when so suspended, he has utterly neglected to attend to them.

He has refused to pass other laws for the accommodation of large districts of people, unless those people would relinquish the right of representation in the legislature, a right inestimable to them, and formidable to tyrants only.

He has called together legislative bodies at places unusual, uncomfortable, and distant for the depository of their public records, for the sole purpose of fatiguing them into compliance with his measures.

He has dissolved representative houses repeatedly, for opposing, with manly firmness, his invasions on the rights of people.

He has refused, for a long time after such dissolutions, to cause others to be elected; whereby the legislative powers incapable of annihilation, have returned to the people at large for their exercise; the state remaining, in the meantime, exposed to all the dangers of invasion from without and convulsions within.

He has endeavored to prevent the population of these states; for that purpose obstructing the laws of naturalization of foreigners, refusing to pass others to encourage their migration hither, and raising the conditions of new appropriations of lands.

He has obstructed the administration of justice, by refusing his assent to laws for establishing judiciary powers.

He has made judges dependent on his will alone for the tenure of their offices, and the amount and payment of their salaries.

He has erected a multitude of new offices, and sent hither swarms of officers to harass our people and eat out their substance.

He has kept among us, in times of peace, standing armies, without the consent of our legislature.

He has affected to render the military independent of, and superior to, the civil power.

He has combined with others to subject us to jurisdiction foreign to our constitution and unacknowledged by our laws, giving his assent to their acts of pretended legislation:

For quartering large bodies of armed troops among us;

For protecting them, by a mock trial, from punishment for any murders which they should commit on the inhabitants of these states;

For cutting off our trade with all parts of the world;

For imposing taxes on us without our consent;

For depriving us, in many cases, of the benefits of trial by jury;

For transporting us beyond seas, to be tried for pretended offenses;

For abolishing the free system of English laws in a neighboring province, establishing therein an arbitrary government, and enlarging its boundaries, so as to render it at once an example and fit instrument for introducing the same absolute rule into these colonies;

For taking away our charters, abolishing our most valuable laws, and altering, fundamentally, the forms of our governments;

For suspending our own legislatures, and declaring themselves invented with power to legislate for us in all cases whatsoever.

A-1

He has abdicated government here, by declaring us out of his protection and waging war against us.

He has plundered our seas, ravaged our coasts, burned our towns, and destroyed the lives of our people.

He is at this time transporting large armies of foreign mercenaries to complete the works of death, desolation, and tyranny already begun with circumstances of cruelty and perfidy scarcely paralleled in the most barbarous ages and totally unworthy of the head of a civilized nation.

He has constrained our fellow-citizens, taken captive on the high seas, to bear arms against their country, to become the executioners of their friends and brethren, or to fall themselves by their hands.

He has excited domestic insurrections among us, and has endeavored to bring on the inhabitants of our frontiers the merciless Indian savages, whose known rule of warfare is an undistinguished destruction of all ages, sexes, and conditions.

In every stage of these oppressions we have petitioned for redress in the most humble terms; our repeated petitions have been answered only by repeated injury. A prince whose character is thus marked by every act which may define a tyrant is unfit to be the ruler of a free people.

Nor have we been wanting in attention to our British brethren. We have warned them, from time to time, of attempts by their legislature to extend an unwarrantable jurisdiction over us. We have reminded them of the circumstances of our emigration and settlement here. We have appealed to their native justice and magnanimity; and we have conjured them, by the ties of our common kindred, to disavow these usurpations, which would inevitably interrupt our connections and correspondence. They, too, have been deaf to the voice of justice and of consanguinity. We must, therefore, acquiesce in the necessity which denounces our separation, and hold them, as we hold the rest of mankind, enemies in war, in peace, friends.

We, therefore, the representatives of the United States of America, in General Congress assembled, appealing to the Supreme Judge of the world for the rectitude of our intentions, do, in the name and by authority of the good people of these colonies, solemnly publish and declare, that these united colonies are, and of right ought to be, free and independent states; that they are absolved from all allegiance to the British crown, and that all political connection between them and the state of Great Britain is, and ought to be, totally dissolved; and that, as free and independent states, they have full power to levy war, conclude peace, contract alliances, establish commerce, and do all other acts and things which independent states may of a right do. And, for the support of this declaration, with a firm reliance on the protection of Divine Providence, we mutually pledge to each other our lives, our fortunes, and our sacred honor.

The Federalist, No. 10, James Madison

The Federalist, No. 10, written by James Madison soon after the Constitutional Convention, was prepared as one of several dozen newspaper essays aimed at persuading New Yorkers to ratify the proposed constitution. One of the most important basic documents in American political history, it outlines the need for and the general principles of a democratic republic. It also provides a political and economic analysis of the realities of interest group or faction politics.

To the People of the State of New York: Among the numerous advantages promised by a well-constructed union, none deserves to be more accurately developed than its tendency to break and control the violence of faction. The friend of popular governments, never finds himself so much alarmed for their character and fate, as when he contemplates their propensity of this dangerous vice. He will not fail, therefore, to set a due value on any plan which, without violating the principles to which he is attached, provides a proper cure for it. The instability, injustice, and confusion introduced into the public councils, have, in truth, been the mortal diseases under which popular governments have everywhere perished; as they continue to be the favorite and fruitful topics from which the adversaries to liberty derive their most specious declamations. The valuable improvements made by the American constitutions on the popular models, both ancient and modern, cannot certainly be too much admired; but it would be an unwarrantable partiality, to contend that they have as effectually obviated the danger on this side, as was wished and expected. Complaints are everywhere heard from our most considerate and virtuous citizens, equally the friends of public and private faith, and of public and personal liberty, that our governments are too unstable; that the public good is disregarded in the conflicts of rival parties; and that measures are too often decided, not according to the rules of justice, and the rights of the minor party, but by the superior force of an interested and overbearing majority. However anxiously we may wish that these complaints had no foundation, the evidence of known facts will not permit us to deny that they are in some degree true. It will be found, indeed, on a candid review of our situation, that some of the distresses under which we labor have been erroneously charged on the operations of our governments; but it will be found, at the same time, that other causes will not alone account for many of our heaviest misfortunes; and, particularly, for that prevailing and increasing distrust of public engagements, and alarm for private rights, which are echoed from one end of the continent to the other. These must be chiefly, if not wholly, effects of the unsteadiness and injustice, with which a factious spirit has tainted our public administrations.

By a faction, I understand a number of citizens, whether amounting to a majority of the whole, who are united and actuated by some common impulse of passion, or of interest, adverse to the rights of other citizens, or to the permanent and aggregate interests of the community.

There are two methods of curing the mischiefs of faction: the one, by removing its causes; the other, by controlling its effects.

There are again two methods of removing the causes of faction: the one, by destroying the liberty which is essential to its existence; the other, by giving to every citizen the same opinions, the same passions, and the same interests.

It could never be more truly said, than of the first remedy, that it was worse than the disease. Liberty is to faction what air is to fire, an aliment without which it instantly expires. But it could not be a less folly to abolish liberty, which is essential to political life, because it nourishes faction, than it would be to wish the annihilation of air, which is essential to animal life, because it imparts to fire its destructive agency.

The second expedient is as impracticable, as the first would be unwise. As long as the reason of man continues fallible, and he is at liberty to exercise it, different opinions will be formed. As long as the connection subsists between his reason and his self-love, his opinions and his passions will have a reciprocal influence on each other; and the former will be objects to which the latter will attach themselves. The diversity in the faculties of men, from which the rights of property originate, is not less an insuperable obstacle to an uniformity of interests. The protection of these faculties is the first object of government. From the protection of different and unequal faculties of acquiring property, the possession of different degrees and kinds of property immediately results; and from the influence of these on the sentiments and views of the respective proprietors, ensues a division of the society into different interests and parties.

The latent causes of faction are thus sown in the nature of man; and we see them everywhere brought into different degrees of activity, according to the different circumstances of civil society. A zeal for different opinions concerning religion, concerning government, and many other points, as well of speculation as of practice; an attachment to different leaders ambitiously contending for preeminence and power; or to persons of other descriptions whose fortunes have been interesting to the human passions, have, in turn, divided mankind into parties, inflamed them with mutual animosity, and rendered them much more disposed to vex and oppress each other, than to cooperate for their common good. So strong is this propensity of mankind, to fall into mutual animosities, that where no substantial occasion presents itself, the most frivolous and fanciful distinctions have been sufficient to kindle their unfriendly passions and excite their most violent conflicts. But the most common and durable source of factions, has been the various and unequal distribution of property. Those who hold, and those who are without property, have ever formed distinct interests in society. Those who are creditors, and those who are debtors, fall under a like discrimination. A landed interest, a manufacturing interest, a mercantile interest, a moneyed interest, with many lesser interests, grow up of necessity in civilized nations, and divide them into different classes, actuated by different sentiments and views. The regulation of these various and interfering interests forms the principal task of modern legislation, and involves the spirit of the party and faction in the necessary and ordinary operations of the government.

No man is allowed to be a judge in his own cause; because his interest will certainly bias his judgment, and, not improbably, corrupt his integrity. With equal, nay, with greater reason, a body of men are unfit to be both judges and par-

ties at the same time; yet what are many of the most important acts of legislation, but so many judicial determinations, not indeed concerning the right of single persons, but concerning the rights of large bodies of citizens? And what are the different classes of legislators, but advocates and parties to the causes which they determine? Is a law proposed concerning private debts? It is a questions to which the creditors are parties on one side, and the debtors on the other. Justice ought to hold the balance between them. Yet the parties are, and must be, themselves the judges; and the most numerous party, or, in other words, the most powerful faction, must be expected to prevail. Shall domestic manufacturers be encouraged, and in what degree, by restrictions on foreign manufacturers? Are questions which would be differently decided by the landed and the manufacturing classes; and probably by neither with a sole regard to justice and the public good. The apportionment of taxes, on the various descriptions of property, is an act which seems to require the most exact impartiality; yet there is, perhaps, no legislative act, in which greater opportunity and temptation are given to a predominant party to trample on the rules of justice. Every shilling, with which they overburden the inferior number, is a shilling saved to their own pockets.

It is in vain to say, that enlightened statesmen will be able to adjust these clashing interests, and render them all subservient to the public good. Enlightened statesmen will not always be at the helm, nor, in many cases, can such an adjustment be made at all, without taking into view indirect and remote considerations, which will rarely prevail over the immediate interest which one party may find in disregarding the rights of another, or the good of the whole.

The inference to which we are brought is, that the causes of faction cannot be removed; and that relief is only to be sought in the means of controlling its effects.

If a faction consists of less than a majority, relief is supplied by the republican principle, which enables the majority to defeat its sinister views, by regular vote. It may clog the administration, it may convulse the society; but it will be unable to execute and mask its violence under the forms of the Constitution. When a majority is included in a faction, the form of popular government, on the other hand, enables it to sacrifice to its ruling passion or interest, both the public good and the rights of other citizens. To secure the public good, and private rights, against the danger of such a faction, and at the same time to preserve the spirit and the form of popular government, is then the great object to which our inquiries are directed. Let me add, that it is the great desideratum, by which alone

this form of government can be rescued from the opprobrium under which it has so long laboured, and be recommended to the esteem and adoption of mankind.

By what means is this object attainable? Evidently by one of two only. Either the existence of the same passion or interest in a majority, at the same time, must be prevented; or the majority, having such coexistent passion or interest, must be rendered, by their number and local situation, unable to concert and carry into effect schemes of oppression. If the impulse and the opportunity be suffered to coincide, we well know that neither moral nor religious motives can be relied on as an adequate control. They are not found to be such on the injustice and violence of individuals, and lose their efficacy in proportion to the number combined together; that is, in proportion as their efficacy becomes needful.

From this view of the subject, it may be concluded, that a pure democracy, by which I mean a society consisting of a small number of citizens, who assemble and administer the government in person, can admit of no cure for the mischiefs of faction. A common passion or interest will, in almost every case, be felt by a majority of the whole; a communication and concert, results from the form of government itself; and there is nothing to check the inducements to sacrifice the weaker party, or an obnoxious individual. Hence, it is, that such democracies have ever been spectacles of turbulence and contention; have ever been found incompatible with personal security, or the rights of property; and have in general been as short in their lives, as they have been violent in their deaths. Theoretic politicians, who have patronized this species of government, have erroneously supposed, that by reducing mankind to a perfect equality in their political rights, they would, at the same time be perfectly equalized and assimilated in their possessions, their opinions, and their passions.

A republic, by which I mean a government in which the scheme of representation takes place, opens a different prospect, and promises the cure for which we are seeking. Let us examine the points in which it varies from pure democracy, and we shall comprehend both the nature of the cure and the efficacy which it must derive from the union.

The two great points of difference, between a democracy and a republic, are, first, the delegation of the government, in the latter, to a small number of citizens, elected by the rest; secondly, the greater number of citizens, and greater sphere of country, over which the latter may be extended.

The effect of the first difference is, on the one hand, to refine and enlarge the public views, by passing them through the medium of a chosen body of citizens, whose wisdom may best discern the true interest of their country, and whose patriotism and love of justice, will be least likely to sacrifice it to temporary or partial considerations. Under such a regulation, it may well happen, that the public voice, pronounced by the representatives of the people, will be more consonant to the public good, than if pronounced by the people themselves, convened for the purpose. On the other hand the effect may be inverted. Men of factious tempers, of local prejudices, or of sinister designs, may by intrigue, by corruption, or by other means, first obtain the suffrages, and then betray the interest of the people. The question resulting is, whether small or extensive republics are most favourable to the election of proper guardians of the public weal; and it is clearly decided in favour of the latter by two obvious considerations.

In the first place, it is to be remarked that, however small the republic may be, the representatives must be raised to a certain number, in order to guard against the cabals of a few; and that however large it may be, they must be limited to a certain number, in order to guard against the confusion of a multitude. Hence, the number of representatives in the two cases not being in proportion to that of the constituents, and being proportionally greatest in the small republic, it follows, that if the proportion of fit characters be not less in the large than in the small republic, the former will present a greater option, and consequently a greater probability of a fit choice.

In the next place, as each representative will be chosen by a greater number of citizens in the large than in the small republic, it will be more difficult for unworthy candidates to practice with success the vicious arts, by which elections are too often carried; and the suffrages of the people being more free, will be more likely to centre in men who possess the most attractive merit, and the most diffusive and established characters.

It must be confessed, that in this, as in most other cases, there is a mean, on both sides of which inconveniences will be found to lie. By enlarging too much the number of electors, you render the representatives too little acquainted with all their local circumstances and lesser interests; as by reducing it too much, you render him unduly attached to these, and too little fit to comprehend and pursue great and national objects. The federal constitution forms a happy combination in this respect; the great and aggregate interests being referred to the national, the local and particular to the state legislatures.

The other point of difference is, the greater number of citizens, and extent of territory, which may be brought within the compass of republican, than of democratic government; and it is this circumstance principally which renders factious combinations less to be dreaded in the former, than in the latter. The smaller the society, the fewer probably will be the distinct parties and interests composing it; the fewer the distinct parties and interests, the more frequently will a majority be found of the same party; and the smaller the number of individuals composing a majority, and the smaller the compass within which they are placed, the more easily will they concert and execute their plans of oppression. Extend the sphere, and you take in a greater variety of parties and interests; you make it less probable that a majority of the whole will have a common motive to invade the rights of other citizens; or if such a common motive exists, it will be more difficult for all who feel it to discover their own strength, and to act in unison with each other. Besides other impediments, it may be remarked, that where there is a consciousness of unjust or dishonourable purposes, communication is always checked by distrust, in proportion to the number whose concurrence is necessary.

Hence, it clearly appears, that the same advantage, which a republic has over a democracy, in controlling the effects of faction, is enjoyed by a large over a small republic—is enjoyed by the union over the states composing it. Does this advantage consist in the substitution of representatives, whose enlightened views and virtuous sentiments render them superior to local prejudices, and to schemes of injustice? It will not be denied that the representation of the union will be most likely to possess these requisite endowments. Does it consist in the greater security afforded by a greater variety of parties, against the event of any one party being able to outnumber and oppress the rest? In an equal degree does the increased variety of parties, comprised within the union, increase the security? Does it, in fine, consist in the greater obstacles opposed to the concert and accomplishment of the secret wishes of an unjust and interested majority? Here, again, the extent of the union gives it the most palpable advantage.

The influence of factious leaders may kindle a flame within their particular states, but will be unable to spread a general conflagration through the other states; a religious sect may degenerate into a political faction in a part of the confederacy; but the variety of sects dispersed over the entire face of it, must secure the national councils against any danger from that source: a rage for paper money, for an abolition of debts, for an equal division of property, or for any other improper or wicked project, will be less apt to pervade the whole body of the union than a particular member of it; in the same proportion as such a malady is more likely to taint a particular county or district, than an entire state.

In the extent and proper structure of the union, therefore, we behold a republican remedy for the diseases most incident to republican government. And according to the degree of pleasure and pride we feel in being republicans, ought to be our zeal in cherishing the spirit, and supporting the character of federalists.

The Federalist, No. 51, James Madison

The Federalist, No. 51, also written by Madison, is a classic statement in defense of separation of powers and republican processes. Its fourth paragraph is especially famous and is frequently quoted by students of government.

To what expedient, then, shall we finally resort, for maintaining in practice the necessary partition of power among the several departments as laid down in the Constitution? The only answer that can be given is that as all these exterior provisions are found to be inadequate the defect must be supplied, by so contriving the interior structure of the government as that its several constituent parts may, by their mutual relations, be the means of keeping each other in their proper places. Without presuming to undertake a full development of this important idea I will hazard a few general observations which may perhaps place it in a clearer light, and enable us to form a more correct judgment of the principles and structure of the government planned by the convention.

In order to lay a due foundation for that separate and distinct exercise of the different powers of government, which to a certain extent is admitted on all hands to be essential to the preservation of liberty, it is evident that each department should have a will of its own; and consequently should be so constituted that the members of each should have as little agency as possible in the appointment of the members of the others. Were this principle rigorously adhered to, it would require that all the appointments for the supreme executive, legislative, and judiciary magistracies should be drawn from the same fountain of authority, the people, through channels having no communication whatever with one another. Perhaps such a plan of constructing the several departments would be less difficult in practice than it may in contemplation appear. Some difficulties, however, and some additional expense would attend the execution of it. Some deviations, therefore, from the principle must be admitted. In the constitution of the judiciary department in particular, it might be inexpedient to insist rigorously on the principle: first, because peculiar qualifications being essential in the members, the primary consideration ought to be to select that mode of choice which best secures these qualifications; second, because the permanent tenure by which the appointments are held in that department must soon destroy all sense of dependence on the authority conferring them.

It is equally evident that the members of each department should be as little dependent as possible on those of the others for the emoluments annexed to their offices. Were the executive magistrate, or the judges, not independent of the legislature in this particular, their independence in every other would be merely nominal.

But the great security against a gradual concentration of the several powers in the same department consists in giving to those who administer each department the necessary constitutional means and personal motives to resist encroachments of the others. The provision for defense must in this, as in all other cases, be made commensurate to the danger of attack. Ambition must be made to counteract ambition. The interest of the man must be connected with the constitutional rights of the place. It may be a reflection on human nature that such devices should be necessary to control the abuses of government. But what is government itself but the greatest of all reflections on human nature? If men were angels, no government would be necessary. If angels were to govern men, neither external nor internal controls on government would be necessary. In framing a government which is to be administered by men over men, the great difficulty lies in this: you must first enable the government to control the governed; and in the next place oblige it to control itself. A dependence on the people is, no doubt, the primary control on the government; but experience has taught mankind the necessity of auxiliary precautions.

This policy of supplying, by opposite and rival interests, the defect of better motives, might be traced through the whole system of human affairs, private as well as public. We see it particularly displayed in all the subordinate distributions of power, where the constant aim is to divide and arrange the several offices in such a manner as that each may be a check on the other—that the private interest of every individual may be a sentinel over the public rights. These inventions of prudence cannot be less requisite in the distribution of the supreme powers of the State.

But it is not possible to give to each department an equal power of self-defense. In republican government, the legislative authority necessarily predominates. The remedy for this inconveniency is to divide the legislature into different branches; and to render them, by modes of election and different principles of action, as little connected with each other as the nature of their common functions and their common dependence on the society will admit. It may even be necessary to guard against dangerous encroachments by still further precautions. As the weight of the legislative authority requires that it should be thus divided, the weakness of the executive may require, on the other hand, that it should be fortified. An absolute negative on the legislature appears, at first view, to be the natural defense with which the executive magistrate should be armed. But perhaps it would be neither altogether safe nor alone sufficient. On ordinary occasions it might not be exerted with the requisite firmness, and on extraordinary occasions it might be perfidiously abused. May not this defect of an absolute negative be supplied by some qualified connection between this weaker department and the weaker branch of the stronger department, by which the latter may be led to support the constitutional rights of the former, without being too much detached from the rights of its own department?

If the principles on which these observations are founded be just, as I persuade myself they are, and they be applied as a criterion to the several State constitutions, and to the federal Constitution, it will be found that if the latter does not perfectly correspond with them, the former are infinitely less able to bear such a test.

There are, moreover, two considerations particularly applicable to the federal system of America, which place that system in a very interesting point of view.

First. In a single republic, all the power surrendered by the people is submitted to the administration of a single government; and the usurpations are guarded against by a division of the government into distinct and separate departments. In the compound republic of America, the power surrendered by the people is first divided between two distinct governments, and then the portion allotted to each subdivided among distinct and separate departments. Hence a double security arises to the rights of the people. The different governments will control each other, at the same time that each will be controlled by itself.

Second. It is of great importance in a republic not only to guard the society against the oppression of its rulers, but to guard one part of the society against the injustice of the other part. Different interests necessarily exist in different classes of citizens. If a majority be united by a common interest, the rights of the minority will be insecure. There are but two methods of providing against this evil: the one by creating a will in the community independent of the majority—that is, of the society itself; the other, by comprehending in the society so many separate descriptions of citizens as will render an unjust combination of a majority of the whole very improbable, if not impracticable. The first method prevails in all governments possessing an hereditary or self-appointed authority. This, at best, is but a precarious security; because a power independent of the society may as well espouse the unjust views of the major as the rightful interests of the minor party, and may possibly be turned against both parties. The second method will be exemplified in the federal republic of the United States. Whilst all authority in it will be derived from and dependent on the society, the society itself will be broken into so many parts, interests and classes of citizens, that the rights of individuals, or of the minority, will be in little danger from interested combinations of the majority. In a free government the security for civil rights must be the same as that for religious rights. It consists in the one case in the multiplicity of interests, and in the other in the multiplicity of sects. The degree of security in both cases will depend on the number of interests and sects; and this may be presumed to depend on the extent of country and number of people comprehended under the same government. This view of the subject must particularly recommend a proper federal system to all the sincere and considerate friends of republican government, since it shows that in exact proportion as the territory of the Union may be formed into more circumscribed Confederacies, or States, oppressive combinations of a majority will be facilitated; the best security, under the republican forms, for the rights of every class of citizen, will be diminished; and consequently the stability and independence of some member of the government, the only other security, must be proportionally increased. Justice is the end of government. It is the end of civil society. It ever has been and ever will be pursued until it be obtained, or until liberty be lost in the pursuit. In a society under the forms of which the stronger faction can readily unite and oppress the weaker, anarchy may as truly be said to reign as in a state of nature, where the weaker individual is not secured against the violence of the stronger; and as, in the latter state, even the stronger individuals are prompted, by the uncertainty of their condition, to submit to a government which may protect the weak as well as themselves; so, in the former state, will the more powerful factions or parties be gradually induced, by a like motive, to wish for a government which will protect all parties, the weaker as well as the more powerful. It can be little doubted that if the State of Rhode Island was separated from the Confederacy and left to itself, the insecurity of rights under the popular form of government within such narrow limits would be displayed by such reiterated oppressions of factious majorities that some power altogether independent of the people would soon be called for by the voice of the very factions whose misrule had proved the necessity to it. In the extended republic of the United States, and among the great variety of interests, parties, and sects which it embraces, a coalition of a majority of the whole society could seldom take place on any other principles than those of justice and the general good; whilst there being thus less danger to a minor from the will of a major party, there must be less pretext, also, to provide for the security of the former, by introducing into the government a will not dependent on the latter, or, in other words, a will independent of the society itself. It is no less certain that it is important, notwithstanding the contrary opinions which have been entertained that the larger the society, provided it lie within a practicable sphere, the more duly capable it will be of self-government. And happily for the *republican cause,* the practicable sphere may be carried to a very great extent by a judicious modification and mixture of the *federal principle.*

The Federalist, No. 78, Alexander Hamilton

The Federalist, *No. 78, written by Alexander Hamilton, explains and praises the provisions for the judiciary in the newly drafted Constitution. Notice especially how Hamilton asserts that the courts have a key responsibility in determining the meaning of the Constitution as fundamental law. Hamilton is outlining here the doctrine of judicial review as we now know it.*

We proceed now to an examination of the judiciary department of the proposed government.

In unfolding the defects of the existing Confederation, the utility and necessity of a federal judicature have been clearly pointed out. It is the less necessary to recapitulate the considerations there urged as the propriety of the institution in the abstract is not disputed; the only questions which have been raised being relative to the manner of constituting it, and to its extent. To these points, therefore, our observations shall be confined.

The manner of constituting it seems to embrace these several objects: 1st. The mode of appointing the judges. 2nd. The tenure by which they are to hold their places. 3rd. The partition of the judiciary authority between different courts and their relations to each other.

First. As to the mode of appointing the judges: this is the same with that of appointing the officers of the Union in general and has been so fully discussed in the two last numbers that nothing can be said here which would not be useless repetition.

Second. As to the tenure by which the judges are to hold their places: this chiefly concerns their duration in office, the provisions for their support, the precautions for their responsibility.

According to the plan of the convention, all judges who may be appointed by the United States are to hold their offices *during good behavior;* which is conformable to the most approved of the State constitutions, and among the rest, to that of this State. Its propriety having been drawn into question by the adversaries of that plan is no light symptom of the rage for objection which disorders their imaginations and judgments. The standard of good behavior for the continuance in office of the judicial magistracy is certainly one of the most valuable of the modern improvements in the practice of government. In a monarchy it is an excellent barrier to the despotism of the prince; in a republic it is a no less excellent barrier to the encroachments and oppressions of the representative body. And it is the best expedient which can be devised in any government to secure a steady, upright, and impartial administration of the laws.

Whoever attentively considers the different departments of power must perceive that, in a government in which they are separated from each other, the judiciary, from the nature of its functions, will always be the least dangerous to the political rights of the Constitution; because it will be least in a capacity to annoy or injure them. The executive not only dispenses the honors but holds the sword of the community. The legislature not only commands the purse but prescribes the rules by which the duties and rights of every citizen are to be regulated. The judiciary, on the contrary, has no influence over either the sword or the purse; no direction either of the strength or of the wealth of the society, and can take no active resolution whatever. It may truly be said to have neither FORCE NOR WILL but merely judgment; and must ultimately depend upon the aid of the executive arm even for the efficacy of its judgments.

This simple view of the matter suggests several important consequences. It proves incontestably that the judiciary is beyond comparison the weakest of the three departments of power; that it can never attack with success either of the other two; and that all possible care is requisite to enable it to defend itself against their attacks. It equally proves that though individual oppression may now and then proceed from the courts of justice, the general liberty of the people can never be endangered from that quarter; I mean so long as the judiciary remains truly distinct from both the legislature and the executive. For I agree that "there is no liberty if the power of judging be not separated from the legislative and executive powers." And it proves, in the last place, that as liberty can have nothing to fear from the judiciary alone, but would have everything to fear from its union with either of the other departments, that as all the effects of such a union must ensue from a dependence of the former on the latter, notwithstanding a nominal and apparent separation; that as, from the natural feebleness of the judiciary, it is in continual jeopardy of being overpowered, awed, or influenced by its co-ordinate branches; and that as nothing can contribute so much to its firmness and independence as permanency in office, this quality may therefore be justly regarded as an indispensable ingredient in its constitution, and, in a great measure, as the citadel for the public justice and the public security.

The complete independence of the courts of justice is peculiarly essential in a limited Constitution. By a limited Constitution, I understand one which contains certain specified exceptions to the legislative authority; such, for instance, as that it shall pass no bills of attainder, no *ex post facto laws,* and the like. Limitations of this kind can be preserved in practice no other way than through the medium of courts of justice, whose duty it must be to declare all acts contrary to the manifest tenor of the Constitution void. Without this, all the reservations of particular rights or privileges would amount to nothing.

Some perplexity respecting the rights of the courts to pronounce legislative acts void, because contrary to the Constitution, has arisen from an imagination that the doctrine would imply a superiority to the judiciary to the legislative power. It is urged that the authority which can declare the acts of another void must necessarily be superior to the one whose acts may be declared void. As this doctrine is of great importance in all the American constitutions, a brief discussion of the grounds on which it rests cannot be unacceptable.

There is no position which depends on clearer principles than that every act of a delegated authority, contrary to the tenor of the commission under which it is exercised, is void. No legislative act, therefore, contrary to the Constitution, can be valid. To deny this would be to affirm that the deputy is greater than his principal; that the servant is above his master; that the representatives of the people are superior to the people themselves; that men acting by virtue of powers do not authorize, but what they forbid.

If it be said that the legislative body are themselves the constitutional judges of their own powers and that the construction they put upon them is conclusive upon the other departments it may be answered that this cannot be the natural presumption where it is not to be collected from any particular provisions in the Constitution. It is not otherwise to be supposed that the Constitution could intend to enable the representatives of the people to substitute their *will* to that of their constituents. It is far more rational to suppose that the courts were designed to be an intermediate body between the people and the legislature in order,

among other things, to keep the latter within the limits assigned to their authority. The interpretation of the laws is the proper and peculiar province of the courts. A constitution is, in fact, and must be regarded by the judges as, a fundamental law. It therefore belongs to them to ascertain its meaning as well as the meaning of any particular act proceeding from the legislative body. If there should happen to be an irreconcilable variance between the two, that which has the superior obligation and validity ought, of course, to be preferred; or, in other words, the Constitution ought to be preferred to the statute, the intention of the people to the intention of their agents.

Nor does this conclusion by any means suppose a superiority of the judicial to the legislative power. It only supposes that the power of the people is superior to both, and that where the will of the legislature, declared in its statutes, stands in opposition to that of the people, declared in the Constitution, the judges ought to be governed by the latter rather than the former. They ought to regulate their decisions by the fundamental laws rather than by those which are not fundamental.

This exercise of judicial discretion in determining between two contradictory laws is exemplified in a familiar instance. It not uncommonly happens that there are two statutes existing at one time, clashing in whole or in part with each other and neither of them containing any repealing clause or expression. In such a case, it is the province of the courts to liquidate and fix their meaning and operation. So far as they can, by any fair construction, be reconciled to each other, reason and law conspire to dictate that this should be done; where this is impracticable, it becomes a matter of necessity to give effect to one in exclusion of the other. The rule which has obtained in the courts for determining their relative validity is that the last in order of time shall be preferred to the first. But this is a mere rule of construction, not derived from any positive law but from the nature and reason of the thing. It is a rule not enjoined upon the courts by legislative provision but adopted by themselves, as consonant to truth and propriety, for the direction of their conduct as interpreters of the law. They thought it reasonable that between the interfering acts of an equal authority that which was the last indication of its will should have the preference.

But in regard to the interfering acts of a superior and subordinate authority of an original and derivative power, the nature and reason of the thing indicates the converse of that rule as proper to be followed. They teach us that the prior act of a superior ought to be preferred to the subsequent act of an inferior and subordinate authority; and that accordingly, whenever

a particular statute contravenes the Constitution, it will be the duty of the judicial tribunals to adhere to the latter and disregard the former.

It can be of no weight to say that the courts, on the pretense of a repugnancy, may substitute their own pleasure to the constitutional intentions of the legislature. This might as well happen in the case of two contradictory statutes; or it might as well happen in every adjudication upon any single statute. The courts must declare the sense of the law; and if they should be disposed to exercise WILL instead of JUDGMENT, the consequence would equally be the substitution of their pleasure to that of the legislative body. The observation, if it prove anything, would prove that there ought to be no judges distinct from that body.

If, then, the courts of justice are to be considered as the bulwarks of a limited Constitution against legislative encroachments, this consideration will afford a strong argument for the permanent tenure of judicial offices, since nothing will contribute so much as this to that independent spirit in the judges which must be essential to the faithful performance of so arduous a duty.

This independence of the judges is equally requisite to guard the Constitution and the rights of individuals from the effects of those ill humors which the arts of designing men, or the influence of particular conjunctures, sometimes disseminate among the people themselves, and which, though they speedily give place to better information, and more deliberate reflection, have a tendency, in the meantime, to occasion dangerous innovations in the government, and serious oppressions of the minor party in the community. Though I trust the friends of the proposed Constitution will never concur with its enemies in questioning that fundamental principal of Republican government which admits the right of the people to alter or abolish the established Constitution whenever they find it inconsistent with their happiness; yet it is not to be inferred from this principle that the representatives of the people, whenever a momentary inclination happens to lay hold of a majority of their constituents incompatible with the provisions in the existing Constitution would, on that account, be justifiable in a violation of those provisions; or that the courts would be under a greater obligation to connive at infractions in this shape than when they had proceeded wholly from the cabals of the representative body. Until the people have, by some solemn and authoritative act, annulled or changed the established form, it is binding upon themselves collectively, as well as individually; and no presumption, or even knowledge of their sentiments, can warrant their representatives in a departure from it prior to such an act. But it is easy to see that it would require an uncommon portion of fortitude in the judges to do their duty as faithful guardians of the Constitution, where legislative invasions of it had been instigated by the major voice of the community.

But it is not with a view to infractions of the Constitution only that the independence of the judges may be an essential safeguard against the effects of occasional ill humors in the society. These sometimes extend no farther than to the injury of the private rights of particular classes of citizens, by unjust and partial laws. Here also the firmness of the judicial magistracy is of vast importance in mitigating the severity and confining the operation of such laws. It not only serves to moderate the immediate mischiefs of those which may have been passed but it operates as a check upon the legislative body in passing them; who, perceiving that obstacles to the success of iniquitous intention are to be expected from the scruples of the courts, are in a manner compelled, by the very motives of the injustice they mediate, to qualify their attempts. This is a circumstance calculated to have more influence upon the character of our governments than but a few may be aware of. The benefits of the integrity and moderation of the judiciary have already been felt in more States than one; and though they may have displeased those whose sinister expectations they may have disappointed, they must have commanded the esteem and applause of all the virtuous and disinterested. Considerate men of every description ought to prize whatever will tend to beget or fortify that temper in the courts; as no man can be sure that he may not be tomorrow the victim of a spirit of injustice, by which he may be a gainer today. And every man must now feel that the inevitable tendency of such a spirit is to sap the foundations of public and private confidence and to introduce in its stead universal distrust and distress.

That inflexible and uniform adherence to the rights of the Constitution, and of individuals, which we perceive to be indispensable in the courts of justice, can certainly not be expected from judges who hold their offices by a temporary commission. Periodical appointments, however regulated, or by whomsoever made, would, in some way or other, be fatal to their necessary independence. If the power of making them was committed either to the executive or legislature there would be danger of an improper complaisance to the branch which possessed it; if to both, there would be an unwillingness to hazard the displeasure of either; if to the people, or to persons chosen by them for the special purpose, there would be too great a disposition to consult popularity to justify a reliance that nothing would be consulted by the Constitution and the laws.

There is yet a further and a weighty reason for the permanency of the judicial offices which is deducible from the nature of the qualifications they require. It has been frequently remarked with great propriety that a voluminous code of laws is one of the inconveniences necessarily connected with the advantages of a free government. To avoid an arbitrary discretion in the courts, it is indispensable that they should be bound down by strict rules and precedents which serve to define and point out their duty in every particular case that comes before them; and it will readily be conceived from the variety of controversies which grow out of the folly and wickedness of mankind that the records of those precedents must unavoidably swell to a very considerable bulk and must demand long and laborious study to acquire a competent knowledge of them. Hence it is that there can be but few men in the society who will have sufficient skill in the laws to qualify them for the stations of judges. And making the proper deductions for the ordinary depravity of human nature, the number must be still smaller of those who unite the requisite integrity with the requisite knowledge. These considerations apprise us that the government can have no great option between fit characters; and that a temporary duration in office which would naturally discourage such characters from quitting a lucrative line of practice to accept a seat on the bench would have a tendency to throw the administration of justice into hands less able and less well qualified to conduct it with utility and dignity. In the present circumstances of this country and in those in which it is likely to be for a long time to come, the disadvantages on this score would be greater than they may at first sight appear; but it must be confessed that they are far inferior to those which present themselves under the other aspects of the subject.

Upon the whole, there can be no room to doubt that the convention acted wisely in copying from the models of those constitutions which have established *good behavior* as the tenure of their judicial offices in point of duration, and that so far from being blamable on this account, their plan would have been inexcusably defective if it had wanted this important feature of good government. The experience of Great Britain affords an illustrious comment on the excellence of the institution.

Presidential Election Results, 1789–2004

Year	Candidates	Party	Popular Vote	Electoral Vote
1789	George Washington			69
	John Adams			34
	Others			35
1793	George Washington			132
	John Adams			77
	George Clinton			50
	Others			5
1796	John Adams	Federalist		71
	Thomas Jefferson	Democratic-Republican		68
	Thomas Pinckney	Federalist		59
	Aaron Burr	Democratic-Republican		30
	Others			48
1800	Thomas Jefferson	Democratic-Republican		73
	Aaron Burr	Democratic-Republican		73
	John Adams	Federalist		65
	Charles C. Pinckney	Federalist		64
1804	Thomas Jefferson	Democratic-Republican		162
	Charles C. Pinckney	Federalist		14
1808	James Madison	Democratic-Republican		122
	Charles C. Pinckney	Federalist		47
	George Clinton	Independent-Republican		6
1812	James Madison	Democratic-Republican		128
	DeWitt Clinton	Federalist		89
1816	James Monroe	Democratic-Republican		183
	Rufus King	Federalist		34
1820	James Monroe	Democratic-Republican		231
	John Quincy Adams	Independent-Republican		1
1824	John Quincy Adams	Democratic-Republican	108,740(30.5%)	84
	Andrew Jackson	Democratic-Republican	153,544(43.1%)	99
	Henry Clay	Democratic-Republican	47,136(13.2%)	37
	William H. Crawford	Democratic-Republican	46,618(13.1%)	41
1828	Andrew Jackson	Democratic	647,231(56.0%)	178
	John Quincy Adams	National Republican	509,097(44.0%)	83
1832	Andrew Jackson	Democratic	687,502(55.0%)	219
	Henry Clay	National Republican	530,189(42.4%)	49
	William Wirt	Anti-Masonic		7
	John Floyd	National Republican	33,108(2.6%)	11
1836	Martin Van Buren	Democratic	761,549(50.9%)	170
	William H. Harrison	Whig	549,567(36.7%)	73
	Hugh L. White	Whig	145,396(9.7%)	26
	Daniel Webster	Whig	41,287(2.7%)	14
1840	William H. Harrison	Whig	1,275,017(53.1%)	234
	Martin Van Buren	Democratic	1,128,702(46.9%)	60
1844	James K. Polk	Democratic	1,337,243(49.6%)	170
	Henry Clay	Whig	1,299,068(48.1%)	105
	James G. Birney	Liberty	63,300(2.3%)	
1848	Zachary Taylor	Whig	1,360,101(47.4%)	163
	Lewis Cass	Democratic	1,220,544(42.5%)	127
	Martin Van Buren	Free Soil	291,163(10.1%)	
1852	Franklin Pierce	Democratic	1,601,474(50.9%)	254
	Winfield Scott	Whig	1,386,578(44.1%)	42
1856	James Buchanan	Democratic	1,838,169(45.4%)	174
	John C. Fremont	Republican	1,335,264(33.0%)	114
	Millard Fillmore	American	874,534(21.6%)	8
1860	Abraham Lincoln	Republican	1,865,593(39.8%)	180
	Stephen A. Douglas	Democratic	1,381,713(29.5%)	12
	John C. Breckinridge	Democratic	848,356(18.1%)	72
	John Bell	Constitutional Union	592,906(12.6%)	79
1864	Abraham Lincoln	Republican	2,206,938(55.0%)	212
	George B. McClellan	Democratic	1,803,787(45.0%)	21
1868	Ulysses S. Grant	Republican	3,013,421(52.7%)	214
	Horatio Seymour	Democratic	2,706,829(47.3%)	80
1872	Ulysses S. Grant	Republican	3,596,745(55.6%)	286
	Horace Greeley	Democratic	2,843,446(43.9%)	66
1876	Rutherford B. Hayes	Republican	4,036,571(48.0%)	185
	Samuel J. Tilden	Democratic	4,284,020(51.0%)	184
1880	James A. Garfield	Republican	4,449,053(48.3%)	214
	Winfield S. Hancock	Democratic	4,442,035(48.2%)	155
	James B. Weaver	Greenback-Labor	308,578(3.4%)	
1884	Grover Cleveland	Democratic	4,874,986(48.5%)	219
	James G. Blaine	Republican	4,851,931(48.2%)	182
	Benjamin F. Butler	Greenback-Labor	175,370(1.8%)	
1888	Benjamin Harrison	Republican	5,444,337(47.8%)	233
	Grover Cleveland	Democratic	5,540,050(48.6%)	168

Presidential Election Results, 1789–2004

Year	Candidates	Party	Popular Vote	Electoral Vote
1892	Grover Cleveland	Democratic	5,554,414(46.0%)	277
	Benjamin Harrison	Republican	5,190,802(43.0%)	145
	James B. Weaver	Peoples	1,027,329(8.5%)	22
1896	William McKinley	Republican	7,035,638(50.8%)	271
	William J. Bryan	Democratic; Populist	6,467,946(46.7%)	176
1900	William McKinley	Republican	7,219,530(51.7%)	292
	William J. Bryan	Democratic; Populist	6,356,734(45.5%)	155
1904	Theodore Roosevelt	Republican	7,628,834(56.4%)	336
	Alton B. Parker	Democratic	5,084,401(37.6%)	140
	Eugene V. Debs	Socialist	402,460(3.0%)	0
1908	William H. Taft	Republican	7,679,006(51.6%)	321
	William J. Bryan	Democratic	6,409,106(43.1%)	162
	Eugene V. Debs	Socialist	420,820(2.8%)	0
1912	Woodrow Wilson	Democratic	6,286,820(41.8%)	435
	Theodore Roosevelt	Progressive	4,126,020(27.4%)	88
	William H. Taft	Republican	3,483,922(23.2%)	8
	Eugene V. Debs	Socialist	897,011(6.0%)	0
1916	Woodrow Wilson	Democratic	9,129,606(49.3%)	277
	Charles E. Hughes	Republican	8,538,211(46.1%)	254
1920	Warren G. Harding	Republican	16,152,200(61.0%)	404
	James M. Cox	Democratic	9,147,353(34.6%)	127
	Eugene V. Debs	Socialist	919,799(3.5%)	0
1924	Calvin Coolidge	Republican	15,725,016(54.1%)	382
	John W. Davis	Democratic	8,385,586(28.8%)	136
	Robert M. La Follette	Progressive	4,822,856(16.6%)	13
1928	Herbert C. Hoover	Republican	21,392,190(58.2%)	444
	Alfred E. Smith	Democratic	15,016,443(40.8%)	87
1932	Franklin D. Roosevelt	Democratic	22,809,638(57.3%)	472
	Herbert C. Hoover	Republican	15,758,901(39.6%)	59
	Norman Thomas	Socialist	881,951(2.2%)	0
1936	Franklin D. Roosevelt	Democratic	27,751,612(60.7%)	523
	Alfred M. Landon	Republican	16,681,913(36.4%)	8
	William Lemke	Union	891,858(1.9%)	0
1940	Franklin D. Roosevelt	Democratic	27,243,466(54.7%)	449
	Wendell L. Willkie	Republican	22,304,755(44.8%)	82
1944	Franklin D. Roosevelt	Democratic	25,602,505(52.8%)	432
	Thomas E. Dewey	Republican	22,006,278(44.5%)	99
1948	Harry S Truman	Democratic	24,105,812(49.5%)	303
	Thomas E. Dewey	Republican	21,970,065(45.1%)	189
	J. Strom Thurmond	States' Rights	1,169,063(2.4%)	39
	Henry A. Wallace	Progressive	1,157,172(2.4%)	0
1952	Dwight D. Eisenhower	Republican	33,936,234(55.2%)	442
	Adlai E. Stevenson	Democratic	27,314,992(44.5%)	89
1956	Dwight D. Eisenhower	Republican	35,590,472(57.4%)	457
	Adlai E. Stevenson	Democratic	26,022,752(42.0%)	73
1960	John F. Kennedy	Democratic	34,227,096(49.9%)	303
	Richard M. Nixon	Republican	34,108,546(49.6%)	219
1964	Lyndon B. Johnson	Democratic	43,126,233(61.1%)	486
	Barry Goldwater	Republican	27,174,989(38.5%)	52
1968	Richard M. Nixon	Republican	31,783,783(43.4%)	301
	Hubert H. Humphrey	Democratic	31,271,839(42.7%)	191
	George C. Wallace	American Independent	9,899,557(13.5%)	46
1972	Richard M. Nixon	Republican	46,632,189(61.3%)	520
	George McGovern	Democratic	28,422,015(37.3%)	17
1976	Jimmy Carter	Democratic	40,828,587(50.1%)	297
	Gerald R. Ford	Republican	39,147,613(48.0%)	240
1980	Ronald Reagan	Republican	42,941,145(51.0%)	489
	Jimmy Carter	Democratic	34,663,037(41.0%)	49
	John B. Anderson	Independent	5,551,551(6.6%)	0
1984	Ronald Reagan	Republican	53,428,357(59%)	525
	Walter F. Mondale	Democratic	36,930,923(41%)	13
1988	George Bush	Republican	48,881,011(53%)	426
	Michael Dukakis	Democratic	41,828,350(46%)	111
1992	Bill Clinton	Democratic	38,394,210(43%)	370
	George Bush	Republican	33,974,386(38%)	168
	H. Ross Perot	Independent	16,573,465(19%)	0
1996	Bill Clinton	Democratic	45,628,667(49%)	379
	Bob Dole	Republican	37,869,435(41%)	159
	H. Ross Perot	Reform	7,874,283(8%)	0
2000	George W. Bush	Republican	50,456,169(48%)	271
	Al Gore	Democratic	50,996,116(48%)	266
	Ralph Nader	Green	2,767,176(3%)	0
2004	George W. Bush	Republican	60,608,582(51%)	286
	John Kerry	Democratic	57,288,974(48%)	252
	Ralph Nader	Independent	400,924(.35%)	0

Presidents and Vice Presidents

1. George Washington (1789)
   John Adams (1789)

2. John Adams (1797)
   Thomas Jefferson (1797)

3. Thomas Jefferson (1801)
   Aaron Burr (1801)
   George Clinton (1805)

4. James Madison (1809)
   George Clinton (1809)
   Elbridge Gerry (1813)

5. James Monroe (1817)
   Daniel D. Tompkins (1817)

6. John Quincy Adams (1825)
   John C. Calhoun (1825)

7. Andrew Jackson (1829)
   John C. Calhoun (1829)
   Martin Van Buren (1833)

8. Martin Van Buren (1837)
   Richard M. Johnson (1837)

9. William H. Harrison (1841)
   John Tyler (1841)

10. John Tyler (1841)

11. James K. Polk (1845)
    George M. Dallas (1845)

12. Zachary Taylor (1849)
    Millard Fillmore (1849)

13. Millard Fillmore (1850)

14. Franklin Pierce (1853)
    William R. King (1853)

15. James Buchanan (1857)
    John C. Breckinridge (1857)

16. Abraham Lincoln (1861)
    Hannibal Hamlin (1861)
    Andrew Johnson (1865)

17. Andrew Johnson (1865)

18. Ulysses S. Grant (1869)
    Schuyler Colfax (1869)
    Henry Wilson (1873)

19. Rutherford B. Hayes (1877)
    William A. Wheeler (1877)

20. James A. Garfield (1881)
    Chester A. Arthur (1881)

21. Chester A. Arthur (1881)

22. Grover Cleveland (1885)
    T. A. Hendricks (1885)

23. Benjamin Harrison (1889)
    Levi P. Morton (1889)

24. Grover Cleveland (1893)
    Adlai E. Stevenson (1893)

25. William McKinley (1897)
    Garret A. Hobart (1897)
    Theodore Roosevelt (1901)

26. Theodore Roosevelt (1901)
    Charles Fairbanks (1905)

27. William H. Taft (1909)
    James S. Sherman (1909)

28. Woodrow Wilson (1913)
    Thomas R. Marshall (1913)

29. Warren G. Harding (1921)
    Calvin Coolidge (1921)

30. Calvin Coolidge (1923)
    Charles G. Dawes (1925)

31. Herbert C. Hoover (1929)
    Charles Curtis (1929)

32. Franklin D. Roosevelt (1933)
    John Nance Garner (1933)
    Henry A. Wallace (1941)
    Harry S Truman (1945)

33. Harry S Truman (1945)
    Alben W. Barkley (1949)

34. Dwight D. Eisenhower (1953)
    Richard M. Nixon (1953)

35. John F. Kennedy (1961)
    Lyndon B. Johnson (1961)

36. Lyndon B. Johnson (1963)
    Hubert H. Humphrey (1965)

37. Richard M. Nixon (1969)
    Spiro T. Agnew (1969)
    Gerald R. Ford (1973)

38. Gerald R. Ford (1974)
    Nelson A. Rockefeller (1974)

39. James E. Carter Jr. (1977)
    Walter F. Mondale (1977)

40. Ronald W. Reagan (1981)
    George H. W. Bush (1981)

41. George H. W. Bush (1989)
    James D. Quayle III (1989)

42. William J. B. Clinton (1993)
    Albert Gore (1993)

43. George W. Bush (2001)
    Richard Cheney (2001)

GLOSSARY

527 groups Interest groups organized under Section 527 of the Internal Revenue Service Code that may advertise for or against candidates. If the source of funding is corporations or unions, they have some restrictions on broadcast advertising. 527 groups were important in the 2000 and 2004 elections.

absentee (or early) voting Period before the regularly scheduled election date, during which voters are allowed to cast ballots. With recent changes in election law, a person does not have to offer a reason for voting absentee.

administrative discretion Authority given by Congress to the federal bureaucracy to use reasonable judgment in implementing the laws.

adversary system A judicial system in which the court of law is a neutral arena where two parties argue their differences.

advisory opinion An opinion unrelated to a particular case that gives a court's view about a constitutional or legal issue.

affirmative action Remedial action designed to overcome the effects of past discrimination against minorities and women.

agriculture commissioner The elected official responsible for administering laws and programs that benefit agriculture.

amendatory veto The power of governors in a few states to return a bill to the legislature with suggested language changes, conditions, or amendments. Legislators then decide either to accept the governor's recommendations or to pass the bill in its original form over the veto.

American dream The widespread belief that the United States is a land of opportunity and that individual initiative and hard work can bring economic success.

***amicus curiae* brief** Literally, a "friend of the court" brief, filed by an individual or organization to present arguments in addition to those presented by the immediate parties to a case.

Annapolis Convention A convention held in September 1786 to consider problems of trade and navigation, attended by five states and important because it issued the call to Congress and the states for what became the Constitutional Convention.

annexation powers Authority of cities to add territory, subject to restrictions set by state law.

Antifederalists Opponents of ratification of the Constitution and of a strong central government generally.

antitrust legislation Federal laws (starting with the Sherman Act of 1890) that try to prevent a monopoly from dominating an industry and restraining trade.

appellate jurisdiction The authority of a court to review decisions made by lower courts.

appraisal district Local agency that determines the value of pieces of property in a county. All local governments are required to use its evaluations, or appraisals, for tax purposes.

appropriations bill Bill that authorizes the expenditure of money for a public program or purpose. In Texas, the general appropriations bill approved by the legislature every two years is the state budget.

Articles of Confederation The first governing document of the confederated states, drafted in 1777, ratified in 1781, and replaced by the present Constitution in 1789.

assessment The valuation a government places on property for the purposes of taxation.

assigned counsel system Arrangement whereby attorneys are provided for persons accused of crimes who are unable to hire their own attorneys. The judge assigns a member of the bar to provide counsel to a particular defendant.

at-large district Legislative or other political district, sometimes called a multimember district because two or more officials are elected from it, that includes an entire county, city, or other political subdivision.

at-large elections Election systems under which officeholders are elected by voters in the entire city, school district, or single-purpose district.

attentive public Those citizens who follow public affairs carefully.

attorney general The state's chief legal officer, who represents Texas in lawsuits and is responsible for enforcing the state's antitrust, consumer protection, and other civil laws.

Australian ballot A secret ballot printed by the state.

bad tendency test Interpretation of the First Amendment that would permit legislatures to forbid speech encouraging people to engage in illegal action.

bicameral legislature A two-house legislature.

bicameralism The principle of a two-house legislature.

bifactionalism Presence of two dominant factions organized around regional, economic, or ideological differences within a single political party. For much of the twentieth century, Texas functioned as a one-party system with two dominant factions.

bifurcated court system Existence of two courts at the highest level of the state judiciary. The Texas Supreme Court is the court of last resort in civil cases, and the Texas Court of Criminal Appeals has the final authority to review criminal cases.

bill of attainder Legislative act inflicting punishment, including deprivation of property, without a trial, on named individuals or members of a specific group.

binding arbitration A collective bargaining agreement in which both parties agree, in case of dispute over the terms of the union contract, to adhere to the decision of an arbitrator.

bipartisanship A policy that emphasizes a united front and cooperation between the major political parties, especially on sensitive foreign policy issues.

blanket primary Primary election open to all voters, who may vote for a candidate from any party for each office.

bloc Group of legislators who act together for a common goal regardless of party affiliation.

bundling A tactic of political action committees whereby they collect contributions from like-minded individuals (each limited to $2,000) and present them to a candidate or political party as a "bundle," thus increasing their influence.

bureaucracy A form of organization that operates through impersonal, uniform rules and procedures.

bureaucrat A career government employee.

Bush doctrine A policy adopted by the Bush administration in 2001 that asserts America's right to attack any nation that has weapons of mass destruction that might be used against U.S. interests at home or abroad.

cabinet Advisory council for the president, consisting of the heads of the executive departments, the vice president, and a few other officials selected by the president.

calendar Agenda or the list of bills to be considered by the house or the senate on a given day.

Calendars Committee Special procedural committee that schedules bills that already have been approved by other committees for floor debate in the house.

candidate appeal How voters feel about a candidate's background, personality, leadership ability, and other personal qualities.

capital murder Murder committed under certain circumstances for which the death penalty or life in prison must be imposed. p. 38

capitalism An economic system characterized by private property, competitive markets, economic incentives, and limited government involvement in the production and pricing of goods and services.

caucus A meeting of local party members to choose party officials or candidates for public office and to decide the platform.

central clearance Review of all executive branch testimony, reports, and draft legislation by the Office of Management and Budget to ensure that each communication to Congress is in accordance with the president's program.

centralists People who favor national action over action at the state and local levels.

charter school A publicly funded alternative to standard public schools in some states, initiated when individuals or groups receive charters; charter schools must meet state standards.

charter City "constitution" that outlines the structure of city government, defines the authority of the various officials, and provides for their selection.

checks and balances Constitutional grant of powers that enables each of the three branches of government to check some acts of the others and therefore ensure that no branch can dominate.

chief of staff The head of the White House staff.

city commission Form of city government in which elected commissioners collectively serve as a city's policy-making body and individually serve as administrative heads of different city departments.

civil disobedience Deliberate refusal to obey a law or comply with the orders of public officials as a means of expressing opposition.

civil lawsuit Noncriminal legal dispute between two or more individuals, businesses, governments, or other entities.

civil service system System under which public employees are hired and promoted on their abilities. It features competitive examinations and offers job security from one election to another.

class action suit Lawsuit brought by an individual or a group of people on behalf of all those similarly situated.

clear and present danger test Interpretation of the First Amendment that holds that the government cannot interfere with speech unless the speech presents a clear and present danger that it will lead to evil or illegal acts. To shout "Fire!" falsely in a crowded theater is Justice Oliver Wendell Holmes's famous example.

closed primary Primary election in which only persons registered in the party holding the primary may vote.

closed rule A procedural rule in the House of Representatives that prohibits any amendments to bills or provides that only members of the committee reporting the bill may offer amendments.

closed shop A company with a labor agreement under which union membership is a condition of employment.

cloture A procedure for terminating debate, especially filibusters, in the Senate.

coattail effect The boost that candidates may get in an election because of the popularity of candidates above them on the ballot, especially the president.

collective bargaining Method whereby representatives of the union and employer determine wages, hours, and other conditions of employment through direct negotiation.

commerce clause The clause of the Constitution (Article I, Section 8, Clause 3) that gives Congress the power to regulate all business activities that cross state lines or affect more than one state or other nations.

commercial speech Advertisements and commercials for products and services; they receive less First Amendment protection, primarily to discourage false and misleading ads.

commissioners court Principal policy-making body for county government. It sets the county tax rate and supervises expenditures.

committee In the legislature, a group of lawmakers who review and hold public hearings on issues or bills they are assigned by the presiding officer. Committees that specialize in bills by subject matter are designated as standing committees. A bill has to win committee approval before it can be considered by the full house or senate. Most bills die in committees, which perform as a legislative screening process.

community policing Assigning police to neighborhoods where they walk the beat and work with churches and other community groups to reduce crime and improve relations with minorities.

comptroller The state's primary tax administrator, accounting officer, and revenue estimator.

concurrent powers Powers that the Constitution gives to both the national and state governments, such as the power to levy taxes.

concurring opinion An opinion that agrees with the majority in a Supreme Court ruling but differs on the reasoning.

confederation Constitutional arrangement in which sovereign nations or states, by compact, create a central government but carefully limit its power and do not give it direct authority over individuals.

conference committee Committee appointed by the presiding officers of each chamber to adjust differences on a particular bill passed by each in different form.

Congressional Budget Office (CBO) An agency of Congress that analyzes presidential budget recommendations and estimates the costs of proposed legislation.

Connecticut Compromise Compromise agreement by states at the Constitutional Convention for a bicameral legislature with a lower house in which representation would be based on population and an upper house in which each state would have two senators.

conservatism A belief that limited government ensures order, competitive markets, and personal opportunity.

constable Elected law enforcement officer who is primarily responsible for executing court judgments, serving subpoenas, and delivering other legal documents.

constitution Legal structure of a political system, establishing government bodies and defining their powers.

Constitutional Convention The convention in Philadelphia, May 25 to September 17, 1787, that framed the Constitution of the United States.

constitutional county court County court created by the Texas Constitution, presided over by the county judge.

constitutional democracy A government that enforces recognized limits on those who govern and allows the voice of the people to be heard through free, fair, and relatively frequent elections.

constitutional home rule State constitutional authorization for local governments to conduct their own affairs.

constitutional initiative petition A device that permits voters to place specific amendments to a state constitution on the ballot by petition.

constitutionalism The set of arrangements, including checks and balances, federalism, separation of powers, rule of law, due process, and a bill of rights, that requires leaders to listen, think, bargain, and explain before they act or make laws. We then hold them politically and legally accountable for how they exercise their powers.

contract clause Clause of the Constitution (Article I, Section 10) originally intended to prohibit state governments from modifying contracts made between individuals; for a while interpreted as prohibiting state governments from taking actions that adversely affect property rights; no longer interpreted so broadly and no longer constrains state governments from exercising their police powers.

council of government (COG) Council comprised of representatives of other governments in a defined region of the state.

council-manager plan Form of local government in which the city council hires a professional administrator to manage city affairs; also known as the *city-manager plan*.

county attorney Elected official who is the chief legal officer of some counties. He or she also prosecutes lesser criminal offenses, primarily misdemeanors, in county courts.

county auditor Appointed officer who is primarily responsible for reviewing every bill and expenditure of a county to assure it is correct and legal.

county chair Presiding officer of a political party's county executive committee. He or she is elected countywide by voters in the party primary.

county clerk Chief record-keeping officer of a county.

county executive committee Panel responsible on the local level for the organization and management of a political party's primary election. It includes the party's county chair and each precinct chair.

county judge Presiding officer of a county commissioners court. This office also has some judicial authority, which is assumed by separate county courts-at-law in most urban counties.

county treasurer Elected officer who is responsible for receiving and disbursing county funds.

court of appeals A court with appellate jurisdiction that hears appeals from the decisions of lower courts.

cross-cutting cleavages Divisions within society that cut across demographic categories to produce groups that are more heterogeneous or different.

crossover voting Voting by a member of one party for a candidate of another party.

de facto segregation Segregation resulting from economic or social conditions or personal choice.

de jure segregation Segregation imposed by law.

de novo In a civil lawsuit or criminal trial, evidence is presented again before an appellate court because no record was kept of the evidence presented to the trial court.

dealignment Weakening of partisan preferences that points to a rejection of both major parties and a rise in the number of Independents.

decentralists People who favor state or local action rather than national action.

defendant In a criminal action, the person or party accused of an offense.

deficit The difference between the revenues raised annually from sources of income other than borrowing and the expenditures of government, including paying the interest on past borrowing.

delegate An official who is expected to represent the views of his or her constituents even when personally holding different views; one interpretation of the role of the legislator.

democracy Government by the people, either directly or indirectly, with free and frequent elections.

democratic consensus Widespread agreement on fundamental principles of democratic governance and the values that undergird them.

demographics The study of the characteristics of populations.

department Usually the largest organization in government; also the highest rank in federal hierarchy.

deregulation A policy promoting cutbacks in the amount of federal regulation in specific areas of economic activity.

devolution revolution The effort to slow the growth of the federal government by returning many functions to the states.

Dillon rule Principle holding that local governments are creations of state government and that their powers and responsibilities are defined by the state.

direct democracy Government in which citizens vote on laws and select officials more directly.

direct primary Election in which voters choose party nominees.

discharge petition Petition that, if signed by a majority of the members of the House of Representatives, will pry a bill from committee and bring it to the floor for consideration.

disclosure A requirement that candidates specify where the money came from to finance their campaign.

dissenting opinion An opinion disagreeing with the majority in a Supreme Court ruling.

distributive policy A type of policy that provides benefits to all Americans.

district attorney Elected official who prosecutes more serious criminal offenses, usually felonies, before state district courts.

district clerk Elected county official who maintains custody of state district court records.

district court Primary trial court in Texas. It has jurisdiction over criminal felony cases and civil disputes.

divided government Governance divided between the parties, as when one holds the presidency and the other controls one or both houses of Congress.

division votes Votes taken on the computerized voting boards in the Texas house but erased without being permanently recorded.

double jeopardy Trial or punishment for the same crime by the same government; forbidden by the Constitution.

dual citizenship Citizenship in more than one nation.

due process clause Clause in the Fifth Amendment limiting the power of the national government; similar clause in the Fourteenth Amendment prohibiting state governments from depriving any person of life, liberty, or property without due process of law.

economic diversification Development of new and varied business activities. New businesses were encouraged to relocate or expand in Texas after the oil and gas industry, which had been the base of the state's economy, suffered a major recession in the 1980s.

economic sanctions Denial of export, import, or financial relations with a target country in an effort to change that nation's policies.

electoral college The electoral system used in electing the president and vice president, in which voters vote for electors pledged to cast their ballots for a particular party's candidates.

elite Small group of people who exercise disproportionate power and influence in the policy-making processes.

elitism Political system in which power is concentrated in the hands of a relatively small group of individuals or institutions.

eminent domain Power of a government to take private property for public use; the U.S. Constitution gives national and state governments this power and requires them to provide just compensation for property so taken.

enterprise zone Inner-city area designated as offering tax incentives to companies that invest in plants there and provide job training for the unemployed.

entitlement programs Government programs, such as unemployment insurance, disaster relief, and disability payments, that provide benefits to all eligible citizens.

enumerated powers The powers explicitly given to Congress in the Constitution.

environmental impact statement A statement required by federal law from all agencies for any project using federal funds to assess the potential effect of the new construction or development on the environment.

environmentalism An ideology that is dominated by concern for the environment but also promotes grassroots democracy, social justice, equal opportunity, nonviolence, respect for diversity, and feminism.

equal protection clause Clause in the Fourteenth Amendment that forbids any state to deny to any person within its jurisdiction the equal protection of the laws. By interpretation, the Fifth Amendment imposes the same limitation on the national government. This clause is the major constitutional restraint on the power of governments to discriminate against persons because of race, national origin, or sex.

establishment clause Clause in the First Amendment that states that Congress shall make no law respecting an establishment of religion. It has been interpreted by the Supreme Court as forbidding governmental support to any or all religions.

ethnicity A social division based on national origin, religion, language, and often race.

ethnocentrism Belief in the superiority of one's nation or ethnic group.

ex post facto **law** Retroactive criminal law that works to the disadvantage of an individual; forbidden in the Constitution.

excise tax Consumer tax on a specific kind of merchandise, such as tobacco.

exclusionary rule Requirement that evidence unconstitutionally or illegally obtained be excluded from a criminal trial.

executive agreement A formal but often secret agreement between the U.S. president and the leaders of other nations that does not require Senate approval.

Executive Office of the President The cluster of presidential staff agencies that help the president carry out his responsibilities. Currently the office includes the Office of Management and Budget, the Council of Economic Advisers, and several other units.

executive order Directive issued by a president or governor that has the force of law.

executive privilege The power to keep executive communications confidential, especially if they relate to national security.

express powers Powers specifically granted to one of the branches of the national government by the Constitution.

extradition Legal process whereby an alleged criminal offender is surrendered by the officials of one state to officials of the state in which the crime is alleged to have been committed.

extraterritorial jurisdiction Power of an incorporated city to control development within nearby unincorporated areas.

faction A term used by the founders of this country to refer to political parties and special interests or interest groups.

fairness doctrine Federal Communications Commission policy that required holders of radio and television licenses to ensure that different viewpoints were presented about controversial issues or persons; largely repealed in 1987.

federal mandate A requirement imposed by the federal government as a condition for the receipt of federal funds.

Federal Register Official document, published every weekday, that lists the new and proposed regulations of executive departments and regulatory agencies.

Federal Reserve System The system created by Congress in 1913 to establish banking practices and regulate currency in circulation and the amount of credit available. It consists of 12 regional banks supervised by the Board of Governors. Often called simply *the Fed.*

federalism Constitutional arrangement whereby power is distributed between a central government and subdivisional governments, called states in the United States. The national and the subdivisional governments both exercise direct authority over individuals.

Federalists Supporters of ratification of the Constitution whose position promoting a strong central government was later voiced in the Federalist party.

felony A serious crime, the penalty for which can range from death to imprisonment in a penitentiary for more than a year.

fighting words Words that by their very nature inflict injury on those to whom they are addressed or incite them to acts of violence.

filibuster A procedural practice in the Senate whereby a senator refuses to relinquish the floor and thereby delays proceedings and prevents a vote on a controversial issue.

first reading Introduction of a bill in the house or the senate and its referral to a committee by the presiding officer.

fiscal policy Government policy that attempts to manage the economy by controlling taxing and spending.

free exercise clause Clause in the First Amendment that states that Congress shall make no law prohibiting the free exercise of religion.

free rider An individual who does not join a group representing his or her interests yet receives the benefit of the influence the group achieves.

full faith and credit clause Clause in the Constitution (Article IV, Section 1) requiring each state to recognize the civil judgments rendered by the courts of the other states and to accept their public records and acts as valid.

gender gap The difference between the political opinions or political behavior of men and of women.

General Agreement on Tariffs and Trade (GATT) An international trade organization with more than 130 members, including the United States and the People's Republic of China, that seeks to encourage free trade by lowering tariffs and other trade restrictions.

general law cities City allowed to exercise only those powers specifically granted to it by the legislature. General law cities have fewer than 5,000 residents.

general obligation bonds Method of borrowing money to pay for new construction projects, such as prisons, mental hospitals, or school facilities. The bonds, which require voter approval, are repaid with tax revenue.

general property tax Tax levied by local and some state governments on real property or personal, tangible property, the major portion of which is on the estimated value of one's home and land.

gerrymandering The drawing of legislative district boundaries to benefit a party, group, or incumbent.

globalization of the economy Increased interdependence in trade, manufacturing, and commerce as well as most other business activities between the United States and other countries.

government corporation A government agency that operates like a business corporation, created to secure greater freedom of action and flexibility for a particular program.

grand jury A jury of 12 to 23 persons who, in private, hear evidence presented by the government to determine whether persons shall be required to stand trial. If the jury believes there is sufficient evidence that a crime was committed, it issues an indictment.

Grange Organization formed in the late nineteenth century to improve the lot of farmers. The Grange influenced provisions in the Texas Constitution of 1876 limiting taxes and government spending and restricting big business, including banks and railroads.

Green party A minor party dedicated to the environment, social justice, nonviolence, and a foreign policy of nonintervention. Ralph Nader ran as the Green party's nominee in 2000.

gross domestic product (GDP) The total output of all economic activity in the nation, including goods and services.

hard money Political contributions given to a party, candidate, or interest group that are limited in amount and fully disclosed. Raising such limited funds is harder than raising unlimited funds, hence the term "hard" money.

Hatch Act Federal statute barring federal employees from active participation in certain kinds of politics and protecting them from being fired on partisan grounds.

health maintenance organization (HMO) Alternative means of health care in which people or their employers are charged a set amount and the HMO provides health care and covers hospital costs.

hold A procedural practice in the Senate whereby a senator temporarily blocks the consideration of a bill or nomination.

home rule City with a population of more than 5,000, which can adopt any form of government residents choose, provided it does not conflict with the state constitution or statutes.

homestead exemption Reduction in property taxes that some local governments grant on a taxpayer's residence.

honeymoon Period at the beginning of a new president's term during which the president enjoys generally positive relations with the press and Congress, usually lasting about six months.

horse race A close contest; by extension, any contest in which the focus is on who is ahead and by how much rather than on substantive differences between the candidates.

ideology A consistent pattern of beliefs about political values and the role of government.

immunity Exemption from prosecution for a particular crime in return for testimony pertaining to the case.

impeachment Formal accusation against the president or other public official; the first step in removal from office.

implementation The process of putting a law into practice through bureaucratic rules or spending.

implied powers Powers inferred from the express powers that allow Congress to carry out its functions.

impoundment A decision by the president not to spend money appropriated by Congress; now prohibited under federal law.

incumbents The current holders of elected office.

independent agency A government entity that is independent of the legislative, executive, and judicial branches.

independent expenditure The Supreme Court has ruled that individuals, groups, and parties can spend unlimited amounts in campaigns for or against candidates as long as they operate independently from the candidates. When an individual, group, or party does so, they are making an independent expenditure.

independent regulatory commission A government agency or commission with regulatory power whose independence is protected by Congress.

independent school district Specific form of special district that administers the public schools in a designated area.

indexing Providing automatic increases to compensate for inflation.

indictment A formal written statement from a grand jury charging an individual with an offense; also called a *true bill*.

individualism Attitude, rooted in classical liberal theory and reinforced by the frontier tradition, that citizens are capable of taking care of themselves with minimal governmental assistance.

individualistic subculture View that government should interfere as little as possible in the private activities of its citizens while assuring that adequate public facilities and a favorable business climate are available to permit individuals to pursue their self-interests.

inflation A rise in the general price level (and decrease in dollar value) owing to an increase in the volume of money and credit in relation to available goods.

information affidavit Certification by a public prosecutor that there is evidence to justify bringing named individuals to trial.

information Document formally charging a person with a misdemeanor.

infrastructure Streets, waste disposal systems, libraries, and other public facilities built and operated by governments.

inherent powers The powers of the national government in the field of foreign affairs that the Supreme Court has declared do not depend on constitutional grants but rather grow out of the very existence of the national government.

initiative Procedure whereby a certain number of voters may, by petition, propose a law or constitutional amendment and have it submitted to the voters.

inquest Examination by a justice of the peace or a medical examiner of unusual circumstances under which someone has died.

Institutionalization In the context of political science, the development of a legislative body into a formally structured system with stable membership, complex rules, expanded internal operations, and the delineation of staff functions.

intent calendar Daily list of bills eligible for debate on the floor of the Texas senate, if the sponsor is recognized by the lieutenant governor.

interest group A collection of people who share some common interest or attitude and seek to influence government for specific ends. Interest groups usually work within the framework of government and employ tactics such as lobbying to achieve their goals.

interested money Financial contributions by individuals or groups in the hope of influencing the outcome of an election and subsequently influencing policy.

interims Periods between legislative sessions.

interstate compact An agreement among two or more states. The Constitution requires that most such agreements be approved by Congress.

iron triangle A mutually dependent relationship among interest groups, congressional committees and subcommittees, and government agencies that share a common policy concern.

issue advocacy Promoting a particular position or an issue paid for by interest groups or individuals but not candidates. Much issue advocacy is often electioneering for or against a candidate and until 2004 had not been subject to any regulation.

issue network A policy making alliance among loosely connected participants that comes together on a particular issue, then disbands.

item veto Right of an executive to veto parts of a bill approved by a legislature without having to veto the entire bill.

Jim Crow laws State laws formerly pervasive throughout the South requiring public facilities and accommodations to be segregated by race; ruled unconstitutional.

joint committee A committee composed of members of both the House of Representatives and the Senate; such committees oversee the Library of Congress and conduct investigations.

judicial activism Philosophy proposing that judges should interpret the Constitution to reflect current conditions and values.

judicial interpretation A method by which judges modify the force of a constitutional provision by reinterpreting its meaning.

judicial review The power of a court to refuse to enforce a law or a government regulation that in the opinion of the judges conflicts with the U.S. Constitution or, in a state court, the state constitution.

judicial self-restraint Philosophy proposing that judges should interpret the Constitution to reflect what the framers intended and what its words literally say.

justice of the peace court Low-ranking court with jurisdiction over minor civil disputes and criminal cases.

justiciable dispute A dispute growing out of an actual case or controversy and that is capable of settlement by legal methods.

Keynesian economics Economic theory based on the principles of John Maynard Keynes, stating that government spending should increase during business slumps and be curbed during booms.

labor injunction A court order forbidding specific individuals or groups from performing certain acts (such as striking) that the court considers harmful to the rights and property of an employer or a community.

laissez-faire economics Theory that opposes governmental interference in economic affairs beyond what is necessary to protect life and property.

land commissioner The elected official who manages the state's public lands and administers the Veterans Land Program, which provides low-interest loans to veterans for the purchase of land and houses.

Legislative Budget Board The panel that makes budgetary recommendations to the full legislature. It is chaired by the lieutenant governor and includes the speaker of the house and eight other key lawmakers.

Legislative Redistricting Board A board created by constitutional amendment charged to redistrict the Texas legislature if it is not accomplished in the regular session following the release of the census.

libel Written defamation of another person. Especially in the case of public officials and public figures, the constitutional tests designed to restrict libel actions are very rigid.

liberalism A belief in the positive uses of government to bring about justice and equality of opportunity.

Libertarian party A minor party that believes in extremely limited government. Libertarians call for a freemarket system, expanded individual liberties such as drug legalization, and a foreign policy of non-intervention, free trade, and open immigration.

libertarianism An ideology that cherishes individual liberty and insists on a sharply limited government, promoting a free market economy, a noninterventionist foreign policy, and an absence of regulation in the moral and social spheres.

lieutenant governor The presiding officer of the senate. This officeholder would become governor if the governor were to die, be incapacitated, be removed from office, or leave office voluntarily in midterm.

limited government Constitutional principle restricting governmental authority and spelling out personal rights.

line item veto Presidential power to strike, or remove, specific items from a spending bill without vetoing the entire package, declared unconstitutional by the Supreme Court.

literacy test Literacy requirement imposed by some states as a condition of voting, generally used to disqualify blacks from voting in the South; now illegal.

lobbying Engaging in activities aimed at influencing public officials, especially legislators, and the policies they enact.

lobbyist A person who is employed by and acts for an organized interest group or corporation to try to influence policy decisions and positions in the executive and legislative branches.

logrolling Mutual aid and vote trading among legislators.

magistrate judge An official who performs a variety of limited judicial duties.

majority leader The legislative leader selected by the majority party who helps plan party strategy, confers with other party leaders, and tries to keep members of the party in line.

majority rule Governance according to the expressed preferences of the majority.

majority The candidate or party that wins more than half the votes cast in an election.

majority-minority district A congressional district created to include a majority of minority voters; ruled constitutional so long as race is not the main factor in redistricting.

malapportionment Having legislative districts with unequal populations.

mandate A president's claim of broad public support.

manifest destiny A notion held by nineteenth-century Americans that the United States was destined to rule the continent, from the Atlantic to the Pacific.

maquiladora program Policies initiated by Mexico in 1964 to stimulate economic growth along the U.S.-Mexico border.

mass media Means of communication that reach the mass public, including newspapers and magazines, radio, television (broadcast, cable, and satellite), films, recordings, books, and electronic communication.

mayor-council charter The oldest and most common form of city government, consisting of either a weak mayor and a city council or a strong mayor elected by voters and council.

means-tested entitlements Programs such as Medicaid and welfare under which applicants must meet eligibility requirements based on need.

Medicaid Federal program that provides medical benefits for low-income persons.

medical examiner Appointed official who is responsible for determining the cause of death of murder victims or others who die under suspicious or unusual circumstances.

medical savings account Alternative means of health care in which individuals make tax-deductible contributions to a special account that can be used to pay medical expenses.

Medicare National health insurance program for the elderly and disabled.

merit selection Proposal under which the governor would appoint state judges from lists of potential nominees recommended by committees of experts. Appointed judges would have to run later in retention elections to keep their seats but would not have opponents on the ballot. Voters would simply decide whether a judge should remain in office or be replaced by another gubernatorial appointee.

merit system A system of public employment in which selection and promotion depend on demonstrated performance rather than political patronage.

metro government Local government in which city and county governments consolidate to avoid duplication of public services.

minor party A small political party that rises and falls with a charismatic candidate or, if composed of ideologies on the right or left, usually persists over time; also called a *third party*.

minority leader The legislative leader selected by the minority party as spokesperson for the opposition.

***Miranda* ruling** Far-reaching decision of the U.S. Supreme Court that requires law enforcement officers to warn a criminal suspect of his or her right to remain silent and have an attorney present before questioning.

misdemeanor A minor crime; the penalty is a fine or imprisonment for a short time, usually less than a year, in a local jail.

Missouri Plan A system for selecting judges that combines features of the appointive and elective methods. The governor selects judges from lists presented by panels of lawyers and laypersons, and at the end of their term, the judges may run against their own record in retention elections.

monetarism A theory that government should control the money supply to encourage economic growth and restrain inflation.

monetary policy Government policy that attempts to manage the economy by controlling the money supply and thus interest rates.

monopoly Domination of an industry by a single company by fixing prices and discouraging competition; also, the company that dominates the industry by these means.

moralistic subculture View that government's primary responsibility is to promote the public welfare and that it should actively use its authority and power to improve the social and economic well-being of its citizens.

movement A large body of people interested in a common issue, idea, or concern that is of continuing significance and who are willing to take action. Movements seek to change attitudes or institutions, not just policies.

municipal court   Court of limited jurisdiction that hears cases involving city ordinances and primarily handles traffic tickets.

national debt   The total amount of money the federal government has borrowed to finance deficit spending over the years.

national party convention   A national meeting of delegates elected in primaries, caucuses, or state conventions who assemble once every four years to nominate candidates for president and vice president, ratify the party platform, elect officers, and adopt rules.

national supremacy   Constitutional doctrine that whenever conflict occurs between the constitutionally authorized actions of the national government and those of a state or local government, the actions of the federal government prevail.

natural law   God's or nature's law that defines right from wrong and is higher than human law.

natural rights   The rights of all people to dignity and worth; also called *human rights*.

naturalization   A legal action conferring citizenship on an alien.

necessary and proper clause   Clause of the Constitution (Article I, Section 8, Clause 18) setting forth the implied powers of Congress. It states that Congress, in addition to its express powers, has the right to make all laws necessary and proper for carrying out all powers vested by the Constitution in the national government.

New Jersey Plan   Proposal at the Constitutional Convention made by William Paterson of New Jersey for a central government with a single-house legislature in which each state would be represented equally.

new judicial federalism   The practice of some state courts using the bill of rights in their state constitutions to provide more protection for some rights than is provided by the Supreme Court's interpretation of the Bill of Rights in the U.S. Constitution.

news media   Media that emphasizes the news.

nolo contendere   Plea of "no contest" to a criminal charge.

nonpartisan election   A local or judicial election in which candidates are not selected or endorsed by political parties and party affiliation is not listed on ballots.

nonprotected speech   Libel, obscenity, fighting words, and commercial speech, which are not entitled to constitutional protection in all circumstances.

North American Free Trade Agreement (NAFTA)   Agreement signed by the United States, Canada, and Mexico in 1992 to form the largest free trade zone in the world.

obscenity   Quality or state of a work that taken as a whole appeals to a prurient interest in sex by depicting sexual conduct in a patently offensive way and that lacks serious literary, artistic, political, or scientific value.

office block ballot   Ballot on which all candidates are listed under the office for which they are running, making split-ticket voting easier.

Office of Management and Budget (OMB)   Presidential staff agency that serves as a clearinghouse for budgetary requests and management improvements for government agencies.

Office of Personnel Management (OPM)   Agency that administers civil service laws, rules, and regulations.

one-party system   Domination of elections and governmental processes by a single party, which may be split into different ideological, economic, or regional factions. In Texas, the phrase is used to describe the period from the late 1870s to the late 1970s, when the Democratic Party claimed virtually all elected, partisan offices.

open primary   Primary election in which any voter, regardless of party, may vote.

open rule   A procedural rule in the House of Representatives that permits floor amendments within the overall time allocated to the bill.

open shop   A company with a labor agreement under which union membership cannot be required as a condition of employment.

opinion of the court   An explanation of a decision of the Supreme Court or any other appellate court.

ordinances   Local laws enacted by a city council.

original jurisdiction   The authority of a court to hear a case "in the first instance."

outsourcing   Contracting of government services to private firms.

override   An action taken by Congress to reverse a presidential veto, requiring a two-thirds majority in each chamber.

oversight   Legislative or executive review of a particular government program or organization. Can be in response to a crisis of some kind or part of routine review.

parliamentary system   A system of government in which the legislature selects the prime minister or president.

parole   Early release of an inmate from prison, subject to certain conditions.

party caucus   A meeting of the members of a party in a legislative chamber to select party leaders and to develop party policy. Called a *conference* by the Republicans.

party column ballot   Type of ballot that encourages party-line voting by listing all of a party's candidates in a column under the party name.

party convention   A meeting of party delegates to vote on matters of policy and in some cases to select party candidates for public office.

party identification   An informal and subjective affiliation with a political party that most people acquire in childhood.

party registration   The act of declaring party affiliation; required by some states when one registers to vote.

patronage   The dispensing of government jobs to persons who belong to the winning political party.

pay-as-you-go   Constitutional requirement that prohibits the legislature from borrowing money for the state's operating expenses.

penal code   Body of law that defines most criminal offenses and sets a range of punishments that can be assessed.

permanent normal trade relations (PNTR) status   Trade status granted as part of an international trade policy that gives a nation the same favorable trade concessions and tariffs that the best trading partners receive.

petit jury   A jury of 6 to 12 persons who determine guilt or innocence in a civil or criminal action.

petition for review   Petition to the Texas Supreme Court claiming that legal or procedural mistakes were made in the lower court.

place system   Form of at-large election in which candidates run for specific positions, or places, on a city council or other governing body.

plaintiff   Individual or party who initiates a lawsuit.

plea bargain   Agreement between a prosecutor and a defendant that the defendant will plead guilty to a lesser offense to avoid having to stand trial for a more serious offense.

plural executive   A fragmented system of authority under which most statewide executive officeholders are elected independently of the governor.

pluralism   Political system in which power is distributed among multiple groups.

plurality   Candidate or party with the most votes cast in an election, not necessarily more than half.

pocket veto   A veto exercised by the president after Congress has adjourned; if the president takes no action for ten days, the bill does not become law and is not returned to Congress for a possible override.

police powers   Inherent powers of state governments to pass laws to protect the public health, safety, and welfare; the national government has no directly granted police powers but accomplishes the same goals through other delegated powers.

policy agenda   The informal list of issues that Congress and the president consider most important for action.

political action committee (PAC)   The political arm of an interest group that is legally entitled to raise funds on a voluntary basis from members, stockholders, or employees in order to contribute funds to favored candidates or political parties.

political culture   The widely shared beliefs, values, and norms concerning the relationship of citizens to government and to one another.

political ideology   A consistent pattern of beliefs about political values and the role of government.

political party   An organization that seeks political power by electing people to office so that its positions and philosophy become public policy.

political patronage   The hiring of government employees on the basis of personal friendships or favors rather than ability or merit.

political predisposition   A characteristic of individuals that is predictive of political behavior.

political question   A dispute that requires knowledge of a nonlegal character or the use of techniques not suitable for a court or explicitly assigned by the Constitution to Congress or the president; judges refuse to answer constitutional questions that they declare are political.

political socialization The process, most notably in families and schools, by which we develop our political attitudes, values, and beliefs.

poll tax Payment required as a condition for voting; prohibited for national elections by the Twenty-Fourth Amendment (1964) and ruled unconstitutional for all elections in *Harper* v. *Virginia Board of Elections* (1966).

popular consent The idea that a just government must derive its powers from the consent of the people it governs.

popular sovereignty A belief that ultimate power resides in the people.

population density Number of residents living within the boundaries of a city, county, or state in relationship to the land area. Population density is a significant factor in determining the level of local public services.

precinct chair Local officer in a political party who presides over the precinct convention and serves on the party's county executive committee. Voters in each precinct elect a chair in the party's primary election.

precinct convention Meeting held by a political party in each precinct on the same day as the party primary. In presidential election years, the precinct conventions and the primaries are the first steps in the selection of delegates to the major parties' national nominating conventions.

precincts Specific local voting areas created by county commissioners courts. The state election code provides detailed requirements for drawing up these election units.

preemption Associated with the Bush doctrine, a belief that a nation is justified in attacking another nation to prevent possible attacks on itself. Also, the right of a federal law or regulation to preclude enforcement of a state or local law or regulation.

preferred position doctrine Interpretation of the First Amendment that holds that freedom of expression is so essential to democracy that governments should not punish persons for what they say, only for what they do.

president pro tempore Officer of the Senate selected by the majority party to act as chair in the absence of the vice president.

presidential ticket The joint listing of the presidential and vice presidential candidates on the same ballot as required by the Twelfth Amendment.

prior restraint Censorship imposed before a speech is made or a newspaper is published; usually presumed to be unconstitutional.

privatization Contracting public services to private organizations, including the power to collect revenues.

pro bono To serve the public good; term used to describe work that lawyers (or other professionals) do for which they receive no fees.

probation Procedure under which a convicted criminal is not sent to prison if he or she meets certain conditions, such as restrictions on travel and associates.

procedural due process Constitutional requirement that governments proceed by proper methods; places limits on how governmental power may be exercised.

progressive tax A tax graduated so that people with higher incomes pay a larger fraction of their income than people with lower incomes.

property rights The rights of an individual to own, use, rent, invest in, buy, and sell property.

proportional representation An election system in which each party running receives the proportion of legislative seats corresponding to its proportion of the vote.

prosecution Conduct of legal proceedings against an individual charged with a crime.

protectionism Policy of erecting trade barriers to protect domestic industry.

public assistance Aid to the poor; "welfare."

public defender system Arrangement whereby public officials are hired to provide legal assistance to people accused of crimes who are unable to hire their own attorneys.

public improvement district Specific area of a city in which property owners pay special taxes in return for improvements to streets and other public facilities in their neighborhood.

public opinion The distribution of individual preferences for or evaluations of a given issue, candidate, or institution within a specific population.

public policy A specific course of action taken by government to achieve a public goal.

quid pro quo Something given with the expectation of receiving something in return.

quorum Required number of the members of a governing body who must be present so that official business, such as voting, can be conducted. In Texas, a quorum of the house and the senate is two-thirds of the membership. For committees, it is a majority of the members.

race A grouping of human beings with distinctive characteristics determined by genetic inheritance.

racial gerrymandering The drawing of election districts so as to ensure that members of a certain race are a minority in the district; ruled unconstitutional in *Gomillion* v. *Lightfoot* (1960).

racial profiling Police targeting of racial minorities as potential suspects of criminal activities.

Radical Reconstructionists The group of Republicans who took control of the U.S. Congress in 1866 and imposed hated military governments on the former Confederate states after the Civil War.

Railroad Commission A three-member, elected body that has some oversight over rail safety but now primarily regulates oil and natural gas production in Texas.

rally point A rise in public approval of the president that follows a crisis as Americans "rally 'round the flag" and the chief executive.

realigning election An election during periods of expanded suffrage and change in the economy and society that proves to be a turning point, redefining the agenda of politics and the alignment of voters within parties.

realignment Major shift in political party support or identification that usually occurs around a critical election. In Texas, realignment took place as a gradual transformation from a one-party system dominated by Democrats to a two-party system in which Republicans became competitive in elections.

reapportionment The assigning by Congress of congressional seats after each census. State legislatures reapportion state legislative districts.

recall Procedure for submitting to popular vote the removal of public officials from office before the end of their term.

recidivist A repeat offender.

record vote Vote taken in the house or the senate of which a permanent record is kept, listing how individual legislators voted.

redistributive policies Governmental tax and social programs that shift wealth or benefits from one segment of the population to another, often from the rich to the poor.

redistricting The redrawing of congressional and other legislative district lines following the census, to accommodate population shifts and keep districts as equal as possible in population.

reduction veto The power of governors in a few states to reduce a particular appropriation.

referendum Procedure for submitting to popular vote measures passed by the legislature or proposed amendments to a state constitution.

Reform party A minor party founded by Ross Perot in 1995. It focuses on national government reform, fiscal responsibility, and political accountability. It has recently struggled with internal strife and criticism that it lacks an identity.

regressive tax A tax whereby people with lower incomes pay a higher fraction of their income than people with higher incomes.

regular session 140-day period in the odd-numbered years in which the legislature meets and can consider and pass laws on any issue or subject.

regulation Efforts by government to alter the free operation of the market to achieve social goals such as protecting workers and the environment.

regulations The formal instructions that government issues for implementing laws.

regulatory taking Government regulation of property so extensive that government is deemed to have taken the property by the power of eminent domain, for which it must compensate the property owners.

reinforcing cleavages Divisions within society that reinforce one another, making groups more homogeneous or similar.

Religious Right Political movement, based primarily in evangelical Protestant churches, that has played an increasingly prominent role in Texas and national politics.

representative democracy Government that derives its powers indirectly from the people, who elect those who will govern; also called a *republic*.

republic Form of government in which representatives of the people, rather than the people themselves, govern.

responsibility contract A welfare strategy adopted by some states in which recipients sign a written agreement specifying their responsibilities and outlining a plan for obtaining work and achieving self-sufficiency.

restrictive covenant A provision in a deed to real property prohibiting its sale to a person of a particular race or religion. Judicial enforcement of such deeds is unconstitutional.

retention elections Elections in which judges run on their own records rather than against other candidates. Voters cast their ballots on the question of whether the incumbent judge should stay in office.

revenue bonds Bonds that are used to finance construction of a public facility and are repaid with income produced by the facility.

revision commission A state commission that recommends changes in the state constitution for action by the legislature and vote by the voters.

revolving door Employment cycle in which individuals who work for governmental agencies regulating interests eventually end up working for interest groups or businesses with the same policy concern.

rider A provision attached to a bill—to which it may or may not be related—in order to secure its passage.

right of expatriation The right to renounce one's citizenship.

right-to-work law Law prohibiting the requirement of union membership in order to hold or get a job.

rollback election Election in which local voters can nullify a property tax increase that exceeds 8 percent in a given year.

rule A precise legal definition of how government will implement a policy.

rule-making process The formal process for making regulations.

runoff elections Elections that are required if no candidate receives an absolute majority of the votes cast in a city council, school district, or party primary race. The runoff is between the two top vote-getters.

safe seat An elected office that is predictably won by one party or the other, so the success of that party's candidate is almost taken for granted.

sales tax General tax on sales transactions, sometimes exempting food and drugs.

school board Governing body of a school district. Its responsibilities include the development or approval of educational policies, approval of the budget, hiring of the superintendent, and other personnel matters.

school superintendent Top administrator of a school district. He or she is hired by the elected school board to direct the district's daily operations.

search warrant A writ issued by a magistrate that authorizes the police to search a particular place or person, specifying the place to be searched and the objects to be seized.

second reading Initial debate by the full house or senate on a bill that has been approved by a committee.

secretary of state The official who administers state election laws, grants charters to corporations, and processes the extradition of prisoners to other states. This officeholder is appointed by the governor.

sedition Attempting to overthrow the government by force or to interrupt its activities by violence.

selective exposure The process by which individuals screen out messages that do not conform to their own biases.

selective incorporation The process by which provisions of the Bill of Rights are brought within the scope of the Fourteenth Amendment and so applied to state and local governments.

selective perception The process by which individuals perceive what they want to in media messages.

senatorial courtesy Presidential custom of submitting the names of prospective appointees for approval to senators from the states in which the appointees are to work.

Senior Executive Service Established by Congress in 1978 as a flexible, mobile corps of senior career executives who work closely with presidential appointees to manage government.

seniority rule A legislative practice that assigns the chair of a committee or subcommittee to the member of the majority party with the longest continuous service on the committee.

separation of powers Constitutional division of powers among the legislative, executive, and judicial branches, with the legislative branch making law, the executive applying and enforcing the law, and the judiciary interpreting the law.

severance tax A tax on the privilege of "severing" such natural resources as coal, oil, timber, and gas from the land.

Shays' Rebellion Rebellion by farmers in western Massachusetts in 1786–1787, protesting mortgage foreclosures; led by Daniel Shays and important because it highlighted the need for a strong national government just as the call for the Constitutional Convention went out.

sheriff Elected official who is the chief law enforcement officer of a county.

single-member district An electoral district in which voters choose one representative or official.

social capital Democratic and civic habits of discussion, compromise, and respect for differences, which grow out of participation in voluntary organizations.

social insurance Programs in which eligibility is based on prior contributions to government, usually in the form of payroll taxes.

Social Security A combination of entitlement programs, paid for by employer and employee taxes, that includes retirement benefits, health insurance, and support for disabled workers and the children of deceased or disabled workers.

social stratification Divisions in a community among socio-economic groups or classes.

socialism An economic and governmental system based on public ownership of the means of production and exchange.

socioeconomic status (SES) A division of population based on occupation, income, and education.

soft money Money raised in unlimited amounts by political parties for party-building purposes. Now largely illegal except for limited contributions to state and local parties for voter registration and get-out-the-vote efforts.

Speaker The presiding officer in the House of Representatives, formally elected by the House but actually selected by the majority party.

special or select committee A congressional committee created for a specific purpose, sometimes to conduct an investigation.

special purpose districts Units of local government created by the state to perform specific functions not met by cities or counties, including the provision of public services to unincorporated areas.

special session A legislative session that can be called at any time by the governor. This session is limited to thirty days and to issues or subjects designated by the governor.

special, or select, committees Special panels appointed to study major policy issues.

split ticket A vote for some of one party's candidates and some of another party's.

spoils system A system of public employment based on rewarding party loyalists and friends.

staggered terms Terms that begin on different dates, a requirement for members of state boards and commissions appointed by the governor.

standing committee A permanent committee established in a legislature, usually focusing on a policy area.

stare decisis The rule of precedent, whereby a rule or law contained in a judicial decision is commonly viewed as binding on judges whenever the same question is presented.

State Board of Education An elected panel that oversees the administration of public education in Texas.

state chair and vice chair Two top state leaders of a political party, one of whom must be a woman. They are selected every two years by delegates to the party's state convention.

state convention Meeting held in June of even-numbered years by each of the two major political parties. Delegates to this convention elect the party's state leadership and adopt a party platform. In presidential election years, the state convention selects the delegates to the party's national nominating convention.

state executive committee Statewide governing board of a political party. It includes a man and a woman from each of the thirty-one state senatorial districts and the state chair and vice chair, who are selected by delegates to the party's biennial state convention.

State of the Union Address The president's annual statement to Congress and the nation.

state treasurer This elective office was created by the Constitution of 1876 to manage state funds. It was abolished by the voters in 1995, and its duties were transferred to the comptroller's office.

states' rights Powers expressly or implicitly reserved to the states and emphasized by decentralists.

statism The idea that the rights of the nation are supreme over the rights of the individuals residing in that nation.

statutes Laws enacted by a legislative body.

statutory county court Court that exercises limited jurisdiction over criminal and/or civil cases. The jurisdiction of these courts varies from county to county.

statutory law Law enacted by a legislative body.

straight ticket A vote for all of one party's candidates.

strong mayor-council form   Form of local government in which the voters directly elect the city council and the mayor, who enjoys almost total administrative authority and appoints the department heads.

subcommittee   A few members of a larger committee appointed to review a particular bill and make recommendations on its disposition to the full committee.

subpoenas   Court orders requiring people to testify in court or before grand juries or to produce certain documents.

substantive due process   Constitutional requirement that governments act reasonably and that the substance of the laws themselves be fair and reasonable; places limits on what a government may do.

sunset   The process under which most state agencies have to be periodically reviewed and recreated by the legislature or go out of business.

tag   Rule that allows an individual senator to postpone a committee hearing on any bill for at least forty-eight hours, a delay that can be fatal to a bill during the closing days of a legislative session.

take care clause   The constitutional requirement (in Article II, Section 3) that presidents take care that the laws are faithfully executed, even if they disagree with the purpose of those laws.

tariff   Tax levied on imports to help protect a nation's industries, labor, or farmers from foreign competition. It can also be used to raise additional revenue.

tax abatements   Exemptions from property taxes granted to certain businesses, usually to encourage them to move to or expand their operations in a city or county. The exemptions are granted for specific periods.

tax assessor-collector   Elected official who determines how much property tax is owed on the different pieces of property within a county and then collects the tax.

tax expenditure   Loss of tax revenue due to federal laws that provide special tax incentives or benefits to individuals or businesses.

Texas Court of Criminal Appeals   Nine-member court with final appellate jurisdiction over criminal cases.

Texas Supreme Court   Nine-member court with final appellate jurisdiction over civil lawsuits.

"The Establishment"   In the days of one-party Democratic politics in Texas, the Establishment was a loosely knit coalition of Anglo business and oil company executives, bankers, and lawyers who controlled state policy making through the dominant conservative wing of the Democratic Party.

The Federalist   Series of essays promoting ratification of the Constitution, published anonymously by Alexander Hamilton, John Jay, and James Madison in 1787 and 1788.

theocracy   Government by religious leaders, who claim divine guidance.

third reading   Final presentation of a bill before the full house or senate.

three-fifths compromise   Compromise agreement between northern and southern states at the Constitutional Convention that three-fifths of the slave population would be counted for determining direct taxation and representation in the House of Representatives.

tort law   Law relating to injuries to person, reputation, or property.

tort reform   Changes in state law to put limits on personal injury lawsuits and damage judgments entered by the courts.

trade deficit   An imbalance in international trade in which the value of imports exceeds the value of exports.

traditionalistic subculture   View that political power should be concentrated in the hands of a few elite citizens who belong to established families or influential social groups. Public policy basically serves the interests of this small group.

transnational regionalism   Expanding economic and social interdependence of South Texas and Mexico.

treaty   A formal, public agreement between the United States and one or more nations that must be approved by two-thirds of the Senate.

trust   A monopoly that controls goods and services, often in combinations that reduce competition.

trustee   An official who is expected to vote independently, based on his or her judgment of the circumstances; one interpretation of the role of a legislator.

turnout   The proportion of the voting-age public that votes, sometimes defined as the number of registered voters that vote.

two-party state   A state in which the two major parties alternate in winning majorities.

two-party system   Political system that has two dominant parties, such as that of the United States.

two-thirds rule   Procedure under which the Texas senate has traditionally operated that requires approval of at least two-thirds of senators before a bill can be debated on the senate floor. It allows a minority of senators to block controversial legislation.

uncontrollable spending   The portion of the federal budget that is spent on programs, such as Social Security, that the president and Congress are unwilling to cut.

unemployment   The number of Americans who are out of work, but actively looking for a job. The number does not usually include those who are not looking.

unicameral legislature   A one-house legislature.

union shop   A company in which new employees must join a union within a stated time period.

unitary system   Constitutional arrangement in which power is concentrated in a central government.

urbanization   Process by which a predominantly rural society or area becomes urban.

value-added tax (VAT)   A tax on increased value of a product at each stage of production and distribution rather than just at the point of sale.

veniremen   Members of a panel from which a petit, or trial, jury is chosen.

veto   Rejection by a president or governor of legislation passed by a legislature.

Virginia Plan   Initial proposal at the Constitutional Convention made by the Virginia delegation for a strong central government with a bicameral legislature, the lower house to be elected by the voters and the upper chosen by the lower.

voter registration   System designed to reduce voter fraud by limiting voting to those who have established eligibility by submitting the proper form.

Voting Rights Act   Federal law designed to protect the voting rights of minorities by requiring the Justice Department's approval of changes in political districts and certain other electoral procedures. The 1965 act, as amended, has eliminated most of the restrictive practices that limited minority political participation.

vouchers   Money provided by the government to parents for payment of their children's tuition in a public or private school of their choice.

ward politics   Term, often with negative connotations, that refers to partisan politics linked to political favoritism.

weak mayor-council form   Form of local government in which the members of the city council select the mayor, who then shares power with other elected or appointed boards and commissions.

weapons of mass destruction   Biological, chemical, and nuclear weapons that can inflict massive casualties in a single event.

whip   Party leader who is the liaison between the leadership and the rank-and-file in the legislature.

whistleblower   A public employee who reports illegal activities or "blows the whistle" on agency wrongdoing.

white primary   Primary operated by the Democratic party in southern states that, before Republicans gained strength in the "one-party South," essentially constituted an election; ruled unconstitutional in *Smith* v. *Allwright* (1944).

winner-take-all system   An election system in which the candidate with the most votes wins.

women's suffrage   The right of women to vote.

workfare   A welfare strategy adopted by some states that gives able-bodied adults who do not have preschool-aged children the opportunity to learn job skills that can lead to employment.

World Trade Organization (WTO)   International organization derived from the General Agreement on Tariffs and Trade (GATT) that promotes free trade around the world.

writ of certiorari   A formal writ used to bring a case before the Supreme Court.

writ of habeas corpus   Court order requiring explanation to a judge why a prisoner is being held in custody.

writ of mandamus   Court order directing an official to perform an official duty.

NOTES

Chapter 1

1. George W. Bush, "President Discusses War on Terrorism," Office of the Press Secretary, 8 November 2001. At www.whitehouse.gov/news/releases/2001/11/20011108-13, 24 November 2003.
2. Robert A. Dahl, *On Democracy* (Yale University Press, 1998), p. 145.
3. Harold Stanley and Richard Niemi, *Vital Statistics on American Politics, 2001–2002* (CQ Press, 2001), pp. 25–29.
4. For a major theoretical work on the principle of majority rule, see Robert A. Dahl, *Democracy and Its Critics* (Yale University Press, 1989).
5. *Reitman v. Mulkey,* 387 U.S. 369 (1967).
6. David B. Magleby, *Direct Legislation: Voting on Ballot Propositions in the United States* (Baltimore: Johns Hopkins University Press, 1984), p. 119.
7. Seymour Martin Lipset, "The Social Requisites of Democracy Revisited," *American Sociological Review* 59 (1994), pp. 1–22.
8. For a discussion of the importance for democracy of such overlapping group memberships, see David Truman's seminal work, *The Governmental Process,* 2d ed. (Knopf, 1971).
9. Joyce Appleby, "The American Heritage: The Heirs and the Disinherited," *Journal of American History* 74 (December 1987), p. 808.
10. Kevin Butterfield, "What You Should Know About the Declaration of Independence," *St. Louis Post-Dispatch,* July 4, 2000, p. F1.
11. Richard L. Hillard, "Liberalism, Civic Humanism and the American Revolutionary Bill of Rights, 1775–1790," paper presented at the annual meeting of the Organization of American Historians, Reno, Nevada, March 26, 1988.
12. Quoted in Charles L. Mee Jr., *The Genius of the People* (Harper & Row, 1987), p. 51.
13. Seymour Martin Lipset, "George Washington and the Founding of Democracy," *Journal of Democracy* 9 (October 1998), p. 31.
14. See the essays in Thomas E. Cronin, ed., *Inventing the American Presidency* (University Press of Kansas, 1989). See also Richard J. Ellis, ed., *Founding the American Presidency* (Rowman & Littlefield, 1999).
15. Charles A. Beard and Mary R. Beard, *A Basic History of the United States* (New Home Library, 1944), p. 136.
16. See Herbert J. Storing, ed., abridgment by Murray Dry, *The Anti-Federalist: Writings by the Opponents of the Constitution* (University of Chicago Press, 1985).
17. On the role of the promised bill of rights amendments in the ratification of the Constitution, see Leonard W. Levy, *Constitutional Opinions* (Oxford University Press, 1986), chap. 6.

Chapter 2

1. Max Lerner, *Ideas for the Ice Age* (Viking, 1941), pp. 241–242.
2. Sanford Levinson, *Constitutional Faith* (Princeton University Press, 1988), pp. 9–52.
3. Richard Morin, "We Love It—What We Know of It," *Washington Post National Weekly Edition,* September 22, 1997, p. 35.
4. Thomas Jefferson, quoted in Alpheus T. Mason, *The Supreme Court: Palladium of Freedom* (University of Michigan Press, 1962), p. 10.
5. Alexander Hamilton, James Madison, and John Jay, *The Federalist Papers,* ed. Clinton Rossiter (New American Library, 1961), p. 301.
6. Justice Brandeis dissenting in *Myers* v. *United States,* 272 U.S. 52 (1926).
7. James L. Sundquist, "Needed: A Political Theory for the New Era of Coalition Government in the United States," *Political Science Quarterly* 103 (1988), pp. 613–635; Robert A. Godwin and Art Kaufman, eds., *Separation of Powers: Does It Still Work?* (AEI Press, 1986).
8. Charles O. Jones, "The Separate Presidency," in Anthony King, ed., *The New American Political System,* 2d ed. (AEI Press, 1990), p. 3.
9. Morris P. Fiorina, "An Era of Divided Government," *Political Science Quarterly* 107 (1992), p. 407.
10. David R. Mayhew, *Divided We Govern: Party Control, Lawmaking, and Investigations, 1946–1990* (Yale University Press, 1991), p. 4. See also James A. Thurber, ed., *Divided Democracy: Presidents and Congress in Cooperation and Conflict* (CQ Press, 1991).
11. Charles O. Jones, *Separate but Equal Branches: Congress and the Presidency* (Chatham House, 1995).
12. Judith A. Best, *The Choice of the People? Debating the Electoral College* (Rowman & Littlefield, 1996).
13. See Alec Stone Sweet, Wayne Sandholtz, and Neil Fligstein, *The Institutionalization of Europe* (Oxford University Press, 2001); Alec Stone Sweet, *Governing with Judges: Constitutional Politics in Europe* (Oxford University Press, 2000); and Anne-Marie Slaughter, Alec Stone Sweet, and J. H. H. Weiler, *The European Court and National Courts—Doctrine, Jurisprudence: Legal Change in Its Social Context* (Hart, 1998).
14. *Marbury* v. *Madison,* 1 Cranch 137 (1803).
15. Dumas Malone, *Jefferson the President: First Term, 1801–1805* (Little, Brown, 1970), p. 145.
16. J. W. Peltason, *Federal Courts in the Political Process* (Random House, 1955).
17. See Eleanore Bushnell, *Crimes, Follies, and Misfortunes: The Federal Impeachment Trials* (University of Illinois Press, 1992), and Michael J. Gerhardt, *The Federal Impeachment Process: A Constitutional and Historical Analysis* (Princeton University Press, 1996).
18. Richard E. Neustadt, *Presidential Power* (Free Press, 1990), pp. 180–181.
19. See John R. Vile, ed., *Proposed Amendments to the U.S. Constitution: 1787–2001* (The Lawbook Exchange, 2003).
20. Ann Stuart Diamond, "A Convention for Proposing Amendments: The Constitution's Other Method," *Publius* 11 (Summer 1981), pp. 113–146; Wilbur Edel, "Amending the Constitution by Convention: Myths and Realities," *State Government* 55 (1982), pp. 51–56.
21. Russell L. Caplan, *Constitutional Brinksmanship: Amending the Constitution by National Convention* (Oxford University Press, 1988), p. x. See also David E. Kyvig, *Explicit and Authentic Acts: Amending the U.S. Constitution, 1776–1995* (University Press of Kansas, 1996), p. 440.
22. Samuel S. Freedman and Pamela J. Naughton, *ERA: May a State Change Its Vote?* (Wayne State University Press, 1979).
23. Kyvig, *Explicit and Authentic Acts,* p. 286; *Dillon* v. *Gloss,* 256 U.S. 368 (1921).
24. Gregory A. Caldeira, "Constitutional Change in America: Dynamics of Ratification Under Article V," *Publius* 15 (Fall 1985), p. 29.
25. Mark R. Daniels, Robert Darcy, and Joseph W. Westphal, "The ERA Won—at Least in the Opinion Polls," *P.S.: Political Science and Politics* (Fall 1982), p. 583.
26. Janet K. Boles, *The Politics of the Equal Rights Amendment: Conflict and Decision-Making Powers* (Longman, 1979), p. 4.
27. Gilbert Y. Steiner, *Constitutional Inequality: The Political Fortunes of the Equal Rights Amendment* (Brookings Institution Press, 1985), p. 64. See also Mary Frances Berry, *Why the ERA Failed: Politics, Women's Rights, and the Amending Process of the Constitution* (Indiana University Press, 1986).

Chapter 3

1. Quoted in Elisabeth Bumiller, "Marriage Amendment Backed," *The New York Times,* December 17, 2003, p. A30.
2. See Nicol C. Rae, "A Right too Far? The Congressional Politics of DOMA and ENDA," in Colton C. Campbell and John F. Stack, Jr., eds., *Congress and the Politics of Emerging Rights* 65 (Rowman & Littlefield, 2002).
3. John P. Feldmeier, "Federalism and Full Faith and Credit: Must States Recognize Out-of-State Same-Sex Marriages?" *Publius* 25 (Fall 1995), p. 126.
4. See Jeremy D. Mayer and Louis-Philippe Rochon, "Gay Rights in the USA: The States Lead the Way," *Federations* 2 (November 2001).
5. *Lawrence* v. *Texas,* 539 U.S. 558 (2003).
6. For background, see Samuel H. Beer, *To Make a Nation: The Rediscovery of American Federalism* (Harvard University Press, 1993).
7. The term "devolution revolution" was coined by Richard P. Nathan in testimony before the Senate Finance Committee; quoted in Daniel Patrick Moynihan, "The Devolution Revolution," *The New York Times,* August 6, 1995, p. B15.
8. See Michael Burgess, *Federalism and the European Union: The Building of Europe, 1950–2000* (Routledge, 2000), and Kalypso Nicolaidis and

Robert Howse, eds., *The Federal Vision: Legitimacy and Levels of Governance in the United States and the European Union* (Oxford University Press, 2001).

9. *United States* v. *Lopez*, 514 U.S. 549 (1995).

10. *Alden* v. *Maine*, 527 U.S. 706 (1999); *Kimel* v. *Florida Board of Regents*, 528 U.S. 62 (2000); *Vermont Agency of Natural Resources* v. *United States ex rel. Stevens*, 529 U.S. 765 (2000).

11. *Saenz* v. *Roe*, 526 U.S. 489 (1999).

12. *Reno* v. *Condon*, 528 U.S. 141 (2000).

13. Martha Derthick, "American Federalism: Half-Full or Half-Empty?" *Brookings Review* (Winter 2000), pp. 24–27.

14. William H. Stewart, *Concepts of Federalism* (Center for the Study of Federalism/University Press of America, 1984). See also Preston King, *Federalism and Federation*, 2d ed. (Cass, 2001).

15. Morton Grodzins, "The Federal System," in *Goals for Americans: The Report of the President's Commission on National Goals* (Columbia University Press, 1960).

16. Thomas R. Dye, *American Federalism: Competition Among Governments* (Lexington Books, 1990), pp. 13–17.

17. Michael D. Reagan and John G. Sanzone, *The New Federalism* (Oxford University Press, 1981), p. 175.

18. Gregory S. Mahler, *Comparative Politics: An Institutional and Cross-National Approach* (Prentice Hall, 2000), p. 31.

19. Frederick K. Lister, *The European Union, the United Nations, and the Revival of Confederal Governance* (Greenwood Press, 1996); Daniel J. Elazar, "The United States and the European Union: Models for their Epochs," in Nicolaidis and Howse, *The Federal Vision*, pp. 31–52.

20. William H. Riker, *The Development of American Federalism* (Academic, 1987), pp. 14–15. Riker contends not only that federalism does not guarantee freedom but also that the framers of our federal system, as well as those of other nations, were animated not by considerations of safeguarding freedom but by practical considerations of preserving unity.

21. The Court, however, ruled in several recent cases that Congress exceeded its power to regulate interstate commerce. See *Printz* v. *United States*, 521 U.S. 898 (1997); *United States* v. *Lopez*, 514 U.S. 549 (1995); *New York* v. *United States*, 505 U.S. 144 (1992); and *United States* v. *Morrison*, 529 U.S. 598 (2000).

22. *Gibbons* v. *Ogden*, 9 Wheaton (22 U.S.) 1 (1824).

23. *Champion* v. *Ames*, 188 U.S. 321 (1907).

24. *Caminetti* v. *United States*, 242 U.S. 470 (1917).

25. *Federal Radio Commission* v. *Nelson Brothers*, 289 U.S. 266 (1933).

26. *Heart of Atlanta Motel* v. *United States*, 379 U.S. 241 (1964).

27. See *United States* v. *Morrison*, 529 U.S. 598 (2000), striking down the Violence Against Women Act.

28. See *New York* v. *United States*, 505 U.S. 144 (1992), and *Printz* v. *United States*, 521 U.S. 898 (1997).

29. Ibid.

30. *Seminole Tribe of Florida* v. *Florida*, 517 U.S. 44 (1996); *Alden* v. *Maine*, 527 U.S. 706 (1999); *Kimel* v. *Florida Board of Regents*, 528 U.S. 62 (2000).

31. See *Franchise Tax Board of California* v. *Hyatt*, 538 U.S.488 (2003).

32. *California* v. *Superior Courts of California*, 482 U.S. 400 (1987).

33. David C. Nice, "State Participation in Interstate Compacts," *Publius* 17 (Spring 1987), p. 70. See also Council of State Governments, *Interstate Compacts and Agencies* (1995), for a list of compacts by subject and by state with brief descriptions.

34. *McCulloch* v. *Maryland*, 4 Wheaton 316 (1819).

35. Joseph F. Zimmerman, "Federal Preemption Under Reagan's New Federalism," *Publius* 21 (Winter 1991), pp. 7–28.

36. Oliver Wendell Holmes Jr., *Collected Legal Papers* (Harcourt, 1920), pp. 295–296.

37. *U.S. Term Limits, Inc.* v. *Thornton*, 514 U.S. 779 (1995).

38. *Garcia* v. *San Antonio Metro*, 469 U.S. 528 (1985).

39. See, for example, *United States* v. *Lopez*, 514 U.S. 549 (1995).

40. *U.S. Term Limits, Inc.* v. *Thornton*, 514 U.S. 779 (1995).

41. *Seminole Tribe of Florida* v. *Florida*, 517 U.S. 44 (1996).

42. *Alden* v. *Maine*, 527 U.S. 706 (1999); *Kimel* v. *Florida Board of Regents*, 528 U.S. 62 (2000); *Vermont Agency of Natural Resources* v. *United States ex rel. Stevens*, 529 U.S. 765 (2000).

43. George Will, "A Revival of Federalism?" *Newsweek*, May 29, 2000, p. 78.

44. *United States* v. *Morrison*, 529 U.S. 598 (2000).

45. John E. Chubb, "The Political Economy of Federalism," *American Political Science Review* 79 (December 1985), p. 1005.

46. Paul E. Peterson, *The Price of Federalism* (Brookings Institution Press, 1995), p. 127.

47. Donald F. Kettl, *The Regulation of American Federalism* (Johns Hopkins University Press, 1987), pp. 154–155.

48. See Paul J. Posner, *The Politics of Unfunded Mandates: Whither Federalism?* (Georgetown University Press, 1998).

49. Joseph Zimmerman, "Congressional Regulation of Subnational Governments," *PS: Political Science and Politics* 26 (June 1993), p. 179.

50. See Jerome J. Hanus, ed., *The Nationalization of State Government* (Heath, 1981).

51. Advisory Commission on Intergovernmental Relations, *Restoring Confidence and Competence* (Advisory Commission on Intergovernmental Relations, 1981), p. 30.

52. Cynthia Cates Colella, "The Creation, Care and Feeding of the Leviathan: Who and What Makes Government Grow," *Intergovernmental Perspective* (Fall 1979), p. 9.

53. Aaron Wildavsky, "Bare Bones: Putting Flesh on the Skeleton of American Federalism," in *The Future of Federalism in the 1980s* (Advisory Commission on Intergovernmental Relations, 1981), p. 79.

54. Peterson, *Price of Federalism*, p. 182.

55. John Kinkaid, "Devolution in the United States: Rhetoric and Reality," in Nicolaidis and Howse, *The Federal Vision*, p. 144.

56. Eliza Newlin Carney, "Power Grab," *National Journal*, April 11, 1998, p. 798.

57. Luther Gulick, "Reorganization of the States," *Civil Engineering* (August 1933), pp. 420–421.

58. David E. Osborne, *Laboratories of Democracy* (Harvard Business School Press, 1988), p. 363.

59. Dye, *American Federalism*, p. 199.

60. Richard A. Oppel and Christopher Drew, "States Planning Their Own Suits on Power Plants: Battle that E.P.A. Quit," *The New York Times*, November 9, 2003, p. A1; and Scott Richards and Yvette Hurt, "States Sue the Federal Environmental Agency," *Federations* 11 (November, 2003).

61. Edward Felsenthal, "Firms Ask Congress to Pass Uniform Rules," *Wall Street Journal*, May 10, 1993, p. B4.

62. John J. DiIulio Jr. and Donald F. Kettl, *Fine Print: The Contract with America, Devolution, and the Administrative Realities of American Federalism* (Brookings Institution Press, 1995), p. 60.

63. Kincaid, "Devolution in the United States," p. 148.

Chapter 4

1. Robert D. Putnam, "Bowling Alone: America's Declining Social Capital," *Journal of Democracy* 6 (January 1995), pp. 65–78. See also Robert D. Putnam, *Bowling Alone: The Collapse and Revival of American Community* (Simon & Schuster, 2000), and Robert D. Putnam, "Bowling Together," *American Prospect* 13 (February 11, 2002), pp. 20–22.

2. See Pippa Norris, "Does Television Erode Social Capital? A Reply to Putnam," *PS: Political Science and Politics* 29 (September 1996), pp. 474–479. See also Everett Carl Ladd, *The Ladd Report* (Free Press, 1999), and Michael Schudson, *The Good Citizen: A History of American Civic Life* (Harvard University Press, 1998).

3. Putnam, "Bowling Together."

4. Clinton Rossiter, *Conservatism in America* (Vintage, 1962), p. 72.

5. Bernard Bailyn, *The Ideological Origins of the American Revolution* (Belknap Press, 1967); Gordon S. Wood, *The Creation of the American Republic, 1776–1787* (University of North Carolina Press, 1969).

6. See Ronald Dworkin, *Taking Rights Seriously* (Harvard University Press, 1977).

7. *Marbury* v. *Madison*, 1 Cranch 137 (1803).

8. "A Nation Challenged: Excerpts from President's Speech: 'We Will Prevail' in War on Terrorism," *The New York Times*, November 9, 2001, p. B1.

9. Robert Coles, *The Political Life of Children* (Atlantic Monthly Press, 1986).

10. Fred I. Greenstein, *Children and Politics* (Yale University Press, 1965).

11. Raymond E. Wolfinger and Steven Rosenstone, *Who Votes?* (Yale University Press, 1980).

12. Franklin Boudotte, "Education for Citizenship," *Public Opinion Quarterly* (Summer 1942): 269–279.

13. Rachel X. Weissman, "The Kids Are All Right—They're Just a Little Converged," *American Demographics* 20, no. 12 (December 1998), pp. 30–32.

14. www.commoncause.org/laundromat/stat/top50.htm.

15. Floyd Norris and Joseph Kahn, "Enron's Many Strands: The Overview; Rule Makers Take On Loopholes That Enron Used in Hiding Debt," *The New York Times*, February 14, 2002, p. A1.

16. www.opensecrets.org/races/summary.asp?ID=NJSI&Cycle=2000.

17. Glen Justice, "Advocacy Groups Reflect on Their Role in the Election," *The New York Times*, November 5, 2004, p. A1.

18. See Michael B. Katz, *The "Underclass" Debate* (Princeton University Press, 1993); Theodore Dalrymple, *Life at the Bottom: The Worldview That Makes the Underclass* (Dee, 2001); and Charles A. Murray, *The Underclass Revisited* (AEI Press, 1999).

19. When adjusted using the consumer price index (CPI), the percentage of households earning over $75,000 a year has risen from 10.1 percent in 1970 to 22.6 percent in 1999. U.S. Bureau of the Census, *Statistical Abstracts of the United States, 2001* (Government Printing Office, 2001), tab. 661.

20. Bailyn, *Ideological Origins.*

21. Robert A. Dahl, "Liberal Democracy in the United States," in William Livingston, ed., *A Prospect of Liberal Democracy* (University of Texas Press, 1979), p. 64.

22. Ibid., pp. 59–60.

23. Franklin D. Roosevelt, State of the Union Address, January 11, 1944, in *The Public Papers of the President of the United States, 1944* (Government Printing Office, 1962), pp. 371–394.

24. Harry S Truman, State of the Union Address, 1949, in *The Public Papers of the President of the United States, 1949* (Government Printing Office, 1964), pp. 1–7.

25. E. J. Dionne Jr., *They Only Look Dead: Why Progressives Will Dominate the Next Political Era* (Simon & Schuster, 1996), p. 13.

26. Quoted in David Brooks, "Need a Map? The Right," *The Washington Post,* October 31, 1999, p. B1.

27. David B. Magleby, *The Outside Campaign* (Rowman & Littlefield, 2001).

28. www.people-press.org/reports/display.php3?PageID=751.

29. Warren B. Rudman, *Combat: Twelve Years in the U.S. Senate* (Random House, 1996), p. 270.

30. David B. Magleby, "Issue Advocacy in the 2000 Presidential Primaries," in David B. Magleby, ed., *Getting Inside the Outside Campaign* (Center for the Study of Elections and Democracy, Brigham Young University, 2000), p. 13. Also at www.byu.edu/outsidemoney.

31. Jonathan Rauch, "The Accidental Radical," *National Journal,* 26 July 2003, 2404–2410.

32. Kathleen Day, *S&L Hell: The People and the Politics Behind the $1 Trillion Savings and Loan Scandal* (Norton, 1993).

33. Sylvia Nasar, "Even Among the Well-Off, the Rich Get Richer," *The New York Times,* March 5, 1992, p. A1.

34. Irving Howe, *Socialism and America* (Harcourt, 1985); Michael Harrington, *Socialism: Past and Future* (Arcade, 1989).

35. Daniel Yergin and Joseph Stainslaw, *The Commanding Heights: The Battle Between Government and the Marketplace That Is Remaking the Modern World* (Simon & Schuster, 1998).

36. www.gp.org/platform/2000/index.html#call.

37. Charles Murray, *What It Means to Be a Libertarian* (Broadway Books, 1997).

38. Center for Political Studies, University of Michigan, *American National Election Study, 1990: Post-Election Survey,* April 1991.

39. Michael Kranish, "Discord Replaced by Desire to Win," *The Boston Globe,* July 31, 2000, p. A10.

40. Earl Black and Merle Black, *The Rise of Southern Republicans* (Belknap Press, 2002).

41. Herbert McClosky and Alida Brill, *Dimensions of Tolerance: What Americans Believe About Civil Liberties* (Russel Sage Foundation, 1983).

42. Nat Hentoff, "Liberal Trimmers of the First Amendment," *The Washington Post,* January 17, 1998, p. A25.

43. Dinesh D'Sousa, *Illiberal Education: The Politics of Race and Sex on Campus* (Free Press, 1991), p. 313.

Chapter 5

1. Franklin Delano Roosevelt, quoted in William Safire, *Lend Me Your Ears: Great Speeches in History* (Norton, 1997), p. 646.

2. Mark Hyman, "Sure, He's Latino. But Don't Expect Salsa at the Park," *BusinessWeek* 3835 (June 2, 2003): 85.

3. Martin Gross, "Homeland Security—Flying High," *The Washington Times,* February 1, 2002, p. A18.

4. "Islam Is Peace, Says President," press release, September 17, 2001, at www.whitehouse.gov/news/releases/2001/09/print/20010917-11.html.

5. Elisabeth Bumiller, "Bush Would Give Illegal Workers Broad New Rights," *The New York Times,* January 6, 2004, p. A1.

6. Albert Einstein, quoted in Laurence J. Peter, *Peter's Quotations* (Morrow, 1977), p. 358.

7. Alexis de Tocqueville, *Democracy in America,* ed. J. P. Mayer, trans. George Lawrence (Doubleday, 1969), p. 278. Originally published 1835 (*Volume 1*) and 1840 (*Volume 2*).

8. "Global Agricultural Trade," at www.ers.usda.gov/BRIEFING/AgTrade/commoditytrade.htm.

9. de Tocqueville, *Democracy in America,* trans. Henry Reeve, eBook at www.netlibrary.com, p. 153.

10. U.S. Bureau of the Census, *Statistical Abstract of the United States, 2003* (Government Printing Office, 2003), p. 269.

11. V. O. Key Jr., *Politics, Parties, and Pressure Groups,* 5th ed. (Crowell, 1964), p. 232.

12. Earl Black and Merle Black, *The Vital South: How Presidents Are Elected* (Harvard University Press, 1992), p. 4.

13. Arthur C. Paulson, *Realignment and Party Revival: Understanding American Electoral Politics at the Turn of the Twenty-First Century* (Westport, 2000), p. 46.

14. Joseph A. Pika and Richard A. Watson, *The Presidential Contest,* 5th ed. (CQ Press, 1996), pp. 80–81.

15. Colbert I. King, "Dean's Faith-Based Folly" January 10, 2004. *The Washington Post,* p. A19.

16. National Governor's Association, *Governor's Political Affiliations,* at www.nga.org/cda/files/GOVLIST2004.PDF.

17. www.cnn.com/ELECTION/2004/results/.

18. U.S. Bureau of the Census, at www.census.gov/population/cen2000/tab01.pdf.

19. www.polstate.com/archives/004713.html.

20. Robert S. Erikson, Gerald C. Wright, and John P. McIver, *Statehouse Democracy: Public Opinion and Policy in the American States* (Cambridge University Press, 1993).

21. U.S. Bureau of the Census, *Statistical Abstract of the United States, 2003* (Government Printing Office, 2003), p. 21.

22. Holly Idelson, "Count Adds Seats in Eight States," *Congressional Quarterly Weekly Report* 48 (December 29, 1999), p. 4240.

23. John M. Broder, "Term Waning, Gov. Davis Reflects on the Battle Lost," *The New York Times,* November 12, 2003, p. A12.

24. *Statistical Abstract, 2003,* p. 28.

25. Ibid., p. 34.

26. U.S. Census Bureau, Current Population Survey, March 2002, Racial Statistics Branch, Population Division. From www.census.gov/population/socdemo/race/black/ppl-164/tab21.pdf.

27. Ibid.

28. *Statistical Abstract, 2003,* pp. 38–39.

29. U.S. Bureau of the Census, *Statistical Abstract of the United States, 2003* (Government Printing Office, 2003) p. 16.

30. Ibid.

31. Ibid.

32. Robert D. Ballard, "Introduction: Lure of the New South," in *In Search of the New South: The Black Urban Experience in the 1970s and 1980s,* ed. Robert D. Ballard (University of Alabama Press, 1989), p. 5; *Statistical Abstract, 2003,* p. 27.

33. Ibid., p. 458.

34. Ibid., p. 463.

35. Ibid.

36. Ibid., p. 458.

37. U.S. Bureau of the Census, at www.census.gov/prod/2003pubs/p70-88.pdf.

38. *Statistical Abstract, 2003,* p. 154.

39. *Statistical Abstract, 2003,* p. 179.

40. *Statistical Abstract, 2003,* p. 15.

41. Jeremy D. Mayer, *Running on Race,* (Random House, 2002) pp. 4, 297. See also Mark R. Levy and Michael S. Kramer, *The Ethnic Factor: How America's Minorities Decide Elections* (Simon & Schuster, 1973). See also Mark Stern, "Democratic Presidency and Voting Rights," in *Blacks in Southern Politics,* ed. Lawrence W. Mooreland, Robert P. Steed, and Todd A. Baker (Praeger, 1987), pp. 50–51.

42. Harold W. Stanley and Richard G. Niemi, *Vital Statistics on American Politics, 2000–2001* (CQ Press, 2001), p. 122.

43. *Statistical Abstract, 2003,* p. 25.

44. See Earl Black, "Presidential Address: The Newest Southern Politics," *The Journal of Politics,* August, 1998, pp. 595–607.

45. "Black Elected Officials: A Statistical Summary 2001," Joint Center for Political and Economic Studies, at www.jointcenter.org/publications/BEO/BEO-01.pdf.

46. Ibid.

47. Rodolfo O. de la Garza, Louis De Sipio, F. Chris Garcia, John Garcia, and Angelo Falcon, *Latino Voices: Mexican, Puerto Rican, and Cuban*

Perspectives on American Politics (Westview Press, 1992), p. 14. See also Richard E. Cohen, "Hispanic Hopes Fade," *National Journal,* February 2, 2002.

48. *Statistical Abstract, 2003,* p. 26.

49. *Statistical Abstract, 2003,* p. 48.

50. Rodney Hero, F. Chris Garcia, John Garcia, and Harry Pachon, "Latino Participation, Partisanship, and Office Holding," *P.S.: Political Science and Politics* 33 (September 2000), p. 529. See also de la Garza et al., *Latino Voices,* p. 14.

51. U.S. Bureau of the Census, at www.census.gov/prod/2001pubs/c2kbr01-3.pdf.

52. Tom Squitieri, "Redistricting Falls Short of Hispanics' Hopes," *USA Today,* August 27, 2002, p. 11A.

53. *Statistical Abstract, 2003,* p. 25.

54. U.S. Bureau of the Census, *Profile of the Foreign-Born Population in the United States, 2000* (Government Printing Office, 2001), at www.census.gov/prod/ 2002pubs/p23-206.pdf.

55. *Statistical Abstract, 2003,* p. 153.

56. Ibid., p. 9.

57. *Statistical Abstract, 2003,* p. 50.

58. James West Davidson, William E. Gienapp, Christine Leigh Heyrman, Mark H. Lytle, and Michael B. Stoff, *Nation of Nations* (McGraw-Hill, 1990), pp. 833–834.

59. G. Thomas Edwards, *Sowing Good Seeds: The Northwest Suffrage Campaigns of Susan B. Anthony* (Oregon Historical Society Press, 1990), p. 136.

60. Paul Kleppner, *Continuity and Change in Electoral Politics, 1893–1928* (Greenwood Press, 1987), p. 172.

61. Margaret C. Trevor, "Political Socialization, Party Identification, and the Gender Gap," *Public Opinion Quarterly* 63 (Spring 1999), p. 62.

62. *Statistical Abstract, 2003,* p. 269; Sue Tolleson-Rinehard and Jyl J. Josephson, eds., *Gender and American Politics* (Sharpe, 2000), pp. 77–78.

63. U.S. Bureau of the Census, "Voting and Registration in the Election of November 2000," at www.census.gov/prod/2002pubs/p20-542.pdf.

64. Tolleson-Rinehard and Josephson, *Gender and American Politics,* (M.E. Sharpe, 2000) pp. 232–233. See also Cindy Simon Rosenthal, ed., *Women Transforming Congress.* (University of Oklahoma Press, 2002), pp. 128–139.

65. Barbara C. Burrell, *A Woman's Place Is in the House: Campaigning for Congress in the Feminist Era* (University of Michigan Press, 1994).

66. Marjorie Connelly, "The Election; Who Voted: A Portrait of American Politics, 1976–2000," *The New York Times,* November 12, 2000, p. D4.

67. Diane L. Fowlkes, "Feminist Theory: Reconstructing Research and Teaching About American Politics and Government," *News for Teachers of Political Science* (Winter 1987), pp. 6–9. See also Sally Helgesen, *Everyday Revolutionaries: Working Women and the Transformation of American Life* (Doubleday, 1998); Karen Lehrman, *The Lipstick Proviso: Women, Sex, and Power in the Real World* (Anchor/Doubleday, 1997); Tanya Melich, *The Republican War Against Women: An Insider's Report from Behind the Lines* (Bantam Books, 1998); and Virginia Valian, *Why So Slow? The Advancement of Women* (MIT Press, 1998).

68. Arlie Russell Hochschild, "There's No Place like Work," *The New York Times,* April 20, 1997, p. 51.

69. The Pew Research Center. *Gay Marriage a Voting Issue, but Mostly for Opponents.* February 27, 2004. www.people-press.org/reports/display.php3?ReportID=204; and Alexis Simendinger, "Why Issues Matter," *National Journal,* April 1, 2000, based on data from a Pew Center Poll conducted March 15–19, 2000.

70. *Statistical Abstract, 2003,* p. 461.

71. U.S. Census Bureau, "Poverty Rate Rises, Household Income Declines, Census Bureau Reports," *United States Department of Commerce News,* September 24, 2002. At www.census.gov/PressRelease/www/2002/cb02-124.html.

72. Wendy Margolis, Bonnie Gordon, Joe Puskarz, and David Rosenlieb, eds., *ABA LSAC Official Guide to ABA-Approved Law Schools, 2005 Edition* (Law School Admissions Council and the American Bar Association, 2004).

73. Anna Quindlen, "Some Struggles Never Seem to End," *The New York Times,* November 14, 2001, p. H24.

74. Elsa Brenner, "The Invisible Population," *The New York Times,* November 14, 1999. See also www.census.gov/population/www/documentation/twps0034.html.

75. Erica Goode. "Sunday Q & A," *The New York Times,* September 2, 2001, p. 16.

76. Rose Arce, "Massachusetts Court Upheld Same-Sex Marriage," see www.cnn.com/2004/LAW/02/04/gay.marriage/.

77. Rachel Gordon, Newsom's Plan for Same-Sex Marriages; Mayor Wants to License Gay and Lesbian Couples, *The San Francisco Chronicle,* February 11, 2004.

78. Adam Clymer, "Senate Expands Hate Crimes Law to Include Gays," *The New York Times,* June 21, 2000, p. A1.

79. *Boy Scouts of America* v. *Dale,* 120 S. Ct. 2446 (2000).

80. David Masci, "The Future of Marriage," *The CQ Researcher Online,* Vol. 14, No. 17 (May 7, 2004), pp. 397–420.

81. *Statistical Abstract, 2003,* p. 76.

82. Laura Vanderkam, "Cities Covet Young Urban Single Professionals," *USA Today,* December 17, 2003, p. 25A.

83. *Statistical Abstract, 2003,* p. 100.

84. Ibid., p. 75.

85. *General Social Survey (GSS) 1972–2000 Cumulative Codebook,* at www.icpsr. umich.edu/GSS/index.html.

86. See Leni Yahil, *The Holocaust: The Fate of European Jewry* (Oxford University Press, 1990).

87. Stephen C. LeSuer, *The 1838 Mormon War in Missouri* (University of Missouri Press, 1987), pp. 151–153.

88. John Conway, "An Adapted Organic Tradition," *Daedalus* 117 (Fall 1988), p. 382. For an extended comparison of the impact of religion on politics in the United States and Canada, see Seymour Martin Lipset, *Continental Divide: The Values and Institutions of the United States and Canada* (Routledge, 1990), pp. 74–89.

89. www.whitehouse.gov/news/releases/2004/01/20040120-7.html.

90. Wesley, Charles. "A Charge to Keep I Have." Text, 1778. Music by Lowell Mason, 1832.

91. "Address of Senator John F. Kennedy to the Greater Houston Ministerial Association," September 12, 1960, at www.cs.umb.edu/jfklibrary/j091260.htm.

92. Jodi Wilgoren, "The 2004 Campaign: Stem-Cell Research," *The New York Times,* January 10, 2004, p. A9.

93. Taylor Branch, *Parting the Waters: America in the King Years, 1954–63* (Simon & Schuster, 1988), p. 3.

94. Douglas Usher, "Strategy, Rules and Participation: Issue Activists in Republican National Convention Delegations 1976–1996," *Political Research Quarterly,* Vol. 53, No. 4. (December, 2000), p. 888.

95. Ronald Inglehart and Wayne E. Baker, "Looking Forward, Looking Back: Continuity and Change at the Turn of the Millennium," *American Sociological Review,* February, 2000, pp. 29, 31.

96. Roper Center for Public Opinion Research, February 27, 2004, at www.ropercenter.uconn.edu/cgi-bin/hsrun.exe/Roperweb/pom/StateId/CYk00u7Ih9k-52Swcm-ofACuZP3lA-.34Ik/HAHTpage/Summary_Link?qstn_i

97. William H. Flanigan and Nancy H. Zingale, *Political Behavior of the American Electorate,* 10th ed. (CQ Press, 2002), p. 131.

98. The Gallup Organization, at www.gallup.com/poll/focus/sr040302.asp.

99. Ibid.

100. *Statistical Abstract, 2003,* p. 67.

101. *Statistical Abstract, 2003,* pp. 21, 67. Also: American Religion Data Archive, at www.thearda.com.

102. Ibid.

103. Ibid.

104. American Religion Data Archive, at www.thearda.com.

105. CNN, at www.cnn.com/ELECTION/2000/results.

106. *2000 American National Election Study* (Center for Political Studies, 2000).

107. Ibid.

108. Lyman A. Kellstedt and John C. Green, "Is There a Culture War? Religion and the 1996 Election," paper presented at the annual meeting of the American Political Science Association, Washington, D.C., 1997, at www.wheaton.edu/polsci/kellstedt.

109. CNN, at www.cnn.com/ELECTION/2000/results.

110. Organization for Economic Cooperation and Development (OECD), at www.oecd.org/dataoecd/48/5/2371372.pdf.

111. Raymond E. Wolfinger, Fred I. Greenstein, and Martin Shapiro, *Dynamics of American Politics,* 2d ed. (Prentice Hall, 1980), p. 19.

112. Thomas Jefferson, "Autobiography," in *The Life and Selected Writings of Thomas Jefferson,* ed. Adrienne Koch and William Peden (Modern Library, 1944), p. 38.

113. Laura D'Andrea Tyson, "Needed: Affirmative Action for the Poor," *BusinessWeek,* July 7, 2003, p. 24.

114. *Statistical Abstract, 2003,* p 189.

115. "Plans to Tackle College Costs Risk Tripping Up Students," *USA Today,* January 5, 2004, p. 12A.

116. Harold W. Stanley and Richard G. Niemi, *Vital Statistics on American Politics, 2003–2004* (CQ Press, 2003), p. 363–364.

117. Stanley Fischer, "Symposium on the Slowdown in Productivity Growth," *Journal of Economic Perspectives* 2 (Fall 1988), pp. 3–7.

118. Robert Gavin, "Q&A Boston Fed Chief Cathy Minehan, On Soaring Productivity Rate," *The Boston Globe*, December 21, 2003, p. E2.

119. Alan B. Krueger. "After 40 Years, What Are Some Results and Lessons of America's War on Poverty?" *The New York Times*, January 8, 2004, p. C2.

120. U.S. Bureau of the Census, at www.census.gov/hhes/poverty/threshld/thresh03.html.

121. U.S. Bureau of the Census, at www.census.gov/prod/2003pubs/p60-222.pdf.

122. *Statistical Abstract, 2003*, p. 465.

123. Ibid., p. 442.

124. "Would You Like Your Class War Shaken or Stirred, Sir?" *The Economist*, September, 6, 2003, p. 46.

125. Ibid.

126. *Statistical Abstract, 2003*, p. 438. "Real" means that inflation has already been taken into account.

127. Daniel Bell, *The Coming of Post-Industrial Society: A Venture in Social Forecasting* (Basic Books, 1973), p. xviii.

128. *Statistical Abstract, 2003*, p. 404.

129. Ibid., p. 438.

130. Ibid., p. 404.

131. Mattei Dogan and Dominique Pelassy, *How to Compare Nations: Strategies in Comparative Politics*, 2d ed. (Chatham House, 1990), p. 47.

132. *Index to International Public Opinion, 1996–97* (Greenwood Press, 1997), p. 397.

133. Seymour Martin Lipset, *Continental Divide: The Values and Institutions of the United States and Canada* (Routledge, 1990), p. 170.

134. U.S. Bureau of Labor Statistics, at www.bls.gov/csx/1999/Aggregate/age.pdf.

135. *Statistical Abstract, 2001*, p. 433, *Statistical Abstract, 2003*, p. 466.

136. CNN, at www.cnn.com/election/2000/results/index.epolls.html.

137. Jose Antonio Vargas, "Vote or Die? Well, They Did Vote," *The Washington Post*, November 9, 2004, p. C1.

138. Seymour Martin Lipset, *Political Man* (Doubleday, 1963), pp. 283–286.

139. Thomas Jefferson to P. S. du Pont de Nemours, April 24, 1816, in *The Writings of Thomas Jefferson*, ed. Paul L. Ford (Putnam, 1899), vol. 10, p. 25.

140. *Statistical Abstract, 2003*, p. 151.

141. Ibid., p. 155.

142. Ibid., p. 154.

143. Herbert McClosky and John Zaller, *The American Ethos: Public Attitudes Toward Capitalism and Democracy* (Harvard University Press, 1984), p. 261.

144. John Gunther, *Inside U.S.A.* (Harper, 1947), p. 911.

145. Carl N. Degler, *Out of Our Past: The Forces That Shaped Modern America*, 3d ed. (Harper & Row, 1984), p. 322.

Chapter 6

1. John E. O'Neill and Jerome R. Corsi, *Unfit for Command: Swift Boat Veterans Speak Out Against John Kerry* (Regnery, 2004).

2. Kate Zernike and Jim Rutenberg, "Friendly Fire: The Birth of an Attack on Kerry," *The New York Times*, August 20, 2004, p. 1.

3. Elisabeth Bumiller and Kate Zeernike, "President Urges Outside Groups to Halt All Ads: But Doesn't Single Out Swift Boat Claims," *The New York Times*, August 24, 2004, p. A1.

4. Zernike and Rutenberg, "Friendly Fire."

5. Jim Rutenberg and Kate Zernike, "Veterans' Group had G.O.P. Lawyer," *The New York Times*, August 25, 2004, p. 1; Zernike and Rutenberg, "Friendly Fire."

6. Bill Sammon, "Bush Raps Anti-Kerry Ads on Vietnam; Rival Urged to Condemn Attacks Funded by Soros," *The Washington Post*, August 24, 2004, p. A1.

7. www.opensecrets.org/softmoney/softcomp1.asp?txtName=wal-mart.

8. www.opensecrets.org/softmoney/softcomp1.asp?txtName=microsoft $$$period.

9. U.S. Bureau of Labor Statistics, at www.bls.gov/cps/cpsaat40.pdf.

10. Michael Podhorzer, Department of Political Research, AFL-CIO, personal communication, June 14, 2002.

11. Brian C. Mooney, "Nation's Two Biggest Unions to Wait on Presidential Endorsement," *The Boston Globe*, September 11, 2003, p. A3.

12. Herbert B. Asher et al., *American Labor Unions in the Electoral Arena* (Rowman & Littlefield, 2001).

13. James MacGregor Burns and Stewart Burns, *A People's Charter: The Pursuit of Rights in America* (Knopf, 1991).

14. William R. Donohue, *The Politics of the American Civil Liberties Union* (Transaction Books, 1985).

15. David B. Magleby, ed., *The Other Campaign: Soft Money and Issue Advocacy in the 2000 Congressional Elections* (Rowman & Littlefield, 2002). See also David B. Magleby, ed., *Outside Money: Soft Money and Issue Advocacy in 1998 Congressional Elections* (Rowman & Littlefield, 2000); and Clyde Wilcox, *Onward Christian Soldiers: The Religious Right in American Politics* (Westview Press, 2000).

16. National Education Association, at www.nea.org/aboutnea.

17. Sam Dillon and Diana Jean Schemo, "Union Urges Bush to Replace Education Chief Over Remark," *The New York Times*, February 25, 2004, p. A15.

18. Robert Salisbury, "Interest Representation: The Dominance of Institutions," *American Political Science Review* 78 (March 1984), p. 66.

19. Ceci Connelly, "Democratic Candidates Criticize AARP," *The Washington Post*, November 19, 2003, p. A12.

20. V. O. Key Jr., *Public Opinion and American Democracy* (Knopf, 1961), pp. 504–507.

21. Jill Lawrence and Susan Page, "Top Candidates Strategize to Pin Down Nomination," *USA Today*, January 5, 2004, p. 1A.

22. "Inside the 2004 Campaign Tool Chest: Blogs and Online Voting," *The Los Angeles Times*, January 5, 2004, p. A10.

23. Joyce Purnick, "One-Doorbell-One-Vote Tactic Re-emerges in Bush–Kerry Race," *The New York Times*, April 6, 2004, p. A1; Glen Justice, "Bush Spent a Record on His Race in March," *The New York Times*, April 21, 2004, p. A18.

24. R. Kenneth Godwin, *One Billion Dollars of Influence: The Direct Marketing of Politics* (Chatham House, 1988).

25. Lucius J. Barker, "Third Parties in Litigation: A Systemic View of the Judicial Function," *Journal of Politics* 29 (February 1967), pp. 41–69; Jethro K. Lieberman, *Litigious Society*, rev. ed. (Basic Books, 1983).

26. Gregory A. Calderia and John R. Wright, "Organized Interests and Agenda Setting in the U.S. Supreme Court," *American Political Science Review* 82 (December 1988), pp. 1109–1127. See also Gregory A. Calderia and John R. Wright, "*Amici Curiae* Before the Supreme Court: Who Participates, When, and How Much?" *Journal of Politics* 52 (August 1990), pp. 782–806.

27. Karen O'Connor, *Women's Organizations' Use of the Courts* (Lexington Books, 1980).

28. Steven P. Brown, *Trumping Religion: The New Christian Right, Religious Liberty, and the Courts* (University of Alabama Press, October 2002), Ph.D. diss.

29. Lee Epstein and C. K. Rowland, "Debunking the Myth of Interest Group Invincibility in the Courts," *American Political Science Review* 85 (March 1991), pp. 205–217.

30. Sam Howe Verhovek, "Police Chief Resigns in Aftermath of Protests," *The New York Times*, December 8, 1999, p. A16.

31. Sam Howe Verhovek, "Talks and Turmoil: The Hosts," *The New York Times*, December 2, 1999, p. A16.

32. See Kenneth Klee, "The Siege of Seattle," *Newsweek*, December 13, 1999, p. 30.

33. David B. Magleby and Kelly D. Patterson, "Campaign Consultants and Direct Democracy: Politics of Citizen Control," in *Campaign Warriors: The Role of Political Consultants in Elections*, eds. James E. Thurber and Candice J. Nelson (Brookings Institution Press, 2000).

34. www.bipac.org/home.asp.

35. For a discussion of the 1998 New Mexico race, see Lonna Rae Atkeson and Anthony C. Coveny, "The 1998 New Mexico Third Congressional District Race," in Magleby, *Outside Money*, pp. 135–152.

36. Ethan Bronner, *Battle for Justice: How the Bork Nomination Shook America* (Norton, 1989), pp. 50–55.

37. Hugh Heclo, "Issue Networks and the Executive Establishment," in *The New American Political System*, ed. Anthony King (American Enterprise Institute, 1978).

38. David Mayhew, *Congress: The Electoral Connection* (Yale University Press, 1974), p. 45.

39. John R. Wright, "Contributions, Lobbying, and Committee Voting in the U.S. House of Representatives," *American Political Science Review* 84 (June 1990), pp. 417–438.

40. www.opensecrets.org/softmoney/softcomp1.asp?txtName=wal-mart.

41. www.clubforgrowth.org/what.php.

42. David B. Magleby and Jonathan W. Tanner, "Interest Group Electioneering in the 2002 Congressional Elections," in *The Last Hurrah*, eds. David B. Magleby and J. Quin Monson (Brookings Institution Press, 2004), p. 81. See also Thomas B. Edsall, "Drug Industry Financing Fuels Pro-GOP TV

Spots; Spending Swamps Donations for Liberal Ads by 3–1 Margin," *The Washington Post*, October 23, 2002, p. A11.

43. Christopher Rowland, "That Spoonful of Sugar Medicare Bids Mollify Makers on a Key Point: No Price Controls," *The Boston Globe*, June 29, 2003, p. H1.

44. Dana Milbank, "Conservatives Criticize Bush on Spending; Medicare Bill Angers Some Allies," *The Washington Post*, December 6, 2003, p. A1.

45. Dana Milbank and Claudia Deane, "President Signs Medicare Drug Bill; Supporters, Opponents Jockey for 2004 Edge," *The Washington Post*, December 9, 2003, p. A1.

46. *McConnell v. Federal Elections Commission*, 124 S.Ct. 621 (2003).

47. For evidence of the impact of PAC expenditures on legislative committee behavior and legislative involvement generally, see Richard L. Hall and Frank W. Wayman, "Buying Time: Moneyed Interests and the Mobilization of Bias in Congressional Committees," *American Political Science Review* 84 (September 1990), pp. 797–820.

48. Edwin M. Epstein, "Business and Labor Under the Federal Election Campaign Act of 1971," in *Parties, Interest Groups, and Campaign Finance Laws*, ed. Michael J. Malbin (American Enterprise Institute for Public Policy Research, 1980), p. 112. See also Gary Jacobson, *Money in Congressional Elections* (Yale University Press, 1980).

49. Open Secrets, at www.opensecrets.org/pacs/index.asp.

50. Kelly Huff, Ron Harris, and Ian Stirton, "FEC Issues Semi-Annual PAC Count," at www.fec.gov/press/20020120124pacno.html and www.fec.gov/press/paccnt_grph.html.

51. Federal Election Commission, at www.fec.gov/press/082101pac.html.

52. Amy Keller, "Leadership PACs 'Not Sinister,' FEC Told," *Roll Call*, February 27, 2003.

53. Federal Election Commission, at www.fec.gov.

54. Ruth Marcus, "Labor Spent $119 Million For '96 Politics, Study Says; Almost All Contributions Went to Democrats," *The Washington Post*, September 10, 1997, p. A19.

55. *Buckley* v. *Valeo*, 96 S.Ct. 647 (1976).

56. David B. Magleby and J. Quin Monson, eds., *The Last Hurrah: Soft Money and Issue Advocacy in the 2002 Congressional Elections*, p. 90; David B. Magleby, ed., *The Other Campaign: Soft Money and Issue Advocacy in the 2000 Congressional Election*, p. 53; David B. Magleby, ed., *Outside Money*, p. 41.

57. David B. Magleby, and J. Quin Monson, eds., *The Last Hurrah*, p. 3; David B. Magleby, ed., *The Other Campaign*, p. 1; David B. Magleby, ed., *Outside Money*, p. 212.

58. David B. Magleby, ed., *The Other Campaign*, p. 149.

59. Ibid.

60. *FEC v. Mass. Citizen's for Life, Inc.*, 479 U.S. 238; 107 S.Ct. 616 (1986).

61. America Coming Together, at http://actforvictory.org/.

62. Ibid.

63. Nicholas Confessore, "Bush's Secret Stash," *Washington Monthly* 36 (May 2004), pp. 17–23.

64. E. J. Dionne Jr., "Fear of McCain-Feingold," *The Washington Post*, December 3, 2002, p. A25.

65. www.campaignlegalcenter.org/press-814.html.

66. Hall and Wayman, "Buying Time," pp. 797–820. A different study of the House Ways and Means Committee found campaign contributions to be part of the representatives' policy decisions, but even more important was the number of lobbying contacts; see Wright, "Contributions, Lobbying, and Committee Voting."

67. Ronald Reagan, "Remarks to Administration Officials on Domestic Policy," December 13, 1988, *Weekly Compilation of Presidential Documents*, vol. 24 (December 1988), pp. 1615–1620.

68. Sylvia Tesh, "In Support of Single-Interest Politics," *Political Science Quarterly* 99 (Spring 1984), pp. 27–44.

69. Howard Dean also turned down the federal matching funds in the 2004 primaries.

70. Ross Sneyd, "Dean First Democrat to Forgo Public Funds," *Associated Press Online*, November 9, 2003.

71. California Commission on Campaign Financing, *The New Gold Rush: Financing California's Legislative Campaigns* (Center for Responsive Government, 1985), pp. 177–197. For a study of state lobby regulation, see Cynthia Opheim, "Explaining the Differences in State Lobby Regulation," *Western Political Quarterly* 44 (June 1991), pp. 405–421.

72. Adam Clymer, "Congress Sends Lobbying Overhaul to Clinton," *The New York Times*, December 16, 1995, p. A36.

73. Legislative Resource Center's Lobbying Section, telephone interview, April 7, 2004.

74. David B. Magleby, *Financing the 2000 Election* (Brookings Institution Press, 2002) p. 11; See also Susan B. Glasser, "George W. Bush's Dash for Cash," *The Washington Post*, April 19, 1999, p. A10.

75. Greg Hitt, "Democrats Move Ahead in Soft-Money Race," *The Wall Street Journal*, August 17, 2000, p. A24.

76. Open Secrets at www.opensecrets.org/industries/indus.asp?Ind+H04.

77. Marianne Holt, "Stealth PAC's Revealed: Interest Group Profiles." Press release, Center for Public Integrity, February 5, 2001.

78. David B. Magleby, ed., *Election Advocacy: Soft Money and Issue Advocacy in the 2000 Congressional Elections* (Center for the Study of Elections and Democracy, 2001), at www.byu.edu/outsidemoney.

79. David B. Magleby and Candice J. Nelson, *The Money Chase: Congressional Campaign Finance Reform* (Brookings Institution Press, 1990), pp. 72–97.

80. Factors that predict the formation of PACs include company size and the degree of regulation for corporations. See Craig Humphries, "Corporations, PACs, and the Strategic Link Between Contributions and Lobbying Activities," *Western Political Quarterly* 44 (June 1991), pp. 353–372.

81. Paul Krugman, "Toward One-Party Rule," *The New York Times*, June 27, 2003, p. A27.

Chapter 7

1. John E. Mueller, "Choosing Among 133 Candidates," *Public Opinion Quarterly* 34 (Fall 1970), pp. 395–402.

2. E. E. Schattschneider, *Party Government* (Holt, Rinehart and Winston, 1942), p. 1.

3. See Scott Mainwaring, "Party Systems in the Third Wave," *Journal of Democracy* (July 1998), pp. 67–81.

4. Joseph A. Schlesinger, *Political Parties and the Winning of Office* (University of Michigan Press, 1994).

5. James A. Thurber and Candice J. Nelson, eds., *Campaign Warriors: The Role of Political Consultants in Elections* (Brookings Institution Press, 2000).

6. Nick Anderson and Jonathan Peterson, "China Trade Vote: House OK's China Trade Bill," *The Los Angeles Times*, May 25, 2000, p. A1.

7. Elizabeth A. Palmer, "Bill to Extend Residency Program Passes House After Six-Month Wait," *Congressional Quarterly*, March 16, 2002, p. 706.

8. Gary W. Cox and Mathew D. McCubbins, *Legislative Leviathan: Party Government in the House* (University of California Press, 1993).

9. David B. Magleby and J. Quin Monson, eds. *The Last Hurrah? Soft Money and Issue Advocacy in the 2002 Congressional Elections* (Brookings Institution Press, 2004).

10. John Bart and James Meader, "The More You Spend, the Less They Listen: The South Dakota U.S. Senate Race," in *The Last Hurrah*, eds. David B. Magleby and J. Quin Monson, pp. 159–179.

11. See three books edited by David B. Magleby: *Outside Money: Soft Money and Issue Advocacy in the 1998 Congressional Elections* (Rowman & Littlefield, 2000); *The Other Campaign: Soft Money and Issue Advocacy in the 2000 Congressional Elections* (Rowman & Littlefield, 2002); and *Financing the 2000 Election* (Brookings Institution Press, 2002).

12. Amy Keller, "FEC Offers Post-BCRA Legislative Ideas," *Roll Call*, April 29, 2004.

13. Federal Election Commission, "The Biennial Contribution Limit," at www.fec.gov/pages/brochures/biennial.htm#Biennial%20Limit, February 2004; and Paul S. Herrnson, *Congressional Elections: Campaigning at Home and in Washington* (CQ Press, 2004), p. 16.

14. *Federal Election Commission v. Colorado Republican Federal Campaign Committee*, 116 S.Ct. 2309 (1996).

15. Federal Election Commission (ftp.fec.gov/FEC/[July 27,2004]).

16. David W. Brady and Craig Volden, *Revolving Gridlock: Politics and Policy from Carter to Clinton* (Westview Press, 1998); James A. Thurber, ed., *Divided Democracy: Cooperation and Conflict Between the President and Congress* (CQ Press, 1991); James A. Thurber, ed., *Rivals for Power: Presidential-Congressional Relations* (CQ Press, 1996); Charles O. Jones, *Separate but Equal Branches: Congress and the Presidency* (Chatham House, 1995), chaps. 5 and 6; and Jon R. Bond and Richard Fleisher, *The President in the Legislative Arena* (University of Chicago Press, 1990).

17. *California Democratic Party et al. v. Jones*, 120 S.Ct. 2402 (2000).

18. Bruce E. Cain and Elisabeth R. Gerber, eds., *Voting at the Political Fault Line: California's Experiment with the Blanket Primary* (University of California Press, 2002), pp. 341–342.

19. "Iowans Flock to Caucuses," *The Associated Press State & Local Wire,* January 20, 2004. Section: "Political News."

20. Arthur Sanders and David Redlawsk, "Money and the Iowa Caucuses," in *Getting Inside the Outside Campaign,* ed. David Magleby (Center for the Study of Elections and Democracy, 2000), pp. 20–29.

21. *The Book of the States, 2000–2001* (Council of State Governments, 2000), pp. 164–165.

22. For an analysis of the potential effects of different electoral rules in the United States see Todd Donovan and Shawn Bowler, *Reforming the Republic: Democratic Institutions for the New America.* Prentice Hall, 2004.

23. William H. Riker, "The Two-Party System and Duverger's Law: An Essay on the History of Political Science," *American Political Science Review* 76 (December 1982), pp. 753–766. For a classic analysis, see Schattschneider, *Party Government.*

24. Robin Toner, "The 1992 Elections: The World–News Analysis; At Dawn of New Politics, Challenges for Both Parties," *The New York Times,* November 5, 1992, p. B1.

25. See Paul S. Herrnson and John C. Green, eds., *Multiparty Politics in America,* 2d ed. (Rowman & Littlefield, 2002); and J. David Gillespie, *Politics at the Periphery: Third Parties in Two-Party America* (University of South Carolina Press, 1993).

26. L. Sandy Maisel and John F. Bibby, *Two Parties—or More? The American Party System* (Westview Press, 1998).

27. Ted G. Jelen, ed., *Ross for Boss* (State University of New York Press, 2001), p. 88.

28. Steven J. Rosenstone, Roy L. Behr, and Edward H. Lazarus, *Third Parties in America: Citizen Response to Major Party Failure,* 2d ed. (Princeton University Press, 1996). See also Xandra Kayden and Eddie Mahe Jr., *The Party Goes On: The Persistence of the Two-Party System in the United States* (Basic Books, 1985), pp. 143–144.

29. Dean Lacy and Quin Monson. "The Origins and Impact of Voter Support for Third-Party Candidates: A Case Study of the 1998 Minnesota Gubernatorial Election," *Political Research Quarterly* 55(2):409–437, 2002.

30. On the impact of third parties, see Howard R. Penniman, "Presidential Third Parties and the Modern American Two-Party System," in *The Party Symbol,* ed. William J. Crotty (Freeman, 1980), pp. 101–117. See also Frank Smallwood, *The Other Candidates: Third Parties in Presidential Elections* (University Press of New England, 1983).

31. Libertarian Party, at www.lp.org/campaigns/candidates.php.

32. Benjamin Franklin, George Washington, and Thomas Jefferson, quoted in Richard Hofstadter, *The Idea of a Party System* (University of California Press, 1969), pp. 2, 123.

33. For concise histories of the two parties, see two studies by Robert A. Rutland, *The Democrats: From Jefferson to Clinton* (University of Missouri Press, 1996), and *The Republicans: From Lincoln to Bush* (University of Missouri Press, 1996).

34. See V. O. Key Jr., "A Theory of Critical Elections," *Journal of Politics* 17 (February 1955), pp. 3–18; Walter Dean Burnham, *Critical Elections and the Mainsprings of American Politics* (Norton, 1970), pp. 1–10; and E. E. Schattschneider, *The Semisovereign People: A Realist's View of Democracy in America* (Holt, Rinehart and Winston, 1975), pp. 78–80.

35. William E. Gienapp, *The Origins of the Republican Party, 1852–1856* (Oxford University Press, 1987).

36. David W. Brady, "Election, Congress, and Public Policy Changes, 1886–1960," in *Realignment in American Politics: Toward a Theory,* eds. Bruce A. Campbell and Richard Trilling (Texas University Press, 1980), p. 188.

37. L. Sandy Maisel, *Parties and Elections in America: The Electoral Process* (Rowman & Littlefield, 2002), pp. 48–49.

38. Gerald Pomper, "Classification of Presidential Elections," *Journal of Politics* 29 (August 1967), p. 538.

39. CNN, at www.cnn.com/ELECTION/2000/results/.

40. V. O. Key Jr., *Political Parties and Pressure Groups,* 5th ed. (International Publishing, 1964). See also Paul Allen Beck and Marjorie Randon Hershey, *Party Politics in America,* 10th ed. (Longman, 2003).

41. "Party Fundraising Escalates," *Federal Elections Commission,* November 3, 2000, at www.fecweb1.fec.gov/press/pty00text.htm.

42. Paul Allen Beck and Marjorie Randon Hershey, *Party Politics in America,* 10th ed. (Longman, 2003).

43. Virginia Sapiro, "It's the Context, Situation, and Question, Stupid: The Gender Basis of Public Opinion," in *Understanding Public Opinion,* 2d ed., eds. Barbara Norrander and Clyde Wilcox (CQ Press, 2001), p. 41.

44. At www.bluedogdemocrats.com/.

45. Zell Miller, "George Bush vs. the Naïve Nine," *The Wall Street Journal,* November 3, 2003, p. A14.

46. GOP.com, "RNC Chairman Ed Gillespie," at www.gop.com/GOPDirectory/LeaderBio.aspx?ID=8, June 15, 2004.

47. Democratic National Committee, "Current DNC Leadership: Terry McAuliffe DNC Chairman," at www.democrats.org/about/bios/mcauliffe.html, June 15, 2004.

48. See L. Sandy Maisel, *From Obscurity to Oblivion: Running in the Congressional Primary,* rev. ed. (University of Tennessee Press, 1986).

49. The early Republican efforts and advantages over the Democrats are well documented in Thomas B. Edsall, *The New Politics of Inequality* (Norton, 1984); and Gary C. Jacobson, "The Republican Advantage in Campaign Finances," in *New Direction in American Politics,* eds. John E. Chubb and Paul E. Peterson (Brookings Institution Press, 1985), p. 6.

50. David C. King, "The Polarization of American Political Parties and Mistrust of Government," in *Why People Don't Trust Government,* eds. Joseph S. Nye, Philip Zelikow, and David C. King (Harvard University Press, 1997); and National Election Study, "Important Difference in What Democratic and Republican Parties Stand For, 1952–2000," at www.umich.edu/~nes/nesguide/toptable/tab2b_4.htm, July 2004.

51. Tom Shales, "Bush, Bringing the Party to Life; From the New Nominee, a Splendid Acceptance Speech," *The Washinton Post,* August 19, 1988, p. C1.

52. Kelly D. Patterson, *Political Parties and the Maintenance of Liberal Democracy* (Columbia University Press, 1996), pp. 30–31.

53. John F. Bibby, *Politics, Parties, and Elections in America,* 4th ed. (Nelson-Hall, 1999). For further data on these roles, see Cornelius P. Cotter, James L. Gibson, John F. Bibby, and Robert J. Huckshorn, *Party Organizations in American Politics* (Praeger, 1984).

54. See James L. Gibson, Cornelius P. Cotter, John F. Bibby, and Robert J. Huckshorn, "Assessing Party Organizational Strength," *American Journal of Political Science* 27 (May 1983), pp. 193–222. See also Cotter et al., *Party Organizations in American Politics.*

55. Paul S. Herrnson, *Party Campaigning in the 1980s: Have the National Parties Made a Comeback as Key Players in Congressional Elections?* (Harvard University Press, 1988), p. 122.

56. Jonathan S. Krasno and Daniel E. Seltz, *Buying Time: Television Advertising in the 1998 Congressional Elections,* report of a grant funded by the Pew Charitable Trusts (1998).

57. On the influence of local parties, see Kayden and Mahe, *The Party Goes On.* See also John C. Green and Daniel M. Shea, eds., *The State of the Parties: The Changing Role of Contemporary Parties,* 3d ed. (Rowman & Littlefield, 1999), which presents recent case studies of parties at the local level.

58. J. Quin Monson, "Get on Television vs. Get on the Van: GOTV and the Ground War in 2002," *The Last Hurrah? Soft Money and Issue Advocacy in the 2002 Congressional Elections,* eds. David B. Magleby and J. Quin Monson, pp. 90–112.

59. Jill Newell, White House staff, personal communication, July 2, 2002. A list of many of these positions appears in *Policy and Supporting Positions* (Government Printing Office, November 9, 1988). For a general discussion of presidential appointments, see G. Calvin Mackenzie, "Partisan Presidential Leadership: The President's Appointees," in L. Sandy Maisel, ed., *Parties Respond: Changes in American Parties and Campaigns,* 3d ed. (Westview Press, 2002), pp. 316–337.

60. *Marbury v. Madison,* I Cranch 137 (1803).

61. See Angus Campbell, Philip E. Converse, Warren E. Miller, and Donald E. Stokes, *The American Voter* (University of Chicago Press, 1960); Norman A. Nie, Sidney Verba, and John R. Petrocik, *The Changing American Voter,* enlarged ed. (Harvard University Press, 1979); and Warren E. Miller and J. Merrill Shanks, *The New American Voter* (Harvard University Press, 1996).

62. Angus Campbell et al., *The American Voter,* pp. 121–128.

63. Bruce E. Keith et al., *The Myth of the Independent Voter* (University of California Press, 1992).

64. See Byron E. Shafer, *The End of Realignment: Interpreting American Electoral Eras* (University of Wisconsin Press, 1991).

65. Michael F. Meffert, Helmut Norpoth, and Anirudh V. S. Ruhil, "Realignment and Macropartisanship," *American Political Science Review* 95 (December 2001), pp. 953–962.

66. Hedrick Smith, *The Power Game: How Washington Works* (Random House, 1988), p. 671.

67. Nine percent of all voters were Pure Independents in 1956 and 1960; Keith et al., *The Myth of the Independent Voter,* p. 51. In 1992, the figure was also 9 percent; *1992 National Election Study* (Center for Political Studies, University of Michigan, 1992).

68. Earl Black and Merle Black, *The Rise of Southern Republicans* (Harvard University Press, 2002).

69. Ibid.
70. For the "optimistic view," see Ralph M. Goldman, *Search for Consensus: The Story of the Democratic Party* (Temple University Press, 1979), pp. 366–373; Kayden and Mahe, *The Party Goes On*; Larry J. Sabato, *The Party's Just Begun: Shaping Political Parties in America's Future* (Scott, Foresman, 1988); Joseph A. Schlesinger, "The New American Political Party," *American Political Science Review* 79 (December 1985), pp. 1152–1169; and David E. Price, *Bringing Back the Parties* (CQ Press, 1984).
71. "Party Unity Background," *Congressional Quarterly Weekly Report* 60 (January 12, 2002), p. 142.
72. Barbara Sinclair, "Evolution or Revolution?" in Maisel, *Parties Respond*, pp. 263–285.
73. Paul S. Herrnson, *Party Campaigning in the 1980s* (Harvard University Press, 1988), pp. 80–81.
74. See Magleby, *Outside Money and The Other Campaign.*
75. *McConnell* v. *FEC*, 124 S.Ct. 516 (2003).
76. See David B. Magleby, "Dictum Without Data: The Myth of Issue Advocacy and Party Building," p. 11 at www.csed.byu.edu/Publications/Dictum.doc.

Chapter 8

1. WisPolitics Press Release, "UW-Madison, BYU: Few Differences Between Voters in Battleground, Other States, Major Study Finds," July 14, 2004, at www.wispolitics.com/printerfriendly.iml?Article=19985.
2. Robert Coles, *The Political Life of Children* (Atlantic Monthly Press, 2000), 24–25. See also Stephen M. Caliendo, *Teachers Matter: The Trouble with Leaving Political Education to the Coaches* (Greenwood, 2000).
3. Robert Coles, *The Political Life of Children* (Atlantic Monthly Press, 2000), pp. 59–60.
4. Pamela Johnston Conover, "The Influence of Group Identifications on Political Perception and Evaluation," *Journal of Politics* 46 (August 1984), pp. 760–785; and Henry E. Brady and Paul M. Sniderman, "Attitude Attribution: A Group Basis for Political Reasoning," *American Political Science Review* 79 (December 1985), pp. 1061–1078.
5. Caliendo, *Teachers Matter*, pp. 16–17.
6. James Garbarino, *Raising Children in a Socially Toxic Environment* (Jossey-Bass, 1995).
7. Russell J. Dalton, "Reassessing Parental Socialization: Indicator Unreliability Versus Generational Transfer," *American Political Science Review* 74 (June 1980), pp. 421–431.
8. Suzanne Koprince Sebert, M. Kent Jennings, and Richard G. Niemi, "The Political Texture of Peer Groups," in *The Political Character of Adolescence*, M. Kent Jennings and Richard G. Niemi (Princeton University Press, 1974), p. 246. See also Richard G. Niemi and M. Kent Jennings, "Issues and Inheritance in the Formation of Party Identification," *American Journal of Political Science* 35 (November 1991), pp. 970–988.
9. National Association of Secretaries of State, *New Millennium Project, Part I: American Youth Attitudes on Policies, Citizenship, Government and Voting* (Washington, D.C.: National Association of Secretaries of State, 1999). See also, "Political Interest on the Rebound Among the Nation's Freshmen." After 3 decades of plummeting political interest among freshmen, political interest has been on the rise since 2001. www.gseis.ucla.edu/heri/03_press_release.pdf.
10. Margaret Stimmann Branson, "Making the Case for Civic Education: Educating Young People for Responsible Citizenship," paper presented at the Conference for Professional Development for Program Trainers, Manhattan Beach, Calif., February 25, 2001.
11. Kenneth Feldman and Theodore M. Newcomb, *The Impact of College on Students*, vol. 2 (Jossey-Bass, 1969), pp. 16–24, 49–56. See also David O. Sears and Nicholas A. Valentino, "Politics Matters: Political Events as Catalysts for Preadult Socialization," *American Political Science Review* 91 (March 1997), pp. 45–65.
12. Robert D. Putnam, "Bowling Together," *American Prospect* 13 (February 11, 2002), pp. 20–22.
13. Robert D. Putnam, "Bowling Together," in *United We Serve*, eds. E.J. Dionne Jr., Kayla Meltzer Drogosz, and Robert E. Litan (Brookings Institution Press, 2003), p. 19. The Putnam data is available at www.ksg.harvard.edu/saguaro/.
14. Benjamin I. Page and Robert Y. Shapiro, *The Rational Public* (University of Chicago Press, 1992), p. 267.
15. Quoted in Hadley Cantril, *Gauging Public Opinion* (Princeton University Press, 1944), p. viii.
16. John G. Geer, *From Tea Leaves to Opinion Polls: A Theory of Democratic Leadership* (Columbia University Press, 1996).
17. Everett C. Ladd and John Benson, "The Growth of News Polls in American Politics," in *Media Polls in American Politics*, eds. Thomas Mann and Gary Orren (Brookings Institution Press, 1992), pp. 19–31.
18. Benjamin I. Page and Robert Y. Shapiro, *The Rational Public: Fifty Years of Trends in Americans' Policy Preferences* (University of Chicago Press, 1992), p. 237.
19. George J. Church, "What in the World Are We Doing?" *Time*, October 18, 1993, p. 42.
20. "Do you approve or disapprove of the way George W. Bush is handling the situation with Iraq?" CBS News/New York Times Poll, May 3, 2003, and May 20, 2004, at www.pollingreport.com/iraq.htm.
21. Jacobs and Shapiro, *Politicians Don't Pander* (University of Chicago Press, 2000), p. 3.
22. David R. Mayhew, *Congress: The Electoral Connection* (Yale University Press, 1974); Richard F. Fenno Jr., *Home Style: House Members in Their Districts* (Longman, 1978).
23. Robert S. Erikson and Kent L. Tedin, *American Public Opinion: Its Origins, Content and Impact*, 6th ed. (Longman, 2001), pp. 272–273.
24. For a general discussion of political knowledge, see Michael Delli Carpini and Scott Keeter, *What Americans Know About Politics and Why it Matters* (Yale University Press, 1996).
25. The 2000 National Election Study, Center for Political Studies, University of Michigan. See the NES Guide to Public Opinion and Electoral Behavior at www.umich.edu/~nes/nesguide/nesguide.htm.
26. Robert S. Erikson and Kent L. Tedin, *American Public Opinion: Its Origins, Content and Impact*, 6th ed. (Longman, 2001), p. 304.
27. Neil S. Newhouse and Christine L. Matthews, "NAFTA Revisited: Most Americans Just Weren't Deeply Engaged," *Public Perspective* 5 (January–February, 1994), pp. 31–32.
28. Center for the Study of Elections and Democracy and Center for the Study of Politics, "2004 Election Panel Study Data," at www.csp.polisci.wisc.edu/byu_uw/.
29. *2002 National Election Study* (Center for Political Studies, University of Michigan, 2002).
30. *2002 National Election Study* (Center for Political Studies, University of Michigan, 2002).
31. Federal Election Commission, "Presidential Election Campaign Fund," at www.fec.gov.
32. For a discussion of the relationship between civic skills and participation, see Sidney Verba, Kay Lehman Schlozman, and Henry E. Brady, *Voice and Equality: Civic Voluntarism in American Politics* (Harvard University Press, 1995).
33. John Balz, "Iorio pushes for national voting reform," *St. Petersburg Times*, May 11, 2001, p. 3B.
34. Juliet Eilperin, "Federal Aid Helps States Fund Election Reform," *The Washington Post*, March 16, 2003, p. A5.
35. Frank R. Parker, *Black Votes Count: Political Empowerment in Mississippi After 1965* (University of North Carolina Press, 1990), p. 3.
36. Bernard Grofman and Lisa Handley, "The Impact of the Voting Rights Act on Black Representation in Southern State Legislatures," *Legislative Studies Quarterly* 16 (February 1991), pp. 111–128.
37. International Institute for Democracy and Electoral Assistance, "Voter Turnout from 1945 to Date: A Global Report on Political Participation," at www.idea.int/voter_turnout/index.html.
38. Raymond E. Wolfinger and Steven J. Rosenstrone, "The Effect of Registration Laws on Voter Turnout," *American Political Science Review* 72 (March 1978), p. 41.
39. Raymond E. Wolfinger and Steven J. Rosenstone, "The Effect of Registration Laws on Voter Turnout," *American Political Science Review* 72 (March 1978), p. 24.
40. Raymond E. Wolfinger and Steven J. Rosenstone, *Who Votes?* (Yale University Press, 1980), pp. 78, 88.
41. Federal Election Commission, "The Impact of the National Voter Registration Act on Federal Elections 1999–2000," at www.fec.gov.
42. See Raymond E. Wolfinger and Ben Highton, "Estimating the Effects of the National Voter Registration Act of 1993," *Political Behavior* (June 1998), pp. 79–104; and Raymond E. Wolfinger and Jonathan Hoffman, "Registering and Voting with Motor Voter," *PS: Political Science and Politics* (March 2001), pp. 85–92.
43. For a discussion of the differences in the turnout between presidential and midterm elections, see James E. Campbell, "The Presidential Surge

and Its Midterm Decline in Congressional Elections, 1868–1988," *Journal of Politics* 53 (May 1991), pp. 477–487.

44. David E. Rosenbaum, "Democrats Keep Solid Hold on Congress," *The New York Times*, November 9, 1988, p. A24; and Louis V. Gerstner, "Next Time, Let Us Boldly Vote as No Democracy Has Before," *USA Today*, November 16, 1998, p. A15.

45. Data from Curtis Gans, "President Bush, Mobilization Drives Propel Turnout to Post-1968 High; Kerry, Democratic Weakness Shown," *Center for Voting and Democracy*, November 4, 2004 at www.fairvote.org/reports/csae2004electionreport.pdf.

46. Raymond E. Wolfinger and Steven J. Rosenstone, *Who Votes?* (Yale University Press, 1980), p. 102.

47. Howard W. Stanley and Richard G. Niemi, *Vital Statistics on Politics, 1999–2000* (CQ Press, 2000), pp. 120–121; CNN, at www.cnn.com/ELECTION/2000/results/index.my.html.

48. The Vanishing Voter, "Election Interest Among Young Adults Is Up Sharply From 2000," March 12, 2004, available at www.vanishingvoter.org/Releases/release031104.shtml.

49. See the classic book on this topic, Angus Campbell, Philip E. Converse, Warren E. Miller, and Donald E. Stokes, *The American Voter* (Wiley, 1960). This volume is a foundation of modern voting analysis despite much new evidence and reinterpretation. See also Warren E. Miller and J. Merrill Shanks, *The New American Voter* (Harvard University Press, 1996); and Eric R.A.N. Smith, *The Unchanging American Voter* (University of California Press, 1989).

50. www.census.gov/prod/2002pubs/p20-542.pdf.

51. Austin Ranney, "Nonvoting Is Not a Social Disease," *Public Opinion*, October–November 1983, pp. 16–19.

52. Thomas Byrne Edsall, *The New Politics of Inequality* (Norton, 1984), p. 181.

53. Steven J. Rosenstone and John Mark Hansen, *Mobilitzation, Participation, and Democracy in America* (Longman, 2003).

54. Frances Fox Piven and Richard A. Cloward, "Prospects for Voter Registration Reform: A Report on the Experiences of the Human SERVE Campaign," *PS: Political Science and Politics* 18 (Summer 1985), p. 589.

55. Ibid., p. 589.

56. Raymond E. Wolfinger and Steven J. Rosenstone, *Who Votes?* (Yale University Press, 1980), p. 109.

57. E. E. Schattschneider, *The Semisovereign People* (Dryden Press, 1975), p. 96.

58. Stephen Earl Bennett and David Resnick, "The Implications of Nonvoting for Democracy in the United States," *American Journal of Political Science* 84 (August 1990), pp. 771–802.

59. Bruce E. Keith, David B. Magleby, Candice J. Nelson, Elizabeth Orr, Mark C. Westlye, and Raymond E. Wolfinger, *The Myth of the Independent Voter* (University of California Press, 1992), pp. 60–75; and 2000 National Election Study, Center for Political Studies, University of Michigan, Ann Arbor.

60. Martin P. Wattenberg, *The Rise of Candidate Centered Politics: Presidential Elections of the 1980s* (Harvard University Press, 1991).

61. David Menefee–Libey, *The Triumph of Campaign-Centered Politics* (Chatham House/Seven Bridges Press, 2000).

62. Barry Goldwater, quoted in Theodore H. White, *The Making of the President, 1964* (Athenaeum, 1965), p. 217.

63. William H. Flanigan and Nancy H. Zingale, *Political Behavior of the American Electorate*, 8th ed. (CQ Press, 1994), p. 173.

64. Tim Graham, "Media-Powered Howard," National Review Online, January 30, 2004.

65. www.cnn.com/ELECTION/2004/pages/results/states/US/P/OO/epolls.O.html.

66. J. Merrill Shanks and Warren E. Miller, "Policy Direction and Performance Evaluation: Complementary Explanations of the Reagan Elections," *British Journal of Political Science* 20 (1990), pp. 143–235; and Warren E. Miller and J. Merrill Shanks, "Policy Direction and Performance Evaluation: Comparing George Bush's Victory with Those of Ronald Reagan in 1980 and 1984," paper presented at the annual meeting of the American Political Science Association, Atlanta, August 31–September 2, 1989.

67. Amihai Glazer, "The Strategy of Candidate Ambiguity," *American Political Science Review* 84 (March 1990), pp. 237–241.

68. Robert S. Erikson and David W. Romero, "Candidate Equilibrium and the Behavioral Model of the Vote," *American Political Science Review* 84 (December 1990), p. 1122.

69. Morris P. Fiorina, *Retrospective Voting in American National Elections* (Yale University Press, 1981).

70. www.cnn.com/ELECTION/2000/results/index.epolls.html.

71. Gerald H. Kramer, "Short-Term Fluctuations in U.S. Voting Behavior, 1896–1964," *American Political Science Review* 65 (March 1971),

pp. 131–143. See also Edward R. Tufte, "Determinants of the Outcomes of Midterm Congressional Elections," *American Political Science Review* 69 (September 1975), pp. 812–826; and Andrew E. Busch, *Horses in Midstream: U.S. Midterm Elections and Their Consequences* (University of Pittsburgh Press, 1999).

72. John R. Hibbing and John R. Alford, "The Educational Impact of Economic Conditions: Who Is Held Responsible?" *American Journal of Political Science* 25 (August 1981), pp. 423–439; and Morris P. Fiorina, "Who Is Held Responsible? Further Evidence on the Hibbing-Alford Thesis," *American Journal of Political Science* (February 1983), pp. 158–164.

73. Robert M. Stein, "Economic Voting for Governor and U.S. Senator: The Electoral Consequences of Federalism," *Journal of Politics* 52 (February 1990), pp. 29–53.

74. www.cnn.com/ELECTION/2004/pages/results/states/US/P/OO/epolls.O.html.

Chapter 9

1. *1994 Census of Governments* (U.S. Government Printing Office, 1995), vol. 1, no. 2, p. 1.

2. United States Senate, at www.senate.gov/general/contact_information/senators_cfm.cfm.

3. See U.S. Term Limits, at www.termlimits.org.

4. In the 1992 and 1994 National Election Studies, approximately 78 percent of Americans favored term limits. *1992 National Election Study and 1994 National Election Study* (Center for Political Studies, University of Michigan, 1992, 1994).

5. *U.S. Term Limits Inc.* v. *Thornton*, 514 U.S. 799 (1995).

6. For an insightful examination of electoral rules, see Bernard Grofman and Arend Lijphart, eds., *Electoral Laws and Their Political Consequences* (Agathon Press, 1986).

7. Arend Lijphart, "The Political Consequences of Electoral Laws, 1945–85," *American Political Science Review* 84 (June 1990), pp. 481–495. See also David M. Farrell, *Electoral Systems: A Comparative Introduction* (Macmillan, 2001).

8. www.fairvote.org/e_college/faithless.htm.

9. As noted, one of Gore's electors abstained, reducing his vote from 267 to 266; CNN, at www.cnn.com/2001/ALLPOLITICS/stories/01/06/electoral.vote/index.html.

10. Paul D. Schumaker and Burdett A. Loomis, *Choosing a President: The Electoral College and Beyond* (Seven Bridges Press, 2002), p. 60. See also George Rabinowitz and Stuart Elaine MacDonald, "The Power of the States in U.S. Presidential Elections," *American Political Science Review* 80 (March 1986), pp. 65–87; and Dany M. Adkison and Christopher Elliott, "The Electoral College: A Misunderstood Institution," *PS: Political Science and Politics* 30 (March 1997), pp. 77–80.

11. See, for example, David R. Mayhew, *Congress: The Electoral Connection* (Yale University Press, 1974); Richard F. Fenno Jr., *Home Style: House Members in Their Districts* (Little, Brown, 1978); and James E. Campbell, "The Return of Incumbents: The Nature of Incumbency Advantage," *Western Political Quarterly* 36 (September 1983), pp. 434–444.

12. Gary King and Andrew Gelman, "Systemic Consequences of Incumbency Advantage in U.S. House Elections," *American Journal of Political Science* 35 (February 1991), pp. 110–137.

13. Alan I. Abramowitz, "Economic Conditions, Presidential Popularity, and Voting Behavior in Midterm Congressional Elections," *Journal of Politics* 47 (February 1985), pp. 31–43. See also Gary C. Jacobson, *The Politics of Congressional Elections*, 5th ed. (Addison-Wesley, 2001), pp. 146–153.

14. See Edward R. Tufte, *Political Control of the Economy* (Princeton University Press, 1978); see also his "Determinants of the Outcomes of Midterm Congressional Elections," *American Political Science Review* 69 (September 1975), pp. 812–826. For a more recent discussion of the same subject, see Jacobson, *Politics of Congressional Elections*, pp. 123–178.

15. Alan I. Abramowitz and Jeffrey A. Segal, "Determinants of the Outcomes of U.S. Senate Elections," *Journal of Politics* 48 (1986), pp. 433–439.

16. This includes the postelection switch of Alabama Senator Richard Shelby to the Republican Party.

17. Paul S. Herrnson, *Congressional Elections: Campaigning at Home and in Washington*, 4th ed. (CQ Press, 2004), pp. 45, 48.

18. Linda L. Fowler and Robert D. McClure, *Political Ambition: Who Decides to Run for Congress* (Yale University Press, 1989); Paul S. Herrnson, *Congressional Elections: Campaigning at Home and in Washington*, 4th ed. (CQ Press, 2004), p. 45.

19. Kathleen Hall Jamieson, *Everything You Think You Know About Politics . . . and Why You're Wrong* (Basic Books, 2000), p. 38.

20. For a discussion of different explanations of the impact of incumbency, see Keith Krehbiel and John R. Wright, "The Incumbency Effect in Congressional Elections: A Test of Two Explanations," *American Journal of Political Science* 27 (February 1983), p. 140.

21. Roll Call, "Roll Call Casualty List," *Roll Call Politics,* November 5, 1998, p. 15; "Senate, House, Gubernatorial Results," *Congressional Quarterly Weekly,* November 11, 2000, pp. 2694–2703.

22. "Financial Activity of Senate and House General Election Campaigns," Federal Election Commission at www.ftp.fec.gov/fec.

23. Albert D. Cover, "One Good Term Deserves Another: The Advantages of Incumbency in Congressional Elections," *American Journal of Political Science* 21 (August 1977), pp. 523–542; Morris P. Fiorina, *Congress: Keystone of the Washington Establishment* (Yale University Press, 1978); and David Mayhew, *Congress: The Electoral Connection* (Yale University Press, 1974), pp. 52–53.

24. Mayhew, *Congress,* p. 61; Richard F. Fenno Jr., *Congressmen in Committees* (Little, Brown, 1973); and Steven S. Smith and Christopher J. Deering, *Committees in Congress,* 3d ed. (CQ Press, 1997).

25. Candice J. Nelson, "Spending in the 2000 Elections," in *Financing the 2000 Election* ed., David B. Magleby, (Brookings Institution Press, 2002), pp. 28–30.

26. Jonathan S. Krasno, *Challengers, Competition, and Reelection: Comparing Senate and House Elections* (Yale University Press, 1994), p. 2.

27. Alan I. Abramowitz, "Explaining Senate Election Outcomes," *American Political Science Review* 82 (June 1988), pp. 385–403.

28. David B. Magleby and J. Quin Monson, eds., *The Last Hurrah?: Soft Money and Issue Advocacy in the 2002 Congressional Elections* (Brookings Institution Press, 2004).

29. David B. Magleby, "More Bang for the Buck: Campaign Spending in Small State U.S. Senate Elections," paper presented at the annual meeting of the Western Political Science Association, Salt Lake City, March 30–April 1, 1989.

30. Associated Press writer, "Edwards Actions Doing Talking Over Possible Presidential Run," *Associated Press State and Local Wire* for North Carolina, June 18, 2001; and Christopher Graff, "Vermont Governor Takes First Step Toward Presidential Campaign," *The Associated Press State & Local Wire* of Vermont, November 19, 2001.

31. www.thegreenpapers.com/P04/tally.phtml.

32. Republican Delegate Selection and Voter Eligibility, at www.thegreenpapers.com/P04/R-DSVE.phtml.

33. The descriptions of these types of primaries are drawn from James W. Davis, *Presidential Primaries,* rev. ed. (Greenwood Press, 1984), chap. 3. See pp. 56–63 for specifics on each state (and Puerto Rico). This material is used with the permission of the publisher.

34. Paul T. David and James W. Caesar, *Proportional Representation in Presidential Nominating Politics* (University Press of Virginia, 1980), pp. 9–11.

35. See Rhodes Cook, *Race for the Presidency: Winning the 2004 Nomination* (CQ Press, 2004), p. 5. See also the Republican National Committee, at www.rnc.org.

36. Nelson W. Polsby and Aaron Wildavsky, *Presidential Elections: Strategies and Structures of American Politics,* 11th ed. (Rowman & Littlefield, 2004), p. 110.

37. The Green Papers, *The Green Papers, 2004 Presidential Primaries, Caucuses, and Conventions: New York Republican,* www.thegreenpapers.com/P04/NY-R.phtml.

38. Costas Panagopoulos, "Election Issues 2004 in Depth," *Campaigns & Elections,* May 2004, p. 48.

39. Jonathan Finer, "No Tea, but Democrats Get the Party Started," *The Washington Post,* July 29, 2003, p. A4.

40. National Association of Secretaries of State, at www.nass.org/issues.html#primaryplan.

41. Federal Elections Commission, "2004 Presidential Primary Dates and Candidates Filing Deadlines for Ballot Access," May 26, 2004, at www.fec.gov.

42. David Redlawsk and Arthur Sanders, "Groups and Grassroots in the Iowa Caucuses," in *Outside Money in the 2000 Presidential Primaries and Congressional Elections,* ed. David B. Magleby, in *PS Online* (June 2001), at www.apsanet.org/PS/june01/redlawsk.cfm.

43. Blake Morrison, "Dean Scream Gaining Cult-Like Status on Web," *USA TODAY,* January 22, 2004, p. 4A.

44. "A Useful Piece of Scream Therapy," *The Economist,* February 14, 2004, United States Section.

45. The viewership of conventions has declined as the amount of time devoted to conventions dropped. In 1988, Democrats averaged 27.1 million viewers and Republicans 24.5 million. By 1996, viewership for the Democrats was 18 million viewers on average and for the Republicans,

16.6 million. See John Carmody, "The TV Column," *The Washington Post,* September 2, 1996, p. D4. Viewership figures improved somewhat in 2000: Democrats averaged 20.6 million viewers and Republicans 19.2 million. See Don Aucoin, "Democrats Hold TV Ratings Edge," *Boston Globe,* August 19, 2000, p. F3.

46. Stephan J. Wayne, *The Road to the White House, 2004: The Politics of Presidential Elections* (Wadsworth, 2004), chap. 5.

47. Jeff Fishel, *Presidents and Promises* (CQ Press, 1984), pp. 26–28.

48. See White House, Education Reform: No Child Left Behind Act, at www.whitehouse.gov/infocus/education.

49. Adam Nagourney, "Kerry Camp Sees Edwards Helping with Rural Vote," *The New York Times,* July 9, 2004, p. 1.

50. John M. Glionna, "The Race to the White House; Nader Bid for Spot on Oregon's Ballot Fails; The State was the First Stop in the Populist Candidate's Quest to Qualify in all 50 States," *Los Angeles Times,* April 6, 2004, p. 14.

51. Arthur Kane, "Reform Party Endorsement Boosts Nader: The Liberal Activist is Now Eligible to Ease onto the Presidential Ballot in Seven States, Including Colorado," *The Denver Post,* May 13, 2004, p. A1.

52. Election Reform.org, at www.ballot-access.org.

53. CNN, "Burden of Proof," August 9, 2000; www.time.com/time/election2004/article/0,18471,641158,00.html.

54. Charles Babington, "Staggering Sum-Raising," *The Washington Post,* June 19, 2004, p. A6.

55. Lisa Getter, "GOP Can't Beat '3rd Party' Groups, So It Forms Them," *Los Angeles Times,* June 6, 2004, p. A20.

56. Sidney Kraus, *The Great Debates: Kennedy vs. Nixon, 1960* (Indiana University Press, 1962). See also Myles Martel, *Political Campaign Debates* (Longman, 1983).

57. "Televised Debate History, 1960–1996," at www.museum.tv/debateweb/html/history/1976/video.htm.

58. Stephen Koff, "VP Debate to Have Free-Flowing Exchange," *Plain Dealer* (Cleveland, Ohio), June 18, 2004, p. A21.

59. Commission on Presidential Debates, at www.debates.org/pages/news_040617_p.html.

60. Robert S. Erikson, "Economic Conditions and the Presidential Vote," *American Political Science Review* 83 (June 1989), pp. 567–575. Class-based voting has also become more important. See Robert S. Erikson, Thomas O. Lancaster, and David W. Romers, "Group Components of the Presidential Vote, 1952–1984," *Journal of Politics* 51 (May 1989), pp. 337–346.

61. David B. Magleby and Candice J. Nelson, *The Money Chase: Congressional Campaign Finance Reform* (Brookings Institution Press, 1990), pp. 13–14.

62. See Senate Committee on Governmental Affairs, "1997 Special Investigation in Connection with the 1996 Federal Election Campaigns," www.senate.gov/~gov_affairs/sireport.htm.

63. *Buckley* v. *Valeo,* 424 U.S. 1 (1976).

64. See Herbert E. Alexander and Monica Bauer, *Financing the 1988 Election* (Westview Press, 1991); & Frank J. Sorauf, *Inside Campaign Finance: Myths and Realities* (Yale University Press, 1992); and Herbert E. Alexander, *Financing Politics: Money, Elections, and Political Reform* (CQ Press, 1992).

65. Federal Election Commission, Public Disclosure Office, personal communication, July 23, 2004; see also Campaign Finance Institute, "Participation, Competition, Engagement: Reviving and Improving Public Financing for Presidential Nomination Politics," September 22, 2003, p. 52.

66. Beth Donovan, "Parties Turned Soft Money Law into Hard and Fast Spending," *Congressional Quarterly Weekly,* May 15, 1993, pp. 1196–1197; David E. Rosenbaum, "In Political Money Game, the Year of Big Loopholes," *The New York Times,* December 26, 1996, p. A1; and "Party Fundraising Escalates," at www.fec.gov.

67. David B. Magleby and J. Quin Monson, eds., 2004. *The Last Hurrah?: Soft Money and Issue Advocacy in the 2002 Congressional Elections* (Brookings Institution Press, 2004), pp. 82–83.

68. See Joseph A. Pika, "Campaign Spending and Activity in the 2000 Delaware U.S. Senate Race," in *Election Advocacy: Soft Money and Issue Advocacy in the 2000 Congressional Elections,* ed. David B. Magleby (Center for the Study of Elections and Democracy, Brigham Young University, 2001), pp. 51–61.

69. David B. Magleby, "Dictum Without Data: The Myth of Issue Advocacy and Party Building," at csed.byu.edu/publications/dictum.doc.

70. David B. Magleby and J. Quin Monson, "Campaign 2002: 'The Perfect Storm'" at www.apsanet.org/PS/july03/magleby.pdf.

71. David. B. Magleby, ed., *The Other Campaign: Soft Money and Issue Advocacy in the 2000 Congressional Elections* (Rowman & Littlefield, 2003); and

David B. Magleby and J. Quin Monson, *The Last Hurrah? Soft Money and Issue Advocacy in the 2002 Congressional Elections* (Brookings Institute Press, 2004), pp. 159–179.

72. Magleby and Monson, *The Last Hurrah?*, pp. 159–179.

73. Craig B. Holman and Luke P. McLoughlin, *Buying Time, 2000: Television Advertising in the 2000 Federal Elections* (Brennan Center for Justice, New York University School of Law, 2001), p. 33.

74. Nicholas Confessore, "Bush's Secret Stash: Why the GOP War Chest Is Even Bigger than You Think," *The Washington Monthly,* May 18, 2004, pp. 117–122.

75. Morton M. Kondracke, "McCain to Lead New Reform Fight for Free TV Time," *Roll Call,* May 30, 2002, at www.rollcall.com/pages/columns/kondracke/00/2002/kond0530.html.

76. Rick Hampson, "Former Banker Was Big Spender," *USA Today,* November 9, 2000, p. A9.

77. Federal Election Commission, "Disclosure Data Base: PAS200.ZIP," at www.fec.gov. See also David B. Magleby and Jason Richard Beal, "Independent Expenditures and Internal Communications," in *The Other Campaign,* ed., Magleby (Rowman & Littlefield, 2003), p. 83.

78. BCRA does allow candidates to pay themselves out of their campaign funds, something that helps less affluent candidates run. But given the high cost of campaign, such a strategy is often not going to be helpful to winning election.

79. Federal Election Commission, "2000–2001 Financial Activity of Senate and House General Election Campaigns," at www.fec.gov. Federal Election Commission, "1999–2000 Financial Activity of Senate and House General Election Campaigns," at www.fec.gov.

80. Federal Elections Commission, at herndon1.sdrdc.com/fecimg/srssea.html.

81. See Todd Donovan and Shawn Bowler, *Reforming the Republic: Democratic Institutions for a New America* (Prentice Hall, 2004).

82. Curtis B. Gans, Director, Committee for the Study of the American Electorate, facsimile to author, September 22, 2004.

83. The President's Commission for a National Agenda for the Eighties, *A National Agenda for the Eighties* (U.S. Government Printing Office, 1980), p. 97, proposed holding four presidential primaries, scheduled about one month apart.

84. Nelson W. Polsby, *Consequences of Party Reform* (Oxford University Press, 1983), p. 118.

85. Thomas E. Cronin and Robert Loevy, "The Case for a National Primary Convention Plan," *Public Opinion,* December 1982–January 1983, pp. 50–53.

86. Barbara Norrander and Greg W. Smith, "Type of Contest, Candidate Strategy, and Turnout in Presidential Primaries," *American Politics Quarterly* 13 (January 1985), p. 28.

87. Neal R. Peirce and Lawrence Longley, *The People's President: The Electoral College in American History and the Direct-Vote Alternative,* 2d ed. (Yale University Press, 1981), describe and advocate the direct-vote alternative. Nelson W. Polsby and Aaron B. Wildavsky, *Presidential Elections: Contemporary Strategies of American Politics,* 10th ed. (Chatham House, 2000), favor the present system.

88. Al Baker, "New York Risking the Loss of Ballot Equipment Money," *The New York Times,* April 29, 2004, p. B05.

89. Ibid.

90. Maha Al-Azar, "Broad Election Reforms Are Urged; Education Called As Crucial As Machines," *The Washington Post,* July 17, 2003, p. T04; Harris N. Miller, "Electronic Voting Is a Solution," *USA Today,* February 4, 2004, p. 14A.

Chapter 10

1. Donna Britt, "Janet's 'Reveal' Lays Bare an Insidious Trend, *The Washington Post,* February 4, 2004, p. B1.

2. Kelefa Sanneh, "During Halftime Show," *The New York Times,* February 2, 2004, p. D4.

3. Frank Ahrens, "Critics Blame Big Media for Sleaze Factor," *The Washington Post,* February 11, 2004, p. E1.

4. Frank Ahrens, "Critics Blame Big Media for Sleaze Factor," *The Washington Post,* February 11, 2004, p. E1.

5. www.cnn.com/2004/US/02/02/superbowl.jackson/.

6. Frank Rich, "My Hero, Janet Jackson," *The New York Times,* February 15, 2004, p. B1.

7. Barabara Meltz, "Kids May Need to Talk about a Revealing Halftime Show," *The Boston Globe,* February 5, 2004, p. D1.

8. Jube Shriver Jr., "FCC Rules Bono Remark Is Indecent," *Los Angeles Times,* March 19, 2004, p. C1.

9. Jonathon Krim, "Congress Acts to Curb Offensive Program; Senate Panel Proposes Fines, Delayed Media Consolidation," *The Washington Post,* March 10, 2004, p. E01.

10. Clear Channel Communications, *Howard Stern Show Taken Off Clear Channel Stations* (San Antonio, Texas: Corporate Communications, 2004).

11. William Rivers, *The Other Government* (Universe Books, 1982); Douglas Cater, *The Fourth Branch of Government* (Houghton Mifflin, 1959); Dom Bonafede, "The Washington Press: An Interpreter or a Participant in Policy Making?" *National Journal,* April 24, 1982, pp. 716–721; Michael Ledeen, "Learning to Say 'No' to the Press," *Public Interest 73* (Fall 1983), p. 113.

12. Leslie G. Moeller, "The Big Four: Mass Media Actualities and Expectations," in *Beyond Media: New Approaches to Mass Communication,* eds. Richard W. Budd and Brent D. Ruben (Transaction Books, 1988), p. 15.

13. Pew Research Center for the People and the Press, "Far More Voters Believe Election Outcome Matters," questionnaire, March 25, 2004. people-press.org/reports/print.php3?PageID=802. One service that e-mails customized news and reminders to subscribers is infobeat.com.

14. U.S. Bureau of the Census, *Statistical Abstract of the United States, 2001* (Government Printing Office, 2001), tabs. 1125 and 1126.

15. Journalism.org, "Evening News Share," at www.stateofthenewsmedia. org/chartland.asp?id=210&ct=line&dir=&sort=&col1_box=1&col2_box=1 &col3_box=1, March 15, 2004.

16. Journalism.org, "Cable TV," at www.stateofthenewsmedia.org/narrative_cabletv_audience.asp?cat=3&media=5, March 15, 2004.

17. David B. Magleby and J. Quin Monson, eds., *The Last Hurrah?* (Brookings Institution Press, 2004); David B. Magleby, ed., *The Other Campaign* (Rowman & Littlefield, 2003); David B. Magleby, ed., *Outside Money* (Rowman & Littlefield, 2000).

18. David B. Magleby, ed., *Dictum Without Data: The Myth of Issue Advocacy and Party Building* (Center for the Study of Elections and Democracy, 2000); David B. Magleby, "Party and Interest Group Electioneering in Federal Elections," in *Inside the Campaign Finance Battle,* eds., Anthony Corrado, Thomas E. Mann, and Trevor Potter (Brookings Institution Press, 2003), p. 147.

19. Magleby and Monson, eds., *The Last Hurrah?*; Magleby, ed., *The Other Campaign;* Magleby, ed., *Outside Money.*

20. Journalism.org, "Local TV," at www.stateofthenewsmedia.org/narrative_localty_contentanalysis.asp?cat=2&media=6, March 15, 2004. See also, Marc Fisher, "TV Stations Offer a Clear Picture of Indifference," *The Washington Post,* September 26, 2000, p. B1.

21. Alliance for Better Campaigns, *Political Standard 4* (March 2001), p. 6.

22. www.localnewsarchive.org/pdf/LocalTV2002.pdf.

23. David B. Magleby, "Direct Legislation in the American States," in *Referendums Around the World: The Growing Use of Direct Democracy,* eds. David Butler and Austin Ranney (AEI Press, 1994), pp. 218–257.

24. U.S. Bureau of the Census, *Statistical Abstract of the United States, 2003* (Government Printing Office, 2003), tab. 1126.

25. Leonard Wiener, "Radio's Future Shock," *U.S. News & World Report,* December 2, 2002, p. 40.

26. *Statistical Abstract of the United States, 2003,* p. 722.

27. Newspaper Association of America, at www.naa.org/marketscope/pdfs/ReaderTrendDaily_Age.pdf.

28. Audit Bureau of Circulations, at abcas1.accessabc.com/ecirc.

29. Elizabeth Weise, "With Dissidents on Board, Net Could See Revolutions," *USA Today,* October 31, 2000, p. 3D.

30. Inktomi, "Web Surpasses One Billion Documents," at www.inktomi.com/new/press/billion.html, January 18, 2000.

31. Pew Research Center for the People and the Press, at people-press.org/reports/print.php3?PageID=748.

32. Amy Poftak, Net-Wise Teens: Safety, Ethics, and Innovation, *Technology & Learning,* August 1, 2002, p. 36.

33. "Inside the 2004 Campaign Tool Chest: Blogs and Online Voting," *Los Angeles Times,* January 5, 2004, p. A10.

34. Mark Singer, "Running on Instinct. Howard Dean's Critics Say He Is Winging It. Can That Get Him to the White House?" *New Yorker,* January 12, 2004, pg. 43.

35. Pew Research Center for the People and the Press, "Web News Takes Off," press release, June 8, 1998, p. 1; Pew Research Center for the People and the Press, Survey Reports, "Public's News Habits Little Changed by September 11," June 9, 2002. See people-press.org/reports.

36. James Fallows, *Breaking the News: How the Media Undermine American Democracy* (Pantheon Books, 1996), p. 3.

37. Paul Starobin, "Heeding the Call," *National Journal,* November 30, 1996, pp. 2584–2589.

38. Howard Kurtz, "Jayson Blair, Continued; With a Story of Lies, The Fallen Writer Hopes to Turn a Page," *The Washington Post,* March 7, 2004, sec. D01.

39. Jacques Steinburg, "Editor of USA Today Resigns; Cites Failure Over Fabrications," *The New York Times,* April 21, 2004, p. A1.

40. See Robert A. Rutland, *Newsmongers: Journalism in the Life of the Nation, 1690–1972* (Dial Press, 1973).

41. Quoted in Frank Luther Mott, *American Journalism,* 3d ed. (Macmillan, 1962), p. 412.

42. During the 1930s, more than 1,000 speeches were made by members of Congress on one network alone. See Edward W. Chester, *Radio, Television, and American Politics* (Sheed & Ward, 1969), p. 62.

43. Frances Perkins, quoted in James MacGregor Burns, *Roosevelt: The Lion and the Fox* (Harcourt, 1956), p. 205.

44. Gannett Corp., at www.gannett.com/map/gan007.htm.

45. "California, Southland Focus; Tribune Gets Antitrust Approval in *Times* Deal," *Los Angeles Times,* April 7, 2000, p. C2.

46. www.pbs.org/wgbh/pages/frontline/shows/cool/giants.

47. Seth Schiesel, "FCC Rules on Ownership Under Review," *The New York Times,* April 3, 2002, p. C1.

48. Paul Davidson, "Spending Bill Settles Two Key Issues," *USA Today,* January 23, 2004, p. B3.

49. Stephen Labaton, "Court Orders FCC to Rethink New Rules on Growth of Media," *The New York Times,* June 25, 2004, p. 1.

50. Shanto Iyengar and Donald R. Kinder, *News That Matters* (University of Chicago Press, 1987).

51. Steven J. Simmons, *The Fairness Doctrine and the Media* (University of California Press, 1978).

52. "Political Fairness on TV," *Christian Science Monitor,* October 17, 2000, p. 10.

53. www.pewinternet.org/reports/chart/asp?. Accessed April 13, 2004.

54. Harvey G. Zeidenstein, "News Media Perception of White House News Management," *Presidential Studies Quarterly* 24 (Summer 1984), pp. 391–398.

55. Elihu Katz and Paul Lazarsfeld, *Personal Influence: The Part Played by People in the Flow of Mass Communications* (Free Press, 1955).

56. See Doris A. Graber, "Say It with Pictures: The Impact of Audiovisual News on Public Opinion Formation," paper presented at the annual meeting of the Midwest Political Science Association, Chicago, April 1987; and Benjamin I. Page, Robert Y. Shapiro, and Glenn R. Dempsey. "What Moves Public Opinion?" *American Political Science Review* 76 (March 1987), pp. 23–43.

57. See, for example, Jack Dennis, "Preadult Learning of Political Independence: Media and Family Communications Effects," *Communication Research* 13 (July 1987), pp. 401–433; and Olive Stevens, *Children Talking Politics* (Robertson, 1982).

58. See Angus Campbell, Philip E. Converse, Warren E. Miller, and Donald E. Stokes, *The American Voter* (Wiley, 1960).

59. Paul Lazarsfeld, Bernard Berelson, and Hazel Gaudet, *The People's Choice: How the Voter Makes Up His Mind in a Presidential Campaign,* 3d ed. (Columbia University Press, 1968); Bernard Berelson, Paul Lazarsfeld, and William McPhee, *Voting: A Study of Opinion Formation in a Presidential Campaign* (University of Chicago Press, 1954).

60. Pew Research Center for the People and the Press, "Scandal Reporting Faulted for Bias and Inaccuracy: Popular Policies and Unpopular Press Lift Clinton Ratings," press release, February 6, 1998, p. 6.

61. Gallup Organization, at www.gallup.com/poll-archives/980926.htm.

62. Stuart Oskamp, ed., *Television as a Social Issue* (Sage, 1988); James W. Carey, ed., *Media, Myths, and Narratives: Television and the Press* (Sage, 1988).

63. Doris A. Graber, *Processing the News: How People Tame the Information Tide,* 2d ed. (Longman, 1988), pp. 107–113.

64. Times Mirror Center for the People and the Press, "Times Mirror News Interest Index," press releases, January 16 and February 28, 1992.

65. John K. Robinson and Mark R. Levy, eds., *The Main Source: Learning from Television News* (Sage, 1986).

66. Graber, *Processing the News,* p. 115.

67. Tides Center, "Internet and American Life," at www.pewinternet.org/reports/reports.asp. Accessed April 13, 2004.

68. Rush Limbaugh, *See, I Told You So* (Pocket Books, 1993), p. 326.

69. See Nelson Polsby, *Consequences of Party Reform* (Oxford University Press, 1983), pp. 142–146. See also Stanley Rothman and S. Robert Lichter, "Media and Business Elites: Two Classes in Conflict!" *Public Interest* 69 (Fall 1982), pp. 119–125.

70. Michael Parenti, *Inventing Reality: The Politics of the Mass Media* (St. Martin's Press, 1986), p. 35.

71. Rick Lyman, "Multimedia Deal: The History; 2 Commanding Publishers, 2 Powerful Empires," *The New York Times,* March 14, 2000, p. C16.

72. David Broder, "Beware of the 'Insider' Syndrome: Why Newsmakers and News Reporters Shouldn't Get Too Cozy," *The Washington Post,* December 4, 1988, p. A21; see also Broder, "Thin-Skinned Journalists," *The Washington Post,* January 11, 1989, p. A21.

73. Daniel P. Moynihan, "The Presidency and the Press," *Commentary* 51 (March 1971), p. 43.

74. S. Robert Lichter, Stanley Rothman, and Linda S. Lichter, *The Media Elite* (Adler & Adler, 1986).

75. Larry J. Sabato, *Feeding Frenzy: How Attack Journalism Has Transformed American Politics* (Free Press, 1991).

76. See Thomas Patterson, *Out of Order* (Knopf, 1993); Paul Weaver, *News and the Culture of Lying* (Free Press, 1993); and Anthony Munro, "Yet Another Conspiracy Theory," *Columbia Journalism Review* 33 (November 1994), p. 71.

77. Maxwell McCombs and Donald Shaw, "The Agenda-setting Function of Mass Media," *Public Opinion Quarterly* 36 (1972) pp. 176–185.

78. Shanto Iyengar, Mark D. Peters, and Donald R. Kinder, "Experimental Demonstrations of the 'Not-So-Minimal' Consequences of Television News Programs," *American Political Science Review* 76 (December 1982), pp. 848–858.

79. Ibid.; Maxwell E. McCombs and Donald L. Shaw, "The Agenda-Setting Function of the Mass Media," *Public Opinion Quarterly* 36 (1972), pp. 176–187; Maxwell E. McCombs and Sheldon Gilbert, "News Influence on Our Pictures of the World," in *Perspectives on Media Effects,* eds. Jennings Bryant and Dolf Gillman (Erlbaum, 1986), pp. 1–15; and Iyengar and Kinder, *News That Matters.*

80. Quoted in Michael J. Robinson and Margaret A. Sheehan, *Over the Wire and on TV: CBS and UPI in Campaign '80* (Russell Sage Foundation, 1983), p. xiii.

81. ABC News, at abcnews.go.com/sections/us/DailyNews/WTC_MAIN010914.html.

82. David B. Magleby, *Direct Legislation: Voting on Ballot Propositions in the United States* (Johns Hopkins University Press, 1984).

83. Randal C. Archibold, "Edwards Tries Personal Touch to Gain in Iowa," *The New York Times,* December 3, 2003, p. A29; and Kathy Kiely, "Clark Catching On With Voters as Contests Near," *USA Today,* January 9, 2004, p. 4A.

84. Maureen Dowd, "Whence the Wince?" *The New York Times,* March 11, 2004, p. A29.

85. Mike Allen, "Ship Carrying Bush Delayed Return," *The Washington Post,* May 8, 2003, p. A29.

86. Paul T. David, Ralph M. Goldman, and Richard C. Bain, *The Politics of the National Party Conventions* (Brookings Institution Press, 1960), pp. 300–301.

87. Richard Davis, *The Press and American Politics: The New Mediator,* 2d ed. (Prentice Hall, 1996), p. 279.

88. Frank I. Lutz, *Candidates, Consultants, and Campaigns* (Blackwell, 1988), chap. 7.

89. www.pewinternet.org/reports/chart.asp?. Accessed April 13, 2004.

90. Larry J. Sabato, *The Rise of Political Consultants* (Basic Books, 1981).

91. See Sabato, *Rise of Political Consultants;* James David Barber, *The Pulse of Politics: Electing Presidents in the Media Age* (Norton, 1980); and Fred Barnes, "The Myth of Political Consultants," *New Republic,* June 16, 1986, p. 16.

92. Quoted in Sabato, *Rise of Political Consultants,* p. 144.

93. Thomas E. Patterson, *The Mass Media Election: How Americans Choose Their President* (Praeger, 1980), chap. 12.

94. John H. Aldrich, *Before the Convention* (University of Chicago Press, 1980), p. 65. See also Patterson, *Mass Media Election.*

95. John Foley et al., *Nominating a President: The Process and the Press* (Praeger, 1980), p. 39. For the press's treatment of incumbents, see James Glen Stovall, "Incumbency and News Coverage of the 1980 Presidential Election Campaign," *Western Political Quarterly* 37 (December 1984), p. 621.

96. Priscilla Southwell, "Voter Turnout in the 1986 Congressional Elections: The Media as Demobilizer?" *American Politics Quarterly* 19 (January 1991), pp. 96–108.

97. William Glaberson, "A New Press Role: Solving Problems," *The New York Times,* October 3, 1994, p. D6.

98. Patterson, *Mass Media Election,* pp. 115–117.

99. Raymond Wolfinger and Peter Linguiti, "Tuning In and Tuning Out," *Public Opinion* 4 (February–March 1981), pp. 56–60.

100. Marvin Kalb, "Financial Pressure Doomed Networks on Election Night," *Deseret News,* December 3, 2000, p. AA7.

101. Lewis Wolfson, *The Untapped Power of the Press* (Praeger, 1985), p. 79.

102. Stephen Hess, *The Government-Press Connection* (Brookings Institution Press, 1984), p. 106.

103. Lloyd Cutler, "Foreign Policy on Deadline," *Foreign Policy* 56 (Fall 1984), p. 114.

104. Michael B. Grossman and Martha Joynt Kumar, *Portraying the President* (Johns Hopkins University Press, 1981), pp. 255–263; and Fredric T. Smoller, *The Six o'Clock Presidency: A Theory of Presidential Press Relations in the Age of Television* (Praeger, 1990), pp. 31–49.

105. Susan Heilmann Miller, "News Coverage of Congress: The Search for the Ultimate Spokesperson," *Journalism Quarterly* 54 (Autumn 1977), pp. 459–465.

106. See Stephen Hess, *Live from Capitol Hill: Studies of Congress and the Media* (Brookings Institution Press, 1991), pp. 102–110.

107. Richard Davis, "Whither the Congress and the Supreme Court? The Television News Portrayal of American National Government," *Television Quarterly* 22 (1987), pp. 55–63.

108. For a discussion of the Supreme Court and public opinion, see Thomas R. Marshall, *Public Opinion and the Supreme Court* (Unwin Hyman, 1989); and Gregory Caldiera, "Neither the Purse nor the Sword: Dynamics of Public Confidence in the Supreme Court," *American Political Science Review* 80 (December 1986), pp. 1209–1228.

109. For a discussion of the relationship between the Supreme Court and the press, see Richard Davis, "Lifting the Shroud: News Media Portrayal of the U.S. Supreme Court," *Communications and the Law* 9 (October 1987), pp. 43–58; and Elliot E. Slotnick, "Media Coverage of Supreme Court Decision Making: Problems and Prospects," *Judicature* (October–November 1991), pp. 128–142.

110. Todd S. Purdum, "TV Political News in California Is Shrinking, Study Confirms," *The New York Times,* January, 13, 1999, p. A11.

111. Times Mirror Center, "Campaign '92," *Times Mirror,* January 16, 1992.

112. Quoted in Herbert Schmertz, "The Making of the Presidency," *Presidential Studies Quarterly* 16 (Winter 1986), p. 25.

Chapter 11

1. See Sarah A. Binder, "Going Nowhere: A Gridlocked Congress?" *The Brookings Review,* Winter, 2000, for an analysis of the growing distance between the two parties and the impact on the national policy agenda.

2. Charles Warren, *The Making of the Constitution* (Little, Brown, 1928), p. 195.

3. Congressional Quarterly, *Origins and Development of Congress* (CQ Press, 1982), pp. 53–54.

4. Richard F. Fenno Jr., *Home Style: House Members in Their Districts* (Little, Brown, 1978), p. 168.

5. *Bush* v. *Vera,* 517 U.S. 952 (1996).

6. *Hunt* v. *Cromartie,* 532 U.S. 234 (2001).

7. Frances E. Lee and Bruce I. Oppenheimer, *Sizing Up the Senate: The Unequal Consequences of Equal Representation* (University of Chicago Press, 1999).

8. Daniel Patrick Moynihan, introduction to Monica Friar and Herman Leonard, *The Federal Budget and the States: Fiscal Year 1994* (Kennedy School of Government, 1994).

9. See David M. Magleby, *Last Hurrah? Soft Money and Issue Advocacy in the 2002 Elections* (Brookings Institution Press, 2004).

10. R. P. Fairfield, *The Federalist Papers* (Doubleday, 1961), p. 160.

11. See Roger H. Davidson and Walter J. Oleszek, *Congress and Its Members,* 8th ed. (CQ Press, 2002).

12. Richard F. Fenno Jr., *The United States Senate: A Bicameral Perspective* (American Enterprise Institute, 1982), p. 1.

13. For discussion of the modern Speakership, see Barbara Sinclair, "House Majority Party Leadership in an Era of Legislative Constraint," in *The Postreform Congress,* ed. Roger H. Davidson (St. Martin's Press, 1992), pp. 91–111; and Ronald M. Peters Jr., ed., *The Speaker: Leadership in the U.S. House of Representatives* (CQ Press, 1995).

14. Newt Gingrich, quoted in Adam Clymer, "Firebrand Who Got Singed Says Being Speaker Suffices," *The New York Times,* January 22, 1996, p. 1.

15. Newt Gingrich, *To Renew America* (HarperCollins, 1995) and *Lessons Learned the Hard Way* (HarperCollins, 1998).

16. Dennis Hastert, quoted in Greg Hitt, "Hastert Is Tapped as House Speaker to Fill Vacuum Created by Livingston," *Wall Street Journal,* December 21, 1998, p. A20.

17. Richard E. Cohen and David Baumann, "Speaking Up for Hastert," *National Journal,* November 13, 1999, pp. 3298–3303.

18. For insightful memoirs by three recently retired U.S. senators, see Bill Bradley, *Time Present, Time Past: A Memoir* (Knopf, 1996); Warren B. Rudman, *Combat: Twelve Years in the U.S. Senate* (Random House, 1996); and Alan K. Simpson, *Right in the Old Kazoo: A Lifetime of Scrapping with the Press* (Morrow, 1997). See also the reflections of Joseph I. Lieberman, *In Praise of Public Life* (Simon & Schuster, 2000); and Adam Clymer, *Edward M. Kennedy: A Biography* (Morrow, 1999).

19. For an insightful set of essays on Senate leadership, see Richard A. Baker and Roger H. Davidson, eds., *First Among Equals: Outstanding Senate Leaders of the Twentieth Century* (CQ Press, 1991).

20. Barbara Sinclair, "Unorthodox Lawmaking in the Individualist Senate," *Extensions: A Journal of the Carl Albert Congressional Research and Studies Center,* vol. 3, no. 2 (Fall 1997), p. 11. See also Sinclair, *Unorthodox Lawmaking: New Legislative Processes in the U.S. Congress,* 2d ed. (CQ Press, 2000), chap. 3.

21. Nicol Rae and Colton Campbell, "The Changing Role of Political Parties in the U.S. Senate in the 104th and 105th Congresses," paper presented at the annual meeting of the American Political Science Association, Boston, September 3–6, 1998, p. 21.

22. Sarah A. Binder and Steven S. Smith, *Politics or Principles? Filibustering in the United States Senate* (Brookings Institution Press, 1997).

23. See David Nather, "Feud with Democrats over Judicial Nominees Keeps Frist's Cloture Score Down," *Congressional Quarterly Weekly,* November 29, 2003, p. 2949.

24. Helen Dewar, "Senate Filibuster Ends with Talk of Next Stage in Fight," *The Washington Post,* November 15, 2003, p. A9.

25. For a criticism of recent confirmation hearings and various reform proposals, see Stephen L. Carter, *The Confirmation Mess: Cleaning Up the Federal Appointments Process* (Basic Books, 1994). See also G. Calvin Mackenzie and Robert Shogan, eds., *Obstacle Course: The Report of the Twentieth Century Fund Task Force on the Presidential Appointment Process* (Twentieth Century Fund Press, 1996); and Michael Comiskey, *Seeking Justice: The Judging of Supreme Court Nominees* (University of Kansas, 2004).

26. Woodrow Wilson, *Congressional Government* (Houghton Mifflin, 1885; reprint, Johns Hopkins University Press, 1981), p. 69.

27. Christopher J. Deering and Steven S. Smith, *Committees in Congress,* 3d ed. (CQ Press, 1997).

28. Joel D. Aberbach, *Keeping a Watchful Eye: The Politics of Congressional Oversight* (Brookings Institution Press, 1990), p. 33. Aberbach's data exclude hearings by Appropriations, Administration, and Rules but do include Budget and the revenue committees.

29. Karen Foerstel, "Chairman's Term Limits Already Shaking Up House," *Congressional Quarterly Weekly,* March 24, 2000, p. 628.

30. Aberbach, *Keeping a Watchful Eye.*

31. "Résumé of Congressional Activity, 105th Congress," *Congressional Record,* Daily Digest, January 19, 1999, p. D29.

32. Ronald Reagan, quoted in Lawrence Longley and Walter Oleszek, *Bicameral Politics* (Yale University Press, 1989), p. 1.

33. For an example of intense bargaining on a major defense appropriation bill, see Pat Towell, "Camouflage-Green Defense Bill Poised for President's Signature," *Congressional Quarterly Weekly,* July 22, 2000, pp. 1819–1822.

34. Davidson and Oleszek, *Congress and Its Members,* p. 307.

35. For a history of the early Congresses, see James Sterling Young, *The Washington Community, 1800–1828* (Columbia University Press, 1966).

36. Davidson and Oleszek, *Congress and Its Members,* p. 30.

37. Polsby, "The Institutionalization of the U.S. House of Representatives," *American Political Science Association* (March 1968), pp. 144–168.

38. Norman J. Ornstein, Thomas Mann, and Michael Malbin, *Vital Statistics on Congress, 1999–2000* (AEI Press, 2000), p. 170.

39. Pew Research Center for the People and the Press, *Washington Leaders Wary of Public Opinion* (Pew Research Center, 1998), p. 30.

40. Herbert Asher, "The Learning of Legislative Norms," *American Political Science Review* 67 (June 1973), pp. 499–513.

41. See the case studies in Richard F. Fenno Jr., *Senators on the Campaign Trail: The Politics of Representation* (University of Oklahoma Press, 1996), p. 331. See also Benjamin Bishin, "Constituency Influence in Congress: Does Subconstituency Matter?" *Legislative Studies Quarterly* (August 2000), pp. 389–415.

42. Statistics from congressional Web sites (www.senate.gov; www.house.gov). See also the Library of Congress Web site (thomas.loc.gov).

43. For a fascinating comparison of two Rhodes scholars, one a liberal from Maryland and the other a conservative from Indiana, and what has

shaped their votes over several terms in the U.S. Senate, see Karl A. Lamb, *Reasonable Disagreement: Two U.S. Senators and the Choices They Make* (Garland, 1998).

44. See Richard Morrin, "Tuned Out, Turned Off: Millions of Americans Know Little About How Their Government Works," *The Washington Post National Weekly Edition*, February 5, 1996, pp. 6–7.

45. A 1999 CBS survey reported in "Poll Readings," *National Journal*, October 9, 1999, p. 2917.

46. Bradley, *Time Present, Time Past*, chap. 4.

47. Jackie Clames, "House Divided: Why Congress Hews to the Party Line on Impeachment," *Wall Street Journal*, December 16, 1998, p. 1.

48. Ornstein et al., *Vital Statistics on Congress, 1999–2000*, pp. 103–106.

49. Lieberman, *In Praise of Public Life*, p. 109.

50. Constance Ewing Cook, *Lobbying for Higher Education* (Vanderbilt University Press, 1998). See also Ken Kolman, *Outside Lobbying* (Princeton University Press, 1998).

51. Jill Barshay, "Bush Starts a Strong Record of Success with the Hill," *Congressional Quarterly Weekly*, January 12, 2002, p. 110.

52. See Jeffrey S. Peake, "Presidential Agenda Setting in Foreign Policy," paper presented at the annual meeting of the American Political Science Association, Boston, September 3–6, 1998.

53. Tim Penny, quoted in Lloyd Grove, "How a Bright Penny Just 'Wore Down,' " *The Washington Post National Weekly Edition*, August 30, 1993, p. 12.

54. Joseph P. Kennedy II, quoted in Clifford Krauss, "How Personal Tragedy Can Shape Public Policy," *The New York Times*, May 16, 1993, p. A16.

55. These figures come from the annual Resume of Congressional Activity, which is published in the Congressional Record at the end of each session; the 2003 resume was published in the *Congressional Record*, December 15, 2003, p. D1361.

56. See David Baumann, "The Heavy Reliance on Riders to the Must-Pass Appropriations Bills as a Crutch to Act on Significant Policy Issues," *National Journal*, January 10, 2004, p. 97.

57. See David W. Brady and Craig Volden, *Revolving Gridlock: Politics and Policy from Carter to Clinton* (Westview Press, 1998). For two case studies on the way bills get treated in Congress, see Janet M. Martin, *Lessons from the Hill: The Legislative Journey of an Education Program* (St. Martin's Press, 1993); and Steven Waldman, *The Bill—How Legislation Really Becomes Law: A Case Study of the National Service Bill* (Penguin, 1996).

Chapter 12

1. Pew Research Center on the People & the Press, "Different Faiths, Different Messages," March 19, 2003.

2. Charles O. Jones, *The Presidency in a Separated System* (Brookings Institution Press, 1994), p. 295. See also Jean Reith Schroedl, *Congress, the President, and Policymaking* (Sharpe, 1994).

3. Richard Pious, *The American Presidency* (Basic Books, 1978).

4. This history of presidential powers draws heavily on Sidney M. Milkis and Michael Nelson, *The American Presidency: Origins and Development, 1976–2000*, 4th ed. (CQ Press, 2003).

5. Letter from Abraham Lincoln to his Illinois law partner W. H. Herndon, February 15, 1848, in *Abraham Lincoln, Speeches and Writings, 1832–1858* (Library of America, 1989), p. 175.

6. Miles A. Pomper, "Bush Hopes to Avoid Battle with Congress over Iraq," *Congressional Quarterly Weekly*, August 31, 2002, p. 2251.

7. Leonard C. Meeker, "The Legality of U.S. Participation in the Defense of Vietnam," *Department of State Bulletin*, March 28, 1966, pp. 448–455.

8. Louis Fisher, *Congressional Abdication on War and Spending* (Texas A&M Press, 2000), p. 184.

9. Ibid., p. 170. See also Louis Fisher and David Gray Adler, "The War Powers: Time to Say Goodbye," *Political Science Quarterly* (Spring 1998), pp. 1–20.

10. Lee Hamilton, "The Role of the Congress in U.S. Foreign Policy," speech delivered to the Center for Strategic and International Studies, Washington, D.C., November 19, 1998.

11. Raoul Berger, *Executive Privilege: A Constitutional Myth* (Harvard University Press, 1974).

12. Mark J. Rozell, "The Law: Executive Privilege—Definition and Standards of Application," *Presidential Studies Quarterly* (December 1999), p. 924.

13. *United States* v. *Nixon*, 418 U.S. 683 (1974).

14. The president's executive orders can be reviewed on the White House Web site at www.whitehouse.gov.

15. *Clinton, et al.*, v. *New York City, et al.*, 524 U.S. 417 (1998).

16. For a recent biography of Washington, see Richard Brookhiser, *Founding Father: Rediscovering George Washington* (New York: Free Press, 1996).

17. See Bradley H. Patterson Jr., *The White House Staff: Inside the West Wing and Beyond* (Brookings Institution Press, 2000).

18. For the views on presidents and the White House staff of a highly placed White House aide in several administrations, see David Gergen, *Eyewitness to Power The Essence of Leadership, Nixon to Clinton* (New York: Touchstone, 2000).

19. See Irving Janis, *Groupthink* (Houghton Mifflin, 1982).

20. See Shelley Lynne Tomkins, *Inside OMB: Politics and Process in the President's Budget Office* (Sharpe, 1998).

21. See Thomas Cronin and Michael Genovese, *Paradoxes of the American Presidency*, 2d Edition (New York: Oxford University Press, 2004), chap. 9.

22. Letter from Kathryn Hughes, secretary of the cabinet in the Clinton White House, February 1997. See also Robert B. Reich, *Locked in the Cabinet* (Knopf, 1997).

23. Alexis Simendinger, James Kitfield, Peter H. Stone, and Kirk Victor, "Just the Ticket?" *National Journal* (February 14, 2004), p. 27.

24. Former Vice President Dan Quayle's views are of interest in *Standing Firm* (Harper, 1995). Three useful general treatments on the vice presidency are Jules Witcover, *Crapshoot: Rolling the Dice on the Vice Presidency* (Crown, 1992); Paul Light, *Vice Presidential Power* (Johns Hopkins University Press, 1984); and Joel Goldstein, *The Modern Vice Presidency* (Princeton University Press, 1982).

25. See Joseph G. Dawson III, ed., *Commanders in Chief: Presidential Leadership in Modern Wars* (University Press of Kansas, 1993).

26. See Paul C. Light, *The President's Agenda: Domestic Policy Choice from Kennedy Through Clinton* (Johns Hopkins University Press, 1999).

27. *United States* v. *Curtiss-Wright Export Corp.*, 299 U.S. 304 (1936).

28. For commentary by analysts who believe the *Curtiss-Wright* ruling is too sweeping, see Harold H. Koh, *The National Security Constitution* (Yale University Press, 1990); Louis Fisher, *Presidential War Power* (University Press of Kansas, 1995); and David Gray Adler and Larry N. George, eds., *The Constitution and the Conduct of American Foreign Policy: Essays on Law and History* (University Press of Kansas, 1996).

29. On the president's major involvement in the budget process, see Allen Schick, *The Federal Budget: Politics, Policy, Process* (Brookings Institution Press, 1995).

30. Richard E. Neustadt, *Presidential Power and the Modern Presidents* (Free Press, 1991).

31. Samuel Kernell, *Going Public: New Strategies of Presidential Leadership* (Congressional Quarterly, 3rd ed., 1997).

32. See the arguments in David Gray Adler and Michael A. Genovese, eds., *The Presidency and the Law: The Clinton Legacy* (University Press of Kansas, 2002); and Louis Fisher, *Congressional Abdication on War and Spending* (Texas A&M Press, 2000).

33. James A. Thurber, "An Introduction to Presidential-Congressional Rivalry," in *Rivals for Power: Presidential-Congressional Relations*, ed. James A. Thurber, (CQ Press, 1996), p. 6.

34. See, for example, former Republican Senator Warren G. Rudman's memoir, *Combat* (Random House, 1996), chaps. 2 and 3. See also former Democratic Congressman Timothy Penny and Major Garrett, *Common Cents* (Little, Brown, 1995).

35. See Paul C. Light, *The President's Agenda: Domestic Policy Choice from Kennedy to Clinton*, 3rd ed., for a discussion of the agenda-setting process.

36. The phrase "power to persuade" is from Richard Neustadt, *Presidential Power and the Modern Presidents: The Politics of Leadership from Roosevelt to Reagan*, (New York: The Free Press, 1990) p. 7.

37. See Paul Light, "The Focusing Skill and Presidential Influence in Congress," in C. Deering, *Congressional Politics* (Dorsey Press, 1989), p. 256.

Chapter 13

1. Andrew Kohut, *Deconstructing Distrust: How Americans View Government* (Pew Research Center for the People and the Press, 1998), p. 124.

2. See Paul C. Light, "To Give or Not to Give," *Reform Watch #7*, Washington, D.C.: Brookings Institution Press, 2003.

3. An exception is a book of essays in praise of innovations by federal agencies, John D. Donahue, ed., *Making Washington Work: Tales of Innovation in the Federal Government* (Brookings Institution Press, 1999).

4. Alexander Hamilton, James Madison, and John Jay, *The Federalist Papers* (New American Library), p. 427.

5. See Stanley Elkins and Eric McKitrick, *The Age of Federalism* (Oxford University Press, 1993), pp. 50–51.
6. See John A. Rohr, *To Run a Constitution: The Legitimacy of the Administrative State* (University of Kansas Press, 1986).
7. Dennis Palumbo and Steven Maynard-Moody, *Contemporary Public Administration* (Longman, 1991).
8. Donald Kettl, *Leadership at the Fed* (Yale University Press, 1986).
9. Tom Ridge, quoted in Maureen Shirhal, "Ridge Hints at Border Agency Consolidation," *Government Executive Daily Briefing*, February 26, 2002, at govexec.com/dailyfed/0202/022602td1.htm.
10. James Fesler and Donald Kettl, *The Politics of the Administrative Process* (Chatham House, 1991).
11. See Paul C. Light, *Thickening Government* (Brookings Institution Press, 1995).
12. See Terry M. Moe, "The Politics of Structural Choice: Toward a Theory of Public Bureaucracy," in *Organization Theory: From Chester Barnard to the Present and Beyond*, ed. Oliver E. Williamson (Oxford University Press, 1990), pp. 140–162.
13. Leonard White, *The Federalists* (Macmillan, 1956), p. 1.
14. For an analysis of the use and abuse of the civil service system in the early twentieth century, see Stephen Skowronek, *Building a New American State* (Cambridge University Press, 1982).
15. See Paul C. Light, "The State of the Federal Service," Brookings Institution Press, October 2001, and "The Troubled State of the Federal Service," Brookings Institution Press, May 2002.
16. See James Eccles, *The Hatch Act and the American Bureaucracy* (Vantage Press, 1981).
17. See Jeanne Ponessa, "The Hatch Act Rewrite," *Congressional Quarterly Weekly*, November 13, 1993, pp. 3146–3147.
18. Theodore J. Lowi Jr., *The End of Liberalism*, 2d ed. (Norton, 1979).
19. Eric Pianin, "EPA Aims to Change Pollution Rules," *Washington Post*, December 5, 2003, p. A2.
20. Kent Weaver, *Automatic Government: The Politics of Indexation* (Brookings Institution Press, 1988), p. 1; updated estimate provided by Paul C. Light.
21. James Q. Wilson, *Bureaucracy: What Government Agencies Do and Why They Do It* (Basic Books, 1989), p. 257.
22. See David E. Lewis, "The Presidential Advantage in the Design of Bureaucratic Agencies," paper presented at the annual meeting of the American Political Science Association, Boston, September 3–6, 1998.
23. Morris P. Fiorina, "Flagellating the Federal Bureaucracy," *Society* (March–April 1983), p. 73.
24. See Steven S. Smith, *The American Congress* (Houghton Mifflin, 1995); see also Joel D. Aberbach, *Keeping a Watchful Eye: The Politics of Congressional Oversight* (Brookings Institution Press, 1990).
25. See Matthew McCubbins and Thomas Schwartz, "Congressional Oversight Overlooked: Police Patrols Versus Fire Alarms," *American Journal of Political Science* 2 (February 1984), pp. 165–179.

Chapter 14

1. Alexis de Tocqueville, *Democracy in America*, ed. Phillips Bradley (Knopf, 1944), vol. 1, pp. 278–280.
2. Harold J. Laski, *The American Democracy* (Viking, 1948), p. 110.
3. See Carol Guarnieri and Patrizia Pederzoli, *The Power of Judges: A Comparative Study of Courts and Democracy* (Oxford University Press, 2002); and C. N. Tate and T. Vallinder, eds., *The Global Expansion of Judicial Power* (New York University Press, 1995).
4. Jerome Frank, *Courts on Trial: Myth and Reality in American Justice* (Princeton University Press, 1949), pp. 80–103. See also Martin Shapiro, *Courts* (University of Chicago Press, 1981), and Robert P. Burns, *A Theory of the Trial* (Princeton University Press, 1999).
5. *United States* v. *Students Challenging Regulatory Agency Procedures (SCRAP)*, 412 U.S. 669 (1973).
6. *Flast* v. *Cohen*, 392 U.S. 83 (1968); *Lujan* v. *Defenders of Wildlife*, 504 U.S. 555 (1992).
7. Philip J. Cooper, *Hard Judicial Choices: Federal District Court Judges and State and Local Officials* (Oxford University Press, 1988), p. 15.
8. *Bordenkircher* v. *Hayes*, 434 U.S. 357 (1978).
9. *Luther* v. *Borden*, 7 Howard 1 (1849).
10. *Bush* v. *Gore*, 531 U.S. 98 (2000).
11. John Roche, "Judicial Self-Restraint," *American Political Science Review* 49 (1955), pp. 762, 768.
12. See Charles Lopeman, *The Activist Advocate: Policymaking in State Supreme Courts* (Praeger, 2000).
13. Eleanore Bushnell, *Crimes, Follies, and Misfortunes: The Federal Impeachment Trials* (University of Illinois Press, 1992); and Mary L. Volcansek, *None Called for Justice: Judicial Impeachment* (University of Illinois Press, 1993).
14. Administrative Office of the U.S. Courts, *Judicial Facts and Figures* (Tables 2.11, 3.1, and 4.1), at www.uscourts.gov (as of February 5, 2004).
15. C. K. Rowland, "The Federal District Courts," in *The American Courts: A Critical Assessment*, eds. John B. Gates and Charles A. Johnson (CQ Press, 1991), pp. 61–80.
16. *Peretz* v. *United States*, 501 U.S. 923 (1991).
17. See Christopher P. Banks, *Judicial Politics in the D. C. Circuit* (Johns Hopkins University Press, 1999); Donald R. Songer and Susan B. Haire, *Continuity and Change in the United States Courts of Appeals* (University of Michigan Press, 2000); David Klein, *Making Law in the U.S. Courts of Appeals* (Cambridge University Press, 2002); and Jonathan Matthew, *Decision Making in the U.S. Courts of Appeals* (University of Michigan Press, 2002).
18. See *Anastasoff* v. *United States*, 223 F. 3d 898 (2000); and Jerome I. Braun, "Eighth Circuit Decision Intensifies Debate over Publication and Citation of Appellate Opinions," *Judicature* 83 (September–October 2000).
19. Neil D. McFeeley, *Appointment of Judges: The Johnson Presidency* (University of Texas Press, 1987), p. 1.
20. Harold W. Chase, *Federal Judges: The Appointing Process* (University of Minnesota Press, 1972); Sheldon Goldman, *Picking Federal Judges: Lower Court Selection from Roosevelt Through Reagan* (Yale University Press, 1997).
21. See David M. O'Brien, "Ironies and Disappointments: Bush and Federal Judgeships," in Colin Campbell and Bert A. Rockman, eds., *The George W. Bush Presidency* (CQ Press, 2004), pp. 133–157; and Brannon P. Denning, "The Judicial Confirmation Process and the Blue Slip," *Judicature* (March–April 2002), pp. 218–226.
22. Lisa M. Holmes and Roger E. Hartley, "Increasing Senate Scrutiny of Lower Federal Court Nominees," *Judicature* (May–June 1997), p. 275.
23. George Watson and John Stookey, "Supreme Court Confirmation Hearings: A View from the Senate," *Judicature* (December 1987–January 1988), p. 193. See also John Massaro, *Supremely Political: The Role of Ideology and Presidential Management in Unsuccessful Supreme Court Nominations* (State University of New York Press, 1990).
24. Barbara A. Perry and Henry J. Abraham, "A 'Representative' Supreme Court? The Thomas, Ginsburg, and Breyer Appointments," *Judicature* (January—February 1998), pp. 158–165.
25. Goldman, *Picking Federal Judges*, pp. 161, 327–336.
26. Sheldon Goldman, "Bush's Judicial Legacy: The Final Imprint," *Judicature* (April–May 1993), p. 291.
27. Eleanor Dean Acheson, quoted in David M. O'Brien, "Judicial Legacies: The Clinton Presidency and the Courts," in *The Clinton Legacy*, eds. Colin Campbell and Burt A. Rockman (Chatham House, 2000), p. 101.
28. As of July 23, 2004, based on data reported by the Federal Judicial Center at www.fjc.gov/newweb/jnetweb.nsf/hisj.
29. Robert A. Carp and C. K. Rowland, *Politics and Judgment in Federal District Courts* (University Press of Kansas, 1996).
30. Sheldon Goldman, "Reagan's Judicial Legacy: Completing the Puzzle and Summing Up," *Judicature* (April–May 1989), pp. 318–330.
31. Robert A. Carp, Donald Songer, C. K. Rowland, Ronald Stidham, and Lisa Richey-Tracey, "The Voting Behavior of Judges Appointed by President Bush," *Judicature* (April–May 1993), pp. 298–302.
32. David G. Savage, *Turning Right: The Making of the Rehnquist Supreme Court* (Wiley, 1992).
33. Naftali Bendavid, "Diversity Marks Clinton Judiciary," *Recorder* (December 30, 1993), p. 11.
34. O'Brien, "Judicial Legacies," pp. 96–117.
35. Helen Dewar, "Senate Democrats Block 3 More Bush Judicial Nominees," *The Washington Post*, July 23, 2004, at A5; Sheldon Goldman, "The Senate and Judicial Nominations," *Extensions* (Spring 2004), pp. 4–12.
36. Neil Lewis, "Deal Ends Impasse Over Judicial Nominees," *The New York Times*, May 18, 2004, p. A17.
37. Jeremiah Smith, quoted in Paul E. Freund, *Understanding the Supreme Court* (Little, Brown, 1949), p. 3.
38. Felix Frankfurter, letter to Justice Hugo Black, December 15, 1939, quoted in David M. O'Brien, *Constitutional Law and Politics*, 6th ed. (Norton, 2005), p. 74.
39. See Benjamin N. Cardozo, *The Nature of the Judicial Process* (Yale University Press, 1921), a classic.

40. William O. Douglas, quoted in David M. O'Brien, *Storm Center: The Supreme Court in American Politics,* 7th ed. (Norton, 2005), p. 184.

41. Ibid., p. 30 (figures as of the end of the 2003–2004 term).

42. William Howard Taft, letter to Horace Taft, November 14, 1929; quoted in Henry Pringle, *The Life and Times of William Howard Taft* (Farrar, 1939), vol. 2, p. 967.

43. See David N. Atkinson, *Leaving the Bench: Supreme Court Justices at the End* (University Press of Kansas, 1999).

44. David M. O'Brien, *Judicial Roulette: Report of the Twentieth Century Fund Task Force on Judicial Selection* (Priority Press Publications, 1988), pp. 10–11.

45. White Burkett Miller Center of Public Affairs, *Improving the Process of Appointing Federal Judges* (Miller Center, University of Virginia, 1996).

46. See Citizens for Independent Courts Task Force on Federal Judicial Selection, *Justice Held Hostage: Politics and Selecting Federal Judges* (Century Foundation, 2000).

47. Donald Santarelli, quoted in Jerry Landauer, "Shaping the Bench," *The Wall Street Journal,* December 10, 1970, p. 1.

48. Michael A. Kahn, "The Appointment of a Supreme Court Justice: A Political Process from Beginning to End," *Presidential Studies Quarterly* 25 (Winter 1995), pp. 26, 39.

49. Ex parte *McCardle,* 74 U.S. 506 (1869).

50. Barry Friedman, "Attacks on Judges: Why They Fail," *Judicature* (January–February 1998), p. 152.

51. William H. Rehnquist, quoted in John R. Vile, "The Selection and Tenure of Chief Justices," *Judicature* (September–October 1994), p. 98.

52. David Danelski, "The Influence of the Chief Justice in the Decisional Process of the Supreme Court," in *The Federal Judicial System: Readings in Process and Behavior,* eds. Thomas P. Jahnige and Sheldon Goldman (Holt, Rinehart and Winston, 1968), p. 148.

53. David M. O'Brien, "The Rehnquist Court's Shrinking Plenary Docket," *Judicature* (September–October 1997), p. 58.

54. O'Brien, *Storm Center,* p. 63.

55. See H. W. Perry Jr., *Deciding to Decide: Agenda Setting in the United States Supreme Court* (Harvard University Press, 1991).

56. Edward Lazarus, *Closed Chambers: The First Eyewitness Account of the Epic Struggles Inside the Supreme Court* (Times Books/Random House, 1998).

57. O'Brien, *Storm Center,* Chap. 3.

58. Lincoln Caplan, *The Tenth Justice: The Solicitor General and the Rule of Law* (Knopf, 1987); and Rebecca Mae Salokar, *The Solicitor General: The Politics of Law* (Temple University Press, 1992).

59. Charles Fried, *Order and Law: Arguing the Reagan Revolution—A First-hand Account* (Simon & Schuster, 1991). See also Rebecca Dean, Joseph Ignagni, and James Meernik, "The Solicitor General as Amicus, 1950–2000: How Influential? *Judicature* 87 (September–October, 2003), p. 60.

60. Jeffrey A. Segal and Robert M. Howard, "How Supreme Court Justices Respond to Litigant Requests to Overturn Precedent," *Judicature* (November–December 2001), pp. 148–157.

61. Gregory A. Caldeira and John R. Wright, "Organized Interest and Agenda Setting in the U.S. Supreme Court," *American Political Science Review* 82 (December 1988), p. 1110; and Donald R. Songer and Reginald S. Sheehan, "Interest Groups' Success in the Courts: *Amicus* Participation in the Supreme Court," *Political Research Quarterly* 46 (June 1993), pp. 339–354.

62. *Webster* v. *Reproductive Health Services,* 492 U.S. 490 (1989); *Roe* v. *Wade,* 410 U.S. 113 (1973); and Susan Behuniak-Long, "Friendly Fire: *Amici Curiae* and *Webster* v. *Reproductive Health Services,*" *Judicature* (February–March 1991), pp. 261–270.

63. *United States* v. *Lopez,* 514 U.S. 549 (1951).

64. Caldeira and Wright, "Organized Interest and Agenda Setting"; Songer and Sheehan, "Interest Groups' Success in the Courts," *American Political Science Review* 82 (December 1988), p. 1118.

65. Tony Mauro, "The Supreme Court as Quiz Show," *Recorder* (December 8, 1993), p. 10.

66. Joyce O'Connor, "Selections from Notes Kept on an Internship at the U.S. Supreme Court, Fall 1988," *Law, Courts, and Judicial Process* 6 (Spring 1989), p. 44.

67. Tony Mauro, "No Comfort for Counsel After Court Review," *Recorder* (November 10, 1997), p. 8.

68. Mauro, "Yipes! Stripes!" *Recorder,* February 8, 1995, p. 8.

69. Joan Biskupie, "Supreme Court Film Offers Glimpse Behind Justices' Closed Doors," *The Washington Post,* June 17, 1997, p. A15.

70. William H. Rehnquist, *The Supreme Court: A New Edition of the Chief Justice's Classic History* (Knopf, 2001), pp. 289–290.

71. Forrest Maltzman, James F. Spriggs III, and Paul Wahlbeck, *Crafting Law on the Supreme Court: The Collegial Game* (Cambridge University Press, 2000).

72. Daniel M. Berman, *It Is So Ordered: The Supreme Court Rules on School Segregation* (Norton, 1986), p. 114; and O'Brien, *Storm Center,* pp. 262–272.

73. Charles Evans Hughes, quoted in Donald E. Lively, *Foreshadows of the Law: Supreme Court Dissents and Constitutional Development* (Praeger, 1992), p. xx.

74. *Brown* v. *Board of Education of Topeka,* 347 U.S. 483 (1954).

75. *United States* v. *Nixon,* 418 U.S. 683 (1974).

76. Gerald N. Rosenberg, *Hollow Hope: Can Courts Bring About Sound Change?* (University of Chicago Press, 1991).

77. J. W. Peltason, *Fifty-Eight Lonely Men: Southern Federal Judges and School Desegregation* (University of Illinois Press, 1971); and Gary Orfield and Chungmei Lee, *Brown at 50: King's Dream or Plessy's Nightmare* (The Civil Rights Project, Harvard University, 2004).

78. See Shawn Francis Peters, *Judging the Jehovah's Witnesses* (University of Kansas Press, 2002); Clyde Wilcox, *Onward, Christian Soldiers? The Religious Right in American Politics* (Westview Press, 1996); Mark Tushnet, *The NAACP's Legal Strategy Against Segregated Education, 1925–1950* (University of North Carolina Press, 1987); and Karen O'Connor, *Women's Organizations' Use of the Court* (Lexington Books, 1980).

79. Cooper, *Hard Judicial Choices,* pp. 347–350.

80. Arthur S. Miller, "In Defense of Judicial Activism," in *Supreme Court Activism and Restraint,* eds. Stephen C. Halpern and Charles M. Lamb (Heath, 1982), p. 177.

81. *United States* v. *Carolene Products,* 304 U.S. 144 (1938). Variations on this basic position have been restated in dozens of books. Halpern and Lamb, *Supreme Court Activism and Restraint,* and Mark Tushnet, *Red, White, and Blue: A Critical Analysis of Constitutional Law* (Harvard University Press, 1988) provide analysis from all perspectives. See also Terri Jennings Peretti, *In Defense of a Political Court* (Princeton University Press, 1999).

82. J. W. Peltason, "The Supreme Court: Transactional or Transformational Leadership," in *Essays in Honor of James MacGregor Burns,* eds. Michael R. Beschloss and Thomas E. Cronin (Prentice Hall, 1988), pp. 165–180; and Valerie Hoeksta, *Public Reactions to Supreme Court Decisions* (Cambridge University Press, 2003).

83. *Planned Parenthood* v. *Casey,* 505 U.S. 833 (1992).

84. Thomas R. Marshall, *Public Opinion and the Supreme Court* (Unwin Hyman, 1989), p. 193. See also William Mishler and Reginald S. Sheehan, "The Supreme Court as a Counter-Majoritarian Institution: The Impact of Public Opinion on Supreme Court Decisions," *American Political Science Review* 87 (January 1993), pp. 87–101; and Helmut Norpoth and Jeffrey A. Segal, "Popular Influence on Supreme Court Decisions," *American Political Science Review* 88 (September 1994), pp. 711–724.

85. See John B. Gates, *The Supreme Court and Partisan Realignment* (Westview Press, 1992).

86. Rosenberg, *Hollow Hope,* p. 343.

87. Rehnquist, *Supreme Court,* p. 98.

88. Gallup Organization, "Confidence in Institutions," June 8–10, 2001, at www.gallup.com; and Herbert Kritzer, "The Impact of *Bush* v. *Gore* on Public Perceptions and Knowledge of the Supreme Court," *Judicature* (July–August 2001), pp. 32–38.

89. Edward White, "The Supreme Court of the United States," *American Bar Association Journal* 7 (1921), p. 341.

Chapter 15

1. Jeffrey Smith, *War and Press Freedom* (Oxford University Press, 1999); and David Cole, *Enemy Aliens: Double Standards and Constitutional Freedoms in the War on Terrorism* (The New Press, 2003).

2. *Felker* v. *Turpin,* 518 U.S. 651 (1996); *Winthrow* v. *Williams,* 507 U.S. 680 (1993); *McCleskey* v. *Zant,* 499 U.S. 467 (1991); and *Stone* v. *Powell,* 428 U.S. 465 (1976).

3. *Rasul* v. *Bush,* 124 S.Ct. 2686 (2004); and *Hamdi* v. *Rumsfeld,* 124 S.Ct. 2633 (2004).

4. *Stogner* v. *California,* 539 U.S. 607 (2003).

5. *United States* v. *Lovett,* 328 U.S. 303 (1946).

6. Neil H. Cogan, ed., *The Complete Bill of Rights: The Drafts, Debates, Sources, and Origins* (Oxford University Press, 1997); Robert A. Rutland,

The Birth of the Bill of Rights, 1776–1791 (University of North Carolina Press, 1955).

7. *Barron* v. *Baltimore*, 7 Peters 243 (1833).
8. *Gitlow* v. *New York*, 268 U.S. 652 (1925).
9. Richard C. Cortner, *The Supreme Court and the Second Bill of Rights: The Fourteenth Amendment and the Nationalization of Civil Liberties* (University of Wisconsin Press, 1981).
10. Dorothy Toth Beasley, "Federalism and the Protection of Individual Rights: The American State Constitutional Perspective," in *Federalism and Rights*, ed. Ellis Katz and G. Alan Tarr (Rowman & Littlefield, 1996); and Charles Lopeman, *The Activist Advocate: Policymaking in State Supreme Courts* (Praeger, 1999).
11. *Witters* v. *Washington Department of Services for the Blind*, 474 U.S. 481 (1986); and *Locke* v. *Davey*, 124 S.Ct. 1307 (2004).
12. *Everson* v. *Board of Education of Ewing Township*, 333 U.S. 203 (1947).
13. *Lemon* v. *Kurtzman*, 403 U.S. 602 (1971).
14. *Capital Square Review Board* v. *Pinette*, 515 U.S. 753 (1995).
15. *Lynch* v. *Donnelly*, 465 U.S. 669 (1984).
16. *Allegheny County* v. *Greater Pittsburgh ACLU*, 492 U.S. 573 (1989).
17. *Bowen* v. *Kendrick*, 487 U.S. 589 (1988); *Lee* v. *Weisman*, 505 U.S. 577 (1992); *Board of Education of Kiryas Joel Village School District* v. *Grumet*, 512 U.S. 687 (1994); and *Zelman* v. *Simmons-Harris*, 536 U.S. 629 (2002).
18. *Mitchell* v. *Helms*, 530 U.S. 793 (2000).
19. *Agostini* v. *Felton*, 521 U.S. 74 (1997).
20. *Lee* v. *Weisman*, 505 U.S. 577 (1992); and *Santa Fe Independent School District* v. *Doe*, 530 U.S. 290 (2000).
21. *Engel* v. *Vitale*, 370 U.S. 421 (1962).
22. *Edwards* v. *Aguillard*, 482 U.S. 578 (1987).
23. *Marsh* v. *Chambers*, 463 U.S. 783 (1983).
24. *Elk Grove Unified School District* v. *Newdow*, 124 S.Ct. 2301 (2004).
25. *Witters* v. *Washington Department of Services for the Blind*, 474 U.S. 481 (1986).
26. *Mueller* v. *Allen*, 463 U.S. 388 (1983); and *Zelman v. Simmons-Harris*, 536 U.S. 639 (2002).
27. *Zobrest* v. *Catalina Foothills School District*, 515 U.S. 1 (1993); *Agostini* v. *Felton*, 521 U.S. 74 (1997); *Mitchell* v. *Helms*, 530 U.S. 793 (2000).
28. *Zelman* v. *Simmons-Harris*, 536 U.S. 639 (2002).
29. Justice Blum, "D.C. School Voucher Applications Fall Short," *The Washington Post*, June 11, 2004, p. A1.
30. *Employment Division of Human Resources of Oregon* v. *Smith*, 494 U.S. 872 (1990).
31. *Church of Lukumi Babalu Aye* v. *City of Hialeah*, 508 U.S. 520 (1993).
32. *City of Boerne* v. *Flores*, 521 U.S. 507 (1997).
33. *Rosenberger* v. *University of Virginia*, 515 U.S. 819 (1995).
34. *Board of Regents of the University of Wisconsin System* v. *Southworth*, 529 U.S. 217 (2000).
35. Oliver Wendell Holmes Jr., in *Abrams* v. *United States*, 250 U.S. 616 (1919).
36. John Stuart Mill, *Essay on Liberty*, in *The English Philosophers from Bacon to Mill*, ed. Arthur Burtt (Random House, 1939), p. 961.
37. Robert Jackson, in *West Virginia State Board of Education* v. *Barnette*, 319 U.S. 624 (1943).
38. *Brown* v. *Hartlage*, 456 U.S. 45 (1982), reversing a decision of the Kentucky Court of Appeals based on the bad tendency test.
39. Oliver Wendell Holmes Jr., in *Schenck* v. *United States*, 249 U.S. 47 (1919).
40. *Dennis* v. *United States*, 341 U.S. 494 (1951).
41. *New York Times* v. *Sullivan*, 376 U.S. 254 (1964).
42. *Yates* v. *United States*, 354 U.S. 298 (1957).
43. *Brandenburg* v. *Ohio*, 395 U.S. 444 (1969).
44. *New York Times* v. *Sullivan*, 376 U.S. 254 (1964).
45. *Hustler Magazine* v. *Falwell*, 485 U.S. 46 (1988).
46. *Masson* v. *New York Magazine, Inc.*, 501 U.S. 496 (1991).
47. *Gertz* v. *Robert Welch, Inc.*, 418 U.S. 323 (1974).
48. Potter Stewart, concurring in *Jacobellis* v. *Ohio*, 378 U.S. 184 (1964).
49. John Marshall Harlan, in *Cohen* v. *California*, 403 U.S. 15 (1971).
50. *Miller* v. *California*, 413 U.S. 15 (1973).
51. *Young* v. *American Mini Theatres*, 427 U.S. 51 (1976); *Renton* v. *Playtime Theatres, Inc.*, 475 U.S. 41 (1986); and *City of Los Angeles* v. *Alameda Books, Inc.*, 535 U.S. 425 (2002).
52. *Barnes* v. *Glen Theatre, Inc.*, 501 U.S. 560 (1991); and *City of Erie* v. *Pap's A.M.*, 529 U.S. 277 (2000).
53. *New York* v. *Ferber*, 458 U.S. 747 (1982); and *Ashcroft* v. *Free Speech Coalition*, 535 U.S. 234 (2002).
54. *General Media Communications* v. *Cohen*, 524 U.S. 951 (1998).
55. See Catharine A. MacKinnon, *Only Words* (Harvard University Press, 1993); and compare another feminist, Nadine Strossen, *Defending Pornography: Free Speech, Sex, and the Fight for Women's Rights* (Scribner, 1995).
56. *Butler* v. *Her Majesty the Queen*, 1 S.C.R. 452 (1992).
57. *Chaplinsky* v. *New Hampshire*, 315 U.S. 568 (1942).
58. *Cohen* v. *California*, 403 U.S. 115 (1971).
59. *R.A.V.* v. *St. Paul*, 505 U.S. 377 (1992). See also *Wisconsin* v. *Mitchell*, 508 U.S. 476 (1993); and *Apprendi* v. *New Jersey*, 530 U.S. 466 (2000).
60. *Virginia* v. *Black*, 538 U.S. 343 (2003).
61. *44 Liquormart, Inc.*, v. *Rhode Island*, 517 U.S. 484 (1996); and *Thompson* v. *Western States Medical Center*, 535 U.S. 357 (2002).
62. *New York Times Company* v. *United States*, 403 U.S. 670 (1971).
63. *Near* v. *Minnesota*, 283 U.S. 697 (1930); ibid.
64. *Hazelwood School District* v. *Kuhlmeier*, 484 U.S. 260 (1988).
65. *R.A.V.* v. *St. Paul*, 505 U.S. 377 (1992). See also *Wisconsin* v. *Mitchell*, 508 U.S. 476 (1993).
66. *Branzburg* v. *Hayes*, 408 U.S. 665 (1972).
67. *Richmond Newspapers, Inc.*, v. *Virginia*, 448 U.S. 555 (1980). See also David M. O'Brien, *The Public's Right to Know: The Supreme Court and the First Amendment* (Praeger, 1981).
68. Oliver Wendell Holmes Jr., dissenting in *Milwaukee Publishing Co.* v. *Burleson*, 255 U.S. 407 (1921).
69. *Lamont* v. *Postmaster General*, 381 U.S. 301 (1965).
70. *Rowan* v. *Post Office Department*, 397 U.S. 728 (1970).
71. *McIntyre* v. *Ohio Election Commission*, 514 U.S. 334 (1995).
72. *Southeastern Promotions, Ltd.*, v. *Conrad*, 420 U.S. 546 (1975).
73. *Federal Communications Commission* v. *Pacifica Foundation*, 438 U.S. 726 (1978).
74. *Turner Broadcasting System* v. *Federal Communications Commission*, 518 U.S. 180 (1997).
75. *United States* v. *Playboy Entertainment Group*, 529 U.S. 803 (2000); and *Denver Area Educational Television* v. *Federal Communications Commission*, 518 U.S. 727 (1996).
76. See and compare *Federal Communications Commission* v. *Pacifica Foundation*, 438 U.S. 726 (1978); and *Sable Communications* v. *Federal Communications Commission*, 492 U.S. 115 (1989).
77. *Reno* v. *American Civil Liberties Union*, 521 U.S. 844 (1997).
78. *Ashcroft* v. *ACLU*, 124 S.Ct. 2783 (2004).
79. *Ashcroft* v. *Free Speech Coalition*, 535 U.S. 234 (2002).
80. Freedom Forum Online at www.freedomforum.org/assembly/1998/9/2/march.asp.
81. *Walker* v. *Birmingham*, 388 U.S. 307 (1967).
82. *Madsen* v. *Women's Health Center*, 512 U.S. 753 (1994); *Schenck* v. *Pro-Choice Network*, 519 U.S. 357 (1997); and *Hill* v. *Colorado*, 530 U.S. 703 (2000).
83. *West Virginia State Board of Education* v. *Barnette*, 319 U.S. 624 (1943).

Chapter 16

1. *Vance* v. *Terrazas*, 444 U.S. 252 (1980).
2. G. Pascal Zachary, "Dual Citizenship Is Double-Edged Sword," *The Wall Street Journal*, March 25, 1998, pp. B1, B15, quoting T. Alexander Aleinikoff of the Carnegie Endowment for International Peace.
3. *Slaughter-House Cases*, 83 U.S. 36 (1873).
4. *Ex Parte Milligan*, 71 U.S. 2 (1866).
5. *Korematsu* v. *United States*, 323 U.S. 214 (1944).
6. *Ex Parte Quirin*, 317 U.S. 1 (1942).
7. *Reid* v. *Covert*, 354 U.S. 1 (1957).
8. *Hamdi* v. *Rumsfeld*, 124 S.Ct. 2686 (2004); and *Rasul* v. *Bush*, 124 S.Ct. 2633 (2004).
9. *Mathews* v. *Diaz*, 426 U.S. 67 (1976); *Shaughnessy* v. *United States ex rel Mezei*, 345 U.S. 206 (1953).
10. *Demore* v. *Kim*, 538 U.S. 510 (2003).
11. *Zadvydas* v. *David*, 533 U.S. 678 (2001).
12. *Yick Wo* v. *Hopkins*, 118 U.S. 356 (1886); *Kwong Hai Chew* v. *Colding*, 344 U.S. 590 (1953); *Zadvydas* v. *Davis*, 533 U.S. 678 (2001); *Rasul* v. *Bush*, 124 S.Ct. 2686 (2004); and *Hamdi* v. *Rumsfeld*, 124 S.Ct. 2633 (2004).
13. *Foley* v. *Connelie*, 435 U.S. 291 (1978); *Ambach* v. *Norwick*, 441 U.S. 68 (1979); and *Cabell* v. *Chavez-Salido*, 454 U.S. 432 (1982).
14. *Plyler* v. *Doe*, 457 U.S. 202 (1982).
15. See Samuel Huntington, *Who Are We?* (Free Press, 2004).
16. Karen De Young, "Bush Lowers Refugee Quota to 70,000," *The Washington Post*, November 22, 2001, p. A45.
17. *Sale* v. *Haitian Centers Council, Inc.*, 509 U.S. 155 (1993).

18. Christopher Marquis, "Census Bureau Estimates 115,000 Middle Eastern Immigrants Are in the U.S. Illegally," *The New York Times*, January 23, 2002, p. A10.
19. Francis X. Clines, "Harsh Civics Lesson for Immigrants," *The New York Times*, November 11, 2001, p. B7.
20. *Chicago Home Building & Loan Association* v. *Blaisdell*, 290 U.S. 398 (1934).
21. *Chicago, Burlington & Quincy Railway Co.* v. *Chicago*, 166 U.S. 226 (1897).
22. *First English Evangelical* v. *Los Angeles County*, 482 U.S. 304 (1987). See Richard A. Epstein, *Taking: Private Property and the Power of Eminent Domain* (Harvard University Press, 1985).
23. *Lucas* v. *South Carolina Coastal Commission*, 505 U.S. 647 (1992).
24. *Tahoe-Sierra Council, Inc.*, v. *Tahoe Regional Planning Agency*, 535 U.S. 302 (2002).
25. *United States* v. *564.54 Acres of Land*, 441 U.S. 506 (1979).
26. *Mathews* v. *Eldridge*, 424 U.S. 319 (1976), restated in *Connecticut* v. *Doeher*, 501 U.S. 1 (1991).
27. *Meyer* v. *Nebraska*, 262 U.S. 390 (1923).
28. *Lochner* v. *New York*, 198 U.S. 45 (1905).
29. *Griswold* v. *Connecticut*, 381 U.S. 479 (1965).
30. Philip B. Kurland, *Some Reflections on Privacy and the Constitution* (University of Chicago Center for Policy Study, 1976), p. 9. A classic and influential article about privacy is Samuel D. Warren and Louis D. Brandeis, "The Right to Privacy," *Harvard Law Review*, December 15, 1890, pp. 193–220.
31. *Roe* v. *Wade*, 410 U.S. 113 (1973).
32. *Planned Parenthood of Southeastern Pennsylvania* v. *Casey*, 505 U.S. 833 (1992).
33. *Stenberg* v. *Carhart*, 530 U.S. 914 (2000).
34. *Bowers* v. *Hardwick*, 478 U.S. 186 (1986).
35. *Boy Scouts of America* v. *Dale*, 530 U.S. 640 (2000).
36. *Lawrence* v. *Texas*, 539 U.S. 558 (2003).
37. *Romer* v. *Evans*, 517 U.S. 620 (1996).
38. But see *Washington* v. *Chrisman*, 455 U.S. 1 (1982).
39. *Katz* v. *United States*, 389 U.S. 347 (1967).
40. *County of Riverside* v. *McLaughlin*, 500 U.S. 44 (1991).
41. *California* v. *Hodari D.*, 499 U.S. 621 (1991).
42. *Bond* v. *United States*, 529 U.S. 334 (2000).
43. *Terry* v. *Ohio*, 392 U.S. 1 (1968).
44. *Hiibel* v. *Sixth Judicial District of Nevada*, 124 S.Ct. 2451 (2004).
45. *Minnesota* v. *Dickerson*, 508 U.S. 366 (1993).
46. *Almeida-Sanchez* v. *United States*, 413 U.S. 266 (1973); *United States* v. *Ortiz*, 422 U.S. 891 (1975); *United States* v. *Arvizu*, 534 U.S. 161 (2002); and *United States* v. *Flores-Montano*, 124 S.Ct. 1582 (2004).
47. *United States* v. *Ramsey*, 431 U.S. 606 (1977).
48. *Coolidge* v. *New Hampshire*, 403 U.S. 443 (1971); and *Arizona* v. *Hicks*, 480 U.S. 321 (1987).
49. *United States* v. *Ross*, 456 U.S. 798 (1982).
50. *Pennsylvania* v. *Mimms*, 434 U.S. 110 (1977); and *Ohio* v. *Robinette*, 519 U.S. 33 (1997).
51. *Thorton* v. *United States*, 124 S.Ct. 2127 (2004).
52. *Chandler* v. *Miller*, 520 U.S. 305 (1997).
53. Randall Kennedy, *Race, Crime, and the Law* (Pantheon Books, 1997), pp. 136–168; and David Cole, *No Equal Justice: Race and Class in the American Criminal Justice System* (New Press, 1999).
54. Quoted in Eric Lichtblau, "Bush Limits Use of Race in Federal Investigations," *International Herald Tribune*, June 19, 2003, p. 5.
55. *Treasury Employees* v. *Von Raab*, 489 U.S. 656 (1989); *Skinner* v. *Railway Labor Executives' Association*, 489 U.S. 602 (1989); *Vernonia School District 47J* v. *Acton*, 515 U.S. 646 (1995); and *Chandler* v. *Miller*, 520 U.S. 305 (1997).
56. *Board of Education of Independent School District No. 2 of Pottawatomie City* v. *Earls*, 536 U.S. 822 (2002).
57. *Mapp* v. *Ohio*, 367 U.S. 643 (1961).
58. Senate Committee on the Judiciary, *The Jury and the Search for Truth: The Case Against Excluding Relevant Evidence at Trial: Hearing Before the Committee*, 104th Cong., 1st sess. (U.S. Government Printing Office, 1997).
59. *United States* v. *Leon*, 468 U.S. 897 (1984); and *Arizona* v. *Evans*, 514 U.S. 1 (1995).
60. *Miranda* v. *Arizona*, 384 U.S. 436 (1966), but see *Yarborough* v. *Alvardo*, 124 S.Ct. 2140 (2004).
61. *Dickerson* v. *United States*, 530 U.S. 428 (2000).
62. Justice Felix Frankfurter, dissenting in *United States* v. *Rabinowitz*, 339 U.S. 56 (1950).
63. *United States* v. *Enterprises, Inc.*, 498 U.S. 292 (1991).
64. *Williams* v. *Florida*, 399 U.S. 78 (1970); and *Burch* v. *Louisiana*, 441 U.S. 130 (1979).
65. *J.E.B.* v. *Alabama ex rel T.B.*, 511 U.S. 127 (1994); *Batson* v. *Kentucky*, 476 U.S. 79 (1986); *Powers* v. *Ohio*, 499 U.S. 400 (1991); *Hernandez* v. *New York*, 500 U.S. 352 (1991); and *Georgia* v. *McCollum*, 505 U.S. 42 (1990).
66. *Ewing* v. *California*, 538 U.S. 11 (2003).
67. *Benton* v. *Maryland*, 395 U.S. 784 (1969). See also *Kansas* v. *Hendricks*, 521 U.S. 346 (1997).
68. *Graham* v. *Collins*, 506 U.S. 461 (1993).
69. Barry Scheck, Peter Neufeld, and Jim Dwyer, *Actual Innocence: Five Days to Execution and Other Dispatches from the Wrongly Convicted* (Doubleday, 2000); and Timothy Kaufman-Osborn, *From Noose to Needle: Capital Punishment and the Late Liberal State* (University of Michigan Press, 2002).
70. *Penry* v. *Lynaugh*, 492 U.S. 302 (1989).
71. *Atkins* v. *Virginia*, 536 U.S. 304 (2002).
72. Jerome Frank, *Courts on Trial* (Princeton University Press, 1949), p. 122. See also Steven Brill, *Trial by Jury* (American Lawyer Books/Touchstone, 1989).
73. Harry Kalven Jr. and Hans Zeisel, *The American Jury* (University of Chicago Press, 1971), p. 57. See also Jeffrey Abramson, *We, the Jury: The Jury System and the Ideal of Democracy* (Harvard University Press, 2000).
74. George Edwards, *The Police on the Urban Frontier* (Institute of Human Relations Press, 1968), p. 28. See also Jerome G. Miller, *African-American Males and the Criminal Justice System* (Cambridge University Press, 1996).
75. Sandra Bass, "Blacks, Browns, and the Blues: Police and Minorities in California," *Public Affairs Report* 38 (November 1997), p. 10.
76. See David Cole, *No Equal Justice: Race and Class in the American Criminal Justice System* (New Press, 1999); and Randall Kennedy, *Race, Crime, and the Law* (Pantheon, 1997).
77. See "Understanding Community Policing" (Bureau of Justice Administration), at www.community_policy.org.
78. Robert H. Jackson, *The Supreme Court in the American System of Government* (Harvard University Press, 1955), pp. 81–82.

Chapter 17

1. Andrew Hacker, *Two Nations: Black and White, Separate, Hostile, Unequal* (Scribner, 1992).
2. *Slaughter-House Cases*, 83 U.S. 36 (1873); and *Civil Rights Cases*, 109 U.S. 3 (1883).
3. *Plessy* v. *Ferguson*, 163 U.S. 537 (1896).
4. *Brown* v. *Board of Education of Topeka*, 347 U.S. 483 (1954); and *Brown* v. *Board of Education of Topeka*, 349 U.S. 294 (1955).
5. *Gomillion* v. *Lightfoot*, 364 U.S. 339 (1960).
6. Michael R. Belknap, *Federal Law and Southern Order: Racial Violence and Constitutional Conflict in the Post-Brown South* (University of Georgia Press, 1987), pp. 128–204.
7. Taylor Branch, *Parting the Waters: America in the King Years, 1954–1963* (Simon & Schuster, 1988). See also Harris Wofford, *Of Kennedys and Kings: Making Sense of the Sixties* (Farrar, Straus & Giroux, 1980).
8. See Charles Whalen and Barbara Whalen, *The Longest Debate: A Legislative History of the 1964 Civil Rights Act* (Mentor, 1985); and Hugh Davis Graham, *The Civil Rights Era* (Oxford University Press, 1990).
9. Aldon D. Morris, *The Origins of the Civil Rights Movement: Black Communities Organizing for Change* (Free Press/Macmillan, 1985); James Farmer, *Lay Bare the Heart: An Autobiography of the Civil Rights Movement* (Arbor House, 1985).
10. National Advisory Commission on Civil Disorders, *The Kerner Report* (U.S. Government Printing Office, 1968), p. 1.
11. Ellen Carol Du Bois, *Feminism and Suffrage: The Emergence of an Independent Women's Movement in America, 1848–1869* (Cornell University Press, 1978); Joan Hoff-Wilson, "Women and the Constitution," *News for Teachers of Political Science* (Summer 1985), pp. 10–15.
12. Susan M. Hartmann, *From Margin to Mainstream: American Women and Politics Since 1960* (Temple University Press, 1989); and Susan Gluck Mezey, *In Pursuit of Equality: Women, Public Policy, and the Federal Courts* (St. Martin's Press, 1992).
13. *United States* v. *Virginia*, 518 U.S. 515 (1996). See also Philippa Strum, *Women in the Barracks: The VMI Case and Equal Rights* (University Press of Kansas, 2002).
14. David M. O'Brien, "Ironies and Unanticipated Consequences of Legislation: Title VII of the 1964 Civil Rights Act and Sexual Harassment," in

Congress and the Politics of Emerging Rights, eds. Colton C. Campbell and John F. Stack Jr. (Rowman & Littlefield, 2002), pp. 27–44.

15. *Meritor Savings Bank, FBD* v. *Vinson,* 477 U.S. 57 (1986).

16. *Oncale* v. *Sundowner Offshore Services,* 523 U.S. 75 (1998); and *Faragher* v. *City of Boca Raton,* 524 U.S. 775 (1998); and *Burlington Industries* v. *Ellerth,* 524 U.S. 742 (1998).

17. Gregory Rodriguez, "The Nation: Where Minorities Rule," *The New York Times,* February 10, 2002, p. WK6.

18. Celia W. Dugger, "U.S. Study Says Asian-Americans Face Widespread Discrimination," *The New York Times,* February 29, 1992, p. 1, reporting on U.S. Civil Rights Commission, *Civil Rights Issues Facing Asian Americans in the 1990s* (U.S. Government Printing Office, 1992).

19. Won Moo Hurh, *Korean Immigrants in America* (Fairleigh Dickinson University Press, 1984).

20. Antonio J. A. Pido, *The Filipinos in America: Macro/Micro Dimensions of Immigration and Integration* (Center for Migration Studies of New York, 1986).

21. Harold L. Hodgkinson, *The Demographics of American Indians: One Percent of the People, Fifty Percent of the Diversity* (Institute for Educational Leadership/Center for Demographic Policy, 1990), pp. 1–5.

22. Charles F. Wilkinson, *American Indians, Times, and the Law* (Yale University Press, 1987); and Vine Deloria Jr. and Clifford M. Lytle, *The Nations Within: The Past and Future of American Indian Sovereignty* (Pantheon Books, 1984).

23. *County of Yakima* v. *Yakima Indian Nation,* 502 U.S. 251 (1992).

24. Theodora Lurie, "Shattering the Myth of the Vanishing American," *Ford Foundation Letter* 22 (Winter 1991), p. 5.

25. Spencer Rich, "Native Americans: They Can Still Get Free Health Care If They're Indian Enough," *The Washington Post National Weekly Edition,* July 14, 1986, p. 34, quoting the Office of Technology Assessment.

26. *Morey* v. *Doud,* 354 U.S. 459 (1957); *Allegheny Pittsburgh Coal Co.* v. *County Commission,* 488 U.S. 336 (1989).

27. *City of Cleburne, Texas* v. *Cleburne Living Center,* 473 U.S. 432 (1985); *Heller* v. *Doe,* 509 U.S. 312 (1993); and *Roemer* v. *Evans,* 517 U.S. 620 (1996).

28. *Roemer* v. *Evans,* 517 U.S. 620 (1996).

29. *San Antonio School District* v. *Rodriguez,* 411 U.S. 1 (1973).

30. *Frontiero* v. *Richardson,* 411 U.S. 677 (1973).

31. *Califano* v. *Webster,* 430 U.S. 313 (1977).

32. *Mississippi University for Woman* v. *Hogan,* 458 U.S. 718 (1982); and *United States* v. *Virginia,* 518 U.S. 515 (1996).

33. *San Antonio School District* v. *Rodriguez,* 411 U.S. 1 (1973); Douglas Reed, *On Equal Terms: The Constitutional Politics of Educational Opportunity* (Princeton University Press, 2001).

34. Matthew Bosworth, *Courts as Catalysts: State Supreme Courts and Public School Finance Equity* (State University of New York Press, 2001).

35. Sandra Day O'Connor, in *Kimel* v. *Florida Board of Regents,* 528 U.S. 62 (2000).

36. Ibid.

37. *Washington* v. *Davis,* 426 U.S. 229 (1976). See also *Hunter* v. *Underwood,* 471 U.S. 522 (1985).

38. Sandra Day O'Connor, concurring in *Hernandez* v. *New York,* 500 U.S. 352 (1991).

39. *Personnel Administrator of Massachusetts* v. *Feeney,* 442 U.S. 256 (1979).

40. *Smith* v. *Allwright,* 321 U.S. 649 (1944).

41. *Gomillion* v. *Lightfoot,* 364 U.S. 339 (1960).

42. *Harper* v. *Virginia Board of Elections,* 383 U.S. 663 (1966).

43. *Report of the United States Commission on Civil Rights* (U.S. Government Printing Office, 1959), pp. 103–104.

44. Harold W. Stanley, *Voter Mobilization and the Politics of Race: The South and Universal Suffrage, 1952–1984* (Praeger, 1987).

45. Abigail M. Thernstrom, *Whose Votes Count? Affirmative Action and Minority Voting Rights* (Harvard University Press, 1987), p. 15.

46. Thernstrom, *Whose Votes Count?* For a contrary view, see Bernard Grofman, Lisa Handley, and Richard G. Niemi, *Minority Representation and the Quest for Voting Equality* (Cambridge University Press, 1992).

47. *Morse* v. *Republican Party of Virginia,* 517 U.S. 116 (1996).

48. *Shaw* v. *Reno,* 509 U.S. 630 (1993).

49. *Hunt* v. *Cromartie,* 532 U.S. 234 (2001).

50. Orlando Patterson, *The Ordeal of Integration: Progress and Resentment in America's "Racial" Crisis* (Civitas/Counterpoint, 1997), p. 67.

51. *Plessy* v. *Ferguson,* 163 U.S. 537 (1896).

52. *Brown* v. *Board of Education of Topeka,* 347 U.S. 483 (1954). See also J. W. Peltason, *Fifty-Eight Lonely Men: Southern Federal Judges and School Desegregation* (University of Illinois Press, 1971), p. 248.

53. *Brown* v. *Board of Education of Topeka,* 349 U.S. 294 (1955).

54. *Freeman* v. *Pitts,* 503 U.S. 467 (1992); and *Missouri* v. *Jenkins,* 515 U.S. 70 (1995).

55. See Gary Orfield, Susan E. Eaton, and the Harvard Project on School Desegregation, *Dismantling Desegregation: The Quiet Reversal of* Brown *v.* Board of Education (New Press, 1996).

56. Raymond Hernandez, "NAACP Suspends Yonkers Leader After Criticism of Usefulness of School Busing," *The New York Times,* November 1, 1995, p. A13.

57. Gary Orfield and Chungmei Lee, *Brown at 50: King's Dream or Plessy's Nightmare?* (The Civil Rights Project, Harvard University, 2004), available at www.civilrightsproject.harvard.edu.

58. See Douglas Reed, *On Equal Terms,* pp. 21–22.

59. William O. Douglas, dissenting in *Moose Lodge No. 107* v. *Irvis,* 407 U.S. 163 (1972).

60. *New York State Club Association* v. *New York City,* 487 U.S. 1 (1988).

61. *Boy Scouts of America* v. *Dale,* 530 U.S. 640 (2000).

62. *Civil Rights Cases,* 109 U.S. 3 (1883).

63. *Heart of Atlanta Motel* v. *United States,* 379 U.S. 421 (1964).

64. Darryl Van Duch, "Plagued by Politics, EEOC Backlog Grows," *Recorder,* August 18, 1998, p. 1; David Rovella, "EEOC Chairman Casellas: 'We Are Being Selective,' " *National Law Journal,* November 20, 1995, p. 1.

65. Charles M. Lamb, "Housing Discrimination and Segregation," *Catholic University Law Review* (Spring 1981), p. 370.

66. *Shelley* v. *Kraemer,* 334 U.S. 1 (1948).

67. Daniel Mitchell, quoted in CQ Researcher, *Housing Discrimination* 5 (February 24, 1995), p. 174.

68. John Marshall Harlan, dissenting in *Plessy* v. *Ferguson,* 163 U.S. 537 (1896).

69. *University of California Regents* v. *Bakke,* 438 U.S. 265 (1978). See Howard Ball, *The Bakke Case* (University Press of Kansas, 2000).

70. Sandra Day O'Connor, in *Richmond* v. *Croson,* 488 U.S. 469 (1989).

71. See *Adarand Constructors, Inc.,* v. *Pena,* 515 U.S. 2000 (1995).

72. *Shaw* v. *Reno,* 509 U.S. 630 (1993); *Miller* v. *Johnson,* 515 U.S. 900 (1995).

73. "Affirmative Action in California Passed," *The Economist,* April 8, 2000, p. 29.

74. "Affirmative Action," *The Economist,* April 20, 2002, p. 30; "Affirmative Action: Moving on, but Very Slowly," *The Economist,* October 4, 2003, p. 29.

75. *Hopwood* v. *Texas,* 518 U.S. 1016 (1996).

76. Jonathan D. Glater, "Diversity Plan Shaped in Texas Is Under Attack," *The New York Times,* June 13, 2004, p. E1.

77. *Gratz* v. *Bollinger,* 539 U.S. 244 (2003).

78. *Grutter* v. *Bollinger,* 539 U.S. 306 (2003).

79. Carol M. Swain et al., "When Whites and Blacks Agree: Fairness in Educational Opportunities," Institute of Governmental Studies, University of California at Berkeley, Working Paper 98–11, 1998, p. 6. See also Lee Sigelman and Susan Welch, *Black Americans' Views of Racial Inequality: The Dream Deferred* (Cambridge University Press, 1994); and Peter Skerry, "The Affirmative Action Paradox," *Society* 35 (September–October 1998), p. 11.

80. James Farmer, quoted in Rochelle L. Stanfield, "Black Complaints Haven't Translated into Political Organization and Power," *National Journal,* June 14, 1980, p. 465.

81. Gary Orfield and Chungmei Lee, *Brown at 50;* and Donald Kinder and Lynn M. Sanders, *Divided by Color: Racial Politics and Democratic Ideals* (University of Chicago Press, 1996).

82. Gregory Rodriguez, "Where the Minorities Rule," *The New York Times,* February 10, 2002, p. WK6.

83. Gary Orfield, "Separate Societies: Have the Kerner Warnings Come True?" in *Quiet Riots: Race and Poverty in the United States—The Kerner Report Twenty Years Later,* eds. Fred R. Harris and Roger W. Wilkins (Pantheon, 1988), p. 103. See also Nicholas Lehmann, *The Promised Land* (Knopf, 1991).

84. Patterson, *The Ordeal of Integration,* p. 54.

85. Gary Orfield and Carole Ashkinaze, *The Closing Door: Conservative Policy and Black Opportunity* (University of Chicago Press, 1991), p. 26.

86. William J. Wilson, *The Truly Disadvantaged: The Inner City, the Underclass, and Public Policy* (University of Chicago Press, 1987), esp. chap. 5; and Kevin Phillips, *The Politics of Rich and Poor* (Random House, 1995).

87. Orfield and Ashkinaze, *Closing Door,* pp. 221–234; and A. Leon Higginbotham Jr., *Shades of Freedom* (Oxford University Press, 1996).

Chapter 18

1. See John Kingdon, *Agendas, Alternatives, and Public Policies* (Boston: Little, Brown, 1984), for a description of the policy-making process.

2. Kingdon, *Agendas, Alternatives, and Public Policies,* p. 3.

3. Anthony Downs, "The 'Issue-Attention Cycle,' " *The Public Interest* 28 (Summer 1972), p. 38.

4. Lester Salamon and Michael Lund, "The Tools Approach: Basic Analytics," in L. Salamon, ed., *Beyond Privatization: The Tools of Government Action* (Washington, D.C.: Urban Institute Press, 1989).

5. Hugh Heclo, "Issue Networks and the Executive Establishment," in A. King, ed., *The New American Political System* (Washington, D.C.: American Enterprise Institute, 1978), pp. 87–124.

6. See "National Debt," at www.jeffords.senate.gov/debt.html.

7. Andrew Taylor, "With Half-Trillion in Red Ink, U.S. Inc. Looks Bad on Paper," *CQ Weekly*, January 17, 2004, p. 132.

8. For a discussion of the budgetary cycle, see Allen Schick, *The Federal Budget: Politics, Policy, Process*, rev. ed. (Brookings Institution Press, 2000).

9. Efforts at past tax reform are described in Jeffrey H. Birnbaum and Alan S. Murray, *Showdown at Gucci Gulch: Lawmakers, Lobbyists, and the Unlikely Triumph of Tax Reform* (Vintage, 1988). See also Timothy J. Conlan, Margaret T. Wrightson, and David R. Beam, *Taxing Choices: The Politics of Tax Reform* (CQ Press, 1990).

10. Quoted in Frederick Lewis Allen, *Since Yesterday* (Harper, 1940), p. 64.

11. W. H. Beveridge, *The Pillars of Security* (Macmillan, 1943), p. 51.

12. The debate over Keynes and his economic theories is still alive in the United States. See Donald E. Moggridge, *Maynard Keynes: An Economist's Biography* (Routledge, 1992).

13. Environmental Working Group, at www.ewg.org.

14. Gary Burtless, Robert J. Lawrence, Robert E. Litan, and Robert J. Shapiro, *Globaphobia: Confronting Fears About Open Trade* (Brookings Institution Press, 1998), p. 29. For more information about GATT and the World Trade Organization, go to www.wto.org.

15. Mary Jordan, "Mexican Workers Pay for Success," *The Washington Post*, June 20, 2002, p. A1.

16. Burtless et al., *Globaphobia*, p. 126.

17. See Robert W. Crandall et al., *An Agenda for Federal Regulatory Reform* (American Enterprise Institute/Brookings Institution, 1997), for a discussion of reasons for the increased activity.

18. Harold W. Stanley and Richard G. Niemi, *Vital Statistics in American Politics, 1999* (CQ Press, 1999), p. 258.

19. Stephen Moore, ed., *Restoring the Dream: The Bold New Plan by House Republicans* (Times Books, 1995), p. 156.

20. *United States* v. *E. C. Knight Co.*, 156 U.S. 1 (1895).

21. On the origins of the Federal Trade Commission and the role of Louis D. Brandeis, see Thomas K. McCraw, *Prophets of Regulation* (Belknap Press, 1984), chap. 3.

22. For a useful history of airline deregulation, see Steven A. Morrison and Clifford Winston, *The Evolution of the Airline Industry* (Brookings Institution Press, 1995).

23. On Southwest Airlines and its longtime chief executive Herb Kelleher, see Kevin Freiberg and Jackie Freiberg, *Nuts!* (Bard Press, 1996).

24. *Reno* v. *American Civil Liberties Union*, 521 U.S. 844 (1997).

25. See Robert W. Crandall and Harold Furchtgott-Roth, *Cable TV: Regulation or Competition?* (Brookings Institution Press, 1996); Richard Klinger, *The New Information Industry: Regulatory Challenges and the First Amendment* (Brookings Institution Press, 1996); and Lawrence Lessig, *Code and Other Laws of Cyberspace* (Basic Books, 2000).

Chapter 19

1. Jackie Koszczuk and Jonathan Allen, "Late-Night Medicare Vote Drama Triggers Some Unexpected Alliances," *Congressional Quarterly Weekly*, November 29, 2003, p. 2958.

2. The Pew Research Center for the People and the Press, *Evenly Divided and Increasingly Polarized: 2004 Political Landscape* (Pew Research Center, November 5, 2003), pp. 39–44.

3. Michael B. Katz, *In the Shadow of the Poorhouse: A Social History of Welfare in America* (Basic Books, 1986).

4. This history draws heavily on Theda Skocpol's wonderful work on the subject, starting with "America's First Social Security System: The Expansion of Benefits for Civil War Veterans," *Political Science Quarterly* 108 (Winter 1993), pp. 64–87.

5. Ibid., pp. 85–86.

6. Joel F. Handler, *The Poverty of Welfare Reform* (Yale University Press, 1995), p. 21.

7. The 2004 guidelines can be found at www.aspe.hhs.gov/poverty/figures-fed-reg.shtml.

8. See U.S. Census Bureau, "Poverty Highlights." www.census.gov/hhes/poverty/poverty-2/pov02hi.html.

9. Gertrude Schaffner Goldberg and Eleanor Kremen, eds., *The Feminization of Poverty: Only in America?* (Greenwood Press, 1990).

10. See, for example, Margaret Weir, "Political Parties and Social Policymaking," in *The Social Divide: Political Parties and the Future of Activist Government*, ed. Margaret Weir (Brookings Institution Press, 1998).

11. Self-employed workers must cover both amounts, and many state and local government workers are not required to participate.

12. These and other simple facts about Social Security can be found at www.ssa.gov.

13. Martha Derthick, "No More Easy Votes for Social Security," *Brookings Review* 10 (Fall 1992), pp. 50–53.

14. For a pessimistic view of the viability of Social Security, see Neil Howe and Richard Jackson, "The Myth of the 2.2 Percent Solution," at www.cato.org/pubs/sspslles.html. Robert D. Reischauer of the Brookings Institution testified before the House Committee on Ways and Means on November 19, 1998, that Social Security will start running deficits by 2021 and that by 2032, "reserves will be depleted."

15. See Theda Skocpol, *Protecting Soldiers and Mothers: The Political Origins of Social Policy in the United States* (Belknap Press, 1992), chap. 9, for a history of the act.

16. Lyndon Johnson, speech at the University of Michigan, May 1964, in *Congress and the Nation, 1965–1968: A Review of Government and Politics During the Johnson Years* (CQ Press, 1969), vol. 2, p. 650.

17. For a history of Medicare and other Great Society programs, see James L. Sundquist, *Politics and Policy: The Eisenhower, Kennedy, and Johnson Years* (Brookings Institution Press, 1968).

18. William J. Clinton, acceptance speech, Democratic National Convention, Chicago, July 6, 1992.

19. Robert Pear, "Judge Rules States Can't Cut Welfare," *The New York Times*, October 14, 1997, p. A1.

20. Isabel V. Sawhill, R. Kent Weaver, Ron Haskins, and Andrea Kane, eds., *Welfare Reform and Beyond: The Future of the Safety Net* (Brookings Institution Press, 2002), p. 19.

21. Centers for Medicare and Medicaid Services, "Health Accounts," at www.cms.hhs.gov/statistics/nhe.

22. U.S. Bureau of the Census, *Statistical Abstracts of the United States*, 1999 (U.S. Government Printing Office, 1999), p. 448.

23. Ibid., p. 93.

24. Laurene A. Graig, *Health of Nations: An International Perspective on U.S. Health Care Reform* (CQ Press, 1993), p. 20.

25. Michael D. Lemonick, "Doctors' Deadly Mistakes," *Time*, December 13, 1999, p. 74.

26. Jennifer Steinhauer, "At Beth Israel, Lapses in Care Mar Gains in Technology," *The New York Times*, February 15, 2000, p. B1.

27. "Medicare Funds Going Up in Smoke," *Deseret News*, May 17, 1994, p. A1.

28. Congressional Budget Office, *How Many People Lack Health Insurance and for How Long?* (Congressional Budget Office, May, 2003).

29. U.S. Bureau of the Census, at www.census.gov.

30. "Measuring the HMOs," *Los Angeles Times*, October 3, 1998, p. B7.

31. Mary Agnes Carey and Rebecca Adams, "Managed-Care Conferees Agree on Appeals Principles; Key Details Remian Unresolved," *Congressional Quarterly Weekly*, April 15, 2000, p. 903.

32. Congressional Budget Office, *How Many People Lack Health Insurance and for How Long?*

33. Institute of Medicine, Committee on Employer-Based Health Benefits, *Employment and Health Benefits: A Connection at Risk*, eds. Marilyn J. Field and Harold T. Shapiro (National Academy Press, 1993), p. 5.

34. The amount permitted for a medical savings account is 75 percent of the maximum total deduction for medical expenses for an individual or couple; see Internal Revenue Service, at www.irs.ustreas.bov/prod/forms_pubs/pubs/p96901.htm.

35. Martin Kady II, "America's Uneasy Mandate for Domestic Security," *Congressional Quarterly Weekly*, April 24, 2004, p. 950.

Chapter 20

1. The complete timeline for the Iraq war, including all links and citations to specific quotes in this section, can be found at www.cooperativeresearch.org.

2. See Glenn Kessler, "U.S. Decision On Iraq Has Puzzling Past Opponents of War Wonder When, How Policy Was Set," *The Washington Post*, January 12, 2003, p. A1, for a detailed history of the increasing interest in Iraq.

3. U.S. Select Committee on Intelligence, *Report on the U.S. Intelligence Community's Prewar Intelligence Assessments on Iraq: Conclusions*, no report number, July 7, 2004, p. 1.

4. Pew Research Center for the People and the Press, "Public Support for War Resilient," June 17, 2004, questions 2a and 52.

5. National Commission on Terrorist Attacks on the United States, *The 9/11 Commission Report*, Government Printing Office, 2004, p. 362.

6. National Commission on Terrorist Attacks on the United States, *The 911 Commission Report*, p. 376.

7. See the entire doctrine explained in *The National Security Strategy of the United States*, White House, September 7, 2002.

8. This reference is contained in the chronology as www. cooperativeresearch.org, which draws from Richard Clarke's *Against All Enemies: Inside America's War on Terror* (Free Press, 2004).

9. Condoleezza Rice, quoted in Glenn Kessler, "Rice Lays Out Case for War in Iraq," *The Washington Post*, August 16, 2002, p. A1.

10. James T. Quinlivan, "Burden of Victory: The Painful Arithmetic of Stability Operations," *RAND Review*, vol. 27, no. 2, 2003, pp. 28–29.

11. United States Senate Select Committee on Intelligence, *Report on the U.S. Intelligence Community's Prewar Intelligence Assessments on Iraq*, Committee print, reported July 7, 2004, Committee summary p. 1, available at www.intelligence.senate.gov/conclusions.pdf.

12. The "slam dunk case" story is reported in Bob Woodward's *Plan of Attack* (Simon & Schuster, 2004).

13. For more information, visit the Peace Corps Web site at www. peacecorps.gov. For a useful study of the Peace Corps, see Elizabeth Cobbs Hoffman, *All You Need Is Love: The Peace Corps and the Spirit of the 1960s* (Harvard University Press, 1998).

14. U.S. Department of Defense, at www.defenselink.mil; U.S. Department of State, at www.state.gov.

15. The case for continued reliance on vital U.S. embassies abroad is well made in Mary Locke and Casimir A. Yost, eds., *Who Needs Embassies? How U.S. Missions Abroad Help Shape Our World* (Georgetown University School of Foreign Policy, 1997).

16. For a fascinating history of U.S. intelligence operations, see Christopher Andrew, *For the President's Eyes Only: Secret Intelligence and the American Presidency from Washington to Bush* (HarperCollins, 1995). See also Rhodri Jeffreys-Jones, *The CIA and American Democracy*, 2d ed. (Yale University Press, 1998).

17. National Commission on Terrorist Attacks on the United States, *The 9/11 Commission Report*, p. 12.

18. See George C. Wilson, *This War Really Matters: Inside the Fight for Defense Dollars* (CQ Press, 2000).

19. Pew Research Center for the People and the Press, *Public Opinion in a Year for the Books* (Pew Research Center, 2002), p. 1.

20. Thomas L. Friedman, "India, Pakistan, and G.E.," *New York Times*, August 11, 2002, sec. 4, p. 13.

21. For an examination of how Japanese companies try to influence foreign policy and trade officials in Washington, see Pat Choate, *Agents of Influence* (Knopf, 1990).

22. "G.O.P. Returns $100,000 Gift," *The New York Times*, January 20, 2001, p. A8.

23. For a useful review of how Congress has occasionally challenged and even more often failed to challenge the White House when it comes to the war power, see Louis Fisher, *Presidential War Power* (University Press of Kansas, 1995).

24. For an analysis that asserts U.S. foreign policy is almost entirely shaped by self-appointed elites, see Eric Alterman, *Who Speaks for America? Why Democracy Matters* (Cornell University Press, 1998). More generally, see Ole Holsti, *Public Opinion and American Foreign Policy* (University of Michigan Press, 1996).

25. Dennis C. Jett, "The U.N.'s Failures Are Everyone's Fault," *The New York Times*, May 22, 2000, p. A23. See also Christopher S. Wren, "Era Waning: Holbrooke Takes Stock," *The New York Times*, January 14, 2001, p. 8.

26. "U.S. Foreign Aid Spending Since World War II," *Public Perspective* 8 (August-September 1997), p. 11.

27. Gallup Poll, May 2000, www.gallup.com.

28. See Sebastian Mallaby, "Why So Stingy on Foreign Aid?" *Washington Post National Weekly Edition*, July 3, 2000, p. 27.

29. Ibid. But see Doug Bandlow, "The Case Against Foreign Aid," *Christian Science Monitor*, September 29, 1999, p. 9; and Eric Schmitt, "Helms Urges Foreign Aid Be Handled by Charities," *The New York Times*, January 12, 2001, p. A4.

30. Richard N. Haass, "Sanctions Almost Never Work," *The Wall Street Journal*, June 19, 1998, p. A14. See also Richard N. Haass and Meghan L. O'Sullivan, eds., *Honey and Vinegar: Incentives, Sanctions, and Foreign Policy* (Brookings Institution Press, 2000).

31. Richard Lugar, in Gerald F. Seib, "Capital Journal," *The Wall Street Journal*, June 17, 1998, p. A18.

32. Gary Hufbauer, "Foreign Policy on the Cheap," *Washington Post National Weekly Edition*, July 20, 1998, p. 22.

33. See Robert Kagan, "The Kerry Doctrine," *The Washington Post*, August 1, 2004, p. B7, for this argument.

34. Gary Hufbauer and Jeffrey J. Schott, "Economic Sanctions and Foreign Policy," *PS: Political Science and Politics* 18 (Fall 1985), p. 278.

35. See Ivo H. Daalder and Michael E. O'Hanlon, *Winning Ugly: NATO's War to Save Kosovo* (Brookings Institution Press, 2000), esp. chap. 6.

36. John Prados, *The President's Secret Wars: CIA and Pentagon Covert Operations Since World War II* (Morrow, 1986); Daniel Patrick Moynihan, *Secrecy: The American Experience* (Yale University Press, 1998).

37. P. W. Singer, "Winning the War of Words: Information Warfare in Afghanistan," *Brookings Analysis Paper No. 5*, October 2001.

38. Norman A. Graebner, "The President as Commander in Chief: A Study in Power," in *Commander-in-Chief: Presidential Leadership in Modern Wars*, ed. Joseph G. Dawson III (University Press of Kansas, 1993), p. 31.

39. Colin L. Powell, quoted in Steven Mufson, "From Soldier to Diplomat," *Washington Post National Weekly Edition*, December 25, 2000, p. 6.

40. Bill Keller, "The World According to Powell," *New York Times Magazine*, November 25, 2001, p. 14.

41. T. M. Destler and Steven Kull, *Misreading the Public: The Myth of a New Isolationism* (Brookings Institution Press, 1998).

42. Eric Schmitt and Thom Shanker, "Army to Call Up Recruits Earlier," *The New York Times*, July 22, 2004, p. A1.

43. Evan Thomas and Gregory L. Vistica, "Falling Out of the Sky," *Newsweek*, March 17, 1997, p. 26.

44. Office of Management and Budget, *Budget of the United States, Fiscal Year 2005* (U.S. Government Printing Office, 2004).

45. Ibid.

46. John Spratt and Hugh Brady, "National Security v. Social Security," *Brookings Review*, vol. 20, no. 3 (Summer 2002), p. 12.

47. See, for example, James Kitfield, "Ships Galore!" *National Journal*, February 10, 1996, pp. 298–302.

48. *Public Papers of the Presidents*, Dwight D. Eisenhower, 1960, pp. 1035–1040.

49. See Renae Merle, "Contract Workers Are War's Forgotten," *The Washington Post*, July 31, 2004, p. A1.

50. Michael Rich, John Birkler, and Mark Lorell, "Defense Industry Goliaths," *The Atlantic Monthly*, July/August, 2003, p. 89.

Chapter 21

1. *The New York Times*, November 11, 1997.

2. Harold Lasswell, *Who Gets What, When, How* (Meridian Books, 1958).

3. Texas Comptroller of Public Accounts, *Fiscal Notes*, June 1998, p. 6.

4. David Easton, *A Framework For Political Analysis* (Prentice Hall, 1965), chap. 5.

5. Louise Cowan, "Myth in the Modern World," in *Texas Myths*, ed. Robert F. O'Connor (Texas A&M University Press, 1986), p. 4.

6. Ibid., p. 14. For an excellent analysis of the concept of the "myth of origin" as integrated into the American mythology, see Robert N. Bellah, *The Broken Covenant: American Civil Religion in Time of Trial* (The Seabury Press, 1975).

7. T. R. Fehrenbach, "Texas Mythology: Now and Forever," in *Texas Myths*, pp. 210–217.

8. Robin Doughty, "From Wilderness to Garden: Conquering the Texas Landscape," in *Texas Myths*, p. 105.

9. Lucian W. Pye, "Political Culture," *International Encyclopedia of the Social Sciences*, vol. 12 (Crowell, Collier and Macmillan, 1968), p. 218.

10. Ellen M. Dran, Robert B. Albritton, and Mikel Wyckoff, "Surrogate versus Direct Measures of Political Culture: Explaining Participation and Policy Attitudes in Illinois," *Publius* 21 (Spring 1991), p. 17.

11. Daniel Elazar, *American Federalism: A View from the States* (Thomas Y. Crowell, 1966), p. 86.

12. Ibid., pp. 86–89.

13. Ibid., pp. 90–92.

14. Ibid., pp. 92–94.

15. Ibid., pp. 97, 102, 108.

16. U.S. Bureau of the Census, Census 2000. Unless otherwise noted, all demographic data are taken from the 2000 census.

17. Ellen N. Murray, "Sorrow Whispers in the Winds," *Texas Journal* 14 (Spring/Summer 1992), p. 16.

18. Terry G. Jordan with John L. Bean, Jr., and William M. Holmes, *Texas: A Geography* (Westview Press, 1984), pp. 79–86.

19. David Montejano, *Anglos and Mexicans in the Making of Texas, 1836–1986* (University of Texas Press, 1987), p. 38.
20. Hispanics can be of any race.
21. Texas State Data Center, Texas A&M University.
22. National Association of Latino Elected and Appointed Officials, *2003 National Roster of Hispanic Elected Officials*.
23. Joint Center for Political Studies, *National Roster of Black Elected Officials, 2001*.
24. Jordan et al., *Texas*, pp. 71–77.
25. V. O. Key, *Southern Politics in State and Nation* (Vintage Books, 1949), p. 261.
26. For an excellent analysis of Key's projections for political change in Texas, see Chandler Davidson, *Race and Class in Texas Politics* (Princeton University Press, 1990).
27. U.S. Bureau of the Census, *Census 2000*.
28. Office of the Governor, Texas 2000 Commission, *Texas Trends*, pp. 5–6; Office of the Governor, Texas 2000 Commission, *Texas Past and Future: A Survey*, p. 6.
29. U.S. Bureau of the Census, *Census 2000*.
30. Ibid.
31. *San Antonio Express-News*, October 1, 2003, p. 1A.; Texas Transportation Institute Texas A&M University, *2003 Mobility Study*, September 2003.
32. Steve H. Murdock, Nazrul Hoque, Martha Michael, Steve White, and Beverly Pecotte, *The Texas Challenge: Population Change and the Future of Texas* (Texas A&M University Press, 1997), p. 29.
33. U.S. Bureau of the Census, *Census 2000*.
34. *Forbes*, Special Edition 2003, "The 400 Richest People in America," pp. 186–284.
35. U.S. Bureau of the Census, *Census 2000*.
36. U.S. Bureau of the Census, *Current Population Survey, 1999*.
37. Murdock et al., *The Texas Challenge*, pp. 64–65.
38. Betsey Bishop and Terry Heller, "Education Reform: Preparing Our Children for the Future," *Fiscal Notes*, March 1991, p. 10.
39. U.S. Bureau of the Census, *Census 2000*.
40. For an expanded analysis of the Texas economy and the dominant role played by larger corporations, see James W. Lamare, *Texas Politics: Economics, Power and Policy*, 7th ed. (Wadsworth, 2001), chap. 2.
41. "Boom, Bust and Back Again: Bullock Tenure Covers Tumultuous Era," *Fiscal Notes*, December 1990, pp. 6–7.
42. Ibid.
43. "Road to Recovery Long and Bumpy, but Positive Signs Begin to Appear," *Fiscal Notes*, March 1989, p. 4.
44. "Boom, Bust and Back Again," p. 7.
45. "Brac'95 Round of Base Closures Will Have a Minor Effect on the Texas Economy," *Texas Economic Quarterly*, September 1995, p. 8; "Texas Economic History and Outlook, for Calendar Years: 1994 to 2000," *Texas Economic Update* (Winter 2000): 2.
46. "Texas Economic Outlook," *Texas Economic Quarterly*, December 1996, p. 2.
47. Texas Economic Development, May 2002, www.bidc.state.tx.us/overview/2-21e.
48. Harry Hurt, "Birth of a New Frontier," *Texas Monthly*, April 1984, pp. 130–135.
49. "Biotechnology: New Science Brings Jobs to Texas as Biotech-Related Efforts Blossom," *Fiscal Notes*, April 1990, pp. 1–8.
50. Texas Department of Economic Development, April 1998.
51. The following discussion of the ten economic regions of Texas is based on reports produced by John Sharp, Texas Comptroller of Public Accounts, in the series *Texas Regional Outlook* (Reports of the Comptroller's Forces of Change Project, 1992); and *Texas Regional Outlook* (2002).
52. M. Delal Baer, "North American Free Trade," *Foreign Affairs* 70 (Fall 1991): 138.
53. Joan B. Anderson, "Maquiladoras and Border Industrialization: Impact on Economic Development in Mexico," *Journal of Borderland Studies* V (Spring 1990), p. 5.
54. Michael Patrick, "Maquiladoras and South Texas Border Economic Development," *Journal of Borderland Studies* IV (Spring 1989, p. 90.
55. Martin E. Rosenfeldt, "Mexico's In Bond Export Industries and U.S. Legislation: Conflictive Issues," *Journal of Borderland Studies* V (Spring 1990), p. 57.
56. Patrick, "Maquiladoras and South Texas Border Economic Development," p. 90.
57. Baer, "North American Free Trade," pp. 132–149.
58. Central Intelligence Agency, *The World Factbook* (CIA), 1997.
59. Chandler Stolp and Jon Hockenyos, "Free Trade over Texas," *San Antonio Light*, September 15, 1991, p. E-1.
60. Augustin Redwine, "A Bureaucracy Is Born: International Departments Being Organized to Oversee NAFTA," *Fiscal Notes*, April 1994, p. 12.
61. Border Environmental Cooperation Commission, Operations Department, "Certified Projects Report," October 2003.
62. Redwine, "A Bureaucracy Is Born," p. 12.
63. Commission for Labor Cooperation, www.NAALC.org, April 2003.
64. Robert S. Chose, Emily B. Hill and Paul Kennedy, "Pivotal States and U.S. Strategy," *Foreign Affairs* 75 (January/February 1996), p. 39.
65. Texas Economic Development, May 2002.
66. David Hendricks, "Security Change Will Discriminate Against Mexico, South Texas," *San Antonio Express*-News, October 25, 2003, p. D1.
67. Joan Anderson and Martin de la Rosa, "Economic Survival Strategies of Poor Families on the Mexican Border," *Journal of Borderland Studies* VI (Spring 1991), p. 51.
68. Howard G. Applegate, C. Richard Bath and Jeffery T. Trannon, "Binational Emissions Trading in an International Air Shed: The Case of El Paso, Texas and Ciudad Juarez," *Journal of Borderland Studies* IV (Fall 1989), pp. 1–25.
69. *San Antonio Express News*, February 18, 1991, p. A-1.
70. Stephen A. Camarota, *Back Where We Started: An Examination of Trends in Immigrant Welfare Use Since Reform*, (Center for Immigration Studies, March 2003), p. 5.
71. Migration Policy Institute, *Immigration Facts, 2003* (Immigration and Naturalization Service).
72. James F. Pearce and Jeffery W. Gunther, "Illegal Immigration from Mexico: Effects on the Texas Economy," *Federal Reserve Bank of Dallas Economic Review*, September 1985, p. 4.
73. Robert W. Gardner and Leon F. Bouvier, "The United States," in *Handbook on International Migration*, eds. William J. Serow, Charles B. Nam, David F. Sly, and Robert H. Weller (Greenwood Press, 1990), p. 342.
74. "Congress Clears Overhaul of Immigration Law," *Congressional Quarterly Almanac, 1986* (CQ Press, 1987), pp. 61–67.
75. Dan Carney, "Law Restricts Illegal Immigration," *Congressional Quarterly Weekly Report* 54 (November 16, 1996), p. 3287.
76. Pearce and Gunther, "Illegal Immigration from Mexico: Effects on the Texas Economy," p. 2.

Chapter 22

1. G. Allan Tarr, *Understanding State Constitutions* (Princeton University Press, 1998), p. 3.
2. Daniel Elazar, "The Principles and Traditions Underlying American State Constitutions," *Publius* 12 (Winter 1982), p. 23.
3. Tarr, pp. 4–5.
4. David Saffell, *State Politics* (Addison-Wesley, 1984), pp. 23–24.
5. Elazar, pp. 20–21.
6. T. R. Fehrenbach, *Lone Star: A History of Texas and the Texans* (Macmillan, 1968), pp. 152–173.
7. Richard Gambitta, Robert A. Milne, and Carol R. Davis, "The Politics of Unequal Educational Opportunity," in *The Politics of San Antonio*, eds. David R. Johnson, John A. Booth, and Richard J. Harris (University of Nebraska Press, 1983), p. 135.
8. Joe B. Frantz, *Texas: A Bicentennial History* (W. W. Norton, 1976), pp. 73, 76.
9. Fehrenbach, *Lone Star*, p. 265.
10. Frantz, *Texas*, p. 92.
11. Fehrenbach, *Lone Star*, p. 396.
12. Ibid., pp. 398–399, 401.
13. J. E. Ericson, "The Delegates to the Convention of 1875: A Reappraisal," *Southwestern Historical Quarterly* 67 (July 1963), p. 22.
14. Ibid., p. 23.
15. Ibid.
16. Ibid., pp. 25–26.
17. Fehrenbach, *Lone Star*, pp. 374, 431, 434.
18. Ericson, "The Delegates to the Convention of 1875," pp. 24–25.
19. Fehrenbach, *Lone Star*, p. 435.
20. Janice May, "Constitutional Revision in Texas," in *The Texas Constitution: Problems and Prospects for Revision* (Urban Development Commission, 1971), p. 82.
21. David Berman, *State and Local Politics*, 6th ed. (Wm. C. Brown, 1991), p. 61.
22. May, "Constitutional Revision in Texas," p. 76.
23. John E. Bebout, "The Problem of the Texas Constitution," in *The Texas Constitution: Problems and Prospects for Revision*, (Institute of Urban Studies, University of Texas at Arlington, 1971), pp. 9, 11.

24. Bill Hobby, quoted in the *Houston Chronicle,* January 8, 1974.
25. Jim Mattox, quoted in the *Houston Chronicle,* July 31, 1974.
26. Quoted in Nelson Wolff, *Challenge of Change* (Naylor, 1975), p. 170.
27. Abner McCall, quoted in the *Houston Chronicle,* September 20, 1973.
28. Dolph Briscoe, reported in the *Houston Chronicle,* October 15, 1975.
29. Lewis A. Froman, Jr., "Some Effects of Interest Group Strength in State Politics," *American Political Science Review* 60 (December 1966), pp. 952–963.
30. "California's Constitutional Amendomania," *Stanford Law Review* 1 (1949), pp. 279–288.

36. Chandler Davidson, *Race and Class in Texas Politics* (Princeton University Press, 1990), p. 24.
37. Secretary of State, Elections Division.
38. Davidson, *Race and Class in Texas Politics,* p. 24.
39. Secretary of State, Elections Division.
40. Ibid.
41. *Houston Chronicle,* December 2, 1997.
42. Associated Press, December 7, 2003.
43. Texans for Public Justice, *Money in Politex: A Guide to Money in the 2002 Texas Elections,* November 2003.
44. Ibid., pp. 9, 17.

Chapter 23

1. *Houston Chronicle,* October 2, 2003, p. 19A.
2. Belle Zeller, *American State Legislatures* (Thomas Y. Crowell, 1954), p. 603; and Clive S. Thomas and Ronald J. Hrebenar, "Interest Groups in the States," in *Politics in the American States,* 6th ed., Virginia Gray and Herbert Jacob, eds. (Congressional Quarterly Press, 1996), p. 152.
3. Harmon L. Zeigler and Hendrik van Dalen, "Interest Groups in State Politics," in *Politics in the American States,* 3rd ed., eds. Herbert Jacob and Kenneth N. Vines (Little, Brown, 1976), pp. 93–136.
4. George Norris Green, *The Establishment in Texas Politics: 1938–1957* (Greenwood Press, 1979), pp. 1, 17.
5. Ibid., p. 30.
6. Chandler Davidson, *Race and Class in Texas Politics* (Princeton University Press, 1990), p. 54.
7. Ibid., chap. 4 and 5.
8. Ibid., p. 83.
9. Ibid., p. 108.
10. See Green, *The Establishment in Texas Politics,* for an excellent analysis of the labor-bashing techniques used by Texas business in the 1940s and 1950s.
11. Ibid., chap. 5.
12. See Davidson, *Race and Class in Texas Politics,* chap. 10.
13. V. O. Key, *Southern Politics* (Vintage Books, 1949), p. 255.
14. Davidson, *Race and Class in Texas Politics,* p. 21.
15. Alexander P. Lamis, *The Two-Party South,* expanded ed. (Oxford University Press, 1988), p. 23.
16. Key, *Southern Politics,* pp. 302–310.
17. Green, *The Establishment in Texas Politics,* pp. 142–148.
18. Lamis, *The Two-Party South,* p. 195.
19. John R. Knaggs, *Two-Party Texas: The John Tower Era, 1961–1984* (Austin: Eakin Press, 1986), p. 15.
20. Davidson, *Race and Class in Texas Politics,* p. 199.
21. For an excellent summary of realignment theory and conditions under which realignment is likely to take place, see James L. Sundquist, *Dynamics of the Party System* (Brookings Institution Press, 1973).
22. James A. Dyer, Arnold Vedlitz, and David Hill, "New Voters, Switchers, and Political Party Realignment in Texas," *Western Political Quarterly* 41 (March 1988), p. 156.
23. Ibid., pp. 165–166; *Texas Poll,* Summer 2003, Fall 2003, Winter 2003, Spring 2004.
24. V. O. Key Jr., *Parties, Politics, and Pressure Groups,* 4th ed. (Thomas Y. Crowell, 1958), p. 347.
25. Wilbourn E. Benton, Texas Politics: *Constraints and Opportunities,* 5th ed. (Nelson-Hall, 1984), pp. 72–73.
26. *Smith* v. *Allwright,* 321 U.S. 649 (1944).
27. *John Terry et al., Petitioners* v. *A. J. Adams et al.,* 345 U. S. 461.
28. Beryl E. Pettus and Randall W. Bland, *Texas Government Today: Structures, Functions, Political Processes,* 3rd ed. (Dorsey, 1984), pp. 85–86.
29. *Beare et al.* v. *Preston Smith, Governor of Texas,* 321 F. Supp. 1100 (1971).
30. *Miller* v. *Johnson,* 115 S.Ct. 2475 (1995); *Bush* v. *Vera,* 116 S.Ct. 1941 (1996).
31. Robert R. Brischetto, Southwest Voter Research Institute, Inc., San Antonio, telephone conversations, November 1, 1991.
32. Ibid. and Robert Brischetto, *The Political Empowerment of Texas Mexicans, 1974–1988* (Southwest Voter Research Institute, Latino Electorate Series, 1988), pp. 1–19.
33. William C. Velasquez Institute news release, March 13, 2002.
34. Texas Municipal League, *Directory of City Officials,* 2004 (Texas Municipal League, 2004); survey conducted by the A.G. Young Institute of County Government, Texas A & M University, 2002.
35. David A. Bositis, Black Elected Officials, 2001 (Joint Center for Political and Economic Studies, 2003), p. 18.

Chapter 24

1. For an extended discussion of legislative functions, see William J. Keffe and Morris S. Ogul, *The American Legislative Process,* 8th ed. (Prentice Hall, 1993), pp. 16–37.
2. On the general concept of institutionalization, see Nelson W. Plosby, "The Institutionalization of the U.S. House of Representatives," *American Political Science Review* 62 (March 1968), pp. 144–168. For a more recent assessment of state legislative development, see Alan Rosenthal, "State Legislative Development: Observations from Three Perspectives," *Legislative Studies Quarterly* XXI (May 1996), pp. 169–198.
3. Thomas R. Dye, *Politics in States and Communities,* 8th ed. (Prentice Hall, 1994), pp. 179–183. In a recent study of state legislatures, Texas ranked thirteenth in terms of professionalization. Other studies place it somewhat lower. See Peverell Squire, "Uncontested Seats in State Legislative Elections," *Legislative Studies Quarterly* XXV (February 2000), p. 143; and James D. King, "Changes in Professionalism in U.S. State Legislatures," *Legislative Studies Quarterly* XXV (May 2000), pp. 327–343.
4. Council of State Governments, *Book of the States, 1998–1999* (The Council of State Governments, 1998), p. 68.
5. Ibid., pp. 78–79; California Legislative Council Bureau.
6. For a comprehensive analysis of the literature on legislative recruitment and careers, see Donald R. Matthews, "Legislative Recruitment and Legislative Careers," *Legislative Studies Quarterly* IX (November 1984), pp. 547–585.
7. *Baker* v. *Carr,* 369 U.S. 186 (1992); *Reynolds* v. *Sims,* 377 U.S. 533 (1964); *Kilgarlin* v. *Martin,* 252 F.Supp. 404 (S.D. Tex. 1966).
8. *Georgia* v. *Ashcroft,* 539 U.S. 461 (2003).
9. *Houston Chronicle,* October 12, 2003, p. 33A.
10. Fred Gantt, Jr., *The Chief Executive in Texas: A Study of Gubernatorial Leadership* (University of Texas Press, 1964), p. 238.
11. *Houston Chronicle,* January 6, 1993.
12. State Senator Bill Ratliff, quoted in the *Houston Chronicle,* June 6, 1999, p. 1E.
13. *Houston Chronicle,* June 6, 2001, p. 1A.
14. For an earlier summary of the scholarly work on legislative committees, see Heinz Eulau and Vera McCluggage, "Standing Committees in Legislatures: Three Decades of Research," *Legislative Studies Quarterly* IX (May 1984), pp. 195–270. For a more recent summary of research on state legislatures, see Malcom Jewell, "Trends in Research on U.S. State Legislatures: A Review Article", *Legislative Studies Quarterly* XXII (May 1997), pp. 265–274.
15. See Malcolm E. Jewell and Samuel C. Patterson, *The Legislative Process in the United States* (Random House, 1966), chap. 11, for a summary of the function of legislative rules and procedures.
16. For a brief overview of the representative problem, see Neil Reimer, ed., *The Representative: Trustee? Delegate? Partisan? Politico?* (D. C. Heath, 1967). For a more comprehensive treatment of the subject, see Hanna F. Pitkin, *The Concept of Representation* (University of California Press, 1967).
17. For an excellent treatment of the relationship of U.S. legislators to their districts and constituencies, see Richard F. Fenno Jr., *Home Style: House Members in Their Districts* (Little, Brown, 1978).
18. There has been a considerable number of studies of these informal norms within the legislative process. Donald R. Matthews's *U.S. Senators and Their World* (Vintage Books, 1960) was the seminal work in this area. For the adaptation of this concept to state legislatures, see Alan Rosenthal, *Legislative Life: People, Process, and Performance of the States* (Harper & Row, 1981), pp. 123–27.
19. The general concepts for this discussion are based on John W. Kingdon, *Congressmen's Voting Decisions,* 2nd ed. (Harper & Row, 1981).

20. For a general discussion of staff in state legislatures, see Rosenthal, *Legislative Life: People, Process, and Performance in the States,* chap. 10.
21. *Fort Worth Star-Telegram,* December 4, 1990.
22. *Houston Chronicle,* December 12, 1990.
23. *Houston Chronicle,* January 1, 1991.
24. Statement issued by Governor Ann Richards, May 1991.

Chapter 25

1. State Comptroller's Office, *Breaking the Mold: A Report of the Texas Performance Review,* vol. 1 (Texas Comptroller's Office, 1991), p. 1.
2. Joseph A. Schlesinger, "The Politics of the Executive," in *Politics in the American States,* 2nd ed., Herbert Jacob and Kenneth N. Vines, eds. (Little, Brown, 1971), chap. 6; Thad L. Beyle, "The Governors, 1988–89." in *The Book of the States, 1990–1991* (The Council of State Governments, 1990), p. 54.
3. Charles F. Cnudde and Robert E. Crew, *Constitutional Democracy in Texas* (West, 1989), p. 90.
4. Fred Gantt Jr., *The Chief Executive in Texas* (University of Texas Press, 1964), p. 116.
5. See James E. Anderson, Richard W. Murray, and Edward L. Farley, *Texas Politics,* 6th ed. (HarperCollins, 1992), pp. 166–191, for an excellent analysis of the leadership styles of Governors Allan Shivers, Price Daniel, John Connally, Preston Smith, and Dolph Briscoe.
6. Gantt, *Chief Executive in Texas,* pp. 229–230.
7. *Dallas Morning News,* April, 1987, p. H-2.
8. *Houston Chronicle,* September 30, 2003, p. 15A.
9. Wilbourn E. Benton, *Texas Politics: Constraints and Opportunities,* 5th ed. (Nelson-Hall, 1984), pp. 164–167.
10. Gantt, *Chief Executive in Texas,* pp. 90–107.
11. Robert S. Lorch, *State and Local Politics,* 3rd ed. (Prentice Hall, 1989), pp. 115–119.
12. Daniel Elazar, "The Principles and Traditions Underlying State Constitutions," *Publius* 12 (Winter 1982), pp. 17.
13. Texas Comptroller of Public Accounts, *Fiscal Notes,* December 1990, pp. 8–9.
14. U.S. Department of Commerce, Bureau of the Census, *Government Organization, 1997,* vol. 1 (Government Printing Office, 1999), table 9.
15. U.S. Census Bureau, *Statistical Abstract of the United States: 2001* (Government Printing Office, 2000).
16. Theodore J. Lowi, *The End of Liberalism,* 2nd ed. (W. W. Norton, 1979), p. 274.
17. Texas Sunset Advisory Commission, *Sunset Review in Texas: Summary of Process and Procedures* (Texas Sunset Advisory Commission, 1991).
18. *Dallas Morning News,* October 24, 1991.
19. Robert Lineberry, *American Public Policy* (Harper & Row, 1977), pp. 84–85.
20. Bill Wells, quoted in Associated Press story, *Dallas Times Herald,* August 14, 1983.
21. *Austin American-Statesman,* June 14, 1993.

Chapter 26

1. *Smith* v. *Allwright,* 321 U.S. 649 (1944).
2. *Miranda* v. *Arizona,* 384 U.S. 436 (1966).
3. Texas Research League, *The Texas Judiciary: A Structural-Functional Overview,* Report 1 (Texas Research League, August 1990).
4. Texas Judicial Council, Office of Court Administration, *Texas Judicial System, 75th Annual Report* (Texas Judicial Council, 2003).
5. Allen E. Smith, *The Impact of the Texas Constitution on the Judiciary* (University of Houston, Institute for Urban Studies, 1973), p. 45.
6. Office of Court Administration, *Texas Judicial System, 75th Annual Report.*
7. Ibid.
8. Ibid.
9. Ibid.
10. Smith, *The Impact of the Texas Constitution on the Judiciary,* pp. 28–31.
11. Texas Research League, *Texas Courts: A Proposal for Structural-Functional Reform,* Report 2 (Texas Research League, May 1991), pp. 1–15.
12. *Fort Worth Star-Telegram,* September 4, 1983.
13. *Houston Chronicle,* April 12, 1986.
14. *Houston Post,* May 18, 1986.

15. Anthony Champagne, "Campaign Contributions in Texas Supreme Court Races," *Crime, Law and Social Change* 17 (1992), pp. 91–106.
16. Kim Ross, quoted in the *Houston Post,* November 10, 1988.
17. *Austin American-Statesman,* December 9, 1993.
18. *Houston Chronicle,* April 30, 2004, page 1A.
19. *Houston Chronicle,* August 21, 2003, p. 24A.
20. Texas Watch, *The Food Chain: Winners and Losers in the Texas Supreme Court, 1995–1999.* (Texas Watch, 1999).
21. Texas Watch press release, May 3, 1999.
22. Texas Watch, *Access Denied, the Texas Supreme Court in 2000–2001.* (Texas Watch, 2001).
23. *Houston Chronicle,* September 18, 2002, p. 25A.
24. Samuel Issacharoff, *The Texas Judiciary and the Voting Rights Act: Background and Options* (Austin: Texas Policy Research Forum, 1989), pp. 2, 13.
25. *Texas Lawyer,* September 18, 1989.
26. *Houston Chronicle,* December 24, 1989.
27. *Texas Lawyer,* September 18, 1989.
28. *League of United Latin American Citizens, et al.* v. *Mattox, et al.,* 501 U.S. 419 (1991); *Chisom* v. *Roemer,* 501 U.S. 380 (1991).
29. *League of United Latin American Citizens* v. *Clements,* 999 F2d 831 (1993).
30. *Houston Chronicle,* January 19, 1994.
31. State Bar of Texas, Department of Research and Analysis, *A Statistical Profile of Texas Judges* (State Bar of Texas, 1998).
32. *Houston Chronicle,* November 13, 1998, p. 1A.
33. Office of Court Administration, *Texas Judicial System, 75th Annual Report.*
34. *Miranda* v. *Arizona,* 384 U.S. 436 (1966).
35. *Texas Lawyer,* November 11, 1991.
36. *Paulson* v. *State,* Texas Court of Criminal Appeals, October 4, 2000.
37. *Furman* v. *Georgia,* 408 U.S. 238 (1972).
38. *Texas Lawyer,* June 3, 1991.
39. *Houston Chronicle,* May 11, 2003, p. 1A.
40. Paul Burka, "Trial by Technicality," *Texas Monthly* (April 1982), pp. 126–31, 210–18, 241.
41. *Houston Chronicle,* August 27, 2003, p. 23A.
42. *Edgewood* v. *Kirby,* 777 S.W.2d 391 (1989).
43. *Fort Worth Star-Telegram,* October 4, 1982; *Brown* v. *Board of Education of Topeka,* 347 U.S. 483 (1954).
44. *Edgewood* v. *Meno,* 893 S.W.2d 450 (1995).
45. Ibid.
46. *Richards* v. *LULAC,* 868 S.W.2d 306 (1993); *Houston Chronicle,* June 16, 1994.
47. *Texas Education Agency* v. *Leeper,* 893 S.W. 2d 432 (1994).
48. *Operation Rescue—National* v. *Planned Parenthood of Houston and Southeast Texas, Inc.,* 975 S.W.2d 546 (1998). See also *Houston Chronicle,* July 4, 1998.
49. *Madsen* v. *Women's Health Clinic, Inc.,* 512 U.S. (1994).
50. *Republican Party of Texas* v. *Dietz,* 924 S.W.2d 932 (1996).

Chapter 27

1. Anwar Hussain Syed, *The Political Theory of American Local Government* (Random House, 1966), p. 27.
2. Ibid., pp. 38–52. Syed presents a summary of Jefferson's theory of local government.
3. Roscoe C. Martin, *Grass Roots* (University of Alabama Press, 1957), p. 5.; Robert C. Wood, *Suburbia* (Houghton Mifflin, 1958), p. 18.
4. *City of Clinton* v. *The Cedar Rapids and Missouri River Railroad Co.,* 24 Iowa 455 (1868).
5. Roscoe C. Martin, *The Cities in the Federal System* (Atherton Press, 1965), pp. 28–35.
6. David B. Brooks, *Texas Practice: County and Special District Law,* vol. 35 (West Publishing Company, 1989), pp. 41–46. A good part of the materials presented on county government rely on this comprehensive work.
7. Advisory Commission on Intergovernmental Relations, *Measuring Local Government Discretionary Authority,* Report M-131 (ACIR, 1981).
8. Advisory Commission on Intergovernmental Relations, *State and Local Roles in the Federal System* (ACIR, 1982), pp. 32–33.
9. For an excellent overview of urban development in Texas, see Char Miller and David R. Johnson, "The Rise of Urban Texas," in Char Miller and Heywood T. Sanders, EDS., *Urban Texas: Politics and Development* (Texas A&M University Press, 1990), pp. 3–29.

10. See Richard L. Cole, Ann Crowley Smith, and Delbert A. Taebel, with a foreword by Marlan Blissett, *Urban Life in Texas: A Statistical Profile and Assessment of the Largest Cities* (University of Texas Press, 1986), for an example of rankings of larger Texas cities on various dimensions measuring aspects of urban quality of life.
11. Texas Municipal League, Austin, Texas, May 2002.
12. Ibid.
13. Ibid.
14. Murray S. Stedman, *Urban Politics,* 2nd ed. (Winthrop Publishers, Inc., 1975), p. 51.
15. Beryl E. Pettus and Randall W. Bland, *Texas Government Today,* 3rd ed. (The Dorsey Press, 1984), p. 347.
16. Telephone calls to budget staff in El Paso and Houston, Texas, December 30, 2003.
17. Wilbourn E. Benton, *Texas Politics,* 5th ed. (Nelson-Hall Publishers, 1984), p. 260.
18. Telephone calls to budget staff in Dallas, San Antonio, and Seguin, Texas, December 30, 2003.
19. Bureau of the Census, *1992 Census of Government, Popularly Elected Officials,* vol. 2, no. 1, table 11.
20. Texas Municipal League, telephone conversation with research staff, Austin, Texas, May 2002.
21. Frank Sturzl, "Fiscal Conditions Survey Shows that Municipal Revenue Is Declining," *Texas Town and City* 89 (March 2003), p. 10.
22. Ibid., pp. 11–12.
23. "Texas Cities Continue to Face Fiscal Squeeze," *Texas Town and City* 79 (March 1991), pp. 26, 32–34.
24. Lawrence E. Jordan, "Municipal Bond Issuance in Texas: The New Realities," *Texas Town and City* 79 (December 1991), pp. 12, 25.
25. Sturzl, "Municipal Fiscal Conditions Remain Strong," pp. 10–11.
26. Miller and Sanders, eds., *Urban Texas: Politics and Development,* p. xiv.
27. Frank Sturzl, "The Tyranny of Environmental Mandates," *Texas Town and City* 79 (September 1991).
28. Robert E. Norwood and Sabrina Strawn, *Texas County Government: Let the People Choose,* 2nd ed. (The Texas Research League, 1984), p. 9. For a sample of Texas court decisions that affirm the general principle of the Dillon rule that the county can perform only those functions allocated to it by law, see pp. 11–12.
29. Texas Association of Counties, *2003 Salary Survey* (Texas Association of Counties, 2003); phone conversation with Office of Budget Management, Harris County, December 5, 2003.
30. *Avery* v. *Midland,* 88 S.Ct. 1114 (1968).
31. Norwood and Strawn, *Texas County Government,* p. 22.
32. Brooks, *Texas Practice,* pp. 331.
33. Texas Commission on Intergovernmental Relations, *An Introduction to Texas County Government* (TCIR, 1980), p. 10.
34. Brooks, *Texas Practice,* pp. 392–393.
35. Ibid., pp. 36, 104–105.
36. Texas Association of Counties, *2003 Salary Survey.*
37. Brooks, *Texas Practice,* pp. 49–50.
38. Ibid., pp. 18–49.
39. Norwood and Strawn, *Texas County Government,* p. 24.
40. Brooks, *Texas Practice,* pp. 273–274.
41. Ibid., pp. 36, 122–23.
42. TCIR, *An Introduction to County Government,* p. 22.
43. Norwood and Strawn, *Texas County Government,* p. 27.
44. Brooks, *Texas Practice,* pp. 273–274.
45. Virginia Marion Perrenod, *Special Districts, Special Purposes: Fringe Governments and Urban Problems in the Houston Area* (Texas A & M University Press, 1984), p. 4.
46. Ibid., p. 34.
47. Woodworth G. Thrombley, *Special Districts and Authorities in Texas* (Institute of Public Affairs, The University of Texas, 1959), p. 13.
48. Robert S. Lorch, *State and Local Politics,* 3rd ed. (Prentice Hall, 1989), p. 246.
49. Ibid., p. 247.
50. Texas Education Agency, *Snapshot 2002:2001–2002 School District Profiles* (Texas Education Agency, 2002).
51. Texas Association of School Boards, Membership Services, telephone conversation on May 14, 2002.
52. Governor's Planning and Budget Office, *Regional Councils in Texas: A Status Report and Directory, 1980–1981,* p. 9.
53. Governor's Budget and Planning Office, *Regional Councils in Texas: Annual Report and Directory, 1990–1991,* p. 8.
54. Texas Association of Regional Councils, "What is a COG?," www.txregionalcouncil.org.
55. Governor's Budget and Planning Office, *Texas Regional Councils: Annual Report and Directory,* 1992–1993.
56. Texas Association of Regional Councils, "What Is a COG?," www.txregionalcouncil.org.
57. Telephone interview by author on March 21, 2000, with governor's office.
58. Brooks, *Texas Practices,* pp. 380–384.
59. For a more detailed discussion of annexation authority, see Wilbourn E. Benton, *Texas Politics,* pp. 264–66.
60. "Texas Legislature Adjourns," *Texas Town and City* 86 (July 1999), p. 10.
61. "Texas Legislature Adjourns," *Texas Town and City* 89 (July 2001), p 11.
62. Norwood and Strawn, *Texas County Government,* pp. 75–81.
63. Joel B. Goldsteen and Russell Fricano, *Municipal Finance Practices and Preferences for New Development: Survey of Texas Cities* (Institute of Urban Studies, The University of Texas at Arlington, 1988), pp. 3–11.
64. Bill R. Shelton and Nancy Ratcliff, "How Cities Organize and Administer Sales Tax Revenues Dedicated to Economic Development," *Texas Town and City* 82 (December 1995), pp. 26–27.
65. Brooks, *Texas Practice,* pp. 229–242.
66. Tom Adams, "Introduction and Recent Experience with the Interlocal Contract," in *Interlocal Contract in Texas,* eds. Richard W. Tees, Richard L. Cole, and Jay G. Stanford. (Institute of Urban Studies, University of Arlington, 1990), p. 1.
67. Tees et al., *Interlocal Contract in Texas,* pp. B1–B7.
68. Vincent Ostrom, *The Meaning of American Federalism* (Institute for Contemporary Studies, 1991), p. 161. Ostrom suggests that advocates of metropolitan government often overlook the "rich and intricate framework for negotiating, adjudicating, and deciding questions" that are now in place in many urbanized areas with multiple governmental units.
69. Ann Long Diveley and Dwight A. Shupe, "Public Improvement Districts: An Alternative for Financing Public Improvements and Services," *Texas Town and City* 79 (September 1991), pp. 6–10, 30, 66.

Epilogue

1. Thucydides, *History of the Peloponnesian War,* trans. Benjamin Jowett (Prometheus Books, 1998).
2. Edith Hamilton, *The Echo of Greece* (Norton, 1957), p. 47.
3. The White House, at www.whitehouse.gov/news/releases/2001/09/20010911-16.html.
4. For a book advocating more direct democracy, see Ted Becker and Christa Daryl Slaton, *The Future of Teledemocracy* (Praeger 2000); for a contrary view, see Richard J. Ellis, *Democratic Delusions: The Initiative Process in America* (University Press of Kansas, 2002).
5. For an extensive list of countries that use some form of proportional representation, see ed.labonte.com/pr.html.
6. For more on the relationship between electoral institutions and party systems, see Maurice Duverger, *Political Parties: Their Organization and Activity in the Modern State* (Wiley, 1954).
7. *Lawrence* v. *Texas,* 539 U.S. 558 (2003).
8. Campaign Media Legal Center, at wwwcampaignlegalcenter.org/BCRA.html; *McConnell* v. *FEC,* 124 S.CT. 619 (2003).
9. Bruce Bimber and Richard Davis, *Campaigning Online: The Internet in U.S. Elections.* Oxford University Press, 2003.
10. John F. Kennedy, *Profiles in Courage* (Pocket Books, 1956), p. 108.
11. Harry S Truman, impromptu remarks before the Reciprocity Club, Washington, D.C., April 11, 1958, as reported by the *New York World-Telegram* April 12, 1958, p. 4. Found at www.bartleby.com/73/1405.html.
12. These three books will give you insight into the life of a politician: Bill Bradley, *Time Present, Time Past: A Memoir* (Knopf 1996); Warren B. Rudman, *Combat: Twelve Years in the U.S. Senate* (Random House, 1996); Mark Hatfield, *Against the Grain: Reflections of a Rebel Republican* (White Cloud Press, 2001).
13. For a contrary view of Madison's presidency, see Gary Rosen, *American Compact: James Madison and the Problem of the Founding* (University Press of Kansas, 1999).
14. Judy Wilgoren, "Dean Spares No Opponent as He Sprints Across Iowa," *The New York Times.* 15 October 2003, p. A17.
15. Richard F. Fenno, Jr., *Home Style: House Members in Their Districts* (Boston: Little, Brown and Company, 1978), pp. 162–169.
16. See Lawrence R. Jacobs and Robert Y. Shapiro, *Politicians Don't Pander* (University of Chicago Press, 2000); Christopher Beem, *The Necessity of Politics* (University of Chicago Press, 1999); and John E. McDonough, *Experiencing Politics* (University of California Press, 2000).

17. See Kareem Abdul-Jabar and Alan Steinberg, *Black Profiles in Courage* (Morrow, 1996).

18. Reinhold Niebuhr, *The Children of Light and the Children of Darkness* (Scribner, 1944), p. xi.

19. See Bernard Crick, *In Defense of Politics,* rev. ed. (Pelican Books, 1983); and Stimson Bullitt, *To Be a Politician,* rev. ed. (Yale University Press, 1977).

20. See Benjamin R. Barber, *A Passion for Democracy* (Princeton University Press, 1998).

21. See Nat Hentoff, *Free Speech for Me—but Not for Thee: How the American Left and Right Relentlessly Censor Each Other* (Harper Perennial, 1993).

22. William J. Brennan, commencement address, Brandeis University, May 18, 1986.

23. Arthur M. Schlesinger Jr., *The Disuniting of America* (Norton, 1993), p. 134.

24. John W. Gardner, *Self-Renewal,* rev. ed. (Norton, 1981), p. xiv.

PHOTO CREDITS

Chapter 1: **xxiv:** Jim Bourg/Reuters America Inc. **1:** AFP Photo/Shawn Thew/Getty Images, Inc.–Agence France Presse **4:** Corbis Digital Stock **5:** The Cartoon Bank/© The New Yorker Collection 1993 Ed Fisher from cartoonbank.com. All Rights Reserved. **9:** Dwayne Newton/PhotoEdit **10:** Chip East/Reuters/CORBIS–NY **12:** Nick Ut/AP Wide World Photos **15:** (*left*) Corbis/Bettmann (*right*) The Granger Collection **16:** Getty Images, Inc.–Liaison **17:** The Cartoon Bank/© The New Yorker Collection 1982 Peter Steiner from cartoonbank.com. All Rights Reserved. **23:** The Granger Collection/Currier & Ives, "Give Me Liberty or Give Me Death!", 1775. Lithograph, 1876. © The Granger Collection, New York

Chapter 2: **26:** CORBIS–NY **27:** Dennis Brack/Dennis Brack **28:** Dunagin/Tribune Media Services, Inc./Reprinted by permission: Tribune Media Services **34:** AP Wide World Photos **35:** The Granger Collection **36:** (*top*) The Granger Collection (*middle*) AP Wide World Photos (*bottom*) Fabian Bachrach/Getty Images, Inc.–Taxi **42:** (*box*) Zigy Kaluzny Photo © Zigy Kaluzny. All Rights Reserved. (*bottom*) Flip Schulke/CORBIS–NY

Chapter 3: **55:** The Granger Collection **57:** Elise Amendola/AP Wide World Photos **58:** Donald McLeod–Pool/AP Wide World Photos **68:** AP Wide World Photos **72:** Dennis Brack **73:** A. Ramey/PhotoEdit **77:** RountreeAdam/Gamma Press USA, Inc.

Chapter 4: **81:** Jeff Greenberg/Painet, Inc. **84:** Stephen Carr/AP Wide World Photos **85:** Enid News & Eagle, Chris Landsberger/AP Wide World Photos **89:** Jean Catuffe/SIPA Press **91:** UPI/Corbis/Bettmann **92:** Gerald Herbert/AP Wide World Photos **95:** AP Wide World Photos **97:** Greg Gibson/AP Wide World Photos **98:** (*box*) Alfred Eisenstaedt/Getty Images/Time Life Pictures (*bottom*) Ric Feld/AP Wide World Photos **101:** Star Tribune/Reprint with permission of the Star Tribune

Chapter 5: **105:** Corbis/Bettmann **108:** Library of Congress/Courtesy of the Library of Congress **110:** Jane Faircloth/Transparencies **114:** Nell Redmond/AP Wide World Photos **115:** (*top*) Ron Edmonds/AP Wide World Photos (*bottom*) Mark Leffingwell/Getty Images/Getty Images, Inc. **116:** Larry Downing/Reuters/CORBIS/Corbis/Bettmann **117:** (*box*) Stan Honda/AFP/Getty Images/Getty Images, Inc. (*bottom*) Pablo Martinez Monsivais/AP Wide World Photos **120:** (*top*) Barry Talesnick/IPOL Inc./Globe Photos Inc. (*bottom*) Arthur Hochstein/Getty Images/Time Life Pictures **126:** © 1982 The New Yorker Collection 1992 Dana Fradon from cartoonbank.com. All rights reserved.

Chapter 6: **130:** Jim Bourg/Reuters America Inc. **131:** Susan Jones/SIPA Press **132:** NRA–ILA Grassroots Division **140:** (*top*) Getty Images, Inc.–Liaison (*bottom*) Celano Lee/Getty Images, Inc.–Liaison **141:** Getty Images/Getty Images, Inc. **142:** AP Wide World Photos **143:** Bob Daemmrich/Bob Daemmrich Photography, Inc. **144:** Montana Democratic Party **146:** Stephen Moore **147:** Corbis/Bettmann **153:** AP Wide World Photos

Chapter 7: **160/161:** Reza Estakhrian/Getty Images Inc.–Stone Allstock **166:** AP Wide World Photos **169:** AP Wide World Photos **175:** Paul Conklin/PhotoEdit **176:** AP Wide World Photos **179:** Ricky Carioti/*Washington Post National Weekly Edition* © 2002, The Washington Post. Photo by Ricky Carioti. Reprinted with permission **182:** The Cartoon Bank © The New Yorker Collection 1986 Tobey from cartoonbank.com. All Rights Reserved. **187:** AP Wide World Photos

Chapter 8: **190:** AP Wide World Photos **191:** Kayte M. Deloma/PhotoEdit **193:** Bob Daemmrich/Bob Daemmrich Photography, Inc. **196:** (*top*) Cartoon Features Syndicate/From *The Wall Street Journal*, December 12, 1990—Permission, Cartoon Features Syndicate. (*bottom*) AP Wide World Photos **197:** UPI/Corbis/Bettmann/© Bettmann/CORBIS **201:** Bob Daemmrich/Stock Boston **202:** Jeff Widener/AP Wide World Photos **207:** Julia Malakie/AP Wide World Photos **210:** Getty Images, Inc.–Liaison

Chapter 9: **216:** G. Fabiano/SIPA Press **216/217:** Justin Sullivan/Getty Images/Getty Images, Inc. **220:** Getty Images, Inc.–Liaison **223:** AP Wide

World Photos **226:** Dunagin's People. Tribune Media Services **228:** Jim Bourg/CORBIS–NY **230:** Bob Daemmrich/The Image Works **233:** (*top*) AP Wide World Photos (*bottom*) Shaun Heasley/Reuters/CORBIS–NY **238:** AP Wide World Photos **239:** Charles Rex Arbogast/AP Wide World Photos **245:** AP Wide World Photos

Chapter 10: **248:** Reuters America Inc. **249:** Douglas McFadd/Stringer/Getty Images/Getty Images, Inc. **250:** Shannon Stapleton/Corbis/Bettmann **251:** Kevin Winter/Getty Images/Getty Images, Inc. **254:** Geostock/Getty Images, Inc.–Photodisc. **255:** Corbis Bettmann **256:** UPI/Corbis Bettmann **257:** Mitchell Gerber/Corbis/Bettmann/Mitchell Gerber/CORBIS **261:** The Cartoon Bank/© The New Yorker Collection 1989 Jack Ziegler from cartoonbank.com. All Rights Reserved. **264:** The Cartoon Bank/© The New Yorker Collection 2000 Dana Fradon from cartoonbank.com. All Rights Reserved. **266:** (*top*) Getty Images Inc.–Hulton Archive Photos (*bottom*) Eric Draper/The White House/CORBIS–NY

Chapter 11: **272:** Grace Davies/Omni-Photo Communications, Inc. **273:** Ron Edmonds/AP Wide World Photos **275:** Corbis/Bettmann **276:** Phil Coale/AP Wide World Photos **277:** Dennis Cook/AP Wide World Photos **279:** Congresswoman Nancy Pelosi **283:** Alex Wong/Getty Images, Inc.–Liaison **284:** Paul J. Richards/Getty Images/Getty Images, Inc. **285:** (*top*) *Knoxville News Sentinel*, J. Miles Cary/AP Wide World Photos (*bottom*) Alex Wong/Getty Images, Inc.–Liaison **287:** Alex Wong/Getty Images, Inc.–Liaison **288:** Mark Wilson/Getty Images/Getty Images, Inc. **291:** Terry Ashe/AP Wide World Photos **293:** (*left*) Office of Congressman Adam H. Putnam (*right*) Reuters/CORBIS–NY **297:** Mark Wilson/Getty Images, Inc.–Taxi **299:** Toles/King Features Syndicate/TOLES © The Buffalo News. Reprinted with permission of UNIVERSAL PRESS SYNDICATE. All rights reserved. **301:** AP Wide World Photos

Chapter 12: **304:** Kul Bhatia/Photo Researchers, Inc. **305:** AP Wide World Photos **307:** Eduardo Verdugo/AP Wide World Photos **308:** AP Wide World Photos **310:** AP Wide World Photos **313:** Reuters/Tyler J. Clements/U.S. Navy photo/CORBIS–NY **319:** Brooks Kraft/CORBIS–NY **322:** AP Wide World Photos **323:** Mark Wilson/Getty Images, Inc.–Taxi **324:** AP Wide World Photos **325:** Rusty Russell/Getty Images/Getty Images, Inc. **326:** ITAR-TASS/Reuters/CORBIS–NY **331:** Getty Images, Inc.–Taxi

Chapter 13: **338:** Roger Ressmeyer/Corbis/Bettmann/© Roger Ressmeyer/CORBIS **343:** U.S. Department of Education **345:** John Neubauer/PhotoEdit **349:** Tom Horan/Sygma/CORBIS/Corbis/Bettmann **351:** Ken Karp/Omni-Photo Communications, Inc. **356:** (*top*) AP Wide World Photos (*box*) AP Wide World Photos **358:** Gail Mooney/Thomas A. Kelly/Corbis/Bettmann/© Kelly-Mooney Photography/CORBIS

Chapter 14: **362:** J. Scott Applewhite/AP Wide World Photos **363:** Joe Sohm/Photo Researchers, Inc. **372:** Damian Dovarganes/AP Wide World Photos **373:** Carol T. Powers/AP Wide World Photos/AP Wide World Photos **374:** (*top*) Reuters/Gary Hershorn/Corbis/Bettmann (*bottom*) Reuters/Steve Jaffe/Corbis/Bettmann **376:** (*top*) Clary/UPI/Corbis/Bettmann (*bottom*) Reuters/Corbis/Bettmann **381:** King Features Syndicate/OLIPHANT © UNIVERSAL PRESS SYNDICATE. Reprinted with permission. All rights reserved **383:** Cartoon Features Syndicate/From *The Wall Street Journal*—Permission, Cartoon Features Syndicate

Chapter 15: **386/387:** Joe Cavaretta/AP Wide World Photos **395:** (*top*) LM Otero/AP Wide World Photos (*box*) Debra Lex/Time Life Pictures/Getty Images/Getty Images, Inc. **396:** Charles Tasnadi/AP Wide World Photos **398:** Tom Uhlman/AP Wide World Photos **399:** AP Wide World Photos **400:** The Report Newsmagazine **403:** Jean Catuffe/SIPA Press **405:** AP Wide World Photos

Chapter 16: **408/409:** Andrew Lichtenstein/Corbis/Sygma **410:** David McNew/Liaison/Online USA/Getty Images, Inc.–Liaison **413:** Corbis/Bettmann **416:** AP Wide World Photos **417:** CORBIS–NY **418:** Joe Marquette/AP Wide World Photos **419:** Blair Seitz/Photo Researchers, Inc. **421:** Bob Daemmrich/Stock Boston **422:** James Wilson/Woodfin Camp &

INDEX

ELECTORAL COLLEGE VOTES IN THE 2004 ELECTION

THE UNITED STATES
A Political Map
States drawn in proportion
to number of electoral votes

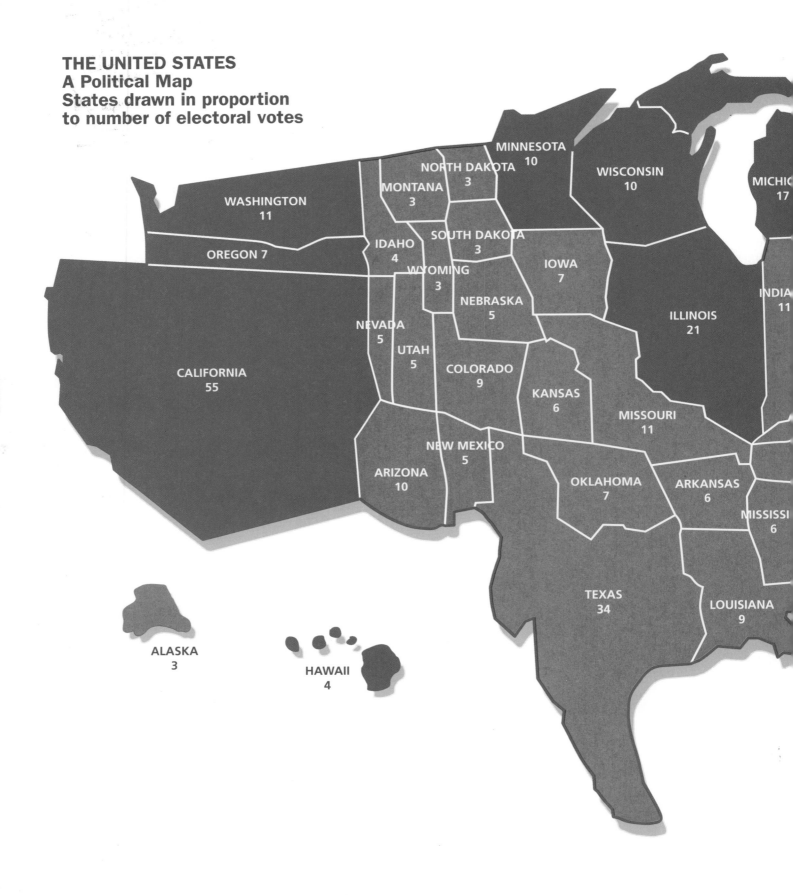